MW01120402

CRITICAL YOUTH STUDIES
READER

Editorial Review Board

This book is part of the Peter Lang Education list.
Every volume is peer reviewed and meets
the highest quality standards for content and production.

PETER LANG
New York • Washington, D.C./Baltimore • Bern
Frankfurt • Berlin • Brussels • Vienna • Oxford

Library of Congress Cataloging-in-Publication Data

Critical youth studies reader / [edited by] Awad Ibrahim, Shirley R. Steinberg.
pages cm
Includes bibliographical references.
1. Youth—History. 2. Youth—Research.
I. Ibrahim, Awad. II. Steinberg, Shirley R.
HQ796.C863   305.235—dc23   2014002273
ISBN 978-1-4331-2120-3 (hardcover)
ISBN 978-1-4331-2119-7 (paperback)
ISBN 978-1-4539-1271-3 (e-book)

Bibliographic information published by **Die Deutsche Nationalbibliothek.**
Die Deutsche Nationalbibliothek lists this publication in the "Deutsche
Nationalbibliografie"; detailed bibliographic data is available
on the Internet at http://dnb.d-nb.de/.

Cover art: Detail of the "I am Hip Hop" mural by Shalak Attack,
painted as part of a participative community mural for the
No Bad Sound Studio in Montreal, Canada, 2009.
www.shalakattack.com

The paper in this book meets the guidelines for permanence and durability
of the Committee on Production Guidelines for Book Longevity
of the Council of Library Resources.

© 2014 Peter Lang Publishing, Inc., New York
29 Broadway, 18th floor, New York, NY 10006
www.peterlang.com

Printed in the United States of America

CRITICAL YOUTH STUDIES
READER

**Edited by Awad Ibrahim
and Shirley R. Steinberg**

LINDSAY HUTTON, ASSISTANT EDITOR

PREFACE BY PAUL WILLIS

PETER LANG
New York • Washington, D.C./Baltimore • Bern
Frankfurt • Berlin • Brussels • Vienna • Oxford

X

Contents

PART II
IDENTITIES: A MÉTISSAGE BETWEEN INDIGENEITY, LGBTQ, WHITENESS, AND DIASPORA

PART III
CULTURES: NAVIGATING MEDIA AND IDENTITIES, SPORTS, TECHNOLOGY, AND MUSIC

PART IV
PRAXIS: PEDAGOGIES AND SCHOOLING, KIDS NOT TALKED ABOUT, AND ACTIVISM

PERMISSIONS

Chapter 8. Willis, P. (2003). "Foot Soldiers of Modernity: The Dialectics of Cultural Consumption and the 21ˢᵗ Century School." *Harvard Educational Review 73* (3), 390–415. Permission from Paul Willis, copyright 2003.

Chapter 9. Giroux, H. (2011). "No Bailouts for Youth: Broken Promises and Dashed Hopes". H. Giroux, *Zombie Politics and Culture in the Age of Casino Capitalism* (pp. 89–94). New York: Peter Lang.

Chapter 23. Meyer, E. J. (2011). "She's the Man: Deconstructing the Gender and Sexuality Curriculum at 'Hollywood High.'" In Carlson, D. & Roseboro, D. L. *The Sexuality Curriculum and Youth Culture* (pp. 231–245). New York: Peter Lang.

Chapter 32. Jones, R. (2009). "Machinima: Gamers Start Playing Director." In Macedo, D. & Steinberg, S. R. *Media Literacy: A Reader* (pp. 486–491). New York: Peter Lang.

Chapter 34. Malott, C. & Porfilio, B. "Punk Rock, Hip Hop, and the Politics of Human Resistance: Reconstituting the Social Studies Through Critical Media Literacy." In Macedo, D. & Steinberg, S. *Media Literacy: A Reader.* (pp. 582–592). New York: Peter Lang.

Chapter 36: Steinberg, S. (2011). "Redefining the Notion of Youth: Contextualizing the Possible for Transformative Youth Leadership." In Shields, C. *Transformative Leadership: A Reader* (pp. 177–206). New York: Peter Lang.

Chapter 44. Gaines, D. (1998). Extracted from *Teenage Wasteland: Suburbia's Dead End Kids.* Chicago: University of Chicago Press. Permission from Donna Gaines, copyright 1998.

Chapter 47. Wegwert, J. (2011). "LGBTQ Youth and the Hidden Curriculum of Citizenship Education: A 'Day of Silence' in a Suburban High School." In Carlson, D. & Roseboro, D. L. *The Sexuality Curriculum and Youth Culture* (pp. 108–121). New York: Peter Lang.

PREFACE

After a generation in educational research besotted with neoliberalism, myopic positivism and self-limiting class practice improvement techniques, at last an international team addresses some of the grand questions again understood through the grain of subordinate experience and cultural form, undertaking theorizing conditioned by an understanding from below dominated positions and their everyday pressures. Big questions, critical perspectives, respect for micro experience, ah the relief! Social science needs generative not reductive theory: an element of radical indeterminacy is always necessary to our understanding of social process; there must always be space for subjective elements allowing felt degrees at least of agentive creativity and choice. Too often for grand theorists these latter were merely illusions to be 'explained' with exemplifications provided of what has already been decided should be there, no 'surprises'. This book reminds and renews the theoretical appreciation of a few simple and open-ended generative mechanisms repeating over and over for different groups in wildly different places with different though not un-patterned outcomes.

I see more clearly than ever that I caught 'the lads' in England described in Learning to Labour perhaps in the last golden age of working class power, culture and organization in one 'core' location and that economic, social, race, nationality and sexual recompositions now sweep through the generations across the nations. I realize how parochial in many ways was my book, a product of its time; that there are quite other ways of ordering, picturing and imagining the giving of labor power, struggling with the need for belonging and the acquiring of identity in many different structural, cultural and institutional contexts. I am struck, though, by a kind of convergence. Desperate the situation may be in poorer countries, but I see in the 'core' countries too that a de facto apartheid is developing with liberal arts, critical discussion, open-ness, high expectations for the elite as opposed to rote learning, standardization, low-flying vocationalism with trappings of progressivism as well as a general cynicism and secret disgust for the rest. Perhaps we need new ways of analyzing the globalizing world based not on traditional national boundaries but on internationally mediated and organized class systems with rungs of abjection strung ever further out at the bottom of social space.

Material and social conditions change at a colossal pace everywhere. This book gives a wide panoramic view. We face a bewildering new world of contradictory influences, profound crises of the old and tumultuous birth of the new. Through what cultural mediations does the necessary now connect with the voluntary under new conditions and at multiple sites across the world? Though I have little direct experience of or understanding of the many sites covered in this book I am sure of one thing. Critical practices and methodologies, reflexive and comparative theoretical work and debate as offered in this book offer a grounds for understanding the human unfoldings of this colossal historical canvas from the position of youth. At the minimum, and as a pre-condition, critical perspectives stress agency and always insist on a role for subordinated groups in the production of their own cultures and understandings. Crudely, we must always ask, what is the meaning-making from below? Too often profound macro changes are seen in a passive way, described from above in gerunds as if merely automatic, agentless processes—globalization, downsizing, urbanization, modernization, etc. Desperately, urgently, there is a need for the human and 'practical sense' view from below. Real social agents live simultaneously, and in the same life space—the dislocations of 'the void' together with the recompositions of the social together with economic transformations and state forms of attempting to grapple with and direct social and economic change. Critical perspectives must encompass the inter-twinings of these too often separated worlds as they constitute the practical field on which agents live and act.

In the train of the new relations and the erosion of traditional cultural forms come new possibilities, emergent forms which must be scrutinized for their social possibilities. The new social agents called forth will not usually declare themselves as new social subjectivities, they will not bear self-made public stamps on their foreheads. Often they will only be known through the insulting stereotypes of their social abjection. But this book reminds us absolutely not to miss the theoretically inescapable but often unobserved moments of meaning-making from below. In this book we are reminded of the whole global range of discursive and symbolic resources—traditional, new and market oriented—which cultural production and penetrations can press into service. This book reminds us not to miss the possible assertiveness and confidence of 'invisible' or 'representationally fixed' groups which produce bottom-end-up, complex changes for all representations of social difference. Social agents can intervene in the symbolic orders of their own social universes. 'Backward', 'anti-social' and 'resistant' cultures or responses can tell us about the larger structural context, of yearnings for social justice and of both the complex creativities and complex submissions of social agents in subordinate and subaltern positions. They teach us about the emerging mismatches and ragged edges between penetrations and reproductions in situated contexts in different parts of the globe.

These issues raise pedagogic questions of the broadest hue. In future circles of these mutual relations how might the balance be switched more to the advantage of the dominated, under what conditions might the penetrations of cultural production be turned into forms of political consciousness/ practice and/or mobilized for the interruption, rather than ironic strengthening, of social reproduction? Not only must young people be equipped technically to face the relentless pressures of changing capitalist labor markets, with renewed agitation to divert scarce resources from the elite to the marginal, they must also be equipped and have the means to equip themselves for the tasks of social becoming with full access to critical tools to understand their present situation in historical context as well as for picturing and imagining what could be in achievably different kinds of worlds.

Read this book, liberation may be some way off but you can liberate yourself from the neoliberal agenda.

Paul Willis, Princeton University

January 2014

Criticalizing Youth, Youth Criticalizing

Shirley R. Steinberg

A short foreword to lead into Awad's introduction to the works of youth workers, teachers of youth, and youth. This book is our first large attempt to reach across disciplines and contexts to bring out those who wish a critical voice in our cultural and pedagogical work with, and for youth. The last phrase is key, for we hope to create a circumstance in which working with youth, becomes a transformative act facilitating empowerment, leadership, and self-efficacy.

When we assembled the book, we realized we had only begun to assemble the voices we want to hear. Starting from our own geographical and personal places, we reached out to scholars whose work reflected the critical and democratic youth work we sought. We acknowledge that much of this volume reflects work and scholarship with North American youth, predominantly English speaking. We acknowledge that for every chapter, there are dozens of chapters that must be written. We acknowledge that for every topic, we did not address many others: caregiver/parental relationships, preparation for youth workers, preparation for youth as workers, romance, wellness and health, and so many genres of culture. We attempted to begin a conversation on how to continue the conversation. This book is the opening sentence to the dialogues, confabs, parlays, tracks, spittin', and yes, scholarship, pedagogy, and research into a field grounded in social justice which recognizes respects youth.

We invited youth poets to contribute to this work. These young men and women wrote their contributions in their later teen years and have generously offered them to this volume. Shout Outs of thanks and love go to each poet, and to their mentors, Bettina Love, Reenah Golden, Fahima Ife, and Hodari Davis of Youth Speaks and Brave New Voices, youth workers with day jobs who spend the other 16 hours a day understanding and building the potential of youth poet/artists. You will find their poetry hidden within the book's pages, as respite of verse and vision.

In opening the book, you turned the cover, the mural, I am Hip Hop, which was taken from the front of Maison des Jeunes, Côte-des-Neiges, Montreal. Painted by Shalak Attack, as part of a participative community mural for the No Bad Sound Studio. The first time I met Shalak was when she was covered I paint at MDJ on a driveway filled with young men and women immersed in learning how to *be* and *do* public art. I often return to that day, meeting this fabulous young woman speaking in multiple languages to each artist as they worked with intensity not often seen in schools, youth centres, or homes. Shalak's work is international, cosmic; feel blessed if you come upon her art—it belongs to us all.

We asked Paul Willis and Donna Gaines to each contribute a piece of their seminal works; they are two writers/youth workers whose work has made a difference—and many, many references in our own work. It is impossible to reconceptualize a critical youth studies without grounding our knowledge with Paul's *lads,* and the contextual understanding that class and place create in our work. Donna's ethnographic/ethnomethodological/hermeneutic/phenomenological journalistic excerpt from *Teenage Wasteland* hits us with the grit, history, and reality we too often find in youth studies. We appreciate Paul's and Donna's time and vision as we put this book together, and Shout them Out with zeal.

We ask you to enter this new conversation, one which demands a criticalization of youth studies, a socially just way in which to engage, facilitate, and promote our most precious resources … our youth.

Critical Youth Studies

An Introduction

Awad Ibrahim

Our aim in this reader is to create an architecture of propositions that is not concerned with the question, "Is this youth studies?" But one which asks, "Why are we conducting youth studies and what do we do with it?" (Deleuze & Guattari, 1987; Deleuze, 1985; Massumi, 1993).

This architecture of propositions for youth studies directly impacts and is impacted by spaces, concepts, intensities and constructs that are found in different fields of study. These include sociology (especially youth culture), cultural studies (media and pop culture), psychoanalysis (desire and seduction), and anthropology (language, cultural maps, norms and values). We are keen on answering our question pedagogically, "Why are we conducting youth studies and what do we do with it?" We emphasize transformative pedagogy, best practices, and leadership as a way to "think through" (Derrida, 2000) this thing, youth studies. The history of youth studies has always been something that is *done to youth*. Instead, this reader approaches youth studies as something that we *can do with youth* (Tilleczek, 2011), or something that youth *can do themselves*. This is why we distinguish between "youth studies" and the "studies of youth."

Traditionally, the studies of youth focus on 'understanding' youth as a special category, as researchers remain outsiders looking in. Starting in the 1950s, most of the studies of youth were done by sociologists, who reached their peak with the work of the Centre for Contemporary Cultural Studies at the University of Birmingham in the 1970s and early 1980s (Amit-Talai & Wulff, 1995). Be it the work of Talcott Parsons (1964), Stanley Cohen (1972), Jock Young (1974), Stuart Hall and Tony Jefferson (1975), Paul Willis (1977) or Dick Hebdige (1979) these studies of youth shifted the ground both epistemologically and empirically from youth as a psychologically categorized deviant group to a group manifesting resistance, rites of passages and temporality. The shift put the study of youth, into a culturally, socially and historically produced category, into a globalized, mediated and creolized category.

However, earlier studies of youth didn't fully explore the intersectionality of gender, class, race, sexuality and ability and how they impact and are impacted by social structure. In other words, the connections between structure and subjectivity, on the one hand, and the significance of subjectivity, on the other, did not receive much attention; hence the emergence of *youth studies*. Following Bourdieu (1978), youth studies involves regarding youth as an evolving concept, layered "with values which reflect contemporary moral, political and social concerns" (Jones, 2009, p. 1). For youth studies, youth is a historical category whose contemporary understanding emerged from twentieth-century welfare capitalism and industrialization. That is, through social and educational reform, when child protection laws began to prohibit child employment and education was extended to upper, middle and working classes, youth became a policy question and a life stage that requires an age range, descriptors, and psychological attributes. This apparently arbitrary age division, youth studies argue, is an expression of both manipulation and intergenerational power struggle. It is manipulation because 'adults' seem to talk about 'youth' as if it were a social unit, with common interests, strengths, and weaknesses at a biologically defined age. It is an intergenerational power struggle because the current negative media representation of young people as dangerous social beings and the resultant moral panic represent the side/site of more powerful and older generations.

A crucial element that is centrally emerging in the literature of youth studies is education. Education is heavily critiqued in youth studies as forcing an "inward movement," in which young people socialize, interact, and create a culture with groups of their own age. The end result of this forced socialization is a stratified, classed, racialized, gendered, age-specific, and dependent culture. We talk about generation X and Y, generations with their own music, clothes, and sub-countercultural practices that began to distinguish youth. As these practices started to solidify, youth studies argue, "the message of consciousness went with it" (Reich, cited in Jones, 2009, p. 16). Keeping this debate on consciousness and sub/counterculture in mind, one of the big questions in youth studies is whether youth are marginalized by society or whether they marginalize themselves.

In the present volume, we want to hold on to these questions, but we also want to flip the script (as Hip Hoppers like to say). Although the volume stands on the shoulders of giants and is grounded on classic and contemporary youth studies, it pushes the field further. This volume is an attempt to criticalize and name a new field in youth studies: Critical Youth Studies (CYS). Epistemologically, CYS sees youth as action; as a performative category; as an identity that is both produced through and is producing our bodies and sense of self; as an agentive, ambiguous, fluid, shifting, multiple, complex, stylized, and forever becoming category. It is more than a transient, dependent, and age-specific category. Socially constructed (much like the term 'adult'), youth in CYS are seen as cultural agents capable of desire, love, hate, hopes, struggles, language, dress, walk, and so many other social and cultural practices. We use *critical* to identify the critical theoretical notion that the study of youth is political; the context of being a youth has everything to do with how agencies of power work, and how this work affects young women and men.

To capture these complexities and contradictions, we invited the authors in this book for their expertise in youth studies, and challenged them and ourselves to push what they/we know further. The book contains an intersectionality of youth studies, sociology, anthropology, education, politics, and cultural studies, creating a theoretical grounding. Readers will gain a comprehensive and complete understanding of what CYS means on the one hand, and an awareness of the complexity of the new field on the other. Strategically, we do not enter the debate on developmental psychology or the traditional notions of adolescence; and we do not pathologize youth. There actually are few existing works addressing the field of a critical youth studies. To address this gap, the volume also includes seminal works by major figures in the field. The reader contextualizes youth critically through globalization, media, identity, leadership, music, fashion, sports, technology, gender, sexuality, religion, race, class, place, critical pedagogy, or decolonization. We adhere to Bourdieu's (1978) notion that youth is not just a concept, and make the presumption that Critical Youth Studies is where it will be fully understood. WORD!

The *Critical Youth Studies Reader* has four major sections, thematically arranged in order to further a conversation on each meta-theme.

Part I
Historical and Contemporary Epistemologies of Critical Youth Studies

Youth, it seems, is a narrative, a strategic, fluid and non-linear story that youth tell themselves and others. It is an organic process of acquiring knowledge about themselves and the world around them, thus making sense of who they are. In a contingent, historicized and postmodern moment, youth is no longer an ascribed identity. No longer, as a result, do youth have to reconcile themselves with their present identities and remain in those identities over their lives, be it through their career, the people they befriend, or the place they live in. Youth is now an identity process in which a story is created about their own lives, where *persons* use the environment around them and, especially, pop culture to create the story of who they are. Attachments to particular aspects of pop culture no longer completely define a young person as that which is loved can be transient. In a 'neo-tribal' spirit, the new social dynamic is now characterized by fluidity, occasional gatherings, and dispersal, especially in a consumer-oriented society (see Maffesoli, 1996). They may be 'punks' during teen years, 'rockers' during their twenties, 'post-rockers' during their thirties, or any number of classifications. This is not a linear process; we can go back and forth. In this process of identity-testing and identity formation, Gill Jones (2009) argues, consumption is an important vehicle for the construction of young people's lifestyles, and it is largely within the context or in relation to pop culture that young people form their identities in the 21st century.

It is significant to note that youth are not dupes who invest completely and blindly in pop culture to the extent that it subsumes their lives. To the contrary, they are able to locate their identities through personal cultural maps where particular kinds of world culture and pop culture interpellate (Althusser, 1971) them. Here, given the vast number of representations they are introduced to, youth enter a process of identity-testing and taste-testing, thus leaving the scene their own tastes in clothing, music, entertainment, etc. Interestingly, with the abundance of social media (Facebook, Twitter, etc.), youth (just like adults) seek groups of people who have the same tastes in popular culture. Michel Maffesoli (1996) calls these groupings 'tribes.' These groupings or tribes are not permanent or fixed. Their transitory nature explains why youth (like anyone else, adults included) are not completely satisfied with sticking to one category. It is not surprising, therefore, that youth will choose or test certain identities (punk, Goth, Hip Hop, hippie, etc.) till they feel loyalty to one brand or identity over another.

This process is situated in a socio-political context where promises are often broken and hopes are dashed. Yet, youth is nothing if not resilient.

Part II
Identities:
A Métissage Between Indigeneity, LGBTQ, Whiteness & Diaspora

Part II is about *how* the process of creolization or *métissage* takes place on the ground; how the global is localized in such innovative ways that it calls for new research and theorization, making the division between the local and the global problematic. *"Pratique de métissage"* or cultural, linguistic, and musical creolization, Édouard Glissant argues, "is not part of some vague humanism, which makes it permissible for us to become one with the other" (cited in Françoise Lionnet, 1989, p. 4). On the contrary, *métissage* is a radical concept which refers to "the constant interaction, the transmutation between two or more cultural components [e.g., Indigeneity and Diaspora; or Whiteness and LGBTQ] with the unconscious goal of creating a third cultural entity—in other words, a culture, a new culture. Lionnet (1989) explains, "each one changes into the other so that both can be transformed" (p. 15). *Métissage* assumes two or more entities that are equally valorized; hence it is an egalitarian hybridity, where ambiguity, multiplicity, fragmentation, and plurality become the new landscape. These entities, however, are not found in complete isolation, as Homi Bhabha (1994) argues, because no form (cultural or otherwise) is "plainly plenitudinous, not only because there are other cultures which contradict its authority, but also because its own symbol-forming activity … always underscores the claim to an originary, ho-listic, organic identity …. [Therefore,] the 'original' is never finished or complete [and the] 'originary' is always open to translation" (p. 210).

Part II deals with horizontal and vertical *métissage*. Dealing specifically with identity, horizontal *métissage* expresses the explicit ways in which identity is performed and expressed on the body, while vertical *métissage* speaks to the intensity and depth of that performance. It is worth noting, as the authors in this section remind us, not all identity performances and testings are conscious. Indeed, most of youth identity negotiation takes place subconsciously, especially when it comes to desire, identification and consumption. That is why, these authors argue, we need an explicit, activist, anti-homophobic, anti-racist and critical pedagogy and politics, in which youth are able to name their own desires and agency, locate themselves in time and space, and at the same time question the adequacy of that loca-tion. Here, communities will not collapse because conscious, contingent, and radical identities are always invented. Identity-building becomes a resilient act when one knows her or his multiple con-tradictory and contingent selves and lives in that liminal space of the rational and the willful and the irrational and the unconscious.

Part III
Cultures:
Navigating Media and Identities, Sports, Technology and Music

Culture, Raymond Williams (1976) tells us, "is one of the two or three most complicated words in the English language. This is so," he continues, "because of its intricate historical development … but mainly because it has now come to be used for important concepts in several distinct intellectual dis-ciplines and in several distinct and incompatible systems of thought" (p. 87). Even though Williams never tells us what the other two or three words are, Part III of this book testifies to the veracity of his conclusion in regard to culture. From media to sports, from technology to music, one can see the four typologies of culture that Chris Jenks (1993) has identified. Jenks sees culture as 1) a cerebral category or a general state of mind; 2) a state of intellectual and/or moral development in society; 3) a descrip-tive and concrete category of arts and intellectual work within any one society; and 4) the whole way of life of a people (pp. 11–12).

As a whole way of life, culture has that ambiguous task of being a producer and a product of media, technology, music, and sports (among other things). As a producer, culture is a map on which things make sense to its participants; as a product, however, the actors control its shapes and contours. Culture is similar to the Hip Hop cipha. In the *Hip Hop cipha*, rules are well known to all participants, but they are unwritten rules. One has to be in the know by either studying or paying very close atten-tion to how dancers dance and battle each other; otherwise, one is doomed to fail. This is also true for students of culture. Culture, Williams (1976) reminds us, is everyday practice and doing; as such, very little is written down. It is a daily, mostly subconscious cultivation of taste, be it in media, sports, music, technology, or anything else.

There is no "nature" or naturalness to the cultivation of taste, especially within Critical Youth Studies. It is a socially and historically produced event, but, Pierre Bourdieu (1984) warns us, since cultivation of taste is also situated within semiotic systems of language, science, and popular arts, it has the potential to be an act of symbolic violence. Whether young people are gamers, Hip Hoppers, or social media users, their bodily and psychic investment is neither neutral nor without a situated politics of desire. This politics creates a double-edged sword: gamers may love gaming, but it is their love of gaming that makes them game. That is to say, similar to Bourdieu's (1984) notion of *habitus*, the cul-tivation of taste becomes the principle that regulates the act, thus creating a direct correlation between the symbolic and the material.

When it comes to Critical Youth Studies, we need to uncover these unwritten rules and better understand that which is taken for granted, the *habitus*. Curriculum, masculinity, disability, bullying, sports, social media, dance, and music all have an epistemic structure of *habitus*. Part III is an attempt to do precisely that. The contributors' intent is to break down the unnatural separation of the different fields discussed herein and to intersect the material and the symbolic so that we can hear the voice of youth and understand what they want us to hear.

Part IV
Praxis:
Pedagogies and Schooling, Kids not Talked About, and Activism

We must dare so as never to dichotomize cognition and emotion. We must dare so that we can continue to teach for a long time under conditions that we know well: low salaries, lack of respect, and ever-present risk of becoming prey to cynicism. We must dare to learn how to dare in order to say no to the bureaucratization of the mind to which we are exposed every day. We must dare so that we can continue to do so even when it is so much more materially advantageous to stop daring —Paulo Freire (1998, p. 3)

There is an urgent need to move from an education that is creating docile, timid, egotistic, and self-absorbed students to an activist education that creates and envisions students as leaders and active citizens who are exceptionally mindful of their local realities yet see these realities as related to global phenomena by which a neoliberal notion of capitalism and global economy is creating casinos out of schools and zombies out of students. We need to envision an education that takes the everyday lived experience of young people seriously and sees the push for testing and standardization as a serious menace that has to be pushed back. Our contemporary system is creating a culturally irrelevant curriculum and prison-like schools. We need students to write and rewrite their own curriculum, that is, their own lives. No one is more of an expert on their lives than young people themselves.

In this sense, as Paulo Freire (1998) reminds us, we need to see teaching as invitational; a form of hospitality where we welcome our students unconditionally; a relation and a labor of love; and a praxis, where the intersection of theory and practice should guide both our teaching and theorizing. Teachers must have humility and be grounded in courage, self-confidence, self-respect, and respect for others. We must live with an insecure security—an existence that does not require absolute answers and solutions—and a lovingness rooted in our commitment to consistently reflect on our practice. This not only requires courage but the willingness to challenge ourselves and others and tolerance founded on respect, discipline, dignity, and ethical responsibility. We must maintain a tension between patience and impatience and sustain the joy of living, for which we need a *pedagogy of humor* in order to genuinely laugh from the bottom of our hearts.

References

Althusser, L. (1971). *Lenin and philosophy and other essays.* London: New Left.
Amit-Talai, V., & Wulff, H. (Eds.). (1995). *Youth cultures: A cross-cultural perspective.* London & New York: Routledge.
Bhabha, H. (1994). *The location of culture.* London: Routledge.
Bourdieu, B. (1978). La jeunesse n'est qu'un mot. Interview with Anne-Marie Métailié. *Les jeunes et le premier emploi* (pp. 520–30). Paris: Association des Ages.
Bourdieu, P. (1984). *Distinction: A social critique of the judgment of taste.* London: Routledge.
Cohen, S. (1972). *Folk devils and moral panics.* St. Albans: Paladin.
Deleuze, G. (1985). *Cinema II: L'image temps.* Paris: Editions de Minuit.
Deleuze, G., & Guattari, F. (1987). *A thousand plateaus: Capitalism and schizophrenia.* London and New York: Continuum.
Derrida, J. (2000). *Of hospitality.* Stanford, CA: Stanford University Press.
Freire, P. (1998). *Teachers as cultural workers: Letters to those who dare to teach.* Boulder, CO: Westview.
Hall, S., & Jefferson, T. (Eds.). (1975). *Resistance through rituals.* London: Hutchinson.
Hebdige, D. (1979). *Subculture: The meaning of style.* London: Methuen.
Jenks, C. (1993). *Culture.* London: Routledge.

Jones, G. (2009). *Youth*. Cambridge, UK: Polity.

Lionnet, F. (1989). *Autobiographical voices: Race, gender, self-portraiture*. Ithaca, NY: Cornell University Press

Maffesoli, M. (1996). *The time of the tribes: The decline of individualism in mass society*. London: Sage.

Massumi, B. (1993). *The politics of everyday fear*. Minneapolis: University of Minnesota Press.

Parsons, T. (1964). *Essays in sociological theory*. New York: Free Press.

Tilleczek, K. (2011). *Approaching youth studies: Being, becoming, and belonging*. Don Mills, ON: Oxford University Press.

Williams, R. (1976). *Keywords: A vocabulary of culture and society*. London: Fontana.

Willis, P. (1977). *Learning to labour: How working class kids get working class jobs*. Farnborough, UK: Saxon House.

Young, J. (1974). New directions in sub-cultural theory. In J. Rex (Ed.), *Approaches to sociology* (pp. 23–34). London: Routledge & Kegan Paul.

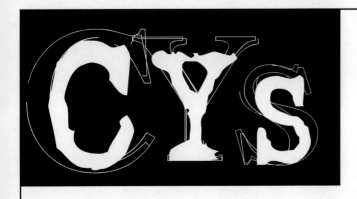

PART I

Historical and Contemporary Epistemologies of Critical Youth Studies

CHAPTER 1

Toward a Critical Theory of Youth

Douglas Kellner

Contemporary youth are major players in the postmodern adventure, because it is they who will enter the future and further shape the world to come.[1] The offspring of the baby boomers born in the 1940s, their identities are indelibly marked as "post"—post-boomer, post-1960s, posthistorical, postmodern. Yet they live in a present marred by extreme uncertainty, facing a future that is murky and unpredictable. For youth today, change is the name of the game, and they are forced to adapt to a rapidly mutating and crisis-ridden world characterized by novel information, computer, and genetic technologies; a complex and fragile global economy; and a frightening era of war and terrorism. According to dominant discourses in the media, politics, and academic research, the everyday life of growing segments of youth is increasingly unstable, violent, and dangerous. The situation of youth is today marked by the dissolution of the family; growing child abuse and domestic conflict; drug and alcohol abuse; sexually transmitted diseases; poor education and crumbling schools; and escalating criminalization, imprisonment, and even state execution. These alarming assaults on youth are combined with massive federal cutbacks of programs that might give youth a chance to succeed in an increasingly difficult world.

Hence, today's youth are at risk in a growing number of ways, and survival is a challenge. Ready or not, they will inherit a social world that is increasingly deteriorating, and a natural world that is ever more savaged by industrial forces. Yet they also have access to exciting realms of cyberspace and the possibilities of technologies, identities, and entrepreneurial adventures unimagined by previous generations. Contemporary youth include the best-educated generation in history, the most technically sophisticated, and the most diverse and multicultural, making generalizations about the youth in the present day precarious.

To illuminate the situation of contemporary youth, we need *a critical theory of youth* that articulates positive, negative, and ambiguous aspects in their current situation. A critical theory delineates some of the defining features of the condition of contemporary youth to indicate the ways that they are encountering the challenges facing them, and to suggest how these might best be engaged. There is obviously a wide diversity of youth experiences of varying genders, races, classes, sexualities, and social groups, and thus major differences within youth today, as well as what they share in common as a generation. Within the present social situation, there are grave dangers for youth, but also some enhanced freedoms and opportunities. More positive futures cannot be created, however, unless youth are able to achieve a variety of forms of literacy, including print, media, and computer skills and enhanced education (Kellner, 2002, 2004). These abilities will enable youth to cope with a rapidly changing environment, and can help the emergent generations to shape their own future and remake the culture and social world they inherit.

Today's youth are privileged subjects of the postmodern adventure, because they are the first generation to live intensely in the transformative realms of cyberspace and hyperreality where media culture, computers, genetic engineering, and other emerging technologies are dramatically transforming all aspects of life (see Best and Kellner, 2001). It is a world where multimedia technologies are changing the very nature of work, education, and the textures of everyday life, but also where previous boundaries are imploding; global capital is restructuring and entering an era of crisis, war, and terrorism; while uncertainty, ambiguity, and pessimism become dominant moods.

Consequently, the youth of the new millennium are the first generation to *live* the themes of postmodern theory.[2] Entropy, chaos, indeterminacy, contingency, simulation, and hyperreality are not just concepts they might encounter in a seminar, but forces that constitute the very texture of their experience, as they deal with corporate downsizing and the disappearance of good jobs, economic recession, information and media overload, the demands of a high-tech computer society, crime and violence, identity crises, terrorism, war, and an increasingly unpredictable future. For youth, the postmodern adventure is a wild and dangerous ride, a rapid roller coaster of thrills and spills plunging into the unknown.

From Boomers to Busters

Perhaps the cruelest joke played on our generation is the general belief that if you went to college, you'll get a job and be upwardly mobile. —Steven Gibb

The prospects for youth have always been problematic, dependent on class, gender, race, nationality, and the concrete sociohistorical environment of the day. *Youth* itself is a social construct that takes on different connotations at different periods in history. What is striking about the contemporary situation of youth is the totalizing and derogatory terms used to describe them. Youth have been tagged with terms such as the "Postponed Generation," the "13th Generation," the "New Lost Generation," "The Nowhere Generation," or most frequently, "Generation X," as well as "the scapegoat generation," "GenNet," "GenNext," and other catch phrases.[3] These terms have mainly been applied to the 80 million Americans born between the 1960s and 1980s who follow the "boomer" generation that emerged in post-World War II affluence and who were the beneficiaries of an unprecedented economic expansion. Howe and Strauss (1993) see all of these young people as one cohesive group, yet they nevertheless draw distinctions between the older "Atari Wave," born in the 1960s and raised on the first video games such as Pac-Man and Space Invaders; the "Nintendo Wave" who played the more advanced Super Mario II and Tetris games; and the "Millennial Generation" born in the 1980s who entered the computer world. While these distinctions serve to distinguish between younger kids and those who are now thirty-somethings and ascending, video games are obviously a poor marker of distinction, and do not adequately delineate important gender, race, sexual preference, and class differences among contemporary youth. Moreover, innovative computer, CD-ROM, and video technologies render video games a decreasingly central aspect of youth culture, hence the term "GenNet" has become a popular phrase to define the current generation. This task of defining today's youth is best left to the generation in question, so I am here just delineating some categories that others can take up and develop.

Contemporary youth embrace a wide array of young people, including those who helped create the Internet and others hooked on violent computer games; the latchkey kids who are home alone and the mall rats devouring fast food in the palaces of consumption; the young activists who helped generate the antiglobalization and emerging peace and antiwar movements; the cafe slackers, klub kidz, computer nerds, and sales clerks; a generation committed to health, exercise, good diet, and animal rights; as well as anorexics and bulimics in thrall to the ideals of the beauty and fashion industries. Today's youth also include creators of exciting 'zines and diverse multimedia; the bike ponies, valley girls, and skinheads; and skaters; gangstas, low-riders, riot grrls, and hip hoppers, all accompanied by a diverse and heterogeneous grouping of multicultural, racial, and hybridized individuals seeking a viable identity.

Certainly, in the age range of fifteen to thirty-something, in young men and women, and in various classes and races, there are important differences to note in an increasingly complex and hybridized "generation," but they also have crucial things in common. In standard media and sociopolitical representations, youth are pejoratively represented as cynical, confused, apolitical (or conservative), ignorant, bibliophobic, scopophilic, and narcissistic. Young people are typically portrayed in media culture as whining slackers and malcontents suffering from severe Attention Deficit Disorder (ADD) induced by MTV, remote-control channel surfing, net cruising, video and computer games, and tempered by Ritalin, Prozac, and the new Drug of the Week. Indeed, the cohorts of American youth over the past couple of decades have been widely stigmatized as "the doofus generation," "the tuned-out generation," "the numb generation," "the blank generation," "a generation of self-centered know-nothings," and "Generation Ecch!" From the Right, Allan Bloom (1987) infamously excoriated youth as illiterate and inarticulate adolescents blithely enjoying the achievements of modern science and the Enlightenment while in the throes of a Dionysian frenzy, drugged by music videos, rock and roll, and illegal substances, and ushering in "the closing of the American mind," the endgame of Enlightenment values. Such jeremiads constitute only the tip of the iceberg of hostility and resentment toward this generation by older generations, reopening a "generation gap" as wide as that between youth of the 1960s and "the establishment."[4]

Such negative labels and characterizations of youth are falsely totalizing. They eliminate, for example, young political activists and volunteers, bright students in opposition to the values of media culture, and the technical wizards who developed much computer software and pioneered the Internet. Moreover, pejorative characterizations of youth fail to understand that whatever undesirable features this generation possesses were in large part shaped by their present and past; and how the younger generation is an unwitting victim of the economic recession, the global restructuring of capitalism, and the decline of democracy. As Geoffrey Holtz (1995) said of his own generation:

> We are, perhaps more than any previous generation, a product of the societal trends of our times and of the times that immediately preceded us. The years in which we were raised—the sixties, seventies, and eighties—saw unprecedented changes in the political, social, and economic environment that, for the first time in American history, have made the future of society's young members uncertain. (p. 1)

There is no widespread agreement concerning what concepts best characterize contemporary youth. During the 1980s and into the 1990s, the term, "Generation X," popularized by Canadian writer, Douglas Coupland (1991), has been widely adopted. The "X" could signify the crossroads upon which the present generation stands between the modern and the postmodern. It suggests an unknown and indeterminate future, a fluidity of identities that are being redefined by new technologies and cultural experiences, and a situation of uncertainty and social chaos. Yet, if one needs a label to characterize this generation, then perhaps not "Generation X," which is vague and widely rejected by those it is supposed to characterize,[5] but "post-boomers" and "millennials" are preferable, because contemporary youth are the successors to those Americans born between 1945 and 1960, and their identities in large part are shaped in reaction to them and their times, and they are now the denizens, products, and potential movers and shapers of a new millennium. Moreover, contemporary youth are the first genera-tion to grow up in the post-1960s Cold-War era, characterized by the unfolding of the postindustrial society and postmodern culture, and have been living in the tensions and conflicts of the "post."

The post-boomer generation could also be labeled as "busters," for with this generation the American dream, enjoyed by many boomers, went bust, and they were thrown into a world of uncertainty, dis-order, and decline. The baby boomers came of age during the optimism which followed World War Two, with the rise of suburbia, cheap education, good job opportunities, abundant housing, the Age of Affluence, and the exciting and turbulent events of the 1960s. Their children, in contrast, matured during more troubled times marked by recession, diminishing expectations, and the conservative reac-tion led by Ronald Reagan and George Bush Senior, an explosion of shallow greed and materialism, followed by the excitement of the explosion of new technologies, and talk of a "new economy" and dot.com boom in the 1990s rapidly followed by a dot.bust and hard times in the Bush-Cheney era.

The e-boom was a boom period for youth and by youth, and quite significant for this reason. In the 1990s, the Internet and the explosion of information technologies created new jobs, almost-unheard-of wealth, and seemingly unlimited possibilities for youth. Though ballooned out of proportion by the financial industries, the Internet boom represented a new economy led by a young vanguard. Yet the economic crisis that came at the end of the Bush-Cheney era dashed many of these hopes, and was accompanied by the mortgaging of a generation forced to take out unprecedented levels of student loans because a Republican antistatist ideology refused to invest in its future, forcing many contempo-rary youth to be slaves of the past.

In retrospect, the Bush II regime can be seen in many ways as a return to the old guard, the old extraction-based economy that sees economic advancement as a win-loss game best advanced through imperialist expansion—a shift from the consumer-, innovation-, and service-driven economy that envisioned (at least) a win-win global economy based on national comparative advantage and world trade. It was big oil and wars fought on its behalf and the almost booming military-industrial sector that characterized the Bush-Cheney Gang, along with stealing billions from federal coffers under the guise of tax breaks for the wealthiest, that constituted an incredible shifting of wealth to the biggest Have Mores, at the cost of stealing possibilities from the young. Thus, the restoration of the old, con-servative order in the opening years of the new millennium is also an attack on contemporary youth, which also has the flavor in many ways of revenge on the young and more progressive on behalf of conservative elders (it is too soon to say if the Obama years can be seen as a revenge of the young in reaction to the attacks on youth of the Bush-Cheney years, or just more of the same under a liberal and multicultural guise).

Moreover, dramatically worsening social conditions in the new millennium emerged following the September 11 terrorist attack on the US and the subsequent "war against terrorism." After declaring war against an "axis of evil" in his 2002 State of the Union speech, in early 2003 Son of Bush assembled his father's Legion of Doom and a gigantic military machine to wage war against Iraq in an unfolding millennium of perennial war, one that will sacrifice another generation of youth, an intervention that intensified a war that went on in Iraq until the Obama administration and a war in Afghanistan still ongoing that has killed hundreds of thousands, cost trillions, and produced paroxysms of blowback (see Kellner, 2003 and Scahill, 2013). Hence, while post-boomer youth faced a life that was more complex, insecure, risky, and unpredictable than boomer youth, today's youth face even more dangerous and anxious times, with threats of terrorism, war, and large-scale apocalypse on the horizon, as the global economy sputters, possibilities for a better life diminish, and climate change and the dangers of ecologi-cal collapse increase to an alarming extent.

To be sure, the 2008 election of Barack Obama and his reelection in 2012 provided some hope for contemporary youth. Youth were involved in the Obama campaign from the beginning, responding positively to his messages of "change you can believe in" and hope. Youth were active in the Obama campaign from the beginning, using new media and social networking to help organize Obama rallies and voters, helping to make him a celebrity and win the presidency (see Kellner, 2009, 2013). Yet the wars, economic crisis, declining polity the Obama administration inherited from the Bush-Cheney Gangs, and political gridlock that set in after the 2010 elections when Republicans took control of Congress have produced new challenges for the political system and for the future of youth.

Post-Boomers, Millennials, and Contemporary Youth

We grew up as America, in many ways, fell down. —Rob Nelson and Jon Cowan (1994)

Post-post boomer youth have lived through the fallout of the rising expectations of the "new economy" and globalization, finding that dotcom.bust, terrorism, and a reactionary U.S. administration bent on a return to the past and threatening unending war have imperiled their future as well as the prospects for survival of the human species. Youth who have come of age during the crisis-saturated 2000s are often referred to as *millennials*, in reference to the new millennium that emerged in the year 2000. Ready for the new age, in 2000, Neil Howe and William Strauss published *Millennials Rising: The Next Great Generation*, making a sharp and contested distinction between the generation born in 1982 and GenX, of whom they had presented a downbeat appraisal in their earlier book, discussed previously (Howe & Strauss, 1993). Howe and Strauss's rosy appraisal of the prospects of millennials, who they touted as the "new great generation," received instant criticism, and provoked a series of books on the millennials, still mushrooming.[6]

Ultimately, it will be up to the contemporary generation to define itself, and it is time for youth and critical social theory to reflect on the Gen-Next that follows the so-called post-boomer generation. While the term, *post-boomer*, helps indicate the experience of coming after the boomer generation, entering the postmodern adventure, and living out the drama of the "post," the new millennium produces novel social conditions for today's youth, who are engaging innovative and challenging cultural forms, a dramatically complex economic and political situation, and an ever more unpredictable life. This generation faces the challenges of forging careers in a declining economy, surviving the threats of war and terrorism, surviving ecological collapse, and overcoming the conservative hegemony that threatens their future.

There were earlier signs that post-boomers were coming to resent the elderly, the "G.I." and "Silent" generations, born respectively between 1901–1924 and 1925–1942, who, through various federal programs, have grown richer as youth have grown poorer, and today's youth were bracing for a shock when 56 million boomers retired in 2010, seeking social and medical benefits that are becoming increasingly costly and scarce.[7] Moreover, the post-boomer, postmodern, millennial generation has been stuck with the highest federal deficit in history that it will be forced to pay off, as well as record high student debts.[8] Despite the efforts of the Clinton administration to cut back on the federal deficit and to produce a surplus for the years to come, future youth face paying off trillions of dollars of debt by the year 2020, more than twenty times what it was in 1960. This enormous mortgaging of the future is arguably the product of unwise and unfair government spending that benefited the upper and middle classes over the lower classes, and the middle-aged and elderly over the young (Nelson & Cowan, 1994, p. 20). During the two Reagan administrations, the national debt doubled, and the Bush I administration managed to further double the deficit in one term. In additon, Bush Junior racked up record $304-billion-dollar deficits for 2003 to pay for his wars, leaving the Obama administration record debts to manage.[9] Consequently, future generations will be forced to pay for the parties for the rich and greedy thrown by the Reagan and Bush administrations, and will have to clean up the mess.

And so the post-generations share in common a difficult future. As Holtz (1995) realized, whatever new freedoms and possibilities are available to contemporary youth—from education to jobs to housing—the opportunities to enjoy them are vanishing. The post-boomers are not only the largest and most diverse of all American generations, they are "the only generation born since the civil war to come of age unlikely to match their parents' economic fortune" (Holtz, 1995, p. 7). The brief exception of the dot.com boom temporarily put Holtz's analysis in question, but unfortunately, his subsequent comment seems appropriate, where he described the 1990s generation as "the only one born this century to grow up personifying (to others) not the advance, but the decline of their society's greatness" (Holtz, 1995, p. 7)—a condition that has continued in the 2000s. Whereas it was once seen as a birthright of American children to inherit a better future, it is now a rite of passage to grow up in an age of decline. Indeed, various statistics add up to a grim picture of decay that shapes the cynicism and pessimism of many post-boomers and contemporary youth. From cradle to the seminar room, their lives have been far more difficult and troubled than past generations. Childhood-poverty rates, family divorces, living and education costs, taxes, violence and incarceration rates, teen pregnancy, mental illness, drug rates, obesity, cigarette smoking, and suicide rates are way *up*, as school performance, job prospects, median weekly earnings, unemployment benefits, and prospects of future home ownership rates are *down*.[10]

By the time the boomers' children reached puberty, optimism had thus given way to pessimism, boom to bust, opportunity to crisis, and they were "lost" in the shuffle. For many, youth was artificially prolonged, as even college graduates could not get good jobs, or lost their jobs after the dot.com bust or the disasters of the post-Enron corporate collapse and the catastrophe of Bushonomics. Many young people have been forced to go back to live with their parents, undergoing a second adolescence,[11] as the perks of adulthood become ever more difficult to achieve.

Yet, for Geoffrey Holtz and others of the post-boomer generation, the situation is not entirely negative. He preferred to call contemporary youth, much too optimistically, the "free generation," because "with the breakdown of many gender-based traditions and racial stereotypes, we enjoy a much broader range of lifestyle and career choices than any generation that preceded us" (Holtz, 1995, p. 3). But he also realized that this generation is "free" of any social, cultural, or political defining generational experience that provides a common, collective identity.

Indeed, in many ways, the current generation of youth is living in an especially depressing socioeconomic environment. Where the boomers had the idealism of the Civil Rights movement, the Vietnam war, the counterculture, solidarity with groups involved in liberation struggles, and dreams of social revolution, their children had Watergate, the Iran hostage crisis, the Iran-Contra affair, CIA wars in Central America, accelerating S&L scandals, cynical conservatism, dreary materialism, anxious narcissism, and the paranoia of additional terrorist attacks and the promise of a cycle of Terror Wars, combined with ongoing economic and ecological crises. Boomers watched Neil Armstrong plant a flag on the moon; post-boomers and contemporary youth witnessed the explosions of the Challenger and Columbia space shuttles. Boomers faced the threat of bullies in the schoolyard; post-boomers pass by metal detectors and security guards on their way into school, and face shootings such as those at Columbine High School, the Virginia Tech college massacre, and the slaughter at Sandy Hook Elementary School in 2013 (see Kellner, 2013). Where the boomers enjoyed Woodstock and the utopia of free love, their children had Woodstock II and then the simulacra of Woodstock III—a soulless, commodified parody of the original orchestrated by MTV—as well as "safe sex" necessitated by the specter of AIDS in a world where Eros and Thanatos are increasingly fused. And while boomers celebrated and multiplied face-to-face encounters and got in the faces of reactionary social forces, post-boomers and millennials are offered the consolation and narcotic of Facebook.

Perhaps most crucially, while boomers enjoyed the luxury of well-funded government services, contemporary youth in the United States must now live with the consequences of the 1996 welfare-reform bill—which began the process of making deep cuts in funding for women, children, and education—followed by continued redistribution of wealth from the poorer and middle classes to the rich under the Bush-Cheney administration, as well as suffer under the burden of the highest student debts in history. Of course, there are gains and advantages shared by the current generation, and generational experience varies according to class, gender, race, region, and individual. While racism continues to fester and racial differences intensify, many youth of color have opportunities today that were denied to their parents. Although sexism continues to prevail, younger women have absorbed feminist consciousness into their everyday lives, and also have more opportunities for independence than their mothers and grandmothers. And while homophobia continues to oppress gays, gay youth are out in record numbers and enjoying solidarity and support denied to previous generations. Also, there are proliferating spaces of youth subcultures, including cyberspace, which provide opportunities for self-expression and participation denied many in the previous generations (Turkle, 1995, 2011; Kahn & Kellner, 2008a).

Crucially, the post-boomers and contemporary youth share a common identity—as products and users of mass media and information technologies—and a common social and political environment. They are not the first TV generation (their boomer parents had that honor), but their media experience is far more intensive and extensive. Where boomers were introduced to a TV world with limited channels in black and white, post-boomers experienced the cornucopia of 50-plus channels in living color transmitted by cable and satellite television, a wealth of video cassettes, remote-control devices, interactive video games, DVDs, and a plethora of material available via Netflix, Amazon, Hulu, and ever-proliferating entertainment sites. Further, whereas much boomer TV watching was rigorously supervised and circumscribed by concerned parents, post-boomers were parked in front of the TV as a pacifier—often with both parents at work—indulging themselves in a media orgy supplemented by video and computer games. And while heavy TV-watching boomers were castigated as couch potatoes, post-boomers and millennials can be active participants in discussion, analysis, and critique of TV as it broadcasts through social networking and interactive websites.

Post-boomers therefore watched much more TV than boomers, competing with the time they spent in school and with other media.[12] The shows post-boomers watch are of a far different nature, filled with images of sex and violence the likes of which were not seen in the 50s and early 60s, substituting in the 1990s *Melrose Place, Beverly Hills 90210*, and *Baywatch* for *Ozzie and Harriet, Dobie Gillis*, and *Lassie*. Younger viewers of the past decades watched shows like *American Gladiators, The Mighty Morphin Power Rangers, Beavis and Butt-Head*, and *Pinky and the Brain*, compared to *The Howdy Doody Show, The Mickey Mouse Club*, and *Mr. Ed* which entertained young boomers. And the current wave of "reality TV" shows feature young contestants struggling for survival, prizes, and celebrity against older players in *Survivor*; locked up in a panopticon of surveillance in *Big Brother*; and subject to the degradations of sexual and social rejection in the highly competitive personality and/or sex contests of *Temptation Island, The Bachelor, The Bachelorette*, or *Joe Millionaire*, in addition to the ever-proliferating new "reality" TV series which feature youth. These latter shows feature narcissism and sadism, depicting a highly Darwinist neoliberal struggle for the survival of the fittest and sexiest, while losers are rejected and cast aside as unworthy.

But post-boomers are also the first generation to grow up with personal computers, the Internet, video and/or computer games, and social networking, providing exciting adventures in cyberspace and proliferating technological skills, making this generation the most technologically literate in history and offering unprecedented opportunities for them to create their *own* culture. Peer-to-peer (P2P) sharing of music, videos, computer programs, and other digitized products represents more communal and social sharing than is evident in the reality-TV shows, and sites like Napster, Kazaa, MySpace, Facebook, Twitter, and YouTube represent social technologies designed by youth to create a participatory and shared digital youth culture, one currently at war against the adult world of copyright litigation and the net police.

By the 1990s, forms of postmodern culture were thus a central part of youth culture. The style of MTV has influenced media culture as a whole, which absorbs and pastiches anything and everything, turning oppositional cultural forms such as hip hop and grunge into seductive hooks for fashion and advertising. The postmodern media and consumer culture is alluring, fragmented, and superficial, inviting its audiences to enter the postmodern game of consumption, style, and identity through the construction of look and image. Postmodern cultural forms are becoming dominant—at least for youth—with genre implosion a recurrent feature of contemporary film and TV, as are pastiche, sampling, hyper-irony, and other features of postmodern culture. Novel forms of electronic music such as techno and rave clubs also produce cultural artifacts where youth can intensely experience postmodern culture, as they indulge in designer drugs, chemical and herbal ecstasy, and psychotropic drinks. Thus, for contemporary youth, postmodernism is not merely an avant-garde aesthetic, or academic topic, but is the form and texture of their everyday lives.

Indeed, the experiences of the Internet and virtual reality have brought postmodern culture into the homes and lives of contemporary youth. Hooking into the World Wide Web, individuals can access myriad forms of culture, engage in discussions, create their own cultural forums and sites, establish relationships, and create novel identities and social relations in a unique cyberspace (see Turkle, 1995). Internet culture is on the whole more fragmented, diverse, and interactive than previous media culture, and as sight and sound become more integral parts of the Internet experience, individuals will increasingly live in a space significantly different from previous print and media culture. Being propelled into a new cultural matrix is thus an integral part of the postmodern adventure with unforeseen results. Contemporary youth constitute the first cybergeneration, the first group enculturated into media and computer culture from the beginning, playing computer and video games, accessing a wealth of TV channels, plugging into the Internet, and creating communities, social relations, artifacts, and identities in an entirely original cultural space for which the term postmodern stands as a semiotic marker.

Youth culture is thus today intersected by ever-proliferating new media and computer technologies and pervasive social networking, plunging the current generation into a new, immersive, postmodern culture. On the downside, youth today have always increasing pressure to participate in new media and social networking, producing anxieties and pressures on youth and often isolation even when they are connected with multiple "friends." Sherry Turkle, in her book, *Alone Together* (2011), pointed to her second thoughts on "life on-line" and a more critical position toward new technologies, in comparison with her 1995 book which celebrated the new, multidimensional, postmodern subjectivities she saw emerging in computer culture. Nicholas Carr, in turn, argued in his 2011 book, *The Shallows: What the Internet Is Doing to Our Brains*, that contemporary youth are subjected to pressures to constantly interact in social networking sites making it increasingly difficult to read books, concentrate, and develop critical subjectivity, producing a new "shallow" generation in thrall to their technologies and pressures to constantly interact.

On the other hand, still pervasive media culture has extended and prolonged youth culture, as 1960s rockers like Mick Jagger and Tina Turner continue to strut their stuff, and youth becomes an ever more obsessive ideal in U.S. culture with enhanced plastic surgery and sophisticated medicine. Yet, in opposition to the dominant media and consumer culture, resistant youth subcultures have emerged which provide autonomous spaces where they can define themselves, creating their own identities and communities. Youth subcultures can be merely cultures of consumption where young people come together to consume cultural products, like rock music, that binds them together as a community. Yet, youth subcultures can also be countercultures in which youth define themselves against the dominant culture, such as in punk, goth, grrrl, or hip hop culture.[13] Youth subcultures can comprise an entire way of life, involving clothes, styles, attitudes, and practices, and be all-involving ways of living. Youth subcultures contain potential spaces of resistance, though these can take various forms, ranging from narcissistic and apolitical, to anarchist and punk cultures, to activist environmental, animal rights, and Vegan groups, to right-wing skinheads and Islamic Jihadists. Thus, although there might be elements of opposition and resistance to mainstream culture in youth subcultures, such counterculture might not be progressive, and must be interrogated in specific cases concerning its politics and effects.

Of course, one needs to distinguish between a postmodern culture produced by youth themselves which articulates their own visions, passions, and anxieties, and media culture produced by adults to be consumed by youth. One also needs to distinguish between youth cultures that are lived and involve immediate, participatory experience, as opposed to mediated cultural experience and consumption, and to be aware that youth cultures involve both poles. Moreover, one should resist either reducing youth cultures merely to cultures of consumption, or glorifying youth cultures as forces of resistance. It is best, instead, to ferret out the contradictions and the ways that youth cultures are constructed by media and consumer culture, and the ways that youth in turn construct their own communities.

The Internet, Technoculture, and New Politics

A community will evolve only when a people control their own communication. —Frantz Fanon

The Internet and multimedia computer technologies and cultural forms are dramatically transforming the circulation of information, images, and various modes of culture, and the younger generation thus needs to gain multifaceted technological skills to survive in the high-tech information society (Best & Kellner, 2001; Kahn & Kellner, 2006; Kellner, 2002). In this situation, students should learn both how to use computer culture to do research and gather information, as well as to perceive it as a cultural terrain which contains texts, spectacles, games, and interactive media that require a form of critical computer literacy. Youth subcultural forms range from 'zines or websites that feature an ever-expanding range of video, music, or multimedia texts to sites of political information and organization.[14]

Moreover, since the 1999 Seattle anticorporate globalization demonstrations, youth have been using the Internet to inform and debate each other, organize oppositional movements, and generate alternative forms of politics and culture (see Best & Kellner, 2001 and Kahn & Kellner, 2008a). In September 2011, a movement called "Occupy Wall Street" emerged in New York, as a variety of people began protesting the economic system in the United States, corruption on Wall Street, and a diverse range of other issues. The project of "Occupy Wall Street" was proposed by *Adbusters* magazine on July 13, 2011; and on August 9th, Occupy Wall Street supporters in New York held a meeting for "We, the 99%." On September 8th, "We are the 99 Percent Tumblair" was launched, and on September 17th Occupy Wall Street protesters began camping out and demonstrating in Zuccotti Park in downtown New York close to Wall Street, setting up a tent city that would be the epicenter of the Occupy movement for some months. Using social media, more and more people joined the demonstrations, which received widespread media attention when police attacked peaceful demonstrators, yielding pictures of young women being sprayed with pepper gas by police. Mainstream media attention and mobilizing through social media brought more people to demonstrate, and by the first weekend in October, there was a massive protest in lower Manhattan that marched across the Brooklyn Bridge and blocked traffic, leading to over 700 arrests.

The idea caught on and during the weekend of October 1st–2nd, similar "Occupy" demonstrations broke out in San Francisco, Los Angeles, Chicago, Boston, Denver, Washington, and several other cities. On October 5th in New York, major unions joined the protest, and thousands marched from Foley Square to the Occupy Wall Street encampment in Zuccotti Park. Celebrities, students and professors, and ordinary citizens joined the protest in support, and daily coverage of the movement was appearing in U.S. and global media.

The Occupy movements were preceded in 2010 by the Arab Spring, in which young people and others used new media and social networking to overthrow dictatorships throughout the Middle East, generating an era of struggle still ongoing (see Kellner, 2012). Facebook, Twitter, YouTube, and other new-media and social-networking resources were used in these struggles, both to inform people concerning social ills and problems and to mobilize people to seek conclusions. Consequently, computer literacy involves not merely technical skills and knowledge, but the ability to scan information, to interact with a variety of cultural forms and groups, and to intervene in a creative manner within the emergent computer and political culture. Whereas youth are excluded for the most part from the dominant media culture, computer culture and social networking provide discursive and political locations in which youth can intervene, engaging in discussion groups, creating their websites, producing multimedia for cultural dissemination, and generating a diversity of political projects. Computer culture enables individuals to actively participate in the production of culture, ranging from discussion of public issues to creation of their own cultural forms, enabling those who had been previously excluded from cultural production and mainstream politics to participate in the production of culture and sociopolitical activism.

Obviously, it is youth that fight and die in wars which often primarily serve the interests of corrupt economic and political elites. Today's youth are becoming aware that their survival is at stake, and that it is thus necessary to become informed and organized on the crucial issues of war, peace, and the future of democracy and the global economy. Likewise, groups are organizing to save endangered species, to fight genetically engineered food, to debate cloning and stem-cell research, to advance animal rights and environmental causes, and to work for creating a healthier diet and alternative medical systems. The Internet is a virtual treasury of alternative information and cultural forms, with young people playing key roles in developing the technology and oppositional culture, and using it for creative pedagogical and political purposes. Alternative courses in every conceivable topic can be found on the Internet, as well as topics such as human rights or environmental education that are often neglected in public schools.

Thus, a postmodern pedagogy requires developing critical forms of print, media, and computer literacy, all of which are of crucial importance in the technoculture of the present and the fast-approaching future. Indeed, contemporary culture is marked by a proliferation of image machines which generate a panoply of print, sound, environmental, and diverse aesthetic artifacts within which we wander, trying to make our way through this forest of symbols. And so we need to begin learning how to read these images, these fascinating and seductive cultural forms whose massive impact on our lives we have only begun to understand. Surely, education should attend to the multimedia culture, and teach how to read images and narratives as part of media, computer, and/or technoculture literacy.

Such an effort would be linked to a revitalized critical pedagogy that attempts to empower individuals so that they can analyze and criticize the emerging technoculture, as well as participate in producing its cultural and political forums and sites. The challenge for education today is thus to promote computer and media literacy to empower students and citizens to use a wide range of technologies to enhance their lives and create a better culture and society. In particular, this involves developing Internet projects that articulate important cultural and political struggles in the contemporary world, and developing relevant educational material (see Best & Kellner, 2001 and Kahn & Kellner, 2008a).

Yet, there is also the danger that youth will become excessively immersed in a glittering world of high-tech experience and lose their social connectedness and ability to communicate and relate concretely to other people. Statistics suggest that more and more sectors of youth are able to access cyberspace, and that college students with Internet accounts are spending as much as four hours a day in the seductive realm of technological experience. The media, however, have been generating a moral panic concerning allegedly growing dangers in cyberspace with sensationalistic stories of young boys and girls lured into dangerous sexual encounters or running away, endless accounts of how pornography on the Internet is proliferating, and the publicizing of calls for increasing control, censorship, and surveillance of communication—usually by politicians who are computer illiterate.

To be sure, there are perils in cyberspace as well as elsewhere, but the threats to adolescents are significantly higher from the danger of family violence and abuse than from seduction by strangers on the Internet. And while there is a flourishing trade in pornography on the Internet, this material has become increasingly available in a variety of venues, from the local video shop to the newspaper stand, so it seems unfair to demonize cyberculture. Indeed, attempts at Internet censorship are part of the attack on youth which would circumscribe their rights to obtain entertainment and information, and create their own subcultures. Devices like the V-chip that would exclude sex and violence on television, or block computer access to objectionable material, are more an expression of adult hysteria and moral panic than genuine dangers to youth—which certainly exist, but much more strikingly in the real world than in the sphere of hyperreality.

Yet there is no doubt that the cyberspace of computer worlds contains as much banality and stupidity as real life, and one can waste much time in useless activity as well as negatively impact one's subjectivity, as Carr (2011) warned. But compared to the bleak and violent urban worlds portrayed in some rap music and youth films such as *Kids* (1995) or *Bubble* (2006), the technological worlds are havens of information, entertainment, interaction, and connection where youth can gain valuable skills, knowledge, and power necessary to survive the postmodern adventure. Youth can create more multiple and flexible selves in cyberspace, as well as alternative subcultures and communities. Indeed, it is exciting to cruise the Internet and to discover how many interesting websites young people and others have established, often containing valuable educational material. There is, of course, the danger that corporate and commercial interests will come to colonize the Internet, but it is likely that there will continue to be spaces where individuals can empower themselves and create their own communities and identities. A main challenge for youth (and others) is to learn to use the computer and information technology for positive cultural and political projects, rather than just for entertainment and passive consumption.

Reflecting on the growing social importance of emerging technologies and cultural sites makes it clear that it is of essential importance for youth today to gain various kinds of literacy to empower themselves for the emerging cybersociety. To survive in a postmodern world, individuals of all ages need to gain skills of media and computer literacy to enable themselves to negotiate the overload of media images and spectacles. We all need to learn technological skills to use the multimedia and computer technologies to subsist in the emerging high-tech economy, and to form our own cultures and communities.

It is therefore extremely important for the future of democracy to make sure that youth of all classes, races, genders, and religions gain access to multimedia technology and critical pedagogies. They need training in media- and computer-literacy skills in order to provide the opportunities to enter the high-tech job market and society of the future, and to prevent an exacerbation of class, gender, and race inequalities. And while multiple literacy skills will be necessary, traditional print-literacy skills are all the more important in a cyberage of word-processing, information gathering, and cybercommunication. Moreover, training in philosophy, ethics, value thinking, and the humanities is necessary now more than ever. Indeed, *how* emergent technologies will be used depends on the overall education of youth, and the skills and interests they bring to the technologies which can be used to access educational and valuable cultural material, or pornography and the banal wares of cybershopping malls.

Of course, cyberlife is just one dimension of experience, and individuals still need to learn to interact in a "real world" of school, jobs, relationships, politics, and other people. Youth—and all of us—need to learn to interact in many dimensions of social reality, and to gain a variety of forms of literacy and skills that will enable the creation of identities, relationships, and communities that will nurture and develop the full spectrum of potentialities and satisfy a wide array of needs. Our lives are more multidimensional than ever, and part of the postmodern adventure is learning to live in a variety of social spaces and adapting to intense change and transformation. Education, too, must meet these challenges, and must use multimedia and information technologies to promote empowering learning and devise strategies to create a more democratic and egalitarian multicultural society.

Notes

1. This analysis was to be included in my book with Steven Best, *The Postmodern Adventure*, but the study was cut from the final version because of space considerations. Examples here are drawn from our studies of youth in the United States, but in an increasingly globalized world, such specificities often have more general relevance. Thanks to Richard Kahn and Andrew Thomas for extremely useful critiques of an earlier version of this text, and to Henry Giroux and Shirley Steinberg for longtime support of my work.

2. On postmodern theory, see Best and Kellner 1991, 1997, and 2001.

3. Coined by Howe and Strauss (1993), the term, "13th generation," refers to the thirteenth generation of American citizens, born in the 1960s. As coincidence would have it, theirs is an unlucky number. "Generation X," popularized by Douglas Coupland (1991), signifies blankness and confusion, and is taken from a British boomer rock band. Mike Males (1996) used the term, "the scapegoat generation," for those youth who are blamed for the social ills which were in large part produced by older generations. Many people, however, do not feel part of either the boomer or post-boomer generation, and are somewhere in between, hence they are baptized "tweeners" (*USA Today*, March 22, 1996). Technically, by their date of birth, they belong to the boomers, but in their cynical and pessimistic mindset, they are much closer to the post-boomers.

4. Exceptions to the negative image of the cynical, apolitical slacker stereotype, include the work of Nelson and Cowan (1994), which featured an analysis of the 1990s debt crisis and suggestions for how youth can intervene politically to help others and shape a brighter future for themselves, moving from unplugged to plugging back in; but their "Lead or Leave" foundation has been heavily funded by conservatives, and they have stressed cutting back on the federal deficit through cutting back on social security and welfare programs—precisely the Republican agenda (see the critique in *Extra!*, Vol. 7, No. 2 (March/April 1994), pp. 6–7). See also Males (1996), who exploded the myth that contemporary youth are themselves responsible for exploding violence, crime, teen pregnancies, and social disorder; and for recent studies and critiques of the escalating attacks on youth, see Giroux 2000 and 2003.

5. A *Newsweek* cover story on "The Myth of Generation X" already by 1994 claimed that "a recent MTV poll found that only one in 10 young people would ever let the phrase 'Generation X' cross their lips" and cited several who rejected the label (*Newsweek*, June 6, 1994, p. 64).

6. See the vast number of books on the millennials listed on Amazon at http://www.amazon.com/s/ref=nb_sb_noss_1/186-8979685-1472818?url=search-alias%3Daps&field-keywords=millennials

7. See Coupland (1991, pp. 181–183), who cited statistics indicating the growing amount of federal wealth and programs directed toward the elderly, and increased tax burdens for younger generations. Third Millennium founder, Jonathan Karl, noted that in 1995, the federal government spent 11 times more on each senior citizen than it did on each child under 18, and warned of generational warfare if the budget deficit and high tax burdens on the young are not dealt with (in *Swing*, September 1996, p. 53f). Obviously, as we note here, the Bush administration has created staggering deficits that will constitute a daunting challenge to future generations.

8. See a video on the *Washington Post* website on June 3, 2013 that explained how "college loan debt has reached a record level just as delinquent payments are surging. The problem could get worse as interest rates are set to double on some student loans on July 1. Wonkblog's Dylan Matthews explains" at http://www.washingtonpost.com/video/thefold/student-debt-hits-record-high-interest-rates-could-double/2013/06/03/d5f1c4f4-cc78-11e2-9f1a-1a7cdee20287_video.html

9. Already by 2003, it was apparent that the Bush-Cheney Gang, with their tax cuts for the wealthy, wars, and high government spending benefiting largely the corporate class, were leading the country to economic ruin. See Elizabeth Bumiller, "Bush's $2.2 Trillion Budget Proposes Record Deficits," *The New York Times* (February 4, 2003). Although the U.S. economy has gone into decline since the 1970s, this skid has hit the young generation the hardest, and they remain the poorest and most exploited. According to the U.S. Bureau of the Census, only 0.3 million Americans over age 65 lacked health insurance in 1990, while 14.8 million between ages 18 to 34 did, as did 8.4 million under age 18 (Howe & Strauss, 1993, p. 108). As Nelson and Cowan (1994) warned, "unless America dramatically shifts our budget priorities over the next 10 to 15 years to create new policies that are fair to all generations, we will confront an unprecedented battle between the baby boomers and everyone born after 1960" (p. 58). The U.S. Bureau of the Census found that childhood poverty rates rose from 15 percent in 1970 to over 20 percent in 1990, as poverty rates for the elderly plummeted from 25 percent to 12 percent during the same period (Howe and Strauss, 1993, p. 35). In the United States today, more than one out of every five people under the age of 18 lives in poverty, a number a Tufts University study predicts will rise to more than one out of four by 2021 (Nelson & Cowan, 1994, p. 40). The U.S. Bureau of Labor Statistics reported that in 1960, only 20 percent of mothers with children under the age of 6 worked, a number that tripled by 1990. For mothers with children ages 6–17, these numbers rose from 43 to 76 percent during the same years (Howe & Strauss, 1993, p. 58). Children born in 1968 faced three times the risk of parental breakup as children born in 1948, and fewer than half of busters reach their mid-teens with two once-married biological parents (Howe & Strauss, 1993, pp. 59, 61). For other relevant statistics found in earlier literature, see Howe and Strauss, 1993; Nelson and Cowan, 1994; Holtz, 1995; and Giroux, 2003 who traced out the growing impoverishment of youth and expanding class divisions in the Bush-Cheney administration, divisions that expanded year by year.

10. See the analyses and statistics on these issues in Howe and Strauss, 1993; Holtz, 1995; Hammer, 2002; and Giroux, 2003.

11. The situation of more youth forced to live with their parents is continuing; see Alan Howe, "Failure to Launch: Adult Children Moving Back Home," *Forbes*, June 6, 2012, at http://www.forbes.com/sites/moneywisewomen/2012/06/06/ failure-to-launch-adult-children-moving-back-home/ (accessed June 14, 2013).
12. By the age of five, boomers had seen little or no TV, compared to the 5,000 hours of viewing by their post-boomer children (Howe and Strauss, 1993). According to some statistics, "the average 14 year old watches on average three hours of television a day, and does one hour of homework" (Howe and Strauss, 1993).
13. For a variety of studies of contemporary youth culture, see the works collected in Epstein, 1998.
14. See Kahn and Kellner, 2008b. Some good sites that exhibit youth voices, participation, and response include http:// www.moveon.org; http://www.raisethefist.com; http://www.tao.com; and the youth blog site at http://www.bloghop. com/topics.htm?numblogs=14566&cacheid=1044419966.3569

References

Best, S., & Kellner, D. (1991). *Postmodern theory: Critical interrogations*. London, UK: Macmillan and Guilford Press.
Best, S., & Kellner, D. (1997). *The postmodern turn*. New York, NY: Guilford Press.
Best, S., & Kellner, D. (2001). *The postmodern adventure: Science, technology, and cultural studies at the third millennium*. New York, NY: Guilford Press.
Bloom, A. (1987). *The closing of the American mind: How higher education has failed democracy and impoverished the souls of today's students*. New York, NY: Simon and Schuster.
Bumiller, E. (2003, February 4). Bush's $2.2 trillion budget proposes record deficits. *The New York Times*.
Carr, N. (2011). *The shallows: What the Internet is doing to our brains*. New York, NY: Norton.
Coupland, D. (1991). *Generation X: Tales for an accelerated culture*. New York, NY: St. Martin's Press.
Epstein, J. S., (Ed.). (1998). *Youth culture: Identity in a postmodern world*. Malden, MA: Blackwell.
Giroux, H. (2000). *Stealing innocence: Youth, corporate power, and the politics of culture*. New York, NY: Saint Martin's Press.
Giroux, H. (2003). *The abandoned generation: Democracy beyond the culture of fear*. New York, NY: Palgrave Macmillan.
Hammer, R. (2002). *Antifeminism and family terrorism*. Lanham, MD: Rowman & Littlefield.
Holtz, G. T. (1995). *Welcome to the jungle: The why behind 'Generation X.'* New York, NY: St. Martin's Press.
Howe, A. (2012, June 6). Failure to launch: Adult children moving back home. *Forbes*. Retrieved from http://www.forbes.com/sites/moneywisewomen/2012/06/06/failure-to-launch-adult-children-moving-back-home/
Howe, N., & Strauss, W. (1993). *13th generation: America's 13th generation, born 1961–1981*. New York, NY: Vintage.
Howe, N., & Strauss, W. (2000). *Millennials rising: The next great generation*. New York, NY: Vintage.
Kahn, R., & Kellner, D. (2006). Reconstructing technoliteracy: A multiple literacies approach. In J. R. Dakers (Ed.), *Defining technological literacy* (pp. 253–274). New York, NY: Palgrave Macmillan.
Kahn, R., & Kellner, D. (2008a). Technopolitics, blogs, and emergent media ecologies: A critical/reconstructive approach. In B. Hawk, D. M. Rider, & O. Oviedo (Eds.), *Small tech: The culture of digital tools* (pp. 22–37). Minneapolis, MN: University of Minnesota Press.
Kahn, R., & Kellner, D. (2008b). Youth culture. In W. Donsbach (Ed.), *The international encyclopedia of communication* (pp. 53–71). Malden, MA.: Blackwell.
Kellner, D. (2002). Technological revolution, multiple literacies, and the restructuring of education. In I. Snyder (Ed.), *Silicon literacies* (pp. 154–169). London, UK: Routledge.
Kellner, D. (2003). *From September 11 to terror war: The dangers of the Bush legacy*. Lanham, MD.: Rowman & Littlefield.
Kellner, D. (2009). Barack Obama and celebrity spectacle. *International Journal of Communication, 3* (2009), 1–20. Retrieved from http://ijoc.org/ojs/index.php/ijoc/article/view/559/350
Kellner, D. (2012). *Media spectacle and insurrection, 2011: From the Arab uprisings to Occupy everywhere*. London, UK: Continuum.
Males, M. (1996). *The scapegoat generation*. Boston, MA: Common Courage Press.
The myth of Generation X. (1994, June 6). *Newsweek*, 64.
Nelson, R., & Cowan, J. (1994). *Revolution X: A survival guide for our generation*. New York, NY: Penguin Books.
Scahill, J. (2013). *Dirty wars: The world is a battlefield*. New York, NY: Nation Books.
Turkle, S. (1995). *Life on the screen: Identity in the age of the Internet*. New York: Simong & Schuster.
Turkle, S. (2011). *Alone together: Why we expect more from technology and less from each other*. New York, NY: Basic Books.

CHAPTER 2

Theorizing Young Lives
Biography, Society, and Time

Kate Tilleczek

The current complication of structural inequalities, and of the forms of self-narration through which they are actively contested and reproduced, clearly requires more sophisticated and empirically grounded accounts …. If we are to do justice to what is at stake in young people's lives, we have to find new ways of integrating empirically grounded and dialogical strategies of youth research within interdisciplinary and theoretically sophisticated frameworks of comparative analysis. (Cohen & Ainley, 2000, p. 242)

The three figures of excess which we have employed to characterize supermodernity—overabundance of events, spatial overabundance, the individualization of references—make it possible to grasp the idea of supermodernity without ignoring its complexities and contradictions, but also without treating it as the uncrossable horizon of a lost modernity with which nothing remains to be done. (Auge, 1995, pp. 40–41)

Introduction

Young people live in the world as experiential beings of the present and past. They also live in possible futures as they move toward becoming adults. In both cases, they seek to belong in and to social institutions and relationships. To capture the complexity of young lives requires theoretically sophisticated modes of interpretation. Over the centuries, artists from the Italian Baroque (such as Caravaggio's *Youth Bitten by a Green Lizard* (1593)), from German Expressionism (such as Munch's *Puberty* (1984)), and from contemporary portraiture (such as Gartner's (2007) *Girl With Siamese Twins*) have attempted to portray the tensions inherent in young lives; in being young and becoming adult while searching for belonging. I have similarly worked to find ways to witness and tell the tales of abundance and tension of youth. In so doing, I have become convinced of the importance of the interconnections of biography (being), society (belonging), and time (becoming) that are inherent in compelling theories and social studies of young lives.

The invitation to submit this chapter derived from an interest in my book, *Approaching Youth Studies: Being, Becoming, and Belonging* (Tilleczek, 2011). Something about the authenticity of the concepts of being, becoming, and belonging caught the attention of the editors. They invited further explication of the theoretical framework I was developing (complex cultural nesting) and in which I had embedded these concepts as fundamental social processes for youth. I had so far simplified my writing about my complex cultural nesting theory, and was pleased to have the space to provide further detail. This more detailed description comes from the vantage point of being embedded in the disciplines of sociology, youth studies, cultural psychology, and human development, and working methodologically in qualitative narrative, visual, and decolonized methods.

I join a long line of scholars and commentators such as C. Wright Mills and Dorothy Smith who have convinced us of the need to find ways to fully interpret both biography and society if we are to proceed with full social analyses. I argue that youth studies seems to require such a re-invocation of a sociological imagination as expressed by Mills: "The sociological imagination enables us to grasp history and biography and the relations between the two in society. That is its task and promise. To recognize this task and promise is the mark of the classic social analyst" (Mills, 1959, p. 6). How do we integrate such classic social analysis into contemporary youth studies to best explicate young lives in time and place? I argue that we must return to dimensions of classic scholarship while providing a more singular focus on young lives so as to witness and "grasp what is going on in the world and to understand what is happening in themselves [*sic*] as minute points of intersection of biography and history within society" (Mills, 1959, p. 7). In this chapter, I therefore begin to recover such theoretical insights for our contemporary work in critical youth studies. In so doing, I am reminded of Mills's conviction for avoiding abstracted empiricism and grand theorizing, and the admonition to "avoid any rigid set of procedures" (Mills, 1959, p. 120) but rather to engage theory as a way of "self conscious thinking" (p. 121). In this case, I am theorizing young lives as the parameter and range of phenomenon. Young lives are lived in historical and societal space so that the parameters widen and some "intellectual craftsmanship" (Mills, 1959, p. 121) is required as part of the process of doing social science *with*, *for*, and *by* youth.

Theorizing Young Lives

> We now live in a culture where 'being young' is paradoxical: while a majority of adults wish to remain forever young, we do not necessarily treat actual young people with respect. Many adults want to preserve the biological aspects of youth (that is, with plastic surgery to look young); they seek lifestyles of freedom from responsibility at the same time that they hold the balance of power in society. Moreover, adults have often chastised youth for being irresponsible and 'young' while they co-opt the posture for themselves. (Tilleczek, 2011, p. 20)

During the time in which I was writing this chapter, I attended the 2013 *Youth Studies Conference* in Glasgow, Scotland. The conference was an important moment in the discipline, as it was hosted by the editor and publisher as a celebration of the 15-year anniversary of the *Journal of Youth Studies*. This has been an important publication venue for scholars across disciplines who investigate the lives and times of young people. The plenary sessions, roundtable discussions, and paper presentations were varied and rich. In a number of sessions, I was intrigued by the explication of the past, present, and future of the field of youth studies. Somewhere along the history of the discipline, the field of youth studies had come to be dichotomized by some commentators and divided into two investigative camps: youth cultures and youth transitions. These camps were described as roughly equivalent to divides in ways of knowing young lives as either structural quantities (the study of transitions over time with statistical methods to track changes), or cultural qualities (the study of cultures and subjectivities as interpretive understanding). The latter sets its focus on being and the former sets its sights on becoming. I was struck by the oversimplification that this dichotomy represents, and the ways in which the tensions and abundant character of young lives and modern society are buried within it. While there was a good deal of lip service paid in the roundtable discussions to an "emerging" importance for youth studies of the concept of "belonging," there was little to no unpacking of the theoretical or methodological depth of what the concept could mean or how to more fully examine it. My earlier work demonstrated what scholars such as Cohen, Willis, Griffin, and Furlong had also been recognizing; namely, that these divides have been well bridged through forms of humanities-infused praxis (Tilleczek & Kinlock, 2013) that include such emergent methods in social science as theatre, narrative, digital story, poetry, and music brought together with philosophical and historical analyses of modernity's most crucial folds.

Many papers and conversations at the *Youth Studies Conference* signalled to me a need to more purposefully return youth studies to classical theoretical roots; to map out more fully some nuanced theoretical contours of the field. It was in this context that I began to re-examine and critique the main arguments and elements of my earlier theoretical framework for understanding both cultures and transitions of youth (complex cultural nesting) as one able to address young lives over time and place. The significant early analysis provided by C. Wright Mills is a call to a social studies grounded in an "intellectual journey" that poses three questions to invoke a sociological imagination required for critical youth studies. First, he insisted that we examine and know the "structure of society as a whole." In this is our knowledge of "essential components" and their interrelations. We must also examine the "meaning of particular features of society to discern what it means for the longevity of society" (Mills, 1959, p. 4). I provide the example of my current work on the social and educational impacts of modern technology on young lives over time and place. I have argued elsewhere (Tilleczek & Srigley, 2012, 2013) that the modern, technological imperative as positioned in modernity is a crucial aspect of knowing young lives. The market, human relational, and educational aspects of society are technological in character, and youth are inheriting and managing technology in myriad ways and on a day-to-day basis. This five-year study of young lives in digital culture examines technology as a form of ruling societal structure within which young people make meanings and practices as it impacts their lives. Much has been written about elements of consumption, fear, individualism, rationality, and the loss of a spirited eros in modern technological cultures (Srigley, 2011), and we analyze these biographical and social shifts in tandem, informed by philosophy and social science. Forms of growing social inequality are also examined as an injurious social context for youth, and examined as both a consequence of the modern technological project and as a form of social reproduction of inequality by social class, gender, and place (Tilleczek, 2012a).

Within this and other projects we also attend to Mills's second imperative question and endeavour to detail the ways in which technological modernity is placed in social and historical context, as both the same as and different from other forms of technology of the past. Here we invoke McLuhan, Baudrillard, Morozov (and others) to further inform our social and historical sketch of the emergence and meaning of modern technology. Most work currently written about technology provides little to no historical analysis, and that written about young people and technology has yet to heed the critical work of sociologists, historians, and philosophers who are attempting to do so. Finally, we also engage Mills's third question relating to understanding the "varieties of men and women now prevailing in this society and time" (Mills, 1959, p. 7) by also examining the everyday lives of young men and women across countries, cultures, and contexts. Here we investigate clues as to the emerging forms that young lives are taking, including an analysis of cyborgian and vampirism aspects of modern technology (Tilleczek & Srigley, 2012). We investigate forms of identity, reproduction, and resistance brought about by modern technology and digital media to examine the paradoxical character of technology that scholars and young people are making plain to us. For instance, the tensions between liberation and repression brought about by modern technological imperatives form one aspect of our investigation and analysis. The utopian, religious, and totalitarian character of modern technological society forms another.

When brought together in this form, the sociological imagination is embedded in interdisciplinary theories which aim to examine many levels of societal influence. The complex cultural nesting approach (Tilleczek, 2011) provides a beginning interpretive framework intended to illustrate how young people and those closest to them are inseparable from these societal structures and shifts. It extends Bronfenbrenner's (1979) work that described levels at which influences and negotiations occur. The concentric systems—chronosystem, exosystem, macrosystem, mesosystem, and microsystem—have come to be well known to those who describe contexts of youth development in which roles and settings constantly change and "every transition is both a consequence and an instigator of developmental processes" (Bronfenbrenner, 1979, p. 27). However, the complex cultural nesting approach attempts an important sociological move beyond general description of levels of influence. This is accomplished by reading and critiquing the work of others who offer direction for theorizing young lives, such as Lerner's (2002) Developmental Contextual model, Elder's (1997) Life Course model, Ungar's (2012) Social Ecology of Resilience model, the socioeconomic gradient and income inequality models (Keating & Hertzman, 1999; Wilkinson & Pickett, 2009), and the sociological insights of Smith (1987, 2002) and Mills (1959). The concept of a nest comes to be used in two ways: as referring to the need for homey comfort to evoke a sense of belonging; and by showing that contexts stack (are nested within one another), each offering different but simultaneous experiences.

These contexts were elegantly defined by Bronfenbrenner (1979), who saw the *microsystem* as a pattern of activities, roles, and interpersonal relations that young people experience in a given setting with particular physical and material characteristics. A young person is involved in several different microsystems at once in which self, identity, and being form the heart of day-to-day human interaction and social relationships. To this I add the centrality of biography, which is socially written and rewritten in the present every day. The *mesosystem* was seen as "a system of microsystems" (Bronfenbrenner, 1979, p. 25) in which relations have indirect or direct bearing on young people's lives. They hold the interrelations among people in two or more settings in which we *actively* participate—a theoretically important point in youth studies since it allows for analyses of negotiation, resistance, and re-enactment. To this I add the conceptual liminality of the mesosystem as it exists between cultures and individuals. The in-between system holds experience and embodiment of intersections such as those of social class, poverty, ethnicity, identity, and age that are played out. The *ecosystem* and *macrosystem* refer to a host of opportunities, constraints, patterns, consistencies, and inconsistencies at the level of society, including the enacting of politics, governance, laws, and ideologies. Processes of globalization, income inequality, technological imperatives, recession, and societal views about young people are forged here. To this I add the profound and expansive anthropological, sociological literature concerning the constitution and negotiation of society and culture. The *chronosystem*—the timing and patterning of lives—provides focus to the analyses of history and time, in all of their currently debated forms.

The ecological models of youth as employed by Bronfenbrenner and others involved the "scientific study of progressive, mutual accommodations between an active, growing human being and the changing properties of the immediate settings" (Bronfenbrenner, 1979, p. 21). Sociological theory has much to contribute by way of understanding social relationships and social relations. The young person is always a social young person, and youth studies must further examine what it means to understand complex nested social relations for young lives over time in shifting global and/or local contexts. Importantly, the notions of bi-directionality and interrelationships among people and systems are of particular relevance. Development and time are not easily determined linear pathways, and time and growth are conceived as non-linear and dynamic (Furlong et al., 2003; Tilleczek, 2012b; Tilleczek et al., 2011) and nested within complex modern and super-modern cultures in which emerging places and non-places require interpretation (Auge, 1995).

We can determine how and why youth live out their complex biographies (Pais, 2003) and avoid characterizing the subaltern as negative without examining the fluidity in biography (Tilleczek,

2012; Ungar, 2012). Such approaches illuminate the liminality of modern young lives and the social, political, and historical contexts that organize them. When we understand young lives in this nuanced way, our methods of work could be more collaborative *with*, *for*, and *by* youth, and analysis could be more grounded in their lives and biographies. Indeed, biography (being), time (becoming), and society (belonging) become fundamental concepts to guide investigation and analyses. Each is further described in the following sections.

Biography and Being

A piece of fiction is a model of the world, but not of the whole world. It focuses on human intentions and plans. That is why it has a narrative structure of actions and of incidents that occur as a result of those actions. It tells of the vicissitudes of our lives, of the emotions we experience, of our selves and our relationships as we pursue our projects. We humans are intensely social and—because our own motives are often mixed and because others can be difficult to know—our attempts to understand ourselves and others are always incomplete. Fiction is a means by which we can increase our understanding (Oatley, 2011, p. ix).

The tale, to be authentic, must always comprehend both the temporal and the timeless elements of reality as they reveal themselves in the cosmic, human and divine realms. (Embry, 2008, p. 142)

Invoking a sociological imagination for youth studies is to examine both biography and society. Biography arises in the work of those devoted to knowing the individual (alone or in social relations with others) through experience, everyday lives, and being. Youth are *being* themselves in their everyday lives in which there are tensions between being and becoming, living in the moment of time and living outside or across this time and into the future. They forge identities through daily negotiations and seek to be valued for who they are today and to find places to simply be and belong. And, young people are also in a state of *becoming* young adults and moving across and through social institutions with physical, emotional, and cognitive development in phases of change and stability in effect. Symbolic integrationists such as Goffman and Mead recognized and theorized these tensions in being and becoming. In attending to the theatre of self in everyday life, and in explicating a philosophy of this present, they continue to offer analytical direction to youth studies.

When one recalls his boyhood days he cannot get into them as he then was, without their relationship to what he has become; and if he could, that is, if he could reproduce the experience as it then took place, he could not use it, for this would involve his not being in the present within which that use must take place. A string of presents conceivably existing as presents would not constitute a past. (Mead, 1959, p. 30)

For Goffman and others, we best capture this tension and presence through the performance of self and character, through self-narration and the biographical story of lives over time. Biography plays a crucial role as a social science of the present, such that biography and narrative portray "accounts which contain transformation (change over time), some kind of 'action' and characters, all of which are brought together within an overall 'plot'—are a central means with which people connect together past and present, self and other" (Lawler, 2002, p. 242). We can trace the powerful use of biography and narrative from oral storytelling practices of indigenous cultures, from literature, and from psychoanalysis. Narrative analysis not only provides a record of what happened, but a manner in which we interpret and reinterpret being and experience. It is the best way to understand 'lived time' (Bruner, 2004, p. 692) and to explore the ways that "social actors interpret the world, and their place within it" (Lawler, 2002, p. 242). Not only does a narrative reveal much about the teller, but it provides insight into the social world that influences individual lives. Groups of narratives can also be analyzed for similarities and differences, while individual narratives are examined for continuities and discontinuities over time. It is a specific type of analysis used to aid in the exploration of ways that "social actors inter-pret the world, and their place within it" (Lawler, 2002, p. 242).

In attending to the biography and being of youth, we form a window of understanding young lives as stories that portray complex, fluid, and flexible characters over time and place. Understanding who moves in and out of troubling social situations, and why and how they do so over time is possible and forms interesting analysis. The use of narrative and biography in youth studies opens the field to deeper description of the abundance of experience and identity processes by providing ways to speak with young people who express experiences and voices. Unlike statistical, thematic, or discourse analysis, narrative analysis attempts to hold experiences in context and without fragmenting, fracture, or reduc-tion (Tilleczek, 2011). Digital storytelling, portraiture, story, and film can unify written and visual means of biography. The complexity of being in the present and its tension with becoming in the future is illustrated in biographical renderings. Storytelling is also a powerful means by which to connect with our social, scientific, and public audiences.

One example of the importance of a theoretical consideration of being and biography is found in the treatment of young lives by educational psychology. These fields of study could well have yielded portraits of young lives as complex, abundant, and agentic (as in the work of Erik Erikson or Glen Elder). However, the opposite effect has taken place, as serious consideration of the abundance of being has been negated in public education. In schools, the guidance from early psychoanalytic and counseling forms of biography and narration was overturned in favour of supremacy for stan-dard and statistical ways of knowing youth. As such, the effects of the labelling and pathologizing of the young has taken hold. The focus of the understanding of being is turned towards rational and bureaucratic forms, ideas, and practices. The tensions we know to theoretically exist between being and becoming and the complexity of living is lost. In its place we find being to be understood as a hollowed-out and simplified form of preparation for becoming. If young people are deemed to be incapable now of meeting a standardized and statistical form of self, they are then also deemed incapable of becoming adults. These faulty measures and interpretations of being both devalue who they are and also wrongly predict them to be failures at living and learning in the future. Both being and becoming are bastardized theoretical and analytical forms in this sense. If educational psychol-ogy has been so wrong in this respect, how will we do better in critical youth studies?

Time and Becoming

> The world of supermodernity does not exactly match the one in which we believe we live, for we live in a world that we have not yet learned to look at. (Auge, 1995, pp. 35–36)

Just as being requires biography for explication, so, too, does becoming require time for analysis. The concept of development as arising in the fields of human development and youth psychology is impor-tant to the discussion, given the primacy of the concept for the treatment of young people. Psychother-apy has shown that metaphors of human change and development range from linear to evolutionary to complex metamorphosis and autopoiesis (Mahoney, 1991). The most used theories of change and time in youth development have generally been tied to Piaget's structural linearity. But non-linear notions of development understand becoming in a different way that investigates how and why biographies move across time as youth become adults (Mahoney, 1991; Pais, 2003; Tilleczek, 2012a). Non-linear development places a focus of study on the tensions between stability and/or change and sameness and/or difference over time. Young lives are therefore characterized by any number of pathways that intersect along levels of social context and influence. Schools do not stand alone, but are nested in social and political contexts of power, and hold numerous contradictions (Bruner, 1996). In the best of this work, problems are not simply individualized, but seen as distributed in social contexts in which young people can act and resist as well as conform. Moreover, analysis of time requires its own historical component insofar as human perception and reactions to time have altered the ways in which everyday lives are lived. "This need to give meaning to the present, if not the past, is the price we pay for the overabundance of events corresponding to a situation we could call 'supermodern' to express its essential quality: excess" (Auge, 1995, p. 29).

Auge argued that our current existence in supermodernity is characterized by excess. Excess is seen in an acceleration of history such that we must access too many events for which we need to make meaning. Time and space are bent in a false sense of familiarity with that which we have not really seen or experienced.

> From the viewpoint of supermodernity the difficulty in thinking about time stems from the overabundance of events in the contemporary world not from the collapse of the idea of progress…; the theme of imminent history, or history snapping at our heels (almost imminent in each of our day to day existences) seems like the premiss [sic] of the meaning or non-meaning of history. (Auge, 1995, p. 30)

The Internet and globalization create societal forms of life, place and non-places such as those in-between here and there. Airports, bank machines, supermarkets, and escalators are examples provided by Auge to which I add the ubiquitous screen presence of computers and phones in the schooling, work, and leisure of young lives. If perceptions of time and space and/or place are in constant change, and these concepts are debated within and across disciplines, critical youth studies must set to the kinds of earlier work of Lee (1998) and others who investigated the problems occurring when

> sociological theory displays a tendency to depict the social world in terms of completed 'beings' … where extant sociologies of childhood have brought children into the 'finished' world of sociological theory, [we must use] childhood's ontological ambiguity to open the door onto an unfinished social world. (Lee, 1998, p. 458)

And, while entering and investigating the tensions between being and belonging (biography and time) in critical youth studies, we require an "ethics of motion" (Lee, 1998, p. 472) that must also recognize and analyze the meaning of interrogating these tensions for (and about) the fundamental human need of youth to belong to and in society and social relations.

Society and Belonging

> *I thought how unpleasant it is to be locked out; and I thought how it is worse, perhaps, to be locked in ….*
> One seemed alone in an inscrutable society. (Virginia Woolf, 1929, p. 31)

> It can be seen from the classical Greek theater, how the personal involvement in certain kinds of narratives can help members of an audience understand the problematic in social life and integrate the understandings with existing models of self and other (Oatley, 1999, p. 110).

Moving an analysis of both biography and time into simultaneous analyses of society is a further challenge levelled by Mills. Notwithstanding Auge's claim that we must continue to find ways and spaces for looking, Dorothy Smith's institutional ethnography has been one way to move us closer to addressing Mills's challenge, particularly if we heed the lessons in her sociological approach for youth studies. Smith's work, and that of her colleagues, provides some way forward to an embedded analysis of biography and time in society. In keeping with Mills's further insistence on avoiding dogma and over-proscribed theory and method in our work, I was pleased to read Smith's insistence that

> institutional ethnography not become a sect, a group of insiders who know how to talk and write it, and insist on a kind of orthodoxy in its practice which puts in hazard its fundamental commitment to inquiry and discovery. Institutional ethnography is distinctive among sociologies in its commitment to *discovering* "how things are actually put together," "how it works." The colloquialisms leave what

"things" are or what "it" is undefined but establish the ideas of encountering the actualities of people's everyday lives, of research that discovers the social as the ongoing coordinating of people's activities, and of the researcher as being changed in the dialogic of research. (Smith, 2006, pp. 1–2)

We therefore have a reasonable place to start the debate in critical youth studies around this sort of analysis as it applies to the lives and times of young people.

Institutional ethnography (Smith, 1987, 2002, 2006) is "an inquiry intended to disclose how activities are organized and how they are articulated to the social relations of the larger social and economic process" (Smith, 1987, p. 151). The important point for our work is the ability of these methods to provide a way of examining the social process by which social inequalities are made problematic and/or resisted (Foley & Valenzuela, 2005; Madison, 2005) as researchers co-locate in the daily lives of youth to discern meaning in conjunction with participants (Campbell & Gregor, 2002; DeVault & McCoy, 2002). I have been able to accomplish such analyses of society through also invoking narrative methodologies of the life-course perspective (Elder, 1997) and life-history narrative interviews (Bruner, 2004; Chase, 2005; Fontana & Frey, 2005; Lawler, 2002) as authentic conversations that elicit retrospective and prospective data. In keeping with a complex cultural nesting approach, this work is designed to examine bi-directional, nested, non-linear and dynamic human and intuitional relationships (Furlong et al., 2003; Tilleczek, 2011; Tilleczek & Ferguson, 2013). Youth life stories also generate "hope and possibility" narratives (Smyth & Hattam, 2001, p. 412) for belonging, and explicate the range of challenges in young lives over time. Most critically at present are those arising in new forms of social inequality, youth marginality, the demise of public education, and the paradox of the technological project in the lives of youth. In each case, young people are in real danger of consistently being pushed out of social relations, social value and social centrality. Social inequalities impact the development of young people and play on the vulnerabilities of the most disadvantaged while rapidly undermining the development of human potential (Woodhead, Dornan, & Murray, 2013).

This social process of marginalization is the topic of investigation and analysis of a recent book (Tilleczek & Ferguson, 2013) in which scholars, young people, youth artists, and practitioners collectively investigate marginalization as the counter-occurrence to belonging in modern society. Andy Furlong's (2013) engagement in analysis of the social and cultural dimensions of exclusion demonstrated how the socio-economic and ethnic exclusion of youth is an embedded feature of modernity. He provided a nuanced conception of the flip side of belonging in that

> if marginalization is about being away from the mainstream, out on the margins of society, exclusion means being more or less cut off from society and in a situation of economic and social isolation. Social exclusion is about being disenfranchisement and about being prevented, through a lack of resources, from being able to participate in the types of activities that are taken for granted by citizens in a given society. (Furlong, 2013, p. 139)

Notwithstanding the crucial work of Mitchell (2013, p. 89), who demonstrated how young, marginal people in both Canada and the southwest Pacific "have things going on"; or that of Smyth (2013), who argued for the ability and propensity to resist and "speak back from the margins" and toward reclamation and belonging; or the work of Boydell (2013) or Tilleczek and Kinlock (2013) on the potential for the arts and humanities-infused work to create new spaces of belonging, the contributors in the book are careful to examine that "inscrutable society" made plain by Virginia Woolf and Dorothy Smith. They also simultaneously maintain a steady focus on the nuance and tension of biography (being) and time (becoming) for contemporary young people. The effect is to offer concrete examples of work and analyses being undertaken by a range of scholars working *for*, *with*, and/or *by* youth in contemporary social sciences, that inform our emerging critical youth studies.

Conclusion

In this chapter, I have developed a cursory response to the call of C. Wright Mills for an intellectual journey in theorizing young lives. The hope embedded in the chapter is that those of us who work in critical youth studies will debate new forms of the sociological imagination as concerned with emerging forms of modernity and biographical narration. We will do so while seeing what is really at stake for young people in emerging forms of societies, in both local and global contexts. I have attempted to demonstrate hinges between biography and being, time and becoming, and society and belonging. These three fundamental social processes of young lives help to organize our investigations and analyses. The hope is that we collectively and more purposefully design and discuss our work as connecting everyday experiences and the folds of modernity in historical context. I have provided direction from a number of scholars who are doing so, and from whom we can learn in our submission of this intellectual journey to critical youth studies.

With the knowledge in place that theorizing young lives is "like the language of the country you live in: it is nothing to brag about that you can speak it, but it is a disgrace and an inconvenience if you cannot" (Mills, 1959, p. 121), I endeavour to open up a way of speaking that informs my work in understanding the folds of modernity and technology in young lives. Knowing also that we should not "allow the public issues as they are officially formulated ... to determine the problems we took up for study" (Mills, 1959, p. 17), I am beginning to embrace the varieties of critique of technology and modernity, and provide space for young people to similarly interrogate difficult lines of questioning. The call-and-response of critical youth studies asks that we take a critical and historical stance arising from our own scholarship across disciplines. In so doing, the path leads towards the making of the private troubles of young lives into public conversations and political debates that work towards the advantage of youth as we invoke a scholarship *with*, *for*, and *by* them.

> Know that many personal troubles cannot be solved merely as troubles, but must be understood in terms of public issues—and in terms of the problems of history-making. Know that the human meaning of public issues must be revealed by relating them to personal troubles—and to the problems of the individual life. Know that the problems of social science, when adequately formulated, must include both troubles and issues, both biography and history, and the range of their intricate relations. Within that range the life of the individual and the making of societies occur; and within that range the sociological imagination has its chance to make a difference in the quality of human life in our time. (Mills, 1959, pp. 7–17)

References

Apple, M., & Buras, K. (2006). *The subaltern speak*. London, UK: Routledge.

Auge, M. (1995). *Non-places: Introduction to an anthropology of supermodernity*. London, UK: Verso Press.

Boydell, K. (2103) Using visual arts to enhance mental health literacy. In K. Tilleczek & H. B. Ferguson (Eds.), *Youth, education, and marginality: Local and global expressions* (pp. 229–239). Waterloo, Canada: Wilfrid Laurier University Press.

Bronfenbrenner, U. (1979). *The ecology of human development*. Cambridge, MA: Harvard University Press.

Bruner, J. (1986). *Actual minds, possible worlds*. Cambridge, MA: Harvard University Press.

Bruner, J. (1996). *The culture of education*. Cambridge, MA: Harvard University Press.

Bruner, J. (2004). Life as narrative. *Social Research, 71*(3), 691–710.

Campbell, M. L., & Gregor, F. M. (2002). *Mapping social relations: A primer in doing institutional ethnography*. Aurora, Canada: Garamond Press.

Chase, S. (2005). Narrative inquiry. In N. K. Denzin & Y. S. Lincoln (Eds.), *The handbook of qualitative research* (3rd ed., pp. 651–680). London, UK: Sage.

Cohen, P. & Ainley, P. (2000) In the country of the blind: Youth studies and cultural studies in Britain. In Jane Pickford (Ed.) *Youth justice: Theory and Practice* (227–246). London: Cavendish Publishing.

Devault, M. L., & McCoy, L. (2002). Institutional ethnography. In J. Gubrium & J. Holstein (Eds.), *Handbook of interview research* (pp. 751–775). Thousand Oaks, CA: Sage.

Elder, G. H. Jr. (1997). The life course and human development. In W. Damon & R. M. Lerner, (Eds.), *Handbook of child psychology* (pp. 939–991). New York, NY: Wiley.

Embry, C. R. (2008). *The philosopher and the storyteller: Eric Voegelin and twentieth century literature*. Columbia, MO: University of Missouri Press.

Erikson, E. H. (1958). *Young man Luther: A study in psychoanalysis and history*. New York, NY: W. W. Norton.

Foley, D., & Valenzuela, A. (2005). Critical ethnography. In N. K. Denzin & Y. S. Lincoln (Eds.), *The handbook of qualitative research* (3rd ed., pp. 217–234). London, UK: Sage.

Fontana, A., & Frey, J. H. (2005). The interview. In N. K. Denzin & Y. S. Lincoln (Eds.), *The handbook of qualitative research* (3rd ed., pp. 695–728). London, UK: Sage.

Furlong, A. (2012). *Youth studies*. London, UK: Routledge.

Furlong, A. (2013). Marginalized youth in education: Social and cultural dimensions of exclusion in Canada and the United Kingdom. In K. Tilleczek & B. Ferguson (Eds.), *Youth, education and marginality: Local and global expressions* (pp. 137–151). Waterloo, Ontario: Wilfred Laurier University Press.

Furlong, A. & Cartmel, F. (2007). *Young people and social change*. Buckingham, UK: Open University Press.

Furlong, A., Cartmel, F., Biggart, A., Sweeting, H., West, P., et al. (2003). *Youth transitions: Patterns of vulnerability and processes of social inclusion*. Edinburgh, Scotland: SESR (Scottish Executive Social Research).

Graham, I. D., Logan, J., Harrison, M. B., Straus, S. E., Tetroe, J., Caswell, W., & Robinson, N. (2006). Lost in knowledge translation: Time for a map? *Journal of Continuing Education in the Health Professions, 26*(1), 13–24.

Keating, D. P., & Hertzman, C. (Eds.). (1999). *Developmental health and the wealth of nations: Social, biological, and educational dynamics*. New York, NY: Guilford Press.

Lawler, S. (2002). Narrative in social research. In T. May (Ed.), *Qualitative research in action* (pp. 242–258). Thousand Oaks, CA: Sage.

Lee, N. (1998). Towards an immature sociology. *Sociological Review, 46*(3), 458–481.

Lerner, R. M. (Ed.). (2002). *Concepts and theories of human development*. Mahwah, NJ: Erlbaum.

Levin, B. (2011). Achieving equity through innovation: A Canada–U.S. dialogue. *Education Canada, 51*(5), 19–25.

Madison, D. S. (2005). Critical ethnography as street performance. In N. K. Denzin & Y. S. Lincoln (Eds.), *The handbook of qualitative research* (3rd ed., pp. 537–546). London, UK: Sage.

Mahoney, M. (1991). *Human change processes: The scientific foundations of psychotherapy*. New York, NY: Basic Books.

Mead, G. H. (1959). *The philosophy of the present*. Chicago, IL: University of Chicago Press.

Mills, C. W. (1959). *The sociological imagination*. New York, NY: Oxford University Press.

Mitchell, J. (2013). Marginal spaces, disparate places: Educational and youth practices in a globalized world. In K. Tilleczek & B. Ferguson (Eds.), *Youth, education and marginality: Local and global expressions* (pp. 75–90). Waterloo, Ontario: Wilfred Laurier University Press.

Oatley, K. (2011). *Such stuff as dreams: The psychology of fiction*. New York: John Wiley & Sons.

Oatley, K. (1999). Why fiction may be twice as true as fact: Fiction as cognitive and emotional simulation. *Review of General Psychology, 3*(2), 101–117.

Pais, J. (2003). The multiple faces of the future in the labyrinth of life. *Journal of Youth Studies, 6*(2), 115–126.

Smith, D. E. (1987). *The everyday world as problematic: A feminist sociology*. Toronto, Canada: University of Toronto Press.

Smith, D. E. (2002). Institutional ethnography. In T. May (Ed.), *Qualitative research in action* (pp. 17–52). London, UK: Sage.

Smith, D. E. (2006). *Institutional ethnography as practice*. Toronto, Canada: Rowman and Littlefield.

Smyth, J. (2013). Young people speaking back from the margins. In K. Tilleczek & H. B. Ferguson (Eds.), *Youth, education, and marginality: Local and global expressions* (pp. 43–58). Waterloo, Canada: Wilfrid Laurier University Press

Smyth, J., & Hattam, R. J. (2001). 'Voiced' research as a sociology for understanding 'dropping out' of school. *British Journal of Sociology of Education, 22*(3), 401–415.

Srigley, R. (2011). *Albert Camus's critique of modernity*. Missouri: University of Missouri Press.

Tilleczek, K. (2011). *Approaching youth studies: Being, becoming, and belonging*. Toronto, Canada: Oxford University Press.

Tilleczek, K. (2012a). *Youth, digital media and social inequality*. Paper presented at the International Sociological Association Forum on Sociology. Session: The New Frontiers of the Digital Divide: Technological Inequalities and Social Justice. Buenos Aires, Argentina.

Tilleczek, K. (2012b). Policy activism *with* and *for* youth transitions through public education. *Journal of Educational Administration and History.* 44(3), 253–267.

Tilleczek, K., Campbell, V., & Rodd, J. (2012, September). *What in the world are we doing with youth? Interrogating international youth-attuned methodologies*. Paper presented at European Conference on Educational Research. Session: New Methodological Approaches to Research on Education, Childhood and Youth: Methodological Advances, Choices and Dilemmas. Cadiz, Spain.

Tilleczek, K., & Ferguson, B. (2013). *Youth, education and marginality: Local and global expressions*. Waterloo, Ontario, Canada: Wilfred Laurier University Press.

Tilleczek, K., & Kinlock, K. (2013). Humanities infused praxis by, with, and for youth: Esoteric hope. In K. Tilleczek & B. Ferguson (Eds.), *Youth, education and marginality: Local and global expressions* (pp. 12–24). Waterloo, Canada, Wilfred Laurier University Press.

Tilleczek, K., & Srigley, R. (2012, August). *Technology's paradox: Theorizing digital media and young lives*. Paper presented at the International Sociological Association Forum on Sociology. Session: Youth Cultures and New Social Movements in the Context of the Digital Revolution. Buenos Aires, Argentina.

Tilleczek, K., & Srigley, R. (2013, April). *Young lives in techno-utopia: Discerning the Borg in youth studies*. Paper to be presented at *Youth Studies Conference*, University of Glasgow, Scotland.

Tilleczek K., Laflamme, S., Ferguson, B., Roth Edney, D., Cudney, D., Girard, M & Cardoso, S. (2011). *Fresh Starts and False Starts: Young People in Transitions from Elementary to Secondary School*. Hospital for Sick Children (Report to the Ontario Ministry of Education). Toronto: Queen's Printer.

Ungar, M. (Ed.). (2012). *The social ecology of resilience: A handbook of theory and practice*. New York, NY: Springer.

Wilkinson, R., & Pickett, K. (2009). *The spirit level*. New York, NY: Penguin.

Woodhead, M., Dornan, P., & Murray, H. (2013). *What inequality means for children: Evidence from young lives*. London, UK: University of Oxford-Young Lives.

Woolf, V. (1929). *A room of one's own*. London, UK: Hogarth Press.

CHAPTER 3

Historicizing Youth Studies

Susan Talburt and Nancy Lesko

S tudies of youth exist in an eternal present, similar to young people themselves. While fields of study, from curriculum to sociology of education to teacher education, are regularly summarized and historicized, with an aim to re-present the conventions, trends, and omissions of scholarship, youth studies, a long-standing interdisciplinary field, has not fallen in line.[1] Following McLeod (2009), we contend that "Youth studies can be usefully understood as itself a kind of international discourse, a body of 'traveling ideas' and truth claims about young people" and, as such, we should inquire not only into its relations to popular discourses, social change, and economic processes but also into how its discourses "impact upon and mediate the experiences and subjectivities of young people" (p. 276).

This chapter initiates a partial *history of the present* of youth studies. By *history of the present* we mean a method of historical analysis that problematizes the very terms and concepts through which we know and understand a topic. A history of the present starts with questions around categories and discourses in use, and interrogates how, where, when, and why they emerged and became popular. Therefore, we ask: Who are the youth that youth studies examines? What are the systems of reasoning that youth studies draws on to know and engage youth? How might we imagine youth and youth studies differently? In creating a history of the present, we do not assume "youth" as a biological reality or age-based category. Rather, we emphasize systems of reasoning, or discourses that circulate across sites and times to create the concepts that produce "youth" as a category to administer through such social and institutional locations as schools, families, the labor market, correctional institutions, popular culture, and scientific expertise (see Tait, 2000, p. 11; Wyn & White, 1997, p. 8). This is a *partial* history, in that we focus on three historical moments and their sedimented discourses that are integral in defining the boundaries of what can be thought or said within youth studies:

1. The "mental hygiene" movement's use of pastoral power to regulate youths' mental and physical health at the end of the nineteenth century;

2. The popularization of psychological developmental stages and sociological studies of adolescent society and deviance of the 1950s and 1960s; and

3. The Birmingham Centre for Contemporary Cultural Studies' turn to subcultural studies of youth in the 1970s.

Discourses produced within these moments assemble in the present to construct youth as defined by age: in a transitional moment to adulthood, they are "at-risk" for deviations from proper development for adult work and family roles; they serve as barometers of societies' and nations' social and economic well-being and future potential; they are enmeshed in peer culture, yet developable through adult administration in formal and informal institutions, such as schooling, scouting, sports, and families.

These discourses incite adults and institutions to orient themselves to youth through systems of reasoning that universalize youth as a unitary category with particular needs at the same time that they differentiate youth according to their alignment with desired developmental norms. An incitement to know and help youth progress and succeed demands a "forgetting" of the dismantled social, political, cultural, institutional, and economic resources that could support their well-being (Duggan, 2003; Quinn & Meiners, 2009). "Young people have not been enfranchised by the research conducted on their lives," concluded Valentine, Skelton, and Chambers (1998, pp. 21–22). We return to this "forgetting" of diminishing resources and supports after first sketching dominant rationalities that animate thought and action in the present.

Creating Systems of Reasoning: Three Historical Moments

Pastoral power, 1880s–1890s

Dramatic changes in the US in the 1880s and 1890s—including industrialization, immigration, urbanization, the rise of science, women's entry into the labor force, and the emergence of consumerism—created changes in family and social life, and accompanying anxieties. Adolescence emerged in this context as scientists and social reformers offered prescriptions for raising the next generation of American boys and girls in an uncertain future. Adolescence became a way of talking about the future of the nation and developing modern citizens who were rational and self-disciplined (Lesko, 2012). Modernization entailed measuring, monitoring, and standardizing time, a zeitgeist applied to civilization and development. As Lesko and Mitschele (2013) pointed out, "Modern ideas of adolescence came into being as clock time became the central way of ordering past, present, and future events and their meaning" (p. 7). With adolescence understood to be a turbulent time, development-in-time became a dominant way of ordering the adolescent. G. Stanley Hall argued that as they develop, individual children recapitulate the same evolutionary steps as do human groups, as they reach toward higher, civilized stages. The job of science was to measure and guide this development.

Systems of reasoning cobbled together in this era emphasized youth as a distinct population, a universal adolescent who was nevertheless gendered, raced, and classed, and whose body proclaimed a healthy, moral status or its dangerous specter, social degeneration. The playground movement, scouting, and the YMCA governed developing bodies to support self-improvement, respectability, and productivity. Central to these practices was the expertise of the "boyologists," who collected data from young people. Their pastoral power merged scientific techniques of knowledge production, an understanding of the importance of peer relations, and an ability to act like a friend (Hunter, 1994; Laqueur, 1976). Teachers were, in turn, admonished to become more like peers and confidants: sensitive, honest, and tactful as they instilled "self-doubt and self-correction" (Hunter, 1994, p. 81). This pastoral power distributed discipline among adult authorities and youthful subjects who internalized regulations to monitor the self.

Teenage markets, 1950s–1960s

The 1950s' emphasis on consumption, style, and leisure and an array of goods and services aimed at a youthful new market inaugurated the "teenager" and, with that invention, the incessant crossing of images between youth-as-fun and youth-as-potential-offender (Valentine, Skelton, & Chambers, 1998, p. 4). As young men were gaining financial independence and cultural spaces apart from their families, moral panics about delinquency and urban gang activity fueled academic study, born in criminology, of youth (Cohen, 1972/2002). Teenage popular culture, especially music and comics, became a target for censors, who railed against the moral corruption of bad uses of leisure (Gilbert, 1986). Rock and roll music, with its clear African American origins and explicit sexuality, was another frightening indicator of wayward and/or rebellious youth. John Waters parodied the hysteria linking racial integration, rock and roll, sexuality, and marijuana in his film, *Hairspray* (Waters, 1988), in which a psychologist is consulted to brainwash Tracy, the central character, into dating White boys. The 1960s free schools and student-centered pedagogy (Cuban, 1984/1993; Graubard, 1972; Neill, 1960) offered reassurances that the "kids were alright" if schools, adults, and textbooks would get out of their way. Romantic ideas of youth—for example, that youth was a creative and generative time—gained ascendancy in these practices, which also dovetailed with marketing spins on the teens as the "best years of one's life."

In a context of anxiety about youth behavior in changing times, legions of psychologists and sociologists identified and resolved youth problems. Erik Erikson (1950/1985, 1968), for example, called for a moratorium on responsibilities for young people, which would allow them to work through the developmental challenges of identity consolidation that he considered an essential task of youth. Erikson's theory of youth identity was important for Cold-War politics, too. Rebellious youth were understood as important bulwarks of a free society, assuming that their rebellion would eventually be modulated (Medovoi, 2005). Magazines in the 1950s were awash with articles on teens, helping adults to understand them and helping businesses to market to them (Osgerby, 2008). The views and behaviors of Cold-War teenagers, from rebellious to revolting, were variously attributed to mothers working outside the home, weak fathers, Negro-influenced rock and roll, too much independence, too much affluence, and the media. The catalogues of concerns were implicitly, and often explicitly, linked to the growth of communist and/or socialist influences that sapped individuals' capacities for self-direction, and to the alleged spike in juvenile crime. Youth studies sought to discern healthy autonomy from deviance in both psychological and political registers.

The Adolescent Society (Coleman, 1961) positioned James Coleman as the preeminent youth sociologist, and his research portrayed youth as preferring to spend time chatting with friends rather than studying for a test. Youth, even those identified as middle class and college-bound, were choosing leisure activities over achievement-oriented ones. Coleman (1974) later focused on reintegrating youth into a society that was in transition, thereby linking psychology and sociology as centers of expertise about youth problems and possibilities.

Youth subcultures, 1970s–1980s

With antecedents in sociological studies of deviance and delinquency from the 1920s to the 1960s, the Birmingham Centre for Contemporary Cultural Studies (CCCS) continued a stage-of-life approach to studying youth (Tait, 2000) in a context of social change. Their Marxist approach to ethnographic and semiotic research of youth subcultures centered a class analysis of how youth resisted, subverted, or appropriated dominant cultures and ideologies as they created their own meanings, styles, and practices. The CCCS positioned youth subcultures' counterhegemonic practices as reasonable responses to their material conditions. At the same time, researchers' "neglect of the young people who conform in many ways to social expectations" (Valentine, Skelton, & Chambers, 1998, p. 24) perpetuated a construction of youth as potentially disruptive, locating youth subculture somewhere between delinquency and normalcy (Tait, 2000, p. 45). Whether conceptualizing youth as a mediated version of or an Oedipal conflict with a parent culture (Halberstam, 2005, p. 160), the emphasis on generational distinction to characterize subculture recirculates ideas of youth as "different" from adults. Moreover, the centering of age to define subculture downplays the significance of popular culture and style in constituting youth as a category (Bennett & Kahn-Harris, 2004, p. 10).

Youth studies surged as mass-market commodity and new scientific specialization in the later decades of the twentieth century. *Reviving Ophelia* (Pipher, 1994) and *Real Boys* (Pollack, 1998) are two examples of crossover books that were read by parents, social scientists, physicians, and Oprah. Part voyeurism, part social science, and part therapy, the books reaffirmed youth as an endangered "separate tribe." Another swath of books focused on analyzing and curbing violent young men and women (e.g., Garbarino, 1999, 2007); one such book, *Queen Bees and Wannabees* (Wiseman, 2002), crossed quickly from the bookshelf to the comic film, *Mean Girls* (Michaels & Waters, 2004).

Neurology has recently discovered the "teenage brain" and its hidden vulnerabilities; medical doctors in white lab coats discuss the undeveloped frontal lobe of the teenage brain, thereby re-working the age-based, biological difference of youth in new language (see http://www.youtube.com/watch?v=RpMG7vS9pfw). Suparna Choudhury (2010) offered one view of this research: "During the last decade brain imaging studies have suggested that cortical development is much more protracted than previously thought, and that beyond childhood the brain manifests significant degrees of malleability, peaking during adolescence and continuing during early adulthood" (p. 160). Thus, brain "wiring" is more experience-based than "hard." The exciting plasticity of adolescents' brains in Choudhury's description becomes biodeterminism in other accounts, with adolescent risk-taking likely to be normative, biologically driven, and, to some extent, inevitable. In this second interpretation, "risk-taking is the product of a competition between the socio-emotional and cognitive control networks" (Steinberg, 2007, p. 56), and teen brains become irrefutable evidence of youth vulnerability. More restrictive policies against young people are proposed and rationalized by these "new scientific discoveries." For example, brain scientists cite evidence that although almost all American high-school students have had courses in drug, sex, and driver education, large proportions of these youth still have unsafe sex, binge drink, and drive recklessly. It must be their undeveloped brains making them act in this way!

In sum, the systems of reasoning identified here continue to produce youth in certain ways. Youth are trapped in "becoming," and their bodies, actions, and emotions are read as evidence of their immaturity. Condensed phrases, such as "raging hormones," "peer pressure," or "teen brain," efficiently telegraph their position. The developmental framework, consumed at a glance in age, requires youth's "less than" status. Researchers, activists, and educators strive to help young people, but on the established terms, which reduce and homogenize them while forgetting the play of power and resources in these representations.

"New" Conditions and "New" Responses

There is a circularity in which established universal discourses of youth and their needs perpetuate a "forgetting" of the diminishing social and economic resources available to them in the present; in turn, this "forgetting" of social dislocations and inequitable material relations perpetuates the sedimentation of systems of reasoning that individualize youth when compared to supposed universal measures in order to make their lives better. For example, the present logic of high-stakes testing adopts a discourse of youth empowerment that seeks to ensure that young people have skills and knowledge to succeed in a global economy and contribute to society. Yet, as the inevitable and inequitable failures and successes created by high-stakes testing reveal, not all youth, particularly poor youth and youth of color, are offered equal institutional resources or are equally empowered (Su, 2009). This individualizing empowerment discourse intensifies a neoliberal "can-do" attitude, or a "belief in [young people's] capacity to invent themselves and succeed" (Harris, 2004, p. 14) that erases the cultural politics of school achievement.

In a context of economic change accompanied by diminishing state and institutional supports and collective social ties, success and risk are individualized. This shift to a privatized, neoliberal present is "forgotten" when experts and popular culture mobilize sedimented systems of reasoning to help youth. As Harris (2004) argued,

> In the modern period of the late nineteenth century, youth were disciplined directly by the state and its agents so that they would develop slowly, under close supervision, to serve a unified and progressive nation. Late modern times, however, are characterized by dislocation, flux, and globalization, and demand citizens who are flexible and self-realizing … direct interventions and guidance by institutions have been replaced by self-governance; power has devolved onto individuals to regulate themselves through the right choices. (p. 2)

Self-governing citizens must "make choices and create life trajectories for themselves without traditional patterns or support structures to guide them. They must develop individual strategies and take personal responsibility for their success, happiness, and livelihood by making the right choices in an uncertain and changeable environment" (p. 4). Youth become individually accountable for being able to adapt, conform, be innovative, be flexible, and be successful—all the while monitoring their own progress toward their future trajectories.

Youth studies offers means of measuring young people's self-government and progress by drawing on familiar developmental discourses. For example, in the guise of attending to socioeconomic changes related to increased educational demands in the information economy, Tanner and Arnett (2009) confidently assigned individuals aged 18–25 to a "new," distinct developmental period, "emerging adulthood," a stage characterized by "identity explorations, feeling 'in-between', instability, self-focus, and possibilities" (p. 39). Emerging adults' three-stage process of "recentering" is reminiscent of the identity crisis, role confusion, and developmental tasks Erikson (1950/1985, 1968) attributed to adolescence half a century ago. Emerging adults move from dependence to mutual responsibility, explore romantic and career roles and opportunities, and end by "making commitments to enduring roles and responsibilities of adulthood (e.g., careers, marriages and partnerships, commitments to the parental role)" (Tanner & Arnett, 2009, p. 40). Like development-in-time a century ago, or the middle school movement that identified specific needs of 10–15 year olds in the 1980s, the young person is inserted into ever more fine-grained segments of *panoptical time* through which to be understood. Panoptical time "emphasizes the endings toward which youth are to progress and places individual adolescents into a temporal narrative that demands a moratorium on responsibility yet expects them at the same time to act as if each moment of the present is consequential" (Lesko, 2012, p. 91). In this prolonged moratorium, the individual continues to be responsible for monitoring and directing her movement forward.

In turning to the present, rather than joining talk of the contemporary "war on kids" (Grossberg, 2005, p. 5) or the "assault on youth" (Giroux, 2000, p. 10) that identifies commercialization and commodification of youth, failed institutional policies and practices, and dwindling spaces and resources to foster youth creativity, we turn to three programs intended to make young people's lives better: teaching emotional resilience, bullying prevention, and "Slumdog Basketball." These programs, which circulate globally, appear to combine "new" psychological and sociological expertise to approach contemporary problems youth face in changing socioeconomic and cultural contexts.

Emotional resilience: "You Can Do It!"

Following the popularization of Goleman's (1995) *Emotional Intelligence*, schools in the UK, the US, Australia, and other countries began to employ curricula to teach emotional resilience to young people to develop their internal strengths and social skills. Justified by "recognition that in the current climate of social, political and economic upheaval young people need to be resilient more than ever"

(Leach, n.d., para. 34), teaching emotional resilience is said to level the proverbial playing field for young people to develop into healthy, productive—and self-governing—adults. Leach (n.d.) explained,

> There is increasing global awareness of the need to improve life chances for all young people. Life chances relate to having autonomy, engaging in positive social and community networks, accessing education and employment opportunities, being economically stable, experiencing health and well-being and living in a safe environment. (para. 1–2)

Rather than pathologizing youth, emotional resilience training claims to mark a shift "from simply fixing what is seen to be wrong with them, to promoting their strengths and potential contribution to society" (para. 4).

Psychologists typically define resilience as individuals' or groups' capacity to cope in the face of risk or adversity (such as poverty, crime, substance abuse, natural disaster); resilience is fostered by "protective factors," such as social or family support, a sense of belonging, and community involvement (Luthar, Cicchetti, & Becker, 2000). Yet "emotional resilience" represents a stripped-down, individualized version of how young people can cope that ignores the social and political. Emotional resilience curricula such as "You Can Do It!" teach a "social-emotional competence called emotional regulation" (Bernard, n.d., p. 1), or "toughness," based on an idea that "with emotional control, one has the calmness to make rational behavioral decisions that are in one's best interest" (Bernard, n.d., p. 5). Because angry students are said to be underachievers (p. 1), young people learn through "You Can Do It!" to control how anxious or angry they become, moderate behavioral impulses, and calm down quickly when upset. The University of Pennsylvania's Penn Resiliency Program, dubbed "Emotional Health 101" in at least one New York City KIPP (Knowledge Is Power Program) Charter School, helps youth to control their reactions to situations by "replac[ing] negative thinking with more realistic and flexible thinking" (Aubrey, 2010, n.p.). The curriculum teaches late-elementary and middle-school students "to detect inaccurate thoughts, to evaluate the accuracy of those thoughts, and to challenge negative beliefs by considering alternative interpretations" ("Resilience Research in Children," n.d., para. 1). A school administrator using this curriculum explained the need for students to develop tools to manage their emotions: "'They're constantly looking for fairness in the world, and they're spotting unfairness in the world' …. This can lead to a lot of hurt feelings, sadness, stress" (Aubrey, 2010, para. 9).

Forgetting the conditions that create "perceptions" of unfairness teaches youth docility and acceptance, and diminishes possibilities for constructive action against injustice. Moreover, teaching emotional resilience as adaptive behavior recirculates discourses of "cultural deficits of inner-city children and/or families rather than the real-life conditions plaguing schools in inner cities" (Su, 2009, p. 22). It is worth noting that KIPP schools have been portrayed as "successful in improving the educational attainment of poor children because of their emphasis on teaching middle-class mores and aspirations" (Theoharis, 2009, p. 202). An emotionally resilient mantra of "You Can Do It!" forgets, and quite possibly supports, the social and material relations underpinning inequitable access and outcomes in stratifying institutions by placing the focus of "corrective" action on youth.

In a reiteration of the mental hygiene movement's construction of the good student, youths' academic achievement and developing emotional control are measured and monitored. Emotional resilience follows the late nineteenth- and early twentieth-centuries' blending of morality, or obedience to rule-based discipline, with a science of skills and utility to promote efficiency and mental health and to reduce social conflict (Boler, 1999, pp. xxii, 31). As a form of pastoral power, emotional resilience individualizes governance so that young people "internalize rules of self-control and discipline" (Boler, 1999, p. 21). Social science can harness this emotional technology to identify types of young people to develop in desirable directions and to address social problems, such as bullying.

Bullying

After the 1999 school shootings at Columbine High School, and a series of publicized shootings in Europe and North America, public concern with school violence stimulated interest in bullying as a potential cause of such violence. A global proliferation of research, school programs, and parenting manuals related to bullying has ensued, focusing on creating types of youth and means for adults to administer them.

A best-selling popularization of bullying discourses that addresses parents, Coloroso's (2003) *The Bully, the Bullied, and the Bystander*, positions all young people as potentially one of "three characters in a tragic play performed daily in our homes, schools, playgrounds, and streets" (p. 3). The book warns of future risks: the bully will continue to have poor social skills and respond aggressively to others; the bullied is at risk of violence against self or others, such as a "rampage" (p. 9); and the bystander risks growing up guilt-ridden or desensitized to violence (pp. 8–9). Concerned that youth have "no opportunity to develop more constructive social skills" (p. 5), Coloroso (2003) urged parental interventions:

> We can re-channel the governing or controlling behavior of the bully positively into leadership activities. The nonaggressive behaviors of the bullied can be acknowledged and developed as strengths. The role of bystander can be transformed into that of a witness: someone willing to stand up, speak out, and act against injustice. (p. 5)

Parents can identify these characters through "assessment tools listing warning signs of possible violent juvenile behavior" (p. 56), and help them to develop skills aligned with emotional intelligence. Not only is the child individualized, but so is the responsible parent, who must listen to his or her child and become more aware of what is happening in the school and playground (see Baez & Talburt, 2008). The text is silent about the social, political, and material contexts of competition, evaluation, and narrowing acceptable social roles that feed school cultures that encourage the formation of exclusionary peer groups. Thus, in another act of forgetting, the individual parent, armed with expert advice, is responsible for monitoring their child and creating the healthy families, caring schools, and community involvement said to be necessary for their children's success.

Slumdog Basketball

The last approach to improving young people's lives that we turn to is Gamechangers, a partnership between Architecture for Humanity and Nike Inc. designed to "encourage community organizations to empower youth through sports by proposing programs that spur social and economic development in a community" ("About Gamechangers," 2008–2010). Bearing the same name as Nike's Jordan Game Changer shoe, Gamechangers awards grants for the construction of facilities that offer youth access to sports and play spaces, improve physical activity, develop social cohesion, and create opportunities for social and economic empowerment in communities lacking resources. The Gamechangers' website announces a featured program: "Slumdog Basketball aiding in the psycho-rehabilitation of slum dwelling youth in Mumbai thru sports!" Slumdog Basketball will bring four basketball courts and a space for computer training to "fill two voids, recreation and education …. This program will create dynamic social change and lifelong learning by arranging daily sports and life training for at-risk slum dwelling children" (Game Changers, 2008–2010, para. 1). Slumdog basketball promotes well-worn discourses of "healthy lifestyles" and "job skills" as resources for youth to move successfully from a life of poverty to self-determination. How the program is to be sustained beyond facilities construction, not to mention how the success of the young people beyond a few rounds of hoops or some internet surfing will be sustained, is unclear. What is clear is that this global program follows an established system of reasoning that impresses adults through the discourse of the underdog who will make it in the world: "Beat Anything. Change Anything" ("Nike Game Changers," 2009). This blend of sports and the swoosh logo with enthusiastic humanitarianism creates a collective forgetting that little sustained scaffolding is available to young people to change the conditions of their lives.

Each intervention—emotional resilience, bullying prevention, and Slumdog Basketball—names itself as a response to cultural worlds and material relations, yet recirculates discourses that universalize youth categorically, employing pastoral power to individualize them as responsible for overcoming obstacles to succeed. Each support incites adults to clear a space for young people, only to position them more firmly in panoptical time where they must govern the self as they develop skills for successful transition to adulthood. The intensification of the ideal of a youthful "can-do" attitude ensures that some youth will not succeed on the terms laid out for them.

Conclusion: Alternative Spatiotemporalities in the Present

What might a more capacious field of youth studies that does not rely on sedimented systems of reasoning and images of youth and adults look like? In her denaturalization of the adult-child binary, Kathryn Bond Stockton (2009) questioned the spatiotemporal developmental metaphor of "growing up," which, she argued, "has been relentlessly figured as vertical movement upward" (p. 4), a process of *"gradual growth* and *managed delay"* (p. 40). She proposed that because delay—and, we would add, the adolescent moratorium—does not allow upward advancement to full adulthood, growth "more appropriately call[s] us into notions of the horizontal—what spreads sideways (p. 11). She reconceptualized growth as:

> a matter of extension, vigor, and volume as well as verticality. And "growing sideways" would likely be an extremely apt phrase for what recent cognitive science recognizes as the brain's growth (throughout a person's lifetime) through the brain's capacity to make neural networks through connection and extension. Hence, "growing up" may be a short-sighted, limited rendering of human growth, one that would imply an end to growth when full stature (or reproduction) is achieved. By contrast, "growing sideways" suggests that the width of a person's experience or ideas, their motives or their motions, may pertain at any age, bringing "adults" and "children" into lateral contact of surprising sorts. (p. 11)

This altered positioning suggests renewed possibilities for understanding young people and for youth and adult contact.

In considering the possibilities of a youth studies that refuses present neoliberal discourses that reframe a public sphere in terms of personal responsibility and moves beyond systems of reasoning that delimit youth in terms of problems and solutions, we draw on several projects that attend to the sociopolitical and material realities of young people's lives in the present. These projects suggest reworked relations of adults and youth along with glimmers of counter-discourses.

Our Schools Suck (Alonso, Anderson, Su, & Theoharis, 2009) centered youth voices in order to counter dominant public discourse of a "culture of failure," offering "an intervention into the adult-driven debates on inner-city youth" (p. 5). The text's emphasis on young people's affect and activism connected their anger, their seemingly "poor choices," and their work against injustices to "the conditions in which they live, work, and attend school rather than essentialized 'cool pose' values" (p. 6). It offered a powerful antidote to emotionally resilient, neoliberal, "can-do" discourses by attending to youth's awareness of and struggles against their positioning via incoherent messages of personal responsibility in the face of systemic material inequalities in their lives: "Despite living in an urban center with a small employment base for low-skilled young workers, attending under-resourced schools, and facing discrimination in their job searches, they were repeatedly told that success rested on their motivation" (p. 25).

Chávez and Soep (2005) presented an analysis of Youth Radio, in which adults and youth coproduce media products, a project of "lateral contact" that pushes against the romanticizing of youth voice as intrinsically emancipatory, a deficit model of youth, or an authoritative role for adults. Youth media projects often position young people as sources for intimate details of their lives, but not as editors or as compensated contributors. But youth media production, they argued, "can provide a resource for young people to rewrite the stories that are told about them, against them, or supposedly on their behalf" (p. 410). In what Chávez and Soep called a "pedagogy of collegiality," adults and youth depend on each others' skills and knowledges to communicate to an audience, which acts as witness, mediating the dialectical power dynamics between students and teacher. Like the authors of *Our Schools Suck*, Chávez and Soep (2005) refused to invoke "youth voice" divorced from political, social, and relational contexts, or in order to establish their own progressive credentials (p. 413). Youth radio intentionally puts "youth development considerations" first, but this policy of "collegial pedagogy" has "baked in" generative tensions (pp. 418–419) that they discussed as "joint framing, youth-led inquiry, mediated intervention, and distributed accountability" (p. 421). The authors noted: "Participating as an adult in collegial pedagogy means always searching for that shifting balance between sufficient mentorship and excessive intervention" (p. 424). And the program's "distributed accountability" refuses the individualized accountability of most pedagogical contexts, and "functions as an iterative process of forming and weighing judgments about the work being produced as it relates to a series of criteria—including those shaped by considerations of accuracy, originality, aesthetics, rigor, and matters of social impact" (p. 430). Chávez and Soep offered a multifaceted portrait of the pedagogy of collegiality that consciously avoids romanticizing, forgetting inequalities, and erasing power differentials. Youths and adults take on many roles and characteristics, and while no one *saves* anyone else, together they produce award-winning programs.

These authors construct youth within social, political, and relational contexts, not as always-already figured by biology, age, and difference. We understand these "breaks" with conventional youth figurations as operating in distinctive temporal imaginaries. While conventional youth studies focuses relentlessly on the future and on "becoming," these authors emphasize the present with its inequalities, limitations, and lines of action in relation to past and future. The temporal imaginary is a dynamic one that not only keeps past, present, and future in relation, but also takes into account space. In other words, this is a spatiotemporal imaginary that does not figure only time as the active figure, but space as well. This is a significant reconceptualization, for time has been the privileged term in conceptualizing adolescence. But time and space are mutually constitutive and are constitutive of our imaginings of the social world and the human. Whether young people "grow up" to be future adults or "grow sideways" in the present in lateral contact with adults offers widely diverging ways of "knowing" and working with youth.

A more supple youth studies attends to youth-adult relations of research or pedagogy in specific, material spaces as well as attending to imaginings of space. For example, at Youth Radio, external audiences and criteria shape the radio stories and the collaborations of youth, peer educators, and adults. Each collaborator interprets the "external" criteria—such as originality or social impact—differently, and the product and process must be negotiated in relation to those interpretations. Alonso, Anderson, Su, and Theoharis (2009) also located themselves with youth in specific urban school spaces, refusing the usual discourses and affects of such locations and working, instead, to establish a good urban school. Yet their work gestures to a more metaphorical understanding of spaces as an effect of relations and connections that represent "*constellations of temporary coherence*" (Massey, 1998, p. 125). This is a political view of space, in which it is not static but dynamic. Space is not a container where youth action takes place (Ruddick, 1998, p. 346) but, like time, is integral to producing youth as a social category. At the same time, space itself is produced through action and interaction. To organize youth spatially, whether by mandating their presence in schools or prohibiting it in malls after dark, is a strategy of "spatial organization [that is] deeply bound up with the social production of identities" (Massey, 1998, p. 127). And this production of identities, imaginations, and actions has much to tell us. For example, Dillabough and Kennelly (2010) explored "the role that particular spatial landscapes and their symbolic assemblages play in framing" the moral-inflected identities of youth groups as "'disgusting', 'superior' and/or 'shameful'" (p. 72). Their ethnography of youths' relational and emotional geographies in Toronto and Vancouver neighborhoods offered phenomenological portraits of shifting urban landscapes, identities, and symbolic resources, as well as the production of discourses of "lost youth." Youth are making themselves and also being made within sedimented and changing locations, economies, and discourses.

In her analysis of the structuring dualisms of local-global in the present "international turn" of youth studies, McLeod (2009) pointed to a tacit, uninterrogated "prevalence of comparative thinking in youth studies research," whether of generations, social and ethnic groups, or national youth cultures' local manifestations of global phenomena (p. 272). To demonstrate difference, these comparisons depend on axes of space and time, with the temporality of generations confirming distinctions and spatial distance illustrating local difference. Space is "mobilized in ways that either privilege the global—with the local either a miniature of the global or acted upon by global forces—or sideline the global and elevate the specificity of the local frame" (p. 272). Although temporalities (history) undergird the production of youth practices in globalizing spaces as distinct, exotic, modern, traditional, and/or globalized, youth studies rarely makes explicit or complicates the spatiotemporal imaginaries guiding its analysis. One exception is Ritty Lukose's (2009) *Liberalization's Children*, in which she studied gendered formations of youth citizenship in Kerala, India, suggesting that

> how young people in Kerala apprehend and negotiate new globally inflected spaces of consumption, particularly the youth-fashion nexus, reveals these spaces to be structured by specifically postcolonial preoccupations about tradition and modernity, public and private that have differential consequences for young women and men. (p. 95)

This careful attention to histories and spatialities enabled Lukose to identify "a complex and contested moment of articulation between the postcolonial and the global that has created a cultural politics of modernity and globalization that young people must and indeed do navigate in a variety of ways" (p. 162). Her focus on young people's negotiations of consumer and political citizenship within and beyond adult society's structures and discourses offered a complex portrait not only of youth, but of the meanings of "liberalization" in India.

Explicit uses of temporality and spatialization in studies of youth offer counternarratives to the biological, developing, and othered youth. They suggest a politics of foregrounding both youth studies' and youths' spatiotemporal imaginings and actions in the production of knowledges, identities, and practices. Whether these theoretical orientations can interrupt conventional progressive practices and the relations of adults and youths in research is an open question.

Acknowledgment

This chapter represents a revised version of Talburt and Lesko (2011), "A History of the Present of Youth Studies."

Note

1. There are exceptions to this generalization. See, for example, Savage (2007), who offered a "prehistory of the Teenager" (p. xv) that intertwined histories of young people in the US, England, and Germany with the rise of popular and expert discourses about youth, programs to administer and educate young people, and youth-targeted massmarketing. It was in the 1940s that Talcott Parsons could coin the term "youth culture" to name what mass culture and youth themselves understood to be a discrete category, the teenager (pp. 452–453). On the creation of historical knowledge about youth, see Reisinger (2011). For a reassessment of research on youth subcultures, see Bennett and Kahn-Harris (2004). For an examination of changes in youth biographies, see Leccardi (2005). Stafseng (2008) historicized the youth theories of Mannheim and Lewin, and Mørch (2003) examined the generations of youth theory and research. Lesko and Talburt's book, *Keywords in Youth Studies* (2011), is an effort to critically historicize youth studies concepts.

References

About Gamechangers. (2008–2010). Retrieved from http://gamechangers.architectureforhumanity.org/about

Alonso, G., Anderson, N. S., Su, C., & Theoharis, J. (2009). *Our schools suck: Students talk back to a segregated nation on the failures of urban education*. New York, NY: New York University Press.

Aubrey, A. (2010, January 18). Emotional training helps kids fight depression. Retrieved from http://www.npr.org/templates/story/story.php?storyId=122526518&ps=cprs

Baez, B., & Talburt, S. (2008). Governing for responsibility and with love: Parents and children between home and school. *Educational Theory, 58*(1), 25–43.

Bennett, A., & Kahn-Harris, K. (2004). Introduction. In A. Bennett & K. Kahn-Harris (Eds.), *After subculture: Critical studies in contemporary youth culture* (pp. 1–18). New York, NY: Palgrave Macmillan.

Bernard, M. E. (n.d.). Emotional resilience: Implications for You Can Do It! Education Theory and Practice. Retrieved from http://www.youcandoiteducation.com/reflectionsonemotional_files/ReflectionsOnEmotional.pdf

Boler, M. (1999). *Feeling power: Emotions and education*. New York, NY: Routledge.

Chávez, V., & Soep, E. (2005). Youth radio and the pedagogy of collegiality. *Harvard Educational Review, 75*(4), 409–488.

Choudhury, S. (2010). Culturing the adolescent brain: What can neuroscience learn from anthropology? *Social Cognitive and Affective Neuroscience, 5*(2–3), 159–168.

Cohen, S. (2002). *Folk devils and moral panics: The creation of the Mods and Rockers* (3rd ed.). New York, NY: Routledge.

Coleman, J. S. (1961). *The adolescent society: The social life of the teenager and its impact on education*. Westport, CT: Greenwood Press.

Coleman, J. S. (1974). *Youth: Transition to adulthood. Report of the panel on youth of the President's Science Advisory Committee*. Chicago, IL: University of Chicago Press.

Coloroso, B. (2003). *The bully, the bullied, and the bystander: From preschool to high school: How parents and teachers can help break the cycle of violence*. New York, NY: HarperResource.

Cuban, L. (1993). *How teachers taught: Constancy and change in American classrooms, 1890–1990* (2nd ed.). New York, NY: Teachers College Press.

Dillabough, J., & Kennelly, J. (2010). *Lost youth in the global city*. New York, NY: Routledge.

Duggan, L. (2003). *The twilight of equality? Neoliberalism, cultural politics, and the attack on democracy*. Boston, MA: Beacon Press.

Erikson, E. H. (1968). *Identity: Youth and crisis*. New York, NY: W. W. Norton.

Erikson, E. H. (1985). *Childhood and society*. New York, NY: W. W. Norton.

Game Changers. (2008–2010). 'Slumdog Basketball' aiding in the psycho-rehabilitation of slum dwelling youth in Mumbai thru sports! Retrieved from http://gamechangers.architectureforhumanity.org/proposals/slumdog_basketball_aiding_in_the_psycho_rehabilitation_of_slum_dwelling_youth_in_mumbai_th

Garbarino, J. (1999). *Lost boys: Why our sons turn violent and how we can save them*. New York, NY: Knopf.

Garbarino, J. (2007). *See Jane hit: Why girls are growing more violent and what we can do about it*. New York, NY: Penguin Group.

Gilbert, J. (1986). *A cycle of outrage: America's reaction to the juvenile delinquent in the 1950s*. New York & Oxford: Oxford University Press.

Giroux, H. (2000). *Stealing innocence: Youth, corporate power, and the politics of culture*. New York, NY: St. Martin's Press.

Goleman, D. (1995). *Emotional intelligence: Why it can matter more than IQ*. New York, NY: Bantam Books.

Graubard, A. (1972). *Free the children: Radical reform and the free school movement*. New York, NY: Pantheon Books.

Grossberg, L. (2005). *Caught in the crossfire: Kids, politics, and America's future*. Boulder, CO: Paradigm.

Halberstam, J. (2005). *In a queer time and place: Transgender bodies, subcultural lives*. New York, NY: New York University Press.

Harris, A. (2004). *Future girl: Young women in the twenty-first century*. New York, NY: Routledge.

Hunter, I. (1994). *Rethinking the school: Subjectivity, bureaucracy, criticism*. New York, NY: St. Martin's Press.

Laqueur, T. W. (1976). *Religion and respectability: Sunday schools and working class culture, 1780–1850*. New Haven, CT: Yale University Press.

Leach, C. (n.d.). Resilient and resourceful young people: A national youth strategy? Retrieved from http://wa.psnews.com.au/BooksFeaturesWApsn0175.html

Leccardi, C. (2005). Facing uncertainty: Temporality and biographies in the new century. *Young, 13*(2), 123–146.

Lesko, N. (2012). *Act your age! A cultural construction of adolescence* (2nd ed.). New York, NY: RoutledgeFalmer.

Lesko, N., & Mitschele, K. (2013). Rethinking adolescence. In P. G. Andrews (Ed.), *Research to guide practice in middle grades education*. Westerville, OH: Association for Middle Level Education.

Lesko, N., & Talburt, S. (Eds.). (2011). *Keywords in youth studies: Tracing affects, movements, knowledges*. New York, NY: Routledge.

Lukose, R. (2009). *Liberalization's children: Gender, youth, and consumer citizenship in globalizing India*. Durham, NC: Duke University Press.

Luthar, S. S., Cicchetti, D., & Becker, B. (2000). The construct of resilience: A critical evaluation and guidelines for future work. *Child Development, 71*(3), 543–562.

Massey, D. (1998). The spatial construction of youth cultures. In T. Skelton & G. Valentine (Eds.), *Cool places: Geographies of youth cultures* (pp. 121–129). London, UK: Routledge.

McLeod, J. (2009). Youth studies, comparative inquiry, and the local/global problematic. *The Review of Education, Pedagogy, and Cultural Studies, 31*(4), 270–292.

Medovoi, L. (2005). *Rebels: Youth and the Cold War origins of identity.* Durham, NC: Duke University Press.

Michaels, L. (Producer), & Waters, M. (Director). (2004). *Mean girls* [Motion picture]. United States: Paramount Pictures.

Mørch, S. (2003). Youth and education. *Young, 11*(1), 49–73.

Neill, A. S. (1960). *Summerhill: A radical approach to child rearing.* New York, NY: Hart.

Nike Game Changers. (2009, June 15). Nike Game Changers. Retrieved from http://www.youtube.com/watch?v=VoVVfCfqcUo

Osgerby, B. (2008). Understanding the 'jackpot market': Media, marketing and the rise of the American teenager. In P. E. Jamieson & D. Romer (Eds.), *The changing portrayal of adolescents in the media since 1950* (pp. 27–58). New York, NY: Oxford University Press.

Pipher, M. B. (1994). *Reviving Ophelia: Saving the selves of adolescent girls.* New York, NY: Putnam.

Pollack, W. S. (1998). *Real boys: Rescuing our sons from the myths of boyhood.* New York, NY: Henry Holt & Co.

Quinn, T., & Meiners, E. R. (2009). *Flaunt it! Queers organizing for public education and justice.* New York, NY: Peter Lang.

Reisinger, A. J. (2011). Histories. In N. Lesko & S. Talburt (Eds.), *Keywords in youth studies: Tracing affects, movements, knowledges* (pp. 86–91). New York, NY: Routledge.

Resilience Research in Children. (n.d.). University of Pennsylvania. Retrieved from http://www.ppc.sas.upenn.edu/prpsum.htm

Ruddick, S. (1998). Modernism and resistance: How 'homeless' youth subcultures make a difference. In T. Skelton & G. Valentine (Eds.), *Cool places: Geographies of youth cultures* (pp. 343–360). London, UK: Routledge.

Savage, J. (2007). *Teenage: The creation of youth culture.* New York, NY: Viking.

Stafseng, O. (2008). *Karl Mannheim & Kurt Lewin on youth research and policy, based on their interests in German-Jewish youth matters before and after World War II.* Paper presented at 1st Forum of Sociology, International Sociological Association, Barcelona, Spain.

Steinberg, L. (2007). Risk taking in adolescence: New perspectives from brain and behavioral science. *Current Directions in Psychological Science, 16*(2), 55–59.

Stockton, K. B. (2009). *The queer child, or growing sideways in the twentieth century.* Durham, NC: Duke University Press.

Su, C. (2009). Introduction. In G. Alonso, N. S. Anderson, C. Su, & J. Theoharis (Eds.), *Our schools suck: Students talk back to a segregated nation on the failures of urban education* (pp. 1–30). New York, NY: New York University Press.

Tait, G. (2000). *Youth, sex, and government.* New York, NY: Peter Lang.

Talburt, S., & Lesko, N. (2011). A history of the present of youth studies. In N. Lesko & S. Talburt (Eds.), *Keywords in youth studies: Tracing affects, movements, knowledges* (pp. 11–23). New York, NY: Routledge.

Tanner, J. L., & Arnett, J. J. (2009). The emergence of 'emerging adulthood': The new life stage between adolescence and young adulthood. In A. Furlong (Ed.), *Handbook of youth and young adulthood: New perspectives and agendas* (pp. 39–45). London, UK: Routledge.

Theoharis, J. (2009). Conclusion. In G. Alonso, N. S. Anderson, C. Su, & J. Theoharis (Eds.), *Our schools suck: Students talk back to a segregated nation on the failures of urban education* (pp. 177–214). New York, NY: New York University Press.

Valentine, G., Skelton, T., & Chambers, D. (1998). An introduction to youth and youth culture. In T. Skelton & G. Valentine (Eds.), *Cool places: Geographies of youth cultures* (pp. 1–32). London, UK: Routledge.

Waters, J. (Producer & Director). (1988). *Hairspray* [Motion picture]. United States: New Line Home Video.

Wiseman, R. (2002). *Queen bees and wannabes: Helping your daughter survive cliques, gossip, boyfriends, and other realities of adolescence.* New York, NY: Crown Publishing Group.

Wyn, J., & White, R. (1997). *Rethinking youth.* London, UK: Sage.

CHAPTER 4

The Symbolism of *Cool* in Adolescence and Youth Culture

Marcel Danesi

Perhaps no other word better evokes images of desirable appearance and lifestyle associated with the period of adolescence than does *cool*. What is *cool*? When did it emerge to designate a new way in which young people saw themselves? The spread of youth culture as a "cool culture" is often explained as a commodification of youth by the media, advertising, and marketing industries (Frank, 1997)—a view that goes as far back as the 1920s to the Frankfurt School of Social Theory (for example, Adorno, 1949), seeing capitalism as an exploitative form of politics that subjugates any form of culture to the profit motive. This interpretation claims that the trends that develop among young people fortuitously provide new commodities for the marketplace, thus tying youth to the political-social arena. This is certainly one way of approaching youth studies and of analyzing the cooption of cool by the media-culture industries. But this tells us nothing about the emergence of cool in the first place, as a state of being. It skirts the psychological, anthropological, and semiotic (meaning-bearing) roots of this phenomenon. These will be discussed here in relation to the origins and evolution of youth culture.

The Birth and Spread of Cool

Birth of the Cool was the title of a jazz album by Miles Davis (recorded 1949–1950, released in 1957), an album that announced a new form of jazz that had been fomenting in previous decades—a form that encapsulated the essence of cool in music (Gioia, 2009; Laughey, 2006; MacAdams, 2001). It also coincided with the coalescence of various trends that led to the establishment of a veritable youth culture in the mid-1950s—a trend that also was envisaged in fiction with J. D. Salinger's novel, *The Catcher in the Rye* (1951), which presented the first ever portrait of the *teenager* as a social category. For the first time in history, a single economic system—the one that took shape after the Industrial Revolution of the nineteenth century—was capable of guaranteeing a certain level of affluence to increasingly larger segments of society. With more wealth and leisure time at their disposal, everyone became more inclined to live the good life. And with the economic capacity to ameliorate the chances of staying healthier, and thus of living much longer than previous generations, a desire to preserve youth for a much longer period of life started to define the collective state of mind. This also led to the perception of the adolescent years as more and more meaningful and as autonomous from adulthood. By the mid-1950s, this led to a new form of culture based on a musical form—rock and roll—that was composed by young people for young people and young people alone, creating the first generation gap in modern times. This meant that teenagers could live separately from adult culture through music and its associated clothing, language styles, and so on, yet, at the same time participate in the institutions of adult culture, such as the school, but in markedly different ways than in the past.

From the outset, being young meant being rebellious, and this meant, in turn, adopting a "cool look" that was openly and evidently different from how adults looked and behaved. This was achieved through clothes, hairstyles, speech patterns, and other such behavioral features. "New" and "different" became the two key concepts espoused by young people for separating themselves from mainstream culture and society. This shocked adults, but it did not threaten them, even though the music of rock and roll was denounced as the "devil's music." As Stan Cohen (1972) has cogently argued, trends introduced into society by young people, and popularized through media structures, are interpreted initially by adults as reflecting a deterioration of the morals of the world around them. But this is short-lived, as the trends lose their transgressive edge and become simply part of mainstream culture (Danesi, 2003; Noxon, 2006). It was in the subsequent counterculture generation of the mid-1960s that the threat became a politically real one, as the hippie movement was much more than a simple form of social rebellion against the status quo—it actually took political actions to bring about change. The generation gap became wider and more acerbic. At that point, society and the business establishment reacted with a clever strategy, which Frank (1997) called a "Culture Trust" that the establishment formed with young people—a trust intended to impart the illusion to them that entry into the world of political dissidence was realized safely through the gates of lifestyle cool. That trust continues unbroken to this day.

To understand why it was able to gain a foothold in the late 1960s, it is necessary to dig a little deeper into the social roots of *cool* as a metaphor for social differentiation. Along with *hip*, it became a primary descriptor of youth trends in the 1950s. But, in actual fact, both terms were coined early on in the twentieth century. The concept of cool came out of the fashionable jazz nightclub scene of the 1930s (or more accurately, the "speakeasy" scene), when relaxing styles of jazz music contrasted with more physically engaging ones, culminating, as discussed, in the emergence of cool jazz as a distinct new genre of music. This trend influenced, in turn, the constitution of youth culture. It also jumped from the music scene to everyday life, becoming a perfect descriptor of the sexual attractiveness of young bodies involved in exhibiting self-control, composure, and poise—all the qualities that were imprinted in the performance of cool jazz. By the 1960s, cool expanded to encompass the impertinent, impudent, and cheeky attitudes exhibited by such counterculture heroes as Bob Dylan (Danesi, 1994).

Hip also came from an earlier era. John Leland (2004) has traced the origin of the word to 1619 when the first Blacks arrived off the coast of Virginia. Without Black culture, Leland maintained, there would be no "hip trends." Hip, he explains, is all about a smooth and ambiguous attitude, which the early slaves had to adopt in order to survive psychologically. This attitude has been adopted, in different ways, by hippies and rap artists, among others. It is something that one feels, rather than understands, and that is why it has always been associated with musical styles—the blues, jazz, rap, and so on. In a 1973 song, the funk group, Tower of Power, defined *hip* as follows: "Hipness is—What it is! And sometimes hipness is, what it ain't." Hip is about portraying through the body a distinct identity. It is about a flight from conformity, a way to put oneself in opposition to it, to stand out, to look and be different. Leland noted that Bugs Bunny—the cartoon character—exemplified hip, with his sassy attitude that always got the better of Elmer Fudd, the ultimate "square." His inimitable line, "What's up, Doc?" is pure hip talk. In the 1960s, hip was recycled to refer to the unisexual clothing style of counterculture rebels, who wore their pants below the waist in such a way as to expose the hip, abdomen, and stomach. The "hippies" even painted these anatomical areas with colorful designs. This gave nonconformity and dissent a label.

Cool and *hip* now designate lifestyle chic, not social protest (Sculatti, 1982), because of the conquest of cool by the business world, as Frank (1997) emphasized. But then, this strategy could not have worked unless there already existed in the social genes of the Western world a built-in tendency towards cool as a metaphor for lifestyle. As the social critic, Stuart Ewen (1988), has observed, the business world discovered accidentally the emotional power of cool and turned it to their advantage. This is why the constant desire for new items of consumption is no longer perceived as an aberration, but as part of the search for happiness, success, status, or beauty. Since the late 1960s, the worlds of advertising, marketing, and entertainment have become totally intertwined with trends in youth culture, both responding and contributing to its rapid fluctuations. The counterculture movement ended in the mid-1970s with a mix of accomplishment and failure, but the marketing of counterculture cool by the media and the business world ensconced it into the imagination of all subsequent generations as a necessity of social life, not an option. The result has been an obliteration of the crucial emotional difference that traditional cultures maintain between the categories of young and old (Danesi, 2010). This is why, nowadays, trends that are started by adolescents are quickly transformed into trends adopted by everyone, regardless of age.

In 1904, the psychologist, Stanley G. Hall, defined *adolescence* not as a socially extended period of childhood, but as a product of the biological processes characterizing pubescence (Hall, 1904). But not all agree with his assessment. Margaret Mead (1928, 1939), for instance, found that in a traditional society, such as the Samoan one of the 1920s, where marriage coincides with the advent of puberty, the kinds of differentiated cultural behaviors that are associated with modern youth in the Western world simply do not emerge. In effect, Mead suggested, adolescence is a culture-specific construction, tied to historical, rather than biological, forces. The debate is still ongoing, and is beyond the purpose of this chapter. Suffice it to say that the cool lifestyle associated with adolescence is certainly not a product of biological forces; it emerged as a cultural construct. By the late 1940s, not only psychologists, but also society at large, had come to view the adolescent period as a "stormy" and "stressful" one that was tied to hormonal and other psycho-physiological changes. Consequently, a growing awareness that adolescents themselves had become a distinct social group on their own had installed itself into groupthink. The term, *teenager*, appeared in print in 1941 in an article in *Popular Science Monthly*, although it may have been coined earlier. Its meaning reverberates with cultural, rather than biological, nuances. Its spread in the 1950s signaled the fact that children entering the pubescent or "teenage" years constituted a distinct social category, united by similar tastes in music and lifestyle (Rice, 1990, p. 79). By the early 1950s, there was no doubt that the teenager lived in a social cosmos separate from the adult one, requiring a special kind of handling in the marketplace, in the media, at home, and at school (Coleman & Hendry, 1990; Côté & Allahar, 1994, 2006; Desjarlais & Rackauskas, 1986). By the mid-1950s the media etched the figure of the teenager into the popular imagination, gearing the ever-growing entertainment industry toward this new and affluent market segment. Music, movies, radio and television programs became increasingly more directed at teenagers. The first teenage icons appeared on the scene. Although there was an initial, well-documented reaction to the emphasis on youth in the mid-1950s, and especially to the perceived "moral danger" of rock and roll music (Grossberg, 1992), eventually it dissipated, as youth culture became an ever-expanding reality.

Already in 1948, *Life* magazine ran a cover story on teenagers, underscoring the fact that, for the first time in American history, young people constituted a distinct demographic category. The article pointed out that, thanks in part to the many extra jobs that were created by World War II, teenagers had plenty of spending money, and it became Madison Avenue's avowed mission to get them to spend it on clothing, dance, and music fads. By 1956, the average American teenager had more pocket money than any young person ever had before. In the mid-1950s, the movies, *Rebel Without a Cause*, with teen idol James Dean, and *The Wild One*, with Marlon Brando as a motorcycle gang leader, made it obvious to one and all that the *Life* article was a prophetic one indeed. Elvis Presley became the "king of rock and roll," symbolizing teenage rebelliousness with his hip-swinging, brash attitude. The growing power of television in the 1950s further cemented the view that the fledgling youth culture was markedly distinct from adult culture, with programs such as *American Bandstand* and the *Adventures of Ozzie and Harriet* gaining enormous popularity. The latter program was, revealingly, the first sitcom to deal with the problems of raising teenage children (two sons, in this case).

The hippie rebellion was hardly seen at first as a threat to the socioeconomic order. It became a concern only after the Chicago Democratic Convention of 1968 turned violent. The manifestation of youth rebellion shown at the Chicago convention was unique in the history of America, and it put a scare into those who had invested the economic future of the world in youth trends. With the threat of adolescents truly growing up and rejecting the capitalist system, cultural cool came to be seen by the establishment as the key to bridging the generation gap. Even the hippies knew that being revolutionary entailed being cool. Already in the early 1970s, cool started to fragment into differential sectors. There was disco, punk, hip hop, alternative, rave, and so on. Each sector was emblematized by music style, and developed its own form and style of cool. Interestingly, one of these involved makeup and cross-dressing. The rock band, Kiss, whose performances on stage were designed to shock adults, symbolized this new type of cool perfectly. Each musician in the band took on a mock comic-book character—a glamour boy, an alien from outer space, a kitty cat, and a sex-crazed Kabuki monster. The stage act included fire-eating, smoke-bombs, hydraulic lifts, and the smashing of instruments. *The Rocky Horror Picture Show* was another manifestation of this new trend. The movie premiered in 1975 and instantly became a cult phenomenon, with hordes of teenagers going to see it week after week, month after month, year after year. It was both a parody of 1950s rock culture and a paradigm of a transgendered lifestyle code portrayed by bands such as Alice Cooper.

Running against the punk and cross-dressing forms of cool was disco culture, epitomized by the 1977 movie, *Saturday Night Fever*. The popularity of disco music and lifestyle with many teens was evidence of youth culture's increasing fragmentation. Disco culture was a throwback to the 1920s and 1930s, when ballroom dancing characterized the first indications that youth culture was starting to become a reality. Punk teens rejected it with the expression, "disco sucks!" So, too, did other teens, who saw the disco scene as too superficial and much too acceptable to the adult world. But disco thrived nonetheless, because it was fun and sexy.

By the early 1980s, snippets of the punk, cross-dressing, and disco cultures remained. But new forms of cool were added to the mix. Two youth icons in particular—Michael Jackson and Madonna—emerged to challenge traditional gender attitudes even more than had Kiss and *Rocky Horror* teens. Michael Jackson incorporated male and female sexual characteristics into his stage persona. His album and video, *Thriller* (1982), were a blend of *Rocky Horror* and Kiss-like gender-bashing. It was right for the times, earning an unprecedented eight Grammy Awards. Madonna's songs, *Like a Virgin*, *Material Girl*, and *Dress You Up* satirized the traditional view of females as sexual objects. She adopted a Marilyn Monroe "sex-kitten" peep-show pose as one of her performance trademarks, heralding the arrival of a new form of female empowerment, known subsequently as "girl power." By the end of the decade, youth culture continued to fragment, as hard rockers, mods, preps, goths, grunge, and other teen lifestyles and subcultures emerged with their own fashion, music, and symbolism. But one trend came to center stage—rap music and the hip hop lifestyle. The term, *rap*, was used for the first time in the mid-1970s to describe an eclectic mix of funk, soul, and hard rock played by disc jockeys in the dance halls of Harlem and the South Bronx. The more enthusiastic members of those audiences would "sing-song" rhymes, exhorting other teens to dance and "get into it." These were called "rapping" sessions.

Rap was the mainstream form of cool until the mid-1990s. Since then, fragmentation has become even more characteristic of trends in youth culture, with rap still remaining cool for specific types of youth. Today, cool is an unconscious pattern in how everyone, regardless of age, dresses, wears their hair, and so on. Cool is really a diffuse attitude that has lost its edge as a form of social differentiation.

The Symbolism of Cool

In the history of youth culture, cool is, as we have seen, an adaptive style attitude, changing in detail over time and across social sectors in order to respond to changes in youth culture. But the basic pattern has not changed. Being cool in the 1950s is similar to being cool today. The difference can be found in the details—in the type of clothing, hairstyle, postures, musical tastes, and so on. Its overall "emotional style" has always been the same (Stearns 1994), and it has, surprisingly, been found at various times across cultures and social classes, coming under various names and interpretations (Connor, 1995; Gold, 1994; Pountain & Robins, 2000). But it is now an almost forgotten fact that without the first generation of teenagers in the 1950s, the spread of cool as an unconscious and ever-meaningful attitude to society at large would never have occurred.

Most of the theories of cool seem to pay little attention to its symbolic power. Symbols of cool have varied throughout youth generations, giving us meaningful insights into the changes undergone by youth culture throughout the twentieth and early twenty-first centuries. It is important to realize how much meaning a single symbol, like a pair of sunglasses, can have in the experience of everyday life and the presentation of the self in it. Symbols of cool characterize specific youth eras and/or subcultures. Although they were not called teenagers yet, the young people of the so-called Roaring Twenties constituted the first true example of young people who engaged in a lifestyle that was different from that of their elders (Palladino, 1996; Savage, 2007). Particularly worrisome to the latter were the young women, called *flappers*, who wore short skirts, rolled-down stockings, short "bobbed" hair, and who frequented the speakeasies, where they drank bootleg liquor, listened to jazz, and danced the Charleston and other sexual musical dances. The bobbed hair in particular became a symbol for the whole flapper lifestyle, being condemned by adults as crude and openly sexual, and highly unsuitable for a young woman. But the flappers ignored the censure, thus setting the tone for the shift in social values that was slowly fomenting—a shift that bestowed upon young people, for the first time in America, a new, semi-autonomous status within the mainstream culture.

The symbol that emerged in the mid-1950s to characterize perfectly the new teen cool was sunglasses—a symbol ensconcing permanently the figure of the rebellious teenager into social consciousness. Sunglasses made their debut into the world of symbolism through rock musicians and actors such as James Dean and Marlon Brando. They perfectly emblemized the rebellious teenager of the era. They did so by hiding the emotionality of the eyes, so that the teen could look and act "cool" (unflustered, in control, and self-confident).

The hippies stood for free love, peace, understanding, and the elimination of all inequities. They adopted the "V" peace sign (made with the index and third fingers) as a symbol for the counterculture movement's "peace-not-war" philosophy. After World War II, the sign was used by Winston Churchill in public to celebrate the victorious outcome for the Allied forces. Aided by the popularity of the 1960s *Star Trek* TV program, where it surfaced (in slightly modified form, made with the third and fourth fingers instead of the second and third) as the Vulcan peace sign, standing for "Live long and prosper," the V-sign caught on with the hippies, who turned its "victory" meaning on its head, using it deliberately as a peace symbol to warn society of the inanity of war. Interestingly, in the mid-1990s, the Spice Girls used it to symbolize a new, emerging trend of teen empowerment—"girl power," as it came to be called.

In the mid-1970s, punks entered the world of symbolism ("stomped into it" might be a better designation). Their demeanor and overall look was intended to be violent and confrontational. Punk band members spat on audiences; mutilated themselves and damaged props on stage; burped and urinated to a basic, rhythmic, pulsating beat, inciting their audiences to do similar things. The fashion symbols they introduced (chains, army boots, "Mohawk" hairdos) were designed to mock society and show insubordination at once. The punks set themselves visibly apart not only from mainstream adult culture, but also from other teen cultures (such as disco teens). The item of punk attire that stood out symbolically in this regard was the reverse dog collar. Dog collars at the time were made with spikes protruding inward, so that if the dog disobeyed a command, the trainer could yank the leash, attached to the collar, thus punishing the dog by driving the spikes into its neck. This method of training was based on the psychology of negative conditioning. Being against all forms of authority and social conditioning, the punks reversed the dog collar in parody of dog-obedience training. The outward-protruding spikes symbolized a reversal of power alignments, signaling that the wearer would never be controlled by mainstream society.

The symbol that perhaps best emblematized the cool lifestyle associated with rap culture was baggy pants, often worn backwards, with the crotch near the knees, and without a belt, along with unlaced sneakers, bandanas, and earrings. The basic message of this dress code is "gangsta savvy," since it is imitative of prison clothes. For safety reasons, prisoners are not allowed to wear belts. So they are expected to wear their pants baggy-style. Hip hop youths have, in effect, embraced this prison-gang symbolism with its "in-your-face" attitude—an attitude that is a throwback to both the ersatz rebellious look of 1950s youths and to the confrontational images associated with punk culture.

The rap movement introduced new fashion trends into general youth culture in the 1990s, including back-to-Africa dashikis, shell necklaces, Kangol caps, sweat suits, unlaced high-top sneakers, gold chains, capped teeth, and beltless baggy pants. But despite the prominence that the movement achieved, it started to fade by the early part of the 2000s, as new trends came onto the scene. Since then, youth culture has continued to develop in a fragmented way, becoming at the same time more and more globalized through technology. This is why many social historians now talk about a "global youth culture" comprising many "national youth cultures." Indeed, as Sherry Turkle (1995) has aptly observed, youth culture is crossing over more and more to cyberspace, where it is developing a new form. Through social networking sites, and related online communities, teen cool has migrated to cyberspace. As Paul Hodkinson (2002, p. 148) wrote, "the Internet can also seem to encourage fabricated or fantasy identities which work to obscure the identities some participants have in real life," thus allowing young people to recreate themselves on their own terms. Similarly, Ken Gelder (2007, p. 147) noted that the Internet offers youths "a realm where one's yearnings for community can at last find their realization," constituting a kind of "extended family, a virtual village, where one can imagine going against the mainstream, the offline world."

But the nature of cool has not changed in the digital universe. It is still about the right dress, hairstyle, and the right language. And it is part of an unconscious history of cool. Consider the word *hot*, as used today to indicate someone sexy (including morphemic variants such as *hottie*). Around 1500, poets started using it to describe passionate love, as in *hot love*, which meant, "excited by sexual desire." This meaning spread in the 1800s, transforming the word into a term for "object of desire," as in "She is hot." In the 1920s, this meaning was attached to celebrities, movie stars, and jazz musicians, all of whom were perceived as living sexy lifestyles. It was used, for example, to describe the New Orleans style of jazz, as exemplified by Louis Armstrong. A 1933 film titled, *Hot Pepper*, featuring a sexy siren, epitomized, and probably ensconced, the use of *hot* as a code word for sexual attractiveness. From the 1930s to the 1960s the expression, *hot pants*, came forward as a slang term for sexy men and women. So, the use today of *hottie* in a sexual sense has really been a part of youth slang for a very long time.

Since the advent of the Internet, social media, and digital devices, the symbolism of cool has migrated to cyberspace and the use of digital devices (Gioia, 2009; Tapscott, 2009). Shifts in youth culture now tend to start and often unfold through the digital universe. Being on Facebook and Twitter and knowing how to manipulate the symbolic resources of these media (images, language styles, and so on) are becoming more and more the only type of cool adopted by youth culture. Social patterns of the past (courtship, hanging out, and so on) are now shifting to online culture more and more (Goodstein, 2007).

Young people have always tapped into technology as a means of interacting with each other and the world. In the 1920s, records and the radio were the media through which young people forged identities and developed a symbolism of cool. They helped to institutionalize emerging musical styles such as jazz and swing beyond the perimeter of youth culture. Young people bought the records and the radio stations played them. Shortly thereafter adults jumped in, modifying the new music to suit their own aesthetics. Radio and records also helped launch the "rock and roll" era of the 1950s, and later the counterculture movement of the 1960s and early 1970s. It thus comes as no surprise that the first massive users of the Internet were young people. Marshall McLuhan (1969) claimed that culture, social evolution, and technology are so intertwined that we hardly ever realize their dynamic, historical interconnection, because the interconnection occurs naturally and without awareness. We can witness this happening practically when a new device comes onto the market. At first, we make little of it. However, young people take to it quickly, and in no time it becomes not just a handy accoutrement in facilitating communication for everyone; in the process, it changes how we communicate. It also changes how we utilize the resources and materials of communication, such as writing style and form.

Because electronic modes of transmission increase the speed at which people can communicate and can reach many more instantly, they have had the effect of altering modes of interaction among youths. Given the historical partnership between youth and technology, it should come as no surprise to find that in the Digital Age young people are among the most active users of new technologies. A new way of congregating, or organizing encounters, has thus crystallized. It may start as either an online or offline mode; but eventually the two fuse into one seamless communicative, social dynamic, providing the means for friends to organize their encounters, events, and simply keep in touch.

Online media are now an integral part of the ways in which people now enact their life schemes. And this has changed the nature of how individuals now experience age and social affinity, altering the ways in which identity is created and managed, and how the sense of self that becomes prominent at adolescence is constructed. In many ways, cyberspace is leading to a complete revision of the theories of identity. In a study of South Korean youth, Kyongwon Yoon (2003) found that there were three kinds of relationships teens maintained via technology. The first was to connect primarily with those who were a part of their daily lives; for example, to keep in touch with school companions and friends in their immediate environment. The second was to maintain relationships with those who were a part of a broader social network, such as friends who attended other schools. The third was to develop and acquire new friendships and to strengthen initial face-to-face encounters. In effect, Yoon concluded, the new technology has allowed young people to become more and more united to each other. A perusal of Facebook sites not only confirms this finding, it also shows that the identity profile posted online reflects diversity in relationships. So on the same profile one would find an identity system that reflected relationships with close friends that was different from presentations of oneself that were directed at others. It would seem that in some areas of behavior, cyberspace is taking over from real space as a context for experiencing reality. As Tilleczek (2011, p. 70) put it, young people today no longer distinguish reality from cyber-reality: "Youth are so completely immersed in a technological world that a technologically unmediated experience of reality seems either false or unreal to them."

The late Jean Baudrillard (1983) used the term, *simulacrum*, to refer to the fact that many today rarely distinguish between reality and hyperreality (what occurs on the other side of the screen). But, it can be argued that social-media sites are appealing to people not because they are part of a simulacrum, but because they allow for a creative construction and management of identity. The sociologist Erving Goffman (1959) drew attention to the idea that everyday life is, in fact, very much like the theater, because it involves a skillful presentation of persona. Online environments are stages of a certain kind, where persona can also be staged and the Self understood. Thus, as Goodstein (2007, p. 12) argued, the online world may have changed where teens "hang out," but it has not changed the nature of the hanging out. The difference is the reach of the social world that the new technologies offer:

> What's different about today's totally wired teens is that the viral and public nature of these new technologies has magnified and publicized, though not changed, what it means to be a teen. Instead of gossiping with a friend and having it travel telephone-style through your school, that gossip can now travel through several schools and include mean pictures posted on a Web site. (Goodstein, 2007, pp. 12–13)

The online world may indeed be a brave, new, hyperreal world. Yet it has many of the same characteristics of the old world order, especially when it comes to fashioning identity and enacting cool. In both the real and online worlds, identity has always been a matter of constructing oneself with the available resources. As Gelder (2007, p. 143) has aptly put it, the Internet offers people "a realm where one's yearnings for community can at last find their realization." In a sense, the Internet has provided the perfect medium for people to write themselves into existence. Fiction is how we come to understand human life. Until recently, most of the fiction came from authors. Now, it is being made by everyone online. But in fiction there is truth. How we forge identity online may be fiction, but it is part of the way in which we envisage ourselves. Technology dictates the languages and the discourse forms in which we speak and think. If we do not use those languages, we will remain mute. And a mute identity is a nonexistent one; it reduces to raw consciousness.

Conclusion

As far back as the first decade of the twentieth century, the sociologist Émile Durkheim (1912) saw the inherent dangers of consumerism. He suggested that the Western world's blatant materialism had created the social conditions that ineluctably induced the all-pervading sense of alienation and of rootlessness that Western people so commonly feel. Durkheim was concerned that materialism had undermined the common values shared by a society, such as morality and religion. In his view, those values were the cohesive bonds that held the social order together. A breakdown of these values due to extreme forms of materialism, Durkheim asserted, led to a loss of social stability and to individual feelings of anxiety and dissatisfaction. It was Durkheim's notion of alienation (derived from Marxism) that initially motivated the countercultural movement of the 1960s. Those participating in that movement felt that they were doing something meaningful to combat alienation. They fought against misery and oppression. They sought to reestablish the spiritual over the material. But as it turned out, the hippies did not pull the plug on consumerism; they merely altered its approach and unwittingly gave it new dynamism.

The concept of cool emerged as part of a display of social rebellion—a placid and tacit form of rebellion. The rebellion was, in part, against alienation. Being cool allowed young people to connect with each other, and thus to combat the sense of angst that the modern world generated, as portrayed in *The Catcher in the Rye*. Cool is no longer an expression of rebellion. It is now simply a way of describing appearance and sociability. As we venture more deeply into the Age of the Internet, the synergy between youth culture, social change, and economics is taking on a new modality for two foreseeable reasons. First, the media stage for youth culture to exhibit itself is shifting away from the traditional electronic one of radio, television, and the movies and becoming more and more virtual. It remains to be seen if this new medium will be shaped by youth, or if youth culture itself will be shaped by it. Second, the social constitution of youth culture is no longer a homogeneous one, with various ethnicities and backgrounds of young people in multicultural and multilingual societies now playing an increasing role in the global village of youth culture. This is changing the meaning of cool and its functions. Many of the schemes put forward for theorizing about youth culture in the past are thus being reevaluated in the light of these emerging forces in world culture.

References

Adams, M. (2009). *Slang: The people's poetry*. Oxford, UK: Oxford University Press.

Adorno, T. (1949). *Philosophy of modern music*. Minneapolis, MN: University of Minnesota Press.

Bakhtin, M. (1981). *The dialogic imagination: Four essays*. Austin, TX: University of Texas Press.

Bakhtin, M. (1986). *Speech genres and other late essays*. Austin, TX: University of Texas Press.

Bakhtin, M. (1990). *Art and answerability*. Austin, TX: University of Texas Press.

Bakhtin, M. (1993a). *Rabelais and his world*. Bloomington, IN: Indiana University Press.

Bakhtin, M. (1993b). *Toward a philosophy of the act*. Austin, TX: University of Texas Press.

Baudrillard, J. (1983). *Simulations*. New York, NY: Semiotexte.

Cohen, S. (1972). *Folk devils and moral panics: The creation of mods and rockers*. London, UK: MacGibbon and Kee.

Coleman, J. C., & Hendry, L. B. (1990). *The nature of adolescence*. London, UK: Routledge.

Connor, M. K. (1995). *What is cool? Understanding Black manhood in America*. New York, NY: Crown.

Côté, J. E., & Allahar, A. L. (1994). *Generation on hold: Coming of age in the late twentieth century*. Toronto, Canada: Stoddart.

Côté, J. E., & Allahar, A. L. (2006). *Critical youth studies*. Toronto, Canada: Pearson Education.

Danesi, M. (1994). *Cool: The signs and meanings of adolescence*. Toronto, Canada: University of Toronto Press.

Danesi, M. (2003). *Forever young: The 'teen-aging' of modern culture*. Toronto, Canada: University of Toronto Press.

Danesi, M. (2010). *Geeks, goths, and gangstas: Youth culture and the evolution of modern society*. Toronto, Canada: Canadian Scholars' Press.

Desjarlais, L., & Rackauskas, J. A. (1986). *Adolescent development*. Toronto, Canada: Ontario Ministry of Education.

Durkheim, É. (1912). *The elementary forms of religious life*. New York, NY: Collier.

Eble, C. (1989). *College slang 101*. Georgetown, CT: Spectacle Lane Press.

Eble, C. (1996). *Slang and sociability*. Chapel Hill, NC: University of North Carolina Press.

Eble, C. (2004). Slang. In E. Finegan & J. Rickford (Eds.), *Language in the USA: Themes for the twenty-first century* (pp. 375–386). Cambridge, UK: Cambridge University Press.

Ewen, S. (1988). *All consuming images*. New York, NY: Basic Books.

Frank, T. (1997). *The conquest of cool: Business culture, counterculture, and the rise of hip consumerism*. Chicago, IL: University of Chicago Press.

Gelder, K. (2007). *Subcultures: Cultural histories and social practice*. London, UK: Routledge.

Gioia, T. (2009). *The birth (and death) of the cool*. Golden, CO: Speck Press.

Goffman, E. (1959). *The presentation of self in everyday life*. Garden City, NY: Doubleday.

Gold, H. (1994). *Bohemia: Digging the roots of cool*. New York, NY: Touchstone.

Goodstein, A. (2007). *Totally wired: What teens and tweens are really doing online*. New York, NY: St. Martin's Press.

Greenwald, T. (1992). *Rock & roll*. New York, NY: Friedman.

Grossberg, L. (1992). *We Gotta Get Out of This Place: Popular Conservatism and Postmodern Culture*. London: Routledge.

Hall, S. G. (1904). *Adolescence*. New York, NY: Appleton-Century-Crofts.

Hodkinson, P. (2002). *Goth: Identity, style and subculture*. New York, NY: Oxford University Press.

Laughey, D. (2006). *Music and youth culture*. Edinburgh, UK: Edinburgh University Press.

Leland, J. (2004). *Hip: The history*. New York, NY: HarperCollins.

Liu, A. (2004). *The laws of cool: Knowledge work and the culture of information*. Chicago, IL: University of Chicago Press.

MacAdams, L. (2001). *Birth of the cool: Beat, bebop, and the American avant-garde*. New York, NY: Free Press.

McLuhan, M. (1969). *Understanding media*. London, UK: Routledge & Kegan Paul.

Mead, M. (1928). *Coming of age in Samoa*. New York, NY: North American Library.

Mead, M. (1939). *From the South Seas: Studies of adolescence and sex in primitive societies*. New York, NY: Morrow.

Noxon, C. (2006). *Rejuvenile: Kickball, cartoons, cupcakes, and the reinvention of the American grown-up*. New York, NY: Three Rivers Press.

Palladino, G. (1996). *Teenagers: An American history*. New York, NY: Basic Books.

Pountain, D., & Robins, D. (2000). *Cool rules: Anatomy of an attitude*. London, UK: Reaktion.

Rice, F. P. (1990). *The adolescent*. Boston, MA: Allyn and Bacon.

Salinger, J. D. (1951). *The catcher in the rye*. Boston, MA: Little, Brown.

Savage, J. (2007). *Teenage: The prehistory of youth culture, 1875–1945*. London, UK: Penguin Books.

Sculatti, G. (1982). *Cool: A hipster's directory*. London, UK: Vermilion.

Stearns, P. N. (1994). *American cool: Constructing a twentieth-century emotional style*. New York, NY: New York University Press.

Tapscott, D. (2009). *Grown up digital: How the net generation is changing your world*. New York, NY: McGraw-Hill.

Tilleczek, K. (2011). *Approaching youth studies: Being, becoming, and belonging*. Oxford, UK: Oxford University Press.

Turkle, S. (1995). *Life on the screen: Identity in the age of the Internet*. New York, NY: Simon & Schuster.

Yoon, K. (2003). 'Retraditionalizing the mobile: Young people's sociality and mobile phone ue in Seoul, South Korea," *European Journal of Cultural Studies* 6, pp. 328–343.

CHAPTER 5

Becoming Revolutionaries
Toward Non-Teleological and Non-Normative Notions of Youth Growth

Michael O'Loughlin and P. Taylor Van Zile IV

Our purpose in this chapter is to seek to articulate ways in which young people might be given critical opportunities to read the discursive contexts of their lives, and thereby be given an opportunity to "imagine themselves otherwise" (cf. O'Loughlin & Johnson, 2010). Young people can experience constraints on their growth for many reasons. Silence in a family and community, for instance, may limit expansive possibilities for imagining self in terms of gender possibilities, racial and ethnic possibilities, class possibilities, or any subaltern subjective identifications. This can impose a sanitary cordon around a young person's imagination and lead to foreclosure of opportunity to imagine life otherwise. Lack of knowledge and lack of opportunity to engage in self-reflection around the socio-historical and socio-political contexts within which individual subjectivity is constituted, and the absence of a critical reading of the ways in which, as Butler (1997) noted, subjectivity is in large part constituted through subjection to pre-existing grand narratives of being, can lead to a lack of self-reflexivity about inter-generationally inherited ghosts, spectral traumas, and unsymbolized experiences, and can produce a re-enactment of foreclosed life scripts and delimited aspirations across generations (O'Loughlin, 2009, 2010a, 2013b). And then, of course, there is the conundrum of structural constraints imposed by hegemonic systems such as unequal schools, and institutionalized ethnic and/or racial and gender discrimination that can foreclose the possibilities of even the most determined young person. In *Ain't No Makin' It*, for example, Jay MacLeod (2008) demonstrated how structural and institutional constraints prohibited even the most diligent and conformist African American children from achieving upward mobility. On the other hand, Paul Willis's (1981) study, *Learning to Labor*, illustrated how the resilience and vigorous oppositionality to hegemonic school practices of a group of working-class adolescent males provoked a fascist response from school authorities and a rejection of schooling by the boys, causing them to fail and then to be consigned permanently to a marginal status. So, if playing the game does not produce results (MacLeod, 2008) and *not* playing the game does not produce results (Willis, 1981), what hope is there for those who are born out of entitlement?

An implicit assumption in this chapter is that critical possibilities for youth are expanded when institutions such as schooling and mass media are rendered less hegemonic through the opening up of rhizomatic possibilities for growth. Such opportunities cannot occur on a grand scale, however, unless the hegemonic systems in place (e.g., schooling, societal gender norms, and institutionalized inequality) are open to critical interrogation and change. The alternative, which the dissemination of the writings in this volume will help facilitate, is the creation of alternate *points de capiton* where new meanings can be defined and individual activists (teachers, youth leaders, youth themselves) can articulate revolutionary speech and action. A good starting point is with those children who, experiencing institutionalized systems as alienating and queer, rather than bowing down in conformity, seek out points of rupture and possibility with which they might re-punctuate their own received experience. However, without adults who can offer up the possibility of multiple and subaltern representations of selfhood, and without a radical expansion of the normative boundaries of selfhood, we condemn many such young people to "the well of loneliness" (cf. Hall 1928/1992) and to potential political paralysis and mutism.

Conceptualizing Subjectivity Otherwise

> With respect to ideology, what if the underlying foundations of the field are built around notions of commodification, i.e., the artful construction of childhood subjectivity to prepare a child for a specific niche in society? What if the articulation of norms for growth and the engineering of children's thought— however carefully orchestrated through inductive processes and "discovery learning" principles—is ultimately designed to produce a child who is a certain way. (O'Loughlin, 2014)

One of the difficulties in developing a critical way of thinking about child growth is that the child development paradigm has achieved canonical status in the field. The essentialist notion of self at the center of "the developing child" is inherently teleological and normative, and perhaps this accounts for its enduring popularity as the central trope of forms of pedagogy that are fundamentally assimilative and didactic in intent. Early childhood education, for example, is constructed entirely around the notion of "developmentally appropriate practice," and it forms the core of a paradigm of pedagogical practice that, while couched in humanistic terms, fundamentally views teachers and parents as socializing children toward attaining predetermined milestones in a linear, cumulative fashion. Backed up by the tyranny of "evidence-based practices" and the disciplining mechanisms of accreditation (cf. Biesta, 2007), developmental notions of "child development" have a stranglehold on educational discourses and practices.[1]

In *The Queer Child* (2009), Kathryn Stockton asked about the fate of the child who cannot or will not follow a predetermined, hierarchical path toward a uniform end. Stockton said that such a child has "nowhere to grow" (2009, p. 3), and she suggested that what is needed are models of growth that accommodate multiple sideways paths to growth, rather than one single, invariant, hierarchical, stage-like process of growing "up." Under our current system, the only way we can conceptualize somebody who refuses to "grow up" is as developmentally delayed, aberrant, deviant, or simply queer.

Central to the teleology of developmental growth, as we noted elsewhere (O'Loughlin, 2014), is a normative notion of the child as innocent, asexual, and inherently bound toward a heterosexual, middle-class, commodified form of "success." The child who fails at this, or at least fails at faking normality, is consigned to a place of misrecognition. While the self-destructive behavior of "the lads" in Paul Willis's study ultimately undermined their political and economic agency, the solidarity they exhibited can be viewed as a form of protection against the annihilation visited on those who refuse to play the game—a game, of course, in which, as they know all too well, the dice is loaded against them from the outset, and upward mobility demands submission to forces of annihilation. How, under such circumstances, might a young person maintain hope, desire, and possibility?

In our work we reject the core epistemological principles of both developmental psychology and prescriptive pedagogy, irrespective of how carefully they are couched in a language of humanism and student-centeredness. We find it disheartening that even though the seminal book, *Changing the Subject* (Henriques, Holloway, Urwin, Venn, & Walkerdine, 1984), was published thirty years ago, and despite a steady stream of critical scholarship on childhood subjectivity since then (e.g., Britzman, 1998, 2003, 2006, 2009, 2010; Burman, 1994; O'Loughlin, 2009, 2010b, 2013a, 2013d, 2014; O'Loughlin & Johnson, 2010; Stainton-Rogers & Stainton-Rogers, 1992; Tobin, 1997; Walkerdine, 1984, 1987, 1990a, 1990b, 2002, 2004), the foundational role of developmental psychology as a basis for thinking about young people's experiences remains unchanged. Clearly the current paradigm serves the status quo very well indeed.

In contrast to an essentialist notion of an intrapsychic developing selfhood, we prefer to think of youth subjectivity as constructed through immersion in the world. The child's entry into prevailing symbolic systems necessitates, as Althusser (1971) observed, that the child become interpellated by culture. As Richards (1984) noted in *Capitalism and Infancy*, it is vital to understand the role of context and ideology in the formation of subjectivity. Thus, contrary to the generic essential child of developmental psychology, we must seek to understand a young person who is coming to be in a particular ideological milieu, as well as embedded in particular familial (cf. Donzelot, 1979) and socio-historical (cf. Fraiberg, Adelson, & Shapiro, 1975) discursive regimes. Considering subjectivity as discursively constructed acknowledges the situationality of subjectivity, and poses the dilemma of assimilation that conventional developmental psychology must brush aside in order to maintain its singular teleology. The dilemma, as Butler (1997) noted, is that becoming a subject necessarily means becoming subject to prevailing discursive practices. It is not that there is a pre-existing subject who is influenced by contextual variables. Rather, it is through entry into symbol systems that we become who we are in the process of becoming. Considering subjectivity discursively, as Henriques, Holloway, Urwin, Venn, and Walkerdine (1984) noted in their seminal critique, therefore, allows us to recognize the dilemma of socialization, and hence to pose the question of where we might identify ruptures and fissures in which subaltern identifications and imaginaries might emerge. In recent writings (O'Loughlin, 2009, 2010a, 2014), the possibility of challenging conventional norms of socialization was explored through the possibilities involved in troubling the spectral origins and genealogical anchors of experience. In this chapter, we will complement that analysis by offering a discussion of the possibility of rhizomatic analysis as another tool that has potential for assisting young people in articulating subaltern visions and imaginaries.

A Rhizomatic Perspective on Youth Subjectivity

Children are slippery movement. They slip and slide through experience, sometimes smoothly, sometimes with great turbulence. Randolph Bourne (1913) wrote that, "youth is always turbulent, but the momentous difference is whether it shall be turbulent in passion or in enthusiasm" (p. 5). Movement can be explosive; it can be subtle. It is dynamic in its ebb and flow—transmutative—it has a sense of randomness and a lack of control that is both exhilarating and frightening. Kathryn Stockton (2009) described one type of movement, sideways growth, which

> refer(s) to something related but not reducible to the death drive; something that locates energy, pleasure, vitality, and (e)motion in the back-and-forth of connections and extensions that are not reproductive. These I will theorize as the moving suspension and shadows of growth. (p. 13)

Stockton spoke to the idea that childhood subjectivity is generative by nature, and she located subjectivity within a back-and-forth, dichotomous movement that extends outwardly in a multiplicitous, yet uniform motion of sideways growth.

An alternative approach, that complements Stockton's formulation, is to conceptualize childhood subjectivity as a deleuzoguattarian, rhizomatic root system: it is unpredictably generative and re/actively creative. A rhizomatic root system is an anti-genealogy; it is defined not by linearity, but by scattered and concentric multiplicities: "In nature, roots are taproots with a more multiple, lateral, and circular system of ramification, rather than a dichotomous one …. The binary logic of dichotomy has simply been replaced by biunivocal relationships between successive circles" (Deleuze & Guattari, 1980/1987, p. 5). A rhizome simultaneously grows into and out of itself, severs and (re)grows, and breaks the confines of the soil by reaching into the air as it is so moved. Childhood subjectivity so grows, severs, explodes, and implodes: it resists and shakes the dichotomies of innocence and corruption, ignorance and knowledge, morality and deviance, and instead "allows for an immanent transformation, a coming into being of a state of life in this world, one that is constantly shifting and producing of new subject/individual positions" (Kuppers, 2009, p. 226). This constant state of becoming and transformation involves an immersion and oneness with the tactile, physical, emotional, and relational. It is constantly sliding like a Lacanian signifier—perpetually (re)defined by the experiences that come before and after. It is ever elusive, yet heading to an end ("I want to be …"). Authoritarian demand can impose an empty end ("Become a doctor … an optician … a heterosexual husband/wife") in an attempt to keep a child's movements restricted and linear, similar to the upright growth of a tree. Yet, like the rhizome, a child's subjective experience has the potential to incorporate and grow into and/or out of linear, causally en-snared, demanding modes of operationalizing experience: "a tree branch or root division may begin to burgeon into a rhizome … a new rhizome may form in the heart of a tree, the hollow of the root, the crook of a branch" (Deleuze & Guattari, 1980/1987, p. 15).

One component of the deleuzoguattarian rhizome is the line of flight, "the abstract line, the line of flight or deterritorialization according to which (multiplicities) change in nature and connect with other multiplicities" (Deleuze & Guattari, 1980/1987, p. 9). Lines of flight connect, break through, and transform multiplicities that co-exist on planes of consistency. A line of flight is a way to pierce through systems of stratification, to escape a "boxed in" way of thinking, and consequently, to sub-vert repression. Lines of flight make the connection of seemingly isolated ideas possible by bridging multiple systems of thought to create new multiplicities, while simultaneously broadening those with which it connects. For example, Marcel Duchamp's *Fountain* constructed a line of flight between the previously existing multiplicities of "urinal" and "art gallery" to create a frenzied expansion of both multiplicities (for image, see Duchamp, 1917).

The mutagenesis of a young person's subjectivity is located within a myriad of assemblages. An assemblage, according to Deleuze and Guattari, is a grouping of lines and movements that are found together within a context. This context is not singular, nor well defined. It contains a multitude of pos-sible outcomes. Deleuze and Guattari described their books as assemblages: they are full of concepts, movements, and possibilities that are located in one context, but that can provoke any number of pos-sible thoughts/(re)actions/movements.

The child's body is one type of assemblage that plays a vital role in children's subjective experience. As Richard Johnson's keen eye observed, the body of the child in relation to itself and other bodies has gone missing in the contemporary discourse surrounding childhood experience: "When and why did the subject of young children, their body(s), them personally, become abject?" (Johnson, 2010, p. 126). The question posed by Johnson here is one that is difficult to answer, but it points to a trend in which young children's bodies are frequently ignored in commercialized and popularized concepts of "child-hood." As James Kincaid (2004) pointed out, when children's bodies are present in discourse, they are often emptied out bodies onto which adults' fantasies and demands are projected. The flattened, min-iaturized body of a child loses its performative significance, and gets replaced by the one-dimensional "idea" of the child (i.e., the innocent child, the out-of-control child, the child as savior). The disem-bodied child is static, linear, totalized. The rhizomatic body of the child, however, is metastatic, and can break free of the ways in which society "orders, controls, and striates bodies as fixed, unconnected, and rooted apart from one another" (Goodley, 2009, p. 260). Petra Kuppers (2003, 2009) conceptualized the body as a place of radical performance and possibility. Despite the body necessarily being read within a system of ideas and constructs (dis/abled, empty/of color), there are spaces of openness where (r)evolution is possible, and constructs can be (re)imagined through the body:

> There is no 'outside' to this system, but moments of openness and difference can be found within it as part of its living, changing nature: knowledge is always in flux and process. 'Performativity' as a term points to the embodied, living quality of knowledge, and its continued production of truth. (Kuppers, 2003, p. 6)

For Kuppers the body is a place from which children can impact the (r)evolution and movement of self-knowledge as it exists within/out of systems of knowledge. A body is a "vibrational movement in which identities are neither essentialized nor compounded, instead, they are in tactile relation to each other" (Kuppers, 2009, p. 229). Children's bodies consume, digest, and produce. By re-integrating children's bodies into our discourse, we can draw more attention to the child's body as a space-of-action, as potentially agentic. Bodies are constantly evolving selves composed of growing and dying cells, and complex neural networks that are ever expanding and connecting in unpredictable ways. Without the skin, the hair, the fluid, and the organs, we have lost the child and the valuable role that their senses play in transforming and interpreting their subjective experiences. Reclaiming the importance of the child's body is a necessary political act of empowerment, as the body is a performative space for the child's re/presentation of subjectivity.

The energy located in bodies is trans-animating. It is passed between journeying objects. Maneuvers, growths, and transferential experiences create friction and heat. Bodies contact each other, shift each other, react to each other, and inform each other ("You're so tall!," "You stink."). Movement is not isolated: it is located within systems of flux and flow in which not all movement is equally mobile. By imposing systems of "childhood" onto children's subjective experiences our goal is to block flight, to guide flow, to contain and confine the ebullient power of experience. We take away paths of wandering: children are not empowered to be citizens in the eyes of the law, children are not qualified to be productive in systems of capital, children's bodies (sexual and/or sensory) are denied: in all of these contexts, children are transformed into ghostly puppets. Children are only allowed to operate in well-defined spaces in ways that adults deem appropriate.

Children are rhizomes growing in permafrost. As Stockton (2009) noted, "adults walk the line—the impossible line—of keeping the child at once what it is (what adults are not) and leading it toward what it cannot (at least, itself) ever be (what adults are)" (pp. 30–31). As Lacan taught us, we limit children's movements before they are conceived: we ascribe meaning to "them" and place "them" in pre-existing systems of being and information by naming them, talking about our expectations and our hopes, and constructing their living quarters to reflect who we expect they will become (a heterosexual boy who likes ships and trains, a heterosexual girl who loves the color pink, teddy bears, etc…). The permafrost begins to harden the instant the child is conceptualized. As a result, children are birthed into a pre-existing system of constructed selves that are immediately superimposed on and/or into the child's body ("You have your father's nose and your mother's eyes"; "He's got the build of an athlete!"). The symbols and expectations are concretized on a body that is now a rigid designator for a system of projected ideas.

As symbols and ideas are imposed, the permafrost gets harder, colder, and more restrictive. Slowly it begins to crush the rhizome. The permafrost funnels movement into particular channels that restrict children's bodies and experiences to certain spaces and modes of being. Compliance is no longer a choice, it is mandated. That is growing up. Adults and children alike are part of structured systems of language and power. These systems are negotiable and fluid, but only when people acquire the meta-analytic tools necessary to be aware of the systems within which they are ensnared. We need to thaw the permafrost to enable free passage and evolving perspectives, to allow children to explode out of the dirt and dive into it, to imbibe moisture from the soil while remaining distinct from it. The movements of the root systems are capable of breaking up the soil: both depend on each other for survival and malleability.

Rhizomatic Possibilities for Youth Growth

In seeking to illustrate the potential of rhizomatic analysis and practices, we offer two brief illustrations, one in the arena of pedagogical practices, and one in the arena of emergent technologies. Both arenas are laden with possibilities for engendering revolutionary thought, but, inevitably, since pedagogy and technology are both powerful societal discourses, embedded in and functioning in relation to capitalism and other hegemonic structures, radical possibilities can only be realized through critical awareness coupled with a willingness to struggle to pursue rhizomatic possibilities which necessarily include assemblages of life narratives that are counter to established master narratives, norms, and expectations.

Rhizomatic possibilities in pedagogical practices

What rhizomatics offers to an already well-established genre of critical pedagogy (cf. Freire, 1969, 1970, 2005; Giroux, 2001, 2011; Hayes, Steinberg, & Tobin, 2011; Kincheloe, 2008, 2010; McLaren, 1999, 2006; McLaren & Kincheloe, 2007) is a set of analytic tools for breaking down the task of pushing back against regimes of signification and establishing what de Freitas (2012) called "an ontology of the social." This, in conjunction with a complementary "psychoanalysis of the social," articulated elsewhere in our work (O'Loughlin, 2009, 2010a, 2010b, 2013a, 2013b, 2014), offers tools for recontextualizing critical pedagogy in ways that are sensitive to the multiple layers of discourse and hierarchy that underlie the power relations of knowledge production and identity formation in contemporary Western societies. Rhizomatics, as noted earlier, allows us to capitalize on the discontinuities, ruptures, fissures, and inconsistencies of prevailing hegemonic practices, and thereby to pose questions about individual desire, social justice, collective good, and shared responsibility for our planet and peoples.

To take a very simple example, Michael O'Loughlin (2009) described spending a year as a consultant in a third-grade classroom in a public school in a very marginalized urban community, and running into student disinterest and opposition as he made futile efforts to engender excitement using classic children's literature as a pedagogical tool. Flailing for a solution, he introduced Matt Groening's (2004) cartoon book, *School Is Hell*, to the students. Drawing on his own experience in school, Groening offered a biting satire of the most oppressive aspects of traditional didactic and authoritarian pedagogy. By providing children with a critical vocabulary and meta-perspectives within which to voice their own daily experiences of oppressive and unjust schooling, the children were able to explore new lines of flight: to escape, enter, and transform assemblages, to construct new maps of the permafrost that surrounded them. The children created their own cartoons that wove together themes from the original book with facets of their own unique histories, which added progressive lines of flight to the discourse of the classroom. "The resulting texts provide windows into some children's constructions of their school lives, as well as into the pedagogical potential of popular culture genres such as cartoons and comics as a means of exploiting the emancipatory possibilities of literacy" (O'Loughlin, 2009, p. 214). By integrating critical voices and perspectives into pedagogical frameworks, we can free up the possibility for youth movement, while at the same time encouraging young people to gain mastery over tools of empowerment such as literacy by, for example, interrogating the relations between popular culture and literacy practices, and moving beyond the mimetic to performative understandings of their own current and possible lives. Literacy interventions by Dyson (1993, 1997, 2003) and Lensmire (1994, 2000) are similarly suggestive of what is possible in this arena.

The power of rhizomatics is that it allows meaning to explode inwards and outwards, and combined with forms of pedagogy that value history, autobiography, and critical questioning, it has the potential to create critical spaces where young people can develop a critical understanding of the intergenerational inheritances and discursive positionings within which their current subjectivity is being created, as well as allowing them to imagine and perform alternate identifications and subjectivities. A critical difference is that rhizomatics upends the canonical, linear, and cumulative notion of curriculum that favors knowledge consumption and that thereby limits access to knowledge-making for young people. Elsewhere we characterized some of the elements of this kind of rhizomatic process that contribute to the pursuit of critical forms of subjectivization.

Turning, then, to pedagogy, a social-historical psychoanalytic approach calls for subjectivization as a primary goal. Pedagogy ought to provide opportunities for an intensive engagement with spoken and unspoken experience, with history, lore, ancestry, and imagination, so that each child can enter into a dynamic relationship with the ruptures and gaps of the past, and with multiple possible futures. A minimal condition of depth pedagogy, therefore, is the reclamation of narrative threads and the location of children as subjects in history—people with genealogical filiations, narrative continuity, and a possibility for becoming that is informed by, but not constrained by, ancestral, historical, and familial legacies. Each child possesses a latent, culturally constituted unconscious that embodies ancestral history and ways of being, as well as inherited traumas due to displacements, wars, genocides, familial trauma, and other forms of unspoken and unmetabolized suffering. Ought not a teacher to be prepared to tap into these resources to help children better understand their locations in history?

> From a pedagogical perspective, in addition to creating an inviting intersubjective and emotionally secure dialogical space, teachers should understand how to evoke the unconscious in children through their own evocative presences. A teacher with a passion for myth, storytelling, drama, memory, and the wisdom of elders will draw these evocative knowledges into the classroom, and will elicit evocative responses from students that allow students to experience their own inner knowledges as namable and addressable. (O'Loughlin, 2009, p. 160)

This kind of work has resonance with the Freirean notion of a pedagogy grounded in generative themes (Freire, 1970), and in the idea of a political literacy embodied in the phrase, "reading the word, reading the world" (Freire & Macedo, 1987). The radical potential of this kind of work is that, in keeping with the liberatory leanings of early psychoanalysis (cf. Danto, 2002; Moskowitz, 1996; O'Loughlin, 2010b; Watkins & Shulman, 2008) and of critical psychoanalytic practice today, it seeks to assist people in learning to question (Freire & Faundez, 1989), rather than giving them the illusion of understanding (O'Loughlin, 2013c, pp. 40–41).

As noted, such a vision is not far removed from Paulo Freire's (1969, 1970) notion of education for critical consciousness, and the use of generative themes to ground pedagogical questions in the lived experience of community members. However, mindful of Myles Horton's deep suspicion of conventional educators, with their instrumental, teleological, and technocratic training, and their insertion into hegemonic systems of social control (cf. Horton, 1997; Horton & Freire, 1990; Jacobs, 2003), perhaps it might be more productive to imagine this kind of critical educational practice taking place outside of school, as part, for example, of a popular education movement for youth, rather than risk its inevitable co-optation and domestication as it became absorbed into conventional pedagogy. The choice of Southern, Black beauty-parlor owners as the linchpin of the Citizenship Schools certainly points to the need for imaginative, grounded thinking in looking to see where the fissures and points of rupture might be identified that can produce critical rhizomatic possibilities. Critical educators, too, need to think rhizomatically, in seeking to advance their strategic causes, as Myles Horton's work at Highlander Folk School illustrated so beautifully.

Rhizomatic possibilities for youth in uses of social media and Internet

> This morning, Erdogan called social media "the worst menace to society," saying it has been used to spread lies about the protests and the government's response. That's probably not the best way to look like you care about what the protesters are saying. (Harkinson, 2013)

Just as with the Arab Spring before it, in many ways the recent social upheaval in Turkey was being shaped significantly by social media. While Prime Minister Erdogan's government muzzled television broadcasters, social media continued to function as tools of political organization and dissemination. Social media provide spaces in which youth are able to hyperlink themselves into and out of multiple concentric circles. The merger of youth and social media opens up a cornucopia of possible becomings that occur so rapidly and move so quickly that they are nearly impossible to constrain. Smartphones offer youth spaces of transgression that can be accessed in an under-desk economy of self-(re)presentations (social media and/or micro blogging), intersubjective de/constructions (texting), and ghostly communications (real-time picture chatting). These spaces allow young people to deconstruct their pre-constructed and individualized subjectivities, and allow them playful spaces in which to explore the possibilities of their inter/subjectivity:

> The role of technology is at the heart of the process of blurring fundamental categorical divides between self and other; a sort of heteroglossia of the species, a colossal hybridization which combines cyborgs, monsters, insects, and machines into a powerfully posthuman approach to what used to be called "the embodied subject." (Braidotti, 2005)

The spaces created by technology allow for transformative experiences of explosive movement, map construction, and the creation of new discourses and languages (emoticons, emojis, initialisms). The transgressive possibilities of technology are often feared by paternalizing and subjugating entities, who have attempted to constrain and even outlaw these lines of flight, with China providing the most heavy-handed example of such censorship. Apart from the computer engineering elite, the people who use social media with the greatest finesse and imagination are youth, and just as rock and roll and hip hop functioned subversively in earlier eras, social media give youth a decided edge in the creation and dissemination of subversive and underground discourses.

In many respects, then, social media spaces are replete with rhizomatic possibility. They permit young people to transcend boundaries of space, time, and chronology, and they have been instrumental in enabling, for example, many queer youth to expand the subjective possibilities of their own becoming and their capacity to affiliate with larger groups. Furthermore, the uses of social media in social uprisings such as the Arab Spring and the recent uprisings in Turkey, as well as the Occupy Wall Street movement in the US, are suggestive of the potential for politically informed collective action. Whether such revolutionary possibilities are realized, however, depends on how critically such media are deployed by youth.

A primary function of social-media companies and distributors of "smart" technologies is to shape consumer demand, and to promote the commodification not only of knowledge, but of social interchange. Technologies are not neutral. Just as surely as our subjectivities are shaped by browsing in a shopping mall, purchasing an automobile, or browsing on the Internet, so, too—but probably to a much greater extent—our subjectivities are shaped by social media and "smart" technologies. In what ways are the tenets of commodification and consumption entering our experience through this process? Social-media spaces are rapidly being co-opted, commercialized, and commodified. For example, YouTube and Facebook, once commercial-free, have become polluted with complex, targeted advertising strategies that are designed to shape people's desire by imposing profit-driven demands. Gmail scans our email to direct suitable advertising our way. These demands are stealthily (or obviously) built into virtual landscapes so that we are sub/liminally bombarded with new demands that limit our lines of flight by funneling our movements into the realm of production and consumption. Those who participate in Internet browsing and social media are simultaneously consumers and commodified products. Consumption and browsing patterns are sold to corporations that then use the data to shape consumer desires and sell yet more products (cf. Smythe, 1988). Dmytri Kleiner (2013) argued that Internet users' experiences are further constrained by the centralized nature of our Web participation. The vast majority of users are only given a handful of tools (run by profit-driven corporations such as Apple, Google, Facebook, Microsoft, and Twitter), inherently limiting choice and constructing experiences in a uniform way. When we perform a Web search on Google, we are implicitly trusting Google to accurately construct and organize the information we seek. This gives the Google results a certain authority, by making their existences and orders a scientifically justified reality. The results are described as "organized," "efficient," and "algorithmically determined." This becomes problematic to users when Google legitimizes and/or normalizes certain aspects of discourse that discourage subjective possibilities, such as, for example, showing results for the term, *worst*, when the term, *gayest*, is entered in a Google search bar (Peitzman, 2013).

With respect to Internet knowledge, while the democratization of knowledge access is to be welcomed, it is possible that many youthful Internet users browse only at the surface level, having neither the desire nor the inclination to acquire the tools that would be necessary to dig deeper. Considerable cultural capital and sophistication are also necessary to discern reasoned opinion from polemic, and in order to go beyond the surface of many complex websites, significant academic preparation is required. While on the surface a cornucopia of democratic and egalitarian knowledge sources are available, in fact, the same mechanisms of cultural sorting are in effect as those that historically delineated those who should read *The Economist* or *The New York Times* from those who were relegated to *the New York Post*. Instead of the kind of pseudo-democratization provided by the conceit that the Internet caters to the lowest common denominator intellectually, a critical project would seek to give youth access to both the intellectual tools to dig deep, and the critical tools, as Paulo Freire notably exhorted, to "read the word and the world."

Conclusion

In an ideal world, the decentralization of information and technology corporations is necessary to rhizomatic growth, in order to promote choice and expand the possibilities of becoming. To do this, Kleiner (2013) argued that alternative work organizations require sufficient funding to compete with monopoly marketing and education programs. The development of filtering software such as ad blockers, and alternative Web browsers may offer some possibility for greater consumer control. If navigated correctly, digital assemblages, unlike the commercially polluted landscapes that necessarily encompass our anthropoidal experience (clothing logos, billboards, etc.), can be decommodified and decentralized. The removal of parental and corporate demand (i.e., advertisements, firewalls, information collection) is a simple hack or line of code away to those in the know. While some of this expertise may pass to generations of youth through the folkways of social media, more likely, it will take a sustained effort around critical media education to produce a generation of young people who can use the immense rhizomatic possibilities of the Internet and social media for critical self-exploration and the establishment of social-justice projects.

Finally, as has been well established in human affairs, tools that can be used for social good also have the potential to be used for social harm. The prevalence of predatory, hateful, and violence-promoting content on the Internet, as well as the increased use of social media for cyber-bullying, all point to the vulnerability of youth to being sucked uncritically into the vortex of the social reproduction of anti-social and even evil acts. These concerns underline even more the importance of critical media and social-justice education in allowing young people to take advantage of the rhizomatic properties of social media for socially good purposes. With freedom comes responsibility, and our greatest responsibility as educators is to devise forums and media that can be used either within formal educational structures or outside of them in popular education venues to give young people the opportunity to develop habits of active participatory citizenship, and to advance the dream of a social revolution. It is the least we can do to preserve the legacy of the critical educators that have come before us, and to offer alternate paths toward active citizenship to future young persons.

Note

1. See O'Loughlin (2013a) for critique of contemporary pedagogy, and O'Loughlin (2009, 2014) for critique of the hegemony of developmentally appropriate practice in early education.

References

Althusser, L. (1971). Ideology and ideological state apparatuses (Notes towards an investigation). In L. Althusser, *Lenin and philosophy, and other essays* (pp. 127–186). New York, NY: Monthly Review Press.

Biesta, G. (2007). Why 'what works' won't work: Evidence-based practice and the democratic deficit in educational research. *Educational Theory, 57*(1), 1–22.

Bourne, R. (1913). *Youth and life*. Boston, MA: Houghton Mifflin.

Braidotti, R. (2005). Affirming the affirmative: On nomadic affectivity. *Rhizomes, 11*. Retrieved from http://rhizomes.net/issue11/braidotti.html

Britzman, D. (1998). *Lost subjects, contested objects: Toward a psychoanalytic inquiry of learning*. Albany, NY: State University of New York Press.

Britzman, D. (2003). *After-education: Anna Freud, Melanie Klein and psychoanalytic histories of learning*. Albany, NY: State University of New York Press.

Britzman, D. (2006). *Novel education: Psychoanalytic studies of learning and not learning*. New York, NY: Peter Lang

Britzman, D. (2009). *The very thought of education: Psychoanalysis and the impossible professions*. Albany, NY: State University of New York Press.

Britzman, D. (2010). *Freud and education*. New York, NY: Routledge.

Burman, E. (1994). *Deconstructing developmental psychology*. London, UK: Routledge.

Butler, J. (1997). *The psychic life of power*. New York, NY: Routledge.

Danto, E, (2002). *Freud's free clinics: Psychoanalysis and social justice, 1918–1938*. New York: Columbia University Press

de Freitas, E. (2012). The classroom as rhizome: New strategies for diagramming knotted interactions. *Qualitative Inquiry, 18*(7), 588–601.

Deleuze, G., & Guattari, F. (1987). *A thousand plateaus: Capitalism and schizophrenia*. (B. Massumi, Trans.). Minneapolis, MN: University of Minnesota Press.

Donzelot, J. (1979). *The policing of families*. New York, NY: Pantheon.

Duchamp, M. (1917). Fountain. Retrieved from http://www.tate.org.uk/art/artworks/duchamp-fountain-t07573

Dyson, A. H. (1993). *The social worlds of children learning to write in an urban primary school*. New York, NY: Teachers College Press.

Dyson, A. H. (1997). *Writing superheroes: Contemporary childhood, popular culture and classroom literacy*. New York, NY: Teachers College Press.

Dyson, A. H. (2003). *The brothers and sisters learn to write: Popular literacies in childhood, school and cultures*. New York, NY: Teachers College Press.

Fraiberg, S., Adelson, E., & Shapiro, V. (1975). Ghosts in the nursery: A psychoanalytic approach to the problems of impaired infant-mother relationships. *Journal of the American Academy of Child Psychiatry, 14*(3), 387–421.

Freire, P. (1969). *Education for critical consciousness*. New York, NY: Continuum.

Freire, P. (1970). *Pedagogy of the oppressed*. New York, NY: Continuum.

Freire, P. (2005). *Teachers as cultural workers: Letters to those who dare teach*. Boulder, CO: Westview Press.

Freire, P., & Faundez, A. (1989). *Learning to question: A pedagogy of liberation* (T. Coates, Trans.). New York, NY: Continuum.

Freire, P., & Macedo, D. (1987). *Literacy: Reading the word and the world*. Westport, CT: Bergin & Garvey.

Giroux, H. (2001). *Theory and resistance in education: Towards a pedagogy for the opposition*. Westport, CT: Praeger.

Giroux, H. (2011). *On critical pedagogy*. New York, NY: Bloomsbury Academic.

Goodley, D. (2009). Bringing the psyche back into disability studies: The case of the body with/out organs. *Journal of Literary & Cultural Disability Studies, 3*(3), 257–272.

Groening, M. (2004). *School is hell: A cartoon book by Matt Groening*. New York, NY: HarperCollins.

Hall, R. (1992). *The well of loneliness*. Cutchogue, NY: Buccaneer Books.

Harkinson, J. (2013, June 3). The protests in Turkey, explained. *Mother Jones*. Retrieved from http://www.motherjones.com/politics/2013/06/instanbul-erdogan-turkey-protests-explained

Hayes, K., Steinberg, S., & Tobin, J. (Eds.). (2011). *Key works in critical pedagogy: Joe L. Kincheloe*. Rotterdam, The Netherlands: Sense.

Henriques, J., Holloway, W., Urwin, C., Venn, C., & Walkerdine, V. (1984). *Changing the subject: Psychology, social regulation, and subjectivity*. London, UK: Methuen.

Horton, M. (1997). *The long haul: An autobiography*. New York, NY: Teachers College Press.

Horton, M., & Freire, P. (1990). *We make the road by walking: Conversations on education and social change*. Philadelphia, PA: Temple University Press.

Jacobs, D. (Ed.). (2003). *The Myles Horton reader: Education for social change.* Knoxville, TN: University of Tennessee Press.

Johnson, R. (2010). Putting myself in the picture: Oppositional looks as sites of resistance. In M. O'Loughlin & R. Johnson (Eds.), *Imagining children otherwise: Theoretical and critical perspectives on childhood subjectivity* (pp. 111–134). New York, NY: Peter Lang.

Kincaid, J. (2004). Producing erotic children. In S. Bruhm & N. Hurley (Eds.), *Curiouser: On the queerness of children* (pp. 3–16). Minneapolis, MN: University of Minnesota Press.

Kincheloe, J. (2008). *Critical pedagogy primer.* New York, NY: Peter Lang.

Kincheloe, J. (2010). *Knowledge and critical pedagogy: An introduction.* New York, NY: Springer.

Kleiner, D. (2013). Dmytri Kleiner: Facebook is Internet reimagined through imagination of network television capitalism [Web series episode]. *SkriptaTV.* Zagreb, Croatia: YouTube. Retrieved from http://www.youtube.com/watch?v=CK319sIWwbA

Kuppers, P. (2003). *Disability and contemporary performance: Bodies on edge.* New York: Routledge.

Kuppers, P. (2009). Toward a rhizomatic model of disability. *Journal of Literary & Cultural Disability Studies, 3*(3), 221–240.

Lensmire, T. J. (1994). *When children write: Critical re-visions of the writing workshop.* New York, NY: Teachers College Press.

Lensmire, T. J. (2000). *Powerful writing, responsible teaching.* New York, NY: Teachers College Press.

MacLeod. J. (2008). *Ain't no makin' it: Aspirations and attainment in a low-income neighborhood.* Boulder, CO: Westview Press.

McLaren, P. (1999). *Che Guevara, Paulo Freire, and the pedagogy of revolution.* Lanham, MD: Rowman & Littlefield.

McLaren, P. (2006). *Life in schools: An introduction to critical pedagogy in the foundations of education* (5th ed.). New York, NY: Pearson.

McLaren, P., & Kincheloe, J. (Eds.). (2007). *Critical pedagogy: Where are we now?* New York, NY: Peter Lang.

Moskowitz, M. (1996). The social conscience of psychoanalysis. In R. Perez Foster, M. Moskowitz & R. Javier (Eds.), *Reaching across boundaries of culture and class: Widening the script of psychoanalysis.* Lanham, MD: Jason Aronson.

O'Loughlin, M. (2009). *The subject of childhood.* New York, NY: Peter Lang.

O'Loughlin, M. (2010a). Ghostly presences in children's lives: Toward a psychoanalysis of the social. In M. O'Loughlin & R. Johnson (Eds.), *Imagining children otherwise: Theoretical and critical perspectives on childhood subjectivity* (pp. 49–74). New York, NY: Peter Lang.

O'Loughlin, M. (2010b, October). Reclaiming a liberatory vision for psychoanalysis. In M. O'Loughlin (Organizer), *The psychologies of liberation: Clinical, critical and pedagogical perspectives.* Symposium conducted at the Annual Meeting of Association of Psychoanalysis, Culture & Society, Rutgers University, New Brunswick, NJ.

O'Loughlin, M. (Ed.). (2013a). *Psychodynamic perspectives on working with children, families and schools.* Lanham, MD: Jason Aronson.

O'Loughlin, M. (2013b). Reclaiming genealogy, memory and history: The psychodynamic potential for reparative therapy in contemporary South Africa. In C. Smith, G. Lobban, & M. O'Loughlin (Eds.), *Psychodynamic psychotherapy in contemporary South Africa: Contexts, theories, practices* (pp. 242–71). Johannesburg, South Africa: Wits University Press.

O'Loughlin, M. (Ed.). (2013c). The uses of psychoanalysis. In M. O'Loughlin (Ed.), *The uses of psychoanalysis in working with children's emotional lives* (pp. 27–46). Lanham, MD: Jason Aronson.

O'Loughlin, M. (Ed.). (2013d). *The uses of psychoanalysis in working with children's emotional lives.* Lanham, MD: Jason Aronson.

O'Loughlin, M. (2014). Still waiting for the revolution. In M. Bloch, B. Swadener, & G. Cannella (Eds.), *Reconceptualizing early childhood care and education: Critical questions, new imaginaries and social activism.* New York, NY: Peter Lang.

O'Loughlin, M., & Johnson, R. (Eds.). (2010). *Imagining children otherwise: Theoretical and critical perspectives on childhood subjectivity.* New York, NY: Peter Lang.

Peitzman, L. (2013, May 22). Google search equates 'gayest' with 'worst.' *BuzzFeed.* Retrieved from http://www.buzzfeed.com/louispeitzman/google-search-equates-gayest-with-worst

Richards, B. (1984). *Capitalism and infancy: Essays on psychoanalysis and politics.* London, UK: Free Association Books.

Smythe, D. (1988). *Communications: Blindspot of Western Marxism.* Quebec City, Quebec, Canada: Presses de l'Université Laval.

Stainton-Rogers, R., & Stainton-Rogers, W. (1992). *Stories of childhood: Shifting agendas of child concern.* Toronto, Canada: University of Toronto Press.

Stockton, K. B. (2009). *The queer child: On growing sideways in the twentieth century.* Durham, NC: Duke University Press.

Tobin, J. (Ed.). (1997). *Making a place for pleasure in early childhood education.* New Haven, CT: Yale University Press.

Walkerdine, V. (1984). Developmental psychology and the child-centred pedagogy: The insertion of Piaget into early education. In J. Henriques, W. Hollway, C. Urwin, C. Venn, & V. Walkerdine (Eds.), *Changing the subject: Psychology, social regulation and subjectivity* (pp. 148–198). London, UK: Methuen.

Walkerdine, V. (1987). *Surveillance, subjectivity and struggle: Lessons from pedagogic and domestic practices.* Minneapolis, MN: University of Minnesota Press.

Walkerdine, V. (1990a). *The mastery of reason.* London, UK: Routledge.

Walkerdine, V. (1990b). *Schoolgirl fictions.* London, UK: Routledge.

Walkerdine, V. (Ed.). (2002). *Challenging subjects: Critical psychology for the new millennium.* London, UK: Palgrave.

Walkerdine, V. (2004). Developmental psychology and the study of childhood. In M. Kehily (Ed.), *An introduction to childhood studies* (pp. 112–123). Maidenhead, UK: Open University Press.

Watkins, M., & Shulman, H. (2008). *Toward psychologies of liberation.* New York, NY: Palgrave Macmillan.

Willis, P. (1981). *Learning to labor: How working class kids get working class jobs.* New York, NY: Columbia University Press.

CHAPTER 6

Youth

Multiple Connectivities, New Temporalities, and Early Nostalgia

Suzana Feldens Schwertner and Rosa Maria Bueno Fischer

People just don't know
that we are not all gangbangers or drugdealers
We are people too
We did not all cross the boarder
for some of us the boarder crossed us
We don't always go looking for truble
truble sometimes comes to us
So you can't say you know me
cause you don't
You don't know where I'm coming from
and you don't know where I'm going.
(Julio, 14 years old, quoted in Leccardi & Ruspini, 2006, p. 98).

Youth: an obscure, uncertain life stage, replete with insecurity and instability? Youth: a phase of irresponsibility, anxiety, alienation, risky experiences and violence? Youth, after all: is youth always a problem? Commonsense seems to insist on a discourse associating the young individual with someone lost in a dark hall with whom only the light of the adult world has been left—a world of balance and autonomy, quite far from the uncertain, tortuous places and times this individual has experienced. From Julio, the Italian student quoted in the epigraph, we can perceive a request, which is probably similar to what many 15-to-25-year-old Brazilians would make, to disrupt such commonsense discursivity. We live at a different moment, and utterances about "being young" should certainly be revised, considering the new temporalities we experience, particularly, in our daily contact with images, media texts, and different kinds of virtual communication.

In this chapter,[1] we explore forms of sociability and digital connectivity among contemporary youth in Brazil, by focusing on the discussion about time and temporalities. First, we discuss some relevant findings of recent studies about youths in Latin America, and highlight findings about cycles, phases, ages, and speeds. Next, we explore the relationship between time and youth, discussing practices of cultural consumption by young students attending a public school in the south of Brazil. The results of our study illustrate the emergence of complex dynamics of sociability among youth, specifically in relation to use of time, their early nostalgia, and desires for constant connectivity.

Youths: A Summary of Some Findings

Over the last 20 years, the young have often been a focus of research, particularly in Latin America. The word, *youth*, was first used in the 1950s,[2] and has oscillated between different meanings: from a simple life phase, often associated with the notions of vitality, optimism, and discovery; to a renovating social force (in certain situations and times, it became a synonym for rebelliousness and even delinquency—classically visible in the figure of the actor, James Dean, and the characters he played in films); or, going beyond a chronological stage, from a time verging on irresponsibility and dependence, to a time to constitute the very way of existence. In discussions about the young, approaching the age group that should delimit this phase, ways to correct what has crystallized as troubled youth (adolescent pregnancy, drug use, violence, apathy, etc.), or even the dominance of themes related to conflict and refusal to replicate prevailing conduct models, among many others, have long been emphasized.

On the other hand, recent studies have taken different theoretical points of view and changed their perspective, in order to think of the young individual as a protagonist, a creator, and even an agent of transformation of the life forms of which he is a part, in different social, economic, and cultural environments. Studies of youth carried out in Brazil have focused—but not exclusively—on areas such as sociology, education, psychology, and psychoanalysis. In an attempt not to become repetitive by reviewing such discussions, we propose a summary of the main research findings about youth. We have selected those that have contributed to our argumentation in this paper.

Widening the youth age range

Much has been discussed about widening the youth age range, but this does not necessarily imply greater prominence of the young: it has to do with considering youth as an increasingly widened age range, by reducing childhood and postponing the entrance into the adult world (Abramo, 2005; Birman, 2005; Carrano, 2000; Guimarães & Grinspun, 2008; Pais, 2003; Sposito, 2005). Several studies have pointed out the recreation of the very generational definitions, including new categories, such as preadolescents (children from 9 to 11), "adultescents" or "kidults"[3] and "third age" (euphemism usually used to denominate people over 70). An increasing juvenilization of society has been noticed, and the "young figure" has almost become a fetish, as if it were an arrival point for children and adults (Fischer, 2008); in parallel, such juvenilization does not necessarily mean an effective valorization of young individuals in their own condition (age and kinds of social life). Anyway, it is worth highlighting that time, as a theme involving relationships between past and future, independent of new delimitations of age groups to define who exactly a young individual is, has been consistently posed as a problem by researchers (in Brazil, since the 1960s, with Marialice Foracchi). Perhaps we could even claim that talking about youth inevitably leads to the theme of time, due to the very condition of this object—a phase in life, the stage "x" in people's lives.

Aesthetic turn

One could say that an "aesthetic turn" took place in studies of youth: the last 10 years have been characterized by a change in the ways of researching into the relationships between youth and culture (Hull, Zacher, & Hibbert, 2009). Greater attention to aspects of popular culture has been equally observed, such as consumption and production by young people in their interaction with different media. According to a recent study (Setton, 2009), considering only research conducted by Brazilian post-graduation programs in the area of social sciences, 74 papers approaching "youth and media" were written between 1999 and 2006. It is a significant number, in comparison to 13 papers about the same theme written from 1980 to 1998. The same could be said of studies in the area of communication, which have tried to go beyond research into the reception of media by children and youths and investigations of the power of means of communication over those audiences, to focus their attention on the action of media in processes of constitution of the categories of adolescence and youth, for instance (Freire Filho, 2008). Such an aesthetic turn is also linked to the growing number of participatory studies committed to listening to youngsters and interested in learning how they live and deal with life situations (Holm, Daspit, & Young, 2006). As an example, the authors mention studies of what young people read and see during school breaks and what they do in their free time. Far from being a (demagogic) methodology of listening without criticism, it searches to understand complex phenomena by addressing the young, who both reproduce social practices and create possibilities as agents.

Young protagonism

Young protagonism has been increasingly approached. In recent years, the effective participation of young people in institutions, social movements, school, family, media, and work has been strongly emphasized (Feixa, 2003; Krauskopf, 2005; Maira & Soep, 2005; Margulis & Urresti, 2000; Melucci, 2001). It is extremely important to see young people as actors, rather than mere reproducers of what they live and experience. Used in a number of knowledge fields, such as law, sociology, psychoanalysis and education, the phrase, *young protagonism*, since the 1990s has appeared in several documents of government and education agencies, as well as in texts of non-governmental organizations, with different interpretations, but with an emphasis: protagonism, for many, has become a synonym for participation, autonomy, citizenship, and social responsibility (Zibas, Ferreti, & Tartuce, 2006).

One of several problematizations of this theme is related to understanding a young individual exclusively as a "pre-project" of the future, as someone that would only be taken into account from the point of "coming to be"; on the contrary, according to Carrano and Dayrell (2002), what young people have already attained as their life experiences should be potentialized. Dayrell (2007) emphasized the importance of symbolic and expressive dimensions of cultural groups of young people as enjoyers and, mainly, producers (of music, videos, choreographies, and so on). In either situation, there are elements that somehow "produce" ways of being young and affirming oneself in society.

However, it is worth highlighting that there is still great polemic on this theme, as the concept has been appropriated by different institutions and has acquired different meanings. Hence, "young protagonism" may be almost becoming a magical or salvation expression, often associated with poorer populations, who are the focus of either public policies or NGOs, for example; or, on the other hand, it may be linked to a certain kind of young activism or entrepreneurship, regardless of important facets of these people's lives, such as those related to art, important community actions, and different forms of sociability. Besides, the expression has been associated with an avant-garde and leadership notion, leaving behind a greater proposal by individuals that may actually become the main subjects of their actions, as the very word, *protagonism*, designates.

Regina Souza (2006) drew attention to the fact that the concept of juvenile protagonism has been equated with the concept of performance; the young individual is seen as an actor that enters the scene of the public space, overcoming adversities, resisting pressures, and, above all, adapting to social requirements—a perspective that is rather different from that claiming more autonomy for this group. Maybe the strongest criticism of the importance of youth protagonism is that made by scholars such as Paulo Carrano. Based on several studies, he pointed out concrete hindrances to the participation of young people in the life of the country, as there would be a strong relationship between material living conditions of most of the young people and their real possibilities to take effective political and social actions (Carrano, 2006).

Time context

Young people have been considered in a very specific time context, that of the interconnected world: young people are said to be on the globalization front line. Innumerable studies have pointed out different relationships and involvements of young people in economic, social, and technological changes that are inherent to this era (Besley, 2003; García Canclini, 2004; Feixa, 2006; Kehily & Nayak, 2008; Krauskopf, 2005; Schwertner, 2010). Here, we refer to the attempt to understand how problematic issues deriving from these times of globalization (such as the emphasis on individualism and consumerism, the different practices of segregation and exclusion, and the understanding of times and spaces) would be producing effects on young people. Furthermore, considering these effects, we think about how young people would be producing ways of coping and alternatives to relate to others. Simultaneously to an evaluation of such changes in contemporary life, it has been argued that young people in the twenty-first century have attained the highest education level ever seen and are technically more sophisticated than their predecessors (Best & Kellner, 2003). It is important to take into account that young people, as "pioneers" in this new way of relating to time and technologies, have abruptly undergone such changes (as they experience a number of other modifications in their own bodies and social lives). They actually seem to be more open to new forms of relationships and, therefore, more apt to deal with changes in the world, sometimes at incredible speed. It is worth reminding that such changes do not affect the young only (although the changes are more intense among them), and that the temporality experience is characterized by a blur between the limits of past, present, and future, which were once "well-defined."

Juvenile Temporalities

Researcher Carmen Leccardi (Leccardi 2005; Leccardi & Ruspini, 2006), sociologist Carles Feixa (2003, 2006), researcher Néstor García Canclini (1995, 2004), and psychoanalyst Joel Birman (2005) are some of many authors interested in investigating the relationships between social changes and temporality as seen by the young in the twenty-first century. For them, young people should be studied and understood in the world where they live, rather than only being compared either to groups that lived in other decades or to certain behavior models and standards that have become hegemonic.

In investigations of contemporary youth, psychoanalyst Joel Birman (2005) underlined the helplessness quantum experienced by young Brazilian people from every social class. According to the author, there is a temporality that is characteristic of the young individual living in the twenty-first century, a temporality that has changed due to the present transformation of both childhood and adult age. Such temporality not only comprehends biological and psychical markers, but also historical, sociological, and institutional traits. With the family order turned "upside down" (for the author, one-parent families are one of the causes of such a turn), adults have devoted new and more intense care to their older children (the young individuals) than to young children; according to the author, an effect of such an attitude would be that children, perhaps left behind, are now precociously concerned about the future, and sometimes are not available (in terms of time and space) for children's games and play that put them in contact with the other; the different; the one that challenges, questions, and makes them think (Kehl, 2008).

If we are to understand contemporary youth in line with Carmen Leccardi, firstly it is fundamental to reformulate the concept of "present time." Daily ruled by uncertainties and constant changes, the young have been subject to the requirement of high performance and great dynamism; they are faced with immediacy, with an undetermined and undeterminable future ahead. According to the author, it would be necessary to enable the inclusion of future and past in an "extended present," or a new space: "a temporal space that wanders over the present, acquiring a growing value, in parallel with the contemporary time acceleration, favored by the speed of technological times and the demand for flexibility which is its corollary" (Leccardi, 2005, p. 45).

In this sense, the great challenge would be designing an "indetermination strategy" and keeping the route despite the impossibility of seeing the final destination, by converting unpredictability into something that has to do with life, self-creation, and protagonism—even in that precarious condition of uncertainties (Leccardi, 2005). Certainly, Leccardi's remark may and should be problematized, by taking into account that the present uncertainties are also related to the fact that today adult life has no longer the seductive power it once had—for many young people, it is not a desirable place at which to arrive; rather, as several authors have written, it is just the opposite: youth is the arrival point itself, the place that seduces and challenges not only children (who look forward to becoming adolescents), but also adults (capable of conducting every possible operation on their bodies to stay beautiful and juvenile).

From another perspective, Carles Feixa's metaphor of the three clocks may help us understand the intergenerational differences and the place young people occupy in contemporary society, besides extending the discussion launched by Leccardi. By using the image of clocks from different times, Feixa leads us to think about life ages and the metaphors of social change, particularly about the relationship between youth and society. Initially, the author invites us to think of a sand clock from the pre-industrial era used by societies that have been usually labeled as primitive and tribal. As the sand clock represents a "natural" or cyclical conception of time, it serves as a metaphor for the demarcation of rites of passage (from youth to adult life) as "natural," i.e., ruled by nature's cycles. Inexactness in time measurement contrasts with the delimitation of phases: we become adults, or not, by passing through the narrow funnel that separates the sand inside the glass.

This means that, like a sand clock, the passage between adult and non-adult in other times seems to have been well demarcated and clearly visualized—something that was concretized in sophisticated rites of passage experienced by young people, as the classical studies by anthropologist, Margaret Mead, showed as early as the first half of the twentieth century by questioning the universality of the concept of adolescence, for example.[4] In primitive societies such as those studied by Mead, non-adults know what their destiny will supposedly be as adults: in principle, it means that they will live exactly like their ancestors did, replicating the behavior of the previous generation, as well as the respective cultural contents inherited. Yet, anthropological studies have long shown that such regularity in generational transmission was and is very complex—certainly different from the one we experience today.

The mechanical or analogical clock, in turn, which is typical of the industrial era and designed with intricate gears, provides us with the metaphor for the linear and progressive conception of time. Regarding the relationships between generational groups, there is a rupture with the culturally monolithic represented by the mechanism of a sand clock (by no means less complex, as we read in Mead). Thus, one can talk about cultural transition, which corresponds to the establishment of different nomenclatures for generations, such as early childhood, adolescence, and adulthood. The precision of time then becomes more evident. Here, the passages from the young world to the adult world no longer announce similarities to be replicated; differentiation processes are started, opening spaces for new expectations and also for making explicit new conflicts between generations. Young individuals aspire to new spaces and positions that are different from those occupied by the previous generation.

In the post-industrial era, marked by the digital clock and time relativity, in this so-called "information society"—Feixa has taught us—we learn another conception of time. (One should say: such different perceptions of temporalities do not occur linearly, at progressive stages, as if one could replace the other; on the contrary, there is superposition of stages, although we can identify the prevalence of one over the others in each period.) Today we perceive a virtual time that bears constant, interchangeable movements for generational roles: for example, parents admit that they learn with their children, and adults do not seem to have a problem in claiming that children and youths teach them new things; the latter, in turn, have means of communication and new information technologies available as an education locus. Generational differentiations have become multiple and complex; categories such as pre-adolescent, adolescent, youth, and young adult are defined in the midst of others that emerge in a very short time period. Counting time has reached ultra precision: "while the sand clock would approximately estimate minutes, and the analogical clock the seconds and tenths, the digital clock can exactly determine hundredths, thousandths, etc." (Feixa, 2003, p. 17).

It seems that the more the time measurement changes, the more precise it becomes; the more millimetrically we can control and measure time, the looser and less precise the generational passage and the demarcation of places between youths and adults become. It appears that the more we try to "hold" time, the more replete with nuances the intergenerational relationship is, the more complex the culture contents become, and the more nebulous the understanding and experience of time are to children, young people, and adults. Historian Eric Hobsbawm (2008) was very clear in his approach to the twentieth century: in our post-industrial times, with the emergence of sophisticated communication and information technologies, it seems that roles related to "the one who knows" and "who teaches whom" are inverted—and examples proliferate, particularly in advertisements, of hyper-intelligent and hyper-informed children teaching adults to buy a car or choose the most delicious chocolate bar.

For García Canclini (1995), social-cultural changes instituted by a globalized economy and culture in the post-industrial era redefine the sense of belonging and identity, as well as the very notion of citizen. Modern identities, characterized as territorial and monolingual, now seem to be defined as trans-territorial and multilingual. More specifically, juvenile identities organize around certain cultural circuits, such as the means of mass communication, and information and communication systems. According to the author, this is the first generation of young people that has grown up in the midst of a simultaneity of visual media and their resources: colored and digital television, remote control and zapping, personal computer and Internet, cell phone, e-book, Twitter, and so on. New public means of communication would be emerging. García Canclini has even suggested the existence of a curious interaction between different media; for instance, he said that TV shows would be posing questions to which the Internet would have the answers.

Young People and Connections: Data From Our Research

Utterances such as "I'm here," "I can't be reduced to a shapeless mass," "I'm Black," "I'm a lesbian," "I'm fat," "I'm of Indian descent," seem to have become strong in our time, and are certainly related to countless achievements by social movements of all kinds, in Brazil and in many other countries. One could say that the discourse affirming difference is associated with the theme of new temporalities and the access to different communication technologies: the spread of images and words in global scale propagates ways of life and political fights at the same time.

In an attempt to understand the use of time by young people, information gathered from a questionnaire applied in a public school in the south of Brazil (Porto Alegre), considering "cultural consumption" practices (reading; Internet usage; habits related to cinema, music, and television), has evidenced disquieting issues related to new ways of socialization, cultural habits, daily use of time, and leisure activities. The age of the research subjects ranged from 11 to 15; most of them were 14 years old (41.8 percent), closely followed by 13-year-olds (36.8 percent), from different social classes in the city of Porto Alegre and its surrounding areas.

Concerning weekly habits of cultural consumption, such as watching TV, reading, accessing the Internet, and listening to music, television and the Internet were the most often accessed media. More than 50 percent of the students watched television for 2–4 hours per day. Almost 30 percent of them invested up to two hours per day to watch soap operas, movies, cartoons, comedies, sports, and musicals. A little less than 50 percent of the students stayed 2–6 hours per day on the computer to access the Internet. By comparing Internet usage to TV watching, it is possible to notice that a large number of students (32 percent) spent more than 6 hours per day on the computer accessing the virtual Web; 14 percent, a much lower percentage, watched TV for more than six hours. Another portion of students (12.3 percent) said they used the Internet for more than eight hours per day. It should be highlighted that several students claimed they performed both activities at the same time: connected to the Internet, they also would take a look at TV shows, sometimes listening to background music. Here, we could use the denomination, "multitask generation" (Rideout, Roberts, & Foehr, 2005), to designate the young that perform multiple practices and use several means of communication simultaneously, almost as a need to fill every space and time, and mitigate a lack of meaning in daily life.[5]

Perhaps, like psychoanalyst Maria Rita Kehl, we could think that this way of occupying time is related to (besides other variables that could be considered) a movement favored by the omnipresence of different media and the multiplication of communication possibilities, especially considering daily practices of younger people. Based on Lacan's theory, Kehl warned us that the more we are guided by the imaginary, i.e., by the images that we see and that crystallize as stable significations, the longer we stay in the comfortable zone of "certainty and totalizing illusions" (Kehl, 2008, p. 127). This analysis can be collated with the American study (Rideout et al., 2005) in which the way that youngsters occupy their time would be directly linked to a greater ability to deal with spatial-visual relations, but also to poor academic performance in school—independent of the students' ethnic and racial origins.

In our research in Southern Brazil, even though the images posted on Orkut profiles and those seen on TV are not necessarily characterized as "totalizing," what has been under discussion, more than school performance, is the problem of production and consumption of discourses that offer easy, magical answers. We refer to occupation of time by youngsters who face an excessive number of images and means of incessant communication as if it were possible to remain in silence, perhaps with no immediate responses to our inquietudes, which are not always negative. The existence of too many answers (Kehl, 2008) may hinder the production of alternative meanings and otherness, as well as the insertion of oneself into the social, by means of artistic and differentiated expression.

Our hypothesis is that spaces that are not occupied by younger people in the social, either because of lack of public education and leisure programs, or because of the fear of the world outside, have been replaced by the lonely and at the same time connected experience of staying in front of a computer accessing the Internet for a long period of time. In general, we have observed that the computer plays an important role in most respondents' lives. Maybe this role is the same that television used to play some time ago. Almost 70 percent of the students claimed that "accessing a computer" was one of the tasks they performed every day as a routine activity. On weekends, this time was significantly extended.

Reading books was less often mentioned: 26 percent of the students (one third of the girls, two thirds of the boys) said they did not perform such activity. Sixty-two students claimed they devoted at most two hours per day to reading. Less than 2 percent ensured they read for more than six hours daily. Only 12 percent pointed to reading as an activity they performed in their free time. What does "reading" actually mean today? This question from the questionnaire may and should be problematized: the question itself separates the traditional reading of books and magazines from reading by accessing the Internet on a computer.

The investigation has proved that almost all the respondents used the Internet for research purposes, i.e., the students always searched for materials, read, and studied on the Internet. Therefore, it is not the case of judging the replacement of *stricto sensu* reading for TV and Internet, but advancing towards new investigations of forms of entertainment, leisure, and study, in a straight connection with multiple forms of communication and reading. Sociologist Silvia Borelli, in an article about youth and the Harry Potter saga, has shown that contemporary reading practices should not ignore the "leakage" of borders, in terms not only of audiences, but of a broader world market of symbolic goods as well (Borelli, 2008, p. 59).

With regard to Internet access, a high percentage of students said they accessed the Web from home: more than 90% had digital connection available at home. The second place where students accessed the Internet more often was at their friends' homes. Cyber cafes and school were also mentioned.

As said before, statistics about access to the digital world and to new forms of communication involve both advancements and problems: at the same time we move toward the democratization of access, we face the exclusion of a huge portion of the population when it comes to the use and possession of those resources. Moreover, we also notice that both situations—possession and privation—involve significant changes in young temporalities: while some enjoy the practices of digital communication on the Internet for hours, others dream about, desire, and aspire to the same right—and this also consumes time, particularly their psychological time.

In the research here considered, we have not investigated every detail of all forms of communication and interaction experienced by the students. However, it is important to remember that the debate about the kind of subject that is constituted in this space of virtual relationships (which are real for most of them) is still open, generating a number of theoretical formulations, either in the specific field of youth studies, or in the fields of psychoanalysis, education, and contemporary communication theories. In a study addressing online sociability, the authors investigated cosplay practices (Internet games in which the participants play the part of chosen characters); according to the researchers, "consumption, competitiveness at school and more sensitivity to both school stress and pressure to start university have led students to close themselves and enter into this fantasy world, as it is more comfortable" (Amaral & Duarte, 2008, p. 278).

It is not the case of judging such facts, but rather of being open to regarding new social complexities and new ways in which younger people use their time. On discussing friendship with them, several remarks characterized by immediacy emerged (thus evidencing the lack of a longer time to develop deeper interpersonal relationships). It is worth highlighting that the ways students spend their time are not apart from a series of utterances about the complex discursivity of new temporalities.

Students viewed the Internet as a place to "meet" people: more than 70 percent of the youngsters pointed out the Web as a place to meet their friends—a privileged place, considering that home was the choice of 54 percent of the respondents, followed by the streets (52 percent). For the American Kelly Boudreau, the Internet provides "a place to which they feel they belong: like a soccer team or a social clique, enabling them to feel connected to each other even when they are physically disconnected" (Boudreau, 2007, p. 77). According to the author, the virtual space would be a new meeting point today, previously occupied by the local snack bar and later by the shopping malls. For the new generations, the online social space would favor a sort of fundamental sense of belonging. This is the reason why the so-called digital exclusion has gained strength, as lots of youngsters in Brazil and in other countries, eager to participate in the large space of digital media, are still excluded from it. Internet usage shown on TV (e.g., in soap operas) announces something that is desirable and fascinating, but it is still unavailable to certain groups, given their social conditions.

Conclusion: New Paths for Thinking About Time and Youths

Different questions appeared while we were organizing the research data. Does the time spent by youngsters on the Internet to maintain their relationships with others evidence their option for isolation or detachment to the detriment of face-to-face relationships, as Bauman (2003) has suggested? This surely does not seem to be the best explanation. In our research, on the contrary, youngsters mentioned the "great adventure" of meeting somebody who is totally different and "strange" through the Internet waves. Furthermore, they told us about the possibilities of keeping friendship alive via social networks. In such situations, they feel neither lonely nor detached from personal relationships: more than half of these youngsters think they cultivate friendships. New investigations could examine more deeply how such relationship networks are experienced by young groups today, and which changes they have provoked in all these daily practices.

The Internet was understood by the respondents as a legitimate meeting network. For them, the Internet is a physically delimited place: the expressions they use, such as "start the computer" or "use the computer," refer to a concrete space that can be accessed, a place where actions are actually taken. "Watching TV/using the computer/hang out and talk with friends" do not exclude each other. They are fundamental forms of leisure and socialization that complement each other, and have become totally compatible with the time of the digital clock.

There is a final issue that summarizes several concerns of researchers addressing youth both in Brazil and abroad. From the students' testimony there is a phenomenon that has emerged as something new in our day: the feeling of nostalgia experienced by younger people—a nostalgia related to "old times," even though they are 11, 13, or 14 years old. The idealization of childhood times and the longing for different phases of their short lives appear strongly, as if they had already lived long, and things experienced in previous phases could disappear and leave them empty. The time of extension and sophistication of digital technologies, a time that is synchronized and speedy, counteracts an individual, or even collective time; anyway, "my time," "my history" are what many of those students attempt to find (by using relationship sites to search for friends they have "lost" in time), or even "reassemble" (by posting their pictures as babies or young children). Past time, despite being so recent, acquires a nostalgic strength, similar to that experienced by older people in relation to their youth when they melancholically say "in my time...." Playing, experimentation, and the easy and simple way that children meet their peers seem to mark childhood time as "one of the best phases in my life"—several students say so. It is worth remembering that in this nostalgic memory the figure of media objects is almost always included (dolls, games, advertisements, and characters from means of communication—all of them associated with "my time"). Would that be a past reification? To what extent would such nostalgia take part in a new culture, in a time that has been called the *homo zappiens* era?[6]

These data might suggest that the new experiences of time by the young deserve further investigation. We refer to the relationship between the occupation of days and hours by youngsters with the use of computer and the Internet, and the instigating way of seeing oneself as someone who passes and disappears in time at uncontrollable speed. This has led many youngsters to become poignantly attached to their recent past, as if it could escape and abandon them irreparably. Ultimately, the issues raised here have led us to think about the strength of the symbolic, going beyond the indiscriminate time consumption, aiming at a more creative action in the social.

Notes

1. The research studies here mentioned have been supported by CNPq with sandwich PhD scholarship and Research Productivity scholarship. We thank CNPq for its support and individual assistance to this research.
2. In Brazil, studies by sociologist, Marialice Foracchi, must be mentioned. Her texts from the 1960s, 1970s, and 1980s were discussed in an important paper by Maria Helena Oliva Augusto: "Resume of an Intellectual Legacy: Marialice Foracchi and the Sociology of Youth" (Augusto, 2005).
3. Expression mentioned by English sociologist, Frank Furedi, in 2004. It refers to university students over 30 who continue to live with their parents and become involved in cultivating childhood heroes, collecting dolls such as Hello Kitty and He-Man. For the sociologist, there is something there hindering the appropriation of (and adherence to) the following stages of life.
4. See Margaret Mead's classic study of adolescents in Samoa, Polynesia (Mead, 1961/1990).
5. In the United States, studies into the effects of the multitasking experience on children and youngsters have proliferated. Several of them have been conducted by groups of investigators from the areas of psychology and neuroscience. In general, those studies replicate a certain disapproving tone towards the use of digital technologies, and establish a sort of hierarchy between classic activities of learning processes and those that are supposedly dispersive and cause poor school performance. In an investigation with almost 500 White and African American students, with an average age of 12, North American researchers showed the relationship between computer and Internet use by the subjects and their academic performance in school. The results, which were published in the journal, *Computers in Human Behavior*, evidenced the emergence of a multitasking generation and the effects of these new practices on the students' school life, especially on their performance (i.e., their grades). See the papers by Kirschner and Karpinski (2010) and Jackson, von Eye, Witt, Zhao, and Fitzgerald (2011), both in the journal, *Computers in Human Behavior*.
6. See the paper, "Juvenile Martyrdom, Music and Nostalgia in Contemporary Cinema", by Angela Prysthon, in which the author discussed the theme of youth and nostalgia in cinema, posing questions that are directly linked to the debate presented here (Prysthon, 2008).

References

Abramo, H. W. (2005). Condição juvenil no Brasil contemporâneo. In H. W. Abramo & P. M. Branco (Eds.), *Retratos da juventude Brasileira: Análises de uma pesquisa nacional* (pp. 37–72). São Paulo, Brazil: Editora Fundação Perseu Abramo e Instituto Cidadania.

Amaral, A., & Duarte, R. R. (2008). A subcultura *cosplay* no Orkut: Comunicação e sociabilidade *online* e *offline*. In S. Borelli & J. Freire Filho (Eds.), *Culturas juvenis no século XXI* (pp. 269–288). São Paulo, Brazil: EDUC.

Augusto, M. H. O. (2005). Retomada de um legado: Marialice Foracchi e a sociologia da juventude. *Tempo Social, 17*(2), 11–33.

Bauman, Z. (2003). *Liquid love: On the frailty of human bonds.* Cambridge, UK: Polity Press.

Besley, A. C. (2003). Hybridized and globalized: Youth cultures in the postmodern era. *Review of Education, Pedagogy, and Cultural Studies, 25*(2), 153–178.

Best, S., & Kellner, D. (2003). Contemporary youth and the postmodern adventure. *Review of Education, Pedagogy, and Cultural Studies, 25*(2), 75–93.

Birman, J. (2005). Tatuando o desamparo—A juventude na atualidade. Retrieved from http://www.eposgsv.org/tatuando.pdf (no longer accessible).

Borelli, S. (2008). Cenários juvenis, adultescências, juvenilizações: A propósito de Harry Potter. In S. Borelli & J. Freire Filho (Eds.), *Culturas juvenis no século XXI* (pp. 59–78). São Paulo, Brazil: EDUC.

Boudreau, K. (2007). The girls' room: Negotiating schoolyard friendships online. In S. Weber & S. Dixon (Eds.), *Growing up online: Young people and digital technologies* (pp. 67–80). New York, NY: Palgrave Macmillan.

Carrano, P. C. R. (2000). Juventudes: As identidades são múltiplas. *Movimento, 1*, 11–27.

Carrano, P. C. R. (2006). Juventude e participação no Brasil—Interdições e possibilidades. *Democracia Viva, Rio de Janeiro, 1*(1), 3–5. Retrieved from http://www.ibase.br/pubibase/media/ibasenet_dv30_artigo1.pdf (no longer accessible).

Carrano, P. C. R., & Dayrell, J. T. (2002). Jovens no Brasil: Difíceis travessias de fim de século e promessas de um outro mundo. Paper presented at the 25th annual meeting of ANPED, GT 3 Movimentos Sociais e Educação. Caxambu, Minas Gerais, Brazil. Retrieved from http://www.anped.org.br/reunioes/25/tp25.htm#gt3 and http://www.uff.br/obsjovem/mambo/images/stories/Documentos/JOVENS_BRASIL_MEXICO.pdf

Dayrell, J. T. (2007). A escola "Faz" as juventudes? Reflexões em torno da socialização juvenil. *Educação e Sociedade, 28*(100), 1105–1128. Retrieved from http://www.cedes.unicamp.br

Feixa, C. (2003). Del reloj de arena al reloj digital—Sobre las temporalidades juveniles. *Revista de Estudios Sobre Juventud, 7*(19), 6–27.

Feixa, C. (2006). Generación XX—Teorías sobre la juventud en la era contemporánea. *Revista Latinoamericana de Ciencias Sociales, Niñez y Juventud, 4*(2), 3–18.

Fischer, R. M. B. (2008). Mídia, juventude e educação: Modos de construir o 'outro' na cultura. *Archivos Analíticos de Políticas Educativas*-AAPE, *16*, 1–20. Retrieved from http://epaa.asu.edu/epaa/v16n2/v16n2.pdf

Freire Filho, J. (2008). Retratos midiáticos da nova geração e a regulação do prazer juvenil. In S. Borelli & J. Freire Filho (Eds.), *Culturas juvenis no século XXI* (pp. 33–57). São Paulo, Brazil: EDUC.

García Canclini, N. (1995). *Consumidores y ciudadanos: Conflictos multiculturales de la globalización.* Mexico City, Mexico: Grijalbo.

García Canclini, N. (2004). *Diferentes, desiguales y desconectados: Mapas de la interculturalidad.* Barcelona, Spain: Gedisa.

Guimarães, G., & Grinspun, M. Z. (2008). Revisitando as origens do termo juventude: A diversidade que caracteriza a identidade. Paper presented at the 31st annual meeting of ANPED, GT Psicologia da Educação. Caxambu, Minas Gerais, Brazil. Retrieved from http://www.anped.org.br/reunioes/31ra/1trabalho/GT20-4136--Int.pdf

Hobsbawm, E. (2008). *Era dos extremos: O breve século XX.* São Paulo, Brazil: Companhia das Letras.

Holm, G., Daspit, T., & Young, A. J. (2006). The sky is always falling. (Un)changing views on youth in the US. In C. Leccardi & E. Ruspini (Eds.), *A new youth? Young people, generations and family life* (pp. 83–102). Hampshire, UK: Ashgate.

Hull, G., Zacher, J., & Hibbert, L. (2009). Youth, risk, and equity in a global world. *Review of Research in Education, 33*(1), 117–159.

Jackson, L. A., von Eye, A, Witt, E. A., Zhao, Y., & Fitzgerald, H. E. (2011). A longitudinal study of the effects of Internet use and videogame playing on academic performance and the roles of gender, race and income in these relationships. *Computers in Human Behavior, 27*(1), 228–239.

Kehily, M. J., & Nayak, A. (2008). Global femininities: Consumption, culture and the significance of place. *Discourse: Studies in the Cultural Politics of Education, 29*(3), 325–342.

Kehl, M. R. (2008). *A fratria órfã.* São Paulo, Brazil: Olho d'Água.

Kirschner, P. A., & Karpinski, A. C. (2010). Facebook and academic performance. *Computers in Human Behavior, 26*(6), 1237–1245.

Krauskopf, D. (2005). Juventudes na América Latina e no Caribe: Dimensões sociais, subjetividades e estratégias de vida. In A. A. Thompson (Ed.), *Associando-se à juventude para construir o futuro* (pp. 149–196). São Paulo, Brazil: Peirópolis.

Leccardi, C. (2005). Por um novo significado de futuro—mudança social, jovens e tempo. *Tempo Social, 17*(2), 35–57.

Leccardi, C., & Ruspini, E. (2006). *A new youth? Young people, generations and family life.* Hampshire, UK: Ashgate.

Maira, S., & Soep, E. (2005). *Youthscapes: The popular, the national, the global.* Philadelphia, PA: University of Pennsylvania Press.

Margulis, M., & Urresti, M. (2000). La juventud es más que una palabra. In M. Margulis (Ed.), *La juventud es más que una palabra: Ensayos sobre cultura y juventud* (2nd ed., pp. 85–101). Buenos Aires, Argentina: Biblos.

Melucci, A. (2001). *A invenção do presente: Movimentos sociais nas sociedades complexas*. Petrópolis, Brazil: Vozes.

Mead, M. (1990). *Coming of age in Samoa: A psychological study of primitive youth for Western civilisation.* New York, NY: Morrow Quill.

Pais, J. M. (2003). Correntes teóricas da sociologia da juventude. In J. M. Pais, *Culturas juvenis* (pp. 47–79). Lisboa, Portugal: Imprensa Nacional, Casa da Moeda.

Prysthon, A. (2008). Martírio juvenil, música e nostalgia no cinema contemporâneo. In S. Borelli & J. Freire Filho (Eds.). *Culturas juvenis no século XXI* (79–92). São Paulo, Brazil: EDUC.

Rideout, V., Roberts, D., & Foehr, U. (2005). *Generation M: Media in the lives of 8- to 18-year-olds.* Palo Alto, CA: Kaiser Family Foundation.

Schwertner, S. F. (2010). *Laços de amizade: modos de relacionamento jovem em tempos de conectividade digital.* 220 f. Tese (Doutorado em Educação) [Doctoral dissertation]. Faculdade de Educação, UFRGS (Universidade Federal do Rio Grande do Sul), Porto Alegre, Brazil.

Setton, M. G. J. (2009). Juventude, mídias e TIC. In M. Sposito (Ed.), *Estado da arte sobre a juventude na pós-graduação Brasileira: Educação, ciências sociais e serviço social* (Vol. 2, pp. 57–86). Belo Horizonte, Brazil: Argvmentvm.

Souza, R. M. (2006). A atividade dos atores sociais e do jovem protagonista. In R. M. Souza, *O discurso do protagonismo juvenil* (pp. 62–105). 351 f. Tese (Doutorado em Sociologia) [Doctoral dissertation]. Faculdade de Filosofia, Letras e Ciências Humanas, USP (Universidade de São Paulo), São Paulo, Brazil.

Sposito, M. P. (2005). Algumas reflexões e muitas indagações sobre as relações entre juventudes e escola no Brasil. In H. W. Abramo & P. P. M. Branco (Eds.), *Retratos da juventude brasileira—Análises de uma pesquisa nacional* (pp. 87–127). São Paulo, Brazil: Editora Fundação Perseu Abramo e Instituto Cidadania.

Zibas, D., Ferreti, C., & Tartuce, G. (2006). Micropolítica escolar e estratégias para o desenvolvimento do protagonismo juvenil. *Cadernos de Pesquisa, 36*(2), 51–85.

CHAPTER 7

An 'Evolving Criticality' in Youth and/or Student Voice in Schools in Hardening Neoliberal Times

John Smyth

At the outset I want to acknowledge a deep debt of gratitude to Joe Kincheloe (2010), from whom I am borrowing the notion of 'evolving criticality'. No one could do it like Joe, but I want to attempt in a modest way I hope Joe would have liked, to build on an important concept to which he alerted us. One of the primary hallmarks of an 'evolving criticality' for Kincheloe (2010), was its commitment to listening carefully to the voices of all who are the object of oppression, so as to enlighten "the critical canon" (p. 27). There is profound respect here, too, for incompleteness, a restlessness for "new theoretical insights … problems and social circumstances" (p. 27), an ever-present threat of "exclusion from the domain of approved research methods" (p. 27), and a need for "a variety of tools" with which to expose any theoretical perspectives that "fail to understand the malevolent workings of power" (p. 28). I hope I am up to the task of addressing these in what follows, in a novel way.

My opening claim in this chapter is that young people, especially those from the most disadvantaged contexts, are being 'consumed' by capitalism within the context of schooling. In pursuing this line I am not endorsing a 'thin' view of consumption, which might be seen as equating to the commercialization and exploitation of schools by the corporate sector, appalling though that is. Rather, I am ascribing a much thicker meaning to consumption, as referring to the ways in which alarming numbers of young people are being constructed as unwitting and complicit consumers of schooling, in the way schools are being swept into the neoliberal project of constructing themselves as unmitigated zones of marketization (mostly of themselves against other schools) in order to secure 'market share'. The consequence is that the sorting, sifting, and displacing that has to occur as the market does its ugly disfiguring work, means that many of these young people are being disposed of or dispensed with as they are pushed to the margins and treated as collateral damage, or at best, being prepared as insecure and menial workers for an increasingly uncaring capitalism.

After discussing briefly what an expanded and somewhat unorthodox view of educational consumption might mean, its features, and implications, I want to proceed then to look at how young people are 'speaking back' to it within the context of their experiences of schooling. In pursuing how young people are actively challenging this diminished construction of their educational lives, I will explore three questions:

1. What has to be spoken back to?

2. What alternative set of conditions has to be spoken into existence?, and

3. How might this occur in and/or through the process of identity formation by young people in and/or through schooling?

The Argument: What Has to Be Spoken Back to?

The central notion I am pursuing of 'being consumed by schooling', I take to refer to the human capital view of schools as existing to satisfy and supply the labor market needs of an ever increasingly voracious and predatory global capitalism. This means making schools and what goes on inside them tame or docile, and I will point to a number of the prominent indicators of this in a moment. There is no delicate or polite way to put it—as they exist in the current phase of capitalism, schools exist primarily to 'ride over' young lives and re-inscribe them with scripts that are considered to be more amenable to the global capitalist agenda. Schools have become deeply implicated in the national and global vocational skills formation agenda, which is given primacy over the educational wishes, desires, and interests of young people, who make it clear that they want an education that will 'get them a job' as well as enable them to make something of themselves while doing it. It need not be an either/or situation, as I will discuss shortly.

The overall point to be made here is that consumers are not, by inclination, people who directly participate in the improvement of a product. By definition, a *consumer* is a person or thing "which squanders, destroys or uses up" something (*New Shorter Oxford English Dictionary*, Vol 1., 1993, p. 490). As such, a consumer does not have a voice, only a right of veto, or the ability to reject a product in order to make a different choice. The lines of communication between a consumer and a producer are impersonal and quite attenuated at best. The framing logic is that the consumer needs to be given what they desire, or there is the risk of the product becoming obsolete as customers change their preferences. Applied to schools, so the logic goes, if schools can be forced to be competitive with one another, and the funding of schools follows 'market share', then schools that are not responsive to savvy consumers are likely to be 'put out of business', or else they have to change their style of operation.

There are a number of fundamental problems with this kind of thinking, sufficient to totally undermine it, even though this is the dominant view that underpins the educational policy trajectory in all Western countries like the US, UK, Australia, New Zealand, and Canada.

First, there is the confusion over who is the real 'consumer'—young people who participate most directly in schooling? Or their parents and/or guardians who are supposed to theoretically shop around for the 'best deal' for them? Clearly, when young people reject what is on offer by schools—largely because of its perceived irrelevance to their lives, backgrounds, experiences, or aspirations—which they do either in part (by truanting, or disconnecting and disengaging while still being present within schools), or in the ultimate case, rejecting schooling completely by leaving or 'dropping out' of school, then this appears to constitute a proxy for 'choice', physically, psychically, and emotionally. The only problem is that schools rarely respond positively to young people who stonewall schools in this way. Schools are quick to blame them and treat them punitively.

Second, if the parents are positioned as the consumer in the way they see what is on offer in a particular school as being unattractive, or they dislike something about the demeanor of the school, then theoretically they are able to exercise mobility on behalf of their children—but this is a fairly crude instrument. It does not work if the parents do not have the means to make their children mobile, for example a car, or if they are not sufficiently apprised as to be able to make an informed decision.

All of this is by way of saying that young people are increasingly becoming caught up and trapped within an ideology that regards them as legitimate pawns to be moved around and sacrificed in some macabre social Darwinist policy game. Without doubt the most scandalous way young people are being 'consumed' and 'used up' is through the international vocational education scam. To put it most directly, vocational education purports to be about providing a viable pathway for young people, who mistakenly, in most cases, have come to regard themselves (with more than a little help from a deeply classed school system), as being 'hands-on people'. The argument put is that vocational education has a democratic intent because of the way it channels these young people into economically rewarding and fulfilling lives they might not otherwise have had. The not-so-subtle subtext is that they are barely educable, at best, and ought to be grateful for being allowed to pursue substandard learning as far as they have. As Nagle (2001) said, the official line is that "The goal of vocational education is to prepare students to go into the workforce as opposed to continuing formal education at a postsecondary level" (p. 9). The barely disguised inference is that these students are ill-suited to academic pursuits, they are not very bright, and besides, they have already made that decision based on their family backgrounds, and therefore rather than disgrace themselves by failing academically, they take the easy exit out.

In the "Introduction" to what is arguably the seminal text on puncturing the myth of vocational education, *Toil and Trouble* (Kincheloe, 1995), Steinberg (1995) noted that the common motif among the tradies she and Kincheloe met in the course of many house renovations, was that they all "hated school, misbehaved, felt like outsiders, and were convinced at an early age that they would be lucky to finish high school, let alone go to college" (p. xi). As to how they got to where they were: "Most of them got into their field through being streamed into vocational education at school, following in the family business, or from a summer job that never ended. Most tell us that their job was not *their* choice" (Steinberg, 1995, p. xi).

After noting how their bosses needed to monitor them, ensuring that they were not taking short cuts, pilfering materials, or slacking off on the job, Steinberg (1995) revealed how these views are deeply sedimented into vocational-education programs early on, where students are given a lesson in 'values'—which is to say, how they are not valued:

> Vocational education is treated like other *special* education—the subject for the misfits—a place to *put* kids that don't fit anywhere else. Many high schools situate their vocational education departments on outer wings, in outside buildings or in the basement (Steinberg, 1995, p. xii).

To borrow a phrase from Brown and Hesketh (2004), what is going on here, notwithstanding that some kids go on from vocational-education programs to work as competent tradespeople, is a huge residual that falls within what might be regarded as a 'mismangement of talent'—they are "residual-ized." A very sizeable portion of kids from vocational educational programs are wasted in low-level studies that end up putting them, at best, into low-paid, insecure, and menial-service jobs in hospitality, customer services, and other low-skill jobs. They are destined to what Standing (2011) labeled the new 'precariat'—although this is by no means a straightforward term.

This kind of fragmented analysis may have a place, but it is still quite limited when it comes to fully explaining the way in which youth of disadvantage and color are consumed by schooling and how this might be changed. We need a deeper analytical approach—but first we need to see where the field of youth studies has come from, and where it is up to. Let me now change tack somewhat.

Ginwright & Cammarota (2002) were helpful in the snapshot they provided us with of three periods. First, the 1980s to the early 1990s was a "problem driven" (p. 84) and "problem prevention" (p. 83) period in which youth studies were undertaken through the lenses of psychological theories of human development that had as their "central focus … identifying youth problems such as delinquency, substance abuse, and violence" (p. 83) and invoked a panoply of fixing devices that largely failed because of their mis-naming of the problem. Second, there was the attempt in the early 1990s to broaden the approach of youth studies through a 'positive youth model' (p. 83), which saw youth as having assets and strengths, emphasizing notions like 'emotional health', well-being, and empowerment. While this was a step forward because of the way it tried to reconstruct and build youth life skills and capacities, it did "not go far enough to account for the powerful social forces that affect young people" (p. 84). As Ginwright & Cammarota (2002) put it:

> Despite the conceptual shift to positive youth development language, low income and urban youth still encounter debilitating effects of poverty, discrimination, drugs in their neighborhoods, police violence, and the burden of supporting their families by earning money and assisting with raising siblings. (pp. 84–85)

The third period, from the early 2000s, has seen the focus shift to the "societal context of young people's experiences," or what Ginwright & Cammarota (2002) called the "social justice development approach" (p. 87) that attempts to understand "how they navigate and respond to the oppressive forces that affect their lives" (p. 85). This social contextual approach provides the opportunity "to examine how their [youth] supports, opportunities, and risks are circumscribed by larger political, economic, and social forces" (p. 85). This is a way of prising apart the forces that produce the "social toxins" (Garbarino, 1999) of "violence, poverty, domestic and sexual abuse, family disruption, and racism" (Ginwright & Cammarota, 2002, p. 86) that manifest themselves in young lives as "apathy, fatalism, and self-destructive behaviors" (p. 86). While pointing to the need to acknowledge the structural constraints that are obviously working on young lives, Ginwright & Cammarota (2002) were careful to warn us to not "discount" the often "resourceful ways" in which young people contest and deal with them (p. 86). The merit of this social-justice approach lies in the way it "encourage[s] youth to address the larger oppressive forces affecting their lives and their communities … [and to] examine the processes by which … youth contest, challenge, respond, and negotiate the use and misuse of power in their lives" (Ginwright & Cammarota, 2002, p. 87). They become "agents of change" (Ginwright & James, 2002).

Speaking This Different Set of Conditions Into Existence

While many students of color, recent immigrants, those of alternative sexual orientations, and backgrounds of disadvantage are clear about the fact that "it's not good to not be in school … [and feel] guilty because you know you need education for a better life" (Romero, Arce, & Cammarota, 2009, p. 217), they also know that they cannot sustain the intolerable conditions they are forced to endure in the way schools are currently organized. As one of Romero's (2008) Chicana informants in her doctoral study put it, when asked to put her feelings in one word:

> the only word I guess is violated. I guess it could be like when women are raped, something is taken from them. In school they take our minds and our souls: they violate us with the way they try to give us school. (Romero, 2008, p. 163, as cited in Romero, Arce, & Cammarota, 2009, p. 217)

Bradley Levinson (2000) made the equally depressing point that our students have grown weary of the non-delivery of the "supposed educative fruits of schooling" to the all-too-familiar refrain: "I get a better education at my job or in the streets. I have to leave school in order to get a real education" (p. 6). There could be no more damning indictment of schooling than these kinds of comments.

Changing the situation I have described and dislodging it will not come about quickly or easily. The current educational policy direction that is gripping young people in schools around the world is deeply embedded, and has powerful and influential friends. The challenge lies in where to start turning it around. Educational anthropologists give us some important clues through the way they look at students who are failing at school. Frederick Erickson (1987) captured it when he said of minority students that they are like any other humans, in that they are learning "constantly" (p. 343):

> To speak of school success or failure is to speak of learning or not learning what is deliberately taught there. Learning is ubiquitous in human experience throughout the life cycle, and humans are very good at it …. Yet in schools, deliberately taught learning seems to be a problem …. When we say [students] are "not learning" what we mean is that they are not learning what school authorities, teachers, and administrators intend for them to learn …. Not learning can be seen as a form of political resistance (pp. 343–344).

For fellow educational anthropologist Levinson (2000), the response must lie in "the possibilities for moving beyond school" (p. 6). Our task as educators, he said, "is to boldly situate the knowledge generated in schools within broader streams of social practices and learning" (p. 6). In doing this, the crucial point made by Daniels, Harnischfeger, Hos, and Akom (2010) is to confront the "hegemonic realities" (p. 17) embedded in the institution of schooling—including power, race, class, gender, sexuality, religion, and place—that operate to marginalize youth.

Some categories that resonate with what might need to occur are ones like "transformational resistance" (Cammarota & Fine, 2008) and "collective radical imagination" (Ginwright, 2008). Focusing on these kinds of positive actions and attributes enables us "to counteract the hegemonic belief that society's senior members are the sole creators of new practice" (Daniels, Harnischfeger, Hos, & Akom, 2010, p. 18). Instead of adults continuing to be 'the problem' because of their narrow and self-interested agenda in education, we need to turn this around so that the question becomes: "How might society's senior members best assist youth in constructing these practices, which are needed for effective means of change?" (Daniels et al., 2010, p. 19). We would be well served in this by paying close attention to the "critically compassionate intellectualism" (CCI) of Romero, Cammarota, and colleagues (Cammarota & Romero, 2006; Romero, Arce, & Cammarota, 2009), as they struggle to come up with a more viable alternative that moves beyond forms of schooling that violate Latina/o students and other marginalized young people.

What, then, is "critically compassionate intellectualism" (Romero, 2008) as it relates to youth, and how might we build upon it and extend it? Of all of the possible directions critical youth studies might take, this is the approach that, in my view, holds the most promise. In many respects, it is not unlike other Freirean-informed endeavors (see, for example, Smyth's critically reflective approach for teachers/teacher educators—Smyth, 1989a, 1989b, 2011).

Coming out of Critical Race Theory and the pedagogy of Paulo Freire, CCI has three main elements, in that it is:

- *critical*—in that it challenges the shibboleths, stereotypes, deficits, pathologies, obfuscations, and other hegemonic occlusions that shroud the way power works to prop up the exploitative status quo, and works at puncturing them.

- *compassionate*—in that it pursues a relational approach around 'authentic caring' (as distinct from 'aesthetic caring' which regards students as objects to be 'inscribed'—Cammarota & Romero, 2006, p. 21).

- *intellectual*—in that it provides young people with the skill and courage to both analyze their situations and how they came to be that way, as well as emboldening them to speak back to institutional processes bent upon silencing them. In other words, it is predicated on the belief that youth is able to think intellectually and act upon things.

If we look for some pervasive themes around which such an emerging critical youth studies litera-ture might begin to coalesce, then as Bucholtz (2002) put it, we need to start by looking to the "anchor points" (Mills, 1959/1971) located within the re-workings of "youth cultures" and "cultural practices of youth" (p. 539), in which marginalized youth are beginning to assert themselves, and I will turn to that now.

Politics of School "Interruption" Around Critical Identity Formation

Stovall (2007) has provided a very helpful orienting architecture around which to argue for and pursue community-engaged forms of accountability that interrupt "theories of social disorganization" that otherwise lead inexorably to forms of "social isolation, social detachment, and culture of poverty used to stereotype working-class/low income … [and ethnic or racial] communities" (p. 681) around young people. Instead, Stovall argued for a form of "community-engaged design" that "interrupts deficit theo-ries" (p. 682) and posits in their place a form of engaged pedagogy that extends the school into the community (p. 685)—thus directly challenging notions of marginalization. Compared with the cur-rent, dominant, emaciated, performative versions of accountability, this version is designed around the notion of "free spaces" (Akom & Shoraka, 2007; Evans & Boyte, 1986; Smyth, Angus, Down, & McInerney, 2009) in which identities can be "recover[ed]" and "rejuvenat[ed]" (Akom & Shoraka, 2007, p. 612) around curriculum as a form of "qualitative community accountability" (Stovall, 2007, p. 687). In other words, the ultimate measure of whether a school is working is not around closing achievement gaps, test performances, out-competing other schools, or any other form of calibration, but the extent to which the school is able to construct a compelling story around how it has reduced the "opportunity gap" (Akom, Ginwright, & Cammarota, 2008, p. 17) between young people and their communities, and the challenges of adversity involved in bringing this about.

From the burgeoning literature beginning to emerge around critical youth studies—much of it in Critical Race Theory, critical pedagogy, and youth community organizing—there seem to be a number of consistently recurring elements that are pointing to what might be called an 'evolving criticality of youth studies'. This is not the place to attempt any kind of exhaustive review of any of these literatures, but even a modest glance reveals the centerpiece to be the notion of 'social justice'—taken to mean, strategies and processes committed to removing disfiguring forms of inequality and recognizing dignity and worth regardless of background, attributes, or social location.

Possibly the most economical way for me to deal with what is arguably still an emerging 'new paradigm' of youth studies (Akom, Ginwright, & Cammarota, 2008), is to do that schematically with a diagram (see Figure 7.1), and then briefly address each component (apologies in advance for non-exhaustiveness, omissions, and overlaps).

This discussion brings me back to my opening argument about youth being 'consumed' by the dominant, neoliberal construction of schooling. What an evolving criticality of youth studies enables us to do, as Ares (2010) noted, is position youth in the much more positive and assertive light as 'pro-ducers, rather than "cultural dopes" (Ares, Hassberg, & YPI, 2010, p. 128), as the prevailing policy and media portrayals would have us believe. That is to say, using notions of social and agentic space enables us to point theoretically, politically, and practically to ways in which young people can construct them-selves as "powerful people" (Smyth & Fasoli, 2007) not beholden to deficit notions that force them into "prefabricated models" (Ares, Hassberg, & YPI, 2010, p. 128). Envisaged as 'producers' of their own cultural practices as learners, they are emboldened to 'speak back' to structural forces, by appropriating quite a different identity for themselves.

What is being advanced through the above elements by the critical youth studies scholars I have invoked, is the possibility of a conceptual design that foregrounds Appadurai's (2004) notion of *ca-pacity to aspire*—something that is not a static psychologistic quality inhering in individuals, but rather an active process worked out in the "disjunctures between economy, culture and politics"

(Appadurai, 1996, p. 33). For Appadurai (1996), capacity to aspire is very context and locale specific and emerges out of "actually existing social forms" (p. 179) in which desires are worked out in contexts of "conjectures" and "refutations" (p. 69) especially around the "global crisis of the nation state" (p. 179). Practically speaking, this means that some young people get to access rich social scripts that provide them with navigational maps (p. 69) that enable them to practice and access opportunities that destine them for rewarding futures, while other young people are denied such scripts, and have to draw on limited familial and neighborhood resources that end up circumscribing their life chances.

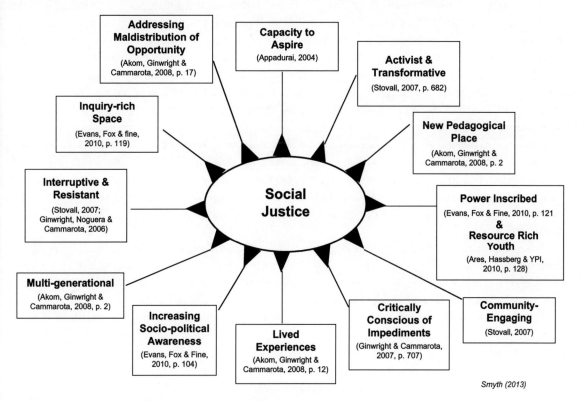

Figure 7.1: An Evolving Criticality of Student Voice

Having a school design that not only permits, but that overtly fosters a "politically relevant pedagogy" (Stovall, 2007) with youth, is to regard teaching as an unavowedly "political act" (Beauboeuf-Lafontant, 1999). This is a perspective that is *activist and transformative* in the way it treats the status quo as having to be usurped so as to dislodge deficit views and replace them with ones more amenable and committed to serving the interests of the least advantaged.

Clearly, this kind of radical thinking and acting is not possible within ossified, sedimented, and degraded places, without considerable courage and a well worked out strategy. Waiting for nirvana to create utopian places will not happen. Rather, this *new pedagogical place* (Akom, Ginwright, & Cammarota, 2008, p. 2) will come about through having the courage to reach out to radical literatures that permit and encourage structures and processes within which youth cultural practices can create "a movement of social justice and equity" (p. 2).

Investing young people with power as students, involves dramatically inverting how we think about expertise. Adults and teachers, while clearly important to the life projects of young people, need to be made subservient (even redundant!). Trusting that young people know how to construct and execute their own learning around projects that are meaningful to them, is not exactly a new idea. Students as researchers (Steinberg & Kincheloe, 1998) and notions of negotiating the curriculum (Boomer, 1982), are ideas that are central to *inscribing young people with power* (Evans, Fox, & Fine, 2010, p. 121), but these ideas are still treated officially with contempt and complete policy deafness. The obvious corollary is that youth are *resource rich* (Ares, Hassberg, & YPI, 2010, p. 128), and have qualities and attributes not always immediately recognizable, that enable them to produce truly remarkable and amazing forms of learning.

Disrupting the pathological and deficit-ridden view of young people who arguably reside in the most complex circumstances in our societies, requires that we allow them the space in which to investigate important *community engaging* forms of knowledge around questions such as: What is good about my neighborhood? What makes it that way? How do people treat one another, and why are these hidden strengths made invisible? What are the problems being struggled against? What are the larger social forces making things this way? How are people collectively contesting their positioning? Stovall (2007), among others, argued that working in these ways with young people is to invoke a "politically relevant pedagogy" in the way learning gets to be constructed around notions of "community account-ability" (p. 682) and community action which invert the deficit stereotype of young people and their communities.

It is obvious by now that pursuing the kind of learning being argued for here requires being *critically conscious of impediments* (Ginwright & Cammarota, 2007, p. 707) that have to be unmasked and punctured so as to change individual circumstances into the context of pursuing wider community change as well. Ginwright & James (2002) said it is "an awareness of how institutional, historical, and systemic forces limit and promote opportunities that lead to collective action to change unjust social conditions" (p. 40).

What has to be foregrounded here is the fact that the *lived experiences* (Akom, Ginwright, & Cammarota, 2008, p. 12) of young people, in all of their unruly untidiness, are crucial to their constructing robust views of themselves, their biographies, histories, and desires. In other words, they have to be empowered to write and speak their lives into existence in order to be able to celebrate them.

Whether in numeracy or literacy, what underpins the educative approach around a voiced approach to youth criticality, is the press to *increasing socio-political awareness* in school learning. Evans, Fox, and Fine (2010) gave an illustration of what this means through highlighting the silencing of the contributions of Black people, even in contexts where they are the majority. In one of the schools they studied: "White people are the minority; despite this, these urban students of color know more about that 'minority' culture (and are expected to conform to its standards) than they do about their own" (p. 102).

Understanding why "the contributions of a few Black" people are acknowledged, while the contributions of the "many are omitted or not given the credit they deserve" (Evans, Fox, & Fine, 2010, p. 102) becomes the starting point for students to investigate how the process of 'invisibling' works. To put it succinctly, it is to pursue Freire's (Freire & Macedo, 1987) notion of "reading the world" as well as "reading the word."

We need to be careful not to position adults as being excluded or squeezed out in this conceptualization. The way Akom, Ginwright, and Cammarota (2008) put it, is in terms of learning experiences that occur in 'real' settings "through *multi-generational* collectives"—which I take to mean, older peers and younger siblings, parents (even grandparents), teachers, and community members in various combinations of formal and informal ways that engage young people in civic engagement.

The terms, *interruptive* and *disruptive* are replete throughout this literature, as a way of making the resounding point that there is no space in here in which oppressive ideas and practices are not troubled and replaced with more just alternatives. As Ginwright and James (2002) noted, this subversive intent goes considerably beyond accommodating to what Kirshner (2006) labeled "a sanctuary from toxic social conditions" (p. 38). Rather, youth need to be seen "as agents capable of transforming their toxic environments, not simply developing resiliency and resistance to them"

(Ginwright & James, 2002, p. 40). Invoking a colleague, they put it that young people who are "not working with others to challenge injustice in his/her or other environments … may be great young people, but they are not fully developed" (p. 40).

The notion of *inquiry-rich spaces* (Evans et al., 2010, p. 119) draws attention to the imperative for young people to be deeply insinuated and implicated in contexts of 'real' and 'authentic' problems which they feel impelled to grapple with—compared to the artificial and 'forced' (p. 120) ones of course requirements. The difference seems to lie in who has the power to determine what is the problem. Authenticity seems to suggest that it has to be young people making the decision as to where and how to "engage in authentic research" (p. 120). The profound difference lies in shifting position from being "passive receivers/refusors of knowledge" to taking on "the identities of producers and spokespersons for critical knowledges" (p. 120).

This really brings us full circle in the discussion of the various elements I have drawn from the critical youth studies literature to point to what I am calling elements of a constellation that comprises an evolving criticality of youth and/or student voice in schooling as experienced by the most oppressed, subordinated, and marginalized. Recall that I started out with the way in which Appadurai's (2004) notion of "capacity to aspire" amounts to having a map with which young people can navigate a future for themselves. But there is a fundamental maldistribution. As Appadurai (2004) put it, "the better off you are (in terms of power, dignity, and material resources), the more likely you are to be conscious of the links between the more and less immediate objects of aspiration" (p. 68). The well-off are by definition able to have a "more complex experience of the relation between a wide range of ends and means" and be better positioned "to explore and harvest diverse experiences of exploration and trial" (p. 68). In other words, they have enhanced "navigational capacity" (p. 69) with which to access opportunities and explore more diverse pathways. The less well-off have "much more brittle horizons" of possibilities, which leaves strategically valuable opportunities less developed, or underdeveloped. All of the elements I have invoked so far in this section have in some way been about addressing *maldistribution of opportunity* (Akom, Ginwright, & Cammarota, 2008, p. 17) because of poverty, familial background, race, gender, or some other socially produced circumstances that circumscribe the capacity to access opportunities—which is really what social justice is all about.

Conclusion: Last Words!

There can of course be no such thing as 'last words' in an evolving criticality, but I want to round out what I have attempted at least in this opening phase. My thesis in this chapter has been that capitalism is voraciously constructing young people as complicit consumers, and that what needs to be spoken into existence is a counter-narrative around them as co-constructors and producers. Furthermore, I have argued that the starting point to this needs to be incubated within their schooling, most notably in positioning them so as to acquire a 'voice' over how, what, when, where, and in what ways they learn. If we are able to start out with this kind of disposition, then young people not only become active agents (Daniels et al., 2010; Smyth & McInerney, 2012) in their own learning identities, but they also take on the role of social activists in refusing to accept the status quo. Such a reclamation not only means constituting learning on their terms (Gustavson, 2007), but it means doing it in "context-renewing and context-creating ways" (Bucholtz, 2002, p. 528) against dominant views of learning that obliterate context. In re-positioning their learning in these wider ways, young people become "global citizens" (Verma, 2010) struggling for self and social justice (Quijada, 2008) in ways that bring them to "lead the way to improved educational and societal equity" (Daniels et al., 2010, p. 18). Envisaged in this kind of refreshing way, young people become collaborators in schools rather than prisoners, they are seen as having strengths and assets rather than being unmitigated bundles of pathologies with a range of deficits, and they are able to enact their rightful role as critically compassionate intellectuals (Cammarota & Romero, 2006) in constructing lives and learning identities committed to hope and change.

Acknowledgments

The thinking contained in this chapter has been made possible through a series of research grants provided to me in recent years by the Australian Research Council, for which I am most grateful.

References

Akom, A., Ginwright, S., & Cammarota, J. (2008). Youthtopias: Toward a new paradigm of critical youth studies. *Youth Study Reporter: The Professional Journal of the Youth Media Field, 2*(4), 1–30.

Akom, A., & Shoraka, S. (2007). Free spaces: Excavating race, class, and gender among urban schools and communities. *International Journal of Qualitative Studies in Education, 20*(6), 611–616.

Appadurai, A. (1996). *Modernity at large: Cultural dimensions of globalization.* Minneapolis, MN: University of Minnesota Press.

Appadurai, A. (2004). The capacity to aspire: Culture and the terms of recognition. In V. Rao & M. Walton (Eds.), *Culture and public action* (pp. 59–84). Stanford, CA: Stanford University Press with the World Bank.

Ares, N. (2010). Introduction. In N. Ares (Ed.), *Youth-full productions: Cultural practices and constructions of content and social spaces* (pp. 1–4). New York, NY: Peter Lang.

Ares, N., Hassberg, A., & with members of Youth as Public Intellectuals (YPI). (2010). Conversation-in-writing. In N. Ares (Ed.), *Youth-full productions: Cultural practices and constructions of content and social spaces* (pp. 125–136). New York, NY: Peter Lang.

Beauboeuf-Lafontant, T. (1999). Movement against and beyond boundaries: Politically relevant teaching among African American teachers. *Teachers College Record, 100*(4), 702–723.

Boomer, G. (Ed.). (1982). *Negotiating the curriculum: A teacher-student partnership.* Sydney, Australia: Ashton Scholastic.

Brown, P., & Hesketh, A. (2004). *The mismanagement of talent: Employability and jobs in the knowledge economy.* Oxford, UK: Oxford University Press.

Bucholtz, M. (2002). Youth and cultural practice. *Annual Review of Anthropology, 19*(4), 525–552.

Cammarota, J., & Fine, M. (2008). Youth participatory action research: A pedagogy for transformational resistance. In J. Cammarota & M. Fine (Eds.), *Revolutionizing education: Youth participatory action research in motion* (pp. 1–11). New York, NY: Routledge.

Cammarota, J., & Romero, A. (2006). A critically compassionate intellectualism for Latino/a students. *Multicultural Education, 14*(2), 16–23.

Daniels, E., Harnischfeger, A., Hos, R., & Akom, A. (2010). Youth as active agents: Counter-narrating the source of reform. In *Youth-full productions: Cultural practices and constructions of content and social spaces* (pp. 17–45). New York, NY: Peter Lang.

Erickson, F. (1987). Transformation and school success: The politics and culture of educational achievement. *Anthropology and Education Quarterly, 18*(4), 335–356.

Evans, D., Fox, M., & Fine, M. (2010). Producing selves and knowledges: Reflections on participatory youth inquiry. In N. Ares (Ed.), *Youth-full productions: Cultural practices and constructions of content and social spaces* (pp. 97–124). New York, NY: Peter Lang.

Evans, S., & Boyte, H. (1986). *Free spaces: The sources of democratic change in America.* Chicago, IL: University of Chicago Press.

Freire, P., & Macedo, D. (1987). *Literacy: Reading the word and the world.* South Hadley, MA: Bergin & Garvey.

Garbarino, J. (1999). *Raising children in a socially toxic environment.* San Francisco, CA: Jossey-Bass.

Ginwright, S. (2008). Collective radical imagination: Youth participatory action research and the art of emancipatory knowledge. In J. Cammarota & M. Fine (Eds.), *Revolutionizing education: Youth participatory action research in motion* (pp. 13–22). London, UK: Routledge.

Ginwright, S., & Cammarota, J. (2002). New terrain in youth development: The promise of a social justice approach. *Social Justice, 29*(4), 82–96.

Ginwright, S., & Cammarota, J. (2007). Youth activism in the urban community: Learning critical civic praxis within community organizations. *International Journal of Qualitative Studies in Education, 20*(6), 693–710.

Ginwright, S., & James, T. (2002). From assets to agents of change: Social justice, organizing, and youth development. *New Directions for Youth Development, 2002*(96), 27–46.

Ginwright, S., Noguera, P., & Cammarota, J. (Eds.). (2006). *Beyond resistance: Youth activism and community change.* New York, NY: Routledge.

Gustavson, L. (2007). *Youth learning on their own terms: Creative practices and classroom teaching.* London, UK: Routledge.

Kincheloe, J. (1995). *Toil and trouble: Good work, smart workers, and the integration of academic and vocational education.* New York, NY: Peter Lang.

Kincheloe, J. (2010). *Knowledge and critical pedagogy.* Dordrecht, The Netherlands: Springer.

Kirshner, B. (2006). Apprenticeship learning in youth activism. In S. Ginwright, P. Noguera, & J. Cammarota (Eds.), *Beyond resistance: Youth activism and community change* (pp. 37–57). New York, NY: Routledge.

Levinson, B. (2000). Introduction: Whither the symbolic animal? Society, culture, and education at the millennium. In B. Levinson et al. (Eds.), *Schooling the symbolic animal: Social and cultural dimensions of education* (pp. 1–11). Lanham, MD: Rowman & Littlefield.

Mills, C. (1971). *The sociological imagination.* Harmondsworth, UK: Penguin.

Nagle, J. (2001). *Voices from the margins: The stories of vocational high school students.* New York, NY: Peter Lang.

The New Shorter Oxford English Dictionary. (1993). Vol. 1. Oxford, UK: Clarendon Press.

Quijada, D. (2008). Marginalization, identity formation, and empowerment: Youth's struggles for self and social justice. In N. Dolby & F. Rizvi (Eds.), *Youth moves: Identities and education in global perspectives* (pp. 207–220). New York, NY: Routledge.

Romero, A. (2008). *Towards a critically compassionate intellectualism model of transformative education: Love, hope, identity and organic intellectualism through convergence of critical race theory, critical pedagogy, and authentic caring. Unpublished doctoral dissertation*. University of Arizona, Tucson, AZ.

Romero, A., Arce, S., & Cammarota, J. (2009). Barrio pedagogy: Identity, intellectualism, activism, and academic achievement through the evolution of a critically compassionate intellectualism. *Race, Ethnicity and Education, 12*(3), 217–233.

Smyth, J. (1989a). A critical pedagogy of classroom practice. *Journal of Curriculum Studies, 21*(6), 483–502.

Smyth, J. (1989b). Developing and sustaining critical reflection in teacher education. *Journal of Teacher Education, 40*(2), 2–9.

Smyth, J. (2011). *Critical pedagogy for social justice*. London, UK: Continuum.

Smyth, J., Angus, L., Down, B., & McInerney, P. (2009). *Activist and socially critical school and community renewal: Social justice in exploitative times*. Rotterdam, The Netherlands: Sense.

Smyth, J., & Fasoli, L. (2007). Climbing over the rocks in the road to student engagement and learning in a challenging high school in Australia. *Educational Research, 49*(3), 273–295.

Smyth, J., & McInerney, P. (2012). *From silent witnesses to active agents: Student voice in re-engaging with learning*. New York, NY: Peter Lang.

Standing, G. (2011). *The precariat: The new dangerous class*. London, UK: Bloomsbury Academic.

Steinberg, S. (1995). Introduction. In J. Kincheloe, *Toil and trouble: Good work, smart workers, and the integration of academic and vocational education* (pp. xi-xiii). New York, NY: Peter Lang.

Steinberg, S., & Kincheloe, J. (1998). *Students as researchers: Creating classrooms that matter*. London, UK: Falmer Press.

Stovall, D. (2007). Towards a politics of interruption: High school design as politically relevant pedagogy. *International Journal of Qualitative Studies in Education, 20*(6), 681–691.

Verma, R. (2010). *Be the change: Teacher, activist, global citizen*. New York, NY: Peter Lang.

CHAPTER 8

Foot Soldiers of Modernity
The Dialectics of Cultural Consumption and the 21st Century School

Paul Willis

School students are unconscious foot soldiers in the long front of modernity, involuntary and disoriented conscripts in battles never explained. Especially subordinate and working class students are the "compulsory" living materials of the future imaginings and mouldings of one generation for the next; institutional imaginings of immense social power but undertaken usually without the rudiments of a sociological or ethnographic imagination. What is crucial but missed is that the waves of attempted economic and technical modernisation "from above" are not synchronised with, often antagonistically related to, associated but usually misunderstood, waves of cultural modernisation "from below." You could say that technical modernisation is fighting, not chaos, the recalcitrant past or the wrong type of future, but its own alter ego of late cultural modernism as articulated in the majority and unprivileged population. Though often standing in the way of, most often the latter tend to believe in 'progress' and certainly profoundly condition how it is played out socially and culturally, oddly especially in ensuring forms of unequal social stability. Schools are one of the principal sites for the dialectical playing out of these connected disjunctions and contradictions. Misunderstandings of them underlie most "urgent" education debates: from traditionalism Vs progressivism to the canon Vs multi-culturism. Though under our very noses, some lessons are never learned.

Youth are always among the first to experience, first hand, the problems and possibilities of the successive waves of technical and economic modernisation sweeping through capitalist societies. Young people respond in disorganised and chaotic ways, but to the best of their abilities and with relevance to the actual possibilities of their lives—as they see them—live and embody them. These responses are actually embedded in the flows of cultural modernisation but may seem to adult eyes to be mysterious, troubling, even shocking and "anti-social." But if we look closely at youth's embedded and embodied strategies and cultural behaviour, we can learn a lot about the social impact and social nature of modernising processes taken in the round as technical and cultural.

Though the activities and processes discussed have currency throughout the western industrialised 'core' countries, and though highly impacted and speeded up versions of them characterise varieties of 'third world' development, England is my particular example and I will be drawing on ethnographic arguments taken, usually, from my own research in England. I will deal with three aspects of what I am calling cultural modernisation. These will be taken in the chronological order of my work on them which does not necessarily reflect their 'real' order in time, certainly not across all countries. Although my main focus will be on the 'third' wave, all aspects and themes of the three waves continue as simultaneous and intertwined forces in play and continue in broad relevance, in different ways, to the current conjunctures in various countries. The basic argument of this paper is that the 'third wave' cannot be understood except within the context of, and dialectical links with, the first two waves

I will deal with three waves of cultural modernisation from below:

1. Working class and subordinate student cultural responses to modernising statist drives within education characterised especially by the development of universal, free, compulsory schooling for all children up to the age of 16.

2. The social and cultural dislocations and crises consequent upon the emergence of "post-industrial" society characterised especially by the rise of mass youth unemployment and the new or extended role of the state in the regulation of the youth labour market and entry to it.

3. Responses to the rise of late or post-modern global "commodity, electronic society" where young people especially are drenched with electronic signals and a plethora of cultural commodities.

First Wave

Part of the political settlement between "capital" and "labour" in the UK after the Second World War was to give "equal" (at least theoretically) education rights to all children of all classes. The raising of the minimum school leaving age to 16 in 1972 marked the coming to full fruition in the UK of the early modernist drive to secure compulsory full time education for all. Durkheim (1956) comments on education as the instrument of modernisation mobilised specifically to raise the skill levels of workers in an internationally competitive industrial world. Always inherent in this drive was the tension between a socially integrative ideology of aspiration and, later, egalitarianism and the obvious practical logic of the delivery of social agents into gendered hierarchies severely divided by skill, remuneration and disposition. This perhaps prepares us to understand that even extended support across the organised left in the UK for the raising of the school leaving age failed to hide the 'disappointing' response of a good section of working class youth to the prospect of another year of enforced attendance at school. Many working class kids did not accept their new 'privilege' with good grace. They simply wanted the earliest possible access to the wage. They did not want to be in school at all, never mind another year of it.

Learning to Labour (1977) describes the informal school culture and modes of bodily interaction of a group of young white working class boys in the mid 1970s in a school in the English industrial midlands. "The lads" resisted the mental and bodily inculcations of the school and rejected students who showed conformist attitudes to the school authorities, calling them "ear'oles" (slang for the exterior bit of the human ear; "the lads" saw them as always listening and never doing). Their culture borrowed and recycled elements of traditional working class culture and was embodied through an assertive masculine style, a particular concrete and sharp way of speaking and devotion to a certain kind of omni-present humour—"having a laugh"—often directed cruelly against conformists and, often, the teachers. They had little or no interest in studying, and were not interested in gaining qualifications. Not all working class students failed then, of course, but, then as now, middle class school students were about six times more likely to go on into Higher Education than were working class pupils: I wanted to get at the inside story of this phenomenon, to try to see the world as they did, to get a feel for their social games and their fields of power from their point of view.

The central vertical dynamic of their lived culture was a vigorous opposition to the authority of the teachers, 'Who are they, tellin' us what to do when they're no better than us'. The central horizontal dynamic was a rejection of conformist pupils labelled as 'ear'oles'—i.e., always listening, never doing: 'They'm prats, they never get any fun do they?' This rejection was felt as a kind of distinction and superiority, 'We can make them laff, they can't make us laff'. These positions and orientations were enacted and embodied through a strong 'rough' masculine set of strategies, embellished in various ways through smoking, drinking and stylish dressing. Also central to the culture was devotion to and deployment of 'the laff', an ubiquitous form capable of turning almost any situation into material for jokes and ribbing, 'it's the most important thing in life, even communists laff'.

From an educationalist and careers work point of view, the strangest thing about 'the lads'' attitudes and behaviour was their low interest in, often hostility towards, academic work and the gaining of qualifications. From a sociological point of view the strangest thing about their culture was the indifference it induced amongst 'the lads' to the actual kind of work they thought of undertaking, in the event, ranging from then readily available factory work, to tyre fitting to brick layers mate. I argued in *Learning to Labour* that their own culture helped induct them, 'voluntarily', in to the low status jobs that most would shun. Their own culture was involved in processes of social reproduction, understood as the generational replacement of individuals in unequal class positions, surprisingly, in more effective ways than produced by any intended ideological mechanism. There was a tragic irony at the heart of their culture.

'Silent' forms of resistance and disaffection are more likely amongst working class girls (see, for instance, Payne, 1980; Llewellyn, 1980; Anyon, 1983) with similarly ironic processes of reproduction to be observed with respect to their destiny in unpaid domestic work and within low paid 'feminised' occupations. In the era of politically driven Diaspora following on from and merging with continuing economic migration (in the UK from the 'new commonwealth, principally the West Indies and the Indian sub-continent), other variants of informal and resistant cultures of school borrow from, recycle and adapt to purpose elements of various traditional race, ethnic and national cultures (see, for instance, Mac an Ghaill, 1988; Raissiguier, 1995; Fordham, 1996, also Portes, 1995).

I argue that although resistant school cultures were, and are, condemned and increasingly seen as "pathological," they actually show some clear elements of rationality. In particular, they supply "life forms" and shields from stigma to blunt the cruel edge of individualism and meritocracy in capitalist societies—ideologies with associated mechanisms and practices that can have only limited meaning for the majority of the working class who cannot all really hope to expect the privilege of well paid and high prestige jobs at the end of the educational process. Individual logic says that it is worth working hard at school to gain qualifications to get a good job and it may be worthwhile for any particular individual to believe in and act on this. A substantial minority from the working class can hope for mobility in this way and their cultures and dispositions are adapted accordingly. But clearly this cannot be the case for all working class individuals and yet all are asked to behave as if it were so. No one else discusses it, but 'the lads'' culture, for instance, despite its disorders and chaos, 'tells' them that no amount of extra qualification will improve the position of the whole class: that would constitute, in fact, the dismantling of the whole class society. Of course the 'empirical' picture in any school is a complex kaleidoscope of cultural adaptation (see 'third wave' section for a systematic treatment with conflicts and instrumental combinations of and between individual and collective logics fought out in the same head and body as well as between cultural forms).

Meanwhile the dominance of the individualistic and meritocratic ideology produces for the middle class (as well as suppressed tensions and guilt) a functional legitimacy for enjoying their privilege—they are there because they have passed exams—and the capacities of the majority are stultified in hopeless obedience to an impossible dream. Prevented from pursuing alternative flowerings of their capacities or subversive courses of growth, credentialism would enslave their powers and trap them in the foothills of human development. From the collective point of view, the proliferation of qualifications is simply a worthless inflation in the currency of credentialism, and advance through it, a fraudulent offer to the majority of what can really mean something only to the few. Meanwhile blanket compliance is demanded from all. The student population is graded in a descending status order, from whose lowest ranks escape is usually impossible. The educational offer is one to join an ever-multiplying classificatory system whose every increase further depresses its bottom layers. 'The lads'' culture exposes some of this, releasing them from collusion in their own exclusion and freeing up their potentials for cultural expressivity, even if in 'anti-social' ways and also ironically ensuring that they will be active in their own domination. Though embattled and ambiguous as never before, informal school cultures continue to sustain zones of humanity and dignity offering alternative evaluations of human powers and potentials.

Oddly, such as 'the lads'' culture also had a real stabilising effect on the hierarchical social order, because in their "tumble out of" and "escape" from what they felt was the oppressive atmosphere of the school, they went into manual work quite voluntarily, so helping the reproduction of the whole social order at its most difficult point. 'The lads'' also found a "culture of the shop floor" on arrival at work, which was welcoming and familiar to them because it displayed many of the same qualities as their own counter-school culture, and gave a collective and human means (even if sexist, anti-intellectual and often racist) of surviving the harsh conditions and authority regimes of work. 'The lads'' 'transition' from school to work was, in part, a cultural vote with their feet for the working class world of work, for what seemed to be its more mature, adult and respectful way of treating them—continuous, of course, with aspects of their own previous cultural experience. You could call all of this a kind of informal socialisation process. There was also an enthusiastic taking up of rights (automatic entitlement now withdrawn) to the only working class inheritance—the wage. Its power released possibilities for which their own culture had already precociously and only too well prepared them: smart dressing, pubbing and clubbing and cross town driving.

Hugely important to understand here is the anti-mental animus of the counter-school culture. Whilst highly relevant in opposing and penetrating the demands of the school, it also becomes a kind of second nature and continues to orient and help direct the attitudes of 'the lads' across the board, during the transition and long after too. This 'locking' impels them towards a certain kind of culturally mediated, experiential form of meaning throughout their lives. There will certainly be future situations in which these attitudes and practices produce worthwhile 'pay-offs', but the danger is that the whole world might, henceforth, be divided up into two—the mental and the manual. This makes hope for 'second chance' return to Higher Education much more difficult and unlikely—the male, white working class continues to suffer from the lowest rate of return of any group even under open enrolment schemes. As part of the tumble out of school their anti-mentalism reconciles 'the lads' and those like them to manual work and often to job hopping between 'dead end jobs' (now interspersed with long spells of unemployment, or even permanent unemployment) for the rest of their lives. It makes all jobs involving mental work, now and for the future, seem to be simply boring 'paper work'—'who wants to spend their day pushing paper around'.

Important to note here also is the importance of gender meanings and resources within the articulation of cultural forces and practices resistant to the school. Symbolic structures of masculinity in 'the lads'' culture, for instance, help to embody and give an extra force to their school resistance. Masculinity gives them an axis of power over and exploitation of women, but it also gives them a realistic basis for feeling at least some ambiguous superiority over other less successful males—teachers as well as 'earholes' (conformists). This has a definite logic and is effective against the attempted domination of the school. It gives alternative non-mental grounds for valuing the self and a whole solid, sometimes formidable presence, to resist belittling. But once formed, 'hard' masculine identities, and the patterning of social relations which follow, prove highly inflexible, intractable and durable. This is perhaps especially so where they have been formed through inescapable institutional tension in the winning back of identity and dignity lost in other sets of relations where you have been 'compulsorily' trapped on the losing/receiving end. Masculinity and its reflexes henceforth help to organise the same repertoire of defensive-offensive responses no matter what the situation—as if all social sites and social relations contained somehow a mandatory threat. This produces an obvious danger for women in and out of the home, where a compensatory masculinity may seek proof and exercise of a felt superiority. Furthermore, shop floor and manual work relations are suffused with masculinity and masculinised social relations which blunt oppositional recognition of specifically capitalist forms of the subordination of labour power.

There is a further twist here where the anti-mentalism and masculinity of 'the lads' become intertwined, fused, in their sense of themselves and of their own vital powers. A manual way of acting in the world is also a manly way; a mental way, effeminate. These two things mutually reinforce and 'lock' each other producing a disposition and sensibility which may, quite literally, last a lifetime. In this final and damning move we can see how, for 'the lads', mental work becomes not only pointless 'paper pushing' but also 'sissy' work. Teachers can be seen as inferior because they are 'sissies'. Even higher paid mental work is not that great because it is still 'sissy' from 'the lads'' point of view. Exhausting and exploited, now increasingly low paid, manual work can still somehow be seen in a masculine register, which prevents its true brutality from showing through.

This account of cultures of white, male, working class resistance in school gives us a perspective for understanding a particular stability in the first 'settlement' of cultural modernisation in the UK, the world's first industrial capitalist society, and its contribution towards the maintenance of a relatively peaceful class divided society. Even after the advent of the Welfare State and formal educational equality for all, there was a settled relation between (very unequal) classes, with no "over-ambition" from the working class threatening either capitalist organisation or the interests of the middle class. At the same time there was some real autonomy allowed to students and young workers, so that their own specifically working class and informal cultural forms and activities—though seen as "anti-social" by some—could take root and flower in inhospitable circumstances. This made those circumstances more "liveable" and provided collective and mutual relations, communications and meanings which sustained working class identity and informal activity on a wider scale.

Though, as we will now pursue, things have changed over the last twenty years, there continue to be very hard and persistent elements of "resistant" culture in school, which despite their sometimes anti-social nature and the undoubted difficulties they produce for classroom teachers, continue to pose in living form, crucial, collective questions from the point of view of the working class: "What is 'progress' for?"; "What can I/we expect from the sacrifice of hard work and obedience in school?" "Why am I compelled to be in school if there appears to be nothing in it for me?"

This long cultural "settlement" is being disrupted in two very important ways, attacked by two further waves of 'modernisation' and 'progress'. The first of these attacks arises at the material level from a series of profound economic and political changes producing a catastrophic secular decline in the demand for industrial manual labour in the 'core' western countries. We can understand this as one aspect of much discussed 'globalisation', in this case a global economic restructuration which sees the brutal arrival of the 'post-industrial' society in the 'first' world just as 'industrial society' finally takes root unevenly in the 'third'.

Second Wave

In the early 1980s the UK was the first industrialised country to experience massive losses of manual industrial work available to the working classes. This trend is now firmly established across the old industrialised world. Since 1979 in the UK over four million manufacturing jobs have been lost with a concomitant and slightly larger reduction in Trade Union membership. At the same time there has been a virtually epochal restructuration of the kind of work available, from the point of view of the working class, essentially away from well paid skilled and reasonably paid semi-skilled industrial work towards lower paid service and usually out of reach white collar work. Taken together, the new call centres around the UK and the hotel and catering industries now employ more than double the number of workers than are employed in the old 'smoke stack' industries (cars, ship building, steel, engineering, coal mining). The whole working class especially young people, older workers and ethnic minorities in particular have been badly effected by the diminution in both the quality and quantity of jobs available. Recently unemployment has dropped considerably to a general rate now of about 7%, but this bald figure conceals both a high turnover in part time, casual, insecure low paid work, and huge geographic variations with large, predominantly middle class areas enjoying virtually full employment and the older industrial areas and inner cities suffering from overall rates of 20% and more, much higher for the continuingly vulnerable groups. One in two less-skilled men are without work and one in five households lacks access to earned income. Clearly not everyone will find a role in the new "weightless" economy, and many continue to expect, against increasing odds, to be remunerated and respected for an ability and disposition to work in traditional manual ways (Willis, 1988; Gregg & Wadsworth, 1999).

So the objective probabilities of a reliable and decent wage through manual work have been radically decreased for substantial parts of the working class, the threat of its removal all together made a permanent condition for all workers. This has to be understood as a threat not only to the wage as an amount of money but also to the wage as a particular kind of social inheritance and cultural, even moral, enfranchisement (Willis, 1990 & 2000). The wage provides access to cultural commodities and services and to the forms of informal meaning-making framed and facilitated by them. The wage also provides the means to independent living, a separate place from the patriarchal dependencies of the parental home, from the vicissitudes of the market place. The wage also enables the formation of the 'the couple' and preparation for the nuclear family. Gaining access, and giving access, to the male 'family wage' is still one of the important material bases for the courtship dance, romance and 'love-pairing'.

In the UK we have been suffering from the breaking of these transitions for getting on for two decades. The old processes and expectations often continue in some form but have been thrown into permanent crisis: truly the teeth grittings of a much less harmonious social balance. There are still plenty of male working class kids like 'the lads', for instance, who are willing, perhaps more willing than ever, to take on exploited manual work in traditional masculine and anti-mentalist way: compelling evidence of the inflexibility and long duree of locked cultural forms. But there is not enough work to go around, so many are left in suspended animation. The lucky ones, at least to start with, feel grateful for any work; though job insecurity or the deceptive lure of job hoping as an antidote to the wearings down of repetitive or heavy labour, threaten at any moment to throw them back into a stagnant pool of labour. Nevertheless simple gratitude and escape from vertiginous despair have become very important reproductive mechanisms for those finding or holding on to work.

These seismic changes have destroyed or substantially weakened the traditional forms of transition from school to work and have shaken the material foundations of traditional forms of working class culture. You could say that successful economic adaptation (unemployment as a 'price worth paying' for competitive economic restructuring) produces continuing social and cultural crisis at the bottom of social space.

Though there are marked race and gender differences, there are some general features of these connected crises which can be described. The following is based, amongst other things, on *The Youth Review* (Willis, 1988), Furlong and Cartmel's *Young People and Social Change* (1997) and Starrin et al.'s, 'In the Wake of Recession—Economic Hardship, Shame and Social Disintegration' (1997). The young unemployed are much less physically mobile than the employed. They cannot afford cars and therefore have no access to the 'cross-town car culture' of visits to pubs, clubs and friends. Half of the unemployed say that their activities are limited by the costs of travel and three quarters by lack of cash. A good proportion of them visits town centres and shopping malls during the day, but then it is to do things which cost no money, principally just hanging about. They are attracted to the consumer meccas but have no role to play there except perhaps to come in to conflict with shoppers, shop owners and the police.

The young unemployed, ironically, have more 'free time' than any other social group but they are, in fact, excluded from 'leisure' which overwhelmingly now requires consumption and commercial power. Take the example of drinking. Whether we like it or not this is by far the most popular activity of young people overall in the UK, around three quarters of whom go to pubs nearly four times a week. Only a third of the long-term unemployed go drinking and then much less often. Sports and outdoor hobbies do not take up the slack of extra time, nor is there any greater take up (than the employed) of activities in the state provided community/sports infrastructure. The dominant experience of the unemployed is one of very limited sociability; they are isolated and homebound, traversing acres of boredom by themselves or in conflict with parent(s) for whom their enforced dependence is often wholly unwelcome dependency. One vivid aspect of this isolation is that, especially for white working class males, 'courtship' seems to lose the absolute centrality it holds for the employed. They are much less likely, generally, to have a 'steady' and thoughts of marriage or settling down seem very far away for most. Generally long-term unemployed young people are prone to alienation, depression and pessimism about their future prospects and plagued by a feeling of social shame and a suspicion that other people blame them for their condition. They are uniquely open to drug abuse, often seen in distorted ways as forms of self-medication.

A whole succession of training programmes and special labour market measures have been developed to bridge the gaping holes left by the collapse of the old transitions. Introduced five years ago in the UK, the 'New Deal' programme for unemployed young people is of two years duration and provides a choice from three options: work experience, training, voluntary work. For the first time on such schemes, refusal to participate is not an option. Benefits are withdrawn if a young person fails to commit to one of these options in an individually signed personal contract. Essentially, the means of subsistence are made contingent upon total flexibility and obedience, a qualitatively new coercive stage in the disciplining of labour power and attitude. A significant minority of people refuse this contractual submission to their own subordination, become 'invisible' and simply do not register in official figures and contact (Unemployment Unit, 1999). Despite such refusal and widespread discontent with 'schemes', there is surprisingly little outright public or organised opposition. This may be explained in part by some bleak, inturned and individualistic additions to the reproduction repertoire whereby many individuals blame themselves for their lack of work and for the lack of success scheme attendance brings. Individualising and internalising a structural problem, they shamefully reproach themselves, singly one by one, for their inability to find work. Having been given so many training opportunities to develop their own individual employability, and having being told repeatedly that finding work is a question of permanent individual job search, it must be their own individual fault when they cannot find work.

These are just some of the corrosive forces eating away at the main elements of the 'first wave' modernist cultural settlement. The pride, depth and independence of a collective industrial cultural tradition, forged from below and neither reliant on patronage nor punished for its cultural impertinences, is giving way to the regulated indignities of client status to a reprimanding, no longer 'mother', state. Young workers are being press-gang recruited to a re-envisioned reserve army of flexible and obedient labour which is supposed to stand ready to occupy, at rock bottom wages, the new menial functions of the 'post-industrial' economy and to service the growing personal and domestic needs of a newly ascendant middle class. As ever, gender registers and plays a part in fundamental social and cultural shifts. In particular, forms of working class masculinity are being thrown into change and crisis by these epochal shifts, uprooted from their secure and central lodgings within proletarian relations of manualism, 'pride in the job' and 'bread winner' power.

There may be new 'under-class' (or more exactly, mutant lower working class) cultural forms developing—exaggerated, and not yet so discontinuous with stressed but still functioning inherited working class forms and experiences—which refuse these indignities and, at a Faustian price, protect their members from working penury interspersed with unreasonable, profoundly contradictory and now 'contracted' official expectations of permanent job search.

For those who refuse to join state schemes and/or the legitimate labour market, 'blagging' from parents and others, 'black' work, crime, drug dealing, prostitution, varieties of hustling and benefit fraud offer some income, as well as entanglements with youth justice systems and possible incarceration—which finally destroys any hope of a 'proper job'. But the highly ambiguous and self-defeating freedoms of the streets may seemingly offer a viable alternative to the mental incarceration of endless state schemes.

It is possible that single mothers may still find some mileage in the manipulation of an increasingly mean, disciplining and coercive state to provide bare housing and subsistence. But various kinds of limitation on total lifetime welfare entitlements mean that they are running out of road on their way to a crossroads of enforced choice between workfare subservience and the dubious freedoms of the street.

The school is and will be a principal site for the early playing out of these contradictions and social tensions, with school questioned and devalued at the level of cultural practice, not only by penetrations of its individualistic and meritocratic ideologies, but also by its inability to practically connect into, or even be honest about, prospects in the world of work. In these conditions it is no longer possible to believe in a universal and positive role for the educational system in promoting benign and emancipatory effects for the popular classes. Are schools to prepare their students for unemployment, are they to engage in remedial programmes to equip individuals to fight each other for the very chance of low paid service work, abandoning altogether any hope of interrupting, rather adding their crushing weight to, all too evident processes of reproduction?

Meanwhile many late adolescent or early adult work-less cultural forms come back into the school importing with them their own hidden and not so hidden injuries and reinforcing attitudes of cynicism, detachment and gender crisis, finding particular articulations and expressions within different school formations bringing increased disorder, violence and attendant social fear (Devine, 1997; Johnson, 1999; Paulle, 2003). Singular oppressions to do with race, exacerbated and magnified through even higher expected unemployment rates, add further impulses of anger and opposition. Within school cultures practices have to be understood within this general context of disaffection, with oppositional forms termed and understood, perhaps, as dis-associated or disaffected resistance. Resistance takes on a kind of futility, even pathology, with disarticulation from traditional 'first wave' cultural resources and their sense of a future. First wave resistance has a kind of solidity in a social bet on capital's need for labour. It is an alternative wager on an access to a future of collective labour free from individualistic and meritocratic distortions and false promises. Even if not fitting the official templates, it has a consequent materiality to be worked on for betterment, economic, social, cultural. Second wave modernisation deconstructs this working class inheritance: resistances spin freely without the context of any socially imagined future and students are immersed in sets of chaotic relations which gradually enter the mind and body. It is hard to detect any link of disaffected or dis-associated resistance with any kind of emancipatory political project.

The undermining of masculinity in general undermines the specific logic of masculinised resistance in school as well as the continuities between male counter-school and what remains of shop floor culture. Further, the 'anti-mentalism' of the counter-school culture cannot be so securely cloaked in traditional proletarian masculinism and loses the counter-pointing of a viable expected future in manual work for and in individual and group trajectories and life courses.

If, for young women, there is no longer the realistic prospect of gaining access to the 'family wage', and to a transition into a separate household through male earning power, then the material base for the courtship dance, passive and subservient respect for the more 'skilled' and 'powerful' male may also disappear. Questions of gender identity may be rendered, at least partly, into matters of immediate attraction or non-attraction to the opposite sex rather than be formed in calculation of longer-term prospect and association. Where a collective apprenticeship to a respectable future fails, for some young men a strategy for maintaining or finding a continuing sense of manhood may entail, even seem to demand immediate gender tributes extracted through physical intimidation or its threat taken up into whole bodily dispositions.

Under conditions of chronic unemployment, it may be functional for social stability and social reproduction that a slice of the young and potentially most disruptive of the unemployed of both sexes should prepare to withdraw themselves into more or less self pacified positions or marginalised positions, excluding themselves permanently from the labour market, so withdrawing from it seeds of non-co-operation and rebellion. The development of an 'under-class' (and especially the degeneracies of its imaginary), vastly expanded prison populations—the new 'welfare' means for the poor—and the further economic victimisation of single mothers, may also provide socially reproductive object lessons in destitution 'pour encourager les autres'. Substantial proportions of the student body may be influenced by oppositional cultures but calculate that a state regulated chance of a low paid job (forget the social democratic ideals of 'wave one') beats incarceration or the tender mercies of the street. But this is a raw and open form of reproduction very different from the more settled, if mystified, forms associated with first wave modernisation.

However, sadly expressed nowhere else again, even through the ambiguous means of dis-associated school cultural forms, collective questions gain cultural articulation: 'What's the point of school if there ain't no jobs to follow?', 'If 'progess' is so great why is all I see at school, and the schemes to follow, increased containment and discipline?'

Third Wave

As well as these upheavals in the material conditions of the subordinate classes and especially of the young in the UK there have been enormous changes at the cultural level bringing about profound change and disorganisation to "settled" forms of working class culture. Old "sensuous" community and face to face communication has been sidelined by new global electronic forms of communication, especially TV, with now literally hundreds of channels available through digitalisation, and also by the huge growth of commercial leisure forms and the mass availability, globally often, of the same cultural commodities. The 'post-modern' cultural epoch is characterised by the qualitative expansion of commodity relations from the meeting of physical needs (food, warmth and shelter) to the meeting and inflaming of mental, emotional, expressive and spiritual needs and aspirations. You could say that the predatory productive forces of capitalism are now unleashed, globally, not only on nature but also on human nature.

Young people are becoming less defined by neighbourhood and class, than they are by these new relations of the "commodity and electronic" culture. Even as their economic conditions of existence falter, most young working class people in the UK would not thank you now for describing them as "working class." They find more passion and acceptable self-identity through music on MTV, wearing baseball caps and designer trainers and socialising in McDonald's fast food joints, than they do through traditional class cultural forms.

We should not underestimate capitalism's cultural offensive against the young consumer. Young people may believe that they are 'free to choose' but the marketers have different ideas. Simon Silvester, executive planning director for Young & Rubicon Europe writes recently in the 'Creative Business' section (that title tells its own story) of the *Financial Times*: 'Marketers have concentrated on youth for 50 years for good reason—they [i.e. youth] are forming their brand preferences and trying out new things (…) In 40 years, there'll be a generation of pierced grannies telling you they're brand-promiscuous and adventurous' (*Financial Times*, 2002).

Ralph Nader begins his *Children First* with:

> A struggle different than any before in world history is intensifying between corporations and parents over their children. It is a struggle over the minds, bodies, time and space of millions of children and the kind of world in which they are growing up.
>
> (1996: p. iii)

He continues a few pages later

> Children are now grown through products. Children are now the Disney Generation, the MTV Generation, the Joe Camel Generation, the Pepsi Generation. Stories used to sell products are being used to raise children. The corporate marketing culture stresses materialism, money, sex, the power of violence, junk food and the status they bring; its power crowds out or erodes the values of the inherent worth and dignity of the human being.
>
> (1996, p. vii):

Such arguments are well known, and oddly enough, made with equal vigour from the left and the right. Though there is much to be agreed with in Nader's pungently expressed views, my purpose is not so much to join a moral crusade, but more to establish the nature of an epochal shift in the symbolic order and its forms which confronts young people and to understand its consequences in a social scientific and ethnographic manner. Leaving aside the important question of age and vulnerability, for middle and late teenagers and early adults it simply has to be accepted that the most attractive and useable symbolic and expressive forms are supplied by the market, which through its electronic forms truly provides an encompassing and saturating cultural environment. We may have wished, variously, for political parties or public cultures or provisions of the public realm or properly functioning educational institutions to have been the principal and principled source of symbolic forms and meanings, and it is certainly necessary to continue to battle for the maintenance of their roles and influence, but as Margaret Thatcher once said, 'You cannot buck the market'. Once penetrating the realm of culture and consciousness, a market economy of commodity relations must exert the same formative powers there as it does in the material realm: driving out craft production and feudal relations of symbolic dependence; bringing in an avalanche of commodity goods for consumers constituted as free citizens to chose and consume as they wish, now with their spirits as well as their bodies. It is not possible to throw out this influence without now throwing our market relations *tout court*.

My position is that the undoubted market power of capitalist cultural provision certainly determines the forms of production of cultural commodities, but that this cannot be seen as necessarily enforcing an isomorphic consumption. The commodity form is certainly dominant, but whilst constricting and structuring the field does not determine it. Within bounds, the commodity forms inbuilt desperation to find use at any price actually indecently incites and provokes certain kinds of appropriation (Willis, 2000). Nor is this necessarily an appropriation along standard lines. No two people look the same, no two living rooms look the same, no two people think the same and yet they are all products of a social existence within a market economy. What the production-oriented pessimists overlook is the other half of the equation: the processes and activities of acculturation, well known by and commented on by cultural anthropologists in other contexts, whereby human beings actively and creatively take up the objects and symbols around them for their own situated purposes of meaning-making. No matter how disreputable their provenance, commodities and electronic messages are still subject to grounded processes, not only of passive consumption but also of active appropriation. It can certainly be argued that young and working class people, especially, are caught up, again, in the front line of engagement here, acculturating the materials of commodity culture almost as a matter of cultural life and death not least because they find themselves with ever diminishing inherited 'folk' cultural resources (passed on safely through the generations) and with little or no access to legitimate and bourgeois forms of cultural capital. In the light of the multiple, complex possibilities of the grounded use of the new environmental resources, commodity and electronic, I think that it can even be argued that there is a strange emergence from below and within subordinate cultural relations of a new kind of 'expressive subject'. Better by far if this had occurred in planned developmental ways with more democratic control at the point of formal cultural production, but our hopes for an institutionally led and mutually co-operative cultural programme for the popular classes have been rendered quaint and parochial by the new relations of desire brokered through the commodity. At any rate, the emergence of the actually existing subordinate expressive subject concerns, if you like, members of the majority popular classes taking for themselves—on the alien and profane grounds of the commodity—something hitherto that only the elites have enjoyed as part of their sacred privilege: the formation of sensibility on relatively chosen or at least autonomous (from the realm of necessity) expressive grounds, rather than automatically ascribed grounds. This is a connection of the 'given self' to variable external symbolic forms, the desire not just to take up social or material space in a way governed by others but to matter culturally (Willis, 2000). Without that you are culturally invisible which means, increasingly, socially invisible. The choice to wear body jewellery may well last a lifetime but it is a choice furnaced in the conditions of a whole experienced life and life stage, a marking of a biography and sense of self and social situation which simply cannot reduced to the successful marketing of earrings.

It is crucial here to recognise the blurring of the lines between production and consumption in what I call 'common culture' (Willis, 1990). Active consumption is a kind of production. Formal production—as in learning to play an instrument through listening to CDs—often arises first in relation to creative consumption. This is part of what separates practices of the acculturation of popular cultural items from the usual notion of popular culture as the provided materials only for themselves. Selecting and appropriating popular cultural items for your own meanings are a kind of cultural production. Though mediated through alien commodity materials, the attachment of an expressive identity to, or its workings through, a socially given 'mere existence' is now a popular and in its own way democratic aspiration. Whereas, in many ways, the early modernist educational question concerns whether state education is a means of liberation or ideological confinement for the "non-privileged" majority, the late modernist question for the same social group concerns whether the commodification and electrification of culture are a new form of domination or a means of opening up new fields of semiotic possibility. Are the young becoming culturally literate and expressive in new ways, or are they merely victims of every turn in cultural marketing and mass media manipulation?

However we judge the general tide of combat on this new front, it is incontestable that all school students are drawn in to the field of force of popular cultural provision. The basic point I want to make with respect to the overall theme of this special issue is that, to summarise, if commodity related expressive consumption (common culture) does not take place in a vacuum or simply repeat the exploited meanings of commodity production, then the acculturations which arise have to be understood as grounded in and informing other inherited social categories and positions as well as antagonisms between them. We must grant the freedoms of consumption that the political economists and anti-humanists deride, but locate them always at material and social interconnections and historical conjunctures which constrain and channel these freedoms in all kinds of ways. In the case of the school this points to the foundational importance of understanding popular cultural consumption with respect to previously existing themes of school conformism, resistance, disaffection, variations and points between them. We must be alive to how cultural commodities are used to 'body out' the nature and practice of previously existent or socially articulated positions still organised ultimately by elementary class, race and gender factors. Of particular importance is how the body oriented and somatic emphasis of common cultural practices chime with, resonate with, show an elective affinity for the manual emphases in working class and subordinate bodily cultures.

It is of note, for instance, that commodity related cultural practices are producing new fields for the expression of gender in and out of the school including the trying on of new 'cloaks' for the expression of masculinised resistance or independence from the school, a masculinity no longer guaranteed by a proletarian industrial inheritance but still often ranged against the school. It is also of note that common cultural practices can wrap themselves up with 'second wave' disaffected resistance supplying a doubly articulated emphasis on 'the now': that of immediate 'consumer' gratification and the extra weight placed on the present by the felt lack of a predictable social future. Where the proletarian inheritance of access to a decent wage and the moral and cultural benefits which flow from that are denied, cultural expressivity through commodities may supply an instant social and cultural imaginary for resistance to find alternatives to the felt oppressions of the school, providing, so to speak, something to resist with, including it has to be recognised, amplifications and resonances of criminal and violent themes. It must be understood that the apparently boundless horizons of consumption have done little to remove the unconscious 'foot soldiers' from their struggles, only added another front on which to contend.

These amplifications and resonances of cultural opposition through common cultural means carry their own marked ironies for social reproduction and negation of subordinate interests, removing students further from what school might offer them and diminishing further the chances of a shot at a 'proper' job. Meanwhile many students from less privileged backgrounds are inexorably drawn to exploited and 'dead end', low paid, intermittent and part-time work in order to gain or maintain access to this world. The interest in any kind of no matter now exploited paid work after school, or the prospect of it, is motivated often not by any intrinsic interest or 'delayed gratification' career plan but primarily for the greater immediate access wages might bring to the things which really energise and impassion beyond the boring world of work. Unemployment, or the prospect of it, produces 'oppression' not because of its social disenfranchisement but for the exclusion it brings from forms of identity making and satisfaction in these new leisure and consumption fields. The old categories of judging a fair wage and a decent job are being capsized.

To put my main point here concerning how to understand the relations of 'popular culture' in another way. I posit, along with many others in this volume, the strong urge by the young to make and maintain a viable informal cultural identity acknowledged by others in shared social space. Commodity consumption and display (trainers, music, appearance) are major 'raw materials' for the development of such expressive subjectivity and for the symbolic public marking of identity for self and others. But these forms of cultural expression are not simply about developing identity but are also about putative comparative and hierarchical social placing of identity (for an interesting parallel argument about the comparative importance of subcultural capital, see Thornton, 1995). But I argue that this comparative social dimension cannot be achieved within consumer relations themselves. In and of themselves, knowledgeable manipulations of symbolic markers of identity do not confer status. For that, a necessary condition, they need to be part of an identity founded on other grounds. The school is a crucial site of such other grounds, so that an over-mapping of distinctions take place with common culture positions and identities mapping onto distinctions within the school, themselves mapping onto wider social distinctions.

This is not to say that there is an automatic connection between the basic social elements (class, race and gender), school resistance or non-resistance (wave one), disaffection (wave two) and particular kinds of common cultural expression (third wave). Within the site of the school each of these factors has a relatively independent life and can attach itself to other elements so that there are certainly possibilities, amongst other things, for 'class and race cross-dressing' (a phrase I heard in a lecture by Cameron McCarthy). There are likely to be some tendencies of strong association, however, which it is the task of ethnography to uncover. For instance, especially in mixed class schools, lower working class (black and white) students are likely to be located at the bottom of the official school status system and be inclined to exploit popular cultural and other resources to embody, with alternative status markers, their resistance or disaffection, mobilising if you like cultural 'positional goods' which can be controlled by them.

Perhaps it is only the singular nature of the modernist school, with its 'compulsory' forcing together of people of exactly the same age into a common arena, which could compel individuals and groups to find a place and identity within a single complex matrix, no matter how heterogeneous their backgrounds and no matter how differently their cultural destinies would have played out without the unnatural social atmospherics of the school. We have looked at some elements of the 'common cultural status system' within the school and some of its points of contact with other systems. There are, in fact, several status systems in play at once in the school. The urgent and sometimes sulphurous social pressures built up in the pressure cooker of the school fuse and force into lived articulation a number of status conferring symbolic relations derived from without and within the school. These include:

a) That based on the internal official academic status measures of the school

b) the related but separate external cultural capital systems which confer likely status and advantage upon middle class students within the internal official system

c) especially in the USA, sport provides a powerful system of status measurement and achievement.

d) status systems based on perceptions of sexual attractiveness

e) systems based on perceived bodily 'hardness' and 'toughness' yielding to working class and black students greater chances for privilege within its terms

f) opposition to authority, derived from both 'wave one' resistance and 'wave two' dis-associated resistance produce their own kinds of status systems.

g) new patterns of popular cultural consumption confer separate bases for evaluation and prestige

Though forced into a common matrix, these schemas are not aligned and do not point uniformly and in the same direction to common high status positions. Conflict is ensured. In the cauldron of the school, students are competing for place and identity with reference to all of these positionalities. To change the metaphor, here is a complex cultural micro ecology, requiring considerable bravery and skill to negotiate and where, on the one hand, failure in navigation skills may lead to victim-hood, suffering and even tragedy, or on the other, to hard to reverse involvements in serious crime and violence stretching beyond the school.

All schools are likely to manifest all or most of the themes discussed, though there is likely to be wide variability in the cultural micro ecologies of particular schools and variation in the combination and alignment of systems. Common cultural systems are likely, in different ways, to become more central to them all. Again, this indicates a wide research agenda for ethnographic study. The predominant social class of students, and mix of social class is likely to be a crucial factor in the formation of such ecologies, as will race and ethnic mix. National differences may play a major part as in the apparently unparalleled importance of sport in social/cultural systems of US schools as well as very possibly the singular hyper-inflation of the 'hardness' dynamic in US ghetto schools. Private schools are likely to show a markedly different dynamic from state supported schools. None of this can be read out automatically, though, from social 'determinants'.

There is a real autonomy and unprefigurable chemistry in how the elements will mix in any given school. Successive, each still churning, waves of modernisation and responses to them have added new layers of pressure and confusion, turning the contemporary school into a strange kind of hybrid, or, in fact, even under the same roof several different kinds of institution, according to past and likely future trajectories of their students and the weightings of their stakes in which kinds of modernisation, and whether 'from above' or 'below'.

In predominantly working class schools there is likely to be a polarisation of the official system and its hierarchies of status from the 'popular' subterranean one. The latter develops and maintains its position by gathering to itself privileged positions within the informal status systems very importantly including the common cultural one so that 'popular' boys, for instance, are likely to be 'tough', opposing the school and also more likely to be seen as stylish in their musical and clothing tastes. To drop one of these attributes would be to drop out of the dominant 'popular'. To a greater or lesser extent other social groups are likely to seek to justify their position vis-à-vis this dominant 'popular' in the magnification of sitemaps beneficial to them. What we can think of as the oxymoron of 'subordinate' dominant 'populars' inverts not only the school's official but also wider social hierarchies so conferring on students dominant roles even where they, or their families, occupy generally subordinate economic and social positions outside the school. Unless, though, they can convert informal skills and knowledges to market advantage in the informal or formal cultural industries, there are likely to be continuingly marked ironic reproductive consequences for the members of such 'inverted' fixings of the official cultural systems of the school. They may enjoy cultural advantage, the ambiguous superiority of symbolic dominance, only as a short prelude to, and through academic under-achievement preparation for, extended economic disadvantage, or relative disadvantage on the labour market. In so far as middle class students in predominantly working class schools take up positions within such subordinate dominant 'populars' interesting competitions of influence will ensue between poor academic performance and attitude and effects flowing from inherited class resources of economic and cultural capital.

In schools with a more or predominantly middle class intake the weight of cultural capital brought into the school system is likely to give a qualitative and quantitative ballast to the official system and its status prizes, with other systems more likely to be more aligned with it, or if out of line, attenuated in their power. In the USA, class derived status systems, internal official systems and common cultural status systems seem to be more aligned (middle class students being 'popular', academic and stylish) in the 'regular' high school, painfully and disjunctively misaligned in the inner city highs. A central point I wish to make is that the contents and meanings of the common cultural status system are likely to be very different when aligned to a dominant 'popular' articulated in line with rather than in opposition to the school. Generally in the USA, and especially for males, the sports system seems to enjoy much more importance and to be more aligned to the official one and to expressive common cultural systems. In the cumulatively rising social atmospheres of the singular institution of the school, there are likely to be very negative social and psychological effects associated with always being on the subordinate end of aligned cultural and status systems no matter what is dominant in their formation (for a biographic and life history ethnographic exploration of some of these issues see Ortner, 2002).

Instrument and Site

The school is the direct instrument of the first, suffers disorientation from the second, and is an important site for the playing out of the third wave of modernisation discussed here. You could say that all cultural forms and experiences now have an element of cultural Diaspora. Even if you stop in the same place, change flows over you. Even when the young are still, symbolic borders pass them.

The combinations of my three themes of cultural modernity 'from below': (1) continuing threads of institutionally based informal cultural resistance; (2) responses of disaffection and depression to the continuing effects of "post-industrial" unemployment and the "tougher" forms of state regulation of much extended "transitions"; (3) the new cultural and bodily relations and possibilities arising from grounded consumption and leisure are unstable and different in their implications for different social groups. Each wave affects the others and has to be understood in the light of the others. In particular, issues of 'popular culture', too often treated for themselves and in their own vectors of effect on identity, can be seen much more productively in the light of a concrete contextualisation dealing with the play and effect of preceding and continuing cultural and structural forces of modernisation playing over particular groups still constituted in traditional categories of class, race and gender. Thus there are multiple possible ways in which resistance (first wave) and disaffection (second wave) effects are given ranges of expression and development by (third wave) common cultural practices.

It is true that in the last wave of modernisation we can see some kind of the pushing back of the cultural unconscious. That which was automatic seems willed. But the tragedy is that what is sometimes called the 'aesthetisation' of experience does not actually change the material relation between freedom and necessity, between the chosen and the determined, a relation that is actually tightening for the worse in the life space of the subordinate classes at the hands of second wave modernisation, even as third wave modernisation indicates symbolic space without border. Cultural and material vectors seem to be out of kilter as never before. We must not overlook that the super-abundance of images and imaginary possibilities of apparently free-floating and 'class-less' forms of consumption intersect with a materially worsening condition especially for the lower working class and with the brute facts of mass youth unemployment and exploitative under-employment in low wage service jobs for masses of young people. The blurring of consumption and production in third wave modernisation might offer hopes to some of the latter for embarking on alternative 'twilight' careers in the provision of cultural goods and services, but second wave conditions also produce heightened attractions to crime and to illegal activities in the informal economy. Meanwhile schools struggle on still formed by the ambitions and illusions of the first wave of modernisation now breaking on very different shores.

In schools we can see a blunt, culturally mediated, form of negotiation (often conflictual) going on between uncomprehending young people and often uncomprehending adults about the meaning and effects of modernity, on the "front line" of change. "Anti-social" behaviour and associated common cultural forms can be vehicles for making points, and taking some real space and autonomy, where words fail or are not available or are not listened to. It must be understood that schooling is not only an instrument for producing modernity, it is also a site for the playing out of its contradictory forces and forms. "Accepting" popular culture does not mean a lazy throwing open of the school doors to the latest fad, but committing to a principled understanding, an enlightenment project, of and into the complexity of contemporary cultural experience.

There are a wider set of issues here concerning the fullest understandings of cultural formations and the determinants of their direction for emancipation or alienation. In so far as the school is a social field as well as an instrument of its development, teachers and educational organisations of the widest kind, as well as allied progressive forces, should speak up unequivocally at last, not for 'leading' interests, but for and on behalf of those majorities in the middle and bottom of social space who are embroiled in the flux of dialectical 'modernisation'. They can take up clues and themes from their emergent cultures, pains and experience. To be direct, if the consciousness, actions and cultures of students need to change, so do the wider conditions and structural possibilities which help to structure those very responses. Rather than ever more individualistic economic competition for 'the good life', where are the means for the majority to find a collective 'place in the sun' free from ideological straight jackets (wave one)? Rather than shaming individualised insecurity and state disciplining for working poverty, where are the guarantees for enhanced security and greater choice that globalised economic advance is supposed to bring (wave two)? Rather than predatory market provision enflaming immediate desire, where are the means for the democratic production of new symbolic production goods (wave three)? The social impulses embodied here may have an ideological and utopian tinge, but no more actually, though in a different vector, than those in the 'progress from the top' imaginary. Otherwise the latter would produce no cultural modernisation 'from below'; all would be as in the official ledger! That the chains of counter effects and folding loops of irony and unintended consequences analysed in this chapter are unleashed from dominant imaginings and mouldings is simply a question of the social power backing them. Maintaining a critique and indicating alternative views of 'progress' are educational issues just as surely (and umbilically connected to) educational questions as are the canon or multi-culturalism, traditionalism or progressivism.

As for the specific questions of how to address issues of 'popular culture' in the curriculum I would argue that we should look beyond the 'things' of popular culture to the popular practices of their uses in context, to the field of what I term, 'common culture'. Educational voices and interests fret over the predatory nature of popular culture, seizing on its exploitation of the vulnerabilities and immoderate desires of the young. I am certainly not endorsing the dominance of market production in scaling away with imaginary relations and desires the remnants of organic community and institutional responsibility. In a more neutral way I am simply trying to understand some of the processes of common culture, to shed light on the grounded forms of the acculturation of commodities in the everyday life of the young. Only then might we be able to separate the predation from the creativity and so entertain a practical hope for practical action beyond the wringing of hands.

For all the predations of popular culture, within common cultural practices is a new growth of awareness and identity within the individual or group, a kind of variable and unpredictable 'mind-full-ness' about the choices, their limits and lodgings within complex social relations and structural determinants. Not dominant, precarious themselves and open to further rounds of commodity exploitation as 'life style' (rather than 'way of life'), they also turn within new complexities and flows of social reproduction in situ. But there is nevertheless, for the attentive, a dialectical site here to be mined for clues to new kinds of public sphere where the subordinate 'mind-full-ness' of practices associated with consumer culture might become a purposeful mindfullness of individual and collective action

Informal educational settings might explore how 'consumption' (and especially its links with production) can take place in less exploitative ways, opening up new 'public realms' which are seen, not as compensating for or attacking commercial imperatives and their 'erosion' of traditional values, but as going along with the flow of actually existing energies and passions, making their conditions of existence more visible and controllable, making what they express, and how, more controllable. Formal settings, perhaps using the resource of critical ethnographic texts, might explore the meanings and 'rationalities' of 'close to home' common cultural practices, and consider popular texts not simply for their (fetishised) immediate identities but for their 'common cultural' histories: how they became commodities and with what effects, how 'in situ' they are 'de-fetishised' and turned into 'cultural possessions', what these express about social position and location, not least with respect to successive waves of 'modernisation'.

Pedagogic voices can be shockingly quiet about issues of social context as if the four walls of the class room, sanctuary making as they can be, contain all that is necessary to understanding and directing what goes on within them. Utilising cultural experience and embedded bodily knowledge as a starting point from which to read outwards to understand their place and formation within flows of cultural modernisation from below can render more conscious what is unconscious to the 'foot soldiers': not least practical grounds for self-understandings of subordinate processes of social reproduction and for appreciation of that most elusive of truths enigmatically presented by Bourdieu: 'Resistance can be alienating and submission can be liberating' (Wacquant and Bourdieu, 1992: 24).

Let us celebrate the 'freedoms' of consumption but remember the front lines where they are exercised.

Acknowledgments

I am extremely grateful for close and detailed critical comments on a earlier draft generously offered by Philip Corrigan and Bowen Paulle and also for comments, support and help from the editors of the *Harvard Educational Review*.

References

Anyon, Jean (1983) 'Intersections of Gender and Class: accommodation and resistance by working class and affluent females to contradictory sex-role ideologies'. In Stephen Walker and Len Barton (ed.s), *Gender, Class and Education*. Lewes: Falmer Press.

Devine, John (1997) *Maximum Security: The Culture of Violence in Inner-city Schools*. Chicago: Chicago University Press.

Durkheim, Emile (1956) *Education and Sociology*, New York: Free Press.

Financial Times, 8th, October, 2002, London.

Fordham, Signithia (1996) *Blacked Out: Dilemmas of Race, Identity, and Success in Capital High*. Chicago: University of Chicago Press.

Furlong, Andy & Fred Cartmel (1997) *Young People and Social Change*. Buckingham & Philadelphia: Open University Press.

Gregg, P. and J. Wadsworth (eds.) (1999), *The State of Working Britain*, Manchester: Manchester University Press.

Johnson, Martin (1999) *Failing School, Failing City: The Reality of Inner City Education*. Chipping Norton, UK: Jon Carpenter Publishing.

Llewellyn, M. (1980) 'Studying girls at school: the implications of confusion', in R. Deem (ed) *Schooling for Women's Work*, Boston and London: Routledge & Kegan Paul.

Mac an Ghaill, Mairtin (1988) *Young, Gifted and Black*. Milton Keynes: Open University Press.

Nader, Ralph (1996) *Children First: A Parent's Guide to Fighting Corporate Predators*. Washington DC: Corporate Accountability Research Group.

Ortner, Sherry (2002) 'Burned Like a Tattoo', *Ethnography* 3.2

Paulle, Bowen (2003) "Contest and Collaboration: Cultural environments of 14–17 year-old students in a 'black' school in the Bronx (New York) and a 'zwarte' school in the Bijlmer (Amsterdam)." In *Moreel-politieke heroriëntatie in het onderwijs*. Leuven: Garant, pp. 14–39

Payne, I. (1980) 'Working Class in a Grammar School', in D. Spender and E. Sarah (eds.) *Learning to Lose: Sexism and Education*, London: Women's Press.

Portes. P. (ed.) (1995) *The Economic Sociology of Immigration: Essays on Networks, Ethnicity and Entrepreneurship*. New York: Russell Sage.

Raissiguier, Catherine (1995) `The construction of marginal identities of working-class girls of Algerian descent in a French school'. In Marianne H. Marchand and Jane L. Parpart (eds.), *Feminism/Postmodernism/Development*. London: Routledge.

Starrin, Bengt & Ulla Rantakeisu & Curt Hagquist 'In the wake of recession—economic hardship, shame and social disintegration', *Scandinavian Journal of Work and Environmental Health* 1997; *23*.4.

Suarez-Orozco, Marcelo M. (2001) "Globalization, Immigration and Eduction: The Research Agenda." *Harvard Education Review* Vol. 71, 3, fall.

Thornton, Sarah (1995) *Club Cultures*. Cambridge: Polity

Unemployment Unit (1999) Working Brief 107 August/September, Poland St, London.

Wacquant, Loic, and Bourdieu, Pierre (1992) *An Invitation to Reflexive Sociology* Chicago: University of Chicago Press.

Willis, Paul (1977) *Learning to Labour*, Aldershot, Saxon House.

— et al. (1988) *The Youth Review*, Aldershot: Avebury.

— et al. (1990) *Common Culture*. Buckingham: Open University Press.

— (2000) *The Ethnographic Imagination*, Cambridge: Polity.

CHAPTER 9

No Bailouts for Youth
Broken Promises and Dashed Hopes

Henry A. Giroux

By almost any political, economic, and ethical measure, Barack Obama's election victory in 2008 inherited a set of problems produced by one of the darkest periods in American history.[1] In the eight years prior to Obama's presidency, not only did the spaces where genuine politics could occur largely disappear as a result of an ongoing assault by the market-driven forces of privatization, deregulation, and unrestrained corporate power, but there was also a radical hardening of the culture that increasingly disparaged democratic values, the public good, and human dignity—and with these the safety nets provided by a once-robust but now exiled social state. George W. Bush, the privileged and profligate son of a wealthy Texas oilman, became the embodiment of a political era in which willful immaturity and stubborn civic illiteracy found its match in an emerging culture of excess and irresponsibility.[2] As the age of casino capitalism reigned supreme over American society, the ongoing work of democratization—along with the public spheres needed to sustain it—became an increasingly fragile, perhaps even dysfunctional, project. Market principles now reached far beyond the realm of the economic and played a formative role in influencing and organizing every domain of human activity and interaction, while simultaneously launching a frontal attack on notions of a common good, public purpose, non-commodified values, and democratic modes of governing.

Yet even in the aftermath of the October 2008 global financial crisis and the historic election of Barack Obama as the 44th president of the United States, the vocabulary and influence of corporate power and hapless governance can still be heard as the expansion of market fundamentalism continues, albeit more slowly, along the trajectory of privileging corporate interests over the needs of the public good, ignoring the rising demands of millions of people struggling for economic, racial, and political justice. Tragically, the Obama administration seems complicit with what has become an element of common sense for a large and noisy segment of the populace—that the market, rather than politics, gives people what they want. President Obama does not talk about a much-needed jobs-creation program to address the massive hardships and suffering many people are experiencing. Instead, he gets his cues from Wall Street and now focuses on taming the budget deficit.[3] Nor does he talk about the crippling poverty, collapsing urban infrastructures, or the general despair that now grips the country. This state of affairs suggests not only a perilous future for the social state and a government willing to intervene on behalf of its citizens but also a dangerous view of governance in which economic priorities dominate and suppress important social needs rather than being carefully adjusted toward the goal of fostering a more just, more democratic society.

It appears ever more unlikely that the Obama administration will undo the havoc wrought by the Bush administration (itself the culmination of a decades-long trend toward market deregulation) or reverse the effects of a rampant free-market fundamentalism now unleashed across the globe. As the financial crisis looms large in the lives of the majority of Americans, government funds are used to bail out Wall Street bankers rather than being used to address either the growing impoverishment of the many people who have lost homes, jobs, and hope of a better future or the structural conditions that created such problems. In this scenario, a privileged minority retains the freedom to purchase time, goods, services, and security, while the vast majority of people are relegated to a life without protections, benefits, and safety supports. For those populations considered expendable, redundant, and invisible by virtue of their race, class, and age, life becomes increasingly precarious.

As I have mentioned youth, in particular, are assaulted by market forces that commodify almost every aspect of their lives, though different groups of young people bear unequally the burden of this market-driven assault. Those who are marginalized by class and power suffer more than the indignity of being endlessly commodified and commercially carpet-bombed. They are also objects of a low-intensity war that now criminalizes their behavior, subjects increasing aspects of their lives to harsh disciplinary practices, and treats them as both dangerous and disposable. In a society in which the social state that has been hollowed out and largely stripped of its welfare functions, youth are no longer provided with the economic, social, and cultural supports that offer them dignity, prosperity, and the promise of a better future. Instead, they are now largely governed by a corporate state that "secures power through the imposition of law, discipline and uncompromising modes of punishment and imprisonment."[4]

As the mechanisms of power, containment, and policing merge, the spaces that young people inhabit become increasingly militarized. At the same time such hyper-militarized spaces, extending from the street to the school, are abetted by a cultural apparatus and public pedagogy that jump at every opportunity to demean and demonize young people, especially poor minority youth, by representing them as an ever-present threat to society. In this instance, it becomes all too easy for the American public to move from the notion of young people being troubled to viewing them as trouble, as a threat to be contained. Newspapers and other popular media treat their audiences to an endless stream of alarming images and dehumanizing stories about rampaging young people who allegedly occupy a domestic war zone. Youth are no longer categorized as Generation X, Y, or Z. On the contrary, they are now defined rhetorically in mainstream media as "Generation Kill," "Killer Children," or, as one CNN special labeled them, "Killers in Our Midst."[5] Capitalizing on shocking and sensational imagery not only swells the media's bottom line; it also adds fuel to a youth panic that insidiously portrays young people as pint-size nihilists and an ever-present threat to public order. Such negative and demeaning views have had disastrous consequences for young people as their lives are increasingly subjected to policies and modes of governance defined through the logic of punishment, surveillance, and penal control. Moreover, under the reign of an expanding punishing state, coupled with the persistent structural racism of the criminal justice system, the situation for a growing number of impoverished young people and youth of color is getting much worse.

These are young people whose labor is unneeded, who are locked out of the commodity market, and who often inhabit the impoverished and soul-crushing margins of society. Too often they fall prey to the dictates of a youth-crime-governing complex that increasingly subjects them to harsh disciplinary controls while criminalizing more and more aspects of their behavior. How else to explain that on any given day "one in every 10 young male high school dropouts is in jail or juvenile detention?"[6] What kind of sense does it make to pass truancy laws in which a student, even when he has a school pass that allows him to be out of classes early, is stopped by the police and issued a \$570 ticket for truancy?[7] How can we reconcile the rise of zero tolerance laws in schools with the presumption that schools should be places where young people can feel safe and receive an education that prepares them to be thoughtful, critical, and socially responsible citizens when such laws impose harsh penalties for often trivial infractions, increase rates of suspension and expulsion, disproportionately target African American youth, push poor young people out of school and often into the criminal justice system? According to the Advancement Project,

> Zero tolerance has engendered a number of problems: denial of education through increased suspension and expulsion rates, referrals to inadequate alternative schools, lower test scores, higher dropout rates, and racial profiling of students .... Once many of these youths are in "the system," they never get back on the academic track. Sometimes, schools refuse to readmit them; and even if these students do return to school, they are often labeled and targeted for close monitoring by school staff and police. Consequently, many become demoralized, drop out, and fall deeper and deeper into the juvenile or criminal justice systems. Those who do not drop out may find that their discipline and juvenile or criminal records haunt them when they apply to college or for a scholarship or government grant, or try to enlist in the military or find employment. In some places, a criminal record may prevent them or their families from residing in publicly subsidized housing. In this era of zero tolerance, the consequences of child or adolescent behaviors may long outlive students' teenage years.[8]

Where is the collective anger over the use of disciplinary policies that share a shameful and close affinity to the legacy of segregated education, slavery, racial targeting, the harsh and ruthless criminalization of poor white and minority youth, and pedagogies of punishment, all of which push young people out of school and into the criminal justice system? In this instance, schools neither educate nor provide even minimal training for the workplace. Instead, they simply mimic traditional lockdown institutions such as the prison and display a disdain for youth that offers no apologies because politicians, school boards, administrators, and some teachers have become too arrogant and ruthless to imagine any resistance. Wedded to the bloodless values of a market-driven society deeply implicated in reproducing the structures of racism, inequality, and exclusion, schools now inhabit a "dead zone" that banishes civic pedagogy, the arts, and different critical modes of intelligibility. Schools now do everything they can to deaden the imagination by defining and framing classroom experiences through a lethal mix of instrumental values, cost-benefit analyses, test-based accountability schemes, and high-stakes testing regimes. These instrumentally- and market-based values and practices drown out, if not repress, those spaces and pedagogical practices that provide the conditions for students to think critically, value their own voices, mobilize their curiosity, engage in shared learning, and—most of all—acquire the knowledge, habits, public values, and social relations necessary for the practice of empowerment necessary for fostering a real democracy and taking responsibility for sustaining it. More and more, it appears that as schools become more militarized and subject to the latest technologies of regulation, surveillance, and control, they are transformed into laboratories in which the limits of new authoritarian tendencies endemic to a corporate/punishing society are tamed, attenuated, and tested.[9]

Where is the moral outrage over a nation that incarcerates one in one hundred adults in its local, state, and federal prisons and jails, fragmenting families, desolating communities, and ruining the lives of millions of children?[10] Where are the intellectuals, parents, teachers, and social movements expressing political indignation over a country that has the onerous and dubious distinction of being the world's leading jailer of young people? Where is the moral wrath over the racist practices that lead to the increasing criminalization of African American youth, particularly those who drop out of schools with "nearly one in four young black male dropouts incarcerated or otherwise institutionalized on an average day?"[11] As one politician noted, "Dropping out of high school [has become] an apprenticeship for prison."[12]

The devastation wreaked by free-market policies has been largely financed in the hard currency of human suffering that such policies have imposed on children, readily evident in some astounding statistics that suggest a profound moral and political contradiction at the heart of one of the richest democracies in the world. The notion that children should be treated as a crucial social resource and represent for any healthy society important ethical and political considerations about the quality of public life, the allocation of social provisions, and the role of the state as a guardian of public interests appears to be lost. Children, for example, make up a disproportionate share of the poor in the United States in that "they are 26 per cent of the total population, but constitute 39 per cent of the poor."[13] Just as alarmingly, prior to the passage of the health care reform bill, over 8 million children lacked health insurance,[14] and millions lacked affordable child care and decent early childhood education. One of the most damaging statistics revealing how low a priority children are in America can be seen in the fact that among the industrialized nations in the world, the United States ranks first in billionaires and in defense expenditures and yet ranks an appalling twenty-ninth in infant mortality.[15] As we might expect, behind these grave statistics lie a series of decisions to favor those already advantaged economically at the expense of the poor and socially vulnerable. Moreover, for the last three decades we have witnessed, especially under the second Bush administration, savage cuts to education, scientific research, and social services such as nutritional assistance for impoverished mothers and veterans' medical care—all of which helped fund tax breaks for the inordinately rich. Sadly, it now seems reasonable to assume that under the current financial crisis non-privileged youth will experience even greater economic and educational hardships, while becoming even more invisible to the larger society.

The toll in human suffering that results from these policies of punishment and neglect becomes clear in shocking stories about poor white and minority youth who literally die because they lack health insurance, often have to fend for themselves in the face of life's tragedies, and increasingly are excommunicated from the sphere of human concern. Too many youth are now rendered invisible and disposable in a world in which short-term investments yield quick profits while long-term social investments in young people are viewed as a drag on the economy. It gets worse. In what amounts to a national disgrace, one out every five children currently lives in poverty. Morever, while 10 percent of white children live in poverty, 34 percent of all black children live in poor families.[16] With home foreclosures still on the rise, school districts across the nation have identified and enrolled almost one million homeless children.[17] There are 1.7 million more children living in poverty today than in 2000. Unfortunately, their numbers are growing at an exponential rate, as 1 in 50 children and teens is now living in crowded rooms in seedy welfare hotels, in emergency shelters, or with relatives, or simply living on the streets.[18]

What is unique about these children and young people is not just the severity of deprivations they experience daily, but how they have been forced to view the world and redefine the nature of their own childhood between the borders of hopelessness and despair. There is little sense of a brighter future lying just beyond the shadows of highly policed and increasingly abandoned urban spaces. An entire generation of youth will not have access to the jobs, material comforts, or social securities available to previous generations. These children are a new generation of youth forced to grow up fast—they think, act, and talk like adults. They worry about their families, which may be headed by a single parent or both parents out of work and searching for a job; they wonder how their parents are going to get money to buy food and what it will take to pay for a doctor. And these children are no longer confined to so-called ghettoes. As the burgeoning landscape of poverty and despair spreads across our cities, suburbs, and rural areas, these children make their presence felt everywhere—there are just too many to ignore or hide away in the usually contained and invisible spaces of disposability. These young people constitute a new and more unsettling scene of suffering, one that reveals not only vast inequalities in our economic landscape but also portends a future that has no claim to a sprited notion of hope, characteristic of an aspiring democracy.

We are treated endlessly to stories in which young people are robbed of their innocence as they are forced to worry about problems that are ordinarily the responsibility of adults. Too many children find themselves living in cars or seedy motels, or even worse, living on the streets. They think about getting jobs to help their parents buy food, put down money for an apartment, or simply get a motel room. Childhood concerns about dating, sports, and hanging out with friends are now replaced with more crucial, if not time-consuming and health-draining, concerns about surviving on a daily basis.

These narratives just scratch the surface of a new social and economic reality, as millions of children now find themselves suffering physical, psychological, and developmental problems that thus far have gone unacknowledged by the Obama administration, as it bails out the automotive industries, banks, and other financial institutions. What kind of country have we become that we cannot protect our children or offer them even the most basic requirements for survival? Where is the public indignation over an administration that provides a multi-billion-dollar gift to Wall Street but cannot develop a public works program to put poor white and minority youth to work? How can the American people put up with a government that is willing to subsidize and rescue the insurance giant American International Group but do virtually nothing to provide assistance for the nearly half of all U.S. children and 90 percent of black youth who will be on food stamps at some point in their childhood?

Everywhere we turn, we see untold amounts of hardship and human suffering among young and old alike. Millions of hard-working people have lost their jobs, homes, hopes, and in some cases their sanity, while Wall Street zombies flourish financially and reward their incompetence, failure, and moral indifference with lavish bonuses, punctuated with renewed efforts to prevent any of the reforms that would put a check on the corrupt practices that produced a global financial meltdown. What does it mean to witness this type of suffering among so many children and not do anything about it—our attentions quickly diverted to view the spectacles and moral indifference that characterize so much of the cut-throat world of reality TV, zombie politics, and a consumer culture that shapes the sensibilities and inner lives of adults and children alike? Obama's attraction to the cultural capital of the rich, his unwillingness to take risks, his Harvard-taught propensity for seeking middle ground, his increasing unwillingness to fight for the people who elected him, and his willingness to disconnect from his own pre-election ideals make him look increasingly not just weak but like a mere puppet of corporate power, an innocent who has been practically eaten alive by the rich and powerful who now treat him with a sense of scorn and derision only matched by their own moral vacuity and arrogance. Of course, this might suggest that I and others initially expected too much from Obama, but that is not the case. I realize that reforming the current problems facing the United States does not lie in the hands of one man but resides in changing the deeply structured economic and social relations of power and interests that inform a mode of casino capitalism that for all intents and purposes is out of control. At the same time, Obama must be held responsible for the decisions he has made—and, for the most part, those decisions that have shaped everything from financial regulation to educational reform are not on the side of working- and middle-class people but on the side of the rich and powerful.

At this moment in history, it is more necessary than ever to enter this debate over the fate of American democracy by registering youth as a central theoretical, moral, and political concern. Doing so reminds adults of their ethical and political responsibility to future generations and will further legitimate what it means to invest in youth as a symbol for nurturing civic imagination and collective resistance in response to the suffering of others. Young people provide a powerful referent for a critical discussion about the long-term consequences of casino capitalism and its hyper-market-driven policies, while also gesturing toward the need for putting into place those conditions that make a democratic future possible. We have been punishing children for a long time in the United States. Removed from the inventory of social concerns and the list of cherished public assets, young people have been either disparaged as a symbol of danger or simply rendered invisible.

Viewed as another casualty of the recession, youth are no longer included in a discourse about the promise of a better future. Instead they are now considered part of a disposable population whose presence threatens to recall repressed collective memories of adult responsibility in the service of a social contract and democratic ideals. Injustice and inequality have a long legacy in the United States, and their most punishing modes and lethal effects have been largely directed against poor white and minority children. The shameful condition of America's youth exposes not only their unbearable victimization but also those larger social and political forces that speak to the callous hardening of a society that actively produces the needless suffering and death of its children. The moral nihilism of a market society, the move from a welfare to a warfare state, the persistent racism of the alleged "raceless" society, the collapse of education into training, the deskilling of teachers and the militarizing of schools, the continued violations of civil liberties, the commodification of knowledge, and the rise of a pernicious corporate state work together to numb us to the suffering of others, especially children.

The crisis of youth is symptomatic of the crisis of democracy, and it calls us to account as much for the threat that it poses as for the challenges and possibilities it invokes. One way of addressing our collapsing intellectual and moral visions regarding young people is to imagine those policies, values, opportunities, and social relations that both invoke adult responsibility and reinforce the ethical imperative to provide young people, especially those marginalized by race and class, with the economic, social, and educational conditions that make life livable and the future sustainable. Clearly, the issue at stake here is not a one-off bailout or temporary fix but concrete structural economic, educational, and political reforms that provide everyone with real social, political, and individual rights and freedoms.

None of the problems facing this generation will be solved unless the institutions, social relations, and values that legitimate and reproduce current levels of inequality, power, and human suffering are dismantled, along with the formative culture that supports them. The very ideal of democracy has been hijacked by casino capitalism and its rampant structures of inequality and power. We catch a glimpse of what this means in Peter Dreier's observation that "Today, the richest one percent of Americans has 22 percent of all income and about 40 percent of all wealth. This is the biggest concentration of income and wealth since 1928."[19] This type of economic inequality is not merely incompatible with a functioning democracy, it makes democracy dysfunctional and corrupt. Just as government can no longer outsource its responsibilities, the American public can no longer allow its political system to be governed by the rich and powerful. Political culture has been emptied of its democratic values and is in free fall, as it is now largely shaped by the most powerful, politically corrupt, socially irresponsible, and morally tainted elements of the society. The widening gap between the rich and the poor has to be addressed if young people are to have a viable future. And that requires pervasive structural reforms that constitute a real shift in both power and politics away from a market-driven system that views too many children as disposable. We need to reimagine what liberty, equality, and freedom might mean as truly democratic values and practices.

Any society that endorses market principles as a template for shaping all aspects of social life and cares more about the accumulation of capital than it does about the fate of young people is in trouble. Next to the needs of the marketplace, life has become cheap, if not irrelevant. We have lived too long with governments and institutions that use power to promote violent acts, conveniently hiding their guilt behind a notion of state secrecy or lofty claims to democracy, while selectively punishing those considered expendable—in prisons, collapsing public schools, foster care institutions, and urban slums. Under the current regime of free-market casino capitalism, children lack power and agency and are increasingly viewed as either commodities or simply rendered disposable. If Barack Obama's call to address the crucial problems facing young people is to be taken seriously, then the political, economic, and institutional conditions that both legitimate and sustain a shameful attack on youth have to be made visible, open to challenge, and transformed. This can only happen by refusing the somnambulance and social amnesia that coincide with the pretense of a post-racial politics and the all-too-easy equation of free-market fundamentalism and democracy, especially given the effects such illusions have on those marginalized by class and color. The road to recovery must align itself with new social movements willing to take risks and that embrace a vision of a democracy that is on the side of children, particularly young children in need. It must enable the conditions for youth to learn—to "grow," as John Dewey once insisted, as engaged social actors more alive to their responsibilities to future generations than contemporary adult society has proven itself willing to be for them.

Notes

1. I have taken up this issue in more detail in my *Against the Terror of Neoliberalism* (Boulder: Paradigm Publishers, 2008). See also Chris Hedges, *American Fascists: The Christian Right and the War on America* (New York: Free Press, 2006); and Sheldon S. Wolin, *Democracy Incorporated: Managed Democracy and the Specter of Inverted Totalitarianism* (Princeton: Princeton University Press, 2008).

2. For an excellent analysis of this issue, see Chris Hedges, *Empire of Illusion: The End of Literacy and the Triumph of Spectacle* (New York: Knopf Canada, 2009). See also George Monbiot, "The Triumph of Ignorance," *AlterNet* (October 31, 2008), http://www.alternet.org/story/105447/the_triumph_of_ignorance:_how_morons_succeed_in_u.s._politics/. For an extensive study of anti-intellectualism in America, see Richard Hoftstadter, *Anti-Intellectualism in American Life* (New York: Vantage House, 1963); and Susan Jacoby, *The Age of American Unreason* (New York: Pantheon, 2008).

3. Paul Krugman, "The Phantom Menace," *The New York Times* (November 23, 2009), p. A27.

4. Judith Butler, *Frames of War: When Is Life Grievable?* (Brooklyn, NY: Verso, 2009), p. 5

5. "Generation Kill" is the name of a seven-part HBO miniseries about what *The New York Times* calls "a group of shamelessly and engagingly profane, coarse and irreverent marines ... that spearhead[ed] the invasion" in the second Iraq war. See Alessandra Stanley, "Comrades in Chaos, Invading Iraq," *The New York Times* (July 11, 2008), p. B1. The term "Killer Children" appears as the title of a *New York Times* book review. See Kathryn Harrison, "Killer Children," *New York Times Book Review* (July 20, 2008), pp. 1, 8.

6. Andrew Sum et al., *The Consequences of Dropping Out of High School: Joblessness and Jailing for High School Dropouts and the High Cost for Taxpayers* (Boston: Center for Labor Market Studies, Northeastern University, October 2009), http://www.clms.neu.edu/publication/documents/The_Consequences_of_Dropping_Out_of_High_School.pdf.

7. Julianne Ong Hing, "Young, Brown—and Charged with Truancy," *Color Lines*, 152 (September/October 2009), www.colorlines.com/article.php?ID=593.

8. NAACP Legal Defense and Educational Fund, *Dismantling the School-to-Prison-Pipeline* (New York: Legal Defense Fund, 2009), http://www.jrclsconference.com/files/SpeakerMaterials/2009/Dismantling_the_School_to_Prison_Pipeline_BW_Version.pdf.

9. This idea comes from Zygmunt Bauman, *Society Under Siege* (Malden, MA: Blackwell Publishers, 2002), pp. 67–68.

10. See Pew Center for Research on the States, *One in 100* (Washington, DC, 2008).

11. Ibid.

12. Ibid.

13. Cesar Chelala, "Rich Man, Poor Man: Hungry Children in America," *Seattle Times* (January 4, 2006), http://www.commondreams.org/views06/0104–24.htm.

14. The Henry J. Kaiser Family Foundation, *The Uninsured: A Primer* (October 2009), http://www.kff.org/uninsured/upload/7451–05.pdf.

15. Marian F. MacDorman and T.J. Mathews, *Recent Trends in Infant Mortality in the United States* (National Center for Health Statistics, October 2008), http://www.cdc.gov/nchs/data/data-briefs/db09.htm.

16. Kenneth C. Land, *The 2009 Foundation for Child Development Child and Youth Well-Being Index (CWI) Report* (May 2009), http://www.fcd-us.org/usr_doc/Final-2009CWIReport.pdf. See also Sarah Fass and Nancy K. Cauthen, *Who Are America's Poor Children?: The Official Story*, National Center for Children in Poverty (October 2008), http://www.nccp.org/publications/pdf/text_843.pdf.

17. Kenneth C. Land, *Education for Homeless Children and Youths Program*, Foundation for Child Development (April 2009). Available online at: http://www.fcd-us.org/usr_doc/Final-2009CWIReport.pdf.

18. National Center on Family Homelessness, *America's Youngest Outcasts: State Report Card on Child Homelessness* (March 2009), http://www.homelesschildrenamerica.org/pdf/rc_full_report.pdf.

19. Peter Dreier, "Bush's Class Warfare." See also Editors, "By the Numbers," *Inequality.Org* (October 14, 2007), http://www.demos.org/inequality/numbers.cfn.

Biological warfare

Shaq (A.O.R) Payne

We are at war with one another
And like war between nation
No one gets special treatment not sisters or brothers.
Cuz we stay at arms
Tatted wit battle scars vaccination
We wear them like purple hearts from vietnam
We step left right left take aim
Bang bang
We dodge STD bullet like we in the matrix
Boom boom a solider down rotting from inside out
He waves his discolored palms
Another man slapped down by syphilis
But I fite on
Humpin a condom vest I am protected
But it seems I managed to acquired immunodeficiency syndrome but there is no one who can come to my AIDS.
Trapped in a ambush
Swarming
Turning antibodies to no-bodies can't get well in one body praying to somebody to break me out this "T" cell
I'm in hell I can't shake the burn between my legs
I clap
It spreads like wild fire
This clap

applauds me on to make others suffer how I do
Cynical sympathetic civilians don't pity me
Your at war too
Look around around your society is breaking
Fissures fractures and crack runs in circulatory
like Ring around a Rosie a pocket full of posies ashes ashes we all fall down
Bubonic bubble bombs blasting casting caskets go fish
This ain't no card game
Girls can't move out the way of anorexic mortars giving a new meaning to poke her face.
They regurgitate cuz the truth is too much to swallow
Insulin infused I will die befor I beat these Mickey D's and Krispy Kreams
While Weight watchers patrol obese-cities.
They Give us bricks and keys to build homes
We pack heat our palms start to moisten
Mislead on a block mine field
Cock back we get lead poisoned
Like chicken pox we walk around draped in inferred dots attracting these red necks bobs and Billy
clubs
Targeted
With a bull's eye
By corporate men who pull strings far away from the front lines
Lusting for our hides
Playing into their concocted plan
we terrorize
Each other
Black on black crime
Die die
Our lifes a gamble
Roll the watch it spin
bak to a time of
Chris columbus and native americans
So Whats the chance that a biological genocide won't happen again
Damn These snake eyes look grim.

Shaq (A.O.R) Payne (18), *SLAM HIGH*, Rochester, NY

ShoutOuts to:
Reenah Golden
Joseph Mangano
Mariana Barry

Target

Anthony Ragler

July 13, 2013
George Zimmerman is not guilty!
My friends are rambunctious bullets in a holster
Who have just realized they have become prey
We are silenced by the hush of a gavel
Through summer air
We trudge our way to the L train
Which on this night,
could stand for Luck.
Or Lost. Or Life. Or Law.
As in:
We are lucky we have not lost our lives
because the law won't protect us
Because the only word that matters now is "suspicious"
How that is the gap between innocent and not guilty
And not guilty and guilty
Mangled thoughts and tears tarred to our faces
my brother is screaming at the top of his lungs to anyone who will listen
About how we are endangered
The older Black man on the Lost train is trying to ceasefire
my Brother only sees red, and thinks it's the shadow of the target on his back
My Sister is roaring the older Black man into a corner
my friends are behind her
The White people on the train are terrified

For they know not how far we are willing to take this protest
I am the only one not outraged
Because I'm not surprised
Post-Racial society, to me
Is just a pretty way to say hope for justice.
Don't expect it
The older Black man is good intentions and horrendous delivery
On the wrong night. On the wrong train.
Trying to tell a group of 12 Black youth
That the system isn't working against us.
And I remember being told that they wouldn't call it a system if it wasn't working
This begins a conversation amongst us
About how being Black in America
Is like being a Grizzly on hunting grounds
Everyone is afraid of your claws
But claws are futile against bullets
We arrive at my Brother's house
Trayvon is the elephant in the room
the chatter is replaced by a silence
that could scare the Grim Reaper back into the shadows
And the desire to drink
Like that would actually numb the numb we already aren't feeling
the night is ugly
I leep because maybe I will wake up from this
And it will all be over
twenty minutes later
I sit by the window sill in my own thoughts
My friends are mahogany carved flasks
In a dark room
They dance like the White night will take them if they don't
The room is plantation humid
My friends
Are trying to dance their targets off
The liquor settles in
This is no longer a preservation dance
It is our last rites
the music is a tone only we can love to
There is sloppy kisses, sloppy sex
gruesome grinding, corpses
Things we would usually regret
To us this is the Black Y2K
Then the clock strikes 5 am
And we realize this is not the end of our lives
But the beginning of the fight for them
We make a pact
That this night never happened
I don't know,

If we meant the partying
Or the verdict.

Anthony Ragler, NYC
Courtesy of Youth Speaks and the Brave New Voices Network

I Have Not Prayed in Years (Bringing the Noise for MLK 2014)

Gabriel Cortez

1.
I have not prayed in years.

The only time I go to church
is when I visit my mother's house.
And even then, my tongue practices
a carefully mimed choreography
when we bow our heads
to say grace.

I say, thank you for your mercy.
For the roof over our heads.
For our silent bellies,
which allow us to have this ritual in peace.

2.
At the homeless clinic where I work,
we do not say grace.
Instead, we gather our plates
around the dinner table like a campfire
and tell each other our stories.

Like about how C—
hopped a freight train

all the way from Minnesota to Berkeley.
How the midnight sky opened up to him
like a belly showing off its scars.

I ask if he'd share some too.
The bags under his eyes
that somehow look heavier tonight
than the pack he hoists over his shoulders.
The bruises speckled along his elbows
from sleeping on the sidewalk last night.

I ask him to tell us of home
and he grows silent.
Staring into his cup
like it's filled with stars.

This is our 13th week together and C—
still guards his stories
as well as I guard mine.
The way we sometimes
reduce our biographies to static motions and gestures.
Write ourselves out of our own poetry
with shallow words and syllables.
Bend our tongues into beautiful, empty shapes,
on stage and around the dinner table.

3.
Mom asks me why I do not go to church anymore.
I point to the stained glass
and vaulted ceilings of our Sunday sanctuary
and ask
why god needs a house
when he does not shiver.
When he does not bruise or sleep at night

When over two-hundred youth
sleep on the streets in Berkeley,
outside a shelter that only has room for twenty-five.

When seven people have frozen to death since November,
here, in the wealthiest metropolitan area in the US.

When even the most powerful entity in the universe
requires a home, what do we do with our runaways?
With our abandoned youth?
The ones with no family or congregation to come home to?
The ones that compete with your Sunday tithes,
your morning Frappuccino, your data plan

and your ability to feed your own
with sullen eyes and dirty collection plates.

4.
It is getting colder outside.
The rainy season is coming.
And my youth ask me
about safe places to sleep at night.

There are two abandoned buildings
standing between my house
and the shelter where I work.
They are the only place that graffiti blossoms
in this neighborhood.
Mercy
is the spray paint of these two buildings
flickering in the headlights of passing cars
like a neon "Enter" sign.

Dr. King says, "I know where we can store that food free of charge"
and I contemplate the bellies of these twin beasts.
These empty edifices.
How best to break into broken windows
without cutting ourselves.
How best to weave caution tape into blankets and welcome mats
without alerting the authorities.
How best to make shelter of abandoned buildings,
vacant lots, couches, hallways, back seats, subway cars.
park benches, closets, street corners and floor boards
fast and free of charge.

5.
When the rain comes, C—
does not come back to clinic.
It is the first week we do not see him in 4 months
I imagine the clouds
disappearing with every mile
his train lurches south.
The night sky opening above him
the color of stained glass.
It is easier than imagining him jailhouse,
back of police car cuffed
for trespassing on deserted property,
for shivving his body
through the boarded windows
of one of the abandoned houses between home and the clinic.
It is easier than imagining him hypothermia,
lips blue and silent

for refusing to push himself
through another shattered window.

6.
At clinic, we hold each other's stories
in our mouths like warm food.
Because it is the closest thing we have
to summoning each other back
when we have become nothing
but distant memory.
Because it is a reminder of how far
some of us have had to run to be here.

Dr. King speaks of millions sleeping in the streets of Bombay, Calcutta.
The millions that go to sleep hungry in Asia, Africa, Latin America,
and even in our own nation.
I speak of the dozens of sleepless youth
that gather round our table in Berkeley
every Monday, 7–9, before stealing back into the night.

Not all of us pray—
But sometimes we bend our tongues
every Monday, 7–9, before stealing back into the night.

Not all of us pray—
but sometimes we bend our tongues
into beautiful shapes,
beckoning each other to enter,
get comfortable and make yourself
home.

Gabriel Cortez (20), Los Angeles, CA
Courtesy of Youth Speaks and the Brave New Voices Network

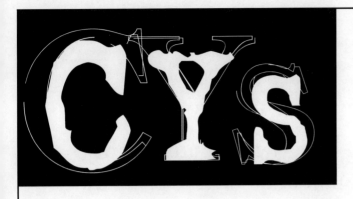

PART II

Identities:
A Métissage Between Indigeneity, LGBTQ, Whiteness, and Diaspora

CHAPTER 10

Abandoning Pathologization

Conceptualizing Indigenous Youth Identity as Flowing from Communitarian Understandings

Dwayne Donald and Mandy Krahn

As a result of their education and socialization, many adults may often view the identity and development of young people from Enlightenment-based perspectives and thus assume that the young are damaged somehow and in need of fixing. This places a heavy burden upon youths to conform to the wishes of adults. As educators, we well know that the contentiousness associated with schooling the young is a persistent and prominent tension in the field of education (Freire, 1993; Apple, 2004; Kincheloe, 2008). Since "conceptions of childhood [and youth] are always culturally and historically conditioned" (Smith, 1988, p. 109) and since young people have been referred to as everything from "subspecies" to "prophets," to representations of "*alternative* epistemolog[ies]" (Kennedy, 2002) to "projection targets for unresolved adult desires and conflicts" (Smith, 2003, p. 44), in this chapter we wonder how and in what ways these understandings of the young have influenced policy conceptions of youth in Canada. More specifically, we wish to explore how these Enlightenment-based cultural and conventionalized understandings of the meaning of youth in the lives of adults has been extended to Indigenous[1] youth in Canada and how this has negatively influenced their well-being.

A key organizing insight of this chapter is that the problems faced by mainstream Canadian youth are also experienced by Indigenous youth in similar ways, except that these problems are often further exacerbated for Indigenous youth due to the influence of colonial frontier logics[2] and the ways in which *Indian*[3] subjectivities have been legislated, marginalized, and pathologized. The purpose of this chapter is to bring focus to the complex realities associated with being an Indigenous youth living today within the political boundaries of the nation-state known as Canada. More specifically, we intend to focus on the policy understandings and discourses that inform how and why Indigenous youth are most typically characterized as damaged (Tuck, 2009) and in urgent need of fixing. Central to this focus is the critical acknowledgement that Canadians in general and the Canadian nation-state in particular maintain troubling colonial relationships with the Indigenous peoples with whom they are mean to live alongside in the spirit of good relations (Alfred, 2005; Barker, 2009; Regan, 2010; Morgenson, 2011;

Johnson 2007). The ongoing betrayal of the spirit, intent, and integrity of treaties is symptomatic of a larger relational psychosis (Donald, 2009; 2011) that has distinctive bearing on how policymakers and educational leaders conceptualize Indigenous youth—who they are—and what they require from adults in order for them to properly conform to normalized and conventionalized understandings of how they should *be*.

We will explore the consequences of this "deficit thinking" (Valencia, 1997) mindset on the well-being of Indigenous youth and suggest that ethical studies of Indigenous youth must begin with unequivocal acknowledgement of their deep-rooted connectivity and belongingness to their home territories—an ecological and natural law sensibility expressed in the Cree language as *nēhīyaw wēyasiwewina* or Cree law.[4] We use this concept to help us express a notion of belongingness that is rooted in the collective memories and communitarian traditions of the people and their relatedness to everything in the world. The implications of this insight are that Indigenous peoples living in Canada belong to the places where they live not according to some official government Act or court ruling originating within an abstract and disembodied notion of legal rights, but because they continue to live amongst and acknowledge their relations according to their own particular version of *nēhīyaw wēyasiwewina*.[5] This is what makes it possible for them to consider themselves 'the real people.'[6] They are the ones who were born into these traditions particular to their territories and seek to live their lives in ways that uphold them. Our point is that a fundamental shift in policy understandings of Indigenous youth could be facilitated if policy leaders and decision makers could begin to understand them as 'real people' in relation to this concept of *nēhīyaw wēyasiwewina* and communitarian traditions rather than as fundamentally damaged and in urgent need of fixing.

We offer this suggestion in an exploratory (rather than definitive) manner with the hope that it may help form a line of inquiry for better understanding Indigenous youth in Canada today. For us, the critical insight for researchers and policymakers comes in recognizing that the various forms of violence (historic and current) endured by Indigenous youth in Canada are not an unfortunate conse-quence of their families' and communities' unwillingness or inability to adjust to change (Francis, 1992, p. 221–222; Bennett & Blackstock, 2007); rather, such violences must be critically understood as a direct consequence of colonial frontier logics that continue to haunt Indigenous-Canadian relations.

Idle No More and the Participation of Indigenous Youth

A poignant example of this relational violence can be seen in the introduction of the controversial Bill C-45 in the Canadian Parliament and the subsequent grassroots response that has become known as the *Idle No More* movement. On October 18, 2012, the Canadian government tabled in the House of Commons a massive omnibus bill with the official title 'A second Act to implement certain provisions of the budget tabled in Parliament on March 29, 2012, and other measures,' but commonly known as Bill C-45.[7] There are many aspects to the Bill, but the provisions of Bill C-45 that have garnered the most critical attention from people living in Canada are those concerned with revisions of the Indian Act, Navigation Protection Act, and the Environmental Assessment Act. In general, the proposed revi-sions to these three Acts are guided by the ruling Conservative Party ideology that is founded on the main tenets of market capitalism and faith in the conviction that government policies are most ben-eficial when they are focused on reducing restrictions and regulations that hinder the entrepreneurial interests of businesses and corporations.

Resistance and protests against the provisions of Bill C-45 quickly coalesced in Canada in the form of the *Idle No More* movement. The *Idle No More* coalition was instigated by four female activists in Saskatoon, Saskatchewan in early November 2012.[8] A short time after this initial teach-in, *Idle No More* quickly became a major social media phenomenon that spread across Canada and soon found allies around the world. The movement spread and gained broad-based support so quickly—largely in the form of flash mob round dances in malls and other public venues across Canada—that within a month of its beginnings, a National Day of Solidarity and Resurgence was organized and held on December 10, 2012. Thus, *Idle No More* has become an influential social movement that has united diverse groups of people together on the basis of their shared impatience with the historic and ongoing marginalization of Indigenous peoples and communities. The impatience stems from a growing realization that Canadian government officials have been creating policies and making decisions that have directly impacted Indigenous peoples and communities without consulting directly with them or their leaders. These approaches effectively violate the main tenets of the numerous Treaties still in effect across Canada that document negotiated legal partnerships between the Crown and First Nations to share the land and resources, as well as to work together for mutual benefit in the spirit of good relations.[9] *Idle No More* supporters view the unilateral introduction and subsequent passage of Bill C-45 by Canadian government officials as the most recent example of this long-time practice of disregarding Indigenous peoples and thus failing to honour the spirit and intent of these Treaties. As the name *Idle No More* implies, supporters of the movement are committed to taking peaceful action to draw public attention to these practices and to promote more balanced and mutually respectful relations between Indigenous peoples and Canadians.[10]

For many observers, one of the more notable and critical aspects of the *Idle No More* movement has been the prominent participation of Indigenous youth. Indigenous youth across Canada are the inheritors of social, political, cultural, and economic realities for their communities that are directly connected to the policies of oppression and assimilation endured by their ancestors for many generations. The legacies of these policies continue to haunt Indigenous communities today. We note that Indigenous youth are often positioned as *the future* (Brendtro, Brokenleg & Van Brockern, 1990; Chiefs of Ontario, 2012; Greenwood, 2003; Townsend & Wernick, 2008) in a redeeming sense (Grumet, 1986), and thus bequeathed the challenge of finding ways to solve the many complex intergenerational problems faced by their peoples. This burdensome inheritance can seem like an unwelcome trap wherein engagement with these challenges requires giving oneself to dispiriting identity politics and thus playing a well-established political and legal game within the confines of a governmental entity commonly known as 'Indian Affairs.'[11] Although most of the original legal and political restrictions governed by 'Indian Affairs' from the high colonial era have been adjusted and have subsequently morphed into updated forms, the colonial relationship remains largely in effect and continues to characterize Indigenous-Canadian relations in damaging ways. Thus, despite some positive broad-ranging policy changes, the lives of Indigenous youth in Canada continue to be deeply influenced by colonial frontier logics and Bill C-45 is one recent example of this.

Idle No More has become an attractive movement to Indigenous youth because it has offered the possibility for them to disengage from the rules, regulations, and restrictions of 'Indian Affairs' and participate as Indigenous peoples on their own terms and by their own means. It has also provided them a venue, both actual and virtual, to draw on communitarian memory and experience—as well as guidance from Elders—and demonstrate how these sources of inspiration are still relevant in the context of their lives today. Under the purview of the *Idle No More* movement, Indigenous youth across Canada connected via Twitter and Facebook and supported each other in imagining policies of peace and respect inspired by the Treaties and not circumscribed by the often divisive and dispiriting language of lawyers and politicians. Since Bill C-45 was introduced, Indigenous youth have been the instigators and leaders of *Idle No More*-inspired events that have drawn many participants and significant media attention.

Perhaps the most inspiring response to this call to action was enacted by the young men from the James Bay Cree—called the Nishiyuu walkers—who trekked 1,600 kilometres from their community of Whapmagoostui First Nation in northern Quebec to the nation's capital city of Ottawa over a sixty-two day period. Their walk was completed in support of the *Idle No More* Movement and to raise public awareness of living conditions in northern Indigenous communities where people often do not have sufficient access to services and resources necessary to meet their basic needs. It is worth noting that the Nishiyuu walkers request to meet with Prime Minister Stephen Harper upon their arrival in Ottawa was unfulfilled; the prime minister decided instead to attend a special ceremony at the Toronto Zoo marking the arrival of two Chinese pandas.[12]

For us, the *Idle No More* movement and the experiences of the Nishiyuu walkers are just a few recent examples of the more complex relational tensions that can get conjured up when Indigenous peoples express ontological self-understandings rooted in communitarian tradition, experience, and memory that Canadians in general are unable to comprehend. The incomprehensibility of Indigenous subjectivities and experiences is the result of a long-term educational program dedicated to telling a story of the Canadian nation and nationality that usually only included mention of Indians as unfortunate remnants from a time before civilization arrived in an empty land (Donald, 2004; Donald 2009; Willinsky, 1998; Clark, 2007). A key feature of this national narrative is the dream of the settler (Veracini, 2008). In summary form, the central vision of this dream is that settlers to a new land called Canada gain access to unprecedented freedom, opportunity, and economic prosperity if they employ the proper habits in the necessary ways (Francis, 1997). Thus, the realization of this dream requires a certain kind of citizen. For the most part, Indigenous peoples and their communities are deemed to be in direct conflict with the realization of this dream because they are considered to be the wrong kind of citizens—largely because they follow sacred, ecological, ethically relational, and communitarian notions of belongingness that do not conform to this dream imaginary (Sheridan & Longboat, 2006). Following the logic of this settler dream, the common perception is that Indigenous peoples need to embrace more modern ways of being if they hope to have the dream extended to them. It is in this way that the twisted rationale of assimilation employed to justify residential schools seems to make good sense. The overwhelming common sense logic that survives from that era is that the best thing an Indigenous person can do is assimilate as quickly as possible and abandon the outdated ways followed by their ancestors. In this way, their success as citizens is understood as dependent on how well they can imitate *normal* Canadians. The message embedded within this logic is that there is really only one viable way to *be*.[13]

We believe that this pattern of pathologizing Indigenous peoples and their children can be understood as deeply rooted in Canadian culture and tremendously influential in the formation of policies and initiatives intended to address the needs of Indigenous peoples and communities (Shields, Bishop & Mazawi, 2005; Waldram, 2004). It is our view that this thinking and these initiatives are generally rooted in Enlightenment-based understandings of the meaning of children in the lives of adults and perceptions of what children need from adults in order for them to be properly prepared to meet the challenges of the future and become valued human beings.

Theories of Child-Youth Development and Notions of Human Being-ness

In Eurocentric thought, there are three prevalent versions of childhood and youth development, and each manifests itself to varying degrees and ways in modern-day home and school life. These understandings arose during the Age of Enlightenment and include thinking of the child as depraved, the child as a blank slate, or the child as inherently good. The *child as depraved* viewpoint is one that has been very influential in Eurocentric thought. This theory posits that children are born evil and thus the role of the adult (and God) is to save the child from eternal damnation. This concept of the child is embedded within Christian theology and views childhood as a period of straightening out, or correcting, the child from their self-interested and impulsive ways. Viewing the *child as a blank slate* is an idea that originated with John Locke, in which he describes the child as a *tabula rasa* and emphasizes the important role of education in shaping who the child will become (Locke, 1968). This view emerged in the late seventeenth century and holds that the child is a malleable entity whose curiosity must be engaged and encouraged. Locke claims that adults can make of the child anything they wish as long as they construct the environment in a manner that is conducive to their learning and growth. The *child as born good* viewpoint is derived from the work of Jean-Jacques Rousseau during the period of Romanticism in late eighteenth century France. He claims that an inherent goodness is present in the child at birth and that exposure to society corrupts the child. Since childhood is viewed as a special, 'ideal' time of life, the role of the parent or teacher is to ensure this idealized outlook is maintained and that they do what they can to ensure that the child receives an education that staves off this corruption. (Rousseau, 1979).

These three theories are founded upon cultural assumptions evident throughout Eurocentric societies like Canada today and are often the basis of governmental policies and public school programming—without them even formally being recognized as such. Each of these views sets up certain pressures for youth today. Despite their differences, these theories are united in the emphasis placed on the central location of the school and schooling as institutions necessary to the proper education of the young. For us, the significance of this realization is in the ways we are trained to accept as normal the well-established intellectual preoccupation with separating the young from the communities in which the purpose and meaning of their lives are contextualized. This preoccupation raises many important questions concerning the study of youth in isolation from the multigenerational realities in which they live and the various influences that flow together to inform who they think they are. This fosters a pathologizing vernacular in which many adults, including those employed in educational circles, tend to predicate their words and actions on their predetermined belief that youth somehow need fixing. Such assumptions imply that the 'fix' that schooling provides results in the production of a certain kind of human being.

Following Nandy (1988, as cited in Smith 2003), there are multiple assumptions made regarding the young, and how they should *be*, that are directly connected to the colonial experience, schooling, and seemingly justify the abuses hidden within those assumptions. Perhaps the most significant of these is

> [w]hen childhood is used in a semantics of dystopia against the utopian logic or development. In such a case, terms like *childish, infantile,* and *immature* are used against an idealized and mythical binary of *adult* maturity as a way to both discipline the young as well as protect adulthood within a static and contained self-definition. This was/is a primary strategy of colonial domination, in which the colonized were/are infantilized within the power logic of the 'adult' colonizer. (Smith, 2003, p. 44, italics original)

These assumptions can also be understood under the general rubric of "adultomorphism" (Kennedy, 1983 as cited in Smith, 2003, p. 46) or the general desire of adults to turn children into replications of themselves to serve their own needs. They can also be generally understood as a product of a culture founded on faith in the validity and veracity of technical, rational, and science-based solutions to human problems. In this cultural preoccupation,

> ...the *idea of childhood* takes precedence over *the real child*. Here a number of things can happen. For example, children become isolated as a sociological variable that can then be used by social engineers within a calculus of social and capital development. Within this set of assumptions, children have no interlocutionary power within the overall social framework. Also under this assumption, the specific flesh and blood needs of specific children can be ignored under generalized theories of childhood... (Smith, 2003, p. 45, italics original)

In connection to these wide-ranging critiques, we note that more and more youth living in affluent societies like Canada have mental disorders, more and more get in trouble with the law, more and more are obsessed with surface consumer concerns at the expense of balance and depth in their lives, and more and more value the consumption of material goods over relationships (Centre for Addiction and Mental Health, n.d.; Giroux, 2004; Buchanan, 2005; Bakan, 2011; Sandlin & McLaren, 2010). Youth are learning "from the new 'central curriculum of childhood'... that life (its meaning and purpose), and people (our identities, worth, happiness, and connections to others) are dependent on relationships to things" (Bakan, 2011, p. 45); a curriculum, both hidden and planned, governed and implemented by adults that teaches the young to seek personal fulfillment in empty consumerism and unsustainable promises of permanent economic prosperity.

A good example of this logic is evident in the Curriculum Redesign project recently initiated by Alberta Education and thus endorsed by the Government of Alberta.[14] For the most part, the Curriculum Redesign initiative is guided by a self-proclaimed state-of-the-art educational approach founded on the concept of 'Competencies for 21st Century Learning.' In this approach, the conceptual framework undergirding the idea of '21st century learning' seems to be largely predicated in economic terms and in relation to a clear faith in the power of technology and innovation to spur economic growth:

> Our education system must both provide an inclusive environment where each student belongs, and equip them with the attitudes, skills, knowledge, and competencies they need to be successful in tomorrow's economy. In addition to helping young Albertans fulfill their individual potential and become self-reliant, contributing members of society, the ECS–12 education system also aligns with and supports key Government of Alberta strategic priorities, such as the Premier's Council for Economic Strategy which will help give an external, big-picture perspective on securing the province's long-term prosperity. The continued development of a highly skilled, knowledgeable, innovative and productive workforce is critical to ensuring that Alberta sustains its competitive advantage in a global economy, allowing the province to attract investment, and high value-added industries. (Alberta Education, 2010, p. 3)

This economics-first educational 'Action Plan' is further guided by this vision: "All students are inspired to achieve success and fulfillment as engaged thinkers and ethical citizens with an *entrepreneurial spirit* (Alberta Education, 2011, p. 6, emphasis ours). While this vision does seem to be student- and competency-focused, we are concerned with the direct link given to an "entrepreneurial spirit" since this wording implies that to be an "engaged thinker" and "ethical citizen" of value requires a business-oriented spirit and outlook. According to this vision statement, an "entrepreneurial spirit" would be exemplified by a student

> who creates opportunities and achieves goals through hard work, perseverance and discipline; who strives for excellence and *earns success*; who explores ideas and challenges the status quo; who is competitive, adaptable and resilient; and who has the confidence to take risks and make bold decisions in the face of adversity. (p. 6, emphasis ours)

For us, the subtle subtext of these policy declarations is that 21st century notions of how best to *be* a human being are largely derived from neoliberal understandings of innovation, entrepreneurship, competition, success, and well-being in the interests of building an economy. Youth are positioned as future generators of economic wealth and their contributing value as citizens is directly dependent on how well they replicate this prescribed value and build it into their emerging identities. Such faith in *muscular* entrepreneurship is a prominent part of the socio-political mythology of Alberta (Harrison, 2005; Lisac, 2004). As earlier stated, we understand this ideological thrust—concealed as common sense (Keil, 2002)—to be a form of ontological violence that has direct impacts on the well-being of youth today.

In light of these policy declarations, a key insight for us is that adults are sending youth the message that it is not necessary for them to consider the problem of how they want to *be* in the world (Fenwick, 2006). The solution to this problem is instead delivered to the young in prescribed forms, and this drives them to *do* more in their already busy lives in order to prove themselves under the watchful eye of adults (Taubman, 2000). As a result of increased pressure to maintain a certain public appearance due to technological advancement and 24/7 plugged-in statuses, many youth are suffering from the oppressive emptiness and ironic poverty of this consumer-based identity (Schor, 2004; Hill, 2011). While there is nothing inherently wrong with attentiveness to such issues—economic issues are a central concern of all human societies—our concerns arise when youth are trained to believe that their emerging identities as human beings are directly connected to neoliberal market logics and consumerism as a necessary lifestyle choice. In the context of Alberta today, a frontier territory with substantial wealth generated from oil and gas resource exploitation, this ideology teaches that a person who is not participating in or benefiting from this prosperity is clearly doing something wrong and needs to be straightened out.

Pathologizing Indigenous Youth: *Homo Economicus* and the Problem of Culture

In keeping with the analytic focus of this chapter, our view is that the problems faced by mainstream Canadian youth concerning how they should *be* are also experienced by Indigenous youth in similar ways, except that Indigenous youth experience these pressures in unique ways. The uniqueness of the pressures experienced by Indigenous youth stems largely from the complex multigenerational historical traumas that haunt their communities (Duran, Duran & Brave Heart, 1998) and are evident in the dismal statistical information that has been compiled concerning the quality of their lives (Blackstock, 2011; Canadian Council of Provincial Child and Youth Advocates, 2010). Our concern is that most policy considerations of Indigenous youth begin with a focus on these intergenerational realities and dismal statistics as a pathologizing characterization of who they are as people.[15] In particular, we consider the phenomenon of the "self-fulfilling prophecy" as relevant here in that a preoccupation with the idea that Indigenous youth are in need of fixing can often result in further marginalization for them (Riley & Ungerleider, 2012). Failure in school is considered a consequence of an individual being a member of a particular community or minority group rather than as an indictment of what schools actually teach and how students *feel* when they are there (Shields, Bishop & Mazawi, 2005, pp. 2–18). Since we know that how a child thinks of him or herself is profoundly influenced by his or her interactions with adults, it should not be a surprising that Indigenous children often struggle to find success in schools. For the most part, they are not exposed to a version of themselves that is comforting, uplifting, enlivening, and rooted in the communitarian experiences and memories of their ancestors. Schools and education systems, rather than aiding Indigenous children to work through the many challenges they might face at home and in their community, can actually contribute to their further pathologization.

In the field of education, the 'fix' for these perceived pathologies of Indigenous youth often comes in the form of policy documents and curriculum initiatives that focus on how they need to become a different quality of person in order to be considered successful. They are two general ways that this is done. For us, the first 'fix' is manifested in the form of the mythical idea of *homo economicus*[16]— a unique form of the human species that is understood to possess a natural propensity to be "rational, individualistic, utilitarian, calculative and instrumental" in economic matters (Houston, 2010, p. 842). In exercising these skills, *homo economicus* is understood as primarily motivated by a self-interested desire for wealth and the accumulation of material goods as a primary measure of success. It is understood that the success pursued by *homo economicus* can really only be achieved via an adherence to the tenets and principles of market capitalism (Williams, 1999). For proponents of these tenets and principles, market capitalism guides human beings to conduct themselves in ways that bring benefits and economic prosperity to the society as a whole. In this view, *homo economicus* is the most natural and most developed form of human being in evolutionary terms. The ontological question of what it means to be a human being is directly connected to the market and the benefits that accrue from it.

What does the concept of *homo economicus* have to do with Indigenous youth in Canada today? Our contention is that much of the policy literature on education and employment for Indigenous youth available in Canada today is predicated upon the conviction that the only viable 'fix' for the many problems faced by Indigenous peoples is produced when "as many young Aboriginals as possible enter the workforce with the highest possible levels of education" (Helin & Snow, 2010, p. 7). This approach was fully endorsed in February 2013 by the Governments of Alberta and Canada when a joint initiative focused on Indigenous youth employment was announced. In the statement, a Member of Parliament stated that

> The Government of Canada's top priorities are job creation, economic growth and long-term prosperity. … Our government's Youth Employment Strategy is helping youth develop the skills and gain the experience they need to get jobs now and prepare for the workforce of tomorrow. (Canada News Centre, 2013)

A minister in the Government of Alberta contributed to the same announcement by stating that "[t]he Alberta government knows that the success of Aboriginal communities is integral to the continued success of our province, and we are committed to ensuring Aboriginal people are able to fully contribute to and benefit from Alberta's diverse economy" (Ibid.). Similar arguments in other studies emphasize the fact that Aboriginal populations in Canada are growing rapidly and that Indigenous youth represent an untapped pool of labour that could address anticipated labour shortages in Canada, especially in the resource extraction industries (Sharp, Arsenault & Lapointe, 2007; Luffman & Sussman, 2007). Such examples demonstrate that governments and policy makers in Canada are increasingly pressured to understand development in terms of the market and thus emphasize that Indigenous peoples must lift themselves out of marginality and take advantage of the abundant opportunities available for them to assume an emerging role in the global economy.

While these economic considerations are indeed very important, and while it seems likely that improved levels of economic well-being for Indigenous peoples would result from this approach, we question the multiple layered assumptions contained within it. The central assumption is that the problems faced by Indigenous peoples and their communities can be resolved if they simply embrace a market-based approach to life and living, realize the potentiality contained in the entrepreneurial spirit, and become their own version of *homo economicus* as quickly as possible. However, as Altamirano-Jimenez (2004) explains, this approach depends on the acceptance of a new form of citizenship for Indigenous peoples in Canada—what she calls market citizenship. She argues that models of development guided by neo-liberal market globalism are insidious because they "deny the legitimacy of communal ownership by separating Indigenous culture from territory," seek to fragment the overall integrity of the communities, and thus undermine the ability of Indigenous peoples to live according to the inherited communitarian ecological sensibilities of their ancestors—something guaranteed through the Treaties (p. 354). In a similar study, Taylor and Friedel (2011) conduct a detailed case study detailing the multiple complications created for Indigenous peoples and their communities when they participate in oil sands operations in their region of Alberta. The authors bring important focus on "*neoliberal* education and training policies" in support of market-based contractual relations with the state that effectively suppress alternative community-based forms of education and training, grow inequities between and amongst Indigenous communities, and generally lessen governmental accountability to Indigenous communities and their rights as Treaty peoples (p. 830). A key neoliberal assumption exposed in this study is that "social exclusion can be remedied by entrepreneurship and employability training and that the market citizen does not require state assistance or protection from structural discrimination" (p. 830). Following the logic expressed in this assumption, then, Indigenous youth need to be educated in ways that position them to shake off the burden of serving communitarian interests and instead take on this emerging economic role in the global economy. This is the crux of the message contained in the first 'fix.'

The second 'fix' for Indigenous youth perceived as damaged comes in the form of culturalist[17] approaches to education and curriculum. Culture-based approaches are viewed by many educators as the key to improving the educational experiences of Indigenous peoples (Archibald, 1995; Archibald, Rayner & Big Head, 2011; Battiste, 2000, 2002, 2010; Demmert & Towner, 2003; McDonald, 2011; Begaye, 2007; Castagno & Brayboy, 2008). Since successful participation in formal schooling has required their adaptation and conformity to Eurocentric cultural values and assumptions, the common belief is that Indigenous students would benefit from curricular and pedagogical approaches that are somehow connected to traditional notions of Indigenous culture and language that are recognizable to them as part of who they are as people. The promotion of culturally relevant and culturally appropriate curriculum developed to spark the interests of Indigenous students has become common practice in Canada. Such work is founded on the assumption that Indigenous students will be more motivated to stay in school and graduate if they are provided opportunities to connect in some way with their own cultures and languages while studying.

However, not all scholars view the focus on particular notions of Indigenous culture to be the cure required to help Indigenous youth become more successful in school. Verna St. Denis, a Cree/Métis scholar working at the University of Saskatchewan, confronts the problem of culturalism in provocative ways and reveals the pathologizing logics they imply. St. Denis (2004) argues that the focus on cultural revitalization in Aboriginal education in the wake of the residential school experiences has led to the predominance of a vexing form of cultural fundamentalism in the field. "Adherence to cultural revitalization encourages the valorization of cultural authenticity and cultural purity among Aboriginal people and has helped to produce the notion and the structure of a cultural hierarchy. 'Authentic' cultural Aboriginal identity has become high currency" (p. 37). The author argues that cultural fundamentalism has created a particular problem for many Indigenous youth who come to feel culturally inadequate as 'Indians' because they cannot perform their cultures or speak their languages in authentic ways. Building on the significance of this analysis, St. Denis contends that the project of cultural revitalization frames Aboriginal peoples as responsible for losing their culture and languages; "they are produced as reckless caretakers of their culture" (p. 43). Importantly, she forwards the view that this emphasis on cultural revitalization in Aboriginal education distracts from and minimizes the historic and ongoing systemic racism and discrimination that has also so deeply affected Indigenous peoples:

> The popular notion that one has lost one's culture, as opposed to having one's culture stolen, places the responsibility for making appropriate cultural adjustments on those who for so long were the target of systemic and individual cultural change. … Describing Aboriginal youth as lost is a benign way to describe the effects of the discrimination, exclusion and sustained violence and aggression they face on a daily basis. (p. 43)

St. Denis (2009) also provides provocative and important insights into the ways in which the culture concept that occupies such a key role in Indigenous education projects is largely derived from the discipline of anthropology and the colonial ventures into new lands that has largely informed its formation. In this insightful analysis, St. Denis shows that educational anthropology—which has had tremendous influence in Indigenous education circles—largely embraced the notion of "cultural essentialism," promoted the idea that culture exists as an entity outside of the people associated with it, concluded that there is a basic incommensurability of different cultures, and held that 'primitive' people are somehow more reliant on culture than more civilized folks (pp. 167–170). "This conceptualization has resulted in the claim that it is 'cultural discontinuity' between the Aboriginal family and community, and the inability of Aboriginal students to make adequate cultural adjustments, that causes high levels of school failure for Aboriginal students" (p. 170).

These points connect to the problem of pathologizing and fixing Indigenous youth by drawing attention to the ways that anthropological and colonial conceptions of culture are used as an explanation for poor academic performance and low school graduation rates. In this understanding, then, the correlating assumption is that the culture of the Indigenous youth is *the* problem in the sense that it makes them unable to comprehend what they are being taught in schools. Once again, the overriding message sent to Indigenous youth is that they need to change themselves in order to achieve in the prescribed ways. This preoccupation with oppressive forms of cultural authenticity imposed on Indigenous youth supports the maintenance of the relational status quo because it ensures that Canadians will not have to consider the ways in which settler culture perpetuates the systemic marginalization of Indigenous peoples and thus fails to acknowledge their deep-rooted belongingness to the lands known as Canada. If we wish to take seriously the challenge to foster qualitative improvements in how Indigenous youth participate in schools and schooling, we cannot frame this challenge as a separate cultural preoccupation of Indigenous peoples.

So, whether the task involves becoming *homo economicus* or becoming a real *Indian*, Indigenous youth are repeatedly inundated with the message that the way they are is simply not good enough and they must become a different kind of person. Educators and policy makers must come to realize that the low level of Indigenous student success in Canadian schools is not necessarily the result of something the students, their families, or their communities are lacking, but is directly connected to the historic and current state of Indigenous-Canadian relations. The pathologization of Indigenous youth that has been exposed in this section must be understood as produced by the institutions of a settler colonial society that is still struggling to come to terms with the fact that it has become wealthy as a result of the displacement and marginalization of the original inhabitants. "…[I]nvasion is a structure not an event…[s]ettler colonialism destroys to replace" (Wolfe, 2006, p. 388).

Conceptualizing Indigenous Youth Identity as Flowing from Communitarian Understandings

If colonialism is indeed a salient aspect of this pathologizing problem, it seems appropriate to wonder how we might begin to decolonize ourselves, and thus relieve Indigenous youth from having to endure this ontological violence. Since colonialism is a shared condition, the task of decolonization must be an endeavor shared by Indigenous peoples and Canadians together. This process of decolonizing in Canada, on a broad scale and especially in relation to the pathologizing of Indigenous youth, can only occur when Indigenous peoples and Canadians face each other across deeply learned divides, revisit and deconstruct their shared past, and carefully engage with the realization that their present and future is similarly tied together. The central challenge of this process is to contest the denial of relationality by paying closer attention to the multiple ways our human sense of living together is constructed on the foundation of communitarian experiences, memories, knowledges shared through stories of ethical interaction set in the places we call home. There is much at stake in working this out in affiliation with these foundations. After all, as *Kainai* Elder Andy Blackwater advises, our tipis are all held down by the same pegs now (Blood & Chambers, 2008).

What might be the guiding inspiration for this decolonizing process? On this point, we wish to assert that *who* you think are cannot be separated from *where* you are. This assertion is derived from a central teaching of Indigenous wisdom traditions that human beings are intimately interconnected to the places they call home as well as the various entities—animals, plants, water, rocks and other creations—that have come to inhabit that place. For most Indigenous peoples, this wisdom arises from deep relationships with significant places in the cultural landscape that are mapped through stories of creation. The people come to know the land and identify with significant places through the stories. The place-stories, as mnemonic triggers, locate and narrate the events of the land called home. Little Bear (2000) notes that this affiliation with place-stories among Indigenous people stems from ways of knowing focused on the relationship to the Earth as the place "where the continuous and/or repetitive process of creation occurs. It is on the Earth that cycles, phases, patterns—in other words, the constant motion or flux—can be observed" (p. 78). Recursive participation in these fluxic movements and renewals is seen as the philosophical and spiritual ideal in this case because such actions serve to honour and respect the knowledge and knowing that grows organically from these relationships (Peat, 1997,

p. 567). Anthropologist Keith Basso (1996), with reference to the culture of the Western Apache, explains the importance of place in these terms:

> For Indian men and women, the past lies embedded in the features of the earth—in canyons and lakes, mountains and arroyos, rocks and vacant fields—which together endow their lands with multiple forms of significance that reach into their lives and shape the ways they think. Knowledge of places is therefore closely linked to knowledge of the self, to grasping one's position in the larger scheme of things, who one is as a person. (p. 34)

So, for example, when the *Kainai* people explain their place in the world, they talk about how the Creator has gifted them with their land, language, culture, ceremonies, resources, stories, and knowledge systems and how their individual and communitarian responsibility is to honour these gifts by using them in their daily lives (Donald, 2003, p. 102). The *Kainai* people believe that all people have similarly been gifted by the Creator and that those gifts are specific to particular places in the world. A temporary balance is achieved when these place-based gifts are honoured and used by the people who were gifted them. This does not mean that peoples and cultures should be closed to each other and that sharing between them should be discouraged. There is recognition that there is value in visiting other places and learning from the people that live there. However, there is clear understanding that the *Kainai* people have a deep relationship to their particular place in the world and they avoid making claims to sovereignty beyond that. Their communitarian understandings of who they are as a people arise from the land and the creation stories that describe its character.

Although things have certainly changed with all that has happened to Indigenous peoples and communities in the recent past, we think such wisdom traditions still have a resonance precisely because we are still living in the places that have been inhabited for millennia prior to now. Thus, acknowledging and honouring this long-term habitation and the knowledge that has grown from it is a critical public policy move in Canada that will have direct implications on the quality and character of future partnerships linking Indigenous people and Canadians. It is these place-based sensibilities that can guide the decolonizing project needed in Canada. This is the spirit and intent of our suggestion to follow the concept of *nēhīyaw wēyasiwewina* as a way to reconceptualize the identities of Indigenous youth in Canada as rooted in the communitarian understandings and imaginaries of their people. The Cree concept, translated directly as 'Cree laws,' is very similar to the *Kainai* understandings described above. Our point in using it here is to bring emphasis on the fact that all Indigenous people in Canada have intimate relationships with their lands that describe Creation and how the people must live in order to survive in their place. This is sacred ecological knowledge that has been acquired and passed on in various forms to the present day. This knowledge is a balance of epistemological, ontological, cosmological, and spiritual understandings that sustains the people and helps keep them strong in the midst of tremendous societal and institutional pressure to become someone else. If you want to know and understand an Indigenous community and how it understands its children, for example, you need to work to comprehend that community's own version of *nēhīyaw wēyasiwewina*. Attentiveness to this concept would help educators and policy makers avoid the problem of starting from an assumption of damage and deficit because it would encourage them to begin instead from the possibility that Indigenous youth are already enmeshed in sacred ecological networks of relations and stories that can support them as they grow.

Such difficult decolonizing work will be challenging and will likely provoke much tension between Indigenous peoples and Canadians. One possible way to imagine such tension as organic and generative is through attentiveness to the idea of "ethical space" as formulated by Cree scholar Willie Ermine (2007). Ermine understands ethics as "our basic capacity to know what harms or enhances the well-being of sentient creatures" (p. 195). As such, ethics concerns our basic humanity and our cherished notions of good, responsibility, duty, and obligation. Ethics constitutes the framework of cultural boundaries that we recognize and respect as part of our daily lives. For Ermine, the ethical space is the area between two entities, the points of contact that entangle and enmesh. Imagine that the two entities are Indigenous and Canadian. Ethical space is a space of possibility—it speaks in the language of possibility—but it can only be created when it is affirmed that there are two different entities, worldviews, and knowledge systems engaging. Once the existence of the other entity is acknowledged, then ethical space emerges as a possibility. The space, as a meeting place where interests intertwine, offers a venue to stretch beyond the limits of our perceived allegiances, detach from the circumscriptive limits and pathologizing tendencies of colonial frontier logics, and enact an ethical theory of human relationality.

To do so, however, requires an ethical desire to defy colonial frontier logics and interface with those who are outside of one's own identifiable group. This requires ecological imagination or the ability to see oneself related to and implicated in the lives of others as a relative. The point here is not to seek the conversion of every Canadian to an Indigenous ecological sensibility founded in the concept *nēhīyaw wēyasiwewina*. Rather, the suggestion is that Indigenous communitarian understandings become a prominent public policy focus so that Canadians are better positioned to comprehend the wishes and goals of Indigenous communities and the hopes and dreams they hold for their children. Canadians "must learn how Creation thinks on this continent" (Sheridan & Longboat, 2006, p. 376). It is the ethical and relational commitments emphasized in Indigenous wisdom traditions and communitarian understandings that can teach a specific form of historical place-based consciousness among Canadians, and thus set the context of decolonization in the interests of relational renewal.

Conclusion

On June 19, 2013, the Canadian Centre for Policy Alternatives and Save the Children Canada released the results of a report that found that half of First Nations children in Canada live in poverty at a rate triple that of non-Indigenous children living in the country.[18] How do average Canadians comprehend a study like this? The argument presented throughout this chapter is that, in the absence of detailed and meaningful contemplation focused on the history of colonialism as an ongoing social, cultural, and educative force that has had deep consequences for Indigenous peoples and their communities, most Canadians will adhere tightly to the belief that there is clearly something wrong with Indigenous peoples that needs to be corrected. This disposition is symptomatic of a deeply learned habit of disregarding the experiences, memories, and knowledge systems of Indigenous peoples and their communities. Our call in this chapter is for educators and policy makers to abandon such pathologizing logics and approaches and begin the complex process of ethical engagement with Indigenous peoples and communities in the spirit of mutual thinking and good relations as imagined by the Indigenous leaders who negotiated the Treaties with government officials generations ago. An ethical approach requires a commitment to explore the ways in which the communitarian traditions and ways of knowing of Indigenous peoples have value in the present context and can offer insights for all of us regarding how to live well today and into the future. If understandings of Indigenous youth are guided by this ethical commitment, it will provide them a chance to imagine themselves as participants in the creation of a qualitatively different kind of society in which the people discover new ways to live in ethical relation with each other— "A Fair Country" as Saul (2009) described it—rather than as unfortunate remnants of a bygone era.

Notes

1. The term Indigenous is preferred in this chapter because it is a better expression of the deep-rooted connectivity of the people to their home territories than other possible names (e.g., Aboriginal, status Indian) derived more directly from colonial impositions and associated identity politics. In using the term with these understandings, we intend to bring emphasis to the point that Indigenous peoples in Canada have unique relationships with their lands and the various entities that comprise them due to the fact that they are indigenous to those territories; they have not come from another place. Their understandings of who they are as distinct peoples are derived from creation stories set in the lands that they call home.

2. Colonial frontier logics are those epistemological assumptions and presuppositions, derived from the colonial project of dividing the world according to racial and cultural categorizations, which serve to naturalize assumed divides and contribute to their social and institutional perpetuation. See Donald (2012) for more.

3. We use this term purposefully. The intent is to draw attention to the tensions associated with the use of the term *Indian* today. These tensions are deeply rooted in the colonial takeover processes experienced by Indigenous peoples which were largely informed by the idea of the Imaginary Indian as a generic social and cultural icon, frozen in time, and incapable of adjusting to change (Francis, 1992). Although the concept of *Indian* has been revealed as a misnomer disrespectful of diverse Indigenous histories, traditions, and subjectivities, it still has surprisingly powerful cultural connotations in Canada today. We use *Indian* in this chapter to acknowledge these ongoing tensions.

4. This concept is taken from the teachings of McAdam (2009) and the summary of insights gained from the Cree Law Gathering of Treaty 6 Elders in March 2011. For more background information on this concept, consult these webpages: http://www.muskeglake.com/services/community-justice/cree-law/. Accessed June 7, 2013 http://intercontinentalcry.org/cree-cultural-teachings-by-sylvia-mcadam/. Accessed June 7, 2013

5. To clarify this point, our argument is that each Indigenous community in Canada has its own version of *nēhīyaw wēyasiwewina* in its own language. For example, we consider the Blackfoot concept of *Kainayssini* to be very similar to *nēhīyaw wēyasiwewina*. For more on *Kainayssini*, visit this webpage: http://blackfootdigitallibrary.com/en/asset/kainaissini-blood-tribe-constitution

6. The names Indigenous peoples have for themselves in their own languages are commonly translated into English as the 'first people' or 'real people.' "…'Real People,' an English term sometimes used to translate Aboriginal ethnic self-designations such as Inuit (known more commonly in the past as Eskimo), Innu (Naskapi), Anishinabe (Ojibwa), or in Alaska, Yup'ik or Inupiaq" (Brown, 1993, p. 24).

7. For more on the specific legislative details of Bill C-45 visit this link: http://parl.gc.ca/HousePublications/Publication.aspx?DocId=5765988. Accessed May 14, 2013.

8. Visit the following link for profiles of these four women as well as some background information on the leadership women have provided in the Idle No More movement: http://www.culturalsurvival.org/publications/cultural-survival-quarterly/being-idle-no-more-women-behind-movement. Accessed May 13, 2013.

9. For more on this understanding of history and background of Treaties in Western Canada, see Price (1999), Hildebrandt, W., Rider, D. F., & Carter, S. (1996), and Johnson (2007).

10. Of course, Indigenous peoples living within the borders of the nation-state known as Canada are also considered Canadians. However, it is important to note that many Indigenous people living in Canada only consider themselves Canadian as an issue of life circumstance. Their affiliations, in terms of identity, place, memory, and belongingness, remain with their Indigenous communities. This is why I maintain the distinctions apparent in this statement.

11. For a good chronological history of the development of this entity, see chapter 1 of Titley (1986). We consider the name 'Indian Affairs' anachronistic in that it arose from the high colonial era and implies the highly paternalistic position that Canadian government officials have held for themselves in relation to those people misnamed as 'Indian.' Vizenor (1999) offers illuminating insight on this:

> The name "Indian" is a convenient one, to be sure, but it is an invented term that does not come from any Native language, and it does not describe or contain any aspect of traditional Native experience or literature. Indian, the noun, is a simulation of racialism, an undesirable separation of race in the political and cultural interests of discovery and colonial settlement of new nations; the noun does not reveal the experiences of diverse Native communities. The name is unbidden, and the Native heirs must bear an unnatural burden to be so christened in their own land. (p. 47)

Today, this governmental entity is officially known as Aboriginal Affairs and Northern Development Canada (AANDC), but the original name and its colonial connotations have proven hard to shake.

12. For more details on this historic walk, see this article: http://www.cbc.ca/news/canada/ottawa/story/2013/03/25/ottawa-walk-nishiyuu-journey-ends-ottawa-parliament-victoria.html. Accessed May 21, 2013.

13. Viable in the sense that this way of being is possible today and being an *Indian* is no longer possible. This point is inspired by Mbembé and Meintje's (2004) concept of "necropolitics" or the understanding of sovereignty, in connection with the modern nation-state, as fundamentally concerned with who or what must live and who or what must die in order for the nation-state to exercise the necessary power and control.

14. The webpage for the Curriculum Redesign project is: http://education.alberta.ca/department/ipr/curriculum.aspx Accessed June 19, 2013.

15. To be clear, we are not seeking to downplay or disregard the importance of historical consciousness and statistical information as insightful ways to better understand all that has happened to Indigenous peoples in Canada and how the consequences of those happenings are lived daily by the people whose families and communities were most negatively impacted by them. They describe lived realities for Indigenous peoples in Canada that are unacceptable and must be addressed before Indigenous peoples can truly feel as though they are living in equal partnership with Canadians. Our point is that Indigenous children are often pathologized and perceived as living in deficit when the statistics are used to determine their subjectivity. We think that there are more hopeful and respectful ways to begin such considerations.

16. See Persky (1995) for more on the origins of this concept. Following insights from Caruso (2012), we intend for this concept to be understood in anthropological and sociological terms rather than in purely economic terms.

17. "Culturalism, in brief, refers to the use of particular anthropological notions of 'culture' by which 'Indigenous culture' enters the field as 'already read'…culturalism incorporates the ideologies and discursive regimes of universalism, cultural racism, and cultural incompatibility in order to construct and perpetuate a 'two race' binary" (McConaghy, 2000, xi). Informed by this definition, I use the term culturalism to denote curricular and pedagogical positions that are founded on static notions of cultural authenticity and codified culture as unquestioned solutions to the problems faced by Aboriginal peoples in the field of education.

18. For more details on this study, see this article: http://www.cbc.ca/news/canada/saskatchewan/story/2013/06/18/f-poverty-first-nations-indigenous-report.html?cmp=rss. Accessed June 21, 2013.

References

Akan, L. (1999). Pimosatamowin sikow kakeequaywin: Walking and Talking—A Saulteaux Elder's view of Native education. *Canadian Journal of Native Education, 23*(1), 16–39.

Alberta Education. (2010). *Alberta Education Action Agenda 2011–2014.* Edmonton, AB: Alberta Education. (Online). Accessed June 19, 2013. http://education.alberta.ca/media/6432073/actionagenda.pdf

Alberta Education. (2011). *Framework for student learning: Competencies for engaged thinkers and ethical citizens with an entrepreneurial spirit.* Edmonton, AB: Alberta Education. (Online). Accessed June 19, 2013. http://education.alberta.ca/media/6581166/framework.pdf

Alfred, T. (2005). *Wasase: Indigenous pathways to action and freedom.* Peterborough, ON: Broadview Press.

Altamirano-Jimenez, I. (2004). North American first peoples: Slipping up into market citizenship. *Citizenship Studies, 8*(4), 349–365.

Apple, M. W. (2004). *Ideology and curriculum.* London: Taylor & Francis Books.

Archibald, J.-A. (1995). Locally developed Native Studies curriculum: An historical and philosphical rationale. In M. Battiste (Ed.), *First Nations education in Canada: The circle unfolds.* Vancouver: UBC Press, pp. 288–312

Archibald, J.-A., Rayner, A., & Big Head, R. (2011). *Community responses to creating a school or model with an Aboriginal focus.* Indigenous Education Institute of Canada.

Bakan, J. (2011). *Childhood under siege: How big business targets children.* Toronto, ON: Penguin Group (Canada), a division of Pearson Canada Inc.

Barker, A. (2009). The contemporary reality of Canadian imperialism: Settler colonialism and the hybrid colonial state. *American Indian Quarterly, 33*(3), 325–351.

Basso, K. (1996). *Wisdom sits in places: Landscape and language among the Western Apache.* Albuquerque: University of New Mexico Press.

Battiste, M. (2000). Maintaining Aboriginal identity, language, and culture in modern society. In M. Battiste (Ed.). *Reclaiming Indigenous voice and vision.* Vancouver: UBC Press, pp. 192–208.

Battiste, M. (2002). *Indigenous knowledge and pedagogy in First Nations education: A literature review with recommendations.* Prepared for the National Working Group on Education and the Minister of Indian and Northern Affairs Canada (INAC).

Battiste, M. (2010). Nourishing the learning spirit: Living our way to new thinking. *Education Canada, 50*(1), 14–18.

Begaye, T. (2007). Native teacher understanding of culture as a concept for curricular inclusion. *Wicazo sa Review, 22*(1), 35–52.

Bennett, M. & Blackstock, C. (2007). The insidious poverty epidemic: Considerations for Aboriginal children, families, communities and other Indigenous Nations. *First Peoples Child and Family Review: A Journal on Innovation and Best Practices in Aboriginal Child Welfare Administration, Research, Policy & Practice, 3*(3), 5–7.

Blackstock, C. (2011). The Canadian Human Rights Tribunal on First Nations child welfare: Why if Canada wins, equality and justice lose. *Children and Youth Services Review, 33,* 187–194.

Blood, N. & Chambers, C. (2009). Love thy neighbour: Repatriating precarious Blackfoot sites. *International Journal of Canadian Studies, 39–40,* 253–279.

Brendtro, L. K., Brokenleg, M. & Van Brockern, S. (1990). *Reclaiming youth at risk: Our hope for the future.* Bloomington, IN: National Education Service.

Brown, J. S. H. (1993). Metis, Half-breeds, and other real people: Challenging cultures and categories. *The History Teacher, 27*(1), 19–26.

Buchanan, I. (2005). Space in the age of non-place. In I. Buchanan & G. Lambert (Eds.), *Deleuze and Space* (pp. 16–35). Edinburgh: Edinburgh University Press Ltd.

Canada News Centre, (2013). Governments of Canada and Alberta invest to help Aboriginal youth get jobs. (Online). Accessed June 20, 2013. http://news.gc.ca/web/article-eng.do?nid=719389

Canadian Council of Provincial Child and Youth Advocates. (2010). *Position Paper: Aboriginal children and youth in Canada: Canada must do better. (Online).* Accessed June 19, 2013. http://www.gnb.ca/0073/PDF/positionpaper-e.pdf

Caruso, S. (2012). *Homo oeconomicus. Paradigma, critiche, revisioni* (Vol. 103). Florence: Firenze University Press.

Castagno, A & Brayboy, B.M.J. (2008). Culturally responsive schooling for Indigenous youth: A review of the literature. *Review of Educational Research, 78*(4), 941–993.

Centre for Addiction and Mental Health. (n.d.). (Online). Accessed May 5, 2013. http://www.camh.ca/en/hospital/about_camh/newsroom/for_reporters/Pages/addictionmentalhealthstatistics.aspx

Chiefs of Ontario. (2012). *Our children, our future, our vision: First Nation jurisdiction over First Nation education in Ontario.* New Agenda Working Group. (Online). Accessed June 7, 2013. http://www.peopleforeducation.ca/wp-content/uploads/2012/02/COO-Education-Report-Feb-8-20121.pdf

Clark, P. (2007). Representations of Aboriginal Peoples in English Canadian history textbooks: Toward reconciliation. In E.A. Cole (Ed.), *Teaching the violent past: History education and reconciliation* (pp. 81–120). Lanham, MD: Rowman & Littlefield and Carnegie Council for Ethics in International Affairs.

Demmert, W. G., & Towner, J. C. (2003). *A review of the research literature on the influences of culturally based education on the academic performance of Native American students.* Portland: Northwest Regional Educational Laboratory.

Donald, D. (2003). *Elder, student, teacher: A Kainai curriculum métissage.* Unpublished Master's Thesis, University of Lethbridge.

Donald, D. (2004). Edmonton pentimento: Rereading history in the case of the Papaschase Cree. *Journal of the Canadian Association for Curriculum Studies, 2*(1), 21–53.

Donald, D. (2009). *The pedagogy of the fort: Curriculum, Aboriginal-Canadian relations, and Indigenous Métissage.* Unpublished doctoral dissertation, University of Alberta.

Donald, D (2011). On What Terms Can We Speak? Aboriginal-Canadian Relations as an Educational Priority. [Broadcast Video]. In *Big Thinking on the Hill Speaker Series.* Ottawa, Ontario: Canadian Federation for the Humanities and Social Sciences. http://blog.fedcan.ca/category/big-thinking/

Donald, D. (2012). Forts, colonial frontier logics, and Aboriginal-Canadian relations: Imagining decolonizing educational philosophies in Canadian contexts. In A. Abdi (Ed). *Decolonizing philosophies in education.* Rotterdam/Boston/Taipei: Sense Publishers, pp. 91–111.

Duran, B., Duran, E., & Brave Heart, M. (1998). Native Americans and the trauma of history. In R. Thornton (Ed.). *Studying Native America: Problems and prospects.* Madison: University of Wisconsin Press, pp. 60–76.

Ermine, W. (2007). The ethical space of engagement. *Indigenous Law Journal,* 6(1), 193–203.

Fenwick, T. (2006). The audacity of hope: Towards poorer pedagogies. *Studies in the Education of Adults, 38*(1), 9–24.

Francis, D. (1992). *The imaginary Indian: The image of the Indian in Canadian culture.* Vancouver, BC: Arsenal Pulp Press.

Francis, D. (1997). *National dreams: Myth, memory, and Canadian history.* Vancouver, BC: Arsenal Pulp Press.

Freire, P. (1993). *Pedagogy of the oppressed.* New York: The Continuum Publishing Company.

Giroux, H. (2004). War on terror: The militarising of public space and culture in the United States. *Third Text, 18*(4), 211–221.

Giroux, H. (2010). Neolioberalism as public pedagogy. In Sandlin, J. A., Schultz, B. D. & Burdick, J. (Eds.). *Handbook of public pedagogy: Education and learning beyond schooling.* New York: Routledge, pp. 486–499.

Greenwood, M. (2003). *BC First Nations children: Our families, our communities, our future.* British Columbia First Nations Early Childhood Development Roundtable. (Online). Accessed June 7, 2013. http://www.designingnations.com/pdf_s/Formatted%20BC%20ECD%20Paper.pdf

Grumet, M. R. (1986). The lie of the child redeemer. *Journal of Education, 168*(3), 87–97.

Harrison, T. (2005). (Ed.). *The return of the Trojan horse: Alberta and the new world (dis)order.* Montreal: Black Rose Books

Helin, C. & Snow, D. (2010). Free to learn: Introduction. In *True north in Canadian public policy (March): Free to learn-Giving Aboriginal youth control over their post-secondary education.* (Online). Toronto: The MacDonald-Laurier Institute for Public Policy. Accessed June 19, 2013. http://www.macdonaldlaurier.ca/files/pdf/FreeToLearn.pdf

Hildebrandt, W., Rider, D. F., & Carter, S. (1996). *The true spirit and original intent of Treaty 7.* Montreal, QC: McGill-Queen's University Press.

Hill, J. A. (2011). Endangered childhoods: How consumerism is impacting child and youth identity. *Media, Culture & Society, 33*(3), 347–362.

Houston, S. (2010). Beyond *homo economicus*: Recognition, self-realization and social work. *British Journal of Social Work, 40*(3), 841–857.

Johnson, H. (2007). *Two families: Treaties and government.* Saskatoon, SK: Purich Publishing.

Keil, R. (2002). "Common–Sense" neoliberalism: Progressive Conservative urbanism in Toronto, Canada. *Antipode, 34*(3), 578–601.

Kennedy, D. (1983). *Toward a phenomenology of childhood.* Unpublished doctoral dissertation, University of Kentucky.

Kennedy, D. (2002). The child and postmodern subjectivity. *Educational Theory, 52*(2), 155–167.

Kincheloe, J. L. (2008). *Knowledge and critical pedagogy: An introduction* (Volume 1). Amsterdam: Springer.

King, T. (2003). *The truth about stories: A Native narrative.* Toronto, ON: House of Anansi Press.

Lisac, M. (2004). (Ed.). *Alberta politics uncovered: Taking back our province.* Edmonton, Canada: NeWest Press

Little Bear, L. (2000). Jagged worldviews colliding. In M. Battiste (Ed.). *Reclaiming indigenous voice and vision.* Vancouver: University of British Columbia Press, pp. 77–85.

Locke, J. (1968). Locke's letters to Edward Clarke on Education. In *The educational writings of John Locke.* Cambridge, UK: Cambridge University Press.

Luffman, J. & Sussman, D. (2007). The Aboriginal labour force in Western Canada. *Perspectives on Labour and Income, 8*(1), 13–27.

McAdam, S. (2009). *Cultural teachings: First nations protocols and methodologies.* Saskatchewan Indian Cultural Centre: Saskatoon, Saskatchewan.

McConaghy, C. (2000). *Rethinking indigenous education: Culturalism, colonialism, and the politics of knowing.* Flaxton, Australia: Post Pressed.

McDonald, R.-A. (2011). *First Nations languages and culture impacts on literacy and student achievement outcomes: Review of literature.* Assembly of First Nations.

Mbembé, J. A., & Meintjes, L. (2003). Necropolitics. *Public culture, 15*(1), 11–40.

Morgensen, S. L. (2011). The biopolitics of settler colonialism: Right here, right now. *Settler Colonial Studies, 1*(1), 52–76.

Nandy, A. (1988). *Traditions, tyranny, and utopias: Essays in the politics of awareness.* Delhi: Oxford University Press.

Peat, F. D. (1997). Blackfoot physics and European minds. *Futures, 29*(6), 563–573.

Persky, J. (1995). Retrospectives: The ethology of *homo economicus. Journal of Economic Perspectives, 9*(2), 221–231.

Price, R. (1999). *The spirit of the Alberta Indian Treaties.* Edmonton, AB: University of Alberta Press.

Riley, T & Ungerleider, C. (2012). Self-fulfilling prophecy: How teachers' attributions, expectations, and stereotypes influence the learning opportunities afforded Aboriginal students. *Canadian Journal of Education, 35*(2), 303–333.

Regan, P. (2010). *Unsettling the settler within: Indian Residential Schools, Truth Telling, and Reconciliation in Canada.* Vancouver, BC: UBC Press.

Rousseau, J. J. (1979). *Emile: or, On Education.* New York, NY: Harper Collins.

Sandlin, J. A. & McLaren, P. (2010) (Eds.). *Critical pedagogies of consumption: Living and learning in the shadow of the "Shopocalypse."* New York: Routledge.

Saul, J. R. (2009). *A fair country: Telling truths about Canada.* Toronto: Penguin Canada.

Schor, J. (2004). *Born to buy: The commercialized child and the new consumer culture.* New York: Scribner.

Sharp, A, Arsenault, J-F & Lapointe, S. (2007). The potential contribution of Aboriginal Canadians to labour force, employment, productivity and output growth in Canada, 2001–2017. (Online). *Centre for the study of living standards: Research report no. 2007–04.* Ottawa, Ontario. Accessed June 19, 2013. http://dspace.cigilibrary.org/jspui/bitstream/123456789/15444/1/The Potential Contribution of Aboriginal Canadians to Labour Force Employment Productivity and Output Growth in Canada 2001 2017 2007.pdf?1

Sheridan, J. & Longboat, R. D. (2006). The Haudenosaunee imagination and the ecology of the sacred. *Space and Culture, 9*(4), 365–381.

Shields, C. M., Bishop, R., & Mazawi, A. E. (2005). *Pathologizing practices: The impact of deficit thinking on education.* New York, NY: Peter Lang.

Smith, D. G. (1988). Review of the dissertation *Young children's thinking: An interpretation from phenomenology,* by D.K. Kennedy. *Phenomenology and Pedagogy, 6*(2), 109–113.

Smith, D. G. (2003). Curriculum and teaching face globalization. In Pinar (Ed.), *International Handbook of Curriculum Research* (pp. 35–51). Mahwah, NJ: Lawrence Erlbaum Associates, Inc.

St. Denis, V. (2004). Real Indians: Cultural revitalization and fundamentalism in Aboriginal education. In C. Schick, J. Jaffe, and A. Watkinson (Eds.). *Contesting fundamentalisms.* Halifax, NS: Fernwood, pp. 35–47.

St. Denis, V. (2009). Rethinking culture theory in Aboriginal education. In C. Levine-Rasky, (Ed.), *Canadian perspectives on the sociology of education* (pp. 163–182). Toronto, ON: Oxford University Press.

Taubman, P. (2000). Teaching without hope: What is really at stake in the standards movement, high stakes testing, and the drive for "practical reforms". *Journal of Curriculum Theorizing, 16*(3), 19–33.

Taylor, A. & Friedel, T. (2011): Enduring neoliberalism in Alberta's oil sands: The troubling effects of private–public partnerships for First Nation and Métis communities. *Citizenship Studies, 15*(6–7), 815–835.

Titley, E. B. (1986). *A narrow vision. Duncan Campbell Scott and the administration of Indian Affairs in Canada.* Vancouver, BC: UBC Press.

Townsend, T. & Wernick, M. (2008). Hope or heartbreak: Aboriginal youth and Canada's future. *Horizons, 10*(1), 4–6.

Tuck, E. (2009). Suspending damage: A letter to communities. *Harvard Educational Review, 79*(3), 409–428.

Valencia, R. (1997).(Ed.). *The evolution of deficit thinking: Educational thought and practice.* London: Falmer Press.

Veracini, L. (2008). Settler collective, founding violence and disavowal: The settler colonial situation. *Journal of Intercultural Studies, 29*(4), 363–379.

Vizenor, G. (1999). Native American Indian literatures: Narratives of survivance. In R. Hulan (Ed.), *Native North America: Critical and cultural perspectives* (pp. 47–63). Toronto, ON: ECW Press.

Waldram, J. (2004). *Revenge of the windigo: The construction of the mind and mental health of North American Aboriginal peoples.* Toronto, ON: University of Toronto Press.

Williams, D. (1999). Constructing the economic space: The World Bank and the making of *homo oeconomicus. Millennium—Journal of International Studies, 28*(1), 79–99.

Willinsky, J. (1998). *Learning to divide the world: Education at empire's end.* Minneapolis, MN: University of Minnesota Press.

Wolfe, P. (2006): Settler colonialism and the elimination of the native. *Journal of Genocide Research, 8*(4), 387–409.

CHAPTER 11

See Me, Hear Me

Engaging With Australian Aboriginal Youth and Their Lifeworlds

Jill Guy and Jon Austin

Research, (neo)colonialism, and alienation sit sinisterly together in the experience of most indigenous peoples (Smith, 1999), and, similarly, researchers working with youth find multiple obstacles in engaging genuinely and transparently with their participants. The compound effect of these two characteristics—indigeneity and youth—means that coming to understand aspects of the life experiences of indigenous youth as an outsider presents as a major methodological and personal challenge. This chapter reports on a form of mixed methods research that has enabled a non-indigenous research team to explore some parts of these worlds that might otherwise have remained difficult, if not impossible, to enter. Here, we explain how a process that draws upon indigenous and non-indigenous ways of knowing has led to valuable insights into aspects of indigenous youth experience.

In this chapter, we draw from a larger research project, and take from it the experiences we have had in utilising a methodological approach that merges the strengths of the visual and oral traditions of Australian Aboriginal cultures with Western (non-indigenous) research approaches. In this chapter, we focus on the power of the visual to open spaces for deeper understandings when trying to understand the life experiences of indigenous youth.

The Larger Project: Indigenous Educational Lifeworlds

The project was motivated by a desire to counter the dominant discourse in Australian education that positioned Indigenous Australians—Aboriginal and Torres Strait Islander peoples—as educationally "behind," deficient, or unable to achieve at the same levels as non-indigenous Australians. As in a number of other countries, and as a significant aspect of the war on youth (Giroux, 2013), this discourse is serviced by the imposition of a national school achievement assessment regimen. In Australia, this is the National Assessment Program-Literacy and Numeracy (NAPLAN), with the annual results of this program posted in various forms for community consumption. Unsurprisingly, indigenous students compare unfavourably with non-indigenous students on all of the test areas. For example, on measures of reading, the relative percentages of students meeting or exceeding the national minimum standard for their age in 2012 is shown in Table 11.1:

	Year 3	Year 5	Year 7	Year 9
Indigenous	74.2%	64.7 %	75.4 %	67.2%
Non-indigenous	94.7%	93.1%	95.1%	92.7%

(Source: http://www.nap.edu.au)

Table 11.1. Percentage of Students Meeting National Minimum Reading Standards

Similar relativities show across the other categories of testing. One of the outcomes of this program of national student testing has been the development of government initiatives such as *Closing the Gap*, drawn from the intergovernmental *Aboriginal and Torres Strait Islander Peoples Education Action Plan* (Ministerial Council for Education, 2010). The language and underlying assumptions of such programs maintain a deficit discourse, and interpellate the Black body as, essentially, uneducable, either through genetics or attitude ("motivation"). In short, indigenous youth are positioned as essentially deficient compared to a purportedly transcendental norm (Yancy, 2013) conveyed ontologically through the power of Whiteness.

What is not apparent in the results of such testing programs is the cultural complexity that attends the schooling process for most Aboriginal and Torres Strait Islander students. In admittedly general terms, non-indigenous students, largely White in the Australian context, inhabit a culture with which the formal school curriculum is consistent, and of which it is supportive and replicative. In broad terms, their educational (schooling) and everyday lifeworlds are almost totally congruent. The educational lifeworlds of most indigenous students, however, is far more complex, and Aboriginal and Torres Strait Islander youth learn to live within and across at least two, if not more, cultures. NAPLAN results leach such details and contexts from the *imago* of indigenous learning outcomes, and reduce the educational achievements of these young people to a single, statistical score against (exclusively) White cultural norms.

The project from which this current chapter is drawn attempted to capture something of this multicultural experience, and in particular the non-school learning Aboriginal and Torres Strait Islander people engage in. The focus of the study is contiguous with an admonition from a local Australian Aboriginal elder at a recent community consultation meeting in which one of the authors (Jon) was involved: "*We've been teaching our kids for thousands of years. Don't tell us how to teach our kids. We've been doing it for thousands of years and we'll go on doing it* [emphasis added]" (McCarthy, May 24th, 2013). The project's focus was on how Australian Aboriginal youth engage with that teaching; of how and where they learn what NAPLAN discounts or ignores.

Researching With Aboriginal Youth: A Different Mixed Methods Approach

In this project, we have conceptualised the current attraction of mixed methods research (Denzin, 2010) to look to a way in which research with indigenous peoples might be more respectfully undertaken. Instead of the more standard "mixing" of quantitative and qualitative methods from within a White, epistemic repertoire, and in addition to attempts to utilise mixed methods for more socially transformative purposes (Mertens, 2010), we have looked to utilise indigenous and non-indigenous addends to better draw on the oral and, particularly in this case, the visual traditions of Australian Aboriginal cultures. We have been working at this development for some time (see Austin & Hickey, 2011; Austin & Williams-Mozley, 2012), not without frustrations, and saw the lifeworlds project as another opportunity to find ways to engage more dialogically and authentically with our indigenous research partners.

We would like to think that our work here demonstrates a concern to embrace the decolonizing methodologies imperative Linda Smith (1999) has written so passionately about, that we might contribute to the reconciliation project of redressing something of what colonial researchers and their methods have wreaked upon colonised peoples: "imperialism and colonialism brought complete disorder to colonised peoples, disconnecting them from their histories, their landscapes, their languages, their social relations and their own ways of thinking, feeling and interacting with the world" (Smith, 1999, p. 30).

This work with Australian Aboriginal youth was an attempt to assist in a process of reconnection with some aspects of these "disordered" cultures. To do so, we attempted to draw in and on the strength and familiarity of forms of visual ways of knowing that are core aspects of Aboriginal and Torres Strait Islander peoples' cultures, but have updated this tradition through the application of contemporary photographic technologies.

Visual ways of knowing and visual research approaches generally have become far more commonplace in research methodology in recent years, but this chapter is not the place to explore the significant literature in this area. The reader is directed to the multiple works of Sarah Pink (2004a, 2004b, 2006, 2007, 2009), Douglas Harper (2005), and Jon Prosser (2011) for inventories of the developments being made here. While being strongly influenced by the critical visual work described by scholar-activists such as these, we are simultaneously cognizant of the role played by various forms of anthropological and ethnographic photography and film in advancing the colonial project through the imposition and naturalizing of the imperial gaze (for specficially Australian perspectives on this, see Connell, 2007; Nakata, 2007). Of particular relevance in the Australian context, Sharp (2010) has explored the ways in which over a century of formal Queensland school-curriculum development drew upon visual representations of Aboriginal Australians that positioned them closer to fauna and nature than human and cultured. Further, we are aware that such colonizing roles are by no means "historical" or "no longer," but that they continue to operate to sustain hegemonic processes of alienation, subjugation, and exploitation. The urgency of "decolonizing methodologies" (Smith, 1999) cannot be ignored.

What might be categorised as a visual tradition within the Western research canon in indigenous cultures worldwide frequently involves far more than the physical and cognitive acts of looking and comprehending. In keeping with the multiple levels of meaning that structure much of the lore of indigenous cultures, the visual also invokes complex intersections of the symbolic, the artistic, the spiritual, and the sacred. For many indigenous cultures, and particularly for those cultures of the Australian Aboriginal and Torres Strait Islander peoples, such visual(ising) processes help *describe the meaning that is beyond words* [emphasis added]" (Lavallée, 2009, p. 30). In our work with indigenous youth, the use of "wordless" research opened up greater participatory possibilities than would have likely been the case with a more standard interview and/or conversation approach. When the power of the visual was merged with an approach to talking that embraced more of the intent and protocols of yarning (Bessarab & Ng'andu, 2010; Carrello, 2009; Power, 2004) as opposed to interviewing, the richness of the dialogic engagement between participants—the formal researcher and the two Australian Aboriginal youth—was significant.

Accordingly, the methodological bricolage (Kincheloe, 2005; Steinberg, 2012) used in this project merged the participatory-research ethos underpinning photovoice (Wang & Burris, 1994), an emic-etic methodological process (Austin & Hickey, 2009), and contemporary digital photographic technologies. In this approach, all participants in the work—the formal researcher and Australian Aboriginal youth in the immediate instance—engaged in the basic photovoice process, capturing images that each individually felt could be used to convey something of how they saw the educational lifeworlds of Australian Aboriginal youth.

The collation of the two types of photographic evidence—the insider or emic material from the young people and the outsider or etic photographs of the researcher—potentially opens up opportunities and reasons for all to engage in discussion about what each party has seen and understood as the significance of their photographic folio. This part of the process allowed a degree of trust and openness to develop between Jill—who was the researcher working with the two young people referred to in this chapter—Jake, and Todd that would have been unlikely to have occurred as rapidly or enthusiastically without Jill opening her "work" to the gaze and interrogation of her "participants." Dialogue aimed at arriving at common understanding and agreement was what ensued, as the three participants here shared, discussed, and interrogated their individual and collective photographic productions. Such oral engagement is very much akin to yarning, where the purpose is often problem-solving through consensus rather than through one-on-one question-and-answer sessions. The use of the photographs here undoubtedly placed the "participants" on a very similar methodological footing as the "researcher." The democratising potential of this approach and attendant agentic outcomes should not be discounted (Austin & Hickey, 2009, pp. 8–9).

Initiating and Maintaining the Work With Indigenous Youth

In working with indigenous communities generally, and Australian Aboriginal groups specifically, there is a need for trust to be built up over a period of time. In locations like ours, inter-generational trauma and memory often mean that many Australian Aboriginal people refuse or very reluctantly complete any sort of formal paperwork. In the recent past and well within living memory, to fill out a government form might mean that you lost your child, that you were taken to jail, or that you were re-located. Such fear and suspicion accounts, for example, for the significant under-reporting of Aboriginal and Torres Strait Islander peoples in national censuses. To have non-indigenous researchers asking to collect information about, from, and even with Aboriginal communities typically throws up a wall of silence, obfuscation, and refusal to participate. To further complicate matters in the current project, it is generally acknowledged that the traditional owners and/or custodians of the area, the Jarowair and Giabal peoples, to all intents and purposes no longer inhabit the land—they have either died out or have been removed to other places over generations. The sizeable Aboriginal and Torres Strait Islander peoples population in the area—estimated at around 20,000—consists of people from many different tribes and countries. As such, the local area houses many elders and respected people, without a single visible Elder authority. This meant that we needed to engage with the local community through a senior Aboriginal man with connections to both the university with which we work and the broader local indigenous community. Having such a trusted source to, in effect, vouch for our motives and intentions—to speak to our hearts—was crucial.

Further, as we are both non-indigenous people and with different, but still relatively limited, cultural competence in matters Aboriginal, we were able to secure cultural support and assistance from a senior Australian Aboriginal woman who acted as cultural advisor to the project. While she was not able to speak to the specifics of groups other than her own in this pan-tribal context, she was able to give us more general advice about more commonly shared protocols and courtesies. Our work with the young people in this project could probably not have proceeded as respectfully and productively without this source of advice and assistance. Even so, we acknowledge that there are many levels of knowledge and insight from which we were prohibited, on ethnicity ("race"), gender, and/or age grounds.

The Participants

From the larger project, we have drawn upon Jill's engagement with two of the youngest participants. Pseudonyms have replaced the names of the two participants and, where appropriate, other details whereby they might be identified have been removed or modified. Where images have been drawn from their contribution to the project, full permission for such use has been granted by them and by their legal guardian. Jill's commentary carries the next part of this chapter.

Jill's story

This data set has emerged from parts of my doctoral project. This project occurred after I had completed my honours project, where I explored an Australian Government Indigenous education program in place in State Schools. I had been quite disheartened with how the government organized and ran the program, and with the eventual dismantling of the program that had appeared to be achieving some worthwhile results. From this I knew that I wanted to continue to research aspects of Indigenous education, but not from a compensatory program perspective. I needed to look at the wider educational lifeworlds of Aboriginal and Torres Strait Islander students. This re-focussing impacted upon a number of methodological and participatory aspects of my work, and influenced a number of decisions I made during the project. I was adamant that I did not want to continue the violence that has often been committed by White researchers against their non-White participants, so it was essential to employ methods that had the potential to reflect the oral and visual ways of knowing of Aboriginal and Torres Strait Islander cultures in an attempt to diminish the potential power differentials of the study. This is how photo elicitation came to be used as one of the methods in the study. Photo elicitation is a very powerful tool that has the potential to allow the development of reciprocal relationships where much deeper data are collected rather than in studies where interviews alone are used.

I also knew that I needed to find participants in situations where they trusted me, and where there was some sort of acceptance of both the project and myself by members of the community. The project was presented to an Elders council from the wider area where it received support and acceptance. I initially worked within a program that was being trialled at some of the local high schools. This program was a mentoring program that grouped Indigenous high-school students with university students. Due to a number of factors, this program was shut down, and I did not continue with the program. Consequently, none of my participants were the high-school students that had participated in this program, as I had imagined they would be. One of my participants was one of the mentors from this program. Two of my participants came from a drop-in centre for disengaged youth that I was affiliated with and who were referred to me by the Director. The other participants were connected to the university's Aboriginal and Torres Strait Islander support centre where I was working.

Eventually I had five participants and they were all male, four of them were youths and aged between 10 and 23, and one was almost 50. Before the participants commenced their data collection, I conducted a racial audit around the town, and took photos of what I thought were sites of learning and Indigenous cultures. Then I gave digital cameras to the participants who did not have access to one, and asked them to take photographs of anything that represented the learning that occurred within their lifeworld. There was no limit put on how many photographs they could take, and I emphasized that there was not a single correct answer, and that the photographs would be a stimulus for us to talk about the learning that they experienced.

Jon's story

As a non-indigenous man, almost a decade older than the typical life expectancy of many Australian Aboriginal men, I came to Jill's project in a collaborator role, providing conceptual, methodological, and (limited) cultural assistance. I had worked on a number of projects in the broad area of indigenous, anti-racist and Whiteness studies over almost three decades of formal academic work. This project drew together a number of threads of personal-professional urgency for me, and allowed me to apply the criterion of criticality embedded in Patti Lather's (2007, pp. 50, 52) questions for critical researchers—*what does it mean to use other people's lives as data?* and *for whom is this work emancipatory?*—in (hopefully) optimistic ways.

Jake's story

Jake is one of five male, Aboriginal participants that are engaged in this study. He is the second youngest participant. Jake was 12 when I first met him at the drop-in centre. Graham, the Director of the centre, introduced me to Jake and Gary, Jake's father, when they dropped in one afternoon. Another participant, who is friends with Jake, spoke to him about my project, and suggested that he do it as well. Jake does not have the phenotypical features of an Australian Aboriginal person. Jake's father is non-Indigenous and his mother is Australian Aboriginal. Jake's parents are not living together anymore, and Jake had lived solely with his father for about a year at the time of this project. Jake has two brothers and a sister who are all significantly older than he. Jake's sister and one of his brothers both have children of their own.

Jake's parents formally separated when he was young, and he was in the custody of his mother. His mother had been very racist towards Indigenous Australians until she learnt, later in life, that she was actually Aboriginal. Since learning of her Aboriginality, she has been very focused on how she has been discriminated against. This, in part, had led to her withdrawing Jake from the school system. She initially moved Jake around a number of schools, and then decided she would homeschool him. Her best friend and the mother of one of my other participants completed this homeschooling. The homeschooling did not consist of the required curriculum or any cultural learning, and consequently Jake spent a number of years without either formal education or cultural education. Eventually, Jake made the decision to go and live with his father. Since moving, he has been going back to school, and is now on track to attend school on a full-time basis.

Jake and his mother's cultural knowledge seems to be quite superficial, and instead focuses on the idea of a homogenous and/or universal 'Aboriginal' culture, rather than demonstrating a genuine understanding of their particular (Australian Aboriginal) country (tribe or clan) and culture. As such, Jake's mother involved Jake in an Aboriginal dance troupe. This troupe consisted of people from many different countries, and seemed to operate more as a commercial enterprise than as a learning and teaching tool, either for those within the troupe or the audiences for whom they performed. If the dances had meaning, rather than being just a collection of moves meant to "be" Aboriginal dancing, then the children-performers did not know it, nor were they aware of what the body painting they applied before performances represented.

Todd's story

When this project first began, I was hoping to recruit participants from an Indigenous high-school mentoring program that I was engaged with. This program was being trialled in several high schools across the region that had Australian Aboriginal and Torres Strait Islander students, and involved, in part, partnering volunteer university student mentors with Indigenous students. Todd was one of the university volunteer mentors, and I met him as we were both attending the program in a particular high school. The program ran once a week after school, and it was unusual to have any of the high-school students attend. As a result, I got to spend some time with Todd, and we got to know each other. After the program had ended, I asked if Todd would like to be a participant in my project, and he readily agreed. Todd was in his very early twenties and completing a degree at university.

Todd is a Bundjalung man and comes from New South Wales and moved from there with his partner. His parents separated when he was a toddler, and the family went through numerous court proceedings, which Todd thinks contributed to his anger-management issues. These anger-management problems surfaced during his school years when Todd was often in trouble for fighting. He would attempt to calm down and control his anger by leaving school and sitting by the river, even though this was against school rules. Although nature, as a whole, is very important to Todd, water has a special place in his soul. This can be quite difficult at times now, as he is living in a town without a river or substantial body of water close by.

Todd's father is Aboriginal, his mother not, and his family identifies very strongly with their Aboriginality and are very connected to nature and the land, and are very passionate about Indigenous education and rights. Todd comes from a family of boys, and they have all had issues with anger management, and he could see that his future was leading him towards jail if he did not make significant changes. He decided to enter the Technical and Further Education stream (TAFE) and complete a Certificate 4 in Community Service Work and then continue on to a university degree. He now works with Indigenous students in a very large high school in the region, and uses his life experiences and knowledge with the aim of encouraging and inspiring students to be proud of their Aboriginality.

The researcher's gaze

Before the participants started photographically documenting aspects of their lifeworlds, I (Jill) conducted a visual racial audit of the town where the research was being conducted. I also asked some senior members of local Aboriginal and Torres Strait Islander communities to complete this process as well, and then I was going to discuss the significance of the photographs collected as a part of the audit with the participants. The purpose of merging both emic and etic perspectives here was to deepen the understanding of the educational lifeworlds of the participants. My initial researcher expectation regarding the likely outcome of the racial audit process was that I would find many examples of representations of indigenous cultures and sites of cultural importance in the town, as there is quite a large population of Aboriginal and Torres Strait Islander people living there. What I found, though, was a very White town. The town is advertised as a place of beautiful gardens, but the gardens represent the colonial invasion, with very few native plants and mostly English-inspired gardens overtaking what were originally important meeting places. Even the names of the parks, street, and landmarks depict colonisation, with examples such as Queens Park and Colonial Way.

For example, I took a photograph of one of a number of sculptures that are situated near the City Art Gallery. I presumed that this might be a place of importance for the local indigenous population, as it was an area in the town that was decorated with contemporary sculptures referencing Australian Aboriginal cultures and was quite central. As I later discovered, this was not an area of importance to my participants. This might be because the council seems to actively discourage the congregation of youths in public places, and implements strategies like playing classical music in public spaces that have 'problems' with youths, particularly Aboriginal youths.

The Australian Aboriginal youths with whom I worked in this project collected images of their own and for the purposes of this chapter, three photographs have been selected because they all stimulated long and involved conversations that ranged from topics that were obviously connected to the content of the photograph to those that seemed only tenuously connected to what the photograph had physically captured. These photographs are an powerful examples of how the use of photo elicitation can mine such deep caves within the life history and experiences of the participants and engage them in deep conversations that would not typically have been possible, particularly when researching across the boundaries of race, gender, and age. Each of the three people involved here—Jill, Jake, and Todd—set off to capture images of where or what they saw as places or sources of indigenous cultural learning. Each person developed a sizeable collection of images. For the purposes of this chapter, we have drawn upon a very small number—one or two from each person—to help demonstrate what we were able to excavate and co-construct by way of shared understandings of aspects of the educational lifeworlds these young people inhabit.

Jake

Jake chose to take what we term a literal photograph, one of his father. When first asked about why he took this particular photograph, he was unsure of the reason. "*And what's happening in that photo? I don't know, I just took a picture*" (Jake, learning conversation, 26/11/12 [November 26th, 2012]). But once we started talking about it, this photograph was a stimulus to a number of topics, including the enormous effect that his father has had on his education, both formally and informally. "*He learnt taught me how to do the time. .... A bit of adding up and taking away ..... He helped put me in school"* (Jake, learning conversation, 26/11/12 [November 26th, 2012]). Jake discussed his experiences with formal education at length. He discussed the long list of schools that his mother had both enrolled him in and withdrawn him from, and his displeasure at being removed from formal education at his mother's request. The photograph also stimulated a detailed discussion of his relationship with his mother and his mother's best friend and her family. *"And then mum's friend Tina and that they threatened to punch me in the mouth and that and I had enough of it cause it was all the time so I ended up saying to dad I want to live with you"* (Jake, learning conversation, 26/11/12 [November 26th, 2012]). His mother and her friend seem to have been negative aspects of his educational lifeworld, and may have actually damaged many of his connections to his identity as an Aboriginal person. This may be because of their limited cultural understandings and their assumption of an identity with a universal or homogenous 'Aboriginal' culture. His mother seems to be at the root of many of the abusive and dangerous situations that he had to endure, and attributed most of Jake's misfortunes to being discriminated against because he was Aboriginal.

Within Jake's educational lifeworld his experiences of Indigenous and non-Indigenous education seem to be in direct competition. His experiences with his mother and the cultural learning with her, place no value on formal (Western) education, whilst his experiences with formal (Western) education do not seem to acknowledge or value his Aboriginality.

Todd

The two photographs that Todd discussed with me were historical or pre-existing photographs, in that instead of using a camera to go out and capture aspects of his educational lifeworld specific to this project, Todd chose to use photographs and artefacts that he already possessed to represent it. His photographs were taken on a trip he recently took back to where he grew up. These two photographs are symbolic photographs, in that he wanted to capture his connection to country and nature and the impact that this has had during his life. *"I have always felt a connection to the land and what some people would deem as nothing I've connected to it, like especially water. Anywhere near the water I feel closer and home so to speak"* (Todd, learning conversation, 22/8/12 [August 22nd, 2012]). Both images he chose depicted scenes of tranquillity, water and trees. Todd spoke about how important the land was to him and his entire family, and of his special connection to water. He made a link between his connection to the water and being able to control and calm his aggressive tendencies during periods of formal education. This was something that was not shared with staff or students at his secondary school, as the ability to have somewhere to collect himself was more important to him than was a concern to ensure his behaviour adhered strictly to school policy.

These photographs stimulated discussions about his family, and how his three brothers and himself were all connected to the land in various capacities, and how being brought up in a proud Aboriginal family that has always been focused on equal rights and education had an enormous impact on his experience in formal schooling as well as his decision to pursue a career within Indigenous education and social justice. *"Pretty much following in the family footsteps in the way of advocating for Aboriginal people. My grandmother is a foundation member of the New South Wales Aboriginal Education Consultancy Group. My dad worked in Aboriginal education, my auntie works at Aboriginal housing head office, so does my cousin. Another cousin of mine, she works at Centrelink as an Aboriginal worker. Her father, my uncle, works at juvenile justice in Wagga as a teacher, teaching mechanics and stuff like that. So I've always had it surrounding me and constantly"* (Todd, learning conversation, 22/8/12 [August 22nd, 2012]). Even though he had issues with anger management at school he was provided with a framework within his family that contradicted the discourse of uneducability, and he was able to make the conscious decision to avoid jail and unemployment and pursue TAFE and university degrees and a career using his experiences to influence Indigenous school students.

In comparing the two sets of photographs—Todd's and Jake's—one of the greatest differences between the photographs that these two participants discussed at such great length was the type of photographs they chose. To help explain their educational lifeworlds, Todd chose symbolic photographs while Jake chose a literal photograph. This may be attributable to the age difference in the two participants and their stage of visual maturity.

Both participants spoke about the influence their families had on their educational lifeworlds. Both Jake and Todd came from families that had separated when they were quite young, and both had one parent who was Indigenous and one who was not, but the cultural and political education that they received within their families was extremely different. Jake has a very limited understanding of his particular Aboriginal culture and will sometimes refer to Indigenous people in seemingly derogatory ways, whilst Todd has been raised by people who are very proud and knowledgeable about their culture. Although both participants have had difficult experiences with formal education and at times faced the labels associated with Aboriginal and Torres Strait Islander students, both have tried to overcome that and re-enter the formal-education setting. For Todd, this has been because of the support and strength of his Aboriginal family, whilst for Jake, it is in spite of his mother actively trying to separate him from the formal schooling system.

Todd spoke at length about his connection to country and particularly water, whilst Jake did not mention these at all. Once again, this might be due to the difference in cultural learning that both participants have experienced within their homes and communities.

Both participants spoke about their experiences with formal education and their position as an outsider, either as someone, like Todd, who had an issue with authority, or like Jake, as someone who has spent many years outside the formal-education system. Both participants have been classified as possibly uneducable and disengaged, but within this project, they were very enthusiastic and eager to participate and use new technologies to discuss their learning with me. Jake was particularly passionate about using the camera to capture aspects of his lifeworld and took large quantities of photographs. It is interesting that despite their experiences in the school setting that both participants still want to participate in the largely Western system, with Jake now transitioning to full-time high-school studies, and Todd working as an Indigenous Education Worker in State secondary schools.

Conclusion: Working With Australian Aboriginal Youth—Lessons From Our Experience

This exploration of indigenous youths' engagement with their wider educational lifeworlds proceeded from three basic presumptions: One, that youth are not only consumers but are also active producers of knowledge (Lankshear & Knobel, 2006); two, that young people typically are or want to be engaged in the construction, analysis, and re-making of their worlds; and three, that there were culturally relevant and respectful ways that indigenous youth might demonstrate these things.

Our experience in this project has led us to re-consider certain facets of our work with Australian Aboriginal youth, and to extract points of enhancement for future engagements. First, the importance of non-indigenous researchers collaborating with a trusted, active, visible, and passionate cultural advisor cannot be overestimated. Without such input to our work, we would have been unlikely to secure the confidence of the local Elders group who endorsed the project, and we would certainly not have navigated the uncertainties borne of ignorance when it came to working with and within unspoken, local cultural protocols. We believe that our open acknowledgement that we were looking to understand things we clearly had little personal knowledge of contributed to the way the project assumed a far more dialogic form. Our repeated insistence on securing appropriate advice from the project's cultural advisors clearly contributed to the development of a relationship with the participants that was based on a collaborative ethos. This is crucial for the success and integrity of any research, but particularly so when non-indigenous researchers are involved with indigenous communities. In this project, it was quite easy to see how information, teaching, and learning were passing in a two-way manner, and the more the young people involved recognised that their knowledge was being valued, the more connected they seemed to be with the overall project.

A related point we have taken from this experience is the value in retaining flexibility in research design and practice. For example, in this case, when the Aboriginal youth involved here felt confidence in the respect being accorded their individual knowledge and interests, they extended the project work or took it in directions that were not initially in the view of the research team. Jake's decision to photograph his father is one example of the perceived agency of the participants to shape aspects of the project in ways they saw appropriate. While we have not dealt in any real depth with the nature and extent of the yarning that took place around this particular photograph, it was considerable, complex, and enlightening. Had Jake not felt the "freedom" to interpret the research activity in his idiosyncratic way, it is doubtful the conversations had with him would have flowed as freely or as intimately.

The importance of family in Australian Aboriginal communities was evident in the research activities, and a number of the more significant (to the research team) engagements occurred when any of the youth participants talked about their photographs with others in their family or kinship group. A development of the methodologies here would see us taking the visual research activities out of individual and into group compositional forms. While the photograph in and of itself is central to project work like this with young Aboriginal people, we suspect that the more long-term impact is to be found in the conversations at home with family triggered by the act of visual researching.

We found that the visual medium employed here allowed the participants to talk about the "wordless." In Todd's case, for instance, the silencing of his voice through his experiences at school has been overturned by his ability to speak to his connections to land, culture, and family through the photographic representations of these things that he entered into the project's evidentiary base. Todd's part of this project provides an excellent example of the power of photographic data to carry and not merely illustrate a case, and in the powerfully (almost blindingly) visual environment that sustains contemporary youth cultures, the opportunity to sit and look, feel, smell, and taste the essence of these images becomes urgent. In many ways, what Todd has done with his more evocatively symbolic image-making comes close to what Sarah Pink (2009) has called sensory ethnography.

Finally, as non-indigenous researchers working with Australian Aboriginal youth, we have experienced first-hand the benefits of demonstrating what George Yancy (2013) has termed "epistemic humility"—of being part of a project where we perhaps came close to "losing our way," to not "feeling at home" epistemologically and methodologically. We were mindful of the potential for our work at the time and in later iterations of it to unthinkingly perpetuate the forms of (neo)colonial violence that the project had set out to expose and deride. Engaging in more collaborative, democratized, and dialogic relationships—while not suggesting these were easily established or sophisticated in their nature—kept us conscious of the need to check our Whiteness at the door.

At this point in the development of our work with young Australian Aboriginal people, we believe the three presumptions that underpinned the project at the beginning were and continue to be powerfully accurate ones.

Acknowledgment

We acknowledge the traditional custodians of the land on which we have conducted the research on which this chapter has been based, the Jarowair and Giabal people of what is now known as the Toowoomba region of Queensland, Australia.

References

Austin, J., & Hickey, A. (2009). Working visually in community identity ethnography. *International Journal of the Humanities, 7*(4), 1–14.

Austin, J., & Hickey, A. (2011). *Indigenizing the research process: Unravelling epistemic and methodological privilege.* Paper presented at the Association of Qualitative Research/Discourse, Power, Resistance 'Down Under' conference: Will the Real Evidence Please Stand Up?: Politicising Qualitative Research, Cairns, Queensland, Australia.

Austin, J., & Williams-Mozley, J. (2012, June). *An alternative view of mixed methods research: Learning with and from Indigenous ways of knowing.* Paper presented at the International Indigenous Development Research conference 2012, Auckland, Aotearoa, New Zealand.

Bessarab, D., & Ng'andu, B. (2010). Yarning about yarning as a legitimate method in Indigenous research. *International Journal of Critical Indigenous Studies, 3*(1), 37–50.

Carrello, C. (2009). Yarning—Aboriginal people's way of doing business. *Journal of Aboriginal Health, 4,* 3.

Connell, R. (2007). *Southern theory: The global dynamics of knowledge in social science.* Crows Nest, NSW, Australia: Allen & Unwin.

Denzin, N. K. (2010). Moments, mixed methods, and paradigm dialogs. *Qualitative Inquiry, 16*(6), 419–427. doi: 10.1177/1077800410364608

Giroux, H. A. (2013). *America's education deficit and the war on youth: Reform beyond electoral politics.* New York, NY: Monthly Review Press.

Harper, D. (2005). What's new visually? In N. K. Denzin & Y. Lincoln (Eds.), *The Sage handbook of qualitative research* (3rd ed., pp. 747–762). Thousand Oaks, CA: Sage.

Kincheloe, J. (2005). On to the next level: Continuing the conceptualization of the bricolage. *Qualitative Inquiry, 11*(3), 323–350.

Lankshear, C., & Knobel, M. (2006). *New literacies.* London, UK: Open University Press.

Lather, P. (2007). *Getting lost: Feminist efforts toward a double(d) science.* Albany, NY: State University of New York Press.

Lavallée, L. F. (2009). Practical application of an Indigenous research framework and two qualitative Indigenous research methods: Sharing circles and Anishnaabe symbol-based reflection. *International Journal of Qualitative Methods, 8*(1), 21–40.

McCarthy, D. (2013, May 24). Community consultation meeting. St Patrick's Cathedral Centre, Toowoomba, Australia.

Mertens, D. M. (2010). Transformative mixed methods research. *Qualitative Inquiry, 16*(6), 469–474. doi: 10.1177/1077800410364612

Ministerial Council for Education, Early Childhood Development and Youth Affairs. (2010). *Aboriginal and Torres Strait Islander education action plan 2010–2014.* Carlton South, Victoria, Australia: Author.

Nakata, M. (2007). *Disciplining the savages, savaging the disciplines.* Canberra, Australia: Aboriginal Studies Press.

Pink, S. (2004a). *Conversing anthropologically: Hypermedia as anthropological text.* In S. Pink, L. Kürti, & A. I. Afonso (Eds.), *Working images: Visual research and representation in ethnography* (pp. 164–181). London, UK: Routledge.

Pink, S. (2004b). *Introduction: Situating visual research.* In S. Pink, L. Kürti, & A. I. Afonso (Eds.), *Working images: Visual research and representation in ethnography* (pp. 1–10). London, UK: Routledge.

Pink, S. (2006). *The future of visual ethnography: Engaging the senses.* London, UK: Routledge.

Pink, S. (2007). *Doing visual ethnography: Images, media and representation in research* (2nd ed.). London, UK: Sage.

Pink, S. (2009). *Doing sensory ethnography.* London, UK: Sage.

Pink, S., Kürti, L., & Afonso, A. I. (Eds.). (2004). *Working images: Visual research and representation in ethnography.* London, UK: Routledge.

Power, K. M. (2004). Yarning: A responsive research methodology. *Journal of Australian Research in Early Childhood Education, 11*(1), 37–46.

Prosser, J. (2011). Visual methodology: Toward a more seeing research. In N. K. Denzin & Y. S. Lincoln (Eds.), *The Sage handbook of qualitative research* (4th ed., pp. 479–496). Thousand Oaks, CA: Sage.

Sharp, H. (2010). *Constructing history: Selective representations of Indigenous Australians and British heritages in Queensland history curriculum* (Unpublished doctoral dissertation). University of Southern Queensland, Queensland, Australia.

Smith, L. T. (1999). *Decolonizing methodologies: Research and Indigenous peoples.* London, UK: Zed Books.

Steinberg, S. (2012). Critical cultural studies research: Bricolage in action. In S. R. Steinberg & G. S. Cannella (Eds.), *Critical qualitative research reader* (pp. 182–197). New York, NY: Peter Lang.

Wang, C., & Burris, M. A. (1994). Empowerment through photo novella: Portraits of participation. *Health Education & Behavior, 21*(2), 171–186. doi: 10.1177/109019819402100204

Yancy, G. (2013). *Whiteness as normative: The Black body as a problem.* Paper presented at the Indigenous Studies Research Network Seminar Series, Queensland University of Technology, Kelvin Grove campus, Brisbane, Australia.

CHAPTER 12

'It Gets Better'

Queer Youth and the History of the "Problem of the Homosexual" in Public Education

Dennis Carlson

The "It Gets Better" campaign organized by LGBT activist, Daniel Savage, in 2010 in the wake of a series of well-publicized suicides of gay teens, consisted of a series of short YouTube videos by well-known gay or gay-friendly adults, including President Obama—all affirming that bullying was developmentally limited to childhood and adolescence, and to the space of schooling (Savage & Miller, 2011). According to the project's website, it "was created to show young LGBT people the level of happiness, potential, and positivity their lives will reach—if they can just get through their teen years." As Tina Majkowski (2011) has argued, the unfortunate message of the "It Gets Better" campaign is that queer youth just need to put up with the bullying and harassment for now, knowing that everything will be great once they are adults (p. 164). The "It Gets Better" campaign also forgets that most bullying occurs in schools or around schools, and that the bullying of LGBT youth is not just a "natural phase" they will outgrow. It is the result of being "schooled" to homophobia in a heteronormative school culture that actively encourages bullying, even when school leaders point with pride to zero-tolerance policies and anti-bullying workshops for teachers. Public schools continue to be primary institutions for the reproduction of heteronormativity, an ethos in which it is assumed everyone is or should be exclusively heterosexual, and where "deviants" are made invisible and unwelcome through stigmatization and exclusion practices. Most public schools in the US, in spite of great change on the "outside," continue to have a *habitus*—Bourdieu's (1984) term for the habits and rules of everyday life, and what is "thinkable" within a cultural site—that is deeply heteronormative and homophobic.

When W.E.B. Du Bois (1903/2009, p. 2) famously asked, "how does it feel to be a problem?" he was referring to the much-researched "Negro problem" in American society, and the tendency of White social scientists to define African Americans as "problems," without recognizing or acknowledging the social construction of the problem and supposedly "objective" scientific research as actually part of a culture of invisible Whiteness, which was, in fact, part of the problem of White racism in America. Understandably, African Americans have reframed the problem as a problem they have, as a problem of taken-for-granted White racism. Much the same, I believe, can be said about the "problem of the homosexual," as it historically has been constructed within modern, professional education discourse and practice, as a health problem, to be assigned to health educators, and more specifically, sex educators.

In this chapter, I review some of the findings from a history of the "problem of the homosexual" in professional educational discourse and the mass media since 1950, as part of a broader study of the history of the "problem" of adolescent sexuality in education (Carlson, 2012).While the mid-20th century was a time in which Kinsey and his associates began to challenge puritanical and moralistic sexual and gender norms, including homosexuality, public schools were spaces of "life adjustment" and "family life education," where young men and women were taught very conforming gender and sexual roles, and where health educators invoked pseudo-scientific psychoanalytic and psychological theories to instill fear of homosexuals and homosexuality, including the fear that homosexuality was contagious. It was not until the 1970s that more enlightened viewpoints entered the health-education curriculum in response to mounting pressure from lesbian and gay rights groups and many professional health educators. The response, however, was most often to adopt a "values clarification" curriculum that at best taught tolerance for homosexuals, and at worst helped young people rationalize their preexisting biases against lesbians and gay men. The AIDS/HIV crisis of the 1980s resulted in reasserting the old connection between homosexuality, sickness, contagion, and sin, along with the trope that separated "innocent" victims from supposedly non-innocent victims. By the mid-1990s, partly in response to public fear mobilized in response to the AIDS/HIV crisis, Christian conservative movements successfully lobbied Congress to fund "abstinence in preparation for marriage" sex-education programs only, in which the sexuality of queer youth was erased and made invisible. I conclude by briefly addressing encouraging signs that public schools are finally beginning to take on homophobia and the bullying of LGBTQ youth, but caution that so long as anti-bullying initiatives individualize the problem and fail to see how homophobia and bullying are ritualized in the *habitus* of the school, things will not get better for queer youth.

"Family Life" Education and the Problem of the Homosexual: 1950–1970

The second half of the 20th century began with the emergence of a new discourse on human sexuality that would radically challenge the prevailing presumption among professional educators and much of the public that homosexuality was "unnatural," and that homosexuals were psychologically "maladjusted." The publication within several years of each other of two books by Alfred Kinsey (1948, 1953) and his associates at the Institute for Sexual Research at Indiana University—*Sexual Behavior in the Human Male* and *Sexual Behavior in the Human Female*—would change everything, although the perspective represented by Kinsey and his associates was still a distinctly minority viewpoint. His research was, and still is, the most extensive interview study of human sexuality ever undertaken, and although the representativeness of his interview sample has been questioned, no one could question the overall findings. Those findings later would be cited by lesbian and gay rights advocates to suggest that approximately ten percent of the population is exclusively homosexual or gay. But Kinsey himself avoided labeling people homosexual or heterosexual, gay or straight. Instead, his interview data led him to reject the sexual identity binary of the modern era as reflecting the reality of people's sexual lives—something that is more consistent with recent perspectives associated with queer studies. He found that 46% of his male subjects had "reacted" sexually to both males and females as adults, and 37% had at least one homosexual experience. Almost 12% of males were rated as being equally heterosexual and homosexual in their experiences and responses; and about 10% were "more or less exclusively homosexual for at least three years." For females, seven percent were rated equally hetero-homo in behaviors and responses, and somewhere between two and six percent were exclusively homosexual. What was clear, and could not easily be avoided, was that homosexuality was a "normal" part of many "normal" peoples' lives, and that exclusive homosexuals also seemed as well-adjusted and happy as exclusive heterosexuals. Of course, it was also clear that such a conclusion would come under attack in the homophobic and heteronormative culture of the early 1950s. On August 30, 1953, Representative Louis Heller, Democrat of Brooklyn, argued before his Congressional colleagues that Kinsey's studies had the effect of "contributing to the depravity of a whole generation, to the loss of faith in human dignity and human decency, [and] to the spread of juvenile delinquency" (*The New York Times*, 1953).

Those who opposed the acceptance of homosexuals and homosexuality as "normal" often relied on religious convictions. However, among professional educators and political leaders, appeals to religious beliefs were generally clothed in a secular and even scientific discourse. The reigning, "normal" science of the early 1950s, at least when it came to human sexuality, was guided by a variation of psychoanalytic theory, grounded in a very conventional interpretation of a Freudian developmental theory, in which the individual moves in the direction of a "mature," "responsible" adulthood, within the framework of a patriarchal, exclusively heterosexual family in which gender roles are clearly differentiated. Anyone who deviated from this expected path of development was presumed to be suffering from psychological disorders, and adolescence was understood as a stage in development in which young people were most likely to become sexual and gender "deviants," who deviate. Ultimately, the problem of the homosexual was blamed on confusing gender roles in the home. But homosexuality, like other problems of sexual adjustment, was also blamed on the persistence of Victorian taboos against talking about sex within the family, or viewing even "normal" sexuality as "dirty" or immoral. The modern, "family life" approach was to talk openly about sexual development with students and their parents so that fears and misunderstandings could be addressed. This was the approach supported by the prestigious Child Study Association (1954) in *What to Tell Your Children About Sex*. The professional experts spoke with one voice in the volume, to encourage parents to help foster their child's "normal development, his later adjustment to the opposite sex, and his ultimate happiness." Everything was at stake, it would appear, in making sure nothing went wrong in "his" (referring to both boys' and girls') "normal" psychosexual development. The problem was that parents, raised in an earlier era, too often "feel strangely uncomfortable, hesitant and inhibited when speaking of sex." Because "sex talk was taboo" when they were growing up, sex educators could help them learn how to talk frankly and openly about what was once taboo but was now to be the subject of an elaborate familial discourse (p. v). In this discourse, according to the text, there must be room to talk about how "natural human sexual functions are sometimes perverted .... No longer is discussion of this subject taboo in the modern home." By understanding the problem better, parents could lessen fears about "the problems of the seamy side of life" (p. 95).

If professional health and sex educators held out little hope for the successful treatment of "committed homosexuals," they did offer hope for adolescents who were not yet committed to the "homosexual lifestyle." In *New Ways in Sex Education: A Guide for Parents and Teachers*, by noted sex educator Dorothy Baruch (1959), the committed homosexual is identified as someone who "stopped in their growing up" (p. 24). But for the un-committed, the "latent homosexuals," if they were identified and counseled in adolescence, and if they were kept from being exposed to "committed homosexuals," the hope was that they might grow out of it. If not, they may become latent homosexuals for life, a condition that results when "so much of the person's emotions stay focused unconsciously on the same sex that not enough of the sex urge is free to attach itself to members of the opposite sex" (p. 219). Like the character, Brick, in Tennessee Williams's *Cat on a Hot Tin Roof*, whose emotional attachment to a buddy from high school supposedly kept him from growing up and sexually satisfying his wife, latent homosexuals were presumed to be chronically unhappy and hurt others.

This controlling psychoanalytic image of the disturbed, chronically unhappy, immature, and selfish homosexual became part of a commonsense, "modern" perspective that was widely circulated in the mass media as well. Homosexuality was not so much a sin as a sickness, and one that was probably contagious. In a front-page editorial in *The New York Times* (1963) titled, "Growth of Overt

Homosexuality in City Provokes Wide Concern," the concern was that tourists, particularly parents with children, would stay away from the city because they did not want to have to be exposed to homosexuals. Recently, in looking back from the vantage point of history, the *Times* felt compelled to offer an apology of sorts. "The article's language, from sources and reporter alike, is outdated at best, derogatory at worst, and many of its assumptions and assertions are long discredited" (*The New York Times*, 2009). The *Times* acknowledged that its 1963 article drew heavily on a study of gay men seeking treatment for their "disorder" by a Dr. Irving Bieber, an influential psychotherapist who believed homosexuality could be "cured," who had now been discredited. Bieber had been the primary "expert" cited in the 1963 articles, and had been quoted to the effect that public acceptance of homosexuals was encouraged when instead of taking a moralistic attitude of condemnation people learned to think of "homosexuality as an illness." Moralistic condemnation might only encourage some rebellious youth to embrace the homosexual lifestyle, so that a reduction in "manifestations of hostility" toward homosexuals is likely to lead to "a gradual, important reduction in the incidence of homosexuality." That is, once homosexuals were understood as sick people who needed medical help, "normal" people could begin to replace hostility with sympathy. Treatment for homosexuals, according to Bieber, must proceed from a scientific analysis of causation, and there was now strong evidence that "a constructive, supportive, warmly related father precludes the possibility of a homosexual son" (*The New York Times*, 1963). The family, particularly the absent father and overly protective mother, were to blame, not the poor homosexual. From such a perspective, the homosexual, by definition, represented a failure in normal gender development.

According to the 1963 *Times* article, while many homosexuals "dream of forming a permanent attachment" to one other person, to give them some sense of "social and emotional stability," the "emotional instability that is inherent in many homosexuals" makes this impossible. Homosexual relationships inevitably flounder on "jealousy and personality clashes." It becomes important to establish that the homosexual cannot be happy, for if that were possible, even thinkable, then the whole theory of the neurotic, developmentally stunted homosexual could be called into question. There can be no happiness for the homosexual, only fleeting acts of sexual pleasure. The *Times'* words in 1963 were eerily similar to those used by Mike Wallace several years later in a CBS Reports (1967) documentary on "The Homosexuals," in which he would report:

> most Americans are repelled by the mere notion of homosexuality …. The average homosexual is promiscuous and not interested in or capable of a lasting relationship like that of a heterosexual marriage. His love life consists of a series of chance encounters at the bars he inhabits.

A psychiatrist, who just happened to be the same Dr. Bieber the *Times* quoted, was then asked by Wallace if he thinks that homosexuals can be happy, to which he replied: "the fact that someone is a homosexual … automatically rules out the possibility that he will remain happy for long." The unhappiness of homosexuals and other "deviates" is once more laid at their own feet (Ring, 2012).

The *Times'* 1963 editorial also relied heavily on a theory of "borderline" cases, adolescents who might be swayed either way—toward a homosexual lifestyle or a "normal" heterosexual adjustment. According to the editorial,"strict enforcement of the law against seduction of minors is important to protect borderline cases from adult influences that could swing them toward homosexual orientation when heterosexual adjustment was still possible." The article concluded by addressing the question of how tourists might minimize their contact with homosexuals (who, according to the article, are also known as "inverts" and "deviates") when visiting the city. According to the *Times*, "inverts are to be found in every conceivable line of work," so it is difficult to avoid them entirely. But they are "most concentrated—or most noticeable" in the fields of the creative and performing arts and in industries serving "women's beauty and fashion needs." Furthermore, just as homosexuals claim that they can identify each other through eye contact, so "most normal persons believe they have a similar facility in spotting deviates." The message to parents was to rely on your intuition. If someone looks homosexual, assume they are, and keep your children away. In this one editorial, it is possible to see a common "commonsense," a unifying and largely taken-for-granted discourse on the "problem of the homosexual" that circulated in the mass media as well as in health education.

The Normalization of the Homosexual: 1970s and 1980s

The commonsense narration of the "problem of the homosexual" in terms of psychological disorder, a failure to develop "normally," and contagion was so hegemonic and pervasive throughout the 1950s and 1960s that it was almost like the air people breathed, or, more accurately, the smog they breathed, obscuring reality. However, the 1960s were also a time of great cultural change, accompanied by the emergence of new counter-discourses and movements of the subaltern, including lesbians and gay men. The emergence of the modern lesbian and gay rights movement in the late 1960s in the US would finally begin to reframe the problem and cut through this hegemonic commonsense, resulting (by the late 1970s) in a rather dramatic discursive shift in the definition of the problem of the homosexual, both among professional health educators and in the mass media. The "homosexual" had been an invention of the medical and psychiatric establishment, so the homosexual had to be reborn as gay, through acts of self-naming and self-affirmation. The lesbian and gay rights movement transformed the problem of the homosexual into a problem of the unequal treatment of lesbians and gay men, the denial of their civil rights, and their victimization within a homophobic culture. Between the Stonewall Riots in New York City in August 1968—the symbolic beginning of the modern lesbian and gay rights movement—and the declassification of homosexuality as a disorder by the American Psychiatric Association in 1973, and by the American Psychological Association in 1975, a seachange would occur in public attitudes about gay people, although a great schism also would be opened up in American culture between those on the side of the lesbian and gay rights movement and those on a growing Christian right who wanted health educators to return to teaching that homosexuality was a perversion and inconsistent with "healthy" family values and lifestyles.

In this culture war, professional health educators slowly began to take sides against the rise of a reactive homophobia on the political right. By the late 1960s, the Sexual Information and Education Council of the United States (SIECUS) had established itself as the new counter-discourse in sex education and health education, one that promised a scientific, value-neutral study of the facts of human and adolescent sexuality, without moralizing or judgment. No science is without its values, however, and SIECUS' values verged on the libertine, at least compared to those of family-life education. SIECUS argued that young people were sexual beings and had rights to sexual lives and access to factual, unbiased information about sexuality so that they could make their own decisions. It preached acceptance, or at least tolerance, of homosexuals, and affirmed that homosexuality has existed throughout human history and is thus natural rather than a perversion, and it supported the idea that homosexuals had rights that needed to be protected and respected in educational institutions.

Meanwhile, the leadership of the American Psychiatric Association and the American Psychological Association was still heavily invested in a psychoanalytic theory of adjustment to traditional gender and sexual roles in which the homosexual was understood to be a failure and riddled with "disorders." This would prove to be an untenable position in an age of lesbian and gay rights. As more lesbian and gay men "came out" publicly or to their family and friends, the myth of the maladjusted homosexual became harder to sustain. And questions were raised about why some homosexuals seemed maladjusted. Were they supposed to "adjust" to a culture that stigmatized and excluded them? Was their failure to adjust the result of internalized oppression and the effects of living in a homophobic environment? Slowly, the framing of the problem began to shift. In the early 1970s, the conventions of the American Psychiatric Association and the American Psychological Association were picketed by lesbian and gay rights supporters, and leadership of the associations faced mounting pressure from within the ranks to change. Lesbian and gay psychiatrists and psychologists mobilized, and began to work effectively to gather support for a resolution to declassify homosexuality as a psychological disorder. At the 1972 convention of the American Psychiatric Association, a gay member was granted permission to address the convention in support of the declassification resolution, although to protect his professional identity, he was not named and wore a mask. By the next year, the masks would come off when the organization rather quickly and rather quietly passed a resolution declassifying homosexuality as a disorder, followed by the American Psychological Association in 1975. Both associations adopted new sets of criteria for defining psychological discourses so that a disorder now had to "regularly cause distress," and "interfere with social effectiveness." Since there was no evidence that non-patient homosexuals suffered from either of these conditions, homosexuality was declassified as a disorder.

Throughout the 1970s and much of the 1980s, sex and health education texts tried to please both sides in the dispute, in effect having it both ways—through a "values clarification" discourse. Teachers were encouraged to present the "facts" and then facilitate a discussion of homosexuality and other controversial topics such as abortion and birth control without interjecting their own values. An article in *Educational Leadership* (Megenity, Megenity, & Barnum, 1973) framed sex education in terms of avoiding the "debate ... about *what* should be taught, [and] *when* the teaching should take place" (p. 26), focusing on "cognitive information" when needed, and on the clarification of "affective domain" values when needed (p. 26). In a sex-education workshop for parents offered as an example, participants were asked to make individual decisions about controversial issues. The instructor began with "Fairly easy decisions such as asking for positions on capital punishment" (p. 28). This was, at that point, still a question often raised and debated in social studies and civics classes. But this "easy" decision was to be followed by taking a position on "legalizing abortions, premarital sex, extramarital sex, homosexuality, masturbation, and sex crimes" (p. 28). This is an odd assortment of crimes and misdemeanors of a sexual nature in the eyes of "normal" society; and if homosexuality may be subcategorized with masturbation as a misdemeanor, it might also be subcategorized with sex crimes. The very placement of homosexuality in this unnamed category of crimes and misdemeanors was itself a decision, and one with consequences for how the participants framed their own decisionmaking. A second activity designed to make participants more comfortable with homosexuals and homosexuality involved viewing "two fully-clothed women embracing, or of one man kissing another on the cheek" (p. 29). Participants were then asked to complete a checklist to reveal how they felt about the pictures, which then provided a basis for small-group discussion. The hope was that "participants [would] become [more] aware of mental and emotional barriers" (p. 29) to "accepting a multiplicity of human sexual behaviors" (p. 29). But the activity needed not be framed as an activity about homosexuality at all, so it is hard to see how it necessarily promoted accepting sexual diversity. What it may have promoted is a bit more comfort in touching someone of the same gender. On the other hand, because it associated homosexuality with touching someone of the same gender, it may have had the opposite effect, of discouraging same-gender contact and reinforcing homophobic fears. Value clarification ironically often ended up accepting and even reinforcing participants' "own" values and interpretations, even when they were homophobic.

By the end of the 1970s, there were signs that health educators and sex educators were ready to move beyond value neutrality to taking sides in the public battle over the normality of gay youth. A groundbreaking text in this regard was *Sex Education: Theory and Practice* (Bruess & Greenberg, 1981), by authors affiliated with the National Center for Health Education. The text incorporated values clarification activities, but used these activities to promote acceptance of homosexuals as about ten percent of the population, and "as individuals with the same rights, responsibilities, and feelings as the other 90 percent." This discourse of homosexual sameness is grounded on the debunking of dominant myths,

> that homosexuals look a lot different than other people. … that homosexual males are effeminate and weak while homosexual females are masculine and physically strong …. that homosexuals lurk at every street corner waiting to pounce on innocent children and seduce them into a life of homosexuality. … [and] that homosexuals obtained their sexual preference because of problems in their early family relationships. (Bruess & Greenberg, 1981, p. 172)

The discourse of homosexual sameness included the facts that physiologically, "homosexuals respond exactly as heterosexuals do … [and] homosexuals are as amenable to treatment for sexual inadequacy as heterosexuals." The text even stated that evidence supports the contention that "among established couples, homosexuals get more pleasure from lovemaking" (Bruess & Greenberg, 1981, pp. 172–173). The homosexual as a social and personal problem had largely vanished in sex-education texts by the end of the 1970s, to be replaced with the problem of heterosexual prejudice. But the "homosexual" was still the preferred category of identification in health education, rather than lesbian and gay youth, but the long era of pathologizing homosexuality and the homosexual had apparently ended and a new era of acceptance had begun. I say "apparently," because the liberal views espoused by health and sex educators in professional journals did not necessarily translate into pedagogical practice in schools, where the culture of heteronormativity was still largely unquestioned and policed daily through bullying practices and other forms of harassment of queer youth. Furthermore, the controlling image of the homosexual, particularly the male homosexual, as sick, sinful, and contagious would resurface with a vengeance in the 1980s with the AIDS/HIV epidemic. At the same time, the AIDS/HIV crisis would provide an opportunity to challenge old stereotypes and reframe the conversation about who owns the problem, as AIDS activists repositioned it as a problem of social stigmatization and homophobia.

From AIDS/HIV Education to Abstinence-Only Education

In June, 1981, the first cases of what the Center for Disease Control (CDC) initially called "GRID," for Gay-Related Immune Deficiency, began to appear in the US, and already it was a term that carried as much implicit, hidden, subliminal meaning as it did clinical, medical meaning. Language has a "hidden curriculum" to it, teaching us both more and less than what it appears to. The clinical marker, GRID, seemed logical enough, since it was designed to capture those aspects of the disease most recognizable, that make it stand out and announce itself as a threat—its emergence within the gay male communities of New York City and San Francisco. Patients were dying of opportunistic infections their bodies should have resisted, and early newspaper reports called it the "Gay Cancer." The CDC's rush to label the disease as GRID was an attempt to be more accurate, but also counter some of the antigay prejudice being stirred up in the media around fear of a Gay Cancer. But "Gay-Related" was not much of an improvement; and gay rights leaders pressured the CDC to come up with a better designation for the disease, one that did not associate the disease with being gay. When the CDC finally settled on "Acquired Immune Deficiency Syndrome" (AIDS), it seemed to remove any politics from a clinical naming process. As Carol Reeves (1999) observed in her history of the language of science, the term, *acquired*, indicated that the disease was not the result of being gay *per se*. The disease was acquired through individual behavior. At the same time, the word, *acquired*, carried an additional meaning, that of behavior causing infection "that placed blame on the infected for 'acquiring' the disease in the first place." For these reasons, the CDC, since the mid-1990s, has encouraged a shift toward a language of AIDS/HIV, or just HIV, which is designed to erase all negative connotations (p. 16). AIDS education has thus slowly evolved into HIV education. Through this naming and renaming (Gay Cancer, GRID, AIDS/HIV, PWA (People with AIDS)), the AIDS crisis has helped us understand that the "truth" about a disease is as much social-constructed as it is medical. It might have once been possible to see language as just a neutral lens for revealing a "truth" already out there. The AIDS crisis and the national response to it demonstrated the power of language to produce what people see and feel when they look into the face of AIDS. Treating the immuno-suppressive disease was one thing. Treating the social disorder—the fear of the new plague and of those groups and individuals perceived to be its carriers—was another.

The Reagan Administration pursued a two-sided (some would say two-faced) educational response to the AIDS catastrophe. On one side of the issue within the Reagan Administration was William Bennett, who served as Chairman of the National Endowment for the Humanities from 1981–1985, when he became Education Secretary, a post he held until 1988. But Bennett was not alone as the voice of religious conservatism in the administration. He formed powerful allies with Gary Bauer, then a domestic affairs advisor to the president (later to lead the conservative Family Research Council and Focus on the Family), and Patrick Buchanan, the president's communication director. Together, they called for sex education grounded in the teaching of traditional "family values" and moral virtues. Theirs would turn out to be the more powerful and persuasive voice within the administration, particularly since it was consistent with the Republican Party's Christian Right constituency that could no longer be ignored. After Bennett resigned his post as Education Secretary to become drug czar in the new Bush administration, Bennett and Bauer (1989) published a booklet, *What You Need to Know About AIDS*, which sought to reattach sex education to traditional family values, and in opposition to what they called "value relativism" among sex educators. In a time of crisis, there was no time for moral relativism, no "safe sex" outside of monogamous marriage—thereby re-territorializing the language of "safe sex" from a usage that implied caring for the self by taking precautions and using condoms, to a usage that implied learning how to "just say no." As for those "intravenous drug users and male homosexuals" who threatened the "contamination of our nation's blood supply," the only virtuous response, Bennett and Bauer argued, would be to protect the public by quarantining those with AIDS (p. 137). The triumvirate of Bennett, Bauer, and Buchanan also tried to position the battle against AIDS as a battle against the moral degeneracy they associated with the "homosexual agenda and lifestyle." Buchanan had written in his newspaper column before he joined the administration that "the poor homosexuals have declared war on nature and now nature is exacting an awful retribution"(as quoted in Feldman, 1994, p. 164). The language of God's retribution infected public policy throughout the Reagan years, even if it had to be officially framed as a secular discourse. God was punishing not only the homosexual, but also the nation as a whole for its permissive attitudes toward the "homosexual agenda." Meanwhile, the president remained silent—and his silence spoke volumes. The word, *AIDS*, was not even spoken publicly by President Reagan until 1987, at the Third International AIDS Conference held in Washington, DC. Textbook publishers, for their part, did revise health and sex education textbooks to highlight AIDS prevention. Unfortunately, this meant that homosexuality and homosexuals were talked about most often in a chapter on sexually transmitted diseases. By linking the AIDS problem with a new version of the homosexual problem (particularly the problem of the hedonistic, sexually promiscuous, young, urban gay male), these texts probably did more to reinforce and legitimize dominant narratives of gayness than to challenge them.

The AIDS crisis shaped the sexual politics of an era, and by the 1990s it had helped galvanize forces on the Christian Right in a moral crusade against any sex-education curriculum that treated homosexuality as "normal," or that preached "value relativism," or that taught anything other than abstinence. By the mid-1990s, Christian and social-conservative groups had amassed enough political power to do just that—through an amendment to the Welfare Reform Act of 1996 that funded abstinence-only sex-education programs in public schools, including programs organized and delivered by religious-based groups. Indeed, the law mandated teaching that "all sexual activity outside the context of marriage is likely to have harmful psychological and physical effects." Behind these health claims lies a puritanical worldview that emphasizes sex as sin (outside "legitimate," procreative purposes in marriage), and that stigmatizes and marginalizes sexual difference. The new abstinence-only guidelines in sex education meant that schools often contracted with Christian conservative groups, like Sex Respect, to deliver the curriculum through a series of slickly produced videos aimed at teens and accompanying curriculum activities and discussion guides. According to an Applied Research Center report, *Sex, Lies, and Politics* (Burlingame, 1997) the Sex Respect curriculum promoted and legitimated homophobia—in not recognizing homosexual behavior as acceptable in any circumstances, and in linking homosexuality exclusively and inaccurately to HIV/AIDS. In one workbook, according to the report, AIDS is described as "the STD most common among homosexuals and bisexuals." Elsewhere, students learn that AIDS is nature's way of "making some kind of a comment on sexual behavior." Abstinence-only sexuality education was modified under the Obama administration to allow "abstinence plus" programs—programs that still taught that abstinence in preparation for marriage was the goal, but that young people needed to learn about condoms and birth control in case they slipped up occasionally. In either form, the sexuality of queer or LGBT youth was rendered either invisible or (when visible) unhealthy. Indeed, sex education, and health education proved to be very limited discursive spaces for advancing a queer-positive agenda or for fighting homophobia in schools. They were limited by the framing of queer sexuality as a health issue, and, implicitly or explicitly, a health problem; and they were limited by the increasing marginalization of health and sex education in a basic skills and standards-driven curriculum.

Conclusion: Reframing the Problem of Queer Youth

Is this history of the "problem of the homosexual" finally over? Have we finally moved out of this dark past into an enlightened age? Certainly, there is reason to celebrate the progress that has been made over the past half century so that the homophobe and the bully have become the problem rather than the "homosexual." Furthermore, the narrower focus on the "homosexual" has shifted to a broad focus on LGBTQ youth, which indicates a growing awareness of both gender and sexual diversity that cannot be understood in terms of neat, binary oppositions, such as homosexual and heterosexual, or even male and female. Anti-bullying campaigns have, in recent years, re-territorialized the problem of the homosexual, from the field of health education to the field of diversity education and multiculturalism. Schools have rushed to implement anti-bullying staff-development programs and curriculum materials and to adopt tough new "zero tolerance" policies for bullying. These are encouraging signs, but I want to issue a word of caution—that mainstream anti-bullying campaigns may not really reframe the problem as much as they appear to at first glance, and may even perpetuate some of the beliefs and attitudes of the old discourse on the "problem of the homosexual." For example, there is much talk of an "epidemic" of bullying in U.S. public schools affecting millions of young people on a daily basis (Wallace, 2011), as if the bully were a viral infection from outside the school that had suddenly infected an otherwise healthy student body. As in earlier discourses on homosexuality as contagious, or persons with AIDS/HIV as a threat to a healthy school environment, the problem is situated in those infected, in this case, infected with the virus of homophobia. If indeed there has been an increase in bullying, the reasons are more complex. First, more cases of bullying are being reported by victims and their parents who had decided to no longer be silent, but rather to fight back. This is related to the fact that as more queer youth are "out" in their schools, they are more visible targets of bullying. At the same time, many young people—no matter what their sexual identity may be—are resisting normative constructions of gender and what it means to act masculine or feminine, and bullying represents an attempt to police heteronormative performances of gender and sexual identity. The rise in incidents of bullying consequently may be interpreted as a reactive response, a mechanism for putting queer and gender-nonconforming youth "back in their places" and restabilizing the heteronormative school culture.

The emergence of an anti-bullying discourse among educators is encouraging from a democratic progressive perspective, because it represents a recognition that there is a problem, and that something needs to be done about the problem. While there is reason to be hopeful about the new anti-bullying discourses in education and in popular culture, it is ironic that in spite of the new visibility of bullying and naming of homophobia and bullying as a problem, they seem more entrenched in theeveryday life of the school than ever before. Anti-bullying discourses are fundamentally limited in their capacity to affect change to the extent that they: *individualize* bullying by treating it as an act of individual students with psychological adjustment problems; they *naturalize* bullying as a case of "boys being boys"; they *developmentalize* bullying as something boys and girls will naturally outgrow, suggesting that nothing much can be done about it in the meantime (the theme of the "It Gets Better" campaign); and they *sympathize* with the victims of bullying, as weak, suicide-prone youth who need to be protected and saved (Carlson, 2013). For these reasons, mainstream anti-bullying and anti-homophobia discourses may represent the latest, seemingly benign versions of the same old problem: What is to be done with the persistent problem of queer youth in the nation's schools, who keep getting beaten up and harassed and require professional intervention to save them?

To get beyond these discursive blockages requires recognizing homophobia as not merely or even primarily an individual psychological disorder, but as something produced and sustained within what Bourdieu (1984) called the *habitus*. As actors unreflectively participate in the "everydayness" of life, with its rituals and commonsense, they produce and reproduce structures and power relations, according to Bourdieu,"without any deliberate pursuit of coherence … without any conscious concentration" (p. 170). A *habitus* is "an adherence to relations of order which, because they structure inseparably both the real world and the thought world, are accepted as self-evident" (p. 471). This micro-world of everyday life is situated in broader worlds of meaning and action, so that changes in the habitus of school are not easily made. Public educators often are quick to point out that they have to adhere to "community values," and avoid controversies at all cost, so that, unfortunately, they cannot do much to promote LGBTQ rights and awareness. The effect of this has been to construct and sustain a school habitus that has not changed dramatically since the 1950s when it comes to queer youth, their invisibility, stigmatization, and bullying. Public schools in a democratic culture must play a decisive role in promoting social justice, equity, and inclusiveness, and the habitus of the school, as John Dewey well understood, had to be constructed as a deliberately democratic, progressive space, so that when young people became adults they would bring the "habits" of democratic public life they learned in schools into their relations with others. Because most anti-bullying discourses fail to address the need for change in the heteronormative habitus of schooling, they cannot be expected to have a transformative effect (Loutzenheiser & Moore, 2009). There will be the appearance of doing much—mandating studies of bullying, instituting zero-tolerance and counseling programs and staff development, and issuing press releases—but the roots of the problem will not be addressed, and incidents of bullying may be expected to continue to rise. But public education can and should play a leading role in democratic social change by helping young people reflect on the heteronormative rituals and beliefs of their everyday lives in schools and other sites in the community, to reconstruct the habitus of schooling through diverse forms of self-reflection, dialogue, resistance, and collective action. Only then will it get better in public schools for LGBTQ youth.

References

Baruch, D. (1959). *New ways in sex education: A guide for parents and teachers.* New York, NY: McGraw-Hill.

Bennett, W., & Bauer, G. (1989). *What you need to know about AIDS.* Ann Arbor, MI: Servant Books.

Bourdieu, P. (1984). *Distinction: A social critique of the judgment of taste.* London, UK: Routledge.

Bruess, C., & Greenberg, J. (1981). *Sex education: Theory and practice.* Belmont, CA: Wadsworth.

Burlingame, P. (1997) *Sex, lies, and politics: Abstinence-only curricula in California public schools.* Oakland, CA: Applied Research Center.

Carlson, D. (2012). *The education of Eros: A history of education and the 'problem' of adolescent sexuality.* New York, NY: Routledge.

Carlson, D. (2013). The bully curriculum: Gender, sexualities, and the new authoritarian populism in education. In D. Carlson & E. Meyers (Eds.), *Gender and sexualities in education: A reader.* New York, NY: Peter Lang.

CBS Reports. (1967). 'The homosexuals.' Retrieved from http://www.advocate.com/politics/media/2012/04/09/mike-wallace-and-homosexuals

Child Study Association of America. (1954). *What to tell your children about sex*. New York, NY: Duell, Sloan & Pearce.

Du Bois, W. E. B. (2009). *The souls of Black folk*. Washington, DC: Library of America.

Feldman, D. (1994). *Global AIDS policy*. New York, NY: Bergin & Garvey.

Kinsey, A. (1948). *Sexual behavior in the human male*. Philadelphia, PA: W.W. Saunders.

Kinsey, A. (1953). *Sexual behavior in the human female*. Philadelphia, PA: W.W. Saunders.

Loutzenheiser, L., & Moore, S. (2009). Safe schools, sexualities, and critical education. In M. Apple, W. Au, & L. Gandin (Eds.), *The Routledge international handbook of critical education* (pp. 150–162). New York, NY: Routledge.

Majkowski, T. (2011). The 'It Gets Better' campaign: An unfortunate use of queer futurity. *Women and Performance: A Journal of Feminist Theory, 21*(1), 163–165.

Megenity, J., Megenity, J., & Barnum, B. (1973). A workshop in human sexuality for parents. *Educational Leadership* (October), 26–29.

The New York Times. (1953, August 30). Postal ban urged on Kinsey's book. p. 78.

The New York Times. (1963, December 17). Growth of overt homosexuality in city provokes wide concern. p. 1.

The New York Times. (2009, April 12). Word for word: 'Deviates' and 'inverts'. p. WK3.

Reeves, C. (1999). *The language of science*. New York, NY: Routledge.

Ring, T. (2012, April 9). Mike Wallace and The homosexuals. *The Advocate*. Retrieved from http://www.advocate.com/politics/media/2012/04/09/mike-wallace-and-homosexuals.

Savage, M., & Miller, T. (2011). *It gets better: Coming out, overcoming bullying and creating a life worth living*. New York, NY: Dutton.

Wallace, J. (2011). Bullycide in American schools: Forging a comprehensive legislative solution. *Indiana Law Journal, 86*(2), 735–761.

CHAPTER 13

Cross-Cultural Reflections on Gender Diversity in the Earliest Stages of Youth Identity Formation

Cathryn Teasley

This is a critical reflection on two powerful and critical "teaching moments" around gender identity in Early Childhood Education, the aim being to contemplate the role that teachers—as significant social agents—play in this initial context of institutionalized learning, and how such dynamics set the stage for the ongoing development of gender identity in youth as they mature. The two instances occurred in my own classroom practice, which has taken place on both sides of the Atlantic. What impressed me in each case was not only the gender identities and relations present in the respective educational contexts, but the self-revelations regarding my own perspectives on gender as a result of such encounters.

This brief study thus represents an exploration, from standpoints at once personal and cross-cultural, of issues related more specifically to gender ambiguity and *queerness* in two geographically and culturally distant—but in other ways, closely related—early learning environments: in Berkeley, California (USA) and in Santiago de Compostela, Galiza (Spain). The focus is on critical self-reflective teaching practice that is committed to promoting social justice through respect for diverse forms of gender identity formation in youth, even in the youngest of schoolchildren; for their experiences and perceptions at this early stage of development stand to influence in significant ways the ease with which gender identity and sexuality are experienced at later stages in their lives. What is ultimately explored here is the crucial role teachers play in the broader critical project of supporting youths' personal and collective emancipation from seemingly neutral or commonsensical notions that may nonetheless prove oppressive.

Scene 1: Berkeley, California, 1984, in a Private "Day Nursery." Age Group: 3- to 4-Year-Olds

As a young adult initiating her teaching career, I took up work at a local nursery school. It was a privately run school, most of the parents (who paid their monthly dues) pertaining to the middle class or higher. And as a university town, Berkeley, by the 1980s, was composed of a highly international and multicultural population, and the children at the school reflected that cultural heterogeneity.

I was in charge of a group of about a dozen three- and four-year-olds, representing a fairly even mix of girls and boys. One of the boys, whose name was similar to Datsun, was brought in and picked up by his young mother, who happened to be of Israeli origin, and spoke English with a slight accent, which I noticed in my brief exchanges with her. She had her own unique style: she kept her hair shaven very close to her head, and generally sported unconventional, well-tailored, understated clothing. Her son, whose hair was quite a bit longer than hers, and curly, usually wore a grey or green sweatsuit to school. He tended to be a bit more distracted than the other children in his group, and to move around more.

About three weeks into my time at the school, my turn for bathroom duty came up. That is when I suddenly realized that Datsun was biologically female. But that fact, although surprising—her/his appearance had in reality always seemed a bit androgynous to me—was not what surprised me the most. What most struck me, in retrospect, was my own reaction.

I fancied myself an egalitarian feminist, who supposedly and consciously treated girls and boys "the same." And yet, the first thought that crossed my mind when I realized Datsun was "a girl" was, "Oh, how *badly* I've treated her all this time!" Then came the next thought: "'Badly'? Why *badly*?" And then, "What does that say about how I systematically treat *boys*?!" And finally, "Oh dear, I'm sexist!!"

Pause. After collecting my thoughts, I came to the conclusion that treating boys "badly," in my case, amounted to interacting with them with less affection, with more distance linguistically, emotionally, and physically. But was that *necessarily* "bad"? I felt it was, or at least it seemed less caring. The mere differential treatment bothered me as well. And was I not patronizing and pampering the girls at the same time? The fact was that Datsun's physical reality clashed with my pre-established notions about her/his gender identity. And I could not recall having ever been corrected by the mother in my usage of male-gendered pronouns when referring to Datsun. Did the mother indeed choose not to "correct" me when I used "him" to refer to her child? In other words, might this mother have been intentionally (or unintentionally) *queering* Datsun's identity by simply not worrying about her child being classified into one of the conventional gender categories of "him" or "her"? Given the fact that the mother's own personal aesthetics could not easily be categorized as typically "feminine," my hunch was that she probably did value the freedom of expression involved in defying classification, both for herself and for Datsun.

I did, too, although the idea of not classifying a child according to fixed gender categories was new to me, and it challenged a whole lifetime of conditioning, in terms of how such categories are constructed, assigned, performed, and interpreted reiteratively—a process that Judith Butler (1990) has referred to as interpellation. Although at first it felt uncomfortable, I sensed that there was indeed something to be gained by overcoming the desire to distinguish female from male, especially in my teaching: it seemed to give rise to a kind of personal and collective emancipation, and, ideally, it represented one more facet of equalitarian practice. On the other hand, it clashed with the feminist in me, always vigilant about the deferential treatment of males over females. These realizations were therefore only the beginning of an ongoing process of reflection about the pedagogical implications of moving gender identity "beyond the binary" (Cho, Laub, Wall, Daley, & Joslin, 2004).

As for Datsun, s/he went about her daily life at school oblivious to this inner conflict of mine. Or so I hoped! I, in the meantime, learned a lot about myself as a teacher and a feminist, thanks to something as simple as interacting on a daily basis in a multicultural educational setting.

Scene 2: Santiago de Compostela, Northwestern Spain, 2012, in a Public Early Childhood Education Classroom. Age Group: 3- to 4-Year-Olds

Twenty-seven years have passed since that eye-opening experience in Berkeley. I am now a teacher educator in Spain, where I have lived since 1991. Recently, I was invited to visit a school where a friend of mine teaches. She is the school's English teacher, and works with children ages 2 to 6. I was able to participate in one of her classes with a group of mostly four-year-olds. All twelve of us sat on the floor in a circle, and following a question-answer session with the kids, my friend started them on a round of songs. Two of the songs placed an emphasis on the words "girls" and "boys." After each song, she invited me, as a native speaker of English, to interact spontaneously with the children. When the first song was over, I decided to elicit from the children a simple "yes" or "no" by asking each one the following question: "Are you a girl?" (or "Are you a boy?"). I proceeded to query each child, and was answered by all but one. The one who chose not to answer just looked at me and squirmed a little. So I shrugged my shoulders and moved on to the next child. My teacher friend, respectfully, did not intervene. Curiously, it was not until that moment that I realized the child could not easily be classified as either girl or boy.

There was another brief song about boys and girls. I was once again asked to interact, and this time, I asked each child to respond to the question, "Are you a girl or a boy?" (These questions were not planned, and were certainly far from ideal, but they were all I could think of on the spur of the moment so as not to break the momentum.) I promptly reached the child who had not answered during the first round, and this time as well s/he remained silent, instead choosing to merely look at me and fidget with his or her shoe. I suspected that my questions were making the child uncomfortable, so with a quick "Okay," I moved on. The rest of the children did respond with "girl" or "boy."

My teacher friend engaged the children in another activity or two to finish her English class. When the children had left, curiosity got the better of me, and I could not resist inquiring about the child who had not responded: could her or his silence be attributed to a lack of knowledge of English, or to feeling uncomfortable answering to one gender or the other? My friend responded to my questions in Spanish, and, in so doing, did not need to use a personal pronoun to refer to the child. Her answer was, "*Es así; va a lo suyo.*" ("[S/he] is like that; does [his/her] own thing.") Still unsatisfied, I asked in Spanish, "*Por curiosidad, ¿es niña o niño?*" ("Out of curiosity, is [s/he] a girl or a boy?") She replied, "*Es una niña.*" ("She's a girl.")

That is when I re-lived the same sensation experienced years earlier in Berkeley: a renewed awareness about my own relationship with gender, and my ongoing desire to classify according to the gender binary. That desire is in fact overwhelmingly present in societies as geographically and culturally distinct from each other as the two addressed here. And yet, as a cross-cultural practice, identifying children according to male-female heteronormativity is increasingly questioned and challenged worldwide by the advocates of *queering* or emancipating our understandings of gender identity and sexuality. Lesbian, gay, bisexual, transsexual, and intersex (LGBTI) individuals, collectives, and theorists have led this movement towards removing such limiting categories in order to make way for an open spectrum of identity expression where gender and sexuality are concerned (Brill & Pepper, 2008; Butler, 1990; Carlson & Roseboro, 2011; DePalma & Atkinson, 2009; Kumashiro, 2004; Preciado, 2000/2011; Rodriguez & Pinar, 2007; Talburt & Steinberg, 2000; Ziga, 2009). The claim is that, as we have seen, normalized, categorical gendering runs the risk of truncating or limiting children's basic rights and freedoms as these relate to their development of a sense of self. Queering identity, then, is all about revealing and disrupting the oppressive facets of what has long been considered "normal" where gender and sexuality are concerned—a critical perspective that is largely indebted to Michel Foucault's (1978) groundbreaking *genealogical* analysis of "normal" sexuality as discursively constructed and institutionally disciplined over time, in arbitrary, questionable ways.

Reflections on the Implications for Socially Just Teaching

These two experiences have allowed me to understand, in more personally meaningful ways,[1] the importance of such identity rights and freedoms in the earliest of educational settings: how central they are to the daily lives of young children; how they can all too easily be overlooked, suppressed, or actively negated through teaching practice; how early gender identities of all kinds—not merely of the heteronormative kind—emerge across cultures and borders; and how carefully and thoughtfully they must be addressed and respected by educators if we are to contribute to youths' smooth transition into adolescence and adulthood, each stage posing its particular challenges to self-representation and sexuality.

At the broadest level of analysis, this is a human-rights issue, one protected by the latest generation of United Nations declarations. Whereas the Universal Declaration of Human Rights of 1948 protected the most basic of human rights, successive declarations have since expanded those rights into civil, political, economic, social, and cultural spheres, which now include reproductive and identity rights. One of the most recent of these is the groundbreaking UN General Assembly Resolution 17/19 on "Human rights, sexual orientation and gender identity" (Human Rights Council, 2011), the first UN resolution to, among other actions, commission a study "documenting discriminatory laws and practices and acts of violence against individuals based on their sexual orientation and gender identity, in all regions of the world" (p. 2). Such a study would also describe how international human-rights law can be used to end violence and related human-rights violations based on sexual orientation and gender identity.

While the emphasis here is on readily identifiable discrimination and "acts of violence," what is still missing from this discourse is a focus on age groups, and on how easily and soon children's self-esteem can be damaged by much more subtly discriminatory interactions with adults and peers (Kumashiro, 2004)—this latter dynamic representing not only a kind of disciplinary social construction of what Foucault (1975) referred to as organic individuality, but also, in my view, yet another component of the symbolic violence theorized by Pierre Bourdieu and Jean-Claude Passeron (1990), one that is all too easily perpetuated through the educational system when left unchallenged. This is where educators, as social agents of change, can fill in the gaps by developing deeper understandings regarding the less obvious constraints that heteronormative assumptions can impose on the development of even the youngest of identities. UN resolutions can only go so far in promoting such awareness, especially considering that institutional recognition and protections of gender-identity rights across state borders are as yet met with opposition from numerous nations around the world. For instance, the aforementioned resolution was adopted by only a slim margin of approval, with 23 states in favor, 19 against, and three abstaining.

And yet, even in countries that embrace emancipative initiatives around gender and sexuality rights, brutal homophobic violence persists. As transgender man and teacher, Loren Krywanczyk (2010), poignantly expressed, asserting gender-diversity rights at school "is sometimes a matter of life or death" (p. 1), in reference to the 2008 murder of Lawrence King—a visibly gender-nonconforming eighth-grade student who was shot to death by a homophobic peer in their California school. In Spain, a major 2012 report has highlighted an urgent need to combat homophobic bullying at school and beyond through the defense and advancement of "affective-sexual diversity," as a transversal concern crossing multiple social and institutional spheres, beginning in schools, but extending into families, social services, and legislative bodies (Generelo, 2012).

Fortunately, gender-diversity rights are increasingly safeguarded and promoted around the world, thanks especially (and initially) to ongoing grassroots activism—Act Up emerging in 1987 New York as one of the largest and most influential of such movements worldwide,[2] while other more recent, local movements and activist collectives continue to emerge, such as the Guerrilla Travolaka of Catalonia,[3] or

Maribolheras Precárias of Galiza.[4] On a more institutional front, queer youth and educational advocacy groups and organizations constitute another line of action, such as Youth Pride Inc.,[5] the Gay, Lesbian & Straight Education Network (GLSEN),[6] or the Safe Schools Coalition[7] in the U.S., and the Federación Estatal de Lesbianas, Gais, Transexuales y Bisexuales (FELGTB)[8] in Spain. There is also a growing body of intellectual activist collectives centered on queer theory and practice,[9] as well as specific legislation throughout the world.

In the legal sphere, for instance, the State of California recently enacted a law requiring, for the first time, that LGBTI perspectives and history be addressed in school curricula (see Khadaroo, 2011). Another unprecedented law was recently passed in California as well, prohibiting subjecting minors to disputed therapies purportedly designed to "cure" homosexuality (see Eckholm, 2012). In Spain, a statewide law was enacted in 2007 to protect and regulate the identity rights of transgender and transsexual citizens (BOE, 2007), while same-sex marriage has been legal in the country since 2005. Nonetheless, just as occurred in California, the right to same-sex marriage in Spain has since been legally challenged in the courts, but has also very recently been upheld by the Constitutional Court, the highest in the country (see Reinlein & Morris, 2012).

A key question, however, is that while such necessary and promising legal, institutional, *glocal*, and grassroots milestones are indeed having positive impact around the world—this often despite their respective and unequal access to the most powerful and highly influential media outlets—*to what extent do these initiatives actually inform or affect the daily decisions teachers need to make where the* youngest *of schoolchildren are concerned?*

One observation from healthcare researchers of early gender nonconformity, Stephanie Brill and Rachel Pepper (2008), is eye-opening. In their book, *The Transgender Child*, they presented extensive research and concluded that "atypical" gender behavior can be observed in children as early as two to three years of age. Moreover, they recommend that such expressions be supported at home and at school in ways that maximize the child's comfort with her or his own sense of self. In fact, they observe that the younger any child is, the more naturally s/he accepts gender diversity, not only in others, but, needless to say, in him- or herself, as long as the child's immediate social environment is also accepting. This is certainly the case in the documentary, *No Dumb Questions* (Regan, 2001), which documented how three daughters, guided by their parents, gradually prepared themselves for their beloved uncle's eventual transformation into an aunt. The youngest, a six-year-old, seemed to have no problem with accepting the change, and embraced her new aunt almost immediately; while the eldest, an eleven-year-old, visibly experienced the most discomfort, and took longer than her two younger sisters to approach and accept her transgender aunt.

Readily embracing and supporting queer gender identities in the youngest of children has not gone, however, without objections from some sectors. Those who question supporting young children's variance from the heteronormative, binary gender categories often base their views on conservative religious, clinical, and psychological analytical traditions that place more emphasis on current levels of social rejection of gender "deviance" than on the positive effects of love and acceptance, or the transformative power of teaching and learning respect for gender diversity in general. One such clinical perspective can be found, for example, in Roberts, Rosario, Corliss, Koenen, and Austin (2012), whose bias was conveyed in the very title of their study: "Childhood Gender Nonconformity: A Risk Indicator for Childhood Abuse and Posttraumatic Stress in Youth." However, the risks they pointed out were due to family members' intolerance, not to a child's gender identity in and of itself. As for psychological approaches, a notoriously polemical method designed and promoted by George Rekers (see Rekers & Lovaas, 1974) as a means of allegedly "curing" homosexuality has since been heavily censured for its homophobic overtones, and for its cruel and dubious means, especially after one of Rekers's proclaimed "success" stories—a young boy who was repeatedly subjected to harsh treatments for "acting homosexual"—committed suicide as an adult (see Bronstein & Joseph, 2011). A more recent version of such therapies is Richard A. Cohen's (2007) method, currently disseminated by Inter-Varsity Press, the publishing wing of the conservative Universities and Colleges Christian Fellowship.

By contrast, the aforementioned handbook for families and professionals by Brill & Pepper (2008) offered an extensive and well-founded critique of such intolerant and potentially devastating approaches to suppressing gender diversity. Moreover, in their groundbreaking study, *Interrogating Heteronormativity in Primary Schools: The Work of the No Outsiders Project*, Renée DePalma and Elizabeth Atkinson (2009) documented how naturally and positively primary schoolchildren in England respond to "interrogating heteronormativity," as engaged not only through interactions with an educator who openly addressed his transsexuality with the children, but through various learning projects centered on—and enacting—queer literature, art, drama, music, and film, through a diversity of media (audio, visual, and textual) at school and on line.[10] Another author, Jennifer Bryan (2012), has recently embarked on a comprehensive educational project in her book, *From the Dress-Up Corner to the Senior Prom*, which teachers from pre-Kindergarten to the 12th grade of high school may turn to as they navigate the intricacies and dynamics of gender and sexuality diversity among students of all ages. In Spain, authors such as Mercedes Sánchez Sáinz et al. (2009, 2010) explored specific pedagogical projects for Early Childhood Education around "affective, sexual, and personal" diversity; while filmmaker Sergi Pérez has produced the poignant and award-winning short film, *Vestido Nuevo* (New Dress), depicting a young boy who insists on wearing his favorite dress to school on *Carnaval* Day (Mardi Gras), despite the teacher's imperative that the whole class dress up as dalmatians (Pérez, 2006).[11] These and many other resources not only offer ideas and tools for addressing gender diversity in an inclusive, straightforward way; they more importantly broaden our critical lens as to the various ways in which reductive "common sense" points of reference around gender needlessly and harmfully condition young people's lives at school and beyond.

Conclusion

One final realm of contention around gender diversity has emerged, nonetheless, from feminist perspectives such as the one I expressed earlier. That is, *might not moving beyond the gender binary eventually run the risk of rendering male privilege less visible?* There is a certain correlation between this question and the critiques of "colorblindness" in the debate over affirmative action (positive discrimination) based on racial classifications. On this latter issue, I have found most convincing Gloria Ladson-Billings's (1994) and Tim Wise's (2010) informed views that, as long as racism persists, then social, cultural, and regulatory practices that attend to color variance and "race"—as a *socially constructed* category—are still a necessary component in the struggle against race-based discrimination. This same logic resonates with the feminist concern around disrupting gender categories. To this challenge, however, queer theorist, Judith Butler (1990), formulated the following response:

> Feminist critique ought to explore the totalizing claims of a masculinist signifying economy, but also remain self-critical with respect to the totalizing gestures of feminism. The effort to identify the enemy as singular in form is a reverse-discourse that uncritically mimics the strategy of the oppressor instead of offering a different set of terms. That the tactic can operate in feminist and antifeminist contexts alike suggests that the colonizing gesture is not primarily or irreducibly masculinist. It can operate to affect other relations of racial, class, and heterosexist subordination, to name but a few. (p. 13)

The upshot of Butler's rebuttal, as I understand it, is that oppressive power (domination, or "the colonizing gesture") can take many forms, and must be identified for what *it* is, and how it is engaged in various contexts and dynamics involving the multifarious expressions of human diversity. In other words, domination is not merely a male trait, although the historic relationship between male privilege and the domination of women is a persistent reality that must never be ignored. On this point, Shirley Steinberg's advancement of a critical theory of sexuality proves powerful. She argues that the kind of pedagogical practice that refuses to address the complexity and the lack of easy correspondence between power and the production of sexuality and gender identity in youth is bound to fail. Thus, a *critical* pedagogy of sexuality must recognize gender identity as a focus of struggle, as an "opportunity allowed by the non-deterministic nature of identity formation, as it opens oppositional locales from which dominant masculinity, patriarchal power, female submission, and privilege can be challenged" (Steinberg, 2011, p. 227).

That said, as we educators assume our role as what Henry Giroux (1988) or Patricia Hill Collins (2012) have respectively referred to as public intellectuals, we gradually gain more nuanced understandings of these complexities of human coexistence and can thus refine our ever-vigilant gaze on the many forms that discrimination, oppression, and inequality can take, at least where equal rights and freedoms are at stake. In other words, in daily interaction at school, children, whether they defy or emulate dominant gender categories, deserve nothing less than acceptance and respect on equal terms, because our potential desire to categorize them against their will may very well prove oppressive. Not only that, but moving "beyond the binary" is indeed, in so many ways, liberating for all of us.

My primary aim, then, with this brief cross-cultural exploration, has been to show how youth identity and culture, even at the earliest stages of personal development, and across cultures, "teach" us adults and educators to open our hearts and minds to the possibilities of a more emancipative, just, and inclusive pedagogy. This is a pedagogy that, in the Freirean (1970) tradition, listens to and learns from youth and other learners, especially those who are socially constructed as subaltern, or as somehow "deviant" from, "defiant" of, or "inferior" to the hegemonic norm. Queer youth clearly endure this form of oppression at much higher rates than do heteronormative youth, and that oppression is only compounded when their social class backgrounds and/or ethnic and racial characteristics further diverge from racist, ethnocentric, and arbitrary elitist standards (Carlson, 2012; Kumashiro, 2004). However, by queering our pedagogical practice, we educators can actively and discursively challenge impositions of the girl-boy or gay-straight identity binaries and hierarchies—thus unmasking the "vocabulary of impoverished oppositions"—to borrow a key notion Henry Giroux (2009) set forth in his book, *Youth in a Suspect Society* (p. 186).

The two children who originally inspired this analysis have progressed through educational systems that—notwithstanding the aforementioned important gains made in the US, Spain, and elsewhere towards loosening the institutional and societal heteronormative grip on youth—nonetheless still overwhelmingly favor heterosexual and dualistic cultural referents and approaches to gender-identity formation and sexuality (Carlson, 2011, 2012; DePalma & Atkinson, 2009; Epstein & Johnson, 2000; Generelo, 2012; Kumashiro, 2004; Meyer, 2007; Rodriguez & Pinar, 2007; Sánchez Sáinz, 2010; Talburt & Steinberg, 2000). Moreover, as children mature, the more likely they are to be conditioned by such dominant sociocultural norms, as was readily apparent in the aforementioned documentary, *No Dumb Questions* (Regan, 2001).

This tendency is further reinforced through a profit-driven, mass-media culture that functions as a parallel, albeit non-formal, educational institution, serving up a commodified and heavily biased *kinderculture* (Steinberg & Kincheloe, 1997) designed to mold kids' tastes, desires, options, and perspectives early on. The mass media's influence on youth culture is in many ways now a global reality, one which Galizan-Spanish scholar, Jurjo Torres Santomé (2008, 2011), has also critically examined within the larger context of globalized neoliberalism and its cultural impact on youth when channeled through the educational institution in general. This is why educational projects that promote, with youth, alternative messages and media outlets, and that critically support those produced by youth themselves, can be so emancipative (Carlson, 2011; Steinberg, 2011). These pedagogical perspectives, coupled with those recommended by other critical educators, envision school as a site of enormous potential for transformation as yet underexplored by educational agents—as are the local school community and cyberspace—for such sites facilitate the *collective* questioning, deconstruction, and denaturalization of "mainstream" messages and dynamics that subordinate, stigmatize, marginalize, or completely exclude gender identities that diverge from the arbitrary, dominant norm. Engaging with youth critically and constructively within these public realms of action is thus one of the central projects of Critical Youth Studies (Cammarota & Fine, 2008).

Notes

1. I am referring here to personally achieving a deeper understanding of queer perspectives as one who has long identified as "female" and "heterosexual."
2. See http://www.actupny.org/
3. A transgender collective active in Catalonia since 2006, but with increasing influence in Spain in general. See http://guerrilla-travolaka.blogspot.com.es/2006/11/manifiesto.html
4. This group's name, loosely translated into English, would be *Precarious Fagdykes*. They have been active since 2007 in the Galizan region of Spain, also referred to as Galicia. See http://maribolheras.blog.com/
5. See http://www.youthprideri.org/
6. See http://www.glsen.org/cgi-bin/iowa/all/home/index.html
7. See http://www.safeschoolscoalition.org/RG-US_GLBTQyouth.html
8. See http://www.felgtb.org/
9. These are most visible on blogs and social networks. See, for example, the Facebook groups, *The COCKTAIL PARTY* or the *Queer Theory Collective: Identities + Ideas*.
10. For instance, one storybook for young children recommended by these authors is *And Tango Makes Three* (Richardson, Parnell, & Cole, 2005), based on the true story about a couple of male penguins at New York City's Central Park Zoo that became mates and formed a family by annually adopting abandoned eggs and hatching chicks. For all its innocence, this storybook has remained among the top ten titles on the American Library Association's list of books most targeted by book-banning publics since 2006, even occupying first place in 2006, 2007, 2008, and 2010. This was allegedly due to its addressing "homosexuality" and "religious viewpoint", and for allegedly being "unsuited to age group." See the American Library Association's "Banned & Challenged Books" webpage at: http://www.ala.org/advocacy/banned/frequentlychallenged/21stcenturychallenged
11. The film can be viewed at: http://www.filmin.es/corto/vestido-nuevo

References

BOE. (2007, March 16). Ley 3/2007, de 15 de marzo, reguladora de la rectificación registral de la mención relativa al sexo de las personas. *Boletín Oficial del Estado* (B.O.E.), No. 65, pp. 11251–11253. Retrieved from http://www.boe.es/buscar/doc.php?id=BOE-A-2007-5585

Bourdieu, P., & Passeron, J-C. (1990). *Reproduction in education, society and culture* (2nd ed.). London, UK: Sage.

Brill, S., & Pepper, R. (2008). *The transgender child: A handbook for families and professionals*. Berkeley, CA: Cleis Press.

Bronstein, S., & Joseph, J. (2011, June 10). Therapy to change "feminine" boy created a troubled man, family says. *CNN*. Retrieved from http://edition.cnn.com/2011/US/06/07/sissy.boy.experiment/index.html

Bryan, J. (2012). *From the dress-up corner to the senior prom: Navigating gender and sexuality diversity in preK–12 schools*. Lanham, MD: Rowman & Littlefield.

Butler, J. (1990). *Gender trouble: Feminism and the subversion of identity*. New York, NY: Routledge.

Cammarota, J., & Fine, M. (Eds.). (2008). *Revolutionizing education: Youth participatory action research in motion*. New York, NY: Routledge.

Carlson, D. (2011). Constructing the adolescent body: Cultural studies and sexuality education. In D. Carlson & D. L. Roseboro (Eds.), *The sexuality curriculum and youth culture* (pp. 4–28). New York, NY: Peter Lang.

Carlson, D. (2012). *The education of Eros: A history of education and the problem of adolescent sexuality*. New York, NY: Routledge.

Cho, S., Laub, C., Wall, S. S. M., Daley, C., & Joslin, C. (2004). *Beyond the binary: A tool kit for gender identity activism in schools*. Gay-Straight Alliance Network/Tides Center, Transgender Law Center, and National Center for Lesbian Rights. Retrieved from http://gsanetwork.org/files/resources/btbonline.pdf

Cohen, R. (2007). *Gay children, straight parents: A plan for family healing*. Nottingham, UK: InterVarsity Press.

DePalma, R., & Atkinson, E. (Eds.). (2009). *Interrogating heteronormativity in primary schools: The work of the No Outsiders project*. Oakhill, Stoke-on-Trent, UK: Trentham Books.

Eckholm, E. (2012, September 30). California is first state to ban gay 'cure' for minors. *The New York Times* (online). Retrieved from http://www.nytimes.com/2012/10/01/us/california-bans-therapies-to-cure-gay-minors.html

Epstein, D., & Johnson, R. (2000). *Sexualidades e institución escolar*. Madrid, Spain: Morata (Original English-language edition: *Schooling Sexualities*. Buckingham, UK: Open University Press, 1998).

Foucault, M. (1975). *Discipline and punish: The birth of the prison*. New York, NY: Random House.

Foucault, M. (1978). *The history of sexuality: An introduction, Volume 1*. New York, NY: Random House.

Freire, P. (1970). *Pedagogy of the oppressed*. New York, NY: Seabury Press.

Generelo, J. (Ed.). (2012). *Acoso escolar homofóbico y riesgo de suicidio en adolescente y jóvenes LGB* (report). Madrid, Spain: Federación Estatal de Lesbianas, Gais, Transexuales y Bisexuales (FELGTB). Retrieved from http://www.felgtb.org/rs/1741/d112d6ad-54ec-438b-9358-4483f9e98868/48e/fd/1/filename/informe-resultados-riesgosuicidio-lgb.pdf

Giroux, H. A. (1988). *Teachers as intellectuals: Toward a critical pedagogy of learning.* Westport, CT: Bergin & Garvey.

Giroux, H. A. (2009). *Youth in a suspect society: Democracy or disposability?* New York, NY: Palgrave Macmillan.

Hill Collins, P. (2012). *On intellectual activism.* Philadelphia, PA: Temple University Press.

Human Rights Council. (2011, July 14). *17/19 Human rights, sexual orientation and gender identity.* Resolution A/HRC/RES/17/19, adopted by the Human Rights Council at the 17th session of the United Nations General Assembly. Retrieved from http://daccess-ods.un.org/access.nsf/Get?Open&DS=A/HRC/RES/17/19&Lang=E

Khadaroo, S. T. (2011). California becomes first state to mandate gay history in curriculum. *Christian Science Monitor.* Retrieved from http://www.csmonitor.com/USA/Education/2011/0714/California-becomes-first-state-to-mandate-gay-history-in-curriculum

Krywanczyk, L. (2010). Transsexuals, teaching your children. *Rethinking Schools, 24*(3). Retrieved from http://www.rethinkingschools.org/restrict.asp?path=archive/24_03/24_03_transsexuals.shtml

Kumashiro, K. K. (2004). *Against common sense: Teaching and learning toward social justice.* New York, NY: RoutledgeFalmer.

Ladson-Billings, G. (1994). *The dreamkeepers: Successful teachers of African American children.* San Francisco, CA: Jossey-Bass.

Meyer, E. J. (2007). 'But I'm not gay': What straight teachers need to know about queer theory. In N. M. Rodriguez & W. F. Pinar (Eds.), *Queering straight teachers: Discourse and identity in education* (pp. 15–29). New York, NY: Peter Lang.

Pérez, S. (2006). *Vestido nuevo* [Shortfilm, 14 mins.]. Spain: Escándalo Films. Retrieved from http://www.filmin.es/corto/vestido-nuevo

Preciado, B. (2011). *Manifiesto contrasexual.* Barcelona, Spain: Anagrama (French edition: *Manifeste contra-sexuel.* Paris, France: Ballars, 2000).

Regan, M. (2001). *No dumb questions* [Documentary, 24 mins.]. USA: Epiphany Productions. Retrieved from http://www.nodumbquestions.com/

Reinlein, I., & Morris, S. (2012, November 6). Same-sex marriage upheld by Spain's highest court. *Reuters* (online). Retrieved from http://www.reuters.com/article/2012/11/07/us-spain-gaymarriage-idUSBRE8A60CK20121107

Rekers, G. A., & Lovass, O. I. (1974). Behavioral treatment of deviant sex-role behaviors in a male child. *Journal of Applied Behavior Analysis, 7*(3), 173–190.

Richardson, J., Parnell, P., & Cole, H. (2005). *And Tango makes three.* New York, NY: Simon & Schuster.

Roberts, A., Rosario, M., Corliss, H. L., Koenen, K. C., & Austin, S. B. (2012, February 20). Childhood gender nonconformity: A risk indicator for childhood abuse and posttraumatic stress in youth. *Pediatrics.* Online publication. doi: 10.1542/peds.2011–1804. Retrieved from http://pediatrics.aappublications.org/content/early/2012/02/15/peds.2011-1804.full.pdf+html

Rodriguez, N. M., & Pinar, W. F. (Eds.). (2007). *Queering straight teachers: Discourse and identity in education.* New York, NY: Peter Lang.

Sánchez Sáinz, M. (Ed.). (2009). *Cómo educar en la diversidad afectivo-sexual en los centros escolares: Orientaciones prácticas para la ESO.* Madrid, Spain: Los Libros de la Catarata.

Sánchez Sáinz, M. (Ed.) (2010). *Cómo educar en la diversidad afectiva, sexual, y personal en educación infantil (orientaciones prácticas).* Madrid, Spain: Los Libros de la Catarata.

Steinberg, S. R. (2011). The celluloid sexuality curriculum: Deconstructing teen films. In D. Carlson & D. L. Roseboro (Eds.), *The sexuality curriculum and youth culture* (pp. 217–230). New York, NY: Peter Lang.

Steinberg, S. R., & Kincheloe, J. L. (1997). *Kinderculture: The corporate construction of childhood.* Boulder, CO: Westview Press.

Talburt, S., & Steinberg, S. R. (Eds.). (2000). *Thinking queer: Sexuality, culture, and education.* New York, NY: Peter Lang.

Torres Santomé, J. (2008). School culture and the fight against exclusion: An optimistic curriculum. In C. McCarthy & C. Teasley (Eds.), *Transnational perspectives on culture, policy, and education: Redirecting cultural studies in neoliberal times* (pp. 183–218). New York, NY: Peter Lang.

Torres Santomé, J. (2011). *La justicia curricular: El caballo de Troya de la cultura escolar.* Madrid, Spain: Morata.

Wise, T. (2010). *Colorblind: The rise of post-racial politics and the retreat from racial equity.* San Francisco, CA: City Lights Books.

Ziga, I. (2009). *Devenir perra.* Barcelona, Spain: Melusina Editorial.

CHAPTER 14

Moving an Anti-Bullying Stance Into Schools

Supporting the Identities of Transgender and Gender Variant Youth

sj Miller

Classrooms today contain students whose identities are constantly shifting and evolving. Often it is the teacher who lacks the embodied knowledge or social expertise to navigate new terrain when teaching students whose identities fall outside of teachers' social, historical, political, and/or gendered networks. Understanding transgender (T) and gender variant and/or gender non-conforming (GV) youth and how to support their burgeoning identities in schools through both curriculum and policy, pose particularized challenges for teachers as they encounter how mythologized gender norms are deeply embedded in the social fabric of schools. Teachers today are being challenged with how to reconcile a binary-gendered past with an ever-evolving, non-binary present and the myriad gendered identities and complex realities of today's students. An unfortunate reality that walks in the shadow of understanding the students' shifting gendered selves is that any deviance from the norm (Miller, 2012) often brings on bullying behavior. This chapter discusses how school-wide policies impacting the school environment, an anti-bullying stance, and queering pedagogy can impact the classroom environment and generate a positive and affirming educational climate for TGV youth.

According to the 2009 GLSEN (The Gay, Lesbian & Straight Education Network) *National School Climate Survey*, secondary students who are either LGBTQ or gender variant and/or non-conforming—e.g., those students whose behaviors, mannerisms, expressions, and gender roles, and/or those whose appearance, whether through clothing, makeup, height, size, or weight, is non-conventional—accrue the worst bullying statistics in schools today. I highlight and hone in on their bullied statistics, because these students incur the highest prevalence of violence and suicidalilty (Markow & Fein, 2005; Sherer & Nickerson, 2010). I refer to bullying against these populations as *queer* bullying. By *queer*, I mean breaking binaries that reinforce compulsory, heteronormative norms for LGBTQ students and those whose gender expressions, mannerisms, roles, behaviors, and appearance are non-conforming, variant, or challenge the dominant gendered narrative.

LGBTQGV[M]

The lesbian, gay, bisexual, transgender, questioning, and gender variant Millennial Generation's history, or the LGBTQGV[M], is deeply embedded in the lives and deaths of the activists who fought for LGBTQGV freedoms of today, and arguably spans back to the 12th century when hostility toward homosexuality began to develop throughout European religious and secular institutions. The LGBTQGV[M] are living in a time and a political climate in which they are now benefitting from the emotional, psychological, and physical labor of the LGBT activists in their quest for equality; for *their* equality. Their history includes once heated discussions about their marginalization in private living rooms (e.g., The Mattachine Society and the Daughters of Bilitis); it includes the pathologization of their sexual orientation in 1952, and later the depathologization in 1973 of homosexuality; it includes the pathologization of transgenderism in 1980, its renaming as a gender-identity disorder in 1984, and the pending repathologization of the diagnosis as gender dysphoria in May 2013; it includes those men who dressed as women at Compton's Cafeteria who fought against the police in 1966; it includes the angry and violent protests by gay activists against police at the Stonewall Inn in 1969; it includes the beginning of Gay Pride marches around the country in 1970; it includes the tragic losses of the too-many-to-name who succumbed to the AIDS Holocaust; it includes the virulent attacks of hate against their population; and it includes the loss of their own to suicide.

The history of the LGBTQGV[M]s also includes an increasing prevalence of more authentic, non-stereotypical representations of LGBT people in the media and on TV. The media help re-frame, represent, and disseminate positive strides made on behalf of the LGBTQGV community and those who identify themselves as members. Examples include an increased attention to same-sex marriage and domestic partnerships, President Barack Obama's 2012 endorsement of marriage equality, political races that are won by openly LGBTQ candidates, TV shows and movies positively depicting non-stereotypical LGBTQGV characters, and a growing number of out actors, musicians, athletes, and politicians. All of these help to provide positive images and an increasing acceptance and recognition of LGBTQGV people as a highly diverse group. Such "outness" provides positive examples of LGBTQGV individuals as normal people living productive lives in ways our society has never been given the chance to see or consider before. It also increases the likelihood that children in the next generation will experience such positive LGBTQGV representations as a normal part of their own worlds as they reach maturity and become leaders in our society.

Why turn to the media to examine their impact on LGBTQGV[M] students? Consider a typical adolescent tuning in to multiple media outlets and experiencing a popular culture that offers nothing but heteronormatively prejudicial beliefs that are validated in those media by celebrities, public officials, and other people in powerful positions. Now consider the impact those ubiquitous representations can have on a young person, how they might play out in an LGBTQGV child's life in school, and how that child's apparent violation of accepted norms is likely to be met with discomfort, fear, confusion, and even (too often) hatred, anger, and resentment.

LGBTQGV people are mostly forced to operate in a social context wherein they may often see, hear, and/or experience nothing but heteronormative messages about who they ought to be, and how they should look, act, feel, think, talk, move, and so forth. That alone leads members of this group to operate out of fear in order to protect their feelings and identities. But at the same time, we are seeing a shift (at least a slight one, but in many ways a dramatic one, given the 2012 elections, for example) wherein media outlets are representing LGBTQGV people in new ways—often very positive ways, and even in ways that make their identity a secondary, tertiary, or even non-existent issue. But because gender typing and heteronormativity are still dominant, members of this group face huge threats to their ways of thinking, feeling, and being in the world, while non-members, who do not access the positive media representations (or who reject them—and are taught to reject—those representations), are going to school with them. That leaves LGBTQGV^M students extremely vulnerable and likely to feel under siege much of the time, and it also leaves the door open for others to bully them because they are different. This ever-present and pervasive media split between representations of heteronormativity and positive portrayals of LGBTQGV people leaves no doubt about why we lack consensus regarding federal anti-LGBTQGV legislation that censures bullying or supports curriculum development.

These historical events have helped to shift public attention to the rights that LGBTQGV people should be afforded, and together, they mark a revolution in social consciousness and values that have shifted the plight for LGBTQGV equality into the national spotlight. Such a history should be part of the elementary- and secondary-school curricula, and should be taught alongside any other civil-rights movement in the search for recognition, equality, and human rights. When these discussions are not part of the daily diet of school curriculum, it sends critical messages to our LGBTQGV^M youth, and their already vulnerable, budding identities, that their history, the positive representations of their lifestyles, and their lives matter less than those of their heterosexual peers. To that end, this chapter addresses a possible blueprint that draws critical attention to how to normalize secondary classrooms for TGV youth—populations who by far, are the most vulnerable to bullying, bullycide, homelessness, drug-use, truancy, and dropping out of school (Greytak, Kosciw, & Diaz, 2009; Kosciw, Greytak, Diaz, & Bartkiewicz, 2010). This work honors those activists whose lived experiences are shaping and informing school curriculum, though they may not be around to see the fruits of their labor today.

School-Wide Policies Impacting the School Environment

Under Title 2, Public Education and the Safe Schools Act, schools are expected to protect students with binding laws and codes that mediate all forms of harassment. A student code of conduct is one common form of providing materials to students and parents, which are expected to clearly delineate the mandates of a respective school district. In the code of conduct, schools are expected to have cited discrimination and harassment policies that reflect both district as well as state policies (and sometimes even national policy), as well as provide reporting policies that are easy to follow. Many codes of conduct also cite current state and national laws so that parents are aware of the possible enforcement of a violation of the stated policies. Most schools require a signature of both the student and guardian as a means to ensure that the handbook has been read. Codes of conduct are expected to be clearly posted so that anyone entering the school is made aware of the school's policies. What we also know is that while codes of conduct are *de jure* law, there is no way to completely surveil an entire school and enforce each and every rule or regulation.

Absences in discourse in codes of conduct about protecting LGBT students or laws that prohibit a positive discussion or portrayal of LGBT people can become largely divisive issues for students whose gender identity or gender expression is non-conforming. Such gaps or even the false representations of LGBT mythologies stigmatize and marginalize LGBT students when schools provide false, misleading, or incomplete information about LGBT people.

Typically, when bullying is based on race, color, national origin, sex, disability, or religion, bullying overlaps with harassment and schools are legally obligated to address it. Under federal law, when bullying and harassment overlap, federally funded schools (including colleges and universities) have an obligation to resolve the harassment. When schools fail to resolve the issue of a protected class, they are likely violating one or more civil-rights laws that are enforced by the U.S. Department of

Education's office or the U.S. Department of Justice. Violations typically fall under one of these civil-rights categories:

- Title IV and Title VI of the Civil Rights Act of 1964,

- Title IX of the Education Amendments of 1972,

- Section 504 of the Rehabilitation Act of 1973,

- Titles II and III of the Americans with Disabilities Act,

- Individuals with Disabilities Education Act (IDEA).

According to GLSEN, due to egregious absences of bullying and discrimination laws that protect students' sexual orientations and gender identities, *some* states have adopted "Safe Schools Laws." These laws are further delineated into two major categories: fully enumerated anti-bullying laws and non-discrimination laws.

Fully enumerated anti-bullying laws prohibit bullying and harassment of students based on sexual orientation and gender identity. According to Stopbullying.gov (2013), fully enumerated means that bullying may include, but is not limited to, acts based on actual or perceived characteristics of students who have historically been targets of bullying. The website provides examples of such characteristics, and it makes it clear that bullying does not have to be based on any particular characteristic.

To date, fifteen states including Arkansas, California, Colorado, Connecticut, Illinois, Iowa, Maine, Maryland, New Jersey, New York, North Carolina, Oregon, Rhode Island, Vermont, and Washington, enumerate protection of students based on sexual orientation and gender identity.

ENUMERATED ANTI-BULLYING LAWS BY STATE

Figure 14.1: Enumerated anti-bullying laws by state that protect students based on sexual orientation and gender identity. (Source: GLSEN, 2013). Fifteen states enumerate protection of students based on sexual orientation and gender identity and thirty-five states have not enumerated anti-bullying laws

Non-discrimination laws by states provide protection from discrimination to LGBT students in public schools, but do not use the words *bullying* or *harassment*. Of the non-discrimination laws, some only protect students from discrimination based on sexual orientation but *not* on gender identity. Thirteen states and the District of Columbia protect students on the basis of sexual orientation and gender identity, and Wisconsin provides protection on the basis of sexual orientation only.

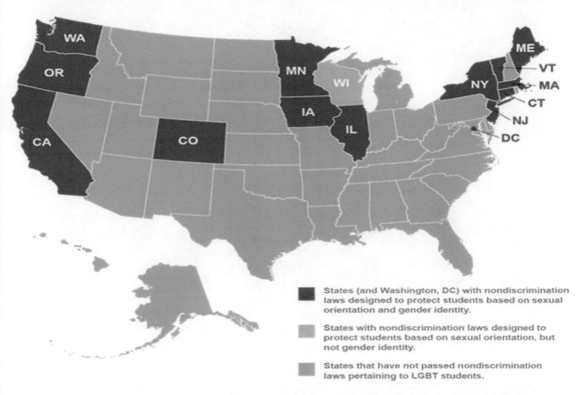

NONDISCRIMINATION LAWS PROTECTING STUDENTS BY STATE

States (and Washington, DC) with nondiscrimination laws designed to protect students based on sexual orientation and gender identity.

States with nondiscrimination laws designed to protect students based on sexual orientation, but not gender identity.

States that have not passed nondiscrimination laws pertaining to LGBT students.

Figure 14.2: This map shows which states have non-discrimination laws that apply to schools and protect students on the basis of sexual orientation or sexual orientation as well as gender identity. (Source: GLSEN, 2013)

There are also states that have laws which purposefully stigmatize LGBT students, and which prohibit local school districts from having enumerated anti-bullying policies. "No promo homo" laws forbid local or state education teachers from discussing gay and transgender issues (including sexual health and HIV/AIDS awareness) in a way that could be viewed as positive. In some states, teachers *must* portray LGBT people in a negative or inaccurate way. Currently, eight states have adopted "no promo homo" laws: Alabama, Arizona, Louisiana, Mississippi, Oklahoma, South Carolina, Texas, and Utah; and Missouri and South Dakota prohibit school districts from having enumerated policies.

So while we have no federal anti-bullying law, LGBT students do have some levels of protection. Title IX and Title IV do not prohibit discrimination based solely on sexual orientation, but they protect all students, including students who are LGBT or those perceived to be LGBT, from sex-based harassment. Likewise, under Title IX, LGBT students are protected from forms of sex discrimination if they experience harassment based on their actual or perceived sexual orientation.

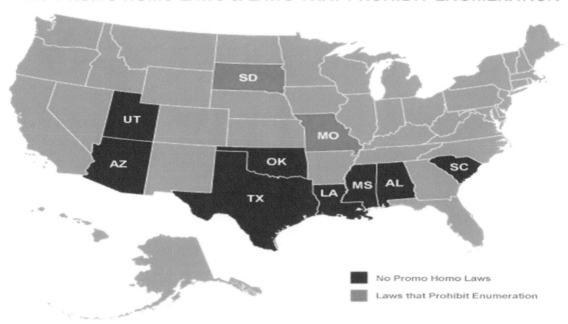

Figure 14.3: This map shows which states have "no promo homo" laws and laws that prohibit enumeration. (Source: GLSEN, 2013)

An Anti-Bullying Stance

Currently, there is no federal anti-bullying law. States must take it upon themselves to create anti-bullying laws. Forty-nine of 50 states have anti-bullying laws in place (Montana is the only state without any anti-bullying laws), and several states have comprehensive anti-bullying laws. Though comprehensiveness varies by state, we are starting to see tough legislative reforms in states such as New York, New Jersey, and Massachusetts. To date, Massachusetts has one of the strictest and toughest anti-bullying laws in the country. It requires teachers and other school staff to report bullying to the principal or another administrator picked to handle reports when they see or become aware of it. It requires yearly training for teachers and staff on prevention and intervention related to all forms of bullying, and it calls for instruction on heading off bullying for students in every grade as part of the curriculum (Miller, 2013). Were tougher anti-bullying laws present in each state, we would likely see a decrease in the number of casualties and bullycides, those who take their own lives due to being bullied.

A comprehensive stance on anti-bullying must be seamlessly tied to law, education, and preventive health care. Miller (2013) enumerated a wish list of interventionist anti-bullying stances, which included:

1. Legislatively preclude it by putting in place a systems-based anti-bullying program in every school in the country.

2. Implement an anti-bullying curriculum in which students take anti-bullying classes every year during their pre-K–16 preparation.

3. Have a federally appointed official serve as a "minister of anti-bullying" who studies and reviews successful models of anti-bullying programs for use in local systems (based on models such as those found in the United Kingdom[1] and Sweden[2]).

4. Fund anti-bullying programs at the federal level and reward states and schools that show reductions in bullying.

5. Tie anti-bullying to preventive mental health and health-care screenings so that prevention/intervention becomes a standard aspect of our citizenry's annual check-ups.

Since these stances have yet to be enacted, states and schools are encumbered with developing stances that can reduce bullying.

What *Schools* Can Do to Support TGV Students

Research does support that some teachers are ably working with the lesbian-gay-bisexual-transgender continuum (Clark & Blackburn, 2009; Meyer, 2007; Miller, 2009; Parker & Bach, 2009; Weinberg, 2009), and are effectively applying it to classroom curriculum and the like, but teachers are likely to be grossly unfamiliar with how current gender theory has rapidly moved into adolescent discourse and is practiced by them each and every day that they enter and exit school grounds. By understanding the current research and conversation related to non-binary representations of gender issues in middle and secondary high school English, math, science, art, physical education, and history classrooms, teachers can challenge normative constructs of gender, masculinity, and femininity that reproduce gender inequities and gendered violence, and that hinder the human development of young people. To be effective and to hold teachers and students accountable, teaching about non-binary representations of gender across curricula must be placed in a social justice and/or human rights context and integrated into an anti-bullying stance in a school's code of conduct—or a *queering* of pedagogy. Such stances must proactively seek to disrupt gender typing and heteronormativity, which have provided limited and narrow lenses for how youth fit into society. By moving beyond the gender binary, the invisibility of those who have once been silenced and marginalized can be decreased, and discourses around gender—which are also privileged, inequitable hierarchies of power and privilege in the classroom—can be reshaped and can inevitably become more equitable.

Moving Beyond the Gender Binary

Discussing laws and exclusionary practices in school curricula that exclude LGBT people can set the tone for how to bridge past to current practices relating specifically to TGV students. Understanding beyond the gender binary can mediate how teachers approach the changing identities of students, and provide them direction for queering pedagogy. *Beyond*, first and foremost, is postmodern and futuristic, and implies and recognizes that there is a foundation from which other ideologies emerge in its location on the binary. Likened to Felski's (1996) work on transexuality, the beyond "remain[s] attentive to disjuncture and nonsynchrony in the experience of temporality while simultaneously acknowledging systematic connections and relationships among discrete cultural practices" (p. 348). For instance, when we consider binary concepts, they are the unspoken and yet agreed upon dominant ideologies that are reinforced institutionally, and exist to maintain popular understandings on myriad topics such as law, education, government, and religion. Often when the binary is challenged in any of these institutions, people become uncomfortable or destabilized because the binary is, in itself, an ideology that can be understood by the masses as it secures and safely localizes dominantly held beliefs and morals. Gender, gender identity, and gender expression tend to conjure destabilization because they do fall outside of, and challenge, the binary.

The binary mediates how relational ideas are often socially constructed as pairs to frame a continuum, but such ideas are not necessarily oppositional. An example of this would be the Jungian symbolic archetype of light versus darkness. These concepts recur and exist in collective unconscious, and reinforce the binary and meaning-making in myriad contexts. *Light* often means good, goodness, faith, right, etc., while *darkness* infers evil, lack of faith, fallen, and wrong. Typically, these archetypes are paired in stories, art, and in various cultural milieus. So while they may be opposite one another, there is an implication of their opposing natures, and they may not be overtly oppositional (though they can be). The same is true for the binary pairing of law and anarchy. *Law* implies right, morally correct, conformity, and acceptance of social norms and mores; while *anarchy* means an abhorrence of law, nonconformity, and rejection of and/or disdain for social norms and mores. These concepts often participate unconsciously opposite one another through acquiescence to social norms that are indoctrinated into people from early in one's life. Like light versus darkness, law and anarchy are not always overtly oppositional, but they do operate on the unconscious mind to maintain order in society.

Applying these examples to the discussion of "beyond the gender binary," the *beyond* recognizes the foundation of its inception, or rather, the institutionalization of the theoretical ideologies from which it emerged, but it also challenges its genesis by constructing emerging ideological language, which cannot fit into neat boxes that will satisfy status quo ideology. And so, the beyond the gender binary is one of the areas that tends to make people uncomfortable, because it is not easily understood, nor is it dominantly accepted.

The word, *queer*, is a transitional word for understanding the movement from the gender binary to the non-binary. Traditionally, *queer* was a pejoratively held term against the LGBT community, but has been reappropriated by activists and academics as a way of taking back power and pivoting this word into a term of empowerment. Though the term itself has become quite normalized within the LGBT community, if one is in the "know," it has become a bridge often synonymously used for the LGBT acronym, but is still on the margin of larger social and heteronormative acceptance. *Queer* can help make sense of moving beyond the gender binary, as it is an umbrella term that many prefer, both because of convenience (easier than gay, lesbian, etc.), and because it does not force the person who uses it to choose a more specific label for their gender identity or sexual orientation.

Although several theories on gender have been fundamental in shaping dominant perspectives on gender, this discussion on understanding moving beyond the gender binary is premised on Judith Butler's (1990) notion that gender is performance, which is an outgrowth of prior feminist theories on gender. Butler suggested that the given identity of the individual is illuminated by the gender that one performs. Butler said, "gender is an identity tenuously constituted in time, instituted in an exterior space through a *stylized repetition of acts*" (p. 140). She went on to suggest that gender is a "surface signification," and that gender "is created through sustained social performances" (p. 141). Butler essentially argued that the individual is a subject, capable of action—not an object to be constructed. Such reasoning infers that people have agency in how they invite and embody an identity. Building from this premise, then, by inviting in discussion about gender in classrooms, we can begin to see how any identity can take on various gender-performed roles.

Gender identity is therefore an individual's personal sense of his or her correct gender along a continuum between normative constructs of masculinity and femininity (Miller, 2009), while *gender expression* is one's choice and/or manipulation of gender cues: such as with hair, clothes, and makeup (Chase & Ressler, 2009, p. 23). Gender expression may or may not be congruent with or influenced by a person's biological sex. *Sexual identity* or *sexual orientation* refers both to how people identify biologically on a continuum between female and male, and to whom they are sexually and/or affectionally attracted. If we are to have a truly pluralistic understanding about gender, gender identity, and gender expression, we must begin to inform ourselves about the emerging politics and discourse on nonnormative representations of gender so that we can inform our own students about current and accurate information that will prepare them for real-world understandings. In fact, bringing them into their own histories of the LGBT movement and the current policies which are and are not in place about state and federal bullying laws can develop into interdisciplinary units that can inform and empower them to become agents of change.

If we move from the stance that gender is socially constructed, we can begin to see how that can inform our observations of gender performance in school contexts. As many of us are aware, students bring with them identities from their lives about which we, as teachers, may lack understanding. Students today perform gender outside of the space-time continuum in which many teachers were socialized. And so, this brings a burgeoning excitement to the classroom that invites close observation from which we can all learn.

Conclusion: Moving Beyond—Adding the TGV and More to the LGB/Straight-Heterosexual Binary

When we talk about non-normative gender, or gender non-conformity, or even gender variance, we enter into territory that students seem to be more comfortable discussing than do their teacher counterparts. In fact, much of our contemporary learning as a society about gender non-conformity has come from peer groups; talking with youth; attending house parties; following Facebook discussions; reading research, magazines, young adult books, and novels; and watching non-mainstream film. In order to add the TGV to the LGB acronym, we need to unpack some of the ideology behind transgender theory.

The word *transgender* entered the English vocabulary in the 1980s from the transsexual and transvestite communities to describe individuals whose gender identity is different from their biological sex (Cromwell, 1997, p. 134). A *transgender person* (refers to the T on the LGBT continuum) is one who has the experience of having a gender identity that is different from one's biological sex. A transgender person does not have to medically transition or have gender-alignment surgery to identify as transgender. *Transgender* has become an umbrella term for non-conforming or non-normative gender identity and gender expression, but a transgender person who does have gender-alignment surgery is referred to as transsexual. Gender-alignment surgery is the actual establishment of one's affirmed sex via legal and medical steps. Other terms often used by the transgender community are *trans woman* or *trans man*, which are informal descriptors used relative to one's affirmed gender. Some variants include trans person and trans folk. *Transsexual people* typically refers to those taking all available medical and legal steps to transition from their assigned sex to their affirmed sex. Transitioning across the sexual binary can go from female to male (FTM) or male to female (MTF), and some people become stealth, hiding their transsexual history (Wenzel, 2007).

Adding transgender to the continuum of LGB suggests that the continuum of LGB/straight-heterosexual is no longer binary, because it disrupts and conflates dominant ideologies of gender. The transgender person has become a contested site where dominant ideologies on gender can no longer be located or codified because

> the gender-ambiguous individual today represents a very different set of assumptions about gender than the gender-inverted subject of the early twentieth century ... and the transgender body has emerged as futurity itself as a kind of heroic fulfillment of postmodern promises of gender flexibility. (Halberstam, 2005, p. 18)

Martin (1995) told us that gender flexibility carries with it "a powerful commodity" (p. xvii) that can be used discriminately against the transgender person or the person whose gender identity and expressions challenge the binary, but that so, too, does it carry powerful social and economic capital which pushes away from being located in the binary.[3] Thus, other expressions of gender will continue to emerge that also lack location on the binary continuum. Subcultures connected to emerging nuances of non-normative gender identities that evolve over space and time will have great power economically and culturally and will continue to push social barriers in new and exciting directions.

We have much to understand when we observe how people identify. Take, for example, a biologically born male who performs masculinity but identifies as a woman; or consider a biologically born female who performs the male gender and wants to transition but wants to be a gay man. One's sexual orientation is no doubt part of this matrix of exciting expressions of non-normative gender. A transgender person may have an orientation that is heterosexual, asexual, bisexual, pansexual, or homosexual, regardless of the person's biological sex. Other identifiers that move us beyond an LGBT/straight-heterosexual non-binary include terms such as label-free, genderqueer, gender creative, pansexual and/or omnisexual, and genderfluid. When we reflect on what we once knew to be binary, i.e., the LGB/straight-heterosexual continuum, we can now locate emerging identities that push us beyond the binary and into spaces where we can begin to shift the discourse and queer pedagogy about gender identity, gender expression, and sexual orientation that support our LGBTQGV^M populations.

This work, I hope, has provided readers with suggestions for ways to move forward with courage and intent as teachers begin to push harder for inclusion of TGV students and their protection in schools. Teachers can be proactive about bullying by queering pedagogy and including the history of LGBTQGV people, by challenging heteronormative discourse, by teaching about gender and gender identity across discipline lines, and by being vigilant when bullying happens. Until we have equal protection for all students across all differences and contexts, we must continue to challenge hegemonic ideology, be on the front lines fighting for the rights of our students, and be relentless in our efforts to not only make change happen but to embody that change.

Notes

1. Schools in England are legally required to have an anti-bullying policy, as stated in the Education and Inspections Act (EIA) of 2006 (Smith, Smith, Osborn, & Samara, 2008).
2. Schools in Sweden are required by law to have an anti-bullying policy (Frisen, Jonsson, & Persson, 2007).
3. Some individuals who transition may not be transitioning from one gender to the other and may balk at gender categories altogether. What is important in working with trans youth is to ask a person how the person would like to be referred to.

References

Butler, J. (1990). *Gender trouble: Feminism and the subversion of identity.* New York, NY: Routledge.

Chase, B., & Ressler, P. (2009). A GLBT/queer glossary. *English Journal, 98*(4), 23–24.

Clark, C., & Blackburn, M. (2009). Reading LGBT literature. *English Journal, 98*(4), 25–32.

Cromwell, P. (1997). Traditions of gender diversity and sexualities: A female-to-male gender perspective. In S-E. Jacobs, W. Thomas, & S. Lang (Eds.), *Two-spirit people: Native American gender identity, sexuality, and spirituality* (pp. 119–142). Chicago, IL: University of Illinois Press.

Felski, R. (1996). Fin de siècle, fin de sexe: Transsexuality, postmodernism, and the death of history. *New Literary History, 27*(2), 337–349.

Frisen, A., Jonsson, A-K., & Persson, C. (2007). Adolescents' perceptions of bullying: Who is the victim? Who is the bully? What can be done to stop bullying? *Adolescence, 42*(168), 749–761.

GLSEN. (2013). *States with safe school laws.* Retrieved from http://www.glsen.org

Greytak, E., Kosciw, J., & Diaz, E. (2009). *Harsh realities: The experiences of transgender youth in our schools.* New York, NY: GLSEN.

Halberstam, J. (2005). *In a queer time & place. Transgender bodies, subcultural lives.* New York, NY: New York University Press.

Kosciw, J., Greytak, E., Diaz, E., & Bartkiewicz, M. (2010). *The 2009 national school climate survey: The experiences of lesbian, gay, bisexual and transgender youth in our nation's schools.* New York, NY: GLSEN.

Martin, E. (1995). *Flexible bodies.* Boston, MA: Beacon Press.

Markow, D., & Fein, J. (2005). *From teasing torment: School climate in America—A survey of students and teachers.* Gay, Lesbian & Straight Education Network. New York, NY: Harris Interactive.

Meyer, E. (2007). But I'm not gay: What straight teachers need to know about queer theory. In N. Rodriguez & W. Pinar (Eds.), *Queering straight teachers: Discourse and identity in education* (pp. 15–29). New York, NY: Peter Lang.

Miller, sj. (2009). (Dis)embedding gender diversity in the preservice classroom. In S. Steinberg (Ed.), *Diversity: A reader* (pp. 193–209). New York, NY: Peter Lang.

Miller, sj. (2012). Mythology of the norm: Disrupting the culture of bullying in schools. *English Journal, 101*(6), 107–109.

Miller, sj. (2013). Where are we now? The current state of bullying in the United States. In sj. Miller, L. Burns, & T. S. Johnson (Eds.), *Generation BULLIED 2.0: Prevention and intervention strategies for our most vulnerable students.* New York, NY: Peter Lang.

Parker, B., & Bach, J. (2009). Gender variant and transgender issues in a professional development book group. *English Journal, 98*(4), 96–101.

Sherer, Y. P., & Nickerson, A. B. (2010). Anti-bullying practices in American schools: Perspectives of school psychologists. *Psychology in the Schools, 47*(3), 217–229.

Smith, P. K., Smith, C., Osborn, R., & Samara, M. (2008). A content analysis of school anti-bullying policies: Progress and limitations. *Educational Psychology in Practice, 24*(1), 1–12.

Stopbullying.gov. (2013). *Key components in state anti-bullying laws.* Retrieved from http://www.stopbullying.gov/laws/key-components/index.html

Weinberg, M. (2009). LGBT inclusive language. *English Journal, 98*(4), 50–51.

Wenzel, R. (2007, December 18). Gay vs. trans in America. *The Advocate,* 999: 48.

Wittig, M. (1983). The point of view: Universal or particular? *Feminist Issues, 3*(2), 63–69.

CHAPTER 15

Reading the Wallpaper
Disrupting Performances of Whiteness in the Blog, "Stuff White People Like"

Nichole E. Grant and Timothy J. Stanley

In everyday culture, including youth cultures, patterns of dominance come to be invisible, even though they are not hidden. Through constant repetition, dominance becomes simply the way the world is; what Hannah Arendt called many years ago, "the organization of a texture of life" (Arendt, 1973, p. 363). Rather than being an underlying, hidden reality, dominance is in plain sight (Abrams, 1988; Stanley, 2009). However, through repetition, its patterns are unrecognized, something in the background that is constantly repeated to the point of banality (Billig, 1995). Patterns of dominance become the wallpaper of everyday culture, invisible to those who re-enact dominance even as they do so. Even for those for whom the resulting physical and psychic violence is all too real, when read against the wallpaper that naturalizes this violence, their experiences can seem unremarkable, their oppression normal, and their resistance solitary, until something makes a hole in the wallpaper or tears it apart. Bumps, holes, and tears; disruptions of the repeating pattern make the wallpaper itself visible. Sharp moments of resistance, voicing excluded knowledges, discoveries of shared histories of exclusion, and resistance, the naming of acts of dominance as dominance, make the wallpaper visible (e.g., see Fanon, 1967/1991; hooks, 1984). Holes create possibilities for tearing the wallpaper down and ending its repetitions (Kumashiro, 2002).

In the following, we explore the wallpaper of popular racism in the form of White supremacy in online social media. We argue that the wallpaper becomes visible in the moments of disruption—the bumps, holes, and tears in the discursive fabric of online social frameworks—and shows it to be papering over relations of dominance. These moments of disruption offer possibilities for antiracist transformation that makes the cultural representations of dominance, in Stuart Hall's words, "uninhabitable" (Hall, as cited in Jhally, 1997). The online world neither "reflects" the "real" world, nor is it free of it. Rather, it is a key place for the creation and exchange of meanings which are constitutive of the "real" (Hall, as cited in Jhally, 1997). The culture of young people who are immersed in social media does not consist of a hierarchy of the offline and online worlds but is made up of the two. Dominance gets enacted through these exchanges in both places, and its patterns in one place articulate (with) the patterns of the other (Hall, 1980; Slack, 1996). Young people's understandings and negotiations of racisms in online exchanges with their peers provide them with meanings through which they negotiate the world.

We build on the work of Lowe (2012) to argue that far from being separate from each other, the relations of dominance found within the racisms of the offline world are articulated in the patterns of representation found online, and that the latter both articulate, and articulate with, the former. Critical examination of the patterns of representation found online helps to illuminate the larger relations of racism that constitute the stuff of everyday contemporary culture.

We make this argument with respect to the blog, "Stuff White People Like," (stuffwhitepeoplelike. com). Started in January of 2008 by a blogger who calls himself *clander*, at the time of writing the site has received over 80 million hits, with individual postings generating between several hundred and several thousand comments each. For example, between February 17, 2008 and November 15, 2012, the first post, "#1 Coffee," generated 2,457 comments. The blog appeared when broadband services were first making the Internet commonplace, and when fears of identity fraud and of people becoming "someone else online" were growing (Gies, 2008). The possibilities of enacting other identities particularly appealed to young people, who were the majority of blog users during this era (Lenhart, Purcell, Smith, & Zickuhr, 2010). The blog also began during a supposed recalibration of racial politics in the United States with the election of President Barack Obama. Thus, this blog about the "White" body was novel and instantly popular. The resulting postings act as a "filter blog" (Wei, 2009), where information and knowledge are politically inclined, filtered, circulated, and shared in a community environment on a large scale. Through people's responses to the original postings, or their responses to others over time, the blog itself creates a kind of conversation in which readers show how they understand the responses of other users. The resulting collective cultural creation makes it an ideal site to study grammars of popular racisms (Rizvi, 1993).

The Patterns in the Paper: Racisms, Discourses, and Antiracist Theory

Our analysis is shaped by an antiessentialist antiracism that builds on the work of a number of theorists of antiracism, and especially that of Robert Miles (1989) and David Theo Goldberg (1993). Rather than individual prejudices or irrational beliefs, within this framework, racisms have no fixed essences, but are analytically identifiable and involve racialization, the organization of these racializations into exclusions, and the enactment of negative consequences for the racialized and excluded. Antiracisms thus resist racialization, organize inclusions, and mitigate consequences, but begin with the resistance of the racialized and excluded to their exclusion. As a result, antiracist scholarship necessarily seeks out and engages the meanings, self-representations, and life experiences of the excluded (Stanley, 2011). Our analysis departs from Miles (1989) by seeing racisms as structuring social relations, rather than as ideologies, and from Goldberg (2009) by insisting on the necessity of naming and documenting racialization. Like Critical Race Theory (CRT), our antiessentialist antiracism begins with the recognition of the ubiquity of racisms in modern, Westernized societies, but unlike at least some Critical Race theorists, we see racisms and all of their constitutive aspects—racializations, exclusions, and consequences—as continually in the process of becoming (On CRT, see Cohen, 2009; Gillborn, Gillborn, & Ladson-Billings, 2009). The results are a researchable agenda that looks for language that racializes, physical and cultural spaces that exclude, and for the lived consequences of exclusion (Stanley 2012).

"Stuff White People Like": A Racialized Blog of White Wallpaper

Typical of blogs, "Stuff White People Like" consists of a posting on a particular subject by the blogger to which users post replies, either directly to *clander*'s original post, or in response to the comments of other users. Each post appears in reverse chronological order, with the newest material at the top of the page, along with a main title banner and several subheadings and side menus. The title banner consists of four pictures representing different "stuff" White people like, where the title of the blog appears in overlay. Therefore, the title banner frames the blog by speaking to its specific worldview and understandings of race and Whiteness. Whiteness becomes a performance of the things in the pictures: liking sushi, small dogs, walks on the beach, and farmers' markets. These performances directly articulate histories of racist privilege, cultural appropriation, and colonization (Lowe, 2012). Something of the yuppie orientation of the blog is suggested by the first posting entitled, "#1 Coffee," where, after describing the ways in which coffee is central to Whiteness, *clander* adds, "If you want to go for extra points—white people really love FAIR TRADE coffee, because paying the extra $2 means they are making a difference" (*clander*, 2008a). Each post is a mixture of text and image, with a title and a short description of how White people exemplify the titled object or practice (e.g., see Figure 15.1). The structure of the postings themselves resembles that of other popular comedy forums such as David Letterman's "Top Ten" lists (*Late Show* Top Ten, 2010), and allows the blog to satirically and unapologetically list performative attributes of Whiteness that are linked to essential understandings of race, of privilege, and of dominance (Leonardo, 2004; McIntosh, 1990). The results create an outline for White racialized membership. The blog's satire make this outline light, playful, and unserious, making racial positionings seem unproblematic in the process—as if they exist as separate statuses, independent of each other, and are shaped by self-expressive choice.

Figure 15.1: "#1 Coffee" post. clander (2008a). #1 Coffee [Web log post]. Retrieved from http://stuffwhitepeoplelike.com/2008/01/18/1-coffee

Our analysis focuses on threads that start in the first three months of responses to two of the posts: the first post, "Coffee" (*clander*, 2008a), and the ninety-second post, "Book Deals," (*clander*, 2008b). Most of the comments are playful, taking on the satirical tone of the blog's framework and creating an in-group of people who "get" the humour of the blog. Indeed, readers often comment negatively on those who apparently do not get the humour. Some responses are too short or too ambiguous to analyze, but in others, users identify their racial positioning, either explicitly within the comment itself or in their user name (e.g., non-white-person, 2008), or implicitly by providing enough information to reveal their positioning in relation to the blog within their comments. It is these last two types of comments that we focus on.

Users who racialize themselves as White enter into the blog by either adding to the "stuff" White people like, or by questioning whether the right list has been identified. For example, in the first post, "Coffee," multiple users debate where coffee comes from, who invented it, and even what kind of coffee is the kind that White people like. They do not, however, question the idea that White people appropriated it (compare *nicole, rachel, and David*, 2008, and *yo mama*, 2009). The overwhelming majority of responses come from people who write from discursive positions that allow them to critique the rules of what gets included in the performances and who celebrate the enactments of whatever they claim are the right performances of Whiteness. The responses are silent on the colonizing effects of the performances themselves or the exclusions that result from these performances. In other words, the majority of comments express a privileged position in which racist oppression does not appear to exist, but in which people have the freedom to establish the boundaries of their identities. These responses enact dominance. They not only physically dominate by occupying the overwhelming majority of the space in the blog, but also through actions that only become evident when fissures appear in the wallpaper.

Bubbles in the Wallpaper: Negotiations of Dominant Discourses

Some comments point to ways of performing race that are outside the framework of the blog, even as they appear to enter into its logic. We understand these comments as bubbles in the wallpaper, momentary eruptions that point to things that the blog papers over through representations of Whiteness as innocent and as independent from other racialized positions. These bumps arise from the comments of people who self-identify as something other than White, and demonstrate how racisms operate in practice. Such comments are either completely ignored or critiqued for being racist themselves, and hence are policed out of the blog. It is as if small bumps are ignored and larger ones flattened.

An example of a small bump is the following post by *Alina*:

> I'm non-white, and you've helped me realize that pretty much ALL the things that I've felt inadequate about over the years (don't snowboard or do yoga, don't drink wine or coffee …) are really just white things! Of couuurse [sic] I don't fit the mold! … I am serious. This has actually affected my sense of self-worth. I feel so much better now. Thank you. (*Alina*, 2008)

Although *Alina's* comment could be read as a genuine expression of gratitude for the blog's effort at revealing the secrets of Whiteness, we read it as sharing in the satiric intent of the blog. Where other users represented Whiteness solely in relation to itself, *Alina's* comment expressed another positioning in which Whiteness exists in relation to being "non-white." If Whites do yoga and drink coffee, non-Whites do not: "Of couuurse I don't fit the mold!" This, however, has negative consequences for her as a "non-white": supposed feelings of inadequacy that have affected her "sense of self-worth." She also articulated a subordinate position in relation to the White authors of the blog. She was grateful to them because they explained something that she supposedly could not possibly understand on her own. In effect, she subordinated herself to Whiteness, while also establishing Whiteness as the norm against which she herself was measured.

However, *Alina* did not merely position herself as a hapless victim who had now been saved from a life of insecurity. She commented that "ALL the things that I've felt inadequate about over the years … are just white things!" For *Alina*, there was more to the world than "just" Whiteness. While on the surface she was positioning herself as benefitting from the blog, she simultaneously offered a counter-text, subverting the importance of the blog in understanding her position of Otherness (Mulkay, 1988). In order for *Alina* to make this comment in this satirical way, she needed to understand the dominant frame, the wallpaper, be in on the joke of the blog itself, and then remake it on her own terms. In so doing, she did not simply critique the blog, she bubbled the wallpaper. She implicitly pointed to dominance being created by explicitly positioning herself as subordinate to Whiteness, as needing enlightenment on how to act White; at the same time, by exaggerating her gratitude, she was pointing to another in-group that sees and recognizes the dominance of Whiteness at work, thus making a kind of counter in-joke. Read satirically, *Alina* is not thankful, or grateful, or even surprised about the epiphanies the blog had brought her. While appearing to enter into a performative text, she in fact was refusing performance. She chose not to write about her sense of identity in contrast or opposition to the discourses of dominance the blog enacts. Whereas for Spivak (1988) the subaltern can only speak within the discursive formations of the dominant, *Alina* chose to speak within the dominant discursive formation, to speak as part of the wallpaper, but bubbled and made the wallpaper known by pointing to her non-white positioning. Significantly, in the four years that her comment has been on the Internet, no one else has picked up on commented on her understanding. Indeed, among the initial comments to the "Coffee" post, such lack of reaction to a comment is the exception. It appears that her bubbling of the wallpaper, simultaneously entering into and yet subverting the dominant framework of the blog, is unanswerable.

Other bubblings of the wallpaper that are less subtle eventually get flattened by other users. For example, on February 16, 2008, *Angry Chinese Driver* congratulated the "whriters (*sic*)" of the site and then commented, "Continue to enlighten us non-whites about your whiteness; I believe many whites like to call that 'integration'" (*Angry Chinese Driver*, 2008). This comment was denounced by *Jonboy* (2008b) as "racist," claiming "that integration as you state, isn't about whites accepting other ethnicities, it's about other ethnicities holding a life time of grudge and resentment for something they never experienced." *Paul Stillman* (2009) stated, "Bravo. I couldn't have said it better my self." For *Jonboy* and for *Paul Stillman*, *Angry Chinese Driver* had nothing valid to say about conceiving integration as becoming White. *Jonboy* and *Paul Stillman* smashed down *Angry Chinese Driver*'s bubble.

Bubbles occur when the structures of dominance are manipulated, even bent, and the wallpaper of the dominant culture pulls away from the structures it covers, but unless closely inspected the surface pattern appears not to be disrupted.

Holes and Patchwork: Policing Oppositions to Dominant Discourse

Dominance, like wallpaper, is always delicate, and works most effectively when it is invisible. But bubbles can lead to holes, and holes emerge where the patterning framework ruptures and the structures carefully hidden under the wallpaper of dominant discourses peek through.

A comment by *a black brother* (2008) created such a hole:

> Hmmmm somehow this website is not racist. Its [*sic*] ok to make fun of one race as long as its [*sic*] white right? Imagine if someone created stuffasianpeoplelike or stuffblackpeoplelike. It would be down within minutes because we would all consider that racist.

In asking whether it is ok to make fun of one race as long as it is White, *a black brother* opened both the politics of humour and the structures of dominance within Whiteness that decide who gets to "make fun" of whom. Unlike *Alina* and *Angry Chinese Driver* who "played along" in an ironic way with the satiric framework of the blog, *a black brother* chose not to adopt the framework. Rather, he seriously questioned the premise that the blog was 'all in good fun' by not only asking a serious question, but also by pointing to the possibility that the blog itself is really racist. In so doing, he critically interrogated the politics of the dominant pattern. In effect, he went against the grain of the dominant pattern, tearing it. It is problematic within a genre of humour to critically engage its premises, as if humour negates critical analysis or thought. However, as Billig (2001) showed, humour can cover over hateful ideologies, making them innocent through denial, with the idiom "it's just a joke" or "I'm just joking." Consequently, *a black brother*'s reading of the blog, as a potential site of racism, and even opening the debate to this line of thinking, created a hole in the wallpaper of dominance and performance the blog upholds.

In responding to *a black brother*, many users reinstated the satirical framework through claims that this site is meant to "be a joke" and that *a black brother*'s claim of racism is consequently ill-founded. A comment by *another white guy* (2008) illustrated this tactic: "this site are [*sic*] so funny ... it's not meant to be racists [*sic*] just funny/so enjoy it don't act like it hurts you are [*sic*] anyone else reading it." Several users followed this tactic to once again physically dominate and to police out the discourse of critical engagement that *a black brother* put forward. In this way, we begin to see the wallpaper come into focus once more, i.e., the repeated, humourous framework of the blog performs Whiteness as dominance. Ironically, this effect to patch over *a black brother*'s hole makes the wallpaper all the more visible, as users must acknowledge the structures of humour in order to reiterate them and recreate the wallpaper.

The opening of the wallpaper created by *a black brother* forged a discursive space that allowed other users to also question the framework of the blog and the racism within it. A comment by *Brian* (2008) showed this opening, as he replied to some of what Michael Billig (2005) called disciplinary humour, like the comment of *another white guy* cited above, by stating, "Guess what a stereotype is ... Yeah, its [*sic*] a bunch of people seeing the same damn thing ... [ellipses in original]." The context of the comment does not allow us to say definitively what *Brian* understood by users "seeing the same damn thing," however, his comment more generally points to how continued discourses, patterns, and repetitions are what lead to stereotypes. These continued discourses and patterns are precisely what the wallpaper of the blog is made up of and what *Brian* was able to draw attention to through the discursive hole started by *a black brother*. Even as some users see the structures under the wallpaper through *a black brother*'s comment, the dominant nature of discourse manages these discourses, and the conversation is repackaged, patched over, and controlled to remind all users that the site is about humour, and that therefore a lack of critical engagement is required. A comment illustrates this: "i [*sic*] don't think the site is racist at all ... but the comments start crossing the line when readers really miss the point of the jokes" (*Anonymous*, 2008c). *Anonymous* did not feel the need to establish what the "point" of the jokes were, assuming that this was understood by the in-group community of the blog. Instead, she or he positioned those who do not get the joke, i.e., the out-group, as defective, and as people whose ideas are not worthy of being considered. In so doing, the discussion of the blog's racism or potential racism is silenced, and the perspectives of people like *a black brother* or *Brian* are excluded. Comments like those of *Anonymous* patch over the hole by reinstating the wallpaper as the "right" discourse; you "get the joke" and are consequently part of the wallpaper, the in-crowd of users, as long as you do not "cross the line" (i.e., critically engage the wallpaper for what it is).

Interesting to note, the reaction to the comment of *a black brother* differed sharply from that of *no* (2008), who posted, "this whole site is so anti-white and anti-american [*sic*]. thats [*sic*] racism. racists [*sic*]." This post drew a single reply, to the effect that the site is not anti-White, it is "anti everything" (*Jonboy*, 2008a). The possible questioning of the site's framework by a self-identified "Black" provoked an assertion of dominance that re-established the pattern of the wallpaper, while that of someone who most likely self-identifies as White caused little concern. In the face of a threat from its racial others, White supremacy was reasserted.

This suggests that the blog is re-enacting social relations found in the offline world. If so, it is not by accident that comments from people who self-identify as other than White rupture the wallpaper. In order to see the structures and the dominant discourse being enacted, in order to know that the wallpaper exists, a position is needed that is aware that the wallpaper is hiding something, and that is aware that it is made up of a repeating pattern. A number of scholars (e.g., Du Bois, 1903; Gilroy, 1993) have noted that people of colour have long occupied positions of alterity where they are part of at least two selves, the mainstream and the marginal. It would seem that the experience of exclusion of *Alina, Angry Chinese Driver*, and *a black brother* in the offline world allowed them to recognize the wallpaper in the blog, while also pointing to the structures underneath that the dominant discourses of the mainstream online environment attempt to silence or ignore. Their efforts at rupture enable us to see the creation of dominance as ongoing. The blog in effect creates a space in which the racism of its overall framework cannot be engaged, and self-identified people of colour and their experiences are ignored or silenced and either way excluded. Despite this, those who are excluded are still able to point to ways of being in the world that differ from those of the dominant.

The Violence of Tearing It Down: Racist Discourses and Dominant Discourses

Racisms, however, are not just systems of symbolic representation and exclusion. They are also systems of direct violence against people. This, too, becomes evident in the blog. As the blog continues from the first post, other moments of bubbling and poking holes rupture the wallpaper. Within these moments we can see the wallpaper covering discursive structures that control ways of talking, performing, and identifying within the blog space. Some of the responses to the ninety-second blog post, "Book Deals," (*clander*, 2008b) point to the direct violence of racisms. "Book Deals" arises at an important moment in the blog's life cycle. At the peak of the blog's popularity, Random House offered the blogger a book contract based on the blog's premise. In "#92 Book Deals," the blogger made his authorship known, and posed in a picture that accompanied the post performing some of the attributes of Whiteness that the blog describes. The picture within the post is reproduced below (see Figure 15.2). Within the comments that accompanied this post, most initial comments were congratulatory and encouraging, but the picture and the wallpaper came to tear apart in a sequence of comments.

Figure 15.2: "#92 Book Deals" [Web log post]. Retrieved from http://stuffwhitepeoplelike. com/2008/03/26/92-book-deals/

In the photograph, the blogger himself appears as a light-skinned, red-haired man wearing a shirt with a Star of David on the front which is usually read as a signifier of Jewishness. For some users, this simultaneous performance of Whiteness and possible Jewishness becomes highly problematic, indeed, sufficient to call the entire blog into question. According to *Henry Blanco* (2008), "This little prick in the picture is not the definition of 'White'. Far from it. Look at the photo again. he's [sic] a jewified weasel" [quotations in original]. *Henry Blanco's* comment tore open the wallpaper's delicate illusion that Whiteness is a light-hearted performance. The comment is anything but light-hearted; it is forceful and demeaning, using two different instances of name-calling: "little prick" and "jewified weasel." The second name also enacts racist violence, as *Henry Blanco* positioned the blogger's possible Jewishness as meaning that he is not really "White" but is also not human. This is as if the performance of Jewishness, flagged by the Star of David on his shirt, transformed him. *Henry Blanco* also revealed that the blogger *was*, at some other point, the definition of "White." Following the pattern of the wallpaper, but *because of* the performance of Jewishness, the blogger was robbed of this title and made less than human. The wallpaper was torn open, as Whiteness came not to be the light-hearted performance of privilege as in *Alina's* comment, or a moment of oppositional questioning as in *a black brother's* comment but rather came to be something that enacts the power to name others in such derogatory terms with little or no concern for a backlash. This type of positioning and the racist logic from a single user and all that it entails appear to be such that it should be policed out and controlled. However, further comments revealed that it was the rupture created by *clander's* embodiment of possible Jewishness and Whiteness that tore the wallpaper, and the discourse in the comments changed to continue enacting oppressive, racist logic to define Whiteness.

It is important to note that Jews of European origins are often excluded from White, racialized identity because in White supremacist imagination their biological heredity is suspect, where many of their historic performances are related, not to dominance, but to being dominated, controlled, and disenfranchised (Goldstein, 2002; Kaplan, 2003). Jews are often also caught between definitions, and their positions are unclear and overlapping between culture, race (read biologically), ethnicity, and religion (Rogoff, 1997). Meanwhile, many Jews in North America continue to experience anti-Semitic violence (e.g., Dowden & Brennan, 2012), while also living the consequences of the Holocaust.

The blogger's questionable or "other White" identity repositioned the blog within a Jewish framework, further tearing the wallpaper. A comment by *Cargill* (2008) described this point: "I called it from the beginning. This site was always about jewified little whites, and now it's right there for all to see. A picture is worth 1,000 words. Unreal. If that's 'White', then what a joke." For *Cargill*, the blog was not about "real" Whites, but had become tainted by Otherness. It is also an ironic use of the "joke," as *Cargill's* comment implied anything but the "joking" manner of the wallpaper of the blog. For *Cargill*, Whiteness here was both tainted by Jewishness and made diminutive in comparison to "real" Whiteness.

Once again, *Cargill* pointed to the "problem" of performing Whiteness as a position that is necessarily dominant, and in which "real" Whiteness is distanced from racialized others attempting to "pass" as White. It is not, therefore, the blogger's performance itself that becomes problematic, but rather the equation of Jewishness with Whiteness and its "passing" for White. Whiteness was threatened, contaminated, and needed to be reasserted as separate from Jewishness. In this sense, the wallpaper tore again as the blog became about Otherness, and not Whiteness, and became itself a "joke." As other users also picked up on this discourse of Jewishness as Other in relation to the blog, the wallpaper tore asunder as the discourse became increasingly hostile, violent, and racist (e.g., *Anonymous*, 2008a). The dominant discourse in relation to the blog's framework of Whiteness as privileged performance was abandoned in favour of racist discourses of White supremacy and the stereotyping of Jews (Lowe, 2012). The blogger's own intervention appeared to tear the wallpaper beyond repair, the structures of dominance and oppression which the comments revealed remained open, and the raw edges of the wallpaper were exposed.

However, *Henry Blanco*'s comment was immediately challenged by others who suggested that he was "way too low-brow for this site" (*Anonymous*, 2008b), that he was "not the right kind of white person," (*Ted*, 2008), or, in the words of one respondent to another post by *Henry Blanco*, "Why don't you just pee your pants and quiet down" (*Hardcastle*, 2008). Significantly, while denouncing *Henry Blanco*, none of these comments took on and exposed the racist repertoire that he was employing, or engaged with the consequences of anti-Semitism. Rather, they were quick to edit him out of the conversation, so that the blog could return to its previously existing framework. Further, these comments picked up on the common-sense understanding of racism as individual, in *Henry Blanco* himself, rather than seeing or admitting to their own positions within racist systems (Lichtenberg, 1998).

Thus, some of the comments in this post directly enact racist violence towards the blogger, but more significantly, towards Jewish people in both the online and real worlds. In effect, these comments shift the discussion away from the wallpaper. The claim never gets taken up and criticized that if *clander* is Jewish, he is therefore not "really" White, and that his blog is consequently a racist attack against "real" White people. This is evidence of two of what Lowe (2012) called the three "registers of whiteness" operating in the blog. One of these registers is that of Whiteness as a light-hearted, self-referential enactment of class privilege. The other, as shown by *Henry Blanco* and *Cargill*, is as a position of supremacy from which violence directed at all others is organized. The third, not directly discussed here, is one of essentialized representations of racialized identities in biological terms. However, in the end, all three registers fail to engage with the realities of exclusion and its consequences that the dominance of Whiteness entails (Leonardo, 2004).

Reading the Wallpaper: Reading Whiteness as Dominance

From the above, we develop the following reading of the wallpaper as a pattern of dominance that keeps repeating. This dominance gets enacted through a recurring representation of Whiteness as first, a racial category that exists on its own, separate from any other category; and further, as a category that is a single thing with a fixed essence. What this essence is may be contested, but the idea that there is an essence is never in dispute. However, the bumps, holes, and tears within the wallpaper reveal something different. First, they reveal that Whiteness is not a single thing, but operates within different registers. The contest over what is the authentic Whiteness demonstrated in the blog, who gets to decide what it is, and who is included in it, if nothing else, points to the social construction of the category—a constant process of labelling, ascribing, and re-inscribing an identity—and to ongoing acts of power that seek to fix difference. None of this would be necessary if in fact racialized identities were natural, fixed, and/or self-evident (American Anthropological Association, 2012). More importantly, these ruptures point to racist realities where Whiteness dominates, and in which the experiences, the meanings, and the lives of people who are racialized differently are excluded, marginalized, and denied. Indeed, some of the ruptures point to the denial of shared humanness that, in the end, all racisms engage in. What began as an inquiry into a humourous website comes to document how all racisms work and how they articulate and articulate with online and offline spaces.

Conclusions and Hopes: Finding the Door

One of the main goals of this chapter was to expose and trouble the everyday and common-sense understandings of race and Whiteness as they appear in popular settings of youth culture. The blog, "Stuff White People Like," became a case study for analyzing these discursive categories in a racialized, real-life setting. What this chapter and its discussions reveal is that people use social media and the Internet to engage discussions of race, racialization, and identity in a real and significant way. They also show the power of visual and discursive cues in the performance of racial categories, and the power of ridicule in the maintenance of these categories. Furthermore, the discussions uncover how the framework of the blog, and the dominant discourses of race that it promotes, has a significant influence about how knowledge of race and racism is perpetuated and produced within the discussion. Therefore, the blog reveals the power of its racialized, discursive structure to act as a framework for knowledge production and understanding of race as a category of essentialized representation and identity. It is this relationship that we illustrate with the metaphor of the wallpaper.

The satire of the blog acts as a separate layer through which knowledges of race and Whiteness are discussed and negotiated. Satire acts as a buffer to allow racist discourses to seem both less harmful and less what they are—racist. It also allows critical discourses that attempt to combat or question essentialist understandings of race to be downplayed and policed out of discussions. Though satire has the power to allow discussions to occur that may seem difficult, such as confronting White dominance and performances of privilege, in its very allowance of these discussions, it also allows them to be denied, ignored, and belittled. The satire within the blog, as taken up within the user comments, makes some discourses difficult to pick apart, as the level of seriousness within the discourse is not entirely self-evident. The effects of these discourses are, however, of the greatest importance. For antiracism, discourses that allow overt, racist expressions to go unquestioned must always be named, pulled apart, and challenged, even if they are "supposed to be a joke."

Thus, our analysis of the blog provides a real-world understanding of how racism functions in popular discourse and how racialization is enacted in those discourses. In particular, it gives a snapshot of where and how people understand racialized identities in relation to power—or, perhaps more importantly, whether they see them as relations of power at all (Dei, 2006; Stanley, 2011). Working through the contextual nature and situatedness of race and power in everyday discourses is vital to larger understandings of how knowledge of race and racism is produced in popular discourses for youth culture. As Dei (2006) pointed out, "understanding the use of power is at the heart of progressive politics for change" (p. 14). So, too, we need continued efforts to stare at the wallpaper and find the bubbles, holes, and tears within it. We need to witness such ruptures in the wallpaper, and make them bigger and more noticeable so as to reveal the structures it covers over. Noticing and pointing out the patterns within the wallpaper, where they are repeated and how often, and finally making such wallpapers so strange that they become uninhabitable (Hall, as cited in Jhally, 1997), will allow us all to turn and walk out of the room.

Acknowledgments

The authors would like to thank Awad Ibrahim for suggesting this collaboration in the first place, and Pamela Rogers, Bryan Smith, and Doug Tateishi for their support in the writing of it.

References

a black brother. (2008, March 25). Re: #1 Coffee [Web log comment]. Retrieved from http://stuffwhitepeoplelike.com/2008/01/18/1-coffee/?cp=all#comments

Abrams, P. (1988). Notes on the difficulty of studying the state, 1977. *Journal of Historical Sociology, 1*(1), 58–89.

Alina. (2008, February 20). Re: #1 Coffee [Web log comment]. Retrieved from http://stuffwhitepeoplelike.com/2008/01/18/1-coffee/?cp=all#comments

American Anthropological Association. (2012). Home. *RACE: Are we so different?* Retrieved from http://www.understandingrace.org/home.html

Angry Chinese Driver. (2008, February 16). Re: #1 Coffee [Web log comment]. Retrieved from http://stuffwhitepeoplelike.com/2008/01/18/1-coffee/?cp=all#comments

Anonymous. (2008a, March 27). Re: #92 Book deals [Web log comment]. Retrieved from http://stuffwhitepeoplelike.com/2008/03/26/92-book-deals/?cp=all#comments

Anonymous. (2008b, March 30). Re: #92 Book deals [Web log comment]. Retrieved from http://stuffwhitepeoplelike.com/2008/03/26/92-book-deals/?cp=all#comments

Anonymous. (2008c, April 6). Re: #1 Coffee [Web log comment]. Retrieved from http://stuffwhitepeoplelike.com/2008/01/18/1-coffee/?cp=all#comments

another white guy. (2008, March 27). Re: #1 Coffee [Web log comment]. Retrieved from http://stuffwhitepeoplelike.com/2008/01/18/1-coffee/?cp=all#comments

Arendt, H. (1973). *The origins of totalitarianism*. San Diego, CA: Harvest HBJ.

Billig, M. (1995). *Banal nationalism*. London, UK: Sage.

Billig, M. (2001). Humour and hatred: The racist jokes of the Ku Klux Klan. *Discourse & Society, 12*(3), 267–289. doi: 10.1177/0957926501012003001

Billig, M. (2005). *Laughter and ridicule: Towards a social critique of humour*. London, UK: Sage.

Brian. (2008, March 30). Re: #1 Coffee [Web log comment]. Retrieved from http://stuffwhitepeoplelike.com/2008/01/18/1-coffee/?cp=all#comments

Cargill. (2008, March 27). Re: #92 Book deals [Web log comment]. Retrieved from http://stuffwhitepeoplelike.com/2008/03/26/92-book-deals/?cp=all#comments

clander. (2008a, January 18). #1 Coffee [Web log post]. Retrieved from http://stuffwhitepeoplelike.com/2008/01/18/1-coffee/

clander. (2008b, March 26). #92 Book deals [Web log post]. Retrieved from http://stuffwhitepeoplelike.com/2008/03/26/92-book-deals/

Cohen, M. (2009). *Critical race theory and education: A Marxist response*. New York, NY: Palgrave Macmillan

Dei, G. J. S. (2006). Introduction. In A. Nuzhat, G. Dei, & M. Lordan (Eds.), *The poetics of anti-racism*. Retrieved from http://www.fernwoodpublishing.ca/website_pdfs/poeticsanti-racism.pdf

Dowden, C., & Brennan, S. (2012). Police-reported hate crime in Canada, 2010. Statistics Canada. Retrieved from http://www.statcan.gc.ca/pub/85-002-x/2012001/article/11635-eng.pdf

Du Bois, W. E. B. (1903). *The souls of Black folk: Essays and sketches*. Chicago, IL: A. C. McClurg & Co.

Fanon, F. (1991). *Black skin, White masks*. New York, NY: Grove Press.

Gies, L. (2008). How material are cyberbodies? Broadband Internet and embodied subjectivity. *Crime, Media, Culture, 4*(3), 311–330. doi: 10.1177/1741659008096369

Gillborn T. E., Gillborn, D., & Ladson-Billings, G. (Eds). (2009). *Foundations of critical race theory in education*. New York, NY: Routledge.

Gilroy, P. (1993). *The Black Atlantic: Modernity and double consciousness*. Cambridge, MA: Harvard University Press.

Goldberg, D. T. (1993). *Racist culture*. Oxford, UK: Blackwell.

Goldberg, D. T. (2009). *The threat of race: Reflections on racial neoliberalism*. Oxford, UK: Blackwell.

Goldstein, E. (2002). The unstable other: Locating the Jew in progressive-era racial discourse. *American Jewish History, 89*(4), 383–409. Retrieved from http://muse.jhu.edu.proxy.bib.uottawa.ca/journals/american_jewish_history/v089/89.4goldstein.html

Hall, S. (1980). Race, articulation and societies structured in dominance. In UNESCO (Ed.), *Sociological theories: Race and colonialism* (pp. 305–345). Paris, France: UNESCO.

Hardcastle. (2008, March 28). Re: #92 Book deals [Web log comment]. Retrieved from http://stuffwhitepeoplelike.com/2008/03/26/92-book-deals/?cp=all#comments

Henry Blanco. (2008, March 27). Re: #92 Book deals [Web log comment]. Retrieved from http://stuffwhitepeoplelike.com/2008/03/26/92-book-deals/?cp=all#comments

hooks, b. (1984). *Feminist theory from margin to center*. Boston, MA: South End Press.

Jhally, S. (Producer & Director). (1997). *Stuart Hall: Race, the floating signifier*. [Videorecording]. United States: Media Education Foundation.

Jonboy. (2008a, June 12). Re: #1 Coffee [Web log comment]. Retrieved from http://stuffwhitepeoplelike.com/2008/01/18/1-coffee/?cp=all#comments

Jonboy. (2008b, December 12). Re: #1 Coffee [Web log comment]. Retrieved from http://stuffwhitepeoplelike.com/2008/01/18/1-coffee/?cp=all#comments

Kaplan, S. (2003). If there are no races, how can Jews be a 'race'? *Journal of Modern Jewish Studies, 2*(1), 79–96. doi: 10.1080/1472588022000070391

Kumashiro, K. (2002). Against repetition: Addressing resistance to anti-oppressive change in the practices of learning, teaching, supervising, and researching. *Harvard Educational Review, 72*(1), 67–92.

Late Show top ten. (2010). *CBS Interactive*. Retrieved from http://www.cbs.com/late_night/late_show/top_ten/

Lenhart, A., Purcell, K., Smith, A., & Zickuhr, K. (2010, February 3). *Social media and young adults*. Retrieved from http://www.pewinternet.org/Reports/2010/Social-Media-and-Young-Adults.aspx

Leonardo, Z. (2004). The colour of supremacy: Beyond the discourse of 'White privilege.' *Journal of Educational Philosophy and Theory, 36*(2), 137–152.

Lichtenberg, J. (1998). Racism in the head, racism in the world. In N. Zack, L. Shrage, & C. Sartwell (Eds.), *Race, class, gender and sexuality: The big questions* (pp. 43–47). Oxford, UK: Blackwell.

Lowe, N. (2012). *'I'm not racist, but that's funny': Registers of Whiteness in the blog-o-sphere* (Master's thesis). Retrieved from uO [University of Ottawa, Canada] Research (http://hdl.handle.net/10393/23233).

McIntosh, P. (1990). White privilege: Unpacking the invisible knapsack. *Independent School, 49*(2), 31–34.

Miles, R. (1989). *Racism*. London, UK: Routledge.

Mulkay, M. (1988). *On humor: Its nature and its place in modern society*. New York, NY: Blackwell.

nicole, rachel, and David. (2008, May 16). Re: #1 Coffee [Web log comment]. Retrieved from http://stuffwhitepeoplelike.com/2008/01/18/1-coffee/?cp=all#comments

no. (2008, June 12). Re: #1 Coffee [Web log comment]. Retrieved from http://stuffwhitepeoplelike.com/2008/01/18/1-coffee/?cp=all#comments

non-white-person. (2008, May 28). Re: #1 Coffee [Web log comment]. Retrieved from http://stuffwhitepeoplelike.com/2008/01/18/1-coffee/?cp=all#comments

Paul Stillman. (2009, September 2). Re: #1 Coffee [Web log comment]. Retrieved from http://stuffwhitepeoplelike.com/2008/01/18/1-coffee/?cp=all#comments

Rizvi, F. (1993). Children and the grammar of popular racism. In C. McCarthy & W. Crichlow, *Race, identity and representation in education* (pp. 126–139). New York, NY: Routledge.

Rogoff, L. (1997). Is the Jew White?: The racial place of the southern Jew. *American Jewish History, 85*(3), 195–230. Retrieved from http://muse.jhu.edu.proxy.bib.uottawa.ca/journals/american_jewish_history/v085/85.3rogoff.html

Slack, J. D. (1996). The theory and method of articulation in cultural studies. In D. Morley & K. Chen (Eds.), *Stuart Hall: Critical dialogues in cultural studies* (pp. 113–130). London, UK: Routledge.

Spivak, G. C. (1988). Can the subaltern speak? In C. Nelson & L. Grossberg (Eds.), *Marxism and the interpretation of culture* (pp. 271–314). Urbana, IL: University of Illinois Press.

Stanley, T. J. (2009). The banality of colonialism: Encountering artefacts of genocide and White supremacy in Vancouver today. In Shirley R. Steinberg (Ed.), *Diversity and multiculturalism: A reader* (pp. 143–159). New York, NY: Peter Lang.

Stanley, T. J. (2011). *Contesting White supremacy: School segregation, anti-racism, and the making of Chinese Canadians.* Vancouver, Canada: University of British Columbia Press.

Stanley, T. J. (2012). Excluded narratives, antiracism and historical representation: Methodological implications. In G. S. Cannella & S. R. Steinberg (Eds.), *Critical qualitative research reader* (pp. 318–328). New York, NY: Peter Lang.

Ted. (2008, March 30). Re: #92 Book deals [Web log comment]. Retrieved from http://stuffwhitepeoplelike.com/2008/03/26/92-book-deals/?cp=all#comments

Wei, L. (2009). Filter blogs vs. personal journals: Understanding the knowledge production gap on the Internet. *Journal of Computer-Mediated Communication, 14*(3), 532–558. doi:10.1111/j.1083-6101.2009.01452.x

yo mama. (2009, January 9). Re: #1 Coffee [Web log comment]. Retrieved from http://stuffwhitepeoplelike.com/2008/01/18/1-coffee/?cp=all#comments

CHAPTER 16

Targeted by the Crosshairs
Student Voices on Colonialism, Racism, and Whiteness as Barriers to Educational Equity

Virginia Lea with Maria Sylvia Edouard-Gundowry

There are times in life when the question of knowing if one can think differently than one thinks, and perceive differently than one sees, is absolutely necessary if one is to go on looking and reflecting at all. (Foucault, 1985, p. 293)

It was Columbus Day, 1992, in a San Francisco elementary school attended disproportionately by children from poor and low-income families. A teacher told her third-grade students that she was going to teach them about Columbus. Ayana listened to the teacher's story and was troubled. Her mother had been sharing with her the journals of the colonizer, Christopher Columbus, edited by Friar Bartolomé de las Casas. The journals described some of the abuses of Native people carried out by Columbus and his men.

Although de las Casas was only nine years old in 1493 when Columbus returned from his first colonizing voyage, de las Casas senior, Bartolomé's father, accompanied Columbus on his second voyage, and Bartolomé traveled to Hispaniola in 1502 to see his family holdings. There he witnessed atrocities, amounting to genocide, wrought by the conquistadores against the Native people, under a system of patronage called *encomienda*. Nevertheless, initially, Bartolomé participated in this colonial system, by which the Spanish monarchy granted Spaniards responsibility over a number of Native people. Eventually, however, he "re-cognized" (Freire, 2001) the nature of the system and his own everyday practice, and decided that he could no longer be a part of the abuse. He spent the rest of his life in the Americas and Spain defending the rights of Native people, albeit as long as they succumbed to the hegemonic authority of the Catholic church. Bartolomé's *History of the Indies* (de las Casas, 1971), completed in 1561, recounted his experience. In it, de las Casas expressed regret for advocating that the enslavement of African people should replace that of the Native people of the Americas. He came to believe that all slavery was against his religion.

Ayana was a child who had also learned of the value of respect for human and civil rights—in her case, without claiming the hegemonic authority and normalcy of a religion—and even at an early age, was able to speak her mind in the face of the abuse of these rights. She had learned that her mother's research contradicted what her teacher was saying. Columbus had not "discovered America."

As governor and viceroy of the Indies, Columbus imposed iron discipline on what is now the Caribbean country of the Dominican Republic, according to documents discovered by Spanish historians in 2005. In response to native unrest and revolt, Columbus ordered a brutal crackdown in which many natives were killed; in an attempt to deter further rebellion, Columbus ordered their dismembered bodies to be paraded through the streets (History.com, 2013).

Columbus's actions with respect to the indigenous people of the Americas made it impossible for Ayana to think of him as a "great man." She told the teacher that her story depicting Columbus as a hero was not true. Columbus had "cut off the legs, and enslaved the Indians" whose land he claimed to have discovered. The teacher tried to silence Ayana by telling her that she "was not back there 500 years ago." Ayana argued, in response, that the teacher was not around in 1492 either, and that she, Ayana, had proof of Columbus's cruelty because she had read the diaries of Columbus with her mother (Seale & Slapin, 2005).

This exchange resulted in the teacher telling Ayana to go away and write something that she had learned about Columbus. Ayana knew what she was going to write. She was going to describe the brutality with which the Spanish invaders of the so-called "new world" had responded to the inhabitants of this land of Hispaniola (the island that is known today as the Dominican Republic and Haiti) into which they had been welcomed. After all, "(the Invaders) thought nothing of knifing Indians by the tens and twenties and of cutting slices off them to test the sharpness of their blades" (de las Casas, as cited in Zinn, 2005, p. 6).

When she had finished, Ayana went to her teacher to show her what she had written. The teacher read the paragraph, and said, "I'm sorry, you must rewrite this because you have to write something nice about Columbus." So Ayana went back to her desk and wrote: "Columbus had three ships: the Nina, the Pinta, and the Santa Maria" (Seale & Slapin, 2005, p. 16).

I tell this story at the start of this chapter to illustrate the intransigence of some adults who inhabit hegemony in the face of the opposition of young people. Hegemony is the process through which we learn to see the social narratives that support the interests of those in power—oligarchies and plutocracies—as normal, natural, and commonsense, even when they do not equate with our interests. Colonialism, racism, and Whiteness are hegemonic processes. In fact, hegemony leads us to vilify poor and immigrant people—disproportionately people of color—and support policies that maintain their economic oppression. We even blame some poor and immigrant parents, who are challenged in terms of economic and language resources and may not share the cultural assumptions of the mainstream, for not helping their children to prepare for and function in school. In other words, we have little sense of the ways in which society was set up by people already socially and culturally advantaged to maintain their own advantage. Even when, as has been the case, certain structural changes were established through federal legislation after the Second World War to redress social inequities—for example, educational rights (*Brown v. Board of Education*, 1954); civil rights (1964); women's rights under Title IX of the Civil Rights Act (1964), and the Educational Amendments (1972)—oligarchies have always looked for ways of reestablishing their privilege and power in a bizarre dance with equity, inclusion, and progress. As recently as 2013, the Supreme Court of the United States had just voted *not* to support DOMA (the Defense of Marriage Act that classified marriage as the union of a man and a woman), opening the way for more states to grant same-sex couples the right to marry. However, at the same time, the court has invalidated key parts of the voting rights act of 1965, potentially allowing states to introduce legislation that will take away hard-won universal voting rights from African American and poor citizens. When advances are made through struggle, as they always will be, oligarchs and plutocrats are afraid of losing their social and economic advantage. The results are uneven and messy, and they tend to maintain the power and privilege of the few. As Harold Berlak (2009) put it:

> The fears that the 1960s movements provoked in the halls of government, big business and culturally right wing sectors of American society are difficult to exaggerate. As the 1970s began, the major US corporations were experiencing what the business pages call a 'profit squeeze.' The World War II enemies of

the US, Germany and Japan, were seriously challenging the economic dominance of the US. All moves toward liberal, social democracy that would restrict corporate power were portrayed by its leaders as serious threats to corporate profitability, economic recovery and growth. (p. 4)

Then, as now, advances in social equity within the social system were met with hostile reactions from those who inhabit the corridors of power and believe in the ancient Platonic ideology that there are essentially different types of people, destined for different types of work. Edited for the modern era, this ideology includes the myth of "race," which was constructed by White oligarchs to justify slavery and colonialism. "Race," as a pseudo-scientific theory, claimed that Whites were superior to other human beings, who could be classified into distinct and separate categories. The theory of "race" resulted in two, bipolar narratives that are very much alive today:

- *Whiteness* in the United States is a complex, hegemonic narrative that has traditionally shaped the cultural identities of White people, and given them legal, symbolic, and cultural advantage (Bell, 1992; 2004). The laws and policies that support Whiteness began to be passed in the second half of the seventeenth century. To legitimize slavery, oligarchs decided that Whites had to see Africans as distinctly different from and inferior to themselves. The law began to offer Whites carrots in the way of small parcels of land, associating their ethnicity with material and legal advantages, as a way of dividing them from Africans. This included Whites who were as poor as their Black peers. It was a way of governing White identities and allegiances, and persuading them that their skin color was more important than the economic interests they shared with people of color (Wise, 2009);

- *Racism* is the vicious expression of the power of Whiteness, given legitimacy by the narrative of "race" over 400 years, and driven by prejudice (Bonilla-Silva, 2006). It may be expressed inter-personally but is also embedded in the dominant culture and social institutions.

Whiteness includes the following practices:

- Defining civilized behavior in terms of certain *Anglocentric*, cultural, symbolic, linguistic, and economic *standards*, including northern European norms of beauty; traditional, direct, individualistic, verbal and nonverbal communication styles; a belief in the superiority of the English language; a belief that hard work will result in social advancement regardless of the structural and cultural barriers that may exist; and a belief in the essential necessity of social hierarchy;

- *Normalizing* these standards, such as the "civilized cultural norm," so that they become invisible—the water we swim in. At the same time, visible, alternative standards are dichotomized and seen as abnormal;

- *Stereotyping* (making simplistic generalizations that are rigid and very hard to change) who and what fall into categories of difference;

- In the context of the above, assuming that one's culture, including norms, values, language, religion, mores, interests, and ideological assumptions, and the unequal structure of one's society are *morally correct, normal, natural and common sense*—the way things are and should be.

Whiteness is a powerful narrative that takes few prisoners. Ayana's teacher was an African American woman who clearly was not advantaged in terms of her skin color, but who nevertheless had bought into the hegemony of Whiteness, in terms of its cultural ideology. Whether through the socialization process in her family or school, or fear of losing her job, this teacher encouraged her students to believe the traditional Columbus story as part of the *normal* history of the United States. Indeed, she questioned any challenge to the validity of Columbus as the "discoverer" of America, in spite of the fact that this narrative justified colonialism and slavery. If she had looked at the story of Columbus through a colonial and/or slavery lens, she might have been encouraged to rethink her acceptance of the story's authenticity. As a White person, albeit with partial Arab ancestry which allowed me an alternative window on the world early in life, I know that I also am deeply entrenched in hegemony, even as I struggle to become more aware of the extent of its ever-moving tentacles. As the mother of Ayana, and as a teacher myself, I feel honored to have been associated with curious, creative, and critical young people motivated to interrupt hegemony and participate in constructing a more socially just world.

In this chapter, I examine a Study Abroad program in the UK, during which my American students were asked to investigate what high-school students from diverse ethnic backgrounds thought about their education in English schools, and the impact of modern English hegemony—the process that ensures the ongoing power and privilege of a disproportionately White elite—in particular, colonialism, racism, and Whiteness, on their identities and perceptions. I include a short narrative from Maria Sylvia Edouard-Gundowry, an immigrant to the UK, whose graduate research highlights the voices of Chagos Island immigrant students on this subject. I compare the narratives shared by the Chagos Island students with those obtained in a study with similar goals, conducted on my Midwest university campus with underserved university students. I argue that a genuinely inclusive, and equitable democracy, built on social justice and caring, requires that we affirm students' voices; encourage solidarity across different identities and racial-ethnic, social class, and gender identities and expressions; and encourage curiosity, creativity, and critique (Freire, 2001).

First, I elaborate on the theoretical framework for these studies.

Colonizing the Norm: An Ancient Agenda

How could you colonize, enslave, and indenture people who you saw as of the same value as your own children, family, and social group, and as having equal human, civil, and labor rights? Colonialism is a practice of domination, a hegemonic practice, which involves oligarchies developing narratives that justify the subjugation of populations they wish to exploit. It usually involves the transportation of people as permanent settlers to a new land where they subjugate the colonized population in the name of the elite in their own society, and retain their allegiance to the home country. Albert Memmi (1965) called the people who directed this mission, "colonizers," and those who carried out the mission, and lived everyday lives in the new territory governing the colonized, "colonials." Colonials had a higher social status than the colonized, but were sometimes almost as economically uncomfortable. Colonizers, and colonials who had been persuaded to identify with the colonizers, validated their conquest of the people whose land they had conquered in terms of a "civilizing mission."

Neocolonialism is a current form of colonialism. It includes the process, described below by Maria Sylvia Edouard-Gundowry, by which the Chagos Islanders came to reside in England. In school, it is an ongoing practice through which "colonials"—some teachers—are persuaded to identify with the oligarchy—some administrations—and maintain school policies and everyday practices that are not in the interest of the colonized—some students—nor necessarily even in their own interest. To social-justice activists in education, the way in which elites have been able to persuade human beings who are low-income or poor themselves that their economic interests lie with the elite and not with the masses of people who are also struggling to get by is a huge road block to developing a more equitable society (Memmi, 1965; Wise, 2009).

Neocolonialism is a framework that helps us to understand the inequities that currently exist in schools, and which relate, to a greater or lesser extent depending on the school, to Whiteness. For example, some language policies result in students' maternal languages being represented as inferior, resulting in extreme culture shock for immigrant and poor students. Culture shock is the emotional experience of recognizing that our familiar cultural markers have moved. This process is exemplified below in Maria Sylvia Edouard-Gundowry's research. Other neocolonial school practices may be recognized in high-stakes testing and language teaching that often draw on texts that are culturally irrelevant to students who are not from mainstream cultural backgrounds as the context for testing comprehension. Moreover, many teachers, disproportionately White and middle-class, contribute to neocolonialism by bringing stereotypes of students and misinformation about their cultural backgrounds to school, resulting in inequitable interactions and expectations.

Public-school teachers are in the difficult position of being agents of the state, with the unstated institutional charge of maintaining the status quo or hegemonic interests. This is a reality many teachers, if not most, take for granted. Most teachers are White and middle-class, and bring their Whiteness to the teaching profession, with the result that some students who are NOT considered part of the racialized and cultural norm often realize that they will only be accepted by some of their teachers if they embrace the academic and cultural mainstream. They realize that they will not be included in institutional programs leading to academic and professional qualifications as long as they claim their cultural difference and insist on emphasizing their racial identities. Monoculturalism (Nieto, 1994) or standardization (Lea, 2012) is the name of this game (Bourdieu, 1994)—standards that have "colonized the definition of normal" (Dyer, 1988), in terms of, for example, religion, language, everyday cultural practices, and superficial physical characteristics such as skin color, hair type, facial features, and body type. These students are "caught in the crosshairs," asking questions like the following from a Hmong university student, who participated in a research project I conducted with my co-researcher, Dang Yang, concerning educational hegemony:

> Where do I fit in? Why am I here? What am I doing? And hence the picture of like, the deer being targeted with like, you know … everyone's always looking at me where … like what am I supposed to do. Like how can I get out of this? (Female Hmong student, 2012)

Standardization as an aspect of Whiteness and hegemony makes it hard for teachers who occupy Whiteness to recognize, value, and include cultural differences in their classrooms; individualism also means that many teachers have a struggle recognizing the social influences on their own teaching and social practice, seeing themselves as autonomous in their own lives (Spring, 2007). If we are part of the majority in our home country, we are often fish who cannot see the water we are swimming in (Maxwell, 2004). The attention of those of us who have not examined our Whiteness is flooded with hegemonic narratives, from the media to the school. Alternative, counter-hegemonic discourses are often drowned out in the process, or disconnected from the hegemonic, so that we continue to be guided by messages that serve economic, political, and cultural oligarchies. We are better able to express "critical capacity, curiosity and autonomy as a learner" (Freire, 2001) when we travel outside our normal environments to a different cultural space that allows us to critique institutional and cultural racism, without feeling that our national and cultural identities are threatened. For our study abroad, this place was England.

The Study Abroad Study

Guided by the theoretical premise that it would be easier for my White female students to understand colonialism, slavery, racism, and Whiteness in a British context than in an American one where their participation in institutional and cultural racism would go unexamined, I recently took a group of four American university students from my Midwest University on an eleven-day Study Abroad to England, with a flying visit to Paris. Our goal was to develop an analysis of the ways in which colonialism, slavery, and racism had impacted students in English schools, so that, on their return to the US, they could better research and re-cognize how colonialism, slavery, racism, and Whiteness had contributed to the development of the institutions in the United States, and Wisconsin and/or Minnesota, in particular. Three of the students were White, and one Hmong. All were eager to participate in the experience and were great companions for the eleven days.

One of the goals of the Study Abroad was to explore racism, particularly "silent racism"—that form of racism "rarely noticed by whites—[that] is instrumental in the production of institutional racism" (Friou, 2008, p. 39). Silent racism, as presented in research by Barbara Trepagnier (2006), is characterized by the tacit acceptance of *stereotypical narratives* about people of color and their cultural practices. It is also revealed in "*a sense of superiority* [emphasis added] found in hierarchical relationships between blacks and whites ... the notion that whites are responsible for blacks, who are seen as in need of protection" (Friou, 2008, p. 39). In addition, silent racism involves

> "passivity," the silence that occurs when one is detached from race matters and believes that racism is limited and rare. Whites are also silent on the issue of race when they are apprehensive about being perceived as racist and confused about what is racist and what isn't. [According to Trepagnier,] [p]assivity endorses and encourages the racist decisions, actions and policies of other white people. (Friou, 2008, p. 40)

Silent racism includes a considerable amount of *misinformation*. In order to challenge our silent racism and misinformation, my American students and I visited several venues in England where the legacies of racism are apparent. One such venue was Bristol, where we retraced the places and spaces where merchant slavers pursued and profited from their ghastly trade. The students, two of whom had had little experience with ethnic diversity, had read a novel prior to coming to England: *A Respectable Trade* by Philippa Gregory (1995). The novel described the horrors of the slave trade in terms of the treatment that a group of enslaved Africans endured in the home of Bristol merchant, Josiah Smith, who aspired to make enough money through the slave trade to move up the social scale. Smith married a woman with more cultural capital than himself and gave her several "slaves" as house servants. The wife subsequently fell in love with one of the "slaves," Mehuru, an African man of aristocratic descent in his own country. In reading the book before we came, I hoped the students would personalize the issue, and bring "a rigorous methodological curiosity" to our study abroad, one that would motivate them to "explore the limits of creativity, persistent in their search, and courageously humble in the adventure" (Freire, 2001). I wanted the students to be inspired enough to explore the economic systems that brought unimaginable horrors to Africans, Native people, and others—and be aware that the practice continues in a different form. The goal was to build emotional empathy with people once seen in negative stereotypical terms so that our ability to passively accept their oppression would be undermined, and we would be propelled to overcome our silence.

In addition to our visits to venues like Bristol, we visited two state (public) high schools, a Sure Start (Head Start) school, and a state (public) elementary school. My students were met with extraordinarily helpful teachers, who facilitated tours of the schools and arranged dialogue with diverse groups of students.

The following narrative, written by Maria Sylvia Edouard-Gundowry, a teacher, PhD candidate, and herself an immigrant to the UK from Mauritius, includes many of the same themes my students identified during their dialogue with immigrant students. She entitles her piece as follows:

Mauritian-Chagossian Adolescents Navigating Their Way Through English Host Society

Britain is Europe's top destination for permanent migrants, according to an OECD report in 2011, making it the second most popular destination in the world after the US. Despite the government's hard-hitting measures to reduce immigration, the latest figures from the Census 2011 revealed that the number of migrants in the UK has reached 3 million in 10 years and that for the first time, British Whites were the minority in London.

About 50 km south of London is a town in the West Sussex called Crawley. This small town near Gat-wick Airport has a very diverse ethnic population, even more diverse now with the arrival of a new group of migrants: people of Chagossian origin, who came to Britain from Mauritius.

Forced displacement

The Chagos Islanders were forcibly uprooted from the Chagos archipelago in the Indian Ocean from late 1960s to 1973 by the British government, which had ceded the largest island, Diego Garcia, to the United States to make way for a military base. The islanders were sent to Mauritius and the Seychelles, where they faced poverty, discrimination, and marginalization. Their fight for a right to return home has long been opposed by the British government. While the fight is still on, the islanders and their children obtained UK citizenship in 2002 when they first started to arrive in the UK in the hope of a better future.

My doctoral research is focused on the acculturation experiences of a group of adolescent students of Chagossian origin and the complexities of their journey to settle in their host country. Eight students, aged 16+, born in Mauritius from at least one parent of Chagossian origin, participated in the study and agreed to be interviewed. They arrived in the UK between five and seven years prior to the interviews and are still in school.

I embarked on this study as an insider researcher. Although I am not of Chagossian origin, we come from the same country (Mauritius), speak the same language, and live in the same town. My contact with and interest in the Chagossian community in Crawley goes back to 2007 when I started to work as a Multilingual Support Assistant in a local primary school, where I support children from Mauritius who arrive in the UK with very little or no English. Within the Chagossian community, I could be considered an outsider researcher, as I am not part of the Chagossian community. From the insider perspective, I had the advantage of knowing the community. I accessed some of the participants through a local secondary school and the rest from the local Chagossian social network.

Educational experiences

The high influx of Mauritian-Chagossian immigrants has increased the diversity in the schools of Crawley. School officials consider adjustment to school the main sociocultural and developmental task for these immigrant children and adolescents (Phinney, Horenczyk, Liebkind, & Vedder, 2001). Although discrimination seems to be a recurrent issue in school environments, I was totally unaware of the extent to which issues of prejudice and intolerance seemed to be normalized in local secondary schools, and the impact this has had on the life of young migrants.

Stereotypes

Speaking Mauritian Creole and walking in groups seems to be a characteristic of the Mauritian-Chagossian pupils in schools, yet it is not always appreciated. This is often accompanied by stereotypes such as "Mauritians are loud" or "Mauritians are trouble makers." While participants in the present study did recognize that some young people from Mauritius are indeed loud, they found it regretful that all the Mauritians seem to bear the blame.

Perceived discrimination

Various forms of discrimination were brought up by almost all of the participants, and the source of discrimination was not simply between peers, but from adults towards students as well. For example, Jamel also perceived discrimination from the administration. He could not understand why a senior member of staff who used to be kind to him suddenly started to show antipathy towards pupils from Mauritius, especially those who would walk in groups and speak their mother tongue.

Powerless and silenced

Not understanding the language and not being able to defend themselves against bullying and discrimination may leave young people feeling powerless and silenced. Although Jennifer had spent five years in school and language was no longer a barrier for her, she remembered how hard it was for her when she first arrived in England.

I would understand but I would not be able to answer them … because I can't answer them—like—it kills me inside.

Eleonore must have experienced a similar feeling when she was bullied at school. She had been in England for about a year and had no friends. A few boys at her secondary school used to bully her and said she smelled of b.o. (body odor). Powerless, Eleonore found refuge in the toilets instead of going to classes.

I couldn't speak English very well. I wanted to say something. … I was scared in case I sound [laughs] like a boy with a big voice when I speak.

Lack of awareness of the history

Another finding that emerged from the interviews was that none of the participants in the present study seemed to know much about what had happened to their grandparents and/or parents on the Chagos Islands. Some of the participants did not even know which island of the archipelago their parents or grandparents were from. This lack of awareness might explain the lack of connection to the Chagossian identity displayed by the adolescents. However, Jamel surprised me when he explained what he would say to someone who might want to know about the Chagossian history.

I would say to that person they took our country … we were angry, then the Queen decided to give us the British passport to come and live here, yeah.

The use of the pronouns 'we' and 'us' revealed a sense of belonging to the Chagossian community, and yet Jamel said he had no connection with the Chagossian history because his father, born in Mauritius from Chagossian parents, was himself unaware of the past. One explanation could be the fact that being a musician in a school drumming group which was comprised of only Mauritian-Chagossian drummers inspired Jamel to identify himself as Chagossian, promote the Chagossian culture, and thus contribute, through music, to the community. Jamel's misunderstanding of the role of the monarch was also instructive.

Anti-English attitude

An anti-English attitude was another result that came from the study. Except for one interviewee, none of the participants had English friends at school, and while Jamel said his group of friends comprised of the 'outsiders' like himself, the others could not explain why they had befriended young people of nationalities such as Portuguese, Sri Lankan, Pakistani, Brazilian, and Romanian, but not English young people.

Racial fights

The racial fights in schools could be one reason for an anti-English attitude. Eleonore gave the example of a fight between a girl from Mauritius and a White English girl after the latter called the other girl "dirty Mauritian." As a result, both girls were excluded temporarily from school. Eleonore described tensions between groups of pupils and said that some English pupils would even avoid physical contact with their peers from Mauritius.

Nostalgia

The Chagossian Islanders in general have lived with nostalgia in their forced exile from Mauritius and Seychelles hoping that one day they would return home. It may be fair to say that nostalgia is all about longing for the loss of the familiar. Losing connection to familiar people, objects, and places can be painful. Jamel realized how homesick he was months after he left his home, Baie du Tombeau in Mauritius. He talked at length about his house, the trees in the garden, and the family car. He also had an elaborated narrative about his dog, with whom the family had a special relationship.

Home

Although the other young participants in the research did not present any nostalgic accounts like Jamel did, some found it hard to articulate where their home was. Eleonore attempted this difficult task.

> *I like here, yeah, but … in Mauritius like I have all my family, this is why I like Mauritius … here like … (smiling) I like it here too … it's hard to explain … I feel home too in Mauritius because I was born there and stuff like that. … I don't know (smiling).*

Good memories are not enough to want to go back home. Jamel, who misses his house, his trees, and his cousins in Mauritius, was not ready to return. Neither were the other participants. They all said they would rather stay in the UK for better prospects.

Power relations at play

The process of developing a coherent sense of identity is one of the main developmental tasks of adolescents who are experiencing a transition to adulthood. It has also been interesting to note how the young Mauritian-Chagossians are confronted with hegemonic social constructions in their efforts to develop a sense of identity in their new "homeland." Language plays an important role in making friendships, but also in the power forces at play here between English speakers and non-English speakers. This dynamic may lead some Chagossians to think their mother tongue is inferior. This is illustrated in the example above where Jamel was trying to understand the reason behind the aversion displayed by the senior member of staff towards Mauritian-Chagossian pupils who spoke their mother tongue in school. Jamel sounded almost apologetic for speaking Mauritian Creole with his peers and stressed that they only spoke their language in short conversations. Yet, Mauritian-Chagossian pupils are adamant that they can communicate better using their mother tongue and they also like switching languages (code-switching); being boisterous could be interpreted as being rude and noisy, whereas the young migrants have always been lively and energetic; walking in groups could be interpreted as not wanting to integrate, whereas the young migrants find their own little groups a comfort zone in a setting where they are a targeted minority group.

Conclusion

The Chagossian community is a unique group of immigrants in the UK, considering their forced displacement by the British government four decades ago. While the older native islanders are still longing for a return, young Mauritian-Chagossians in the UK are trying to make a way into adulthood while confronting daily challenges that may affect the process of getting to know themselves. Schools may be able to help young Mauritian-Chagossians examine their history and value their collective memory.

On the University Campus

Maria Sylvia's research underscores the ways in which colonialism, silent racism, and Whiteness play out in the experiences of the students she interviewed. These same themes were apparent in the research I have been undertaking with Dang Yang at my Midwestern university. We developed a unique "edu-cultural" methodology to try to help the small groups of Asian (Hmong), African American, Latino, and White university students, who volunteered for the research project, identify hegemonic barriers to equity and inclusion in their educational experience. The students created collages, inspired by hegemonic terms such as "racism" and "standardization." They then used the collages to engage their minds and emotions in telling us about their educational experiences. With their permission, we recorded their narratives, and used critical discourse analysis to identify the ways in which they felt hegemony had impacted their educational lives. The students identified the many micro-aggressions they experienced at the hands of well-meaning faculty and White students, including feeling targeted by the surveillance measures that White students saw as protective. They experienced being singled out by teachers to represent their entire ethnic group; and they endured stereotyping. The students shared feelings of alienation in the classroom, as they felt they had no alternative but to accept the imposition of cultural norms that they did not embody, felt obliged to embrace these norms to be successful, and felt marginalized by daily incidences of White privilege.

Stereotypes

Like the Chagos Island students, the students in the university study felt that they were stereotyped by the White majority. Referring to his collage, one of the African American students put his experience as follows:

> Underneath "black" I have "the few, the proud, the broken." I cut it out of GQ magazine. Umm, I feel like that sums it up in itself … because … umm, the people of the Black culture, and basically any minority cultures, that … actually understand what the word pride means are limited … And I feel like that their definition is really messed up because it's about being, ah … the stereotypical Black person.

The pain embedded in this statement is palpable, and reminds me of the anguish with which a young Pakistani student described his own stereotyping experiences growing up in England. During a Study Abroad circle dialogue with my students and other high-school students from the Chagos Islands, Ghana, Sri Lanka, and India, the Pakistani student talked about stereotyping related to his religion, Islam. I had taken my students to the largest mosque in Europe to break down their own stereotypes about Islam, and this experience allowed them to better hear and understand what the Pakistani student was saying. As they shared with me, they, my students, had also received misinformation about Islam, which is a religion of peace. Indeed, during our time in England, a group of right-wing people painted hate symbols on the walls of a mosque in Reddich, bringing more poignancy to the ways in which non-Muslim people's perceptions of Islam have become synonymous with terrorism. Indeed, the act of hateful vandalism is itself an act of terror, illustrating how perceptions of terrorism are responded to with terrorism, reproducing a vicious cycle of hate.

Conclusions: What Student Voices Tell Us

The voices of many of our immigrant, migrant, and marginalized students in the United States and Britain tell us that while some schools are doing better than others in addressing their needs, we need to listen much more closely to what they have to say if we are to create genuinely equitable educational spaces. England now offers EAL (English as an additional language), instead of the American ESL (English as a Second language). EAL acknowledges that we live in a multilingual world, and that many of our students speak more than two languages. This is a strong advance on the U.S. reductionist approach but requires a host of additional educational practices to be meaningful, including culturally responsive, critical, and creative pedagogy. The two high schools we visited in England certainly went to different lengths to include these practices. It was also clear that in both schools certain departments were much more committed than others to moving away from the one-size-fits-all curriculum to support innovations that met all students' needs, and that these innovations depended on individual teachers. At one school it was the Music teacher; and at another, the EAL teacher. My long-term relationship with the schools supports these findings.

The university study also suggested a lack of consistent and coherent commitment to critical multicultural curricula and pedagogy across departments and programs. The students in this study also indicated an institutional failure to provide culturally relevant services and/or disseminate information about their existence, and a dependence on individual teachers to recognize alternative students' voices and support their needs.

In terms of silent racism, my Study Abroad students have certainly had their stereotypes challenged, and whatever tendencies they held towards patronizing the "Other" with a missionary approach, and expressing passivity in the face of oppression may have been interrupted. They are certainly better informed about ethnic differences in the world.

Perhaps the greatest challenge my Study Abroad students experienced was their own culture shock. Research does tell us that human beings can recover from culture shock with knowledge of what is happening to them, familiarity with the new cultural markers, and knowledge of the target language. My students only had a small taste of this during the Study Abroad, but their initial reflections certainly indicate that they gained an appreciation of what immigrants and students who do not come from the mainstream culture go through. They claim a deeper understanding of the impact of colonialism, slavery, and racism on the extremely diverse students they met. Part of the reflection from one of the students sums up this experience:

> This trip really stretched my thinking. It made me open my eyes and look at the world from a different perspective. It forced me to think critically about what I was actually seeing among the people and places we saw. It almost made my brain hurt at certain points because there was so much information for me to be first taking in, then understanding, and then analyzing in a way that was more multicultural. Going to France was one of the most frustrating days by far, but it definitely made me feel for the students who are coming to England and can't speak English at all and know nothing. Everything is different and new. It takes a lot of effort and patience to be able to overcome this type of culture shock and these students are forced to do it. They have no other option. A final piece that really affected me on the trip was the amount of diversity in language spoken all around …. Everywhere I turned there was another language being spoken. The students are able to bring a piece of home with them when they come, and hold on to, which makes them so unique. What an amazing talent to be able to speak two, three, or even four languages. Having been in the school and seen how an EAL classroom works, I have some more of an understanding as to how I should be relating to students who are learning English as another language and where to start in teaching them the language. (Tessa Krueger)

References

Bell, D. (1992). *Faces at the bottom of the well: The permanence of racism.* Basic Books.

Bell, D. (2004). *Silent covenants:* Brown v. Board of Education *and the unfulfilled hopes for racial reform.* New York, NY: Oxford University Press.

Berlak, H. (2009). Education policy 1964–2004: The No Child Left Behind Act and the assault on progressive education and local control. Rouge Forum. Retrieved from http://www.pipeline.com/~rougeforum/PolicyandNCLB.htm

Bonilla-Silva, E. (2006). *Racism without racists: Color-blind racism and the persistence of racial inequality in the United States* (2nd ed.). Lanham, MD: Rowman & Littlefield.

Bourdieu, P. (1994). Structures, habitus, power: Basis for a theory of symbolic power. In N. B. Dirks, G. Eley, & S. B. Ortner (Eds.), *Culture, power, history: A reader in contemporary social theory* (pp. 155–199). Princeton, NJ: Princeton University Press.

de las Casas, B. (1971). *History of the Indies.* New York, NY: Harper & Row.

Dyer, R. (1988). White. *Screen, 29*(4), 44–65.

Foucault. M. (1985). *The use of pleasure: The history of sexuality* (Vol. 2; R. Hurley, Trans.). New York. NY: Pantheon Books.

Freire, P. (2001). *Pedagogy of freedom: Ethics, democracy, and civic courage.* Lanham, MD: Rowman & Littlefield.

Friou, A. (2008). Silent racism: How Whites perpetuate the racial status quo. *Hillviews, Fall/Winter,* 38–41. Retrieved from http://www.liberalarts.txstate.edu/about/news/hillviews/contentParagraph/01/document/HV_fw08_racism.pdf

Gregory, P. (1995). *A respectable trade.* New York, NY: Touchstone.

History.com. (2013). Columbus controversy. Retrieved from http://www.history.com/topics/columbus-controversy

Lea, V. (2012). Controlled by the corporate narrative: Obama's education policy, the shock doctrine, and mechanisms of capitalist power. *Journal of Inquiry and Action in Education, 4*(1), Article 7. Retrieved from http://digitalcommons.buffalostate.edu/jiae/vol4/iss1/7

Maxwell, K. (2004). Deconstructing Whiteness: Discovering the water. In V. Lea & J. Helfand (Eds.), *Identifying race and transforming Whiteness in the classroom* (pp. 153–170). New York, NY: Peter Lang.

Memmi, A. (1965). *The colonizer and the colonized.* Boston, MA: Beacon Press.

Nieto, S. (1994). Affirmation, solidarity and critique: Moving beyond tolerance in multicultural education. *Multicultural Education, 1*(4), 9–12, 35–38.

Phinney, J. S., Horenczyk, G., Liebkind, K., & Vedder, P. (2001). Ethnic identity, immigration, and well-being: An interactional perspective. *Journal of Social Issues, 57*(3), 493–510.

Seale, D., & Slapin, B. (2005). *A broken flute: The native experience in books for children.* Walnut Creek, CA: AltaMira Press.

Spring, J. (2007). *The intersection of cultures: Multicultural education in the United States and the global economy.* New York, NY: Routledge.

Trepagnier, B. (2006). *Silent racism: How well-meaning White people perpetuate the racial divide.* Boulder, CO: Paradigm.

Wise, T. (2009, September 15). On White privilege. YouTube. Retrieved from http://www.youtube.com/watch?v=Y9-96xMLvkc&feature=related

Zinn, H. (2005). *A people's history of the United States: 1492 to present.* New York, NY: HarperCollins.

CHAPTER 17

Politics of Urban Diasporized Youth and Possibilities for Belonging

Marlon Simmons

The unabated influx of Diasporized youth within the flotsam of colonial empire has given rise to a range of complex experiences regarding youth, Diaspora, and the interplay of colonial modernities. Diaspora and youth studies have emerged as disciplines that critically engage these politics. These disciplines also contribute to understanding how diverse bodies, spaces, and lived experiences of the 'Other' have come to be textually framed through counter-narratives. This chapter seeks to understand the experiences of diverse Urban Diasporized youth that have historically emerged through the Caribbean Diaspora, and who, through struggle and resiliency, have worked to change social conditions that carry the vestiges of colonialism. As part of the larger fields of Diaspora and youth studies, this chapter queries the transatlantic experiences of Urban Diasporized youth who emerged from the Caribbean Diaspora in order to understand the particular cultural practices they engage to come to know the self and to understand what it means to be human as they negotiate their contemporary political and cultural landscapes within schooling and education. The study of these Urban Diasporized youth provides alternative ways of knowing and understanding how youth come to actualize the self, and what it means to belong to the nation-state that are relevant for youth studies and critical social theory. It offers different ways of interpreting citizenry as experienced in Western culture, which could inform transformative practices for social science research. Understanding this diverse form of knowledge can help educators and policymakers re-conceptualize learning in the context of conventional education in order to promote inclusive schooling. Holistically, the discussion is meant to engender critical discernment concerning youth leadership as contextualized within the everyday, Diasporic, public-sphere life of youth culture. My purpose is to suggest theoretical sensibilities germane to schooling and education. Ultimately, my research interests concern the questions: How do diverse youth come to know the self? And what does it mean for diverse youth to be human?

Learning Objectives and Research Questions

As noted, this chapter seeks to understand the lived experiences of Urban Diasporized youth, and how these experiences are shaped by concepts of race, culture, nationalism, and ethnicity. My learning objectives concern the ways in which these youth come to understand race within the public sphere of the Western nation-state, and center on the following questions: What are the ways in which Urban Diasporized youth come to understand race and ethnicity through their transatlantic histories? By what means does the understanding of race and ethnicity by Urban Diasporized youth organize and inscribe their political identities? In particular, I am concerned with how the social desires, cultural discontinuities, and embodied ways of knowing of these diverse Urban Diasporized youth come to be shaped through the Diaspora, and simultaneously become organized and configured through the governing cultural terrain of the Western public sphere. From the outset, let me say that my interest in the Diaspora is less about the etymological construct; nor am I speaking about a totalizing experience of exile, though at moments exile is part and parcel of the Diasporic experience. With Diaspora, I am thinking of process, I am thinking of the movement of people to different geographies, such as transatlantic, transoceanic movement from Britain to Africa to the Caribbean and Euro-Americas, a movement whereby historically people come to know themselves through the margins of their contemporary public sphere. Consequently, I am interested in a sociocultural reading of the different political identity formations of urban youth, particularly, how urban youth come to know and understand the historical, discursive racial constellations of the Diaspora. I am concerned with understanding how, in the context of schooling and education, through the Diaspora, the national subject emerges and continues the project of civility as her or his own within the context of the colonial settler nation-state, and how this process aids with entrenching North-South imperial relations. I am more concerned about how urban youth experience citizenry-sovereignty, and how this experience forms the conditions of insertion within the nation-state, and in what way this sense of insertion comes to govern the integrative potentiality of Diasporized peoples.

Diaspora as Method

I foreground the discussion by writing autoethnography by way of Diaspora as method (Ellis, 2009; Ellis & Bochner, 2000; Pinar, 1994; Reed-Danahay, 1997; Richardson, 2000; Roth, 2005; Wolcott, 2004). Through this method, I intervene by way of Diasporic sensibilities that speak to the colonial specificities that ethnocentrically privilege power within historical schooling institutions. I am particularly concerned with how contemporary, Diasporized national-subjects come to be regulated. What are the contemporary polities of resistance to Diasporized citizenship? Writing autoethnography through Diaspora as method involves disembedding the complex cultural practices of urban youth that have been historically silenced through the colonial racial schema (Fanon, 1967). In our contemporary epoch, to write Diaspora suggests speaking through particular constellations of imperialism, transnationalism, the nation-state, the national-subject, race, culture, ethnicity, sexuality, religion, migrant, refugee, and, given the events of 9/11, the emerging classification of terrorist. What we are left with is a series of discontinuities, as these discontinuities continue themselves through particular cultural predilections. My interest is with understanding how Urban Diasporic youth make sense of their cultural affiliations as discursively produced through its ontology.

Thinking about Diasporic subjectivities involves understanding how power, knowledge, and privilege come to be enacted and simultaneously circumscribed through the spatial procedures of race. The challenge here is with finding ways that Urban Diasporized bodies come into some sense of agency, in particular, how local, historic ways of knowing the Diaspora come to engage, come to dialogue with Euromodernity. My interest, too, has been with the everyday conceptualization of desire by urban youth, with the way desire comes to be maneuvered, and concomitantly, the producing of urban subjectivities, that is, to think about how the variant life choices of Diasporic bodies come to be contingent upon or mutually exclusive of colonial modernity. Needless to say, these moments speak to questions of accessibility, about cultural memories of Indigenous ways of knowing. They speak to the contradictions of the culturally mediated past and present, to the movement of African peoples in which ontological histories encounter the colonial modalities of modernity, an encounter which coalesces the Indigeneity of the Diaspora (Dei & Simmons, 2012; Kincheloe, 2005, Kincheloe & Steinberg, 2008; Scott, 1995), the colonial-civility of Euromodernity into this national-subject, that of sovereign citizen within settler nation-state (Bauman, 2004; Foucault, 2007; Giddens, 1991; Habermas, 1998).

I want to locate this encounter as ambivalent to the Diaspora. In that, if we are speaking about race-racism and the ensuing relations of the imperial state and how power-privilege becomes ascribed to the dominant bodies, Diaspora as method becomes central to discussing these lived moments as they come to be navigated and contoured through race and everyday racism, thus calling for a specific theorizing that wills an understanding of what it means to be human, as historically circumscribed through the congeries of colonial modernity. It means ethnographically engaging these abject spaces-places, which undoubtedly are rife with uncertainty, transgression, spirituality, pedagogies, and regularities of the human. It involves coming to know, coming to make sense of one's complicity within local performatives of domination. Essentially, I am writing to come to situate what spaces-places are made possible for Urban Diasporized youth through these subjectivities of desire as they come to be racially underpinned to the material, to expressions, to attitudes and cultural dispositions of the Diaspora, ultimately culminating in an identity that disrupts the Manichean confines of what it means to be human (Fanon, 1967; Hall, 1997, 2000, 2007).

There always already exist historical conditions of affect immanent within the experiences of urban youth. I turn my attention to Fanon (1963), *The Wretched of the Earth*, where he engaged questions of national consciousness, and decolonization through particular ineffable conditions of affect, such as alienation and abjection. Fanon suggested that these moments in their coloniality have been uneven, insofar as they have been embodied through a historical perception of time that speaks concomitantly to the past-present. I am suggesting that these moments of national consciousness, abjection, alienation, and decolonization, as constituted through the Diasporic spatiality of urban youth, are part and parcel of urban youth modernities (Gilroy, 1993; Wolcott, 2004; Wynter, 1995). Yet, capitalism necessitates the continued colonial production of modernity, and saturates itself throughout North-South geographies (Giroux, 2009; Hardt & Negri, 2000; Jameson, 2005). I am suggesting, then, that Diasporized subjects come to avow, and congruently disavow, their location within capitalist-modernity through embodied polities of the archetype abject-urban youth as lived through essentialism-anti-essentialism, authenticity, cultural homogeneity-heterogeneity and ethnic sameness-difference. At the same time, I am writing less with reducing the Caribbean Diaspora as to always already being fashioned through the permanence of change, I am suggesting that Urban Diasporic culture immanent within the political sites of resistance calls for recognizing the everyday sociality of intertextual histories as they culminate in the lived experiences of modernity. I am evoking critical educational discursive practices imbued through Diasporic sensibilities that have the potential to resist and disrupt hegemonic patterns of knowledge about Diasporic identity, which have historically subverted possibilities for transformative work, including ethical relations and solidarities in local, national, and transnational academic spaces. My aim is, in a sense, to provide a particular conceptualization for schooling and education that, in effect, provides a peopling for the decolonized future of urban youth.

Placing historical trajectories to Diaspora is key to understanding contemporary questions concerning Diasporized youth, in that local knowledges about community, settler, immigrant, race, and nation-state ought to be engaged dialectically when talking about youth citizenship and belonging to a particular urban space. Diasporic sensibilities allow for an articulation of youth citizenry that moves the hegemonic discourse of nation-state citizenry beyond that of its binary confines, from dislocation and belonging or home and exile, to invite more of a historical reading that takes into account enslavement, imperialism, expropriation of Indigenous lands, extermination of local peoples, genocide, settlement, and migration. In that there are multiple embodied bio-histories at play within urban spaces, bio-histories that ought to recognize shared experiences of colonial affect which makes alternative possibilities for urban solidarity. Historically, sovereignty concerned colonial conquest of Indigenous lands. Cartographized through territories and borders, and legitimized through legal constitutions, the acquisition of land through time has continued to a broader economic sphere. At the same time, the historical procedures of sovereignty have refashioned themselves from colonial conquest of Indigenous lands to a sense of bio-sovereignty in which Urban Diasporized youth engage in particular performative procedures as inculcated through militarized, capitalist, transnational cultures of modernity and as culminating in this subject of citizenry. Sovereignty of urban youth then becomes dependent on the performative, which surreptitiously forms integrative platforms within the governing system of urban production. It involves understanding the variant ways that urban youth, individually and collectively, move through their surroundings by way of primordial knowledge to traverse their modernities of the present. Much of the conversation about urban youth within media and public sphere concerns the problematic of youth, a problematic that ultimately culminates in the desiring of final solutions. Hence, the pedagogical requisite to trace these primordial knowledge experiences of urban youth to understand how these primordial moments become discursively refashioned to meet the needs of contemporary society. And how this refashioning of the primordial comes to relocate and reimagine alternative ways of reinserting Diasporized youth within the governing capitalist public sphere.

Diasporized Youth and the Race to Modernity

The cry from the capitalist print (see Anderson, 1991) is that long gone are systems of enslavement, legal institutionalizing of apartheid, Civil Rights movements, anti-racism and/or anti-colonial struggles, and that racism has retracted itself. But historically, racism has always already been a transhistorical experience. Historically, racism involved relations to the 'Other'. Historically, racism concerned modes of production, exploitative social relations, capitalism, and global territorialization. In contemporary neocolonial times, we are presented with different articulations of racism through state policies that work to exclude and position certain customs, values, and cultures that have historical, epistemological roots within Eurocentric traditions. The experience of racism, then, may not be in the sense of acquisition of colonies, but more so through particular modes of production that move Urban Diasporized youth into different spaces of the capitalist public sphere, thereby producing and reproducing the unfreedoms of desire in the form of aestheticized commodities waiting to be consumed. Race and capital have been vital invariants to the movement of urban youth within the myriad constellations of Diaspora, and remain critical for urban youth to come into the spirit of post-human sovereignty in a time when power and privilege have been embedded in the commodification of state-culture. Having an invested interest in these polities allows for Diasporized youth to transport their subjectivities into a particular quality of civic life. Yet the race to modernity involves relocating subjectivities within the colonial capillaries of the technological nation-state in which the racialization of space approaches its fecundity through public-sphere, socio-politico culture that historically has its epistemes anchored in Euro-Enlightenment forms of knowledge. Modernity, then, in and of itself, becomes dependent on this sovereign, Diasporized subject in ways in which Diasporized youth take up the imperial subject position of the national-subject, insofar as the coloniality contingent to urban spaces circumscribes these said Diasporized bodies. This, in a sense, speaks to the embodiment of transhistoric territorialization, in that urban youth, as propertized through sovereignty, become the local territory of the nation-state and concomitantly endowed with the governing politics of capitalist, socio-cultural modes of production.

Supposedly, we are in the post-racial epoch, yet the proteanism of coloniality articulates itself through institutions, schooling and education, capitalist media, citizenry, and state governance, tacitly mediating translocal communicative exchanges of Diasporized youth. The resurgence of class debates has centered the post-racial. Urged through the discourse of militarized, imperial globalization, mass media conversations do well to place and locate conversations about exploitation, poverty, employment, housing, and issues concerning social justice as ontologically spatial to all bodies, trumpeting in a sense that within the governing democracy we all face oppression as discontinuous from colonial histories. Hence, the post-racial is inserted into, and, to some extent, is contiguous to the post-colonial, allowing for the economic disposition to become the determining variant regarding what it means to be human, what it means to be this re-scripted, post-modern citizen as constituted through the pluralization of difference and as materializing through fragmented communities. The paradox here, and what I have come to frame as the ambivalence of the Diaspora, is that as urban youth of the Diaspora come to claim their humanism by contesting the systemic forms of discrimination through race, gender, class, religion, ableism, and language as such, they have willingly participated and continue to participate in these hegemonic relations of the West in which Diasporized youth come into power and privilege as they oath themselves into being this sovereign national-subject, where ultimately the transformed Diasporic youth benefits through the active complicity of the coloniality of capitalist-citizenry. Today, with the retooling of globalization, we are faced with pointed questions about human rights and the redistribution of material goods, where ultimately, I think the call suggests reparation. There has been an urgent engagement for social-justice needs within the nation-states of the West. My concern is that while we engage in contesting the location of equity within the Western metropolis, the imperial agendas between North-South countries are left well in place. Presently, part and parcel of being human is about belonging, that is, identifying with a particular nation-state. It is about borders and territories imperially marking and inscribing the human condition through the culture of bounded geographies.

Historically, primordialism has resided within and beyond these imperial contours, and continues to resist these scripted material enticements of the coloniality of globalization. As constituted through the primordial (see also Allahar, 1994), Diasporic sensibilities allow for the movement of peoples as governed through the coloniality of globalization to be counter-hegemonic by the same neo-liberal humanitarianism of the Western nation-state. In a sense, then, I am arguing that colonial forms of citizenry can come to be underwritten through Diasporic movement. However, by no means is this some naïve, utopian claim to citizenry without a sum critical read concerning the interplay with different histories, about the politics of resistance, self-determination, and survival, that for different bodies these desires play out differently. Citizenry and sovereignty, within the capitalist production of nation-state, concern legitimized insertion through secured, militarized borders, while at the same time producing Diasporic movement that has come to be discursively contoured through the tropes of immigrant, refugee, illegality, and foreigner. Keeping with the culture of the imperial order, these tropes are essentially racialized, and continue through histories of colonial time to mark the 'Other'. To invite Diasporic citizenry through a particular thinking of a post-national humanism is to then have to work with the colonial historical trajectories of Indigenous expropriation, transatlantic conditioning of African enslavement, and the desires of difference.

Pedagogy of Diaspora and the Search for Youth Citizenship

Diaspora provides the impetus to usurp historical questions of settler nation-state citizenry by centering complicit capitalist flows of movement, be it labour, goods, services, or commodities. Yet, what historical trajectories constitute this settler national-subject and concomitantly invite Diasporic inclination to permanently participate within these Northern constellations of the human condition? Isin and Wood (1999) amplified certain variants of sovereignty, those of *territoriality*, *autonomy*, and *legality*, arguing that these variants, as underpinned through militarized violence, assign rights, power, and privilege to certain bodies, insofar as the body becomes interpellated into the human condition of citizenship. Where the Diaspora intervenes is through a particular primordial governmentality that is not readily organized and inscribed, as the historical settler nation-state subject came to be reified through the said *territoriality*, *autonomy*, and *legality* of sovereignty. Diasporized youth come into the variegated forms of the human condition as located within the public sphere of the metropole, transformative of a divergent mode of socializing; one inculcated through the dispositions, expressions, articulations, practices, perceptions, and attitudes (Bourdieu, 1991) of the Enlightened-subject.

Yet, these newly found dispositions, immanent to the West, offer no guarantee for the Enlightenment public sphere, such that to say the urban youth becomes circumscribed and enveloped in ways that stabilize and render fecund the colonial desire of the West is by no means finite and totalizing. Diasporic youth carry with them across space and time histories of resistance, histories of colonial encounters, embodied knowledges that anachronistically speak through the lived experience of transatlantic plantation life. Depending on the degree of decolonization, different polities emerge that can help dissipate entrenched colonial attitudes. However, while the Enlightenment public sphere struggles to reconfigure itself through these transplanted Diasporic-polities, the imperial lacuna between the West and Southern countries expands itself in ways that further dependency on the West, one of which is through increased migration. Migration as capitalistically imbued, allows for Diasporized youth to move into the status quo of power and privilege through education, occupation, and skilled labour. At the same time, education has delimited certain spaces for the 'Othered' body that have come to mark the participatory process of youth citizenship. This demarcation speaks very much to a necessary class analysis of the social field, which, more often than not, becomes discursively pinned to debates concerning equality and meritocracy.

My interest, however, concerning youth citizenry as constitutively formed through the Diaspora is about accountability and responsibility; it is about the quality of civic life as negotiated through difference. It is about questions regarding the redistribution of Indigenous land. It is about understanding how a series of political configurations, a series of nation-state policies, come to self-regulate citizenry and/or sovereignty in particular spaces, and at the same time, how these spaces come to be resisted and contested by urban youth of difference. But, historically, citizenry has been fixed, homogenous, and always already relational to the nation-state. However, with the emergence of Diasporic-fields, Diasporic-domains in their material presence come to articulate social inquires which speak to the broader colonial experience as reified through the inter-intra policies of the imperial formations of the nation-state. The social of the public sphere comes to coalesce itself through cultural difference, thereby formulating new polities of representation, which variably culminate into a disquiet predicated about the sum historical, indissoluble, ethno-racial, embodied property. Yet, the Diaspora disseminates knowledges in which institutionalized recognition has been a struggle. Coming to belong, or to identify with a particular nation-state, often places Diasporized youth in contradictory relations to which they have claimed sovereign membership. My interest is with finding ways to challenge the way of being/becoming/performing the national-subject as a bounded relationship with the state.

Perhaps, too, we should consider how urban youth come into being the national-subject, and think about the particular socio-cultural variants being resisted, and the particular variants being desired and performed within present-day society. But what are the contemporary forms of desire, resistance, and orientations of belonging? In Toronto, in the summer of 2010, during the occasion of the G20 Summit, there were historical forms of resistance in the downtown public sphere of Toronto. Various interest groups, including youth, marched together for a collective call for social change and/or social justice. At the centre of the disquiet was bringing about critical awareness of the urgent need to de-imperialize concurrent transmissions of globalization. Put another way, to undo neocolonial forms of inter-intra state policies that work to maintain particular geographies in impoverished axes, and also problematize the quality of life, the quality of what it means to be human for particular bodies deemed illegal, refugee, terrorist, foreigner, undocumented worker, as such. Yet, resistance to the G20 Summit was taken up broadly through different political locals, accorded by different bodies, underpinned through race, class, gender, sexuality, and ability, in which the irreducible question invariably speaks to the relationship with human rights and becoming the subject of the sovereign citizen. I am thinking about these points of engagement, these points of resistance culminating through shared experiences of the Diaspora, in that the Diaspora is a politics of doing, a politics of becoming, a politics of action.

I think it is important to note that the G20 was well steeped in violence. My politics is not about condoning violence, but more so with placing a historical vector on violence to understand how citizenry of youth, and the settler nation-state, materialized through this index, and how violence plays out in the contemporary moment to will youth citizenry into being. How might we read a pedagogy of violence as a political act of resistance that ultimately works to de-interpellate the youth subject into the human? How do we come to understand the legitimized, protective forces of the state as constitutive of violence? Moreover, the G20 protests marked spaces of youth resistance that endowed belonging differently, that called attention to the unequal distribution of goods, to the question of rights, justice for all, and the need to articulate a critical sense of citizenship that necessitates resistance. Watching this violence play out on my television screen was quite appalling, for I was watching two competing forms of violence—legitimized violence as installed through the state and as inaugurated through various apparatuses, from uniforms, badges, horses, batons; and de-legitimized violence, forms of resistance as imbued through critical memory of histories of anti-colonial, anti-imperial, and/or anti-racist revolutions. What I was witnessing was, in a sense, the contestation of privilege, in which the diverging forces form themselves through the interests of human rights, social justice, equality, and some sense of freedom. For me, these performative acts of illegitimized violence speak to histories of transformation, histories of resistance for oppressed peoples. Interestingly enough however, the dominant, mass-media articulation, in its presumably neutral, objective, omnipresent posture, worked quickly to frame the uncertainties and unresolved tensions of the G20 protests. Yet, in many ways, the G20 protest was about the material. My concern, however, is with the location of the material—that the contestation of the material as imbued locally might not necessarily speak to the *ownership of the means of production*, but more so to the equitable distribution of commodities, goods, and services, and contemporary questions about civil rights, which systemically leave imperial transmissions well in place. If the collective responsibility of the protest spoke to the interest of global equity, then I am suggesting critical dialogue as engendered through Diasporic sensibilities that can speak to the necessity of de-imperializing North-South relations.

I am proposing that contemporary forms of desire, resistance, and orientations of belonging precipitate the alterity of the Diaspora (Bhatt, 2004; Pinar, 2000), in ways in which the practices of Urban Diasporized youth cultures—even when commodified and packaged—become primordially endowed through transoceanic embodiment, which inherently conveys transhistorical and/or transatlantic expressive meanings of emancipation, freedom, and/or liberation of oppressed peoples. What I am suggesting here is that these forms of desire, resistance, and orientations of belonging, as immanent to the alterity of Diasporized youth, are not mutually exclusive, but more so dependent, constitutive on the immutable, ethnocentric, Euro-Enlightened subject. What I am interested in is the primacy of the "counter-culture of modernity" (Gilroy, 1993); that these said Urban Diasporized youth cultures develop polities of the present where, through socially stratified spaces of occupation, Diasporized youth come into spaces of privilege which then become ahistorically performed as their own. So if we are thinking about the spatiality of race and the way in which currency and/or capital is accorded to the abject-body, or as Cheryl Harris (1995) aptly noted, *Whiteness as property*, I am thinking about how these embodied, privileged spaces of the Diaspora speak to the delimitation of Diasporic communities as they become colonially uncertained through racialized difference. I would imagine that this calls for a discussion concerning the complexities with the colonized body of difference, historic specificities of colonialism, and the production of Whiteness as privileged, gendered, and classed within the congeries of globalization and the nation-state. My concern here is with knowing how these disjunctures come to be Whitened and simultaneously Blackened through Diasporic-alterity (Ladson-Billings, 2000).

I also think it is important to discuss the tropes of emancipation, liberation, and freedom in the context of the Diaspora, as these tropes become situated in the West. Too often, urban youth becomes framed as the consumer of post-modern capitalism, as ahistorical, de-political, as turning one's back from the native homeland, as co-opting with the imperial gender, as being complicit with contributing to the impoverishment of Southern countries, as all but desiring to be this Enlightened national-subject (Appadurai, 1996; Gilroy, 1993; Jameson, 2005; Scott, 1995). Part and parcel of my writing is in a sense working to reclaim the Diasporic youth from these enclaves, to instead re-frame the discussion differently concerning the transatlantic experience of the Diaspora and what it means to be human, while at the same time working with the politics and ethics of these essentialist notions that come to totalize the experience of the Diaspora. In doing so, I am not dismissing these essentialist claims. I am, however, marking them as some of the possibilities, and I am willing to work with them dialectically as they come to configure the social, the lived experiences of Diasporized peoples. I am framing these spaces as distinctive, for I believe these spaces need to be understood through specific histories that situate the colonial differently as the colonial comes to reside within the West and the imperialized South. I also recognize that these colonial histories are interwoven and constitutive. However, I am arguing that the colonial comes to be nuanced in the West in ways that are arguably distinguishable from how the colonial comes to be located in the South. In this regard, the matter of culture-and-decolonization is of the utmost importance to this discussion, in that culture and decolonization can help articulate a theory concerning the socio-cultural experiences of the Diaspora as these synchronistic experiences become embodied within urban youth.

Conclusion

Notably, theory ought to be specific to particular historical conditions as contingent across place, time, and space. Given the geography of Urban Diasporized youth, we must then speak about certain constitutive variants such as transatlantic-Blackness, indentureship, post-independence, race, and culture. However, with the congeries of White settler nation-state differing itself in ways in which the inauguration of this event called Independence ushered in a form of governance where the body historically designated as the abject-plantation-subject becomes relocated in the public sphere as citizen, as national subject, as human. I am asking, then, and as precipitated through these specific histories of colonialism, what does it mean to have this sense of a collective national consciousness for urban youth as emerging from these colonial designated spaces of enslavement and plantation? Frantz Fanon (1967), in his *The Wretched of the Earth*, essentially broached this question. Fanon spoke about the necessity of having a national consciousness that engaged the histories of colonialism. For urban youth to have some emancipatory sense would entail having the critical consciousness to engage daily in lived colonial modernities. Fanon cautioned about the pitfalls of such, that the colonial can re-present itself in ways in which the local takes up the subject position of the privileged, thus repeating the colonial through different practices and different bodies. Hence, belonging, unbelonging, migrancy, and Diasporic conditions become ontologized within a given geographical domain (Ahmad, 2008).

I am suggesting that the dominant mode of political orientation within the spatial communes of urban youth as lived, refashioned, and performed, congeals and forms itself ahistorically through cultural memories of transhistorical peoples, discursive inscriptions of the governing edicts of capitalism, and the myriad neocolonial procedures of globalization. This concomitantly works to constitute what it means to be human for urban youth, that is, incited through the interests of self-determination, and as Fanon (1963) noted, the demiurge has been colonially assimilated; that said, self-determination of urban youth becomes procured through the material conditions of colonialism. Fanon was quite careful to distinguish between nationalism and national consciousness: that national consciousness becomes conditioned through culture; that for colonized peoples, culture ought to be determined through decolonization; that decolonization can come to qualitatively frame local peoples with de-imperializing attitudes. Having said that, my politics concern the manner in which contemporary, material, sociocultural artifacts of Urban Diasporized youth become an organizing vector through transhistorical understandings of ontological belonging. What I am interested in is the experience of urban youth concerning these contemporary questions of understanding the self through ontological belonging, as they come to be historically shaped through the social conjunctures of the many cultural formations of modernity. I am considering, then, a necessary theory that speaks to this present Diasporic contiguity. I am imagining a theory that dialectically intervenes through Diaspora as method, one that speaks with the complex histories immanent to the lived social world of Urban Diasporized youth.

References

Ahmad, A. (2008). *In theory: Classes, nations, literatures*. New York, NY: Verso.

Allahar, A. L. (1994). More than an oxymoron: Ethnicity and the social construction of primordial attachment. *Canadian Ethnic Studies, 26*(3), 18–33.

Anderson, B. (1991). *Imagined communities: Reflections on the origin and spread of nationalism*. London, UK: Verso.

Appadurai, A. (1996). *Modernity at large: Cultural dimensions of globalization*. Minneapolis, MN: University of Minnesota Press.

Bauman, Z. (2004). *Wasted lives: Modernity and its outcasts*. Cambridge, UK: Polity Press.

Bhatt, C. (2004). Contemporary geopolitics and 'alterity' research. In M. Bulmer & J. Solomos (Eds.), *Researching race and racism* (pp. 16–36). London, UK: Routledge.

Bourdieu, P. (1991). *Language and symbolic power*. Cambridge, MA: Harvard University Press.

Dei, G. J. S., & Simmons, M. (2012). Writing diasporic indigeneity through critical research and social method. In S. Steinberg & G. Cannella (Eds.), *Critical qualitative research reader* (pp. 296–306). New York, NY: Peter Lang.

Ellis, C. (2009). *Revision: Autoethnographic reflections on life and work*. Walnut Creek, CA: Left Coast Press.

Ellis, C., & Bochner, A. P. (2000). Autoethnography, personal narrative, reflexivity: Researcher as subject. In N. K. Denzin & Y. S. Lincoln (Eds.), *Handbook of qualitative research* (pp. 733–768). Thousand Oaks, CA: Sage.

Fanon, F. (1963). *The wretched of the earth*. New York, NY: Grove Press.

Fanon, F. (1967). *Black skin, White masks*. New York, NY: Grove Press.

Foucault, M. (2007). *The politics of truth*. Los Angeles, CA: Semiotext(e).

Giddens, A. (1991). *Modernity and self-identity: Self and society in the late modern age*. Stanford, CA: Stanford University Press.

Gilroy, P. (1993). *The Black Atlantic: Modernity and double consciousness*. Cambridge, MA: Harvard University Press.

Giroux, A. H. (2009). Dirty democracy and the new authoritarianism in the United States. In A. H. Itwaru (Ed.), *The White supremacist state: Eurocentrism, imperialism, colonialism, racism* (pp. 157–184). Toronto, Canada: Other Eye.

Habermas, J. (1998). Modernity—An incomplete project. In H. Foster (Ed.), *The anti-aesthetic: Essays on postmodern culture* (pp. 1–15). New York, NY: New Press.

Hall, S. (1997). Subjects in history: Making diasporic identities. In W. Lubiano (Ed.), *The house that race built: Black Americans, U.S. terrain* (pp. 280–299). New York, NY: Pantheon Books.

Hall, S. (2000). Cultural identity and diaspora. In N. Mirzoeff (Ed.), *Diaspora and visual culture: Representing Africans and Jews* (pp. 21–33). London, UK: Routledge.

Hall, S. (2007). The global, the local, and the return of ethnicity. In S. Hall, D. Held, D. Hubert, & K. Thompson (Eds.), *Modernity: An introduction to modern societies* (pp. 623–629). Oxford, UK: Blackwell.

Hardt, M., & Negri, A. (2000). *Empire*. Cambridge, MA: Harvard University Press.

Harris, C. (1995). Whiteness as property. In K. Crenshaw, N. Gotanda, G. Peller, & K. Thomas (Eds.), *Critical race theory: The key writings that formed the movement* (pp. 276–291). New York, NY: New Press.

Isin, E. F., & Wood, P. K. (1999). *Citizenship and identity*. London, UK: Sage.

Jameson, F. (2005). *Postmodernism, or, the cultural logic of late capitalism*. Durham, NC: Duke University Press.

Kincheloe, J. (2005). Critical ontology and auto/biography: Being a teacher, developing a reflective teacher persona. In W. M. Roth (Ed.), *Auto/biography and auto/ethnography: Praxis of research method* (pp. 155–174). Rotterdam, The Netherlands: Sense.

Kincheloe, J., & Steinberg, S. (2008). Indigenous knowledges in education: Complexities, dangers and profound benefits. In. N. K. Denzin, Y. S. Lincoln, & L. T. Smith (Eds.), *Handbook of critical and indigenous methodologies* (pp. 135–156). Los Angeles, CA: Sage.

Ladson-Billings, G. (2000). Racialized discourses and ethnic epistemologies. In N. K. Denzin & Y. S. Lincoln (Eds.), *Handbook of qualitative research* (pp. 257–277). Thousand Oaks, CA: Sage.

Pinar, W. (1994). *Autobiography, politics, and sexuality: Essays in curriculum theory, 1972–1992*. New York, NY: Peter Lang.

Pinar, W. (2000). Strange fruit: Race, sex, and an autobiography of alterity. In P. P. Trifonas (Ed.), *Revolutionary pedagogies: Cultural politics, instituting education, and the discourse of theory* (pp. 30–46). New York, NY: RoutledgeFalmer.

Reed-Danahay, D. E. (1997). Introduction. In D. E. Reed-Danahay (Ed.), *Auto/ethnography: Rewriting the self and the social* (pp. 1–17). Oxford, UK: Berg.

Richardson, L. (2000). Writing: A method of inquiry. In N. K. Denzin & Y. S. Lincoln (Eds.), *Handbook of qualitative research* (pp. 923–948). Thousand Oaks, CA: Sage.

Roth, W. M. (2005). *Auto/biography and auto/ethnography: Praxis of research method.* Rotterdam, The Netherlands: Sense.

Scott, D. (1995). Colonial governmentality. *Social Text, 43*(2), 191–220.

Wolcott, H. F. (2004). The ethnographic autobiography. *Auto/Biography, 12*(2), 93–106.

Wynter, S. (1995). The pope must have been drunk, the king of Castile a madman: Culture as actuality, and the Caribbean rethinking modernity. In A. Ruprecht & C. Taiana (Eds.), *The reordering of culture: Latin America, the Caribbean and Canada: In the hood* (pp. 1–41). Ottawa, Canada: Carleton University Press.

CHAPTER 18

Conocimiento

Mixtec Youth *sin fronteras*

Fabiola Martinez and Elizabeth Quintero

C onocimiento, for Anzaldúa, is

> an overarching theory of consciousness … all the dimensions of life, both inner—mental, emotional, instinctive, imaginal, spiritual, bodily realms—and outer—social, political, lived experiences … the awareness of facultad that sees through all human acts whether of the individual mind and spirit or of the collective, social body. (Hérnandez-Ávila & Anzaldúa, 2000, p. 177)

In this chapter, we explore examples of Conocimiento Theory through the interactions of a senior-level university student working with migrant youth from Mixtec backgrounds (from Oaxaca, Mexico) in an urban high school in southern California. A segment of a conversation between Fabiola Martinez and a high-school student she tutors hints at the need for a theoretical approach such as Conocimiento according to Anzaldúa. This is a way to view and support the strengths and challenges of youth in migrant situations. Fabiola noted in her journal:

> A young tenth grader approached me asking about my own living situations. "Maestra, usted vive sola?" she said. I went on to say I had a roommate, then I had to explain what a roommate was, and that I take care of my personal things.

> She asked if I missed my family, but specifically, she asked if my missed my mother. At the moment this wasn't awkward, later I made the connection. A while later that day … she went on to share with me that she had lived in Mexico while her mother lived in California. This student had to go to school, work, and maintain a home for her eight younger siblings. Three years ago her mother brought her here to California and here she is. She is a straight "A" student speaking English very well, soaking in information and was well on her way to college and to being a success story.

> But … now, she is being taken out of my program. Worse than that, she is being taken out of school as a whole. Her mother is moving her to Las Vegas with no plans to enroll her in school. (Martinez, 2013)

We discuss the strengths of the youth from this group of students, the challenges they face, and the multidirectional learning between the university student and the high-school youth she interacts with in a student-support program. Critical literacy will be a framework within the theory of Conocimiento to view this work.

This research story addresses issues of access and quality in education for children of migrant farmworkers. Migration, language, culture, power, ethnicity, race, and class enter into the complex consideration of how education serves the needs of this population. Fabiola Martinez is graduating from an Early Childhood Studies program in a State University in California. The students in the program approach curricula from a participatory critical theory framework study, and work to create responsive, high-quality education for children and youth of migrant farmworkers. The university students rethink curriculum for children and youth through their university coursework by learning from the families and children of the migrant workers in Southern California. Research has shown that quality early care and education positively influence children's success in school and later in life (Loeb, Fuller, Kagan, & Carrol, 2004; Schweinhart, Barnes, Weikart, Barnett, & Epstein, 1993; Shonkoff & Phillips, 2000). This is true for all children and particularly important for children of recent immigrants, who are often beginning to learn English, and who have a rich cultural history as well as diverse needs.

From Conocimiento as Theory to Critical Theory

As stated earlier, Conocimiento Theory, for Anzaldúa, is

> an overarching theory of consciousness … all the dimensions of life, both inner—mental, emotional, instinctive, imaginal, spiritual, bodily realms—and outer—social, political, lived experiences … the awareness of facultad that sees through all human acts whether of the individual mind and spirit or of the collective, social body. (Hérnandez-Ávila & Anzaldúa, 2000, p. 177)

Anzaldúa urged the generation of theories based on those whose knowledges are traditionally excluded from and silenced by academic research. She further asserted that beyond creating theories, "we need to find practical application for those theories." Anzaldúa advised that "we need to de-academize theory and to connect the community to the academy" (Anzaldúa, 1990, p. xxvi). Anzaldúa (2002) also noted that "Change requires more than words on a page—it takes perseverance, creative ingenuity and acts of love." (p. 574)

Family History and De-Academization of Theory

Through the persona of Fabiola Martinez, her own historical and cultural influences, and her dedication to working with youth from migrant families, we see illustrations of the de-academization of theory. Multiple examples of Conocimiento Theory appear as all the dimensions of the lives of migrant students and their tutor interconnect. Fabiola Martinez has documented memories from her childhood that influenced her strong feelings about her home language, her family, and her passions and interests. These experiences reflect the importance of viewing family, learning, and opportunities through Conocimiento Theory and point to her passion for supporting Latino youth, from all backgrounds, and especially those from migrant families.

Martinez wrote a summary of memories about maintaining home language. When asked what influenced her to nurture and use her home language, complete her education, and persevere in general, she said:

> My dad! He always made it a point to (insist that we) keep our Spanish. He would always complain about cousins that spoke Spanish with an accent or didn't know how to conjugate properly while speaking. I definitely have him, and my mom, to thank for my not forgetting Spanish.…

> Also, ever since I can remember it was imprinted in my head that college was not an option. It was elementary, middle school, high school, and college. NO OPTIONS! … And all that is due to my parents.

Now that I have moved out and I see the graduation light so close, I definitely have to thank my parents. I appreciate them more now that I am away from them compared to when I saw them every day.

In a class focusing on methods for teaching multilingual students, Fabiola wrote an "I Am … " poem (Christensen, 2003) that reflects Conocimiento Theory in her own life:

Where I am From …
I say I am from a breeze
From a golden globe that warms my every step
From a place where mountains decorate my surroundings
With their white tops on hot summer days
From a place where dreams are supposed to come true
With white picket fences
From a place where people run on their own clock
Places to be and people to see
From a place where gold started it all
And diamonds are a girl's best friend
From a place where stars decorate the floor we walk on
And the stars in the sky hide behind our bright lights

But this is all a lie …
Where I am really from is from a place full of spirit
And culture is everything
From "Donde esta Fabiola?"
And "Todo el mundo es un coral …."
From a place where family is priority
And priority means leaving them behind to better their life
Like my father …
So now I can say I am from a breeze.…
(Martinez, 2012)

Fabiola explained that California Mini-Corps is a migrant tutoring service provided through Butte County Schools. It began in 1967 and was designed after the Peace Corps program. While working for the program she has been able to go to different districts each school year and work with the migrant students and their families. She noted, "We do assessments, SMART goals and make home visits in order to help us better understand our students." (Martinez, 2013, n.p.)

During the summers, Fabiola Martinez had the honor of attending Mini-Corps Professional Development sessions in Sacramento. Travel expenses were covered as well as lodging at Sacramento State University for the weekend. All summer tutors were offered educational and informational workshops. Martinez says, "This has helped me grow as an individual and as a future educator. Through Mini-Corps I received a well-rounded experience in all levels of K-12 in different districts in California."

Fabiola Martinez, her family, her tenacity, and her dedication to what we have come to see as Conocimiento Theory illustrate what many critical and postmodern scholars call transformation. Critical theory encourages the production and application of theory as a part of the overall search for transformative knowledge. Paulo Freire (1985) promoted critical theory, which emphasizes participation through personal histories, the sharing of multiple ways of knowing, and transformative action.

Critical Race theorist, Gloria Ladson-Billings (2009), stated that the critical turning point of transformation might be the stage educators would be most interested in seeing their students achieve. This is a stage where the student becomes qualitatively renewed, with a commitment to compassionate understanding; in some ways, it shares affinities with the goals of culturally relevant pedagogy, in that educational work should be transformative (Ladson-Billings, 2009).

When this happens in students, what are the factors that contribute to it? We believe that this transformation is multidirectional and can occur for both the learner and the tutor or teacher. We believe that by approaching Conocimiento through critical theory and critical literacy, participants in learning situations have the opportunity to fully participate, knowing that their history and languages will be respected, and that they will become an integral part of all learning, sharing multiple sources of knowledge—traditional and nontraditional—and will have the opportunity to make decisions about transformative knowledge. We also believe that until approaches such as these are instituted with youth from backgrounds rich in diversity and experience; their struggles will remain very difficult.

In our work, we use critical theory and critical literacy as processes of both reading history (the world) and creating history. Whose stories are important, and in what ways? In what ways can we learn from the stories? Whose background knowledge will we respect and include, and in what ways? Whose and which knowledge is power, and in what ways? In what ways can we use literacy for specific transformative action? (Quintero, 2009).

Context of Current Study

The contemporary poet, Francisco X. Alarcón, asks us if we can "hear the voices between these lines" (Alarcón, 1997, p. 28). Scholars, dedicated teachers, and community activists have documented the fact that many immigrant students come from a variety of backgrounds with different "funds of knowledge" (Moll, Gonzalez, & Amanti, 2005; Quintero & Rummel, 2010; Steinberg & Kincheloe, 2009) for contributing to our communities and educational programs. Acculturation and language acquisition are impacted by the process of aligning new societal expectations and requirements of immigrants with previous cultural norms, individual perceptions, and experiences preeminent in their lives; yet, these urgent issues are often ignored. By virtue of the fact that many immigrant students come from a variety of backgrounds with different "funds of knowledge" as Moll, Gonzalez, and Amanti (2005) reported, it is urgent that university education students learn the complicated practice of recognizing, acknowledging, and incorporating learners' background knowledge while providing them access to new and necessary knowledge for successful participation in the 21st century. The research described provides a focus on this work in ways that currently are not often discussed in literature in the field.

Agricultural workers in our county include families from Mexico and Central America, and a large, close-knit, indigenous group of families from Oaxaca and Mexico, known as the Mixtecs. The Mixtecs are indigenous inhabitants of southern Mexico whose language and culture predate the Spanish conquest by hundreds of years. There are an estimated 500,000 Mixtec speakers today; almost one-fifth live in the United States for at least part of their lives. Mixtec language and culture are as different from Spanish as Navajo is from English. The Mixtecs' beliefs about health, religion, and family include many traditional concepts, and are often at odds with Western concepts. Along with other indigenous cultures, the Mixtec's unique language, art, and culture are in danger of being lost forever. Many of the immigrant families who arrived in the United States in the 1970s and 1980s raised their families here—and now have children in college or who are successfully employed. Many have become U.S. citizens (Fox & Rivera-Salgado, 2004).

However, there are barriers for many of the Mixtec people living in California. Many are illiterate, and some speak neither Spanish nor English but only their native language, Mixteco, or another indigenous language. As a result, they face exploitation and discrimination in labor, housing, and everyday life. Most live in extreme poverty and lack basic provisions such as adequate housing, food, clothing, and other necessities of life. Central to their struggle is the fact that they cannot communicate with people beyond their own indigenous community, thus impeding their ability to obtain appropriate health care, educate themselves and their children, negotiate with their employers to improve their work situation, and exercise their basic civil rights (Wright, 2005).

Fabiola explains her work with this group of learners from infant-toddler programs through middle school and high school:

Working with migrant students ages three to eighteen has been an experience unlike any other. When I was focusing solely on the younger ages, I had been witness to children struggling to identify a language to speak. What is going to happen to the children when they enter the elementary years and are expected to read a language that no one in their home speaks?

I am the oldest sibling and from my experiences with younger children, I wonder who do these kids go to for help? How are parents supposed to be involved parents if this language barrier also stops them? With this, I believe that a well thought out literacy plan will greatly impact these kids and their families. (Martinez, 2013)

A migrant child is defined as a child who has parents or guardians that are migratory agricultural workers. Due to this lifestyle the child is at risk of possible health problems, poverty, constant relocation, discrimination, and language barriers. The problems can have an intense influence on the educational accomplishments of children of migrant laborers. These are not new elements of struggle to any one of us in this society. Some of these conditions happen to many of the poor populations here in the United States. However, having to constantly move and readjust creates a new set of obstacles and consequences for the child and for their education. Migrant students may attend as many as six or seven schools per year (Jachman, 2002).

Fabiola, as a part of her university study, read "Classroom Teaching and Instruction "Best Practices": for Young English Language Learners" by Linda M. Espinosa (2010). She reflected:

Something new that stood out to me right away is that the number of programs for students who are learning to speak another language other than English is increasing. Due to my tutoring with migrant students I have gotten the chance to meet these students. When I think of students learning a second language my mind automatically jumped to students learning English. However, I had students that were learning Spanish as a second language and English as a third. As simple as the idea is, I had never seen it from that point of view. And the number of these students is increasing? It is something amazing to me.

She goes on to reflect:

When I was learning English, around the age of 4 or 5 (still young), I would go back to my Spanish to make connections. I would say a Spanish word and put an awkward accent to it and call it "English." Then as I grew up I used my knowledge of Spanish to learn how to spell. Since in the English language we don't pronounce every single letter in a word (i.e., Wednesday/because) and in Spanish we do, I would say "w-e-D-n-e-s-d-a-y" or "b-e-C-A-U-s-E" just to make sure I got all the letters down. This article by Espinosa states that ELL students make relationships between the language they are learning and their primary language. And it is true. I think that this is something important to keep in mind when working with children.

I had a student last week ask me "how do you spell tender?" They were writing sentences about the colonial times so I was confused as to how the word "tender" fit in her sentences. So I asked her how she was trying to use it. She said "In the morning I tender my bed." I honestly couldn't help but laugh a little bit. She was using the Spanish word "tender" which means "to make." So she translated the Spanish verb over to English. She went to her Spanish knowledge to figure out her sentence. She was a fourth grader learning English and the fact that she's trying to use what she knows is a good step.

Tying the information from Espinosa's article to her personal history and her work with children and youth from the migrant community, Martinez said:

Knowing how kids think and accepting it as a positive step forward I think is a key lesson for teachers. Being patient and accepting that each child will slowly accept and grasp the new language at her/his own pace is important. I've had students that refused to communicate with me in English (given these were kids that first spoke Mixteco, while learning Spanish in a bilingual classroom). I had to ask questions and converse in Spanish. Only later I learned that the parents of one boy pushed learning Spanish so much that he didn't want to learn English. (Martinez, 2013, n.p.)

Anzaldúa might have smiled at Martinez's final thoughts about the article she had been thinking about. Martinez said, "Reading articles makes us knowledgeable and it is important to learn what others have found and concluded. But nothing beats personally working with these kids and first hand verifying that what one is reading in academia is true" (Martinez, 2013, n.p.).

So What? Conocimiento Literacy

Martinez found that some children are introduced to the school system when they have not had any school knowledge at all. She comments,

> Being introduced to math, how to read, a schedule is something new and unnatural to these kids. Then after they are getting settled in a school, it is time to move and time to readjust to a new curriculum and procedures.

If we think about Conocimiento Theory, "all the dimensions of life, both inner—mental, emotional, instinctive, imaginal, spiritual, bodily realms—and outer—social, political, lived experiences … the awareness of facultad that sees through all human acts whether of the individual mind and spirit or of the collective, social body" (Hérnandez-Ávila & Anzaldúa, 2000, p. 177), then we have to really interrupt assumptions about "school readiness" and other stereotypical expectations for performance and narrow approaches to knowledge. Children who are migrating with their families not only are disrupted in the typical school processes and expectations, but they must also make new friends and learn to trust again. Again, some of the children are learning English as a third language. This inconsistency and the many challenges set the tone for the child's reading readiness and their ability to retain knowledge, or not.

The complexity of all of it, in particular the overarching theory as an important lens for viewing complex strengths and struggles, is illustrated through the brief segment of Fabiola's notes about working with two brothers, one in 10th grade (Student A) and one in 11th grade (Student B). Martinez writes,

> Having a set of brothers gives me the opportunity to see how two different students raised in the same household, with similar experiences does not necessarily mean the same outcome will occur.

> Student B tries hard to do his work even though I can see in his eyes that he knows that he can't do it without me. It takes a lot of guidance and one-on-one attention to help him do the work instead of just letting him work with a group and simply copy answers. Having him in a group causes the group to slow down because then I have to work with students that are in two different places. (Martinez, 2013, n.p.)

She notes that teachers often do not have the time to slow down for that one student who needs more attention, because then the other 25 students are not given attention. She says, "Student B slides by and copies work if I do not sit with him and allow him to slowly but surely work out the homework" (Martinez, 2013, n.p.).

Martinez noted a disturbing experience with this student:

> While working on a packet for his English 101 class I was made aware of something huge that even made me feel guilty for assuming. The page consisted of fixing what was wrong with the sentence: "There are **33** seconds in a minute." All students had to do was correct the bold word. I ASSUMED he could do this much on his own and simply translated the sentence expecting him to know the answer in Spanish. To my surprise the first answer he gave me was "One?" and the guessing just continued from

there. After I told him that this was "easy" I was made aware that at 11th grade, he had never been taught his numbers in Mexico.

Then she describes his brother, Student A, who, on the other hand, has given up as a whole. "Para que maestra? Si voy a reprovar." "Why bother? I'm going to fail anyways." She says,

I know the correct response to that is supposed to be something positive, but what do I do when even I know that this student will most likely not graduate? Do I lie? All I can do is to my best to set up this student to be motivated. I know the student is involved in gang related activity. He does turn in homework, but only when I sit with him and help him. While reading short stories in English it takes him a good while to get through it and with a lot of errors along the way. (Martinez, 2013, n.p.)

Martinez went on to say,

Student A did confide in me one day that their mother and four sisters are in Mexico while they live here with their father. The dad wasn't working so it made me wonder how things were getting paid. A few months later the student stayed after school for tutoring for the first time in 8 months. I couldn't help but ask why. Looking down and hesitant, he told me that due to their dad not working they had to leave their small house and rent a room in a stranger's home. Now the 3 men live in one room. He said that the owner told them that they can't do their homework in the living room, so now he stays after school with me for 3 hours to make sure his work is done before he goes home. This is helping his grades! I hope this is the beginning of a positive ending. (Martinez, 2013, n.p.)

Heartfelt Questions for Teachers

Through critical approaches to how things are and how things could be and/or should be for this population of students, Martinez says,

I have noticed from teachers teaching Specially Designed Academic Instruction in English (SDAIE) that often they seem to forget what it is that they signed up for. While tutoring a US History class, a boring subject for students right from the beginning, I noticed the teacher not even teach. The class was full of English Language Learners (ELL's) and with them the migrant students I tutor. The teacher never left the desk, never lectured the chapters and never controlled the class. This alone made the class a problem for me, making me be the disciplinarian when that is not my job, it's hers.

Eventually I decided to just focus on my migrant students and made sure they got ahead. The teacher would randomly show a Power Point on a television screen up on one corner of the room that was hardly visible. Power Points don't work for my students and they can't keep taking notes. They are at a huge disadvantage with "teaching" techniques like this. She would pass out packets about chapters and simply put a due date, give a test on that day and move on to next chapter. Needless to say, all students were failing. As a tutor I can only do so much to attempt to help them understand a chapter and translate for them along with translating the packet. Why take a SDAIE class if one isn't prepared for what it takes to make those students succeed? It is documented that "The SDAIE teacher is a facilitator of learning; the teacher is the essential expert in a classroom typified by social interaction and the construction of meaning" (Sobul, 1995).

Martinez asks, "How will the Common Core affect ELL's and migrant students that are learning Spanish as a second language and English as a third?"

Conclusion: What Can We Do?

Martinez suggests that we can support migrant youth in spite of the struggles beyond their control by creating a positive environment and displaying respect for diversity and values. Her suggestions reveal work she has considered and internalized based on Critical Theory and Critical Literacy, with the overlap of exploring the knowledges of Conocimiento Theory. Critical theory stresses participation by all in the learning process, multiple sources of knowledge, and transformative action. Conocimiento Theory stresses the merging of the individual and the collective, the academic and the social … the whole person. Martinez suggests having older students mentor the younger ones. This would give them a chance to be mentors and share experiences and demonstrate trust. She notes that the teacher can personalize lessons based on the student's experiences. This can help the learners feel confident in the classroom. The teacher can implement assessments based on language proficiency that are appropriate to the student's academic needs. (This would be transformative for the teacher as well as the students.) It is also important that the teacher does some research about the learners' culture and language. This can help open the communication between parents and the teacher.

Linking community resources (such as adult-education programs or existing parenting programs) and schools has the potential of creating positive learning environments for both children and families (St. Clair, Jackson, & Zweiback, 2012). It is no secret that parent involvement is a huge factor in any child's education. Parents of migrant children suffer from the same challenges as their children: language and education barriers, and lack of confidence. Programs that help the parent are useful and necessary.

Despite all of the challenges that migrant students go through due to their lifestyle, they also gain many advantages from the experiences of their lifestyle. The necessity of having to adapt to new environments is a skill that many people cannot grasp. These students also have the ability to solve problems on their own. They meet new challenges and are able to problem-solve and adapt with ease. Migrant students also have wide-ranging knowledge in cultural and geographical diversity. Using this knowledge and these skills, these students can develop confidence and a sense of self that can lead them toward a successful academic future.

According to Anzaldúa (1999, p. 195), our muse for this work,

To survive the Borderlands
you must live sin fronteras
be a crossroads.

References

Alarcón, F. X. (1997). *Laughing tomatoes and other spring poems / Jitomates risueños y otros poemas de primavera*. San Francisco, CA: Children's Book Press.

Anzaldúa, G. (1990). *Haciendo caras/making face, making soul: Creative and critical perspectives by women of color*. San Francisco, CA, Aunt Lute Press.

Anzaldúa, G. (1999). *Borderlands: The new mestiza/La frontera* (2nd ed.). San Francisco, CA: Spinsters/Aunt Lute Press.

Anzaldúa, G. (2002). Now let us shift … the path of conocimiento … inner work, public acts. In G. Anzaldúa & A. Keating (Eds.), *This bridge we call home: Radical visions for transformation* (pp. 540–578). New York, NY: Routledge.

Christensen, L. (2000). *Reading, writing and rising up: Teaching about social justice and the power of the written word*. Milwaukee, WI: Rethinking Schools.

Espinosa, L. M. (2010). Classroom teaching and instruction "best practices" for young English language learners. In E. E. Garcia & E. C. Frede (Eds.), *Young English language learners: Current research and emerging directions for practice and policy* (pp. 143–164). New York, NY: Teachers College Press.

Fox, J., & Rivera-Salgado, G. (Eds.). (2004). *Indigenous Mexican migrants in the United States*. Stanford, CA: Center for Comparative Immigration Studies.

Freire, P. (1985). *The politics of education: Culture, power, and liberation*. Granby, MA: Bergin & Garvey.

Hérnandez-Ávila, A., & Anzaldúa, G. (2000). Interview. In A. C. Elenes (Ed.), *Transforming borders: Chicana/o popular culture and pedagogy* (p. 177). Lanham, MD: Rowman & Littlefield.

Jachman, A. (2002). SEDL letter: Putting reading first. *Reading and the Migrant Student*. Retrieved from http://www.sedl.org/pubs/sedl-letter/v14n03/4.html

Ladson-Billings, G. (2009). *The dreamkeepers: Successful teachers of African American children* (2nd ed.). San Francisco, CA: Jossey-Bass.

Loeb, S., Fuller, B., Kagan, S. L., & Carrol, B. (2004). Child care in poor communities: Early learning effects of type, quality, and stability. *Child Development, 75*(1), 47–65.

Martinez, F. (2012). Unpublished manuscript.

Martinez, F. (2013). Unpublished manuscript.

Moll, L. C., Gonzalez, N., & Amanti, C. (2005). *Funds of knowledge: Theorizing practices in households, communities, and classrooms*. Mahweh, NJ: Lawrence Erlbaum.

Quintero, E. P. (2009). Young children and story: The path to transformative action. In S. Steinberg (Ed.), *Diversity and multiculturalism: A reader* (pp. 161–173). New York, NY: Peter Lang.

Quintero, E. P., & Rummel, M. K. (2010). Problem posing, reflection, action: Literature and our lives. In C. Rhodes & L. Wolf (Eds.), *Children's literature and social justice*. Newark, DE: International Reading Association.

Schweinhart, L. J., Barnes, H. V., Weikart, D. P., Barnett, W. S., & Epstein, A. S. (1993). Significant benefits: The High/Scope Perry Preschool study through age 27. *Monographs of the High/Scope Educational Research Foundation, No. 10*. Ypsilanti, MI: High/Scope Press.

Shonkoff, J. P., & Phillips, D. (2000). *From neurons to neighborhoods: The science of early childhood development*. Washington, DC: National Academies Press.

Sobul, D. (1995). *Specially designed academic instruction in English*. Alexandria, VA: ERIC Reports (ED391357).

St. Clair, L., Jackson, B., & Zweiback, R. (2012). Six years later: Effect of family involvement training on the language skills of children from migrant families. *School Community Journal, 22*(1), 9–19.

Steinberg, S., & Kincheloe, J. (2009). *Christotainment: Selling Jesus through popular culture*. Boulder, CO: Westview Press.

Troia, G. A. (2004). Migrant students with limited English proficiency: Can Fast ForWord Language? make a difference in their language skills and academic achievement? *Remedial and Special Education, 25*(6), 353–366.

Wright, A. (2005). *The death of Ramón González*. Austin, TX: University of Texas Press.

CHAPTER 19

From Hijabi to Ho-jabi
Voguing the Hijab and the Politics
Behind an Emerging Subculture

Saba Alvi

Hijabi and the City

In the closing scenes of *Sex and the City 2*, the feisty Carrie and her loyal sidekicks take on the exotically portrayed streets of Abu Dhabi in the United Arab Emirates. Their provocative and colourful clothing is starkly contrasted with the long, black cloaks of the Emirati women. As the lead characters make their way through markets and side streets, there is repeated emphasis on their sexual liberation, while the local men and women are depicted as stern and asexual. It is on one of these streets that the women, while making a comedic getaway from an angry mob of men who want to persecute them for being so open about their sexuality, are pulled into a secret tent. Here, a mysterious group of veiled women unveil themselves to reveal what lies beneath their cloaks: the women proudly show off the latest trends and most coveted names off the runway—not so modest and not so monotone. To the surprise of Carrie and her friends, the fashion was so stunning that it not only exceeded their expectations, but it was beyond anything that *Sex and the City* put on.

Revealing what is worn underneath the veil, it seems, shifts the meaning behind the veil as a sign of the 'other' to the more familiar. Clothing here plays a powerful role in how one can use objects to create new meanings. One's clothes become a tool through which interactions with the world can be made and relationships formed. Al-Saji (2010) recognized clothing as intimate pieces that deeply inform one's sense of self, noting, "clothing is no longer felt as an object apart from the lived body, but comes to form an integrated part of one's body schema. Bodily extensions ... become themselves dimensions through which the subject perceives and interacts with the world and others" (p. 890). This inevitably implicates the role clothing can play in shaping and performing one's identity.

Butler's (1999) notion of *performativity* is exceedingly significant here in examining how clothing can be performative. Butler (1999) used the term to describe how gender is constructed through discourse rather than actually existing as a part of nature. Therefore, 'being' a man or woman is consolidated by learned and repeated behaviours. Gender performativity challenges constructed expectations of gender. Blaise's (2005) study demonstrated that as early as the age of four, children become aware of how to perform gender through what they put on their bodies. Young girls and boys become aware that the colour pink is a socially constructed female colour, while blues and greens are constructed as male colours. They use this understanding to engage in acts that are categorized as either 'masculine' or 'feminine'.

Similarly, Zine (2000) and Willett (2008), in their respective studies, illustrated how women gender their clothing as a way of asserting their sexual identity. For the Muslim women in Zine's (2000) study, dressing modestly and covering the body is a strategic way of controlling the outsider's gaze, of determining who can have access to their bodies. In Willett's (2008) study, participants dressed provocatively to accomplish just the opposite. Dressing in revealing clothing gives the women the power to assert control over their sexuality. In both scenarios, clothing is used as the primary marker of gaining a sense of ownership over one's sense of self. Clothing thus becomes performative. It is used by the subject to communicate ideologies about one's own subjectivity.

It is for these very reasons that many subcultures rely on various fashion trends, or what Hebdige (2003) referred to as 'style' as a way to perform identity. Clothing is more than the mere objects on their bodies, rather, articles of clothing are the "mundane objects which have double meanings" (p. 2). Hebdige (2003) and other cultural theorists such as Hall and Jefferson (2003) have explored how simple articles of clothing can take on new meanings. These authors theorize that within some subcultures, clothing and the objects put on them become a means of resistance to mainstream society. By withdrawing from what are considered the norms of a culture, subcultures further demonstrate how the clothing they put on can be performative acts, as it is primarily through clothing that these groups identify themselves as part of a subculture.

In this chapter, I seek to explore how the Muslim veil as represented through articles of clothing is used not as a religious symbol, but rather, as a fashion accessory that informs and performs the identity formation of young Muslim women. Furthermore, I seek to explore how the veil as a sign becomes fixed in sources such as the news media, and how some young Muslim women are constructing new meanings that contest the dominant discourse and the politics that lie within this internal discourse.

Redefining the Veil

The term, *hijab*, has roots in the Arabic language, meaning to cover or to screen. While this may be a broad definition of *hijab*, the word itself has come to mean much more. It is most often associated with just the head covering, but based on its origins, I define the *hijab* to mean the same thing as the veil, that is, *any* covering that visibly identifies a woman as Muslim. Within the context of the veil as a fashion accessory, I expand this definition to further include the objects and accessories Muslim women use to complement their veils. Therefore, the veil is not limited to just the cloth that covers a woman's hair or body, it also includes the object she uses to adorn her clothes. These objects—be they shoes, a purse, or jewellery—all make up her veil.

The veil continues to be shrouded with a complex discourse, particularly in the West. The post 9/11 representation of the veil has brought under scrutiny its function as a religious symbol. Several scholars note that the Muslim woman's veil continues to be portrayed as a tool of oppression and backwardness (Alvi, 2008; Aswad & Bilge, 1996; Haddad, Smith, & Moore, 2006; Kincheloe & Steinberg, 2004; McDonough, 2003; Rezai-Rashti, 1994). The media repeatedly focus on the veil as a marker of gender inequality within the religion of Islam, at times accusing those who wear it of being victims to a practice enforced not by God but by men.

Despite the controversy shrouding the veil, especially in the West, it appears to be on the rise (Hoodfar, 2003; Meshal, 2003). While the assumption may be that the recent increase in representation is a result of immigration trends, the majority of youth choosing to wear the *hijab* in a North American context, Meshal (2003) argued, are actually those born and raised in non-Muslim countries.

Many Muslim women are choosing to veil as a way of asserting their identities as Muslims, and to exercise their political rights to veil in any manner they choose. As much as it is a political statement, in my earlier study (Alvi, 2008), I found that it is also an identity marker. Here, feeling alienated and rejected by the dominant society and groups, women veil because they "seek to bond and belong" (as one participant put it) to a safe space where they feel themselves and community. Zine (2000) identified Muslim clubs as one such particular space where Muslim youth can go to interact with "their own kind" (p. 306).

Voguing the Veil

As a Muslim woman who was born and grew up in the West (Toronto, in particular, among other various cities across Ontario, Canada), I have a difficult time relating to both sides of the spectrum. I do not relate to the images that are represented of Muslims in the media, such as the images I see of Muslim women residing in Muslim countries, nor the silenced Muslim women I see in movies such as the ones described in the introduction. I also cannot relate to those individuals who feel the need to segregate themselves from what I now recognize as 'mainstream Canadian' society and seek refuge amongst 'Muslim spaces'.

I am a second-generation Canadian Muslim woman who veils, and I have seldom felt any less 'Canadian' because of it. This is partially because of the way I veil. The way I dress is inspired by the trends that dominate the malls and boutiques of Canadian cities. While my veil is meant to communicate an unspoken unity between God and myself, the way I style it also adheres to the cultural influences of fashion. The Muslim women that are part of my social circle are also like me, and many of the veiled women I walk past on campus where I work appear to be similar. Their head coverings are adorned with the names of Gucci and Chanel, their shoes are Coach, and their purses are Michael Kors. These images of how the veil is worn and adorned are more representative to me of Canadian Muslim women than the images I see in the news media. Why, then, are these images missing?

In an effort to understand the veil in a space removed from the dominant discourse, I sought to explore the Muslim veil, not as a religious symbol, but as a fashion accessory. I was seeking women who fashion their veils in new and untraditional ways; women who 'vogue the veil'. By wearing the veil as such, I was curious to learn how the veil becomes performative, and how fashioning oneself in untraditionally represented ways resignified the veil as a sign within the West, Canada in this case. The following section strives to address these issues by sharing select findings of a study I conducted (Alvi, 2013). My curiosity led me to ultimately discover a whole subculture of women who veil in ways that defiantly 'vogue the veil' and break stereotypical images of the veil as represented in the media.

Introduction to the Study

During the summer of 2011, I recruited a group of young, dynamic, Canadian Muslim women who wore headscarves and self-identified as *hijabi*-fashionistas. They were all middle-class, came from different cultural heritages, and attended a public university in northeastern Ontario, Canada, at the time of this research. As mentioned above, I re-worked the definition of *hijab* to include any type of veil that identified a woman as Muslim. This included not only the headscarf, but other ways of veiling. More specifically, it included the overall apparel worn in conjunction with the headscarf, such as the accessories and fashion trends followed by Canadian Muslim women. I asked the women to share stories as women who contested the mainstream understanding of the veil. We explored various websites, blogs, and social-media outlets such as Facebook, Instagram, Twitter, and YouTube that engaged Muslim women who were interested in '*hijabi* fashion'. What emerged was a dialogue that revealed the complex agenda behind veiling fashionably, and the hidden politics amongst the women who veiled.

At the beginning of the project, the women assigned themselves pseudonyms that also described their personal styles. Therefore, Imaan was the 'British Hipster *Hijabi*'. Her style was influenced by the

British rock-music scene as well as the prominent styles of the 1960s era. Aleena was the 'Chiq-*Hijabi*', influenced by the latest trends of the runway. Anna was the 'Mod-Muslim', a title given to her by her family, describing her style as modest yet 'à la mode'. Finally, Mina was the 'Avant-Garde *Hijabi*', a look she described as consciously unconventional. The women felt that these titles accurately described their personal fashion philosophies.

Using a cultural studies conceptual framework, the women and I examined the veil as a sign. Through interviews, focus groups, and journal entries, accompanied by photographs taken personally by the women—a process called Photovoice (McIntyre, 2008)—the women and I co-constructed narratives of their stories and the meaning-making process behind the veil.

One of the main themes discussed in our focus groups and interviews was the concept of modesty in Islam and the participants' understanding of what it means to 'be' modest. The women agreed that modesty is an important element of the veil; however, the women also agreed that the meaning of modesty shifted between various geographical spaces. 'Muslim spaces' such as organized Muslim associations, the Mosque, and Muslim countries, warranted different degrees of modesty, while moving around in spaces within Canada, such as the campuses the women attended and the parties they went to for social gatherings, meant being modest in different ways.

Mina recognized the importance of reading the social cues of one's surrounding to help one adapt. For her, modesty meant respecting the culture one was moving within without compromising one's religious beliefs. Therefore, she wore a traditional black gown when visiting her parents in the Middle East, to respect the norms of the country, while in Canada, she often wore a hat in place of a traditional headscarf and her clothing reflected current trends. "My *hijab* changes so I can adapt," she stated, emphasizing that the "point of *hijab* is to get the right attention," meaning, the veil should not be a source of discomfort or unease for those around her. Mina implicated Muslim women who wore veils she described as 'traditional'; these were women that avoided wearing colour, kept mostly to themselves, and wore clothes that deterred interaction with those around them.

Anna, a Muslim convert, believed that clothing and fashioning the veil in particular ways played an important role in establishing relationships with those around her. She used her veil as a way to show others that one could be fashionable and modest at the same time. In her experience, her trendy ensembles often became an icebreaker for her colleagues and co-workers. Many of the women she interacted with felt they could relate to Anna immediately based solely on her clothing. They were impressed by how Anna managed to colour-coordinate her headscarf perfectly with her shoes and purse on a daily basis. For this reason, Anna felt dressing well went beyond wanting to look and feel good; it broke barriers between the two seemingly competing communities she moved within. That 'competition', Anna argues, is more invented than real, and it certainly has an 'antagonistic' and long history.

Social spaces such as parties also impacted the women's understanding of modesty. In particular, all-women parties, popular amongst the *hijabi* community, allowed women an opportunity to forego the veil and wear clothing they normally did not. In this context, modesty meant saving their revealing clothing for select, private spaces such as the all-women's party; however, often there was nothing modest physically about the clothing they wore. The women admitted that anything was fair game at these parties, which is also why participants such as Anna chose to invite her female colleagues to the parties she hosted. She felt it was an important opportunity to share with those less familiar with the veil that Muslim women had a fun and 'sexy' side.

However, modesty was a slippery signifier when it came to defining its perimeters. When I asked the women to share any negative feedback they received about their veils, I was surprised to learn that the women had more stories to share about the criticism they received from within the Muslim community regarding the veil than from outside. The women shared how moving within the Muslim spaces of their communities informed their understanding of the messy politics of modesty. There appeared to be a debate about what it meant to 'be' modest and how to veil modestly or the 'right' way. Some individuals from within the community criticized the ways in which the women veiled. For example, Aleena often wore her headscarf slightly pulled back, revealing her bangs. She noted that this was a cultural influence that was acceptable within most of the Pakistani community; however, amongst other Muslim communities, this was frowned upon. Some individuals even told her "that's not *hijab*." Aleena disagreed, stating that the point of the headscarf was to cover the hair, but not necessarily all the hair. As long as her head was 'mostly' covered, it served as a sufficient amount of modesty.

Mina shared that some women in the Arab community criticized her for showing her neck. This was because of the way she often styled her headscarf, either wearing a hat or tying her headscarf in the back of her head in the shape of a bun. She retorted by stating, "some girls cover their necks but everything else is sticking out." Mina felt that it was more modest to cover her chest, and that showing a little neck was less of an issue. Imaan defended both Aleena and Mina's decision to veil in particular ways by stating, "nothing will ever be good enough for the 'religobots' of the community." She regarded 'religobots' as those individuals who believed the veil should only look one way, and that fashion had no part to play in the matter.

It was through these types of exchanges within the community that the women went from being labelled *hijabi* to ho-*jabi*. Ho-*jabi* is, of course, a play on the word, *hijabi*, and suggests that women who wear their veils in 'provocative' ways are morally inferior and thus 'hos'. Bold ways of veiling were seen by some, especially other *hijabis*, as 'wrong' ways of veiling. Although the women agreed that there were no set guidelines for veiling the 'right' way, they were often treated by other *hijabis* as though they were straying from the rules.

The women were aware that the ways in which they fashioned their veils pushed the conventional boundaries of what is expected of the veil by many. While the term, ho-*jabi*, may not be a desirable title, the women recognized that the act of exploring new ways of veiling is an important one for the future of the veil in Canada. As Mina stated earlier, the *hijab* has to "adapt", not in ways that compromise religious identity, but as a strategy, so that the veil as a sign can be resignified from the binary other to one of Canadianness.

While the women disapproved of the critique they received about particular ways of veiling, they also had their own perspectives on right and wrong ways to veil. This was meant to be dually interpreted. First, there were certain elements of veiling that the women believed to be fashion faux pas and therefore 'wrong'; secondly, some styles of the veil, according to the women who partook in the study, compromised the integrity of the veil 'too much'. It is the latter that is of particular interest. It was unclear who and what defines the boundaries of 'too much'. This was a point of contention. According to Anna and Imaan, there was a fine line between wearing clothes that were modest yet fit well, and clothes that were 'too tight'. For Aleena, showing some hair was acceptable, but showing 'too much' hair was not. Mina believed certain prints could make a woman look sexy, but it was important that she not look 'too sexy', and all the women believed makeup was an acceptable way of enhancing one's beauty, but 'too much' makeup would risk taking away the modesty of the veil.

The imaginary line between 'enough' and 'too much' was undefinable, yet it was this same line that determined which *hijabi* was a ho-*jabi*. It is important to note that the women, myself included, did not regard being labelled a ho-*jabi* as a negative thing. It is recognized as a slang that loses its meaning across time and space. A ho-*jabi* in one space is considered a *hijabi* in another, and vice versa. What some of the women wore to the mall would, by many, be considered *hijab*, but were they to wear it to a religious gathering, the same outfit transformed them into ho-*jabis*. The two terms are completely informed by one's construction of what the veil 'should' look like.

The women discussed that within the *hijabi* community, some women believed that wearing a headscarf and a long, black gown was the most modest way of veiling, and therefore the 'real' way of veiling. There also seemed to be a misconception that women who veiled in this manner were 'more' religious than others. "*Hijab* should not be a litmus test," stated Imaan, who, like the other women in the study, did not believe that the way one veiled determined modesty. The women all agreed that one could be modest and a 'good Muslim' and not wear any type of veil at all, while some women they knew wore traditional gowns and face coverings, yet lacked modesty in their character. These were often the women who judged others, and pointed fingers at those who were wearing the veil the 'wrong' way. "The article of clothing itself isn't oppressive," noted Imaan, "it's some people's interpretation of it." The desire to regulate the *hijab* within Canada was a problematic issue for the women in the study, who believed that as Canadians, they had the privilege of escaping rigid rules that were enforced in other countries.

While the women in the study did not always agree with the ways the other participants veiled, they did agree that within Canada, veiling was open to interpretation and not subject to regulation. Therefore, while Anna admitted that she did not think it was appropriate to show one's hair intentionally while veiling, such as Aleena did, she respected Aleena's decision to express her personal style in this way. She defined the variety of the ways in which young women were fashioning the veil in Canada today as a "good clash," stating, "What you get as a result, is us four girls sitting around a table recognizing that there is wiggle room, that there is this individuality, that that's allowed by the veil."

The women and I recognized that by blurring the line between fashion and religion, Muslim women such as ourselves were reshaping the meaning of 'modest' (internally), and in doing so redefining the meaning(s) behind the veil (externally). This was important for two reasons. First, it inspired other Muslim women to see that the veil is a dynamic piece that did not have to reinforce the stereotypes shown in the media. Secondly, it demonstrated to non-Muslims and those who may regard the veil as a limitation that the women who practice it are active members of the community, their veils never constraining them. As depicted by the women, the veil does not mean one thing; it has many meanings and continues to take on multiple meanings. While the women held their own opinions on 'wrong' ways of veiling, they recognized that truly, there was no one 'right' way of veiling either.

Fashioning the Veil as an Emerging Subculture

As part of the study, the women and I collaboratively explored the *hijabi* fashion world. It was much larger than we ever anticipated. Through the use of the World Wide Web, we discovered thousands of YouTube videos, fashion blogs, Twitter and Instagram accounts, Facebook pages, and online businesses that catered to the 'modern' Muslim woman. By the time the study was complete, a two-year time frame, I had to update those numbers into the *hundreds* of thousands. On YouTube alone, I found over 113,000 tutorials on how to tie a headscarf. These are just videos of Muslim women showing other women creative and intricate ways of tying a scarf. These styles range from braided headscarves to layered, draped, and 'volumized' ones.

This abundance of representation informed the women and myself in profound ways. While at many times the women felt that their roles as fashionable *hijabis* in the community were independent and insignificant acts, becoming aware that fashioning the veil was in fact a global movement was deeply empowering. For the women, it reinforced that their effort to fashion their veils in new ways was making a positive difference in the community around them. The veil had the potential to be a tool that opened up new and welcoming spaces for Muslims and non-Muslims alike. By continuing to fashion the veil in new and exciting ways, the women recognized that their style could open up a dialogue about the veil for those unfamiliar with it. Styling the veil to reflect current trends demonstrated to people that the veil is not an oppressive piece of clothing, and that the women who wear it have as much freedom of choice as other non-veiled Canadian women. They, too, are interested in fashion, have a desire to look beautiful, and want to feel feminine—many of the characteristics that have been snatched away from Muslim women through the representations of the veil in the media.

It is through this process that the women demonstrate how the act of veiling can be performative. On the one hand, through the various ways the women veil, they are asserting their identities as

Canadians. Canadianness, these women are saying, does include veiled women. On the other hand, by using these fashion trends of the West as part of their veil, they are also attempting to fashion a new identity as Canadian Muslims; an identity that does not require them to choose between 'being Muslim' and 'being Canadian'. Through the use of fashion, the women in the study demonstrate how they can be, and indeed are, both simultaneously. As they move through their everyday lives, they share the positive interactions they have with those around them. They all shared personal stories of the people who have approached them curious about their style. This was one of the necessities of veiling in fashionable ways, according to Mina, who stated that traditional ways of veiling intimidated outsiders, while new and modern ways encouraged dialogue. Some non-Muslim women even asked participants for tutorials on how to tie the scarf in different ways. They were interested in wearing one as a fashion statement. The women were encouraged by the idea that their veil could be seen beyond the scope of religion, and that their identities as Muslims could be more than the previous, limited interpretations.

As the women recognized the vital role they played in performing the veil, I theorize that these women are part of an emerging subculture in Canada, as I continue to see an increase in Muslim women 'voguing the veil'. While subcultures have traditionally used particular types of clothing and objects to identify themselves as part of a subculture, this subculture is distinct in many ways. First, the styles they rely on are never static. They continuously change every season with the fashion trends of the West. Therefore, there is no particular article of clothing that remains constant, except, of course, the headscarf, for those who wear it. However, as the YouTube videos explored demonstrate, the veil itself as a cultural factor is also evolving as new ways of wearing it are being created by those who practice it. Even the women who partook in my study evolved, in particular Aleena, who started off wearing a headscarf that was often draped loosely around her head and evolved to a new style she discovered in an online tutorial that is similar to a turban. She aptly named this style, 'turban *hijab* swag'. Most recently, she visited Turkey, and came back donning another style that is a combination of wrapping a scarf around her hair in a bun and allowing the leftover material to flow on the side, as hair would. Aleena calls this style, 'Turkish swag'. But of course!

Veiling fashionably is also unique from the subcultures that dress in particular ways to segregate from society and build community only amongst others within the subculture. In fact, I argue that the women who participated in the study are doing just the opposite. Their subculture relies on using style to be seen as an integral part of society. The women are using fashion to demonstrate their place in Canadian society. If the women are using style to step away from the mainstream at all, it is within their own communities. Participants did not want to be associated with women who wore traditional veils and frowned upon the mixing of fashion and religion.

The women resemble a subculture, in that their numbers are increasing steadily, as depicted by the sheer growth of online representation over the past two years. The women are consciously using fashion as a "mediated response" (Hebdige, 2003, p. 73) to the current discourse around the veil. They are actively seeking to challenge the images and actions that are dominantly portrayed of the Muslim woman. They are entering into spaces they are not expected in, and in doing so, creating welcoming spaces for other marginalized groups.

Conclusion

The women who participated in the study parted ways with a renewed sense of motivation. They recognized, more than ever before, that their roles as *hijabi* fashionistas played an important part in the discourse around the veil. Despite the politics that existed within the Muslim community, the women embraced the fact that they were a representation of the new, modern modest, one that opened up much needed spaces for those who cannot relate to the current representation of the veil. They accepted that being a ho-*jabi* is a much needed addition to the discourse around the veil.

The women demonstrated how moving within and between spaces informs their understanding of the veil, and how the veil continuously shifts and adapts to the spaces it enters. The women are consciously adapting the latest fashion trends, and by doing so, they are building connections to those around them. By engaging in such strategies, the women are ultimately striving to re-signify the veil as a sign in the West, namely in Canada. Through the use of fashion, the women, provocatively and consciously, are seeking ways to normalize the veil, not as the 'other', but as a deeply Canadian signifier. They do not want to segregate themselves from the society; rather, they desire to be active members within it. Staying within the margins of 'Muslim spaces' is limiting not only for them, but for everyone; it deters any progress being made in the area of anti-racism and critical multiculturalism within Canada.

Through fashion, the women illustrate how the veil as a piece of clothing can be performative. They challenge people's perceptions and expectations of what veiling is. They rebel against the static images of the veil that surround them. The women repeatedly proved that the veil as a text is indeed a complex sign. It is disheartening, however, to continue to see the veil being represented in limited ways within the media. Perhaps what is needed is an urgent appeal for the necessity of improving our literacy as a society. For us to recognize that images need to be unpacked and critically questioned; for us to become more media literate, socially literate, and culturally literate.

As I theorize the women to be part of an emerging subculture, I also call for society to engage with those around us and be a proactive part of opening new and welcoming spaces. As the women's narratives demonstrate, often it can be within our own communities that we shun and judge one another. The possibilities are endless when we can truly accept differences and respect that we are each on an ongoing journey of discovering our subjectivities.

References

Al-Saji, A. (2010). The racialization of Muslim veils: A philosophical analysis. *Philosophy and Social Criticism, 38*(8), 875–902.

Alvi, S. (2008). *An analysis of how hijabi youth experience social activities in Ottawa secondary schools* (Unpublished masters thesis). University of Ottawa, Ottawa, Canada.

Alvi, S. (2013). *Voguing the veil: Exploring an emerging youth subculture of Muslim women fashioning a new Canadian identity* (Unpublished doctoral dissertation). University of Ottawa, Ottawa, Canada.

Aswad, B. C., & Bilge, B. (Eds.). (1996). *Family and gender among American Muslims: Issues facing Middle Eastern immigrants and their descendants.* Philadelphia, PA: Temple University Press.

Blaise, M. (2005). A feminist poststructuralist study of children 'doing' gender in an urban kindergarten classroom. *Early Childhood Research Quarterly, 20*(1), 85–108.

Butler, J. (1999). *Gender trouble: Feminism and the subversion of identity.* New York, NY: Routledge.

Haddad, Y. Y., Smith, J. I., & Moore, K. M. (2006). *Muslim women in America: The challenge of Islamic identity today.* New York, NY: Oxford University Press.

Hall, S., & Jefferson, T. (Eds.). (2003). *Resistance through rituals: Youth subcultures in post-war Britain* [Taylor & Francis e-library version].

Hebdige, D. (2003). *Subculture.* London, UK: Routledge.

Hoodfar, H. (2003). More than clothing: Veiling as an adaptive strategy. In S. S. Alvi, H. Hoodfar, & S. McDonough (Eds.), *The Muslim veil in North America: Issues and debates* (pp. 3–41). Toronto, Ontario, Canada: Scholar's Press.

Kincheloe, J. L., & Steinberg, S. R. (Eds.). (2004). *The miseducation of the West: How schools and the media distort our understanding of the Islamic world.* Westport, CT: Praeger.

McDonough, S. (2003). Perceptions of hijab in Canada. In S. S. Alvi, H. Hoodfar, & S. McDonough (Eds.), *The Muslim veil in North America: Issues and debates* (pp. 121–142). Toronto, Ontario, Canada: Scholar's Press.

McIntyre, A. (2008). *Participatory action research.* London, UK: Sage.

Meshal, R. A. (2003). Banners of faith and identities in construct: The hijab in Canada. In S. S. Alvi, H. Hoodfar, & S. McDonough (Eds.), *The Muslim veil in North America: Issues and debates* (pp. 72–104). Toronto, Ontario, Canada: Scholar's Press.

Rezai-Rashti, G. (1994). Islamic identity and racism: Muslim students and Ontario education. *Orbit, 25*(2), 37–38.

Willett, R. (2008). 'What you wear tells a lot about you': Girls dress up online. *Gender and Education, 20*(5), 421–434.

Zine, J. (2000). Redefining resistance: Towards an Islamic subculture in schools. *Race, Ethnicity and Education, 3*(3), 293–316.

The Dark Room Dance

G!rL Fr0m D0wN Und3r

I've been practicing slow dancing in my living room
With no music to dance to
If you would
Just let me serenade you
With words of why I think you're so wonderful
And what really makes you beautiful
Except you're not here
You never were
And I doubt you ever will be
So I guess I'll slow dance alone in my living room
With no music to dance to

The Journey

Leave the light on for me
I'll be home soon
I have traveled through the dusty back roads of breath
Wondered the hallways of living
Living to live life
Right and true
This journey has turned to an expedition
It has jaded me
My inhale is labored
My exhale is heavy
I lay in ruins

Awaiting some type of peace
But I feel as though there is none
Wait on me
I'll be home soon
Leave the light on
As a sign that you have not lost faith in me
Have faith in me
I will not been gone for long
Leave the light on
Leave the light on

My Hands

And my hands
They shake like tremors
When no one is there to hold them
Age Written: 16
Name: G!rL Fr0m D0wN Und3r
Brothers
You are young men now
Grown in many ways
But I know you're all still figuring it out
It was love that bonded us
Men, take that to your graves
Know that there is nothing greater than family
Nothing greater than my love for each one of you
Nothing greater than the time times we have shared
And memories we've accumulated
Blood has never defined us
Time will never decline our love
Past mistakes are behind us
Know that we are one

G!rL Fr0m D0wN Und3r (17)
Dedicated To: Donny, Joshie Pooh Bear, E-man, and Eric

The Cutting Piece

LaVerne Thompson

I'm in constant pain because of you.
I have to rub myself all over to soothe the ache
Because of your aches
Our aches.
I need to put an end to this.
I don't know how to tell you
I'm much more righteous than your metal redemption,
Your stainless steel deity firm in your grasp,
Ready to smite my blasphemy—
I am sick and fucking tired of you cutting me.

How many tonight?
One for each time your mother called you a bitch, a whore, a slut?
I was there.
I felt it too when she left that bruise on both of us,
I covered it up for you.
Just how long will those scars be today?
Is that just long enough to pass as your 10,000ᵗʰ cat scratch,
Just long enough to be covered by sleeves,
Or maybe something as long as it took to get your first boy meets girl,
The first slit you made in me when he saw another girl,

When you first found your religion.
A God you could hold in your hand, or your back pocket,

Or better yet, wedged in the middle of me
Cleaving the flesh from your bones.
Do me a favor and convert to something less cold,
Cause I'll be damned if I let you keep going to church,
Say your galvanized prayers,
Sip communion of your own blood.

I have been and grown with you since our birth.
Took physical stress until I've broken and stretched,
Protected you from every element from helium to beryllium
But I've failed you in the face of iron.
I couldn't save you from yourself
Or a metallic holy ghost that got you high.
You remember that night.
My memory turns over
Cause at that point, you get tipsy.
Things get really upside-downsy when
You're on your back and
Another tipsy turvey stranger is on top you,
His penis walking in and out like happiness
Coming for a visit, but never to stay.
I was there for that.
You were too busy moaning to notice
Your womanhood wept.
Despite being attached, we've never felt farther from you.

Of course, once your vagina stopped bleeding, you decided it was my turn.
So tell me, how many tonight.
A cut for each party,
Each dixie cup,
Each penis,
There isn't one for daddy
He was never there.

Your worship is more than I can bear.
Your faith twisted,
You pray to him for deliverance,
Take punishment as forgiveness.
They've stopped bloodletting
But you continue your masochism,
Batter yourself into sacrilegious salvation
In the name of a razor blade.

He's not divine,
He's mundane.
After all we've been through, I'm disgusted that you've
Let us become a bloody God forsaken mess.
Truth is … I'm so sorry.

I can't ease all your aches, but if you give me a chance,
I can heal.
Stop offering me to your sacrificial idol.
You won't need him to love you
If you just love yourself
Then I'll be warm again,
Your switchblade savior will no longer feel like a cross in your hand
I'm begging you
Please denounce your religion.

LaVerne Thompson (16), *SLAM HIGH*, Rochester, NY

Straight Girl

Aaliyah Jihad

Straight girl run like Usain Bolt
Straight girl volleyball like Misty Mae
Straight girl soccer like Mia Hamm
Straight girl cheer like "Bring It On"
Straight girl not athletic
See, straight girl always trip herself
Straight girl tell her little sisters always keep trying
Straight girl tried anorexia
Got hungry
Straight girl tried veganism
Got hungry
Tried again
Straight girl so over-confident
Think she so pretty without make-up
Flirt with boys who don't even look at her
Straight girl eye-fuck the shit out of straight boy
Straight boy say, "Goddamn, girl"
Straight girl virgin
Straight girl just wanna fuck
Straight girl
Single
Lonely
Can't masturbate
Eat Nutella and watch Netflix instead

Straight girl like boys
Straight girl like … girls?
Straight girl: bisexual tendencies
Straight girl drink Henny
Straight girl drink girls who drink Henny when she's drunk
Straight girl — no chaser
Straight girl chases no one chases straight girl
Straight girl girl crush
Straight girl, straight path
Straight girl don't curve
Straight girl got curves
Don't got much ass though
Straight girl still want you to grab her non-ass anyway
Straight girl eat affection like it got caramel in it
Straight girl eat anything with caramel in it
Straight girl wanted caramel boy
Straight girl
Socially inept
Strange friends
Strange pranks
Straight girl no caramel boy
Same old story
Straight girl need a re-write
Straight girl love assholes
The kind that like to remind her she's an idiot
Straight girl love the assholes that only wanna make her cry
Straight girl love a challenge
Straight girl lose every challenge
Straight girl only got love for what can't love her back
Straight girl taste girls who are curvy
Straight girl still straight the next day
Straight girl wholesome
Mom say straight girl still wholesome, long as she straight
Straight girl
Won't burn in Hell long as she bubble "Straight" on her questionnaires
Straight girl don't know her God yet
But know your God say she better be straight
Straight girl rather just be straight than have to explain why she don't wanna fuck EVERY girl she meet
Straight girl too straight for your gay pride
Straight girl too stuck on her straight path
Straight girl
So warm in this closet

Aaliyah Jihad, Ann Arbor, MI
Courtesy of Youth Speaks and the Brave New Voices Network

Tip of the Flame

Natalie Cook

Rub kerosene around your lips
to burn open the mouth.
Rip the flesh from its hinges.
Your teeth are doors
that will never return
to your language.

Make a wish,
and blow your skin like a dandelion.
Watch the sun scatter into the wind.

Children will snatch your yellow like fireflies.

Look at yourself in the jar
how you shine
too bright to not be covered.

Everyone will see
you as the lantern in
a white man's palm.
Not a mango
picked from the tree
in your grandmother's backyard.

The dog inhales wet air
left from the slave's back.

Children will gaze upon your fur in awe.

Look at the mut!
Look at the way
she chases after her father
to sink her teeth in his
flesh!

Your teeth are yellow, gal.
why make them brown
They are already dirty enough.

Mixed breeds are often
not chosen to be loved.
Blackness
is not contained to
skin,

but

you have the sand of an island for a mother

and

a father that grew up in the shell of a bomb.

Your color is not that of a tree.
No one can see your roots.
Your hair is the ocean
between
Trinidad and Africa/America,
but waves can only be named
once a master colonizes his land.

You are only breasts
under a moonlit chest.
the inside of a house
a cage where the bird
squawks in display

Exotic, she is, says the parrot.
Touch her.
The world is a freak show,
and she is the main attraction.

too light to be black
too black to be american
too american to be where she is from

what is the black girl's name

The children
that carry you home
in their palms
say,
you are
darkie
or high yella
or colored
or nigger girl
or anything that isn't your name.

You break in their hands like glass.
Parents throw the jar away
without cleaning
the blood
from their children's
hands.

Natalie Cook (21), Atlanta, GA

Obasi Davis

Restlessly propelled bus tour through poverty's playpen
Inhaling the vile stench of minimum wage and food-stamps
An unholy concoction of $8/hr in a $960 cramped studio apartment fed by cal fresh's moldy
government cheese
You can't see your reflection in these dark waters

Poor packed blacks on boats
But these ones float
Above neglected concrete
Journeying through the flatlands
Where row house windows bear constricting iron bars and beat with the melodic music of despair like
imprisoned hearts

Tattooed reflections display poverty like full screen settings on flat screen TVs
Rolling over restless seas
roiling with potholes like whirlpools where crackheads are caught in the undertow

The block conductor at the head of the snake
Piloting us to overcrowded buildings, clogged ventricles, new Virginias and street corners

The girl next to me
Blackberry skin
Hair more plastic than the bus seat snacking on hot Cheetos and guzzling a Pepsi
She's Loud

Claps hands
Smacks lips
I want to help her
She's confused
Swallowing manufactured poison
trying to glimpse her face in troubled lakes

A man
slumped drunk across the aisle
Mouth smothered with muttered fuck yous
Moaning with the ghosts of the city's lost sons
He floats
Immersed in a pool of toxic regrets
Stirring up the will to drown
Wailing his throat-gauging sorrows like a banshee to his transparent deities
refusing to let them drown with him he holds them aloft
Buoys them on bent head
swims with a cigarette
two drags like white flags
float above him
Surrendering to his closeted demons

In the shadows
Black boys relapse to times when the back of the bus
and the bottom of the ship
were home
Engraving their names into the metallic flesh of this death trap
Hoping to be remembered
Littering pieces of themselves onto buses that last longer than their bones so they won't be forgotten
future generations will know … we sank here

I sit silent in the crows nest of a mad sanctuary
Etching my thoughts onto a crinkled brown paper bag
Documenting demise
Peering down at flailing limbs
My people
Not my direction
Torn between a plummet and survival
There is a piece of me
in the confused girl (ignorantly, voluntarily, willingly) consuming her poison
In the lost husk of a man
Adrift in lonely waters
Scripted onto the bleeding echoing walls of a wrecked ship

Born into consciousness
Surrounded by a violent, leeching ignorance
How far have we really come
When we live like slaves to our own misfortune

When we search for salvation in the shadowed irises of our oppressor
We're so backwards that we've been engineered to oppress ourselves
We rob our own communities in mobs of hopeless heathens
Where is this progress you flaunt like a new coat of ebony flesh
There is no happy ending
This line ends at 107 and Mac
Where black and brown boys reach the end of the line at the barrel of a Mac 11
Where they pave concrete over our wandering souls
Hardly a promise land
But ironically the land we were promised

Obasi Davis (17), Oakland, California
Oakland 2013 Youth Poet Laureate
Courtesy of Youth Speaks and the Brave New Voices Network

A Taste of Home

Monica Mendoza

Every time my family and I visit tias, tios, y compadres, the first question we're asked
"Quieres una coca?"

Send their children to the liquor store on the corner of the block, with two crinkled dollars and coins rattling in their pockets

We laugh about who was passed out drunk at the last family fiesta and update each other about nuestra familia in Guerrero, while sipping on carbonated poison

It just isn't polite to not have soda when visitors are over

Reject it and you'll be labeled as a malcriado

Accept everything that is offered to you

Coca, papitas fritas con chile, limon, y sal, los dulces Mexicanos que triamos de Mexico la ves pasada

We use sweets as a way of showing we care

Diabetes and obesity is the last thing in our minds

Pansa llena, Corazon content

Our heartbeats beat at the rhythm of cumbia, as mom cooks her sopes and enchiladas

It just doesn't feel like a meal without that coke bottle

Without the gas bubbles drowning our noses and mouths

That gargling feeling that takes over our throats

Coke in glass bottles from Mexico

That gives us that taste and sensation of home

We think this possibly can't hurt us without realizing that we can't even read the ingredients on the label

Forget that home is the number one obese country in the world and we're here in the U.S. living up to the same legacy

Walk into Mi Pueblo and stock up on this week's special of four two liter coke bottles for a dollar

Throw in the cheap Tampico juices and sabritas for the kids to eat after school for the next two weeks

Mom and dad are too busy working 10 hours or more to limit the intake of junk food

No desperdieces la comida, eso me costo

Too busy trying to make a living than live healthily

Any kind of nourishment that keeps us moving

Even if we're moving a bit slower than the rest of the world or struggling to complete everyday tasks

We are still moving, and that is all that matters

Desperately looking for home in our plates and cups

Dinner has become into an expedition

Where we lick our plates clean and swallow cups of nostalgia

Nostalgia that isn't even from our country

Our tongues have been colonized with the belief that this cup of coke is home

Forget that those before us only drank water

We are literally killing ourselves trying to find parts of us in a two liter plastic coke bottle

We've forgotten the days when we use to grow our own fruits on Guerrero soil and walk to the closest river for our next cup of water

Dinner in Mexico was always cooked and served under the moonlight

But now we're more than a thousand miles away, finally having that one hour we've been looking forward all day, family dinner

All the women call their children away from the TV

Coca Cola polar bear commercials playing in the background for the fourth time that hour

The clinks and clatter of plates and forks drown out all the commercials

The sound of laughter at childhood stories de Mexico fill up our bellies

We find home in each one of our stories

There's no need to pull out that coke bottle anymore

There's no need to almost kill ourselves, looking for memories of home.

Monica Mendoza, 20, Oakland, California
Courtesy of Youth Speaks and the Brave New Voices Network

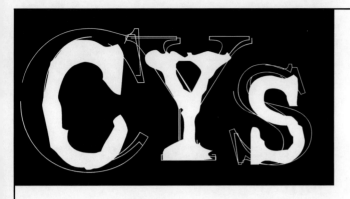

PART III

Cultures:
Navigating Media and Identities, Sports, Technology, and Music

CHAPTER 20

Living Hyph-E-Nations
Marginalized Youth, Social Networking, and Third Spaces

Nicholas Ng-A-Fook, Linda Radford, and Tasha Ausman

> We are not fated to choose those great apparatuses of mediation that structure our symbolic world.
> —Homi K. Bhabha, 1999, p. xii.

Since 2008, over 200,000 migrants from the Philippines, India, and China have made their way to Canada and are now living here as permanent residents. In the last two years, Canada has accepted almost 25,000 refugees from countries such as Nigeria, Sri Lanka, and China (Citizenship and Immigration Canada, 2012). Tagalog, Urdu, and Mandarin are listed as some of the dominant mother tongues spoken at home among Canadian permanent residents. In turn, for many displaced youth, social networking has become the new, mediated apparatus for communicating and representing the hyphenated symbolic worlds of temporary foreign workers, permanent residents, and citizens in a new country. Unlike the generations before them, immigrant and diasporic youth are plugged in to the digital world, its technologies, and respective literacies.

Indeed, youth are now referred to by some, like Prensky (2001), as Digital Natives. At the turn of the 21st century, Prensky put forth this particular metaphor to distinguish "the attitudes of younger and of older people regarding digital technologies" (p. 1). However, as Prensky recently (2011) warned in response to his critics, "Digital Native is *not*, at its core, about capabilities, or even knowledge, regarding all things digital" (p. 17). Instead, "it is about growing up in a digital country or culture, as opposed to coming to it as an adult" (p. 17). Therefore, digital natives, as Prensky suggested, have a kind of "growing up with it" knowledge that digital immigrants would not. The metaphor of digital natives is both useful and problematic for understanding the trials and tribulations of immigrant and non-immigrant youth navigating the school corridors, while also attempting to mediate and/or appropriate different kinds of institutionally legitimized "social and culture capital" in relation to an increasingly technologically driven curriculum here in Canada.

As educational researchers working within the field of Critical Youth Studies, we are particularly interested in how immigrant youth seek to perform, enunciate, and represent their subjectivities through and with digital technologies, like social networking, within the contexts of a nation like Canada, which has the ideological concept of multiculturalism built into the fabric of its very constitution and respective schooling systems (see Ghosh & Abdi, 2004). Whether multicultural policies encourage cosmopolitanism (Banks, 2009), are interpreted by the far right as a threat to "traditional" Anglosaxon cultures (Pinar, 2009), represent a positive openness to difference, or are used politically through the rhetoric of social cohesion depends on the country, locale, and historical context in question. Regardless of the historical debates, the notions of "nation" and "multiculturalism" are themselves unstable categories. On account of the ongoing economic, political, and environmental crises, nationalism seems to have increased around the world, threatening to break up organizations like the European Union, or provoke the overthrow of governments through movements such as the Arab Spring. Social networking played a role in such revolutionary movements either here (like *Idle No More*), or abroad in places such as Iran (the *Green Movement* after the 2009 presidential election).[1]

In response to such transnational geopolitical movements, curriculum scholars have drawn upon concepts such as "globalization," "transnationalism," and "third space" to understand how immigrant and non-immigrant youth engage each others' subjectivities and respective symbolic representations—of gender, culture, nationality, etc. These representations, in the form of YouTube, Facebook, Myspace, online gaming, and so on, are ways of social networking (see Levy, 2011; Thomas, 2008). Moreover, scholars such as Roland Sintos Coloma (2009) assert that "fram[ing] research beyond the nation as [the] main unit of analysis can yield rich insights regarding the imbricated inter-relatedness of nations and the border-crossing flows of people, ideas, goods, cultures, and institutions" (p. 497). For example, the term, *multiculturalism*, is an interpellation of the classroom—it names the classroom as a certain kind of Canadian cultural space, importantly, one made official by being wrapped up in a term coined by the Canadian government. It is a certain kind of Canadian learning space that has traditionally taken up the concepts of equity and inclusiveness through the use of migrant hyphenated communities: Lebanese-Canadian, Chinese-Canadian, Indo-Canadian, and so forth. Employing the multidimensional space of the Internet and cyber-social communities, this chapter seeks to re-work the boundaries that define multiculturalism as a series of homogeneous, hyphenated spaces from which immigrant students are expected to speak. We ask, "what is at play in the hyphen?" and "how might the networked classroom space be considered a hyph-e-nation?" To theorize this curriculum inquiry, we invoke a research project that employs a reading of Third Spaces (Bhabha, 1994) and quantum physics to re-read representations of immigrant student subjectivities. We examine how students might open up dual Third Spaces through self-representations in a social-networking space used for various assignments: first through the social network, and second, as certain kinds of learners caught between the hyph-e-nated middles of Canadian multiculturalism in an Ontario classroom.

Networking Subjectivities Within Quantum Third Spaces

After all, if the subject is always differentiated, we have to understand precisely what that means. —Judith Butler, 2009, p. 142.

And by exploring this Third Space, we may elude the politics of polarity and emerge as the others of our selves. —Homi Bhabha, 1994, p. 56.

The students in our study came from differing ethnic backgrounds—some migrants who have travelled and lived in many countries, some born here within one of the numerous diasporas that make up the cultural tapestry of this part of Ontario. Through their participation in the social network, they enter the open domain of cyberspace—one that is undefined, and that is able to absorb the changing and constantly updated and redefined self-identifications of its users. Students within the educational context of a plugged-in classroom name and symbolically represent themselves both within and against traditional educational structures. Thus, the social network is an optimal locale from which a discussion of Third Spaces in relation to identity can begin. Before talking about the larger social-action project from which some of our curriculum theorizing emerges, we offer the following experimental theoretical model of "quantum (third) space" to understand and disrupt essentializations of identity (Moon, 2010). Although culturally responsive theory initially framed the design and implementation of the larger project (Gay, 2000, 2002), we have since moved our theoretical framework toward the concept of quantum (third) spaces, in order to understand the complexities of immigrant students' hyphenated, symbolic enunciations on the social networking site.

In our theoretical model of quantum (third) space, we situate identity as a continuous re-shaping of the self based upon identification, desire, and subsequent symbolic representations (see Figure 20.1). We draw upon quantum theory to reconceptualize (third) spaces within the representational and special contexts of three dimensions. In this model, each circle represents multiple potential identifications and in relation to their respective desires. Moreover, once those representations are conceived, they are in turn pushed to the outside of the "shell"[2] of one's unconscious, like Freud's mystic pad, or the outer perimeter of the circle, and these different potential enunciations are perhaps what self and others eventually see—whether as filmic performative representations, as writings, as symbolic representations on social-network sites, or any other form of representation (Ausman, 2012).

In this model, representations pushed to the outside after each moment of individual identification (shown by the arrows within each circle) are a way of thinking about the things we see and consume. Within this conceptual framework, individuals can produce, recognize, and consume simultaneous representations at once. Our understanding of quantum (third) spaces includes the existence of several spaces at the same time, in varying dimensions. This is an attempt to break free from the essentialization of stereotypical identities, affording us capacities to think of (third) spaces as both places and the spaces between places. Hyphenated cultural identities do not volley from one stable or determined space to another (India-Canada, Guyana-Canada, Scotland-Canada, Italy-Canada, for example), emotionally or physically. Being in a (third) space, at least for hyphenated subjectivities, includes experiencing constant change, with multiple contradictory feelings of belonging and not belonging, of appropriation and alienation (Ng-A-Fook, 2009). Therefore, drawing on quantum theory, the original theoretical conceptualization of quantum (third) spaces began with one of us (Tasha Ausman) attempting to explain her autobiographical experiences of living such differing differences, where it is both possible and probable for a self to inhabit two or more places at the same time, the spaces between such places, and the transient, enunciated hyphens (either symbolically or peformatively) that link such places within (third) space.

In this picture, the different circles imply that quantum (third) spaces can be a number of things, all of which are evolving and shifting. They can be referential—a circle that emerges from a moment of identification and desire to be another circle, another (third) space—and we see this in real life, with fads, knock offs, movies similar to other movies, T-shirts that copy pictures and logos from other cultural artifacts, etc. In turn, the frames of reference in quantum (third) spaces are always shifting, as well. But the originary object (or identity) is fleeting and gone in the next instant. And, unlike in Bhabha's theory, the originary object does exist, just in another time. In quantum theory, our autobiographical differences with the past, present, and future can co-exist, and we see this in cultures that try to hold on to values and traditions held deeply for generations while living in a Canadian cultural milieu.

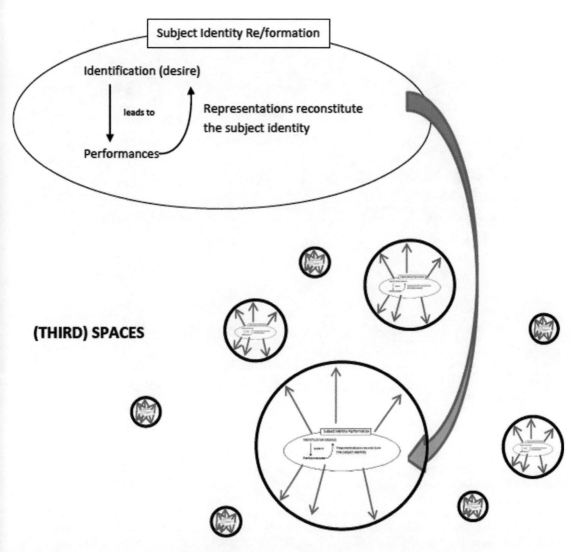

Figure 20.1: A subject identifies with something or someone, desires to be like it or them in part or in whole, and this leads to (re)actions. These actions can be considered performances by the subject, and are observed or consumed by those in space and time (others in a social network, viewers of a film, readers of a book). This subject who has represented herself publicly in some way (through speech, film, written text, online posting), is personally changed by this act of representation

Social networking affords curricular and pedagogical opportunities for multiple self-identifications that are linked to others' life experiences, playing off the multiple hyphens that momentarily trans/ connect to and with each sphere. Some students' journeys from Canada to homelands abroad and returning are similar to others, and so students find their own stories mirrored, yet transformed, in the journeys of others. This model for representing and recognizing identity formations as fluid, dynamic, ambivalent, and changing on account of reading the self through others' experiences, forms an evolving social network of self-identifications (see Figure 20.2).

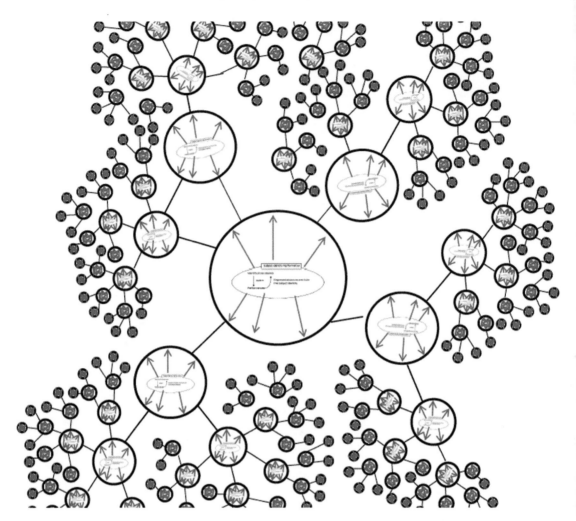

Figure 20.2: The self-representations people put forth in the digital space, on their home pages, are seen, read, appropriated, deflected, ignored, or passed on by any number of other people in the network. Because of this, identities within the social network are mediated through fluid quantum (third) spaces that are temporally dynamic and geographically defy fixity, yet are inextricably linked to the rest of the network. Although such links are represented in the model through what we might call hyph-e-nations (–), they remain transient, always having the capacity and potential to make multiple spontaneous as well as structured connections through time and space

Engaging a Social Action Curriculum Project With Marginalized Youth

> This ability to speak publicly and to pool our capabilities is so different from what we're used to that we have to rethink the basic concept of media; it's not just something we consume, it's something we use. As a result, many of our previously stable concepts about media are now coming unglued.
> —Clay Shirky, 2011, p. 327.

We began implementing our social action curriculum project (SACP) in September 2008 and ended it in June of 2010. During these two years, two of us (Nicholas Ng-A-Fook and Linda Radford) were at the school teaching the courses we created with graduate and teacher education students almost every day. There were three phases in the project:

1. Building a sense of community;

2. Developing and implementing a culturally responsive media-studies curriculum (this concept is problematic today); and,

3. Analyzing and synthesizing the impacts of the design and living the implementation of this project with marginalized youth.

Students involved in the program were selected by a steering committee to reflect the diversity of their school community, and then invited to participate within the project in order to complement the overall team dynamic. Some students had behavioural issues and were deemed "at-risk" by the administration.[3] These students were part of the school's special behavioural unit. Some students had ADHD. Other students had difficulties negotiating the dominant literacies of schooling, such as reading and writing formal English. The organizational structure of our collaborative partnership and its flexibility enabled our research team to embed the Ontario Ministry of Education (2008) Character Development Initiatives within a Communications and Technology course and later a locally developed English curriculum. There were forty-six students in five Grade 10 courses over the two years of the project. The participating students' ages ranged from 15 to 18 years old.

Figure 20.3: Social network sites

Initially, the curriculum was designed to address the bigger picture of the school, community, and environment. However, we quickly saw that the students wished to focus on their individual struggles, in terms of how to address issues of equity within the contexts of public schooling. In attempting to give students the necessary technological skills, we observed that while many adults view today's youth culture as the most "plugged in," students were unfamiliar with the Apple software and popular websites such as YouTube, Myspace, Facebook, Ning, etc.

Following this observation, the teaching team created a social networking site for students to share their work. Across Canada and in school boards like this one in Eastern Ontario, administrators are making their infrastructure wireless and implementing policies that support the eventual facilitation of a computer or laptop for every student enrolled within the public schooling system. Outside schools, politicians are increasingly reaching the public through social networking sites such as Facebook. Consequently, schools must provide a space for students to engage the different competencies for becoming responsible cyber citizens (Bennett, 2008). However, when we initially began our program, sites like Facebook, Myspace, and YouTube were censored by the school board. As a result, we set up our social networking site with www.ning.com. During the program's first year, the site was called *Engaging Youth Activism*. And in year two, the name was revised to *Digital Youth Activism* (see Figure 20.3). Within a few weeks of establishing the site, it became a central and integral component of the curriculum design for future units of study with students.

The students were encouraged to develop their social networking site pages, and were provided with technical support. The field coordinators periodically took and incorporated screen captures of students' web pages into their daily journals, as a form of virtual ethnography to track each student's development toward becoming responsible cyber citizens within our larger virtual classroom community. For many students, the social network remained a preferred medium for both performing and sharing their newfound online literacies and narratives. The teaching team and students also discussed how social-network sites in general now serve the political needs of various local, national, and international organizations as a preferred medium for engaging social-justice issues. In turn, the students discussed the relationships among popular culture, social justice, and youth activism (see Buckingham, 2008).

Regardless of what kind of curriculum inquiry projects that were created with and for students, they were asked to reflect on their capacities to engage youth activism as a key component of their lived curriculum while enrolled in our program. Let us consider the following two examples of the ways in which immigrant students used the social networking site to produce different cultural representations. We will then return to the concept of lived curriculum as hyph-e-nations in relation to multicultural education, diversity, and equity.

Little Moe

Little Moe, as he calls himself, was an 18-year-old student who chose to enroll in our program. At the time, he described his youth as somewhat "hectic" because of the continuous migrations of his family. He was born in Carleton Place, Canada, and attended school there until second grade. His family then moved back to Lebanon, where he spent the next three years. When he returned to Canada, he attended three different middle schools before entering the vocational high school in Grade 9. Even while Moe was in our program, his family moved houses at least one more time. Moe explained that when he returned to Lebanon, he had a lot of social and cultural capital at the schools he attended because he could speak English. His background in Canada provided him with an advantage, and he told us, "I aced the English classes." However, upon his return to Canada, his classmates often teased him because of his apparent accent. Nonetheless, when Moe describes his linguistic interactions with his family, he considered both English and Arabic to be "equal" in terms of what constituted his "first" language. His struggles with performing the cultural, accentuated norms of the English language within the contexts of public schooling often made him a target for bullying. He told us:

> When …. what's it called … in Grade 6 when I was first in Carleton Place, I was shorter than most of the kids in my class, so they'd make fun of my height and stuff, like oh, you don't know how to speak English, go back to your country and stuff. So ….

He does not remember exactly how he reacted, but his sister has recounted to him that in response to this, he "freaked out and started, like, running and punching kids in the head." These experiences of bullying changed the way he performed academically, and had a lasting effect so much so that the defeat he experienced as a child was repeated through his schooling experience. Consequently, when Moe began high school, he was put into an English as a Second Language stream (ESL) where he was now dwarfed by the curriculum.

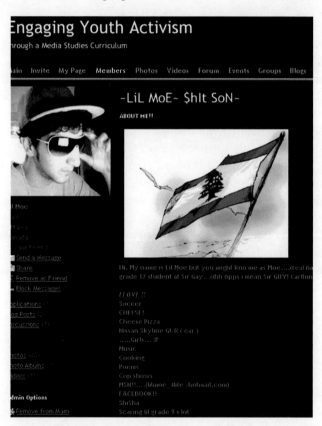

Figure 20.4: Moe's Social Network My Page

During this first year, he was unable to achieve any Grade-9 credits, and had to redo the entire year. Moe also struggled with the Ontario Grade 10 Literacy Test, failing it twice prior to his Grade-12 year. He was well aware that it is a hurdle to overcome in order to graduate. "If I don't pass it this time I don't graduate so I am kinda nervous." He identified the essay portion as the hardest part of the test, in that "some kids, they don't think that much, not that they don't think that much, they don't have enough thoughts to fill up the whole page." Moe also struggled with his language skills outside of school. When he originally took the written test for his driver's license, he failed. During his second attempt, he requested the help of an Arabic translator. He did not get a single question wrong. Moe was one of the only students enrolled in our program to highlight on the ning.com website national and cultural representations that were important to him, like the Lebanese flag (see Figure 20.4). Moe's struggle is mildly exemplified in what Banks (2009) describes as a gap between democratic ideals and the experiences of minority students. Banks argues that visible minorities are often marginalized, both in their own communities and in national cultures. By adopting the dominant language and culture, they may become isolated from their community culture, yet are also denied full participation and structural inclusion in mainstream society.

Moe's and other students' postings of international symbols on ning.com, flagged us, as teachers and researchers involved with the program, to reconsider the complexities of living a cross-cultural curriculum as both immigrants and non-immigrants, native-born and foreign-born within the multicultural contexts of Canada. Moe, whose audience is both his peers and teachers, signifies and symbolically represents himself in a new space. His hyphenated, lived experiences speak to what Kirsten Drotner (2008) called the restructuring of "dominant educational thinking about knowledge" (p. 171) through a space of multidimensional dispersal that the Internet affords its users. Morever, Moe's story locates him in multiple spaces simultaneously, a hyph-e-nation between the dual geopolitical nations of Canada and Lebanon, and in the linguistic spaces between each.

In Lebanon, Moe was identified by his ability to speak English, and in Canada, by his lack of that same ability. Reading Moe's journey through quantum (third) spaces, his experiences as part of the Lebanese diaspora in Canada are about simultaneous geographical movement and dispersal, and also about his experiences with Canadian multiculturalism through the dimension of time. As an adult learner, Moe experiences a temporal return to the space of the Canadian classroom that has not changed from his elementary experience years before. Moe's subjectivities are symbolically mediated as a Canadian ESL student through the institutional apparatus of public-schooling spaces of a vocational secondary school in Ontario. The social network affords Moe a place to speak from the abundances of "between" places: the liminal zones between Lebanon and Canada where his linguistic identity does not have to be the dominant marker of his social identity. On the ning.com site, Moe is able to speak his own multidimensional language of self-identity. He puts up images, phrases, and flags that are meaningful to him, and which change over the course of the term. His home page is a site where self-identification occurs, but one that remains fragmented, rather than totalizing the fluid, enunciated dynamics of his subjectivity. As a quantum (third) space, the content of the page constantly changes, the language shifts, and images substitute one representation for another, again and again.

When asked about how the overall social action curriculum project impacted Moe's life at school, inside and outside the classroom, he responded in relation to creating news broadcasts and public-service announcements for both the social-networking site and larger school community:

> *It taught me how to uh, like, how to do, like, questions, how to make up my own questions right on the spot. … So, yeah, it helped me, like, work faster with people, and talk to people faster. You know, it gave me more confidence. … The teachers in the program taught me how to work with groups of people. Like me and Sara would work mostly together. But before the program, me and Sara would never work together. Like, I barely talked to her. Like I used to barely talk to her, but now we talk a lot. Now I walk around the hallway and say to people, "this Friday we are putting out a news cast." Right after the news cast, we'd be walking down the hall, they'd be, like, "Oh, good job, Moe, good job, Moe." So yeah, the program gave me more confidence to make another one. Yeah, yeah. It's like … it showed me, that at school it's not only a bully Moe, it's not only a Moe that doesn't say much. It showed people that I'm, a different side.*

In a sense, the social networking site, as well as the other dimensions of the program, provided opportunities for teachers and students to call forth our capacities as a cosmopolitan praxis to imagine unexpected cross-cultural flows and transnational mobilities. To a large extent, the narratives students offered represented autobiographical inter-subjective accounts of what Miller (2006) aptly calls the "shifting and rapidly changing discursive and material effects of globalization" (p. 31). Moe's story represents a lived curriculum inhabited by the hyphenated spaces between alienation and appropriation, becoming and happening, and being and not being Canadian—living a social-networking curriculum of hyph-e-nations within a quantum (third) space.

Kiko

Kiko was a 17-year-old student enrolled in the program. In class, he was one of the quieter students. Not until he started posting cultural representations of his family on the site did we learn that he spent his formative years growing up in the Philippines. He created several videos that documented what it meant for him to be a Filipino student living in Canada. Prior to his postings, there were many times, both inside and outside of class, when other students referred to him as "Spanish" or "Chinese." In one instance, when Kiko corrected one of his peers about being Filipino, the student responded, "whatever, same thing." In "Theorizing Asian Canada, Reframing Differences," Coloma (2012) situated the concept of Asian Canadian as a "formation within the simultaneous and negotiated process of interpellation and identification that name and bring together a racialized coagulation of diverse ethno-national cultural groups" (p. 122). Such hyphenated coagulations provide spaces of agency for subjectivities originating and associating their differing individual and collective symbolic representations at a strategic moment in time for solidarity to then work together and against institutional violence. On the downside, however, as Coloma (2012) asserts, this same interpellation is utilized by mediated apparatuses like "the Canadian government in the form of census and other technologies of surveillance and management to sort, regulate, and allocate resources to various populations by race and ethnicity" (p. 122). Following Coloma's argument, on one side, we see Kiko's ability to form alliances with others in his class that self-identify as Asian, and alternatively, we observe how his individual identity can be erased or misrepresented by others in this pan-Asian conceptual framework. In either case, a quantum (third) space model affords us opportunities as educational researchers and teachers to understand Kiko's temporal existence in both of these spaces simultaneously, and at different times, and at different locales, depending on the political, historical, or cultural context of his engagement of others within the classroom.

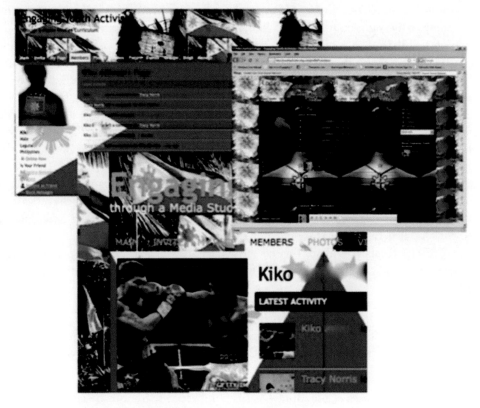

Figure 20.5: Screenshots of Kiko's Evolving "My Page"

Once we acknowledged this student's national and cultural identifications in class, he then asked to be called by his Filipino name (Kiko), rather than by his "Canadian" name, Peter[4]—the given, baptismal, Anglicized "English" name registered to him by the school and in use by the school administration, most students, and the education system in general. On ning.com and in his video assignments, he went by his birth name for the first time in a Canadian school. Out of all of the students enrolled in the program, Kiko's cultural representations were the most prominent on the social networking site (see Figure 20.5). Like Moe, he posted the flag of the Philippines, and featured many famous Filipino artists and athletes on his site. He created a video for his culminating task that spoke to his experiences both of living in the Philippines and of leaving. Consider the following letter that Kiko wrote for one of his course assignments:

Leaving the Philippines, kinda hard cos thats where we all grew up at and so much memories fading from back then i really miss the long days of summer all year round, the beautiful beaches and the home cooked meals sutch as Tinola, Sinigangnahipon, Champorado [chocolaate rice], Nilaga but the best parts of the foods were the frech grown vegitabals and/or fruits, they are really diffrent from the fruits and vegitabls here, becuse in the Philippines its more tropical so the fruits are more juicyer and there are alot more variets to choes from i could go on but it would take forever and i'll make my self hungery. Another awsome place is where all the mountains are, tropical water falls with unbeleavobly clean n' fresh water and the people are very nice even if they are living on the streets they always find a way to find happyness and make money, by making bags, hats, cooking food they are jsutreall friendly people. Ghetto houses in the Philippines are huge compared to the houses here the called a project homes but they all still sell for a lot of money. They builed them big because usally there are more then 5 children in the family my grandmother had 13 kids so they had to have a big house to fit them all in, but alog time ago it wasnt really like that you would have to build your own home witch was really tiny and catch your own meals its gotten a bit better now but im still hoping to go back to the Pomis Land again someday.

Considering Kiko in relation to Moe, here we try to begin to work with and perhaps extend Coloma's call for comparative multiculturalism, to look through one student's experiences to read another's. And like Coloma (2008), we try to "understand the postcolonial conditions of peoples of color both in their "native" countries and in the diaspora" (p. 37). Thus, in taking Kiko's site as its own utterance, we find his home page to be a different place from which to speak about geographical movement and growing up in different countries. Formerly silenced when lumped in with being Spanish or Chinese in the eyes of others, Kiko uses the quantum (third) space of social networking to represent memories and future desires of the "Promis[ed] Land," rich with colours, smells, tastes, and geography, while also negotiating the reorientations of such desires and their emerging multiple literacies within the structures of public schooling.

After Kiko's family immigrated to Canada, like many other immigrant families, they moved around frequently, seeking employment opportunities. One of Kiko's Grade-8 teachers recommended that he attend vocational school because of his academic struggles with math and English. Kiko mentioned on several occasions that he did not find the work at the school challenging, and often expressed that certain teachers underestimated the capacities of the student body in general. During an interview, when asked what he thought students or teachers could learn from his experiences, Kiko responded:

"They could learn how to treat the students better, respectful. And, like, change the work, 'cause, we need a challenge." He went on to say, *"I think I am getting stupider. No, it's true,"* and then, *"When I was back in grade school the work there was much harder than here."*

Kiko's desire to belong, and in some ways to return to the joys of his youth in the Philippines is not addressed by the structures of schooling. As his family moves around the city and the world, he seems to be left desiring stability and academic challenges. And yet, when symbolically represented as a Filipino permanent resident, a hyphenated Canadian citizen, Kiko now somehow "feels stupider." The Ontario schooling system labeled him as an ESL student struggling with language and mathematics, placing his present and future lived experiences of the curriculum within the spaces of an adaptive vocational school.

The aim of creating social cohesion through multiculturalism policies that target so-called "at-risk" students, has, in Kiko's case, left him feeling marginalized, on the outside. Kiko's perceived under-education, alongside his colonial re-naming as Peter, left him caught between the "Canadian dream" of migration for higher education, political stability, acceptance, and perhaps even economic prosperity, and the actual symbolic and material reality of his schooling experience in Ontario. Without our capacity to hear his voice as a hyphenated Canadian citizen occupying several fluid spaces, Kiko is not understood by the mainstream schooling system, which has streamed him mainly into the wrong public-school program.

In the social network, Kiko is able to describe the imaginative spaces that return him to a different time and place—a (third) space which is both memory and desire. He is able to articulate his position from within the class, but outside the structured classroom. In the liminal space of hyph-e-nations, Kiko was able to enunciate different representational possibilities for his hyphenated subjectivity, beginning with the revelation to researchers and teachers that his real name was not Peter—his first steps toward caring about, and participating in our class, marked by a desire to shed the institutionally mediated and colonial, symbolic name assigned to him.

Through participating in the program, things did begin to turn around academically for Kiko near the end of the year. He was more open during conversations in the class, he shared his ideas, and he became more comfortable in front of a video camera. Moreover, he expressed excitement about the different projects he was able to create and develop over the course of our program. His voice emerged through the media he was able to use, as his critiques of schooling, responses to literature and media, and reminiscences of his personal histories became ways of finding his place between the Philippines and Canada—living a social-networking curriculum of hyph-e-nations within a quantum (third) space. Kiko teaches us here what multiculturalism means from his perspective. One of the inherent limits of any study which explores student engagement through new classroom techniques is that we cannot account for future student success, but Kiko's work, along with what we have shared of Little Moe's, would be examples of the potential these projects have for supporting the work of self-formation and affirmation, essential elements in literacy development with marginalized youth.[5]

Throughout the program, other students also expressed their hyphenated identities on the social network, in terms of gender, class, popular culture, sexuality, etc. What is evident in our research is that the social networking site provided a space for some students to enunciate and perform their multiple identities in relation to their differing lived contexts, either inside or outside the institution of public schooling. Living a social-network curriculum afforded their teachers, the researchers, and volunteers in the program the opportunity to learn more about the complexity of students' lived experiences outside the classroom, and then make subsequent changes to the curriculum developed for the Communication and Technology course. In a sense, we attempted to create spaces for students to both see and express their lived experiences in the school curriculum.

Many of the students in the program improved their overall attendance, worked to foster a sense of community, created spaces for both their voices and others to be heard, represented their differing literacies, and became politically engaged citizens within the larger school community. For example, two students who were expelled from the school the year before for being a physical risk to peers and teachers, were able to pass all of their courses while enrolled in our program that school year. However, there were also students who had extenuating circumstances that continually overshadowed what we were trying to accomplish in the program (incarcerated or being kicked out of their parents' homes). Indeed, our project did not facilitate the typical, feel-good Hollywood ending.

Conclusion: Living A Curriculum of Hyph-e-Nations

The social network affords students a quantum (third) space where they are able to bring forth their personal histories, across continents, and within the diasporas in Canada to articulate their identities beyond stereotypes that demand cultural intelligibility by teachers. Moe's and Kiko's identities were constantly in flux on the social network, where their home pages become symbolic cultural representations of these students' constant evolution, their "coming into being" as subjects whose cultural identities might have particular roots and/or routes, but are not fixed in any given time and place (see Butler, 1999). Furthermore, access to the Internet and social-networking forums provided students like Moe and Kiko civic opportunities to engage with what mattered to them while living within the apparatus of public schooling.

What we learned during this social action curriculum project is that the concepts of authority and institutional legitimacy, of who has the power to validate knowledge production (cultural, epistemic, social, etc.), are in a constant state of flux within a public-schooling system that is becoming more wireless. Students, or digital natives, if you will, can now access information outside the classroom in fundamentally different ways from how they are asked to "learn" within the institutional structures of a classroom while still inside the school. "For perhaps the first time in human history," as Lankshear and Knobel (2008) make clear, "new technologies have amplified the capacities and skills of the young to such an extent that many conventional assumptions about curriculum seem to have become inappropriate" (p. 8). Here the theoretical and poetic works of Canadian Poet Laureate, Fred Wah (1996, 2000), have also helped us to (re)conceptualize the thoughtful and playful spaces between cross-cultural hyph-e-nations, of curricular doublings, taking place within the intellectual theorizing of our research on multicultural education within the contexts of curriculum studies and social networking.

Lingering within the poetics of the hyph-e-nated spaces of social networking, as one example, is where the temporal hyphens among nation, culture, and subject, both bind and divide (Wah, 2000). But even when it is notated through the symbolic representation of a flag, a song, or popular culture, as Wah (2000) reminds us, the hyphen "is often silent and transparent" (p. 73) within the contexts of public school. In our work within such cross-cultural hyph-e-nations within quantum (third) spaces, as teachers and educational researchers working within Critical Youth Studies, we must attune ourselves toward alternative curricular possibilities that break through such silences and erasures toward understanding curriculum, or ideologies (left, right, neo, and so on) of multiculturalism within the context of public schooling, in what Aoki (2005) has called a "curriculum in a new key." Much like the poetic bio-texts of Fred Wah (1996), our curriculum theorizing, designs, implementation, and evaluation for this particular project can make the interstices at the margins of the hyphen (and in-between its connective spaces) more audible, and their cross-cultural pigmentations more visible. Here the transparency of the hyphen thus becomes a thorn—an aporia, a perpetual deferral of signs, signifiers, and signified—in the side of what we might call "predetermined" colonial configurations (Stanley, 2009). And within this hyphenated quantum (third) space of infinite discursive and symbolic representational possibilities, we in turn can then create alternative interpretations of concepts such as diversity, equity, and critical multicultural education while working with marginalized youth within the contexts of public schooling.

Such conceptual navigations and reconceptualizations of multicultural policies and education as a temporary temporal assemblage of curricular hyph-e-nations might then play with what Wah (2000) calls the contradictions, paradoxes, and theoretical assumptions active at the edges of the hyphen, in our classrooms, of our hyphenated Canadian students. "This constant pressure that the hyphen brings to bear against the master narratives of duality, multiculturalism, and apartheid," Wah (2000) tells us, "creates a volatile space that is inhabited by a wide range of voices" (p. 74). Here our curriculum theorizing and its respective curricular designs would then involve the geopolitical, cultural, and psychic play with the "poetics of the 'trans,'" methods of translation, transference, transposition, or poetics that speaks of the awareness and use of any means of occupying" (p. 90) the diverse narrative locations that immigrant, non-immigrant, and Aboriginal youth here in Canada choose to produce and occupy either within our classrooms or on social-network sites such as www.ning.com. It is at the interstitiality of these narrative locations—students' lived hyph-e-nated locations, whether recognized as digital natives, immigrants, foreigners, or original inhabitants—that we as policymakers, administrators, teachers, and educational researchers can then perform the recursive questioning of concepts such as curriculum, social networking, quantum (third) space, equity, diversity, and multicultural education. Our critical (re)readings of differing symbolic representations offer insight into the past, present, and future of marginalized youth, and the multiplicities of their lived experiences.

Notes

1. In "How Much Did Social Media Contribute to Revolution in the Middle East," Evgeny Morozov (2011) troubled what he called cyber-utopian claims that social networking itself actually summoned up the Arab Spring. Instead, he emphasized that social networks like Facebook and/or Myspace are simply another (digital) tool available to policitians and/or social-justice orientated citizens associated with revolutionary movements.
2. The use of the term, *shell*, is linked to chemistry as well, as in the shell of the Bohr model of the atom or the idea of a nucleus. In quantum physics, particles are only contained by probabilities, not strict "shells" as in earlier models of the atom. This idea of probabilities allows for multiple positions at once—in other words, just as a particle changes through the act of observation (Heisenberg's Uncertainty Principle), the act of interaction within a social network, the act of being observed because of self-representation and interaction on one's homepage, can change the networker's behaviour (our students in the classroom). The defining of the self in this space is fluid and multiple, simultaneously and ambivalently an attempt at self-definition and deferral.
3. Labels such as "at-risk," "special needs," "vocational," etc., can often decontextualize the problems experienced by marginalized students, and thus lead to misinterpretation. We are conscious of how these labels often work as a homogenizing discursive force to frame the experiences of millions of complex individuals coming from diverse contexts under one catch-all banner. Therefore we are referring to such marginalized youth as individuals who are in danger of not graduating from the public-schooling system with a high-school diploma.
4. Moe, Peter, Kiko, and Sara are pseudonyms.
5. To read more about the lived experiences of other students enrolled in the program, dealing with similar but different dimensions of the project, see Ng-A-Fook, Radford, Norris, and Yazdanian (2013) in the *Canadian Journal of Action Research*.

References

Aoki, T. (2005). Toward curriculum in a new key. In W. F. Pinar & R. Irwin (Eds.), *Curriculum in a new key: The collected works of Ted T. Aoki* (pp. 89 –110). Mahwah, NJ: Lawrence Erlbaum.

Ausman, T. (2012). *Indian diasporic films as quantum (third) spaces: A curriculum of cultural translation* (Unpublished master's thesis). University of Ottawa, Ottawa, Canada.

Banks, J. (2009). Diversity and citizenship education in multicultural nations. *Multicultural Education Review, 1*(1), 1–28.

Bennett, W. L. (2008). (Ed.). *Civic life online: Learning how digital media can engage youth.* Cambridge, MA: MIT Press.

Bhabha, H. K. (1994). *The location of culture.* New York, NY: Routledge.

Bhabha, H. K. (1999). Arrivals and departures. In H. Naficy (Ed.), *Home, exile, homeland: Film, media, and the politics of place* (pp. vii–xii). New York, NY: Routledge.

Buckingham, D. (Ed.). (2008). *Youth, identity, and digital media.* Cambridge, MA: MIT Press.

Butler, J. (1999). *Gender trouble: Feminism and the subversion of identity* (2nd ed.). New York, NY: Routledge.

Butler, J. (2009). *Frames of war: When is life grievable?* London, UK: Verso.

Citizenship and Immigration Canada. (2012). *Immigration overview: Permanent and temporary residents.* Retrieved from http://www.cic.gc.ca/english/resources/statistics/facts2010/permanent/10.asp#countries

Coloma, R. S. (2008). All immigrants are Mexicans, only Blacks are minorities, but some of us are brave: Race, multiculturalism, and postcolonial studies in U.S. education. *Journal of Curriculum Theorizing, 24*(1), 32–46.

Coloma, R. S. (2009). "Destiny has thrown the Negro and the Filipino under the tutelage of America": Race and curriculum in the age of empire. *Curriculum Inquiry, 39*(4), 495–519.

Coloma, R. S. (2012). Theorizing Asian Canada, reframing differences. In N. Ng-A-Fook & J. Rottmann (Eds.), *Reconsidering Canadian curriculum studies: Provoking historical, present, and future perspectives* (pp. 119–136). New York, NY: Palgrave Macmillan.

Drotner, K. (2008). Leisure is hard work: Digital practices and future competencies. In D. Buckingham (Ed.), *Youth, identity, and digital media* (pp. 167–184). Cambridge, MA: MIT Press.

Gay, G. (2000). *Culturally responsive teaching: Theory, research, and practice.* New York, NY: Teachers College Press.

Gay, G. (2002). Preparing for culturally responsive teaching. *Journal of Teacher Education, 53*(2), 106–116.

Ghosh, R., & Abdi, A. (Eds.). (2004). *Education and the politics of difference: Canadian perspectives*. Toronto, Canada: Canadian Scholar's Press.

Joshee, R., & Sinfield, I. (2010). The Canadian multicultural education policy web: Lessons to learn, pitfalls to avoid. *Multicultural Education Review, 2*(1), 55–75.

Lankshear, C., & Knobel, M. (Eds.). (2008). *Digital literacies: Concepts, policies, and practices*. New York, NY: Peter Lang.

Levy, R. (2011). Young children, digital technology, and interaction with text. In M. Thomas (Ed.), *Deconstructing digital natives: Young people, technology and the new literacies* (pp. 151–166). New York, NY: Routledge.

Miller, J. (2006). Curriculum studies and transnational flows and mobilities: Feminist autobiographical perspectives. *Transnational Curriculum Inquiry, 3*(2), 31–50.

Moon, S. (2010). Rethinking culturally responsive teaching: Toward new (im)possibilities of curriculum studies and policy. *Multicultural Education Review, 3*(2), 69–102.

Morozov, E. (2011). *How much did social media contribute to revolution in the Middle East?* Retrieved from http://www.bookforum.com/inprint/018_01/7222

Ng-A-Fook, N. (2009). Inhabiting the hyphenated spaces of alienation and appropriation: *Currere*, language, and postcolonial migrant subjectivities. In J. Nahachewsky & I. Johnson (Eds.), *Beyond presentism* (pp. 87–103). Rotterdam, The Netherlands: Sense.

Ng-A-Fook, N., Radford, L., Norris, T., & Yazdanian, S. (2013). Empowering marginalized youth: Curriculum, digital media, and character development. *Canadian Journal of Action Research, 14*(1), 38–50.

Ontario Ministry of Education. (2008). *Finding common ground: Character development in Ontario schools, K–12*. Toronto, Ontario, Canada: Queen's Printer for Ontario.

Pinar, W. F. (2009). Hand in hand: Multiculturalism, nationality, cosmopolitanism. *Multicultural Education Review, 2*(1), 25–53.

Prensky, M. (2001). Digital natives, digital immigrants. *On the Horizon, 9*(5), 1–6.

Prensky, M. (2011). Digital wisdom and Homo sapiens digital. In M. Thomas (Ed.), *Deconstructing digital natives: Young people, technology and the new literacies* (pp. 15–29). New York, NY: Routledge.

Shirky, C. (2011). Means. In M. Bauerlein (Ed.), *The digital divide: Arguments for and against Facebook, Google, texting, and the age of social networking* (pp. 318–334). New York, NY: Jeremy P. Tarcher.

Stanley, T. (2009). The banality of colonialism: Encountering artifacts of genocide and White supremacy in Vancouver today. In S. Steinberg (Ed.), *Diversity and multiculturalism* (pp. 143–159). New York, NY: Peter Lang.

Thomas, D. (2008). KPK, Inc.: Race, nation, and emergent cultures in online games. In A. Everett (Ed.), *Learning race and ethnicity: Youth and digital media* (pp. 155–173). Cambridge, MA: MIT Press.

Wah, F. (1996). *Diamond grill*. Edmonton, Alberta, Canada: NeWest Press.

Wah, F. (2000). *Faking it: Poetics and hybridity, critical writing, 1984–1999*. Edmonton, Alberta, Canada: NeWest Press.

CHAPTER 21

A Fat Woman's Story of Body-Image Politics and the Weighty Discourses of Magnification and Minimization

Susan Beierling

I have always been female. I have always been Caucasian. I have NOT always been "fat." In fact, I was a "healthy and normal" (by that I mean average-sized—or an appropriate size for my age) girl for the first ten years of my life. Then, in grade five, I hit puberty, or, perhaps, puberty hit me. As if instantaneously responsive, my body began to re-shape itself in ways I was, at the time and for many years afterward, not able to understand. For example, I began, at ten years old, to develop breasts; or rather, one breast. Unlike most girls during this becoming-a-woman developmental stage who develop both breasts more or less simultaneously, mine seemed to be developing one at a time. I can still remember a close family member commenting about me that, "it looks like she has been hit in the chest with a soccer ball." This was my first—well … first time consciously remembered, but unfortunately never really questioned or understood—glimpse of myself as an alien "other." I learned from, in fact was taught by this experience, at that vulnerable age of ten—and a learning and/or teaching that I wrestle with to this day—that I was not "normal." I was and continue to be actually a "freak," and I needed then and now to hide my hideous, corrupt, betrayer of a body so that no one would notice how "abnormal" I was.

Between ten and thirteen years old, I discovered that one breast was the least of my issues—I began to gain weight at an accelerated pace, even compared to my hormone-awakened girl peers who also had rapidly changing bodies. However, their bodies seemed to be conforming into the visually stimulating, stereotypical "standards" of what was "girlishly-womanly" and noticeably desirable to males (Bordo, 1993). In comparison to my peers, again, here I was—a rapidly weight-gaining, one-breasted freak. An aside: Yes, the other breast did arrive later. I was feeling so badly about my changing and oddly shaped body, I even remember stealing money from my mom's coin jar so that I could go to the neighborhood convenience store on my way to school and bring treats such as potato chips, or bubble gum, or candy to share with my classmates. I guess I thought that if I supplied treats to my peers, maybe they would like me and not notice how big I was becoming and how oddly shaped I was. Then, one day, in grade five, one of my classmates told me straight out, no whispering, that I was "fat." That statement was followed up with the comment that I needed to lose at least twenty pounds. It was then I realized that my secret—O.K., I was in kid denial—was out. The silence had been broken and the elephant in the room (me) was available for abuse. People lined up to tell me I had gained significant weight and that I was not "normal" like them. It is here, at ground zero, with these pile-on, emphatic declarations of being an overweight female, that I begin my lifelong struggle. Today, I am currently approaching 45, and I am still wrestling with a large body and with my compromised body image, and thus, my struggle, as well, with my sense of identity.

This chapter will not provide answers to all the questions regarding a categorically overweight woman's issues in a thin-ness obsessed Western society. Nor will the chapter focus on a statistical, data-driven analysis of the "obesity epidemic" that has invaded most First World nations. Nor is this chapter a rant or diatribe against the late-capitalist media. This chapter is a first-person voiced narrative journey of discovery and recovery from a fat, middle-aged, and single woman who is still trying to make hermeneutic sense of what it means to phenomenologically experience contemporary Western society and its consumptive cultures as just that—a fat, middle-aged, and single woman.

Let me begin by noting that coming to use the term, fat, was something I needed to wrestle with. I am still physically troubled, that is, my stomach turns, when I say the word—"fat." At various periods in my life, I could have chosen, and often did, the more politically correct terms such as overweight or obese, but these terms tend to have medical or health-care discourses associated with them, and actually increase the objectification, categorization, and marginalization. In my search to re-name myself as "other"/"fat person," I could have chosen any number of social descriptors, such as "beached whale," "tubby," "lard ass," "fatso," "pig," "cow," or "chubby." However, these sticks-and-stones words have particular hurtful and objectifying connotations as well, and the use of any of these words would be prescriptive and overly derogatory, and actually becomes another word-association game of language and linguistic hide-and-seek. On it goes, until all meaning and any sense of subjectivity is obliterated in the name of medical, or health, or slang clarity. Therefore, I chose to use the term, fat, to describe myself and others with similar body sizes and types to mine. Why? Because the word, *fat*, needs to be shouted out where until now it has only been whispered. It needs to be brought out of the closet and its intentionality explicitly held open for a while so some meaning may be gleaned from the word itself and its referential representations.

Despite descriptions of the denotative meaning of the word, fat—which seems to be non-definable except via connotative comparisons, or examples, or through the use of medicalization references—it has also come to be a very negative descriptor for the persecution of some bodies in Western societies. The word, fat carries with it political, medical, social, sexual, and professional historicity, and, therefore, contemporary implications. The use of the word, fat, is more than a descriptor for me; it is also a statement of intent. That word holds personal and political power and control—over me. It has become such a shutdown, that it is almost taboo to speak the word, fat. By using it here, in a public text, I am hoping to re-introduce the word and simply not accept it being pushed into the politically correct background, where it lives well in the shadows, yet is still influential for those of us who are fat. The absence is still presence, and yet the absence seems to appease the normalizing sensibilities of the semi-concerned but mostly frightened "normals." By bringing the word and its simply complex lived experience meanings into a talking space, I seek to hopefully help my readers and myself deflate the power and control that comes along with both the presence and absence of that word—FAT.

While I still cringe at the mere utterance of the word, *fat*, my writing mission here is not to become an advocate for "fat" or "fatness" per se, but the reality of my situation is that I am fat, and I live in a society that over-privileges "thinness." As such, I must find a way to navigate and live within this society. It is this learning to navigate that I seek to share with you, the reader. I am selfish here, in that this writing is a way for me, and hopefully for you as a reader, to deepen the societal conversation regarding (mis)understandings of what it actually means to not just be named "fat," but to live "fat." That is, to be fat every moment of every waking day, and to then to be held up, again in every way possible, as the negative confirmation that "thinness" is the right, true, proper, healthy, and godly sanctioned way of being a (Western) woman.

So, some background … to the narrative at hand. Transitioning from elementary school to junior high school was particularly difficult for me. Most of my peers would be going to a different junior high school than I would, due to school zoning changes in my neighborhood that located my house in a different school catchment zone. Already realizing that I was different from most other kids my age, I was incredibly anxious to be venturing into a new and different school—and to do so alone. Fortunately, for me, I met a new best friend in grade seven; we even shared the same first name. My friend was barely five feet tall, and likely not even one hundred pounds (sorry, I do not do the metric system, although I have heard I would be smaller if I counted weight in kilograms) when we met. I, on the other hand, was already quite tall at about five feet, six inches, and weighing a whopping 130 pounds. I towered over my new friend, and yet, in some weird way, as I think back now, I lived in her shadow. People were always drawn to her, and often I felt that some even befriended me just to get closer to her. So, how come, then, my bigger body seemed to be casting me into the shadows?

Why, with my large presence, did people seem to gravitate to my tiny friend and others who were small like her? You see, I entered junior high school during the early 1980s, at a time when the mass media was exploding with images—such as MTV (music videos), magazines, advertisements, movies, and television—illustrating just how girl-teens and young women should (must really) look and behave. As hungry consumers, most of us—young girls at the time—literally ate up these new "go-girl" images. We were literally consumed, and perhaps metaphorically, by these product-consumption images. What we did not realize at the time was that these magazines and other visual media, in particular, were perpetuating what feminist, Naomi Wolf (1990), called the "beauty myth," which, she explained, "is a backlash against feminism that uses images of female beauty as a political weapon" (p. 10). Who knew? I did not at the time, with my desire to be normal, and the girls around me did not. If sales of glorifying and objectifying female products and services were any indication, then most other girls and women did not either. Transitioning from our sculpted Barbie dolls, which had already begun conditioning our young minds with societal desires for specific body images and beckoning sexuality and female "trophyism," we now faced a visual overload of hundreds upon hundreds of images every day. All these images taught us all how to look, how to behave, and what we must be capable of—really. These images began to teach us who we were, and they became part of who we were. If we did not see ourselves in them, then we were doing something wrong or we were abnormal, or weird, or a tomboy, or, perhaps, a lesbian. We knew of no such thing as "media propaganda literacy" at this time, and we knew no better than to buy into the "norms" being set by these powerful industries and reinforced by the consumer inside us as conforming, good little girls. I tried very hard to conform, but my size and weight resulted in even more disappointment, and deeper issues were surfacing with my identity—if I was not and never could be Barbie, then who was I?

Between the ages of 19 and 20, I began to gain even more weight and at an accelerated pace. My body was becoming bigger and bigger and I was getting larger and larger. I was now too big for the clothing in the mainstream fashion shops where the popular thin styles were evident in every window, and so I had to source out new shops that catered to my increasing size. There was only one "plus-sized" shop in the entire mall in the city where I lived. The clothing they carried was very pricey. I guess it costs more in fabric and labour to build large-size clothes. I could not help but feel the walls of my world closing in on me—or perhaps it was I closing in on them. Either way, the pressure on me regarding my size was mounting. I could no longer express myself through fashion in a way that I had grown accustomed to as the proverbial little girl. I had to re-define who I was based on what I was able to find to fit me, rather than being able to define who I was, and then dress to express that belief. My options, even my visual identity, were becoming more and more limited, ironically, as my body seemed to know no bounds as it expressed itself.

In addition to this body expandability, my visibility or value as a human being, again ironically, decreased in a negative, direct correlation to the growth of my body. Although I now took up more physical space than ever before, I was actually treated by those around me with less respect and validity and, at times, dignity. Simply, the larger I became, the less noticeable and more invisible I was becoming as a person—how is it possible for a very large woman to become, in social settings, the incredible shrinking woman? I just could not understand why I was becoming so unacceptable within my social and personal relationships and my personal-family-friends and schooling environments; in fact, I was no longer able to even accept myself. I had lost myself in my desire to be small. I became a self-hater. This is not what I was used to as a little girl, and I could not make sense of it at the time as an adolescent and then as a young adult.

Despite several doctor, health, and weight-specialist appointments, and a trail of several reduced caloric diets combined with intense exercise regimens, I ended up gaining just over one hundred pounds in about eight months. Obviously, my problem was bigger than initially suspected. How does a person gain weight starving themselves and exercising like a want-to-be Olympic athlete? Later it was discovered that I had an extreme hormonal imbalance, which could have been a contributing factor to my massive increase in weight and size. So, a diagnosis of a hormonal imbalance. Still, I was at least 130 pounds overweight—this gave me a completely new perspective on what it means to be hormonally fat. What I had thought was fat in high school was a dream body compared to the one I now had to navigate as a youth or young adult through this increasingly noticeable, cruel, unaccepting, and body-prejudiced world. In addition to this new fat body, my breasts, now fully developed, had never really evened themselves out, and there was a several cup-size difference between them—ouch. Never before had I been so ashamed of who I had become. I was nothing other than a huge, freakish, de-formed, and bloated body; I hated myself for becoming the "thing" I had learned to fear.

Still, deep down, I could not give up on the belief that I could, if I just found the right thing or the right way for me, achieve a smaller body, and so I immersed myself into fad diets, long-term eating plans, extreme low-calorie diets, learning about exercise and proper meal planning, and so on. When I read my journals from this time of my life, I am disturbed at how much of my life was defined by the discourses of weight loss, health, beauty, and ideal body images. Every journal entry has some reference to my bigger-than-average body and my desire (or dreaming) of what life would be like if only I had a smaller body. The only thing holding me back from this so-called perfect life, confirmed by my journals, which I knew anyway, was my big body. I felt as though I was doing everything right in adhering to these ways of reducing my mass, and yet I kept coming up short, and, in fact, I just kept reinforcing the belief that I was a failure, and eventually I just gave up trying—at least, to some extent.

I had just completed an unfulfilling undergraduate degree, and I was living on my own and working in retail. My education, an unfulfilling intellectual experience, was being wasted in retail, but my eroded self-confidence would not allow me to believe I was deserving of a job better than a retail-service-industry, minimum-wage job. So, I was struggling—personally, professionally, financially, socially, and so on. Most females of the same age seemed to be going out to nightclubs, meeting men, getting married, and having babies—moving through their "normal" lives. When I went to nightclubs, I felt literally invisible, again ironic, considering how large I was. People must have seen me, but people refused to make eye contact with me. If they did not acknowledge or see me, then I did not exist. If I caught a glimpse of them sneak-looking at me, I knew they would turn me into a pity-her conversation piece over which to laugh and joke. Sometimes, people in the bars would try to trip me; seemingly, everybody loves a fat person falling and struggling to get up. Others would call out to me over the bar noise using derogatory words, or they would imitate animal sounds that I later repeated over and over in my head. I have always tried to process these experiences, but I did not realize that through this rehearsal, I was buying into what they were saying. I was internalizing their harsh, cruel, and defining words, sounds, and gestures. I was unable to stand up for myself, and because I surrounded myself with people who were all too willing to stand up for me, I was re-victimized with negativity and judgment.

Really, what would I be standing up for—fatness, or the trapped little girl in me? I could not understand, at the time, that I was being told to just accept the fat identity society was telling me that I am regardless of what I increasingly was trying to know to be otherwise untrue.

Because I could not accept my space, place, and life, I believed that there must be something wrong with me. But then, would not there be something wrong with me if I accepted my life as it existed? I realize now that I was trying to stand up for myself, but I had not yet been introduced to any discourses that would equip me with the language and action to do so. I grew increasingly desperate to meet and maintain friends who would see past my ever-growing body and realize there was a good person under all that dis-connecting fat. However, not many people are willing to get close enough to discover the Oprah "inner beautiful child." I severely lowered—and I mean lowered—my expectations for white-knight, suitable mates, and I found myself in some very negative and hurtful relationships with trolls masquerading as men—actually they were trolls masquerading as trolls. I had practically surrounded myself with people who did nothing but reinforce the terrible feelings I had towards myself. My self-hatred and dis-engagement with my typical but atypical social life continued, and I hit some all-time lows—emotionally, psychologically, and mentally, as well as socially. In fact, some lows I reached are still too painful to even put in words to this day (somehow I think putting them into words lets them come back to life, and I am afraid to have that happen), but suffice it to say that it was between the ages of 23 and 26 that I hit my "rock bottom." I had become so "controlled" by my body and society's image-driven media, and since I had failed miserably to achieve any approximations of an ideal body size, I was a failure. I conducted my life as if that were true.

During this time, fortunately, I was able to make some new friends through my place of employment. These new friends were actually accepting of me. They accepted my big, lopsided body, which did not seem to be a problem for them. Why so? You see, they were all gay. They knew already what it was like to face marginalization during their youth, and so their criteria for acceptance looked beyond social labels and superficial images. Also, to these gay men, I was not competing for the attention of the same desirable mates as they were. This created an environment for different kinds of friendships to begin, ones not based on the superficiality of outer images. This was the first time in a long time that I finally began to feel better about myself. If my body was not an issue to them, why should it remain such an issue for me? All of this dieting and focusing on food consumption and exercise was completely exhausting, and I was interested in other things.

Despite my new supportive community of friends, I did not take long before I returned to perceiving myself as a complete failure. When it came to taking care of myself—inside and out—I realized that I had committed much of my life to educating myself about the "right way" to live, but I could not stick to something long enough to have much success. Something had to change. I could not keep trying to meet an ideal that I would likely never achieve. I also could not keep giving myself over to this ideal, in believing that unless I look a certain way, I am not able to feel, or experience, happiness. I realized that I needed to start changing some of the discourses that played so heavily into my early and youth identities and my body-obsessed life experiences—such as the positivistic discourses of the natural sciences, the health-care system, the capitalistic marketplace, the entertainment media, and medicine generally and specifically. While these discourses are useful in measuring, controlling, and manipulating, they are inadequate in bringing forth a deeper understanding of what it is like and what it means to be a complete human being. The dominant discourses of positivistic science and medicine support the notion of "fat phobia," and it is through these harsh, dissecting, and categorizing discourses that I have come to name and know myself. So, I started to read new and different kinds of books, and with the support of my new gay-lesbian friends, and investing in myself as a valuable and valued human being, I moved forward. Despite being advised by all who "cared" about me to just lose the weight and that would fix my troubles—little did they know that I had all but killed myself trying—I knew the truth. Doing without understanding is doomed for failure. By the time I was reaching my late 20s and early 30s, I began to find some courage and began making some positive life changes. I discovered that meaning-making required an intellectual effort.

These steps on the path of my life journey were some of the hardest for me. I felt that most of the time, I walked this learning journey alone, with very few people to turn to who could help me understand and make meaning of my life struggles, intellectually and meaningfully.

At the age of 28, while I was learning more about myself and the discourses that shaped me, and equipped with an improving self-confidence and the support of a new community of friends, I decided to have elective reconstructive surgery to deal with my uneven breasts. That was not very intellectual, but it was meaningful to me. I chose to have a reduction done, and other than minor complications and some permanent nerve damage, the process was a "success." Can anything ever be easy for me? I then had even distribution—at least regarding my breasts—for the first time in my life. It was wonderful to be able to buy a "normal" bra, something I had never really been able to do—simply, I had to wear sports bras for most of my youth. This physical change spurred me on to focus even more on my understandings of the determining discourses regarding girls and/or women and body images and identity.

In regards to my own identity, I realize now that I never did reconcile my "self" with a "bigger" body, and before the age of 30 I had gone through some incredible changes. I had yet to ever even consider what that might mean in relation to my desired embodied life, my live-strong hopes, and my life-fulfilling dreams. Until quite recently, I had believed that somehow this fat body is what I actually deserved, because I longed so hard to be otherwise—this was my punishment; a life of struggle, challenge, and desperation. I realize now that despite my best efforts to rid myself of the operationalizing, oppressive dialogues that had consumed so much of my youth, I was just too embedded in them to even be aware of them and how they were manipulating and controlling almost every aspect of my life.

During my early 30s, then, I had the opportunity to pursue a thesis-based graduate degree. I was fortunate to find a graduate supervisor who was willing to work with me to create a program that would allow me to wrestle with some of the very dialogues and ideologies that I had downloaded into my personal, daily life. Through exploring the grand, socializing, positivistic meta-narratives, I realized that they frame the diet and/or weight-loss industry, the health and beauty industries, the medical industry, and the exercise and fitness industries—to name just a few. I was able to realize that I am not alone in wrestling with issues of the body and body image, and the questions of appropriate size and shapes of our bodies. The more I spoke about my life and what I was reading (for example, Susan Bordo, 1993; Naomi Wolf, 1997; M. G. Lord, 2004) with others, the more I became aware of the magnitude of this thinly disguised, weighty issue in our contemporary society, and how heavy-handedly the body is dealt with. Through my graduate studies, I had the unique opportunity to speak to other women self-defined as "overweight" about their experiences of being large women, and especially in relation to their thoughts and feelings regarding their bodies. The stories and experiences that we shared in our conversations, as core to my graduate research project, deepened my and my participants' collective understandings of the issues around the large female body and those massive, mediated, predefined images of what counts as a culturally appropriate and useful—slender and/or thin—female body. As an inquiry talk circle, we cracked open the surfaces of body issues, realizing the depth of the power and control that operates within the dominant cultural industries. Gathering all of the stories together—mine and those of the research-study participants who became my co-researchers—and analyzing them, allowed me to realize some of the macro and micro themes that underpin the capitalistic-driven foundations of the industries mentioned above. There were three distinct meta-themes that emerged, and they were:

1. The bigger you are, the less you are seen,

2. Weight prejudice really does exist, and

3. Square pegs in round holes (this theme dealt with "fitting in"—literally, physically, and socially) (Beierling, 2009).

The first major theme emerging from my research was a focus on an ever-increasing sense of invisibility directly related to the size of one's body. The women I spoke with in my study, and myself included, experienced a feeling of "fading away" as our bodies grew larger. Our body-conscious culture has taught Western society members that a bigger female body has no value; in fact, it is to be feared (unless one were an elite athlete; then the body needs to be large but muscular—no fatties need apply). Therefore, regardless of any other attributes a fat girl may possess, she is still, first and foremost, fat, and thus less valuable. Often, participants expressed feeling as though "people would look right through them," or as though "people just ignore me completely." Others felt that because they were trying to "hide" their big bodies, it meant that they were able to hide their "selves," further perpetuating the feelings of invisibility. In hiding their bodies, maybe they could still exist in society without the painful interactions that their too-large bodies seemed to invite. Other participants were so embarrassed to be walking around in their bigger bodies that they chose to hide from the public as much as possible. We all learned early on that a big body invites ridicule, scorn, and disgust. I can recall many times from my own past instances where derogatory comments or rude looks were given regarding my big presence in social situations. Some persons were discrete and some were blatant and bold, but all provided looks, gestures, or words that were hurtful, and each one built upon the other, casting my own self-worth deeper into the shadows. This social out-casting added to the feeling of invisibility, as women of size feel that they need to avoid social settings in order to avoid the abuse and humiliation that is cast upon them by seemingly offended and righteous others. Hearing these stories and reflecting back on my own youth and young adult past experiences has allowed me to realize the magnitude of the issue of oppressive body image in North American culture.

The negative attention and perception towards fat women go deeper than just looks and comments. Unfortunately, in many cases the difficulties transgress into outright prejudice and discrimination. This leads me to theme two from my graduate work: Weight prejudice really does exist. Weighty women do earn lower wages and have fewer employment opportunities. They, at times, face inhumane treatment from the medical community, and experience higher costs for clothing, and there are physical limitations fat women in North America face, in terms of shopping, transportation, and so on. These are additional challenges in their lives that their thinner "sisters" do not face (Beierling, 2009). At the moment, there is no "anti-being fat" legislation to protect the overweight woman from fat discrimination, and there are strong discourses at play "educating" us all about the good (slim) and bad (fat) of our bodies. This is the perspective supported by the dominant discourses of positivistic-governed science and medicine. For example, when I was about 33 years old, I decided that it was time to be responsible and get a life-insurance policy. When the medical professional came to my house to record my medical statistics, I was horrified to find out that the scale she brought did not even go up high enough on the point scale to measure me. In addition, the blood-pressure cuff used was "average" sized, and it gave an inaccurate reading of "high" blood pressure. Despite sending over all of my medical records showing I did not have any history of high blood pressure, my premium was based on their inaccurate readings—and so I immediately canceled my policy with them and found another insurance company which was able to accurately assess me. In a country that provides health care for its citizens, and with a growing percentage of the population being labeled "obese," I cannot understand why medical equipment and medical opinions have not changed to keep up with the reality of the situation at hand. We, fat women, are human beings with feelings and rights. We need to find a discourse that enables us to explore these weight-prejudice factors, and then bring into the open new conversations regarding what it really is like to live as a fat person in North America, especially if you happen to be a girl or young adult woman.

The third theme emerging from my research attended to the idea that finding one's "fit" (socially and physically) as a woman becomes increasingly more difficult the bigger or larger you are. Every participant in my study mentioned several incidences of not "fitting in"—literally and metaphorically.

These incidences encompassed issues regarding physically fitting one's body into spaces, or fitting in socially and in social situations, or fitting in in the sense of societal belonging and acceptance generally. From fashion, to bathroom stalls, to bus and airplane seats, to stadium- and university-theatre seating, to exercise equipment, to medical equipment, the findings from my research showed that there are many physical spaces and situations that we "fat" women just cannot partake in or experience. For example, I remember that in my thirties I had bought a bicycle, and I was getting to the point that I could go for longer rides, and so I was shopping for a hydration backpack (a backpack with water bottles and a tube so that you can drink while riding without having to stop). The backpack fits over your shoulders like any normal backpack, and it has straps that close around your waist. Even including an online search, I have yet to find a manufactured hydration pack with straps big enough to fit around my waist (and I am not that big).

Fitting in socially also becomes quite a problem for those of us who are fat. Let us be real, who wants someone like me on their baseball team or as a dance partner? What can I contribute to a cycle club or pretty much anything requiring physical stamina? I am just going to hold everyone back. If fat women are not able to define themselves through fashion, or activities, and they are generally marginalized from society, and they are hearing messages everyday about how they do not fit into mainstream society, then they need to find somewhere else to be. In some cities across North America, fat women have come together and have built communities of support. Some of these are exercise classes geared towards overweight bodies, or fashion shows and clothing swaps, or clubs—gatherings of women of local and national stature and from private and/or social clubs—that organize engagement in political movements and attempts to influence discrimination policies. My graduate research is helping me to understand my self-image and self-identity, and allowing me to help others, and to become increasingly aware or conscious of the social meta-discourses or "grand narratives" (Lyotard, 1984) that have come to dominate our Western culture. These discourses are accepted as the "norm." and are rarely questioned, remaining the pillars that they are, and upholding social views of what is appropriate regarding the size and shape of our bodies. Realizing that there were forces in operation that were out of my control, and coupled with realizing that my home life as a child and youth did not promote a healthy lifestyle or body image, I was able to liberate myself and my body from the fat-phobic dominant discourses, and to begin to see myself as more than an object to be measured and categorized. I was a product of my environment, and though my family and I made some bad choices about how to deal with my body development, I was not a bad person. I agree, health-wise, my body is probably at risk more so than some others, but I also think that thinner people have their own health risks, and that body size is not an accurate indicator of health. Knowing that most health professionals (and most of society in general) have subscribed to the belief that thin equals good and fat equals bad helps me navigate in this world. When I am held up against these discourses or have to navigate my way within them, I can do so now, and I find I no longer internalize it; I no longer allow it to become part of how I identify myself. I keep it safely contained within the context in which it operates, and I take it for what it is. I use different discourses now, interpretive ones, that allow me to process the more dominant ones, and this has helped me remain independent (mostly) of their power and control.

Conclusion

The defining grand narratives of modernity are foundationally about establishing regimes of order, rationality, and rationalization, and, of course, always creating controlling and empowering order out of chaos—the ultimate terror. The greater the regimes of rationality, the greater the societal order. The more ordered a society is, the better it functions. As such, anything named as "disorder" (and disorder has micro and macro manifestations within our society), which might disrupt order, is problematic. Therefore, our society is relentless in its necessary violence to continuously re-establish a metaphysics of the binary opposition between "order" and "disorder." In addition, the superiority of "order" must be the "winner."

Yet, in a sense, the binary requires "disorder"; indeed, the binary often manufactures it in order to perpetuate a rational response. In our Western society, disorder often becomes, then, image-body located in an identifiable "other." That means that those objectified "things" that are non-White, non-male, non-heterosexual, non-rational, and so on are "the" disordering presence. I am that disordering presence. My body represents the threat to order control of that which a minded society hates most—its own body. Again, as such, I—my representational body—must be eliminated, and the minimization-magnification tensions that I have pressed upon my body, being, and identity are manifestations of my necessary "otherness." My purpose here, then, is to proclaim—loudly—that I am also a mini-narrative. This is what it feels like to be a mini-narrative. I am that mini-narrative facing the meta-narratives of a society filled with loathing and self-hate for our physical bodies—those smelly, disintegrating, and diseased forms that retard our human destiny; which is to be pure abstraction, perfect spirit, or sublime-minded entity.

Again, my purpose in this showing and telling of my story and my research is that I want to share with others what I have learned. I want to open up conversations around the topic of the body and its images. In addition, I know that most people are just not ready for that encounter, and so when a large woman brings out the topic of large-ness, the resulting conversations generally turn defensive and critical. And, why would they not? The disorder has a voice, and dealing with it often reveals an inability to bring order to that voice.

I am still trying to find ways to deal with questions such as "what now?" What do I do with this deeper and new awareness I have found regarding the discourses of order? Although I was able to share my research findings with high-school students in different contexts, I still felt as though there was a message or lesson that I had missed through this work. I still had so many unanswered questions.

As an educated fat woman—I have an undergraduate degree and a Master of Arts degree, and I am finishing my doctorate—I am aware of the "beauty myth" (Wolf, 1990) and our society's foundational meat-narratives. Still, knowing that intellectually, I continue to wrestle with understanding the depths of how our North American society has been taught to fear "fat." Much of that stereotyping has been induced by the media, advertising, and health and marketplace industries. These industries have depicted overweight and larger women in a very negative light. We are often cast as clumsy, lazy, unmotivated, stupid, greedy, prone to over-consumption, and dirty—while thin people seem to be happily normal in every advertisement, on every television show, and in every music video. Thin persons seem to have every opportunity—travel, employability, relationships, and so on—afforded to them. The thin who are privileged in our society are depicted as having "perfect" lives, which I know is not true, but why let reality get in the way of perpetuating big lies. Especially, big—huge—lies that sell. Well, I am the collateral damage of those lies.

Having had some time since the completion of my first graduate degree, I can now recognize the dominant discourses of modernist science and medicine, and from their perspectives, they are not wrong; I am fat, and that likely has some negative impact on my health. However, what I also now understand is that there are other (sub- and/or counter-) discourses that when woven together make up a counter-narrative that questions the fabric of the ordering privilege pole of a binary oscillating between images of order and disorder. Science and medicine have their space in that fabric, and when I am sick, I certainly appreciate that they do what they do. Nevertheless, when it comes to understanding complex human beings and relationships, there are other, quieter, and non-dominant discourses that are more adequately equipped to wrestle with such a task. Beginning my doctoral program brought me to a rocky terrain on my personal academic journey. After a couple of false starts—following well-intended advice and aiming to meet funding expectations—I realized that I needed to return to this work around the female body and the relationships we women have with our own bodies within the contexts of the modernist discourses. The battle I am dealing with, between my own mind and body, is not in isolation. Women everywhere are struggling to understand their bodies, their identities, and the relationships between the two in a society seemingly and increasingly out of control, and out of control in its attempts to re-establish order.

I realize now that the dominant modernist discourses, by which I have come to mis-understand and mis-know myself, will never bring me to the answers I seek. These discourses have stripped me of a necessary visibility, they have silenced my voice, and they have created confusion and a powerlessness in my fundamental being, knowing, and doing. Until now, my mission was to "fix" myself so that I could again have value as a human being. My research has shown me that there are many discourses and counter-discourses I may select to re-activate my voice, to increase my visibility, and to create conversations that will explode the minimization-magnification tensions I live with every day.

References

Beierling, S. (2009). *Living large: A hermeneutic inquiry into what it means to live as an overweight woman* (Unpublished master's thesis). University of Calgary, Alberta, Canada.

Bordo, S. (1993). *Unbearable weight: Feminism, Western culture, and the body.* Los Angeles, CA: University of California Press.

Lord, M. G. (2004). *Forever Barbie: The unauthorized biography of a real doll.* Fredericton, New Brunswick, Canada: Goose Lane.

Lyotard, F. (1984). *The postmodern condition: A report on knowledge* (G. Bennington & B. Massumi, Trans.). Minneapolis, MN: University of Minnesota Press.

Weaver, J. (2010). *The posthuman: Biosciences, fiction, and curriculum studies.* Boston, MA: Sense.

Wolf, N. (1990). *The beauty myth.* Toronto, Ontario, Canada: Random House of Canada.

CHAPTER 22

"Breaking" Stereotypes
How Are Youth With Disability Represented in Mainstream Media?

Dana Hasson

Individuals now have more viewing choices than ever before in deciding how to spend their time with television. With the explosion of cable programming channels, many different genres of programming are competing for niche market audiences. (Hiebert & Gibbons, 2000)

I wish to draw from a theory helpful in forming an understanding of the influence that television viewing has on its audience: Information Processing Theory. This supports the argument that as individuals watch television, they use various cognitive schemas to organize the observed phenomena (Lemish, 2007). Lemish (2007) stated,

The relationship between "new" information is combined with the previously held beliefs and in other cases, the schema is modified to accommodate new information. These schemas are formed and modified throughout life; media serves as a likely influence, as the previously held schema "guides interpretation of encounters with ... TV characters. (p. 102)

Based on Lemish's notion, I began uncovering the many themes and intricacies found in characters with disability recurring in two prime-time television shows. Through thorough analysis, I was able to see patterns and relationships emerge. For the purposes of this chapter, I will be analyzing the themes, bullying and stereotyping, as they appear in *Breaking Bad* and *Glee*.

A methodological approach that was useful in helping to guide my analysis was bricolage. In his work, *The Savage Mind*, Claude Lévi-Strauss (1962) defined *bricolage* as a way to be resourceful with any materials made available. French for the verb, *bricoler*, "to fiddle" or "tinker with," this term has evolved in the world of qualitative research as a way to utilize previous ideas and theories and create new methods of interpretation. Lévi-Strauss compared the Engineer (the scientific mind) with the Bricoleur (the savage mind), as a way of depicting two modes of acquiring knowledge: concrete and abstract. Kincheloe (2001) stated, "In particular, critical bricoleurs employ historiographical, philosophical, and social theoretical lenses to gain a more complex understanding of the intricacies of research design" (p. 679).

Bricolage From an Historical Perspective

The evolution of bricolage began with post-1950 positivistic modes of research. Within the constructs of most research discourses, a standard empirical approach is taken. In their book, *Rigour and Complexity in Educational Research: Conceptualizing the Bricolage*, Kincheloe and Berry (2004) addressed, in the "traditional" sense, how the researcher is limited to a more standard way in which to approach his or her area of study. This generally consists of a sequence of questions regarding:

1. Identification and questions for study,

2. Review of previous theories and research related to research field,

3. Chosen methodology (how data will be collected, organized, and researched),

4. Report and analysis of findings from data collection, and

5. Implications and further research in said area (Kincheloe & Berry, 2004, p. 103).

On the other hand, the bricoleur rigorously follows along with a list of useful traits that helps to solidify its position in the research sphere (Kincheloe, 2008):

• To imagine things that never were

• To see the world as it could be

• To develop alternatives to oppressive existing conditions

• To discern what is lacking in a way that promotes the will to act

• To understand that there is far more to the world than what we can see.

The term, *bricoleur*, was first used by Denzin and Lincoln (2000) to describe the more modern approach taken by the qualitative researcher. They hoped that the expression, *bricoleur*, rather than, *qualitative researcher*, would paint a more succinct picture of qualitative research as a whole. Working within the trend of blurred genres in the 1970s, Denzin and Lincoln felt that including multiple methodologies and theoretical frameworks within the context of research was an additional benefit to the researcher embarking on the long and winding road of study.

Within this complex, multifaceted world of bricolage, the formation of identity from the bricoleur is critical. Schwandt (2001) quoted Denzin and Lincoln, stating that the bricoleur must be:

> Adept at performing a large number of diverse tasks ranging from interviewing to observing, to interpreting personal and historical documents, to intensive self-reflection and introspection ... [and must be one who] reads widely and is knowledgeable about the many interpretive paradigms ... that can be brought to a particular problem" (Denzin and Lincoln, 1994, p. 2). As a bricoleur, the qualitative researcher is capable of donning multiple identities—researcher, scientist, artist, critic, and performer—and engaging in different kinds of bricolage that consist of particular configurations of (or ways of relating) various fragments of inherited methodologies, methods, empirical materials, perspectives, understandings, ways of presentation, situated responsiveness, and so on to a coherent, reasoned approach to a research situation and problem. What the bricoleur produces is bricolage—a kind of pieced

together (in contrast to algorithmically guided) but structured solution to a problem. (Schwandt, 2001, pp. 20–21)

The crux of bricolage is to take apart various ideas and theories and connect them in ways useful to the bricoleur. Taken from Derrida:

Bricolage doesn't worry about the coherence of the words or ideas it uses. For example, you are a bricoleur if you talk about penis envy or the Oedipus complex and you don't know anything about psychoanalysis; you can use the terms without having to acknowledge the whole system of thought that produced these terms and ideas. (Klages, 2001, n.p.)

How I Used Bricolage

Stemming from Kincheloe and Steinberg's (1997) work on critical multiculturalism, bricolage uses an interdisciplinary approach to cultivating research. It offers a way to research a discipline without reducing it to a narrow, monolithic result.

The bricoleur uses a host of backgrounds and institutions in order to gain a more fair and balanced perspective. This becomes especially important when studying a marginalized group that is often underrepresented or misunderstood. Kincheloe discussed the significance of this approach, in terms of the researcher gaining positionality and a more democratic perspective as he or she travels the bumpy road of research. As the bricoleur supports multiple disciplines, and applies different forms of understanding to a group of individuals, he or she creates a deeper dimension of knowledge and construction (Kincheloe, 2008).

The ongoing process of asking questions and not necessarily expecting answers is what sets the bricoleur apart from other researchers. Kincheloe (2008) eloquently stated,

Appreciating research as a power-driven act, the ethnic studies researcher-as-bricoleur abandons the quest for some naïve concept of realism, focusing instead on the clarification of his or her position in the web of reality and the social locations of other researchers and the ways they shape the production and interpretation of knowledge.

As a bricoleur, I have used a wide range of tools in order to create a picture of disability and representation as a means of inhibiting identity formation. To go along with the many other theories I looked at to help inform my work, a solid definition of media culture and its overall impact on society was acutely important as a means of guidance.

The attempt to delineate a universal research method for the study of the culture curriculum and cultural pedagogy is a futile quest. The critical research of cultural studies and cultural pedagogy can make no guarantee about what questions will be important in different contexts; thus, no one method should be promoted over others—at the same time, none can be eliminated without examination. (Steinberg, 2006, p. 119)

The rapidly growing discourse of media and popular culture is taking the world of academia by storm. Nearly impossible to define, popular culture absorbs much of the responsibility for taking part in the shaping and dissemination of values on our youth. Popular culture is looked upon as the teacher and a reliable source of information; to ignore its position of power in society would be unjust.

In terms of researching the media, there are countless ways in which to compile information to prove a given theory. Whether it be through content analysis, surveys, questionnaires, or ethnographic observation, the criticality of weaving together the various disciplines in the media field will ultimately provide a rich body of work. For the purposes of my area, disability representation on popular television, I will use the bricolage approach in order to negotiate a fair and balanced study that attempts to answer some pending questions and address current ideological frameworks.

Characters and Description of Disability

The disabilities that I looked at particularly dealt with physical (wheelchair-bound or on crutches) to intellectual disabilities (Down Syndrome). The characters were between the ages of 9–18 and were attending school (elementary, high school). The majority of the characters were male coming from suburban, predominately White, middle-class neighborhoods.

1. *Glee*—Arty Abrams—Paralysis of legs (wheelchair-bound)

2. *Glee*—Becky Jackson—Down Syndrome

3. *Breaking Bad*—Walt Jr. White—Cerebral Palsy (uses crutches to walk).

Television Show	Character	Disability	Age	Types of Actor Playing Role
Glee	Arty Abrams	Paralysis of legs due to spinal-cord injury (uses wheelchair)	16	Able bodied
Glee	Becky Jackson	Down Syndrome	16	Disabled
Breaking Bad	Walt Jr. White	Cerebral Palsy (uses crutches to walk)		Disabled

Both Arty Abrams from *Glee* and Walt Jr. from *Breaking Bad* are characters with physical impairments; they are integrated fully into their classes at school.

It is not clear if the character with Down Syndrome (Becky) is integrated fully into her classes at school. She is mostly shown assisting another character (the school's cheerleading coach) and participating in extracurricular activities organized by the school (i.e., cheerleading).

Although Becky's character plays an important role on *Glee*, she does not enter until mid-way through the first season and is only featured in three episodes, "Wheels," "The Power of Madonna," and "Home."

Looking at the aspect of parental involvement, Walt Jr.'s parents from *Breaking Bad* are present and included. Walt Jr. attends the same school where his father Walt teaches.

On *Glee*, the parents of Arty Abrams and Becky Jackson never appear on the show and are not spoken of much.

Sampling and Data Collection

The shows I chose to look at for my study are all contemporary, prime-time shows airing on major cable networks, generally bringing in a high amount of viewers. According to the *Nielsen* ratings system, Fox and NBC have continuously dominated the television market, in their respective time slot, bringing in a high number of viewers on a weekly basis with shows such as *Glee* (Fox).

As of May 19th 2010 Results Time Net Show 18–49 Rating 18–49 Share Viewers Live+SD (million)
8:00
FOX American Idol 6.6 18 18.309
CBS NCIS 3.2 9 15.569
NBC The Biggest Loser 2.7 8 7.145
ABC Dancing with the Stars Results 2.5 7 13.058
CW 90210 (finale) 0.8 2 1.604
9:00
FOX Glee 4.8 12 11.588 ABC Lost 4.1 10 10.393

NBC *The Biggest Loser* 3.5 9 9.403 CBS *NCIS: LA* 3.1 8 15.230
CW *Life Unexpected* (repeat) 0.4 1 0.960
10:00
NBC *Parenthood* 2.6 7 6.238
CBS *The Good Wife* 2.3 6 12.165
ABC *V* (finale) 2.3 6 5.867
As the above chart presents, the top television show in its time slot was *Glee* (Fox, 9:00)

It is critical to emphasize the ratings that these shows brought to the networks, as this best reflects the popularity and importance of these shows on their intended audience, thus reiterating the significance of studying the particular shows I chose and their relationship to disability being distributed to a wider audience.

In each of the shows viewed, I concentrated on the first season. The reason for this was that it helped to condense the sample size, and it gave me a solid basis for grasping the early writing of the disabled character, and for watching the progress or regress as the show developed.

Each show had a varied amount of episodes in the first season, due either to the writer's strike or because of uncertainty from the networks on whether or not the show would be successful enough to merit subsequent episodes.

I looked predominantly at dramatic television series airing for 60-minute intervals. The reason for this format was that it allowed for the plot devices to be more involved and intricate. I did not look at any sitcoms (e.g., *Malcolm in the Middle*), or cartoons (e.g., *Family Guy, South Park*) because of the satirical nature of their characters and story lines. These shows oftentimes use very explicit language and are poking fun at the disabled character, creating more of a caricature rather than an "accurate" portrayal of what might be going on in the individual's life.

After looking through the various journals, books, articles, and websites related to disability studies and media, I found that much of the studies done on representations of disability in the media were done in Great Britain. There has not been much analysis done from the North American perspective on this particular topic, especially with shows that are now current and considered popular by Nielsen ratings standards, but they are discussed widely through the Internet on various social-media networks (i.e., Facebook and Twitter).

This study does not attempt to cover the whole spectrum of disability and its representations on television; rather, it looks at current images and how they have evolved more inclusively over the last fifty years or so.

I viewed the episodes on DVD and transcribed them. I stopped and started them several times in order to pick up the verbal and nonverbal cues expressed by the characters. The scenes featuring disabled characters or discussion of disabled characters were particularly sought out and noted.

I chose television as my focus because it plays a major role in households worldwide. It is both contemplative and persuasive. Because of its nature, it becomes pivotal to assess the messages generated by the programs being aired on a nightly basis. "Today's consumers are watching more TV than ever, which makes understanding what and how they're watching an essential part of any marketing campaign" (Nielsen Media Research, 2012). As the viewing audience continues to drive the direction that television programming goes in, the model of what is relevant in today's culture is set. The three shows selected for my study are in large part reflective of what is significant in our present-day philosophies. *Glee* and *Breaking Bad* have both brought in high numbers in the ratings. In 2012, *Breaking Bad* brought in its highest ratings during its finale, with 2.8 million viewers—a large showing for cable networks such as AMC in the adult 18–49 demographic (Nielsen Media Research, 2012). In 2012, *Glee* ranked #3 in the ratings for adults 18–49 with 5.43 million viewers. It was important to include this information in my study, as it is indicative of the wide spectrum of viewership for the shows analyzed over the last few seasons.

Breaking Bad

The series first premiered on cable network *AMC* in January 2008, and follows protagonist Walter White, an ordinary high-school chemistry teacher who lives in New Mexico with his wife who is expecting a child, and teenage son who has cerebral palsy (CP). Early on in the show, White is diagnosed with Stage III cancer and given a prognosis of two years to live. With a new sense of fearlessness based on his medical prognosis, and a desire to gain financial security for his family, White wearily chooses to enter the perilous world of drugs and crime and ascends to power in this world. The series follows the exploits of White, and shows his transformation from ordinary family man to a risk-taking drug lord, seeking power and control in such a treacherous environment.

Throughout the show's first season, White is trying to stay true to his family and go about his everyday life as if nothing major is going on. It takes many episodes before White reveals his cancer diagnosis to his wife and son.

The relationship between White and his son, Walt Jr., who has cerebral palsy, is strained at times because of what White is privately battling with. Walt Jr. looks up to his father, but is often shown becoming frustrated with his father's secrecy and reserve.

The bullying theme runs rampant on all of the shows I examine. *Breaking Bad*, the first episode of the series, captures this particular theme quite powerfully.

The major difference between the bullying scenes on *Breaking Bad* in comparison with *Glee* is that the parents are present as the verbal abuse is taking place, thus allowing for the intervention from the parents to occur in order to protect their son. As a result, Walt Jr. is left powerless and undermined because his father steps forward in an attempt to glamorize his role as the patriarch of the family and regain control of his family and his manhood.

This can be seen in one of the last scenes of the pilot episode. Walt Jr. is in a dressing room with his parents trying on jeans. He is clearly having some difficulty pulling the jeans on and off. His mother asks if he needs help from his father, to which he hesitantly replies, "Yes." White enters his son's dressing room and begins to help him pull his pants up. There is an intimate father-son moment revealed here and some insight of the types of difficulties Walt Jr. has faced over the years due to his CP.

When Jr. finally gets his jeans on, he steps outside of the dressing room to show his mother and look in the mirror to see if he likes the pants. This is when the themes of Bullying, Emotional Angst and Stereotyping enter the analysis. There is a group of teenage boys loudly making comments in a derogatory voice meant to mimic the speech impediment held by Walt Jr.

Both Jr. and his parents are trying to ignore the boys, but they are becoming more and more inappropriate as the scene goes on.

Walt Jr.'s mom, Skylar, wants to go over to speak to the boys and ask them to stop, but in a quiet fit of rage, Walt Senior tells her to stay put, and he walks out of the store, leaving both Skylar and Jr. in a confused state.

As the scene narrows in on the boys continuing to degrade Walt Jr., White enters the store and walks directly over to the main bully and begins kicking him in the leg. He furiously states, "What's wrong, chief, having a little trouble walking?"

(This is clearly done for the purposes of being made to, pardon the expression, "walk in someone else's shoes".)

The boy who is being attacked is shocked and angry by what Walt Senior is doing to him as his other two cohorts watch frozen in a panic.

The mood of the scene shifts into that of Walt Senior being turned into a hero of sorts and truly acting like the patriarch of his family, displaying "authentic" masculinity for defending his son. Through analysis, the themes that continuously emerged during the episode were:

Breaking Bad subthemes

> **Role of Mother/Wife (femininity)**
> **Patriarch/Role of Gender (masculinity)**
> **Visible Disability Portrayed**
> **Disability not Visible but Audible**
> **Family Acceptance**
> **Requiring Assistance From Others**
> **Emotional Angst**
> **Internal Struggle**
> **Emotional Bullying**
> **Stereotyping**
> **Relating to Others**

Below, the scene plays out as follows:

37:12 New Scene (Dressing Room of a clothing store)

Visible Disability Portrayed
(Walt Jr. is in the dressing room trying on a pair of jeans. His crutches are leaning up against the wall as he sits in a chair pulling his pants up)
(Skylar and Walt are waiting outside the dressing room … the audience hears Skylar's voice from outside the room)

Role of Mother/Wife (femininity)
SKYLAR: How is it going in there?

Visible Disability Portrayed
JR: (sounding frustrated, struggling to pull up pants) Fine …

Role of Mother/Wife (femininity)
SKYLAR: (having gone through this before) Do you want me or your dad?

Visible Disability Portrayed
JR: (sighing and defeated) Dad …

Patriarch/Role of Gender (masculinity)/Family Acceptance/Visible Disability Portrayed/ Requiring Assistance From Others
(Walt enters the dressing room picking Jr. up by the waist and helping him to pull up the jeans …. Jr. holds Walt around the neck allowing him to assist)
(Scene cuts to outside the dressing room where Jr. is standing in front of a mirror as his parents ask him how the jeans fit)

Role of Mother/Wife (femininity)
SKYLAR: So how are those feeling in the waist? Are they too tight cause you don't want to get them if they are too tight.

Relating to Others/Visible Disability Portrayed
JR: (stuttering slightly) They … they are pre-shrunk.

(In the background of the store are a group of high school boys Jr.'s age looking at him as he is standing in front of the mirror with his parents' help to figure out if the jeans he is wearing are comfortable … they are smiling and making comments)

Role of Mother/Wife (femininity)
SKYLAR: Are you sure you don't want to get a different kind … like the skinny jeans cause those are really supposed to be in style now. The skaters wear them.

Emotional Angst
(The volume of the boys' laughter and harassment is getting louder and more apparent …. Walt starts to take notice while Skylar and Jr. continue discussing his jeans, not taking notice)

Internal Struggle/Visible Disability Portrayed
JR: (irritated) Do I look like a skater?

Role of Mother/Wife (femininity)/Emotional Angst
SKYLAR: (gently) All right …
(She begins to hear the boys and looks toward them)

(The camera zooms in on one of the boys making blatant fun of Jr., holding up a pair of jeans to his waist and mimicking his voice)

Emotional Bullying/Stereotyping
BOY 1: (making his voice sound distorted) Look at my big boy pants …
(Laughter from friends)
(Skylar gives them the look of death and Jr. bows his head down in frustration as Walt is fuming, about to confront them)
Mommy, could you zip up my big boy pants …
(More laughter)

Internal Struggle
(Skylar turns toward them, about to go talk to them, and Walt grabs her by the hand, stopping her)

Patriarch/Role of Gender (masculinity)/Emotional Angst
WALT: Don't … don't.

Role of Mother/Wife (femininity)
SKYLAR: (not understanding) Walt!
(Jr. and Skylar watch as Walt walks away angrily … confused as to where he is going)

Internal Struggle/Relating to Others
JR: Where …?

Role of Mother/Wife (femininity)/Emotional Angst
SKYLAR: I have no idea … (walking over to Jr. and putting her hand on his back).
You know what you don't even have to look at them. They are obviously very stupid.
(Jr. nods his head in agreement, distributing his weight around on either crutch/leg … Skylar is still standing behind him)

Internal Struggle/Emotional Angst

I think that um … I think those jeans look really good on you … I think you should get them if you like them … (Jr.'s head is still tilted down). Okay. You know why don't you just hang out here for a second. I'll be right back.

Emotional Bullying/Stereotyping

BOY 1: (with impediment) Oh no …. Hey mommy I think I pinched a loaf in my brand new big boy pants.

(Skylar starts to walk toward the boys as Jr. remains standing in front of mirror near dressing room, at the same time Walt comes charging through the front doors of the store)

(Skylar sees him looking angry and watches him as he charges at the boy making fun of Jr. Walt pushes him down to the floor and begins stomping on his leg. The boy is totally taken by surprise and asks … the other store patrons look on quietly)

BOY 1: (in shock) What the hell are you doing?

Patriarch/Role of Gender (masculinity)/Emotional Angst

WALT: (with a deep look of rage on his face) What's wrong, chief, having a little trouble walking? (Walt continues to step on the boy's leg with all his strength)

BOY 1: (in agony) Get off me … get off me now!
(Walt finally stops and the boy gets up quickly, facing Walt with anger … he is clearly much bigger and taller than Walt … his peers are behind him speechless)
I will mess you up, man.

Patriarch/Role of Gender (masculinity)/Emotional Angst

WALT: (not backing down) Well, you will have one shot … you better make it good.
(The boy contemplates hitting him)
What are you waiting for, your girlfriends? You better go … you better go … take it … take your shot … (loudly) take it!
(Skylar and Jr. look at Walt and how he is acting in complete shock)
Come on … come on.
(The boy is continuing to look into Walt's eyes, clearly backing down … his friend puts his hand on his shoulder to pull him away)

BOY 2: Come on, let's get out of here.
Let's go …

BOY 1: (getting in the last word … shocked he was stood up to) Psycho!

Emotional Acceptance

(The three boys walk out of the store together, constantly looking back at Walt, totally taken aback by what he has just done …. Skylar and Jr. are without words, their eyes big … pride creeping up to their faces.

Walt has a satisfactory smile plastered on his face as he watches the boys exiting the store)
POWERFUL MOMENT

39:48 Scene Ends

GLEE

The premise of *Glee* features a group of high-school students (the majority are outcasts) who have a love of singing and performance. The focus stays primarily on the glee club students; they are The New Directions, and the audience watches the students' many trials and tribulations while in high school competing on the choir competition circuit. As the show weaves in musical performances of everything from old standards, popular and/or contemporary music, and Broadway tunes, its members deal with issues pertaining to disabilities, relationships, race, sexuality, and social issues. The first season officially ran from September 9, 2009 to June 8, 2010.

Bullying and stereotypes

During Season 1, the story lines concerning bullying and stereotyping are prevalent in the first few episodes. In the pilot, the audience is introduced to Arty Abrams's character, a submissive, quiet adolescent who is confined to his wheelchair. Intellectually, Arty functions at a "normal" level with his peers. What helps integrate Arty into the mix with his peers is his love for music and performing.

Overall, the status of the glee-club students is low, and they are not received well by the other students at the school (i.e., football players, cheerleaders, "popular" students). Therefore, bullying is prevalent for all of the students involved in the club.

There are substantial representations of other marginalized groups such as homosexuals and African Americans. In addition, the glee-club students are constantly bombarded by bullies, and often get slushy drinks thrown in their faces.

In the scene below, the transcript illustrates Arty at the center of a bullying tirade by one of the stars of the football team, Puck and his posse. There is a strong sense of helplessness and entrapment, as Arty is being held violently inside a port-a-potty.

The basis for the bullying at this point stems from Puck's anger toward Finn, a former teammate of Puck's, who quit the football team to join the glee club; the rest of the team looks at this as weak and effeminate. Arty is used as the bait, because he is in the most vulnerable position, physically. When Puck expresses to Finn that they have the "wheelchair kid inside" the port-a-potty and that he plans to flip it over with Arty still inside, Finn recognizes the danger and attempts to alert Puck, but Puck ignorantly makes the statement, "he's already in a wheelchair." The exchange between Puck and Finn over Arty's well-being puts them in positions of power and authority over Arty because he is in a wheelchair and unable to break free of confinement.

Ignoring Puck's threats, Finn finally opens the door to an extremely grateful Arty. Arty is overwhelmed with fear and disgust at the smell of the toilet where he was trapped. Puck continuously refers to Arty as a loser, as are the other glee-club members, referring to the club as a "Homoexplosion." The scene is laced with derogatory slurs and intolerance. Arty feels a sense of empowerment with Finn by his side, and as the scene ends, he hisses at Puck and the other members of the football team, able to finally retaliate with the support of an able-bodied person by his side.

Glee subthemes

Visible Disability Portrayed
Associated Disability Portrayed
No Mention of Disability
Negative View of Disability
Stereotyping
Submitting to Negativity
Educator: Submitting to Negativity
Implicit
Intolerance

Sense of Belonging
Role of Educator
Helplessness
Needs Rescuing
CONFIDENCE BUILDS
Effect of Music
Fear of Being Bullied
Integration
Negative Association
Frustration
Empathy From Others
Demeaning
Submitting to Negativity
Other Disabilities Mentioned
Administration
Discrimination
Peers: Insensitivity
Using Disability as a Means to Own Advantage
Accessibility
Needs Rescuing
Empathy
Misusing Disability
Creating Awareness
Personal Connection
Frustration
No Mention of Disability
Associated Disability Portrayed: Deafness
RACE
MARGINALIZATION
POWER

(New Scene: Football field)

(Finn and other teammates are outside at practice. One of Finn's teammates (Puck) is trying to get Finn back onto the football team since he quit glee club.

Empathy From Others
FINN: I quit, anything else?

Discrimination/Peers: Insensitivity
PUCK: That's it and as a welcome back to the world of the normal, I got you a present.
(Finn looks on as Puck walks over to port-a-potties in the back of the bleachers ... close up of Arty squeezed into one of the bathrooms struggling to get out. Moaning and pleading while the rest of the football team look on with pleasure)

Helplessness
ARTY: Help!! Help!!

Empathy From Others
FINN: Is someone in there?

Helplessness/Needs Rescuing/Stereotyping/Demeaning
PUCK: We got that wheelchair kid inside. We are going to flip it.

Empathy From Others
FINN: Isn't that kind of dangerous?

Helplessness/Needs Rescuing/Stereotyping/Demeaning
PUCK: He's already in a wheelchair. Come on, we saved you the first role.

Empathy From Others
FINN: (shakes his head no, and opens door where Arty is. Gasps at smell)

Helplessness/Needs Rescuing
ARTY: (Relieved) Thank you, thank you so much. Thank you. My god, the smell.

Helplessness/Needs Rescuing/Stereotyping/Demeaning
PUCK: What the hell, dude? I can't believe you are helping out this loser.

Empathy From Others
FINN: Don't you get it, man? We are all losers. Everyone in this school. Everyone in this town. Out of all the kids that graduate maybe half will go to college and two will leave the state to do it. I am not afraid of being called a loser cause that is what I am. But I am afraid of turning my back on something that actually made me happy for the first time in my solid life.

Discrimination/Peers: Insensitivity/Stereotyping/Demeaning
PUCK: So what are you quitting to join, Homoexplosion?

Empathy From Others
FINN: No, I am doing both. You can't win without me and neither could they.

CONFIDENCE BUILDS
ARTY: Hiss (exuding more confidence with Finn by his side. Finn wheels him away)
(Jocks look on)

Comparison of Bullying Scenes

In both of the shows researched for this study, there is at least one scenario that involved bullying of the disabled character. In *Breaking Bad* and *Glee*, the characters are rescued by an able-bodied individual, and the bullying starts off with slurs. The disabled character is already in a weakened position, because he is either caught off guard or physically unable to defend himself.

The bullying scenarios in *Breaking Bad* and *Glee* differ because of the acute awareness the characters have of what is going on toward them when they are being targeted.

Discussion

The purpose of this study was to examine the various themes related to disability, particularly youth with disability, in order to get a better sense of how popular television programs include this population in their repertoire. This work builds upon previous work in the field of disability, media, and critical youth studies.

For the sample, two prime-time television programs, one airing on a major network (Fox) and the other one on a cable network (AMC) were chosen. I looked specifically at episodes featured in season one, each an hour long. Through thematic analysis, major themes related to depictions of contemporary disability emerged in these dramas. After rigorous note-taking and episode-viewing, I sorted through the many themes that continuously emerged.

The first of the major themes focused on bullying and stereotyping; inclusively depicting situations involving a disabled adolescent. Bullying and stereotyping were particularly touched upon in all of the shows looked at for this study. Under the bullying umbrella, the subthemes included:

Breaking Bad—visible disability portrayed, relating to others, requiring assistance from others, emotional angst, internal struggle, stereotyping, emotional acceptance, empathy from others

Glee—discrimination, peers: insensitivity, helplessness, needs rescuing, demeaning, confidence builds.

Looking at the two shows, the one common thread in each of the bullying subthemes is the internal struggle faced by each character being bullied. The sense of helplessness and emotional angst from their situation is visibly displayed by facial expressions and body language. The two characters, Arty (*Glee*) and Walt Jr. (*Breaking Bad*), who have visible disabilities for which they are being ridiculed, share a common experience. Both characters are assisted by an able-bodied third party to get out of their toxic situation. For Arty (*Glee*) it is another peer from the glee club, and for Walt Jr. (*Breaking Bad*) it is his father.

Both shows clearly articulate the effect bullying has on their ability to develop peer relationships and feel secure in their own skin.

Another common theme found while viewing was the role that education and educators play in relation to the problems faced by the disabled individual. The subthemes are: *Glee*—role of educator, administration, negative view of disability, stereotyping, discrimination, integration, visible disability portrayed, helplessness, insensitivity, submitting to negativity.

In *Glee*, the character, Arty, is not only being mistreated by his peers, but at times the school administration is responsible for the injustices seen at the school. For example, the school does not have the proper accommodations for Arty and his wheelchair, therefore, the principal is spoken to by a concerned teacher. Due to lack of funds, there is no way to provide the proper ramps for Arty to comfortably get around in certain areas of the school, and, more importantly, to ride on the bus with the other students in glee club.

Glee addresses the role that educators and educational institutions play in the potential for success of the disabled student. The decisions being made by the administration can create an ample learning environment for the student. Through their disabled characters, *Glee* attempts to address the subject of education and functionality within the school setting.

A third theme looked at was that of inclusion and a building of relationships between the disabled character and their "able"-bodied peers. Both shows examined represented this theme in different forms; the subthemes somewhat overlap with the themes found when discussing the role of education and educational institutions. In *Glee*, the character, Becky Jackson, adds another dimension to the study, because she is an actress who has Down Syndrome. The topic of inclusion is best exhibited during the scene where Becky is trying out for the cheerleading squad. She is receiving no special treatment from the coach, which at first upsets one of the teachers sitting in on the auditions. The initial reaction is that the coach is insensitive and unfeeling, but the audience later learns that she has a sister also living with Down Syndrome who she adores and looks up to. *Glee* never harps on Becky's Down Syndrome as a negative thing, nor does the show go into any depth as to how living with Down Syndrome in a mainstream school may affect her ability to fit in or learn.

In *Breaking Bad*, Walt Jr. attends a mainstream school, and has no known learning problems. Due to his cerebral palsy, visibly, Walt Jr. walks with crutches and has some facial disfigurement when he speaks. There is little discussion about his disability. It does come up in a scene where there is a family meeting about his father's cancer diagnosis. Other than that, Walt Jr.'s character has an inclusive role in the show, and his disability is not the main focus.

A fourth theme appearing on *Glee* and *Breaking Bad* was misusing disability for the purposes of gaining. This theme considered the subthemes: *Glee*—role of educator, misusing disability, educating (teachable moments); *Breaking Bad*—visible disability portrayed, sense of belonging, acceptance from peers, stereotyping, demeaning, inauthentic peers, power struggle.

In *Glee*, the students in the glee club decide to come together in the episode, "Wheels," to help raise money for a wheelchair-friendly bus that would allow Arty to ride to sectionals with his fellow classmates instead of separately. Will, the glee-club teacher, attempts to make this a teachable moment, instructing his students to try getting around in a wheelchair for a week, in order to get a sense of what Arty goes through on a daily basis. This addresses the issue of inaccessibility in the public domain. Finn takes advantage of the opportunity he has with his wheelchair, and decides to demand a job that at one time was not available, using the wheelchair as a ploy to get the manager to agree to hire him, exploiting his temporary handicap in order to gain a position and empathy from others.

In the same episode, a similar situation occurs when the character, Puck, fakes a spinal-cord injury and uses his wheelchair to get medical marijuana from another teacher. Once again, the character is looking for a false sense of compassion in order to benefit from his temporary handicap.

The theme entitled building relationships ties in with the misuse of disability theme. Once again, *Glee* illustrates an able-bodied student who is faking a disability in order to get attention. The character, Tina, fakes having a stutter, in order to push others away so they do not judge her for being a "weird" person. Her fake stutter empowered her to be judged for something others can actually grasp, giving them an excuse to make fun of her.

In *Breaking Bad*, Walt Jr. is standing outside of a convenience store with two "friends." The boys are underage and scoping out a willing adult who would buy them alcohol. As the boys continuously get turned down, Walt Jr.'s visible crutches become a potential source of gaining. The boys seek to misuse Jr.'s disability as their source of power to obtain their desired outcome. When one of the store patrons tricks them into thinking he is on board and turns out to be an undercover police officer, the able-bodied boys let Walt Jr. take the fall, not caring about what might happen to him.

In both *Glee* and *Breaking Bad*, the misuse of disability for the purposes of gaining seeks to expose the many injustices facing the disabled individual, who does not have the choice of turning their disability off.

In the shows analyzed, disability is not a mainstay of the shows' story lines. While the characters play a significant role in the shows' content, they are not central to the shows' plot lines; they play supporting roles, and are featured intermittently throughout season one.

Limitations

While conducting any type of study using a proposed methodology, there are limitations that will arise. One of the first stipulations found while conducting my study was that there was a limited ability to make general assumptions about each program viewed. Only the first season of each show was viewed for content, therefore, the future story lines featuring those characters with disability are not known. The main purpose of this study is to provide a substantial overview of the overarching themes, messages, and representations of youth living with disability on television. This study also delves deeper into how television transmits messages about disability during a short period of time (a season's worth lasting a few months), allowing the audience to get a brief but albeit ample look at disability and the many issues that arise for young individuals (ages 13–18) with disability. The sample of the television shows chosen were hour-long dramas, with the exception of *Glee*, which is considered a musical comedy-drama. Keeping the focus on youth with disability eliminated other television shows with characters in different age ranges living with disability. The popular genre of reality-television programs was not included in the study, limiting some important dialogue and trends featuring youth with disability in a "real" sense. The individuals on programs such as *Little People Big World*, *The Littlest Couple*, and *The Biggest Loser* do live with disability, and would be able to provide a more accurate and authentic view of living with disability on a daily basis. Future research could analyze the portrayal of disability across a wide variety of programming types, including depictions from other countries. Another aspect of research that could be looked at further, is character development in subsequent seasons. Limiting my research to Season 1 of the three shows chosen negates some of the more intricate writing and situations featuring disability later on in the shows' future seasons. It is imperative to note that a global view of disability is not a stated goal of qualitative research, which seeks instead to provide an in-depth analysis of a situation. This study does not intend to provide a generalized understanding of how disability is portrayed on television, it attempts to provide an analysis of how youth with disability are presented at one distinct point in time in one popular genre of a TV show.

Conclusion

The current chapter has identified multiple themes and character-driven situations related to disability on popular prime-time television programs. Such representations of disabled youth transmit both positive and negative messages about their place in society. These messages are consistent with the difficulty producers and writers are faced with while attempting to fairly and accurately represent a marginalized group of individuals in the mainstream media. It is important to note that the television shows used for this study are doing their best to highlight recurring issues such as the ones described above. These perhaps are the most obvious forms of dealing with a subject matter as sensitive as disability in the mainstream, but at least some attempt is being made. There is always a flawed sense of accuracy, and it is difficult to fully encompass the different areas of disability worthy of depiction.

Mainstream television has come a long way from the days of the telethon. Although negative images of disability still do exist through characters such as Timmy on *South Park*, who is wheelchair-bound and has a speech impediment, there has been a more concerted effort to start a dialogue about disability and represent youth, a population so easily swayed by what is considered popular culture. To include characters with various disabilities shows a concentrated effort to balance a usually marginalized group and illustrate a type of acceptance.

References

Americans with Disabilities Act of 1990, Pub. L. No. 101–336, 104 Stat. 328 (1990).

Barnes, C. (2003). What a difference a decade makes: Reflections on doing 'emancipatory' disability research. *Disability & Society*, *18*(1), 1, 3–17.

Barnes, C., & Mercer, G. (2003). *Disability*. Malden, MA: Blackwell.

Barnes, C., Mercer, G., & Shakespeare, T. (1999). *Exploring disability: A sociological introduction*. Cambridge, UK: Polity Press.

Barthes, R. (1992). The structuralist activity. In H. Adams (Ed.), *Critical theory since Plato* (Rev. ed., pp. 1128–1133). New York, NY: Harcourt Brace Jovanovich.

Berry, G. L., & Asamen, J. K. (Eds). (1993). *Children and television: Images in a changing sociocultural world*. Newbury Park, CA: Sage.

Betts, R. (2004). *A history of popular culture: More of everything, faster and brighter*. New York, NY: Routledge.

Bourdieu, P. (1984). *Distinction: A social critique of the judgement of taste*. London, UK: Routledge.

Braun, V., & Clarke, V. (2006). Using thematic analysis in psychology. *Qualitative Research in Psychology*, *3*(2) 77–101.

Butler-Kisber, L. (2010). *Qualitative inquiry: Thematic, narrative and arts-informed perspectives*. Thousand Oaks, CA: Sage.

Clogston, J. (1990). *Disability coverage in 16 newspapers*. Louisville, KY: Avocado Press.

Cook, D. (1996). *The culture industry revisited: Theodor Adorno on mass culture*. Lanham, MD: Rowman and Littlefield.

Corker, M. (1999). 'Disability': The unwelcome ghost at the banquet … and the conspiracy of 'normality.' *Body and Society*, *5*(4), 75–83.

Corker, M., & Shakespeare, T. (2006). *Disability/postmodernity: Embodying disability theory*. London, UK: Continuum.

Dahl, M. (1993). The role of the media in promoting images of disability—Disability as metaphor: The evil crip. *Canadian Journal of Communication*. Retrieved from http://cjconline.ca/index.php/journal/article/view/718/624

Dansforth, S., & Gabel, S. (2006). *Vital questions facing disability studies in education*. New York, NY: Peter Lang.

Davies, J. (1996). *Educating students in a media saturated culture*. Lancaster, PA: Technomic.

Davis, L. (2006). *The disability studies reader*. New York, NY: Routledge.

Denzin, N. K., & Lincoln, Y. S. (Eds.). (2000). *Handbook of qualitative research* (2nd ed.). Thousand Oaks, CA: Sage.

Disability. (n.d.). In the World Health Organization. Retrieved from http://www.who.int/en/

Doob, C. B. (1994). *Sociology: An introduction*. Boston, MA: Harcourt.

du Gay, P. (1997). Organizing identity: Making up people at work. In P. du Gay, *Production of culture/cultures of production* (pp. 285–345). Thousand Oaks, CA: Open University.

du Gay, P., Hall, S., James, L., Mackay, H., & Negus, K. (1997). *Doing cultural studies: The story of the Sony Walkman*. Thousand Oaks, CA: Open University.

Flecha, R., Gomez, J., & Puigvert, L. (2001). *Contemporary sociological theory*. New York, NY: Peter Lang.

Foucault, M. (1992). *The uses of pleasure*. In M. Foucault, *The history of sexuality: Volume two* (R. Hurley, Trans., pp. 10–11). Harmondsworth, UK: Penguin.

Gangrene. (n.d.). National Library of Medicine. Retrieved from http://www.nlm.nih.gov/databases/

Gardner, J. M., & Radel, M. (1978). Portrait of the disabled in the media. *Journal of Community Psychology, 6*(3), 269–274.

Gebner, G., Gross, L., Morgan, M., Signorielli, N., & Shanahan, J. (2002). Growing up with television: Cultivation processes. In J. Bryant & D. Zillmann (Eds.), *Media effects: Advances in theory and research* (2nd ed., pp. 43–67). Mahwah, NJ: Lawrence Erlbaum.

Gilligan, V. (Writer & Director). (2008, January 20). Pilot [Television series episode]. In V. Gilligan (Producer), *Breaking Bad*. Santa Monica, CA: High Bridge Productions.

Guest, G., MacQueen K., & Namey, E. (2012). *Applied thematic analysis*. Thousand Oaks, CA: Sage.

Haller, B. (2006). *Disability and mass communication*. Retrieved from www.natcom.org

Hiebert, R. E., & Gibbons, S. J. (2000). *Exploring mass media for a changing world*. Mahwah, NJ: Lawrence Erlbaum.

Houston, B. (2000). Viewing television: The metapsychology of endless consumption. In M. T. Caroll & E. Tafoya (Eds.), *Phenomenological approaches to popular culture*. Bowling Green, Ohio: Bowling Green State University Popular Press.

Johnson, S. (2006). *Everything bad is good for you*. New York, NY: Penguin.

Kellner, D. (1994). *Media culture: Cultural studies, identity, and politics between the modern and the postmodern*. London, UK: Routledge.

Kincheloe, J. L. (2001). Describing the bricolage: Conceptualizing a new rigor in qualitative research. *Qualitative Inquiry, 7*(6), 679–692.

Kincheloe, J. L. (2005). *Critical constructivism*. New York, NY: Peter Lang.

Kincheloe, J. L. (2008). Bricolage and the quest for multiple perspectives: New approaches to research in ethnic studies. In T. P. Fong (Ed.), *Ethnic studies research: Approaches and perspectives* (pp. 313–352). Lanham, MD: AltaMira Press.

Kincheloe, J. L., & Berry, K. S. (2004). *Rigour and complexity in educational research: Conceptualizing the bricolage*. Maidenhead, UK: Open University Press.

Kincheloe, J. L., & Steinberg, S. R. (2007). *Changing multiculturalism*. Philadelphia, PA: Open University Press.

Klages, M. (2001). *Structure, sign, and play in the discourse of the human sciences*. Retrieved from http://www.webpages.uidaho.edu/~sflores/KlagesDerrida.html

Kroeber, L., & Kluckhohn, C. (1952). *Culture: A critical review of concepts and definitions*. New York, NY: Random House.

Leder, D. (1990). *The absent body*. Chicago, IL: University of Chicago Press.

Lemesianou, C., & Grinberg, J. (2006). Criticality in education research. In K. Tobin & J. Kincheloe (Eds.), *Doing educational research: A handbook* (pp. 211–233). Rotterdam, The Netherlands: Sense.

Lemish, D. (2007). *Children and television: A global perspective*. Malden, MA: Blackwell.

Lévi-Strauss, C. (1962). *The savage mind*. London, UK: Weidenfeld and Nicolson.

Longmore, P. (2003). Screening stereotypes: Images of disabled people in television and motion pictures. In P. Longmore, *Why I burned my book and other essays on disability* (pp. 131–146). Philadelphia, PA: Temple University Press.

McLuhan, M. (1962). *The Gutenberg galaxy: The making of typographic man*. Toronto, Canada: University of Toronto Press.

McLuhan, M. (1964). *Understanding media: The extensions of man*. Cambridge, MA: MIT Press.

McLuhan, M., Fiore, Q., & Agel, J. (1967). *The medium is the massage: An inventory of effects*. New York, NY: Bantam Books.

McRuer, R. (2006). We were never identified: Feminism, queer theory, and a disabled world. *Radical History Review, 94*, 148–154.

Merrin, W. (2005). *Baudrillard and the media*. Cambridge, UK: Polity Press.

Mittell, J. (2004). A cultural approach to television genre theory. In R. C. Allen & A. Hill (Eds.), *The television studies reader* (pp. 171–181). London, UK: Routledge.

Murphy, R. (Writer & Director), Falchuck, B. (Writer), & Brennan, I. (Writer). (2009, May 19). Pilot [Television series episode]. In V. Gilligan (Producer), *Glee*. USA: Brad Falchuk Teley-Vision, Ryan Murphy Productions, 20th Century Fox Television.

The National Institute of Child Health and Human Development. Retrieved from http://www.nichd.nih.gov

Nielsen Media Research. (2012). *TV measurement.* Retrieved from http://www.nielsen.com/us/en/nielsen-solutions/nielsen-measurement/nielsen-tv-measurement.html

Oliver, M. (1996). *Understanding disability: From theory to practice.* Houndmills, UK: Palgrave.

Overboe, J. (1999). "Difference in itself": Validating disabled people's lived experience. *Body and Society, 5*(4): 17–29. Thousand Oaks, CA: Sage.

Philosophy. (n.d.). *Stanford Encyclopedia of Philosophy.* Retrieved from http://plato.stanford.edu/

Pointon, A., & Davies, C. (Eds.). (1997). *Framed: Interrogating disability in the media.* London, UK: BFI.

Postman, N. (1979). *Teaching as a conserving activity.* New York, NY: Delacorte Press.

Postman, N. (1985, December 4). Commentary: Learning in the age of television. *Education Week.* Retrieved from http://www.edweek.org/ew/articles/1985/12/04/06120030.h05.html

Postman, N. (1994). *The disappearance of childhood.* New York, NY: Vintage/Random House.

Roper, L. (2003). Disability in the media. *The Media Education Journal.* Retrieved from http://www.miusa.org/idd/resources/files/mediaresources/disabmedia/view

Ross, K. (1997). But where's me in it?: Disability, broadcasting and the audience: Commentary. *Media Culture and Society, 19*(4), 669–677.

Rothenberg, P. (1998). The construction, deconstruction, and reconstruction of difference. In L. Harris (Ed.), *Racism* (pp. 281–296.) Amherst, NY: Humanity Books.

Sardar, Z., & Van Loon, B. (2010). *Introducing cultural studies: A graphic guide.* London, UK: Totem Books.

Schwandt, T. A. (2001). *Dictionary of qualitative inquiry.* Thousand Oaks, CA: Sage.

Schwoch, J., White, M., & Reilly, S. (1992). *Media knowledge: Readings in popular culture, pedagogy, and critical citizenship.* Albany, NY: State University of New York Press.

Share, J. (2009). *Media literacy is elementary: Teaching youth to critically read and create.* New York, NY: Peter Lang.

Siebers, T. (2008). *Disability theory.* Ann Arbor, Michigan: University of Michigan Press.

Sprafkin, J., Gadow, K. D., & Abelman, R. (1992). *Television and the exceptional child: A forgotten audience.* Hillsdale, NJ: Lawrence Erlbaum.

Steinberg, S. (2006). Critical cultural studies research: Bricolage in action. In K. Tobin & J. Kincheloe (Eds.), *Doing educational research: A handbook* (pp. 117–138). Rotterdam, The Netherlands: Sense.

Steinberg, S. (2011). *Kinderculture: The corporate construction of childhood* (3rd ed.). Boulder, CO: Westview Press.

Steinberg, S., & Cannella, G. (2012). *Critical qualitative research reader.* New York, NY: Peter Lang.

Steinberg, S., & Kincheloe, J. (2004). *Kinderculture: The corporate construction of childhood* (2nd ed.). Boulder, CO: Westview Press.

Storey, J. (2001). *Cultural theory and popular culture: An introduction.* Essex, UK: Pearson.

Storey, J. (2003). *Cultural studies and the study of popular culture.* Atlanta, GA: University of Georgia Press.

Sullivan, M., & Lysaker, J. T. (1992). Between impotence and illusion: Adorno's art of theory and practice. *New German Critique, 57,* 87–122.

Talbot, M. (2007). *Media discourse: Representation and interaction.* Edinburgh, Scotland: Edinburgh University Press.

Tobin, K., & Kincheloe, J. (2006). Doing educational research in a complex world. In K. Tobin & J. Kincheloe (Eds.), *Doing educational research: A handbook* (pp. 3–13). Rotterdam, The Netherlands: Sense.

Wallach Bologh, R. (1991). Learning from feminism: Social theory and intellectual vitality. In C. Lemert (Ed.), *Intellectuals and politics: Social theory in a changing world* (pp. 31–46). London, UK: Sage.

CHAPTER 23

She's the Man

Deconstructing the Gender and Sexuality Curriculum at "Hollywood High"

Elizabeth J. Meyer

Movies about the high school experience are popular at the box office and influential in constructing cultural notions about what constitutes normal and ideal high school experiences. From John Hughes' popular films such as *Sixteen Candles* (1984), *The Breakfast Club* (1985), *Ferris Buehler's Day Off* (1986a), and *Pretty in Pink* (1986b), to more contemporary examples such as *Bring It On* (Bendinger, 2000), *10 things I Hate about You* (Lutz & Smith, 1999), the *High School Musical* franchise (Barsocchini, 2006), and the *Twilight* (Rosenberg & Meyer, 2008) saga, these films present scripts and expectations for teen relationships and high school life and exemplify the concept of "Hollywood High." With few exceptions, these films focus exclusively on heterosexual relationships based in suburban schools with predominantly White students. These representations of adolescent sexuality create and perpetuate the dominance of suburban White heterosexual experiences as ideal and iconic. As a result, the stories and characters in these films contribute to the construction of the gender and sexuality curriculum at "Hollywood High."

Masculinity and femininity are ideals that are carefully constructed, performed, and enforced in North American society (Bem, 1993; Butler, 1990; Meyer, 2008, 2009; West & Zimmerman, 1987). Films and television shows that focus on adolescence and the high school experience teach and reinforce dominant notions of valued masculinity and femininity through the scripts, casting, and costuming of characters (McKinley, 1997; Meyer, 2007b; Resnick, 2008). Although many teen films could provide an interesting text for a deeper analysis of gender codes and how they relate to sexual ideals and identities, this chapter will focus on two films that explicitly play with gender: *She's the Man* (Leslie, Lutz, & Smith, 2006) and *Just One of the Guys* (Feldman & Franklin, 1985). In both of these films, a female protagonist chooses to change schools and cross-dress in order to pass as a male student for a short period of time. This decision is motivated by a feminist goal of proving her competence in historically male-dominated domains: athletics and journalism. This chapter will explore how these films present masculinity, femininity, and heterosexuality in order to better understand how cultural codes work to police gender conformity and punish those whose gender or sexuality exist in the "outer limits" of the sex hierarchy (Rubin, 1984/1993). By deconstructing and making explicit this curriculum, my aim is to provide educators a sample of how critical media literacy (Steinberg, 2004) combined with queer pedagogy (Britzman, 1995; Meyer, 2007a) can work to support the objectives of a democratic sexuality curriculum and make explicit these messages in order to dismantle the hegemonic power embedded in these pop culture texts.

Although these films were made almost 20 years apart, they share several common themes. These themes and excerpts from the films will be presented from a post-structural feminist and queer lens to illustrate how heteronormativity and post-feminism in mainstream Hollywood films limit and marginalize diverse gender and sexual expressions and identities. Post-structural feminism is used as the primary lens for analysis as it encourages a reading of gender that questions the existing binaries of masculinity and femininity as fixed and tied directly to one's sex as male or female. As Norman Denzin explains, "Poststructuralism is that theoretical position which asks how the human subject is constructed in and through the structures of language and ideology" (1993, p. 204). He explains what this means in the context of gender and sexuality:

> Gender and sexuality arise out of the complex interactions that connect the texts, meanings, and experiences that circulate in everyday life, with the things the members of our culture tell one another about being men and women. Stories in the daily newspaper, in social science articles, comic books, daytime TV soap operas, nighttime family comedies, and melodramas, and in large box-office-drawing films … reproduce the gender stratification order. (Denzin, 1993, p. 202)

Queer theory builds on post-structuralism and pushes readers to question how practices of normalcy are repeated and maintained—particularly in regards to gender and sexuality. These two theoretical approaches encourage viewers to read against the grain and question taken-for-granted assumptions about masculinity, femininity, and sexuality in these and other texts. How these approaches differ from post-feminism will be discussed at the end of the chapter.

By making these messages more explicit to audiences, educators can help develop students' abilities to more critically engage with media texts and decide what influence these texts will have over their own lives. To introduce viewers to the characters and their challenges, these Hollywood-produced (Columbia & Dreamworks) films frame their stories in similar ways: first they establish the heterosexual desirability of the lead female character and then present the crisis of gender injustice that she must face.

Bikinis and Boyfriends: Establishing "Het Cred"

In the opening sequence of both films the viewers are introduced to the lead female protagonist's body in various states of undress. In the opening sequence of *Just One of the Guys* (*JootG*), the camera slowly pans up a pair of naked, fair, thin, hairless legs to reveal our heroine, Terry, sleeping in lacy, two-piece lingerie. Within the first two minutes the audience is also introduced to her White, blonde, college boyfriend, who picks her up in his sports car to take her to school. In *She's the Man* (*StM*), the opening sequence focuses on a beach scene where the lead character, Viola, is shown playing soccer in a string bikini and celebrating a goal with a kiss from her White, blonde, athletic boyfriend. These two sequences position the heroine as feminine and a source of heterosexual desire by presenting her thin, hairless, mostly naked body and immediately pairing her with a Hollywood version of the ideal male. According to Mulvey, we the spectators are being forced to identify with the 'male gaze.' She explains,

> In a world ordered by sexual imbalance, pleasure in looking has been split between active/male and passive/female. The determining male gaze projects its fantasy onto the female figure which is styled accordingly. In their traditional exhibitionist role, women are simultaneously looked at and displayed, with their appearance coded for strong visual and erotic impact so they can be said to connote *to-be-looked-at-ness* (1989, p. 19).

Ironically, both of these films are clearly targeted at an adolescent female market, however, the male gaze is still the frame created for the viewer. The director's use of the male gaze normalizes the passivity associated with femininity and situates Terry and Viola and their "to-be-looked-at-ness" as objects of desire. This establishes them as successful producers of feminine heterosexuality. This conformity and presentation as all-American heterosexual girls offers the audience an opening through which they might identify with them as sympathetic. This is an essential first step in the storyline of these films. When Terry and Viola both experience sexism the viewers can sympathize with their situations. The criteria for successful performance in the category of "teenage girl" is not always explicitly addressed; however, when Terry and Viola choose to cross-dress, the gender codes that mark them as feminine are exposed for more careful analysis and will be discussed throughout this chapter.

Within the first ten minutes of each film, injustice emerges and Terry and Viola both decide to take action against the sex-based discrimination they experience. In *JootG*, Terry's journalism teacher doesn't submit her essay for a competition that could earn her an important internship. While reassuring her that he had good reasons he explains, "I had to pick kids who have a real shot. It's nice that you have something to fall back on, you're a pretty girl. You could be a model" (Feldman & Franklin, 1985). This line positions her teacher as sexist, and motivates Terry to prove that her article was overlooked because she was "cute." She vents her frustration to her best friend by remarking, "It's as if women's lib never existed" (Feldman & Franklin, 1985). This statement explicitly marks her actions as being informed of the women's liberation, or feminist, movement.

In Viola's story, she returns to school in the fall to learn that the girls' soccer team has been cut and the boys' soccer coach won't let the girls try out for the boys' team. He cements his sexist position by stating, "Girls aren't as fast, as strong or as athletic, it's a scientific fact" (Leslie, Lutz, & Smith, 2006). The blatant discriminatory treatment towards these two female characters is used to justify the extreme measures they each decide to take in order to achieve their individual goals. In both films, they have a two-week window in which they can assume a masculine identity in a new school to prove themselves in their respective disciplines.

Walk Like a Man

The make-over sequences in both films identify basic elements that are essential for these adolescent females to successfully pass as masculine. The basic physical elements are short hair, flat chest, lower voice, and a different walk. In *StM*, the walk is described as a "strut" whereas in *JootG*, Terry uses gym socks to pad her[1] crotch and is coached by her brother, Buddy, to de-feminize her walk. He explains, "Guys take up space, you gotta look tougher ... you got balls now, use them" (Feldman & Franklin, 1985)! Both characters initially "pass" as male, however, they fail in effectively performing a valued, or hegemonic masculinity (Connell, 1995), and are subjected to teasing, exclusion, and hazing. Viola describes herself in a low moment as a "huge geek, loser, deviant" (Leslie et al., 2006). In addition to changing their hair, voice, and clothes, both characters try to express other normative masculine behaviors in order to distance themselves from their femaleness and to successfully pass as a teenage boy.

In *StM*, her male confidante, Paul, assures Viola that he can improve her social status. He orchestrates this by situating her masculine persona, Sebastian, as a womanizer and an object of feminine heterosexual desire. Paul recruits some of Viola's friends to stage a scene in a popular pizza joint that presents Sebastian as a person who is successful at attracting desirable, feminine, girls and who isn't emotionally involved with any of them. The girls in this scenario are presented in revealing, form-fitting clothes, have long hair, wear make-up, jewellery, and high heels—all symbols of successful femininity in these films and mainstream North American society. In this scene, Viola as Sebastian dismisses three different young women who are vying for her attention and objectifies them in front of her more popular male peers. Viola as Sebastian mutters, "I'd tap that" then grabs the buttocks of one of the young women, then grabs her own crotch. After this public display of apparent heterosexual dating prowess, and emotional detachment from sexual relationships, Viola as Sebastian is suddenly accepted by the popular guys on the soccer team, and receives applause, admiration, and greatly improved social status at school.

In *JootG*, Terry spends less effort in gaining social status, but still has to work to establish her masculine credibility. In various situations, she tries to speak as she imagines a hegemonic male would speak. She is initially coached by Buddy to practice the following phrase: "Say, baby, what's happenin'? I'm a lean, mean, sex machine and that be the way it is" (Feldman & Franklin, 1985). The tone, body language, and inflections of this phrase are an appropriation of Black urban masculinity. This is an indicator of how Hollywood, and young suburban White males, often look to urban communities of color for models of hegemonic masculinity (Katz, 2002). At other moments when Terry is embodying her masculine persona she says things such as: "Yo Rick, how they hangin'?" and "We're rapping. Man-to-man, about chicks and shit like that" (Feldman & Franklin, 1985). This last statement was made in an attempt to recuperate her "tough guise" (Katz, 2002) after a tender moment visiting the home of her new male best friend, Rick. Terry's friendship with Rick and Viola's friendship with her roommate Duke lead to several queer moments in both films. These relationships lead to homoerotic tensions that trouble the characters' and the audience's understandings of sexuality and desire, yet clearly teach the dominant curriculum of heterosexism and homophobia at "Hollywood High."

Queer Heterosexuality and Threats of Homoerotic Desire

In both films, Viola and Terry become objects of feminine desire when presenting as their masculine selves. They also each experience desire for a man. These situations provide opportunities for examining moments of same-gender[2] desire and how they are represented in Hollywood teen films. These texts are not violently homophobic, but they demonstrate how heterosexism and homophobia operate. In both films, these love interests provide comic moments for the audience who are "in the know" about the female sex of each character, but also illuminate how same-gender desire is marked as scary, gross, or threatening and is to be avoided at all costs. These situations are acceptable and presented as comedic to the audience because Terry and Viola's feminine "het cred" was established in the first frames of their respective films and was never in question; therefore, there is never a real "threat" of queer desire or behaviors. However, using same-gender desire as a comic device that encourages the audience to laugh at these situations exposes the homophobia in the text. These moments of apparent same-sex intimacy are presented as inherently frightening and uncomfortable. Thus, these films situate any deviation from heterosexual desire and relationships as negative and teach viewers that it is to be avoided at all costs.

In *JootG*, Terry as teen boy is placed in several situations where she is actively admiring her fellow masculine peers in school. At one point, she is in the locker room for gym class and is checking out the naked legs, buttocks, and chests of the guys going to and from the showers. In another moment, she is consoling her friend Rick after he had food dumped on him by the school bully. These moments hint at homoeroticism, but since the viewers know that Terry is not male-identified, these scenes can be read as Terry's true feminine heterosexual nature emerging through her masculine drag.

Similar moments happen between Viola and Duke. At one point they are lifting weights together and Viola as Sebastian is caught admiring Duke's physique. In another conversation back at the dorm, Duke confesses that he doesn't feel confident speaking to girls because he doesn't know what to say. Viola reacts by saying, "[high pitched voice] why not? You're hot! [pause—clears throat—lowers voice]—I mean you're an appealing guy ... man, guy-man" (Leslie et al., 2006). She quickly catches herself from expressing desire for Duke in ways that would not be valued by him or their peers, so she changes the pitch of her voice and the content of her message to conform to the hegemonic masculine curriculum of appropriate man-to-man expression. These moments of self-policing by Terry and Viola indicate the powerful role of this gendered curriculum and how each person actively plays a role in monitoring the boundaries of acceptable gendered behaviors.

These acts of surveillance are rooted in Michel Foucault's concept of the panopticon—an all-seeing, yet completely invisible source of power and control (1975). This type of surveillance and control is effective because we all unknowingly contribute to it unless we actively work to question and challenge it. These films represent how schools teach and reinforce heteronormativity and homophobia through the surveillance and policing of bodies and language. These structures promote heterosexuality among students and teachers and work to exclude identities and experiences that queer this social order (Meyer, 2010).

In *StM*, when Viola is living as Sebastian, she attracts the eye of Olivia, a popular girl in school. Terry, in *JootG*, is also pursued actively by a girl named Sandy. Terry agrees to go out with Sandy on the condition that she brings a friend for Rick so they can double-date. When preparing to leave, Terry's brother Buddy jokes about her evening plans, "at least my date is someone of the opposite sex." This joke makes clear that it is neither desirable nor acceptable to go on a date with someone of the same sex.

The fact that both Olivia and Sandy are interested in girls-in-drag points to the potential for sexual fluidity and that initial desire is a product of attraction to a gender performance—not one's sex category assigned at birth. They are attracted to aspects of Viola and Terry that are appealing—regardless of the sex of their bodies. Viola and Terry's persistent attempts to avoid intimate moments with Olivia and Sandy, respectively, underline the devalued and humoristic aspects of same-sex desire. In Gayle Rubin's article, *Thinking Sex: Notes for a Radical Theory of the Politics of Sexuality* she argues that good, natural and normative sex forms the "charmed circle" which is defined as being "heterosexual, marital, monogamous, reproductive and non-commercial" and anyone who engages in activities outside of this "charmed circle" exists in the "outer limits" of sexuality (Rubin, 1984/1993). During these scenes, Viola and Terry work hard to stay within the charmed circle by avoiding flirting and intimate contact with other girls, in order to avoid the scrutiny and marginalization that come with being placed in the "outer limits."

These moments of sexual tension and confusion are the driving conflicts in the film that require resolution. In both films, Viola and Terry end up confessing their love for Duke and Rick, respectively, while still living in their masculine drag. In order to demonstrate their heterosexual affection, avoid rejection, and escape perceptions of queerness, both Terry and Viola reject their carefully crafted masculine personae, abandon the pursuit of their feminist goals, and re-assert their femininity. All actions communicate the importance of following the gender and sexuality curriculum.

Proving It: Re-asserting Feminine Legitimacy

"I love you, Duke" Viola as Sebastian declares on the soccer field in the middle of the big game. He appears disgusted, confused and angry until she lifts her shirt and flashes her breasts. She then removes her wig, fake eyebrows, and sideburns and explains why she went to these lengths by saying, "I wanted to prove I was good enough" (Leslie et al., 2006). Terry makes a similar declaration to Rick at their prom and then kisses him. In this scene, they are both wearing tuxedos, and so other students observing this interaction read it as a gay kiss. Rick initially starts to distance himself from the kiss, yet accepts his friend Terry as gay, until she opens her shirt and flashes her breasts. He then walks away in anger and confusion telling the bystanders, "It's okay, he has tits" (Feldman & Franklin, 1985). In both of these situations, the female character's breasts and her desire for a male are the defining features of her femininity. Thus, these anatomical features, combined with her "het cred" are the essential criteria at Hollywood High for being marked as feminine. The message this sends to young women is that if you have small breasts or no breasts, you are marked as failing at femininity. Also, if you experience desire for and intimacy with someone other than a masculine male, this will also call your femininity into question.

The narrow codes that are presented in these high school films, along with many others, reinforce limiting notions of gender and sexuality that are repeated in high schools and popular culture images across North America. These codes essentially confine youth to carefully marked boxes of masculine and feminine and those whose behavior, dress, walk, extra-curricular interests, or vocal expression somehow vary from their prescribed category are generally punished through jokes, exclusion, bullying, harassment, and violence (California Safe Schools Coalition, 2004; Kosciw, Diaz, & Gretytak, 2008; Meyer, 2009). The final message in each of these films is one that is post-feminist in nature: feminism is no longer relevant and women can achieve anything as long as they conform to the codes of femininity within the matrix of heterosexual relationships (Butler, 1990).

A Post-feminist Happily Ever After

Post-feminism is a response to the feminist movement that makes claims that actions to achieve gender equity are not necessary and calls for a return to more traditional heterosexual gender roles. Angela McRobbie describes post-feminism as, "an active process by which feminist gains of the 1970s and 80s come to be undermined" (2004, p. 265). Post-feminism has gained some popularity with a younger generation of women who want to distance themselves from the politics of second-wave feminism which is perceived as "out of date" (McRobbie, 2004). Its popularity also may be linked to the concept that many young women feel that they have never been subjected to harassment or discrimination on the basis of sex. Many young women want to believe that full equality between the sexes has been achieved therefore, feminism is no longer necessary. Post-feminism is also attractive to marketers in the magazine, fashion, and beauty industries that target adolescent and young women as key consumers, since these messages enable them to successfully sell a certain kind of femininity that supports a multi-billion-dollar industry.

In these films the injustices that Terry and Viola experienced early in the stories are explained as not related to systemic discrimination, but due to other individualized reasons. For Terry, she discovered that her news article and writing style was indeed sub-par when her new journalism teacher gave her feedback that matched what her previous teacher had told her. She only secured the coveted summer internship when she wrote and submitted a new piece about her experience living as a teenage boy. In Viola's case, her new soccer coach clearly announces that his team does not discriminate on the basis of gender and that she is welcome to continue playing as Viola. This public statement communicates to the audience that the sexism she experienced at her previous school was a result of an isolated sexist coach and did not indicate broader systems of sexual oppression that are enacted and enforced through various social structures (Bartky, 1990; Frye, 1983; Young, 1990).

These explanations show viewers that sexism no longer exists, feminism is no longer necessary, and although life is sometimes unfair it does not mean that it is related to larger systems of power and oppression. We are encouraged to believe that through individual effort and free choice, young women can achieve anything. This message is post-feminist as it de-politicizes and de-contextualizes the struggles that these characters and other young women experience. It presents the false lesson that sexism and other forms of discrimination are just historical facts that are no longer relevant today.

The second post-feminist element of these films is embedded in the heterosexual coupling and return to traditional male-female relations at the conclusion of each film. In *StM*, Viola is presented in a debutante ball being escorted by her new boyfriend, Duke. She has her hair down, is wearing make-up, jewellery, high heels, and a floor-length gown. The historic roots of such balls were for high society families to formally present their daughters as ready for marriage and to display them to eligible bachelors for their consideration (Harrison, 1997). This finale builds on elitist White heteronormative traditions and celebrates Viola's successful return to normalized and valued femininity while simultaneously erasing the earlier version of a feminist, cross-dressing soccer player.

The final scene of *JootG* also reclaims Terry's lost femininity by dressing her in a white dress with a lace collar that ties in a bow at the front. She is wearing make-up, jewelry, and her short hair is styled into soft curls that frame her face. As she exits her internship she notices Rick waiting for her outside. They have the following conversation:

Rick: You look very good in a dress."
Terry: Why don't we go out dancing or something?"
Rick: Wait a minute, I'm the guy. Let me just try this: why don't we go out dancing?"
Terry: Sounds good. You want to go for a ride?" (in her car) Rick: Yeah. As long as I get to drive."

This interaction clearly shows Rick establishing himself as the dominant male to reassert the codes of traditional heterosexual relationships. The message is that it is not appropriate for girls to ask guys out, nor is it acceptable for guys to be seen in a car driven by a girl. Who is in the driver's seat, literally, is often seen as proxy for who is in control of that relationship.

The gender and sexuality curriculum of Hollywood High presented in these films can be summed up in four post-feminist points:

1. Gender discrimination doesn't exist systemically. There are a few bad individuals, but society as a whole isn't oppressive, therefore, feminism is no longer relevant and patriarchy is a myth.

2. Hegemonic masculinity is the only valued form of maleness and is achievable through asserting dominance over women (sexually and physically) and distancing oneself from feminine signifiers.

3. Heterosexual femininity which is signified through boyfriends and breasts, long hair, make up, jewellery, high heels and dresses can bring girls all they could ever dream of and hope to achieve.

4. Same-sex and same-gender desires are laughable, awkward, threatening, and uncomfortable and must be avoided at all costs.

So what can educators do to help students make sense of this Hollywood curriculum, and is it possible to counteract or undo the impact that these pervasive images have on youth cultures?

Enacting Critical Media Literacy and Queer Pedagogy

This analysis of *She's the Man* and *Just One of the Guys* is influenced by what Barthes refers to as the "triple context": "the location of the text, the historical moment and the cultural formation of the reader" (Storey, 1993, p. 80). It is important to acknowledge that people bring different contexts to their interpretation of media texts. Youth are becoming more technologically savvy and are active readers of the media texts in their worlds. Through interacting with film, TV shows, fan 'zines, and other opportunities offered by technology, viewers can create their own meanings and interpretations of the messages presented to them in popular cultural texts. But, as McKinley pointed out in her a study of fans of the popular 1990s high school TV show *90210*: "viewers positioned themselves as authors and sources of television-centered behaviors; in the process, cultural norms could be naturalized and uncritically perpetuated" (1997, p. 152). What we need to do as educators is to teach critical media literacy skills and provide students with the tools and the knowledge to become savvier in reading these texts. This example of democratic sexuality education can empower youth to create their own meanings and cultural artifacts rather than being passive consumers of corporate entertainment. By initiating discussions about gender, race, and sexuality, and asking students to reflect critically on the representations that they see in their favorite shows, films, and music, we will be better able to teach, learn, and interact with them about how they experience and act in the world. These kinds of conversations can be informed by and grounded in existing progressive pedagogical approaches such as feminist and queer pedagogies (Meyer, 2010).

Advocates of a queer pedagogy have grounded many of their assertions in critical and post-structural feminist theories. Queer theory's most significant achievement is to specify "how gender operates as a regulatory construct that privileges heterosexuality and, furthermore, how the deconstruction of normative models of gender legitimates lesbian and gay subject-positions," (Jagose, 1996, p. 83). Queering seeks to disrupt and challenge traditional modes of thought around gender and sexual identity and, by standing on the boundaries or "borderlands" (Anzaldúa, 1987/2007) drawn by dominant culture, can more effectively examine and dismantle them. Deborah Britzman, a leading theorist in this field, explains how she understands queer theory and its role in learning:

> Queer Theory offers methods of critiques to mark the repetitions of normalcy as a structure and as a pedagogy. Whether defining normalcy as an approximation of limits and mastery, or as renunciations, as the refusal of difference itself, Queer Theory insists on posing the production of normalization as a problem of culture and of thought (1995, p. 154).

While marginalized groups employ new strategies to challenge dominant ideologies, these entrenched discourses push back. Resistance is offered up by the dominant structures of society to forces that try to change them. Britzman presents the queer theoretical approach to understand this opposition in outlining three forms of resistance to sexuality: structural, pedagogical, and psychical. She defines these terms as follows: (a) structural resistance is "the very design or organization of education," (b) pedagogical resistance, "worries about Eros between students and teachers [and] considers sexuality as the secret of an individual's nature," and (c) psychical resistance is "the conflict within" (p. 34). She asserts the need to challenge all forms of resistance. She specifically addresses how sexuality is currently inserted into the school curriculum. She notes, "this has to do with how the curriculum structures modes of behaviour and orientations to knowledge that are repetitions of the underlying structure and dynamics of education: compliance, conformity, and the myth that knowledge cures" (2000, p. 35).

In discussing how to challenge *pedagogical* forms of resistance, Britzman encourages educators to recognize the power that *Eros* can play in teaching. By understanding sexuality as a force that, "allows the human its capacity for passion, interests, explorations, disappointment, and drama" and "because sexuality is both private and public—something from inside of bodies and something made between bodies—we must focus on sexuality in terms of its contradictory, discontinuous, and ambiguous workings" (2000, p. 37). Finally, in addressing *psychical* forms of resistance, Britzman advocates working through internal conflicts and ambivalence towards sexuality in order to, "raise rather serious questions on the nature of education and on the uses of educational anxiety" (2000, p. 35). This means that educators need to explore and understand their own conflicted experiences and understandings of gender and sexuality in order to be able to facilitate and support students' explorations of these difficult topics.

Discussing previously silenced issues in school settings can be a very difficult challenge for teachers to initiate and navigate. Feminist and queer pedagogies empower educators to open up traditionally silenced discourses and create spaces for students to explore and challenge the hierarchy of identities that is disseminated by mass media and repeated in schools, such as: jock-nerd, sciences-arts, male-female, Black-White, rich-poor, disabled/able-bodied, and gay-straight. In order to move past this, media texts can be valuable teaching tools to promote critical thinking and schooling can be a place to question, explore, and seek alternative explanations rather than a place where knowledge means "certainty, authority, and stability" (Britzman, 2000, p. 51). Although the term queer pedagogy might seem difficult for some educators to embrace, it can help creatively and effectively work to transform hostile and oppressive environments and meet the needs of all students.

Historically, schools have been institutions that have filled an important cultural role of teaching children to learn what has been deemed important by the people in power. In North America, these people have been overwhelmingly White, European, heterosexual, male, English-speaking, able-bodied and Christian. As a result, children emerge from school having learned only the language, the history, and the ideals of this dominant culture. Shifts towards critical, feminist and queer pedagogies since the civil rights movement and the second-wave feminist movements of the 1960s have begun to question this type of schooling in search of a way to create students and citizens who will be critical, engaged, independent thinkers in order to move our society in a more egalitarian direction. In understanding how the forces of oppression, privilege, and social power work, educators will be better equipped to create classrooms that enact the ideals of a public education system designed to teach all students.

Queer theory offers a further application of ideas introduced by democratic education, critical pedagogy, multiculturalism as well as anti-oppressive theories, by calling on educators to question and reformulate through a queer pedagogical lens: (a) how they teach and reinforce gendered practices in schools, (b) how they support traditional notions of heterosexuality, and (c) how they present culturally specific information in the classroom. In so doing, we will be able to reduce and eventually remove all forms of discrimination from schools and consequently, most realms of society. Schools should be doing more to challenge and disrupt traditional ways of knowing and encourage students to question and "trouble" all that is normally assumed and taken for granted in society so that all students have a fair chance to learn and succeed (Kumashiro, 2002). Institutions of learning must redefine themselves in order to move towards a truly democratic, socially just, and emancipatory learning experience.

By doing away with the docile, submissive style of learning in schools, we can open up more educational possibilities and socially just experiences for future citizens rather than confine them with ideologies of traditional hegemonic, heteronormative gender roles. In order to move in this direction, it is important to understand the psychical, pedagogical, and structural resistance that prevent teachers from challenging these strict codes and police their own language and behavior in addition to that of their students and continue to question and deconstruct the gender and sexuality curricula consistently taught at "Hollywood High."

Notes

1. Throughout this chapter I will use feminine pronouns to refer to Terry and Viola regardless of which gender they are currently expressing. I have made this choice because both characters consistently identify as women and despite their masculine drag, never take on a coherent masculine identity.
2. I use the term "same-gender" desire here instead of "same-sex" since neither Viola nor Terry identify as members of the male sex. Therefore, when they are dressed and living as their masculine selves, their gender presentation is masculine and thus when they have romantic feelings for other masculine characters, the films' narratives show how same-gender desire is read and managed.

References

Anzaldúa, G. (1987/2007). *Borderlands/La Frontera The New Mestiza*. San Francisco: Aunt Lute Books.
Barsocchini, P. (Writer) (2006). *High School Musical* [film]. USA: Disney Channel.
Bartky, S. (1990). *Femininity and Domination: Studies in the Phenomenology of Oppression*. New York and London: Routledge.
Bem, S. (1993). *The Lenses of Gender: Transforming the Debate on Sexual Inequality*. New Haven: Yale University Press.
Bendinger, J. (Writer) (2000). *Bring It On* [film]. USA: Beacon Communications.
Britzman, D. (1995). Is there a Queer Pedagogy? Or, Stop Reading Straight. *Educational Theory, 45*(2), 151–165.
Britzman, D. (2000). Precocious Education. In S. Talburt & S. Steinberg (Eds.), *Thinking Queer: Sexuality, Culture, and Education* (pp. 33–60). New York: Peter Lang.
Butler, J. (1990). *Gender Trouble*. New York: Routledge Falmer.
California Safe Schools Coalition. (2004). *Consequences of Harassment Based on Actual or Perceived Sexual Orientation and Gender Non-conformity and Steps for Making Schools Safer*. Davis: University of California.
Connell, R. W. (1995). *Masculinities*. Sydney: Allen and Unwin.

Denzin, N. K. (1993). Sexuality and Gender: An Interactionist/Poststructural Reading. In P. England (Ed.), *Theory on Gender/Feminism on Theory* (pp. 199–221). New York: Aldine de Gruyter.

Feldman, D., & Franklin, J. (Writer) (1985). *Just One of the Guys* [film]. USA: Columbia Pictures.

Foucault, M. (1975). *Surveiller et Punir: Naissance de la Prison*. Paris: Gallimard.

Frye, M. (1983). Oppression. In *The Politics of Reality: Essays in Feminist Theory* (pp. 1–16). Freedom, CA: The Crossing Press.

Harrison, L. (1997). 'It's a Nice Day for a White Wedding': The Debutante Ball and Constructions of Femininity. *Feminism & Psychology, 7*, 495–516.

Hughes, J. (Writer) (1984). *16 Candles* [film]. USA: Channel Productions.

Hughes, J. (Writer) (1985). *The Breakfast Club* [film]. USA: A&M films.

Hughes, J. (Writer) (1986a). *Ferris Beuhler's Day Off* [film]. USA: Paramount Pictures.

Hughes, J. (Writer) (1986b). *Pretty in Pink* [film]. USA: Paramount Pictures.

Jagose, A. (1996). *Queer Theory: An Introduction*. New York: New York University Press.

Katz, J. (Writer) (2002). Tough Guise: Violence, Media, and the Crisis in Masculinity. Northampton, MA: Media Education Foundation.

Kosciw, J., Diaz, E., & Gretytak, E. (2008). *2007 National School Climate Survey: The Experiences of Lesbian, Gay, Bisexual, and Transgender Youth in Our Nation's Schools*. New York, NY: GLSEN.

Kumashiro, K. (2002). *Troubling Education: Queer Activism and Antioppressive Pedagogy*. New York: Routledge Falmer.

Leslie, E., Lutz, K. M., & Smith, K. (Writer) (2006). *She's the Man* [film]. USA: Dreamworks SKG.

Lutz, K. M., & Smith, K. (Writer) (1999). *10 Things I Hate about You* [film]. USA: Touchstone Pictures.

McKinley, E. G. (1997). *Beverly Hills, 90210: Television, Gender, and Identity*. Philadelphia: University of Pennsylvania Press.

McRobbie, A. (2004). Postfeminism and Popular Culture. *Feminist Media Studies, 4*(3), 255–264.

Meyer, E. J. (2007a). "But I'm Not Gay": What Straight Teachers Need to Know about Queer Theory. In N. Rodriguez & W. F. Pinar (Eds.), *Queering Straight Teachers* (pp. 1–17). New York: Peter Lang.

Meyer, E. J. (2007b). Masculinities on the OC: A Critical Analysis of Representations of Gender. In S. Steinberg & D. Macedo (Eds.), *Handbook of Media Literacy* (pp. 454–462). New York: Peter Lang.

Meyer, E. J. (2008). A Feminist Reframing of Bullying and Harassment: Transforming Schools through Critical Pedagogy. *McGill Journal of Education, 43*(1), 33–48.

Meyer, E. J. (2009). *Gender, Bullying, and Harassment: Strategies to End Sexism and Homophobia in Schools*. New York: Teachers College Press.

Meyer, E. J. (2010). *Gender and Sexual Diversity in Schools*. New York: Springer.

Mulvey, L. (1989). *Visual and Other Pleasures*. Basingstoke: Macmillan.

Resnick, D. (2008). Life in an Unjust Community: A Hollywood View of High School Moral Life. *Journal of Moral Education, 37*(1), 99–113.

Rosenberg, M., & Meyer, S. (Writer) (2008). *Twilight* [film]: Summit Entertainment.

Rubin, G. (1984/1993). Thinking Sex: Notes for a Radical Theory of the Politics of Sexuality. In H. Abelove, M. A. Barale & D. M. Halperin (Eds.), *The Lesbian and Gay Studies Reader* (pp. 3–44). New York: Routledge.

Steinberg, S. R. (2004). Reading Media Critically. In S. R. Steinberg & D. Macedo (Eds.), *Media Literacy* (pp. xiii–xv). New York: Peter Lang.

Storey, J. (1993). Roland Barthes. In *An Introductory Guide to Cultural Theory and Popular Culture* (pp. 77–85). Athens, GA: University of Georgia Press.

West, C., & Zimmerman, D. H. (1987). Doing Gender. *Gender and Society, 1*(2), 125–151.

Young, I. M. (1990). *Justice and the Politics of Difference*. Princeton, NJ: Princeton University Press.

CHAPTER 24

Learning Filipino Youth Identities

Positive Portrayals or Stifling Stereotypes?

Eloise Tan

Throughout their careers, identities can function as points of identification and attachment only *because* of their capacity to exclude, to leave out, to render 'outside', abjected. Every identity has at its 'margin', an excess, something more. (Hall, 1996, p. 5)

The inscription of the minority subject [lays] *somewhere between the too visible and the not visible enough*. (Bhabha, 1996, p. 56)

Introduction

In 2010 the Philippines became Canada's largest source of short- and long-term migrants, edging out both India and China (Sintos Coloma, McElhinny, Tungohan, Catungal, & Davidson, 2012). Similarly, in the United States, the Philippines has been the largest provider of occupational immigrants since the 1960s (Espiritu, 2001). Despite the growing and already substantial Filipino population within these two countries, the Filipino community has been described as "forgotten" (Espiritu, 2001), "lost" (Horn, 2007), and "disturbingly invisible" (Sintos Coloma et al., 2012). This tag of invisibility has been suggested in relation to the sparse representation in the media, history books, and public spheres such as the government.[1] So if we see little and learn little about this growing population of Filipinos in Canada and the United States, in what spaces can we seek out representations of Filipina/o[2] youth? How might these representations come to bear on the multiple identities of Filipino youth?

The edited collection in which this chapter sits is the ideal space to critically map out media representations and scholarly interrogations of Filipino youth. As researchers of, with, and/or for youth,[3] we must work against the portrayal of a homogeneous youth experience, or indeed a homogeneous immigrant youth experience. Suarez-Orozco and Todorova (2003) offered what can be taken as words of caution for researchers of youth: "Because immigrant youth are extraordinarily diverse, their experiences resist facile generalizations" (p. 19). While immigrant youth collectively occupy "in-between spaces" where they negotiate processes of hybridity, they do so in contradicting and sometimes competing ways (Asher, 2008). As well, the more research available about specific immigrant youth communities, the better we can understand the diversity of experiences within those groups. We can begin to work against a singular representation of the Filipino immigrant youth experience, the Asian immigrant youth experience, or other binding constructs. Focused study on specific immigrant youth communities adds to the richness of understanding of youth experiences accessible through both critical youth studies and critical immigrant youth studies.

This chapter attempts to seek out representations of Filipino youth[4] in North American primetime television, and to uncover what these portrayals 'teach' about what it means to be a Filipino youth in Canada or the US. I find that among the limited representations of Filipino youth in the media, they are consistently framed as active cultural producers. As the chapter title suggests, throughout I work through the ways in which this portrayal might simultaneously open up and shut down spaces for Filipino youth identities. Before I seek out representations of Filipino youth in the media and in the literature, I frame the chapter by discussing identity as a fluid process rather than a fixed construct, and how this relates to what it might mean to be a Filipino youth in Canada and America.

In what follows, I undertake a review of Filipino youth representations in North American primetime television. This is not a quantitative content analysis of Filipino youth representations, but rather, a portraiture of narratives of Filipino youth in the media. I examine the inclusion of Filipino youth in three mainstream television series: *America's Best Dance Crew* (Simon, 2008), *Degrassi: The Next Generation* (Moore & Schuyler, 2001), and *Glee* (Murphy, Falchuk, & Brennan, 2009). *Degrassi: The Next Generation* and *Glee* are fictional series; *America's Best Dance Crew* is a reality competition show. I examine how within these three series the archetype of the Filipino as youth cultural producer is being sustained within both fictive television series and reality television. I question what this consistent and exclusive message of Filipino youth as cultural producers might mean for Filipino youth who are not engaged in these activities.

In the discussion of the recurring representations of Filipino youth as cultural producers, I attempt to draw comparisons with other positive racial stereotypes to tease out how positive stereotypes exclude. Within the discussion, I highlight research that explores Filipino youth engaged in cultural production around hip hop culture (see Bischoff, 2012, pp. 13–14, for a rundown of academic studies on Filipino youth and hip hop culture). What does the emergence of multiple theses and/or dissertations on the relationship between Filipino youth and hip hop have to say about the seeming 'invisibility' of Filipino youth in youth cultures outside of hip hop?

When I turn my eye to two seemingly distinct spaces—prime-time television and academic publication venues—I find the recurring thread of the Filipino youth as performer, as youth cultural producer. We find Filipino youth singing (*Glee*), acting (*Degrassi: The Next Generation*), breakdancing (*America's Best Dance Crew*), DJing, or emceeing (Bischoff, 2012; Harrison, 2009; Wang, 2012), in various places we turn to as youth researchers. What does this focus on performance and Filipino youth mean for how Filipino youth construct and negotiate their identities? Does research on other immigrant youth cultures also focus on youth within those cultures that engage in performative activities? I conclude the chapter by attempting to map possible future directions within the emerging field of Filipino youth studies.

Youth Identities[5] and Media Representations

Though they [identities] seem to invoke an origin in a historical past with which they continue to correspond, actually identities are about questions of using the resources of history, language and culture in the process of becoming rather than being: not 'who we are' or 'where we came from', so much as what we might become, how we have been represented and how that bears on how we might represent ourselves. Identities are therefore constituted within, not outside representation. (Hall, 1996, p. 4)

Radio, television, film, and the other products of media culture provide materials out of which we forge our very identities; our sense of selfhood; our notion of what it means to be male or female; our sense of class, of ethnicity and race, of nationality, of sexuality; and of "us" and "them." ... Media stories provide the symbols, myths, and resources through which we constitute a common culture and through the appropriation of which we insert ourselves into this culture. (Kellner, 2011, p. 7)

The quotes from Hall and Kellner draw out the complexities of how youth identities and media representations of youth intersect and can possibly create new spaces for identities. As Hall mentioned, identities are not solely about continuing a kind of 'authentic' narrative grounded in origin stories from the past. Identities are equally about what we *might* become, as they are about what we *are*.

Building upon this notion of identity as possibilities, Côté (2006) argued for an end to phrases such as 'having an identity', as identity is not something one can possess, or lose, for that matter. Similarly, Sfard and Prusak (2005) drew attention to how researchers concerned with identity must turn from a conceptualization of identity as a static, externalized object and instead embrace identity-making as a "communicational practice" that involves negotiating with the world about how we come to recognize ourselves and be recognized by others. These researchers went on to call for a narrative definition of identities: "In concert with the vision of identifying as a discursive activity, we suggest that identities may be defined as collections of stories about persons or, more specifically, as those narratives about individuals that are *reifying, endorsable,* and *significant*" (Sfard & Prusak, 2005, pp. 16–17). Thus, in this way, identities come to be about the stories we tell about ourselves. So if youth identities are about stories they tell about themselves, then what meaning can we make out of the stories that mainstream media tell about youth?

Media Representations of Immigrant Youth

If we accept that media representations contribute to our narrative identities, then what does it mean for immigrant youth identities when there is a lack of media representation? As one of the epigraphs that opened this chapter stated, minorities seem to hover between "too visible and not visible enough" (Bhabha, 1996, p. 56). Immigrant youth are *visible*, as their ethnic identities are often visually inscribed upon their bodies, yet they are not *seen*, in the sense that there is little understanding or representation of their diverse experiences.

Drawing on the work of Fleras and Kunz (2001), Canadian mediawatch agency, Media Action Media (Cho et al., 2011, p. 24), offered the following framework for how minorities are represented in Canadian media:

1. Invisible and irrelevant,

2. Race-role stereotyping,

3. Promulgators of social problems,

4. Decorative tokens for entertainment.

Within this framework of minority media representation, immigrant youth are denied the possibilities of identities; they are either absent from the discussion or they are one-dimensional in nature. The important report published by Media Action Media (Cho et al., 2011) illustrated, through a thematic content analysis of various Canadian television shows, how diversity on Canadian television is constructed around a heterosexual, White centre of power (p. 8). That is, while White characters are abundant, they are also open to diverse storylines that portray multiple and competing identities. I will draw upon this framework throughout the chapter.

Filipino Youth Identities

People of Filipino heritage have experiences very different from those of other Asian American groups who are part of the fabric of this country. Not dominated by Confucian philosophy, oral in tradition, coming from societies that have matriarchal structures and bilateral kinship systems, intersected and invaded by seafarers, traders, military, missionaries, and colonizers, Filipinos of America are seldom accurately situated in history or culture and are therefore often misinterpreted. (Root, 1997, p. xiii)

As critical youth researchers working with immigrant youth identities, we must step outside binary constructs of immigrant versus non-immigrant youth. We must also take care to avoid the temptation to rely on research under the banner of 'Asian American' or 'Asian Canadian' when researching immigrant youth populations. As Root (1997) suggested above, Filipino cultures have many key factors that distinguish them from other Asian nations. We cannot speak of a singular Filipino-Canadian youth identity that stands alongside (or in opposition to) a singular Canadian youth identity; "rather than conceiving of minority individuals as simply buffeted between the wider society and their co-ethnics ... see them as agents who actively negotiate their desired ethnic identities in relation to both insiders and outsiders in a multitude of contexts" (Song, 2003, as quoted in Ang Chiu Li, 2006, p. 23). Ang Chiu Li (2006) suggested that immigrant youth have agency in their ethnic identities; that immigrant youth are active participants in the construction of their identities—they are not passive recipients of a predetermined set of characteristics and narratives that constitute their lived ethnicity. The role of 'desire' in this active negotiation of identities is important, as it highlights that immigrant youth are not aimless in this negotiation; there may exist identity goals or yearnings, however changeable they may be. These desired ethnic identities shift over a lifetime and through generations (Espiritu, 2001). Hall (1996, p. 5) referred to the "career" of an identity that has a longitudinal dimension. In keeping with Hall's notion of identity careers, a longitudinal study on the identities of Filipino youth over time into adulthood might highlight how this particular ethnic youth population shifts or maintains identities over a period of time.

As well, these desired identities are not constructed in a vacuum: "the making of a Filipino American culture and identity is not done in isolation, but in dialogue with and in opposition to the racist ideologies and practices within the United States" (Espiritu, 1994, p. 268). Filipino immigrant identities are also constructed in relation to other immigrant identities and in relation to dominant American or Canadian identities. We see from Espiritu's work with Filipino female youth that participants defined their lived experience of being a Filipina as distinct from how they construct what it means to be a 'White girl', which for them equated to having multiple sexual partners (Espiritu, 2001). Also, we see narratives of how Filipino youth construct their identities alongside Black American youth identities in the growing body of research on Filipino youth hip hop cultural producers (Bischoff, 2012).

The research on Filipino immigrant youth is disparate, but there are some common themes that emerge from studies on Filipino youth. The prominence of family is a common theme in the literature around Filipino youth in the US, particularly how the family unit socializes and regulates gender roles and expectations (Espiritu, 2001, 2003; Wolf, 1997). Much research on Filipino immigrant youth acknowledges that the family unit and structure present an alternate conception of family than a nuclear family. I would argue that one cannot conduct research with Filipino immigrant youth without deconstructing and discussing the role of the family in Filipino immigrant families. Another theme that emerges is the tension between the invisibility of being 'another Asian' and the history of American colonization of the Philippines. As mentioned at the beginning of this chapter, Filipinos are often characterized as being invisible or forgotten. While they constitute a large number of immigrants in Canada and the US, and while they have distinct historical narratives from most Asian countries, they are often lost under the silencing label of 'Asian'. The history of American colonization of the Philippines is an interesting starting point for understanding Filipino immigration to North America. Colonial remnants of America in the Philippines, such as the English language and the school system, create an impression for some Filipinos that they are Americanized even before setting foot in America (Espiritu, 2001). However, while American colonization is a good starting point for understanding Filipino immigration to the US, I question whether in Canada we require examination of factors influencing immigration to Canada, and also how Filipino Canadians negotiate their identity in relation to the narrative of American colonization.

Recently, there have been great strides in the area of study on Filipino immigrant youth populations in Canada. The book, *Filipinos in Canada: Disturbing Invisibility* (Sintos Coloma et al., 2012) contained a section on youth subjectivities, and represents the most cohesive collection to date of published works on Filipino immigrant youth. As well, the Filipino Youth Transitions in Canada (FYTiC) is a three-year, mixed-methods research funded by the Social Sciences and Humanities Research Council (SSHRC) and based in York University, Toronto (Filipino Youth Transitions, 2013). It is collating data from Winnipeg and Toronto on Filipino youth populations, specifically in relation to education achievement, identity, and social support structures. With these two recent achievements in Filipino youth studies, perhaps we will see a growth in the study of this particular immigrant youth population in a Canadian context. These scholarly works on the Filipino youth community are particularly welcome in the context of the Filipino populations consistently referred to as 'lost' and 'invisible', as cited earlier in this chapter.

Reviewing Representations of Filipino Youth in Prime-Time Television

Searching for Filipino youth in the media

My requirements for inclusion here were such:

1. The show must be aired to a prime-time North American audience,

2. The character must have at least a recurring role in the series,

3. The show must have aired sometime between 2010 and 2013.

I was familiar with the character of Sunshine Corazon on *Glee*, so I included this character based on personal knowledge. I conducted an Internet search of 'Filipino characters on television', and searched the archives of Filipino American entertainment Internet news outlet, ABS-CBN, that regularly highlights the appearance of Filipinos in North American media. I also canvassed members of the Filipino Canadian community to ensure that I was not overlooking a relevant show. From this, I came to discover the character of Manny Santos on *Degrassi: The Next Generation*.

I also came across references to minor appearances (at times not speaking roles) of Filipino adult characters in series such as *Desperate Housewives*, *Will and Grace*, and *House*. However, because these characters were depictions of Filipino adults, I did not include them here. A comprehensive examination of the portrayal of Filipinos in American and/or Canadian prime-time television would be beneficial in uncovering possible archetypes of Filipino characters.

I watched six episodes of *Degrassi: The Next Generation* (DTNG) and three episodes of *Glee*. I chose six, as it would allow me to watch episodes over the course of various series and it was feasible. There were only three episodes of *Glee* that featured Sunshine Corazon. I selected the episodes by reading synopses of each episode to ascertain if the relevant character had a major storyline (for example, when Manny in DTNG decides to have an abortion). While watching, I made note of how Sunshine and Manny were portrayed, in terms of their personalities, interests, and social networks. The following analyses are character portraitures of Filipino youth in the media, and focus on the interests and talents of the characters. This portraiture treatment was preferred over a content analysis or critical discourse analysis because I ask how Filipino youth are portrayed in the media as cultural producers.

Degrassi: The Next Generation

Degrassi: The Next Generation (DTNG) is a Canadian television franchise that has had various series incarnations since its creation in 1979 by Linda Schuyler and Kit Hood (Levine, 2009). The Degrassi franchise is an iconic Canadian teen television series that has managed to achieve successful viewerships in its local context as well as global markets. It has been discussed in relation to its role in representation of Canadian youth and its role in shaping Canadian youth identities (Byers, 2005; Levine, 2009; Rintoul & Hewlett, 2009). Its latest incarnation, DTNG, is the fourth series to emerge from the franchise (Moore & Schuyler, 2001). DTNG focuses on high school students attending a fictional high school in Toronto, and also includes storylines on their teachers and families. Past characters who were once teens on previous *Degrassi* series return to play the roles of parent or teacher in this series. The show follows the ensemble cast as they experience various storylines, such as teen pregnancies, school shootings, as well as the mundane. *Degrassi* is known for its diverse representation of characters. For example, within the show there have been teens with disabilities and teenage moms. However, in her Critical Discourse Analysis of Season 9 of DNTG, Godo (2011) found that two-thirds of the characters are Caucasian, and that among the Black characters depicted, the characters are brothers. Godo stated that, "Degrassi is couched in a framework of Whiteness as the benchmark for Canadian identity" (Godo, 2011, p. 108).[6]

Manny Santos

Manny is a regular character on the show who is portrayed as being from a Filipino background. Her Filipino background is rarely referenced, in keeping with the treatment of race and ethnicity on *Degrassi*. Manny is brown-skinned; has long, dark hair; brown eyes; and is short. Manny appears in seasons one to nine of *Degrassi*, and she is arguably one of the most developed characters on the show. During her appearance on the show her major storylines include: a teen pregnancy and subsequent abortion in the dual part episodes, 'Accidents will happen parts one and two' (Eastman & Potter, 2004a, 2004b); various heterosexual love interests; her transformation from 'cute' to 'sexy'; and her journey to becoming an actress.

We witness a transformation in Manny from a shy girl who dresses in baggy clothes to a sexualized young woman who often wears provocative clothes. In the episode that marks her transformation, Manny states, "I don't want to be cute, I want to be sexy" (in the episode, 'U got the look') (Eastman & Potter, 2003). Manny's character is often embroiled in storylines related to her hyper-sexualized image, for example, she takes a naked picture of herself in one episode, and in another, she is reprimanded by the principal for visibly wearing a thong. Manny's character is also heavily involved in the Spirit Squad, which is a cheerleading squad at the fictional high school.

Manny comes from a conservative family that comes to support her decisions even if they clash with their own. For example, in the episode, 'Accidents will happen part two' (Eastman & Potter, 2004b), Manny's mother takes her to get an abortion, which surprises Manny, because she thought she would be shipped to a convent in the Philippines like her cousin. The only other explicit reference to Manny's Filipino heritage is the storyline around her debut, in the episode, 'We got the beat' (Earnshaw & Scain, 2008). The debut is analogous to a cotillion, and is a Filipino traditional party hosted by parents when their daughter turns 18. Manny's parents are portrayed as strict, especially her father, who at first is resistant to her desire to be an actress. In the later years of the portrayal of Manny, her storyline becomes tied to her desire to become an actress, beginning in season five and culminating in a move to Hollywood by season nine.

Glee

Glee is a popular comedy-drama-musical that is set in Ohio and follows the lives of high-school students who participate in an afterschool Glee club where they sing and dance. Three episodes of *Glee* within season two feature the character of Sunshine Corazon, who is an international student from the Philippines: 'Audition' (Brennan & Falchuk, 2010), 'A night of neglect' (Brennan & Banker, 2011) and 'New York' (Falchuk, 2011). Sunshine is short; has long, dark hair; brown eyes; and brown skin.

Sunshine Corazon

Sunshine's character is a powerhouse singer whose singing talent rivals that of the Glee leader, Rachel Berry. Throughout the recurring storyline of Sunshine she is depicted as a star, someone to watch out for. In our first glimpse of Sunshine, she is seen watching the Glee club perform outside. The first proper introduction to her character occurs in the episode, 'Audition', when Sunshine is discovered singing in the bathroom while Rachel overhears her. Rachel immediately feels threatened, and gives Sunshine a fake address so that she will not be able to audition for Glee. Within this episode, Sunshine decides to sing for a rival high school, as they offer her a Green Card.

Unlike Manny Santos on *Degrassi*, Sunshine's character is not fully developed outside her singing and stage prowess. At no point do we see Sunshine in the context of friend to another character, or romantic interest of or romantically interested in another character. We do not see her interacting with friends or family, and her storyline is mostly connected to her presence as a lead singer in the singing competitions. She is given three solos, where she wows the crowd in singing competitions with powerhouse ballads. However we do learn that she has 600 Twitter followers, which suggests that she is far from socially isolated. She also is seen as academically gifted, as she is seen in the episode, 'A night of neglect', on the academic decathlon team. From this we can infer that Sunshine is academically gifted as well as artistically talented.

Filipino youth in reality television

I also decided to include here mention of Filipino youth as represented in *America's Best Dance Crew*. The decision to include *America's Best Dance Crew* (ABDC from here on) was based on two reasons:

1. The lack of Filipino youth in fictional characters, and

2. The notorious presence of Filipino youth within this particular reality show.

Reality shows are media constructions with directors and studio executives deciding on the direction of character portrayals and storylines, as well as exercising editorial control over what is shown and when. In this way, reality shows can be seen as a mix of "authentic and inauthentic elements" (Rose & Wood, 2005, p. 287). Despite this behind-the-scenes construction, reality shows are presented as reality—as a mirror to ourselves, our communities, and our youth. In this way, the depictions of youth in reality television necessitate deconstruction and reflection, because they claim to present to us our truth, when it is a negotiated truth designed to gain viewership. I recognize that the Filipino youth are not constructed characters, as in *Glee* and *Degrassi: The Next Generation*. However, they are representations of Filipino youth in prime-time television. Given ABDC's status as a reality competition show, I do not analyze their 'characters', but rather, comment on the representations of race on the show.

If we look to reality shows related to dancing and singing, we see what could be considered an overrepresentation of Filipino youth, considering their near invisibility in fictive television shows. The reality show, *America's Best Dance Crew*, is one such example which regularly featured Filipino youth during its run from 2008 to 2012, a total of seven seasons. ABDC is a reality competition show that pits dance crews from across America against each other to battle in front of celebrity judges. Hip hop is overwhelmingly the most common form of dance in the show, though occasionally, dance crews will showcase other types of dance, such as clogging, the jig, or modern dance. Of the seven seasons of ABDC, the winning crews have consisted of Filipino youth in seasons one, two, three, and five.

Some have remarked that the Filipino youth are 'dominating' the competition ("Asian Americans/ Filipinos Taking Over," 2008; Bunoan, 2012). Other Asian nationalities are also represented on competing dance crews, such as Vietnamese and Korean.

Filipino Youth as Cultural Producer: Positive Portrayal or Stifling Stereotype?

While the first- and second-generation Filipino population continues to grow in North America, the representation of Filipino immigrant youth in public spaces such as the media has not. As discussed earlier, identity at any stage is not fixed, nor is it tangible. However, what we are seeing more and more in the media is a singular Filipino immigrant youth representation: the Filipina/o as youth cultural producer. Within Manny's character on *Degrassi*, we see a complex character that is explored in relation to sexuality, family relationships, romantic relationships, and career ambitions. In the final seasons in which Manny appears, she is consistently seen pursuing and achieving her dream of being an actress. Manny Santos represents the most complex Filipina character in North American prime-time television and the longest standing through nine seasons. However, there was only one other Filipino youth character discovered in this review of prime-time television. In contrast to Manny, Sunshine Corazon appears to be more one-dimensional in nature. She is primarily known in the series for her singing ability. While we are given hints that she has friends (through the reference to her 600 Twitter followers), we never actually see her engaging in a social context. Her role is to sing and perform. This image of Filipino youth as cultural producer is further reproduced within reality television shows such as *America's Best Dance Crew*.

If we return to the framework Fleras and Kunz (2001) offered for understanding representations of minorities in Canadian media, we can conclude that the portrayal of Filipino youth in prime-time North American television fits to a great extent. Within that framework Fleras and Kunz suggested that minorities are portrayed as

1. Invisible and irrelevant,

2. Race-role stereotyping,

3. Promulgators of social problems, and

4. Decorative tokens for entertainment (Cho et al., 2011).

Filipino youth are overwhelmingly 'invisible', as evidenced by their lack of appearance in this review. Where they are portrayed, there is a strong degree of race-role stereotyping as cultural producers. In relation to being portrayed as 'promulgators of social problems', Manny is depicted as having a teen pregnancy and subsequent abortion, and she is portrayed as sexually deviant. Within *Glee*, Sunshine is seen as taking an illegal offer for a Green Card, although she later declines. In this way, the two representations of Filipina characters on television are seen to be working against the norms of society. In one case, Manny is sexually deviant, and in the other, Sunshine is seen as an opportunistic immigrant. Finally, it is clear in both cases (and in the reality show appearances) that Filipino youth are decorative tokens for entertainment. This is shown most clearly with Sunshine, whose sole role on *Glee* is to perform. While *Glee* is a show focused on show choir, the remaining cast are given multiple storylines and a backstory that fills out their character as more than just a performer.

Many sections of society are subject to positive stereotyping (Morrison & Bearden, 2007; Ngo & Lee, 2007). Ngo and Lee (2007) argued that the model minority myth masks the complexity of experiences among Asian American students, and that a more nuanced approach is needed. Related to the stereotype of Filipino youth as cultural producers, Black populations worldwide are stereotyped as gifted performers in song and dance (Sotiropoulos, 2006). Sotiropoulos's (2006) book described the tension between the intention of Black performing artists to contribute to 'racial advancement' and the reception of Black cultural production by most as a form of 'minstrelsy' (p. 7). Thus, we see that a primary reason that positive stereotypes harm the populations they target is because they present subjects as one-dimensional beings—political intentions, nuances within the target population, and those that are excluded from the population—are all swept away. All we are left with is the certainty that Filipino youth equates with cultural production, specifically in song, dance, and stage.

Within scholarly research on Filipino popular youth culture there has been some interest in the community's affiliation with hip hop culture and identity construction (Bischoff, 2012; Deleon, 2004; Harrison, 2009; Wang, 2012). Given the emergence of the study of hip hop affiliated youth in youth studies (see this edited collection, for example), perhaps the volume of work on Filipino youth and hip hop is to be expected. However, I ask what this means for Filipino youth not affiliated with hip hop culture—what could we gain by working with Filipino youth who are not cultural producers or who work outside of the hip hop culture? I posit that exploring other youth cultural affiliations—and indeed, those who choose not to affiliate with such cultural activities—will do much to provide a nuanced representation of Filipino youth in this growing body of research.

Conclusion: Learning Filipino Youth Identities

I conclude with where I began, with a quote from Hall's essay, "Why Identity?": "identities can function as points of identification and attachment only *because* of their capacity to exclude, to leave out, to render 'outside', abjected. Every identity has at its 'margin', an excess, something more" (Hall, 1996, p. 5). To date, there is a dismal representation of Filipino youth within prime-time North American television. While the first- and second-generation population of Filipinos continues to be one of the largest immigrant populations in Canada and America, we can point to two fictional characters who are Filipina on television. From those characters we gather that Filipinos are naturally talented performers. This is further supported by the overrepresentation of Filipino youth on reality dance shows. To use Hall's words, what is 'left out' of these portrayals of Filipino youth? Almost everything: where are the Filipino youth athletes, the shy Filipino youth, the goth Filipino youth, the Filipino youth who are disabled? We have yet to see Filipino youth represented in the media in a way where they are not performing, singing, or dancing.

Throughout this chapter, I have talked about identity in relation to processes of negotiation, desire, and fluidity. In this way, our identities are narratives that we can take an active part in shaping and telling. Yes, identities are not purely fixed, nor are they imposed upon us against our will, and indeed, audiences are not passive recipients of the stories we consume through the media. As well, we must acknowledge the power of youth media as spaces where youth can tell their own stories.[7] However, I find that while we can negotiate our identities and can respond to how our identities are told in the media—we always negotiate or respond to a fixed representation. Thus, while Filipino youth can of course construct identities outside of this singular representation of the 'performer', they are already doing so 'outside' of something, they are seen as 'not being the performer'. As Howarth (2002) stated:

> there are limits to how far we can opt in and opt out of identities. However one makes sense of one's sexed body or the colour of one's skin, our identities have to incorporate, negotiate and/or contest representations of gender and skin-colour. The gaze of the other makes these identities unavoidable. In some senses, therefore, identities are imposed onto us. 'We are not left to define ourselves as we see fit', Ryan recognizes (1999, p. 146). (Howarth, 2002, p. 158)

This perhaps is the greatest tension surrounding representation of immigrant youth identities in mainstream media. While, as a critical youth scholar, I argue that immigrant youth identities should be included and represented in the media, their very inclusion creates identity narratives that impose certain norms onto the youth they represent. In this way, representations of Filipino youth in mainstream media become an active site of learning a particular narrative of what it means to be a Filipino immigrant youth in Canada or the US. In response, as critical youth scholars, we can undertake co-research with immigrant youth, where we can amplify the diversity of narratives available to immigrant youth.

Notes

1. For a critical historiography of Filipino Canadians, see Sintos Coloma et al., 2012; for Filipino Americans, see Espiritu, 2003.
2. *Filipina* refers to the feminine, *Filipino* to the male subject. The terms *Pinay/Pinoy* are also used within the Filipino community. *Pin@y* has also emerged from various community-based organizations to encompass both genders as well as those who are questioning or transgender. *Pin@y* is an attempt to not privilege one gender over the other when writing using these descriptive terms. Recently there has been argument for the term, *Pilipino*, as a politicized Filipino, as the 'F' is a colonial artefact from the Spanish (Harrison, 2009).
3. For the remainder of this chapter, I revert to the term, 'researchers of youth'. However, I use the term in a way that encompasses a spectrum of participatory research relationships within youth research that highlight the role of youth within youth research.
4. I draw a necessary distinction between Filipino youth studies that focuses on first- and second- generation Filipino youth in the diaspora, and the existing field of youth studies in the Philippines that focuses on the study of youth growing up in the Philippines. While both fields contribute to and learn from each other, they are distinct in nature.
5. Much of this discussion draws upon my previous treatment of identities in youth cultures, in Tan, 2009.
6. See Cho et al. (2011, p. 26) for a representation of the evolution of multiculturalism in Canada as conceived by Fleras and Kunz.
7. However, see Fleetwood (2005) for a discussion of how youth media can be romanticized as youth telling their stories unmediated and unencumbered by narratives imposed by adults and mainstream media.

References

Ang Chiu Li, W. (2006). *Negotiating spaces of belonging and social support in Filipino immigrant youth* (Unpublished master's thesis). McGill University, Montreal, Canada.

Asher, N. (2008). Listening to hyphenated Americans: Hybrid identities of youth from immigrant families. *Theory Into Practice, 47*(1), 12–19.

Asian Americans/Filipinos taking over *America's Best Dance Crew* and hip hop scene. (2008). [Web log post]. Retrieved from http://www.bboyworld.com/forum/showthread.php?70158-Asians-Filipinos-Taking-Over-America-s-Best-Dance-Crew-and-HipHop-Dance-Scene

Bhabha, H. K. (1996). Culture's in-between. In S. Hall & P. Du Gay (Eds.), *Questions of cultural identity* (pp. 53–60). London, UK: Sage.

Bischoff, S. (2012). *Expressions of resistance: Intersections of Filipino American identity, hip hop culture, and social justice* (Unpublished doctoral dissertation). Washington State University, Pullman, WA.

Brennan, I. (Writer), & Banker, C. (Director). (2011, April 19). A night of neglect [Episode 17, Season 2]. In R. Murphy, B. Falchuk, & I. Brennan (Creators), *Glee*. Los Angeles, CA: 20th Century Fox.

Brennan, I. (Writer), & Falchuk, B. (Director). (2010, September 21). Audition [Episode 1, Season 2]. In R. Murphy, B. Falchuk, & I. Brennan (Creators), *Glee*. Los Angeles, CA: 20th Century Fox.

Bunoan, V. (2012, May 24). Pinoy success in US reality TV. *ABS-CBN News*. Retrieved from http://www.abs-cbnnews.com/lifestyle/05/24/12/list-pinoy-success-us-reality-tv

Byers, M. (Ed.). (2005). *Growing up Degrassi: Television, identity and youth cultures*. Toronto, Canada: Sumach Press.

Cho, H., Bhatty, F., Godo, E., Jenicek, A., Klein, R., Luka, M., & Ward, M. (2011). *Representations of diversity in Canadian television entertainment programming: Case studies*. Unpublished report. Toronto, Canada: Media Action Media.

Côté, J. (2006). Identity studies: How close are we to developing a social science of identity?—An appraisal of the field. *Identity, 6*(1), 3–25.

Deleon, L. (2004). Filipinotown and the dj scene: Cultural expression and identity affirmation of Filipino American youth in Los Angeles. In J. Lee & M. Zhou (Eds.), *Asian American youth: Culture, identity, and ethnicity* (pp. 191–206). New York, NY: Routledge.

Earnshaw, P., & Scain, S. (Directors). (2008, February 18). We got the beat [Episode 7, Season 7]. In Y. Moore & L. Schuyler (Creators), *Degrassi: The next generation*. Toronto, Canada: Epitome Pictures.

Eastman, A., & Potter, A. (Directors). (2003, October 1). U got the look [Episode 1, Season 3]. In Y. Moore & L. Schuyler (Creators), *Degrassi: The next generation*. Toronto, Canada: Epitome Pictures.

Eastman, A., & Potter, A. (Directors). (2004a, January 26). Accidents will happen, part one [Episode 14, Season 3]. In Y. Moore & L. Schuyler (Creators). *Degrassi: The next generation*. Toronto, Canada: Epitome Pictures.

Eastman, A., & Potter, A. (Directors). (2004b, February 9). Accidents will happen, part two [Episode 15, Season 3]. In Y. Moore & L. Schuyler (Creators). *Degrassi: The next generation*. Toronto, Canada: Epitome Pictures.

Espina, A. (2012, August 15). The representation of Asians and LGBT in North American youth television. *Huffington Post Gay Voices*. Retrieved from http://www.huffingtonpost.com/alfonso-espina/minority-diversity-tv_b_1784532.html

Espiritu, Y. L. (1994). The intersection of race, ethnicity, and class: The multiple identities of second-generation Filipinos. *Identities: Global Studies in Culture and Power, 1*(2–3), 249–273.

Espiritu, Y. L. (2001). 'We don't sleep around like White girls do': Family, culture, and gender in Filipina American lives. *Signs: Journal of Women in Culture and Society, 26*(2), 415–440.

Espiritu, Y. L. (2003). *Home bound: Filipino American lives across cultures, communities, and countries*. Berkeley, CA: University of California Press.

Falchuk, B. (Writer & Director). (2011, May 24). New York [Episode 22, Season 2]. In R. Murphy, B. Falchuk, & I. Brennan (Creators), *Glee*. Los Angeles, CA: 20th Century Fox.

Filipino Youth Transitions in Canada (FYTiC). (2013). Retrieved from http://www.yorku.ca/ycar/programmes_projects/FYTiC_home.html

Fleetwood, N. R. (2005). Authenticating practices: Producing realness, performing youth. In S. Maira & E. Soep (Eds.), *Youthscapes: The popular, the national, the global* (pp. 155–172). Philadelphia, PA: University of Pennsylvania Press.

Fleras, A., & Kunz, J. (2001). *Media and minorities: Representing diversity in a multicultural Canada*. Toronto, Ontario, Canada: Thompson Educational.

Godo, E. (2011). Case study: *Degrassi: The next generation*. In H. Cho, F. Bhatty, E. Godo, A. Jenicek, R. Klein, M. Luka, & M. Ward (Eds.), *Representations of diversity in Canadian television entertainment programming: Case studies* (pp. 99–112). Unpublished report. Toronto, Canada: Media Action Media.

Hall, S. (1996). Who needs identity? In S. Hall & P. Du Gay (Eds.), *Questions of cultural identity* (pp. 1–18). London, UK: Sage.

Harrison, A. K. (2009). *Emcee authenticity and post-colonial consciousness within Filipino American hip hop*. Paper presented at the 2009 International Association for the Study of Popular Music. San Diego, CA.

Horn, M. (Director). (2007). *Lost in America* [Documentary]. Retrieved from http://www.youtube.com/watch?v=oiQcuWkxZ38

Howarth, C. (2002). Identity in whose eyes?: The role of representations in identity construction. *Journal for the Theory of Social Behaviour, 32*(2), 145–162.

Kellner, D. (2011). Cultural studies, multiculturalism, and media culture. In G. Dines & J. M. Humez (Eds.), *Gender, race, and class in media* (3rd ed., pp. 7–18). Los Angeles, CA: Sage.

Levine, E. (2009). National television, global market: Canada's *Degrassi: The next generation*. *Media, Culture and Society, 31*(4), 515–531.

Low, B., Tan, E., & Celemencki, J. (2013). The limits of 'keepin' it real': The challenges for critical hip hop pedagogies of discourses of authenticity. In M. Lamont Hill & E. Petchauer (Eds.), *Schooling hip hop: Expanding hip hop based education across the curriculum* (pp. 118–136). New York, NY: Teachers College Press.

Moore, Y., & Schuyler, L. (Creators). (2001). *Degrassi: The next generation* [Television series]. Toronto, Canada: Epitome Pictures.

Morrison, T., & Bearden, A. (2007). The construction and validation of the homopositivity scale: An instrument measuring endorsement of positive stereotypes about gay men. *Journal of Homosexuality, 52*(3–4), 63–89.

Murphy, R., Falchuk, B., & Brennan, I. (Creators). (2009). *Glee* [Television series]. Los Angeles, CA: 20th Century Fox.

Ngo, B., & Lee, S. T. (2007). Complicating the image of model minority success: A review of Southeast Asian American education. *Review of Educational Research, 77*(4), 415–453.

Rintoul, S., & Hewlett, Q. Z. (2009). Negotiating Canadian culture through youth television: Discourse on *Degrassi*. *Jeunesse: Young People, Texts, Cultures, 1*(1), 125–147.

Root, M. P. P. (Ed.). (1997). *Filipino Americans: Transformation and identity*. Thousand Oaks, CA: Sage.

Rose, R. L., & Wood, S. L. (2005). Paradox and the consumption of authenticity through reality television. *Journal of Consumer Research, 32*(2), 284–296.

Sfard, A., & Prusak, A. (2005). Telling identities: In search of an analytic tool for investigating learning as a culturally shaped activity. *Educational Researcher, 34*(4), 14–22.

Simon, M. (Director). (2008). *Randy Jackson presents America's best dance crew* [Television series]. Los Angeles, CA: Warner Horizon.

Sintos Coloma, R., McElhinny, B., Tungohan, E., Catungal, J. P. C., & Davidson, L. M. (2012). *Filipinos in Canada: Disturbing invisibility*. Toronto, Canada: University of Toronto Press.

Sotiropoulos, K. (2006). *Staging race: Black performers in turn of the century America*. Cambridge, MA: Harvard University Press.

Suarez-Orozco, C., & Todorova, I. (2003). The social worlds of immigrant youth. *New Directions for Youth Development, 100*, 15–24.

Tan, E. (2009). *Participatory and critical out-of-school learning for urban youth: Building community through popular culture* (Unpublished doctoral dissertation). McGill University, Montreal, Canada.

Tiongson, A. T., Jr. (2006). *Filipino youth cultural politics and DJ culture* (Unpublished doctoral dissertation). University of California-San Diego, La Jolla, CA.

Wang, O. (2012). Rapping and repping Asian: Race, authenticity, and the Asian American MC. In M. Forman & M. A. Neal (Eds.), *That's the joint!: The hip hop studies reader* (2nd ed., pp. 199–224). New York, NY: Routledge.

Ward, L. M. (2004). Wading through the stereotypes: Positive and negative associations between media use and Black adolescents' conceptions of self. *Developmental Psychology, 40*(2), 284–294.

Wolf, D. L. (1997). Family secrets: Transnational struggles among children of Filipino immigrants. *Sociological Perspectives, 40*(3), 457–482.

CHAPTER 25

Surprising Representations of Youth in *Saved!* and *Loving Annabelle*

Kerri Mesner and Carl Leggo

Introduction

The lived experiences of teachers and learners are often represented in films. Nevertheless, even though there are more than one thousand (mostly Hollywood produced) films about schools and teachers and learners, education scholars have paid little attention to the narrative depictions of educators and youth in films. Informed by arts-based research, cultural studies, and critical pedagogy, we examine how two films focused on narratives of school experiences contribute to representations of youth. We discuss the films, *Saved!* (Dannelly, 2004) and *Loving Annabelle* (Brooks, 2006), with a focus on how understandings of diversity are constructed, constrained, and challenged, especially regarding issues of gender, sexuality, bodies, spirituality and morality, and queer studies.

It is surprising that film study is not a more integral part of research in education. In our university a few years ago, a former associate dean with responsibility for research dismissed popular films as having no value for education research. We are glad to note that at the annual meeting of the American Educational Research Association (AERA) in April, 2013, there was an inaugural film festival. While the focus was mostly on documentary films, the AERA film festival is a clear indication of the growing enthusiasm for researching experiences of education in film.

One of the most useful books about films and schools is Mary Dalton's (2004) *The Hollywood Curriculum*. As Dalton (2004) noted, "we borrow from the stories of the films we see to help us create ourselves as characters and organize the plotlines of our daily lives" (p. 2). Dalton offered many thoughtful observations and themes, but her book is most useful because it raises numerous questions. For Dalton, "popular film, rich in meanings both fluid and diverse, offers an intersection for the theoretical and the everyday" (p. 7). Like Dalton, we are interested in exploring how the theoretical and the everyday intersect, especially because we understand that education is always a process of learning how to attend to the intersections of everyday experiences informed by theoretical perspectives.

We began this filmic research with a review of the breadth of textual research already undertaken around filmic portrayals of teachers and learners. We noted the wonderful array of writing articulating the various tropes in these films (for example, the heroic teacher motif, the bad teacher movie, and the teacher as buffoon).[1] We also noted just how often films about teachers and learners tend to be so blatantly didactic that there is very little space for an aesthetic response or an alternative interpretation. In our investigations, we wanted to move beyond these more obvious analyses—indeed, to ask different questions. One such question that has arisen with great resonance for us throughout this project is, quite simply, "what is this film good for?" Somehow, this question opens up possibilities, controversies, edges ... opening up opportunities to look at the filmic stories that are overlooked, silenced, marginalized ... that are evocatively exciting to explore—both in terms of filmic interpretation, as well as in terms of their pedagogical implications.

To further open up this question, we present our writing as a conversation, a double-voiced braiding, a métissage (Hasebe-Ludt, Chambers, & Leggo, 2009; Hasebe-Ludt, Chambers, Leggo, et al., 2008; Hasebe-Ludt, Chambers, Oberg, & Leggo, 2008) that we hope will open up many questions and issues from diverse perspectives. Carl comes to this conversation as a professor with long-standing research interests in pedagogy, curriculum, creativity, popular culture, narrative inquiry, life writing, and arts-based education research. While he recognizes the many privileges he enjoys as a White, heterosexual man with a middle-class socio-economic status and the authority of tenure and fullness in the professoriate, he is always eager to question his own privileges and the social-political-eonomic dynamics that have produced and continue to sustain his privileges. Kerri comes to this conversation as a queer Christian minister and theologian, noting the complex (and often hegemonic) influences of Christian belief systems in secular education systems, as well as the need for a more nuanced discussion of queer sexualities within educational films. Kerri's professional theatre background also informs her perspectives in this filmic analysis. We are intrigued to see what this unusual conversation will help us to discover about teachers' and students' identities in contemproary films. Indeed, as Leavy (2011) put it, "Given the complexity around 'identity' ... transdisciplinary approaches to research, which embrace messiness and paradox, are often useful in projects informed by intersectionality theories and may produce additional theories" (pp. 38–39). Our hope is that this dialogue—between the aesthetic and the critical, the artistic and the theological—will enable us to open up new pedagogical insights that attend closely to particular films while extending beyond the scope of specific films. In a conversation with Ondaatje (2002), Walter Murch, one of Hollywood's most successful film editors, promoted "the concept of polyphony—multiple musical lines playing at the same time" (p. 50). This is what we pursue in our collaborative writing. Like Murch, we understand that every specific film "engages each member of the audience as a creative participant in the work" (p. 46).

While there are more than a thousand films that address educational identities in a variety of ways, we have, by necessity, focused this conversation on two films in particular: *Saved!* (Dannelly, 2004) and *Loving Annabelle* (Brooks, 2006). Both films were chosen for their nuanced and complex explorations of issues of identity, as lived by both teachers and students, especially regarding spirituality and sexuality. By bringing each of our disciplinary lenses to bear on these two films, we hope to open up a more complex conversation about youth and teacher identities as portrayed in popular films. Both *Saved!* and *Loving Annabelle* stand out because they are connected to so many other films. As Hutcheon (2006) wrote, "adaptation is how stories evolve and mutate to fit new times and different places" (p. 176). There are only a few stories, and those few stories are composed and presented in diverse ways, sometimes with startling aesthetic and political innovation. But even clichéd or formulaic films can be viewed and interpreted with critical and creative attention.

Dalton (2004) surmised that "Hollywood ... has its own model of curriculum theory, a model that exalts personal experience in a broad aesthetic-ethical-political sweep, making curriculum and teaching one" (p. 11). While we do not disagree with Dalton's claim that many films about teachers and youth focus on the personal and the individual, especially as a hero or a villain, we are encouraged by the complex representations of teachers and youth in *Saved!* and *Loving Annabelle* that extend beyond the merely personal. Dalton was convinced that "there is no prophetic voice in Hollywood's teachers" (p. 149). She was concerned that movies do not present teachers and learners as "consciously political" and committed to promoting "social change instead of individual change" (p. 149). In our responses to *Saved!* and *Loving Annabelle*, we are encouraged by the ways that both films challenge dominant ideologies and connect the personal to the political. Both films resonate with Brueggemann's (2001) call for a prophetic imagination which seeks to "nurture, nourish, and evoke a consciousness and perception alternative to the consciousness and perception of the dominant culture around us" (p. 3).

Opening the Conversation

Kerri: I think both movies offer intriguing takes on narratives that are traditionally silenced (Adams, 2008), and indeed, challenge the viewer to wrestle with contradictory ways of knowing (Adams & Jones, 2011, p. 108)—to sit with the productive learning engendered by discomfort (Kumashiro, 2002). I am intrigued, too, by the possibility that this kind of "social acupuncture" (O'Donnell, 2006) might be particular to the arts—in this case to the filmic arts—here, I find myself thinking of Kirkland and Leggo's (2008) discussion of the value of mythopoetics as uniquely able to tackle taboo subjects. As Adams and Jones (2011) put it,

> stories can be insurrectionary acts if we make room for our (all of our) selves and their desires, for making trouble and acknowledging the implications of doing so, for embracing the texture of knowing without grabbing on to sure or fast answers. (p. 114)

I am particularly interested here in how queer theological perspectives might help us to voice more of these silenced stories; Althaus-Reid (2002) reminded us that *every* theology has some kind of sexual and political praxis—whether conscious or unconscious. Indeed, (as we see in both these films) sexual stories are never just private—they also impact our economic, political, and societal lives (p. 131). I think both these movies offer some marvelous opportunities to challenge traditional theology's tendency to function as "a sexual ideology performed in a sacralising pattern: it is a sexual divinised orthodoxy (right sexual dogma) and orthopraxy (right sexual behaviour)" (p. 87).

I find resonance with arts-based research goals in Althaus-Reid's (2002) suggestion that "indecent acts in theology demand of us creatively to see the unseen, but also courage to denounce what does not work" (p. 78). I am reminded here of Pryer's (2011) discussion of the "ob-scene" as that which is relegated "off-stage", and her declaration that "the true liminar will repeatedly abandon the center, asserting instead her right to speak from the margins, and in so doing, continuing to challenge the hegemony of the mainstream culture" (p. 7). Leavy's (2011) discussion of transdisciplinary approaches to research as intersectionally theorized, and as embracing messiness and paradox, seem exciting to the approaches we are taking here, as well.

Carl: I have been watching films enthusiastically for at least fifty years. I still remember vividly the excitement of Saturday matinees at the Majestic Theatre in Corner Brook, Newfoundland. I continue to go to the cinema at least once a week. Film is a way of narrating and understanding life experiences. I have spent a long life devoted to immersion in Baudrillard's (1997) "gossamer-thin difference between illusion and the real" (p. 63). I have seen many films in my life. I like Fulford's (1999) notion that "stories are how we explain, how we teach, how we entertain ourselves, and how we often do all three at once" (p. 9). Certainly, this is my experience in composing stories and in responding to the stories of literature, research, and film. But while I enjoy viewing films immensely, I am not sure I have yet learned to ask the tough questions that need to be asked. I am especially concerned that the narratives of many films present stories that are too neat, culturally sanctioned and sanitized, stories that lack complexity, ambiguity, even mystery and wonder.

Sexuality and Spirituality

Kerri: While I think both movies tackle intersections of sexuality and spirituality in bold ways, I find their differing approaches delightful. *Saved!* offers a lovely satirical mixture of sex and the sacred right from the start, with Mary's vision, in the swimming pool, of "Jesus" instructing her to have sex with Dean. For Mary, sex is a tool to save Dean from the spiritual toxicity of gayness. Not only that, but Jesus, divinely ordaining this act, can also restore her virginity and make her pure again. Despite her vision, she is still unsure, asking Pastor Skip in sex-ed class ("sex is about procreation and waiting til you're married") if it is possible that Jesus needs us to do his will by not waiting. Satirical humor allows *Saved!* to push some edges … perhaps one of the most outrageous—and, I would suggest, intriguing!—moments in the movie, is when we see the teens performing Jesus Christ Superstar and their clear sexualization of Roland's Jesus on the cross.

Sexual morality is a running thread—not just the obvious satirical condemnations of homosexuality (Hilary's "you're not born a gay, you're born again", as well as her desire to pray away Dean's unnatural perversions); but also the clear double standards with Pastor Skip's and Mary's mother's infidelity (and their children's awareness of it). For Skip, there is "no room for ambiguity" in his black and white Bible; following this logic, Skip believes that God must be punishing their sin with Mary's pregnancy. In this rigid world of moral certitude, I am reminded of Jakobsen's (2002) work looking at how the connections between Christianity and sexual regulation bolster the religious right.

In contrast, in *Loving Annabelle*, the issues of sexuality are centered on the relationship between a student and her teacher in a girls' Catholic boarding school. The movie evades easy "villainization" of the teacher, however; the student, Annabelle, instigates the relationship, pursuing Simone at length until the relationship is finally consummated. While it is clear that this relationship is both scandalous and forbidden (both legally and in the eyes of the school), it is less clear how much of that is informed and/or influenced by its also being a lesbian relationship. I am reminded here of Cavanagh's (2007, 2008) work exploring the complex issues around lesbian teachers, their students, and relationality. Also in contrast to *Saved!*, the viewer is deliberately left unsettled at the end of the movie—do we root for the relationship to survive, or condemn it for its moral and ethical transgressions? Intriguingly, there is also an alternate ending to the movie, released with the DVD version, that shows Annabelle reading a headline that no charges have been laid in Simone's case, and it ends with Annabelle heading down the stairs to Simone's beach house. I am also curious how (or if) this different ending might change our answers to these questions.

I would suggest that in both films, sexual transgression (whether by students or by teachers) serves as a flashpoint for institutional and social boundaries; whether in Mary's rejection of Christian hypocrisy, or Annabelle's and Simone's choice to engage in an illicit relationship, the transgressor seems to function as what Wilcox (2010) referred to as a kind of "freak" who serves as the canary in the coal mine for social boundaries (p. 7).

Carl: I once planned to be an evangelical Christian pastor, and I attended a conservative Christian seminary in Toronto where I completed a graduate Certificate in Biblical Studies. I have been a part of various evangelical Christian communities all my adult life. I have taught young people who remind me of the characters in *Saved!*, and I know many Christians who would be lividly offended with the film, who would certainly not find it funny, and would not promote it as appropriate for others to view. And this is the heart of the dilemma that drives so much pedagogy. Are schools places where teachers and learners are engaging in experiences of conforming or in experiences of transforming? Linda Hutcheon (2000) wrote about the transgressing impulses of parody (p. xvii), and called for "changing the focus of attention from aesthetic merit (however determined) to instructional value" (p. 3). Hutcheon was not denying the value of attending to the aesthetic value of literature or film or life writing, but she acknowledged the importance of attending to how texts instruct. So, when I view *Saved!*, I am unsettled.

I laugh, and feel a little guilty that I am laughing about characters who remind me vividly of people I have known and continue to know, and I even feel some need to defend evangelical Christians from parodic dismissal. But mostly, I am caught up in the subversion of *Saved!*, the way that humour connects me again to the humus of the earth, to humility and humanity. So many perspectives, emotions, and experiences that are taken for granted, that are ignored in the embrace of what is called common sense or normal or common, are unsettled and contested. Humour is central to the classroom that is imaginative and critical. McMahon (2000) reminded us that "humor is an incredible pedagogical tool" (p. 93). *Saved!* reminds me, even compels me, to ask questions I have simply not considered. I need to be unsettled in order to engage with the kind of self-conscious and self-critical recognition (seeing myself again and again) that can subvert all the places I linger in as a privileged, White, economically successful man. Surely, research in education must support this kind of subversion.

In many ways, *Loving Annabelle* is even more subversive than *Saved!* because *Loving Annabelle* confronts its taboo subjects without parody or without the usual social opprobrium brought to bear on topics that transgress social norms, ethics, and laws. As educators, how do we practice a thoughtful engagement with complex human experiences without drawing conclusions and morals so quickly that an insightful conversation is not even possible? So many school experiences are constrained by a legalistic impetus for rules and standards that everybody is expected to know and obey. *Loving Annabelle* does not provide an argument for sanctioning teacher and student romantic and sexual relationships. Educators understand well the need for legal and ethical rules that acknowledge the power differences between people in complex positions of authority and care. A film narrative like *Loving Annabelle* is pedagogically valuable because it reminds us that human experiences are full of nuances and mysteries, and therefore human experiences need to be addressed in stories that are full of nuances and mysteries. In that regard, the alternative ending provided in the DVD version of *Loving Annabelle* raises even more issues and questions for conversation.

Kerri: I love *Saved!*'s subplot dealing with Roland's disability and his sexuality. Early on, Hilary voices a familiar, culturally normative (and silencing) approach when she remonstrates with Roland ("why do you have to make everyone so awkward about your differently abledness?"). Roland and Cassandra's relationship offers a wonderful challenge to traditional discussions of disability and sexuality—perhaps summarized most clearly in Roland's declaration that he *wants* Cassandra—rather than that he needs her. Again, we find a really subtle and poignant moment with Roland sitting on the grass at the foot of Jesus. Throughout this thread, I am reminded of Betcher's (2007, 2010) work on disability, the body, and sociocultural and/or theological relationships with the body in pain.

Carl: Perhaps the most significant theme in both *Saved!* and *Loving Annabelle* is how sexuality is presented as pleasure. Michael Bronski (1998) claimed that "pleasure and sexuality are vital tools in creating a society and culture that is humane, celebratory, and life-sustaining" (p. 3). He also claimed that "for the dominant culture, the threat of homosexuality is that it embodies and prioritizes the pleasure principle" (pp. 13–14). When I think about a long life devoted to learning and teaching, I confess that there has been little of pleasure or bliss or joy in much of my extensive educational experience. Instead, I have been controlled and constrained and conserved. Teachers and learners need opportunities to tell their stories, whatever stories they desire and choose to tell, so we can learn from one another. So much of contemporary education is not about calling out in prophetic voices, but about conforming to dominant perspectives. *Saved!* and *Loving Annabelle* are still significantly constrained by the conservative cultural norms and expectations that govern censorship and the "appropriateness" of content for viewers. Still, within these constraints each film opens up possibilities for discussion about pleasure, repression, contemporary culture, Christian culture, heteronormativity, and lesbian and gay visibility.

Notions of Christianity, Christian Imagery

Kerri: As a Christian minister, and with no disrespect intended to my evangelically oriented friends and colleagues, I have to say I quite enjoyed the movie's satirical take on evangelical Christianity. Many of these moments functioned as comedic storytelling whilst simultaneously highlighting religious issues through the use of satire … from Pastor Skip's "let's get our Christ on … let's kick it Jesus style!", to the irreverent inner thoughts revealing the teens' real prayers, to the Jewels attempting to follow Skip's request that they be "spiritually armed warriors for Christ" by kidnapping and exorcising Mary. *Saved!*'s usage of Christian stories and imagery is also fascinating—both the clear lines drawn between Mary and the Christian Mary ("I don't think she made it [the virgin birth] up but I can understand why she would"), and the recitation of the "blessed are those who are persecuted …" beatitude just as Mary is about to confess her pregnancy to Cassandra. Perhaps the most poignant (and, I would suggest, theologically laden) moment might be when a pregnant Mary stands at the foot of the cross, unable to say anything more than "shit … fuck … goddam".

In contrast, I thought *Loving Annabelle*'s use of religious imagery was subtler, but no less powerful. I did not realize, for instance, that we were even in a Catholic boarding school until the camera showed a crucifix on Mother Immaculata's office door as Annabelle was about to meet her for the first time. I thought the juxtaposition of the Father's recitation of the Mariological prayer with Simone's dread-filled walk to Mother Immaculata's office (after the discovery of the affair) served to powerfully highlight the movie's conflicting themes of Christian spirituality and forbidden sexuality.

In both movies, I am intrigued by the potential for theological discussion that arises from these controversial "edges"; for example, how might our discussion of youth engagement (and disengagement) with Christianity be informed by Althaus-Reid's (2005) statement that "In Jesus as *el Tocado*, what is touchable is his untouchability" (p. 403). Indeed, a provocative challenge to liberation theologians might be found in Althaus-Reid's (1999) declaration that

> the Christ of liberation theology cannot compete with the late Paulo Freire when the Brazilian educator was 30 years old and working on conscientization processes. Between that Christ and Freire, many of us would like to choose Freire, who had more awareness, consciousness and critical strategic thinking than the constructed un-dialogical Christ of current theology, in spite of the fact that Freire was not a Messiah. (p. 42)

I wonder: what are the places of untouchability—in pedagogy, spirituality, and sexuality—that movies like these highlight?

Carl: Kerri's references to Freire are personally poignant. As a young man pursuing teacher education at Memorial University of Newfoundland in the mid-seventies, I first read Freire, and of all the words I read and heard in that year of study, Freire's words are the ones that most readily resonated with me. Freire has been informing my teaching practice for almost four decades. In *Pedagogy of the Heart*, Freire (1997) wrote: "I do not feel very comfortable speaking about my faith. At least, I do not feel as comfortable as I do when speaking about my political choice, my utopia, and my pedagogical dreams" (p. 104). I have shared Freire's reluctance for much of my academic life. I have often felt pulled by an eagerness to acknowledge that my Christian faith is integral to my ways of living in the academy in relationship to others, and a concern that I would be ridiculed for simplistic thinking, or worse still, held accountable for all the horrors that have been and continue to be perpetrated in the world by Christianity and Christians. Freire reminds me that a spiritual commitment can be a mighty motivation for addressing oppression and inhumanity. I am learning to speak out in a spiritual language that includes concepts such as love and hope. At the annual meeting of the American Educational Research Association in 2013, I heard colleagues I eagerly respect express their suspicions about hope and love in the contexts of education. My initial response was surprise, but I now realize that the articulation of suspicion is pedagogically significant. As Freire (1997) suggested, "only an education of question can trigger, motivate, and reinforce curiosity" (p. 31). We need more narrative texts like *Saved!* and *Loving Annabelle* to shake up our assumptions and ignite more lively conversations about romance, love, sex, spirituality, fundamentalism, relationships, and possibilities.

Interreligious and Postcolonial Issues

Kerri: In both movies, I am fascinated by the subtle nod to interreligious and postcolonial issues as well; I am reminded of indecent theology's explicitly intersectional analysis of sexuality, gender, race, and global economics. In *Saved!*, we know that everyone wants to save Cassandra, the "only Jewish" (at the school's assembly altar call, everyone automatically looks at Cassandra to go forward). Cassandra's "speaking in tongues" at this moment offers a lovely, irreverent (and sexual) jab back at this kind of Christian colonialism. We also see a more poignant side to this issue in Mary's struggle to find a new religion to help her with her pregnancy ("they [other religions] can't all be right but they can't all be wrong, right?"). I note, too, *Saved!*'s satirical explorations of White Christian colonialism, in the discussion at the start of the movie about the White Jesus on the school sign, the discussion with Veronica and the Jewels about her parents saving the godless in Vietnam, and Hilary Faye's desire to "save the heathens".

In *Loving Annabelle*, a significant part of Annabelle's rebellion (aside from her sexual transgressions) emerges in her steadfast determination to wear her Buddhist prayer beads in spite of the school's dress code. While for Annabelle this may be more about the emotional import of the beads than their religious significance, they clearly serve as a flashpoint in the school, beautifully illustrated visually as Annabelle is required to don multiple heavy crucifix necklaces in order to realize "how heavy a burden denying Christ can be". I note, again, a moment of quiet complexity, however, in the Father's later sermon in the chapel, wherein he talks about his youthful realization that there are many paths to God—likely a revolutionary notion within his current context.

Carl: Both *Saved!* and *Loving Annabelle* remind me of Miller's (2005) proposal for a pragmatic pedagogy which provides students with "the opportunity to speak, read, and write in a wider range of discursive contexts" than is typically available to them in schools where they often live and learn under "codes of silence and manufactured consent" (pp. 140–141). In turn, Miller promoted institutional autobiography, where students and teachers can locate their emerging and evolving and ever changing narratives within "the range of institutional contexts, shifting attention from the self to the nexus where the self and institution meet" (p. 138). By attending to a wide range of individual and idiosyncratic stories, schools can become places where more critical and creative discussions of the ways stories are shaped and sustained, subverted and shaped anew take place. Teachers and learners need to avoid formulaic and generic understandings of identity, relationship, and possibility. These film narratives are not fables with clear moral themes that can be expressed in simple declarative sentences. Instead, they invite questions about what one holds to be "true", and why one holds those particular views, and how others hold other views. And perhaps most significantly, both *Saved!* and *Loving Annabelle* refuse simplistic resolutions. Lived experience is seldom, if ever, simplistic, and finding ways to address complex understandings of complex stories ought to be the heart of contemporary and cosmopolitan pedagogy.

Ruthven (2004) noted that "fundamentalists are nothing if not selective about the texts they use" (p. 15), and "fundamentalists everywhere tend towards a literalist interpretation of the texts they revere" (p. 59). Teachers and learners need a wide range of texts. Since the text of the universe is vast and complex beyond explanation and narration, teachers and learners need texts that defy simple interpretation. Instead of a fundamentalist claim that I can know the systematic interpretation that connects all the parts in a coherent and cohesive story, I confess my agnosticism, my questions, my suspicions. I want humility. I want to stand in the humus, the earth, the beautiful and wild heart of the earth.

Fundamentalism always rears its loud mouth urgently as a response to cosmopolitanism. Cosmopolitanism reminds me of all I do not know, did not even know I did not know. We need more reverence, more humility, a dynamic sense of mystery and wonder. Like Miller (2005), I seek stories that can generate "a greater sense of connection to the world and its inhabitants", stories that move out "from the mundane, personal tragedies that mark any individual life into the history, the culture, and the lives of the institutions that surround us all" (p. 25). Both *Saved!* and *Loving Annabelle* present stories that refuse easy consumption or dismissal. Here are stories that startle and unsettle like good art and good pedagogy ought to.

Artistic Imagery and/or Arts-Based Research

Kerri: In terms of arts-based research lenses, I was intrigued by the use of art and poetry in *Loving Annabelle*; poetry actually served as a thread weaving together many of the complex issues under discussion. Simone's reading and discussion of Walt Whitman's "Song of Myself" and of poems by Rilke serve as backdrop to highly charged discussions between Annabelle and Simone; there is lots of fascinating potential here to explore these dual layers between the poetic and the controversial. I note, too, the movie's choice to end with a quote about love from Rilke: "For one human being to love another; that is perhaps the most difficult of all our tasks ... the work for which all other work is but preparation."

Visual imagery is also a key revelatory tool in this movie; I note that the movie starts and ends with Annabelle and Simone (respectively) staring at very similar landscapes of sunlight through trees from the confines of jail-like cars. Water imagery also recurs at key, significant moments throughout the movie, including the pair's critical conversations by the ocean, Simone's private moments of revelation and grief in her bathtub, and the images of rain at the dance and shadowed on the walls when the two consummate their relationship.

I wonder if artistic approaches like these (or even like the artistic use of satire in *Saved!*) might be one way, as Althaus-Reid (2001) described it, to move to God at the margins, and to become tougher without losing our tenderness (p. 29). I am reminded here of Snowber's (2004) striving for a "spirituality of messiness" (p. 134), to "imagine yourself wild with words" (Leggo, 2006, p. 75), to continue "seeking the shapes that have not been named" (Leggo, 2008, p. 11).

Carl: Brueggemann (2001) claimed that "human transformative activity depends upon a transformed imagination" (p. xx). According to Brueggemann, prophetic imagination "is concerned with matters political and social, but it is as intensely concerned with matters linguistic (how we say things) and epistemological (how we know what we know)" (p. 21). Brueggemann then spun the intriguing phrase, "prophetic imagination", into the resonant phrase, "poetic imagination", which he argued "is the last way left in which to challenge and conflict the dominant reality" (p. 40). In much of my writing and pedagogy, I am seeking to recognize with Brueggemann "how singularly words, speech, language, and phrase shape consciousness and define reality" (p. 64). Film can be an *act* of transformation and an *art* of transformation, because film is always minding and mining the possibilities of language and discourse for translating the stories we live by and in. I agree with hooks (2003) that "the struggle to transform education" is a struggle "to find a new language of spirit" (p. 183). I am reminded of Hillman's (1999) wisdom that "the aesthetic imagination is the primary mode of knowing the cosmos, and aesthetic language the most fitting way to formulate the world" (p. 184).

I linger artfully in the world by seeking an ethics that is fired in the heart of aesthetics. Too often, ethics is understood as *morals*, construed in binary oppositions of right and wrong behaviour, good and bad character, high and low status. With a similarly simplistic disposition, English teachers often ask students to state the moral of the story or poem or film, but the heart of aesthetics refuses binary oppositions, simple judgements, and epigrammatic solutions. Instead, the heart of aesthetics pulses with questions, curiosity, openness, and imagination. Above all, the heart of aesthetics is devoted to a lively hopefulness.

My ongoing problem with many films about teaching and schools is that they are not aesthetically successful. So many films about teachers and learners are formulaic, predictable, idealized, sentimentalized, and sanitized. *Saved!* and *Loving Annabelle* are, happily, not those kinds of films. In a prophetic voice, both films avoid the simplistic by acknowledging an aesthetic awareness of alternative possibilities for storying identities and living. Dalton (2004) recommended that "giving students the tools to interpret their lives and the world outside them is central to the aesthetic classroom" (p. 43). So, when I ask, "what is this film good for?", I am hoping for films that will not recapitulate what I already know. Instead, I am looking for films that will shake me awake, and turn me around and around so I must see from new perspectives.

Teacher Formation and/or Identity

Kerri: I appreciated the nuanced exploration of teacher identity in *Loving Annabelle*, particularly with regards to Simone's grief and her sexuality. Clearly, the sexual relationship with a student is a critical issue throughout the movie; I am intrigued, however, by the subtler questions the movie hints at in terms of teacher formation and identity. I wonder, for instance, about Simone's own historical relationship with Mother Immaculata. Clearly, theirs is a charged history (see, for example, their awkward exchange around a half hour into the film), and, in some way, it parallels that of Simone and Annabelle, but we never find out exactly why.

I also appreciated that Simone's past was not just simplistically reduced to her having had a prior lesbian relationship; this prior relationship was in fact portrayed as complex and difficult, offering a beautiful opportunity to explore the impact of Simone's grief process (or lack thereof) on her current vocational and personal life. I would suggest that these more nuanced investigations of teachers' grief are fairly scarce in most of our filmic research—*Akeelah and the Bee* (Atchison, 2006) is one notable exception. I am reminded here of Betcher's (2007) evocative challenge to "unhinge" religion, and to rethink our relationships with pain and suffering (p. 47).

Carl: Teachers in movies remind me how my subject positions have been constructed and constrained by schools. As Dalton (2004) noted, "the Hollywood version of the 'good' teacher merely tugs a little at the cornerstone of the institutional hierarchy" (p. 15). Dalton presented a compelling argument that the idealized teachers in many movies are presented as inspirational heroes who "do not present a serious challenge to the dominant ideology of our cultural institutions" (p. 26). I see my own stories as a teacher well represented in films about schools and universities. I have had some impact in the lives of many students, but I have been a dutiful and obedient member of the teaching class that has been largely responsible for sustaining the status quo, the conservative agenda, "the dominant ideology of our cultural institutions." Instead of prophetically challenging schools as culturally constrained institutions, I have contributed to legitimating the institutions. When I reflect on *Saved!* and *Loving Annabelle*, I am reminded that there are other possibilities—personal, political, pedagogic, and prophetic.

As Dalton (2004) contended, "a more radical approach would be to directly challenge the validity of the curriculum itself instead of merely trying to make the curriculum more manageable for their students" (p. 41). *Saved!* and *Loving Annabelle* represent this kind of radical and innovative challenge to pedagogical and curricular practices.

Conclusion: Closing Thoughts

Kerri: I am aware that our braided conversations interweave an expansive range of issues; perhaps a linking thread throughout, however, is the intention to look for those places of unsettledness (Regan, 2010), of productive discomfort (Kumashiro, 2002), of indecency (Althaus-Reid, 2002), and to see what those edges might have to teach us. I wonder if this work is not dissimilar to Althaus-Reid's (2002) statement that "theology has its own deconstructive forces, its own instabilities and imprecisions which always create tensions and open new ways of understanding … [making of] theology something still worth the effort" (pp. 148–149). Perhaps in exploring these evocatively disruptive moments in our filmic research, we might come closer to answering that question, "what is this film good for?"

Carl: Lynch (2006) noted that "cinema is a language. It can say things—big, abstract things" (p. 17), but cinema also performs and offers specific, concrete stories that invite viewers to critically and creatively respond with other personal, political, and pedagogical stories. David Gilmour, the Canadian novelist, decided that his fifteen-year-old son, Jesse, could drop out of school if he watched three films a week with his father. For three years, Gilmour and his son watched films. I am intrigued by the notion of a curriculum of film. Gilmour (2007) wrote: "I knew I wasn't giving him a systematic education in cinema. That wasn't the point" (p. 107). Instead, the films provided "an occasion to spend time together, hundreds of hours, as well as a door-opener for all manner of conversational topics" (pp. 107–108). I am beginning to imagine a curriculum of film where teachers and learners engage in conversation about the many films that compose and construct and constrain and challenge our identities as human beings in relationships with one another and with others. I am beginning to imagine a curriculum of film where we ask the question, "what is this film good for?", as a way of opening up possibilities for more creative and critical pedagogy.

Acknowledgments

The research for this chapter was funded by the Social Sciences and Humanities Research Council of Canada (SSHRC). We wish to thank SSHRC for the generous support of our research program.

Note

1.   See, for example: Breault (2009), Bulman (2002, 2005), Dalton (2004), and Farhi (1999).

References

Adams, T. E. (2008). A review of narrative ethics. *Qualitative Inquiry, 14*(2), 175–194.

Adams, T. E., & Jones, S. H. (2011). Telling stories: Reflexivity, queer theory, and autoethnography. *Cultural Studies/Critical Methodologies, 11*(2), 108–116.

Althaus-Reid, M. (1999). On wearing skirts without underwear: 'Indecent theology challenging the liberation theology of the pueblo': Poor women contesting Christ. *Feminist Theology, 7*(20), 39–51.

Althaus-Reid, M. (2001). The divine exodus of God: Involuntarily marginalized, taking an option for the margins, or truly marginal? In W. Jeanrond, C. Theobald, S. Freyne, & G. Ruggieri (Eds.), *God: Experience and mystery* (pp. 27–33). London, UK: SCM.

Althaus-Reid, M. (2002). *Indecent theology: Theological perversions in sex, gender and politics*. New York, NY: Routledge.

Althaus-Reid, M. (2005). El tocado (le toucher): Sexual irregularities in the translation of God (the word) in Jesus. In Y. Sherwood & K. Hart (Eds.), *Derrida and religion: Other testaments* (pp. 393–405). New York, NY: Routledge.

Atchison, D. (Director). (2006). *Akeelah and the bee*. USA: Lions Gate.

Baudrillard, J. (1997). *Fragments: Cool memories III, 1991–1995* (E. Agar, Trans.). London, UK: Verso.

Betcher, S. V. (2007). *Spirit and the politics of disablement*. Minneapolis, MN: Fortress Press.

Betcher, S. V. (2010). Becoming flesh of my flesh: Feminist and disability theologies on the edge of posthumanist discourse. *Journal of Feminist Studies in Religion, 26*(2), 107–118.

Breault, R. (2009). The celluloid teacher. *Educational Forum, 73*(4), 306–317.

Bronski, M. (1998). *The pleasure principle: Sex, backlash, and the struggle for gay freedom*. New York, NY: St. Martin's Press.

Brooks, K. (Director). (2006). *Loving Annabelle*. USA: Big Easy Pictures; Divine Light Productions.

Brueggemann, W. (2001). *The prophetic imagination* (2nd ed.). Minneapolis, MN: Fortress Press.

Bulman, R. (2002). Teachers in the 'hood: Hollywood's middle-class fantasy. *Urban Review, 34*(3), 251–276.

Bulman, R. (2005). *Hollywood goes to high school: Cinema, schools, and American culture*. New York, NY: Worth.

Cavanagh, S. L. (2007). *Sexing the teacher: School sex scandals and queer pedagogies*. Vancouver, British Columbia, Canada: University of British Columbia Press.

Cavanagh, S. L. (2008). Sex in the lesbian teacher's closet: The hybrid proliferation of queers in school. *Discourse: Studies in the Cultural Politics of Education, 29*(3), 387–399.

Dalton, M. M. (2004). *The Hollywood curriculum: Teachers in the movies*. New York, NY: Peter Lang.

Dannelly, B. (Director). (2004). *Saved!*. USA: MGM.

Farhi, A. (1999). Hollywood goes to school: Recognizing the superteacher myth in film. *Clearing House, 72*(3), 157–159.

Freire, P. (1997). *Pedagogy of the heart* (D. Macedo & A. Oliveira, Trans.). New York, NY: Continuum.

Fulford, R. (1999). *The triumph of narrative: Storytelling in the age of mass culture.* Toronto, Ontario, Canada: Anansi.

Gilmour, D. (2007). *The film club: A true story of a father and son.* Toronto, Ontario, Canada: Thomas Allen.

Hasebe-Ludt, E., Chambers, C., & Leggo, C. (2009). *Life writing and literary métissage as an ethos for our times.* New York, NY: Peter Lang.

Hasebe-Ludt, E., Chambers, C., Leggo, C., Hurren, W., Oberg, A., & Donald, D. (2008). Métissage. In A. L. Cole & J. G. Knowles (Eds.), *Handbook of the arts in qualitative social science research* (pp. 141–153). Thousand Oaks, CA: Sage.

Hasebe-Ludt, E., Chambers, C., Oberg, A., & Leggo, C. (2008). Embracing the world, with all our relations: Métissage as an artful braiding. In S. Springgay, R. Irwin, C. Leggo, & P. Gouzouasis (Eds.), *Being with a/r/tography* (pp. 57–67). Rotterdam, The Netherlands: Sense.

Hillman, J. (1999). *The force of character: And the lasting life.* New York, NY: Random House.

hooks, b. (2003). *Teaching community: A pedagogy of hope.* New York, NY: Routledge.

Hutcheon, L. (2000). *A theory of parody: The teachings of twentieth-century art forms.* Urbana, IL: University of Illinois Press.

Hutcheon, L. (2006). *A theory of adaptation.* New York, NY: Routledge.

Jakobsen, J. R. (2002). Can homosexuals end Western civilization as we know it? Family values in a global economy. In A. Cruz-Malave & M. F. Manalansan, IV (Eds.), *Queer globalizations: Citizenship and the afterlife of colonialism* (pp. 134–148). New York, NY: New York University Press.

Kirkland, K., & Leggo, C. (2008). A grim fairy tale: Taboo, mythopoetics, and truth-telling. In J. G. Knowles, S. Promislow, & A. J. Cole (Eds.), *Creating scholartistry: Imagining the arts-informed thesis or dissertation* (pp. 245–258). Halifax, Nova Scotia, Canada: Backalong Books.

Kumashiro, K. (2002). *Troubling education: Queer activism and antioppressive pedagogy.* New York, NY: Routledge.

Leavy, P. (2011). *Essentials of transdisciplinary research: Using problem-centered methodologies.* Walnut Creek, CA: Left Coast.

Leggo, C. (2006). Learning by heart: A poetics of research. *JCT: Journal of Curriculum Theorizing, 22*(4), 73–96.

Leggo, C. (2008). Autobiography: Researching our lives and living our research. In S. Springgay, C. Leggo, R. Irwin, & P. Gouzouasis (Eds.), *Being with a/r/tography* (pp. 3–23). Rotterdam, The Netherlands: Sense.

Lynch, D. (2006). *Catching the big fish: Meditation, consciousness, and creativity.* New York, NY: Jeremy P. Tarcher/Penguin.

McMahon, J. (2000). *Seinfeld,* subjectivity, and Sartre. In W. Irwin (Ed.), *Seinfeld and philosophy: A book about everything and nothing* (pp. 90–108). Chicago, IL: Open Court.

Miller, R. E. (2005). *Writing at the end of the world.* Pittsburgh, PA: University of Pittsburgh Press.

O'Donnell, D. (2006). *Social acupuncture: A guide to suicide, performance and utopia.* Toronto, Ontario, Canada: Coach House Books.

Ondaatje, M. (2002). *The conversations: Walter Murch and the art of editing film.* Toronto, Ontario, Canada: Vintage Canada.

Pryer, A. (2011). *Embodied wisdom: Meditations on memoir and education.* Charlotte, NC: Information Age.

Regan, P. (2010). *Unsettling the settler within: Indian residential schools, truth telling, and reconciliation in Canada.* Vancouver, British Columbia: University of British Columbia Press.

Ruthven, M. (2004). *Fundamentalism: The search for meaning.* Oxford, UK: Oxford University Press.

Snowber, C. N. (2004). Leaning absolutes: Honoring the detours in our lives. In D. Denton & W. Ashton (Eds.), *Spirituality, action and pedagogy: Teaching from the heart* (pp. 124–135). New York, NY: Peter Lang.

Wilcox, M. M. (2010). Freaks and queers in the study of religion. *Bulletin for the Study of Religion, 39*(4), 4–9.

CHAPTER 26

"He Seemed Like Such a Nice Guy"

Youth, Intimate Partner Violence, and the Media

Lynn Corcoran

On December 15th, 2011, I glanced at the morning news on television. I saw a scenario unfolding whereby in the middle of the night, one car rammed another car just outside of Claresholm, a small Canadian prairie town. A violent shooting spree had ensued. It sounded as though it had been a targeted attack. The obligatory tarps were covering the bodies of several young people who had been shot to death. I thought to myself, "Gang stuff. Gang violence. Weird. Weird how it has now spread out to the rural areas." I live in Calgary, Canada's fourth largest city, a city of one million people in the province of Alberta. I had thought gang violence was generally contained to big cities like Calgary. The thought of this level of gang violence in the rural town of Claresholm, 110 kilometers south of Calgary was disturbing but, in all honesty, I did not give it much more thought at the time. As it turned out, this was not gang violence. Later that day, the story unfolded that a young man had stalked a car with four young people in it, including his ex-girlfriend, from their hometown, Lethbridge, to Claresholm. The young man was a jealous ex-boyfriend of one of the young women in the other car. He rammed their car with his car, causing the driver to stop, get out of the car, and see what was going on. The ex-boyfriend shot all four of the young people who were in their early 20s, killing three, wounding one; and then he shot and killed himself. He allegedly murdered his ex-girlfriend, as well as two young men who were in the car. He shot one other young woman seriously wounding her; she eventually recovered from her physical injuries.

The stories in the media unfolded over the next week. For the first few days after the shootings, interviews showed images of young people who knew both the victims and the gunman. These young adults looked completely surprised by what had occurred. Many of them, in reference to the gunman, said, "He seemed like such a nice guy." Within a week of the incident, in-depth reporting indicated that this young man had access to weapons (he was a hunter and he owned several guns). He had exhibited stalking behaviors (obsessive texting, checking up on his ex-girlfriend's whereabouts). He was also seen pushing his ex-girlfriend off a chair in a crowded bar frequented by university and college students just hours before he shot himself and the other four young people at the side of the highway in rural Alberta on that cold December night.

When I learned the details of what had occurred that night, I felt sick to my stomach. I had worked as a public-health nurse in schools, and I thought about the past 20 years of anti-bullying education and dating-violence classes in Alberta elementary, junior high, and high schools. I had worked in a shelter counseling men and women living in or breaking away from violent relationships, and I thought to myself, "Those young adults had no idea of the potential danger that they were in; any professional informed about risk assessment and intimate partner violence could easily see that the gunman possessed several significant risk factors. How is it that these young adults had no idea of the risk they faced?"

The details of this incident also had an impact on my work life. Most recently, I had worked in the area of universal screening for intimate partner violence. The premise behind this is that if all health professionals (nurses, physicians, midwives, dentists, dental hygienists, x-ray technicians, physiotherapists, occupational therapists) accurately and consistently screened all individuals for intimate partner violence across all settings where delivery of health care takes place (hospitals, community clinics, physicians' offices, homes), the violence will ultimately be identified and prevented. While universal screening for intimate partner violence can result in identifying those at-risk for or experiencing violence in their relationship, many cases are undetected. I realized that one of the flaws in this thinking about universal screening relative to the Claresholm murders is that the likelihood of a health professional assessing and ultimately screening these healthy young people was slim. These young people would have had little or no contact with the health system; they were healthy young adults with little or no reason to see a physician or nurse. There was little or no *access* to these young people for screening, assessment, or education regarding intimate partner violence.

It was through this realization that I began to understand that if young people were to be screened, they needed to screen themselves and each other. I also felt strongly that the messages (about intimate partner violence) and the messengers (those delivering these messages) need to change. The messages about intimate partner violence need to be different, new, and somehow catchy enough for young adults to take notice, for themselves and their friends. Although there may be some utility in the traditional messengers (e.g., teachers in the classroom, public-health nurses), it needs to be acknowledged that media is a messenger, and as such, it needs to be involved in this shift. Furthermore, youth themselves need to accept some responsibility in becoming media literate in a world where text and images of violence are mixed in with text and images of love and loving relationships. These mixed messages bombard youth daily and in sheer numbers. Youth need to be and become critical in their scrutiny of text and images related to intimate partner violence. It is important for youth to accept this responsibilty, but, it is also in the hands of the adults—parents, educators (school teachers, university professors, teachers of teachers), and policymakers to also join youth in this process.

Youth and Intimate Partner Violence

Youth and young adults (those between the ages of 18 and 25 years) in particular are in a developmental stage whereby they are forming their beliefs about education, work and/or working, and love and/or relationships (Arnett, 2000). Images and text from books, newspapers, magazines, television, and radio, as well as websites, Facebook, Twitter, and Instagram are a few of the rich data sources from which young adults are accessing both actively and passively as they formulate these beliefs. As participants in North American popular culture, youth are bombarded by graphic images and explicit messages portraying violence between men and women in intimate partner relationships. "Humankind may have had more bloodthirsty eras but none as filled with images of violence as the present" (Gerbner, 2009, p. 103). To get a sense of where we are now, it is always interesting to look back and see where we have come from.

Youth and Media: My Experience

I read the newspaper every day. I have done this since I was 10 years old when I started reading the Ann Landers column. Ann filled in the blanks for me and answered many of the questions that I could not ask my parents. Eventually, I took an interest in the other parts of the newspaper to learn about what was going on in the world. I scanned the front page and city and/or region sections, ignored the business section, spent some time examining the entertainment section, read about fringe topics (e.g., high-school and/or university sports) in the sports section, and depending on what was being covered, I had a pretty good look at the lifestyle section. *Reader's Digest* was also an exceptional source of information about people and the world for me. I remember the weekend I read the "Drama in Real Life" section of *Reader's Digest*. I quickly became hooked. I ventured down to the basement to find the back issues, and I read every single "Drama in Real Life" that I could get my hands on. I was fascinated about the details of rescues of humans and the occasional pet from frigid waters, industrial accidents where appendages were somehow caught in a menacing machine and quickly moving toward a spinning blade, and all other manner of excruciating edge-of-my-seat unfolding human disaster. I was 11 years old. I was in my youth and I was completely connected with the (mostly print) media available to me at the time.

As a teenager, I remember when I first saw music videos on television. Suddenly, pictures had been added to the music we had been listening to on the radio, and it was as though each new song now was also accompanied by a miniature movie. Music Television (MTV) came into being in the early 1980s. My friends and I could now watch music videos virtually non-stop. We nearly lost our minds in 1983 when Michael Jackson's *Thriller*, a 14-minute-long music video was released.

I learned about intimate partner relationships as an observer of my parents' marriage, by reading print media in the newspaper, watching television, and through song lyrics and music videos. I do not remember text or images of violence between men and women in much of what I consumed as a youth. While I would agree that my children are also learning about intimate partner relationships by observing my marriage to their father, the rest is history; their relationship with media is vastly different from mine when I was their age.

Youth and Media: My Teenagers' Experience

I am a mother of two teenagers, aged 13 and 16 years. Their access to and consumption of text and images is much different than mine was at their ages, although I do recognize the all-consuming nature of their relationship with media. They are very interested in the world around them, and they are looking to make sense of it, just as I did when I was teenager. They are constantly bombarded by images and messages about themselves and the world in which they live. My experiences with Ann Landers, *Reader's Digest*, music videos, and MTV are laughable, and should be archived in the bricks and mortar (not digital, not online) library using the Dewey Decimal System. Facebook, Twitter, and Skype are social-networking spaces that I use, which makes them almost irrelevant to my teenagers. Indeed, my son has told me about teenagers' *fake* Facebook pages, where they friend their parents, and their *real* Facebook pages, where these same teenagers interact, avoiding the watchful eye of their parents. As soon as I learn the name of the social-networking platform or an app that my teenage children are using, it is over for them, and they are on to the next one. Adults (or perhaps parents in particular) are meant to be excluded from the world that youth occupy; that much has not changed over time and generations.

We were recently enjoying a family holiday when my daughter said, "Well, when Ashley kicked me…" I did not hear much else, and I did not *get it*. I thought to myself, "How could Ashley kick her?" We were on a vacation, thousands of kilometers away from Ashley, who, at the time, was at home with her family enjoying the holidays. More importantly, Ashley is a gentle soul and a close friend of my daughter's. I was having some difficulty conjuring up the circumstances whereby she would actually kick my daughter. Kick was actually Kik Messenger, and it is free, it is instant messaging, and Ashley does not have a phone (yet), so she and my daughter instant messaged each other on their iPod touch devices. On holidays, we had access to a wireless network, and Ashley had indeed *Kiked* my daughter. Ashley had sent several messages, and they were keeping in close contact even though they were thousands of kilometers apart.

Not long after the Kiking incident, my daughter accidentally slipped up and let me in on an app called SnapChat. She was laughing uproariously as she gazed into her iPod touch. Her friend, who lives about 150 kilometres north of our city, had sent a picture of herself making a funny face. The image appeared for 10 seconds and then disappeared. They spent a good portion of their time that evening doing this back and forth—making a face, taking a picture, and then sending it to one another in a 10-second flash. I said, out loud, with my 16-year-old son within earshot, "That seems like a pretty good app for sexting." My daughter replied, "This app is just used for funny faces," in a tone of righteous indignation. My son did not say a word, but the subtle shift of the look on his face indicated that he knew exactly what I was talking about. By the time this chapter is published, SnapChat and Kik may well be artifacts of social media.

My teenagers and most youth have access to an insurmountable amount of information in an equally unimaginable number of forms. The old stand-bys of books, newspapers, magazines, television, and radio still exist, and assume some importance in informing them about their world. Added on top of that are computers, phones, and all types of mobile devices as portals to an exploding number of digitized texts and images. In order to navigate the world, they need some strategies to filter through the barrage of this media in order to make their own meaning. This task, I believe, is becoming increasingly challenging.

Youth, Violence, and the Media

The effect of exposure to violent images and text in the media, and the influence of this on attitudes and behaviors of children, adolescents, and youth have been studied at length and through a variety of disciplines such as psychology (and specifically, developmental psychology), public health, behavioral science, pediatrics, and communications. Although it is exceedingly difficult to establish causal or correlational relationships, there is some agreement in the predominantly quantitative literature of the past 10 years that exposure to violence in the media is related to increases in aggression and hostility, and that this can translate into violent attitudes and behaviors. Children, adolescents, and youth exposed to violence in music and/or music videos, computer and/or video games, movies, television, and television news reports are influenced by these images and texts (American Academy of Pediatrics, 2009; Brady, 2007; Brodeur, 2009; Browne & Hamilton-Giachritsis, 2005; Gentile, Saleem, & Anderson, 2007; Huesmann & Taylor, 2006; Krug, Dahlberg, Mercy, Zwi, & Lozano, 2002; Murray, 2008).

Youth, violence, and the influence of media is a complex and layered issue. The influence of media on youth and intimate partner violence in particular is less clear. However, there is agreement among researchers that this issue should be explored in greater detail (Brady, 2007; Browne & Hamilton-Giachritsis, 2005; Escobar-Chaves et al., 2005; Krug et al., 2002; Marcus, 2005). There is support in the literature for enacting strategies to address the challenge of youth and violence in all its forms, from intimate partner violence to aggression, hostility, and criminal behavior (American Academy of Pediatrics, 2009; Brady, 2007; Browne & Hamilton-Giachritsis, 2005; Escobar-Chaves et al., 2005; Foshee & McNaughton Reyes, 2009; Krug et al., 2002). In the next section of this chapter, I will present two strategies and discuss how they might be viable in addressing the issue of youth and intimate partner violence.

Addressing the Challenge: Media Mindfulness and Media Literacy

There is no one answer or single strategy to address the personal, political, social, cultural, and deeply textured issue of the influence of media on youth and intimate partner violence. Regardless of what strategies might be offered to address this issue, the thinking grounding the strategies needs to be creative, energetic, and situated in acknowledging the changing contexts of the developmental tasks of young adulthood and the evolution of communication and media (e.g., apps, social-networking platforms). The two very broad strategies I suggest to address the concerns around youth, media, and intimate partner violence are *media mindfulness* and *media literacy*. Equally importantly, I advocate that these strategies engage the following groups of people:

- Youth (individually and collectively);

- Caring adults engaged in the lives of youth (parents, grandmothers and grandfathers, aunts and uncles, and close family friends);

- Educators (classroom teachers, college and/or university professors, and those who develop curriculum);

- Policymakers and those who work to interpret and enact policy in their work with governmental and non-governmental organizations.

Media mindfulness

Mindfulness involves being in and appreciating the present moment as well as questioning our view of and place in the world (Kabat-Zinn, 1995). Media mindfulness builds on this concept, and involves being actively engaged in the moment, regarding the media being consumed. Serafin (2009) conceptualized media mindfulness as involving "the ability to read texts more meaningfully, being motivated to do so regularly, and practicing mindful attendance to our consumption of media" (p. 180). Rather than being a passive consumer of media, a mindul approach involves taking a critical look at media using a cognitive-response approach to the message (image and/or text) being processed. The cognitive-response approach can occur in one of two ways, the peripheral route or the central route. Serafin (2009) advocated the cognitive-response approach using central route processing. In this approach, when a message in the media is received by an individual, the person thinks about it critically, thoughtfully, and contextually. The person receiving the message must be capable of this task and motivated to carry it out. In essence, the mindful media consumer processes the message by paying close attention to it, relating it to what is already known, and elaborating on it by generating new meanings and implications (Serafin, 2009).

I offer an example of the media mindfulness in my work as a nurse educator. I teach a class to third-year undergraduate nursing students about assessing and screening for intimate partner violence in hospital and community settings with pregnant and parenting families. While I cover *the basics* in terms of risk factors and screening questions that nurses might ask patients and/or clients in the hospital and during home visits, this content information is always delivered near the end of the 90-minute class. I spend well over half of this class offering examples from the media—such as news stories covering domestic homicides and music videos portraying intimate partner violence—to set the ground work for the meaningful consideration of this topic in the context of their nursing practice. Lately, in class, I have been showing the music video by Rihanna and Eminem, "Love the Way You Lie," to illustrate the cycle of violence. The images used to represent the lyrics provide impetus for substantive class discussions regarding: the ambivalence (of a woman or a man) choosing to remain in or leave an abusive relationship, the use of alcohol to manage powerful feelings, and the isolating nature of a violent relationship. In this way, I am inviting the nursing students (many of whom are young adults themselves in the midst of sorting out their beliefs regarding intimate relationships) to critically examine the meaning of the texts and images in the context of their own lives. This sets the stage for receptivity of the nursing students to content information such as risk assessment and choices of questions to be used when screeening for intimate partner violence in their nursing work with individuals and families. Mindfulness focuses on the process of the learning rather than the outcome. "Mindfulness theory ... lies at the heart of what it means to be media literate" (Serafin, 2009, p. 179).

Media literacy

"Reading the media is never easy. It is precisely the nature of media to often appear innocent, benign, yet to be incredibly complex and often insidious" (Steinberg, 2009, p. xiii). I agree with Steinberg's assertion; like a series of optical illusions intertwined with auditory hallucinations, what is seen and heard in the media is not always as it appears. This underscores the importance of media literacy as a broad strategy to address the concerns around youth, media, and intimate partner violence.

"Literacy involves gaining the skills and knowledge to read, interpret, produce texts and artifacts, and to gain the intellectual tools and capacities to fully particpate in one's culture and society" (Kellner & Share, 2009, pp. 4–5). Critical media literacy stretches this definition to include cultivation of skills to analyze media codes and conventions, and to question stereotypes, dominant values, and ideologies presented in media. It is important to recognize that media have the power to liberate, dominate, manipulate, or enlighten (Kellner & Share, 2009). Youth need to become active and discerning in their consumption of media. "Students and youths are often more media savvy, knowledgeable, and immersed in media culture than their teachers, and can contribute to the educational process through sharing their ideas, perceptions, and insights" (Kellner & Share, 2009, p. 17). In a formal education setting, such as a classroom or lecture theatre, a strategy involving media literacy needs to be open, fluid, and relevant. Media literacy educators need to take the lead, caring adults involved in the lives of youth need to follow this lead, and the youth themselves are integral to the process.

Media Mindfulness, Media Literacy, and the Discourse of Intimate Partner Violence: Revisiting the Claresholm Murders

As an extension of the strategies of media mindfulness and media literacy, the media itself—those reporters and journalists who scoop, develop, and ultimately share news stories of youth and intimate partner violence—have a responsibility for their role in shaping the public discourse of violence. "All messages are influenced by the subjectivity and biases of those creating the message" (Kellner & Share, 2009, p. 12). Those who write, direct, and produce media, and those who provide coverage of incidents of intimate partner violence, also share the responsibility for engaging in the strategies of media mindfulness and media literacy. "Mass media form the convening systems of modern societies ... mass media host the public discourse that influences public opinion" (Ryan, Anastario, & DaCunha, 2006, p. 210). Coverage of intimate partner violence stories in the news has a significant impact on the public and youth, who are consumers of the news media (Benedict, 1993; Ryan et al., 2006; Vives-Cases, Torrubiano-Domínguez, & Alvarez-Dardet, 2009; Walma van der Molen, 2004).

In this final section, I will revisit the Claresholm murders described earlier in this chapter. I will highlight and critically analyze significant aspects of the news coverage of this incident of intimate partner violence involving young adults. I will end this section by taking another look at the strategies of media mindfulness and media literacy in the context of news coverage of the Claresholm murders.

For the first few days after the Claresholm murders, television interviews and news clips showed images of young people who knew both the victims and the gunman. These young adults looked utterly perplexed and were at a loss to explain these murders. The headlines in national newspapers reinforced these images and texts:

- "Claresholm Highway Killer's Friends Had 'No Sign This Was Coming'" (*National Post*, December 17, 2011 [Tetley, 2011a];

- "Despite Signs of Rage, Friends Couldn't Have Foreseen Alberta Rampage" (*The Globe and Mail*, December 19, 2011 [Walton & Waldie, 2011].

As the more detailed stories in the media unfolded over the next week, all was not quite as it had initially appeared. The young man who allegedly shot the four young adults possessed significant risk factors, placing him at risk of acting out violence toward his ex-girlfriend. He owned several guns; he threatened his ex-girlfriend, and was physically violent toward her in public. Often, these details were downplayed in newspaper articles describing friends' reactions of shock and disbelief over the gunman's violent actions. It was as though the news coverage needed to conceal the horrific violence by somehow softening it with details proving that the gunman was a "nice guy":

> He was a quiet Mormon man, just out of his teens and on the verge of working in a life-saving role as a paramedic, his friends say. And while more details emerge about the frightening events leading up to the murderous roadside rampage carried out south of Calgary, friends of the killer … are reeling from the shock. They say they are heartbroken and confused. (Tetley, 2011b, p. 1)

In the months following the Claresholm murders, news coverage focused initially on funerals and memorial services. Following that, updates on the recovery of the young woman who survived the shootings were periodically reported. The reports regarding the two murdered young men often focused on their athletic achievements. Images of two young men in baseball uniforms were shown on the screen and they were often described as "promising young baseball players" attending the Prairie Baseball Academy. The young woman who survived the shootings was referred to as the "sole survivor" and "an amazing young woman." Interestingly, the gunman's ex-girlfriend did not seem to be specifically labelled in ways similar to that of the other young adults. She was referred to as a "shooting victim," "female passenger in the car," or simply "ex-girlfriend." The tragedy of this violent incident was palpable in these reports; it is always sad when young people die, and these deaths are often tragic and unexpected. However, the fact that this was an incident of intimate partner violence was strangely absent from much of the news coverage. Generally, this incident was referred to as a "Murder-Suicide." This language conceals what was actually the result of a jealous ex-boyfriend stalking his ex-girlfriend with what seemed to be intent to shoot her and those close to her.

On March 16th, 2012, three months after the Claresholm murders, Global National television news provided an update on the young woman who survived the shootings. She was being discharged from hospital and returning to her home in Prince Edward Island. She spent three months in the hospital in Calgary, Alberta, undergoing and recovering from surgeries to remove the bullets in her stomach, shoulder, and leg. Watching the news report, it was evident that her physical injuries persisted. One news clip showed her in a wheelchair, but she got out of it and was able to walk. Her left hand hung limply by her side, and media reports indicated that she would need more physiotherapy to help return function. Her psychological injuries were haunting. Tears streamed down her face as she spoke in an apprehensive tone of voice, "Everyone keeps telling me that it's going to be OK. I guess at some point it will be for *everybody*." She shrugged her shoulders and looked away, and as her voice trailed off, she said, "*I* don't know…" (Global National News, 2012). This two and a half minutes of coverage again failed to connect her injuries and long, painful recovery with a horrific incident of intimate partner violence involving young adults. The phrases, "domestic violence," "domestic abuse," "intimate partner violence," or "dating violence" were not uttered. The story was of the remarkable recovery of the sole survivor of the shootings and her hopeful new life in Prince Edward Island.

Interestingly, one year later, on the anniversary of the Claresholm murders, there was little news coverage. The story dominating the news was the Sandy Hook Elementary School shootings in Connecticut, in which 20 students and 6 teachers were murdered on December 14th, 2012. The media has a short attention span; it is always looking for and showing eager viewers the next big human tragedy.

In February of 2013, the television program, W5, an investigative reporting news show, aired "Road to Murder." This program was an in-depth report of the Claresholm murders. Airing a show of this nature 14 months after the murders was an admirable undertaking; it made me think that people did not want to forget about the deaths of the young people. I was optimistic that in the 60-minute duration of this program, the layers would be peeled back, and the depth of intimate partner violence would be revealed. I had a secret hope that a few key messages related to how young adults might recognize intimate partner violence in their own lives and those of their friends might be offered. I was wondering if part of the program might be used as a public-education segment.

"Road to Murder" (Day, 2013) was narrated by Lloyd Robertson, a trusted, grandfatherly, suit-wearing figure in Canadian news reporting. To me, choosing this White, older male to narrate this program signaled from the beginning that the old guard was present and the public discourse around intimate partner violence might be protected and reinforced. The show was broken down into four segments: a chronological recounting of the events of the night of December 14th, 2011, with a focus on the young woman who survived the shootings telling her story; a report on the life of the gunman and an exploration of his character; a focus on the lives and accomplishments of the three murdered young people as well as the parents of these youth; and a conclusion featuring footage from the male Royal Canadian Mounted Police (RCMP) lead investigator and a female RCMP domestic violence expert. The long interview with the survivor of the shootings at the beginning of the program evoked nothing but sympathy from the viewer toward this pleasant-looking, articulate, and vulnerable young woman with tears streaming down her face. The two young men who were victims were portrayed as decent young men with promising careers in baseball. The gunman's ex-girlfriend was shown as a good-looking, fun-loving, and generous young woman. In contrast, pictures of the gunman portrayed a less flattering image—he looked either intense and angry or aloof and disengaged. This presentation of contrasts was a misguided note to the viewer that surely they will recognize intimate partner violence when they see it.

However, toward the end of the program, there was a shift and a legitimate attempt was made at showing what intimate partner violence really looks like, in real life, right here and right now. The gunman's text messages to his girlfriend during their on-again, off-again relationship and in the critical time period just prior to the murders were clearly shown to viewers and read aloud. The texts were littered with threats, swear words, and put-downs. These real-life examples were illustrative to viewers in terms of psychological abuse. Major risk factors were clearly listed (access to guns, controlling behavior, excessive jealousy, anger and threats, alcohol abuse, and abuse directed at pets) on the television screen in bold letters. That the gunman possessed these risk factors was made apparent. Relevant public education was provided by a nondescript, uniformed, female RCMP officer. She stated that victims should not feel embarrassed and should seek help. However, bolstering these messages, in plain language, was the mother of one of the murdered young men, as she acknowledged that young women often have no basis of comparison for their first intimate relationship. She added that controlling is not normal, and that young women need to be aware that they deserve to be treated with respect. This message from this mother was powerful.

There is a good chance that the demographic of young adults just gaining life experience with intimate partner relationships (around the ages of 18 to 25 years) would not have been watching W5: "Road to Murder." However, those involved in the lives of this demographic, such as caring adults engaged with youth (parents, grandmothers and grandfathers, aunts and uncles, close family friends, teachers, college and/or university professors, and guidance counsellors), quite likely were watching this show. Media mindfulness is evident in that an in-depth report on this horrendous incident of intimate partner violence was undertaken 14 months after this incident. Those invested in the strategy of media literacy might pose the question, "Was the public discourse of '*he seemed like such a nice guy*' supported and reinforced or disrupted through the W5 program, 'Road to Murder'?" There were elements of support and reinforcement for this discourse, as seen in the images of beautiful young adults, kind and fun-loving young women, athletic and decent young men, gunned down before their time with nary a mention of the context noted by the absence of the phrases "domestic violence," "domestic abuse," "intimate partner violence," or "dating violence" in this program. However, a beginning of some disruption was evident for a full 10 minutes toward the conclusion of the program when how violence is manifested in text messages was shown, risk factors were boldly presented, and a mother appealed to all young women to recognize violence in their relationships. This was a good start, in terms of informing youth and those who live with, educate, and work alongside youth as they begin to navigate intimate partner relationships in their lives.

In summary, those involved with constructing and delivering media, as messengers with the power to shape the public discourse, need to accept this responsibility and embrace the strategies of *media mindfulness* and *media literacy* in order to shift the public discourse. The news coverage of the Claresholm murders, both immediately after they occurred and in the months following, fell short of disrupting the public discourse around youth and intimate partner violence. Those who produced this coverage did not practice media mindfulness or consider media literacy, as the shock, surprise, and rhetoric of "he seemed like such a nice guy" was paraded out followed by heart-wrenching coverage of memorial services, mass grieving, and personal recovery. However, the investigative news report, *W5: "Road to Murder,"* was a watchable and compelling program. Although much of the show seemed to also highlight the shock of the tragedy and loss of young lives, the display of actual obsessive and abusive texts sent by the gunman to his ex-girlfriend clearly revealed the raw material of intimate partner violence, and the messages shown regarding being aware of risk factors were loud and clear. This is a good beginning where the media are becoming media mindful and media literate.

Concluding Thoughts

Youth, violence, and the influence of media is a loaded topic, a bouncing ball, and a constantly moving target. Media mindfulness and media literacy are two broad strategies that need to be seriously considered when addresssing this problem. As more youth, (as well as those who love and care about youth, those who create, produce, and direct media) become media mindful and media literate regarding images and texts of intimate partner violence, a shift in the public discourse from unexpected tragedy to preventable incident, becomes conceivable.

References

American Academy of Pediatrics. (2009). Media violence: Policy statement. *Pediatrics, 124*(5), 1495–1503. doi: 10.1542/peds.2009-2146

Arnett, J. J. (2000). Emerging adulthood: A theory of development from the late teens through the twenties. *American Psychologist, 55*(5), 469–480. doi: 10.1037//0003-066x.55.5.469

Benedict, H. (1993). *Virgin or vamp: How the press covers sex crimes.* New York, NY: Oxford University Press.

Brady, S. S. (2007). Young adults' media use and attitudes toward interpersonal and institutional forms of aggression. *Aggressive Behavior, 33*(6), 519–525. doi: 10.1002/ab

Brodeur, J. (2009). Media violence: Why is it used to abuse children? How to oppose it and win. In D. Macedo & S. R. Steinberg (Eds.), *Media literacy: A reader* (pp. 667–686). New York, NY: Peter Lang.

Browne, K. D., & Hamilton-Giachritsis, C. (2005). The influence of violent media on children and adolescents: A public health approach. *Lancet, 365*(9460), 702–710.

Day, L. (Writer, Director). (2013, February 15). Road to murder [Television series episode]. *W5.* Toronto, Canada: CTV.

Escobar-Chaves, S. L., Tortolero, S. R., Markham, C. M., Low, B. J., Eitel, P., & Thickstun, P. (2005). Impact of the media on adolescent sexual attitudes and behaviors. *Pediatrics, s116*(1), 303–326. doi: 10.1542/peds.2005-0355D

Foshee, V. A., & McNaughton Reyes, H. L. (2009). Primary prevention of adolescent dating abuse perpetration: When to begin, whom to targe, and how to do it. In D. J. Whitaker & J. R. Lutzker (Eds.), *Preventing partner violence: Research and evidence-based intervention strategies* (pp. 141–168). Washington, DC: American Psychological Association.

Gentile, D. A., Saleem, M., & Anderson, C. A. (2007). Public policy and the effects of media violence on children. *Social Issues and Policy Review, 1*(1), 15–61.

Gerbner, G. (2009). Television violence at a time of turmoil and terror. In D. Macedo & S. R. Steinberg (Eds.), *Media literacy: A reader* (pp. 103–115). New York, NY: Peter Lang.

Global National News. (2012, March 16). Calgary, Canada: Author.

Huesmann, L. R., & Taylor, L. D. (2006). The role of media violence in violent behavior. *Annual Review of Public Health*, *27*(1), 393–415. doi: 10.1146/annure.publhealth.26.021304.144640

Kabat-Zinn, J. (1995). *Wherever you go, there you are: Mindfulness meditation in everyday life*. New York, NY: Hyperion.

Kellner, D., & Share, J. (2009). Critical media literacy, democracy, and the reconstruction of education. In D. Macedo & S. R. Steinberg (Eds.), *Media literacy: A reader* (pp. 3–23). New York, NY: Peter Lang.

Krug, E. G., Dahlberg, L. L., Mercy, J. A., Zwi, A. B., & Lozano, R. (2002). *World report on violence and health: Youth violence*. Geneva, Switzerland: World Health Organization.

Marcus, R. F. (2005). Youth violence in everday life. *Journal of Interpersonal Violence, 20*(4), 442–447. doi: 10.1177/0886260504267550

Murray, J. P. (2008). Media violence: The effects are both real and strong. *American Behavioral Scientist, 5*(8), 1212–1230. doi: 10.1177/0002764207312018

Ryan, C., Anastario, M., & DaCunha, A. (2006). Changing coverage of domestic violence murders: A longitudinal experiment in participatory communication. *Journal of Interpersonal Violence, 21*(2), 209–228. doi: 10.1177/0886260505282285

Serafin, G. M. (2009). Media mindfulness. In D. Macedo & S. R. Steinberg (Eds.), *Media literacy: A reader* (pp. 178–196). New York, NY: Peter Lang.

Steinberg, S. R. (2009). Preface: Reading media critically. In D. Macedo & S. R. Steinberg (Eds.), *Media literacy: A reader* (pp. xiii–xvi). New York, NY: Peter Lang.

Tetley, D. (2011a, December 17). Claresholm highway killer's friends had "no sign this was coming." *National Post*. Retrieved from http://news.nationalpost.com/2011/12/17/claresholm-highway-killers-friends-had-no-sign-this-was-coming/

Tetley, D. (2011b, December 17). Friends of killer Derek Jensen shocked at his actions. *Calgary Herald*. Retrieved from http://www.theguardian.pe.ca/News/Local/2011-12-17/article-2840358/Friends-of-killer-Derek-Jensen-shocked-at-his-actions/1

Vives-Cases, C., Torrubiano-Domínguez, J., & Alvarez-Dardet, C. (2009). The effect of television news items on intimate partner violence murders. *European Journal of Public Health, 19*(6), 592–596.

Walma van der Molen, J. H. (2004). Violence and suffering in television news: Toward a broader conception of harmful television content for children. *Pediatrics, 113*(9), 1771–1775.

Walton, D., & Waldie, P. (2011, December 19). Despite signs of rage, friends couldn't have foreseen Alberta rampage. *The Globe and Mail*. Retrieved from http://www.theglobeandmail.com/news/national/despite-signs-of-rage-friends-couldnt-have-foreseen-alberta-rampage/article4248010/

CHAPTER 27

We Don't Need Another Hero

Captaining in Youth Sport

Tracy D. Keats

I am not even sure if he was the official captain of the swim team, but what I saw and admired in my inaugural sporting experience was the tall, fair-skinned, beautifully lithe boy with the wonderful smile who swam like a fish and collected all the medals. The boys wanted to be him, the girls wanted to date him—he was the aspiration of that particular sport.

That image has been repeated incessantly in each and every sport I have encountered as a player, coach, and teacher. The captain has been the measure within a team; if you were named captain, you knew you had made it.

Although I excelled at most sports in junior high and high school—soccer, volleyball, basketball, softball—I was never quite pretty enough, charismatic enough, skilled enough, or popular enough to claim captain status. But I always wanted to be. Being captain was so obviously a status that everyone involved in team sport aspired to. It meant you were the best, and who did not want to be the best?

The sport captain is a team member designated as the leader of the group. Roles and responsibilities of a captain vary according to the particular sport, and sometimes according to each individual team, but captaining is an honored, respected, and accepted practice in sport culture around the world. Captains are recognized as peer leaders, and certain sports identify them publicly in different ways; for example, a "C" on the left chest of the jersey of an ice hockey captain, a bar beneath the jersey number of a volleyball captain, and an upper armband on a soccer captain. Such practices are commonly employed to ensure that these designated players are the only members of a team permitted to interact with game officials during a match. When the captain leaves the game for any reason, this responsibility often falls to an alternate: ice hockey teams designate two alternate "A" captain jerseys, and another player must be designated "floor captain" in volleyball should the captain require a substitution. Captains therefore have the responsibility of discussing the application and interpretation of rules, and may be required to relay information between officials and the coach. In addition to these and other practical roles within sport, many coaches agree that the leadership provided by the captain is important for team cohesion and success, yet there is a marked absence of research examining peer leadership in sport. Much of the existing literature discussing leadership in athletics centres on the coach; however, coaches conventionally depend on athletes as a vital source of leadership within teams. Captains provide motivation and direction to their teammates, and play an important part of teams coming together to work hard and achieve their goals (Dupuis, Bloom, & Loughead, 2006; Glenn & Horn, 1993; Todd & Kent, 2004; Weese & Nicholls, 1986).

Good Captains

By my senior year of high school, I had sacrificed all other sporting opportunities to specialize in volleyball, and had become quite skilled in my 6'2" frame, thanks to summer Provincial Team training. I learned that if I were to ever really achieve anything big in sport, I had to specialize. I became one of the two best players on my high school volleyball team. Not *the* best. The best player was named captain. The captain, Jane, was the star. She was beautiful, confident, enthusiastic. She was the undisputed team leader; the team was "hers" and she was responsible for its successes. Since the team *was* successful, she was never criticized for failure. Jane led the team into the gym during pep rallies, and took the mic to proudly address the student body. She was quoted in the newspaper, and was referred to as "Captain Jane," while others who may have been mentioned were only distinguished by the position they played, not by their leadership status or importance to the team. Although I was envious of the advantages she enjoyed as captain, Jane was a positive leader, and nobody disputed the appropriateness of her designation.

Certainly, there must be some magical combination of personality, motivation, and behaviour that makes a good captain; maybe something that I was missing. What are the requirements of a good team leader? Sport leadership research suggests that athletes possess greater leadership tendencies than non-athletes (Dobosz & Beaty, 1999; Snyder & Spreitzer, 1992), but what makes a captain a good leader?

Imagine that star athlete with the bold "C" on the left chest. A number of identifiers may come to mind: Skilled. Knowledgeable. Confident. Hard-working. Well-spoken. Communicator. Motivator. Motivated. Consistent. Honest. Respected. Respectable. Disciplined. Dedicated. Personable. Charismatic. Play-maker. Game-changer. Additionally, Hollywood portrayals of captains in sports films may elicit glorified images: Tall. Blond. Rugged. Good-looking. Sexy. Heterosexual. Male. Popular. Strong. Fit. Poised. Cool. But are these identifiers not available to all athletes, regardless of captainship?

Initial peer-leadership studies aimed at identifying traits and/or behaviours that distinguish leaders from non-leaders on sport teams. Researchers attempted to identify leaders as a result of their centrality of position, interaction frequency, and position specificity (e.g., Gill & Perry, 1979; Tropp & Landers, 1979). Starter status and previous experience also play a large role in predicting peer leadership; players who are more involved in competition (starters) are more likely to be leaders of a team than non-starters or less-experienced players (e.g., Gill & Perry, 1979). Others have found correlations in sport leaders who are able to integrate both task-related and relationship-oriented functions (Rees & Segal, 1984; Yukelson, Weinberg, Richardson, & Jackson, 1983); players who are considered leaders by their peers are ranked high in popularity. These findings indicate that peer leaders of sports teams are highly instrumental to the physical success of the team through skill, experience, and knowledge of the game, but also contribute to team cohesion and teammates' performance through interpersonal attraction, likeability, and relationship building. Rees and Segal (1984) suggested that sports-team leaders are charismatic leaders, and that part of their leadership role includes relational tasks:

> It may be that in goal-directed groups, such as sports teams, expressive behavior is perceived as part of task leadership, since having members get along with each other is essential for the successful coordination of task activities and through this the realization of group goals .... Failure to provide expressive leadership by instrumental team leaders may be perceived by group members as violating the group norm of 'being a team player'. (p. 121)

Just as there are many definitions and understandings of leadership, there are many interpretations of what makes a good leader in team sport. Early research rarely distinguished between team leaders and captains, and those studies that did often indicated that players identified as leaders by their peers were *not* those chosen as captains by their coaches. In a study of female field-hockey players, Tropp and Landers (1979) found that goalies were rated highest in leadership by their peers, and yet represented only 25% of team captain positions. Similarly, Gill and Perry (1979) noted in their women's intercollegiate softball study, "The player who was consistently ranked highest on leadership ... was not the team captain" (p. 89). These early studies are examples of the prevalence of coach-appointed leaders as captains. While coaches rely on captains as team leaders who contribute to team cohesion as well as team performance, they often select such leaders based primarily on skill (Glenn & Horn, 1993; Moran & Weiss, 2006). Although sport competence is important, athlete self-ratings and peer-ratings of leadership tend to encompass factors beyond skill, including the demonstration of both instrumental and expressive behaviours. Athletes identify peer leaders based on psychological (perceived competence, instrumentality, expressiveness), social (peer acceptance, friendship quality), and ability (actual skill) variables (Moran & Weiss, 2006). Glenn and Horn's (1993) examination of self-ratings, peer-ratings, and coach-ratings of leadership in female soccer players revealed that players have an "androgynous conception of an effective team leader (i.e., one who is assertive, confident and aggressive but is also friendly, nurturant [*sic*], and empathetic)" (p. 30), while coaches rated leaders based solely on their level of actual skill competence. Other factors that are important to team members include work ethic in games and practice, respect for fellow teammates, low competitive trait anxiety (calm and cool under pressure), and high self-esteem (Dupuis et al., 2006; Glenn & Horn, 1993; Todd & Kent, 2004).

Coaches traditionally select captains without team-member input, and it is common for the "best" player to receive the "C" jersey. Weese and Nicholls (1986) indicated that a

> coach wants a team captain to possess several talents, including: knowledge of the rules, ability to make decisions that will maximize strategic advantage, skill in performance, and an ability to keep his cool in pressure situations. As well, he would like this captain to be influential with the other players, popular, respected and a solid motivator of good performances from his teammates. (p. 270)

Therefore, based on the existing research, it is possible to identify a set of leadership identifiers in athletics. Leaders of sports teams generally occupy a highly specialized or central position, through which they can perform particular task functions because they are an experienced, skilled, starting, and contributing member of the team. Although they are primarily concerned with goal-attainment roles, effective peer leaders also maintain effective relationships with teammates in order to ensure team cohesion and goal achievement. This is a tall order to fill, and a coach would need to get this decision right for the best fitted player among all team members to fill the captaincy position.

In "Follow the Leader: Beyond Captain Selection," Springfield College women's volleyball coach, Joel Dearing (2012), described a process by which team members select the captain based on specific qualities and characteristics they deem necessary for that particular team. In this process, players can take some ownership in electing the teammate that will lead them. Captain selection by vote has become a popular practice in many sports, particularly at younger ages. While team involvement in the peer-leadership decision may have its benefits, it is also problematic for a number of reasons, including individuals voted by popularity rather than leadership "skill," and disagreement within the group regarding appropriateness of selection.

Regardless of which player is chosen as captain, there is no guarantee that they will lead effectively. While the above offers a description of identified peer leaders within sports teams, it does not delineate *effective* leaders. Do all team members who meet these criteria serve leadership roles (formal or informal)? Do these leaders effectively *lead* their teams?

Bad Captains

In university, I experienced the negative effects of a poor captain selection. The team voted. As a rookie with little experience at that level of training and competition, and having known my teammates for all of two weeks at that point, it was obvious who to vote for: the oldest, most skilled, most experienced, most vocal, and most take-charge person on the team. Throughout the season, Captain Kelly enjoyed many benefits as team leader. Although she was indeed talented, she was never pulled from games for performing badly. She received positive feedback when others were criticized. She was exempted from punishment when she made mistakes that would earn teammates a set of suicides. She appeared on game-night advertising posters around campus. And she proudly wore the bar beneath her jersey number, a bright beacon to all that she was Top Dog of that team. These things may have all gone unnoticed—or at least unquestioned—if Captain Kelly were able to lead her team positively. But coupled with her inability to inspire trust and respect from her teammates, these things led to dissention. She rarely contributed insightful or motivational words to team meetings or locker-room talks. Instead, her comments were negative, accusatory, and self-promoting. Teammates respected her less and less as the season went on, and it turned into a destructive, manipulative, clique-type leadership that ended up dividing the team further. Neither team cohesion nor performance goals were achieved.

This is not a rare occurrence in sport. I have encountered many athletes, coaches, and teachers in my career with anecdotes similar to mine. Recently, in a second-year teacher-education class, I inquired about negative captain experiences. More than half the audience reported having played on a team whose captain was not an appropriate designation. What is astounding is that most of the students in that class would not even self-identify as accomplished athletes (only three played post-secondary sport), and their negative experiences occurred during early-development and recreational youth sports programs. But these negative experiences cannot be blamed on young athletes who have little experience in sport and therefore do not know how to lead a team. Bad captains exist at all levels of sport. During the 2012 National Football League (NFL) season, New York Jets coach, Rex Ryan, did not name a team captain because of a disastrous experience with receiver, Santonio Holmes, as captain during the previous season. According to *New York Post* reporter, Brian Costello (2012), "Holmes seemed emboldened by having the "C" on his chest, referencing it several times while making remarks critical of some teammates. His implosion at the end of the season forced Ryan to reconsider the idea of captains" (para. 5). The 2011 Jets were a talented squad with Super Bowl aspirations, but instead they lost the last three regular-season games and failed to even make the playoffs for the first time since 2008. Players attested to poor team chemistry, and Holmes was blamed for "poisoning the locker room" throughout the season. During the last game, Holmes was benched for the final two minutes after fighting with teammates, and even had to be restrained from going after a teammate in the huddle (Cimini, 2012).

This sounds like a case of a superstar professional athlete who has allowed fame to "go to his head." How and why does that happen? Why would a coach nominate such an individual to the most powerful position within the team? Fans and media personnel speculated that Coach Ryan hoped to make a leader out of Holmes. Many will describe a captain as a confident, yet humble individual, who understands the importance of team unity and the contribution of each team member towards a common goal. Such an individual will often deflect his or her own significance or status, much like Chinese philosopher Lao Tzu's description of good leadership as a process of interpersonal influence:

> A leader is best
> When people barely know he exists
> Not so good when people obey and acclaim him
> Worse when they despise him
> But of a good leader, who talks little,

When his work is done, his aim fulfilled,
They will say:
We did it ourselves.
(Lao Tzu, as cited in Bolden, Hawkins, Gosling, & Taylor, 2011, p. 21)

A "bad" captain, or an ineffective leader, is potentially just the opposite: someone who claims the limelight and commands without respect; like New York Jets' Santonio Holmes in 2011. But does our society not promote the confident, best player as best leader? How can we blame individual athletes who have been bolstered throughout their careers into an over-confidence that is often celebrated? Some athletes may end up feeling as though they can compare themselves to famous, heroic leaders who were 'born to lead,' and therefore do not require any type of leadership development or learning. Others, like Holmes, may have had their leadership positions thrust upon them in hopes that they would grow into the position. However, can we expect leadership skills and behaviours to develop naturally simply because one occupies a particular leadership position? Are certain athletes born to lead while others are not?

Leadership Development

Given the importance assigned to adult leadership, it would be advantageous to understand the early development of leadership behaviour. Adolescents display leadership characteristics and behaviour in a variety of settings, including school, student council, academic clubs, athletic teams, family situations, and social settings; yet there is a need to explore dimensions that contribute to youth acquisition of these leadership positions.

According to Todd and Kent (2004), drawing correlations between adolescent leadership tendencies and adult behaviours has been difficult due to a lack of longitudinal research in this area, but some studies have found positive associations between adolescent leadership and self-esteem, locus of control, parental examples in the home, and academic success. In their study of developmental and negative experiences in organized activities, Hansen and Larson (2007) found that adolescents who engaged in lead roles such as a starter on a sports team experienced greater developmental benefits but also more frequent negative experiences during the activity. The authors suggested that a higher level of immersion and investment would facilitate greater responsibility and increased likelihood for learning, whereas stress and an increased pressure to perform could characterize negative experiences. It was hypothesized that these challenges may also be part of the developmental process and an additional stimulus for growth (Hansen & Larson, 2007).

In a qualitative investigation of leader development, Wright and Côté (2003) identified four components that contributed to the early leadership experiences of six male university athletes: high skill and/or ability, strong work ethic, advanced sport knowledge, and good rapport with others. Athletes acknowledged a number of similar experiences that influenced their development in these areas, such as exposure to competition with older peers, roles in play activities as well as organized sport, mature conversations with adults, and receiving feedback, support, and acknowledgement (Wright & Côté, 2003).

In their interviews of six former Canadian university male ice hockey team captains, Dupuis, Bloom, and Loughead (2006) attempted to show the importance of athletes designated as formal leaders of their teams. Participants described their experiences, including the process by which they became captains (learning from the mentorship of other captains; their selection by coach appointment or teammates' voting), the qualities that made them effective leaders (communicating honestly and respectfully; having a positive attitude; having a strong work ethic; controlling their emotions), and their task roles as captains (interacting with teammates, coaches, and referees; managing team dynamics and dealing with team problems; representing the team during various functions). In describing the interactional role of a captain, Dupuis et al. (2006) mentioned a hierarchy that exists between coach, captain, and other team members: "Due to their formal leadership status, team captains appeared to have a strategic hierarchical position that served as the communication bridge between coaches and players" (p. 74). The authors speculated that effective athlete leaders acquire and hone their leadership abilities at a young age through early athletic involvement; skills learned from sources such as mentors, clinics, and books; and athlete leadership positions in youth sport. The notion of mentorship continued in the participants' roles as captains in the study, as most of them stressed the importance of leading by proper example, both on- and off-ice. The authors suggested that these exemplary behaviours also have immense impact on team culture (norms and atmosphere): "While the team captain (i.e., mentor) makes an effort to set the right example, young players (i.e., protégés) will follow their footsteps, and the team (i.e., organization) should perform better" (Dupuis et al., 2006, p. 75).

The limited research of captain and leadership development in sport reveals that athletes who gain early access to skill and knowledge development are more likely to become leaders, particularly after learning and competing with older athletes who model advanced levels of play. These early developers achieve a higher level of competence than peers who begin sport participation later, or who do not have access to advanced skill and knowledge acquisition. Roles in play activities as well as organized sport are also important for high competency, particularly considering the number of practice or training hours necessary for athletic skill mastery. Canadian Sport for Life's Long-Term Athlete Development (LTAD) model outlines the various stages through which an athlete must venture in pursuit of elite sport performance. LTAD stated:

> Research has shown that it takes 10,000 hours of quality training for athletes to achieve their full potential and perform at an elite level. In most examples of top-ranked athletes and other star performers, their 10,000 hours are usually accumulated over at least 10 years of training and competing. (Canadian Sport for Life, 2011b, "Excellence Takes Time" section, para. 1)

The early stages of physical literacy provide a foundation for elite training, and should consist of a blend of free play and structured activity. Athletes who partake in playground activities as well as organized sport will potentially accumulate "training and competing" hours more quickly than those who do not. Furthermore, feedback, support, and encouragement from knowledgeable adults are essential to athlete development. These adults not only provide the skill and tactical correction and guidance required, but also play a vital role in maintaining interest, motivation, and engagement for young athletes.

Captain Power

While these considerations are presented in an attempt to explain how captains attained their leadership status, absent from athletic leadership scholarship is the notion of power and privilege within a team. The existence of a team captain as leader in a hierarchical conceptualization of team sport implies that non-captains are subjugated and marginalized as non-leaders. This dominant ideology asserts that peer leadership in sport is available to only a select, privileged few. The power dynamics that exist between the captain and non-captains have yet to be examined, although such dynamics are vital to peer relationships and team cohesion. Players' understanding and acceptance of their roles within the team dictate their ability to interact effectively with each other in order to perform and achieve success.

Hollywood is complicit in the perpetuation of a hegemonic understanding of captains in sport. Movies such as *Varsity Blues* (Robbins, 1999), *Remember the Titans* (Yakin, 2000), and *The Longest Yard* (Segal, 2005) depict hyper-masculine, hyper-heterosexual, and hyper-attractive team leaders who command respect and authority simply by their existence. In a society where the dominant ideology of leadership is male, heterosexual, White, middle-class, and attractive, film representations confirm to the viewer that this is a normalized and appropriate interpretation of team captains. Furthermore, the captain is nothing less than heroic. He is unparalleled in talent and ability, or in his contributions to the team. No other team member could ever be as good, or ever hope to live up to all that he is, or was, to the team.

Captain Lance Harbor, played by Paul Walker in *Varsity Blues* (Robbins, 1999), makes his film entrance in slow motion to a glorious instrumental chorus of strings. The camera angle captures his radiance from below, implying that he is a god-like individual—someone to be revered. The scene continues to the school pep rally where Captain Lance takes the podium to address his admiring student body, which consists mainly of screaming, swooning, sex-crazed teenage girls. The film's producers glorify this one team member above all others; he is the only one with such heightened status within the team, school, and community. He enjoys privileges such as coach favouritism; teammates who carry his bags; the attention of the prettiest, most popular cheerleader as his girlfriend; and a personal billboard on his front lawn.

In *The Longest Yard* (Segal, 2005), the main character, Paul Crewe (Adam Sandler), sums up the nature of his role within the football team: "I'm Paul Crewe. I'm gonna be your coach, your captain, your quarterback." The implication here is that the leadership roles associated with these three distinct positions (coach, captain, quarterback) are similar, and can be assumed by the same individual. The power dynamics associated with these titles give the bearer an unquestioned ability to enforce team procedures and strategies, but also the ability to control other members of the team in both subtle and overt ways. Since the coach typically dictates how much or how little each player will enter into competition, players are forced to comply with directions they are given, and to make every effort to satisfy the coach's expectations in order to first become a member of the team, and then a starting and contributing member. Furthermore, there is an element of identity in Crewe's statement; he is essentially saying, "This is who I am, and who you are not." In fact, the scene continues as someone questions why he cannot be quarterback. Faced with this challenge to authority, Crewe humiliates the other player, putting him in his place and solidifying the established hierarchy that puts himself at the top.

It is apparent that captains have achieved a powerful and prestigious position, but what role does societal privilege play in captaincy? The existing peer-leadership model in sport is heroic, patriarchal, and militaristic. The captain is the hero, *the* leader—while all others are merely followers—and often implicitly male or possessing inherently masculine qualities (Haslam, Reicher, & Platow, 2011). There are a few investigators who compare male leaders to female leaders in sport (e.g., Moran & Weiss, 2006), but research has not delineated race, sexual orientation, economic status, or other factors of social oppression. Hollywood's depictions are predictably White, male, and heterosexual. Even in the racially charged script of *Remember the Titans* (2000), where the controversially appointed head coach is Black, the team captain is White. It can be hypothesized that, comparatively, female, non-heterosexual, non-White, and/or lower-income athletes would have diminished access to sport-development opportunities, particularly at early stages when it is apparent that focused, quality attention from coaches is paramount to advanced sport competency. Without a skill advantage, athletes have little hope for captaincy.

Regardless of social marginalization, *all* players on a sports team are marginalized as non-captains. While it can be argued that every individual possesses leadership potential, the captain title officially recognizes only one.

Conclusion: New Approaches to Captaining

Scholarship focused on defining and measuring leadership aims to predict who will emerge as leaders; however, leadership development is essentially dynamic, unpredictable, and moulded by societal, cultural, historical, political, and contextual influences. While it is clear that leadership development occurs in adolescence, research has not been able to identify major differences between youth leaders and non-leaders, or at least, adolescents identified as such. Adolescents lead in many ways that are typically unrecognized—working a job, volunteering, or standing up for what they believe. Attempts to predict and identify the strongest leaders early detract from opportunities to develop the leadership potential of *all* adolescents. In *Youth Leadership: A Guide to Understanding Leadership Development in Adolescents*, van Linden and Fertman (1998) identified three stages of leadership development: awareness, interaction, and mastery. However, most youth do not see themselves as leaders, likely due to society's stereotypical view of what constitutes leadership. Individuals who do not fit this narrow interpretation of a leader are not aware of themselves as leaders.

On a sports team, many types of leaders exist in many diverse situations. The Utah Jazz named three different leaders to share the captain role in the 2012–2013 National Basketball Association (NBA) season, as described by *Deseret News* sports writer, Jody Genessy (2012, para. 6, 9–11):

> The Voice. The Mentor. The Example. … Williams, entering his 10th season in the NBA, is the most outspoken player and one who dishes out tough love and support alike while directing the team from his floor-general position. Jefferson, now in his third season in Utah, is the lovable leader who's taken the young bigs under his wing and occasionally dispenses guidance. Millsap, the longest-tenured Jazzman going into year No. 7, is the classic soft-spoken do-as-I-do type who also picks his moments to speak up now and then.

Even these three leader descriptions are typical of particular leadership styles, but do not encompass the countless leadership approaches available to athletes.

Experienced and intuitive coaches may recognize the leadership potential that exists in many, if not all, members of their team. Leadership skill and behaviour may be as diverse as each individual occupying a role on the team. Some players may emerge naturally as leaders, or may be recognized as captains or alternate captains. Others may lead in more subtle ways—never missing a practice, offering quiet encouragement to a struggling teammate, or alerting the coach to an unresolved conflict. Still others may feel limited in their abilities to lead or exert influence within the group, particularly if they are unaware of leadership roles beyond the typical. Coaches who identify leadership based primarily on the team hero limit their team's leadership benefits. On the other hand, coaches who recognize the scope of leadership among team members unlock a whole new team dynamic in which leaders are not defined by their physical contributions, but instead by their abilities to think, communicate, act on their knowledge and beliefs, and influence others in ethical and socially responsible ways (van Linden & Fertman, 1998). These skills, behaviours, and attitudes can be learned and practiced; indeed, sports teams provide an ideal environment to do so.

Captain-less teams are extremely rare in North American professional sport, and teams that do compete without their captains usually do so because those players are missing from the line-up due to injury, trade, or retirement. Only the Minnesota Wild stands out as a long-term example, using a rotating captain system for their first nine years in the National Hockey League (NHL). At all levels of sport, however, coaches have begun to experiment with different forms of athletic leadership. What happens when a team has more than one emergent leader who is deserving of the captain title? Or when there is a voted tie? Co-captains. Or a captain cohort. Occasionally, a leadership committee is formed from the most senior players, or perhaps from a representation of various parts of the team, offense and defence for example. In each of these models, the notion of captain has simply been stretched to include a few more individuals among the privileged elite. Does captaining have to be hierarchical? Can an equitable model of leadership exist in team sport?

While existing sport culture and specific organizational regulations govern the existence of captains during competition, it is possible for coaches to reconceptualize the captaincy within their teams. Rotating captain roles and responsibilities between players would de-emphasize the importance of the title while promoting communication and conflict-resolution skills in multiple athletes. Indeed, assigning this role to a less vocal, more reserved athlete, rather than the typically confident communicator, produces potential benefits: an increase in the athlete's self-confidence and ability to communicate with game officials and the coach; enhanced teammates' perceptions of the athlete; and absence of a boisterous, potentially offensive captain in such an interactional role. Identifying the duties of the "game captain" or "floor captain" during competition as merely one of many forms of peer leadership would allow athletes the opportunity and confidence to perform leadership duties in areas to which they are better suited, such as group organization, vocal motivation, or team promotion during media or community events. Emphasizing the importance of a multitude of leadership roles among team members increases athletes' sense of ownership for the team and team accomplishments.

Of course, implementing a democratic model of peer leadership in sport requires the coach to know and understand each player and to manage the team differently. Without a specific captain liaison between coach and team, players are empowered to interact personally with coaching staff and other team members. Each athlete is responsible for relationship building and for seeking appropriate avenues for guidance, clarification, and conflict resolution. In this way, mentorship roles would increase in significance and meaningfulness; mentorship would exist based on knowledge and experience at multiple levels for multiple purposes.

A criticalized pedagogy of sports leadership is needed to gain a richer understanding of leadership and the power dynamics involved in the existing heroic peer-leadership model. Specific captain traits, skills, behaviours, attitudes, and functions should be available to everyone involved. Various team members' contributions should be encouraged, recognized, and celebrated, so that the entire team may benefit from the leadership influence of each individual, and each individual may grow as an athlete, an individual, and a leader. A more democratic notion of captaining will allow focused leadership development among *all* athletes, resulting in more well-rounded and effective individuals contributing to teams, communities, and society.

References

Bolden, R., Hawkins, B., Gosling, J., & Taylor, S. (2011). *Exploring leadership: Individual, organizational, and societal perspectives*. New York, NY: Oxford University Press.

Canadian Sport for Life. (2011a). *LTAD stages*. Retrieved from http://www.canadiansportforlife.ca/learn-about-canadian-sport-life/ltad-stages

Canadian Sport for Life. (2011b). *Ten key factors*. Retrieved from http://www.canadiansportforlife.ca/learn-about-canadian-sport-life/ten-key-factors

Cimini, R. (2012, January 2). Rex Ryan: No more captains for Jets. *ESPN.com: NFL*. Retrieved from http://espn.go.com/new-york/nfl/story/_/id/7415765/new-york-jets-rex-ryan-says-think-had-pulse-team

Costello, B. (2012, July 5). Rex's Jets like not having captains. *New York Post*. Retrieved from http://www.nypost.com/p/sports/jets/no_more_captains_L9QDxDxvyxLTASzZINzN8O

Dearing, J. B. (2012). Follow the leader: Beyond captain selection. *Coaching Volleyball, 29*(5), 8–11.

Dobosz, R. P., & Beaty, L. A. (1999). The relationship between athletic participation and high school students' leadership ability. *Adolescence, 34*(133), 215–220.

Dupuis, M., Bloom, G. A., & Loughead, T. M. (2006). Team captains' perceptions of athlete leadership. *Journal of Sport Behavior, 29*(1), 60–78.

Genessy, J. (2012, October 29). Utah Jazz: Mo Williams, Al Jefferson and Paul Millsap will be team's three-headed captain. *Deseret News*. Retrieved from http://www.deseretnews.com/article/865565602/Utah-Jazz-Mo-Williams-Al-Jefferson-and-Paul-Millsap-will-be-teams-three-headed-captain.html?pg=all

Gill, D. L., & Perry, J. L. (1979). A case study of leadership in women's intercollegiate softball. *International Review for the Sociology of Sport, 14*(2), 83–91.

Glenn, S. D., & Horn, T. S. (1993). Psychological and personal predictors of leadership behavior in female soccer athletes. *Journal of Applied Sport Psychology, 5*(1), 17–34.

Hansen, D. M., & Larson, R. W. (2007). Amplifiers of developmental and negative experiences in organized activities: Dosage, motivation, lead roles, and adult-youth ratios. *Journal of Applied Developmental Psychology, 28*(4), 360–374. doi: 10.1016/j.appdev.2007.04.006

Haslam, S. A., Reicher, S., & Platow, M. (2011). *The new psychology of leadership: Identity, influence, and power*. New York, NY: Psychology Press.

Moran, M. M., & Weiss, M. R. (2006). Peer leadership in sport: Links with friendship, peer acceptance, psychological characteristics, and athletic ability. *Journal of Applied Sport Psychology, 18*(2), 97–113. doi: 10.1080/10413200600653501

Rees, C. R., & Segal, M. W. (1984). Role differentiation in groups: The relationship between instrumental and expressive leadership. *Small Group Behavior, 15*(1), 109–123.

Robbins, B. (Director). (1999). *Varsity blues* [Motion picture]. USA: MTV Films.

Segal, P. (Director). (2005). *The longest yard* [Motion picture]. USA: Paramount Pictures.

Snyder, E. E., & Spreitzer, E. (1992). Social psychological concomitants of adolescents' role identities as scholars and athletes: A longitudinal analysis. *Youth and Society, 23*(4), 507–522.

Todd, S. Y., & Kent, A. (2004). Perceptions of the role differentiation behaviors of ideal peer leaders: A study of adolescent athletes. *International Sports Journal, 8*(2), 105–118.

Tropp, K., & Landers, D. (1979). Team interaction and the emergence of leadership and interpersonal attraction in field hockey. *Journal of Sport & Exercise Psychology, 1*(3), 228–240.

van Linden, J. A., & Fertman, C. I. (1998). *Youth Leadership: A guide to understanding leadership development in adolescents.* San Francisco, CA: Jossey-Bass.

Weese, J., & Nicholls, E. (1986). Team leadership: Selection and expectations. *Physical Educator, 44*(1), 269–272.

Wright, A., & Côté, J. (2003). A retrospective analysis of leadership development through sport. *Sport Psychologist, 17*(3), 268–291.

Yakin, B. (Director). (2000). *Remember the Titans* [Motion picture]. USA: Jerry Bruckheimer Films; Run It Up Productions.

Yukelson, D., Weinberg, R., Richardson, P., & Jackson, A. (1983). Interpersonal attraction and leadership within collegiate sport teams. *Journal of Sport Behavior, 6*(1), 28–36.

CHAPTER 28

Decolonizing Sport-Based Youth Development

Renee K. L. Wikaire and Joshua I. Newman

I t has been suggested in some quarters that sport, as we know it, is a uniquely modern phenomenon. It is a cultural formation that places emphasis on efficiency, spatial conquest, discipline, adherence to rules, training and regimentation, physical strength and competition, calculability, spectacles, and commercialization. It is a civilizing apparatus unlike any other, the argument goes, metonymically bound in equal parts to the pathologizations of Henry Ford, Adam Smith, Edward Wakefield, and Vince Lombardi (to name but a few key patriarchs).

In recent years, scholars have paid considerable attention to "concrete techniques" imbedded in sport, "whereby individuals and their bodies are subjected to control and whereby individuals discipline themselves into docile, productive bodies and peak performers" (Heikkala, 1993, p. 398); asking, in what ways does the individual participant, by engaging in sport, give themselves, their bodies, and the corporeal freedoms over to modern systematics? This line of critical inquiry seeks to explicate and raise awareness about how—through regimes of Muscular Christianity in the United States, public school sport in the United Kingdom, Eastern European callisthenic and German Turner movements, and Victorian Government school sport systems found in many Southern hemisphere Commonwealth outposts—the sporting body has been transformed into a site of surveillance, control, and productivity. In short, how sport offers a way to produce modernity's right bodies.

Here we join a number of critical physical educators and sport scholars in extending these considerations to contemporary sport's disciplinary utility over youth (see Giardina & Donnelly, 2008). We follow a number of sport studies scholars who have clearly illustrated the ways in which sport has long served as a site of installing in youth proper "leadership education, a means of constructing masculinity, femininity, and demarcating social status" as well as an "instrument of colonialism and imperialism" (Kirk & Twigg, 1995, p. 3). In what follows, we argue that sport's civilizing programmatics, as enacted in the present as in the past, raise a number of micropolitical concerns, particularly when advocates and practitioners use sport for youth 'development.' Specifically, we turn our attention to "sport-based youth development" programs in indigenous communities.

While we assume that coaches, administrators, and activists within the sports-based youth development movement are acting from a well-intentioned, politico-moral position, we want to consider a number of problematics arising from common implementation strategies shared by many programs. In particular, we look at the *praxes*—or dialectic formations of practice and ideas—that often undergird sport-based youth development programs; namely the assumptive bases *about culture* (as common), *about youth* (as source of 'the problem'), and *about sport* (as remediating apparatus). With respect to these multifarious initiatives, we ask:

Who defines the uses of sport?
Who defines development?
Development toward what end?
Development away from what starting point?

We argue that in many underprivileged communities, and in many underserved indigenous communities in particular, the sport-based youth development programmatic—as a research and interventionist trajectory—holds the potential to intercede in ways already fraught with epistemological and praxical contradictions: contradictions emerging from divergent conceptions of 'development,' from the intervening agents' lack of deference to cultural and historical placings, and from formulaic approaches to, if not actively working against, the critical pluralities of local indigenous ways of being and knowing.

Drawing directly from Renee's experiences as the co-founder and co-president of the University of Otago Physical Education Māori Association (which will from now be referred to as PEMA) during the years of 2010–2011, and her role as the coordinator of the *waka ama*—an outrigger canoe modeled after the sacred water vessel, the *waka* (canoe) that many Māori used to migrate to Aotearoa/ New Zealand)—component of a three-day Positive Youth Development (PYD) weekend run by the University of Otago, Division of Sciences, we explore decolonizing strategies for Sport for Youth Development programs. In so doing, we seek to break from conventional, modern ontologies and definitions of "youth development," and instead explicate the critical place indigenous world views and body ontologies might have in establishing and sustaining more holistic and community-grounded sporting engagements. We then conclude with a broader discussion about the politics of sport-based youth development program implementation—with consideration of how participants of sport for development programs, young and old, might use sporting praxis[1] to flip traditional modern, colonial notions of 'development' on their proverbial heads.

"Developing" Youth Through Modern Sport

Amongst many Western researchers, (physical) educators, and community organizers, sport has long been seen as a mechanism for bringing about ('corrective') behavioral change within certain youth populations. Western psychologists in particular have been overly keen to demonstrate and operationalize sport's socializing (see Brustad, 1988; Fraser-Thomas, Côté, & Deakin, 2005; Fredricks & Eccles, 2004) and 'developmental' potentialities (see Larson, 2000; Le Menestrel, Bruno, & Christian, 2002; Perkins & Le Menestrel, 2007; Perkins & Noam, 2007; Petitpas, Cornelius, Van Raalte, & Jones, 2005).

Often referred to as "developmentally focused youth sports programs" or "positive youth development through sport," and largely captured within broader framings such as "Sport for Development" (SFD) and "sport for health," these initiatives have proliferated around the world in recent years. For instance, in 2009 the United Nations formed a "Sport for Development and Peace International Working Group" and soon thereafter pledged financial and political support to the group's three strategic priority areas: child protection in sport; sport to strengthen child and youth education; and sport to enhance transferrable skills and employment opportunities (United Nations Office on Sport for Development and Peace, 2009). In turn, a number of Western agencies took the lead in establishing or expanding programs in both underserved communities in the Global North and the Global South. As laid out in the *Action Plan*, a vast network of advocates, activists, and community-development practitioners began to codify and territorialize various projects and programs, all under the director of a Europe-based Executive Board.

In essence, these UN programs, like many others, look something like this: facilities and other resources are secured, and program administrators enter into communities that are deemed disadvantaged, marginalized, at-risk, or requiring development, including: at-risk youth, indigenous communities, and refugees (Coalter, 2010; Kidd, 2008). These administrators then introduce new, or expand upon, existing sport-based activities. The programs are often offered after school or as an alternative to other, seemingly deviant social behaviors. Over the course of weeks, months, and in some cases years, program developers work with local community members and local youth to establish teams, leagues, and other structured forms of play.

According to the Center for Sport-Based Youth Development website, these initiatives seek to use

> sports to provide the supports and opportunities youth need to be healthy contributing citizens now and as adults. A sports-based youth development program offers youth an experience in which they learn and master sports skills along with life and leadership skills in a safe, fun, supportive, and challenging environment. This experience involves caring relationships, facilitated learning, experiential learning, and vigorous physical activity. (Center for Sport-Based Youth Development, 2013)

In this and other sport for development organizations, activists engage in undertakings ranging from program development and implementation, government advocacy, fundraising, research, and policy-planning—often with the basic assumption that by modeling and rationalizing everything from coaching strategies to types of game play, and by adapting those models to multiple contexts, sport participation can bring about relief, motivation, and well-being to youth in underprivileged and disparate areas. Using "best practice approaches," these sport-based youth development practitioners share effective strategies for program development and implementation—sharing strategies of reformative success and applying those to the next community in need. In these contexts, sport is observed as a medium to exert "positive influence on public health, socialization of children, youths and adults, the social inclusion of the disadvantaged, the economic development of regions and states, and on fostering intercultural exchange and conflict resolution" (Lyras & Welty Peachey, 2011, p. 311).[2]

Sport's basic developmental ontology goes something like this: by introducing competition, structure, team-based social relationships, and 'challenging' physical activity to a youth population which might not otherwise have access to sport, the intervening party can instill certain values; achieve certain health outcomes; and improve social, educative, and even economic conditions for an 'underserved' community. In short, and to draw upon the quote above, through these programs, sport can help produce "healthy contributing citizens."[3]

In the introduction to his edited book, *Positive Youth Development Through Sport*, Holt (2008) argued that 'youth development' has historically been predicated on the notion that youth are "problems" that need to be solved. Under this guise, there has been a tendency for youth development to be oriented around a deficit-model approach, one that uses a problem (such as type II diabetes, obesity, crime, teen pregnancy, smoking, etc.) to devise and implement youth development programs (rather than a strengths-based approach). Kegler, Rodine, Marshall, Oman, and McLeroy (2003) have posited that within a deficit-model approach to youth development, little attention is given to building the strengths and assets of the youth. Whereas, in a strengths-based approach, program organizers and participants more actively acknowledge and work toward cultivating a variety of person-specific assets such as positive peer influences, involvement in organized activity, strong relationships, culture, and aspirations for the future (Kegler et al., 2003).

Given the predominance of the deficit-model approach in most youth development programs, it is perhaps not surprising to the reader of this volume that many programs have seen limited success. However, in recent years, critical scholars have pushed for a shift toward a strengths-based approach. Thus, a new vision of youth development known as 'positive youth development' (PYD) has emerged. Indeed, for the boundaries of this chapter, we build upon Roth, Brooks-Gunn, Murray, and Foster's (1998) definition of PYD as "the engagement in prosocial behaviors and avoidance of health compromising and future-jeopardizing behaviors" (p. 426).

Furthermore, as many other scholars (Holt, 2008; Larson, 2000) have noted, sport is viewed as a vehicle through which PYD can occur. Therefore, the goal of this chapter is to look at PYD through sport in indigenous communities and highlight the need to adopt a de-colonizing praxis when conducting these programs. To date, there has been limited research that has looked at the dominance of the Western world view in PYD programs, and subsequently, this dominance as a form of neo-colonialism. Given this, in the next section we shall review PYD through sport as part of the broader field of Sport for Development (SFD).

As we noted in the introduction, sport is widely seen as a vehicle for positive social change—a way forward and out of conditions of war, violence, poverty, malnourishment and starvation, and deviance (Kidd, 2008). MacIntosh and Spence (2012) entertained the notion that the concept of using sport for developmental purposes is premised on two approaches. The first approach is denoted as the 'development of sport,' whereby the development of sport is centered on developing the sport itself—this approach is particularly concerned with elite, amateur sport. The second approach looks at 'sport for development'; in this way, sport is seen as a vehicle to achieve positive social change amongst individuals and communities—it is the second approach that this chapter is concerned with, the use of sport for development (Darnell & Hayhurst, 2011).

As Black (2010) contended, the concept of 'development' itself is a ubiquitous term. As many development theorists such as Pieterse (2010) have also argued, development and development theory have been largely couched as an offshoot of Eurocentric Western notions of progress and evolution. However, if we are to look critically at the genealogy of development, and the paradigm from which it has been engineered, this perspective can be questioned. In fact, numerous critics including Black (2010), and Hartmann and Kwauk (2011), have questioned the Eurocentric and modernistic discourse that pervades development and development practices. Given the dominance of Western thought in the field of development, and more recently, in the field of SFD, we shall adopt a critical approach to the study of SFD. Rather than looking for a homogenous SFD paradigm, we propose that there are multiple paradigms from which SFD can be conceived.

Burnett (2009) suggested that SFD is a "contested social construct which encapsulates a wide range of movement phenomena and activities that present various degrees of institutionalization, reflecting unique individualized and cultural meanings as it finds expression in diverse social contexts" (p. 1193). Within this statement, "social change" is viewed as being achieved in the "in-field" application of the SFD program—and this social change is usually viewed as positive. In relation, the term, *development*, is usually reflected in the perception of progress for the recipients. Consequently, the success of SFD programs is usually measured on 'tangible evidence' (health factors or social factors), and as a result, SFD programs become majorly results-driven, with a strong focus on outcomes, rather than on the process.

Darnell (2010) highlighted the historic use of sport to produce healthy bodies for the labor force (see also Ingham & Hardy, 1984). He prescribed that SFD initiatives use sport to support the uptake of "competitive and hierarchical culture and the political economy" by marginalized groups (p. 85). In understanding this point, one must question the true objectives of SFD and whether it is truly empowering, or whether it is just a way to encourage active "citizenship" within the increasingly global free market. By adopting these dominant free-market ideologies, the SFD rhetoric emulates the capitalist economic system that proposes that "human wellbeing can be best advanced by liberating entrepreneurial freedoms and skills within an institutional framework characterized by strong private property rights, free markets and free trade" (Harvey, 2005, p. 2). Although, as we know, not all sport forms are good, and not all forms of corporeal liberation are in fact, liberating (Newman, 2013). Indeed, to play sport often means to give oneself over to systems of surveillance, exploitation, and regimentation. Saavedra (2009) took a similar tack, arguing, "Sport carries historical and cultural baggage, especially from its hegemonic core" (p. 131).

The use of modern sport in SFD programs carries many contentious issues, as it constantly transmits Western norms and ideologies in the name of progress. Newman (2013) cautioned against the lure of modernity's hyper-competitive and hyper-rationalized system, and the place of SFD within this system. If we are to accept that SFD does in fact equal progress, as a function of free-market (late) modernization, then we also accept that those peoples (usually the developing) are in need of acculturation into the dominant framings of "productive" citizenship. So, the question really becomes, are we merely reconstructing colonial power relations through these SFD programs? If the true premise of SFD is to develop and empower communities, then there is a need to drastically rethink the boundaries of what does, and what does not, constitute development.

Jay Coakley (2011) has been particularly critical of what he and others refer to as the dominant neoliberal axioms that pervade youth-focused SFD programs. He claimed that a dominant notion amongst "sport evangelists" is that sport is an effective activity for solving problems and improving the quality of life for individuals, communities, and disadvantaged groups within society. According to these sport evangelists, PYD through SFD falls under three common categories:

1. Personal character development,

2. Reforming "at-risk" populations, and

3. Fostering social capital leading to future occupational success and civic engagement (adapted from Coakley, 2011, p. 307).

Under these key categories is the functionalist belief that sport can teach (dis)advantaged youth

> indispensible developmental lessons, although individuals must integrate these lessons into their lives to enhance their own life chances. Only when these lessons are internalized by enough people will the positive qualities, decisions, and choices of individuals benefit the communities in which they live. (Coakley, 2011, p. 309)

Although this rhetoric is negated by some SFD organizations, it is majorly prevalent throughout SFD organizations that are conducted from the Global North (Northern Americans and Northern Europeans). However, as many scholars have shown, including Black (2010); Catalano, Berglund, Ryan, Lonczak, and Hawkins (2004); Coakley (1996, 2002); Holt (2008); Kane and LaVoi (2007); Weiss (2008); Weiss and Wiese-Bjornstal (2009), youth SFD is widely contingent on the SFD initiative's praxis.

Indigenous Youth Development Through Sport

Moreover, many SFD and PYD initiatives have used sport as a context for transmitting information about broader health and wellness objectives in indigenous communities (Maro, Roberts, & Sørensen, 2009). Despite the positive potential SFD and PYD programs have to enhance indigenous communities, in many instances there has been a lack of co-creation in the development of these initiatives.

Given the lack of co-creation, there has been a tendency for SFD and PYD initiatives working in indigenous communities to perpetuate Western ideas and measures of development, modernization, and progress—or what some critics might point to as the key tenets of (neo)colonialism. This is, we argue, a consequence of many SFD and PYD initiatives having been developed and implemented within the parameters of a Western world view, rather than within the world view of the indigenous communities.

However, in the last few years, we have seen an increase in "culturally relevant,"[4] strengths-based approaches (coming from the indigenous community and/or culture) as the bases for the SFD and PYD programs in indigenous communities. This shift is important because it addresses the colonial histories of these communities while taking steps toward enabling an empowering space in which indigenous communities are taking ownership over their own development, rather than having the "appropriate development" being decided for them. In a number of contexts, including Australia, New Zealand, and North America, there have been cases of using the strengths of the indigenous culture in the genesis of PYD programs. For example, in New Zealand, a sport-based intervention program entitled the 'Hokowhitu program' has been designed in New Zealand by Māori, for Māori. As Theokas, Danish, Hodge, Heke, and Forneris (2008) stated, "The program used Māori language and culture in the program development, implementation and evaluation. This approach was known as 'Kaupapa Māori Research' and appropriates Māori preferred learning and investigation styles" (pp. 75–76). Similarly, in Australia, surfing programs with a strong alignment to indigenous culture have been used with Aboriginal youth to promote "community involvement; contribute to personal development and positive social outcomes; support professional development and provide potential employment opportunities; enhance connections to country and Indigenous communities" (Ryne & Rossi, 2012).

For example, the 'our games, our health' PYD through sport initiative was developed as a culturally relevant sport program with two indigenous communities in Queensland, Australia. The project, based in Stradbroke Island and Cherbourg, was underpinned by a holistic approach to well-being, which emphasized the importance of relationships and connectedness at the family, community, and societal levels. Like the Hokowhitu program, and the surfing programs, the 'our games, our health' utilized indigenous knowledge through the use of indigenous games and indigenous culture from Australia as a vehicle for physical activity. Indigenous games were chosen due to their cultural relevance to the indigenous communities that were involved, and the potential they hold for strengthening cultural identity. The program was operationalized through three interconnecting stages:

1. Community engagement,

2. Community mobilization, and

3. Capacity building.

An underlying theme to the entire project was the privileging of an indigenous world view throughout the process (Parker et al., 2006).

And while we are certainly not suggesting here that these groups share common colonial histories, nor do we seek to homogenize the pluralisms of local indigenous PYD and SFD programs, in these strengths-based, culturally relevant approaches we find some common qualities: a strong alignment with indigenous culture and beliefs; development of connections between indigenous people, indigenous communities, and the wider community; connection to the natural environment; acknowledgement of the spiritual component involved in physical activity, health, and well-being; and privileging an indigenous world view. It is our belief that by putting these three PYD through sport programs in conversation with each other, their common bases illustrate what we believe is the need in SFD and PYD programs within indigenous communities: to be devised and implemented in radically contextualized and deeply localized ways.

To further make our case, we now turn to Renee's work with a sport-based youth development program (though we might shy away from calling it that) that took place in Ōraka Aparima in the South Island of New Zealand in 2011. In doing so, we are not

1. Prescribing that this one case offers a "how to do development in all indigenous communities" formula, nor

2. Suggesting that Renee's work and role within this setting is without complexity.

Rather, we introduce Renee's experiences as a point from which to start a conversation about the role of the advocate and/or practitioner as she or he emerges from, comes into, and works with (young members of) an indigenous community. By putting Renee's experiences as PYD practitioner in conversation with those indigenous and SFD and/or PYD activists' accounts, we might find some common epistemological and praxical ground upon which to further decolonize development sport's ongoing power dynamics.

Decolonizing PYD Through *Waka Ama*, Ōraka Aparima, New Zealand

In what follows, we will describe a case study that elucidates the successful implementation of youth SFD programs in *Aotearoa*/New Zealand. Throughout the program, you will notice that there is an emphasis on healthy relationships between the participants, the environment, Māori culture, and the four walls of *te whare tapa wha* (spiritual, family, mental, and physical) (Durie, 1998). The *wānanga* that Renee worked with in Ōraka Aparima was part of a partnership between the University of Otago and Māori communities, in the form of science outreach *wānanga* (Campbell-Price, 2011). These *wānanga* are run over three days, and involve Māori and *Pākehā* (non-Māori) scientists working with high-school students on a variety of experiential science projects. Science projects are taught alongside *mātauranga* Māori that is provided by local *kaumātua* and *kuia* (Māori elders) of respective communities. Before the *wānanga* take place, there is an extensive planning period, in which the *wānanga* organizers enter into a high level of consultation with the *iwi* (tribe). During this consultation period, organizers work with the local *iwi* to identify environmental or health issues that are affecting the community. These issues are then used to develop the outreach program, so that *rangatahi* (young people) have the opportunity to connect and learn about the issues affecting the local areas in which they live.

Māori visionary, Dr. Paratene Ngata, with the University of Otago enacted these *wānanga*, because he wanted to increase the involvement of Māori youth in the field of the sciences and health sciences in his *iwi* (tribe), Ngāti Porou. Since these early days, *wānanga* have spread and now take place in a variety of communities around *Aotearoa*/New Zealand. In particular, the science *wānanga* function to bridge the gap between Māori students and science, in order to break down the dominant rhetoric that sciences and health sciences are for "white men in lab coats" (Campbell-Price, 2011, p. 90).

In regard to youth sport for development, we would like to speak to a specific *wānanga* set in Ōraka Aparima in the South Island of *Aotearoa*/New Zealand in 2011.[5] The *wānanga* was centered on connection to the local Jacob's River estuary and connecting students through science to the health of the river. The *waka ama* instruction was predicated on connecting the students to the "four walls of health" through the use of a holistic Māori health model, *te whare tapa wha*: *te taha tinana* (physical well-being), *te taha wairua* (spiritual well-being), *te taha hinengaro* (mental well-being), and *te taha whānau* (social well-being) (Durie, 2004). In particular, the connection between the *waka*, the river, and the students was emphasized, by highlighting how the students are *kaitiaki* (caretakers) of the environment. Furthermore, through a holistic approach to health and well-being, the students were shown how their health is connected to the health of the river. This connection was a key component of the sessions. The session was led by the founder of *waka ama* in *Aotearoa*/New Zealand, a lecturer at the University of Otago School of Physical Education, and six undergraduate students from the University of Otago School of Physical Education, Sport and Exercise Sciences 'Physical Education Māori Association.'[6]

The *waka ama* session was comprised of five components:

1. *Mihimihi*, or introductions between the instructors and the students;

2. The recollection of a history of *waka ama* in *Aotearoa*/New Zealand, as a way to connect students to *waka ama* by showing how it is interwoven within their own *whakapapa* (genealogy), given that *waka* (canoe) are the vehicles of the Māori ancestors (Wikaire, 2011);

3. The land-based session, which involved the water-safety session, the students getting their life jackets and gear on, and the assembling of the *waka ama*;

4. Moving the *waka ama* out onto the water, and the recitation of *karakia* (prayer) to the god of the ocean, Tangaroa, and then the practical water session; and

5. The end of the session, working together to move off the water, breaking down the equipment together, and then coming together to finish the session.

Throughout the session, the emphasis was on relationships and connections between people, the environment, Māori culture, *whakapapa* (genealogy), and the spiritual realm.

1. *Mihimihi* is an important part of Māori culture; getting to know each other and the places where people have come from is important in making connections between people, their *whakapapa* (genealogy), and their *whānau* (family). From *te whare tapa wha* (holistic Māori health model), we can observe that *te taha whānau* (social well-being) is at work in this practice. By placing importance on getting to know each other instead of launching straight into the practical paddling parts of the session, this encouraged *whānaungatanga*, or the building of relationships. This also privileges Māori identity and culture throughout the session, and helps the students to connect to each other, the environment, their *whānau* (family), and culture.

2. The recitation of a history of *waka ama* in *Aotearoa*/New Zealand was devised between Renee and the founder of the revitalization movement of *waka ama* in New Zealand during the 1980s, Matahi Whakataka Brightwell (Wikaire, 2011). This was an important part of the decolonizing process of the session, by recollecting a history of *waka ama* in *Aotearoa*/New Zealand and the influences that colonization has had upon the cultural practice of the indigenous Māori people of *Aotearoa*/New Zealand. In this way, *waka ama* becomes a pedagogical vehicle enabling students to develop a broader understanding of colonial processes in *Aotearoa*/New Zealand and the subsequent impacts of colonization on Māori culture and identity.

3. Part three was the land-based part of the session. In this part of the session, the instructors and students assembled a *waka ama* together, through lashing techniques. As Campbell-Price (2011) noted, the session was taught as a *tuakana/teina* (older sibling/younger sibling) approach. A *tuakana/teina* approach is an approach that sees both the instructor and the students in a collaborative learning situation, in which the instructor can be both the 'teacher' and the 'learner.' Once the *waka ama* were assembled, the instructors went through paddling techniques with the students, with an emphasis on working together and timing while the students were in the *waka*, can also be referred to as *kotahitanga* (please see Table 28.1 for further explanations of *kotahitanga* and *manaakitanga*). Additionally, this part of the session was also where students put on safety gear, and were orientated to the *waka ama* apparatus.

Value	Description	What it looks like	How to incorporate it into your *waka ama* session
Whānaungatanga	A sense of belonging; relationships between people and the wider environment.	Getting to know one another. *Whānau* support. Inclusiveness. Connections.	Start each session with a brief *mihimihi*, and then proceed with name games. Encourage involvement with teams—such as giving teams Māori names.
Manaakitanga	A measurement of people's ability to extend *aroha* (love) to each other.	Students helping each other, during the session. *Tuakana/Teina* approach.	Encourage helping and sharing. Show how *manaakitanga* can be applied through *waka ama* in teamwork and doing tasks for others.
Kotahitanga	Oneness, working together as one.	Everyone doing the same thing at the same time.	Encourage unity and explain how in the *waka*, when all people work together as one, the *waka* will move more smoothly. This can then be applied to many other tasks throughout life.
Kaitiakitanga	Acknowledging our roles as caretakers of traditional Māori practices, culture, and natural resources and/or environment.	Reciprocity (Giving back).	Ensure the grounds are in the same condition or better than upon arrival. For example, pick up all rubbish.
Atuatanga	Paying respect to the Māori Gods.	*Karakia* (Prayer); knowing and respecting the realms of each God and their roles in our everyday lives.	Learning around the Māori Gods and the roles they play in the Māori world. Emphasize how this knowledge can be used practically to connect us to the ancestors, and the environment. Being aware of individuals' different beliefs and respecting those. Sharing *karakia* (prayer). Demonstrate the respect of the paddles, and not to step over them as they have come from Tāne Mahuta (God of the Forest). *Karakia* (prayer) to Tangaroa (God of the Ocean) before paddling.

Table 28.1. Key Māori Values Incorporated Into Waka Ama *Sessions*

4. Part four was the water-based part of the session. Before moving out onto the water, the students and instructors performed *karakia* (prayer) to Tangaroa, the god of the ocean. Then, the students and instructors launched the *waka ama* and completed their paddling session. Throughout the session, there was an emphasis on *kotahitanga*, or working together as one. For example, when the paddling was out of time, the *waka ama* became disjointed. Conversely, when everyone paddled in unison, the *waka* would glide. As shown in Table 28.1, *kotahitanga* (oneness) within the *waka ama* could be used as a metaphor for life. Through the practice of *karakia* (prayer), students held up the wall of health, *te taha wairua* (spirituality or spiritual well-being).

5. In part five, the students moved off the water and returned the *waka ama* and paddles to the bank, hung the paddles, and got changed. The entire area was cleaned, and the students and instructors made sure to take any rubbish or belongings that they had brought there, exemplifying the concept of *kaitiakitanga* (see Table 28.1). The session finished with a thank you and a *hongi* (pressing of noses), which signified the coming together of the students and instructors and an expression of *te taha whānau* (family or social well-being).

The Body as Locus of Praxis

We believe that from Renee's experiences with the *waka ama* session of the Ōraka Aparima University of Otago Science *wānanga* we can begin to glean a few decolonizing *praxes* for youth sport for development. In the first instance, Renee and her collaborators (participants of all ages) were deeply engaged in holistic corporeal praxes. According to a Māori world view,[7] the world is holistic and cyclic, one in which everything is connected to every other living thing and to the ancestors and gods through *whakapapa* (genealogy) (Wikaire & Newman, 2013). Numerous scholars have written about a predominantly Māori philosophical approach to health, notably the Honourable Mason Durie. Durie could be regarded as the cornerstone in developing the concept of *hauora* in an academic context. To return to one of the most commonly used references of *hauora* in *Aotearoa/*New Zealand society—*te whare tapa wha* (four walls of health)—health can be likened to the four walls of a house.[8] With deference to Durie's *te whare tapa wha*, in order to have a healthy body, and to 'develop' as an individual (as some Westerners might put it), one must be healthy in all other aspects of one's life. By conceptualizing health in this way, one understands that if one wall is affected, then the rest of the walls will also be affected. It is this concept of *hauora* (health) that we contend is an appropriate way to actuate youth SFD praxis. We will now unpack *te whare tapa wha* in more detail, and relate it to the praxis of youth SFD.

Firstly, *te taha tinana* denotes the physical well-being of a person as it relates to the body or *tinana*. For Māori, the body and all things that touch the body are *tapu* (or sacred); an example of this could be considered the touching of the head. Under a Māori world view, the head could be considered one of the most sacred parts of the body. Thus, Māori will not go around touching each other's heads, or mixing utensils that are used in conjunction with the head, such as a hairbrushes or hats, near things that are associated with food.[9] The *tinana* suffers when a person is injured or sick, therefore, it is important that SFD programs with youth are aware of *te taha tinana*, and can take appropriate steps to ensure that youth are not put in danger of hurting *te taha tinana*.

The second wall is *te taha wairua*, which encapsulates the spiritual well-being of a person. This wall has been acknowledged as the most important for the health of a person. It is believed that when a person is lacking in spiritual awareness, they are lacking in well-being and will be more prone to illness. *Te taha wairua* extends beyond the individual, and also incorporates a person's relationship with other people, the environment, heritage, and genealogy. The breakdown of this wall can often be interpreted in terms of lacking well-being or personal identity. An example of *te taha wairua* as *praxis* is that when Māori are confronted with a problem, they often put that problem in dialogue with the larger context that it is working in—for example, they see the problem in relation to past, present, and future generations. This may mean that the conversation diverges from its original purpose, but the answer that is found may address the overarching contextual issues affecting the problem.

The third wall, *te taha hinengaro*, refers to psychological well-being. In a Māori world view, thoughts, beliefs, emotions, and behavior are vital to well-being. It is important to understand that under a Māori world view, the body and mind are inseparable, and communication through non-verbal communication can often be just (if not more) important than verbal communication. For example, someone that is unhappy in his or her current circumstance (school or work) could manifest this unhappiness in physical sickness. In particular, Māori thought processes are very holistic, meaning that a healthy mind is a mind that thinks about the whole circumstance of being, rather than just their individual needs. For instance, a Māori approach to youth SFD would think through how the program may affect future generations, and the environment.

The fourth wall, *te taha whānau*, is the most fundamental idea in Māori society: the concept of the family. For Māori, the *whānau* (family) provide care for the person both culturally and emotionally. Rather than the Western concept of a 'nuclear family,' under a Māori world view, the *whānau* encompasses the extended family, which can span over many generations. Moreover, the maintenance of family relationships is of paramount importance to Māori. That means caring for both younger and elder *whānau* members. Every person in a *whānau* has his or her role in the healthy functioning of the *te taha whānau*. In terms of youth SFD praxis, it is important to devise practices that can incorporate all generations of the *whānau*, both young and old. This is especially pertinent for the transmission of cultural knowledge throughout the generations.

Conclusion

We can envision that a Māori philosophy of PYD and SFD is premised on holism. Through the four walls of Durie's *te whare tapa wha*, we have explicated that the idea of Māori *hauora* (health) is multifaceted and multilayered. It is an approach that is based on the interrelation of the spiritual, cultural, family, physical, environmental, and mental facets of health. Like those we described above, this approach is predicated on the epistemological bases of an indigenous (in this case, Māori) world view. Therefore, when devising youth SFD programs to be used in indigenous communities, and particularly, indigenous Māori communities, the whole genesis of these programs should be from a deeply Māori world view.

In summary, our aim here has been to point toward some epistemological bases—bases shared by successful SFD and PYD programs in Māori communities. Renee's experiences and her work in the South Island of New Zealand offer but one very small contribution to a wider discussion, a conversation, which has yet to be had regarding the place of epistemology and culturally relevant praxis in recentering sport programs around the body and its spiritual and historical articulations. These conversations might in some ways move us away from the prescriptions and formulae that have come to dominate many Western, modern, arguably neocolonial SFD initiatives, and along the way, practitioners might find new ways of conceiving strengths-based approaches to using sport to raise and share radically spiritual, critical consciousness and corporeal experiences with youth in indigenous and non-indigenous communities.

Notes

1.   Our use of this term, *praxis*, is meant to align with Paulo Freire's use of the term. Specifically, we are calling for embodied and practiced theory and critical consciousness; the act of engaging, applying, exercising, realizing, or practicing radically democratic ideas.

2.   Although many of these *Sport for Development* initiatives claim to have a significant impact on society, to date, there is little empirical evidence to support such claims (Coalter, 2010; Kidd, 2008). Coalter (2010) has also suggested that there has been little research into the effectiveness of the conditions and processes of Sport for Development. Nevertheless, the scope of the use of Sport for Development is broad, with programs being conducted in regions ranging from Africa to South America, Australia to Southeast Asia, the United States, and throughout Europe.

3. More critically, a number of sport sociologists have consistently argued that sport must be critically interrogated for its subjectifying tendencies as well (see Coakley, 1986; McPherson, Curtis, & Loy, 1989).
4. Here we are referring to Gloria Ladson-Billings's (1995) notion of culturally relevant pedagogy. We are calling for a sort of bodily practice that evokes and generates a pedagogy that integrates and respects the historical multiplicities and perspectival complexities that come from the common, and diverse, practices, shapes, corporealities, and identities constructed on, and through, the body. We encourage students to "develop a critical consciousness through which they challenge the status quo of the social order" (Ladson-Billings, 1995, p. 160), and perhaps more importantly, dialectically generate pedagogical encounters that oppose, or *stand down*, the uses of 'bio-power' (both institutionally and individually wielded) to culturally, economically, or politically marginalize or oppress 'non-normative' individuals or groups.
5. Another important aspect of the *wānanga* was from the Chair of the Ōraka Aparima Rūnaka, who presented on the 12-year collaborative project with the University of Otago on the sustainability of traditional harvesting of local *titi* (mutton birds) by local Māori. The traditional harvesting project was predicated on oral histories of birding and harvesting from over many generations of local Māori. Overall, the talk was designed to emphasize the connection between the past, present, and future, exemplifying how traditional Māori knowledge can be merged with science. As Campbell-Price (2011) has shown, throughout the talk students were encouraged to think about their place within the future of the local community, and to see the connections between the past, present, and future. However, for the remainder of this section we will speak specifically to the *waka ama* component of the *wānanga*.
6. The first-author of this chapter (Wikaire) is the co-founder of the Physical Education Māori Association at the University of Otago, School of Physical Education, alongside another Māori student within the school. Wikaire was also the student leader of the *waka ama* component of the Division of Sciences *wānanga* in Ōraka Aparima, and one of the key members in the devising of the program that was delivered to high-school students. Of the utmost importance was the privileging of *tikanga Māori* (Māori culture) and a decolonizing history of *waka ama* in *Aotearoa*/New Zealand.
7. Te Ahukaramū Charles Royal offered a definition of the word, *indigenous*, based on what he calls "world views"—he prescribed that *indigenous* be used for those cultures that subscribe to an ecological world view, in which humans are interconnected with the natural world. Upon acknowledging this world view, we will speak to a predominantly indigenous Māori world view in relation to *hauora* (health) and youth SFD.
8. Other notable Māori health models have been Rose Pere's *Te Wheke* (the octopus) and Mason Durie's (2013) *Te Pae Mahutonga* (The Southern Cross). From all of these Māori models of hauora (health) it can be devised that health is a very holistic practice, one that is deeply connected to the spiritual, social, family, culture, mental, physical, and environmental aspects of life.
9. This follows the Māori cultural belief of *tapū* or *noa* that needs far more elaboration than we can allow in this chapter (for additional reading, see Ka'ai, Moorfield, Reilly, & Mosley, 2004).

References

Black, D. R. (2010). The ambiguities of development: Implications for 'development through sport'. *Sport in Society*, *13*(1), 121–129.

Brustad, R. J. (1988). Affective outcomes in competitive youth sport: The influence of intrapersonal and socialization factors. *Journal of Sport and Exercise Psychology*, *10*(3), 307–321.

Burnett, C. (2009). Engaging sport-for-development for social impact in the South African context. *Sport in Society*, *12*(9), 1192–1205.

Campbell-Price, M. (2011). School curriculum and outdoor education: Part 2: Secondary school. In D. Irwin, J. Straker, & A. Hill (Eds.), *Outdoor education in Aotearoa New Zealand: A new vision for the twenty first century* (pp. 84–103). Christchurch, New Zealand: CPIT.

Catalano, R. F., Berglund, M. L., Ryan, J. A. M., Lonczak, H. S., & Hawkins, J. D. (2004). Positive youth development in the United States: Research findings on evaluations of positive youth development programs. *Annals of the American Academy of Political and Social Science*, *591*(1), 98–124.

Coakley, J. (1986). Socialization and youth sports. In C. R. Rees & A. W. Miracle (Eds.), *Sport and social theory* (pp. 135–147). Champaign, IL: Human Kinetics.

Coakley, J. (1996). Socialization through sports. In O. Bar-Or (Ed.), *The child and adolescent athlete* (Vol. 6 of the *Encyclopedia of Sports Medicine*, pp. 353–363). London, UK: Blackwell Science.

Coakley, J. (2002). Using sports to control deviance and violence among youths: Let's be critical and cautious. In M. Gatz, M. A. Messner, & S. J. Ball-Rokeach (Eds.), *Paradoxes of youth and sport* (pp. 13–30). Albany, NY: State University of New York Press.

Coakley, J. (2011). Youth sports: What counts as 'positive development?' *Journal of Sport & Social Issues*, *35*(3), 306–324.

Coalter, F. (2010). The politics of sport-for-development: Limited focus programmes and broad gauge problems? *International Review for the Sociology of Sport*, *45*(3), 295–314.

Cunningham, J., & Beneforti, M. (2005). Investigating indicators for measuring the health and social impact of sport and recreation programs in Australian indigenous communities. *International Review for the Sociology of Sport*, *40*(1), 89–98.

Darnell, S. C. (2010). Power, politics and 'sport for development and peace': Investigating the utility of sport for international development. *Sociology of Sport Journal*, *27*(1), 54–75.

Darnell, S. C., & Hayhurst, L. M. (2011). Sport for decolonization: Exploring a new praxis of sport for development. *Progress in Development Studies*, *11*(3), 183–196.

Durie, M. (1998). *Whaiora: Maori health development* (2ⁿᵈ ed.). Auckland, New Zealand: Oxford University Press.

Durie, M. (2004). Understanding health and illness: Research at the interface between science and indigenous knowledge. *International Journal of Epidemiology, 33*(5), 1138–1143.

Durie, M. (2013). *Te pae mahutonga* (southern cross Māori model of health). Retrieved from http://www.health.govt.nz/our-work/populations/maori-health/maori-health-models/maori-health-models-te-pae-mahutonga

Fraser-Thomas, J. L., Côté, J., & Deakin, J. (2005). Youth sport programs: An avenue to foster positive youth development. *Physical Education & Sport Pedagogy, 10*(1), 19–40.

Fredricks, J. A., & Eccles, J. S. (2004). Parental influences on youth involvement in sports. In M. R. Weiss (Ed.), *Developmental sport and exercise psychology: A lifespan perspective* (pp. 145–164). Morgantown, WV: Fitness Information Technology.

Giardina, M. D., & Donnelly, M. K. (Eds.). (2008). *Youth culture and sport: Identity, power, and politics.* London, UK: Routledge.

Hartmann, D., & Kwauk, C. (2011). Sport and development: An overview, critique, and reconstruction. *Journal of Sport & Social Issues, 35*(3), 284–305.

Harvey, D. (2005). *A brief history of neoliberalism.* London, UK: Oxford University Press.

Heikkala, J. (1993). Discipline and excel: Techniques of the self and body and the logic of competing. *Sociology of Sport Journal, 10*(4), 397–412.

Holt, N. L. (Ed.). (2008). *Positive youth development through sport.* New York, NY: Routledge.

Ingham, A., & Hardy, S. (1984). Sport: Structuration, subjugation and hegemony. *Theory, Culture & Society, 2*(2), 85–103.

Ka'ai, T. M., Moorfield, J. C., Reilly, M. P. J., & Mosley, S. (2004) *Ki te whaiao: An introduction to Māori culture and society.* Auckland: Pearson Education.

Kane, M. J., & LaVoi, N. M. (2007). *The 2007 Tucker Center research report: Developing physically active girls: An evidence-based multidisciplinary approach.* Minneapolis, MN: University of Minnesota Press. Retrieved from www.tuckercenter.org/projects/tcrr

Kegler, M., Rodine, S., Marshall, L., Oman, R., & McLeroy, K. (2003). An asset-based youth development model for preventing teen pregnancy: Illustrations from the HEART of OKC project. *Health Education, 103*(3), 131–144.

Kidd, B. (2008). A new social movement: Sport for development and peace. *Sport in Society, 11*(4), 370–380.

Kirk, D., & Twigg, K. (1995). Civilising Australian bodies: The games ethic and sport in Victorian government schools, 1904–1945. *Sporting Traditions, 11*(2), 3–34.

Ladson-Billings, G. (1995). But that's just good teaching! The case for culturally relevant pedagogy. *Theory Into Practice, 34*(3), 159–165.

Larson, R. W. (2000). Toward a psychology of positive youth development. *American Psychologist, 55*(1), 170–183.

Le Menestrel, S., Bruno, M. L., & Christian, D. (2002). *Sports as a hook: An exploratory study of developmentally focused sports programs.* Washington, DC: Academy for Educational Development.

Lyras, A., & Welty Peachey, J. (2011). Integrating sport-for-development theory and praxis. *Sport Management Review, 14*(4), 311–326.

MacIntosh, E., & Spence, K. (2012). An exploration of stakeholder values: In search of common ground within an international sport and development initiative. *Sport Management Review, 15*(4), 404–415.

Maro, C. N., Roberts, G. C., & Sørensen, M. (2009). Using sport to promote HIV/AIDS education for at-risk youths: An intervention using peer coaches in football. *Scandinavian Journal of Medicine & Science in Sports, 19*(1), 129–141.

McPherson, B. D., Curtis, J. E., & Loy, J. W. (1989). *The social significance of sport: An introduction to the sociology of sport.* Champaign, IL: Human Kinetics.

Newman, J. I. (2013). Arousing a [post-]Enlightenment active body *praxis. Sociology of Sport Journal, 30*, 380–407.

Parker, E., Meiklejohn, B., Patterson, C., Edwards, K., Preece, C., Shuter, P., & Gould, T. (2006). Our games our health: A cultural asset for promoting health in indigenous communities. *Health Promotion Journal of Australia, 17*(2), 103–108.

Perkins, D. F., & Le Menestrel, S. (2007). *Sports-based youth development.* New York, NY: Jossey-Bass/Wiley.

Perkins, D. F., & Noam, G. G. (2007). Characteristics of sports-based youth development programs. *New Directions for Youth Development,* (115), 75–84.

Petitpas, A. J., Cornelius, A. E., Van Raalte, J. L., & Jones, T. (2005). A framework for planning youth sport programs that foster psychosocial development. *Sport Psychologist, 19*(1), 63–80.

Pieterse, J. N. (2010). *Development theory* (2ⁿᵈ ed). London, UK: Sage.

Roth, J., Brooks-Gunn, J., Murray, L., & Foster, W. (1998). Promoting healthy adolescents: Synthesis of youth development program evaluations. *Journal of Research on Adolescence, 8*(4), 423–459.

Ryne, S., & Rossi, T. (2012). *Abridged report on findings, the impact of indigenous community sports programs: The case of surfing.* Retrieved from http://www.ausport.gov.au/__data/assets/pdf_file/0011/507989/FINAL_The_Impact_of_Indigenous_Community_Sports_Programs_Abridged_Report.pdf

Saavedra, M. (2009). Dilemmas and opportunities in gender and sport-in-development. In R. Levermore & A. Beacom (Eds.), *Sport and international development* (pp. 124–155). New York, NY: Palgrave Macmillan.

Theokas, C., Danish, S., Hodge, K., Heke, I., & Forneris, T. (2008). Enhancing life skills through sport for children and youth. In N. L. Holt (Ed.), *Positive youth development through sport* (pp. 71–81). London, UK: Routledge.

Thomas, D. R. (2002). Evaluating the cultural appropriateness of service delivery in multi-ethnic communities. *Evaluation Journal of Australia, 2*(2), 50–56.

United Nations Office on Sport for Development and Peace (2009). *Sport & Child & Youth Development Thematic Working Group, Action Plan 2010–2012*. Available at: http://www.un.org/wcm/webdav/site/sport/shared/sport/pdfs/SDP%20 IWG/Action%20Plan_Sport%20and%20Child%20%26%20Youth%20Development_FINAL_New.pdf. Geneva.

Up2Us Center (2013). *Featured research brief: Sport-based youth development*. Available at: https://0ea29dd9a16d63 dcc571-314f1dcf5bee97a05ffca38f060fb9e3.ssl.cf1.rackcdn.com/uploads/center_resource/document/341/SBYD.pdf. Boston, MA.

Weiss, M. R. (2008). 'Field of dreams': Sport as a context for youth development. *Research Quarterly for Exercise and Sport*, *79*(4), 434–449.

Weiss, M. R., & Wiese-Bjornstal, D. M. (2009). *Promoting positive youth development through physical activity*. Retrieved from http://presidentschallenge.org/informed/digest/docs/september2009digest.pdf

Wikaire, R. K. L. (2011). *Ko te haerenga o te waka ki Aotearoa: Waka ama and the reconstruction of Māori identity and culture through the Māori female body* (Unpublished honors thesis). University of Otago, Dunedin, New Zealand.

Wikaire, R. K. L., & Newman, J. I. (2013). Neoliberalism as neocolonialism?: Considerations on the marketisation of *waka ama* in *Aotearoa*/New Zealand. In C. Hallinan & B. Judd (Eds.), *Native games: Indigenous peoples and sports in the postcolonial world* (pp. 59–84). University of Florida: Emerald Group.

CHAPTER 29

Posthuman(ist) Youth

Control, Play, and Possibilities

Nathan Snaza and John A. Weaver

What Came After Postmodernism?

I n the last two decades of the twentieth century, the style, substance, and meaning of the postmodern condition was intensely debated. Was the postmodern a moment in time, an era, or a concept that rejected modern notions of segments of time? Was it a new architectural form, a new writing style, or a novel way to think about the world? In Jean-François Lyotard's (1984) prescient report to the French speaking universities in Canada, he highlighted some key issues that will define the postmodern condition. Besides raising an incredulous suspicion of all metanarratives that claimed to hold the key to all the answers humans seek, and predicting the decline of nation-state power, Lyotard also noted intense transformations in institutions of learning and the nature of knowledge. Replacing nation-states as the major arbiter of knowledge would be multinational corporations, and knowledge would be better defined as information. As a result of these changes, important questions were raised concerning the possibility for a democratic society to thrive in a postmodern world. In order for democracies to remain vibrant and viable, Lyotard believed that access to information was crucial, since those who were able to define what is valuable information and what is not would control the conditions of possibility for a democracy.

Moreover, as universities and nation-states were beginning to experience a transformation of meaning, the notion of performativity was also being redefined. In the traditional humanist and liberal arts approach, performativity referred to the interpretation of texts, the creation of worldviews, and the use of the arts to create human character. In the postmodern condition, performativity was becoming defined more by an economical definition of usefulness. Knowledge, now readily referred to as information, was defined as that which could secure an individual a high paying career so that individual could buy more and more goods and become the model consumer, born in a specific nation, but beholden to no boundaries but their whims and fancies. Performativity was now a measure of economic buying power, and democracy came to be defined by the principle of one dollar, one vote: The more you have, the more relevant and important you are. This, of course, has taken hold of the thoughts of school leaders and policymakers, and public schools have now become the primary site in which young people are trained in their preparation to become full-fledged consumers ready to perform their duty as wage earners and economic entities.

In a not-so-postmodern, ironic twist, what survived the debates about postmodernity was certainly not modernity, but one last meta-narrative: Homo economicus. Everything is reduced to economics. In other words, while postmodernity proclaimed the end of meta-narratives, its implicit acceptance of another specific (and ultimately humanist) meta-narrative leads us to recognize that the potentials of "post" thinking have yet to be realized. Just as Marxism was expunged from the public discourse for being too deterministic and too much of a meta-narrative, up from the ashes arose Homo economicus. Now public schools are defined by their test scores, universities by their ability to entertain the students and place them in future careers, corporations by their profit margins, sports teams by their branded names, and political leaders by their job creation policies. Youth have not escaped these debates, whether they have heard the term, *postmodern*, or not. They are part of neo-liberal discourses and the Homo economicus metanarrative. They are future workers, current test-takers, and as a result, they are the first complete generation of posthumans. Before the current generation of youth, posthumans did exist, but never in the abundance in which they today roam the schools, streets, and virtual spaces of these multi-corporate, patent pending, privately owned lands we formerly called earth and now refer to as an investment opportunity and entrepreneurial dreamscape.

While the postmodern debates may linger, and the remnants of modernity certainly do still exist, we live in times that have passed through the postmodern moment. In regards to youth, we submit that while they may be considered posthumans, they are also potential posthumanists. In the rest of the chapter, we want to address how and why young people can be considered posthuman, what the cost of the posthuman condition is, how Bernard Stiegler's ideas can help us to reclaim play as a means to overcome the posthuman condition, how youth are also potentially posthumanist, and how posthumanism can shape curriculum in schools and life experiences of youth.

Look Around! You Are Surrounded by Fellow Posthumans

Briefly, the posthuman condition may be understood as the merger of humans with machines that extends, supplements, and enhances human capabilities, including extended life expectancies, enhanced learning capabilities, supplemented body forms and conditions, and extended capabilities for control of bodies and minds (Weaver, 2010). To find examples of the posthuman takes little time, and mere observations in any public space will suffice. We live in a time of war, although without the clear "enemies" of older, modern wars between nation-states. The current moment is marked by the "war on terror" in which youth kill and die, or are maimed, or are incarcerated in (increasingly) for-profit prisons. As a result of this war, strategies such as the use of Improvised Explosive Devices (IEDs), coupled with new medical techniques of treating wounded military and civilian casualties, mean that there is a rise in the number of youth who survive their war wounds. Because of these factors, more people are fitted with state-of-the-art prosthetic limbs that allow them to walk, run, kick, write, wave, and lift as if they never lost a limb. These war veterans and civilians are posthuman. The prosthetic limbs extend their life expectancy and enhance their capabilities as machine merges with the human body.

We can also visit any hospital or some doctors' offices to find patients there with genetically fatal sequences that will cause breast cancer, various other forms of cancers, Huntington's disease, Parkinson, and many other disorders. With a small amount of blood, our DNA can be read; threatening sequences can be removed, and if need be, replaced with a healthier combination of As, Ts, Cs, and Gs. Of course, all of these tests and sequences cost money, so in order to be posthuman, one must either have good insurance or a good amount of disposable income to pay for the treatment. Today there are more young people walking the earth born from Preimplantation Genetic Diagnosis than ever before, allowing them to live a life of vanity with the eye color and hair color their parents always wanted them to have, but also for some, a life, period, because a deadly genetic sequence was removed in vivo or in vitro.

By far the largest population of posthuman youth are the pharmaceutically enhanced. By Peter Breggin's (2001) estimations, there are anywhere from seven to ten million young people in the United States alone on psychotropic drugs pushed by the multinational pharmaceutical drug companies, who see public schools as prime market sites. The most common label piled on young people is Attention Deficit Hyperactivity Disorder, or, for you attentionally challenged, ADHD. Conveniently labeled a neurological disorder so that anxiety-ridden parents can sleep at night knowing their child's condition is not their fault, the creators of the wonder pharmaceuticals still do not exactly know how ADHD is neurological, how it is causal in nature, and whether there is a known causality between neurological development and youths' actions. What the pharmaceutical drugs do besides give parents peace of mind is to give public schools a legal avenue to label students as disruptive in class, in order to control them as young people sit through boring, mind numbing testing preparation and eventually testing. ADHD is the tool school officials utilize to assure future businesses and corrupt politicians that the future work force, one way or another, will be ready to accept any challenge and submit to any order a boss gives. The posthuman condition for these millions of youth has enhanced their ability to pay attention to testing strategies and bits of information disconnected from any reality, but there is often a high non-monetary cost to be paid. Once a young person is placed on a stimulant (Ritalin or Adderall, for instance) or non-stimulant (Strattera, for instance), they often report to their physician a loss of appetite. To alleviate this side effect, a doctor gives them another pill to help them eat. If the youth report a feeling of listlessness, or what is often referred to as the Zombie Effect (many still falsely believe Zombies do not exist), the pharmaceutical representative, formally known as your physician, gives them another pill. And on the cycle goes. Filling youth up with a whole regimen of pills is referred to as the cocktail effect, because what these psychotropic pills are doing to the long-term development of the young brain is still not completely known. Indeed, such pharmaceutical interventions may be considered properly posthuman, in that they re-organize the body's molecular and chemical makeup in the service of an abstract sociality: "symptom management modulates subjectification by deterritorializing potential conjunctions between neurochemical processes and abstract social facialities, working at a neurobiological ground zero of social being and becoming" (Griggers, 1997, p. 121). By intervening in the organic body at a neurobiological level, this body's hardware is re-tooled to disenable some behaviors and encourage others.

In spite of the unknowns involved in the pharmaceutical posthuman condition, it is clear that the justification for the use of these drugs is to enable young people to pay attention and take a battery of tests that literally batter their brains and creativity. As a result of this overt policy of control in the name of testing done in the name of preparing the young for a workforce, anything associated with creative and imaginative development of the mind is often eliminated from the schooling experience. Play, which is not simply frolicking, as a way of exploring, imagining, and creating has been expelled for most young people in schools.

Before moving on, we want to note that our concern is not with the use of drugs per se. As Stengers (1997) has noted, the "war on drugs" obfuscates ethical issues in the name of "moral consensus." While youth are taught, on the one hand, to "just say no" to recreational drugs (a category that includes potentially lethal as well as relatively harmless substances), they are encouraged, on the other hand, to ingest anything and everything ordered by their physicians. Thus, doctors and pharmaceutical corporations attain the status of priests, leaving everyone else without a properly *ethical* claim in deciding their own actions, behavior, and psychic or neural functioning. Everyone implicated in recreational drug markets and use is inserted into an increasingly profitable carceral system where prisoners work for only nominal pay for global corporations. The problem of "drugs" (a category that conflates radically heterogeneous substances) has to be dealt with *ethically*, which means giving everyone affected some say in policy. Youth, today, are either *forced* to say no to recreational drugs or *forced* to take prescription drugs, and both are great for business. While there are many problems associated with the widespread use of *any* drugs, the problem with the drugging of youth in schools is that the particular drugs given in order to control the attention and testing skills of students transform youth into posthuman hybrids of humanimal and chemical, in ways that are totally in the service of the Homo economicus meta-narrative. Put more simply, our present system turns youth into posthumans in the name of a completely "humanist" end. Or perhaps more simply still, humanism has had to *abandon* the human in order to achieve its aims.

Playing With Bernard Stiegler

To be a youth is to live in perilous times, surrounded by a media industrial complex that encourages adults to skirt their responsibilities as the mature leaders of the young in order to relive their fantasies, infantile adults who no longer seem to know how to educate children, and an educational system that is completely corrupted by a multinational corporation system that reduces all learning to job training and consumption. As a result, youth are unable to develop in a healthy, mature manner. Youth are lost in a world that provides them with nothing but shallow alternatives for development. As Stiegler (2010) noted in a lengthy passage:

> Only by thinking the evolution of the psychic apparatus organologically (i.e., as a cerebral organ inter-acting with other vital organs, forming a body), in relation to both evolving social structures (qua social organ-izations) and the technical and technological configurations constructing tertiary retention (qua artificial organs), can the psyche's process of inherited internalization—which is called education—be properly assessed. (p. 7)

Without an educational system that provides youth with challenging and imaginative ways in which to process the worlds around them—both a world found through the bodies' senses and artificially constructed worlds via technology—there is no potential for the young to create a world that fits their intellectual, societal, political, and psychological needs. The present system produces youth who do not know how to grow up and become independent thinking adults. What Stiegler called education is defined not only by an institution of learning called schools, but also by the techno-entertainment industry and parenting. The techno-entertainment industry, according to Stiegler (2010, p. 9), fails in educating the young in any productive manner—other than in a selfish, bottom line, profit motive way—by "diverting primary identification and capturing the attention of young minds, [which] purely and simply destroys the psychic apparatus's resistance to the pleasure principle," the very pleasure principle found in the techno-entertainment educational plan, not in books, public debates, familial discourses, or any meaningful dialogue. It is a pleasure principle found in the market created by and for the entertainment industry. As a result, the educational process is designed to create players and/or gamers who will not grow up and out of adolescent pleasures (pleasures which can be harnessed quite productively in the computerized world of global capitalism). In order to do this, the entertainment industry has to redesign—or as Stiegler said, "short-circuit"—the educational system and parental influences.

First parental influences

Parental roles in developing youth into adults are subverted by the same principle used towards youth. Stiegler (2010) asserted that the short circuiting of parental roles does not oblige

> adults to submit to their children's *desires*; the apparatus of attention control is aimed at soliciting and exciting not only desires but *drives*. The goal is the stimulation of immature drives, making them prescriptive for adults as well by inverting intergenerational relations. (p. 12)

In other words, create a techno-entertainment economic structure that educates the adults the same way it does youth. At stake is not the specific objects of attention (the desires) but the *how* of attention (the drive). For Stiegler, adults have forsaken their generational responsibility to educate the young in cultural ways that will help them to understand their relations to past generations and raise the next. Instead, what the present system produces are adults and youth who just want to have fun. There are no longer "adults" or "youth," just thrill seekers. "Short-circuiting generational inheritance," Stiegler (2010, p. 13) suggested, "effaces both what differentiates children, parents, grandparents, and at the same time, cultural memory, consciousness, and attention to what is passed down through the myriad human experiences accumulated as secondary and tertiary retentions underlying cultural knowledge." To complete the short-circuiting process, educational institutions have to be redesigned. "This short-circuiting is consistent with 'job skills' and 'life skills' … chief characteristics of hyperindustrial, service societies that lead to consumers not being in charge of their very existence" (Stiegler, 2010, p. 13).

What are the consequences of this redesigning? Stiegler (2010) asked:

> What do … children deserve; what do "our" children deserve; what do children deserve, who(so)ever they are? Do they not deserve, at least, to have fathers, grandfathers, and a family … within which they can *play*, and through doing so learn to respect, that is, to love and not merely to fear? What does it mean to play with one's daughter or grandson? (p. 14)

When play is removed from the schools, it is also removed from the family. Play is now commodified as a consumer act, rather than an act of bonding and the transmission of culture, as Stiegler believes is necessary for adult responsibility. Play is more of a move on a game board undergirded by economic principles. Play has become the game of Life without much life involved. To play, for Stiegler and us, is to think as an always already social individual, connected to machines and other sentient beings, and it holds the potential to create a world different from the one constructed for us by the techno-entertainment enterprise. To play is to create your own games (video, virtual, sporting, or imaginative). To play is to demand a voice in imagining a future in which humans and other species are not treated as focus groups, targeted audiences, or potential workers. To play is to explore the past, present, and future, not alone but *with* parents, grandparents, and others, as they transmit important historical and cultural knowledge to the young. Finally, to play is to accept responsibility as adults (perhaps especially parents and teachers) to move beyond the pleasure principle, and raise the young to become thoughtful, caring, intelligent young people ready to educate the next generation.

How do we become posthumanists?

It is our contention that youth are not only posthumans, but that they are posthumanists as well. Just as it was the case with the posthuman condition, youth did not become posthumanists by accident or overnight. What follows in this section is our outline of how youth became posthumanists.

To be posthumanist is to live in ways that limn or even outstrip the habits of thought, action, becoming, dreaming, and playing that were developed in humanistic social and intellectual formations. While humanism has passed itself off as the most universal, most lofty set of values ever created by civilization, the emergent field of posthumanism argues, in a stunning variety of ways, that humanism and all its claims about human exceptionalism are "errors." As Pettman (2011) noted, the most tenacious error of all is believing in "the existence of 'humanity' as an autonomous, discrete, sovereign species" (p. 36). While posthuman youth experience bodily configurations that combine humanimal matter, technological prostheses, and synthetic-chemical-altered neural functioning, they increasingly also inhabit a world that cannot be adequately conceptualized in humanist terms. Posthuman youth have trouble understanding human uniqueness and exceptionalism, and are more open to recognizing the continuity between humans and other animals, and between living organisms and "postvital" forms of mechanized and computerized life. Unlike the generation of scholars currently producing the posthumanist research that is en vogue in theoretical circles at universities (research that is driven by helping us figure out how to move beyond thinking about ourselves as "humans"), these students *are not buying into humanism in the first place.* While this may be a matter of concern for some (including Stiegler, whose vision of a future polity is, finally, quite humanist), for us it is a matter of celebration.

N. Katherine Hayles (1999) ended her study with this sentence:

> Although some current versions of the posthuman point toward the antihuman and the apocalyptic, we can craft others that will be conducive to the long-range survival of humans and of the other life-forms, biological and artificial, with whom we share the planet and ourselves. (p. 291)

While the posthuman youth wandering zombie-like through the halls of contemporary schools face an increasingly dystopian world of authoritarian biopolitics, this experience also provides a possible point of departure from the humanist ideologies that trap them. This may be conceptualized in relation to the logic of consciousness-raising associated with Marxism and feminism. To be a woman, or working-class, or posthuman is a matter of the social capture of an ontological condition. To be a feminist, or a communist, or a posthumanist is a matter of *the politicization of attention*, one that may be grounded in that socially given identity, but which transforms it through imaginative fabulations of alternative futures. The posthuman is a condition; being posthumanist is a politico-ethico-intellectual orientation.

Pressing Play

Although many educators and curriculum theorists have been interested in play—especially those associated with so-called "child-centered" pedagogies in the wake of philosophers such as Rousseau—recent work in ethology opens up new ways of understanding the political, and specially posthumanist, import of play. Gordon Burghardt (2005, p. xii) insisted that "human play is continuous with nonhuman animal play in many respects." In other words, what contemporary animal studies reveal is that the human's need for play is not something "immature" that can be schooled out of youth, but a fundamental drive of the *human animal*'s being-in-the-world. All animals, including human animals, play, and this play is increasingly understood as *necessary* for processes of psychological and social becoming. At stake in play, for ethologists like Burghardt, is a specific distanciation from the material necessities of survival and compulsion. At the end of a long chapter outlining five criteria needed to recognize play, he offered this one sentence definition: "*Play is repeated, incompletely functional behavior differing from more serious versions structurally, contextually, or ontogenically, and initiated voluntarily when the animal is in a relaxed or low-stress setting*" (p. 82). Play may look like "serious" work, but its difference is found in its relation to purpose and context. Crucially, for posthuman youth forced to compulsively take tests, the school setting has become determined by a constant state of over-stressing (and not just by tests: schools are heavily militarized zones today, with the most advanced forms of surveillance equipment and armed guards). Without breaks from stress, without enabling youth to exist in relation to, but at a distance from, the dizzying demands of postmodern neo-liberal capitalism, there is no play.

In the penultimate paragraph of his book, Burghardt (2005) wrote that "play may be something that creates a spark, lighting a candle where there was darkness" (p. 405). *This* is precisely why play may open onto the posthumanist future. In a world so determined by the *humanist* demands of a neo-liberal economy and its organization of the production of our very subjectivities, the potential to *see something new*, to imagine alternatives, is paramount. The humanist vision has become so totalizing that today's youth are being drugged in order to make them serviceable employees and consumers. While such drugging zombifies them, they are also given a unique opportunity to theorize the gap between the humanist ideology into which they are indoctrinated and the posthuman *ontology* they experience. Play, for us, is the condition of possibility for this ability to see and think the contradictions of the present in ways that enable different forms of action, relation, and becoming.

Returning to Stiegler (2010), we may say that the posthumanist potential inhering in today's post-human youth is something we must *care for* as part of the "battle for intelligence" (p. 65). If the post-human youth are to grasp their potential, they will need us adults to care for them, to be *with* them in ways that are not reducible to control, discipline, and indoctrination. We need to affirm their play, and we need to play with them. Stiegler (2010) wrote:

> Reason as freedom, to critique, discern, analyze, and resynthesize after having analyzed—freedom to *reinvent*, the basic power of rational imagination—this reason is synthesized in its potential capacity to project ideal objects that do not ex-ist but con-sist, as protentions, and as the double desire for knowledge as such and the infinite expansion of ideal knowledge. (p. 67)

In the present moment, such protentions have been short-circuited by the media entertainment complex. Crucially, entertainment is not the same as play; in fact, they may be usefully understood as opposed. Play, by activating a shared, social, inter-generational set of frameworks for making sense of life, necessarily mobilizes "reason as freedom," especially in the way this reason imagines futures currently unthinkable. Entertainment, by contrast, disenables reason by substituting distraction for sustained attention.

We may usefully re-phrase "the battle for intelligence" as the battle for attention. In today's world, we can no longer afford to understand attention as a mere biological faculty. Attention is political, even biopolitical: in attention, the social networks of power relations and the biological, neural, and/or cognitive networks of a given being are inextricably bound. In sum, attention is situated at the precise intersection of "nature" and "culture," revealing the fallacy of this very binary. Posthumanism names a particular kind of attention, one that is attentive to the continuities among humans, animals, machines, and things, and that recognizes the many material relations linking them together. This world—a non-anthropocentric world in which the human does not have logical or political priority over other inhabitants of the world—is potentially accessible through play. Play, understood in the sense offered by Burghardt, also opens onto another sense of play, that from engineering and carpentry. "Play" refers to the flexibility or "give" of any structure. Posthumanist play forgets to take humanism and its ideologies as rigid, given structures, and seeks to ascertain their "play." It stretches humanism, bending and re-forming it. In the process, it transforms its sense. Spinoza famously thought that we do not know what a body is until we know what it can *do*. We have been so used to being "human" for so long that we have stopped trying to *play* with ourselves, taking for granted that we already know what we can "do," what we are capable of. But what if we are capable of so much more than we know? What if we cannot begin to imagine what our future holds because we have been tricked by humanism's oversimplifications and stupid certainties? And what if today's posthuman youth are less certain? What would happen if instead of drugging them to make them good humanist workers, we cared for them and let them play?

Curricular Play

One way to turn to play is to return to a naturalist's approach to learning. Today much of science is done in a laboratory and through computer simulations. Economics is done through modeling, as is population ecology; genetic and molecular biology are done through statistical probabilities. What this approach to science has done, however, is remove the scientist from nature (Prigogine & Stengers, 1984). The same thing has happened in public schools: science teachers and youth rarely leave the classroom to explore and reconnect with nature. Because of testing, science has become yet another discipline that feeds students tidbits of information to be regurgitated on command by Educational Testing Services (ETS). At the same time, science teachers have reduced science to a process of replicating an experiment done thousands of times by previous classes, rather than have students do as scientists always do: invent their own protocol to discover the best way or ways to understand a natural phenomenon or societal problem. What we propose is the return of the naturalists in the science classroom.

Or, as Stengers (1997) put it, we call for science to take the "risk" of its object surprising the scientist, speaking for itself, becoming a subject.

Although Darwin may be the most (in)famous naturalist today, Alexander von Humboldt inspired Darwin to become a naturalist and explore the worlds on earth. Humboldt had a simple method for approaching nature. First, the scientist has to explore. In 1799, Humboldt set out to explore the Americas. What resulted was a deeper understanding of what Humboldt called the Kosmos or the interrelationship between humans, other sentient beings, nature, and the universe. During his five-year saunter through the Americas, Humboldt explored the ways the lands and the peoples of those lands merged into a whole. While his contemporaries in Europe were pontificating on the superiority of Western Culture, Humboldt was formulating a different view in which he condemned slavery and imperialism and came to the conclusion that all people, no matter how different in culture and beliefs, were equal. He warned a deaf North America that slavery was evil, and an equally deaf Europe that colonialism was a sign not of superiority but of inferiority. Second, while exploring, the naturalist must collect; we might even say that Humboldt began the era of collection. Like so many other cases in the history of Western science, Humboldt's notion of collection was misunderstood. While many scientists collected in order to collect, Humboldt only collected in order to make sense of the world. "One must collect samples," said Laura Walls (2009), "and bring them back to a central location for description and comparison. … Collecting is not a mindless grabfest, but an effort of intelligence that creates, in effect, new organs of perception" (p. 127). Third, once the collection is in process, one must measure. Like collection, measurement is not done for the sake of measuring, as we do today in educational testing in schools: measurement is done in order to help the naturalist understand the patterns of the Kosmos. The final part is drawing connection, today almost a dead art. Students today merely collect because someone says they should, and what they collect are disconnected bits of information that have no meaning or purpose. Yet, to connect is to see and listen to the many ways parts of nature are linked to humans, other sentient beings, nature, and the universe. "The smallest of things," Walls (2009) suggested, "could, collectively, lead to the largest of ideas. Humboldt's method led to extraordinary conceptual leaps" (p. 127). Such leaps are undecidable in advance. Humboldt's approach inspired Adolphe Quetelet to invent statistical approaches and Darwin to understand natural selection, but it also guided Louis Agassiz as he developed a more specialized science that he used to justify racism.

What Agassiz seemed to ignore in Humboldt's naturalist approach was the poetics of Humboldt's vision. For Humboldt, science was not what we know it to be today. Science was not rigidly divided up into various subfields such as genetics, molecular biology, biochemistry, and countless others that exist under the abstract category of science. As Laura Walls (2009) noted, the wonder and beauty of science for Humboldt was found in the

> excitement of discoveries, of "mysteries to be unfolded" and the "inextricable net-work of organisms."…
> Wonder and the pleasure of discovery feed the desire to know, and knowledge leads back to wonder,
> in an ascending spiral fed by imagination at every turn that ever enlarges and will never end. (p. 224)

Science is not separate from history, poetry, politics, and religion, as so many believe today (something Alfred North Whitehead never tired of arguing). They combine to spark the human imagination to see the worlds of nature and to listen to them. This is what is missing from science today in schools. Youth cannot see the worlds of nature merely through a simulation or a model. They need to see nature for themselves. They need to explore, collect, measure, and connect for themselves. Youth need to *listen to* nature, and this cannot be done through an ETS standardized examination, or simply by memorizing a textbook that ignores the fact that other disciplines such as history and poetry shape the sciences. As Stengers (1997, p. 165) explained of scientific invention, what is at stake for the scientist is learning how to speak in the name of natural phenomena, to bring nature into discourse. To see and listen to nature is to play with(in) nature. To explore, by its very nature, is to play, and through play hopefully youth will see the many ways all humans are connected to other sentient beings and the rest of nature. Given a chance to play, hopefully youth will listen to what other sentient beings and nature are saying. To see and listen, however, they have to leave the classroom and reconnect with the world.

As it stands, many youth are not encouraged to explore, collect, measure, and connect. Instead, they are encouraged to demand: demand more natural resources no matter how finite they may be, demand more goods to consume, and demand more of the pleasures of life without giving to others and the one earth we inhabit. This attitude of demand, Robert Harrison (2008) believed, is a mark of "extreme ingratitude. For the ingrate, nothing is ever enough … we want more of everything that promises to perpetuate the cycle of unending consumption" (p. 164). Seeing and listening to nature with the right adult care can help youth remove themselves from a culture of ingratitude, and develop a more playful, gracious, poetic, and naturalist approach to the world.

Conclusion: Posthumanist Ethics

A posthumanist ethics grows out of and is cultivated by the rich soil of play and a poetic, naturalist approach lived by people such as Humboldt and Darwin. If we begin to interact with the Kosmos again, and if posthumanism is ultimately the return of humans to other sentient beings and nature, then we can ask, how does this return shape our lives and how do our interactions with other beings and nature change? Once we enter into the realm of posthumanist ethics, we begin to see how play means a rethinking of concepts and ideas. Calarco (2008) analyzed how twentieth century philosophers approach the question of the animal or the other Others. In this questioning of the human-animal relation, Calarco found that although the philosophers he covered—Heidegger, Levinas, Agamben, and Derrida—attempted to question the boundaries established to separate and elevate humans from animals, there are dimensions of their philosophies that reestablish this boundary. Calarco's (2008, p. 149) conclusion and suggestion was stunningly compact, but radical. Instead of trying to justify how humans are different and superior to other sentient beings, he wondered what would happen if "we could simply let the human-animal distinction go or, at the very least, not insist on maintaining it." What if we humans did not see ourselves as superior to all other species because we can think, have a soul, can reason, or experience death rather than just die? What if we did not try to draw distinctions, but worked from the assumption that humans are animals and are just as much the Other as other sentient beings? What kind of thinking would this provoke?

Once again, we are encouraged to play with concepts and ideas that are not as concrete or universal as we supposed. We find ourselves returning to Stiegler, who asked adults to assume the role of adults. We must pass on inherited traditions of our culture passed down through the generations, and simultaneously pass on a new way of thinking about our culture to the youth. In turn, if we pass on a new way of thinking, it will require youth to rethink their own position in the Kosmos and their own relationship with other sentient beings. Eventually, such questioning will require youth to play with concepts and ideas, no longer understood as natural. After all, while it may feel "natural" that humans are superior to animals given our humanist and modern education of the last five hundred years, this superiority is pure fiction indoctrinated into us, causing us to entirely mis-recognize ourselves and our relations to the world. To play within these embedded traditions and replace them with counter-intuitive belief systems is disconcerting. Yet this is exactly what we should expect from adults and eventually from youth. To play with concepts and ideas is a serious business that never should be a business, but rather, a way of living and honoring those that came before us, other species, and the Kosmos. To play with the concept and idea of human-animal relations is not to continue a modern tradition of what Harrison (2008) referred to as a frenzy: an aimlessness that pervades modern capitalism. Instead, play encourages a cultivation that requires each individual to give more than it takes. It requires individuals to be caretakers of the earth, and to take care of one another and other species. Humanism, under the heading of "dominion," insisted that to care for other sentient beings means humans must be responsible owners of animals and stewards of the land. This, however, is not what we mean. To take care in a posthumanist way is to recognize that other sentient beings are our companions on earth. Each being has a sanctity and right to dignity, to be treated with respect. It is to move beyond the limitation of subject status to humans, and experiment with political and ethical relations that acknowledge the *subjectivity* of non-human animals, ecosystems, and perhaps even things. This does not mean we are proclaiming that everyone should become a vegetarian, and/or proclaiming that to own a pet is immoral. What a posthumanist ethics means, to start, is to ponder this question Calarco (2008, p. 136) posited: "the ethical question should not be 'How do I achieve an ethically pure, cruelty free diet?' but rather, 'What is the best, most respectful, most grateful, and also most giving way of relating' to animals and other Others?" How should we show our gratitude to animals who die so we can eat? Does it often take the shape of the ingratitude Harrison mentioned? How do we give respect to all life, and the non-living entities enmeshed with living beings on earth? Do we really respect life, or do we play zero-sum games with some species and willfully cause species to go extinct in the name of economic progress? How should we relate to animals and other Others? Are they ours to do with as we please?

These questions cannot even be asked in our present milieu, where unanswered or unanswerable questions have been muted in schools where students are chemically and/or neurologically modified to make them into the kinds of being humanism *presupposes* they must be. Against the standardization of curricula, the absolute domination of standardized testing, and the forced "humanization" of students (which, paradoxically, produces posthuman youth), we would do well to invoke Nietzsche's distinction between civilization and culture. Civilization—which for him is coterminous with humanism—is a degeneration of the work of culture, a process that is in no way uniquely human. As Vanessa Lemm (2009) explained, "Civilization's attempt to awaken and enlighten the human being is, here, inseparable from the attempt to keep the animal within the human being asleep" (p. 26). Civilization is only possible as a forced domestication of the human animal's cultural potential. Against civilization, Nietzsche imagined the Übermensch:

> Becoming over-human, therefore, does not reflect an attempt to stabilize human life into some sort of ideal superhuman form, but, rather, to provoke a counter-movement against that which stabilizes itself into a fixed identity and nature. It does not entail remaining identical to oneself, but altering oneself, becoming unfaithful to oneself. (Lemm, 2009, p. 23)

In other words, becoming over-human requires a re-awakening of the animality *of the human*, an awakening that produces experiments with becoming-other-than-one-is, experiments we can only call "play."

References

Breggin, P. R. (2001). *Talking back to Ritalin: What doctors aren't telling you about stimulants and ADHD*. Cambridge, MA: Da Capo Press.

Burghardt, G. M. (2005). *The genesis of animal play: Testing the limits*. Cambridge, MA: MIT Press.

Calarco, M. (2008). *Zoographies: The question of the animal from Heidegger to Derrida*. New York, NY: Columbia University Press.

Griggers, C. (1997). *Becoming-woman*. Minneapolis, MN: University of Minnesota Press.

Harrison, R. P. (2008). *Gardens: An essay on the human condition*. Chicago, IL: University of Chicago Press.

Hayles, N. K. (1999). *How we became posthuman: Virtual bodies in cybernetics, literature, and informatics*. Chicago, IL: University of Chicago Press.

Lemm, V. (2009). *Nietzsche's animal philosophy: Culture, politics, and the animality of the human being*. New York, NY: Fordham University Press.

Lyotard, J-F. (1984). *The postmodern condition: A report on knowledge.* Minneapolis, MN: University of Minnesota Press.

Pettman, D. (2011). *Human error: Species-being and media machines.* Minneapolis, MN: University of Minnesota Press.

Prigogine, I., & Stengers, I. (1984). *Order out of chaos: Man's new dialogue with nature.* New York, NY: Bantam Books.

Stengers, I. (1997). *Power and invention: Situating science* (P. Bains, Trans.). Minneapolis, MN: University of Minnesota Press.

Stiegler, B. (2010). *Taking care of youth and the generations* (S. Barker, Trans.). Stanford, CA: Stanford University Press.

Walls, L. (2009). *The passage to cosmos: Alexander von Humboldt and the shaping of America.* Chicago, IL: University of Chicago Press.

Weaver, J. (2010). *Educating the posthuman: Biosciences, fiction, and curriculum studies.* Rotterdam, The Netherlands: Sense.

CHAPTER 30

Mediated Youth, Curriculum, and Cyberspace

Pivoting the In-Between

Donyell L. Roseboro

Without question, youth are using digital technologies to construct identities, make connections, and challenge the world they inhabit. The statistics among teens are unsurprising—93% report having home Internet access, just 22% do not have a cell phone, and 47% of those who do possess a cell phone actually have a smart phone. Approximately 25% of teens who have smart phones report using that device to access the Internet more often than using a computer or tablet (Madden, Lenhart, Duggan, Cortesi, & Gasser, 2013). Increasingly, teens are wired on mobile devices, with older teen girls more likely to surf the Internet using a smart phone. The steady rise in mobile-device ownership and usage among teens represents a clear shift in digital-technology usage. Instead of using a fixed device to bring the world to them, teens are carrying the world with them using portable technologies.

Historically, researchers have examined the ways that youth use digital technologies, the influence of those technologies on youth, and the ways that parents and teachers might use similar tools to educate young people. This research explored the effects of emerging technologies (cell phones, computers) on the lives of young people, and their evolution as the "net generation" (Tapscott, 1998). Important critiques emerged as well, with some researchers challenging the portrayals of youth as one homogenous entity with similar access to technology (McKay, Thurlow, & Zimmerman, 2005). Clearly, the ways that urban youth of color might access technology might differ from the ways that rural White youth might access. Equally important, researchers began to question the quest for technology absent any meaningful discussion about why and how such technology might improve humankind (Russell & Russell, 1997; Schwarz, 1996; Smethers, 1998). These researchers suggested that the acquisition of technology could not be an end unto itself. Such challenges shifted the questions being asked from "why don't more teachers use technology" to "why should technology be used and why?" (Schwarz, 1996, p. 78). In this shift, educators would move outside of the rhetoric of technology to a place of critical thought with and in response to technology.

More recent scholarship has extended this debate to nuanced examinations of the ways that identity and learning intersect in and with cyberspace. The substance of cyberspace and the learning it inspires (or undoes) has emerged as a point of debate. Questions of truth and authenticity complicate cyberspace usage—who has access and what individuals can access affects the construction of and dissemination of knowledge online. Race and gender still matter online (Bellamy & Greenfield, 2009; Jones, Johnson-Yale, Millermaier, & Pérez, 2009; Nakamura, 2002). The stories told and histories recreated online are shaped by other identity markers (i.e., sexuality, ability, nationality, etc.), all of which translate from face-to-face realities to virtual ones. Despite claims that cyberspace is a tabula rasa, it can reify existing stereotypes, extend misperceptions, and provide ample space for the spread of misinformation.

Yet, its potential as a different kind of space remains present. As young people have found their public educational spaces increasingly constrained (Fine & Ruglis, 2009), the Internet has become a third space of possibility. Third spaces are spaces for oppositional language and identity construction. They are spaces for the development of counter-narratives that can resist and/or reject mainstream ideologies (Bhabha, 1994; Meyers, 2009). The Internet, in as much as it functions as a third space for the exploration of different discourses and/or realities, is also a space tempered by the capacity of the technologies that sustain it. Its perceived unlimited scope stands in direct contrast to its tangible limits as a space entirely dependent on the hardware and software that support the connections. It is this tension between unlimited possibility and limited reality that undergirds my analysis of cyberspace as curriculum.

This chapter will explore the cyberspace curriculum as a third space between face-to-face and virtual realities—it is the in-between that emerges when these realities connect. In this examination, I start with Russell and Russell's (1997) definition of cyberspace curriculum as "an approach to teaching and learning which involves all those planned and unplanned learning activities and outcomes which result from the integrated use of computers in school for the purposes of communication, interaction, information retrieval, and knowledge construction" (p. 584). I will extend this definition to include any mobile device on which the Internet can be accessed. Ultimately, this conceptual analysis of the Internet as curriculum explores the nexus between language, technology, and space. It is a nexus that generates a distinct discourse, one that shapes what and how we know.

Theoretical Framework

As a learning medium that also affects identity building, the Internet creates different possibilities for the construction of kinship networks, the performance of varied roles, the assumption of particular forms of sovereignty, and the reconstitution of experience. Thus, the Internet presents a possible third space (Bhabha, 1994; Wright, 2012; Zaver, 2013) for the expression of identity, a space somewhere between legitimate and illegitimate spaces. Third spaces represent dynamic spaces, spaces in which ambiguity and conflict etch new meaning onto each exchange. They are spaces in which every identity marker is a floating signifier (Jhally, 1997) that resists the confines of discourse. Indeed, they are spaces in which the typical dichotomies that function in first and second spaces unravel. They are spaces in which legitimacy and illegitimacy can occupy the same space, switch roles, or change meaning. They act as spaces of discovery and exploration, spaces for the embracing of conflict, acceptance of the unknown, and delay of punitive consequences (those that we would normally receive for abnormal behavior in first or second spaces).

Understanding Culture and Cyberspace

Manovich (2002) used the concepts of montage, transcoding, interface, compositing, telepresence, and illusion to create a framework for understanding how culture and cyberspace interact. With montage, editors piece together different frames. This is particularly important for us to consider when done as temporal montage. In temporal montage, different points in time are pieced together, yet each image maintains its distinctiveness. In transcoding, we switch formats. A newspaper in cyberspace is still a newspaper, albeit in a different format. What we tend to forget in transcoding is that we often maintain the same interpretive lens after the item has changed formats. In doing so, we fail to consider the distinct differences that may arise simply because of the re-formatting. Interface represents the human-computer interface (HCI) that occurs each time we connect to cyberspace using a device. HCI demands a certain suspension of disbelief. Each time we interface, we allow ourselves to enter a virtual world, despite the prospect of identity theft, hyper-surveillance, and tracking. In compositing, editors piece together different images, and blur the boundaries that distinguish them to make them appear as one reality. Boundaries become fluid, as spatial barriers lose their permanence. Cyberspace allows us to be telepresent—in different spaces at the same time. Finally, illusion suggests that our perceptions are always not quite what they seem.

Curriculum as Marked by Technology

With this framework, we can consider cyberspace as a curriculum marked by technology (rather than technology that delivers a curriculum). Indeed, the Internet has remarkably changed the nature of political activism (i.e., the evolution of democratic upheaval in the Middle East), social networking (i.e., Facebook, Instagram, Twitter), and professional work (i.e., online meetings, resource sharing, research). As a curriculum, it has generated new ways of considering artifacts in cyber anthropology (Svilicić, 2012), social currency (Rainie, Brenner, & Purcell, 2012), and historical narrative (Rigney, 2010). To illustrate, with cyber-anthropology, anthropology has profoundly changed. Svilicić (2012) suggested,

> Hypermediality enables the researcher to manage the information in a non-linear manner in the context of investigating the visual anthropology domain to such a degree that in the development of this profession a point will soon be reached when the researcher's presence on the spot will not be imperative any more. (p. 272)

This transformation in the way anthropology is done demonstrates that cyberspace is more than a curricular medium. It does more than facilitate the transmission of knowledge. As a third space, it generates curricula and stimulates new epistemologies. With social networking, cyberspace represents a constantly connected curriculum. Claiming over one billion users as of July 6, 2013, Facebook poses its mission as "to make the world more open and connected." While the content that Facebook pages extend is extraordinary in sheer volume, the importance of online social networking as a curriculum has clearly emerged—cyberspace has altered the way we initiate contact, maintain that contact, and end that contact. In this way, it has changed the way we know others. Perhaps most important, it has changed the way we exercise our creative and curatorial abilities. With 46% of adult Internet users posting images they have taken online (creating), and 41% sharing images they have found online (curating), cyberspace has fundamentally changed what is considered social currency (Rainie et al., 2012). In this way, it has generated a curriculum of social interaction that shapes our face-to-face exchanges.

Finally, cyberspace has shifted historical narrative. No longer is history presumed to be a singular narrative bound to a specific author's interpretation and/or representation. Historical narrative online forces us to understand history as always bound to multiple representations. Rigney (2010) argued,

> Beyond their practical implications, the digital media also provide a new theoretical model for viewing historical narrative in terms of its social production by multiple agents across different platforms, and this changes our understanding both of past and of future practices. (p. 100)

The interactivity that cyberspace allows interjects an exchange process in historical narrative that is unlike the exchange that occurs when a reader reads a narrative in a bound volume. The interactivity of cyberspace not only changes the interaction between the narrative and the reader; it alters the production of the narrative such that all narratives are potentially co-constructed. With news stories accompanied by open commentary blogs, readers contribute to the interpretive possibilities of the original narrative, and as each reader adds a comment, they extend the narrative. Because narrative shapes much of our understanding of history, this shift in its production changes the core of how we do historical inquiry. Such a change suggests that cyberspace creates a different history curriculum; one not bound by fixed texts, but one in which overlapping additions, subtractions, multiplication, and division make narratives anew in seconds.

The Curricular Nexus

Curriculum has been defined as a permanent body of knowledge and entirety of learning experiences (Marsh, 2004); the means and ends of education (Posner, 2004); educational purposes, experiences, and assessment of learning (Tyler, 1949); a collective story (Grumet, 1981); and currere—running the course or journey (Pinar & Grumet, 1976). It is the subject of teaching and learning, that which we attune ourselves to for particular amounts of time. More recently, curriculum has also been examined along with identity. What we study is invariably affected by who we are and the collectivities with which we identify (Kincheloe, 2004; McLaren, 2006; O'Malley & Roseboro, 2010; Stanley, 2009). These identities in turn shape how, when, why, and in what manner we access the Internet.

Cyberspace curriculum therefore refers to the interaction between identity, teaching, and learning across face-to-face, virtual, and cultural dimensions. The unique spatial dimensions and technological possibilities of cyberspace have created a curricular platform that defies the bounds of time and space. Van Manen & Adams (2009), in their discussion of how new media have changed the way we write, offer an important contribution to how we consider the effects of cyberspace on curricula:

> Over a century ago, Nietzsche, inspired by his new typewriter, wrote, "Our writing instruments contribute to our thoughts". Typewriting, and more particularly writing with keyboard and mouse, changes how we write, and the way our words look as we write. But how do the writing instruments contribute to our (writing) thoughts? Jacques Derrida, the philosopher of writing, was hesitant: "People often ask me, 'Has your writing changed since you have been writing on the computer?' I'm incapable of replying. I don't know what criteria to measure it by. There's certainly a change but I'm not sure that it affects what is written". (p. 10)

Van Manen and Adams (2009) suggested that "writing public," "writing the distance to the other," and "entering the page" are specific ways that cyberspace has altered what we do as writers. If we apply these same concepts to cyberspace curriculum, we turn our attention to place and perception, relationships, and access to the Internet.

In writing public, we lose the visual distinctiveness of individual handwriting. Each person who authors in cyberspace does so in a pre-set font, one that lacks the individual characteristics of handwriting. With public fonts, writing appears as a finished product at the same time as it appears easily manipulated. Once typed, the writing assumes a life separate from the author. It stands alone, finds its own place. In writing the distance to the other, words help us traverse the distance from I to they. In asynchronous communication, we lose much of the non-verbal language that might affect our communication. In many ways, writing online calls us in, demands us to respond across space and time. Finally, writing online requires us to enter the page. Cyberspace pages clearly mimic the pages of hardback books. But, cyberspace pages also invite a different kind of interaction, one that can be erased or changed immediately by multiple authors. Applying these concepts to cyberspace curriculum forces us to consider the cyberspace curriculum as a series of simultaneous paradoxes—finished product/perpetually editable, distance/proximity, and familiarity/newness.

Just as it sits at the nexus of face-to-face and virtual worlds, the cyberspace curriculum operates at the interstices, the "in-between reality" of extremes (Bozeman, 2003, p. 63) and the "dialectical tensions" inherent in those seemingly oppositional spaces (Mason, 2009, p. 22). It is a curriculum that constantly works the other, requires simultaneity, and speaks hybridity. As such, it resists singularity in thought and action. It is a consistently evolving and operationalized curriculum, never confined to the purely theoretical space and always defined in the exchanges that take place in cyberspace. Perhaps most important, it is a curriculum that comes imbued with a certain currency, a newness that invigorates, inspires, and challenges. This currency, in social, political, and cultural dimensions, sustains a belief in infinite possibility. With infinite possibility at the core of its curricular distinctiveness, the cyberspace curriculum stands apart from traditional print curricula.

A Topology of the Cyberspace Curriculum

Schmidt and Cohen (2013) made several compelling arguments about the impending effects of the new digital age. Amidst the dizzying statistics they presented (5 billion more people connected to the Internet over the next 10 years), they also predicted that this connectedness will exacerbate existing social problems. Schmidt and Cohen (2013) argued,

> the vast majority of the world will be net beneficiaries of connectivity … despite these almost universal benefits … a digital caste system will endure well into the future, and people's experience will be greatly determined by where they fall in this structure. (p. 254)

Though the virtual and physical worlds will intersect, extend, and challenge one another, they will create two distinct policy arenas—what a state allows in one space it may not admit in another. Virtual revolutions and virtual honor killings may both find space online, proving that cyberspace can enhance our capacity for collective action in compelling and deeply troubling ways. Indeed, Schmidt and Cohen suggested that the lure of cyberspace is so tantalizing that ordinary folks accept cyber surveillance, forego privacy in the sharing of deeply personal events, and ignore security issues in online exchanges.

These sacrifices become embedded in the ways we interface with cyberspace, and complicate the existing paradoxes (finished product/perpetually editable, distance/proximity, and familiarity/newness) that shape the cyberspace curriculum. In accepting cyber surveillance, foregoing privacy, and ignoring security issues, Internet users are actually adding a fourth paradox to the cyberspace curriculum—visible/invisible/hypervisible. There is an implicit assumption that one can be all three in cyberspace, and that this being is entirely contingent on which settings one chooses. Equally important, cyberspace, to some extent, does allow for the movement between visibility, invisibility, and hypervisibility. Movement between these spaces is driven by the actions of the individual, others with whom she or he interacts, and the unseen entities that control cyberspace (i.e., corporations).

In the remaining pages, I will examine these four paradoxes as they relate to the cyberspace curriculum—finished product/perpetually editable, distance/proximity, familiarity/newness, and visibility/invisibility/hypervisibility. Using this examination, I will construct a topology of the cyberspace curriculum, a way of analyzing cyberspace as curriculum. It is an analysis that will challenge the dichotomy of cyberspace as either an innovative technological medium or a cultural product, as either an epistemological courier or a constitutive space of knowledge construction. In this vein, the cyberspace curriculum emerges from the in-between of medium and product, courier and space.

Finished Product/Perpetually Editable

The editorial capability in cyberspace has given rise to a generation of media users who assume a level of authorship heretofore impossible with print media. Not only can individuals construct and add their own content online, they can alter the content of others. There are, of course, inherent problems with such authorship. Publishing one's work or editing the work of others online requires no third-party approval, no particular review process to assess the quality of such work or changes. This issue of authorship and editorial ability stands seemingly at odds with the Internet's ability to make a product look finished or complete. Presentation alone enhances the believability of online documents—the more polished the website, the more possible it is to lure readers in, to make them believe, to diminish the possibility of questioning.

Manovich's concepts of montage and compositing undergird this tension between finished and perpetually editable product. In cyberspace, we have the ability to collectively author our lives, to construct families, friendships, and work online in ways that provide what seem to be complete representations. Perhaps most striking, we constantly work at making these representations appear complete, yet to do so, we are constantly revising, adding, or deleting. We work consistently in the nexus between the complete and in process, always in response to a collective Other that will read, judge, and edit our self-portraits. Understanding the in-between of finished and perpetually editable product also requires us to redefine finished. With cyberspace, complete or finished cannot convey the same meaning. At best, we can say that a finished product, document, or image is presentable or publishable. It is believed worthy of being on display, being shared, or being centered.

Indeed, cyberspace has given birth to a new language, a new way of communicating that changes the ways we present ourselves, respond to others, and work towards completion. Bilton (2013) suggested that individuals are using their creative and curatorial abilities with images to communicate online. Used in this manner, images complete thoughts and sentences, disseminate ideas, and inspire dialogue. The use of photos as historical memory is quickly being replaced by the use of photos as discourse. With mobile applications like Snapchat, Bilton argued that people can use an image to communicate an idea for a finite amount of time. The image then disappears. To provide some perspective, Bilton (2013) added,

> Evan Spiegel, Snapchat's co-founder, who built the service two years ago while at Stanford, recently said that Snapchat users sent 200 million images a day, up from 50 million images a day in December. Instagram said last week that people shared 45 million photos a day on the site, and 16 billion in total since it began less than three years ago. On Facebook, people share 300 million images each day, or 100 billion photos a year. (para. 9)

Using photos as a way to communicate erases language barriers, allows us to witness others ideas, and inspires emotional exchanges across borders, time zones, and belief systems. This shift in communication captures the nexus between finished and perpetually editable—in as much as the image is losing its permanence, it is simultaneously being adopted as a more complete representation of questions, ideas, hopes, or feelings. The cyberspace curriculum thus demands a language that traverses traditional linguistic barriers and provides a way to communicate more completely, while simultaneously allowing us to continuously edit.

Distance/Proximity

Part of what makes cyberspace so inviting is its promise to erase temporal, physical, and cultural borders. As Manovich argued, it creates the illusion that distance, time, and cultural difference do not exist, at least not as barriers to the exchange of ideas. With telepresence, we can exist in multiple spaces at once, exchange ideas, and retain significant physical distance. We can create virtual identities, interact as those identities, and return to a very different F2F (face-to-face) reality. In this way, distance and proximity refer not only to our relationship with others, but they also refer to our relationship to ourselves. The self online is collectively constructed using transferable identity markers that can, at any given time, belong to someone else. While such transferability also exists in the physical world, online it becomes a cut-and-paste exercise that resists the permanence inherent in physical identities. It is an exercise that loops identities, images, and realities.

As we consider the in-between of distance and proximity, we must examine the tension between the anonymous and the identifiable. Distance affords individuals a certain privacy that may not exist online. Navigating between the anonymous and identifiable forces us to consider how we purposefully use distance or proximity to further ideas, causes, or movements. It forces us to examine how, why, and when we use distance or proximity to our advantage. Smethers (1998) foreshadowed these issues by suggesting,

> And while the new media forms fostered by interactive computer technology bear some resemblance to more traditional prototypes, the peculiarities associated with cyberspace—the anonymity of its users, the ease with which sensitive information can be accessed, and the complexities involved in creating meaningful regulation—have bred complex new twists to old legal and ethical problems, and those complications seem to defy the parameters of accountability that have traditionally governed print and broadcasting. (p. 16)

The in-between of distance and proximity has created new ethical and moral dilemmas with regard to what we know, how we know, and how we share information. Our ability to divorce the message from the messenger, to create pockets of anonymity online, represents the paradox inherent in the distance/proximity nexus—just as we use cyberspace to connect, so do we also use it to protect and to hide. And while this protection and hiding might be necessary to challenge oppressive structures, it also removes the identity of the messenger which, in turn, eliminates much of the context of the message. It is this context which shifts as we navigate between proximity and distance.

Clearly, the sheer volume of people linked through social-networking sites suggests that people desire connection. What is also clear, however, is that our use of privacy settings represents a re-creating of distance within cyberspace. The layers of privacy settings within social-networking sites like Facebook suggest that we can personalize our privacy; create distinct hierarchies of friends, family, and acquaintances; and construct a public self-portrait that shapes who we are just as much as we think we shape what that portrait is. On January 24, 2012, Facebook announced that it would release Timeline, a replacement for its Wall and Profile features. Users would not be able to opt out of Timeline (Duffy, 2012). When the announcement hit the Internet, one Yahoo news columnist warned,

> Left untouched, your Timeline may remind you of breakups, job troubles, or even a few unfortunate party photos that you have long since buried. Depending on your settings, these black marks on your digital past could allow new followers—including friends or business associates—to see a side of you that was better kept tucked away. (Wehner, 2012, para. 3)

Wehner's warning captured the tension between distance and proximity while it simultaneously depicted a fundamental assumption in cyberspace—that the identities and relationships we construct are always infinitely public though we work to make them private. Those who join our social-networking spaces are followers, a word that connotes a public persona, one that (as Wehner described) encompasses friends, or business associates. It is a word that connotes distance and implies a level of control of how that distance operates for different followers. Thus the nexus between distance and proximity is more about relationship than space, more about connection than geography.

Familiarity/Newness

Cyberspace comes imbued with an aura of currency, an expectation of newness that stems from the speed of information that travels through it. Since pages and sites are perpetually editable, we assume that the Internet captures the most recent and relevant information. In a functional sense, however, cyberspace has to operate as the familiar. While it is the new that might draw us in, it is the familiar that keeps us there. This power to mimic the physical world creates a certain level of safety, as individuals take risks, innovate, and challenge online. We create profiles, friend people, and access pages. We use the language of old media in a new media reality. Mark Fitzgerald (1995) captured this tension between the new and the familiar when he argued, "One big problem for newspapers in the online world is that anyone—or any business—can be a publisher of something that at least looks like a newspaper" para. 9). Though he was specifically referring to the migration of print newspapers to cyberspace, his point can be generally applied to the transfer from old media to new. Indeed, some level of familiarity helps to facilitate individuals' interpretation of the document, source, or product in cyberspace.

In cyberspace, the power of mimicry undergirds every exchange. Interactions appear, in small or large part, similar to their physical world counterparts. And though we recognize this mimicry when faced with security threats—emails that seem to come from our bank, notices to change our passwords (all attempts to steal information), the Internet functions as a deceptively safe mimetic space, one in which we re-create the physical world using its familiar language. When we switch from old to new media formats but use the same language and interpretive lenses, we are transcoding, as Manovich (2002) described. This transcoding allows us to work in the nexus between two disparate media forms, to make connections, interpretive leaps, and necessary transitions. The familiar helps us to make sense of the new, but the new simultaneously changes our interpretation of the familiar.

It is the mimetic actuality of cyberspace and our transcoding of it that warrants extended discussion. Alan Shipman's (2001) delineation of the term, *sovereignty*, from old media to new media language is a solid example. In old media language, sovereignty was more concerned with producers, while in new media discourse, the focus is on consumers. He said,

> Instead of commanding a "supply chain" producing to configurations and quantities set in advance by statistical inference and market research, firms now wait at the end of a "demand chain," not able to set the presses or roll the production lines until an order has been placed. (pp. 331–332)

The immediacy of cyberspace, its ability to provide layers of complex information that can be readily accessed by consumers across international borders, has, in effect, changed the way we define consumer sovereignty. We cannot simply superimpose the physical world conceptualization of consumer sovereignty over the new media actualization of it. It is a familiar term fashioned differently in new space. Cyberspace thus represents a working of the familiar and the new simultaneously, an acceptance of both as our translation matrix for cyberspace.

Visibility/Invisibility/Hypervisibility

Cyberspace demands a persistent navigation between the visible, the invisible, and the hypervisible. Though this has cultural implications, those are primarily discussed with regard to distance and proximity. In this section, I highlight the technical operation of the Internet, the software and the hardware that support it, and the ways those affect what we see and how we are seen. Gibson (1984) conceptualized cyberspace in this way,

> Cyberpace. A consensual hallucination experienced daily by billions of legitimate operators, in every nation .... A graphic representation of data abstracted from the banks of every computer in the human system. Unthinkable complexity. Lines of light ranged in the non-space of the mind, clusters and constellations of data. (p. 69)

What is visible to us in cyberspace is the familiar. We see the documents, the web pages, the old media transferred to new media form. What is hypervisible to us are the navigational tools that help us move from site to site. What is invisible to us, however, are the complicated ways that data is constructed, transmitted, and hidden in cyberspace. What we miss are the lines of code that make it work, the embedded commands from software engineers, and the internally wired connections that facilitate it all.

In essence, we see what we are supposed to see. We are inundated with what others want us to see. Yet typically, we cannot see how it all works together. This invisibility of exactly how cyberspace functions prevents the vast majority of Internet users from understanding how it works to store, retrieve, disseminate, ignore, and/or bury information. Yet this *how* is particularly important, because it does not function value-free. Cyberspace and the technology that support it are ultimately connected to the physical world. It is connected to people who write the programs, connect the wires, and troubleshoot the problems. But its invisibility disrupts our ability to question, challenge, or undo it. Its absence from our line of sight relegates it to a very real place of omniscience—in truth, we believe in its infinite capabilities even though we have no way of testing this infinity. In this way, cyberspace demands a particular kind of faith, a degree of trust in an unseen system.

Equally important, cyberspace tests this trust each time we interface with it. Upgrades, daily changes to web pages, and the integration of new software represent faith tests. Each time we move on despite the upgrade, changes, and/or integration of new software, we demonstrate a faith in the system, faith that it will work in the familiar and with the new, in close proximity yet while maintaining distance, and with finished products in perpetual editing. Despite the security risks present with cyberspace's mimetic ability, we continue to interface. Despite the bugs, viruses, and otherwise suspicious agents online, we continue to interface. In this way, the invisibility of cyberspace fosters a faith-based response. We interface despite what we do not know and cannot see.

Conclusions

The purpose of this chapter was to delineate a topology of the cyberspace curriculum, a way to begin thinking about cyberspace as a curriculum. It is a curriculum grounded in hybridity, teaching and learning in the nexus, the in-between space(s) of finished product/perpetually editable, distance/proximity, familiarity/newness, and visibility/invisibility/hypervisibility. As such, it is a curriculum not bound by content, but bound to process. It is a curriculum that resists and mimics permanence while it embraces the communicative process as fundamental to the innovative possibilities of cyberspace. The evolution of *how* thus becomes the basis for the cyberspace curriculum—it is a curriculum that speaks change. Ultimately, it is a curriculum that operates at the pivot, which works in the turn from one space to another.

For mediated youth, this curriculum networks their lives. The ways that mediated youth learn through cyberspace directly contrast the traditional print curricula of schools. While the cyberspace curriculum speaks change, process, and pivot points, traditional school curricula represent static, product-based, linear forms. Traditional curricula cannot respond to change, inspire new language, or work in contradictory spaces in the same speed that the cyberspace curriculum can—the former would dichotomize learning as complete or incomplete, in proximity or at a distance, while the latter works the multiplicity in simultaneity. Perhaps most important, for youth who were "born digital" (Palfrey & Gasser, 2008), they learn in the moment, in relation, with an expectation of currency, and using an evolving discourse that transcends cultural barriers. Their nativity, their sense of place and home, is bound to the intangible, the seen and unseen, the known and unknown. Their curriculum is indeed in the in-between.

References

Bellamy, A., & Greenfield, M. C. (2009). Examining African American and Caucasian communication patterns within computer-mediated communication environments. *Journal of Technology Studies, 35*(2), 2–13.

Bhabha, H. K. (1994). *The location of culture.* London, UK: Routledge.

Bilton, N. (2013, June 30). *Disruptions: Social media images form a new language online.* Retrieved from http://bits.blogs.nytimes.com/2013/06/30/disruptions-social-media-images-form-a-new-language-online/?ref=facebookinc

Bozeman, T. S. (2003). Interstices, hybridity, and identity: Olaudah Equiano and the discourse of the African slave trade. *Studies in the Literary Imagination, 36*(2), 61–70.

Duffy, J. (2012, January 25). *12 things you should know about Facebook Timeline.* Retrieved from http://www.pcmag.com/article2/0,2817,2393464,00.asp

Fine, M., & Ruglis, J. (2009). Circuits and consequences of dispossession: The racialized realignment of the public sphere for U.S. youth. *Transforming Anthropology, 17*(1), 20–33.

Fitzgerald, M. (1995). First job in cyberspace: Establish trust. *Editor & Publisher, 128*(9), 34. Retrieved from EbscoHost.com

Gibson, W. (1984). *Neuromancer.* New York, NY: Ace Books.

Grumet, M. R. (1981). Restitution and reconstruction of educational experience: An autobiographical method for curriculum theory. In M. Lawn & L. Barton (Eds.), *Rethinking curriculum studies: A radical approach*. London, UK: Croom Helm.

Jhally, S. (Producer & Director). (1997). *Stuart Hall: Race, the floating signifier* [Videorecording]. Northampton, MA: Media Education Foundation (MEF).

Jones, S., Johnson-Yale, C., Millermaier, S., & Pérez, F. S. (2009). U.S. college students' Internet use: Race, gender, and digital divides. *Journal of Computer-Mediated Communication, 14*(2), 244–264.

Kincheloe, J. (2004). *Critical pedagogy*. New York, NY: Peter Lang.

Madden, M., Lenhart, A., Duggan, M., Cortesi, S., & Gasser, U. (2013). *Teens and technology 2013*. Washington, DC: Pew Center's Internet & American Life Project. Retrieved from http://www.pewinternet.org/~/media//Files/Reports/2013/PIP_TeensandTechnology2013.pdf

Manovich, L. (2002). *The language of new media*. Cambridge, MA: MIT Press.

Marsh, C. J. (2004). *Key concepts for understanding curriculum* (3rd ed.). London, UK: RoutledgeFalmer.

Mason, A. (2009). Shifting shapes: The complicated interstices of imagining other America(s) and the collapse of race/nation in Arab identity. *Making Connections: Interdisciplinary Approaches to Cultural Diversity, 11*(1), 22–32.

McKay, S., Thurlow, C., & Zimmerman, H. T. (2005). Wired whizzes or techno slaves? Young people and their emergent communication technologies. In A. Williams & C. Thurlow (Eds.), *Talking adolescence: Perspectives on communication in the teenage years* (pp. 185–203). New York, NY: Peter Lang.

McLaren, P. (2006). *Life in schools: An introduction to critical pedagogy in the foundations of education* (5th ed.). Boston, MA: Pearson/Allyn and Bacon.

Meyers, S. V. (2009). So you don't get tricked: Counter narratives of literacy in a rural Mexican community. *Community Literacy Journal, 3*(2), 19–35.

Nakamura, L. (2002). *Cybertypes: Race, identity, and the Internet*. New York, NY: Routledge.

O'Malley, M. P., & Roseboro, D. (2010). Public pedagogy as critical educational and community leadership. In J. A. Sandlin, B. D. Schultz, & J. Burdick (Eds.), *Handbook of public pedagogy: Education and learning beyond schooling* (pp. 639–647). New York, NY: Routledge.

Palfrey, J., & Gasser, U. (2008). *Born digital: Understanding the first generation of digital natives*. Philadelphia, PA: Basic Books.

Pinar, W. F., & Grumet, M. R. (1976). *Toward a poor curriculum*. Dubuque, IA: Kendall/Hunt.

Posner, G. J. (2004). *Analyzing the curriculum* (3rd ed.). Boston, MA: McGraw-Hill.

Rainie, L., Brenner, J., & Purcell, K. (2012, September 13). *Photos and videos as social currency online*. Washington, DC: Pew Center's Internet & American Life Project. Retrieved from http://pewinternet.org/Reports/2012/Online-Pictures.aspx

Rigney, A. (2010). When the monograph is no longer the medium: Historical narrative in the online age. *History & Theory, 49*(4), 100–117.

Russell, G., & Russell, N. (1997). Imperatives and dissonances in cyberspace curricula: An Australian perspective. *Education, 117*(4), 584–591.

Schmidt, E., & Cohen, J. (2013). *The new digital age: Reshaping the future of people, nations, and business*. New York, NY: Alfred A. Knopf.

Schwarz, G. (1996). The rhetoric of cyberspace and the real curriculum. *Journal of Curriculum & Supervision, 12*(1), 76–84.

Shipman, A. (2001). Privatized production, socialized consumption? Old producer power behind the new consumer sovereignty. *Review of Social Economy, 59*(3), 331–352.

Smethers, S. (1998). Cyberspace in the curricula: New legal and ethical issues. *Journalism & Mass Communication Educator, 52*(4), 15–23.

Stanley, W. B. (2009). Curriculum theory and education for democracy. *Journal of Curriculum & Pedagogy, 6*(1), 44–56.

Svilicić, N. (2012). Cyber anthropology or anthropology in cyberspace. *Collegium Antropologicum, 36*(1), 271–280.

Tapscott, D. (1998). *Growing up digital: The rise of the net generation*. New York, NY: McGraw-Hill.

Tyler, R. W. (1949). *Basic principles of curriculum and instruction*. Chicago, IL: University of Chicago Press.

Van Manen, M., & Adams, C. (2009). The phenomenology of space in writing online. *Educational Philosophy and Theory, 41*(1), 10–21.

Wehner, M. (2012, January 24). *Facebook Timeline mandatory rollout: You have 7 days to scour your past*. Retrieved from http://news.yahoo.com/blogs/technology-blog/facebook-timeline-mandatory-rollout-7-days-scour-past-185456598.html

Wright, S. (2012). From third "place" to third "space": Everyday political talk in non-political online spaces. *Javnost—The Public, 19*(3), 5–20.

Zaver, A. (2013). Recreating third spaces in the classroom: Using dialogue to understand faith. *Journal of Religion & Spirituality in Society, 2*(3), 9–20.

CHAPTER 31

Why Is My Champion so "Hot"?
Gender Performance in the Online Video Game, *League of Legends*

Kelsey Catherine Schmitz

"You've got dangerous eyes …. I like that." —Miss Fortune the Pirate Hunter, *League of Legends*

Gaming Discourse: An Introduction to the Power of Avatars

Through imitation and simulation in video games, gamers are learning a range of cultural roles, both negative and positive in nature. When it comes to gender, more specifically, which games we are attracted to can depend strongly on our gender, and the agency we are given when it comes to learning gaming discourse. For example, with four brothers, my need to adapt and thrive on video games directly related to my brothers' being willing to play with me. Looking past the notions that 'boy games' and 'girl games' exist, and that gender is the only influence for choosing the kind of game with which one interacts, a difference in gaming interaction becomes more prevalent. While many female gamers play 'boy games,' their interaction with these male-centric games, and the male gaming world as a whole, involves a great deal of reinterpreting digital identities. This chapter will explore the complicated space of gender representation in gaming, and how girls and women learn to negotiate the creation of digital identities when designing an avatar themselves is not an option. Exploring the online 'real time strategy' game, *League of Legends*, I argue that when gaming, female gamers are forced to interact with a male-created gender identity far different from their own self-image. When game creators allow players selected options of representation in the game, players, both male and female, must negotiate the images of their avatars with the strategic benefits of the character they have chosen. By including the idea that "the body is the inscribed surface of events" (Foucault, 1980), the female game characters, and their digital representation of individual players, are spaces of exclusion that expose gamers, young and old, to distorted views of digital identities and the physical representation of those identities. Here, I suggest that the female 'champions' or avatars within the game become a surface upon which gaming culture's stereotypes and discourses are inscribed. The following is a deconstruction of the semiotics of avatars within the gameplay, with a gendered focus which is performed via an auto-narrative reading of gameplay. By selecting one champion from the twenty odd 'female' champions from the game, as well as sayings and/or quotes from others, and examining the artwork and digital bodily representation, a thread of common themes will begin to emerge that will demonstrate how female digital representation in this space is held hostage by game creators and designers.

Representation and Gender in Gaming: How Do We Approach It?

Feminism and digital bodies

Gender is simultaneously the body's variable modes of cultural articulation, as well as the site or surface upon which cultural forms are imposed or written. It is a continual modality of bodily interpretation within or partially outside the shifting paradigms of ordinariness. Bodies are texts, "bodies can be read insofar as our experiences are invariably written on the body" (Cavallaro, 2003, p. 115). However, one cannot be a sex or gender; there is only an engagement with hegemonic language and ideas from which we perform and act out gender. Sex and gender are not biologically determined, but rather, are a juridical concept and a means of cultural production of identity. Butler (1990) argued that the body exists prior to the circumstances of lived history; I would argue that we must engage in research that forces us to break down the meanings placed on the body (sexuality, wealth, worth, shape, colour), and enact Foucault's idea of the destruction of the body in order to view the cultural impacts on that body when looking at the body as a representation. Culture and history inscribe on a newly minted body, and inform how that body is shaped. Man's disembodiment is reliant on the condition of women occupying their bodies as their absolute and essential identities. If women are their bodies, i.e., if women are only their bodies, this implies that they are not "existing" or living their bodies as a "project and bearer of created meanings." Women subsequently "monopolize the bodily sphere" as their freedom and consciousness are merely permutations of bodily need (Butler, 1990; de Beauvoir, 1989; Foucault, 1980). As a researcher examining the digital gendered body, I seek to deconstruct the representation of the body within the culture in which it is presented.

Butler (1990) asked,

> if there is no recourse to a "person", a "sex" or a "sexuality" that escapes the matrix of power and discursive relations that effectively produce and regulate the intelligibility of those concepts for us, what constitutes the possibility of effective inversion, subversion, or displacement within the terms of constructed identity? What possibilities exist by virtue of the constructed character of sex and gender? (p. 44)

This would be an interesting question to begin answering in the exploration of gender and gaming, examining the matrix of power of the gaming culture and/or world within which the players learn to produce and/or construct their identities, and the various possibilities that could exist in those productions would be demonstrated through performance. Bury (2005) borrowed from Haraway's (1992) feminism and technology discourse of *the cyborg* to ground her own online ethnography. Haraway's (1992) notion of *the cyborg* suggested that "technologies are 'crucial tools recrafting our bodies' and as such they 'embody and enforce new social relations for women world-wide'" (Haraway, 1992, p. 164; see also Bury, 2005, p. 12).

Many storyline-based games with a first-person interaction do not usually give you the option of playing as a female. The gaming industry has a very specific target audience of young adult males (the average male gamer, according to consumer reports, being 30), with a propensity for first-person shooter and sports games. This is made obvious by simply stepping into any local gaming store and examining the shelf content of games. Not only are game genres and storylines catering to a more 'male' style of gaming, the industry itself has a distinct disregard for female gamers and their desired game experience. Because, for the most part, games are created by males for males, much of what players interact with is hetero male-centric. Player and/or computer dialogue involves responses and commentary male gamers respond to. On the other hand, computer-controlled female characters are shaped and designed to visually please hetero male gamers. The gaming world toys with the image of gender by creating a fantasy interpretation of what is and is not allowed in gender representation. Specifically, gender is hypersexualized and dictated by a male-centric fantasy line. Building on my lengthy experience with gaming, female gamers must negotiate a new sense of self each time they game, because of gender-specific storylines or character models they are exposed to in each video game. Though male gamers may not always face similar issues with gender (depending on their own orientation), they, too, negotiate multiple identity experiences. It is in this atmosphere of indifference and shunning that female gamers are forced to create a new gender identity from their own gender when gaming. This is done in two different ways: first, girls and women playing video games must negotiate a game more often than not as a male character. This representation forces these gamers to navigate a games' storyline and character interactions as a man would, and choosing from actions designed to cater (usually) to heterosexual males. For example, should I wish to play any of the *Grand Theft Auto* games, I would have to interact with the story as a male character who regains health points by having sex in the back of his car with a female prostitute, whom he can either pay, or force at gun point and then simply kill a woman to conclude the act of sex. While this example is highly controversial, because the game itself is extremely questionable for its content value, its extreme misogyny is typical of many mainstream games.

Second, women gamers, when given the option in mainstream games of creating a female avatar, almost always have to negotiate the production controls that have been created by a male designer. As a result, the typical female avatar in games such as *World of Warcraft*, or our focus game, *League of Legends*, have a very cookie-cutter design of the female body: curvy, large-breasted, big-eyed, and appealing to the number of hetero male gamers who will interact with said avatar. Even in games such as *Tomb Raider*, which features a female main character named Lara Croft, the visual representation of the female body caters to one representational dimension of female identity; namely, her body, in order to stimulate the (misogynistic) desires of hetero male gamers. Further, in *League*, players are not even able to customize their appearance; instead they select a 'champion' with a pre-set design and back story, along with colourful sayings and jokes they voice over the game while playing. This narrowed representation, and how these champions are designed, will be the specific parts of the game analyzed in this chapter.

Auto-narrative and semiotics

My narrative of experience playing with my chosen champion, Miss Fortune, will serve as the data through which I examine how gender is represented within the online game, *League of Legends*. Through narrative the normalized discourse becomes troubled. Hasebe-Ludt, Chambers, and Leggo (2009) introduced autobiography as theorizing lived experiences through a method called literary métissage: "métissage requires researchers to craft pieces of autobiographical writing in which they research and teach themselves" (p. 9). Métissage as an interactive scholarship asks researchers and educators to interact with, and play off of each other's lived experiences and writing, the "echolocation" (p. 3) of educational discourse. Using autobiography, Hasebe-Ludt et al. suggested life writing as a method where researchers can 'braid' gender, race, sexuality, etc., into studies. Autobiography can be an effective way to tease out meanings behind everyday occurrences and experiences, which can then allow us to examine and even question our understanding of social construction. When examining Giddens's writings on postmodern thought and how it impacts gender, Gauntlett (2008) postulated that

> self-identity becomes a reflexive project—an endeavour that we continuously work and reflect on. We create, maintain and revise a set of biographical narratives—the story of who we are, and how we came to be where we are now. (p. 107)

Lather (2001) put it best, suggesting that "we are inscribed in what we struggle against" (p. 20). How I negotiate game play as Miss Fortune, in her pirate hat and bustier, as well as my interaction with her ascribed 'dialogue,' the gameplay quotes she expresses while I do combat, will serve as an example of dwelling between a positive and negative cultural interaction with digitalized gender.

Beyond an auto-narrative, we must also examine the signs of representation that make up our understanding of avatars and gender. However, videogames are not simply semiotic images that we can analyze for representation and truths. More significantly, games are *played*; therefore, the representations that these images project are both the response of the player to the narrative and interpretation of the designer. Gonzalo Frasca (2004) suggested that "narrative is based on semiotic representation, while videogames also rely on simulation, understood as the modeling of a dynamic system through another system" (p. 86). While avatars in their design are the result of the game designers construct, the actions and interaction of the avatars are the sole representation of the gamer (or representations through engagements and/or encounters with other gamers' avatars—sign exchange system-fluid, evolving, spontaneous, etc.).

"Learning in videogames," wrote Jenson and de Castell (2009), "is not accomplished through the delivery of content, understood as abstracted 'facts'; rather meaning and significance arise through the player's activation and negotiation of images, objects, events, and so on, in specific situations of challenge" (p. 2). Here, Stuart Hall's deconstruction of the relationship with language and the *meaning* behind representations is pivotal, as I think about the learning that takes place in video games. According to Hall (1997), "all cultural objects convey meaning, and all cultural practices depend on meaning, [thus] they must make use of signs" (p. 36). One may conclude, therefore, that the cultural object in question, *League of Legends* (or even online games as a whole), conveys a representation of real-world culture blended with fictional storylines and fantasy role playing. In order for us, the gamers, to comprehend the story and expectations while playing through the game, it must encompass at least some 'signs' to which we can relate and through which we can develop meaning.

However, I would argue that learning in videogames goes beyond signs and signifiers; the gamer's actions become a sign which reflects the meaning, too. What do I mean by this? Signs, by Hall's (1997) description, are images, objects, or text which we then interpret into signifiers, or meanings, based on our previously learnt engagement with social norms. Within a game, however, an avatar is not the only image we must learn to interpret; we must also find the meaning behind the avatars' movements and actions, which are visually represented using their bodies (arms, clothes, eyes, colors, breasts, hair, movement, etc.), whose meaning is *purposely constructed* by the player behind them. Gee (2007) explained the importance of critical engagement with the semiotic learning that occurs in interacting with images controlled either by game designers or other players:

> For active learning, the learner must, at least unconsciously, understand and operate within the internal and external design grammars of the semiotic domain he or she is learning. But for critical learning, the learner must be able consciously to attend to, reflect on, critique, and manipulate those design grammars at a metalevel. That is, the learner must see and appreciate the semiotic domain as a design space. (pp. 31–32)

Therefore, true learning in gaming happens not only with the literal learning of the game, but on the ability to reflect upon and deconstruct the engagement one has within the game. *League of Legends* may not always offer players the opportunity to deconstruct their learning process, but through a series of group gameplay, I believe that it encourages players to reflect on practice as a team, to become more successful as they progress. Further, Gee (2007) suggested that the semiotic domains of videogames, when we learn to negotiate them in a more active manner, are spaces "usually shared by groups of people who carry them on as distinctive social practices," and "we gain the potential to join this social group, to become affiliated with such kinds of people (even though we may never see all of them, or any of them, face to face)" (p. 24).

In many games, semiotics, or reading the meaning behind images, evolves into simulation. Simulation recreates our cultural and social representations of objects, people, and even institutions such as governments, nations, borders, wars, etc., and allows players to reinterpret them using their own meaning and values. Gee and Hayes (2009) explained simulation as an act of play and control:

> [P]layers 'play' (control) a character … in game simulations …. The player is, in a sense, both outside and inside the simulation. This can give rise to an important educational effect if used properly. Players can be encouraged to combine two perspectives, a top-down, big-picture consideration of simulation as a whole and the insider perspective from the point of view of the character they control. (pp. 171–172)

League of Legends is not a true simulator such as *The Sims*, as it does not fully simulate 'real' life; in fact, as a real-time strategy game, the only simulation to real life is the need to learn to negotiate team play with others in order to win. However, the historical values of our society are represented in the social structure of the game, the interaction of players with other players, and the connection to everyday images and objects.

Using Stuart Hall's (1997) concepts of representation and semiotics, and Frasca's (2004) simulation and gaming, my examination takes a close look at how gender is exchanged or signified as a sign and/or signifier within the world of gaming. I believe that gamers, and more significantly, female gamers, must negotiate a new sense of representation each time they 'game,' because of gender-specific storylines or character models. *League of Legends* affords opportunities for the player to choose either sex—though there is a limited and highly sexualized female representation to select from—but many games do not. As such, many female gamers are now used to immersing themselves in storylines and gameplay that are male-centric. Young female gamers can only gain the respect of the gaming community if they identify with the more popular, more male games such as *Halo* and *Call of Duty*, two popular online combat shooting games. While gender-specific avatars exist within *League of Legends*, the representation of gender has a very specific, male-centred agenda. These representations demonstrate different 'fantasy' types of women, from the sexy warrior woman that follows along the male hero's side (*The Witcher*, *Fable*, *DragonAge*, etc.), to the overly sexualized female in distress stereotype (*Metal Gear Solid*, *Grand Theft Auto*, etc.). Using a semiotic approach to examine avatars of the signified female champions, I argue that *the visual images of avatars are shaped to engender a male response rather than to represent female gamers.*

> Games are powerful contexts for learning because they make it possible to create virtual worlds, and because acting in such worlds makes it possible to develop the situated understandings, effective social practices, powerful identity, shared values, and ways of thinking of important communities of practice. (Shaffer, Squire, Halverson, & Gee, 2005, p. 105)

Discourse of *League of Legends* Female Avatars

How do gamers go about creating, distinguishing, and defining gender in relation to their digital identities? Is it any different than the experiences of racism in gaming? I would argue that distinguishing one's gender is somewhat easier in an online role-playing game, where there are only two representational options for us to construct our avatar's gendered identities. However, in online games where all avatars are male and all players are virtually identified as male, it becomes much more difficult. The gaming world toys with the image of gender that Haraway (1997) promoted by creating a fantasy interpretation of what is and is not allowed in gender representation.

When another player blows you a kiss, the symbol for flirting in everyday society is now translated through your avatar. "In interactive media a user is not simply exposed to images that may contain representations of things and actions. The user is trained in the inaction of behaviours in response to images, and images appear in response to behaviours" (Penny, 2004, p. 80). Therefore, the ability to read the signs in a simulated world becomes even more important when dealing with how individuals represent their identity within the world. Significant to note, these identities are gendered. Put more broadly, through imitation and simulation in video games, we are learning a range of cultural roles, both negative and positive in nature. Quoting Jansz and Martis (2007), Gauntlett (2008) suggested that characters and avatars within the gaming industry are trapped within a stereotype of gender and representation:

> By their nature, video games are typically about action rather than reflection, and male characters in games are often brutal gangsters or grunting soldiers. Female *player* characters are not weak—which would make for boring gameplay—but are usually fighters who are meant to have a particular 'sexy-feminine' allure. (Jansz & Martis, 2007, as quoted in Gauntlett, 2008, p. 68)

I play video games. Not simple word games or strategy games typical of most girl gamers (Gee, 2007; Jenson & de Castell, 2009), but 'hardcore' (more intricate, demanding) games such as *Knights of the Old Republic* and *Dragon Age Origins*. Yes, the infection of gaming seeped from the minds of my brothers into my unassumingly little head, and drives me to this day to playing. Alberti (2008) noted the popular use of the phrase, "to play videogames," prompting him to question the verb *to play*. "While the verb 'play' is used in reference to other art forms," he wrote, "it usually applies to the producers of artistic texts—musicians, actors—rather than their audiences, *play* video games" (p. 262). This brings into question the role of the person *playing* videogames. Alberti suggested that video gaming is a discursive situation where the processes of "creation" and "reception" mesh together (Alberti, 2008, p. 262).

However, who takes part in the creation of this 'text'? Is it only the player, or is the game designer also a creator? Are most women like me, or is my affinity for gaming simply a by-product of my environment, the 'infectious' nature of belonging and togetherness I felt from participating with my brothers? Jenson and de Castell (2009) would suggest that my gender is still desperately underrepresented in this modern literacy, that "Girls and women … continue to be under-represented as players and are woefully few in the industry (latest figures from the International Game Developers Association (IGDA) put the number of women working in the commercial games industry at 11.5%)" (p. 2). The danger in this lack of gender discourse, the male-oriented targeting of the industry, is apparent if one simply examines the games that sit at the top of the gaming ranks: Overtly sexual, often misogynistic. As primary targets of the gaming industry, most games will cater to their interests, heroes, favourite sports, and overall social roles. As a result, the general environment, or discourse, of the gaming industry is exclusively bent to a hetero-normative male narrative.

The game: League of Legends

It is in this discourse that the popular, real-time strategy game, *League of Legends*, arises. Created in 2009 by Riot Games, it is described as a multiplayer online battle arena video game. It has millions of players across the globe ("*League of Legends* Players Summit a New Peak," 2013), from the lowly amateur gamer, to the professional gamers. The more elite players' battles are showcased on the game's main page, where other gamers may upload and view the battle between players. *League* is a strategy game played in real time (online within a set time) that pits two teams of 5 or 3 against each other. Players can elect to play with friends, or be queued for the game alone to be grouped with other players. These combinations of friends and strangers can result in fun, successful team play, or outright anarchy. The game is won by destroying the defences (towers) of the other team to reach their home base (Nexus) first, whilst defending your own base. Each Nexus releases computer-controlled minor characters called minions, which help in deterring the opposite team from reaching their goal. Each player selects a champion to use during the battle; the champions are gifted with different skills, powers, and abilities. A good team negotiates in the chat screen during selection about who will play which champions, and what constitutes a great makeup for success. These discussions can be highly successful and engaging, or discouraging mayhem, depending on the grouping. Throughout the game, a dialogue box and series of map 'pings' are used to communicate with your team. As a real-time strategy game, your success depends on your ability to work together, to communicate, and on a knowledge of the skills your champion possesses. Someone unfamiliar with a champion who can heal, for example, can let their teammates down (and die) if they are not quick enough. Champions deal damage to the opposing champions with their skills, and should your champion die from that damage, you spend a certain number of seconds removed from gameplay. There is certainly much more to the gameplay strategies, item building, champion skills, and abilities that are described here, but the basics should be enough to understand the game analysis which follows. This style of game attracts many different gamers, because it is free to play and download, and is accessed through an Internet connection. As a result, it is a game you can hear fourth-grade boys discussing, or McDonald's employees arguing over while they prepare your order. I have a few girlfriends who play, who are serious gamers like I am, but the population is predominantly male. I was introduced to the game in 2011 by my younger brother, but only became a more active player in 2012. Now comfortably sitting at a level 28 (of 30), I can safely say I have a good understanding of gameplay, strategy, code words, and etiquette when in the game.

Who plays who? Gender selection in the game

From the moment you are queued to play the game, you are immediately given the opportunity to select a champion. From the number of friends I have played the game with over the years, I can safely say that usually the gender of the champion has little impact on whether or not you choose to play them. Perhaps female gamers are more likely to choose a female champion, and males a male champion, but there is certainly plenty of crossover. Some gamers like to play a variety of champions to hone their skills. Personally, I learned the game playing a few key champions, and turn to them most often when playing the game; I will note: they are all construed as female champions.

Miss Fortune: A Gendered Discourse

My favourite champion selection is Miss Fortune, the pirate hunter. Armed with two musket pistols and a variety of long ranged attacks, she has quick movements and the ability to deal serious damage to an opponent. I have been guilty of signing out of champion selections when teammates would not let me play as her, I will admit. The game designers, however, have armed her with a few other details that trouble me as a gamer who also happens to be a woman: an avatar that is blatantly sexualized and 'desirable'; witty and suggestive one-liner gameplay sayings, and the passive skill of 'strut,' signified by a leather, high-heeled boot that allows her speedy movement, trailing hearts as she walks.

As the image in Figure 31.1 shows, here we have a champion dressed as a pirate, created thin at the waist, with round hips and large breasts barely contained by her top. The actual gameplay champion is a little harder to examine without a video of gameplay, but even standing still, she exudes 'womanly sexuality,' swaying her hips, holding both pistols in the air. We are also given the ability to access in-game dialogue and actions using keystrokes. /d in the text box, for example, will set my champion to dancing. While several champions have very silly dances, from the Macarena to one that closely resembles the chicken dance, Miss Fortune's dance again is highly suggestive and sexualized. Her in-game quotes, suggestive laughter, and flirtation methods all seem highly outrageous; her death moans could easily be mistaken for an x-rated video sound clip, a fellow gamer once suggested to me during a match. However, game designers have given her some credit, in my mind, by giving her several quotes that are directly related to famous sayings by the character, Han Solo, from Star Wars (*I always shoot first*), in a sense bringing balance to the at times questionable content of this champion.

The description of our champion is not enough in itself to demonstrate what is the problem with a virtual avatar being sexualized in a game. Reading her virtual body and what that says to male and female gamers alike shows why we should be troubled by champions and avatars like hers.

Figure 31.1: "Are you sure you can handle me, Summoner?"—Miss Fortune

In *Gender Trouble*, Butler (1990) asked, "Does being female constitute a 'natural fact' or a cultural performance, or is 'naturalness' constituted through discursively constrained performative acts that produce the body through and within the categories of sex?" (p. xxxi). What does it mean to perform gender? And can our bodies be the site of a performance projected by others? Do our skins become a stage for the enactment of a cultural performance? As previously mentioned, gender is simultaneously the body's variable modes of cultural articulation, as well as the site or surface upon which cultural forms are imposed or written. I would suggest that the performance of gender on the body of Miss Fortune is in fact a projection of cultural ideals of the female form, and site of performance of gender; but not as a performance in the way that I, the gamer, articulate my gender in the real world, or even within the gamers' culture; it is the game creators' and designers' projected beliefs of gender and the female form which are enacted on her body. Drawing from their cultural beliefs of what a female avatar should look like in a game, which is itself constructed from the male heteronormativity of the larger community of video games, Riot Games imposes their interpretation of what it means to be a female. Her body (as well as those of the majority of the female champions created for the game) then becomes the site of my struggle against this cultural stereotype that permeates the gaming world, and the objectification of other players. The performance of her gender, hypersexualized and created to please and entice, projects onto my understanding of the female form and desire. It also becomes the site of player aggression; issues regarding language centred around such things as sexuality and rape, something one would think far removed from a battle arena strategy game, are engaged with in a regular fashion. Recently, a teammate's champion malfunctioned during gameplay and attacked my champion, who happened to be Miss Fortune. The teammate, after expressing shock that this had happened, typed "HAH! I just tried to rape you. Man, who wouldn't try to rape that?" At that moment, though I am not Miss Fortune, and her body is not mine, the aggression and perceived violence made towards that body became a site of aggression towards me. Her digital body represents a history of gender in gaming, as well as the story of gamers, female and male, who must continually navigate a discourse that is negative and highly sexualizes the female form.

In my experience, in online gaming communities there exists a level of language which can alienate based on gender, race, and sexuality; and a better understanding of the cultural and gender stereotypes gamers are learning in these spaces is necessary. Gee (2007) suggested that the semiotic domains of videogames, when we learn to negotiate them in a more active manner, are spaces "usually shared by groups of people who carry them on as distinctive social practices," and "we gain the potential to join this social group, to become affiliated with such kinds of people (even though we may never see all of them, or any of them, face to face)" (p. 24). While I have highlighted one champion in particular, I will note that many of the champions are designed in a similarly disturbing manner. Champion Ahri, for example, a petite, racialized, Asian character who also changes into a fox, taunts, "Should I make your pulse rise? Or … STOP (giggles)." Janna, a blond, large-breasted sorceress whose main power is to harness the wind, jokes, "Yes, it's true. For only 2.95 a minute, I will leave you … breathless." Women who play *League of Legends* must learn to negotiate a body with which they do not identify, projecting cultural ideas and dialogue which is imposed on them by game designers who aim to play to a discourse that often completely excludes women.

Conclusion: Victory or Defeat?

In *League*, Miss Fortune's female form and my identity as a woman become bodies graffitied with conflict, violence against women, rape culture, and hypersexualization of women. However empowering having multiple female champions within a game setting can be for a gamer who is a woman, when they become stages for hetero-male fantasies, they also project the many issues with gender the gaming community continues to face. Here I must return to Butler's (1990) questions, "what constitutes the possibility of effective inversion, subversion, or displacement within the terms of constructed identity? What possibilities exist by virtue of the constructed character of sex and gender?" (p. 44), and suggest that performance of identity, the social construction of gender in the culture of *League of Legends*, is a displacement of any identity felt by the gamers themselves; it becomes solely a constructed ideal of others, with no opportunities for disruption, protest, or change by those whose online identity is enveloped, for a battle match, by the body of their champion.

References

Activision. (2003). *Call of duty*.

Alberti, J. (2008). The game of reading and writing: How video games reframe our understanding of literacy. *Computers and Composition, 25*(3), 258–269.

Atari, Inc. (2007). *The witcher*.

BGM Interactive/ASC Games. (1997). *Grand theft auto*.

Blizzard Entertainment. (2010). *World of warcraft: Cataclysm*.

Bury, R. (2005). *Cyberspaces of their own: Female fandoms online*. New York, NY: Peter Lang.

Butler, J. (1990). *Gender trouble: Feminism and the subversion of identity*. New York, NY: Routledge.

Butler, J. (1991). Contingent foundations: Feminism and the question of 'postmodernism.' *Praxis International, 11*(2), 150–165.

Butler, J. (1993). *Bodies that matter: On the discursive limits of sex*. New York, NY: Routledge.

Butler, J. (2004). Bodies and power revisited. In D. Taylor & K. Vintges (Eds.), *Feminism and the final Foucault* (pp. 183–194). Urbana, IL: University of Illinois Press.

Cavallaro, D. (2003). *French feminist theory: An introduction*. New York, NY: Continuum.

de Beauvoir, S. (1989). *The second sex*. New York, NY: Vintage Books.

Edios Interactive. (1996). *Tomb raider*.

Electronic Arts. (2000). *The Sims*.

Electronic Arts/Bioware. (2009). *Dragon age* (2011) *Dragon age origin*.

Foucault, M. (1978). *The history of sexuality: The will to knowledge.* London, UK: Penguin Books.

Foucault, M. (1980). *Power/knowledge: Selected interviews and other writings, 1972–1977* (C. Gordon, Ed.; C. Gordon, L. Marshall, J. Mepham, & K. Soper, Trans.). New York, NY: Pantheon Books.

Frasca, G. (2004). Videogames of the oppressed. In N. Wardrip-Fruin & P. Harrigan (Eds.), *First person: New media as story, performance, and game* (pp. 85–94). Cambridge, MA: MIT Press.

Gauntlett, D. (2008). *Media, gender and identity: An introduction* (2nd ed.). London, UK: Routledge.

Gee, J. P. (2007). *What video games have to teach us about learning and literacy* (Rev. ed.). New York, NY: Palgrave Macmillan.

Gee, J. P., & Hayes, E. (2009). *Women and gaming: The Sims and 21st century learning.* New York, NY: Palgrave Macmillan.

Hall, S. (1997). The work of representation. In S. Hall (Ed.), *Representation: Cultural representations and signifying practices* (pp. 1–74). London, UK: Sage.

Haraway, D. J. (1992). *Simians, cyborgs, and women: The reinvention of nature.* New York, NY: Routledge. Retrieved from http://www.amazon.com/Simians-Cyborgs-Women-Reinvention-Nature/dp/0415903874

Haraway, D. J. (1997). *Modest_Witness@Second_Millennium. FemaleMan©_Meets_OncoMouse: Feminism and technoscience.* New York, NY: Routledge.

Hasebe-Ludt, E., Chambers, C., & Leggo, C. (2009). *Life writing and literary metissage as an ethos for our times.* New York, NY: Peter Lang.

Jansz, J., & Martis, R. (2007). The Lara phenomenon: Powerful female characters in video games. *Sex Roles, 56*(3–4), 141–148.

Jenson, J., & de Castell, S. (2009). From simulation to imitation: New controllers, new forms of play. In *Breaking new ground: Innovation in games, play, practice and theory.* (Proceedings of DiGRA 2009, pp. 1–7). Retrieved from http://www.digra.org/wp-content/uploads/digital-library/09287.28053.pdf

Lather, P. (2001). *Getting smart: Feminist research and pedagogy with/in the postmodern.* New York, NY: Routledge.

League of Legends players summit a new peak. (2013). Riot Games. Retrieved from http://www.riotgames.com/articles/20130312/700/league-legends-players-summit-new-peak

LucasArts/Bioware. (2003). *Star wars: Knights of the old republic.*

Microsoft Game Studios. (2004). *Fable.*

Microsoft Studios. (1998). *Metal gear solid.*

Microsoft Studios. (2001). *Halo: Combat evolved.*

Palfrey, J., & Gasser, U. (2008). *Born digital: Understanding the first generation of digital natives.* New York, NY: Basic Books.

Penny, S. (2004). Representation, education and the ethics of simulation. In P. Harrigan & N. Wardrip-Fruin (Eds.), *First person: New media as story, performance and game* (pp. 73–84). Cambridge, MA: MIT Press.

Riot Games. (2009). *League of legends.*

Shaffer, D. W., Squire, K. R., Halverson, R., & Gee, J. P. (2005). Video games and the future of learning. *Phi Delta Kappan, 87*(2), 104–111. Retrieved from http://www.academia.edu/3219371/Video_Games_and_The_Future_of_Learning

CHAPTER 32

Machinima

Gamers Start Playing Director

Robert Jones

Despite early claims of being a short-lived fad, video games have proven they are here to stay. With revenues surpassing those of Hollywood box office receipts, the video game industry has emerged as a predominant fixture on our media landscape. As with previous new forms of media, the initial impulse has been to protect our children from the seemingly dangerous and addictive qualities of a medium we do not yet fully understand. Much of the rhetoric surrounding the dangers of video games (originating largely from the religious right and the various conservative watchdog groups) aims at categorically vilifying the medium as a threat to family values which celebrates violence and sex. The reality is that only 15 percent of games sold in the United States receive an M rating, which identifies a title as only suitable for ages 17 and older due to graphic violence or language.[1] While games like *Grand Theft Auto* and *Doom* embody the high profile games that get covered by the media as cases of how violent video games have become, they actually represent only a fraction of the gaming market. The vast majority of video games being produced and sold look a lot more like *Mario Kart* and *The Sims 2*. So when we talk about *video games*, it is important to clarify that we cannot talk about them as a single form.

Refusing to adopt the popularly held opinions of video games as violent and addictive, media literacy scholars like Buckingham et al. (2006) and Squire and Jenkins (2003) have made strong arguments for the educational qualities many games offer. From the development of organizational skills and cognitive abilities to teambuilding, video games do much more than threaten the moral fabric of our youths, despite what much of the popular media would have us believe. Therefore, developing a critical media literacy about this emerging form requires that we examine both the larger discourse about video games set forth by reactionaries as well as actually look at the different types of games available and how they are being used.

Machinima, one of the more recent developments within video game culture, demonstrates a classic example of how literacy in a certain medium can transform the relationship between consumers and their media. Put simply, *machinima* is an art form that uses the 3D graphics power of video games to create short animated films. By controlling the avatars on the screen, these *machinimators* act out scenes and add their voices to the characters or use subtitles to tell stories ranging from parody of the game worlds in which they are created to pointed political commentaries on current affairs.[2]

A video game's interactive nature distinguishes it from other traditional media and therefore invites a requisite amount of play on the behalf of the player. It is this level of control and freedom to play that makes video games so compelling. *Machinimators* merely take the agency granted to them by designers and go beyond it, transforming the medium from an interactive game to a filmmaking tool. Once they have created their films, they distribute them online either through Web sites they develop themselves or through the ones dedicated to the distribution of *machinima*. The volume of traffic varies from film to film and site to site, but at its highest point the numbers are quite surprising; the best known *machinima* series *Red vs. Blue* recorded nearly one million downloads a week at its peak (Thompson, 2005).

Though it began over a decade ago, *machinima* has only recently transitioned from a tiny subculture among hardcore gamers to a more widely known online phenomenon. In its earliest days *machinima* required a relatively high level of computer literacy for *machinimators* to get their game-play footage in a video format that could be edited and made into a movie. As game design technology advanced, designers saw that this sort of play by gamers served their interest. Upon realizing that these films served as promotional ads for the branded characters of the games, designers began developing games with built in tools for moviemaking. Will Wright's *The Sims 2* and Peter Molyneux's *The Movies* serve as prime examples of how the penchant for storytelling in gamers has changed the approach to game design. In the case of *The Sims 2*, a simulation game where players control the social interactions of their avatars, a record function was added to the game that allowed players to record their game-play as a video file.

Coupled with the control of the in-game camera, this record function provided the basic tools for making *machinima* available to a large market. *The Movies*, a simulation game where the player controls the success of a movie studio, took this one step further by making a core part of the game-play based on user created films that could then be exported as video files. Through the use of user-friendly controls, *The Movies* allows for the full control over creating short animated films.

In both cases, designers adapted the game design to cater to a growing need in players to use media as a means of creation and expression.

Video Games as Tools

In order to understand exactly what *machinima* is, it is important to know how video games work in general. Much of the literature on video game theory has made varying attempts at defining precisely what distinguishes video games from other media. The most obvious as well as most common correlation draws a connection to other audio/visual media like film. Because so many of the production elements in contemporary games derive from filmmaking techniques, it is easy to see that this could provide an entry point into understanding video games. However, video games fundamentally differentiate from film in that they are an interactive medium, requiring a constant exchange of information between the user and the game. So while video games appear to look mostly like films (and this is actually really only a portion of games because a lot of games like *Teris* look nothing like films), they actually function as another medium we do not often think of: software.

Despite the various debates as how to best categorize video games, at their primary level all video games function as software. Every video game consists of a certain amount of code that forms sets of rules known as *algorithms* that a player has to then navigate and try and overcome. For example, the basic algorithm of the arcade classic *Pac-Man* would be: consume all the small dots on a level without eating the ghosts, unless you first power up with one of the larger dots. Like most software, user input has some sort of impact on the processes taking place within the computer. Just as keystrokes create text on the screen within word-processing software, so too does the input of information through a joystick change the outcome on the screen in *Pac-Man*. For that reason, new media theorist Lev Manovich (2001) insists that we must always think of software as tools that allow the manipulation of data. In the case of video games, the software is creating either 2D or 3D graphics in real time, responding to the input of the player.

To create those graphics, all video games have what are called *engines* as a core part of their software. These engines are a series of processes that create the graphics as well as govern how the avatars and environment interact with each other, including the nature of the physics with which they interact. When Mario jumps onto one of the pipes in a level of *Super Mario Brothers*, the game's engine creates an avatar that can be moved toward a portion of the environment, making it bound through the air with a gravity that resembles cartoons. The purpose of creating engines is to minimize the amount of code that would be needed for every possible action within the game. In the case of *Mario*, the avatar could be changed to whatever the game designers want; it could be Luigi, Princess Peach, or some other character. The engine just knows that it is moving an avatar through the environment; the form that avatar takes does not matter. Similarly, the pipe is a rectangular object which could easily be replaced by a building or a mushroom. When gamers play a game, their input serves as the instructions to the engine to create the necessary graphics to allow them to play the game.

What makes game engines unique from other forms of software that can create 3D graphics like Maya and 3D Studio Max, is that they create the graphics in real time. In a common example of 3D animation like *Shrek*, which is created using high-end software, the detail in the lighting and the textures is what makes it look so impressive. It requires tremendous computer resources to create those graphics. Just to have Shrek walk down the hall of the castle requires that each frame (24 per second) be *rendered* before motion is even possible.[3] Video game engines do the same things as part of the rendering process in order to create their 3D animations; they simply do them with less detail which allows for them to do it in real-time. Looking at the difference between *Shrek* the movie and *Shrek* the video game, anyone can see that the graphics in the movie are far more detailed and photorealistic than those of the game. Because the images in the movie are *pre-rendered* (meaning hours or days were spent creating the files), they are more detailed. The engine, on the other hand, allows for a player to choose wherever she wants Shrek to go in the environment, and the avatar of Shrek immediately responds. Therefore, since the graphics within games are created in real-time by the game engines, the ability to manipulate those graphics demonstrates Manovich's point of software functioning as a tool. What on the surface may appear to be simply a game, purchased for $50, is actually very powerful software capable of creating vivid 3D graphics in real time. *Machinimators* have recognized this potential in games and have chosen to harness that power by using it to create their own 3D animated films. Traditionally creating 3D animated films requires a number of skills and expensive resources. *Machinima*, however, appropriates a technology already widely available to consumers and uses it in an act of creation that could be best described as virtual puppetry whereby the controlling of avatars on the screen forms the characters of the stories they choose to tell.

Consumer/Producers

According to a recent survey done by the Pew Center of Internet Life, 57% of teens who use the Internet were considered media creators, defined as using the Internet to distribute either original or remixed content.[4] Through the convergence of digital technologies a new landscape has emerged where media consumers are seeking opportunities to become media producers. Media literacy scholars have always noted the importance of an active relationship with media. Whether critically engaging the text by asking the important questions (Who is creating this text? For whom is this text created?) or appropriating the text to serve their needs, an active relationship with media empowers consumers in ways that passive consumption does not. As media technologies become more varied and ubiquitous the importance of critical media literacy becomes an imperative part of citizenship. Moreover, the growing dependency upon information as the most valuable global commodity demonstrates that media literacy is not simply about becoming more responsible consumers. Much in the same way that print literacy enabled and nourished the principles of a democratic society, a comprehensive literacy in media and information systems becomes a requisite part of navigating a world run not by nations but transnational media corporations. Being media literate does not simply mean that students have the ability to access, analyze and evaluate media in multiple forms. They must also possess the capacity to communicate in those forms as well. The convergence of digital technologies not only suggests that students must be adept at comprehending messages that come in multiple variations, but they must now have a capacity to use those same channels. The growth of the Internet is probably the single biggest contributor to the expansion of the channels of distribution available to consumers. From peer to peer networks to servers that house millions of forums, the Internet provides an incentive to produce some form of media because there is a means of distributing it. While the development of *machinima* is largely dependent upon the rising popularity of video games in general, without the online Web sites dedicated to distributing *machinima*, it would have likely remained the hobby of only hardcore gamers. Through these networks of distribution, *machinima* found a larger audience than just gamers. The *Red vs. Blue* series in particular has been shown at various film festivals in addition to its wide-spread popularity.

This new generation of students, with access to so many digital technologies, is driven by the need to create. Although the trend of consumers producing their own texts is hardly a new phenomenon (from students writing stories about their favorite shows to clipping pictures from magazines to make their own collages), the relative availability of digital technologies has expanded the variety of what can be created. Students can create their own online diaries in the form of a *blog*, they can make their own music by remixing their favorite songs, they can perform their own talk show and distribute it as a *podcast*, they can make their own films with inexpensive digital cameras and free editing software, and now they can make 3D animated films using the engines of the video games they already play and enjoy.

Gamers have always enacted a certain amount of agency as media consumers due to the interactive quality of video games. The ability to control an avatar in a virtual environment grants the type of control that traditional media simply do not provide. *Machinima's* origin can then easily be attested to the type of play and exploration that games foster. The earliest forms of *machinima* derived from those gamers who grew tired of just playing the game and started playing around with the software. By realizing that those early First Person Shooter games like *Doom* and *Quake* gave the user the ability to control 3D characters on the screen, those gamers made a dramatic shift from a player to a director.[5] They took control of what was actually a very powerful piece of software and used it to tell their stories. Now, more and more games are being designed with this very purpose in mind. Some game developers have even built it into the way that they market their games by creating filmmaking contests and creating Web sites dedicated to *machinima* distribution, acknowledging the fact that gamers prefer having total control over their media. As new media technologies become further integrated into the lives of students, marked by more interaction and user control, this need to create will only develop. In the case of *machinima*, students can become the directors of their own stories and create a text that looks rather professional. The fact that gamers discovered this use of a media technology speaks to our growing desire to be creators and not just consumers of media. For media literacy scholars it provides yet another example of how a certain amount of authorship and power can come from understanding how media work, rather than just consuming them. As for now *machinima* may be a small blip on the radar of mainstream culture, but as the inevitable growth in the popularity of video games flourishes, so too will this new form of consumer production.

Notes

1. For this and more statistics on video game software go to http://www.theesa.com/facts/top_10_facts.php.
2. For an example of parody see the *Red vs. Blue* series and for an example of political commentary see *The French Democracy*. Both are available for download at www.machinima.com.
3. Rendering is a complex process by which every piece of the three dimensional image must be put into its place, adding the proper texturing and lighting. This is very time consuming in that the computer is literally taking many tiny files and bringing them together into a single video clip that can be played.

4. See *Teen Content Creators and Consumers* at http://www.pewinternet.org/PPF/r/166/report_display.asp
5. The First Person Shooter genre, made famous as the "shoot'em ups" vilified in the media due to the violent content, is unique in that it was the first type of game that allowed the player to navigate through three-dimensional space. The importance to *machinima* is that players of these games quickly began to see that the first person perspective of their avatar provides the same view as a camera; therefore, they would move their character through the environment and act as the camera while the other players served as the actors of the movie.

References

Buckingham, D., Burn, Carr, & Schott, (2006). *Computer games: Text narrative and play.* Cambridge, UK: Polity Press.

Manovich, L. (2001). *Language of new media.* Cambridge, MA: MIT Press.

Squire, K., & Jenkins, H. (2003). Harnessing the power of video games in education. *Insight, 3.*

Thompson, C. (2005, August 7). The Xbox auteurs. *The New York Times,* 6.21.

Further Reading

Jones, R. (2006). From shooting monsters to shooting movies: Machinima and the transformative play of video game fan culture. In K. Hellekson & K. Busse (Eds.), *Fan fiction and fan communities in the age of the Internet* (pp. 261–280). Jefferson, NC: McFarland.

Marino, P. (2004). *3D game-based filmmaking: The art of machinima.* Scottsdale, AZ: Paraglyph.

Morris, D., Kelland, M., & Lloyd, D. (2005) *Machinima.* Course Technology PTR.

CHAPTER 33

Hip Hop Pedagogies in/for Transformation of Youth Identities

A Pilot Project

Angel Lin

You want to know why I don't pay attention in English lessons? You really want to know? Okay, here's the reason: NO INTEREST!! It's so boring and difficult and I can never master it. But the society wants you to learn English! If you're no good in English, you're no good in finding a job! (said by a 14-year-old school boy in Hong Kong to the author in an informal interview; original in Cantonese)

Why Hip Hop Pedagogies? Hong Kong: The Setting of the Story

Despite its international, cosmopolitan appearance, Hong Kong is ethnically rather homogeneous. Over 90% of its population is ethnic Chinese, and Cantonese is the mother tongue of the majority. English native speakers account for a small proportion of the entire population. They had constituted the privileged class of the society until July 1, 1997, when Hong Kong's sovereignty was returned to China and Hong Kong became a Special Administrative Region (SAR) of China. The English-conversant, bilingual Chinese middle class has, however, remained the socioeconomically dominant group in Hong Kong.

Notwithstanding its being the mother tongue of only a minority, English has been the language of educational and socioeconomic advancement; that is, the dominant symbolic resource in the symbolic market (Bourdieu, 1991) in Hong Kong. Even in the post-1997/colonial era, English has remained a socioeconomically dominant language in Hong Kong society. For instance, English remains the medium of instruction in most universities and professional-training programmes.

It can be seen that the symbolic market is embodied and enacted in the many key situations (e.g., educational and job settings) in which symbolic resources (e.g., certain types of linguistic skills, cultural knowledge, specialized knowledge and skills) are demanded of social actors if they want to gain access to valuable social, educational, and eventually, material resources (Bourdieu, 1991). For instance, a Hong Kong student must have adequate English resources to enter and succeed in the English-medium professional-training programmes, and in order to earn the qualifications to enter high-income professions. Hence, access to English in schooling acts as a crucial gatekeeper for socioeconomic mobility, and helps to reproduce class structures in Hong Kong. However, such access has been constrained by a number of factors, including government legislation in 1998 that reduced the number of English-medium public schools, as well as the varying quality of English instruction in both English-medium and Chinese-medium schools (Evans, 2008; Lin, 2000). Public secondary schools in Hong Kong are generally classified into three bands that are based on competitive entry requirements. Band 1 schools admit the approximately top 33% of primary school leavers, Band 2 schools admit the middle 33%, and Band 3 schools admit the lowest 33%. The banding label has been criticized, but it has been a well-established administrative fact of the Hong Kong schooling system. This chapter tells the story of a hip hop project piloted in a Band 3 school located in a working-class housing complex in a rural area Hong Kong. We focus on the ways in which hip hop in English provided working-class students with new spaces (or, in Bourdieu's terms, a new habitus) for developing their identities as English speakers. In the next section, a quick outline of Bourdieu's notions of cultural capital and related terms is presented. Then we continue with the story of our journey of piloting hip hop pedagogies in a working-class school in Hong Kong. Implications for further work in exploring hip hop pedagogies for youth empowerment and identity transformation are discussed.

Theoretical Notions for Understanding Youth Identities and Hip Hop Pedagogies: Cultural Capital, Habitus, Structure, and Agency

Cultural capital is a concept from Bourdieu (Bourdieu, 1973, 1977, 1984, 1991; Bourdieu & Passeron, 1977) referring to language use, skills, and orientations, dispositions, attitudes, and schemes of perception (also called *habitus*) that a child is endowed with by virtue of socialization in her or his family and community. Bourdieu's argument is that children of the socioeconomic elite are endowed by their familial socialization with both more and the right kind of cultural capital for school success (i.e., their habitus becomes their cultural capital in the social field of the school). A recurrent theme in Bourdieu's works is that children from disadvantaged groups, with a habitus incompatible with that presupposed in school, are not competing with equal starting points with children of the socioeconomic elite, and thus experience the reproduction of social stratification.

While Bourdieu has sometimes been accused of being a theorist of reproduction rather than transformation (e.g., Canagarajah, 1993; Jenkins, 1992), Luke (2009) remarked that Bourdieu's concept of habitus does allow for the possibility of transformation, and Bourdieu seemed to have managed to find a way between structural determinism and an over-emphasis on individual agency. Giddens's (1984) structuration theory also seems to provide a solution for overcoming the sociological macro-micro, structure-agency theoretical divide by seeing the macro and micro, social structures and agency, as mutually constitutive and shaping. Giddens (1984) saw social action and interaction as tacitly enacted social practices, and discussed how they become institutions or routines and reproduce familiar forms of social life:

The basic domain of study of the social sciences, according to the theory of structuration, is neither the experience of the individual actor, nor the existence of any form of social totality, but social practices ordered across space and time. Human social activities, like some self-reproducing items in nature, are recursive. That is to say, they are not brought into being by social actors, but are continually recreated by them via the very means whereby they express themselves *as* actors. In and through their activities, agents reproduce the conditions that make these activities possible (Giddens, 1984, p. 2).

With structuration theory, Giddens attempted to integrate human social action with the larger systems, structures, and institutions of which we are a part. It is the continual repetition of social action and interaction in more or less routines or repeated practices that constitutes what may appear to be the larger social forms or systems. Under structuration theory, structure is not outside of and imposed on social action, but is both constituted and/or structured by, and shaping and/or structuring, social action. This is in line with Bourdieu's notion of habitus, which is postulated as a 'structuring structure.'

Both Bourdieu's theory and Giddens's structuration theory thus seem to converge in helping to overcome the structuralist determinism that is sometimes attributed to studies which emphasize too much the reproduction tendency of social structures (e.g., Willis, 1980). Precisely because structures and social actions are seen as mutually constitutive and shaping or structuring, there is the possibility of transformation of social structures (such as habitus) through creative, situated social actions. However, this kind of creative agency is not to be over-celebrated, as it does not happen easily. In this chapter, we tell of the attempts of some education researchers to use an innovative hip hop programme to help change the habitus of some children in a secondary school situated in a working-class residential area in Hong Kong, and how the project met with both shares of success and difficulties.

In terms of identity formation, the project aimed to introduce Hong Kong students to a prestigious new English-speaker identity, *the young emcee*, by creating an alternative and extracurricular curriculum based on hip hop. This identity offered the students an opportunity to enhance their English abilities by identifying themselves as capable learners, and, more importantly, as artists who were using their voices to connect with others. We wanted to motivate students to work hard at learning the English rapping, timing, and rhyming skills necessary to become good emcees, rhymers, storytellers, and lyricists—all positive and trendy English-speaker identities for teenagers unavailable to them before (cf. Lin, 1999). In the following sections, we shall outline the setting, the programme, and our findings. In the concluding section, we discuss what we have learnt that might help us to achieve more success if we are to embark on a similar project in the future.

Piloting an English-Language Teaching (ELT) Rap Project

We invented the name, ELT Rap, to indicate to school principals and educational funding bodies that it is a kind of hip hop rap adapted or written for English-language teaching (ELT) purposes. Working with a team of English-language educators in the Faculty of Education at The Chinese University of Hong Kong from 2006 to 2008, we designed the project as an innovative way of drawing on youth popular cultural resources for English-language education.

The linguist, Geneva Smitherman, has highlighted eight features of signification (i.e., meaning-making) in rap lyrics:

1. Indirection, circumlocution

2. Metaphorical-imagistic

3. Humorous, ironic

4. Rhythmic fluence and sound

5. Teachy but not preachy

6. Directed at person or persons usually present in the situational context

7. Punning, play on words

8. Introduction of the semantically or logically unexpected
   (as cited in Perry, 2004, p. 62)

A glance at the list will show that when adapted, rap has great potential in English-language teaching. The rhythmic nature of rap lyrics facilitates the acquisition of the stress-timed rhythm of English. This has special significance in Hong Kong, where the majority of learners speak Cantonese, a syllable-timed language, as their mother tongue. The play on words that is often a part of rap has great appeal for students when they repeat raps for practice. The rhyming nature of rap lyrics can also heighten learners' phonetic skills and phonological awareness, and practice rapping has the potential to build confidence among these students as English-language users.

Why is ELT Rap potentially appealing to young people?

In English-language education, jazz chants (e.g., Graham, 2000) have been some of the activities advocated for improving learners' pronunciation, especially in terms of rhythm and intonation. ELT Rap differs from jazz chants in that it has a much richer musical dimension that appeals to young people: the rhythm is provided by hip hop music in the background. This popular, musical dimension should make ELT Rap especially appealing to teenage students, since it is infused into the global popular culture that they consume on a daily basis. Though many of the students in this project were relatively new to hip hop music, it became clear over the course of the project that the appeal of participating in a globally popular youth culture that could easily be localized to represent their experience in Hong Kong struck a chord with the learners.

In addition to the entertainment element, what can also attract teenage students to ELT Rap is its lyrical content: rap is a channel for (young) people to speak out, to unload their personal worries and frustrations, and to speak to and against scenarios of social injustice (Morrell & Duncan-Andrade, 2002; Rose, 1994). The use of rap as a vehicle for voicing one's frustrations or concerns about social problems has been well-documented in rap around the world (cf. Alim, 2006; Mitchell, 2001), but little has been explored with regard to the context of Hong Kong. Given that social class divisions in Hong Kong are often shaped by access to English through education, rap in English became an appealing prospect for connecting to working-class students in Hong Kong's secondary schools. Disassociated from the English of their classrooms, and the *ideoscapes* (Appadurai, 1990) that govern the centralized education system, we felt that ELT Rap had the potential to offer them new avenues for creative expression. We developed the project with the idea that many students would find in ELT Rap a space to reconcile their mixed feelings about English: on the one hand, they understand the importance of English to their future; on the other hand, they resent the sense of frustration brought by their perceived inability to master a foreign language that is deemed so necessary for socioeconomic mobility. ELT Rap provided them with the potential to reconstruct and transform their society-given identities of 'deficient' English speakers by using the language for creative expression that melded their interest in music with opportunities for language learning.

What is an emcee?—Building positive English-speaker identities among Hong Kong teenagers

The title of our ELT Rap lyrics booklet used in the project is, "The Young Emcee Scrolls". This title is modeled on the trendy title of the hip hop poetry collection of the famous American urban poet, Saul Williams (2006): *The Dead Emcee Scrolls: The Lost Teachings of Hip Hop*. In hip hop music culture, the emcee[1] embodies a prestigious identity. An emcee is not only a rapper, but also a talented artist and storyteller who specializes in using poetic language with rhythm and music to liven up the atmosphere of a party or a concert. A skilled emcee has to go through rigorous language and music training. A skilled hip hop emcee is also sometimes called a "rhymer", as they are good at spontaneously coming up with "cool" rhyming verses to go with the rhythm of the music on the spot (called "freestyling"). In hip hop music culture, it is important for emcees to frequently engage in animated "battles" (i.e., competitions) to test their spontaneous linguistic, poetic, and music talents, as good emcees are skillful in using poetic, verbal signifying (meaning-making) techniques which can be traced back to the oral cultural storytelling discourse practices of African Americans (Lee, 1993). To become a good hip hop emcee, one needs to work on expanding one's speaking vocabulary, remembering a vast number of rhyming words, and needs to read newspapers and books every day to increase one's knowledge about the world so as to be able to rap about a wide range of interesting, contemporary topics. Through introducing Hong Kong students to the concept of the young emcee in our ELT Rap teaching materials, we wanted to provide them with an identity that would resonate with them and which would lead them to invest in English-language learning.

Piloting ELT Rap as an extracurricular activity in a school in Hong Kong

With the support of the school principal and vice-principal, we piloted a project entitled, "ELT Rap Resident Artist Project", in one Band 3 school from September 2006 to June 2007. We started the project with the following set of research objectives:

1. To provide a context in which students would improve their English-language proficiency;

2. To enhance students' interest in and attitude towards learning English; and

3. To improve students' self-image and self-confidence through positive interactions with hip hop artists and an English tutor.

Programme implementation

To introduce the project to the students and to recruit participants, an "Artists' Demonstration Session" was organized in September. Though there were more students interested in hip hop dance, a joint decision between the school and the research team was made to keep the original class arrangements for promoting ELT Rap. Over the course of the project, 68 high-school students volunteered to join the programme. The students were divided into groups according to grade, and met on different days to focus on either ELT Rap or Hip Hop Dance. On Thursdays, Group A (comprised of 28 Secondary (S)4–S7 students) met after school to participate in the ELT Rap workshops. On Fridays, Group B met (23 students from S3–S6 participated in the ELT Rap workshops, eight of whom also participated in the dance workshops on Thursdays). Group C (25 S3–S6 students) met on Thursdays to learn hip hop dance styles.

The workshop team consisted of a team of local hip hop artists as instructors (MC Yan, MC Chef, MC ADV, MC Double T). A research team member, Ms. Margaret Ting, served as the English-language tutor, working closely with the local artists. Together they led a series of afterschool ELT Rap workshops during which they taught seven rap songs (see Table 33.1). Another local breakdance artist, Big Mouth, served as the instructor of dance workshops for students.

RAP Focus	ELT Focus	Description of Group Interaction
Workshop 1: Rapped "How are you?" and Group Names.	<u>Lecture</u>: Introduced letter-sound relationships, and the "Final E" Phonics Rule as in "How are you?"	Used "How are you?" to greet each other.
Workshop 2: Rapped "Bee-lee-blah-lah Boom Boom"; watched "Freestyle" DVD; introduced hip hop components (rapping, breaking, DJ-ing, Graffiti).	<u>Lecture</u>: Introduced "26 Letter Sounds" as in "BLBLBB". Worksheet with letter shape design was used.	Awarded letter shape design winners for motivation; distributed Halloween sweets to create a relaxing atmosphere.
Workshop 3: Students rehearsed previous raps and created their own lyrics.	<u>Group Work</u>: Reviewed the 26 letter sounds with groups of 3–4 students. Students read out some nonsense words to practice blending.	Arranged group practices of letter sounds.

Table 33.1. English-Language Learning During Rap ELT

RAP Focus	ELT Focus	Description of Group Interaction
Workshop 4: Rapped "B-A-Bay".	<u>Lecture</u>: Introduced the "Two Vowels Go Walking" Phonics Rule as in "B-A Bay".	Encouraged students to use their body as metronome to feel the beats.
Workshop 5: Students rehearsed previous raps and designed ELT Rap logo.	<u>Worksheet</u>: Finished long vowel worksheet while tutor conducted focus-group interviews.	Conducted focus-group interviews.
Workshop 6: Rapped "Rapper's Delight" and "Chinese Poems Can We Rap?"	Lyrics of "Rapper's Delight" and "Chinese Poems Can We Rap?"	Moved to the hall and joined the dance group to feel more about rhythm.
Workshop 7: Watched "Def Society" and "Make You Look" DVDs; rapped "I Have Promises To Keep".	Lyrics of "I Have Promises To Keep".	Brainstormed with students about the performance; provided snack to create a relaxing atmosphere.
Workshop 8: Reviewed all raps and confirmed programme rundown.	Reviewed programme.	Awarded ELT Rap button design winner for motivation.
Workshops 9–11: Rehearsals for finale.	Reviewed programme.	Distributed ELT Rap buttons and performance props to student performers.

Table 33.1. English-Language Learning During Rap ELT

As the project progressed, the students worked with the workshop team to develop a finale performance programme. The finale show was hosted in February in the school hall, and was attended by over 800 students, teachers, and parents. A final count of 38 students performed in the February finale show. Based on the focus-group interviews, the 56% participation rate could be attributed to conflicts in scheduling with other school activities and different expectations of the programmes. The performers enjoyed and took pride in their work, while the audience gave positive and encouraging feedback.

Research Methodology

We used a battery of research instruments for collecting data that would allow us to both assess students' linguistic competence in English and to understand the identities they were developing in response to the ELT Rap project. Pre- and post-workshop questionnaires were completed by the students in October 2006 and February 2007, respectively. We conducted mid- and post-workshop focus-group interviews with high-, medium-, and low-involvement students in November 2006 at the fifth rap and sixth dance workshops, and subsequently in March 2007 at the reunion gathering. Based on the data collected in the mid-workshop interviews, some programme implementation strategies were adjusted. For example, we integrated groups of students who were focusing on raps with those focusing on hip hop dance styles in order to create a more authentic experience. We also modified the original curriculum by adding Sugarhill Gang's "Rapper's Delight" to the workshop, with less language focus and more focus on music appreciation, in order to engage students in the project more fully.

Language-Learning Benefits of ELT Rap

For the many limited-English-proficiency participants at the school, rapping seemed to be easier to approach as a "speaking" rather than "listening" activity, as it requires "speaking" or "spitting the words" at a fast speed; hence, words are often not very clear and comprehension can be difficult. Students with higher English proficiency would take less time to rehearse and could rap at a much faster pace, whereas students with lower English proficiency would have a much slower pace in rapping. Some felt discouraged seeing others rapping so fast when they rapped together.

In spite of these difficulties, the rap songs created a fun, meaningful context for the use of English, and seemed to be appealing to the students. The artists' demonstrations had a strong modeling effect, both in learning ELT raps and in creating positive attitudes towards learning. It became clear throughout the project that the students bonded well with the artists and showed respect for their talents. It was also clear that the English tutor was only able to build credibility if she expressed knowledge about hip hop and rap. Since she lacked knowledge about these musical styles, students would only seek language support from the ELT tutor; however, they identified more closely with the artists as role models for their own language learning.

The participating students expressed positive views towards ELT Rap as a way of learning English. Some said that they learned useful phonics skills which they can transfer to their regular English learning (e.g., they can now sound out new English words). Most reported that they increased their self-confidence through performing their songs in the finale show. After the project ended, some students continued their friendships with the artists, regularly joining in the artists' local hip hop gigs in community centres. A few of them continue to write Chinese and bilingual raps on their own. Some students have also asked the English tutor to teach them more rhyming words so that they can have more words to write their rap lyrics.

Constructing Positive Identities as English Learners Through Lyrics

In this section, excerpts from the workshop participants' lyrics will be illustrated to see how emergent positive identities are being constructed. These are corroborated by excerpts from interview data to illustrate how the experience through the hip hop programme has helped some participants construct identities as better English learners.

Excerpts (1) through (3) are taken from lyrics produced by the students during their third workshop, which was the first time they had the opportunity to create their own raps. The lyrics demonstrate how the students are experimenting with rhyme, syllable structure, and beats per line. In addition, these three examples show some positive expressions of identity. In (1), the students voice their enthusiasm for hip hop and their extracurricular activities connected to this 'school' practice; (2) reveals how the students link writing hip hop lyrics to an act that requires them to "use your brain"; and (3) arguably presents an attitude of confidence with English through their chosen alias "C-A-N" and their ability to "scare" others with their raps (and with their English).

(1) Workshop 3: Ka-hei & Friends
We all like hip hop
Always go to the CD-shop
When I go back home
The door is tightly locked.

(2) Workshop 3: Tom, Key, & Kin
Pick up your pen and
Use your brain!

(3) Workshop 3: Carrie, Apple, & Nadia
My team name is C-A-N
Carrie, Apple and Nadia Tang
Double T is our friend
We are making a horrible plan
Hey! Are you scared?

In the finale show, a group of workshop participants had written a "Thank you Artists" song to express thanks to the artist instructors of the workshops. The song was written mainly in Cantonese and performed in the finale show by the students. Below are excerpts from the song lyrics, which illustrate their newfound confidence about their campus and school life. English translations of the lines are provided in the right column:

(4) "Thank You Artists!"
電腦設備又係度   There are computer facilities here
不斷更新   Always upgrading
…   …
呢個地方唔可以缺少嘅一份子   They (referring to students) are all
                                         indispensable here
努力認同求學習就個個都   All are working hard studying diligently
…   …
唔再俾人砌低   No longer beaten by others
唔再做一頭縮頭烏龜   No longer chicken out like a shy tortoise
…
Thank you Artists!

The expression of confidence and self-worth in these lyrics is very significant, given the habitus of these working-class students. Traditionally, in Hong Kong, students from low-banding schools, which are frequently in low-income housing areas, are stigmatized in society and labeled as 'losers' in general. In this song, the students are expressing a message of self-assertion—both asserting the good facilities of the school (the ever-upgrading computer equipment) and the new self-image of students: everyone is hardworking and hence becoming indispensable; they are no longer feeling like losers beaten by others nor chickening out like a shy tortoise who has to hide its head in its shell. They are using metaphors to express a new powerful identity that they are constructing both for their own school and the students in this school. It is significant that they are not referring to themselves directly, but addressing this message to everyone in the school, as they are performing this song to all students and teachers in the finale show in the school hall. Coming from the students' own creative self-expression, this message is significant.

It might be said that the hip hop music and the rap genre and the self-reliant, self-assertive attitude as embodied by hip hop culture and the artists themselves seem to have inspired these students to feel a renewed confidence about their own school and the students in this school. This newly found confidence is echoed by some other participants in the interview data, which were done right after the finale show by a research team member. The interviews were done in Cantonese, and below are English translations of excerpts of the interview data.

Many excerpts illustrate how the students recognized their own learning, and that they felt their English had improved over the course of the project. Though some of them had not previously been familiar with hip hop, their comments show that they found this medium for learning to be highly motivating and beneficial to their command over English.

(5)
Interviewer: What do you think of ELT Rap?
S6 student: It was fun!
Interviewer: Fun …
S6 student: I've learnt English …
Interviewer: Learnt English …
S6 student: And got to know hip hop culture.

(6)
S4 Student: At first I'd no idea about hip hop and rap. But after attending these sessions, I learnt that hip hop and rap are so broad! As we usually rap in English, so I also have learnt more English.

(7)
S4 Student: I think I'm much better now (勁咗). When we first tried to rap "How are you?" I couldn't even rap one sentence! But now I can even rap the more difficult ones.

Excerpt (8) also acknowledges the linguistic benefits of the programme, but perhaps more importantly, documents the sense of an empowering habitus that came into being as a result of the project. As an 'alternative' curriculum carried out in the form of an extracurricular programme, ELT Rap provided the students with a new space for identification. In contrast to their 'deficient' identities in their mainstream classrooms, ELT Rap gave them the chance to identify positively as members of an English-speaking community who enjoyed each other's company and formed close social bonds.

(8) (A Group of S5 students becoming good friends)
Girl 1:   We've learnt so much!
Girl 2:   The most important thing is Margaret teaching us English.
Girl 3:   We've learnt more about phonics.
Girl 4:   It was fun! Really fun!
Girl 2:   Yeah! It was fun! And we also got to make new friends! I didn't know them before. And now we've known each other and could even hug each other!
Girl 3:   And even to share the same piece of cake! (girls laughing)

Excerpt (9) shows how the students gained confidence by performing in front of their peers, which also enhanced their sense of agency over their learning, since they witnessed the practical benefits of "involving themselves" in what they were learning.

(9) (A group of students who performed hip hop dance in the finale show; the students are from different grade levels, from S4–S6):
Dancer 1:   At first I wanted to stop dancing because I didn't want to perform on stage. But actually it's not that frightening on stage. It was fun!
Dancer 2:   It's us who are benefitting … it's like learning a new skill and you feel good if you can perform.
Dancer 3:   I think if you involve yourself in dancing, you'll enjoy it. And have fun with these good tutors.
Dancer 4:   At first when I started practicing it was a mess. But it's ok at the end. Even today's performance wasn't a perfect one, but it's not like [as bad as] the rehearsal.

The artists were also interviewed (together with some of their workshop students who hung around them) right after the finale show. Below are English translations of excerpts from the interview data. Many of the excerpts show that the workshop team observed changes in the students' willingness to express themselves across time, an important factor in both rapping and speaking English. In (10), MC Chef points out how the students seem to have developed a new sense of self through the project as they cultivated a hip hop persona.

(10)
MC Chef: I've noticed the students … because of hip hop, they would actually pick up a pen and start writing their own raps. And they've changed so much! Maybe this thing [rap]. … Because hip hop has changed my whole life, so I want more people can get to know it. In the first lesson, they knew nothing, and now, after the tenth lesson, they had a show, and create raps at home; I noticed that they've put hard work into it. They are not playing but serious about it. They can express their feelings and opinions through raps. It's good … it's a means to let others get to know them. Sometimes teachers don't understand their students' feelings. But through this chance now … the teachers can notice that the students have turned into someone else on the stage, becoming more confident … Although the time given was limited, the students showed great dedication and effort. Their performance … you can see the result! I really think they are superb!

This new, more confident self showed up in classrooms as well, as reported by the students. Importantly, the students felt they improved not only in their English literacies, but also their abilities in Chinese. One of the Secondary 5 student mentees reported that he received praise from his English teacher, which afforded him the important opportunity to identify as a "good" English speaker in the context of school, as well as in the extracurricular ELT Rap programme.

(11)
S5 mentee: After learning raps from MC Chef, my Chinese composition improves. And now during the English lessons, when there are words that are a bit challenging, because of the phonic skills learnt in the programme, I know how to decode the words. And get more praises from teachers! My English teacher ... I used to be unable to decode the words and pronounce them correctly, but because of the method (referring to phonics) I learnt, I know how to pronounce the words and my teacher praises me for this improvement.

The students frequently reported that they worked very hard once they committed to the project, a behaviour often not attributed to working-class schoolchildren from low-banding schools. It appeared that the ELT Rap project provided the students with the chance to identify as very capable learners, an identity that is not commonly attributed to working-class children (Lin, 1999; Willis, 1980). By receiving steady encouragement from the artists, whom they admired, they invested in their learning, despite it being "hard work."

(12)
S4 student: Extremely hard work! When they (referring to the artist instructors) comment, "Your rap isn't good enough, go home and practice many times", and I went home and practiced a hundred times! I almost died because of it! (laughing as she spoke this)

(13)
S4 student: At first my friends wanted to join it, so I joined it. But after really joining it, I'm the only one who has stayed on, not wanting to quit. I have become the one who doesn't want to quit most.

(14)
S6 student: When the programme first started, we were with the lower form students. I didn't know them and I feel strange and bored about it. But after the show, because all of us have put in many efforts and worked together, the bonding became strong, and it was fun!

This hard work was also noted by the workshop team artists, who were impressed with the students' capacity to learn new things in a relatively short period of time. Their comments characterize the students as 'quick learners', 'hard workers', and 'highly capable' English speakers and rappers.

(15)
Big Mouth: At first the students were not attentive and they only came to play. But when time progressed ... Some of them got more serious and could keep on [practicing]. I could notice the result of practice between the workshops. Not just breaking for a while during the workshops, but practicing outside of the workshops. I could notice their improvement in the following session.

(16)
KDG: I've watched them rehearse, and I noticed their hard work. What a big difference between the first rehearsal and the show! They've shown high collaboration. I just hope more schools can accept this kind of teaching programme, letting more people understand hip hop.

(17)
MC Yan: It involved many students this time. ... The more people the harder to control. But as they worked together as a team, working very hard. ... It shows that students in

Hong Kong have great learning capacity, apart from memorizing textbooks or rote learning! Actually, their skills can improve in a short period of time … they can absorb and learn much faster and better than we can imagine. They have benefitted a lot from it in the end.

One of the artists who worked on the project, MC Double T, linked the students' progress with their confidence in "speaking up" in English, an important factor in identifying as English speakers who have the "power to impose reception" (Bourdieu, 1977a, p. 648) despite exhibiting working-class language features.

(18)
MC Double T: It's very important not to be afraid of speaking English. After the workshops, I noticed they are more willing to speak up. They realize that isn't difficult. They might be shy. Their pronunciation might be incorrect. But now through raps and music, they can rap with ease or speak English with ease.

The school's teachers and administrators were also interviewed after the finale show, and their comments revealed similar observations regarding the students' growing confidence and their willingness to express themselves in English. Below are English translations of excerpts from the interview data:

(19) School Vice-Principal
Mr. Poon: I'm so proud of my students. They gave their best performance. Although the abilities of our students are not that high, they might not be very good in language or other aspects, but you can notice their confidence on stage and I'll give me 100 marks for their performance. What makes me the happiest is their self-confidence!

Though Mr. Poon draws attention to what the student lacks academically, which potentially constructs an identity for them as 'deficient', he remains proud of what they have achieved, noting growth in their confidence. More praise comes from the teachers, who noted the quality of the students' performances and the importance of performing successful academic identities in front of their school population.

(20) School Teacher
Mr Hon: It's like working very hard all the times and getting paid off now. The students performed very well, and I expect a good show but I didn't expect that excellent! Very coherent, and very confident! I'm so happy about the show.

(21) School Teacher
Miss Jie: During the whole event, the students were so engaged, much more engaged than their usual behaviour. To them, English poems are quite difficult, but they tried very hard to master the lyrics and rap with rhythm. It's so encouraging for the students. And it gave them a sense of achievement. They can show themselves to others.

Importantly, the principal acknowledged the benefits of ELT Rap as a productive space for the students to perform their linguistic skills and to be treated as successful learners.

(22) School Principal
Mr. Yan: I believe teenagers need channels to express themselves, and we need to give them room for building self-confidence. So raps, hip hop, performing on stage, are really good opportunities. We really hope that our teaching professions can support this kind of teaching approach, letting more students benefit from it.

Conclusion: Coda—Transforming Youth Identities Through the Hip Hop Experience

Upon the completion of this pilot project, 10 students of the school were invited to perform their ELT Rap songs at the English Festival 2007 kick-off ceremony. They performed rapping three English songs and one Chinese song. This was a glorious moment for the school and the students, and has boosted the overall morale of the school. The school had originally been selected by the Hong Kong Education Bureau for consideration of closing down due to decreasing new student enrollments. However, this event enhanced the school's public image and has partially contributed to the cancelation of the government's plan of closing down the school.

Overall, the direction of using hip hop pedagogies to engage students in using English to express their own voice, and to enhance their phonological awareness and rhyming and creative verbal skills is promising. Further research is needed to refine the pedagogy for different learning styles and interest levels of students and different school contexts. Based on the data, however, we have come to realize both the potential and challenges of capitalizing on students' desire for and investment in pop cultural artistic identities in transforming their habitus, in particular, their attitude towards and relationship with English. The central difficulty experienced in this pilot project seems to be that the local hip hop artists participating in this project themselves have limited English capital. Our research team has sought to compensate for this with the provision of an English tutor who has worked closely and collaboratively with the artists. However, when it comes to identification with their role models, students tend to identify much more readily with the "cool" local artists than with the English tutor.

This difficulty notwithstanding, three of the Form 7 (Grade 13) female workshop participants were highly motivated to learn rapping, and started to write their own lyrics for the artists to comment on. They have stayed in contact with the artists even long after the end of the programme, and have joined in the artists' music gigs in community centres. Two Form 4 (Grade 10) boys, notwithstanding their limited English proficiency, were eager to rap for fun in their daily conversations with their friends (although mainly Cantonese is used), and expressed an interest in joining an ELT Rap Society at school if such a society is formed. Some students also tried to freestyle on their own (i.e., to come up with rap lyrics on the spot, without pre-drafting them), for instance, by rapping and adapting paragraphs from their geography textbook.

It thus seems that some of the students are acquiring a new identity of a creative language user through developing a hip hop rapper identity—in Cantonese, English, or bilingual rapping. The transformation and development of such new self-identities and self-understandings seem to be a result of their informal interactions with the artists and the modeling of such new, trans-local, hip hop identities by the artists. We argue that when these working-class students are doing hip hop, they are also acquiring new, empowered, youth rapper selves that hip hop culture seems to be offering to them. When learning and honing their creative verbal skills in writing and performing Chinese, bilingual, and English raps, they also seem to be transforming their social class habitus, and are acquiring new cultural capital (e.g., rhyming and rapping skills, knowledge of letter-sound relationships, new attitudes and dispositions towards English).

However, the actual translation of these ideas into feasible, workable, youth-empowering hip hop pedagogies in the schools still needs further research, exploration, and trial and error. These challenges notwithstanding, the observations and lessons that we have learnt from this pilot project have led us to believe that if given the right role models and scaffolding (e.g., hip hop artists with bilingual cultural capital who can share with students both rapping and creative bilingual verbal skills), students coming from working-class backgrounds can be helped to break through the learned helplessness acquired through years of negative experience with language learning in the local schooling system that tends to favour students already endowed with the kind of family habitus for school success (Lin, 1999, 2005).

Through transforming their own identities and acquiring empowered identities such as those of creative rapper-artists, working-class students can engage enthusiastically in language learning, including learning English, which is, otherwise, not a daily language for them. We, therefore, need to continue to research and explore the possibilities that trans-local hip hop cultures and pedagogies can offer to young students—especially those coming from social classes without the habitus and cultural capital required by mainstream schools for literacy success—so that they can exercise their agency to change their habitus and acquire new cultural capital and new identities for empowerment.

Note

1.   Emcee is a word derived from the acronym, MC (Master of Ceremony, or Microphone Controller).

References

Alim, H. S. (2006). *Roc the mic right: The language of hip hop culture.* New York, NY: Routledge.

Appadurai, A. (1990). *Disjuncture and difference in the global cultural economy.* Middlesbrough, UK: Theory, Culture and Society.

Bourdieu, P. (1973). Cultural reproduction and social reproduction. In R. Brown (Ed.), *Knowledge, education and cultural change* (pp. 56–68). London, UK: Tavistock.

Bourdieu, P. (1977a). The economics of linguistic exchanges. *Social Science Information, 16*(6), 645–668.

Bourdieu, P. (1977b). *Outline of a theory of practice* (R. Nice, Trans.). Cambridge, UK: Cambridge University Press.

Bourdieu, P. (1984). *Distinction: A social critique of the judgement of taste.* London, UK: Routledge and Kegan Paul.

Bourdieu, P. (1991). *Language and symbolic power.* Cambridge, MA: Harvard University Press.

Bourdieu, P., & Passeron, J-C. (1977). *Reproduction in education, society and culture.* London, UK: Sage.

Canagarajah, A. S. (1993). Critical ethnography of a Sri Lankan classroom: Ambiguities in student opposition to reproduction through ESOL. *TESOL Quarterly, 27*(4), 601–626.

Evans, S. (2008). Classroom language use in Hong Kong's reformed English-medium stream. *Journal of Multilingual and Multicultural Development, 29*(6), 483–498.

Giddens, A. (1984). *The constitution of society: Outline of the theory of structuration.* Cambridge, UK: Polity Press.

Graham, C. (2000). *Jazz chants old and new.* New York, NY: Oxford University Press.

Jenkins, R. (1992). *Pierre Bourdieu.* London, UK: Routledge.

Lee, C. D. (1993). *Signifying as a scaffold for literary interpretation: The pedagogical implications of an African American discourse genre.* Urbana, IL: National Council of Teachers of English.

Lin, A. M. Y. (1999). Doing-English-lessons in the reproduction or transformation of social worlds? *TESOL Quarterly, 33*(3), 393–412.

Lin, A. M. Y. (2000). Lively children trapped in an island of disadvantage: Verbal play of Cantonese working-class schoolboys in Hong Kong. *International Journal of the Sociology of Language, 143*(1), 63–83.

Lin, A. M. Y. (2005). Doing verbal play: Creative work of Cantonese working class schoolboys in Hong Kong. In A. Abbas & J. Erni (Eds.), *Internationalizing cultural studies: An anthology* (pp. 317–329). Oxford, UK: Blackwell.

Luke, A. (2009). Race and language as capital in school: A sociological template for language education reform. In R. Kubota & A. Lin (Eds.), *Race, culture, and identities in second language education: Exploring critically engaged practice* (pp. 286–308). New York, NY: Routledge.

Mitchell, T. (Ed.). (2001). *Global noise: Rap and hip hop outside the USA.* Middletown, CT: Wesleyan University Press.

Morrell, E., & Duncan-Andrade, J. (2002). Promoting academic literacy with urban youth through engaging hip hop. *English Journal, 91*(6), 88–92.

Perry, I. (2004). *Prophets of the hood: Politics and poetics in hip hop.* Durham, NC: Duke University Press.

Rose, T. (1994). *Black noise: Rap music and Black culture in contemporary America.* Hanover, NH: University Press of New England.

Williams, S. (2006). *The dead emcee scrolls: The lost teachings of hip hop.* New York, NY: Pocket Books.

Willis, P. (1980). *Learning to labour: How working class kids get working class jobs.* Aldershot, Hants: Gower.

CHAPTER 34

Punk Rock, Hip Hop, and the Politics of Human Resistance

Reconstituting the Social Studies Through Critical Media Literacy

Curry Malott and Brad Porfilio

Nearly one hundred years ago, the social studies discipline was formally introduced in North America as a possible school subject. Business leaders and corporate leaders saw social studies as an avenue for indoctrinating the millions of immigrants, who were entering North America from predominantly European countries, with values conducive to becoming a *productive* worker as well as beliefs that promoted American and Canadian patriotism and colonialism (Russell, 2002). Progressive educators, on the other hand, had a quite different vision of the discipline. They viewed it as a way of fostering within students the ability to critically reflect on their world and take action for social justice. Unfortunately, business and governmental leaders used their privileged position to ensure their vision for this discipline came out victorious; consequently, it became the official model for the social studies curriculum across the educational landscape. We have been left with the legacy that has, while serving the interests of capital, which include fostering the development of an uninformed spectator-oriented citizenry, failed to meet the intellectual needs of the majority of its populace.

Despite the ongoing struggle and subsequent attempts over the past several decades made by progressive educators/activists to revamp the social studies curriculum for creating a more socially just education and wider social structure, the discipline, officially, has not strayed from its state-building, pro-capitalist function. For instance, in classrooms across North America, youths rarely learn about "the contributions, perspectives, or talents of women or those outside the mainstream culture" (Nieto, 2002, p. 9). Consequently, the social studies curricula, textbooks, and standardized examinations still reflect the values and beliefs of North America's economic and political leaders. In-service teachers in contemporary classrooms frequently alienate and thus fail to engage youths by centering their curriculum on historical narratives that valorize the lives of dead white men as well as the conquests and expeditions of western society.

Likewise, the test-driven environment within public schools and teacher education programs has limited teachers' sense of empowerment and thus willingness to engage in critical multicultural social studies

(Malott & Pruyn, 2006). Unable or willing to take the risks needed to spark student interests, teacher educators, and classroom teachers often turn to the "banking model" of education. The pedagogy is inextricably linked to promoting a passive type of citizenship, where the great majority of students become apathetic toward social, political, and economic issues, but become complicit in internalizing dominant beliefs, values, worldviews, and social practices (Case & Clark, 1997, p. 20).

It would not be a stretch to say the social studies curriculum "seems meaningless to almost every student, regardless of race, class or gender" (Kornfeld & Goodman, 1998, p. 306). Contemporary youths have been positioned to lack what Paulo Freire (2005) refers to as "a passion to know"; therefore, they are without the drive to develop the self-discipline needed to learn to not only read the word, but the world as well, a process designed to lead to critical consciousness and ultimately a sense of empowerment needed to transform our dull reality, that is, the material world. For Freire (2005) and others (see Freire & Macedo, 1987; McLaren, 1995) this is what it means to be fully literate and thus equipped with the intellectual tools to participate in the production and reproduction of our world. In short, this is critical literacy. This chapter is a foray into critical media literacy. For us, critical media literacy (Kellner & Share, 2005) is a pedagogical tool that provides us with the theoretical ballast needed to uncover the liberatory potential of countercultural formations and puts forth possible ideas of intervention for teachers, pre-service teachers, professors (including ourselves), and other community and cultural workers interested in reinforcing the more transgressive moments in our cultural manifestations—punk rock and hip hop serving as primary examples in this chapter.

To revitalize the social studies for the purpose of ensuring it has the potency to be a viable part of the move toward creating a more democratic social order—a society predicated on the principles of equity, social justice, freedom, and diversity—we believe critical theory must be central in this mission. Within critical theory, we can still find examples of unwavering resistance that are withstanding the corporate takeover of higher education. It is within these examples of vibrant militancy that we theoretically depart. These traditions continue to help educators "link learning to social change and education to the imperatives of a critical and global democracy" by focusing our critical lens on cultural artifacts such as music (Giroux, 2005). Current transformative educators also provide us with the theoretical tools necessary for both knowledge construction and action, assisting our awareness of how educational policies and practices are linked to the social production of labor, the lifeblood of capital, and how we can teach against these draconian formations through a revitalized critical/revolutionary pedagogy (McLaren & Jaramillo, 2005; Allman, McLaren, & Rikowski, 2005). In other words, critical theory provides us with the theoretical tools to not only analyze countercultural formations for their transformative potential against the process of value production, but also challenges us to unearth the unjust practices and social formations that foster economic and social injustices across the globe. In the following analysis, we take a critical approach guiding our analysis and pedagogical project. It is our intent in the pages that follow to provide a theoretically rich project for a critical multicultural social studies (Malott & Pruyn, 2006).

Specifically, we will document how two alternative subcultures—punk rock and hip hop—at their most radical moments, have the potency to provide in-service and pre-service teachers with a critical reading of the word and the world and opportunity to be a part of changing the relationships that define our lives through conscious intervention, to paraphrase Paulo Freire (1998, 2005). By examining these youth subcultures within the context of teacher education programs, we argue schoolteachers will begin to take inventory of the economic, social, and historical forces creating social inequalities within schools and the wider social world, recognize the urgency to develop critical forms of pedagogies for the purpose of ensuring that today's youths are equipped to make sense of the constitutive forces causing injustice and oppression in their own social worlds, take action as empowered agents of change, and understand the importance of linking their pedagogical projects with their students and other global citizens to excavate various forms of injustice in our increasingly morally bankrupt society.

What follows is, therefore, first an overview of punk rock and hip hop lyrics that provide a critical analysis of the contemporary social historical world. What is more, we pay particular attention to how the politics of these artists transcends the forum of music. Next, we discuss pedagogical implications for how this body of work and movement can be used by teacher educators, in-service teachers, administrators, and other cultural workers for the purpose of revitalizing the social studies, empowering youths, and transforming the world.

Subcultures in Context

Both punk rock and hip hop emerged during the 1970s and 1980s in the United States as a response to the increasing success of the economic elites' ability to wage warfare on working people through economic policies and a highly skilled propaganda machine (Chomsky, 2005; Giroux, 1994; McLaren & McLaren, 2004; Malott & Peña, 2004; Porfilio & Malott, 2007) (see Malott & Peña, 2004, for a discussion on the British punk rock movement). That is, policies that have ultimately led to deindustrialization, the increasing globalization of capital through policies such as the North American Free Trade Agreement (NAFTA), the militarization and privatization of everyday life, and a mean-spirited discourse blaming young people for their own dispossessed conditions, which resulted in a material reality that left many youths alienated from the dominant society, and therefore searching for meaning in a seemingly meaningless world. Armed with a largely intuitive response to the downsizing of their futures, many youths took to their creative impulses. They forged what is now known as punk rock and hip hop.

Both hip hop and punk rock first drew breath in New York City's European American and Afro-American, Latin, and Afro-Caribbean working-class communities, while punk rock was simultaneously born out of the rubble of Los Angeles' "white" and Latina/o barrios (Dancis, 1978; Cohen, 1980; Dimitriadis, 1996; Malott & Peña, 2004). Existing on the fringes of cultural life, both subcultures, at their more critical moments, gained strength and credibility through a creative process of building something out of nothing.

For punk rockers, this pedagogical approach has come to be known as DIY, or Do It Yourself, that is, creating something new within the remains of the old, such as small fanzines, record labels, bands, styles, modes of analysis, and ultimately a movement and way of life. DIY has, therefore, served as a rallying cry for those punk rockers who take pride in surviving against an economic social structure that does not serve their own interests, a system that grows more powerful the more surplus value or unpaid labor hours it is able to extract from the majority of the world's working people.

Similarly, the more progressive elements of hip hop draw on an identity of independence often manifesting itself as a "fight the power" sentiment, which is imbued with Afro-centric pedagogy, as expressed by New York City's Public Enemy (PE). For example, in "Fight the Power" on the *Fear of a Black Planet* (1990) record Chuck D of PE exclaims:

… I'm Black and I'm proud …
Most of my heroes don't appear on stamps
Nothing but rednecks for 400 years if you check …
Power to the people no delay …

Contemporary radical hip hop groups such as Dead Prez and Immortal Technique have built on pro-black counterhegemonic messages from PE and other groups such as the Poor Righteous Teachers and X Clan. Their music has added a more sophisticated class analysis to the hip hop scene. Brooklyn's Dead Prez (DP), emerging as one of the leading voices in hip hop's cultural and material revolution, identifying themselves as "revolutionary but gangsta, RBG," has upped the radical ante. For instance, the group's song "it's bigger than hip hop" refers to the social revolution they argue is needed at this particular social juncture, an epoch marred by growing global poverty, hunger, a resurgence in white supremacy, among many other indicators of an out-of-control transnational capitalist elite. In the following lyric, like Public Enemy, DP assumes an Afro-centric stance while advocating for a humane social and economic system:

Organize the wealth into a socialist economy
Cause the world is controlled by the white
male
Dead Prez (2000). "Police State." *Let's Get Free.*

DP often refers to the Black Panther Party as a source of pedagogical inspiration. Their music is informed by community activism, Black pride and power, and a desire to create a society predicated on symmetrical power relationships (discussed below). They postulate their music is a cross between PE and NWA, and if they had come of age during the 1970s, they would have been Panthers. Coming from Oakland, California, where Huey P. Newton and Bobby Seale started the Black Panther Party for Self-Defense, The Coup stands as an exemplary example of today's African American revolutionary West Coast U.S. hip hop. Although offering anti-racist sentiments through their songs, The Coup offers a more class-based perspective on what causes systemic oppression. They have also successfully melded their social commentary with political satire in songs such as *Wear Clean Draws* and *5 Million Ways to Kill a CEO* that, respectively, address the issue of African American female body image and how to create the conditions whereby oppressors, motivated by greed, are lured into self-destructing. In the introduction to their album *Party Music* (2001), The Coup chants "every broke motherfucker gonna form a gang, and when we come we're takin everything." In this song The Coup presents a non-racially specific message to working and poor people in general. In another track, "Ghetto Manifesto," The Coup offers a serious yet slightly humorous rallying call against the state and capital. Consider their words:

This is my resume slash resignation
A ransom not with proposed legislation
A fevered ultimatum you should take it verbatim ...

The class analysis and anti-racism offered by The Coup and other hip hop artists highlighted above have also been prevalent in the lyrics of many punk rock bands from early groups such as the Dead Kennedys and Bad Religion to more contemporary artists like Anti-Flag, Leftover Crack, and the Fartz. Rising out of San Francisco's underground punk and hardcore scene in the late 1970s and early 1980s the Dead Kennedys (DK) emerged as a leading satire-infused unity punk band with overtly leftist political messages. For example, in their first release, "Nazi Punks Fuck Off" (1979/1980) Jello Biafra, DK lead vocalist, takes a stance against white supremacist infiltrations into the punk scene, exclaiming:

You still think swastikas look cool
The real nazis run your schools
They're coaches, businessmen and cops ...

Rather than taking aim at hegemonic/counter-revolutionary elements within the scene, Anti-Flag, more recently, offers a devastating blow to the corporate-dominated military complex, which, they allude, usurps both the labor power and physical bodies of working people as cannon fodder. These are key forces in promulgating U.S. imperialism across the globe. Consider their words:

Isn't everybody tired of the
killing? Isn't everybody tired of
the dying? Isn't everybody tired
of the hatred?
Anti-Flag, 2002, "911 for Peace," *Mobilize.*

In another song Anti-Flag extends their plea for peace with a solid analysis of the deleterious effects of the alienating nature of selling one's ability to labor for a wage, thereby contributing to the creation of a world that benefits the few at the expense of the many.

> *To join the corporate army*
> *For god and country give up your life,*
> *Don't try to figure out what's wrong or*
> *right*
> Anti-Flag, 2002, "Their System Doesn't Work for You," *Mobilize.*

Coming from a similar theoretical/political perspective as Anti-Flag and the Dead Kennedys, although employing a more reggae-dub/punk/hardcore sound, New York City's Leftover Crack in "Super Tuesday" connects the North American legacy of colonization and slavery with current economic policies of the World Bank and the International Monetary Fund:

> *It ain't a mystery, that US History*
> *Was built upon the graves*
> *Of Native ways and beaten slaves …*

Beyond the Lyrics

Beyond the messages transmitted through their songs, teacher educators, teachers and students can look to the community activism of hip hop and punk artists as guideposts for possible *paths of dissent.* Here we will detail the activism of several key figures highlighted above. They are actions that can lead us beyond our unjust social and economic systems and their hegemonic manifestations, such as patriarchy, white supremacy, and homophobia. Lead singer of Leftover Crack, Stza Sturgeon, has been vociferous in his condemnation of North America's mass media and Bush's presidency. Over the past several years, Sturgeon has conducted several interviews for the purpose of unveiling the mass media's role in concealing how U.S. global policy spreads violence and injustice across the globe, while concomitantly, throwing light on how the Bush regime and the mass media espouse "ultranationalist propaganda to squelch dissent" aimed at their unjust policies and practices (McLaren, 2005, p. 198). He has urged his fans to reflect critically upon the dominant narratives generated by the media and state, and to support political movements designed to bring about a democratic state. On September 11, 2005, he brought his messages to the stage by performing a protest concert with Choking Victim. He made it clear to over 2000 fans that western imperialism, neoliberal economics, and xenophobia are to blame for the 9/11 attacks. Here he implicates Bush and the media for creating false narratives about the causes of terrorism:

> George Bush's brother Marvin Bush was head of security at the World Trade Center up until 9–11, and they were doing nefarious things, … They wanted another Pearl Harbor to install the Patriot Act and take us to war. Don't listen to the media; the media is there for maximum security—to tell you lies! (Ferguson)

Likewise, the *raison d'être* of Anti-Flag's work and social projects is to "play the role of educator to fans" about U.S. government and business leaders' 'current war on terrorism' (Usinger, 2004). In contrast to many artists who have taken part on the Warped Tour, Anti-Flag has openly renounced the United States' involvement in Iraq. Not only were the band's shows geared to raise young people's consciousness about 9/11, terrorism, and U.S. imperialism, but they were designed to encourage action against unjust policies perpetuated by greed. Offstage, band members have worked to empower youths alongside U.S. Representative Jim McDermott, who, in 2004, "gave a speech in the House of Representatives, praising Anti-Flag for working to encourage young people to register and vote" (http://en.wikipedia.org/wiki/Anti-Flag). The group has been actively involved in several endeavors that they feel will bring about a more just and humane society. They have taken part in anti-war demonstrations in Washington, DC, and Pittsburgh, backed PETA's stance for humane treatment of animals by bringing members from the organization to its shows, as well as taking part in interviews surrounding animal rights, and started a campaign http://militaryfreezone.org/ to end military recruitment in public schools.

Anti-Flag's central theme of social protest and change is representative of a long tradition of punk rock pedagogy, at its most critical moments. Perhaps one of the most influential punk rock activists since the 1979/1980 release of the aforementioned song, "Nazi Punks Fuck Off," is Jello Biafra and the establishment of Alternative Tentacles Records. Beyond the turbulent and controversial legacy of the Dead Kennedys, wrought with internal conflict that persists to this day (see Malott & Peña, 2004), is the existence and focus of Alternative Tentacles itself, which sarcastically boasts of "25 years of cultural terrorism" (www.alternativetentaclesrecords.com). In 1983 the Dead Kennedys were taken to court and charged with the "distribution of harmful matter to minors," for an insert on their "Frankenchrist" record of a reproduction of a painting by Swiss artist H. R. Giger, "Penis Landscape." However, the prosecution's case did not focus on the insert of "Penis Landscape," but rather on the legacy of the Dead Kennedys, considering it was presented to the court through such tactics as blowing up DK lyrics on large poster boards. The case was eventually overturned, but the trial tore the Dead Kennedys apart and nearly bankrupted Alternative Tentacles as a result of costly court fees and the banning of Dead Kennedys records in most retail outlets with the exception of small independent record stores.

As a result, Jello Biafra, a self-proclaimed "information junky," engaged in a series of spoken word tours, resulting in over 10 spoken words records on Alternative Tentacles. Biafra continues to tour and lecture at colleges and universities throughout the United States and elsewhere on issues from censorship to unjust imperialist wars. In addition to publishing Biafra's lectures, AT also continues to put out original independent music through its many signed artists who, brags Biafra, have 100% artistic freedom, which is antithetical to how mainstream corporate labels tend to be run. Making AT especially significant is its publishing of the lectures of noteworthy radical academics, writers, and activists such as Jim Hightower, Angela Davis, Noam Chomsky, Howard Zinn, Mumia Abu-Jamal, and Ward Churchill, to name a few. The coexistence of such radical thinkers with independent musicians under one label provides the opportunity for many AT music fans to be exposed to political ideas of critique and the possibility for large-scale social change otherwise not happening (Malott & Peña, 2004). Embracing the notion that punk rock is more of an ideology than a style, AT has signed critical artists from Earth First!, folk singers, hillbilly country acts, schizophrenic eccentrics, and radical rappers.

However, beyond the efforts of AT, one of the most influential Rap music icons, Public Enemy, continue in their quest to "fight the power" for the sake of forging a democratic society. PE founder Chuck D has utilized the radio and television airwaves to condemn the United States' involvement in Iraq. On his (co-hosted with Gia'na) Air America show, *On the Real*, he provides a space for youths and other progressive speakers to be heard on "how life, politics and the history of the American culture work (and who gets sacrificed for it)" (http://shows.airamericaradio.com/onthereal/about). For instance, the show helped to educate youths about the racist and classist response by Washington in the aftermath of Hurricane Katrina, one of the biggest crises, faced primarily by working people, in this country. Along with providing a space for discussion on this crisis, he composed a poem for his listeners, which was eventually turned into the band's song "Hell No We Ain't Alright," to express his outrage at today's "new world order:"

New Orleans in the morning, afternoon, and night
Hell No We Ain't Alright
Now all these press conferences breaking news alerts

Chuck D has also shared his insight in relation to social issues at college campuses across North America. In his discussion, "Race, Rap, and Reality," he has "lambasted America's anti-intellectualism and its obsession with celebrity. He criticized the lack of substance in today's rap music and suggested that technology distances us from our fellow man" (Rivers, 2006). His social commentary has spilled over to film. In the short documentary, *Bling: Consequences and Reproductions*, Chuck D's narration illustrates how the Revolutionary United Front has killed between 50,000–75,000 people and amputated many other individuals' limbs to secure Sierra Leone—the most diamond-rich country in the world (Cornish, 2005). The question remains: how can the music, messages, and movements highlighted above be used to enhance and make relevant a social studies curriculum that is if not dead, terminally ill?

Making Connections and Creating Passion
Through Music: CMSS

Pedagogically, what role can punk rock and hip hop play in the formation of revolutionary praxis? Drawing on critical media literacy, in the following paragraphs, we put forth the beginnings of a revitalized K-12 social studies education, a possible pedagogical and curricular place of departure.

More so now than ever, students who enter our classrooms, be it classrooms in universities, elementary schools, or high schools, are bringing with them the cultural commodities of punk rock and hip hop. Within these cultural artifacts are embedded ways of understanding and viewing the self and the larger world (as demonstrated within the examples of punk and rap outlined above). It is imperative for educators to understand how our students know. Honing in on this pedagogical necessity Freire (2005) argues:

> … our relationship with learners demands that we respect them and demands equally that we be aware
> of the concrete conditions of their world, the conditions that shape them … Without this, we have no
> access to the way they think, so only with great difficulty can we perceive what and how they know.
> (Freire, 2005, p. 58)

Understanding the ways in which students perceive the world enables teachers to begin to create a culturally relevant and engaging education, which are key components in fostering *a passion to know*. For example, in our work teaching high school social studies and teacher education social studies methods courses, we have had students bring in songs that relate to particular social issues such as racism, sexism, among countless other foci. Discussing the messages presented within these songs has offered our classes a focus of critique and an opportunity for us to share more revolutionary/critical examples from the genres, as outlined above.

Such an approach has also provided a powerful and engaging method to teach students about the internal workings of capitalism. Focusing on the commodification and cooptation of punk rock and hip hop has provided our students with a critical lens to better understand the predatory nature of capital, as well as other social forces creating injustices in society. Using critical media literacy in this way has consistently led many of our students to more informed visions of their own subjectivities and the ways in which they are shaped by market forces and capital's divisive hegemonies such as white supremacy. However, because "… we are programmed but not predetermined, because we are conditioned but, at the same time, conscious of the conditioning, that we become fit to fight for freedom as a process and not as an endpoint …" (Freire, 2005, p. 70). In other words, our approach does not focus on awareness alone, but calls for action.

The activism of the artists described above has allowed many of our students to, first, envision themselves as agents of change, and then, once empowered, be able to overcome their own fear of freedom and to take action for social justice. For example, some of our students have begun with actions such as writing letters to record companies and politicians. While such actions, it can be argued, are ultimately ineffective in their attempts to convince the powers that be to change their policies, they are effective at providing students with that first step at seeing themselves as participants rather than observers. This step is fundamental in their development as critically literate global citizens. Actions our students have taken are by no means limited to letter writing. Other examples include, but are not limited to, joining activist organizations and groups, attending demonstrations, publishing critical work/becoming radical scholars, and developing progressive curricula.

Given the current trends in privatization and standardization, which, together, threaten the democratic potential of the social studies curriculum in particular, and education in general, critical theory, along with critical media literacy, must assist us to meet the democratic challenge put forth by humanity's relentless demand for dignity and respect.

References

http://shows.airamericaradio.com/onthereal/about). Retrieved, January 22, 2006.

Allman, P., McLaren, P., & Rikowski, G. (2005). After the box people: The labor-capital relation as class constitution and its consequences for Marxist educational theory and human resistance. In P. McLaren (Ed.), *Capitalists & conquerors: A critical pedagogy against empire* (pp. 135–165). New York: Rowman and Littlefield.

www.alternativetentaclesrecords.com Retrieved, January 28, 2006 *Anti-Flag: Biography.* Retrieved, January 28, 2006, from http://en.wikipedia.org/wiki/Anti-Flag.

Case, R., & Clark, P. (1997). Four purposes of citizenship education. In R. Case & P. Clark (Eds.), *The Canadian anthology of social studies: Issues and strategies for teachers* (pp. 17–28). Vancouver, BC: University of British Columbia Press.

Chomsky, N. (2005). *Imperial ambitions: Conversations on the post-9/11 world.* New York: Metropolitan Books.

Cohen, P. (1980). Subculture conflict and working-class community. In S. Hall, D. Hobson, A. Lowe, & P. Willis (Eds.), *Culture, media, language: Working papers cultural studies 1972–1979* (pp. 78–87). Birmingham: The Center for Contemporary Cultural Studies, University of Birmingham.

Cornish, M. J. (2005, December 9). *Chuck D narrates 'bling: Consequences and repercussions.'* Retrieved, February 7, 2006, from www.nobodysmiling.com.

The Coup. (2001/2004). *Party music* [CD]. Los Angeles, CA: Epitaph Records.

Dancis, B. (1978). Safety pins and class struggle: Punk rock and the left. *Socialist Review, 8* (39), 58–83. Dead Kennedys. (1979/1980). Nazi punks fuck off. *In God We Trust, Inc.* San Francisco, CA: Alternative Tentacles Records.

Dead Prez. (2000). "Police State." *Let's Get Free.* New York: Loud Records.

Dimitriadis, G. (1996). Hip hop: From live performance to mediated narrative. *Popular Music, 15*(2), 179–194.

Ferguson, S. (12 September 12, 2005). 9–11 Conspiracists invade Ground Zero. *The Village Voice.* Retrieved, February 6, 2006, from http://www.villagevoice.com/news/0537, fergusonweb2,67726,2.html

Freire, P. (1998). *Pedagogy of the oppressed.* Boulder, CO: Continuum.

Freire, P. (2005). *Teachers as cultural workers: Letters to those who dare teach.* New York: Westview Press.

Freire, P., & Macedo, D. (1987). *Literacy: Reading the word and the world.* South Hadley, MA: Bergin and Garvey.

Giroux, H. A. (1994). Doing cultural studies: Youth and challenges of pedagogy. *Harvard Educational Review, 64*(3), 278–308.

Giroux, H. A. (2005). Cultural studies in dark times: Public pedagogy and the challenge of neoliberalism. *Fast Capitalism, 1*(2). Retrieved, January 22, 2006, from http://www.henryagiroux.com/.

Kellner D., & Share J. (2005). Politics of education towards a critical media literacy: Core concepts, debates, organizations and policy. *Discourse: Studies in the Cultural Politics of Education, 26*(3), 369–386.

Kornfeld, J., & Goodman, J. (1998). Melting the glaze: Exploring student responses to liberatory social studies. *Theory into Practice, 37*(4), 306–314.

Malott, C., & Peña, M. (2004). *Punk rockers' revolution: A pedagogy of race, class, and gender.* New York: Peter Lang.

Malott, C., & Pruyn, M. (2006). Marxism and critical multicultural social studies. In W. Ross (Eds.) *The social studies curriculum: Purposes, problems, and possibilities* (3rd Edition) (pp. 157–170). Albany: State University of New York Press.

McLaren, P. (1995). *Rethinking media literacy: A critical pedagogy of representation.* New York: Peter Lang.

McLaren, P. (2005). *Capitalists & conquerors: A critical pedagogy against empire.* New York: Rowman and Littlefield.

McLaren P., & Jaramillo, N. (2005). God's cowboy warrior: Christianity, globalization, and the false prophets of imperialism. In P. McLaren (Ed.), *Capitalists & conquerors: A critical pedagogy against empire* (pp. 261–334). Lanham, MD: Rowman and Littlefield.

McLaren, P., & McLaren, J. (2004). Afterword: Remaking the revolution. In C. Malott & M. Peña (Eds.), *Punk rockers' revolution: A pedagogy of race, class, and gender* (pp. 123–127). New York: Peter Lang. www.militaryfreezone.org/ Retrieved, January 22, 2006

Nieto, S. (2002). Affirmation, solidarity and critique: Moving beyond tolerance in education. In E. Lee, D. Menkart, & M. Okazawa-Rey (Eds.), *Beyond heroes and holidays: A practical guide to K-12 anti-racist, multicultural education and staff development* (pp. 7–18). Washington, DC: Teaching Change.

On the real: About the show. Retrieved, January 25, 2006, from http://shows.airamericaradio.com/onthereal/about.

Porfilio, B., & Malott, C. (2007). Neoliberalism. In G. L. Anderson & K. G. Herr (Eds.), *Encyclopedia of activism and social justice*. New York: Sage.

Rivers, K. (2006, February 4). *Chuck D finds a new public enemy*. Retrieved, February 6, 2006, from www.SouthBendTribune.com.

Russell, R. (2002). Bridging the boundaries for a more inclusive citizenship education. In Y. Hebert (Ed.), *Citizenship in transformation in Canada* (pp. 134–149) Toronto: University of Toronto Press.

Usinger, M. (2004, July 8). *Anti-Flag backs up its bashing*. Retrieved, January 24, 2006, from www.straight.com.

CHAPTER 35

The Breaking (Street Dance) Cipher

A Shared Context for Knowledge Creation

Haidee Smith Lefebvre

Figure 35.1: Ciphering at Circle Industry 2012 (International Breaking Competition). Photograph posted at The BBoyspot.com (http://www.thebboyspot.com/circle-industry-2012-wrap-up/). Every effort has been made to trace copyright holders and to obtain their permission for the use of copyright material. The author apologizes for any errors or omissions and would be grateful if notified of any corrections that should be incorporated in future reprints or editions of this chapter

I jumped inside the ring, all of me. Dance, then, and I danced,
till the room blurred like water, like blood, *dance*,
and I was leaning headlong into the universe,
Dance!
(Naomi Shihab Nye, "The Whole Self," 1995)

Funk beats bounce 4/4 time from the deejays' speakers, ricocheting off walls, reverberating up
and down the ceiling. Music dominates the basketball court on the ground floor of the Montréal
Downtown YMCA. The only place to sit is on the floor. Movement requires stepping over, between,
among the huge crowd attending Montréal's sixth annual Braggin' Rites, a hip hop dance competition
designed for "b-girls and b-boys" (BGBBs). The first round takes nearly two hours; gradually humidity
saturates the room. Eventually, the host announces intermission.

In a flash, improvisational dance circles pop up from one end of the court to the other. Spectators'
bodies create the boundary that separates onlookers from the alternating soloist at the center. From the
sidelines I observe dancers flow back and forth from soloist to spectator through some imperceptible
signal. A sudden uproar from across the room; dancers run over, pushing into that circle's periphery. As
the circle expands and contracts, I catch partial views of alternating performances. Soloists *Bronx Rock*
the beat, then *Corkscrew* drop to *floor work* for a classic *6-Step*, some transition to *Zulu Spins*, others
snap off a *Coffee Grinder*, eventually a *power move* flares, flips, springs into a *Lotus freeze*, the concluding
static pose. Often, spectators hoot, holler, gesture their opinions about a soloist's performance; usually
in these instances the energy intensifies as spectators crowd the dancer. In such instances, the circumfer-
ence shrinks, a hair's breadth separating soloist from onlookers.

By now, if you envisioned an overheated, crowded, closed space; shouted conversations; individuals
seated, standing, walking, running, dancing; if what comes to mind is recess with disorganized clusters of unstructured dance circles, unidentifiable dance moves, and esoteric turn-taking—chaos!—then
you have a fairly good idea what the cipher appears like to the uninitiated (see Figure 35.1). BGBBs
often describe thecipher as a performance arena for the dance; as a competitive, yet collaborative, act
expressed through improvisational dance performances; and as a flow or transcendental state.

I consider BGBBs youth or adults who perform the street dance known as breaking. Although
some may practice other elements of the hip hop culture, the term, b-boy and/or b-girl, does not
describe graffiti writers, emcees, and deejays (Fogarty, 2012). Rather than refer to dancers as"b-boy,"
"b-girl," and "b-girl/b-boy," I use: "BGBB," "dancer," "breaker," and "b-youth." In deference to hip hop
standards, I refer to the dance as "breaking," "break," or "b-boying." Also, I use "cipher" for "the quint-
essential b-boy environment" (Schloss, 2009, p. 98); however, if "cypher" appears in original sources,
I cite it without commenting on stylistic differences.

Generally, education researchers inquire into the ways youth mobilize hiphop to make meaning
(Dimitriadis, 2001; Tan, 2010), construct identity (Ibrahim, 1999, 2003), and produce ways of doing
and being (Petchauer, 2009, 2012a). Education professionals use hiphop to develop classroom activities (Emdin, 2010; Low, 2011, Petchauer, 2012b). Authors also emphasize the fact that youth produce
hiphop. Chang (2006) acknowledged that hiphop was created by and for Black and Latino youth in
response to the socioeconomic conditions in the Bronx, New York, during the 1970s. Petchauer (2012a)
portrayed college students as "hiphop collegians" whose active participation in hiphop informs and shapes
their educational interests, motivations, and practices. Alim (2011) mapped emerging local and global
"ill-literacy" practices, where "ill" signifies youth's skilled literacies, and not a lack of (dominant forms of)
literacy. Finally, Fogarty (2006) traced the production, distribution, and circulation of "underground"
video documentaries and travel video "magazines" that sustained the breaking culture from the mid-
1980s to the late 1990s, a period when the dance had practically disappeared from public view. I argue
that BGBBs are an innovative knowledge community (Smith Lefebvre, 2011) that since the late 1970s

has created and refined an extensive body of knowledge that includes dance moves and sequences, competition strategies and choreographic processes, and a philosophy about the dance and the b-boying way of life (Schloss, 2009). I ask: What actual processes do b-youth enact to create and advance knowledge that sustains their dance?

I suggest that the cipher (an improvisational dance circle) is one place where b-youth create aesthetic knowledge. Most dancers cipher, and then, sometimes for decades, they discuss cipher performances, "construct[ing them] in like miniature ways ... right down to the moves, the attitudes, to the timing, to the personality, and to the crowd's response" (S. Leafloor, personal communication, December 2, 2010). In the cipher hub, dancers think on their feet, improvise, draw on strengths under pressure, face inner fears, and cope with the self (Schloss, 2009). These are but a few examples of possible ways BGBBs have evolved through self-transcendence to innovate dance moves, construct a code of conduct (Dyzee, 2011), and author a foundational philosophy (Schloss, 2009).

The general claim that for nearly four decades dancers created and refined a unique knowledge domain can be supported by Ikujiro Nonaka's (1991/2007) organizational knowledge creation theory (Nonaka & Konno, 1998; Nonaka, Konno, & Toyama, 2001; Nonaka & Toyama, 2003; Nonaka, Toyama, & Hirata, 2008; Nonaka, Toyama, & Konno, 2000. See also, Nonaka & von Krogh, 2009, for their comments on the debate about the theory of organizational knowledge creation). The theory traces the knowledge-creation process that arises during face-to-face interactions situated in a particular time and place. Nonaka called such space *ba*, a Japanese word that denotes physical space, a specific time and space, and the space of interpersonal relationships. Although Nonaka's theory contains several key components because *ba* and the cipher are similar, I limit the discussion to three features they have in common:

1. They occur in a shared context in motion, in a space for emerging relationships (Nonaka & Toyama, 2002);

2. They rely on human interaction; and

3. They provide opportunities for transcendence.

I describe transcendence as a continuous process through which one transcends both the boundary of self and the boundary between self and the other. When individuals transcend their limited boundaries and understand that they are part of a larger perspective, they are engrossed in the knowledge-creation process (Nonaka et al., 2001). This chapter includes a rationale for the method of inquiry—participation observation; a description of the cipher; and a discussion of features shared by *ba* and the cipher.

Shared Traits: Breaking and Participant Observation

Long before I began to study street dance, I researched breaking in my role as a mother. My participation in the Montréal street-dance scene dates back to 2004 when, as a parent of a pre-adolescent with a deepening investment in the b-boying culture, I accompanied my son on his journey of apprenticeship into Montréal's breaking community. Gradually, my curiosity transformed into a commitment to document the educational practices I witnessed at local hip hop and breaking events. Typically, apprentices observe for two purposes:

1. To learn and refine dance moves and sequences; and

2. To identify or act as a member of the community.

Therefore, choosing participation observation appeared to match both a cultural norm and the community's familiarity with me as a non-dancing observer.

Participant observation aims to immerse the researcher in the community so that the research site is situated inside the lives of those under study. Many b-youth plunge into the hip hop culture to emulate the b-boy aesthetic (Schloss, 2009). In this manner, they begin to comprehend implicit rules and make them explicit by learning the community's vocabulary, cultural grammar, and discourse modes. Likewise, engrossed in community life, researchers learn to construct a "thick description" (Geertz, 1973, p. 9) of a human activity in a natural setting using the community's own language and everyday concepts (Conteh, Gregory, Kearney, & Mor-Sommerfeld, 2005). My qualitative, interpretive research design relied on participant observation as the central tool of inquiry that structured activities at thirteen breaking events and four instructional episodes. A few are listed below to provide a general idea of the variety of observation sites.

From winter 2009 to winter 2011, I attended public and private breaking events. Some of the organized public events include Montréal's annual urban arts festival, *Hiphop You Don't Stop*, and the *House of Paint* in Ottawa. Some insider events include a battle that spun off from the 2010 *Hiphop You Don't Stop* and open practice sessions at three Montréal dance studios. During the Montréal urban arts festival, local dancers discovered that Iron Monkey, a legendary breaker from San Francisco, was on site and willing to compete; so, they spontaneously organized an informal competition. The battle was not publicized; for the most part, word-of-mouth invitations were limited to people at the festival. Located in a downtown dance studio housed in the Belgo Building, the dancers ciphered before, in between, and after the battles. Most breakers would consider the event one long cipher revolving in cycles: battling and freestyling. The open practice sessions occurred in three different locations (Shauna Roberts Dance Center, Studio Sweatshop, and Café Graffiti). During open practice, no one was officially in charge. Attendance was unpredictable with staggered arrivals; often, the musical selection depended on who attended and for what purpose (e.g., rehearsal, regular training, meet friends). Toward the middle or end of practice, ciphers emerged. For the most part, the only times I noticed the cipher *did not appear* was in educational settings where BGBBs were in the minority (i.e., two or more dancers delivering a workshop or class to non-street dancers).

B-youth claim that researchers who do not break lack a significant understandingof the dance, so in 2013 I signed up for instructional events held at the Diss Torsion Studio and organized by B-girl Lynx, active in Montréal since the late 1990s. Theyinclude: *B-boy/B-girl Classes with Lynx: Fall Session*; *Rocking Workshop with Wary the Warrior*; and *Top Rock Workshop with Crazy Smooth*. Although a class session and two workshops are inadequate to develop skill for the demanding dance, I experienced several traditions elaborated by Joseph Schloss (2009) in *Foundation: B-boys, B-girls, and Hip hop Culture in New York*. His study documented the ways b-boying traditions and aesthetic expressions have been passed down since the 1970s to create and further a profound art form. He explained that the term "foundation" refers to an "almost mystical set of notions" transmitted from teacher to student that contains more than "the actual physical movements, it includes the history of the movements and the form in general, strategies for how to improvise, philosophy about the dance in general, musical associations, and a variety of other subjects" (p. 12). Dancers' pedigree often depends on how well they master the foundation's breadth, depth, and nuances.

In 2009, at the *International Symposium on Hip Hop Culture* held at Concordia University, I met B-boy Buddha for the first time. After explaining my inquiry, he suggested himself as an interview candidate based on a lifelong commitment to the dance dating back to 1975 and his unique perch as the co-founder of Canada's oldest b-boy crew, Canadian Floor Masters. To better understand the symbolic interactions characteristic (Deegan, 2001/2007) of the breaking subculture, Buddha and I engaged in three two-hour, semi-structured interviews that occurred in his home. Additional sources include text from hip hop- and breaking-related websites.

I gathered a flood of information that helped me understand the freestyle or improvisational cipher from my lived experience. Cipher dynamics are tightly bound to a specific social context; it is difficult to understand the dynamics without actually experiencing the activity. The only way I could gain this knowledge was through participant observation based on the notion that newcomers evolve from peripheral to full participation in a community organized around an activity occurring in a particular social context (Lave & Wenger, 1991/2006). Peripheral participation conceptualizes learners' participation as a way "—of both absorbing and being absorbed in—the 'culture of practice.'" (p. 95). By combining interviews and text with peripheral participation in the Montréal breaking scene, I met the research goal to describe the cipher from a variety of sources.

The Cipher: Definite and Indefinable

Only the people in the Cypher can see it. There are no rules or time limits.
(Dyzee, 2011, Bboy Etiquette Don't Do's, #2)

The term, *cipher* or *cypher* originates from the Nation of Gods and Earths (NGE), also known as Five Percenters, who formed in the 1960s after separating from the Nation of Islam (Johnson, 2009; Schloss, 2009). The term represents circles or cycles, such as the zero or the letter "o" and "especially the circles of people in which their [NGE's] lessons are propagated" (Schloss, 2009, p. 98). Johnson (2009) explained, "Ciphering among Five Percenters also refers to standing or sitting in a circle and speaking with one another to 'build' intellectually among those schooled in their 'Lost-Found' lessons" (p. 4). Building means to add on to or elevate knowledge, the physical body, finances, and institutions; to build on to the cipher is to complete a 360-degree circle.

The cipher typifies a competitive dance space built by a circle of onlookers that has been used historically throughout the African diaspora for dance, religious rituals, and martial arts (Schloss, 2009). It traverses several elements of hiphop: breaking, emceeing, and knowledge.[1] In broad terms, ciphering involves participants performing as both spectator and soloist; onlookers commenting on the performances, and equal turns taken by all as performer and observer. When at the centre, dancers open themselves to the spectators' assessment of their improvised performance. From the periphery, onlookers evaluate the progress of the individuals' dance moves and sequences. These interactions contain intrinsic educational experiences where, under the watchful gaze of qualified breakers, participants can choose to refine or innovate dance moves and sequences, mimic or mock cultural norms, fortify or undermine the breaking ethos. On such occasions, BGBBs share, further, and create individual and/or communal knowledge. So far, academics have written little about this crucial feature of the hip hop culture. Generally, most hip hop artists are acquainted with ciphering, and may practice its principles in some form or another; dancers, however, consider ciphering the centerpiece of breaking (Osumare, 2002).

B-boying or breaking, the archetype of hip hop dance, customarily happens in the cipher, an improvisational circle where the soloist showcases her or his skills "while encoding gestural messages into the executed movement phrases ... these messages often comment with bravura on other dancers' perceived lack of skill, while extolling one's prowess as a performer" (Osumare, 2002, p. 33). As BG-BBs battle to be the best, the group also creates a choreographic performance piece much like the party game where one person starts a story that develops according to each person's contribution. The cultural criterion—compete and co-create—emerges as dancers respond to the song that happens to be played by the deejay in that moment; in this manner, the group creates a sophisticated pantomimic narrative (Banes, 2004; Schloss, 2009), while individuals rival to be the best in that particular cipher set in that specific place and time. At the same time, informed spectators validate whether or not dancers qualify as breakers; their recognition confers membership or acknowledgement that a dancer has advanced to a new level (Stevens, 2008). Thus, BGBBs utilize, share, and create individual and collective knowledge set in the local space from which the cipher materialized.

The cipher depends on fluidity. Driven by the music, moved by the emerging dance narrative, provoked by a competitor, dancers flow back and forth from the periphery to the interior. Typically, participants are expected to enter and leave the centre, to build the cipher energy from the sidelines and the limelight. The cipher forms at the unequivocal moment when the crowd spontaneously moves into the shape of a circle, creating "a dance space in the middle that spans about 16'x20'. Audiences are usually more than two people deep …. Individual breakers take turns, an average of 30 seconds to three minutes long, 'freestyle' dancing or improvising in the circle" (Stevens, 2008, p. 123–124). Unlike the proscenium stage, the cipher does not require advance booking, staff, technicians, and nearby parking. The bare necessities are a minimum of two dancers, some spectators, and music (Johnson, 2009). The musical source does not necessarily rely on playback devices, or electricity. For example, once, during a pit stop on a trip to the Ottawa urban art festival, *House of Paint*, in the parking lot of a coffee and donut shop, a short-lived cipher between three breakers popped up to the accompaniment of a beat-boxer. (The art of creating beats and rhythms using the human mouth, beatboxing, or vocal percussion, consists of a range of drum, bass, and sound effects.)

Schloss (2009) indicated that BGBBs presume the space, dance, and relationship between the two constitutes the entire cipher experience; when conceptualized as a verb, the social and spiritual nuances associated with the cipher emerge. He summed up the space and energy BGBBs often ascribe to the freestyle or raw cipher:

> [The cypher] does not require a stage, an audience, a roof, or a dance floor, or even a designated block of time. The cypher's very informality and transience are part of its power; it appears when and where it is needed, then melts away. Rhetorically, it is often referred to as "the" cypher, rather than "a" cypher, which suggests that all cyphers are, in some abstract way, connected. B-boys and b-girls view the cypher with an almost mystical reverence, befitting its status as the most authentic, challenging, and raw environment for b-boying. (p. 99)

Johnson (2009) developed the meaning of raw:

> *Raw* speaks to ciphers as uncooked or unprocessed—i.e. the freshness of improvisation. Or it can suggest that the performances are raw, as in unrestrained or unbridled. The rawness is eternally present tense, an unrepeatable combination of overt yet controlled performative aggression. (p. 6)

According to Buddha, raw means "you feel it" and are driven by the music into the cipher core (S. Leafloor, personal conversation, November 2, 2010). For him, this becomes a moment of transcendence, because the dancer neither shows off, nor seeks approval. Instead, the music evokes feelings that are expressed through the dance. The feeling expressed at the core in turn taps into and accentuates those feelings experienced by the dancers forming a circle around the soloist. As mentioned earlier, when individuals transcend their limited boundaries and understand that they are part of a larger perspective, they are engrossed in the knowledge-creation process (Nonaka et al., 2001).

A Perceptible Likeness: The Cipher and *Ba*

> The cipher is a microcosm of both the dance itself and the social movement it represents. Like b-boying, it creates a dialog of both competition and collaboration. And like hiphop, it's a way for practitioners to impose a new interpretation onto their surroundings—to remix the environment, effectively, into a space of their own. (Wilburn, 2010, final paragraph)

The cipher fluctuates as both a source of energy and as a repository for the dancers' energy, while serving as a platform for competition and collaboration. The interactions between the dancers and between the dancers and the environment influence the cipher's nature. For example, there are several types: warm-up, rehearsal, competitive, or raw. Often, depending on the interaction between dancers and spectators, the cipher begins as one type, then in a beat becomes another, then another. The interplay determines whether the cipher remains a rehearsal or teeters into a competition then totters into a dance narrative, or simply fades away as another pops off in a different area of the same place. Consequently, the cipher resonates with the description of *ba* as a shared context in motion, a space for emerging relationships.

Ba is context-specific; it fuses time, space, and human interactions; it provides opportunities to create knowledge in situated action (Nonaka & Toyama, 2002). When knowledge and *ba* interpenetrate, a new boundary for human interaction occurs. For Nonaka and Konno (1998), knowledge creation distinguishes *ba* from ordinary human interaction. When individuals with multi-viewpoints interact in a shared context, then *ba* exists. As a shared space, *ba* contains a worldview that guides creative interaction and organizes the social conditions for participation. Therefore, *ba* sets a boundary that influences interactions among individuals, yet remains open.

We acquire knowledge embedded in these shared spaces either through reflecting on our own individual experience or by reflecting on the experience of others. In *ba*, we recognize the self in all; thus, interaction is the most important aspect in *ba*. As a shared space, *ba* "serves as a foundation for knowledge creation" (Nonaka & Konno, 1998, p. 40). As mentioned in the chapter outline, here, I discuss three features *ba* and the cipher have in common:

1. They occur in a shared context,

2. They rely on human interaction, and

3. They provide opportunities for transcendence.

First, *ba* and the cipher are not bound to an actual geographical location anda scheduled time; instead they unify people, space, and time in a shared context. *Ba* provides individuals the energy, quality, and places to create knowledge (Nonaka & Toyama, 2002). The cipher appears anywhere at any time, and so, too, does the knowledge embedded in this social practice. The cipher is built with the dancers' bodies and charged with their energy; it does not depend on the material world (e.g., live or recorded music, indoor or outdoor, day or night). In many ways, BGBBs decide when to dance, when to observe, all the while constantly negotiating and renegotiating a cipher entry with the encircling spectators. The opportunity to act in the world as a spectator and a soloist exemplifies some of the ways BGBBs interact with one another and their environment. When ciphering, b-youth gain experience in places that serve as a foundation to create knowledge. Perhaps, time spent immersed in these shared contexts contributes to their ability to view themselves and their peers as artistic innovators.

Second, interaction is key to understanding *ba* and the cipher. For Nonaka et al. (2000), "participants of ba cannot be mere onlookers. Instead, they are committed through action and interaction" (p. 15). In the cipher, all participants are expected to engage, to enact both roles—that of the soloist and of the spectator. In general, the rotating soloists build the performance that exists independent of each individual contribution. Simultaneously, onlookers influence the performance's direction through their criticisms and cheers, which may be expressed vocally or through pantomime. The overall dance performance belongs in the cipher and not to any one dancer. When ciphering, BGBBs learn new understandings of the aesthetic, themselves, and the breaking culture as a whole. For instance, novice dancers learn to enter and exit the cipher. Onlookers learn how others personalize basic dance moves, or see a move for the first time. Uninformed spectators learn the various hand gestures and vocal responses that indicate disapproval or approval. Performers learn the difference between their appreciation and the audience's of their dance moves and sequences (Schloss, 2009). B-youth learn to inhabit the music, to let the dance in while looking out. Everyone learns to look each other in the eye.

The group disperses, and when individuals regroup in different places with different folk, they diffuse their knowledge throughout the breaking culture.

Involved in *Ba*: The Cipher as Transcending Limited Boundaries

> To participate in a ba means to get involved and transcend one's own limited perspective or boundary.... . Ba is the world where the individual understands him- or herself as a part of the environment on which his or her life depends. (Nonaka et al., 2001, p. 19)

Most advanced BGBBs are quite articulate about the cipher's multiple meanings. They often claim that the cipher offers spiritual connection or transcendence (Johnson, 2009; Schloss, 2009). Buddha's cipher definition resembles their definitions in its complexity and perspective on spirituality. The following quote from Buddha demonstrates a probable way that individuals transcend their own limited perspective when ciphering. First, I summarize Buddha's intricate description of the raw cipher; then include an excerpt from the middle of his comprehensive definition, followed by possible interpretations of his meanings.

To summarize, first and foremost, Buddha defines the cipher as "Yeah, I'm feeling it. I'm feeling that cipher" (S. Leafloor, personal communication, November 2, 2010). He then emphasizes the magnetic pull of the music that draws him into the cipher despite an intention not to dance; thereby showing a reciprocal relationship between the music, transcendence, and "engagement tools." When driven by the music, Buddha enters a zone where his authentic self flows here and now. In this transcendent zone, barriers dissolve that inhibit a heartfelt sensitivity to gifts received in the cipher. For him, the gifts are "a repertoire of engagement tools" for life beyond the cipher that becomes "the lens that you're going to reflect on the world through. I use that to look at capitalism, to look at global economies, all this stuff." Buddha's intricate cipher description as a place where breakers connect to the heart of the dance concludes with his belief that it bestows engagement tools that can be used to guide a mindset for participating in the world.

> Buddha: I would say when I feel the most spiritual about my dance is when I totally felt I was totally there. There was no self-consciousness about it. Whatsoever. At that point, I am the most connected to the music …. I'm in the zone and I'm not doing it to impress you …. I'm just becoming one with the music …. We would all define spiritualism differently, but I think connectivity through music and dance is a way of feeling kind of transcendent in some ways. In that I'm not worried about my day troubles that have gone on, I am not thinking about anything now. So I am giving my unbridled attention directly to feeling the music and feeling like it's flowing through me and coming back out …. When you see b-boys who actually do that [transcendence], the audience recognizes it. You feel that. You feel the heart of it. And you know this is, well, we often talk about 'what is it?' Heart is really what makes it a dance and not just bendies and Chinese-circus-something. Heart …. Heart comes out in the look in the eyes, comes out in the smile that you give, the wink over here, a lot of the subtleties …. I seldom remember dance moves and combos; I remember the heart. The ideal b-boy has both. They call them breakdancers in a derogatory way as opposed to a b-boy. (S. Leafloor, personal communication, November 2, 2010)

Standing on the edge, the music's centripetal force pulls Buddha inward to dance at the cipher's centre. Here, equipoise shows as his full immersion in the activity balances his energized focus (Csikszentmihalyi, 1990/2008). Unbound from his own limited perspective, represented here as unworried about day troubles, Buddha becomes a conduit: feelings flow through and from him. Nonaka, Toyama, and Hirata (2008) link *ba* to Csikszentmihalyi's flow theory, "where others have observed a loss of self-consciousness in flow" (p. 36). As a flow activity, the cipher pushes Buddha to higher levels of performance that lead to previously unimagined states of consciousness. Csikszentmihalyi (2008) explained, "When the flow episode is over, one feels more 'together' than before, not only internally but also with respect to other people and the world in general" (p. 41). The cipher becomes a place of discovery imbued with a creative feeling that transports Buddha into a new reality. The face-to-face cipher interactions transform him into a self more complex than he was before.

The cipher synthesizes real time, physical and acoustical space, people and their communal knowledge. In *ba*, devoid of the atomistic self, existence is in relationship to others in a given time and place that organically concentrates resources (i.e., people and their communal knowledge). According to Buddha, this occurs when the physical and acoustical space consecrates the cipher (Schloss, 2009) and the dancer transcends selfhood, feeling the heart of the moment. The audience recognizes a heartfelt response to the music; they relate emotionally to those who vibe to the music. Buddha and Johnson (2009) specified that preplanned sets and performance crutches are irrelevant in ciphers. Also, both called attention to a bias or criticism that prevails in the breaking culture. Johnson (2009) observed:

> [Many breakers are critical of dancers] who can "rock the battle" in front of a panel of judges but cannot "rock the cyphers" after the competition is over. Despite that there are those for whom the reverse is true, those who can perform better in cyphers than at competitions or on stage, such breakers maintain a degree of respect that the former do not, though all concur that those who are able to shine in both arenas are extremely talented. (p. 203)

Johnson explained that ciphering demands integration of kinesthetic knowledge and imagination that must give rise to a raw performance; therefore, ciphering "carries greater cultural weight." The bias implies an underlying expectation that eventually b-youth will attempt to excel as artistic innovators.

For Buddha, BGBBs with heart harmonize aesthetic superiority with spiritualism. It follows that heart makes breaking a dance. He cites immaterial connections such as looking into each other's eyes, smiling, winking, flowing to or united to the music. Above all, heart is the genuine, unmasked self motivated by a willingness to "lose oneself to be open to others .... [to connect to people engaged in] real human activities, concretely present in space and time" (Engeström, 1999, pp. 28, 36). Buddha's explanation is predicated on heart as an important criterion to internalize the understandings grasped in the cipher. In some ways, the cipher forges engagement tools that breakers use to reflect on alternatives to the future. It stands that heartfelt dancing indicates a state of readiness to traverse new boundaries that open onto the unstable future. In this way, humans do more than create knowledge, they exercise creativity when choosing alternatives to create their future (Nonaka et al., 2001).

Conclusion

All things considered, the cipher produces and contains intrinsic interactions; these resemble interactions that occur in *ba*. Thus, the cipher and *ba* can be described as a shared context in motion. The cipher has neither a beginning, nor an end; rather, it is a process where individuals may experience spiritual connection, lose self-consciousness to open to others. This resembles the self-transcending process that Nonaka et al. (2001) argued permeates the knowledge-creation process. During this process, dancers understand a larger perspective of the dance that transcends their limited boundary. The cipher overlaps with practices and philosophies that form the spectrum we refer to as the breaking culture. Thinking of the cipher as *ba* illuminates one possible way BGBBs have created knowledge that continues to refine and advance a particular dance aesthetic.

For nearly four decades, BGBBs have created an aesthetic by quilting together material from a variety of sources, then integrating it into their own self-created, self-driven youth culture. The aesthetic conventions model a relationship between music, place, and spirituality that offers an array of choices for personal transformation (Schloss, 2009). The breaking culture "trains [b-boys and b-girls] to project confidence, discipline, and preparedness for any eventuality as they go forth into the future" (Schloss, 2009, p. 116). By interpreting the breaking culture as an innovative knowledge community, we have an opportunity to view teaching and learning as individual and collective processes that represent education in a unique fashion. Future studies may shed light on how, with little or no institutional support, youth educate themselves in ways that profoundly shape their sense of self and place, as well as greatly influence their social interactions and worldviews. In particular, Nonaka's knowledge theory may contribute to better understanding how breaking's intrinsic educational experiences and processes have matured from a neighborhood activity to a worldwide practice that appears to have institutionalized educative methods and philosophies. In many ways, the b-boying aesthetic provides opportunities to conceptualize the ways humans learn and teach in places with people who may not come to mind when conceptualizing educational approaches, settings, or teachers.

As a hiphop pedagogical site, the cipher takes place away from school. It is a communal, circular space where we learn and perfect dance moves, construct our individual and communal identities, collaborate in a competitive context, as well as use, share, and create knowledge. The cipher pulls us inward. We jump inside the ring, all of us. Wholly present in all totality, we feel the circle.

Acknowledgments

This research was supported by: Social Sciences and Humanities Research Council: 766-2009-4094 Joseph-Armand Bombardier Canada Graduate Scholarship Master's Scholarship, 2009–2010 and the Fonds québécois de la recherche sur la société et la culture:139678 Bourse de maîtrise en recherché (B1, 10A), 2010–2011.

Note

1.   Hiphop expressions are often referred to as the four elements: emceeing (i.e., rapping), deejaying (i.e, turntablism), forms of street dance (i.e., locking, popping, etc.), and writing (i.e., graffiti) (Chang, 2006). Afrika Bambaataa, the Godfather of hiphop, consistently adds on the fifth element, knowledge. These expressions have expanded to include spoken-word poetry, theater, fashion, language, and some forms of activism (Chang, 2006; Petchauer, 2009).

References

Alim, H. S. (2011). Hip hop and the politics of ill-literacy. In B. A. U. Levinson & M. Pollock (Eds.), *A companion to the anthropology of education* [Online edition]. Retreived from http://onlinelibrary.wiley.com/doi/10.1002/9781444396713.ch14/summary

Banes, S. (2004). Breaking. In M. Forman & M. A. Neal (Eds.), *That's the joint!: The hip hop studies reader* (pp. 13–20). New York, NY: Routledge.

Chang, J. (2006). *Can't stop, won't stop: A history of the hip hop generation.* New York, NY: Picador.

Conteh, J., Gregory, E., Kearney, C., & Mor-Sommerfeld, A. (2005). *On writing educational ethnographies: The art of collusion.* Stoke-on-Trent, Staffordshire, UK: Trentham Books.

Csikszentmihalyi, M. (2008). *Flow: The psychology of optimal experience.* New York, NY: Harper Perennial.

Deegan, M. (2007). The Chicago School of ethnography. In P. Atkinson, A. Coffey, S. Delamont, J. Lofland, & L. Lonland (Eds.), *Handbook of ethnography* (pp. 11–25). Thousand Oaks, CA: Sage.

Dimitriadis, G. (2001). *Performing identity/performing text: Hip hop as text, pedagogy, and lived practice.* New York, NY: Peter Lang.

Dyzee (2011, January 27). Bboy etiquette 101. [The Bboy Spot Forums>Breakboy Discussions>Bboy Life]. [Online forum comment]. Retrieved from http://www.bboy.org/forums/word-up/141688-bboy-etiquette-101-a.html

Emdin, C. (2010). Affiliation and alienation: Hip hop, rap, and urban science education. *Journal of Curriculum Studies, 42*(1), 1–25. doi: 10.1080/00220270903161118

Engeström, Y. (1999). Activity theory and individual and social transformation. In Y. Engeström, R. Miettinen, & R-L Punamäki (Eds.), *Perspectives on activity theory* (pp. 19–38). Cambridge, UK: Cambridge University Press.

Fogarty, M. (2006). *Whatever happened to breakdancing?* (Unpublished master's thesis). Brock University, Ste-Catherines, Ontario, Canada.

Fogarty, M. (2012). Breaking expectations: Imagined affinities in mediated youth cultures. *Continuum: Journal of Media & Cultural Studies, 26*(3), 449–462. doi: 10.1080/10304312.2012.665845

Geertz, C. (1973). Thick description: Toward an interpretive theory of culture. In C. Geertz, *The interpretation of cultures: Selected essays* (pp. 3–30). New York, NY: Basic Books.

Ibrahim, A. (1999). Becoming Black: Rap and hip hop, race, gender, identity, and the politics of ESL learning. *TESOL Quarterly, 33*(3), 349–369.

Ibrahim, A. (2003). 'Whassup, homeboy?' Joining the African diaspora: Black English as a symbolic site of identification and language learning. In S. Makoni, G. Smitherman, A. F. Ball, & A. Spears (Eds.), *Black linguistics: Language, society, and politics in Africa and the Americas* (pp. 169–185). London, UK: Routledge.

Johnson, I. K. (2009). *Darkmatter in b-boying cyphers: Race and global connection in hip hop* (Unpublished doctoral dissertation). University of Southern California, Los Angeles, CA. Retrieved from http://digitallibrary.usc.edu/search/controller/view/usctheses-m2598.html

Lave, J., & Wenger, E. (2006). *Situated learning: Legitimate peripheral participation* (15th ed.). New York, NY: Cambridge University Press.

Low, B. E. (2011). *Slam school: Learning through conflict in the hip hop and spoken word classroom*. Stanford, CA: Stanford University Press.

Nonaka, I. (2007). The knowledge-creating company (Best of HBR: November–December, 1991). *Harvard Business Review, 85*(7–8), 162–171.

Nonaka, I., & Konno, N. (1998). The concept of 'ba': Building a foundation for knowledge creation. *California Management Review, 40*(3), 40–54.

Nonaka, I., Konno, N., & Toyama, R. (2001). Emergence of 'ba': A conceptual framework for the continuous and self-transcending process of knowledge creation. In I. Nonaka & T. Nishiguchi (Eds.), *Knowledge emergence: Social, technical, and evolutionary dimensions of knowledge creation* (pp. 13–29). New York, NY: Oxford University Press.

Nonaka, I., & Toyama, R. (2002). A firm as a dialectical being: Towards a dynamic theory of a firm. *Industrial and Corporate Change, 11*(5), 995–1009.

Nonaka, I., & Toyama, R. (2003). The knowledge-creating theory revisited: Knowledge creation as a synthesizing process. *Knowledge Management Research & Practice, 1*(1), 2–10.

Nonaka, I., Toyama, R., & Hirata, T. (2008). *Managing flow: A process theory of the knowledge-based firm*. New York, NY: Palgrave Macmillan.

Nonaka, I., Toyama, R., & Konno, N. (2000). SECI, ba and leadership: A unified model of dynamic knowledge creation. *Long Range Planning, 33*(1), 5–34.

Nonaka, I., & von Krogh, G. (2009). Tacit knowledge and knowledge conversion: Controversy and advancement in organizational knowledge creation theory. *Organization Science, 20*(3), 635–652. doi: 10.1287/orsc.1080.0412

Nye, N. S. (1995). The whole self. In *Words under the words: Selected poems/Naomi Shihab Nye*. Portland, OR: Far Corner Books.

Osumare, H. (2002). Global breakdancing and the intercultural body. *Congress on Research in Dance, 34*(2), 30–45. Retrieved from http://wwwjstor.org/stable/1478458/116

Petchauer, E. (2009). Framing and reviewing hip hop educational research. *Review of Educational Research, 79*(2), 946–978.

Petchauer, E. (2012a). *Hip hop culture in college students' lives: Elements, embodiment, and higher edutainment*. New York, NY: Routledge.

Petchauer, E. (2012b). Sampling memories: Using hip hop aesthetics to learn from urban schooling experiences. *Educational Studies: A Journal of the American Educational Studies Association, 48*(2), 137–155. doi: 10.1080/00131946.2011.647148

Schloss, J. (2009). *Foundation: B-boys, b-girls, and hip hop culture in New York*. New York, NY: Oxford University Press.

Smith Lefebvre, H. (2011). *B-boy (dance) cipher: An innovative knowledge community's shared activity* (Unpublished master's thesis). McGill University, Montréal, Québec, Canada.

Stevens, L. (2008). *Breaking across lines: An ethnography of a Montreal hip hop street dance [Breaking à Montréal: Ethnographie d'une danse de rue hip hop]* (Unpublished master's thesis). Université du Québec à Montréal, Montréal, Québec, Canada. Retrieved from www.archipel.uqam.ca/1063/01/M10318.pdf

Tan, E. (2010). *Participatory and critical out-of-school learning for urban youth: Building community through popular culture* (Unpublished doctoral dissertation). McGill University, Montréal, Québec, Canada.

Wilburn, T. (2010, July 14). B-boy year one: Cypher up [Web log comment]. Retrieved from http://www.milezero.org/index.php/music/performance/dance/by1_cypher_up.html

13 ways at looking at 13 (abridged)

Donte Collins

1) At night, when heat rakes skin raw and you become aroused
at the sound of thunder/ your bed will beacon company
your palms, glowing pink, pulsing like the red bellies of
hungry wolves/ will want to migrate south, between steaming
thighs/ the thought of sin has settled/ something here is growing/
your heart is sweating/ your chest is a rising river
ready to release/ your bed is rocking to the
rhythm of you/ your face/ wine red/ drunk on steam and
simulated sex/ your body thrusting at the thought of her/
she is in your english class/ wears her smile soft/ her
touch a torch and you are sawdust/ you a cotton sky
ready to rain/ trembling like flood water/ like salted
skin/ like thunder/ roar/ rage/ release/ again, then, sleep.

2) At school, heat rakes skin raw and you find yourself lost in
mirror trying to make Mona Lisa out of flakey
flesh resting on the dirt road of your reflection, your
face/ a pimple stained glass window wearing a million
tiny puss filled reasons to leave/during lunch you bring
bottles of chemical cottage cheese to paint into
the sidewalk of your cheeks/ learn words like ugly; crater;
they creep into scabbing skin and stick like some sort of
kick-me sign/ cold water relaxes the skin/ school bath
room tissue could be mistook for cardboard but you use

it anyway/ learn to dab not wipe/ hot water kills
the germs/ rinse your fingers/ relearn words like love/ it is the
best adjective for beauty/ and you were born perfect.

3) In class, when called on like a thief and something
on you stiffens/ hardens and hangs like an ornament/ like
a wooden plank/ and you must walk it to the front of
the room/ your heart will become a drum/ you will forget
the reason of your feet/ your face will call your bluff/ this
is the fifth time week your body has become
a bus and swallowed you under it/ there is no
equation for correcting an unwanted erection/
walk with hands hammered into the stitching of your
pockets/ pretend to be searching for the sun/ set your
binder before your zipper and tap your thumb / play it
cool/ cock your chin back/ break no sweat/ you soldier of study/
you bucket of brave/ you boy of panic/ got this.

4) Somewhere they're sagging their skin and their language into slang
they're resting their tongues in the mouths of a daughter/ Somewhere
a mother becomes a bitch by definition of
decedent/ Somewhere they're singing sin like gospel hems
Somewhere a son is being given a name and a
gun/ Somewhere there is liquor licking a daughters breasts
Somewhere there is smoke stealing the breath of youth/ Somewhere
There is a white pill being placed in the punch bowl/ Somewhere
there is a sister sneaking out an open window
Somewhere there is a brown boy/ wrestling with the
war weeping in his chest/ a blank page awaiting his breath
Somewhere there is a poem hiding in his heart/ scattered
like glass/ he is more beautiful when broken/ Somewhere…

5) Donte, do you still perform autopsies on conver /
sations you've had lives ago / Are you still wondering
what gender the voice in your head is / is it still asking
for a name / Because today, you watched him? thought his
voice soft candy melting beneath your tongue / thought his hand
the best piece of jewelry on the playground / today
you don't want your hands, think them too rough too big for your
wrist / bend and dangled / 8th grade & god hates the gays? / you
don't know words like spectrum / fluid / weren't taught their taste they
too sweet & mother never allowed her boys too much sugar /
so you shift / alter taste at the altar / become
something worthy to call man / boy / swallowed your flame / your
insides are scorched in secret / your tongue can't tell / the difference

Donte Collins, St. Paul, MN
Courtesy of Youth Speaks and the Brave New Voices Network

(13 stanzas, 13 lines per stanza, 13 syllables in each line)

Flipping Switches

Anna Sun

I have a friend who's afraid of spiders. He's completely terrified. It's hilarious.
If I don't feel like talking to him, I'll send him a picture of one and he leaves me alone for the rest of the day.

I had a teacher who was afraid of heights. He was completely terrified. It was hilarious; he was about 6 foot tall and lived on the 7th floor of him building. I never questioned him when he came to school looking nervous.

I am afraid of the dark. I am afraid of soulless rooms where no matter how still I stand
I am falling into nothing,
And no matter where I look, the darkness is crawling everywhere.

Every night is a reminder that there is nowhere to run. Our entire hemisphere is being swallowed by black.
It is the most violent quiet I have ever known.
And even at that…
The worst parts of my life are not when he sun is gone.
It's having to watch it leave.

I grew up knowing that we are supposed to love sunsets.
Embrace the sun bleeding its last bursts of light
Over the horizon
Like wildfire on the ocean.

But when I see burning water, parts of me want to follow.

Life isn't easy for a nyctophobic;
It is not cute being afraid of the dark.
I have always been scared of charred oceans and smoke black skies.

When I was a kid, we used to play hide and seek in the dark.
One night, I reached to my right and exclaimed that I found my sister.
She thought would be funny to slowly stand up and, in a gruff voice, say, "Who said I was your sister."

I screamed at the top of my lungs!
Ran through he whole house, throwing all of the lights on,
And landed in my living room
In the fetal position.

It was hilarious.

It was hilarious because it was over.
It was hilarious because the lights were on.
If fear has taught me anything,
It's that sometimes, all you have to do is flip a switch
Or stomp your feet
Or don't look down.

The red, yellow and orange of sun sets
Still make it look like the earth is burning.
But it is also a reminder that there is a second ignition.
I may be afraid every night of my life
But I can never forget that there is a sunrise coming.
And it is going to light the world
On fire.

Anna Sun
Courtesy of Youth Speaks and the Brave New Voices Network

Elias

Gabrielle Isabella Grace

I met him in 7ᵗʰ grade.
Big head, pimples, big feet, real goofy
He wasn't that important
Just another guy in my class.
I didn't even notice him …. Someone else was already, in the words of his friends
"Tappin' dat ass!"
8ᵗʰ grade was different.
I still didn't know him but we kinda became friends
Didn't talk all that much
I just needed someone to replace those bad ends
I needed someone just to be my friend
We clicked! Just like that
We were compatible, no questions asked.
He was my brother, I was his sister
Strange how it all worked out
Because sooner than later
I was his lover and he was my mister
We walked together, talked together
Took breaths together
Slept together
Loved each other
He was mine and I was his
Nothing could go wrong
As long as my heart was connected to his

People stared, people judged
But it didn't matter to us
We had an amazing relationship
I couldn't believe that I put him with the group of misfits
I'll never forget that first kiss
It was filled with so much bliss
It was more of a dare but I'll never forget his stare
He pulled me close and he wasn't letting go
I wrapped my arms around his neck
And stared into his hazel eyes
I don't know how I knew
But from that day forward…
I knew he would always and forever
Be mine
I kissed him like I had never kissed anyone before
I can't remember how long but time was passing on and on
The next day ….. I woke up feeling happier than I had ever felt in my life
I just knew he was mine
The bell rang for dismissal and I was at my locker
He pressed his body against mine and I just knew he was my stalker
He kissed my neck and I melted in his arms
I turned around and he pulled me into the middle of hallway
I was sort of shocked because nothing like that had ever happened in my day
Behind his back was a bouquet of flowers
He put one in my hair
One on my dress
One in his is mouth
He gave me the rest
And said these are ours
He said "You are mine and I'm never letting go."
I said "I love you more than you will ever know."
I dropped the flowers as he smashed his lips against mine
Right then and there …. He was mine until the end of time
Mrs. McCauley didn't really appreciate our public display of affection
But she didn't understand our connection
I kissed him over and over
I wasn't ever letting go
He wasn't going to escape like Red Rover
Up against the locker
Up against the wall
It's a wonder we didn't fall
McCauley was trying to break it up
But we weren't letting her get in the way of our love
I wanted him and he wanted me
I think that was obvious for everyone to see
Finally we had to stop
Because the clock was ticking
Tick Tock

I had to go home
He had to stay
But it was difficult without him
Because I couldn't spend every minute of everyday
In his arms where I really felt safe
I wanted to have sex with him everyday since our first kiss
He did too but he had more self restraint than I ever did
I had already made that mistake in 8th grade
Over and over again and it wasn't worth the headache
He helped me see the value I possessed
And for the first time, I knew I was loved for who I was
And I wasn't pressured for sex
It felt good to be with him
To know that he was mine
If only things were still the same
Between He and I
I think I could've been a good wife
He could've been a great husband too
But when our goals changed
I didn't know what else to do
I had to say something because
We weren't compatible anymore
He wanted the promise I tried desperately to keep
And when I refused, I guess he found someone else to fulfill his desire, his need
It took me a long time to find my happiness again
I didn't know how to live life without my best friend
Some time passed by and now he calls me everyday
I wondered for a while if I would ever love anyone the way
I loved him
He tells me all the time that I'm gonna be his wife soon
He says "You are the most beautiful flower that I have ever seen bloom."
He was the nicest guy I ever called mine
My sweet Elias
My love for you will never die

Gabrielle Isabella Grace (16), Lithonia, GA

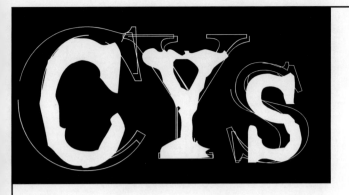

PART IV

Praxis: Pedagogies and Schooling, Kids not Talked About, and Activism

CHAPTER 36

Redefining the Notion of Youth
Contextualizing the Possible for Transformative Youth Leadership

Shirley R. Steinberg

Introduction: What's Wrong with You?

When I was hired as a high school drama teacher in 1987, it was expected that I "bring" back a dying program by producing and directing an enormous musical production. Creating a theatrical community while mounting *Grease* was part of my own personal mandate. The students, musicians, stagehands, all of us, became parts of a dynamic whole. The group was a social and artistic organism, enjoying one another. Jeremy was cast as Kenickie, the hell-raising greaser who becomes the potential father attached to Rizzo's possible pregnancy. Lanky, funny, and flexible, Jeremy had a dynamite voice, he was perfect for the part. Early one morning, following the previous evening's run-through of "Greased Lightning," my office phone rang:

Hello
I'm looking for Ms. Steinberg *You found me, can I help you?* This is Reverend Erb.
I'm so glad you phoned, Jeremy is doing so well, he is amazing.
That is why I am calling. I have a problem with you.
In what way?
I don't like the play you are directing, I don't like the part Jeremy is playing, I think it sends the wrong messages to our children, and I don't like what I hear about you.
Is there anything else?
I don't like that these young adults are doing, what I think you call, improvisation. Drama games. They are not following scripts. The whole play and the drama program are not what we want them to be learning. This is a school, and your values are not appropriate.
What is it you want me to do?
My son refuses to quit the play. I think you should tell him he can't have the part.
I can't do that. Jeremy deserves the part, it is his decision.

That's precisely the problem, you are teaching a program which allows students to make the decisions.

I'm sorry you feel that way, you are welcome to discuss it with the administration; however, they approved this production.

Obviously, I can't get anywhere discussing this with you.

Thank you for calling.

Wait, just one more thing ... this is what I really want to ask you ....

(pause)

What is wrong with you, Ms. Steinberg?

Wrong with me?

There has to be something wrong with you. The students stay late after school; you take them to plays; you all go out for dinner.

Yes.

No one likes teenagers. Only someone with something wrong inside wants to be around them that much.

Reverend Erb was right. Most people (grownups) don't like teenagers, they don't trust them, and certainly wanting to be around them is suspect. It was then that I decided to devote my career to facilitating young adults to become leaders, to be viewed as worthwhile, trustworthy, and brilliant. The old boy was speaking the language of the dominant North American parent: *kids are bad, kids are sneaky, kids raise hell, kids are not capable of making good decisions.*

Our son, Ian, and his best friend, Nathan, were hanging out a few years later, I was working on a book about schools and wanted to ask the boys a few questions. Nathan was up to answering my questions:

You are 16. You are in school. What do you think the purpose of school is for you?

To keep us in.

In?

Yeah, to keep us out of trouble, off the streets until we learn how not to get into trouble. They just want to keep us in.

Fear of Youth

Historically, adolescents and youth were not a distinct societal subculture. Indeed, until the twentieth century, North American 'teens' were often working at a young age, and certainly few were educated. In the 1950s, the notion of the rebel youth appeared, poster child James Dean became a grown-up's nightmare, along with rock n' roll, the hell-raising 50s led into the tune in, turn on, drop out 60s. Popular images of youth created a suspect society driven by desire and the ability to terrify adults. Psychologists and sociologists struggled to deal with youth; psychologizing, pathologizing, and institutionally marginalizing youth became the practice. What was wrong with youth? Everything.

Schools attempted to balance out youth subcultural movements by counter images of *the good girl* and *the manly, responsible boy.* Certainly, the Cleavers never had problems with Wally or the Beaver; Patty Duke complied; Father always knew best, and popular television created images of teens who did not question, did not rebel, and certainly, did not emulate Kenickie on the stage. Notions of drag racing, hoods, loose girls and back talking to parents were lower class behaviors, by the kids from across-the-tracks. Leadership by teens was reduced to two categories: *Preppies* (my word), the Paul Petersonesque kids with starched shirts and ties: and *Hoods*, those from lower or blacker/browner social classes who ran in gangs. Popular culture throughout the first thirty years of television did not portray empowered, functional youth as leaders.

Empowerment was not discussed. Schools did not address the possibility of creating a curriculum of leadership for youth ... sort of like they don't do this now. Historically, and presently, the idea of youth leadership is not engaged. Youth are to be feared, controlled, contained, and, as Nathan noted, "kept in."

A fear of youth is part of our fabric. Woven between the threads, young men and women are un-loved, often not understood, and often feared. Academics, school, and parents address issues *about* youth in constant discussions about:

- eating disorders

- bullying

- teen mothers

- gangs

- youth suicide

- homelessness

- disrespect for parents

- boredom in school

- failure to succeed

- lack of initiative

- sexualities

- identities

- language (as in slang, crude, or non-standard)

Conversations about youth reveal that *they are a problem.* Yet we do not have the conversations about why *we* perceive a problem. Curricula are designed to make sure youth know that they need to change, they need to take responsibility, and yes, Nathan was right, they need to be kept in.

All this to say, that in this chapter, I will not look at the "youth problem" nor articulate any confir-mation that youth are "at risk." I will engage in a conversation about youth leadership, its possibilities and challenges. Bottom line, youth are not a deficit in our culture or educational system. The deficit vision of youth is psychologized, pathologized, institutionalized, and marginalized... in a phrase, adults fear youth.

How Do We Discuss Youth Leadership If We Don't Want Youth to Lead?

Leadership is a clumsy term to deal with, the non-transformative kind. I'm not sure how to replace it, but want to state upfront, I don't like it much. It implies a hierarchy with the leader at the top, and then the leadees following below. Some may be given tasks or delegated responsibility, but leadership tends to expect that the leader will ultimately have the power. As a critical theorist, leadership for me becomes problematic. In a critical pedagogical world, noting how power works and replicates itself, how does one become a leader without assuming power? And, how do we work with youth to become leaders who do not intend to wield power? This is a tough one, and I want to keep it in mind in this discussion.

The notion of transformative youth leadership must be grounded in the articulation that youth are distinct beings and citizens, with specific needs, cultures, and views of the world. Instead of seeing youth as mini us, we need to redefine youth by seeing how youth define themselves—they are not a subculture; they are young men and women with cultures. Within these youth cultures, subcultures are created (usually by the youth themselves). I have observed in my work with youth, that many adults are reluctant to name youth cultures, instead discuss them with disdain, pathology, or marginalization: *She's in her Goth phase. Facebook has taken them over. World of Warfare is just his way of avoiding being with the family. I was the same way, I hated all adults. She just needs to understand that her appearance is not acceptable in our home. This music is out of control. He thinks he is gay; we are ignoring it; he will grow out of it. This hip hop thing, it is violent; we don't allow it in our home.* Rarely are young women and men given credit and respect for the decisions they make on a daily basis. Issues of identity become points of ridicule, and many teachers and caregivers view choices as phases, stages, or unimportant fads.

Certainly, teacher education does not prepare secondary and middle school teachers to facilitate youth leadership and empowerment; most parents and caregivers are not wired to assist empowerment, rather to squelch it. Often citing yellowed memories from their own lives, adults forget that they somehow made it through adolescence and teen years and actually did lots of good things during that time. Memories from adults are often categorized in two ways:

1. I did it, regret it, and don't ever want my kids to know I did it or to do "it" themselves: or

2. When I was that age, I did what I was told, what was expected, did not ask for my own "space," I was part of a family.

Incanting the term, *youth leadership*, most educators and parents speak out of both sides of their mouths, giving the term, and taking the power … no one seems to want kids to lead, to make responsible decisions, and to eventually replace a stagnant status quo. Ironically, it will happen. Thirty years ago, no one would have ever guessed that a presidential nominee's theme song would be one by Fleetwood Mac. There is almost a 'get over it' pedagogy that we must enact in order to overcome the youth phobia shared by many adults … especially those who design curriculum and create pseudo leadership roles for youth.

What We Need to Know

Creating a socially just youth leadership curriculum has obstacles, and the more urban the area, the more disenfranchised, the harder the challenge becomes. However, we must use the dialectic of challenges and opportunities. We must view our youth as novel entities, who may be similar or dissimilar from other young men and women. We rid ourselves of assumptions and create a space and pedagogy of leadership for schools and students, researching and observing each group on its own. We must focus attention on:

• The socio-cultural context of a school or community organization

• The backgrounds of each young man and woman

• The positions of empowerment and disempowerment from which each youth operates

• The knowledges youth bring to the classroom or organization

• The languages spoken by the youth, both cultural and sub-cultural

• The ways these dynamics mold teaching and learning

Keeping in mind the complexity and contradictions of the category of youth leadership, we must look at the unique features in creating a transformative youth leadership program. These are features which be kept in the forefront, especially in working with urban and marginalized youth.

- What are the considerations of population density as it applies to where youth live?

- Sizes of schools, availability of community centers. Are large suburban and rural counterparts more prepared to serve higher numbers of lower socio-economic class students? Are many students likely to be ignored and overlooked in the crowds of an urban area? In this context, it is difficult for urban and marginalized students to create and feel a sense of community. This creates an alienation which often leads to low academic performance, high dropout rates, and unanticipated leadership, gang affiliation, and negative subculture associations.

- What does the examination of geographic areas marked by profound economic disparity reveal? Disproportionate percentages of minority students and their families are plagued by centralized urban poverty, which hampers their quest for academic success on a plethora of levels. In urban schools and drop-in community centers (if they exist), there is an appalling lack of resources, financial inequalities, horrendous infrastructural violations, dilapidated buildings, and no space … no space for youth to just be… to be trusted, to make decisions.

- Urban areas have a higher rate of ethnic, racial, and religious diversity. In densely populated urban locales, people come from different ethnic, racial, and religious backgrounds, not to mention economic, social, and linguistic arenas, and they live close to one another. Nearly two-thirds of these urban youth do not fit the categories of white or middle class, and within these populations high percentages of students receive a free or reduced price lunch. Achievement rates for poor minority youth consistently fall below those of whites and higher socio-economic classes, and often their failures are the final proof that quitting school, engaging in illegal activity, is success.

- How does our work reach gay, lesbian, bisexual, transgendered and questioning youth?

- Where do indigenous youth fit into a closed definition of youth? Immigrant and migrant youth?

- Adults who sit on school boards, city councils, and on youth task forces, experience and factionalize infighting over issues on resources and influence, and often fighting is reduced to the youthphobia notion, that they are not to be leaders … as the reverend told me, *there has to be something wrong with me.* How could I tolerate and trust youth? There are no attempts to incorporate the voices of youth within these boards, councils and task forces. Youth are discussed as the societal deficit … the youth problem.

- Often administrators and leaders who work with teachers are undermined by ineffective business operations. The facilities rely on basic resources, especially in urban settings, and no one has the ability to change the reality. I am working with youth in East New York (Brooklyn) now and have made it a point to count the amount of play yards with functioning hoops for basketball, basketballs, and a minimum of jump ropes and hand balls. Youth drop centers are often in the cast-off basements or temporary buildings of a past era, and groups are reluctant to add financially to the structure of a soon-to-be condemned building and space.

- Work with youth does not tend to include initiatives for health and well-being. Naturally, the more socially deprived the youth, the worse the health and safety issues. School administrators will be more concerned with providing a warm building on a cold day, than fixing unsanitary and disease-producing bathrooms—poor spaces for youth, if any are provided for them to meet. The community fears youth meeting in groups; malls are closed during certain hours, or kids must be accompanied by adults. Street corners, steps of stores, these become the places for youth to meet.

- A mobility issue also haunts disenfranchised and urban schools. Students, teachers, and community leaders, and especially administrators, leave frequently. Good work may be being done but halts when an adult is replaced. Analysts have noted that the poorer the student, the more moves he or she is likely to make. High teacher turnover, one out of every two teachers in urban and poor schools leaves in five years ... community organizers are volunteers or so poorly paid that they are unable to advocate for even a minimal raise.

- Urban and poor schools serve higher immigrant populations. Each group experience has needs particular to their own ethnic group, yet they have little governmental or educational help to get them started.

- Urban schools have characteristic linguistic challenges. In New York City, for example, over 350 languages and dialects are spoken. Because the leaders and teachers are white or middle class, it is hard to have the general sense of heritage and educational backgrounds to make use of linguistic diversity. Indeed, linguistic diversity is seen as a problem, rather than a unique opportunity.

- Context is important. We know the responsibilities many young men and women carry. Once again, in lower socio-economic strata, or in specific cultures, youth take on adult roles as small children. Minding baby brothers and sisters/nieces and nephews, tending to aged grandparents, translating personal and medical knowledge between adults and doctors or social workers... these conditions throw youth into powerless leadership positions of translation and decision making.

- Mentors, teachers, and social workers are less likely to live in a community, which is profiled economically or culturally. Consequently, youth do not have consistent leadership models upon which to build or seek advice.

Eschewing the Modernist Constructions of Youth

Along with contextualizing the above thoughts is a short deconstruction of previous notions and definitions of youth. Keep in mind that 'teenager,' as a separate designation of *an older kid*, started to appear in literature in the late 1930s, early 40s. No historical reference launches fireworks for *the* day that the word first was used. Originally, it described literally, kids who were in the teens, 13–19. Most who work in adolescent and youth studies have different definitions. I loosely look at the ages between 11 and 21 but also can see that teenager and youth are tentative words, and along with them come expectations both cognitively and performatively. Jean Piaget addressed the notion of adolescence, observing that sometime around the age of 12, adolescents began to enter the formal operational stage, a more enlightened and sophisticated cognitive developmental stage. He saw that scientific, logical, and abstract thought was enacted by this age group and understood that many young people could stretch concrete thought to abstractions. He saw them as able to uderstand words and ideas in meaning-making terms, consider relationships, and have an operating knowledge of concepts like justice, morals, fairness, etc. My criticisms of Piaget have been discussed in the work done with Joe Kincheloe in postformal thinking (Kincheloe & Steinberg, 1993). Our main issue was that Piaget as the final word in youth construction was exactly that ... and there are no final words. Piaget's developmentalist approaches are limited, essentialistic, and not capable of considering the nuances of youth ... especially in a postmodern era. We cannot work with youth, teach youth, or facilitate youth empowerment for leadership using the tired methods of developmentalism... with a redefined notion of youth, adulthood, and the cultural capital of technology and cyberspace, the development of youth has changed (of course, I would argue that the Piagetian model never created the appropriate read on youth).

Youth development is not in stages: it is culturally and socially defined by the surroundings and experience of each young adult. Facilitating youth to become socially aware and ethical leaders requires a deep read of the lived world of each young man or woman. There are no Coveyesque or Tony Robbinsian ways to methodologize youth, no applicable Fullanization that can take place to acknowledge the importance of working with youth to create individualized and contextualized leadership empowerment. The discussions with youth on empowerment and leadership must be tentative and on-going, and they must be done with those who *like* youth, who are not afraid of youth, and who are committed to a vision of engaged youth leadership.

A Transformative Critical Pedagogical Youth Leadership

We must ask, in the Freirean fashion of dialogue: *what can be done in youth leadership?* What is it we are trying to facilitate and enact? Freire (1970) reminds us that empowerment cannot be taught; rather, we can act as conduits to creating safe spaces and opportunities for empowerment/enlightenment to take place. As critical educators, we learn first to view the world from the eyes of those who are not part of the dominant culture. In this case, we view from the perspectives and ways in which youth see the world. How do youth see power? Do they identify with their place in the world, in the web of reality? Do they recognize opportunities? Are they comfortable with becoming leaders and mentors? What is it like to be a young man or woman today? How can one organize? Can character be built? What are the ethics of leadership? How does trust fit in with leadership? What communication skills are needed in leadership? Is there an *attitude* of leadership? Leaders are not born, they develop, and it is our mandate to secure dialogue and place in which to mentor and usher in development. Youth leadership in a critical sense includes character, responsibility, respect, and knowledge. Those who work with youth to create viable leadership opportunities acknowledge each of these traits ... and in this context, I would assert that respect is paramount in youth engagment. Our work with youth should be committed to facilitating the development of a democratic citizen, one who is conscious of being part of a whole, of society.

We encourage and mentor the notions that a young leader learns to articulate vision and understands her or his place within power structures and society, in general. We encourage leadership by doing and modeling and by seeking/researching those who lead but may not be known as *leaders*. I often use the example of the Canadian athlete, Terry Fox, a young amputee with cancer, who determined to run the width of Canada in order to bring awareness to cancer research. Fox began in Newfoundland with little fanfare, just a kid with a metal leg and a vision. Momentum gathered, and he became a symbol of persistence, faith, and leadership. Fox was a leader who did not seek to lead but to do good work. Leadership can be created by good works. This is not to confuse the notion of leader with role models or heroes. Often media-driven, those who are defined as role models are part of the Hollywoodization of leadership. Many are called heroes but incorrectly. A hero is one who does not seek to do heroic deeds but is thrust into being a hero through altruistic motivation and selflessness. It is an important pedagogical act to differentiate between a leader and a role model or hero. A leader does not aspire to be 'followed,' but she or he aspires merely to do, as I said earlier, *good work*. Paulo Freire also serves as an example of a leader, a quiet intellectual with political indignation, who was imprisoned and exiled; Freire didn't seek fame; he sought to create socially just dialogue which would serve to open paths to empowerment. Engaging in a conversation about youth leadership demands that youth identify those who serve to define leadership and good work. Part of a critical pedagogy of youth leadership asks that young men and women deliberate upon what characteristics a youth leader needs and who exemplifies those characteristics.

Youth can be engaged in defining youth leadership; discussions about listening, respect, desire to learn, sharing, delegation, lifetime learning, are all part of coming to terms with leadership qualities. We ask when one should lead and when a leader supports another to lead. Leadership also means giving up the lead if necessary. Youth should be leaders; they are leaders, however, with the decades of seeing youth as hoodlums, ganstas, thugs, and reprobates, it will take time to change, not only society's view of youth, but the self-identity of young men and women themselves.

Only a Beginning

Avoiding the platitude-laden liberal tripe about youth, we name the needs, issues, and social conditions surrounding our youth. We act as mentors and treat youth as young leaders... younger colleagues, engaging in respect and collegiality as we create a safe and healthy leadership vision. We ask that youth contribute to the vision, that it is not imposed upon them, and that we assist them in discovering their abilities and potentials as leaders. We do not create a defined *leader* but a flexible view of one who leads; some will be tacit leaders, some will be overt, some will share leadership, and some will support it... youth leaders are not the new curricular thing, the new black of pedagogical lexicons; youth leaders are necessary to nurture in order to create a healthy and optimistic environment.

A critical pedagogy of transformative youth leadership can impact youth in a global context, creating a space for youth leadership studies, research, mentorship, internships, and empowerment.

References

Freire, P. (1970). *Pedagogy of the Oppressed.* London: Continuum Books.

Kincheloe, J. L., & Steinberg, S. R. (1993). ""A Tentative Description of Post-Formal Thinking: The Critical Confrontation with Cognitive Theory." *Harvard Educational Review, 63,* 3, Fall.

CHAPTER 37

Cultural Studies of Youth Culture Aesthetics as Critical Aesthetic Education

Michael B. MacDonald

Introduction

Instead of choosing between instilling youth with an appreciation of artistic culture (art history) or training youth for professional life in art production (performance), youth art educators might choose *conscientização* through critical aesthetic education. Paulo Freire's *conscientização* "can be literally translated as the process used to raise somebody's awareness" (Cruz, 2013, p. 171) but is richer than this. It is

> the process in which men [and women], not as recipients, but as knowing subjects, achieve a deepening awareness both of the sociocultural reality that shapes their lives and of their capacity to transform that reality. (Freire, 1970, p. 519)

From Plato, to Matthew Arnold, to Theador Adorno, it has been understood that youth are molded by cultural education. Plato encouraged art education that would influence the development of youth taste in ways that would support the state. Arnold worried about the loss of culture with the rise of cultural industries. Adorno, relatedly, worried about cultural industries transforming people into empty-headed consumers powerless to tell good art from bad. Thinkers in this school all champion aesthetic education by way of cultural appreciation. It is thought that youth taught to appreciate the masterworks of European culture will come into possession of *culture*. I am going to suggest a different approach: that youth are already fully engaged in culture, and that in a democracy, we do not need to instill culture from positions of power, but instead to provide teachers and youth opportunities and capacities to make decisions about their participation in the formation of their culture. Instead of making aesthetic decisions for youth, we might develop an approach to art education that is a 'critical' study of aesthetic. I believe this will lead to what we really want, *conscientização*, and there is good reason for this hunch.

Since at least the 1950s, but perhaps since the jazz age of the 1930s, progressive youth art cultures have been engines of individual and social transformation. At the center of these transformations (think jazz, counter-culture, festival culture, DIY, Punk, Riot Grrrl, HipHop Kulture, EDM) are processes of consciousness-raising related to art production, aesthetic *conscientização*. To understand how this occurs, we need to develop a *cultural studies of aesthetics*.

But why do this? What is wrong with the current form of aesthetic education? First, there is little in the way of aesthetic education actually being offered. Nearly all art education is either art production (doing it) or art history (what has been done), and little time is placed on the hows and whys of art practice. Practices that are little studied are seldom taught. This means, in the North American context, that youth are surrounded by generations of popular music forms, many of them historically significant, that are still not taught in school. There is no point waiting for school curriculum and school text books to catch up. Instead, I propose teaching students to do cultural studies of aesthetics, to transform art appreciation classes into cultural studies of aesthetics classes.

In the first part of this chapter, through a discussion of aesthetics, I will illustrate the way that cultural studies of aesthetics reframes what we currently have, a colonial aesthetic education. Traditional art educators should not read this as an attack on European Fine-Art Culture (EFA); I am not proposing that we elevate popular practices over fine-arts practices, but that we level the playing field by developing a cultural approach to the study of all forms of art culture. Cultural studies of aesthetics begins by recognizing fine-art culture as one culturally informed aesthetic approach among many. To expand on this point, a short history of aesthetics is necessary to appreciate the hurdle that we are about to collectively jump.

The next step is to see youth culture as important sites of informal learning from which formal education can learn. To do this, I will do a cultural study of HipHop Kulture aesthetics. I will conclude with a call for doing cultural studies of aesthetics work together with students, teachers, and community arts practitioners, as a practice of critical aesthetic education. I think that this is our best chance to develop *conscientização* in aesthetic education, to build bridges with youth and the cultures that they bring with them to school, and is a model of art education that educators, policymakers, communities, and administrators can get behind.

Aesthetics

bell hooks (1990) told us that "many underclass black people who do not know conventional academic theoretical language are thinking critically about aesthetics. The richness of their thoughts is rarely documented in books" (p. 112). I want to expand on this and say that many *people* are thinking critically about aesthetics, but do not have access to Aesthetics, an elite philosophical practice of writing about art. But aesthetics does not need to be something only philosophers are permitted to do. Quite the contrary: philosophical aesthetics is not the only discourse on aesthetics.

In fact, an exhaustive study of all academic aesthetics may still not prepare you to understand the HipHop Kulture concept of *flow*, or the jazz concept of *swing*. If you wish to study fine-arts culture, then you may delight in reading philosophical aesthetics. But if you delight in the deep throb of an electronic kick drum, those books may not be the place for you. Much popular music culture is not related to European notions of creativity or expressiveness. These cultural forms developed in North American urban contexts and are distinct. So, if, as Plato and Adorno noted, aesthetic education informs consciousness, what is at stake by not recognizing that popular culture is aesthetically distinct from Fine-Art Culture? To answer this question, we need to have a definition of aesthetics.

In his question about understanding reason's role in the Enlightenment, 18th-century philosopher Alexander Baumgarten began to puzzle over a complex relationship between intellect and perception. Baumgarten noted that the senses work to acquire information from the environment, fed to the brain by way of perception. The senses provide complex information that the mind works to sort out. The mind sorts sense information into meaning.

Baumgarten recognized that art meaning emerged from the crossroads of conceptual, emotional, historical, and physical information. He and others recognized this as a new and interesting subject area that he called Aesthetics, the science of how things are cognized by means of the senses. Unfortunately, this tidy definition would not last long. By 1790, Immanuel Kant redefined aesthetics as the study of the beautiful, a definition that has exerted far greater impact and limited the subjects practitioners might be equipped to survey. Perhaps if aesthetics had remained a scientific study of the relationship between perception and meaning in relation to art, it may have become a cross-cultural study of expressive practices. But this was not to be so.

A Cultural Definition of Aesthetics

In recent years, there have been some signs of a return to Baumgarten's ideas. German complexity sociologist Niklas Luhmann (2000) has suggested a redefinition of aesthetics: the study of perception and communication in relation to art. Luhmann began with the premise that the inner world of each human is separated from other inner worlds. Within each inner world, a constant flood of information is registered by the nervous system. These data are registered by the brain and understood by the mind. The mind, what Luhmann called the psychic system, deals with information by treating it as communication resources. For Luhmann, human experience is made possible by communication. We understand the world by first internalizing a communication system; only then can we 'understand' the world. Learning, therefore, the acquisition of communication resources, opens up ways of knowing the world. Further, he argued that social groups are formed by and through communication. From here it can be said that aesthetics is the study of art as a *special form of communication* that plays with familiar or unfamiliar communication resources in familiar or unfamiliar ways; that meddles with the links that bind perception to meaning.

Separate from Luhmann, but similar in important ways, Gayatri Spivak, in *An Aesthetic Education in the Era of Globalization* (2012), suggested that aesthetic education is the preparation of the imagination for epistemological work. 'Epistemological work' is the meaning process, and 'preparing the imagination' is the teaching and learning process that works with learners, often youth, to become 'aware' of the processes of imagination behind, or underneath, meaning.

In his 2009 book, *Framing Consciousness in Art*, Gregory Minissale suggested two processes of consciousness at work in art: a lower and higher order. In everyday life, the lower order is concerned with perception, while the higher order is interested in the meaning of the perceptions and of acting upon them. Minissale argued, much like Luhmann, that art frames these processes so that the viewer (in visual art) becomes aware of the act of perception, a process called reflexivity. Reflexivity occurs when a viewer recognizes that the viewer has recognized a frame that surrounds and separates 'a thing' from everyday life. This separation draws the viewer into a self-consciousness about the viewer's perception-meaning process.[1] Perception as a lower-order consciousness usually just functions routinely in the basement of experience, then enters into higher-order consciousness. Suddenly and surprisingly, perception emerges from the shadows into the full light of consciousness. Consciousness and perception in an engagement with art get locked in a recursive process where consciousness reflects on the act of perception, and perception feeds consciousness, consciousness reflects on this new information, and perception feeds these to consciousness. John Dewey called this the aesthetic experience, and Arnold Berleant, the aesthetic field. Why do humans do this? Why do we enjoy it? In what ways does this occur in other cultural groups? These are exciting questions, certainly. So it is a source of great disappointment that aesthetic education is limited to art appreciation.

Aesthetic Education as Art Appreciation

A great deal of aesthetic education in formal schooling, when it contends with aesthetics at all, continues to rely upon the disciplinary model. Sometimes this begins with an outright dismissal of aesthetic education in favor of art education. Many young people's first introduction to music education is a teacher writing symbols on a white board saying, "ta-ta-tete-ta, this is music." But of course this is not music, it is a form of literacy developed in the Western Art Music tradition as a social technology to communicate and store musical ideas. In this literary tradition, youth were trained to listen, to read, to perform, to dance to, and ultimately, to appreciate the beautiful. When this cultural group began to expand their sphere of influence, they brought with them art and aesthetic education. The problem is not aesthetics necessarily; in fact this is quite an important discovery. The problem is that Enlightenment-era Europeans mistook a cultural aesthetics for universal aesthetics. The study of the beautiful was not understood to be one expression of aesthetics, but the only approach to the study of perception-meaning. Europeans have art, and everyone else has generalized culture. In *The Darker Side of Western Modernity*, Walter Mignolo (2011) explained:

> That foundation was crucial in the sixteenth century, when European men and institutions began to populate the Americas, founding universities and establishing a system of knowledge, training Indians to paint churches and to legitimize artistic principles and practices that were connected with the symbolic in the control of authority and with the economic in the mutual complicity between economic wealth and the splendor of the arts. From the seventeenth century, European colonies provided the raw material for the foundation of museums of curiosities (Kunstkamera), which later on divided pieces from the non-European world (museums of natural history, of anthropology) from museums of art (primarily European, from the Renaissance on). (pp. 20–21)

This framework gets applied in all colonial situations. Authorities make it their mission to intercede into indigenous symbolic processes.[2] Aesthetics and aesthetic education play a role in this, and continue to do so. From my perspective, that of a European Canadian male, I can see the continuation of cultural colonization at work in the century-long use of residential school education to "kill the Indian in the child."[3] A photographic record of residential school musical bands shows generations of aboriginal youth playing concert band and wind band instruments, symbols of their cultural possession.[4] Plato's observations on aesthetic education as discipline take a sinister turn. The pedagogy of Music appreciation, for instance, works to create young listeners who *appreciate* the masterworks of the dominator culture—youth willing to be disciplined as the "mark of an aesthetically prepared and culturally elevated individual" (Dell'Antonio, 2004, p. 3). Terry Eagleton and Luc Ferry have pointed out that aesthetics is really about an Enlightenment conception of individual and/or personal development and bourgeoisie morality (as cited in Guyer, 2005, p. 30), and less about an inquiry into human practices of expression and reception. Walter Mignolo (2011) has argued that the very notion of Art, upon which Kant's aesthetics is based, is itself a social construction, used as a tool to establish hierarchies of expression that allowed European bourgeois expression to dominate the rest. This strategy elevated European cultural output and defined it as art, which thereby cast aspersions on the expressive practices of other cultural groups, terming them folklore, craft, popular culture, etc. Mignolo termed this technique colonial difference.

Cultural Studies of Aesthetics: Black Arts Movement and HipHop Kulture

For the better part of the last century, we have been living through what might be called a struggle for the democratization of aesthetics. I mark this period at the advent of audio recording and the rise of jazz and popular music industries. Aesthetic education was no longer reserved for formal educational institutions. Networks of artists engaged with youth culture and formed informal learning processes that fed into cultural industries. Although little understood and little researched, informal learning practices provided the educational basis for culturally located processes of art education rich enough to power the emergence of popular culture. This was not a product of disciplined youth listeners, but rebellious cultural creators. Youth culture, supported by cultural industries, successfully toppled the cultural dominance of European Fine-Arts culture everywhere except perhaps in state-sponsored institutions. It seems sensible that a transformed aesthetic education in formal educational institutions would begin by learning more about the informal learning practiced in youth culture.

The beginning of this process is going to be difficult, because the colonial difference is so deeply engrained in our social fabric that its existence often has the feel of 'common sense.' Take Hip Hop for instance: even jazz musicians enact the colonial difference in discussion of HipHop Kulture:

> Formally trained musicians criticize rap music DJs' assumed lack of knowledge of basic Western music theory, which, for some is the sine qua non of a composer. The musician-composer and Pulitzer Prize winner Wynton Marsalis summarizes this popular opinion: 'When you get to rap music, you can't reduce anymore. When you get past that, it's not music anymore'. (Keyes, 2002, p. 5)

As Hip Hop emerged into popularity in the 1980s, the response to it by the dominant classes was framed along the colonial difference, and used similar moral concerns that would have been familiar to Matthew Arnold in the late 19th century. Ronald Reagan's conservatism was a return to "old fashioned Republicanism" (Dallek, 1984, p. vii) that "functioned as the cultural and historical sign, for many whites, of the 'real' America" (Gray, 1995, p. 16). Few outside of HipHop Kulture could see the rising popular success of Hip Hop as a challenge to colonial difference, an aesthetic emerging from the lived urban realities of its practitioners.

HipHop Kulture challenges the colonial difference. In a 2004 Temple University lecture, KRS-ONE remarked that dominator culture tries to convince you that "everything that you have has no value." The only way to get validated is to buy into the commodities, practices, and institutions of dominator culture. But as he explained, these same institutions have created frameworks designed to exclude, thus making cultural validation impossible.

Gregory Bateson (1972) called this impossible situation a double bind (pp. 271–278). He explained that it is a technique of domination without its outward appearance. It works when a social actor, as a functionary of a system, makes two contradictory demands. This strategy is powerful because, as KRS-ONE illustrated, there is no way to solve the dilemma of the double bind within the system. Inside the system you will forever remain trapped in its double pincers.

KRS-ONE explained that Hip Hop was a movement to "create an entirely different community." In this sense, HipHop Kulture is the emergence of a postcolonial aesthetic culture. The emergence and success of HipHop Kulture are proof of cultural aesthetics. As long as the system of dominator culture refuses to validate cultural aesthetics, it remains possible to live in the fiction of a universal aesthetics. But this fiction is being deconstructed. While bell hooks argued that black people's aesthetics ideas were not documented in books, this is not exactly the case.

Inspired by Civil Rights and Black Power discourses of the 1960s, the Black Arts Movement was radically opposed to any concept of the artist that "alienates him from his community," (Neal, 1968), and was "the period extending somewhat beyond the defining decade of 1964 (the year of Malcolm X's rupture with the Nation of Islam) to 1974 (the year of Amiri Baraka's renunciation of absolute Black nationalism), during which the category of 'Blackness' served as the dominant sign of African American cultural activity (Benston, 2000, p. 3). Black Arts built on Alain Locke's 1925 publication, *The New Negro*, and upon the Harlem Renaissance concept of 'Blackness.' Kimberly Benston (2000) observed:

> Blackness … a term of multiple, often conflicting, implications which, taken together, signal black America's effort to articulate its own conditions of possibility. At one moment, blackness may signify a reified essence posited at the end of a revolutionary 'meta-language' projecting the community toward 'something not included here'; at another moment, blackness may indicate a self-interpreting process which simultaneously 'makes and unmakes' black identity in the ceaseless flux of historical change. (pp. 3–4)

By encouraging African American artists to seek inspiration from an ancestral heritage as well as from the ghetto community, Locke believed a unique art "would emerge" (Fine, 1971, p. 374). Black Arts joined with Black Power for political and cultural empowerment within ghetto communities:

> The Black Art Movement artists are linked to Black separatist politics and Black Nationalism. The social, political and economic conditions of the country during the 1960's gave birth to the latter group of young, militant artists, who, disdaining the traditions of Western art, seek to communicate with their brothers and sisters in the ghetto. (Fine, 1971, p. 374)

This was the emergence of a powerful cultural aesthetics, and its success depended on creating an alternative, what Spivak (2012) has called, doing aesthetics 'from below.' This occurs with the cultural and sometimes militant elevation of "African-derived American Culture" (Caponi, 1999, pp. 17–31) that should be understood as an emerging into consciousness of a new paradigm. The Black Arts Movement was postcolonial cultural aesthetics education designed to liberate oppressed Black youth. Black Arts mentors supported young and mostly African American artists to look for inspiration in their home communities; to recognize their unique perspective, their unique imagination; and to use their arts to help rejuvenate their community culture. Often this would take the shape of "boldly patterned murals painted on the decaying walls of ghetto buildings" (Fine, 1971, p. 374), community theatre, or literature based on street art and inner-city life, emerging from place-based imagination, that does not require acceptance from (colonial) fine-art institutions.

As the political elements of the Black Power Movement were finding their aesthetic expression in Black Arts, they found new expression "in the aesthetics of Afro-American dramatists, poets, choreographers, musicians, and novelists" who were defining "the world in their own terms" (Neal, 1968, p. 39). These elements, championed by a Black, inner-city avant-garde, posed a challenge to aesthetics, stripping it of any illusion that it could claim universality:

> In critical theory, Baraka was instrumental in the creation of what became the 'black aesthetic' of the 1970s, as well as the 'vernacularism' of the 1980s, demanding that African American literature and music be examined in the context of the culture that gave rise to it, with particular focus on the oral traditions of storytelling, sermonizing, and music of all sorts—sacred and secular. (Caponi, 1999, p. 21)

Black Arts works to undo the aesthetics double bind, and creates a new aesthetic order rooted in local expressive practices that lead to critical awareness and liberation: *conscientização*. We see this in the words of Baraka, writing about Black Arts aesthetics in a language that would resonate with Paulo Freire and Augusto Boal (2006):

> Our theatre will show victims so that their brothers in the audience will be better able to understand that they are the brothers of victims, and that they themselves are blood brothers. And what we show must cause the blood to rush, so that pre-revolutionary temperaments will be bathed in this blood, and it will cause their deepest souls to move, and they will find themselves tensed and clenched, even ready to die, at what the soul has been taught. We will scream and cry, murder, run through the streets in agony, if it means some soul will be moved, moved to actual life understanding of what the world is, and what it ought to be. (in Baraka & Harris, 1991, p. 76)

Baraka's lifelong interest in showing "what the world is" is echoed in the street logic of HipHop Kulture. Marvin Gladney (1995) characterized this heritage:

> Black art has always been rooted in the anger felt by Afrikan-Americans, and hiphop culture has remained true to many of the convictions and aesthetic criteria that evolved out of the Black Arts Movement of the '60s, including calls for social relevance, originality, and a focused dedication to produce art that challenges American mainstream artistic expression…. Public Enemy's Chuck D refers to hiphop as the "CNN" of the Black community. (p. 291)

The Black Arts movement helped to prepare a political "movement poetics" (Smethurst, 2003, p. 268) that helped create a symbolic politicization of the HipHop Kulture voice that as Rachel Sullivan (2003) pointed out, has subjective impact: "African American rap fans are not arguing that rap leads them into social protest, they seem to be indicating that it offers a counter-dominant message that they use as an affirmation of their experience" (p. 616). It is precisely this self-affirmation that characterizes critical aesthetic education, and why I think the study of cultural aesthetics like HipHop Kulture is an important basis for developing a culturally informed approach to music education that I call Critical Aesthetic Education.

Cultural Studies of Aesthetics as Critical Aesthetic Education

A critical aesthetic education begins with the cultural studies of aesthetics. This requires that you and your students (or teachers) develop relationships with local arts practitioners 'to do' cultural studies together. I follow Handel Wright's (2003) assertion that cultural studies is more than theorizing, it is "the idea of articulating theory, empirical research, and service learning as interrelated elements of cultural studies work … cultural studies as social justice praxis" (p. 807). Wright suggested that we begin by "taking cultural studies personally" (p. 809), as an epistemological mission of sorts, dedicated to understanding our lives within our cultures, and our societies.

The work of documenting cultural aesthetics and then of building critical aesthetic education is only going to happen with a variety of partnerships. Moreover, it is through the developing of these partnerships—between professors, teachers, students, cultural aesthetic community members, government agencies, boards of education—that we begin to re-write and undo colonial difference. Critical Aesthetic Education, because of our colonial history, necessarily begins with recognizing the impact of colonization upon our imaginations. This is a personal commitment to decolonization that will help us develop the epistemological curiosity (Freire, 2001, p. 35) necessary for this difficult intellectual work. Taking cultural studies personally will help to build the type of imagination and/or consciousness necessary for rigorous critical work. As Freire (2001) wrote:

> To think correctly demands profundity and not superficiality in the comprehension and interpretation of the facts. It presupposes an openness that allows for the revision of conclusions; it recognizes not only the possibility of making a new choice or a new evaluation but also the right to do so. (p. 39)

I have suggested above that a place to begin is the deconstruction of the colonial difference, a starting point Freire (2001) would approve: "it is equally part of right thinking to reject decidedly any and every form of discrimination. Preconceptions of race, class, or sex offend the essence of human dignity and constitute a radical negation of democracy" (p. 41). And it is with this concern for the development of epistemological curiosity that I conclude with three concerns that you might take up in your cultural studies of aesthetics.

Conclusion: Three Topics for Cultural Studies of Aesthetics

The first is a concern about the reification of culture. Even as I wrote about the Black Arts Movement foundations of HipHop Kulture, I am self-conscious about participating in the cementing of a fixed historical narrative for a culture. HipHop Kulture is constantly informed and constantly in flux. In the HipHop Kulture community in Edmonton, Canada, where I live and work, there are a variety of histories, and a variety of staring points, that weave a richly textured and complex culture together. It is not homogeneous, nor even a single community. When I use the word, *culture*, I mean a symbolic learning network of individuals connected by shared communication. Culture is a learning system, and a system that learns, changes. When culture stops being a learning system it becomes a fixed form, a commodity, and stops being an engine of human development. Black culture in the Black Arts

Movement is therefore different from the Black culture that Mark Anthony Neal 2002) discussed as the post-soul aesthetic:

> In the post-soul aesthetic I am surmising that there is an aesthetic centre within contemporary black popular culture that at various moments considers issues like deindustrialization, desegregation, the corporate annexation of black popular expression, cybernization in the workforce, the globalization of finance and communication, the general commodification of black life and culture, and the pro-liferation of black "meta-identities," while continuously collapsing on modern concepts of blackness and reanimating "Premodern" (African?) concepts of blackness. I am also suggesting that this aesthetic ultimately renders many 'traditional' tropes of blackness dated and even meaningless; in its borrowing from black modern traditions, it is so consumed with its contemporary existential concerns that such traditions are not just called into question but obliterated. (pp. 2–3)

A cultural studies of youth aesthetics will have to maintain a focus on the dynamic qualities of culture and resist the reification of youth culture, and of race, of sex.

The second concern is what Tim Wise (2010) called post-racial liberalism, that he defined as a "rhetoric of racial transcendence and a public policy agenda of colorblind universalism" with

> adherents dating back at least forty years, and which emerged after the civil rights revolution had largely accomplished its immediate goals ... and following several years of violent uprisings in urban centers thanks to frustration at the slow pace of change—especially with regard to economic opportunity—some of the nation's scholars and public intellectuals began to turn against race-specific remedies for lingering social inequalities. Beginning in the late 1970s ... and extending through to the Obama campaign for presidency, post-racial liberalism has advocated a de-emphasis of racial discrimination and race-based remedies for inequality, in favor of class-based or "universal" programs of uplift: from job creation politics to better education funding to health care reform. (p. 16)

Post-racial liberalism threatens to return us, perhaps ironically (but not humorously), to the very same Enlightenment values that Walter Mignolo identified as the basis of colonial difference. As I have tried to show, universalism is a cover for cultural hegemony. Colourblind universalism is the dismissal of cultural diversity, the turning back of the gains we have made. What is left after post-racial liberalism is not an absence of culture, but a false cultural universalism, a singular identity by which to dismiss all others. A cultural studies of aesthetics will need to grapple with communities of difference; how people can be together in community and in culture *and* also recognize their diversity.

Finally, my third concern, one already well documented in cultural studies, is the impact of neolib-eral cultural production on local culture. Henry Giroux (2009) warned that, "in the society of consum-ers no one can become a subject without first turning into a commodity" (p. 31). The production of a cultural commodity transforms culture from a learning system into a thing. Cultural appreciation is based upon this fixed view of culture. Neoliberal cultural production changes the framework of cultural appreciation because of cultural value to cultural appreciation based on commodity success. Central to the concern about neoliberal cultural production is the impact that it has on individual consciousness. It has been shown, time and again, that these cultural commodities, produced for sale by the popular music industry, target young people to "deal with their lack of self-confidence, powerlessness, and the endless indignities heaped upon them in a consumer society" (Giroux, 2009, p. 59) by buying products produced by corporations "which use magnetic resonance imaging (MRI) to map brain patterns and reveal how consumers respond to advertisements or products" (Giroux, 2009, p. 59). This process is called neuromarketing, and it attests to precisely what Plato, Baumgarten, Arnold, and Adorno have suggested, a connection between aesthetics and consciousness.

Instead of working to elevate consciousness in prosocial ways, corporations tend to target and exploit weaknesses, often using ploys that tend towards the anti-social and anti-cultural. It is not their fault; their job is to produce consumers. Youth need critical aesthetic education, not in order to dismiss cultural production, but to 'critically' engage it. Educators need to make it our mission to provide youth the necessary skills to resist a very prepared and equipped sales machine working to create better consumers, not better people. Educators play a frontline role in working with youth to develop *conscientização*, the critical awareness necessary to simultaneously disempower mass marketing and support local cultural production. It is my contention that this cultural resistance is currently being practiced in youth cultures in your community. Instead of 'educated' adults telling youth how to resist, I would suggest making it an educational commitment to work with youth to document existing youth culture resistance movements happening right now in your community. This is cultural studies of aesthetics as aesthetics education.

Notes

1. This draws upon a history of work in phenomenology.
2. Aesthetics is an expression of culture understood as a possession until as late as the 1950s and 1960s. This is now changing. Culture is now more likely to be understood as "The ideas and values, the cosmology, morality, and aesthetics, [that] are expressed in symbols, and so—if the medium is the message—culture could be described as a symbolic system" (Kuper, 2003, p. 227). In the colonial system, the possession of culture was to hold membership in White supremacist-capitalist-patriarchy (hooks, 2003, p. 11).
3. 'About the Commission.' Truth and Reconciliation Commission of Canada, accessible at http://www.trc.ca/websites/trcinstitution/index.php?p=39
4. I would like to thank musicologist, Professor David Gramit, at the University of Alberta, who shared these photographs at a 2012 conference on Intersensory Approaches to the Study of Music in Canada.

References

Adorno, T. W. (1984). *Aesthetic theory* (C. Lenhardt, Trans.). Boston, MA: Routledge & Kegan Paul.
Adorno, T. W. (1991). *The culture industry: Selected essays on a mass culture*. New York, NY: Routledge.
Adorno, T. W., Benjamin, W., Bloch, E., Brecht, B., & Lukacs, G. (1977). *Aesthetics and politics*. New York, NY: Verso.
Alcoff, L. M. (2007). Mignolo's epistemology of coloniality. *CR: The New Centennial Review, 7*(3), 79–101.
Attali, J. (1999). *Noise: The political economy of music* (B. Massumi, Trans.). Minneapolis, MN: University of Minnesota Press.
Baraka, A. (Ed.). (1973). *Black art*. New York, NY: Morrow.
Baraka, A., & Harris, W. J. (1991). *The LeRoi Jones/Amiri Baraka reader*. New York, NY: Thunder's Mouth Press.
Bateson, G. (1972). *Steps to an ecology of mind*. Chicago, IL: University of Chicago Press.
Becker, H. S. (1984). *Art worlds*. Berkeley, CA: University of California Press.
Benjamin, W. (1968). The work of art in the age of mechanical reproduction (H. Zohn, Trans.). In H. Arendt (Ed.), *Illuminations* (pp. 219–253). New York, NY: Harcourt Brace & World.
Benston, K. W. (2000). *Performing Blackness: Enactments of African-American modernism*. New York, NY: Routledge.
Berleant, A. (1991). *Art and engagement*. Philadelphia, PA: Temple University Press.
Berleant, A. (1992). *The aesthetics of environment*. Philadelphia, PA: Temple University Press.
Berleant, A. (1999). Getting along beautifully: Ideas for a social aesthetics. In P. Von Bonsdorff & A. Haapala (Eds.), *Aesthetics in the human environment* (Vol. 6, pp. 12–29). Lahti, Finland: International Institute of Applied Aesthetics.
Berleant, A. (2000). *The aesthetic field*. New York, NY: Cybereditions.
Berleant, A. (2002). Notes for a cultural aesthetic. In V. Sarapik, K. Tüür, & M. Laanemets (Eds.), *Koht ja paik/place and location* (pp. 19–26). Tallinn, Estonia: Eesti Kunstiakadeemia (Estonian Academy of Arts).
Berleant, A. (2004). *Re-thinking aesthetics: Rogue essays on aesthetics and the arts*. Aldershot, UK: Ashgate.
Berleant, A. (2010). *Sensibility and sense: The aesthetic transformation of the human world*. Charlottesville, VA: Imprint Academic.
Bérubé, M. (2005). *The aesthetics of cultural studies*. Malden, MA: Blackwell.
Boal, A. (2006). *The aesthetics of the oppressed* (A. Jackson, Trans.). New York, NY: Routledge.
Bourriaud, N. (2002). *Relational aesthetics* (S. Pleasance, F. Woods, & M. Copeland, Trans.). Dijon, France: Les Presses du réel.
Caponi, G. D. (1999). *Signifyin(g), sanctifyin', & slam dunking: A reader in African American expressive culture*. Amherst, MA: University of Massachusetts Press.
Chamberland, R. (2001). Rap in Canada: Bilingual and multicultural. In T. Mitchell (Ed.), *Global noise* (pp. 306–323). Middletown, CT: Wesleyan University Press.
Cruz, A. L. (2013). Paulo Freire's concept of conscientização. In R. Lake & T. Kress (Eds.), *Paulo Freire's intellectual roots* (pp. 169–182). New York, NY: Bloomsbury.
Dallek, R. (1984). *Ronald Reagan: The politics of symbolism*. Cambridge, MA: Harvard University Press.
Deleuze, G., & Guattari, F. (1983). *Anti-Oedipus: Capitalism and schizophrenia* (R. Hurley, M. Seem, & H. R. Lane, Trans.). Minneapolis, MN: University of Minnesota Press.
Deleuze, G., & Guattari, F. (1987). *A thousand plateaus: Capitalism and schizophrenia* (B. Massumi, Trans.). Minneapolis, MN: University of Minnesota Press.

Dewey, J. (1916). *Democracy and education*. New York, NY: Free Press.

Dewey, J. (1934). *Art as experience*. New York, NY: Capricorn Books.

Dewey, J. (1938). *Experience and education*. New York, NY: Macmillan.

Driscoll, M. P. (1994). *Psychology of learning for instruction*. Boston, MA: Allyn and Bacon.

Du Bois, W. E. B. (1994). *The souls of Black folk*. New York, NY: Dover.

Fine, E. H. (1971). Mainstream, Blackstream and the Black Art Movement. *Art Journal, 30*(4), 374–375.

Forney, K. & Machlis, J. (2007). *The enjoyment of music: An introduction to perceptive listening* (10th ed.). New York, NY: W.W. Norton.

Freire, P. (1970). *Pedagogy of the oppressed* (M. B. Ramos, Trans.). New York, NY: Continuum.

Freire, P. (2001). *Pedagogy of freedom: Ethics, democracy, and civic courage*. Lanham, MA: Rowman & Littlefield.

Freire, P. (2010). *Education for a critical consciousness*. New York, NY: Continuum.

Giroux, H. A. (1997). *Pedagogy and the politics of hope: Theory, culture, and schooling: A critical reader*. Boulder, CO: Westview Press.

Giroux, H. A. (2000). Public pedagogy as cultural politics: Stuart Hall and the 'crisis' of culture. *Cultural Studies, 14*(2), 341–360.

Giroux, H. A. (2003). *The abandoned generation: Democracy beyond the culture of fear*. New York, NY: Palgrave Macmillan.

Giroux, H. A. (2004). Public pedagogy and the politics of neo-liberalism: Making the political more pedagogical. *Policy Futures in Education, 2*(3–4), 494–503.

Giroux, H. A. (2009). *Youth in a suspect society: Democracy or disposability?* New York, NY: Palgrave Macmillan.

Gladney, M. J. (1995). The Black Arts Movement and hip hop. *African American Review, 29*(2), 291–301.

Gray, H. (1995). *Watching race: Television and the struggle for Blackness*. Minneapolis, MN: University of Minnesota Press.

Guyer, P. (2005). *Values of beauty: Historical essays in aesthetics*. New York, NY: Cambridge University Press.

hooks, b. (1990). *Yearning: Race, gender, and cultural politics*. Boston, MA: South End Press.

hooks, b. (2003). *Teaching community: A pedagogy of hope*. New York, NY: Routledge.

Horkheimer, M., & Adorno, T. W. (2002). *Dialectic of enlightenment: Philosophical fragments* (E. F. N. Jephcott, Trans.). Stanford, CA: Stanford University Press.

Jones, L. (1968). *Black music*. New York, NY: William Morrow.

Kerman, J., & Tomlinson, G. (2008). *Listen*. Boston, MA: Bedford/St. Martin's.

Keyes, C. (2002). *Rap music and street consciousness*. Urbana, IL: University of Illinois Press.

Krims, A. (2000). *Rap music and the poetics of identity*. New York, NY: Cambridge University Press.

Kuper, A. (2003). *Culture: The anthropologists' account*. Cambridge, MA: Harvard University Press.

Luhmann, N. (2000). *Art as a social system*. Stanford, CA: Stanford University Press.

MacDonald, M. (2012). Hip hop citizens: Local hip hop and the production of democratic grassroots change in Alberta. In B. J. Porfilio & M. J. Viola (Eds.), *Hip hop(e): The cultural practice and critical pedagogy of international hip hop* (pp. 95–109). New York, NY: Peter Lang.

Marple, H. D. (1975). *The world of music*. Boston, MA: Allyn and Bacon.

Martinez, T. A. (1997). Popular culture as oppositional culture: Rap as resistance. *Sociological Perspectives, 40*(2), 265–286.

Mignolo, W. D. (2000). *Local histories/global designs: Coloniality, subaltern knowledges, and border thinking*. Princeton, NJ: Princeton University Press.

Mignolo, W. D. (2011). *The darker side of Western modernity: Global futures, decolonial options*. Durham, NC: Duke University Press.

Minissale, G. (2009). *Framing consciousness in art: Transcultural perspectives*. New York, NY: Rodopi.

Neal, L. (1968). The Black Arts movement. *The Drama Review: TDR, 12*(4), 28–39.

Neal, M. A. (2002). *Soul babies: Black popular culture and the post-soul aesthetic*. New York, NY: Routledge.

Plato. (2000). *The republic*. (B. Jowett, Trans.). New York, NY: Dover.

Rancière, J. (2000). What aesthetics can mean (B. Holmes, Trans.). In P. Osborne (Ed.), *From an aesthetic point of view: Philosophy, art, and the senses*. London, UK: Serpent's Tail.

Rancière, J. (2005). From politics to aesthetics? *Paragraph, 28*(1), 13–25.

Rancière, J. (2007). *The politics of aesthetics: The distribution of the sensible* (G. Rockhill, Trans.). London, UK: Continuum.

Rancière, J. (2010). *Dissensus: On politics and aesthetics*. New York, NY: Continuum.

Robson, M. (2005). Jacques Rancière: Aesthetic communities. *Paragraph, 28*(1), 77–95.

Smethurst, J. (2003). 'Pat your foot and turn the corner': Amiri Baraka, the Black Arts movement, and the poetics of a popular avant-garde. *African American Review, 37*(2–3), 261–270.

Spivak, G. C. (2012). *An aesthetic education in the era of globalization*. Cambridge, MA: Harvard University Press.

Sullivan, R. E. (2003). Rap and race: It's got a nice beat, but what about the message? *Journal of Black Studies, 33*(5), 605–622.

Tuhiwai Smith, L. (2012). *Decolonizing methodologies: Research and indigenous peoples*. New York, NY: Zed Books.

Werner, C. H. (1994). *Playing the changes: From Afro-modernism to the jazz impulse*. Urbana, IL: University of Illinois Press.

Williams, L. (2010). Hip hop as a site of public pedagogy. In J. A. Sandlin, B. D. Schultz, & J. Burdick (Eds.), *Handbook of public pedagogy: Education and learning beyond schooling* (pp. 221–232). New York, NY: Routledge.

Wise, T. (2010). *Color-blind: The rise of post-racial politics and the retreat from racial equity*. San Francisco, CA: City Lights Books.

Wright, H. K. (2003). Cultural studies as praxis: (Making) an autobiographical case. *Cultural Studies, 17*(6), 805–822.

CHAPTER 38

"Too Young for the Marches but I Remember These Drums"
Recommended Pedagogies for Hip Hop–Based Education and Youth Studies

Bettina L. Love

The first function of education is to provide identity. —Akbar (1998)

I Don't Know Much, But I Know What Moves Me!

My mother and father never really shared much with me about how they met, where they grew up, who my great-grandparents were, or how two people with Southern roots landed in upstate New York. Similarly, my teachers never discussed my culture or heritage, and never linked my experiences at school to my community or home life. Of course, in school, we discussed the usual Black History events and icons—The Underground Railroad, Dr. Martin Luther King, Jr., Rosa Parks, and the Civil Rights Movement. As a youth, I respected those events and viewed those freedom fighters as heroes, but I could not emotionally connect to such larger-than-life figures. I had trouble comprehending how my life and struggles as an urban youth linked to that of Parks or King—perhaps because they were only discussed during Black History Month, or maybe because I was never told the full story of their brilliance, sacrifice, and humanity. Moreover, the process of schooling and the marginalization of Black History left me less connected to my history as an urban youth, someone of African descent, and an African American. I had little understanding of who I was in relation to my community and heritage. While I was not completely lost—as my skin, speech, and body movements connected me to my local community—I ultimately had no sense of who I was outside of my zip code.

When I was around twelve or fourteen years old, something happened to my view of the world that changed my relationship to my culture completely. I had listened to Hip Hop music throughout my childhood through my older brother, who is fourteen years my senior, but as I reached adolescence, Hip Hop became more than just music to me. I began to view Hip Hop as my culture, my teacher, and, most importantly, my way of grasping concepts that adults claimed eluded my young mind.

444

For example, in the late 1980s and early 1990s, my working-class neighborhood fell to drugs and crime, one corner at a time. Rappers like Chuck D, Nas, Queen Latifah, Jay Z, and KRS-One boldly explained to me the nature of this transformation, and all its consequences. KRS-One taught me about my African and African American history, Jungle Brothers and De La Soul introduced me to jazz and Afrocentrism, and Lauryn Hill became my big sister with powerful advice to conquer the social ills of my community.

For me, Hip Hop connected my everyday life and the lives of my friends to the greater contributions and struggles of African people and African Americans living in the United States. Furthermore, Hip Hop's sound—influenced by the African drums, slave songs coded in metaphors and euphemisms, jazz, soul, rhythm and blues, funk, and Civil Rights freedom songs—sonically transported me to the Motherland, the March on Washington, the L.A. janitors' strikes, the 1968 Chicano student walkouts, and the 1992 L.A. riots (Love, 2012). Thus, in the words of Common (2007), I was, "too young for the marches but I remember these drums" (track 12). Hip Hop gave me a sense of identity and an emotional wholeness filled with love, anger, hope, and youthfulness.

Thus, I know first-hand the transformative power of Hip Hop. It is an unflinching culture of urban youth rooted in the principles of democracy. Hip Hop represents youths' "critical modes of self-expression," reflective of their yearning to be heard, recognized, and included in the democratic process (Prier, 2012, p. xxxv). From an educational perspective, when Hip Hop merges with the pedagogies of "cultural connectedness" (Paris, 2012), the "funds of knowledge" (Moll & Gonzalez, 1994) and everyday realities of students, a form of education arises that "recognizes and celebrates how youth move, speak, think, create, and relate to the world" (Love, 2012, p. 109).

This chapter will explore the significance of merging the field of youth and Hip Hop studies with the transformative and empowering teaching methods of culturally sustaining pedagogy (CSP) and reality pedagogy (RP). The integration and amalgamation of pedagogies like CSP and RP within the field of youth and Hip Hop studies builds on the long-standing use of critical pedagogy in the field to position the culture, social context, learning styles, and experiences of students at the center of the learning experience. More specifically, I will argue that Hip Hop music and culture can be a catalyst for ensuring that Black and Brown youth know their rich African, African American, and Latina/o heritage, which is the foundation of Hip Hop and the fight against oppression. In that same vein, I contend that before youth can attempt the critical endeavor of examining issues of race, class, power, and place, they must first understand their cultural heritage and its significance, as well as their everyday realities as urban youth.

Theory

In 2009, Christopher Emdin introduced the teaching framework of RP to the field of science education. Emdin (2011) defined RP as a teaching method that "focuses on the cultural understandings of students within a particular social space, like a science classroom" (p. 286). RP consists of what Emdin (2011) called the "5 C's": cogenerative dialogues, coteaching, cosmopolitanism, context, and content. Cogenerative dialogues, the first C, are structured dialogues that build on students' Hip Hop identities and familiarity with the Hip Hop communal tradition of cyphers. Cyphers are one of the most long-standing cultural rituals of Hip Hop (Love, 2013). The second C, coteaching, encourages students to be the "expert at pedagogy ... while the teacher is positioned as a novice who is learning how to teach" (Emdin, 2011, p. 288). Coteaching allows teachers to study how students learn from one another in order to better understand students' learning styles, and provides an opportunity for students to learn in ways that reflect their realities.

The third C, cosmopolitanism, is based on the philosophical construct that human beings are responsible for each other, and that individual differences should be valued. Context, the fourth C, connects students' home lives and culture to their classrooms through community and culture artifacts.

Context allows students to bring to the classroom artifacts that represent who they are and where they come from. Emdin (2011) wrote, "[w]hen students can physically see and examine artifacts both in the classrooms and in their home communities, the divides between the school world and their real lives are broken down" (p. 291). Finally, content, the fifth C, evolves out of the willingness of the teacher to acknowledge his or her limitations with academic content, and to explore and learn with students.

As a teaching framework, RP sets the stage and tone for constructing classrooms where both teachers and students are co-creating and learning from the realities of students' lives and cultural knowledge. Although Emdin's work is situated for urban science classrooms, his five C's can transform education through all disciplines. However, I recommend combining RP with CSP, as explained in further detail below, due to the dire need in the field of youth studies to embrace the realities of students, while maintaining and enhancing students' knowledge of their culture, history, and traditions. Only then can educators begin the process of examining oppression, especially in the field of Hip Hop and youth studies.

Turning now to CSP, Django Paris introduced this teaching method in 2012 with his article "Culturally Sustaining Pedagogy: A Needed Change in Stance, Terminology, and Practice." Paris (2012) wrote that CSP "seeks to perpetuate and foster—to sustain—linguistic, literate, and cultural pluralism as part of the democratic project of schooling" (p. 93). CSP embraces students' heritage while recognizing that culture is fluid and ever-changing. Furthermore, CSP is rooted in the ideological premise of cultural pluralism and schooling as a fundamental component of democracy. Establishing a teaching framework that embraces cultural pluralism is vital, because U.S. schools, more than ever before, are multiethnic and multilingual spaces. Schools are vibrant with culture, yet indolent with curriculum and teaching practices that reflect the diversity of students.

Both RP and CSP are outgrowths of "culturally relevant pedagogy" (CRP), inspired by the seminal work of Gloria Ladson-Billings, who coined the term in 1995. CRP "produce[s] students who can achieve academically, produce[s] students who can demonstrate cultural competence, and develop[s] students who can both understand and critique the existing social order" (Ladson-Billings, 1995, p. 474). However, Paris (2012) contended that CRP does not explicitly support the "linguistic and cultural dexterity and plurality necessary for success and access in our demographically changing U.S. and global schools and communities" (p. 95). Today's schools are filled with Black and Brown faces, especially in urban areas. Overall, more than 45% of school-age students are minorities, according to the Pew Research Hispanic Center (2013). In 2011, the Hispanic student population among grades pre-k through 12 reached 23.9%. Furthermore, in 2011, there were more than 2 million Hispanics aged 18–24 years old enrolled in college, a record high. Put another way, Hispanics make up 16.5% of college enrollment. By the year 2043, Hispanics will be the majority, and Whites will be the minority in the population (Pew Research Hispanic Center, 2013). Moreover, Hip Hop is the common culture of Black and Brown students. Cohen, Celestine-Michener, Holmes, Merseth, and Ralph (2007) found that 97% of Black youth and 88% of Hispanic youth listened to rap music. Their research also uncovered that youth of various ethnicities were using Hip Hop to express their cultural identity. Watkins (2005) explained that:

> Whatever social or political impact hip hop has had on young people has come primarily in the world of popular culture. Hip hop's evolution launched a revolution in youth culture. All the things that traditionally matter to young people—style, music, fashion, and a sense of generational purpose—have come under the spell of hip hop. (p. 148)

Based on the above statistics and research, there is a clear need for a pedagogy that meaningfully responds to the cultural and linguistic diversity of our youth. For too long, educators have responded to diversity through deficit approaches that ignore cultural pluralism, cultural equity, and the day-to-day realties of urban youth from multiethnic and multilingual backgrounds. Both RP and CSP teaching theories have focused on using the customs, traditions, and the language of students who identify with

Hip Hop music and culture to explicitly link students' culture to schooling. Hip Hop can at once build solidarity among youth and represent modes of cultural expression that give them a sense of purpose and knowledge about who they are. My own story that I shared at the beginning of this chapter reflects how Hip Hop can inform youth and youth culture. In light of that power, educators need to help youth question that influential "spell" of Hip Hop. However, there is not necessarily one pedagogy that captures the heritage of all youth (at times both fluid and fixed), corporate America's media attack on youths' humanity by way of Hip Hop, and the oppressive social structures that complicate the lives of urban youth. Therefore, I suggest a hybrid of RP and CSP as a starting point to begin transforming the field of youth studies, since both pedagogies build upon the work of critical pedagogy, which is the foundation of critical youth studies. In short, these two pedagogies serve as a fitting starting place to engage in real educational reform which cannot take place unless it is rooted, I believe, in the principles of critical pedagogy.

This Has Been Done Before

Critical pedagogy and Hip Hop share two very important common principles:

1. Raising the critical consciousness of people who have been or who are being oppressed (Ginwright, 2004; Morrell, 2002; Williams, 2009), and

2. Firmly acknowledging that schools are places that maintain the status quo.

For example, KRS-One (1989) rapped that, "[i]t seems to me in a school that's ebony, African history should be pumped up steadily, but it's not and this has got to stop" (track 8). Freire (1970/2003) suggested that education could be transformative and empowering if poor and oppressed people had the pedagogical space to understand how their lived experiences have been shaped by social institutions (Akom, 2009). Yet, Freire (1970/2003) noted that many schools rely on the "banking method of education" (p. 71) that turns students into passive receptacles of knowledge and fails to make a connection between school and their lives.

Akom, Cammarota, and Ginwright (2008) contended that traditional and nontraditional educational spaces that are "youth driven cultural products" can be places "that embody a critique of oppression, a desire for social change, and ultimately lay the foundations for community empowerment and social change" (p. 4). The authors called for Youth Participatory Action Research (YPAR) in the field of critical youth studies. The authors defined YPAR as a "research methodology in which young people study their own social contexts to understand how to improve conditions and bring about greater equity" (p. 4). They argued that YPAR must be linked to critical race theory and critical media literacy in order to "develop pedagogical spaces for resistance, resiliency, hope, and healing" (p. 4). I am inspired by the work of Akom, Ginwright, and Cammarota—individually and jointly—because they conduct their research within the field of youth studies with the actual youth. Thus, their merging of theories is rooted in their understanding of the needs of youth on the ground. I witnessed this approach first-hand in the spring of 2013, when I attended a presentation by the organization Speak Out in Oakland, California. Akom partnered with human-rights activist, Ninotchka Rosca, through Speak Out to work with a group of students and examine their community, media, and oppressive social structures through traditional research methods (quantitative and qualitative data collection, and analysis). However, they also disrupted traditional research methods by using Spoken Word and Hip Hop to report their findings.

That experience solidified for me the power of integrating theories to shape youth studies grounded in critical pedagogy. Therefore, combining CSP and RP is in no way an alternative to YPAR; it is another powerful pedagogical tool to transform our society through the experiences and culture of youth. Thus, I am proposing a hybrid pedagogical method that can reach similar goals of YPAR through a different format. Teachers, community organizers, youth, Hip Hop studies scholars, and all individuals concerned with the body, mind, and spirit of youth must engage them with empowering pedagogies. If not, we are simply maintaining the status quo by not equipping students with the tools to effectively fight injustice.

Moving From Theory to Practice: RP and CSP

I believe that traditional and nontraditional educational spaces that are anchored by the experiences of youth will fundamentally transform education for the better. However, in implementing new classroom practices that address how educators begin to value and maintain the languages and cultures of urban youth, traditional youth learning spaces must meet the needs of innovative pedagogies like Paris's CSP. In short, CSP cannot be an effective pedagogical resource if learning structures do not provide the space for innovation. It is for that reason that a merger of Paris's CSP and Emdin's RP is necessary to afford teachers the time, space, and classroom procedures to effectively create a classroom where cultural pluralism and cultural equality are possible.

The five C's of RP provide the learning structure for CSP to function in a classroom on a daily basis. For example, taking from Emdin's (2011) classroom cyphers concept,

> a small group of students are given the opportunity to reflect on their classroom experiences, critique the instruction, discuss the inhibitors to the classroom learning, and most importantly, provide teachers with insight into what can work well in the classroom from the students' perspective. (p. 287)

Cyphers provide a space for students to not only critique instruction, but also society, in ways that reflect their language and cultural understanding of social structures, which is fundamental to CSP. I have written in the past on the way in which cyphers can be culturally relevant spaces for urban youth to express themselves and their culture (Love, 2013). Through the work of Paris, I contend that cyphers can be culturally sustaining spaces as well. Likewise, Emdin's work is the foundation for my premise of using cyphers to encourage youths' social-emotional learning and community-building skills (Love, 2013). Educator and youth advocates attempting CSP need, first and foremost, to create spaces that provide opportunities for youth from various ethnicities and "linguistic realities" to discuss inequities and how to value people's differences in hopes of creating "cultural pluralism" (Paris, 2012). CSP can only function if the learning spaces allow it to do so. Emdin's RP provides this space.

Emdin's (2011) notion of students possessing a "cosmopolitan ethos" that cultivates youth who are invested in sustaining "each other's livelihoods and happiness" (p. 290) is also fundamental to CSP. Cosmopolitism and cultural pluralism go hand in hand, but traditional and nontraditional learning structures must engage differently with youth to create youth-driven spaces. Furthermore, Emdin's fourth and fifth Cs, context and content, help define Paris's CSP in ways that allow students to develop and sustain school curriculum and pedagogy that is co-created by students and teachers. When students are allowed to change the physical space where they learn to reflect their lives, this act affirms youths' culture, and allows youth to take ownership of the space. The final C of Emdin's RP, content, amplifies Paris's CSP, because it involves teachers acknowledging what they do not know in relation to science. By extending context to culture, language, and the everyday realities of youth, it could be transformative if educators acknowledged to students that they actually knew very little about the languages that were spoken by youth every day, or their cultural backgrounds, but at the same time demonstrate a willingness to learn about that language and culture. Thus, content allows CSP to form organically from the community of youth. Lastly, Emdin (2011) stressed that for RP to be successfully implemented, educators must develop the "appropriate mind-set" (p. 292) for creating learning spaces that value diversity and social justice, matched with instructional practices that allow for this mind-set to flourish. That mind-set is transformative when teachers, community members, youth advocates, and researchers enter into students' culture and teach from a place of cultural pluralism that unites all youth. This concept demonstrates the pedagogical power of CSP and RP. Additionally, the amalgamation of CSP and RP—inspired by youths' Hip Hop identity—can create a pedagogical third space where classroom activities are informed by the lives of students and official school curriculum (Gutiérrez & Stone, 2000; Kirkland, 2008, 2009; Love, 2013).

Teaching in the Third Space

A conglomeration of Hip Hop, CSP, and RP frameworks offers a complex space for critical reflection by allowing educators and students to examine students' lives and communities within the ever-changing cultural practice of Hip Hop. However, Hip Hop education, coupled with the principles of RP and CSP, which are rooted in democratic education, moves beyond the official and unofficial dimensions of pedagogical space into a "third space" (Dyson, 2001; Kirkland, 2008, 2009) where youth counternarratives are reflective of youths' social, economic, political, and cultural realities and conditions.

In the third space model, educational text, discussion, and activities emerge from students' lives. The third space creates a reciprocal relationship between school and out-of-school practices, values, and beliefs of students because instruction and classroom procedures are so closely tied to the everyday realities of youth (Dyson, 2001; Gutiérrez & Stone, 2000; Love, 2013). The elements of CSP and RP assist educators in creating classrooms that are pedagogical third spaces, while embracing students' heritage. For example, when students coteach, learn in classrooms that resemble their communities, and have artifacts present in the classroom that are of importance to their cultural identity, traditional classroom ways are then overshadowed by new configurations of instruction informed by youth. Further, when educational spaces are informed by youth who identify with Hip Hop music and culture, critical dialogue concerning racism, sexism, love, language, cultural differences and pride, sexual orientation, capitalism, classism, drugs, crime, hard work, and violence are at the center of the curriculum. Hip Hop is rich with examples of society's ills and what uplifts us all. Tupac Shakur is a great example of how a Hip Hop artist can inspire, educate, and express what it means to be young and full of life. Moving the topics discussed in Hip Hop, mentioned above, to the center of the curriculum is key to fostering CSP and RP.

Apple and Beane (2000) emphasized that democratic education must not be consumed within "glossy political rhetoric" (p. 105), but within the everyday realities of youth. Put another way, democratic education must acknowledge that young people learn from their everyday sociocultural activities (Cole, 1996; Moll, 2000) in and outside of school walls. A combination of CSP and RP—rooted in Hip Hop—provides educators committed to democratic education and cultural pluralism with a pedagogical space to understand the importance and educational value of situating instruction within the realities of their students' lives. Furthermore, curriculum focused on students' lives is "supported by cognitive research demonstrating that learning is a process of making meaning out of new or unfamiliar events in light of familiar ideas or experiences" (Darling-Hammond, 1997, p. 74). This ideological and pedagogical shift recognizes that urban youth consume Hip Hop as a site of epistemological development linked to youths' everyday language and literacy practices (Mahiri, 2004; Richardson, 2006, 2007). Alim (2006) argued that, "Hip Hop is a cultural practice embedded in the lived experiences of Hip Hop-conscious beings existing in a home, street, hood, city, state, country, continent, hemisphere near you" (p. 12). Educators have used Hip Hop to help students make sense of the classics (Morrell & Duncan-Andrade, 2002), the academic writing process (Cooks, 2004), and teach literacy interpretation (Hill, 2006).

As empowering as Hip Hop education is for students and educators alike, Hip Hop is created and disseminated in the contested and ever-shifting space of Black popular culture. Although Hall (1993) contended that Black popular culture represents the culture of Black folks, it is still created in the space of homogenization and formulaic narratives of Black life fueled by cultural, social, economic, and technological conditions of today. David Kirkland (2008) added that Hip Hop, which is grounded in Black popular culture, operates within postmodern Blackness. He wrote:

> Postmodern blackness reiterates the idea that cultural, social, economic, and technological conditions of our age are constantly shifting. These shifts have given rise to a decentralized, multimedia dominated society in which norms are continuously revised, ways of living are continually improvised, and new technologies for communication and meaning making are regularly being devised…. Human conditions, or human experiences, are rich and diverse, elaborated on in tension through texts and conversations that take into account the contexts in which they are composed. (Kirkland, 2008, p. 72)

For youth to successfully grapple with the sly and shifting landscape in which Hip Hop is created and disseminated, they must engage in pedagogical practices that are fluid, dexterous, and rich in critical discussion that teaches youth how societal norms are reinvented to maintain the status quo, perpetuate stereotypes, and label Black and Brown youth as society's problem. RP and CSP combined is a ripe teaching framework for promoting and sustaining a classroom that is fluid enough to teach youth how to enjoy Hip Hop as consumers and critique the music and its culture as intellectuals.

Never Too Young

> Must be a bond, a connection between us here and us what are across the sea. A connection, the last of the old, first of the new. —Nana Peazant in *Daughters of the Dust* (Dash, 1991).

I have never been to Africa, but I am African. I cannot rap, dance, or DJ, but I am Hip Hop. As a teenager, I grew angry when I began to learn about my culture, my history, and my language outside of school, because in school I was forced to deny those aspects of my humanity every day. I found solace in Hip Hop, along with knowledge of self. I define knowledge of self as "[t]he study of Hip Hop culture, music, and elements, alongside the examination of issues within one's surroundings to create positive change in one's community" (Love, 2013, p. 19). More broadly, Akbar (1998) argued that knowledge of self is part of an effective education that allows students to understand who they are and the dilemmas they may face in life. In short, knowledge of self is empowerment. To empower youth through schooling, students must know where they come from, feel connected to their heritage, and be able to then link that heritage to that of others, thus forming cultural connectedness. Joining the structured principles of RP to the teaching framework of CSP creates a structure for CSP to flourish. In my experience, most teachers who are concerned with integrating RP or CSP into their classrooms feel overwhelmed by the task. While they possess the fortification to transform how we teach, research, and work with young folk, they lack the knowledge base as to how to accomplish that goal on a grand scale and on a day-to-day basis. However, when incorporated, the 5 C's of RP provide a daily structure for CSP. Merging these two theories together will create the structure needed for adults to learn and see "the brilliance the students bring with them in their blood" (Delpit, 1992, p. 248). As an educator and scholar in Hip Hop and youth studies, I am encouraged by the work of Paris and Emdin, as both of these scholars push the boundaries of the youth studies field and education to create new ways of thinking and teaching urban youth. Through such work, Hip Hop Education is alive and well.

References

Akbar, N. (1998). *Know thyself*. Tallahassee, FL: Mind Productions & Associates.

Akom, A. A. (2009). Critical hip hop pedagogy as a form of liberatory praxis. *Equity and Excellence in Education, 42*(1), 52–66.

Akom, A. A, Cammarota, J., & Ginwright, S. (2008). Youthtopias: Towards a new paradigm of critical youth studies. *Youth Media Reporter, 2*(4), 1–30.

Alim, H. S. (2006). *Roc the mic right: The language of hip hop culture*. New York, NY: Routledge.

Apple, M. W., & Beane, J. A. (2000). Democratic schools: Lessons from the chalk face. Buckingham, UK: Open University Press.

Cohen, C. J., Celestine-Michener, J., Holmes, C., Merseth, J. L., & Ralph, L. (2007). *The attitudes and behavior of young Black Americans: Research summary.* Retrieved from http://www.resourcelibrary.gcyf.org/node/290

Cole, M. (1996). *Cultural psychology: A once and future discipline.* Cambridge, MA: Belknap Press of Harvard University Press.

Common. (2007). Finding forever. On *Finding forever* [CD]. New York, NY: G.O.O.D. Music.

Cooks, J. A. (2004). Writing for something: Essays, raps, and writing preferences. *English Journal, 94*(1), 72–76.

Darling-Hammond, L. (1997). *The right to learn: A blueprint for creating schools that work.* San Francisco, CA: Jossey-Bass.

Dash, J. (Writer & Director). (1991). *Daughters of the dust* [Motion picture]. USA: Kino International.

Delpit, L. D. (1988). The silenced dialogue: Power and pedagogy in educating other people's children. *Harvard Educational Review, 58*(3), 280–299.

Delpit, L. D. (1992). Education in a multicultural society: Our future's greatest challenge. *Journal of Negro Education, 61*(3), 237–249.

Dyson, A. H. (2001). Donkey Kong in Little Bear country: A first grader's composing development in the media spotlight. *Elementary School Journal, 101*(4), 417–433.

Emdin, C. (2009). Reality pedagogy: Hip hop culture and the urban science classroom. In W. M. Roth (Ed.), *Science education from people for people: Taking a stand(point)* (pp. 72–90). New York, NY: Routledge.

Emdin, C. (2011). Moving beyond the boat without a paddle: Reality pedagogy, Black youth, and urban science education. *Journal of Negro Education, 80*(3), 284–295.

Freire, P. (2003). Pedagogy of the oppressed (Rev. ed.). New York, NY: Continuum.

Ginwright, S. (2004). *Black in school: Afrocentric reform, urban youth, and the promise of hip hop culture.* New York, NY: Teachers College Press.

Gutiérrez, K. D., & Stone, L. D. (2000). Synchronic and diachronic dimensions of social practice: An emerging methodology for cultural-historical perspectives on literacy learning. In C. D. Lee & P. Smagorinsky (Eds.), *Vygotskian perspectives on literacy research: Constructing meaning through collaborative inquiry* (pp. 150–164). Cambridge, UK: Cambridge University Press.

Hall, S. (1993). What is this 'Black' in Black popular culture? *Social Justice, 20*(1–2), 104–114.

Hill, M. L. (2006). Using Jay-Z to reflect on post-9/11 race relations. *English Journal, 96*(2), 23–27.

Kirkland, D. E. (2008). 'The rose that grew from concrete': Postmodern Blackness and new English education. *English Journal, 97*(5), 69–75.

Kirkland, D. E. (2009). Standpoints: Researching and teaching English in the digital dimension. *Research in the Teaching of English, 44*(1), 8–22.

KRS-One. (1989). You must learn. On *Ghetto music: The blueprint of hip hop* [CD]. New York, NY: Jive Records.

Ladson-Billings, G. (1995). Toward a theory of culturally relevant pedagogy. *American Educational Research Journal, 32*(3), 465–491.

Love, B. L. (2012). *Hip hop's li'l sistas speak: Negotiating hip hop identities and politics in the new South.* New York, NY: Peter Lang.

Love, B. L. (2013). Urban storytelling: How storyboarding, moviemaking & hip hop-based education can promote students' critical voice. *English Journal.*

Mahiri, J. (2004). *What they don't learn in school: Literacy in the lives of urban youth.* New York, NY: Peter Lang.

Moll, L. (2000). Inspired by Vygotsky: Ethnographic experiments in education. In C. Lee & P. Smagorinsky (Eds.), *Vygotskian perspectives on literacy research: Constructing meaning through collaborative inquiry* (pp. 256–268). New York, NY: Cambridge University Press.

Moll, L. C., & Gonzalez, N. (1994). Lessons from research with language-minority children. *Journal of Reading Behavior, 26*(4), 439–456.

Morrell, E. (2002). Toward a critical pedagogy of popular culture: Literacy development among urban youth. *Journal of Adolescent and Adult Literacy, 46*(1), 72–77.

Morrell, E., & Duncan-Andrade, J. M. R. (2002). Promoting academic literacy with urban youth through engaging hip hop culture. *English Journal, 91*(6), 88–92.

Paris, D. (2012). Culturally sustaining pedagogy: A needed change in stance, terminology, and practice. *Educational Researcher, 41*(3), 93–97.

Pew Research Hispanic Center. (2013). *A nation of immigrants.* Retrieved from http://www.pewhispanic.org/files/2013/01/statistical_portrait_final_jan_29.pdf

Prier, D. C. (2012). *Culturally relevant teaching: Hip hop pedagogy in urban schools.* New York, NY: Peter Lang.

Richardson, E. (2006). *Hip hop literacies.* Hoboken, NJ: Taylor & Francis.

Richardson, E. (2007). 'She workin' it like foreal': Critical literacy and discourse practices of African American females in the age of hip hop. *Discourse and Society, 18*, 789–809.

Watkins, S. C. (2005). *Hip hop matters: Politics, pop culture, and the struggle for the soul of a movement.* Boston, MA: Beacon Press.

Williams, A. D. (2009). The critical cultural cypher: Remaking Paulo Freire's cultural circles using hip hop culture. *International Journal of Critical Pedagogy, 2*(1), 1–29.

CHAPTER 39

No Bystanders in Authentic Assessment

Critical Pedagogies for Youth Empowerment

Valerie J. Janesick

*Problem posing education affirms men and women
As beings in the process of becoming—as unfinished
uncompleted beings in and with a likewise unfinished reality.
… The unfinished character of human beings and the
transformational character of reality necessitate that
education be an ongoing activity.*
(Paulo Freire, 1970/2000, *Pedagogy of the Oppressed*)

Introduction

Paulo Freire (1970/2000) wrote these words in his groundbreaking text, *Pedagogy of the Oppressed*, in the section following his carefully crafted description of the banking concept of education. He was trying to explain that there are alternatives to the banking model. The banking model basically is a robotic approach to education which consists of the teacher making a deposit into a student's head and then the student withdraws that knowledge on command. It is in effect an anti-model. For me as a teacher educator, I have witnessed firsthand the failed educational policy of high-stakes testing, which is a banking approach to education. In this chapter, I wish to describe and explain how authentic assessment is a critical pedagogical problem-posing approach to learning. As a result, and in place of high-stakes testing, I once again encourage educators to use authentic assessment as a more dependable and trustworthy approach to assessing what a student can do and what a student has learned.

Many have written (Horn & Kincheloe, 2001; Janesick, 2006, 2010) about the dangers, problems, and outright quackery of high-stakes, corporatized testing and what might replace reliance on high-stakes testing. Subsequently, I continue to write about and think about authentic assessment as a critical tool for engaging youth in the educational experience and process and the power of authentic assessment. Through authentic assessment as opposed to high-stakes testing, the learner is an active agent in the learning process. In contrast, drilling for and memorizing answers for bubbled-in, high-stakes tests simply avoids and erases the learner in the learning process. In this chapter, I would like to describe how authentic assessment strategies can lead to more powerful, reflective, active agency in youth culture. I begin with the notion of critical authentic assessment, then describe possible strategies for demonstrating performance-based activities that place learners in a space that is creative, practical, and empowering. In addition, a short review of the hazards of high-stakes testing as national policy in the current form as Race to the Top, and previously as No Child Left Behind will be addressed. In the end, there is no more wooden-headed policy than high-stakes testing. A good way to view authentic assessment is as a way to avoid the banking model of education so well described by Freire (1970/2000). By using Freire's construct of the banking system as a starting point, we look to a critical pedagogical approach to authentic assessment.

Critical Authentic Assessment

Critical Authentic Assessment is an approach to authentic assessment which recognizes the importance of the learner as actively engaged in the learning process and as a problem poser. In addition, any authentic performance task can and most likely should be part of critical authentic assessment. Historically, authentic assessment requires authentic tasks that show a learner's ability to do something, and therefore is evidence of what the learner can do in any given area of study. I wrote of this earlier (Janesick, 2006, 2010), and many other writers in the mid-1990s also wrote of authentic assessment in their disciplinary areas, such as Science and Math, Language Arts, and Social Studies, for example. Furthermore, the learner receives feedback and is redirected to push further in the area of study. Feedback is meant to be ongoing. It is not a one-shot mechanism. It is organic, continual, and includes the learner in the discussion when appropriate, and therefore is unfinished, as Freire put it so elegantly. This allows for a great deal of growth on the learner's part, and requires a deep engagement in whatever is being studied. Thus, you can never be a bystander in the process. *Critical authentic assessment is a term I use to identify a deep engagement in the learning process, with the learner and the teacher taking ownership of the authentic assessment process. It is impossible to be a bystander in the process. The learner gives evidence of what the learner can do and there is a continual feedback loop.* An easy way to think about authentic assessment is by contrasting it to traditional high-stakes tests.

Traditional Typical Test	**Authentic Assessment Task**
Requires one correct answer.	Requires quality performance or product.
Is disconnected from student's life.	Is connected to the student's life.
Is simplified.	Is multilayered.
Is one-shot.	Is continuing, with multiple tasks.
Provides one score.	Provides complex feedback.
Looks for one level of thought.	Looks for higher-order thinking and a demonstration of knowledge.

You may be asking, why aren't we doing this instead of high-stakes testing? That is an excellent question. Given that even if you thought testing measured learning, such as in the international charts of comparison which seem to be driving this nonsense, you the reader might be amazed to know a few facts on this topic. For example, of the countries that rank at the top in reading and math, typically Japan, China, and Korea, in their own educational system, young children are not even tested until about the age of 12.

Furthermore, higher-performing countries such as Scandinavian countries also respect young children enough not to test till an appropriate age. They pay attention to the research in the area of child and youth development. In other words, children are not little robots memorizing potential answers for a poorly constructed test. Still further, internationally, top-performing nations do not use test scores to punish learners, such as the USA so regularly and so recklessly does. To close public schools, for example, because test scores went down over time, without a thorough investigation into the social forces at play in a given neighborhood, only adds to the messiness of a wrong-headed approach to judging what a student can do.

Definitions

To begin, we must look at a few definitions so that we have a common language. *High-stakes testing* refers to standardized, corporate-made tests whose results are the basis of critical decisions, such as retaining a student in a particular grade level, cutting funding to a school, or even closing a school. Ever since the heavy focus on high-stakes testing, there has been and continues to be an uproar of dissent and disagreement about testing in the educational research community, the evaluation community, and most directly, teachers and parents. Historically, all this focus on testing began in the 1980s with the Reagan administration and the systematic and relentless attack on public education. High-stakes tests are quick, cost a great deal in school budgets, turn the teacher into a test-prep coordinator and/or robot, and unnerve many a student. A great deal of the curriculum in any grade level is pushed aside, as nearly an entire semester is spent just on prepping for the test. Often, the test is not connected to the grade level curriculum of the school. In addition, test items are created and scored by hourly workers, some of whom may not be prepared to take on this type of work. If one looks at the amount of money spent on the high-stakes testing adventure, one can easily see that the only group benefitting from high-stakes testing are the test-making groups, often housed in a corporate entity geared for making profits.

Authentic assessment refers to an approach to assessment that requires students to perform authentic tasks to demonstrate what they can do and what they know with real-world problems. Teachers have used authentic assessment regularly, and through these tasks, have been able to more realistically and over time assess a student's work and progress. The authentic tasks require thinking, comparing, learning, and evaluating on the part of the learner. Some of the wide range of authentic assessment tasks might be something like writing a story, creating a video, writing poetry, taking photographs and writing about the meaning of the photographs, painting, writing a song, performing a play, keeping a portfolio of the learner's work, and doing a dramatic reading. The numerous options would take up this entire chapter, and I am listing here some of the well-used and well-proven authentic tasks that are workable in just about every area of study. Basically, authentic assessment is an alternative to teaching to the test and spoon-feeding answers to be memorized. As someone put it so wisely, spoon-feeding in the end only teaches us the shape of the spoon. To avoid spoon-feeding answers to youth, and to avoid the banking model, authentic assessment offers strategies for demonstrating critical thinking. If a learner is to become a critical thinker, the learner needs to go deeply into authentic tasks. The result can assist in higher-order thinking skills, such as:

1. Examining assumptions.

2. Examining alternative positions.

3. Creating conclusions based on evidence.

4. Gathering evidence to make a photo, a story, a dance, a portrait, etc.

5. Connecting knowledge to actual experience and practice.

6. Connecting knowledge to the area under study.

7. Synthesizing information.

8. Reevaluating data.

9. Problem-posing and problem-solving.

In other words, rather than focus student energy on drill-and-kill models for passing a test, have the student engage deeply with material, and create a product or performance that indicates what was learned. Because the use of authentic tasks is nearly endless, I wish to concentrate here on three approaches suited to youth culture that may assist in the learning process, engagement in the school and community, and which will demonstrate the level of knowledge and experience of any learner. The three authentic assessment tasks are

1. Writing the pedagogical letter,

2. Creating poetry from textbooks being studied in the form of found-data poetry, and

3. Photography as Photovoice.

Each of these approaches is a powerful tool for any learner. Furthermore, they are a perfect fit with critical pedagogical theory and practice.

Writing the Pedagogical Letter

Freire often used the pedagogical letter to write to friends, family, and students about a critical idea or problem with which he was wrestling. The letter is a personal communication tool. In my Critical Pedagogy classes, I ask students to craft a pedagogical letter to someone alive today or someone in history to talk about a problem they are wrestling with in the area of critical curriculum studies. Some write to presidents, governors of states, elected officials such as senators or council members; and some write to family or friends. What the pedagogical letter allows for as an authentic task is the opportunity for a learner to take control of the topical area of the learner's choice. My classes have students in various departments, and each departmental curriculum varies as to focus. For example, in Science Education, socio-scientific issues remain a key topic. In Measurement and Evaluation, the ethical issues of testing and test bias, for example, are critical issues. Regardless of the discipline involved, the writer of the letter takes a real-world classroom experience—for most are classroom teachers in service at the time—deconstructs that experience through our readings in Critical Pedagogy, and invites the person reading the letter to think about these issues. See this description of the assignment and a short section of a pedagogical letter as an exemplar.

Sample assignment

The Pedagogical Letter: 7–10 pages. Based on your readings from our first text, Curriculum Pedagogy: Where Are We Now?

One of Paulo's favorite formats of communication was letters. He described in these letters his political, sociological, ideological, philosophical, and contextual beliefs, values, and ideas. Most of his final text, *Pedagogy of Indignation*, evolved and is generated from these pedagogical letters over the course of a lifetime. These letters contained his hope, his emotions, and his sensibility.

The Letter

a) Select someone you would like to write to and explain your critical pedagogical beliefs regarding an educational issue you care about, and how you apply these beliefs in your everyday world. Let this evolve from your favorite selected chapter from our textbook. Include the most significant idea found in the chapter of your choice and write about how it relates to your current work experience. What surprised you in the chapter? Can you think of ways you can use the knowledge gained from this chapter? For example, some students have written to their own children, their grandparent, a spouse, a significant other, another student, political leaders, or some historical figure, like Mother Jones or Eleanor Roosevelt, or someone who has inspired the writer. Some have written to Paulo Freire himself or one of the authors in our text, *Critical Pedagogy: Where Are We Now* (McLaren & Kincheloe, 2007). Spend time thinking and writing.

b) Share your letter with your group or someone in class.

c) Be prepared to have a one-page handout for distribution to the class stressing the major points of your letter, and how this relates to our readings, and the references to our text when appropriate. Be prepared to share the ideas from this letter if you like with the class in your in-class presentation. Your one-page handout for all in class should include name, title of the work, etc., and of course, your own name and email. Consider sending it to the person you are writing to if it makes sense.

Example of an excerpt of a pedagogical letter

Here in this letter, the student, Silvia, wrote to Jan Brewer, Governor of Arizona, upon reading of the harsh immigration proposals of the governor. Silvia was inspired by many of the chapters in the McLaren and Kincheloe (2007) text we read.

> *Dear Governor Brewer:*
>
> *I am writing this letter because several things have compelled me to urge you to reconsider your recent House Bill (2281). Foremost, I would like to tell you a bit about myself. I am a Cuban born doctoral student…. I am reading and studying about Critical pedagogy…. I think it is important to share my views on the subject.*
>
> *I do not mean to disrespect your opinion. I welcome your feedback. To begin, I wanted to share my understanding of what critical pedagogy means. I think it is a complex concept worth understanding. It entails teaching students that meaningful dialogue could be part of their world…. It goes beyond teaching students to learn dates and "historical" facts. Actually critical pedagogy's aim is to instill an intellectual curiosity in children through the art of communication and argument. It calls for students not to accept easy formulas; it calls for them to question concepts and to be willing to actively engage in public discourse. Critical pedagogy postulates that it is difficult to separate what happens in the classroom from the economic and political conditions of our world.*

Silvia then goes on in her letter to make a case for the governor to reconsider her bill banning "ethnic studies." Since Silvia is an educator, she goes on to explain that this will harm students, particularly Mexican American students and others. She concludes the letter by asking why should the 30% or more of Mexican American students be banned from learning their own history.

Thus, in using this authentic assessment task, we have the opportunity to enable students to find their voice, and to use it effectively when it comes to being active in the political arena of education. In addition, here you can see how a student may use her own experience to accomplish an authentic task. Furthermore, the teacher then can see the progress the student has made, and is able to provide feedback for the student to advance even further. Here is a good example of the student being an active agent, and in the current world of youth culture, how powerful this technique can be.

Found-Data Poetry as an Authentic Assessment Task

Put your ear down close to your soul
And listen hard.
(Anne Sexton)

Youth culture today embraces music, poetry, drama, dance, and visual arts, and appears to embrace many forms of alternative art. Learners use the Internet, social networks, and blogging to make their voices known, to connect with others, and to find their way on the information highway, so to speak. I enjoy the use of poetry for tapping into a learner's love for the beautiful. While many students will protest when asked to write a poem, in fact they eventually get in the spirit of finding data poems in any of the readings they are currently mastering. Since I use, in both my research courses and curriculum courses, an activity to find poetry and to make poetry, I want to share this authentic assessment technique in the context of and spirit of Freire's problem-posing and active engagement in learning. Found-data poetry is a technique where the poet or prospective poet reads a narrative passage and creates a poem using the words of the writer of the passage. Found poetry is often used as a research technique, and basically, it is a way of seeing the world with a new lens. It forces the learner to think poetically, to sift through the words (data) and come up with something new. This is like the process of analysis they will use in writing their own theses or dissertations. The heart of analysis is taking something apart, and then putting it back together to tell a story of one kind or another. I would like to share this found-data poetry assignment, and then display a sample found poem.

Sample poetry assignment

Create a poem found in the text you are reading to capture its meaning. Use any style and format, and title the poem.

Example of a found poem

The basic tenets of critical pedagogy resonate with today's youth, and you can clearly see this in terms of their digital stories and autobiographies on the Web, on social-media sites, and on their own websites. In the fast-paced world of texting, instant messages, non-stop email, and connection to a digital world, why not step into another kind of creativity by tapping into poetry? Here the learner must settle down and focus on a particular idea and write about it in a poetry style of their own choice. Many students already appreciate the poetry of hip hop and rap. Many have attended or performed at an open microphone poetry night or even made short video stories on YouTube of themselves ranting poetically. Taking the baby step of trying one's hand at poetry, found poems are a good strategy for easing into poetry.

In addition to using the critical pedagogy textbook mentioned earlier, I have students read Fowler's (2006) book, *A Curriculum of Difficulty*. As an example, I share this poem I wrote (Janesick, 2011) to indicate how anyone can pore over any narrative writing and create a poem from the words of that narrative.

Difficulty

A curriculum of difficulty
Emerges from a writer's memory and perception.

Bumping into the text
Fearing a blank pedagogical form to be filled,
Like waves hitting the break wall.
A curriculum of difficulty is like quantum teaching
Radiant and splendid.

Calling us to go to the root of it all
To get power over is to block out the light.

Signify your narrative
Stronger than Hermes.

Step into it.
Watch the rays of light
Incandescent and true.

In other words, for anyone trying to find a way to create a poem from a narrative, the learner actually opens the mind and heart to take in the material in a new form, and generates a found-data poem. Poetry then becomes a pedagogical tool for extending a history both of the learner and of the writer of the narrative from which the poem was designed. Poetry also helps clarify our being and existence, and what could be more educational? Currently, there is a renewed interest in poetry in the social sciences, education, and the health sciences (see Furman, 2007; Prendergast, 2006; Richardson, 1993). It is a good time for using poetry to engage youth in a creative way in the educational process. One certainly cannot be a bystander when shaping a poem.

So we have two solid pedagogical tools described thus far: the pedagogical letter, and the found-data poem. A third strategy to consider as a strong authentic assessment task is that of photography as Photovoice. This technique offers us a vehicle for student advocacy that is so in line with the notion of problem-posing.

What Is Photovoice?

You don't make a photograph just with a
Camera. You bring to the act of photography all
The pictures you have seen, the books you have read,
The music you have heard, the people you have loved.
(Ansel Adams)

Photovoice is a technique that grew out of participatory research projects such as participatory action research. It is a wonderful technique for critical pedagogues, in that participants are not bystanders, but active agents taking photographs of a given social context and writing about it. Particpants and/or photographers bring attention to inequities and other conditions in a community through photography. The well-known writers in this area, Wang and Burris (1997), have written extensively in this area, focusing on its importance for critical engagement, reflection, and empowerment. Briefly, Photovoice is like a double-jointed acrobat. It gives voice to the critical agent taking the photo, and also gives voice to the subjects of the photos. The major goals of Photovoice include:

1. Empowering people to reflect upon personal and social concerns of a given community,

2. Encouraging people to construct a dialogue around the photograph in question, and

3. Opening up access to voice from individuals or groups on the edges of a community.

The gist of Photovoice is that it is a means for a community (or an individual) to assess its (or his or her) own problems and needs. It has been used widely in disability studies and health studies, but easily resonates with critical pedagogy and the issues related to youth culture. Photography then becomes the vehicle for documenting underrepresented groups and the challenges they face. Learners have the opportunity to supply the photograph as evidence of a problem, challenge, or issue facing them. It is a natural technique for problem-posing.

Advantages of Photovoice

Give someone a camera and they usually enjoy documenting some activity, event, or person in active, everyday life. Photovoice facilitates greater involvement of participants, usually participants who have been outsiders. In Education, second-language learners, students classified as special-education students, homeless, etc., have been active agents in documented studies of Photovoice. Goodhart et al. (2006) have written about this and about the value of Photovoice as a means of empowering students. The students become more aware of their own surroundings, their social context, and ultimately see themselves as active agents. Photovoice is a solid authentic assessment tool for student advocacy. In addition to actually taking documentary photos, the learner then usually writes about that picture descriptively and interprets the photo. Previously, in some circles this was known as photo elicitation, and from time to time, the terms Photovoice and photo elicitation are used interchangeably. You may already be wondering about the costs involved in using this technique. Since many learners already have an iPhone, BlackBerry, or smart phone of some type, often this allows for ease in terms of taking photographs. Many schools have technology centers where one may borrow digital cameras, or one way or another, someone finds a digital camera to use for a short term.

Sample Photovoice assignment

Take at least five photos of the social context of campus. Photograph any person (get verbal permission), or place, or section of a setting. Come back to the class and discuss your photo with a partner. Relate our readings to the photo.

Summary of examples

As you might imagine, in a class of 15 learners, the depth and breadth of the types of photographs varies, and the explanations of their meanings vary widely. What happens with using an actual photograph is that the photographer has a deep emotional attachment to the photograph. Consequently, the intensity of the discussion escalates as a critical partner offers alternative or like interpretations and may also offer possibilities for competing interpretations. For example, I recently conducted a workshop on digital oral history at an international conference, and used this Photovoice assignment as an activity for using the iPad to document any person or context of the conference. One of the participants was from South Africa, and photographed a statue in the entrance of a building. It was a beautifully rendered bronze likeness of Abraham Lincoln. At the moment she was doing this, coincidentally, visitors to the building were also taking photographs, including a photograph of Lincoln. They then began comparing and discussing their respective work spontaneously. Upon returning to the workshop, the photographer described this event as a preparation for sharing the photo in the workshop.

From this set of photos, a discussion was then generated about the act of taking the photographs, and about the subject of the photograph, Abraham Lincoln. The photographer emailed the photo to anyone who requested it. A lengthy discussion ensued on Lincoln, his place in history, and the recently released Steven Spielberg movie, *Lincoln*, and a new discussion took shape. The completely new discussion centered around slavery, minority status, and voluntary and involuntary minorities, and that led to a discussion on the meaning of democracy. All this is to say that Photovoice is a vigorous authentic assessment task. Following all this, members in the workshop wrote short reflections on the process and the content of their photographs.

Within the context of a workshop, timed for a specific number of hours and a short time frame, there are constraints. However, as educators in the course of a semester, or the course of an entire school year, there is much more flexibility and continuity, in terms of providing feedback on authentic tasks such as this one. Likewise, using rubrics for writing, for example, makes it possible to allow for a maximum of creativity in documenting a social setting through Photovoice.

Conclusion and Discussion

In this chapter, I have introduced the problem-posing technique of authentic assessment as an antidote and alternative to high-stakes, one-shot, corporatized testing of youth. Authentic assessment offers youth the opportunity to become active agents in the learning process, rather than bystanders. Three powerful authentic assessment tasks were described and examples given to indicate the potential of the three approaches. These three approaches, which include the pedagogical letter, found-data poetry, and photography as Photovoice clearly show that a learner can be an active agent. The discussion, writing, reflection, and action of a learner can be facilitated through tasks such as these. Furthermore, this shows what a learner can actually do, and feedback is always available to help the student go even further in the educational process.

Currently, this administration (like previous ones) still clings to the old model of relying on standardized, one-shot tests. These tests, in many cases, are seriously flawed, are scored by hourly workers, are constructed out-of-context relative to the learners' lives, and are certainly aimed at making profits for the test-makers. I began this chapter with the words of Freire, who anticipated the authentic assessment alternative to our current logic. We know that high-stakes testing is hazardous to our children, not only from current research, but just from plain common sense. We know that high-stakes, one-shot testing is profitable for corporate test-makers. We know that high-stakes testing gets learning, growth, and child development wrong. We know that high-stakes testing leaves students on the outside, especially students who have special needs, are second-language learners, and/or who are minorities in need of assistance. We know that high-stakes testing does not allow for creativity, imagination, or authentic artistic expression.

In closing, the following words of Freire's capture for me the importance of youth becoming active agents in their educational process, rather than bystanders. The mindlessness of high-stakes testing makes no sense. When we have an effective, solid, and valid alternative, such as authentic assessment, and given that we are practicing critical pedagogy, what are we waiting for?

Education either functions as an instrument which is used to facilitate integration of the younger generation into the logic of the present system and bring about conformity or it becomes the practice of freedom, the means by which men and women deal critically and creatively with reality and discover how to participate in the transformation of their world.
(Paulo Freire, 1970/2000, *Pedagogy of the Oppressed*)

References

Brock, R., Malott, C. S., & Villaverde, L. E. (Eds.). (2011). *Teaching Joe Kincheloe*. New York, NY: Peter Lang.

Fowler, L. (2006). *A curriculum of difficulty*. New York, NY: Peter Lang.

Freire, P. (2000). *Pedagogy of the oppressed* (30th anniversary ed.). New York, NY: Continuum.

Furman, R. (2007). Poetry and narrative as qualitative data: Explorations into existential theory. *Indo-Pacific Journal of Phenomenology, 7*(1), 1–9.

Goodhart, F. W., Hsu, J., Baek, J. H., Coleman, A. L., Maresca, F. M., & Miller, M. B. (2006). A view through a different lens: Photovoice as a tool for student advocacy. *Journal of American College Health, 55*(1), 53–56.

Horn, R. A., Jr., & Kincheloe, J. L. (2001). *American standards: Quality education in a complex world: The Texas case*. New York, NY: Peter Lang.

Janesick, V. J. (2006). *Authentic assessment primer*. New York, NY: Peter Lang.

Janesick, V. J. (2010). How can assessment work in urban schools? In S. R. Steinberg & A. Darder (Eds.), *19 urban questions: Teaching in the city* (2nd ed., pp. 69–86). New York, NY: Peter Lang.

Janesick, V. J. (2011). Teaching critical pedagogy through poetry and the pedagogical letter. In R. C. Brock, S. Malott, & L. E. Villaverde (Eds.), *Teaching Joe Kincheloe* (pp. 63–75). New York, NY: Peter Lang.

McLaren, P., & Kincheloe, J. L. (2007). *Critical pedagogy: Where are we now?* New York, NY: Peter Lang.

Prendergast, M. (2006). Found poetry as literature review: Research poems on audience and performance. *Qualitative Inquiry, 12*(2), 369–388.

Richardson, L. (1993). Poetics, dramatics, and transgressive validity: The case of the skipped line. *Sociological Quarterly, 34*(4), 695–710.

Steinberg, S. R., & Darder, A. (Eds.). *19 urban questions: Teaching in the city*. New York, NY: Peter Lang.

Wang, C., & Burris, M.A. (1997). Photovoice: Concept, methodology, and use for participatory needs assessment. *Health Education and Behavior, 24*(3), 369–387.

CHAPTER 40

Schools as Prisons

Normative Youth Pedagogies

P. L. Thomas

Writing in August of 2004, poet Adrienne Rich (2009) "wondered *why now*" about a commemorative James Baldwin postal stamp, leading her into a consideration of the value of Baldwin's words during his life and career spanning the decades around the Civil-Rights era as well as the time contemporary to her piece: "His country has put his face on a first-class postage stamp. Has named a black president candidate. But has yet to face its own confusions in his art's unsparing mirror" (pp. 49, 56). These words sit between the largest federal education legislation in the history of the US, No Child Left Behind (NCLB), and the election of the first African American president, Barack Obama, in 2008. Yet, as Rich declared, Baldwin's words from 1972 remain powerful and provocative in the second decade of the twenty-first century:

> The truth is that the country does not know what to do with its black population now that the blacks are no longer a source of wealth, are no longer to be bought and sold and bred, like cattle; and they especially do not know what to do with young black men, who pose as devastating a threat to the economy as they do to the morals of young white cheerleaders. (Baldwin, 1998, pp. 432)

Despite claims that Obama's election was a harbinger for postracial America, and despite over thirty years of school reform characterizing public "education as the one true path out of poverty—the great equalizer that overcomes differences in background, culture and privilege…. the only way to secure our common future in a competitive global economy" (Duncan, 2009, n.p.), two facts remain about the role of education in the American pursuit of democracy—schools mirror the inequity of the society, and schools perpetuate inequity (Tavernise, 2012). Education in the US has failed most directly American youth among the Other, those marginalized because of their race, class, gender, sexual orientation, and any status not honored by the mythical middle-class norm.

Rich (2001) recognized this failure against the promise of public schools, a promise often invoked by political leadership as a mask for their corporate and neoliberal commitments: "Universal public education has two possible—and contradictory—missions" (p. 162), choosing not its democratic and liberatory possibilities, but instead allowing schools to perpetuate inequity remaining in society. Education reform has failed Freire's (1998) argument that education should be a mechanism for social change: "If education cannot do everything, there is something fundamental it can do. In other words, if education is not the key to social transformation, neither is it simply meant to reproduce the dominant ideology" (p. 110).

Yet, traditional education structures, the current era of high-accountability education reform, and the rise of zero-tolerance and "no excuses" ideologies in school policies and practices have merged with the New Jim Crow era of mass incarceration (Alexander, 2012) to trap children in poverty and children of color in both the school-to-prison pipeline (Bahena, Cooc, Currie-Rubin, Kuttner, & Ng, 2012; Christensen, 2011/2012) and schools as prisons. Just as Baldwin's charges remain relevant to contemporary concerns about the failures of universal public education, Carter Godwin Woodson (1933) also spoke to the mis-education of not just African Americans, but all students in America, although the situation was most stark among those children cast as Others: "The Negro thus educated is a hopeless liability of the race" (p. 5).

Public education in the US traps students in normative youth pedagogies, especially in the context of education reform, when marginalized youth—children of color, children in poverty, English-language learners, special-needs students—are disproportionately targeted with "no excuses" and zero-tolerance policies and practices that create schools as prisons.

Students as Prisoners of ZIP Codes in an Era of High Accountability

Secretary of Education, Arne Duncan, represents both the discourse and policy currently driving education reform in the US. Associating civil rights with education reform and federal policies, Duncan (2009) explained: "King had to convince them as well, that they could not wait. As he told them, justice too long delayed is justice denied. Opportunity too long delayed is opportunity denied. Quality education too long delayed is education denied" (n.p.). Building on the framework for reform endorsed by Obama and Duncan, self-appointed reformers—including Joel Kline, Michelle Rhee, Paul Vallas, and many others—directly announced an education-reform manifesto that asserted: "As President Obama has emphasized, the single most important factor determining whether students succeed in school is not the color of their skin or their ZIP code or even their parents' income—it is the quality of their teacher" ("How to Fix Our Schools," 2010).

Despite the overwhelming evidence contradicting such claims, "We like to believe all students have an equal opportunity to learn," explained Liz Dwyer (2012), "regardless of the color of their skin or the amount of money their families have" (n.p.). Several components of "no excuses" education reform, however, are likely to increase the current problems with social and educational equity for American youth, instead of addressing them. For example, Pedro Noguera explained: "[E]vidence of blatant disparities amount to Apartheid-like separations that have been accepted in New York for far too long" (Holzman, 2012, p. vi).

The patterns exposed in New York are typical across the US in public education, a system currently under siege by "no excuses" reformers from the White House to statehouses across the country. The data connecting housing prices with school attendance and measurable outcomes for those students reveal that the home and community of children determine their access to quality education. Broadly, then, Holzman (2012) concluded research "documents not only where de facto education redlining occurs in New York City communities, but also the devastating impact inequitable educational opportunity has on New York City's public school students" (p. 4).

These findings reinforce the broader issue of in-school inequity exposed by Peske and Haycock (2006), who examined patterns of teacher assignment based on student characteristics most strongly associated with measurable student outcomes—family income, race, native language, special needs—and revealed: "The very children who most need strong teachers are assigned, on average, to teachers with less experience, less education and less skill than those who teach other children" (p. 2). Educational inequity, however, is not unique to New York: "Nationwide, the average low-income student attends a school that scores at the 42nd percentile on state exams, while the average middle/high-income student attends a school that scores at the 61st percentile on state exams" (Rothwell, 2012, p. 1).

Patterns of in-school inequity linked to social inequity pose significant problems for current education-reform narratives and initiatives coming from political and public leaders in the US. If American children are experiencing growing inequity of income in their homes and communities, as well as inequity of opportunity in their community schools, how do the current education-reform commitments match the weight of evidence concerning what sort of reform public education needs? Rothwell (2012) offered an answer:

> While all of these [reform] efforts deserve careful consideration, none directly addresses one of the central issues that limit educational opportunity for low-income and minority children: their disproportionate concentration in low-performing schools. In particular, limiting the development of inexpensive housing in affluent neighborhoods and jurisdictions fuels economic and racial segregation and contributes to significant differences in school performance across the metropolitan landscape. (p. 2)

Traditional patterns and current reform commitments in public education show that, as Woodson and Baldwin argued decades ago, goals of democracy, equity, and liberation are not being met for America's youth—not in society, not in the schools they are zoned to attend, not in the charter schools they seem to choose. American youth remain prisoners of their ZIP codes, especially if those youth are African American, Latino/a, and/or impoverished, resulting in their being "doubly disadvantaged" by their communities and their public schools (Gennetian et al., 2012), as well as in their access to college (Fruchter, 2013; Fruchter, Hester, Mokhtar, & Shan, 2012). Yet, a number of reform commitments remain robust in the political and public discourse, despite all of them failing to address issues of equity, as well as many of them perpetuating and reinforcing inequity:

- *Charter Schools*. The advocacy behind charter schools appears more focused on school choice than on reforming education or addressing equity of educational opportunity for marginalized youth in the US. Charter schools remain no better at academic outcomes than public schools (CREDO, 2009), and offer nothing unique about "charterness" that trumps public schools (Di Carlo, 2011), but have shown patterns of segregating and isolating children by race and class (Miron, Urschel, Mathis, & Tornquist, 2010). Charter schools also disproportionately target ethnic minorities and impoverished students with "no excuses" and zero-tolerance policies.

- *School Choice*. In the past few years, choice, vouchers, and other forms of choice (charter schools) have all regained popularity, despite the lack of evidence that choice itself addresses social equity, educational equity, or educational outcomes. Choice and, specifically, parental choice, is a powerful argument again refuted by, for example, reviews of Milwaukee's extensive voucher program (Cobb, 2012).

- *Teach for America (TFA)*. Like charter schools, TFA has gained a great deal of support from the Obama administration as well as states and school districts across the US. Since TFA recruits are college graduates without teacher education or teaching experience, commitments to TFA fail to address the inequitable distribution of quality teachers to high-needs populations of students (Heilig & Jez, 2010). In fact, TFA perpetuates the inequitable practice of assigning inexperienced and un- or under-qualified teachers to high-poverty, minority, ELL, and special-needs students (Peske & Haycock, 2006).

The reality of "no excuses" reform is that political and public leaders ignore poverty and inequity by repeating slogans such as "poverty is not destiny" to mask policy that fails to address and often increases inequity. Part of the current reform language includes persistent references to the "achievement gap," but as Gardner (2010) explained, even if in-school equity were realized (and currently it is not), "Don't forget that advantaged children are not standing still in the interim. They continue to benefit from travel and other enriching learning experiences. As a result, the gap will persist" (n.p.).

Ample evidence that youth are prisoners of their ZIP codes (Fruchter et al., 2012; Gennetian et al., 2012; Holzman, 2012; Reardon, 2011; Rothwell, 2012) shows that US social and education reform must be reimagined in order to address not an achievement gap based on test scores that tell us what we already know—the out-of-school factors of a child's life are more powerful than that child's school (Berliner, 2009)—but the equity gap (Carter & Welner, 2013). Until education reform focuses on social and school policies aimed at equity, liberation, and genuine revolution, the institution of education will remain a social force that reflects and further entrenches inequity, particularly for disadvantaged children who exist as the Others—"other people's children" (Delpit, 2006).

The Rise of the Police State in the Schools of "Other People's Children"

James Baldwin (1966) proclaimed, "The law is meant to be my servant and not my master, still less my torturer and my murderer" (n.p.). Much could be said about public schools, as I will address further below. A common pattern to how both the legal-penal and education systems characterize, treat, and marginalize children as Others can be found in literature, specifically Ralph Ellison's (1952) *Invisible Man*, Richard Wright's (1940) *Native Son*, and Stieg Larsson's (2009a, 2009b, 2009c) Millennium trilogy—works that confront how a culture of control and surveillance (Foucault, 1984), always in a state of reform (Deleuze, 1992), reduces marginalized people to criminal states. Here, briefly, Larsson's central character, Lisbeth Salander, is examined against Kathleen Nolan's (2011) ethnography of zero-tolerance school policies in urban high schools.

While the mesmerizing narrative of Larsson's novels, specifically the character, Lisbeth Salander, can be discounted as mere fiction, the life and career of Baldwin and the lives of the urban youth chronicled by Nolan (2011) must not be ignored. It is at this intersection of history, literature, and ethnography that I want to build a case that schools and prisons work within a similar dynamic of control (Deleuze, 1992; Foucault, 1984) that creates marginalized populations as children, and then perpetuates that pattern for them as adults; education, then, functions as school-to-prison pipelines *and* as schools as prisons (Carr, 2013; Nolan, 2011).

Larsson's trilogy is more than crime or mystery novels; the narrative is an important and serious venture into how cultures identify and marginalize the Other. Lisbeth Salander is a case study in social norms creating contexts that distort perception; she is rendered an Other because of her *abnormal* intelligence and sexuality, as well as her gender. Throughout the three novels, Salander's history and behavior are carefully assembled for the reader against how Salander is manipulated and judged by powerful cultural institutions from many different perspectives throughout her life. Further, Larsson's (2009a, 2009b, 2009c) trilogy achieved an international pop-culture status, and the novels can be framed within a literary history paralleling Ellison's invisible man, Wright's Bigger Thomas—modern-classic novels exploring African American males as Others—and Mersault in the existential classic, *The Stranger*, by Albert Camus (1988), which examined the mechanisms of judicial marginalizing.

In the context of a police state and social norms of justice and authority, Salander's behavior is either incomprehensible or evidence of mental deficiency or derangement. For those having read the novels, of course, the truth about Salander is that she is neither randomly violent nor unethical; in fact, *Salander is compulsively ethical*, an ironic source of her Otherness. She has developed stringent guidelines for what is just and unjust, and takes it upon herself to serve as judge, jury, and executioner. In the climactic court case of the trilogy, Palmgren explains the context of Salander's behavior:

Our client on principle does not speak to the police or to other persons of authority, and least of all to psychiatrists. The reason is simple. From the time she was a child she tried time and again to talk to police and social workers to explain that her mother was being abused by Alexander Zalachenko. *The result in every instance was that she was punished* [emphasis added] because government civil servants had decided that Zalachenko was more important than she was. (Larsson, 2009a, p. 733)

Salander embodies the power of institutions to impose onto humans the shackles of justice in the name of justice. Salander, like journalist Mikael Blomkvist, must work above and around the law in order to maintain her ethical groundings.

The trilogy's narrative details the enormous weight of evidence unmasking the corruption of agents of social institutions (secret police, lawyers, psychiatrists), and *justifies* Salander's distrust and refusal to cooperate with official authority. In that context, Michel Foucault's (1995) examination of the power of surveillance offers a powerful and disturbing question: "Is it surprising that prisons resemble factories, schools, barracks, hospitals, which all resemble prisons?" (n.p.). Through mere observation, Salander is cast as deviant, an Other, due to her looks (doubly damning, since she appears different from most people as well as different from social norms for women), and her behavior is repeatedly, throughout her life, *associated with her own agency*, without regard to the contexts that provoke that behavior. The use of observation by formalized institutions represents the arbitrary but codified influence of who can be marginalized.

Salander becomes more than a fictional character against Nolan's (2011) ethnography of a high-poverty urban high school that has incorporated pervasive surveillance techniques, including metal detectors and police in the hallways, all built on zero-tolerance policies that mirror "get tough on crime" and the "war on drugs" slogans that pervade American culture. Nolan detailed how and then concluded that the nearly seamless blending of school and justice system has created not a school-to-prison pipeline, but something far more disturbing:

These findings highlight that, although the oft-used metaphor of the school-to-prison pipeline is helpful (and real), the lived experience of many students at UPHS can be better understood through a *nuanced description of daily life* [emphasis added] rather than the pipeline metaphor.... The school, where they are by law required to spend most of their day, becomes an auxiliary to the criminal-justice system. These findings show that urban youth get subjected to levels of surveillance and repression that are not the same as long-term incarceration, but nonetheless, as the school merges with an ideology of street policing, the courts, and even the prison, a particular culture of penal control becomes an aspect of everyday life at school and beyond. (Kindle edition)

Urban youth learn, like Salander, that the exact agents of power who surround them—administrators, teachers, police officers, judges—are not to be trusted, and the result is that student after student experiences not just school discipline, but criminal discipline, due to how they react to the circumstances that are created for them and around them. Nolan (2011) explained: "Their contestations during interactions with police and agents contained within them a decisive critique of disciplinary practices. Policing practices, especially the demand to see ID, conflicted with students' sense of justice and fairness and their imagined ideal of schooling" (Kindle edition). The culture of control that Nolan recognized and catalogued in this urban high school is an intensified version of the larger culture of control that typifies America, or at least the American middle-class norm that both accepts and perpetuates the nearly perpetual social surveillance that allows their idealized middle-class cocoon to exist—a cocoon of safety *from the Other* and the freedom to amass and protect possessions.

Zero-tolerance policies are the province of an idealized, middle-class norm imposed on "other people's children" (Delpit, 2006), creating not a school-to-prison pipeline, but schools as prison.

The parallels between schools and prison detailed in Nolan's (2011) ethnography are also reflected in the data surrounding in-school discipline as that mirrors mass incarceration (Alexander, 2012):

- Pre-kindergarten expulsions are disproportionately male and African American students: "Rates were highest for older preschoolers and African-Americans, and boys were over 4½ times more likely to be expelled than were girls" (Gilliam, 2005, p. 1).

- As a snapshot but typical urban school setting, Chicago represents the merging of law enforcement and education, twin systems that punish children of color: "In 2010, Blacks represented 74 percent (4,737) of total school based arrests (of people of all ages) and Latinos accounted for 22 percent (1,438)" (Kaba & Edwards, 2012, p. 13).

- Often ignored, punitive actions such as retention must be considered within the dynamic of control that disproportionately impacts children by race, class, and gender: "New nationwide data collected by the U.S. Department of Education's civil rights office reveal stark racial and ethnic disparities in student retentions, with black and Hispanic students far more likely than white students to repeat a grade" (Adams, Robelen, & Shah, 2012, n.p.).

- Children of color are labeled as criminal Others in schools, again as represented in Chicago public schools: "While the total numbers of school-based arrests are declining, Black youth continue to be disproportionately targeted" ("Fact Sheet: Arrests of Youth," 2013, n.p.).

- Labeling as criminal Others is powerfully contrasted with labeling as elite for children of color in schools, especially in zero-tolerance schools, as Lewin (2012) reported: "Although black students made up only 18 percent of those enrolled in the schools sampled, they accounted for 35 percent of those suspended once, 46 percent of those suspended more than once and 39 percent of all expulsions" (n.p.).

- These patterns in school, then, must be framed against 2010 incarceration rates (number of people incarcerated per 100,000 people in that group):

  Incarceration rates by race/ethnicity
  White 330
  Latino 966
  African American 2207
  Male incarceration rates by race/ethnicity
  White 678
  Latino 1775
  African American 4347
  Young male incarceration rates
  White 1437
  Latino 3892
  African American 8932. (Wagner, 2012)

Schools function, then, as both school-to-prison pipelines and schools as prison, particularly within zero-tolerance policies (Nolan, 2011). The codified systems of labeling students—through disciplinary and academic processes—in order to sort the Others from middle-class and affluent students work within a larger culture of control, one that Alexander (2012) has identified as the New Jim Crow.

Schools as Prison in the New Jim Crow Era

In the US, the intersection of the criminal-justice system and public schools has intensified in the wake of school shootings, prompting similar policies from opposite ends of the political spectrum, as noted by an editorial in *The New York Times*: "The National Rifle Association and President Obama responded to the Newtown, Conn., shootings by recommending that more police officers be placed in the nation's schools" ("Criminalizing Children at School," 2013). As the editorial explained, however, research tends to show that having police in the hallways creates schools as prisons and students as criminals (Nolan, 2011), increasing, thus not eliminating, the problems. Chloe Angyal (2013) highlighted the disturbing connection between incarceration and education: "Punishment rates in schools mirror the rates in the 'real world'—though what could be more real than entrenched discrimination in our schools?—and in fact, contribute to those real world figures" (n.p.).

While the phrase, "a nation at risk" tends to be associated with the 1983 report on US education from the Reagan administration (NCEE, 1983), the early 1980s also spawned an era of mass incarceration (Jones & Mauer, 2013), built on claims that the US was also a nation at risk because of illegal drug sales and use, identified by Alexander (2012) as the New Jim Crow: "In October 1982, President Reagan officially announced his administration's War on Drugs.... By waging a war on drug users and drug dealers, Reagan made good on his promise to crack down on the racially defined 'others'—the undeserving" (p. 49).

Within a year of each other, then, the Reagan administration launched a *war on drugs* and a *crisis response to public education*. Just as Alexander detailed about the racialized, masked intent behind the war on drugs, John Holton (2003) exposed *A Nation at Risk* as less about education reform and more about political agendas. For three decades, the war on drugs has led to mass incarceration, primarily impacting African American males (see above), "the racially defined 'others,'"; and the education-reform movement based on high-stakes accountability has targeted "other people's children" (Delpit, 2006) in ways that suggest that market-oriented education reform is a school-based component of the New Jim Crow, grounded in the criminal-justice system.

Mass incarceration and market-oriented education reform share more than their genesis in the 1980s, since both have been shown to cause far more harm than good and to marginalize further African American and impoverished youths and adults. The education-accountability era begun in the early 1980s focused on implementing curriculum standards and high-stakes testing, first at the state level and then over the decade since NCLB, increasingly at the national level. The evolution of the education-reform movement has included some central ideological commitments—focusing on in-school-only reform, and relying on slogans such as "no excuses" and "poverty is not destiny," as expressed in a 2010 manifesto ("How to Fix Our Schools," 2010) from several key figures in reform, as noted above. At first, education reform was driven by revolutionary promises and often unverified claims of public school failure, but over the past thirty years, ample evidence now suggests that political education reform has failed to fulfill its promises, and, like the negative consequences of the mass incarceration, has harmed the exact students those reforms were designed to help. The "no excuses" era of reform is an extension of the zero-tolerance era examined by Nolan (2011).

The Broader, Bolder Approach to Education has resisted market-oriented, in-school-only reform championed by Secretary Duncan, Bill Gates, Rhee, Vallas, and Klein, calling instead for social and educational reform seeking equity of opportunity for all families and students. Weiss and Long (2013)—examining test-based teacher evaluations, school closures, and expanded charter schools in Chicago, New York City, and Washington, DC—concluded:

> The report finds that the reforms delivered few benefits and in some cases harmed the students they purport to help. It also identifies a set of largely neglected policies with real promise to weaken the poverty-education link, if they receive some of the attention and resources now targeted to the touted reforms. (p. 3)

Market-oriented education reform has depended on claims of addressing inequity *indirectly*, trusting mechanisms such as choice and business models of managing teachers as well as schools to initiate social change. This reform has specifically targeted goals such as closing the achievement gap, better serving impoverished and minority students, and raising international indicators of educational quality. As Weiss and Long (2013) showed, however, test-based teacher evaluations, school closures, and expanded charter schools have not succeeded; test scores and achievement gaps remain identified problems, many success stories by reformers have proven to be misleading, teachers and schools have come under unsubstantiated assault, charter schools and other choice mechanisms have not accomplished what advocates claim, and social inequity and poverty continue to be ignored.

Further, additional evidence reveals that unintended consequences of market-oriented reform have included increased segregation by race and class in charter schools (Miron et al., 2010) as well as traditional public schools (Siegel-Hawley & Frankenberg, 2012), and a widening gap between the type of educational experiences affluent children receive compared with the authoritarian and test-prep focused "no excuses" schools for minority and impoverished students, notably as detailed by Sarah Carr (2013), exploring the post-Katrina rise of charter schools in New Orleans:

> The reformers approach students they perceive as disadvantaged in much the same way they do struggling teachers…. [L]ow income children must be taught, explicitly and step-by-step, how to be good students. Staff at a growing number of "no-excuses" charter schools … are prescriptive about where new students look (they must "track" the speaker with their eyes), how they sit (upright, with both feet planted on the ground, hands folded in front of them), how they walk (silently and in a straight line, which is sometimes marked out for them by tape on the floor), how they express agreement (usually through snaps or "silent clapping" because it's less disruptive to the flow of class), and, most important, what they aspire to (college, college, college). This conditioning (or "calibration" or "acculturation" …) starts with the youngest of students. (pp. 42–43)

Carr's narrative and analysis reveal that market-oriented reform tends to replicate and even perpetuate inequity instead of eradicating it: students in New Orleans sit in "no excuses" schools as prisons that are both authoritarian and segregated, while the post-Katrina Recovery District reduced the African American teacher workforce from 75% to 57% of the city's teachers.

Despite the slogans and the rhetoric, schools implementing market-oriented education-reform policies have shown that, as examined above, *home and community characteristics do predict educational opportunities*, mirroring the historically greatest challenge facing traditional public schools. Ultimately, like the war on drugs, current education reform exists as a key element in America's New Jim Crow era. Just as the education-reform movement was spurred by a "manufactured crisis" (Berliner & Biddle, 1995), as exposed by Gerald Bracey (2003) and Holton (2003), the war on drugs grew out of a racially divisive political agenda, a drug crisis that did not yet exist, but created "mass incarceration in the United States … as a stunningly comprehensive and well-designed system of racialized social control that functions in a manner strikingly similar to Jim Crow," as Alexander (2012) detailed (p. 4).

Since market-oriented education reform is producing evidence highlighting the ineffectiveness and even negative outcomes associated with those policies, that the agenda remains robust suggests, again like mass incarceration, that education reform fulfills many of the dynamics found in the New Jim Crow. Just as mass incarceration from the war on drugs continues institutional racism once found in slavery and Jim Crow (Alexander, 2012), education reform, especially the "no excuses" charter-school movement and zero-tolerance policies in urban schools, resurrects a separate-but-equal education system that is separate, but certainly is not equal. The double-disadvantage (Gennetian et al., 2012) of masked racism in mass incarceration and education reform share many parallels, including the following:

- Both depend on "racially sanitized rhetoric," according to Alexander (2012, p. 43), that thinly masks racism. "Getting tough on crime" as a war on drugs (not people) justifies disproportional arrests, convictions, and sentencing for African Americans; "no excuses" and "zero toler-ance" justify highly authoritarian and punitive schools disproportionately serving high-poverty children of color.

- Both depend on claims of objective mechanisms—laws for the war on drugs and test scores for education reform—to deflect charges of racism. Alexander (2012) recognized that "[t]his system is better designed to *create* crime, and a perpetual class of people labeled criminals, rather than to eliminate crime or reduce the number of criminals" (p. 236), just as test-based education reform creates the achievement gap.

- Both depend on racialized fears among poor and working-class Whites, which Alexander (2012) identified in the Reagan drug-war agenda:

  In his campaign for the presidency, Reagan mastered the "excision of the language of race from conservative public discourse" and thus built on the success of the earlier conservatives who devel-oped a strategy of exploiting racial hostility or resentment for political gain without making explicit reference to race. (p. 48)

The charter school movement masks segregation within a progressive-friendly public school choice.

- Both depend on either current claims of postracial America or the goal of a postracial society: "This system of control depends far more on *racial indifference* ... than racial hostility," Alexander (2012, p. 203) noted.

- Both depend on a bipartisan and popular commitment to seemingly obvious goals of crime eradication and world-class schools.

- Both depend on the *appearance* of African American support. Alexander (2012) explained about the effectiveness of the war on drugs: "Conservatives could point to black support for highly punitive approaches to dealing with the problems of the urban poor as 'proof' that race had nothing to do with their 'law and order' agenda" (p. 42).

This last point—that African Americans seem to support the war on crime, "no excuses" charter schools, and zero-tolerance policies—presents the most problematic aspect of charges that mass incar-ceration and education reform are ultimately racist, significant contributions to the New Jim Crow. For example, Carr (2013) reported that African American parents not only choose "no excuses" charter schools in New Orleans, but also actively cheer and encourage the authoritarian policies voiced by the schools' administrators. But Alexander (2012) explained, "Given the dilemma facing poor black com-munities, it is inaccurate to say that black people 'support' mass incarceration or 'get tough' policies" because "[i]f the only choice that is offered blacks is rampant crime or more prisons, the predictable (and understandable) answer will be 'more prisons'" (p. 210). New Orleans serves as a stark example of how this dynamic works in education reform: Given the choice between segregated, underfunded, and deteriorating public schools and "no excuses" charters and zero-tolerance policies—and not the choice of the school environments and offerings found in many elite private schools—the predictable answer is "no excuses" charters and zero-tolerance policies.

Conclusion

Educational and social reform grounded in liberatory and democratic goals have failed to gain traction within the American consumer and/or capitalist system; however, critical pedagogy has offered a vision of schooling that confronts, instead of replicates, social norms (hooks, 1994; Kincheloe, 2004, 2005;

Pahomov, 2013). Yet, market-oriented education reform continues to produce evidence that it fails against its own goals and standards. But more disturbing is that current education reform also shares with the war on drugs evidence that the US is committed to the New Jim Crow, about which Alexander (2012) quoted Martin Luther King, Jr.: "'Nothing in all the world is more dangerous than sincere ignorance and conscientious stupidity'" (p. 203). The war on drugs and highly punitive, segregated charter schools are creating an underclass, significantly among young African American males and populations labeled as Others—facts that must be acknowledged before equity of opportunity can be secured. About this intersection of the criminal justice system and education reform, where marginalized youth experience schools as prison, Angyal (2013) asked, "But the real question is, what will it take for us to fix this system that punishes students and citizens for no other reason but their membership in marginalized groups?"

Acknowledgments

Sections of this chapter have been adapted from Thomas 2012a, 2012b, and 2013.

References

Adams, C. J., Robelen, E. W., & Shah, N. (2012, March 6). Civil rights data show retention disparities. *Education Week, 31*(23). Retrieved from http://www.edweek.org/ew/articles/2012/03/07/23data_ep.h31.html

Alexander, M. (2012). *The new Jim Crow: Mass incarceration in the age of colorblindness* (Rev. ed.). New York, NY: New Press.

Angyal, C. (2013, April 19). Punishing students for who they are, not what they do. *Truthout.* Retrieved from http://www.truth-out.org/opinion/item/15840-punishing-students-for-who-they-are-not-what-they-do

Bahena, S., Cooc, N., Currie-Rubin, R., Kuttner, P., & Ng, M. (Eds.). (2012). *Disrupting the school-to-prison pipeline.* Cambridge, MA: Harvard Educational Review.

Baldwin, J. (1966, July 11). A report from occupied territory. *The Nation.* Retrieved from http://www.thenation.com/article/159618/report-occupied-territory

Baldwin, J. (1998). *James Baldwin: Collected essays.* New York, NY: Library of America.

Berliner, D. C. (2009). *Poverty and potential: Out-of-school factors and school success.* Boulder, CO: Education and the Public Interest Center & Education Policy Research Unit. Retrieved from http://epicpolicy.org/publication/povertyand-potential/

Berliner, D.C., & Biddle, B. J. (1995). *The manufactured crisis: Myths, fraud, and the attack on America's schools.* New York, NY: Perseus Books.

Bracey, G. W. (2003). April foolishness: The 20th anniversary of *A Nation at Risk. Phi Delta Kappan, 84*(8), 616–621.

Camus, A. (1988). *The stranger* (M. Ward, Trans.). New York, NY: Vintage.

Carr, S. (2013). *Hope against hope: Three schools, one city, and the struggle to educate America's children.* New York, NY: Bloomsbury Press.

Carter, P. L., & Welner, K. G. (2013). *Closing the opportunity gap: What America must do to give every child an even chance.* New York, NY: Oxford University Press.

The Center for Civil Rights Remedies. (2013, January). *A summary of new research. Closing the school discipline gap: Research to policy.* Los Angeles, CA: The Civil Rights Project. Retrieved from http://civilrightsproject.ucla.edu/events/2013/summary-of-new-research-closing-the-school-discipline-gap-research-to-policy/Research_Summary_Closing_the_School_Discipline_Gap.pdf

Center for Research on Education Outcomes (CREDO). (2009, June). *Multiple choice: Charter school performance in 16 states.* Stanford, CA: Author. Retrieved from http://credo.stanford.edu/reports/MULTIPLE_CHOICE_CREDO.pdf

Christensen, L. (2011/2012, Winter). The classroom-to-prison pipeline. *Rethinking Schools, 26*(2). Retrieved from http://www.rethinkingschools.org/restrict.asp?path=archive/26_02/26_02_christensen.shtml

Cobb, C. (2012, April 19). *SCDP Milwaukee Evaluation Report #29, #30, #32.* Boulder, CO: National Education Policy Center. Retrieved from http://nepc.colorado.edu/thinktank/review-Milwaukee-Choice-Year-5

Criminalizing children at school. (2013, April 18). [Editorial]. *The New York Times.* Retrieved from http://www.nytimes.com/2013/04/19/opinion/criminalizing-children-at-school.html

Deleuze, G. (1992). Postscript on the societies of control. *October, 59,* 3–7. Retrieved from https://files.nyu.edu/dnm232/public/deleuze_postcript.pdf

Delpit, L. (2006). *Other people's children: Cultural conflict in the classroom.* New York, NY: New Press.

Di Carlo, M. (2011, November 16). Explaining the consistently inconsistent results of charter schools. *Shanker Blog* [Web log]. Retrieved from http://shankerblog.org/?p=4229

Duncan, A. (2009, September 24). *Reauthorization of ESEA: Why we can't wait.* U.S. Department of Education. Retrieved from http://www.ed.gov/news/speeches/reauthorization-esea-why-we-cant-wait

Dwyer, L. (2012, April 8). Why America's education system is like Apartheid. *Good Education.* Retrieved from http://www.good.is/post/why-america-s-education-system-is-like-apartheid/

Ellison, R. (1952). *Invisible man*. New York, NY: Vintage.

Fact sheet: Arrests of youth (18 and under) on CPS grounds, 2011 & 2012. (2013, April 29). [Web log]. Policing Chicago Public Schools. Retrieved from http://chiyouthjustice.files.wordpress.com/2013/04/cps-arrests-2011-2012.pdf

Foucault, M. (1984). *The Foucault reader* (P. Rabinow, Ed.). New York, NY: Pantheon Books.

Foucault, M. (1995). Panopticism. *Discipline and punish: The birth of the prison* (A. Sheridan, Trans.; 2nd ed.; pp. 195–228). New York, NY: Vintage. Retrieved from http://foucault.info/documents/disciplineAndPunish/foucault.disciplineAndPunish.panOpticism.html

Freire, P. (1998). *Pedagogy of freedom: Ethics, democracy, and civic courage* (P. Clarke, Trans.). Lanham, MD: Rowman & Littlefield.

Fruchter, N. (2013, January 6). Demography & destiny: College readiness in New York. *City Limits*. Retrieved from http://www.citylimits.org/news/articles/4677/demography-destiny-college-readiness-in-new-york

Fruchter, N., Hester, M., Mokhtar, C., & Shan, Z. (2012). *Is demography still destiny?: Neighborhood demographics and public high school students' readiness for college in New York City*. Providence, RI: Anneberg Institute for School Reform. Retrieved from http://www.citylimits.org/multimedia/2012/is-demography-still-destiny#.UYK7Lyt36BU

Gardner, W. (2010, September 20). Poverty rate and the achievement gap. *Walt Gardner's Reality Check* [Web log post]. *Education Week*. Retrieved from http://blogs.edweek.org/edweek/walt_gardners_reality_check/2010/09/

Gennetian, L. A., Sanbonmatsu, L., Katz, L. F., Kling, J. R., Sciandra, M., Ludwig, J., … Kessler, R. C. (2012). The long-term effects of moving to opportunity on youth outcomes. *Cityscape: A Journal of Policy Development and Research, 14*(2), 137–167. Retrieved from http://www.huduser.org/portal/periodicals/cityscpe/vol14num2/Cityscape_July2012_long_term_effects_youth.pdf

Gilliam, W. S. (2005, May 4). *Prekindergarteners left behind: Expulsion rates in state prekindergarten systems*. Yale University Child Study Center. Retrieved from http://www.hartfordinfo.org/issues/wsd/education/NationalPreKExpulsionPaper.pdf

Heilig, J. V., & Jez, S. J. (2010). *Teach For America: A review of the evidence*. Boulder, CO: Education and the Public Interest Center & Education Policy Research Unit. Retrieved from http://epicpolicy.org/publication/teach-for-america

Holton, G. (2003, April 25). An insider's view of "A Nation at Risk" and why it still matters. *The Chronicle of Higher Education, 49*(33), B13. Retrieved from http://chronicle.com/article/An-Insider-s-View-of-A/20696

Holzman, M. (2012, April). *A rotting apple: Education redlining in New York City*. Cambridge, MA: Schott Foundation for Public Education. Retrieved from http://schottfoundation.org/drupal/docs/redlining-full-report.pdf

hooks, b. (1994). *Teaching to transgress: Education as the practice of freedom*. New York, NY: Routledge.

How to fix our schools: A manifesto by Joel Klein, Michelle Rhee and other education leaders. (2010, October 10). *The Washington Post*. Retrieved from http://www.washingtonpost.com/wp-dyn/content/article/2010/10/07/AR2010100705078.html

Jones, S., & Mauer, M. (2013, April 29). Ronald Reagan made the war on drugs a race to incarcerate. *Truthout*. Retrieved from http://www.truth-out.org/opinion/item/16065-ronald-reagan-made-the-war-on-drugs-a-race-to-incarcerate

Kaba, M., & Edwards, F. (2012, January). *Policing Chicago public schools: A gateway to the school-to-prison pipeline*. Project NIA. Retrieved from http://policeinschools.files.wordpress.com/2011/12/policing-chicago-public-schools-final2.pdf

Kincheloe, J. (2004). *Critical pedagogy primer*. New York, NY: Peter Lang.

Kincheloe, J. (2005). *Critical constructivism primer*. New York, NY: Peter Lang.

Larsson, S. (2009a). *The girl who kicked the hornet's nest* (R. Keeland, Trans.). New York, NY: Vintage Crime/Black Lizard.

Larsson, S. (2009b). *The girl who played with fire* (R. Keeland, Trans.). New York, NY: Vintage Crime/Black Lizard.

Larsson, S. (2009c). *The girl with the dragon tattoo* (R. Keeland, Trans.). New York, NY: Vintage Crime/Black Lizard.

Lewin, T. (2012, March 6). Black students face more discipline, data suggests. *The New York Times*. Retrieved from http://www.nytimes.com/2012/03/06/education/black-students-face-more-harsh-discipline-data-shows.html

Miron, G., Urschel, J., Mathis, W. J., & Tornquist, E. (2010, February 5). *Schools without diversity: Education management organizations, charter schools, and the demographic stratification of the American school system*. Boulder, CO: Education and the Public Interest Center & Education Policy Research Unit. Retrieved from http://epicpolicy.org/publication/schools-without-diversity

The National Commission on Excellence in Education (NCEE). (1983, April). *A nation at risk: The imperative for educational reform. A report to the nation and the Secretary of Education, United States Department of Education*. Washington, DC: Author. Retrieved from http://datacenter.spps.org/uploads/SOTW_A_Nation_at_Risk_1983.pdf

Nolan, K. (2011). *Police in the hallways: Discipline in an urban high school* [Kindle edition version]. Minneapolis, MN: University of Minnesota Press.

Pahomov, L. (2013). Building a collective understanding of prisons. *English Journal, 102*(4), 38–44.

Peske, H. G., & Haycock, K. (2006, June). *Teaching inequality: How poor and minority students are shortchanged on teacher quality*. Washington, DC: Educational Trust. Retrieved from http://www.edtrust.org/sites/edtrust.org/files/publications/files/TQReportJune2006.pdf

Reardon, S. F. (2011). The widening academic achievement gap between the rich and the poor: New evidence and possible explanations. In G. J. Duncan (Ed.), *Whither opportunity?: Rising inequality, schools, and children's life chances*. New York, NY: Russell Sage Foundation. Retrieved from http://cepa.stanford.edu/sites/default/files/reardon%20whither%20opportunity%20-%20chapter%205.pdf

Rich, A. (2001). *Arts of the possible: Essays and conversations*. New York, NY: W.W. Norton.

Rich, A. (2009). *A human eye: Essays on art in society 1997–2008*. New York, NY: W.W. Norton.

Rothwell, J. (2012, April). *Housing costs, zoning, and access to high-scoring schools*. Washington, DC: Brookings. Retrieved from http://www.brookings.edu/~/media/research/files/papers/2012/4/19%20school%20inequality%20rothwell/0419_school_inequality_rothwell.pdf

Siegel-Hawley, G., & Frankenberg, E. (2012, September). *Southern slippage: Growing school segregation in the most desegregated region of the country*. Los Angeles, CA: Civil Rights Project. Retrieved from http://civilrightsproject.ucla.edu/research/k-12-education/integration-and-diversity/mlk-national/southern-slippage-growing-school-segregation-in-the-most-desegregated-region-of-the-country/hawley-MLK-South-2012.pdf

Tavernise, S. (2012, February 9). Education gap grows between rich and poor, studies say. *The New York Times*. Retrieved from http://www.nytimes.com/2012/02/10/education/education-gap-grows-between-rich-and-poor-studies-show.html

Thomas, P. L. (2012a, May 15). Studies suggest economic inequity is built into, and worsened by, school systems. *Truthout*. Retrieved from http://truth-out.org/news/item/8993-studies-suggest-economic-inequity-is-built-into-and-worsened-by-school-systems

Thomas, P. L. (2012b, August 9). James Baldwin, Lisbeth Salander and the rise of the police state in some children's schools. *Truthout*. Retrieved from http://truth-out.org/opinion/item/10804-james-baldwin-lisbeth-salander-and-the-rise-of-the-police-state-in-some-childrens-schools

Thomas, P. L. (2013, May 17). Education reform in the New Jim Crow era. *Truthout*. Retrieved from http://truth-out.org/opinion/item/16406-education-reform-in-the-new-jim-crow-era

Wagner, P. (2012, August 28). Incarceration is not an equal opportunity punishment. *Prison Policy Initiative*. Retrieved from http://www.prisonpolicy.org/articles/notequal.html

Weiss, E., & Long, D. (2013, April 22). *Market-oriented education reforms' rhetoric trumps reality: The impacts of test-based teacher evaluations, school closures, and increased charter school access on student outcomes in Chicago, New York City, and Washington, D.C.* Broader, Bolder Approach to Education. Washington, DC: Economic Policy Institute. Retrieved from http://www.epi.org/files/2013/bba-rhetoric-trumps-reality.pdf

Woodson, C. G. (1933). *The mis-education of the Negro*. New York, NY: Tribeca Books.

Wright, R. (1940). *Native son*. New York, NY: Harper & Row.

CHAPTER 41

Youth Writing

Rage Against the Machine

Jeff Park

It has been fashionable for policymakers, educators, and the media to criticize and judge young people for decades. "Our schools are in crisis." "Young people lack skills and initiative." "Students don't read anymore; students don't know how to write." Worse, students are often blamed for being apathetic and failing or doing poorly in large-scale assessments. In terms of writing, students are said to consider writing to be old-fashioned and out of style in this new cyber world of constant visual and informational literacy. But how true are these claims? Is it true that students do not engage in writing as fully as they once did? And if true, are there reasons for their disengagement?

In this rapidly changing world of visual literacy and cyber interaction, maybe educators and their students are not completely aware of what is going on. Writing, and being able to create and manipulate word text, is a form of power, of control, and a means of navigating in a world where individual voice is constantly undermined.

Yet students often feel that there is no need to write, or they think that writing is outdated; however, young people constantly text, keep journals, write and act in their own digital videos, post on Facebook and other forms of social media, write and perform their own music in a DIY world of self-sufficiency, as well as engage actively in relatively new ideas such as spoken-word poetry and YouTube creations. Clearly, the situation regarding writing is a bit more complex than many have stated. Is it possible that students are simply involved in different forms of writing and literacy in general? Maybe schools and educators are the ones that are slightly behind the times in relation to new literacies.

In fact, schools have never been particularly interested in getting students to write, despite the research that suggests that writing would be beneficial on a number of levels. There have been very few overviews of writing in North American school systems. In the last major study of writing in high schools in the United States, Applebee (2000) noted that "only 3 percent of class work and of homework involved composing original text" (p. 1). The majority of writing activities in school involved writing without composing: fill in the blank and completion exercises, direct translation, or other seat work in which the text was constructed by the teacher or textbook, and the student supplied missing information that was, typically, judged as right or wrong. (p. 1)

With such a paucity of original writing being asked of students, it is not difficult to see why students often perceive writing as a meaningless activity, or a waste of time. In addition, writing is often used as a form of punishment, ranging from such old forms of discipline as writing lines, to asking students to write extra essays because of behavioral issues.

In my nearly forty years of experience of teaching high school, undergraduate, and graduate students, I have found that it is really not that difficult to get young people to write, as long as you keep several things in mind. In order to truly engage students in writing, a teacher must acknowledge the significance of student knowledge and experience, as well as be aware of youth culture and their interests. It is probably best if an educator takes a critical pedagogical approach in class, in order to facilitate student learning and engagement. The shift goes far beyond simply befriending students, and making them feel comfortable. Kincheloe (2008) stated:

A critical pedagogical vision grounded as it is in social, cultural, cognitive, economic, and political contexts understands schooling as part of a larger set of human services and community development. Any viable vision of critical education has to be based on larger social and cognitive visions. In this context, educators deal not only with questions of schooling, curriculum, and educational policy, but also with social justice and human possibility. (p. 7)

This shift is quite profound, especially in how the relationship radically changes between students and teachers. In a critical pedagogical sense, teachers and students work together on common goals. In a traditional educational situation, there is often a perceived hierarchical difference. Students are often disengaged in today's schools, and do not feel that they have any self-determination in their own education. Writing especially suffers, because students perceive it as not being relevant, or as being unimportant to them. A critical pedagogical approach helps them see that their perceptions and expressions have value. Once students are truly engaged, improvement in style and specific skills can be rapid because of the deeper student involvement and faith in what they are doing. If we begin to see literacy as a social practice, and not just as a set of neutral skills, education suddenly becomes central to the development of each individual in society, and in fact, leads to a sense of community within society. In this way, we are all involved and part of society, not simply passive consumers in society.

Writing, from this perspective, becomes a way of knowing and a means of identity construction. Freire (1998) maintained literacy always involves "an attitude of creation and re-creation, a self-transformation producing a stance of intervention in one's context" (p. 86). If students are treated to a meaningful, dialogic relationship with their teachers, they become engaged in their own learning because they have a stake in it.

For teachers of writing it is helpful to have a background in writing and composing theory in order to better understand students, as well as to help conceptualize their writing assignments. The writing theories of James Britton (1970, 1982a, 1982b, 1982c), especially his concept of the three writing functions—transactional, poetic, and expressive—have been vastly underestimated in the last few years.

Expressive writing uses language that is "close to the self" (Britton, 1982a, p. 96) and verbalizes the writer's consciousness. Britton maintained that all writing begins in the expressive function, and from there develops into transactional writing (persuasive, argumentative) and poetic forms (where the language and structure become part of the meaning, including various forms of fiction, poems, and drama). Yet expressive writing is the type of writing that is done least in schools, according to his studies (Britton, Burgess, Martin, McLeod, & Rosen, 1975). In *Writing at the Edge* (Park, 2005), I maintained that:

Utilizing expressive writing ... would allow a writer to explore complex social, political, cultural, and historical concepts through the filter of a personal lens of a self, even though that self is both in a state of being and an ever-shifting state of becoming. In this sense, learning and writing become meaningful acts of critical thinking and integration that acknowledge the self as a complex matrix. Expressive writing is a way of negotiating that matrix. (p. 161)

Teachers need to understand that students need to be able to play with language casually in the expressive function before they develop more formalized types of writing.

In addition, teachers and students need to have a basic understanding of writing-process theory in order to facilitate a classroom where writing is perceived as a meaningful act. It is essential to get students to understand that writing is a process with many options, and that they need not fear creating a finished product immediately. Writing-process theory allows students to explore and gather ideas in their work through a variety of means (Atwell, 1987; Calkins, 1983, 1986; Elbow, 1973/1998, 1981; Emig, 1971; Graves, 1973, 1975; Macrorie, 1970, 1974; Moffett, 1968, 1973; Murray, 1968, 1984). Writing becomes much more immediate and significant to students when they feel that they have time to develop their ideas without the immediate pressure of a finished product, such as an essay or report.

A simple summation of the writing process is that writing is not a one-step activity resulting in a final product; rather, a writer develops a piece of writing through a series of steps including prewriting (gathering ideas, brainstorming, clustering, discussing), draft writing, revision [or re-writing, or re-visioning as Murray (1984) maintained], editing (proofreading, correcting spelling, grammar, sentence structure), and finally, publishing (considering an audience, and the ultimate production of the writing).

Once students understand that 'real' writers undergo a series of writing activities (or a writing process), they feel less threatened to produce a finished product that is flawless. For the teacher, understanding this process helps them facilitate writing with their students on a number of levels simultaneously. In addition, students need to be able to pick their topics at least some of the time. This creates ownership of their work, and they are able to explore issues and ideas that are important to them.

A writing workshop approach provides students with a venue to write together in a social situation (showing that writing is a social activity and not an act of isolation, as is often demonstrated in schools), and to share ideas and concepts, as well as critique peers' work in a community of writers.

Teachers can teach specific writing formats and genres, but always with a discussed explanation of the value of the genres and the social implications of each. In other words, do not just demand a blind, obedient compliance from students—for instance, show them how and why a business letter, or resume, or essay is structured the way it is. In fact, grammatical issues can also be taught this way using sociolinguistics as a foundation. The students then begin to realize that they are part of an ever evolving world of language when they realize that there are social and political reasons for structure. They also become active learners, rather than passive and bored recipients.

The major change is one of attitude—teachers work with students and engage them as sentient, intelligent beings, and listen to and value their ideas and feelings. Another advantage of this shift is that the classes become much more interesting, both for the students and for the teachers—teachers have much to learn from their students,

Best known for his ideas on freewriting, Elbow's (1973/1998) formulation of two types of writing to monitor two types of thinking is of great potential to all educators:

First-order thinking is intuitive and creative and doesn't strive for conscious direction or control.... Second-order thinking is conscious, directed, controlled thinking.... Second-order thinking is what most people have in mind when they talk about 'critical thinking.' (Elbow, 1986b, p. 55)

Elbow (1986b) maintained that there is a link between the writing process and these two kinds of thinking:

I link first-order intuitive or creative thinking with freewriting and first-draft exploratory writing in which one defers planning, control, organizing, and censoring. I link second-order thinking with slow, thoughtful rewriting or revising where one constantly subjects everything to critical scrutiny. (pp. 57–58)

Elbow noted that the two types of writing correspond to the two types of thinking, but operate at different times in the writing process. Far too often, teachers impose critical and judgmental thinking on the writing when students are trying to creatively gather ideas and construct thoughts.

In this sense, the act of writing becomes an act of knowing. Writing could be used in schools as a means of learning and understanding—not just as a means of taking notes, recording content, or demonstrating what they have learned on exams and by writing essays and projects. Murray (1984) maintained that,

> Writing, in fact, is the most disciplined form of thinking. It allows us to be precise, to stand back and examine what we have thought, to see what our words really mean, to see if they stand up to our own critical eye, make sense, will be understood by someone else. (p. 4)

This type of writing as a form of thinking is far more exploratory and expressive, and students become far more engaged in their own work.

How the various, theorized writing approaches can be utilized, in perhaps an anti-hegemonic fashion, can be shown in the following example from my own teaching career. I once taught at a New York City university where all students were required to write an entrance and exit essay. The entrance essay was a persuasive essay arguing a point of view, and was scored by a team of three markers, and students were basically sorted into four levels according to English-language proficiency based on the 'score' of the writing of the essay, both in skill and development of a cogent, coherent argument. At the end of the degree, the lower levels were required to write an exit exam to demonstrate language proficiency and the ability to persuade and argue a point of view. The exam questions were based on a quotation that was quite complex and often based on an aspect of constitutional law, or a complicated social issue. Being able to decode the quotation and question was a challenge, and writing a coherent response was often overwhelming for the students. On the first day of class, I read my students a few sample questions from previous exams, and we talked about the ramifications and format of the exam. Most of the students felt hopeless about passing and/or were overwhelmed with the language and the topics. They did not know where to start, and for the first few minutes, just sat silently in class.

After a short break, some of the class, composed mainly of young males, started talking about the new baseball season and arguing who was better, the Mets or the Yankees. This led to a lively discussion about the various pros and cons of each team and their overall merits. Instead of getting them back 'on task,' I used the discussion in a pedagogical sense to apply some of my ideas about writing to the classroom situation. I asked them to provide more specific reasons for their choices. For instance, they could mention better pitching, or hitting, or even coaching, but they had to provide reasons and evidence for what they were arguing. Slowly they began to build a persuasive argument for their viewpoint. At this point, I asked them to put their ideas on paper. In many ways, the writing started as expressive writing, where the writer was simply expressing their thoughts with no thought of an audience; however, once they realized that they had to convince others of their argument, they began to carefully build an argument.

To me, this is an excellent example of what Freire described as a *generative theme*—an idea that has special significance to that person in the specific social context. Baseball, in this case, and it was not an irrelevant topic, and the resulting discussion was not pandering to the students, or lowering 'standards.' Rather, it should be seen as an example of a generative theme, something that was of significance to these young men. Suddenly the class was transformed from a stodgy and inactive academic space into an active Bahktian playground of carnival where ideas were generated, expressed, and respectfully debated in a dialogic format. As Kincheloe (2008) stated,

> Critical pedagogy is enacted through the use of generative themes to read the word and the world and the process of problem solving…. The reading of the word and the world helped students connect what they decoded on the printed page to an understanding of the world around them. Thus a synergistic relationship emerged between the word and the world. (p. 15)

The students were actively involved in constructing a viable, strong, persuasive argument, and the skills they developed in this exercise could be transferred to the more formal exit exam. But other events were occurring that would later add to the success of the class over the term. We were building a pedagogical space where individual ideas were respected and listened to. Not that all ideas were always agreed upon, and the point of the discussion was not to build consensus, but rather to generate ideas and organize them in a persuasive argument—ultimately in a piece of writing. With the building of community, other benefits occurred—for instance, attendance was never an issue in these classes. Students wanted to engage and to be part of a class where they could express their ideas in a safe, pedagogical space. In addition, I could teach grammatical and writing skills more easily because the students always saw a purpose to what I was teaching and would buy in much more easily. By explaining why as well as how, the confrontational nature that sometimes occurs in classrooms completely disappeared.

I introduced writing skills constantly throughout the term, but always within the context of better expressing their ideas, thoughts, and feelings, rather than randomly imposing the skills in an abstract way with no context. That shift in focus is vital and central to the success of any writing program with young people. It is not a top-down, hierarchical approach that often disenfranchises students. Instead, students feel connected, valued, and significant. Trust is important. For instance, if students constantly feel that they are being judged, criticized, and 'put down,' they will often just shut down. But if they feel that the teacher is working with them, and for them, they are much more willing to try new things, including working on sentence structure and grammatical, spelling, and punctuation issues, as well as more complex genre structural issues. All of these 'issues,' concepts, and specific skills can be taught more easily if students feel they have value and significance in helping them express their thoughts, feelings, and ideas that are often in the process of being constructed and formulated.

Later in the term, we addressed the exit exam format, and wrote complex, persuasive essays on drugs in the streets, gun laws, women's rights, constitutional and legal issues—but it all began with an interest in the generative theme of baseball, something that meant something to them.

Conclusion

All meaningful writing engages the self and others in the world into complex, dialogical relationship—meaning is always contextual. The self constantly constructs itself and negotiates meaning with others in a series of social agreements. A writer, in creating a text, negotiates a meaningful relationship between a self and a culture, with text acting as the interface. (Park, 2012, pp. 552–553)

Writing is a way of knowing—and a means of learning, not just the demonstration of what has been learned (the basis of examinations, tests, quizzes, and most writing assignments, including essays). Rather, the act of writing is a way for students to begin conceptualizing complex ideas.

Youth writers need to be connected with something relevant and meaningful in their lives—and this means their real, everyday lives, not simply their constructed, academic lives. Home life, street life, work life—including interests such as movies, music, sports, politics, friends, pop culture, life goals, world issues, as well as emotional turmoil, and domestic issues—need to be acknowledged, rather than ignored. An education system that has an infinite need to measure, quantify, and rank students is largely irrelevant—a silent revolt and student withdrawal is the consequence. Acceptance and encouragement are important, while at the same time, it is equally important that the teacher always asks more in manageable, incremental amounts. Education is usually a contradictory process and rarely linear and as sequential as many would assume.

Students need and want to write, to express themselves—it is often the case that they do not want to be judged so quickly on what they do not do. Ironically, the best way to get youth involved is to enter their world and value their world, and push them to be better while at the same time acknowledging and valuing where they are. Do not be so quick to judge, measure, value, sort, and quantify.

References

Applebee, A. (2000). Alternative models of writing development. In R. Indrisano & J. Squire (Eds.), *Writing: Research/Theory/Practice*. Newark, DE: International Reading Association. Retrieved from http://www.albany.edu/cela/publication/article/writing.htm

Atwell, N. (1987). *In the middle: Writing, reading and learning with adolescents*. Portsmouth, NH: Boyton/Cook.

Britton, J. (1970). *Language and learning*. Coral Gables, FL: University of Miami Press.

Britton, J. (1982a). Writing to learn and learning to write. In G. M. Pradl (Ed.), *Prospect and retrospect: Selected essays of James Britton* (pp. 94–111). Upper Montclair, NJ: Boynton/Cook.

Britton, J. (1982b). Notes on a working hypothesis about writing. In G. M. Pradl (Ed.), *Prospect and retrospect: Selected essays of James Britton* (pp. 123–139). Upper Montclair, NJ: Boynton/Cook.

Britton, J. (1982c). Shaping at the point of utterance. In G. M. Pradl (Ed.), *Prospect and retrospect: Selected essays of James Britton* (pp. 139–145). Upper Montclair, NJ: Boynton/Cook.

Britton, J., Burgess, T., Martin, N., McLeod, A., & Rosen, H. (1975). *The development of writing abilities (11–18)*. London, UK: Macmillan.

Calkins, L. M. (1983). *Lessons from a child: On the teaching and learning of writing*. Exeter, NH: Heinemann.

Calkins, L. M. (1986). *The art of teaching writing*. Portsmouth, NH: Heinemann.

Elbow, P. (1981). *Writing with power: Techniques for mastering the writing process*. New York, NY: Oxford University Press.

Elbow, P. (1986a). Embracing contraries in the teaching process. In P. Elbow, *Embracing contraries: Exploration in learning and teaching* (pp. 142–159). New York, NY: Oxford University Press.

Elbow, P. (1986b). Teaching two kinds of thinking by teaching writing. In P. Elbow, *Embracing contraries: Exploration in learning and teaching* (pp. 55–63). New York, NY: Oxford University Press.

Elbow, P. (1998). *Writing without teachers* (2nd ed.). New York, NY: Oxford University Press.

Emig, J. (1971). *The composing processes of twelfth graders. Research Report no. 13*. Urbana, IL: National Council of Teachers of English.

Freire, P. (1985). Reading the world and reading the word: An interview with Paulo Freire. *Language Arts, 62*(1), 15–21.

Freire, P. (1998). Education for critical consciousness. In A. M. Freire & D. Macedo (Eds.), *The Paulo Freire reader*. New York, NY: Continuum.

Freire, P., & Macedo, D. (1987). *Literacy: Reading the word and reading the world*. Westport, CT: Bergin and Garvey.

Graves, D. H. (1973). *Children's writing: Research directions and hypotheses based upon an examination of the writing processes of seven year old children* (Unpublished doctoral dissertation). Buffalo, NY, SUNY Buffalo.

Graves, D. H. (1975). An examination of the writing processes of seven year old children. *Research in the Teaching of English, 9*(3), 227–241.

Kincheloe, J. (2008). *Critical pedagogy* (2nd ed.). New York, NY: Peter Lang.

Macrorie, K. (1970). *Telling writing*. New York, NY: Hayden.

Macrorie, K. (1974). *A vulnerable teacher*. Rochelle Park, NJ: Hayden.

Moffett, J. (1968). *Teaching the universe of discourse*. Boston, MA: Houghton Mifflin.

Moffett, J. (1973). *A student-centered language arts curriculum, grades K–13: A handbook for teachers*. Boston, MA: Houghton Mifflin.

Murray, D. (1968). *A writer teaches writing: A practical method of teaching composition by Donald M. Murray*. Boston, MA: Houghton Mifflin.

Murray, D. (1984). *Write to learn*. New York, NY: Holt, Rinehart, and Winston.

Park, J. (2005). *Writing at the edge: Narrative and writing process theory*. New York, NY: Peter Lang.

Park, J. (2012). Writing as critical literacy engagement: Outliers and the recursive nature of critical qualitative research. In S. Steinberg & G. Cannella (Eds.), *Critical qualitative research reader* (pp. 548–554). New York, NY: Peter Lang.

Park, J. (2013). How can English language arts teachers get students to 'buy into' the value of engaging in a process-based approach to writing. In K. James, T. Dobson, & C. Leggo (Eds.), *English in middle and secondary classrooms: Creative and critical advice from Canada's teacher educators* (pp. 212–216). Toronto, ON: Pearson.

CHAPTER 42

I hope I don't see you tomorrow

L. A. Gabay

"Everything has beauty, but not everyone can see it." —Confucius

I suppose that every occupation has a variable that keeps it fresh. Doctors see new patients, painters use different canvases and plumbers have to operate on different toilets. As a teacher at Passages Academy, a school that caters to students awaiting trial, I have one glaring variable. The building is the same. The books are the same. I am the same. But my students are always different and their tenure is most often brief.

More than just a high turnover rate, all of the students in my class must be attended to, regardless of their learning discrepancies, their unstable court-involved lives and their prior learning experiences. It is the definition of a heterogeneous group. Some students walk through my doors reading at a second grade level; some can breeze through Melville in a week. Some have been arrested for violent crimes, while others have arrived in my classroom because of minor cafeteria skirmishes. These differences are irrelevant to me. They have to be. I am there to teach and to focus exclusively on their progress.

It is impossible to stagnate in this environment. Some of the lessons stay the same year to year, but I am constantly in flux. I take inspiration from the lessons I teach, from the teaching methods of my colleagues and, most of all, from my students.

Transparency

"The fate of one individual invariably fits the fate of the other, and each is the hero of his own drama while simultaneously figuring in a drama foreign to him." —Arthur Schopenhauer

In this chapter, I present an auto-ethnography of my experiences as a teacher at Passages Academy, a school that tailors its curriculum to the needs of court-involved youth under the age of seventeen. I use this study of my experience working with the students of Passages Academy to examine how my personal experience of teaching is affected by this unique pedagogical environment and the myriad ways that this environment both complicates curriculum and structures educational experiences for detained youth.

I began working as an English teacher at Passages Academy in August of 2002. From that time I have kept a journal. If the writing has been sporadic and occasionally soporific, it has been pursued with the intention of allowing for reflection on my teaching and lesson planning, as well as my evolution as a pedagogical practitioner. For the purposes of this dissertation, I have formalized this process of documenting my teaching experience and life as an employee of the Passage Academy school program. What follows are excerpts and entries from the last decade. Some are personal and informal while others are more structured and academic. I have purposefully omitted exact dates in an attempt to more accurately reflect my experience—to misquote Alphonse Karr, "The more things change the more they stay the same."

I borrow this method from Willard Waller who made use of journal writing in his research; many of Waller's studies were lifted directly from his own experiences, particularly from the disappointments of his early days as a teacher. He also drew insights from the personal experiences of his colleagues and students, which at the time was hardly a traditional procedure. Waller observes, "If you believe that the way to research is to split hairs concerning what is and what is not scientific, you create a market for methodological disputations and that is all that you get" (1970, p. 59). In this way, my journals are not only personally relevant to me but I hope that they may also be scientifically relevant to a community of teachers.

Willard Waller pioneered the ethnographic analysis of schools as miniature societies with problematic relationships to the larger community. In his direct, perceptive, and often cynical style, Waller penetrated the facades of schools as social institutions. In such a framework, many things that often seem contradictory can be true at once, specifically when working with identity development, knowledge and emotional healing.

Waller's depiction of his own emotional experience is important to this chapter. When I first started writing about my teaching experiences, I tried to remove myself from the text in order to convince the reader, or myself, that I had not become entangled in a way that might affect my objectivity. I would unconsciously edit out any aspect of my emotional life. I realized, however, that it is impossible to remain uninvolved and that, as much as I tried, I was never really neutral. Further, and more importantly, I have found that what I learn about myself becomes part of the study. A study of a place, event or practice is also a "study of self-in-relation to other" (Bullough & Pinnegar, 2001, p. 13). Connelly and Clandinin (1990) note that sometimes our own "stories come to light as much as do those of our participants" (p. 2). In accordance with Waller's tradition and expertise I position this part of the study in narrative journal form.

In this chapter, I implement Waller's technique of using personal narrative by paying close attention to epistemological and ethical issues. The aim is to provide a detailed account of my teaching at the school. Applying Waller's art of sustained fieldwork, I was provided with an insightful overview of changes in the empirical and theoretical aspects of my teaching practice. My panegyric of non-fictive discourse includes self-analysis and self-evaluation, examining the issues I have confronted in my work as a teacher at Passages. It is important for me to discuss my personal experiences because they illustrate a world that is, to many, not only unfamiliar, but also unimaginable. I have become inured to circumstances that many would find disheartening at best and statutorily egregious at worst. It is important to personalize the academic because, ultimately, the policies and history of Alternative Schooling have affected individuals, not just institutions.

I'm watching the trial of a sixteen-year-old boy, charged with vandalism and trespassing. From the open courtroom window across Leonard Street I can barely see the local high school, where kids are pouring out into the spring day. The sounds of their laughter drift into the stuffy courtroom while, on the stand, a witness points out the frightened young man sitting at the defense table. Idling on the corner is a Department of Corrections van, waiting to transport this young man to the Bridges Intake Center, where he will endure a medical examination and academic and emotional diagnosis before being shipped off to an unfamiliar new home and school.

I imagine that, upon entering Passages, students must feel like they are slipping into an altered reality where time and space shifts. The world they knew—whether it was comfortable and homey or unpredictable and tumultuous—is gone. What follows is a tale of what happens on the other side.

A Captive Audience

I am not supposed to have favorite students, but it is impossible to avoid. One Friday, just before a long weekend and a day before my birthday, Stacey solidified her place in my memory.

The girls' class is waiting for the van to take them back to their group home and I am headed downstairs from my office on the fourth floor. Stacey sees me from the art room doorway and calls me over. We shake hands, formally, as is the norm for greeting someone at Boys Town and she leans against the dark blue door-jamb, her dyed orange-blonde-brown hair in stark contrast to her backdrop. I make myself comfortable in the chair across from her, eager, even after school hours on a Friday, to hear whatever stories she tells because her stories are funny, sometimes shocking and always revealing. For the shortest second ever recorded, it is silent, while Stacey searches for something to say; as much as she likes me, I realize that I'm just an excuse for her to avoid the art teacher.

All of a sudden, her face lights up. There is fire behind her eyes, and words tumble out of her mouth like a waterfall. "You neva' axed why I'm here!" she exclaims, her Queens accent beautifully mutilating her words. "Aren't chu curious? It doesn't make you scared? What if I wuz in here for killin' my English teacher?"

Tongue-in-cheek as ever, Stacey grins as she crinkles her eyes and forehead. I have learned that this is her version of a wink. She continues, half a breath later. "I got arrested. That wuz when I wuz at Passages before. Four months. Got let out on probation. I started smoking cigarettes cuz I couldn't smoke weed."

When I show my distain for cigarettes, Stacey jumps on it: "I know. I know! But I couldn't smoke weed! I was doin' good for a while, but then I broke probation. That's what really got me in trouble. I wuzn't keeping curfew an' I missed two drug tests ... nah, three. But the third wuz cuz I wuz in a fight. Bitch pulled out a knife! Cops came before she swung though, so ain't nuthin' happened. 'Cept I got locked up again. But I broke probation, so I guess I'm not that surprised.

"I tol' you I got sentenced?" A strange energy infuses her voice, excitement and sadness intertwined. "Yea, they supposed to take me today. I don't know when tho-- Damn ... oh well. Anywayz, I'm glad they waited 'til later in the day, cuz I wanted to take your test."

The fire returns to her eyes as the sadness leaves them.

"I aced it, Mista! I studied real hard. Did you grade it yet?" She looks disappointed as I shake my head, but remains upbeat. "Well ... when you do ... you'll see! A+... Anyways, I got 18 months, Cayuga Homes. Supposed to be kinda nice. I guess. And don't worry, Mr. G, I'm not down wit' the way I wuz. I'm gonna get my GED there. They got this program, you know?"

The front door opens downstairs and Stacey hears her name.

"What?!" she calls, standing to take a couple steps to the top of the stairs. "Oh ... okay ... I'm coming." She turns back to me: "I gotta go, Mista. Eighteen months if I'm good. Four years if I'm not. I'll be good." She smirks, shakes my hand, and heads back into the hallway.

Two seconds later, Stacey barges back into the classroom, her hair trailing behind her: "Oh yeah. Happy birthday, Mista. I'll holla at 'chu."

Les Misérables

"You can learn a lot about a society by looking at its prisons." —Fyodor Dostoyevsky

I have taught many Staceys. She, like many of the pre-adjudicated students at Passages, had made mistakes and was struggling, like most young adults, to figure out the world and her burgeoning place in it. In my role as educator, I feel it is inappropriate to pry into why my students have been detained. Instead, I focus on teaching individuals, irrespective of whatever brought them into my classroom. This offers them an opportunity to transcend the labels and allegations that are likely weighing on them and gives them a chance to interact with a sense of normalcy during this time of crisis.

Like Stacey, some students are academically motivated. Others, as I discovered early on, will read their first sentence on the premises. Some are shy, seeming to hide a secret life, and others extremely boisterous. Some thrive in these smaller classes, taking advantage of the extra attention we can provide, and some are recalcitrant, likely feeling exposed in a classroom setting for the first time. Some are explicit about their dreams of becoming architects, lawyers or dancers, while others project a nihilism that seems tragically premature or are deeply entrenched in gang life. They tell me stories of life on the streets, of a Fresh-Air-Fund summer in upstate New York, or the terror of being locked up during the Blackout of 2003.

One of the encouraging cases was a fifteen-year-old girl named Tammi, who was extremely motivated. She was the kind of student who sits up front, as though this will allow her to receive the information slightly before those sitting in the back. But she was not selfish; she helped other students and, when there was a distraction in class, she became annoyed, seemingly on behalf of all of us. Tammi's eagerness to learn motivated me to be a better teacher. I would specifically think about her as I planned my lessons. For example, in prior years, I would bring in Ginsberg's poem *Howl*, and while the students were reading it, I would write five lines on the board for a post-reading discussion. However, anticipating Tammi's elastic interpretation of structure, I instead asked the students to select five lines from the poem for our discussion. This proved to be more interesting because choosing the lines forced them to engage with the poem more deeply.

I was surprised, then, to find out that Tammi was barely passing in her community school. According to her, she had excelled throughout elementary school but when she got to middle and high school her social life took priority over academic work. With her strong personality, Tammi found herself in one fight after another, a pattern that ultimately brought her into my classroom. In private discussions, Tammi acknowledged that the small classes and constant supervision at Passages had gotten her back on track. When she finally left us, she was studying for the Global History Regents Exam.

Unlike Tammi, fourteen-year-old Martin could barely read. When he first arrived at Passages, he was extremely disruptive in class. Martin did not do any work and he was often written up and sent to the correctional officers. The reading teacher, Ms. Burwell, was the first to realize that Martin was a non-reader and she began tutoring him after school, a luxury unheard of to Martin. She also referred him to the reading specialist, Ms. Carris, who visited our site twice a week. After a few weeks of one-to-one tutoring, Martin made small but significant improvements. He seemed to develop a new trust for teachers and even began to settle down during class. Though he couldn't read very well, he was able to get involved in discussions. He especially thrived when we listened to music as part of the lesson. I particularly remember during a drama unit (Victor Hugo's *Les Misérables*) that he enjoyed when I played the *Eroica* symphony, which Beethoven wrote to honor Napoleon.

The staff at Passages not only helped to demystify reading and writing for Martin, but we helped to simplify and elucidate the confusing and intimidating world of school. It is both encouraging and disheartening to see kids like Martin, Tammi and Stacey pass through my classroom. It is painfully clear that students like them thrive in our system, which promotes individual attention and inspired, unique lessons. But our system is not a permanent solution; Passages is a temporary artery that they pass through on their way back to an overcrowded public school or a stifling detention center classroom. I always value the little time we have together, struggle to make it sustainable after they are gone and, ultimately, wish it could be longer.

A Culture of No Expectations

"Our worst fear is not that we are inadequate; our deepest fear is that we are powerful beyond measure. It is our light, not our darkness that most frightens us." —Marianne Williamson

In order to meet the vastly different needs of my revolving door of learners, I have to create lesson plans elastic enough to suit each student. More specifically, I have to find ways to challenge those who are working above grade level and remediate those below—one lesson plan that accommodates both the Martins and the Tammis. For example, one lesson plan that seems to successfully span all learning levels is the analysis of the Tupac Shakur song "Me Against the World." For the lower level learners, a discussion of rhyme scheme might be sufficient, while the higher-level learners can focus on the sociopolitical philosophies behind Tupac's words. In this way, the following two lines can provide a full lesson for almost any student: "Can't reach the children cause they're illin'/Addicted to killing and the appeal from the cap peeling."

The lower-level learners can examine the way Tupac plays with rhyme scheme and alliteration —"illing" rhymes with "killing" and is a half rhyme with "peeling" and "appeal" is alliterative with "cap peeling." The higher-level learners can analyze Tupac's lament of the difficulties of educating those who are stuck in a cycle of violence. Furthermore, an even more in-depth discussion can relate Tupac's words to the students' own lives, creating a self-reflective discourse that is both academically relevant and personally valuable. Therefore, in one forty-five minute class period that focuses on two lines of a rap, our lesson could span a genuinely high-level discussion of identity as well as a more simple analysis of poetry, alliteration and rhyme scheme. We are able to carry on this varied discussion without alienating any students; everyone feels integrated because each of them can relate and participate in at least one part of the lesson. And, more importantly, the lower level-learners are exposed to high-level discussions, which may accelerate their academic experience.

As a teacher at Passages Academy, it is important for me to not only know my students, but to understand the complicated environments in which they have been raised. Paulo Freire's (1970) work bluntly calls upon educators to understand the worlds of their students before addressing them: "Often, educators and politicians speak and are not understood because their language is not attuned to the concrete situation of the people they address. Accordingly, their talk is just alienated and alienating rhetoric" (p. 77).

For this reason, I believe it is important for me to understand where my students have come from. I have been able to do this in a few ways: I have visited the four group homes that house the non-secure detention (NSD) residents on Thanksgivings, I have done personal walking tours of the neighborhoods that my students mention in class and I have spoken to the parents of students, either over the telephone or in-person at parent-teacher nights. But the most important interaction I have had with students was simply speaking to them.

What initially inspired me to bring in the Tupac Shakur piece is that my students often refer to him. However, I also had an interesting conversation about the Tupac lesson from a student who suggested I bring in some alternative resources. She said to me, "Gabay, I get enough negativity at home and I like you and your class, but I like it best when you keep the lessons positive. I like 'Me Against the World,' but it wouldn't hurt you to also find something happy." This student taught me that I had failed to acknowledge the beauty and positivity in their worlds and the dialectic between difference and deficiency. That is, in my attempt to connect with the students, I had brought in songs, magazine articles and books that all shared a heightened sense of urban drama and an element of sensationalized danger. I found myself playing into hackneyed imagery of violence and adversity as a means to capture their attention and win them over. Therefore, my student's request that I "lighten up" the classroom discourse made me realize that their worlds are as varied as anyone else's, despite their current unique situation.

This theme of not exoticizing the students was further hammered home when I was teaching at Crossroads and a guard, Ms. Howard, pulled me aside and said, "When you write your book, don't exploit us or the students. Don't make it Hollywood. Don't forget the beauty! You got to keep it real ... but isn't beauty part of keeping it real?" The student and Ms. Howard reframed the way I taught at the school. Obviously, despite the students' incarceration, there are hope and love, and productive things are happening in the areas where these students live. By omitting their rich cultural, social and even economic histories I limited the students' classroom learning experience. Not surprisingly, as I began this shift to lessons of elevation or positivity, I noticed improvements in behavior during class time and even a rise in the number of students doing homework assignments that appealed to their more positive experiences.

Speak up, but don't shout!

As detailed above, my students' feedback is invaluable. In fact, it is the most important feedback I receive. Nonetheless, working in the tight quarters of the Boys Town building at Passages Academy, it is impossible not to take inspiration from my colleagues. In particular, the late Devon Smalls, who was the Music and Creative Writing teacher, was a perfect model for me. Specifically, I remember one scene where Mr. Smalls helped me grow:

There are two Mac computers, a bass guitar, a microphone and two students with headphones and pre-occupied looks, holding marble writing books. Three other students are sitting at the table and compulsively thinking; brainwaves seem to be humming vertiginous sensations of recognition of something familiar. What I am observing is exactly how one might imagine a hip hop recording studio in Brooklyn to be as opposed to a classroom in a juvenile detention center.

When Mr. Smalls addresses the students, expounding on the historical significance of today's beat, which they will be singing and rapping over, they look at him as teenagers often do—bored and unimpressed. Billy, the poet and apparent raconteur of the group, complains, "Who cares about the history of rap? We're running out of time and need to finish!" Mr. Smalls looks at the candid student with the 'I don't give a damn what you think' mouth. He pauses, for effect. "Music and art are history, Billy" he proceeds, "and this is part of the program. Though your fortitude is humbling, you will not be rude and cut me off, especially when I am about to talk about the Cold Crush Brothers." Mr. Smalls and Billy make quick eye contact and both smile knowingly, both aware of the other's games.

In the scenario above, Mr. Smalls deftly does a dozen good things at once. His academic lesson is as important as his social one and his candor is as valuable as his kindness. He is able to use his student's creativity to teach them about history and, when he is challenged, he immediately and, with sly humor, draws a correlation between art and history. Frankly, I was in awe.

I would often find myself like a fly on the wall in Mr. Smalls' classroom. We were co-teachers but I sometimes felt like another student, furiously taking mental notes with the intention of emulating. His teaching was not subtle and his lessons were implicit. He freely employed street terms—"let's get *crunk*," "make sure your mind's *brollick*"—to let students know where he came from. But more than just words, Mr. Smalls was able to seamlessly connect our students' lives with their work. He once told me, "I wanted to try a different thing. I wanted to bring in the culture of their neighborhood in a stronger way, so I decided to have them narrate their stories in song, using their voice, persona, and elements from their neighborhood. Many of our students have been alienated from serious academic work; theirs is a culture of disenfranchisement. Education needs to respect identity by allowing the students to express their own emotional reality as opposed to one driven or prescribed. A teacher who can connect self and community has provided an honest exchange between people. The way I gauge it is, if at the end of the class I end up exhausted and the students are not, I am doing too much of the work."

Mr. Smalls taught me that our students' reality is something to be questioned and analyzed and is a subject as important to our curriculum as math and science. I have always felt that my hip hop unit with Mr. Smalls was an example of the purest form of telling a story because we were opening up the schematic of literacy by using various forms of expression. We were employing in-class writing, music and oratory collaboration in a deeply calculated attempt to offer a technical examination of this school and a conversation about life, art, philosophy, and even incarceration. In our own way, we were writing a mini-ethnography with music.

When I asked him how he had so skillfully quieted Billy, his answer surprised me:

"Don't underestimate the sophistication of that kid. While his antics may seem reckless, I think they are intentional and part of a broader and complicated psychology: to motivate and inspire his peers and himself, and to disorient and annoy his opponents (like us teachers). This street psychology is a large part of why he is here, but it can also lead to success at this level. It's also why he has been able to maintain an incredible level of intensity and consistency in this classroom."

Though Mr. Smalls is no longer with us, his voice stays with me every day because of his insightful analyses of students like Billy. Mr. Smalls forced me to practice thinking in a way that was, for him, instinct. He was able to see so many things at once—e.g., Billy's recklessness and calculation, his supportiveness and antagonism—and the more I am able to acknowledge and reconcile these apparently conflicting motivations, the more like Mr. Smalls—and the better teacher—I become.

Straight Out of Comp. 101

At the beginning of every school year, I am faced with an almost humorous conflict: what to do with the dense, two-inch thick *Curriculum and State Standards* tome? I have the simultaneous urge to frame and memorize it and also use it as a doorstop or seat cushion. The *Curriculum and State Standards* is a guidebook designed to take teachers through an entire year of teaching. It is replete with lesson plans, learning materials such as articles, short stories and poems and a "Pacing Calendar" that instructs teachers what and when to teach various subjects. It is valuable, but primarily as a point of departure, not a destination carved in stone. The Curriculum I am given is specifically designed for my unique school and rightly accounts for the average twenty-three day stay of our students; my administration has suggested either telescoping or spreading out the concepts and activities over two or three days, as new students are constantly rotating through my classroom.

Fortunately, the scripted framework of the *Curriculum and State Standards* has encouraged me to experiment and personalize strategies to make them my own. With provisions for a certain degree of improvisation and spontaneity, many of my lessons follow a self-developed format: I begin to learn about the students on a personal level, evaluate their needs as writers, and assess their personal passions as a means of seeking to broaden their learning parameters. During a lesson on onomatopoeia that felt rote and stagnant, a student suggested that a hip hop group, the Roots, used this literary technique to create words based upon sound and effect. With each successive lesson on language, more hip hop songwriters were being referenced: Tupac Shakur for imagery (as explained in the previous section), Notorious B.I.G. for narrative, and Jay-Z for metaphor. I started bringing these songs into the classroom and asking students to analyze the lyrics as well as to use what others had written as a model for their own writing. With such an approach, my once-stagnant lesson was given new life and intimacy, celebrating creativity, history, diversity, intelligence and personal power.

Another time, during a mandated lesson on "Symbolism in Writing," a student referenced the use in popular culture of iconic symbols such as Nike's "Swoosh" logo and McDonald's' famous yellow Arches. This fun and transformative moment ultimately led to an exploration of trends in media consolidation by understanding basic principles of advertising and describing images and symbolism. The following semester, I continued with this analysis when teaching imagery by examining how the media influences self-conceptions of body image and how this affects social attitudes and behaviors. In this way, my methodology is such that lesson plans are rooted in traditional academic customs but are ultimately designed to grow out of departure points and expand into further educational exploration.

The most successful application of a unique teaching method to a more formal mandate was a non-traditional approach to our unit on theater. In this unit, the *Curriculum and State Standards* provides teachers with passages from Arthur Miller's *Crucible* and August Wilson's *Fences*. While these texts can be enjoyable and engaging for students, I wanted to take advantage of being in New York City and my personal connections to those in the theater arts community.

I asked a professional actor friend to take on the role of my co-teacher by visiting my class once a week over the course of a semester. She taught and administered various acting games that inspired students to learn in a totally new way. For example, one of the games she played with students was called "Taxi." In this exercise, one student is assigned the role of Taxi driver and his/her job is to pick up various passengers, who are played by the other students, and make casual conversation. Entirely improvised, this game asks students to create characters and use their imaginations to project those characters onto an entirely fictional set of circumstances. More than just fun, this exercise forced students to empathize, because they had to immerse themselves in the mind of someone else. It also brought typically shy students out of their shells because they were encouraged to speak without the often-intimidating feeling of being judged—after all, it was "just a character."

Furthermore, though the acting project is not formally part of the curriculum, it is pedagogically reflective by nature as the learners look at characters and explore issues of self in relation to society. Evidence of its efficacy was found in a free-writing journal entry of a student, who expressed this very sentiment with great insight and aplomb:

> When I'm alone I try to finally relax and think about the struggle of my parents and what it means for me. I can't just relax though, I need something to twist up or drink down. Just like Hubble [from Runaways], anger has built up in me. Performing keeps me safe because when I'm bored I do stupid things. It is better for everyone if I just chill when I'm alone, I don't know what else to do. (Jonathan, student, age 16)

Jonathan's piece demonstrates different forms of reflectiveness and empowerment. During the theater unit, students have opportunities to play out their situations, emotions and feelings while hiding behind the safety of a costume and character. In this case, Jonathan is able to think about himself in a roundabout way—through the character of Hubble—and this likely a more palatable experience for someone unaccustomed to confronting his inner turmoil.

By condoning my use of such a methodology, my school's administration has provided both its teachers and students the opportunity for agency while simultaneously offering a curriculum that is focused upon breaking the built-in structural antagonisms. In doing so, I feel that they were able to successfully alter the traditional hegemonic dynamic often found in schools without compromising the legitimacy of school as a place to learn.

No Child Left Behind—But Are They Moving Forward?

"An individual has not started living until he can rise above the narrow confines of his individualistic concerns to the broader concerns of all humanity." —Martin Luther King, Jr.

I have described above the many ways I am inspired by my colleagues and students. But it is important for me to remember that, while emulating those who I think are great, I also must emphasize what I believe I do well as a teacher. For this reason, I would like to explore my own style, how it has evolved and what I learned from each experience. In retrospect, it seems that my trajectory to Passages Academy was inevitable and, in hindsight, it is easy to see that I have always been attracted to teaching. Long before I had formalized any concrete thoughts of educating, I regularly volunteered to teach. Not surprisingly, this behavior led to more official teaching opportunities.

In eleventh grade, I was standing outside my school when I saw my teacher's daughter trying to ride her bicycle. She was struggling to stay balanced in the parking lot while waiting for her mother to exit the school. Instinctively, I ran over and, as I'm wont to do, gave her some advice: "Keep your head up, relax your hands and trust it." It was advice that I would have wanted to hear.

Several weeks later, Ms. Quintos, my teacher and the mother of the budding cyclist, recommended me to be a counselor at the Helen Keller Day Camp for the Blind. When I asked her why she thought I would be a good fit, she said, "My daughter said you were the only one who taught her how to ride a bike." Ironically, I hadn't thought much about helping her daughter. I was just doing what came naturally.

At the Helen Keller Day Camp, I discovered, in a more structured way, I had a skill set that I really enjoyed. The camp was comprised of young people with visual and hearing disabilities and I was assigned to be the counselor of the older boys group. Though my campers were disabled, they were also typical boys—rambunctious, competitive and curious about girls. In this way, I had to simultaneously temper their enthusiasm and protect them. It never occurred to me that this might be a difficult task because I always felt at ease. In retrospect, it seems that my comfort in this unique situation meant that I belonged; I excelled because I felt challenged but not overwhelmed. I spent the following three summers at the Helen Keller Day Camp.

After finishing my undergraduate degree at USC, I was in Los Angeles with an English degree and little direction. I attended a USC job fair to explore possible career opportunities and was struck by the results of a questionnaire: I was on track to be either a photographer, a beautician or a youth care worker. Though I was handy with an aperture and a hairbrush, I was most interested in teaching, so I was given the contact information for a group home in North Hollywood.

The Eddie Lee Home for Youth was an emancipation home for students transitioning out of incarceration. As a youth care worker, I worked twelve hour shifts with various responsibilities: I made sure the students went to school everyday, did their homework, cleaned their rooms, did their chores, held a job and maintained a bank account. I felt immediately comfortable and, more importantly, valuable. I had grown up in a nice suburb of New York City, but I realized that the only thing separating me from these kids who just got out of detention was opportunity and access. At Eddie Lee, I felt I was providing them with that missing link.

Determined to become a teacher in earnest, I decided to enroll in NYU's Graduate English Education Program. At NYU, I learned the trade of teaching—lesson planning, classroom management and creating a personal philosophical disposition as a teacher—and I also studied the formal history of education. After receiving my Masters degree, I went to Geneva, Switzerland and taught English at an International School. Though I loved teaching and, in many ways, this experience confirmed my decision to pursue it as a career, I became a little homesick and vowed to begin teaching in the New York City public school system.

After returning home from Switzerland, I taught in two traditional New York City Public Schools: MS 321 and Columbus High School, both in the Bronx. Though many of my students were dealing with difficult personal circumstances, they were not in need of the kind of special attention that I had been asked to provide at the Helen Keller Day Camp and Eddie Lee. I felt like I was missing something, as though I was only doing half of what I wanted to be doing and decided to seek out a school setting that allowed me to reconcile my interest in teaching English with my interest in helping those in need. When a friend suggested Passages Academy, I became immediately inspired. Passages seemed like the perfect fit and I expected that it would give me an opportunity to teach in an environment where I would thrive. Of course, this transition was not initially easy.

The first few months at Passages were very uncomfortable for me. I found myself far out of my comfort zone, as the students were unused to this environment and the turnover rate was alarmingly brief and high. Still, I knew enough about myself to know that I was on the right path, just in a difficult part of it. I decided to stick it out, be resourceful and pretend I was confident until I actually was.

It is a cliché at Passages to talk about "reinvention," because the teachers are always telling the students that this is a safe place to create their new lives. But at the risk of perpetuating a cliché, Passages reinvented me. Although the stakes for each student were higher than in my previous teaching environments, just by virtue of their more dramatic circumstances, I felt paradoxically at ease. Similar to my experiences at Helen Keller and Eddie Lee, I felt more valuable in a room that cried out for extra attention. More significantly, I was able to reframe teaching for myself by trying everything from repeating a lecture to exploring and questioning.

Over the next several years, my teaching style evolved, although the core has not really changed. Though I am shaped by great colleagues like Mr. Smalls and insightful and outspoken students like Tammi, I am also the same teacher I was so many years ago with Ms. Quintos' daughter: "Keep your head up, relax your hands and trust it." In an attempt to characterize my teaching style, I like to emulate a marginally original quote from the movie *Hoosiers*: "Don't show them what you're not, just share who you are. Don't waste time hiding bad stuff, just let your good parts shine through." Mr. Smalls called me, "The Lady Gaga of teachers: assured, excessive, self-important and ridiculous beyond belief." My boss called my class "a masterpiece of under- and overstatement." In a classroom evaluation, my students referred to me as gentle, ironic, self-deprecating and tough.

When I started teaching at Passages, I tried to suppress my personality or tailor my behavior to my students. But I discovered I was far happier and more successful emphasizing what made me unique. I've learned how to reconcile who I am with what my students need: that is, how to be both boisterous and reserved, sympathetic and brutal, how to talk about life in general while simultaneously talking about the subject at hand and, finally, how to walk the fine line between frivolous conversation and formal instruction.

Most importantly, I try to reaffirm a positive message. I know that these students' lives are exceedingly difficult and that they are often surrounded by negative and discouraging examples. In this way, I have several mantras that I try to communicate, whether implicitly or explicitly. Many of my Passages students are either remarkably intelligent but unmotivated, or garrulously confident but bored. Instead of meeting these reluctant students with frustration or admonition that they are not living up to their potential, our classroom becomes place of acceptance and promise. My students are tiptoeing in a world of insecurity and it is my role to create a safe space for them to open up and experiment. The students do not want my pity, but rather they want me to be good at what I do; I can be firm and encouraging at the same time. Finally, I tell the students (and, in many ways, I tell myself) that if they are not making mistakes, they are not trying. It is only when we overcome the inevitable frustration of trying and failing that we can begin the very satisfying journey of trying again and succeeding.

Never Get in Their Face, but Get in Their Head

"All young people are looking for the same thing: a pat on the back for doing something well."
—Joe Namath

As this chapter focuses on my experiences teaching, I think it is fitting to end with the most important part of my job: the students. As such, below is the complicated and all-too-common story of Aiden:

Aidan should have been in eighth grade, but he was stuck in seventh. The teachers and I agreed that this young Haitian boy was the sweetest student we had seen in years and we were all inclined to believe his story: He had taken the fall for a parole violation that his brother committed. His brother ran their family; Mom was crazy and Dad was heavily gang related, with ties going back to Haiti.

Aidan was fourteen years old but looked twelve and, when you asked him his name, he would always give you his first and last name, like there was a stenographer in the room. He was one of those students that arrives every few months: the kind that makes teachers want to go above and beyond to help. Aidan's problems were profound and institutional but we did the little we could to make his brief time at Passages as beneficial as possible:

- *Aidan liked to paint, so we made sure he an unlimited stock of art supplies. I even went to Pearl Paint on Canal Street to get him the specific acrylic paints he liked.*

- *He mentioned he liked "Street Lit," so I went to the Strand Bookstore to pick up a few books by K'wanFoye.*

- *I rearranged the schedule to give Aidan extra time with the school social worker in an attempt to give him a feeling of safety structure.*

These little gestures had an impact, but I felt like I was pushing water back into the ocean. I knew that there were much larger waves sweeping him deeper in and, after a few weeks of minor progress, he was washed back into the system. Aidan was sent up to Rikers one night with no warning and no explanation. I just showed up for work and his seat was empty. And this is the way my job works: You get attached to students, and want to help, and then the thing you were making progress with is gone. It's the most frustrating feeling; like any good I do is going to be discouragingly temporary.

But even more discouraging is hearing about what happened to Aidan. His story is unfortunately all too common and all too baffling. After he mysteriously leaves Passages, he was brought to Intake at Riker's Island Prison, the largest Penal colony in America, to live under the same roof as murderers, high profile felons and the generally dangerous. Through the Passages social worker, I find out the following about Aidan:

Just before his sixteenth birthday, he is released from Rikers and gets sent back home. He is enrolled in a GED program, GED Plus, in Midtown Manhattan and is listed as being in seventh grade even though he was taking high school level classes at Island Academy, the school at Rikers. Presumably, because Aidan feels old and out of place amongst the seventh graders, he stops going to the GED program. Unhelpfully, his parole officer says, "I don't care if you go to school or not. Just don't get busted for having drugs in you." The PO means this colloquially, implying that the most important thing for Aidan is staying clean, but Aidan, taking advantage of the PO, stops going to school. A few weeks later, he is called in front of a judge and, too nervous to discuss his academic truancy, skips the hearing and is eventually sent upstate to Oswego Prison. Seven months later, he is released and sent to Community Prep in East Midtown. Still trying to help, I call the Principal to tell him how great Aidan is. He says, "We had no idea, all he does is hang out with other kids from jail." About to be eighteen, he still has not a single high school credit to his name and can't read above a fourth grade level. I feel powerless and wish he was back here at Passages, where we able to let him paint and write and read and grow.

But before I can fully mourn Aidan and his unfortunate circumstances, a new kid has taken his place.

References

Bullough, R. V., Jr., & Pinnegar, S. (2001). Guidelines for quality in autobiographical forms of self-study research. *Education Researcher 30*(3), 13–21.

Connelly, F. M., & Clandinin, D. J. (1990). Stories of experience and narrative inquiry. *Educational Researcher, 19*(5), 2–14.

Freire, Paulo (1970). *Pedagogy of the oppressed*. New York: Continuum Publishing Co.

Shakur, T. (1995). *Me against the world*. Interscope Records.

Waller, W. W. (1970). *Willard W. Waller on the family, education and war: Selected writings* (W. J. Goode, Jr., F. F. Fustenberg, & L. R. Mitchell, Eds.). Chicago: University of Chicago Press.

CHAPTER 43

Where Are the Mockingjays?
The Commodification of Monstrous Children and Rebellion

William M. Reynolds

The information, entertainment, and cultural pedagogy disseminated by massive multimedia corporations have become central in shaping and influencing every waking moment of children's lives—all toward a lifetime of constant, unthinking consumptions (Giroux, 2011b, p. 73).

[In consumer society,] culture and aesthetics blended with production and advertising to create a way of life focused on consumption of goods, services, mass images and spectacles. (Kellner, 1989, p. 146)

Marketing is now the instrument of social control and produces the arrogant breed, who are our masters. (Deleuze, 1995, p. 181)

Introduction

It is appropriate that I am writing a portion of this chapter on consumption, commodification, and dystopic youth fiction on a yellow legal pad stamped with a Staples logo in Starbucks next to shelving stacked with Starbucks merchandise, almost all of which contains the Starbucks logo. I'm drinking Sumatra-blend coffee from a Starbucks to-go cup with the logo emblazoned on it. No one stands outside this postmodern consumer culture. But it is also a time of activism with students in the streets and dystopic novels about resistance by youth. The times demand our attention. Giroux (2012a) and others have written extensively on student activism, particularly in the case of the global protest against increasing tuition fees and austerity measures.

> Counter-public spheres and modes of resistance that we once did not think young people could mount have erupted in a rush of emotional and political expressions and scattered demonstrations. Mass demonstrations have been organized through emergent screen cultures of a generation well versed in new technologically assisted forms of social networking and political exchange. (Giroux, 2012a, p. 2)

I will turn my attention to the fictional manifestations of monstrous and threatening wild children and their violence, resistance, and refusal.

I have always enjoyed reading novels, which is probably the primary reason I became an English major as an undergraduate and for my master's degree. Nothing was better than curling up in a comfy chair and reading a novel. I read all the novels I could get my hands on from the Western canon of authors like Dickens to the pulp novels of Stephen King. I also read many dystopic novels and watched many dystopic films. *Do Androids Dream of Electric Sheep?* (1968/1996) by Philip Dick (the basis of the film *Blade Runner*, 1982), *Animal Farm* (1945/1996) by George Orwell, *Lord of the Flies* (1963) by William Golding and *Brave New World* (1931/1989) by Aldous Huxley and many others made my reading list. Not only were these novels dystopic views of a possible future, they were a critique of the present society. I think one of the sources of my present critical perspective(s) were these novels that I read as a young kid. These readings and my studies of literary criticism also led to my keen interest in cultural studies, youth culture, and critical media literacy. Of course, reading novels curled up in a chair or couch is a position of privilege of which I am acutely aware. So, for me the question becomes how we make this activity of reading current dystopic youth fiction a place for developing social consciousness and moving towards issues of social justice. At the very least we should be able to make youth question the taken-for-granted consumerist mentalities.

At the present historical moment reading books in schools has become a quantified and standardized activity. Reading (whether classics or pulp fiction) has become a question of accountability and measurement. When students do read it is often to satisfy some testing requirement. In most schools in the United States, the only reason students read is to take a test for the Accelerated Reader Program (AR), a software program that provides tests on a wide range of books. Schools buy into the AR program and then can purchase additional book tests as needed. On the Accelerated Reader website the producers discuss how reading success is easy: Students just read a book and then take a computer test on that book. A high score earns the students points on the way toward the cumulative point score for the particular grade level. Read a book, take a test on trivia, and acquire points. It depends on the teacher, of course, but there is little discussion of the books. Usually there is none. The students read the books individually, not collectively, and learn that reading is attached to evaluation (test-taking) and accountability. And they begin to focus all their reading toward that end. Critical engaged reading does not have a place in this scheme. It is reminiscent of the now-defunct Book It program in which students read a certain number of books to win a free Pizza Hut pizza. Read so many books, acquire so many points, and you can take a trip to the local chain pizza place and get a pizza for your efforts. Some kids may have learned to love reading through this program, but it is more than likely they learned that the purpose of reading is, like most things in schooling, accumulation and consumption. But, it is possible to use readings, particularly of dystopic youth fiction, as opportunities for critical complicated conversations about society, politics, and social justice. Giroux (2002) discusses this possibility in regard to films.

> The decline of public life demands that we use film as a way of raising questions that are increasingly lost to the forces of market relations, commercialization, and privatization. As the opportunities for civic education and public engagement begin to disappear, film may provide one of the few media left that enables conversations that connect politics, personal experiences, and public life to larger social issues. (Giroux, 2002, p. 7)

I would suggest that the same possibility exists for current dystopic youth fiction.

I have spent two summers teaching critical literacy, graphic novels and youth fiction at McGill University. In the summer of 2010 the students and I discussed ideas about critical literacy, ecological literacy, and graphic novels (see Reynolds, in press). In 2011 I returned to teach a course in Children and Youth Literature. In this course we discussed pulp fiction like *Crank* (2004) by Ellen Hopkins, *Push* (1997) by Sapphire and *The Film Club* (2008) by David Gilmore. These novels were not the usual canonical texts that the students anticipated and had interesting portraits of postmodern youth as monstrous in some ways. There was Kristina, a high school junior dealing with methamphetamine (crank), Precious, an illiterate sixteen-year-old black girl, the victim of abuse and incest, and Jesse, a fifteen-year-old who (after making a deal with his dad to watch and discuss three movies a week) drops out of school. This popular fiction produced many discussions of contemporary youth culture, visions of the postmodern child, and the ways in which these books could foster critical perspectives on society. Those critical perspectives included issues of dystopic youth fiction and commodification.

Commodification: The Shopocalypse[1] of Dystopic Youth Fiction

Most of the blood and tribulations of the revolutionary spirit of *Battle Royale* (2010) and *The Hunger Games* (2010) are laid on the altar of the consumption of commodities in our postmodern society. I want to analyze the phenomenon of dystopic fiction within a bricolage of critical perspectives. Revolutionary spirit can be blunted by purchasing and displaying our rebelliousness by wearing Che Guevara t-shirts or demonstrating on social networks like Facebook with a type of slacktivism which replaces activism. A politics of hope (Giroux, 2012a, p. 28) is faced with the real economics of consumer culture. This does not make me lose hope for critical change. A critical media analysis of cultural artifacts such as dystopic pulp fiction can allow us to face our nightmare times and engage them. Indeed, youth have been instrumental in the Occupy Movement in facing police in riot gear and armed with extreme pepper spray. Despite the slacktivism of various social networks, there is also a real activism.

Of course, not only do dystopic pulp novels and their film adaptations have potentially critical dispositions and troubling content, they also are enmeshed within the corporate culture of marketing and production. These are not to be taken as either the epitome of critical work or the pawns of corporate marketing though they manifest the potential for both. Horkheimer and Adorno analyze this in "The Culture Industry: Enlightenment as Mass Deception" (1944/2010). Their thesis is that even popular cultural productions (lowbrow) have the potential to create cracks in the "common-sense," taken-for-granted perceptions of everyday life or to demystify some forms of ideological blindness. They also commented, however, on the paradox that any cultural production (neither Horkheimer nor Adorno comment specifically on pulp fiction) not only has the potential to critique the socio-economic milieu while because of its commercial nature can be often co-opted to maintain the very same milieu. Capitalism is recuperative, and any artifact or cultural phenomenon that manifests resistant or critical potential is eventually co-opted/reified for the market's benefit. Pulp fiction novels and their film adaptations become objects to be consumed.

Horkheimer and Adorno discuss the recuperative power of the capitalist market.

> Marked differentiations such as those of A and B films, or of stories in magazines in different price ranges, depend not so much on subject matter as on classifying, organizing, and labeling consumers. Something is provided for all so that none may escape; the distinctions are emphasized and extended. The public is catered for with a hierarchical range of mass-produced products of varying quality thus advancing their rule of complete quantification.... Consumers appear as statistics on research organization charts, and divided by income groups into red, green, and blue areas; the technique that is used for any type of propaganda. (Horkheimer & Adorno, 1944/2010, p. 97)

This concept of the power of the market and consumer culture to counteract the critical potential of any cultural artifact was also discussed by Gilles Deleuze.

> Even art has moved away from closed sites and into open circuits of banking. Markets are won by taking control rather than establishing a discipline, by fixing rates rather than by reducing costs by transforming products rather than by specializing production. Corruption takes on a new power. The sales department becomes the business center or 'soul' (Deleuze, 1995, p. 181).

So, the status and function of dystopic youth fiction can be placed into this critical postmodern context of potential and problematic. Perhaps, dystopic fiction occupies or can negotiate a space between potential and problematic as it can be characterized as manifesting varying degrees of "accommodation contestation and resistance" (Freire & Macedo, 1987, p. 17). Products such as these dystopic pulp fiction books and the numerous consumer products generated from the books and film adaptations swirl in this potential and problematic. Just as youth are enmeshed in buying all the products, the products are produced because the youths desire them or at least the desire for these products has been manufactured for the youth. Let us turn to the books.

Battle Royale and The Hunger Games

After returning from McGill in the fall of 2011, inspired by the ideas and conversations the students and I had about critical literacy and various forms of fiction, I was eager to read more of the literature that was designated as youth (teen) fiction. I went to the local bookstore and found a plethora of choices in the many aisles devoted to "teen" fiction—the evidence of consumption. I also had discussions with my 20-something son about what people were currently reading. Of course I also consulted the *New York Times*, etc. to discover the hot-ticket books. It didn't take long to realize that the best-selling and critically acclaimed Hunger Games trilogy had replaced the Harry Potter series and the Twilight series.

The Hunger Games series, including *The Hunger Games* (2008), *Catching Fire* (2009), and *Mockingjay* (2010), was written by Suzanne Collins and published by Scholastic, Inc., a major corporation. According to the Scholastic, Inc. website, "Scholastic has approximately $2 billion in annual revenues, employs about 9,500 employees worldwide, is the largest publisher and distributor of children's books in the world, is a leader in educational technology and service, children's media and has a global reach, serving customers in 45 languages and more than 150 countries" (Robinson, 2013, p. 1). The Hunger Games joins the tradition of the Harry Potter series (which Scholastic also publishes) and the Twilight Series, which is about a love triangle of a human, a vampire, and a werewolf.

After reading The Hunger Games series and watching the film, I discovered a Japanese precursor to these novels about children being picked by a type of lottery to become tributes who fight each other to the death to maintain the system of the Capitol. It was *Battle Royale* by KoushunTakami (2010). Takami, a pro-wrestling fan, derived the title from an event in the pro-wrestling world.

After reading four books and watching two films on youth, in which the plot was primarily about rebellion initially gave me hope. I thought perhaps, at last, we have left the world of wizards and quidditch, vampire lovers and teenage angst. But maybe President Snow in *The Hunger Games* movie was correct. "A little hope is effective; a lot of hope is dangerous" (Bissell & Collins, 2012). So we transition to threatening youth competing in survival games in which they murder each other and move away from Twilight's love relationships and love triangles.

Killing for Your Country—Battle Royale

As you are well aware, our nation has no conscription system. The Army, Navy, and Air Special Defense Forces all consist of patriotic souls, young volunteers every one of them, passionate fighters for the Revolution and the building of our nation. They are risking their lives every day and night at the frontlines. I would like you to consider the Program [Program 68] as a conscription system unique to this country. In order to protect our nation…. (Takami, p. 26)

Battle Royale is a much darker novel and film than anything in The Hunger Games series. The setting is described in the introduction to the film, which follows the novel closely.

At the dawn of the millennium the nation collapsed. 15% unemployment, 10 million out of work—800,000 students boycotted the schools—the adults lost confidence and fearing the youth eventually passed the Millennium Educational Reform Act—called the (Battle Royale) BR Act. (Fukasaku & Fukasaku, 2000)

Under the provisions of the BR act, 42 junior high students, chosen by lottery, are hijacked from their school bus and taken to a deserted island. Each student is outfitted with an electronic collar, which enables tracking and detonates if the student commits any infraction. There are rules to the game. Every hour a different section of the island is designated as a danger zone, and if a student is in that danger zone the collar explodes. If there are no fatalities within a 24-hour period, all the collars explode. The head of the enforcement team is a former junior high school teacher, who was previously stabbed by one of the students in the game (Ruined Endings, 2013, p. 1).

The book and the film portray the graphic murders of students by fellow students with guns, scythes, knives, rocks, etc., and a record is kept of how many students remain. It is *Survivor* to the extreme.

> Although he might not have particularly realized it, or more appropriately, perhaps because he was incapable of coming to such realization, this is what it came down to: Kazuo Kirimaya felt nothing; no guilt, no sorrow, and no pity toward the four corpses, including Mitsuru's; and ever since the day he was dropped into this world the way he was, he had never once felt a single emotion.
> **34 STUDENTS REMAINING** (Takami, 2010, p. 83)

During the battle there is resistance. Three male students discover that the collars have microphones which enable constant surveillance. So they join forces to resist the government and escape the island. In true 21st-century technological resistance, the leader, Shinji, hacks into the mainframe computer on the island and infects it with a virus, disrupting all surveillance and disabling all the danger zones. Additionally he has had his two compatriots round up fertilizer, pesticide, charcoal, sulfur and kerosene so that they can make bombs, Molotov cocktails, and various other destructive devices. Shinji, interestingly enough, traces his rebellious roots back to his uncle who was an activist in the 1960s. He has pictures of his uncle holding a gun and smiling: "My uncle was an activist in the 60s. Taught me stuff they never teach you in school. He is still fighting in some corner of the world. Someday you will smile like this" (Fukasaku & Fukasaku, 2000). The rebellious group succeeds in momentarily disrupting the game, but as they are about to deliver the explosives, a youth who has been recruited by the government opens fire on the group with an automatic weapon, killing all of them.

Shuya (male) and Norika (female), the survivors/"winners" of the *Battle Royale*, confidants, and lovers, are on the run from authorities at the novel's end.

> But still he (Shuya) thought this:
>
> *Together Norika we'll live with the sadness.*
> *I'll love you with all the madness in my soul.*
> *Someday girl I don't know when*
> *We're gonna get to that place*
> *Where we really want to go*
> *And we'll walk in the sun*
> *But till then tramps like us*
> *Baby we were born to run.* (Takami, 2010, p. 576)

Terrible monstrous children, despite attempts to fight back or escape, are dealt with. Readers and viewers understand that any resistance is futile. Running is, perhaps, the only choice possible in this novel and film. Despite the attempts at youth resistance, the message of the book and film is conservative and reifies the conclusion that resistance to the system is foolhardy.

Not only is there a conservative warning in this dystopic youth novel and film, but the film is commodified through the merchandise available from the *Battle Royale* franchise. Most of these items are only available in Japan, but since the DVD of the film had a March 2012 release in the United States, the merchandise will eventually follow. There are mousepads, card games, toys, books, an entire clothing line (including copies of the school uniforms the children wear), documentaries, and soundtrack(s). Since there is a sequel, the items will, no doubt, increase in number.

So as I reflect on this example of dystopic fiction and film, I can see the potential for increased commodification of youth consciousness. Any discussion of freedom, camaraderie, resistance, and rebellion is muffled by the prodigious output of the market. It is not about discussing the critical possibilities of the literature but about buying the artifacts associated with the cultural phenomenon. Buying the *Battle Royale* t-shirt becomes both a sign and status symbol that signifies that the consumer has either read or watched the film—a form of cultural capital. Possibly the consumer has neither read the book nor viewed the film but realizes that the purchase of these artifacts puts him or her within a particular group much the way buying a Lexus puts adults into a certain group, or at least they hope others view them as belonging to that group [Deleuze (1995), Bourdieu (1984), and Corrigan (1997)[2]].

A Little Hope—The Hunger Games Trilogy

President: Why do we have a winner? Hope.
Seneca: Hope?
President: It is the only thing stronger than fear. A little hope is effective; a lot of hope is dangerous. A spark is fine as long as it is contained. (Bissell, Collins & Ross, 2012)

The rules of the Hunger Games are simple. In punishment for the uprising, each of the twelve districts must provide one girl and one boy, called tributes, to participate. The twenty-four tributes will be imprisoned in a vast outdoor arena that could hold anything from a burning desert to a frozen wasteland. Over a period of several weeks, the competitors must fight to the death. The last tribute standing wins. (Collins, 2009, p. 75)

In the case of The Hunger Games trilogy, I will discuss the series as a whole along with the film. For the purposes of this chapter a survey of the novels will have to serve. There seems to be a critical love affair with these books, and since the film had opening weekend box office receipts of $155 million as well as critical acclaim, There is a love affair with the film as well. In *The Hunger Games and Philosophy: A Critique of Pure Treason* (2012), the editors stated their love for the series in this way.

We love the Hunger Games trilogy for many reasons. It offers us a strong and resourceful heroine, Katniss Everdeen, whom we all can admire and aspire to be like; it constantly leaves us on tenterhooks with its blend of thrilling action and captivating romance; it gives us the opportunity to grow alongside the main characters as they come to understand themselves and their world more deeply; and memorable scenes that touch our emotions and stay with us long after we put the books down. (Dunn & Michaud, 2012, p. 1).

Setting

Panem, comprised of the remains of the United States and Canada, is the setting for the dystopic trilogy. The ruling district, the Capitol, is supported by all the other districts.

The result was Panem, a shining Capitol ringed by thirteen districts, which brought peace and prosperity to its citizens. Then came the Dark Days, the uprising of the districts against the Capitol. Twelve were defeated, the thirteenth obliterated. The threat of Treason gave us the new laws to guarantee peace and, as our yearly reminder that the Dark Days must never be repeated, it gave us the Hunger Games. (Collins, 2008, p. 18)

Interestingly the Hunger Games were developed and employed as a means to prevent further resistance and rebellion to the rule of the Capitol. The Capitol is set in contrast to the other twelve districts, particularly District 12 where Katniss and Peeta are from. The Capitol is a city with all possible wealth and comforts, while the other districts that support the Capitol with their labor exist on a meager survival level. The lavish dining tables of the Capitol are in stark contrast to the daily struggle to find food in the other districts. There is an undercurrent of resistance and resentment to the Capitol, which is mollified by the Hunger Games. Control and compliance rule the day in Panem. Youth are selected as tributes to go and die in the games. They are all fearful but must participate. Again, there is a solution to the potential of rebellion—the games. The games that cost many youth their lives solve the issue.

Race in *The Hunger Games*

The issue of race is relevant to the phenomenon that is *The Hunger Games*. Engaging students in discussions of the racial differences of characters in *The Hunger Games* through critical media literacy could elicit insights into positionality and privilege. It is most interesting that hours after the showing of *The Hunger Games* in theaters the blogs were alive with reactions to the film. Some of the most troubling reactions were to the characters of Rue (played by Amandla Stenberg) and Cinna (played by Lenny Kravitz).

In the books Cinna's race is not clearly defined.

> Cinna's close-cropped hair appears to be its natural shade of brown. …The only concession to self-alteration seems to be metallic gold eyeliner that has been applied by a light hand. It brings out the flecks of gold in his green eyes. (Collins, 2009, p. 63)

Rue's description is a bit more specific. "She has bright, dark eyes and satiny brown skin" (Collins, 2009, p. 98). Her fellow tribute Thresh has "the same dark skin as Rue, but the resemblance stops there" (Collins, 2009, p. 126). Regardless of the character descriptions, the casting of black actors in the roles generated racist tweets on the Internet. Four people tweeted at the website Jezebel.

> Why does rue have to be black not gonna lie kinda ruined the movie—Maggie Macdonnell

> Cinna and Rue weren't supposed to be black—Marie

> Why did the producer make all the good characters black smh—Marie

> EWW Rue is black?? I'm not watching—Joe Longley

> Kk call me racist but when I found out Rue was black her death wasn't as sad—Jashper paras

> The posts go on and on and on. It's not just a couple of tweets, it's not just a coincidence. There's an underlying rage, coming out as overt prejudice and plain old racism. Stenberg is called a "black bitch," a "nigger" and one person writes that though he pictured Rue with "darker skin," he "didn't really take it all the way to black." It's as if that is the worst possible thing a person could be. (Jezebel, 2013)

Critical discussions of the books and films can elicit thinking that reads the world and the word. The issue of race in these reactions to the film and the discussions of those reactions can lead to confronting the global issues of race in the 21st century. "Racist and sexist remarks have to be drawn out as legitimate objects of study, as authentic parts of student consciousness. How can you study anything kept silent?" (Shor & Freire, 1987, p. 183). Of course, the reactions to race are linked to issues of gender and class.

Gender Issues

It is crucial to realize that the hero in The Hunger Games series is an adolescent female. This seems to be a common theme or characteristic of these dystopic youth novels and films including *Battle Royale, The Hunger Games,* and an interesting new addition to the genre, the Divergent series (Roth, 2011, 2012, 2013). A young woman as a leader of resistance is an encouraging development. Women who refuse to be totally immersed in a suffocating system provide openings for discussion of women's role in critical analysis. Women are not only resisting but at the same time accommodating a suppressive system in *The Hunger Games*. Katniss realizes that complicity and discusses Effie, a member of the Capitol, and the ways in which she is instrumental in perpetuating the games. Effie starts the conversation.

> But I have done my best with what I had to work with. How Katniss sacrificed herself for her sister. How you have both successfully struggled to overcome the barbarism of your district.

> Barbarism? That's ironic coming from a woman helping to prepare us for slaughter. And she is basing our success on? Our table manners? (Collins, 2008, p. 74)

As in many cases women are blamed for helping to prepare other women for their demise and can be blamed for the entire situation, while the men in positions of power are not. These issues which arise in a critical analysis of dystopic fiction are applicable to our own present system.

These independent adolescent women revolutionaries are shown as strong, thoughtful, and self-sacrificing individuals who resist a dystopic future, and Katniss is a leader in the revolution against the Capitol. The troubling aspect of the strong female protagonist is that in the end, even after cataclysmic struggles, the resolution/solution is a return to a traditional romantic relationship. In *Mockingjay* (Collins, 2010), Katniss is most concerned with that relationship and her role as mother to two children.

> That what I needed to survive was not, is not Gale's fire, kindled with rage and hatred. I have plenty of fire myself. What I needed was a dandelion in the spring. The bright yellow that means rebirth instead of destruction. The promise that life can go on no matter how bad our losses. That it can be good again and only Peeta can give me that. (Collins, 2010, p. 388)

It is reminiscent of all the stories of Disney princesses and fairy tales where there is always a Prince Charming. It is not an either/or in the case of these dystopic novels but the discussion of these issues that can illuminate the current milieu.

Class Issues

> Class issues are the most evident in *The Hunger Games*. The contrast between the Capitol's abundance and the other districts' meager existence is blatant. Collins makes the class differences stark. Katniss describes the electric power that is available to the poor. "The Capitol twinkles like a vast field of fireflies. Electricity on District 12 comes and goes; usually we only have it for a few hours a day. Often the evenings are spent in candlelight." (Collins, 2008, p. 80)

Not only electricity but the contrast in the quality and availability of food is discussed by Katniss.

> I watch the sun rise over the Capitol. I have a second plate of hot grain smothered in beef stew. Finally I fill a plate with rolls and sit at the table breaking off bits and dipping them into hot chocolate, the way Peeta did on the train.

> My mind wanders to my mother and Prim [in District 12]. They must be up. My mother getting their breakfast of mush. (Collins, 2008, p. 87)

Abundant bread in the Capitol is contrasted to the bread lines in the other districts. These two examples illustrate the class differences in the books, and the film accentuates the difference with the stunning visual portraits.

The complicated conversations about these differences can move critical classroom discussions toward the analysis of our present period of cruelty and punishment.

> This culture of cruelty is especially evident in the hardships and deprivations now visited upon many young people in the United States. We have 13.3 million homeless children; one in five lives in poverty;

too many are now under the supervision of the criminal justice system, and many more young adults are unemployed and lack any hope for the future. (Giroux, 2011b, p. 13)

We have the 1% in contrast to the 99%, and the Capitol and its contrast with District 12 can lead to discussions of the vast inequities in our 21ˢᵗ-century world.

The Commodification of *The Hunger Games*

Again any message of resistance can be dissolved in the plethora of merchandise for *The Hunger Games*. There are commentaries, a strategy board game, umbrellas, movie guides, guides to the series, a Hunger Games and philosophy book, figurines, trading cards, t-shirts, cookbooks, stickers, magnets, journals, notebooks, pins, necklaces, keychains and on and on. Youth can purchase their indications of being in the know about *The Hunger Games*. Some youth will admit that they never read the books; maybe they saw the film but wanted to be "in," so they have purchased the merchandise. Thus, the purchase of merchandise becomes more important than reading the books. As stated previously, capitalism is extremely recuperative and any challenges to its hegemony are easily coopted by the market. Any resistant messages the books may contain are commodified. Let me repeat, no one stands outside the lure of capitalist consumption.

Despite this commodification, the books are widely read, and because of that a critical media analysis of this dystopic youth fiction could still provide openings to critical discussions of important issues of race, gender and class.

The Challenge of Critical Media Analysis, Critical Pedagogy, and Youth Culture

Given our current economic crisis, a growing authoritarian populism, the rise of religious dogmatism, the failure of democratic governance, a political system largely controlled by bankers and corporations, and a massive education deficit in the United States, critical pedagogy becomes a reminder not only of something precious that has been lost under a regime of casino capitalism, but also of a democratizing project that needs to be reclaimed, reconfigured, and made a central part of our current political lives and those of future generations. (Giroux, 2013, pp. 204–205)

In our present historical context, we are witnessing the resurgence of youth activism against the effects of postmodern casino capitalism, and the overly violent responses by authorities to this questioning. There has also been an encouraging trend to resist and refuse the elaborate skill, drill, test, and hold accountable our education system. Students, parents, and teachers are refusing to give and take the high-stakes tests. When we can get beyond this accountability schooling scheme, we can seek to understand and critique what youth are watching and reading. It is crucial to have those young people question and critique what they are reading, watching and buying. A critical pedagogy/literacy reads the world as well as the word (Freire & Macedo, 1987). It is not enough to simply bring dystopic youth fiction into the curriculum just to demonstrate how hip we are. I remember how my teachers would bring in Simon and Garfunkel to demonstrate their "with-it-ness." My friends and I would then question how revolutionary Simon and Garfunkel actually were. I am suggesting that we give students a chance to bring their knowledges into a classroom that recognizes and legitimates them. The legitimation of student knowledges is a significant issue in the present educational system given its deficit of critical thinking. Youth knowledges are seldom given credence if a system is mainly concerned with accumulation for accreditation and producing a consuming populace, not a critical citizenry. Even books and films that legitimate student knowledge and interests can be absorbed and co-opted by an overbearing system that serves the present social order. It is easy to imagine, for example, an Accelerated Reader test for the *Battle Royale* and *The Hunger Games*.

Despite the fact that many of the messages of critique, resistance and rebellion are lost in the haze of an overabundance of merchandise generated by this dystopic fiction, critical reading/media analysis could help to provoke questions centering not only on the themes and structures of the novels and the movies but on their commodification and issues that arise from analysis. Critically discussing issues of contemporary youth knowledges and their interests in this type of reading can lead us to the development of critical thinking and questioning missing from our educational system. May the odds be in our favor?

Notes

1. In Sandlin, J. A. & McLaren, P. (2010) the editors discuss the term "Shopocalypse"

    The 'Shopocalypse'—a combination of "Shopping" and "Apocalypse"— is a term coined by anti-consumption social activist Bill Talen, who takes on the persona of "Reverend Billy." Reverend Billy, along with the "Stop Shopping Gospel Choir" stage "Retail Interventions" in big-box stores, chain stores, traffic jams and other monuments of our current mono-culture. (Sandlin & McLaren, 2010, p. 16).

2. There is an excellent discussion of various approaches to conceptualizations of consumption in the introduction to the Sandlin and McLaren text, pp. 1–19.

References

Bissell, R., & Collins, S. (Producers) & Ross, G. (Director). (2012). *The hunger games* [Motion picture]. United States: Lionsgate.

Bourdieu, P. (1984). *Distinction: A social critique of the judgement of taste* (R. Nice, Trans.). Cambridge, MA: Harvard University Press.

Collins, S. (2008). *The hunger games*. London: Scholastic.

Collins, S. (2009). *Catching fire, book two*. New York: Scholastic Press.

Collins, S. (2010). *Mockingjay*. New York: Scholastic Press.

Corrigan, P. (1997). *The sociology of consumption: An introduction*. Thousand Oaks, CA: Sage Publications

Deleuze, G. (1995). *Negotiations: 1972–1990* (M. Joughin, Trans.). New York: Columbia University Press.

Dick, P. (1968/1996). *Do androids dream of electric sheep?* New York: Del Rey Books.

Dunn, G. A., & Michaud, N. (Eds.). (2012). *The hunger games and philosophy: A critique of pure treason*. Hoboken, NJ: John Wiley and Sons.

Fancher, H., & Kelly, B. (Producers) & Scott, R. (Director). (1982). *Blade runner*. [Motion picture]. United States: Warner Brothers.

Freire, P., & Macedo, D. (1987). *Literacy: Reading the word and the world*. Westport, CT: Bergin and Garvey.

Fukasaku, K. (Producer) & Fukasaku, K. (Director). (2000). *Battleroyale* [Motion picture]. United States: Anchor Bay Films.

Gilbert, J. (2008). Against the commodification of everything. *Cultural Studies, 22*(5), 551–566.

Gilmore, D. (2008). *The film club*. New York: The Hachette Book Group.

Giroux, H. A. (2002). *Breaking into the movies: Film and the culture of politics*. Malden, MA: Blackwell Publishers, Inc.

Giroux, H. A. (2009*). Youth in a suspect society: Democracy or disposability?* New York: Palgrave Macmillan.

Giroux, H. A., (2011a, August 12). How Disney magic and the corporate media shape youth identity in the digital age. *Truthout*. Retrieved (5/19/13) from http://www.truth-out.org/opinion/item/2808:how-disney-magic-and-the-corporate-media-shape-youth-identity-in-the-digital-age

Giroux, H. A. (2011b). *Zombie politics and culture in the age of casino capitalism*. New York: Peter Lang.

Giroux, H. A. (2012a). *Twilight of the social: Resurgent publics in the age of disposability*. Boulder, CO: Paradigm Publishers.

Giroux, H. A. (2012b). *Education and the crisis of public values: Challenging the assault on teachers, students, & public education*. New York: Peter Lang.

Giroux, H. A. (2013). *America's education deficit and the war on youth*. New York: Monthly Review Press.

Golding, W. (1963). *Lord of the flies*. London: Faber and Faber.

Hopkins, E. (2004). *Crank*. New York: Simon Pulse.

Horkheimer, M., & Adorno, T. (2010). *The culture industry: Enlightenment as mass deception*. Retrieved from www.marxists.or/reference/archive/adorno/1944/culture industry.

Huxley, A. (1931/1989). *Brave new world*. New York: HarperPerennial.

Jezebel. (2013, May). *Racist Hunger Games fans are very disappointed*. Retrieved from: http://jezebel.com/5896408/racist-hunger-games-fans-dont-care-how-much-money-themovie-made.

Kellner, Douglas. (1989). *Critical theory, Marxism, and modernity*. Baltimore: Johns Hopkins University Press.

Orwell, G. (1945/1996). *Animal farm*. New York: Signet.

Renaissance Learning. (2013). *Accelerated Reader enterprise*. Retrieved (5/11/13) from http://www.renlearn.com/ar/

Reynolds, W. M. (in press). Neo-post-urban-noir graphic novels and critical literacy: The hard connection. In P. Paugh, T. Kress, *Critical and new literacies: Teaching toward democracy with/in/through post-modern and popular culture texts*.

Robinson, D. (2013, May). *Welcome*. Retrieved from: http://www.scholastic.com/aboutscholastic/index.htm.

Roth, V. (2011). *Divergent*. New York: HarperCollins Publishers.

Roth, V. (2012). *Insurgent*. New York: HarperCollins Publishers.

Roth, V. (2013, in press). *Allegiant*. New York: HarperCollins Publishers.

Ruined Endings. (2013, May). *Battle Royale*. Retrieved from: http://ruinedendings.com/film3666plot.

Sandlin, J. A., & McLaren, P. (Eds.). (2010). *Critical pedagogies of consumption: Living and learning in the shadow of the "shopocalypse."* New York: Routledge.

Sapphire. (1997). *Push: A novel*. New York: Vintage Contemporaries.

Shor, I., & Freire, P. (1987). *A pedagogy for liberation: Dialogues on transforming education*. South Hadley, MA: Bergin and Garvey Publishers, Inc.

Takami, K. (2010). *Battle Royale: The novel*. San Francisco, CA: Viz.

CHAPTER 44

Youth against the Wall

Donna Gaines

While this seminal piece in early critical youth studies was written in the 1990s, Gaines' work resonates with today, and unfortunately tomorrow. We have included this piece from Teenage Wasteland: Suburbia's Dead End Kids *(1998) as a classic example of criticalizing the narrative of cultural work with and for youth. We ask … how far have we come? How far do we have to go to remove kids from against the wall? S. Steinberg.*

When I heard about the suicide pact, it grabbed me in the solar plexus. I looked at the pictures of the kids and their friends. I read what the reporters said. I was in my apartment looking out on Long Island's Jericho Turnpike thinking maybe this is how the world ends with the last generation bowing out first.

In Bergenfield, New Jersey, on March 11, 1987, the bodies of four teenagers were discovered inside a 1977 rust-colored Chevrolet Camaro. The car, which belonged to Thomas Olton, was parked in an unused garage in the Foster Village garden apartment complex, behind the Foster Village Shopping Center. Two sisters, Lisa and Cheryl Burress, and their friends, Thomas Rizzo and Thomas Olton, had died of carbon monoxide poisoning.

Lisa was sixteen, Cheryl was seventeen, and boys were nineteen—they were suburban teens, turnpike kids like the ones in the town I live in. And thinking about them made me remember how it felt to be a teenager too. I was horrified that it had come to this. I believed I understood why they did it, although it wasn't a feeling I could have put into words.

You could tell from the newspapers that they were rock n' roll kids. The police had found a cassette tape cover of AC/DC's *If You Want Blood, You've Got It* near the bodies. Their friends were described as kids who listened to thrash metal, had shaggy haircuts and wore lots of black and leather. "Dropouts," "druggies," the papers called them. Teenage suburban rockers whose lives revolved around their favorite bands and their friends. Youths who barely got by in school and at home and who did not impress authority in any remarkable way. Except as fuck-ups.

My friends, most of whom were born in the 1950s, felt the same way about the kids everyone called "burnouts." On the weekend following the suicides, a friend's band, the Grinders, were playing at My Father's Place, a Long Island club. That night the guys dedicated a song, "The Kids in the Basement," to the four teens from Bergenfield— "This is for the suicide kids." In the weeks following the suicide pact, a number of bands in the tri-state area also dedicated songs to them. Their deaths had hit close to home.

Long Island is a lot like New Jersey. City people make fun of suburbia, but I have lived here for most of my life and I like it. My social life has revolved around music. The Grinders have played around in various incarnations since the middle 1970s. The guys have good union jobs in shipping, sanitation, and one owns an automotive repair business. As wives and girlfriends, we have jobs in glamour trades, careers in software engineering, and one of us is a guitarist with a band of her own.

We all grew up hanging out, but now, some fifteen years after high school, most of us are involved in our jobs, married, having children, and saving up to buy homes. We still dress with big rock and roll hair and full black leather regalia. For years, we have looked forward to band practice or to seeing shows at downtown New York clubs and on the Island. For a long time after high school, some of us drank, others got high, then went into detox, stayed on methadone maintenance, or joined A.A. programs. Basically, we still consider ourselves rockers.

Sometimes, in the passionate pursuit of pleasure and danger, our friends died in car crashes or drug overdoses. Only rarely did anyone commit suicide intentionally. We, too, were known as "fucked-up kids."

Like many of my peers, I spent a lot of my early adulthood recovering from a history of substance abuse, family trauma, school failure and arrests. With most of that behind me, I wanted to help "troubled" teenagers. First I was a big sister with junior high school kids in Brooklyn. Then I worked on a suicide-prevention hotline. I became a New York State certified social worker, employed mainly in child welfare, investigating allegations of abuse and neglect, later organizing self-advocacy groups for parents. I also worked in special adoptions and youth services.

For a while I had a job as a street worker in the nearby community of Levittown. Some of my colleagues also had outlaw "pasts" that helped to prepare them for this work. Our earlier careers as identified outcasts in our families, at school, and in the neighborhoods we grew up in enriched what we now thought of as "social work practice skills."

More like 1950s gang workers than agency-based outreach workers, street workers were to provide "positive role modeling" and concrete services for "alienated youth at risk." We did this exclusively on the kids' turf, and on their terms. We were there as a resource, to help negotiate with police, parents, schools, employers. We were there for the kids—like an older friend to walk them through the wasted years. I think we wanted to make "growing up" easier for them, less painful than it had been for us.

My office was the parking lot of a small shopping center known commonly as a village green. "Therapeutic interventions" took place in cars, spontaneously—on the streets, as needed. The kids could seek us out for emotional support or quick advice, hit us up for rides, small cash loans, whatever. Sometimes we arranged baseball games, "rap groups," small trips. Since many of the kids' parents had moved out to Long Island hoping to protect their children from urban life, some kids were a little phobic about "the city." So once I took the girls to Little Italy for one of the feasts.

By the beginning of the 1980s, like many of my colleagues, I had moved into indirect services: research and program evaluation. I began picking up consulting jobs. Hoping to compete for bigger contracts, I wanted to become computer literate, and to learn advanced statistics.

A week or two after the suicide pact, *The Village Voice* assigned me to go to Bergenfield. Now this was not a story I would've volunteered for. Usually I write about things I enjoy: computers, guns, pornography, tattoos, rock and roll, and cars. I don't like the idea of "research subjects" or getting vulnerable people to trust me with their secrets so I can go back and tell about them. Generally, I prefer leaving people alone. By now I fully embraced the sociologist's ethical commitment to the "rights of the researched," and the social worker's vow of client confidentiality. As far as suicidal teenagers were concerned, I felt that if I couldn't help them, I didn't want to bother them.

But I was really pissed off at what I kept reading. How people in Bergenfield openly referred to the four kids as "troubled losers." Even after they were dead nobody cut them any slack. "Burnouts," "druggies," "dropouts." Something was wrong.

From the beginning, I believed that the Bergenfield suicides symbolized a tragic defeat for young people. Something was happening in the larger society that was not yet comprehended. Scholars spoke ominously of "the postmodern condition," "societal upheaval," "decay," "anomie." Meanwhile, American kids kept losing ground, showing all the symptoms of societal neglect. Many were left to fend for themselves, often with little success. The news got worse. Teenage suicides continued, and still nobody seemed to be getting the point.

Now, in trying to understand this event, I might have continued working within the established discourse on teenage suicide. I might have carried on the tradition of obscuring the picture, psychologizing the Bergenfield suicide pact, interviewing the parents of the four youths, hounding their friends for the gory details. I might have spent my time probing school records, tracking down their teachers and shrinks for insights, focusing on their personal histories and intimate relationships. I might have searched out the individual motivations behind the words left in the note written and signed by each youth on the brown paper bag found with their bodies on March 11. But I did not.

Because the world has changed for kids. We also engaged in activities that adults called self-destructive. But for my generation, "doing it" meant having sex; for them it means committing suicide.

"Teenage suicide" was a virtually nonexistent category prior to 1960. But between 1950 and 1980 it nearly tripled, and at the time of the Bergenfield suicide pact it was described as the second leading cause of death among America's young people; "accidents" were the first. The actual suicide rate among people aged fifteen to twenty-four—the statistical category for teenage suicide—is estimated to be even higher, underreported because of social stigma. By 1987, we had books and articles on "copycat" and "cluster" suicides. Teenage suicide was now described as an epidemic.

Some kids do it violently: drowning, hanging, slashing, jumping, or crashing. Firearms are still the most popular. Others prefer to go out more peacefully, by gas or drug overdose. Boys do it more than girls, though girls try it more often than boys. And it does not seem to matter if kids are rich or poor.

Throughout the 1980s, teenage suicide clusters appeared across the country—six or seven deaths, sometimes more, in a short period of time in a community. In the boomtown of Plano, Texas. The fading factory town of Leominster, Massachusetts. At Bryan High School in a white, working-class suburb of Omaha, Nebraska. A series of domino suicides among Arapaho Indian youths at the Wind River Reservation in Wyoming. Six youth suicides in the county of Westchester, New York, in 1984; five in 1985 and seven in 1986.

Sometimes they were close friends who died in pacts of two. In other cases, one followed shortly after the other, unable to survive apart. Then there were strangers who died alone, in separate incidents timed closely together.

The Bergenfield suicide pact of March 11 was alternately termed a "multiple-death pact," a "quadruple suicide," or simply a "pact," depending on where you read about it. Some people actually called it a *mass* suicide because the Bergenfield case reminded them of Jonestown, Guyana, in 1978, where over nine hundred followers of Jim Jones took poison fearing their community would be destroyed.

As experts speculated over the deaths in Bergenfield, none could recall a teenage suicide pact involving four people dying together; *it was historically unique.*

I wondered, did the "burnouts" see themselves as a community under siege? Like Jim Jones's people, or the 960 Jews at Masada who jumped to their deaths rather than face defeat at the hands of the Romans? Were the "burnouts" of Bergenfield choosing death over surrender? Surrender to what? Were they martyrs? If so, what was their common cause?

Because the suicide pact was a *collective act*, it warrants a social explanation: a portrait of the "burn-outs" in Bergenfield as actors within a particular social landscape.

For a long time now, the discourse of teenage suicide has been dominated by atomizing psychological and medical models. And so the larger picture of American youth as members of a distinctive generation with a unique collective biography, at a particular moment in history, has been lost.

There were specific sociocultural patterns in Bergenfield through which a teenage suicide pact became objectively possible. Yes, there were particular conditions that influenced how the town reacted to the event. There were reasons—that unique constellation of circumstances congealed in the lives of the four youths in the years, weeks, and days prior to March 11—that made suicide seem like their best alternative.

Given the four youths' personal histories, their losses, their failures, their shattered dreams, the motivation to die in this way seems transparent. Yet, after the suicide pact, in towns across the country, on television and in the press, people asked, "Why did they do it?" This was a suicide pact that involved close friends who were by no accounts star-crossed lovers. What would make four people want to die together? Why would they ask, in their collective suicide note, to be waked and buried together? Were they part of a suicide cult?

If not, what was the nature of the *social* bond that tied them so closely? What could be so intimately binding that in the early morning hours of March 11 not one of them could stop, step back from the pact they had made to say, "Wait, I can't do this"? Who were these kids that everybody called "burnouts"?

"Greasers," "hoods," "beats," "hippies," "punks." From the 1950s onward, these groups have signified young people's refusal to cooperate. In the social order of the American high school, teens are expected to do what they are told—make the grade, win the prize, play the game. Kids who refuse have always found something else to do. Sometimes it kills them; sometimes it sets them free. Everybody knows you don't call somebody a burnout to their face unless you are looking for a fight. At that point, the word becomes synonymous with "troubled loser," "druggie"—all the things the press and some residents of the town called the four kids who died in Tommy Olton's Camaro.

How did kids in Bergenfield become "burnouts"? At what point were they identified as outcasts? Was this a labeling process or one of self-selection? What kinds of lives did they have? What resources were available for them? What choices did they have? What ties did these kids have to the world outside Bergenfield? Where did their particular subculture come from? Why in the 1980s, the Reagan years, in white suburban America? What were their hopes and fears? What did heavy metal, Satan, suicide, and long hair mean to them? Who were their heroes, their gods? What saved them and what betrayed them in the long, cold night?

And what was this "something evil in the air" that people spoke about? Were the kids in Bergenfield "possessed"? Was the suicide pact an act of cowardice by four "losers," or the final refuge of kids helplessly and hopelessly trapped? How different was Bergenfield from other towns?

Could kids be labeled to death? How much power did these labels have? I wanted to meet other kids in Bergenfield who were identified as "burnouts" to find out what it felt like to carry these labels. I wanted to understand the existential situation they operated in—not simply as hapless losers, helpless victims, but also as *historical actors* determined in their choices, resistant, defiant.

From the beginning, I decided I didn't want to dwell too much on the negatives. I wanted to understand how alienated kids survived, as well as how they were defeated. How did they maintain their humanity against what I now felt were impossible odds? I wondered. What keeps young people together when the world they are told to trust no longer seems to work? What motivates them to be decent human beings when nobody seems to respect them or take them seriously?

The radical educator begins by validating the dominated person's local, intuitive knowledge of the world. Likewise, the therapeutic intervention must reinforce this knowledge, acknowledge it, constitute it as a truth. That means—to borrow my neighbor's words—"calling out the bullshit" when and how you see it coming down. I wanted to do that for every kid who survived "the decade of greed," and for all the ones who didn't.

> *You* made your children what they are…. These children that come at you with knives, they are your children. You taught them. I didn't teach them. I just tried to help them stand up. —Charles Manson

Shortly after the suicide pact, this was how one Bergenfield resident, a middle-aged man, described the kids who hung around the streets of his town: "Those kids, the look in their eyes, their eyes are empty, like they weren't going anywhere. Their idea of the future was next week. They have given up on life." Why were some American kids giving up on life before it even got started? What had chilled their young spirits and wiped out their hopes and dreams?

Face-to-face, young people in Bergenfield as elsewhere appear rather sober about life, less inflated by ideals, less encouraged to dream. They work hard for anything they've got, money, dignity, serenity, morality. Racial and ethnic lines of difference keep them apart. The variety of youth subcults reflects and reinforces this distance. Turf wars in neighborhoods, at shows, and in schools divide them, and the future seems grim: no jobs, no security, no world, no future. Generally, they ask for very little. Often, they try to do their best. Usually, their positive actions go unrecognized.

Somewhere during the 1980s, our social contract with our youth became null and void. Adults lost their legitimacy as trustworthy authority figures.

Then there is teenage suicide. I watched as experts trivialized this phenomenon, neatly packaging teenage suicide as another social problem, one more "crisis" to perk up afternoon talk shows. Teen suicide soon became new grist for the mills of professional helping industries. It meant new jobs and contracts. Special task forces, research projects, seminars, programs, and pamphlets. Yet under the law, and in the public eye, kids remained powerless and voiceless.

As I have said, kids are now coming of age when "doing it" means suicide, not premarital sex. Nobody has ever been able to understand suicide, especially among teenagers. Being young is associated with being happy and carefree. You go to high school, you socialize with friends, you get a part-time job. How bad can life be? Why give it up before you start? Why is suicide so appealing?

In the scientific imagination, suicide is viewed as a disease, like drug addiction or depression. But when people talk about teenage suicide, the word "romance" is often invoked. Supposedly, suicide is not real to young people. They are anesthetized to life and desensitized to death. They don't understand that it is final, irreversible. The poetics of suicide appeal to those most vulnerable to influences, and the young lack the resources needed to buffer the violence of an emergent self.

It is also believed that young people kill themselves to get attention or revenge. Suicide is now hip, dangerous, the final resistance to adult authority, a last stand against conformity. To some kids, suicide is death before dishonor, heroism over defeat. Because attempts so outnumber actual suicide is as much a statement of the desire to control life as it is to end it.

Death has taken on new meaning. To the postmodern imagination, suicide is titillating. It is the last great taboo. Having exhausted sex, death—by suicide or homicide—becomes the final frontier of sensate experience. New pleasures. People disagree on whether the taboo on suicide should be strengthened or deconstructed. Are we better able to suppress the urge by making it unthinkable or by thinking it through?

For young people, suicide promises comfort. It is a violent seductive release, a means to an end, a soothing and delicious deep sleep. In the context of young lives lived like rapid fire but focused nowhere, suicide seems intoxicating, contagious. Death and suicide become eroticized, as terror and rapture, self-loathing and self-gratification.

In fashion we invoke an iconography of decline, celebrating life in the "kingdom of death." We gorge on post-apocalyptic art; we see ourselves as dissipated road warriors on an exhausted, depleted emotional landscape. Armageddon, doom and gloom, death and destruction—these themes are localized, internalized. We play it out in everyday life, this simulation of The End—in music, in painting, in film, in new forms created explicitly to contain our emergent psychosis. It makes for compelling art. Millenarian rock.

When he gave the eulogy at his godson's funeral, Tommy Olton's uncle Richard was quoted as saying, "When I held you in my arms at your baptism, I wanted it to be a fresh start, for you to be more complete than we had ever been ourselves, but I wonder if we expected too much. In thinking only of ourselves, maybe we passed down too great a burden."

Trans-historically, cross-culturally, humans have placed enormous burdens on their young. Sometimes these burdens have been primarily economic: the child contributes to the economy of the family or the tribe. Sometimes the burden has been social: the child is a contribution to the immortality of our creed. Be fruitful and multiply. But the spiritual burden we pass on to the child may be the most difficult to bear. We do expect them to fulfill an incompleteness in ourselves, in our world. Our children are our vehicle for the realization of unfulfilled human dreams; our class aspirations, our visions of social justice and world peace, of a better life on earth.

Faith in the child, in the next generation, helps get us through this life. Without this hope in the future *through the child* we could not endure slavery, torture, war, genocide, or even the ordinary, everyday grind of a "bad life." The child-as-myth is an empty slate upon which we carve our highest ideals. For human beings, the child is God, utopia, and the future incarnate. The Bergenfield suicide pact ruptured the sacred trust between the generations. It was a negation.

On the surface the ending of the four kids' bad lives can be explained away by the "case history" approach. Three of the four had suicidal or self-destructive adult role models: the suicide of Tommy Olton's father, the drug-related death of the Burress sisters' father. Tommy Rizzo, along with his three friends, had experienced the recent loss of a beloved friend, Joe Major. Before Joe, the death of three other local "burnouts." Then there was the chronic drug and alcohol abuse, an acknowledged contributing factor in suicide. Families ruptured by divorce, death, estrangement. Failure at school.

But these explanations alone would not add up to a suicide pact among four kids. If they did, the teenage suicide rate would be much, much higher. The personal problems experienced by the four kids were severe, painful, but by the 1980s, they were no longer remarkable.

As I felt from the beginning, the unusually cloying geography of Bergenfield seemed somehow implicated in the suicide pact. The landscape appeared even more circumscribed because of the "burnouts'" lack of legitimate space in the town: they were too old for the Rink, and the Building was available for criminal trespass only. Outcast, socially and spatially, for years the "burnouts" had been chased from corner to parking lot, and finally, to the garage bays of Foster Village. They were nomads, refugees in the town of their birth. *There was no space for them.* They felt unloved, unwanted, devalued, disregarded, and discarded.

But this little town, not even two miles long from north to south, was just a dot on a much larger map. It wasn't the whole world. Hip adults I know, friends who grew up feeling like outcasts in their hometown, were very sympathetic to the plight of the "burnouts." Yet even they often held out one last question, sometimes contemptuously: "Why didn't they *just leave?*" As if the four kids had failed even as outcasts. My friends found this confusing. "No matter how worthless the people who make the rules say you are, you don't have to play their game. You can always walk and not look back," they would argue. People who feel abject and weird in their hometown simply move away.

But that has always been a class privilege. The townies are the poor kids, the wounded street warriors who stay behind. And besides, escape was easier for everyone twenty years ago. American society had safety nets then that don't exist now—it's just not the same anymore.

In a now famous footnote in *Suicide*, written almost a hundred years ago, the French sociologist Emile Durkheim described fatalistic suicide as "the suicide deriving from excessive regulation, that of persons with futures pitilessly blocked and passions violently choked by oppressive discipline." Where there is overregulation, explains Durkheim, "rule against which there is no appeal, we might call it fatalistic suicide."

But as far as young people are concerned, fatalistic suicide is not the whole story. True, young people are among the most regulated in our society. With the exception of people in total institutions, only the lives of animals are more controlled. Yet most experts attribute youth suicide to anomie—the opposite of fatalistic suicide in Durkheim's thinking.

In an anomic suicide, the individual isn't connected to the society—the glue that holds the person to the group isn't strong enough; social bonds are loose, weak, or absent. To be anomic is to feel disengaged, adrift, alienated. Like you don't fit in anywhere, there is no place for you: in your family, your school, your town—in the social order.

Where fatalistic suicide may result from overregulation, anomic suicide is attributed to nonintegration. Young people are in the peculiar position of being overregulated by adults, yet alienated from them. Many are integrated only into the world shared with their peers—some may be overly integrated into that world, as in gangs or subcults. Young people are always somewhere on a continuum between overregulation and nonintegration. In the eighties, both ends of this continuum grew to extremes.

In recent years many American kids have had their dreams taken from them. Their vision has been blocked, unable to move beyond next week, because the world outside is simply too much. Suicide is known as the disease of hope. Helplessness and hopelessness. Hopeless because you see no choices. Helpless because you feel that nothing you can do will ever make a difference. You feel powerless and trapped. This makes you feel worthless; you can't defend yourself. Adolescence continues to serve as a psychic holding pen for superfluous young people, stuck in economic and social limbo, in between childhood dependency and adult autonomy. In killing time in teenage wasteland, some kids end up killing themselves too.

But most kids are not committing suicide. In writing my book, I was as much concerned with why they weren't doing it as I was with why they were. I knew that kids fought back symbolically; articulated their dissent culturally, in their clothes, language, music, and attitudes. They looked for the truth in unorthodox knowledge, created autonomous spaces for self-expression, carved out a place for themselves on their own terms, and they survived.

The kids' role in my research was crucial, since the discourse of suicide as it pertains to young people has totally overlooked the social context they live in. While I could never "speak for them," I could translate. Since young people's experience of the world around them is largely discontinuous from that experienced by adults, the kids were my informants, consultants, decoders of cultural signs and symbols. Young people move within social enclaves, just like everybody else. The autonomous history of each new generation operates a lot like an ethnicity. Kids are a priori marginal. They live in a historically specific moment of their own, making sense of the world in new ways, different from the parental generation.

Today's young are not only trying to control media misrepresentation and adult misinterpretation of their activities and goals, they are fighting back. Many are engaged as activists—as fascists, anarchists, separatists, nationalists, feminists, and Greens. Some now struggle for their civil rights as homosexuals or petition for their reproductive rights, and also for the rights of the unborn. It is true that many of the kids in America are alienated and apathetic. Often, just getting through the day may be heroic. And it is also true that like all Americans, kids bear divergent class agendas. They come in all shapes and colors, from different regions, with varied cultural histories and orientations.

Margaret Mead once described our culture as "prefigurative" because she believed that it was the child—not the parent or grandparent—that represented what was to come. In such a culture, one's peers must predominate because they are the only carriers of new understandings of the world. Our world is changing rapidly, and in some ways, the kids do understand it *better* than adults. It is often the kids who carry the news. We have failed to acknowledge that. Many adult educators and "progressive," intellectuals who came of age in the sixties, find contemporary American kids disappointing. These "political correctness police" want the working class according to Bruce Springsteen not Axl Rose; they love "the masses" theoretically while abhorring them socially and culturally. Believing some cultural practices are better than others, this self-appointed orthodoxy dismisses and condemns American kids— "They never read." But these same adults will marvel at the kids' prowess with video games, innovating style and sound, and computer technology. Everyone knows that if you want to know how something works, ask a kid. Often their manual dexterity and visual accuracy far exceed ours.

There will be no Marcuse to enlighten this generation. Often college kids don't read books except to cram for tests. Many young people do read, in or out of school, but books are now only one form in our country's vast knowledge-production network. To many, "electronic text" is as valid as static text (books, magazines). Videos, television, and film can no longer be dismissed as anti-intellectual "low" culture. Mentalities are changing. We have to recognize this if we are to move forward.

But in the midst of all these massive transformations, kids still do need our help. In everyday life, they need adults as allies. Talking about her relationship to adults, one eighteen-year-old from Selden, Long Island, remarked, "We'll be the ones running this country someday. You'd think they'd try and help us out." So far we haven't, but I think we can.

I always figured I would go back to Bergenfield someday. I wanted to see what went up in place of the Building, to show off my new tattoo. I missed the kids and wanted to know how their lives were turning out. But as I got more involved with the young in the town I live in, I realized my place was here, where I am known and trusted as a neighbor and a friend. By now, they are permanently part of my life.

It takes more than love to motivate people out of teenage wasteland. As adults, we control the resources and we make the rules. We can do things to help young people get ahead while we also help them to fight for better economic and legal participation. Wherever we are, we can offer support—at the workplace, in the schools, the community, and on the streets. Regardless of our own ideological convictions, we can help to empower young people. We can empower kids by validating their perceptions of the world instead of dismissing or trivializing them. By creating arenas for kids to speak on their own terms, for themselves, we help foster their self-confidence.

At the political level, we can also fight the laws and practices that keep kids down. We have to question our assumptions about young people's unreadiness to participate in the world, to recognize and value their demonstrated competence. We can no longer assume that most kids will go on to college, or that our vocational programs are preparing them adequately for jobs. We can no longer expect American youth to subsist on below-minimum-wage "training salaries" because we can no longer take for granted that parental support is supplementing this income.

The kids' wasted years are based on the obsolete assumption that these years are preparation for adulthood. Often, they aren't being prepared for anything. At twenty-four, many kids still have the jobs they held in high school. They get married, start families, and are stuck in jobs that do not offer any growth or security.

We especially have to rethink the wasted years from seventeen to twenty-one, between high school and the traditional age of majority. We can find a more efficient economic organization to absorb our superfluous young people—those not effectively absorbed by the schools we created at the turn of the century for that purpose. In cities, and in suburbs, American youth are being wasted, getting wasted, subsisting, marking time as troublesome artifacts. We speak of them as redundant. They have no place to fit in; by seventeen, many are stranded, dead-end kids, all dressed up for the future with no place to go.

In the information age, kids need real education, not banal, custodial schooling. In an ideal world, adults would provide "minors" with knowledge, skills, love, support, security, and care until they could go out into the world on their own. Parents can no longer bear this burden alone. It is a societal responsibility.

But we can't have it both ways. If we fail in our societal responsibility to our young, we have no reason to "protect" them with infantilizing rules and regulations. In a worst-case scenario, adults would recognize and admit that they are ignoring the needs of young people. Young people would be fully emancipated at, say, sixteen. The social organization of young people's time would revert back to what it was prior to the reforms that took a century ago (labor laws, mandatory schooling). Young people could earn livable wages, vote, fight wars, drink, and be legitimately responsible for themselves. Many already are de facto, and some are de jure.

But if we renewed our social contract with young or had a robust national policy for them, if American education and family life did actually prepare kids for autonomous living instead of warehousing and infantilizing them, the somewhat cynical words above would not have to be articulated.

But my book is mainly intended as a dialogue with other baby boomers, with my generation. Many of us are now making the laws. We are setting agendas for the kids at home, in school, at work. We have the power, and the choice to use it for positive motion. Some of us have lost loved ones to teenage wasteland; some of us have survived it ourselves. We know what is at stake here.

As "adults" we must also recognize that strategies now used by us to regulate young people are rooted in class struggle as well as intergenerational conflict. Rules were made to control people during large-scale societal transformations. Populations were moving around and the nature of production was changing. To some extent, this is happening again. We have to rethink where young people fit into this, and how we can integrate them, not alienate them.

Margaret Mead once said, "In the past there were always some elders who knew more than any children in terms of their experience of having grown up within a cultural system. Today there are none. It is not only that parents are no longer guides, but that there are no guides, whether one seeks them in one's own country or abroad. There are no elders who know what those who have been reared within the last twenty years know about the world into which they were born." She said that in 1969. It's still news.

For some time now, kids have been able to create their own meanings, to make sense of the ruptures of the social order. Despite the media porn, and the teen casualties, many contemporary American youth have gone a lot further with a lot less than others before them. They are stronger and braver for it. More than ever, kids now coming of age deserve our respect. They earn it every day. Remember, it is much harder to live up to ideals, to strive for excellence, to be moral, loving, and strong during decline than in ascendancy.

The twenty-first century promises a harmonic convergence in the resolution of cold war ideologies, racial conflict, and social inequalities. It also threatens war, disaster, and despair. This is what living in the world means. As we move forward, we are exploring new forms of economic organization, experimenting in new modes of production. We are rethinking the nature of the nuclear family, organized religion, the world order, and the fate of our most powerful technologies.

We don't know what's coming next: the most glorious or most hideous of human possibilities. Afraid of the new, we hold fast to the old. Often we don't even know who or what we can believe in. Sometimes the world seems like a fragmented whirling mass, reeling out of control. We feel scared, angry, sad. We give up, we say we don't care, but we do. So we stand together, as human beings before us have done, and we survive, we get by.

"Life Ain't So Bad"—anonymous graffiti Garage door #74, Foster Village, March 1987

CHAPTER 45

Reclaiming Our Public Spaces
Wall of Femmes as a Grassroots, Feminist, Social Action Project

Michelle Harazny, Lisa Sproull, and Cat Terleski

W̶e are living in an increasingly privatized world, where many aspects of our daily lives occur in spaces that are neither fully public nor fully private. Think of the shopping mall or the coffee shop. These are spaces where people meet and socialize, but the ultimate purpose is the selling of products and services. Think of the movie theatre, where people also gather socially, but do so while paying for the privilege of absorbing content. The massive private entities that create these media spectacles have an interest in instilling wants and desires in audiences for products and content made by these firms' subsidiaries or affiliates. Think of the Internet, which is becoming an increasingly important "public space", where our communication is facilitated by even more private companies who collect our personal information and browsing tendencies in order to market to us in ever more sophisticated and personalized ways. Think of our schools and universities, where more than ever, the content of our curricula is being designed and shaped by corporate entities.

All of the spaces above are generally publicly accessible, but still require some type of access fee—money to shop, buy coffee, pay for admission, or for tuition. One of the only remaining spaces that is accessible to almost everyone is the street. In fact, the street is often overlooked as a space. It is not a destination—it is a transitional space, which we use to get from one destination to another (Castells, 1989; Voronkova & Pachenkov, 2011). Yet, even this space, the most public of them all, is controlled. When we step outside, we need only to look around to see the myriad of messages that vie for our valuable attention. Some are directive: Walk or Don't Walk. Parking $3/h. Stoop and Scoop. These messages remind us that there is an authority, and that we must follow the rules. Other messages are commercial: Buy this hair dye! Buy this beer! Buy this condo! These messages remind us that we are consumers, and their very presence indicates that consuming is an activity approved by the authorities that administrate our public space.

We use public space everyday: we walk in our neighbourhoods, we take public transportation, we use public restrooms. In these spaces, we are forced to see images that reinforce consumerist behaviour, messages that represent the viewpoint of a dominating fraction of society. Public wall space has been sold as advertising to companies which prioritize corporate interests to make a profit. When doing so, they do not ask for public opinion, therefore silencing the voices of all but a select few.

The media we are forced to see is not constructed objectively, and much more space is allotted for messages that maintain the status quo. We recognize patterns and variations of the same messages in our public spaces: in advertisements and cultural content that portray women in negative ways, and in which consumerism and other tendencies that are damaging to women are encouraged. Unsurprisingly, due to the cultural obsession with youth and the purchasing power of this demographic, they are the targeted audience of most content and advertising.

Young people experience an endless barrage of messages advertised through television and the Internet that encourage consumer behaviour and impact their self-image. Through advertising, corporations capture a youth's attention using powerful messages that shape attitudes, motivation, behaviour, and ultimately, one's identity. This buy-and-consume mentality directed at youth causes serious physical, emotional, and social suffering when they are flooded with stimuli from television, computers, or video games (Hill, 2011). Young people also learn at an early age to define their self-worth by what they own, seeking happiness through the acquisition of material goods. Hill (2011) found that "children have fewer opportunities to learn to initiate action or to influence the world they inhabit, and less chance to exercise creativity" (p. 352). According to Deutsch and Theodorou (2010), consumption is used to create identity among youth. Appearance is paramount to self-definition, especially for many women and girls in consumer cultures, as they are the targets of marketing campaigns that sell lines of products they "need" to emulate a feminine ideal. Girls are pressured into performing gendered appearances, which are based on socially constructed and fashionable perceptions of femininity. This performance results in feelings of insecurity, as youth anathematize those attributes that place them outside the narrow confines of "the beautiful", and develop insatiable longing for the brand names and products that could place them inside the exclusive club of "the cool". When so much mental energy is focused on what they do not have, there is not much left to devote to celebrating their strengths and developing their own unique identities (Tokuhama, 2011). As such, youth compensate for their feelings of anxiety, and substitute them with superficial value and prestige found in wearing brand-name clothing.

In our media-dominated culture, it is important to acknowledge the cultural landscape as a type of public space, insofar as people share common cultural experiences in much the same way as people share a physical public space. These shared cultural experiences help shape individuals' attitudes and ideas about a variety of facets of everyday life, to such an extent that the values portrayed in our mass cultural content are internalized, normalized, and adopted by consumers of this content. Through this process of cultural hegemony, the ideology of the dominant group in society is accepted by civil society at large (Gramsci, 1971).

The mass-media machine contributes to the reinforcement of the dominant ideology in society by exerting control through cultural hegemony. As people consume mass-media content and internalize the ideas embedded within, the status quo is organically upheld, facilitating the continuation of divisive and oppressive power structures. The dominant ideology of our culture is damaging to women, as content produced by the major media conglomerates portray women as sexual objects and use narratives to place them in subordinate positions. When the viewing public accepts these portrayals uncritically, people accept these constructed representations of reality as truth.

The lack of realistic representations of women (and other marginalized groups) in the media, and the lack of access that these groups have to the channels of distributing their own content, results in their symbolic annihilation from our cultural landscape (Tuchman, Daniels, & Benét, 1978). The constant sexualization and trivialization of women by the mass media serve to reinforce negative stereotypes about women, and establish a limited framework for the collective imagination of the roles for women in society.

The learning in which we engage, both about ourselves and about our public spaces, primarily takes place through our everyday experiences, as lessons are unconsciously ingrained (Duncum, 1999).

Many people are not aware of this incidental learning that is taking place. As a captive audience and as critical viewers of these advertisements and media, we grew increasingly frustrated with the images available to us, realizing that alternatives to dominant messages are rarely given space. We learned of how we are embedded in social networks, as we engaged in dialogue through informal conversations in response to the mainstream bombardment of sexist advertising.

Griff Foley (1999) acknowledged that something has to happen in people's consciousness for them to become actively involved in social movements; he urged that people "have to learn that social action is necessary and possible" (p. 5). Through our individual experiences throughout our lives, something happened to our consciousness: we developed a greater awareness of the possibilities for asserting our agency in public spaces.

Our growing, politicized response to the images in our visual landscape necessitated urgent action. This desire for mobilization and the urgency we felt to take action compelled us to collectively "work to reclaim, reimagine, and rebuild our own home" (Berger & Dixon, 2009, p. 162). The idea that our "home"—an urban public context—was saturated by corporate advertising and messages that we did not ask for, became resonant for us.

The more we began to pay attention to the spaces we occupy, the more we noticed the disjuncture between our lives and the airbrushed hyper-reality presented in our common culture. We began to talk amongst ourselves and with our friends, discussing the images and their lack of positive messages for and about women.

Through our discussions, informal learning was taking place. Our learning could be viewed as "a complex process whereby individuals, embedded in social networks, develop a political analysis of their situation while they develop strategies of response" (Baltodano et al., 2007, p. 100). These moments served as catalysts for action, as we realized how we all have a responsibility, not only to inform ourselves and to view our media critically, but also to respond. What public response did these corporate-sponsored images call for? In what ways could we offer a counter-narrative or alternative to the mainstream messages invading our public spaces? As an act of resistance, we decided to launch a project as a way to actively contribute to the existing intersectional struggles against racism, capitalism, and patriarchy. *Wall of Femmes* was born.

Awareness to Action

People learn in practice that they have the power to disobey laws and social normality, and people learn that they can exert their own power much more effectively when they establish some control over the streets. (Kinsman, 2006, p. 153)

Wall of Femmes is a collective of feminists based in Montréal, established to execute a project, which is part street-art and part social action. We found common ground in a shared rejection of the messages available to us—about us—in our public spaces. Our primary intentions involve engaging others in our analysis of mainstream media by providing alternatives to the negative messages that dominate our spaces. We bring our politics to the streets, through stenciled images and high-contrast stickers of inspirational women. With these images, we aim:

- To promote a wider recognition and knowledge of the women we admire and find inspirational.

- To assert the people's ownership of public space.

- To counter the bombardment by mainstream media of negative, unhealthy, unattainable, sexist and/or objectified images of women in our public space.

- To engage in public discourse and contribute to the unique culture of our city in a meaningful way.

Figure 45.1

The *Wall of Femmes* project took inspiration from the book, *Revolutionary Women: A Book of Stencils*, edited by the *Queen of the Neighbourhood* collective (2010). After our discovery of this book, we began to generate ideas for our own vehicle for activism, incorporating their stencil format into a broader platform of communication involving both street art and web-based content. Like the *Queen of the Neighbourhood* collective, we also wanted to share the stories of revolutionary and radical women with a wider audience. We made a list of women who represent many different ideas and approaches, but who all took control of their own lives, never asked permission, and strove to eliminate inequality wherever they found it. After developing a course of action, we cut out stencils of the faces and names of women from the list we made.

In addition to asserting our message in the street, the *Wall of Femmes* project also etches out an online presence through a companion blog that elaborates on women that are highlighted. It extends the conversation through the Web with people from outside the group. The companion website, wall of femmes.org, and Facebook page of the same name, highlight and expand upon issues that are relevant to the aims of the collective.

The women that we select to highlight come from all over the world, and are situated in diverse social, political, and economic locations. Some are well known, some obscure, and some controversial. With the project, we want to acknowledge the way these women have improved our lives through their courage and hard work, in a way that encourages others to reflect, discuss, and mobilize in their own way. We try to carve out a space for these women in a public place that is too often saturated with messages that do not resonate with our own lives.

The *Wall of Femmes* collective primarily consists of students, educators, working people, and activists who are committed to the struggle for social justice and its manifestation in the public space.

Many of us were already actively engaged in work within community organizations and social movements. We shared common goals and had overlapping political and social locations. The *Wall of Femmes* emerged from this intersection of each collaborator's background and trajectory. When we meet informally, in coffee shops or in our homes, these places become intentional spaces for critical, collective reflection where we discuss issues that we want to address (Berger & Dixon, 2009). The conversations that we have with each other, in response to messages in our public spaces, became the foundation for collective action.

We locate ourselves with people who share our desire for change and who, like us, are unwilling to accept that we do not have control over what we see in our day-to-day activities. We each bring differing experiences and skills to share, and each devotes varying amounts of time to the project, as other commitments allow. Each member takes initiative on their own terms, from researching women to be highlighted, to making the stencils or stickers, to taking action in the streets, to writing articles for the blog. Rather than ask permission from one another for guidelines about how to engage in the project, we share our thinking and ask questions, respecting each others' autonomy within the framework of the collective. We recognize that participation can occur in many different forms and from different locations.

Building Solidarity Through Public Discourse

For the collective, street art is a way of showing support for local and global social movements that we are participating in, of building solidarity among struggles, and of contesting the capitalist system's control over our public spaces. As the project has evolved, our actions have become more focused on responding to and supporting social action and political events taking place in our city. For example, in response to the student movement that gained momentum in Montréal in the spring of 2012, we made stencils of Madeleine Parent and Léa Roback, both of whom actively worked to gain equal rights to education. With these stencils, we demonstrate our support for accessible education and for the work that women have done to advance the movement. Similarly, when an Indigenous rights activist-scholar working within the collective shared her knowledge about Natividad Llanquileo, Chilean Indigenous rights activist for the Mapuche people, it was decided to highlight her work on the streets of Montréal. Llanquileo's activist efforts have concentrated on fighting the criminalization of the struggles of her people and the militarization of their Indigenous territories.

Members of the *Wall of Femmes* collective are constantly seeking out learning opportunities relating to the aims of the project. In this spirit, many of us attended an event that featured readings from Audre Lorde's (1984) book, *Sister Outsider: Essays and Speeches*. The readings were followed by a film screening, *Audre Lorde: The Berlin Years 1984–1992* (Schultz, 2012), highlighting the life of Audre Lorde. This event was organized by Montréal-based social-action group, *Politics & Care* (a project that works to make explicit the links between the process of creativity through holistic healing, street art practices, and an integrated political discourse around well-being and self-care in activism and organizing), with assistance by *C-UniT* (Community-University Talks, a collective of students and community members committed to the pursuit of accessible education informed by anti-colonial and critical race discourse). As a way of promoting and supporting the critical work of the *Politics & Care Project*, and the *C-UniT* collective, we were inspired to make a stencil of Audre Lorde.

We draw from powerful examples of street art, born out of acts of resistance within the context of social movements around the world. Throughout the Arab Spring movements across the Middle East and North Africa, street art and social media have played extremely important roles in organizing and mobilizing people. Egypt saw an explosion in street art of all kinds. Some depicted martyrs, or people who were killed during the initial protests. Some portrayed raised fists and other rebellious symbolism. As we watched a popular revolution unfold in Egypt, we were inspired by the powerful actions of the millions of people demanding social change. Among them was Nawal El Saadawi, a resilient activist fighting for equality for women and against political, imperial, and class-based oppression of all people.

The international publication of her actions and speeches at the rallies in Tahrir Square informed us about her and her lifelong body of work. Depicting her in our stencils was a way for us to demonstrate solidarity with the Egyptian people and share her ideas with others in our own city.

The *Wall of Femmes* project has opened up an opportunity to learn, in greater detail, about the women we feature. Along with the learning that takes place in social movements, we attend events and talks hosted in our community. In the winter of 2013, members of the collective attended a talk by Angela Davis as part of the Fro Festival in Montréal hosted in concert with Black History Month. At the talk, Davis emphasized Martin Luther King Jr.'s idea of the indivisibility of justice, that "an injustice anywhere is a threat to justice everywhere". In this spirit, she expressed solidarity with a wide variety of current struggles in North America and around the world. In the previous year, we attended a talk presented by the grassroots campaign, *Justice for Missing and Murdered Indigenous Women* (Missing Justice) and the 2110 Centre for Gender Advocacy in Montréal. The talk featured Andrea Smith, a Cherokee scholar, feminist, and anti-violence activist who spoke about systemic violence against Native women and First Nations land struggles. From those events, we take our learning further to inform our actions in the collective.

Our collective and individual experiences assure us that the learning that takes place through social action is a crucial appendage to that which occurs within conventional educational institutions. As participants in this project and members of the collective, we have discovered how experiences of art as social action in the community can provide opportunities for meaningful learning to take place. The project is an opportunity for members of the collective to not only learn about the women featured, but also to participate in social movements by embedding symbols of support for them into the public discourse with stencils of women who are and have been drivers of social change. We also learn more about our community's attitudes towards these women and the project in general through reactions online and in the street.

As a space for communication and interaction, street art is used by artists to talk to each other. Unlike commercial advertising, one of the goals of many street artists is to encourage communication among viewers of their art by highlighting power struggles in the community. The artists and viewers, who do not know one another, may constantly interact with each other by leaving messages and interpreting these messages. Therefore, in addition to projecting a one-way message at viewers, street art also communicates dialogue among artists and members of the community (Christen, 2003).

Wall of Femmes takes action in a way that establishes some control over the streets when we insert our own images in the public domain. The images that are stenciled on walls cause a reaction, and call for a conversation or reconsideration of what kinds of messages are available to people in our public spaces. It has been interesting to see how the community has responded: critically, supportively, and in a few cases, negatively. A few days after the stencils went up, some responses appeared on the wall itself, as people in the community began to communicate with each other through the project. Below a stencil of Jane Addams, someone painted words, "HOLYFUCK ILOVEYOU." Additionally, next to the stencil of Amelia Earhart, someone wrote, "The world was amazing with you, keep flying", and added to the *Wall of Femmes* collection by drawing their own portrait of Emily Carr beside our stencil of Earhart. In a different location, someone wrote, "LA FEMINISME, C'EST PUNK", under the stencils, which we interpret as a positive message. However, negative responses also appeared on the wall. In one location, someone painted an X over the face of each woman, and wrote, "FUCK DEEZ FOOLS" next to them. Though the positive responses still outweigh the negative responses by far, seeing negative responses like this reminds us that feminism is still a polarizing idea. Engaging in feminist action remains critical because hostile attitudes towards women continue to persist. All of these responses represent the public's interest in participating in this conversation in physical space. They call for further reaction, response, and action.

In addition to the response to the artwork in the streets, people also give feedback and suggestions, and express support and solidarity online through the Facebook page or through the companion blog. We use the companion blog to write articles that provide more information about the women we highlight, detail upcoming events, promote social-action projects we support, analyze current events and popular culture, and critically review mass-media images and content, all from a feminist perspective. Since its launch, the blog has grown from being simply a forum for us to express ourselves to becoming a new avenue to extend our own learning when readers post links to additional information and resources. On the Facebook page, due to the extensively social nature of the platform, we have been able to further expand our local connections to global ones. People share our posts and page so that the project is proliferated across the Web.

When the conversation is extended, through responses to our work in the streets or online, we welcome the possibility to make connections and alliances among other social-action and community groups on local and global levels. Through our online presence, we have connected with groups in other parts of the world, such as global network, *Guerilla Feminism*; Brooklyn-based political graphic-arts archive, *Interference Archive*; and Montréal-based collective, *Maille à Part*. Together, we have shared each other's updates and articles, resulting in a global community of knowledge building. Taking up online space, in addition to physical space, is necessary to counteract the bombardment of negative messages we see on the Internet, while building a network of support with similar interest groups.

These conversations construct a place to connect struggles to help build solidarity among groups. When we come together in a spirit of political solidarity, we build stronger alliances. As Kinsman (2006) explained, global justice movements are most effective when a series of different social forces and modes of struggle intersect. For example, feminist, anti-racist, ecological groups and others can, and must, work together to create a louder voice against current power structures. For the collective, the project is about showing support for local and global social movements that we are participating in, building solidarity among struggles, and asserting our own agency to reclaim our public spaces.

Challenges and Possibilities

As the public responds to the project with newly developing conversations in the street and online, some challenges emerge; we question ourselves, wondering how the project will evolve and develop over time. These challenges have been difficult to address, because by publicizing our ideas, we open our ideas up for critique, and by extension, ourselves. We acknowledge that not everyone will agree with the messages we share, or the way in which we choose to share them.

As a collective, we have struggled to critically identify how we might be contributing to the very systems of oppression that we are trying to challenge from within the group. We have taken up questions around the iconicization of women we highlight. With the project, we intend not to render specific women as icons, but rather to provide positive alternatives to the potentially damaging images that the corporate media chooses to make available to us in our public spaces.

Tui Gordon, a member of the *Queen of the Neighbourhood* collective, described her thoughts on singling out female revolutionaries as icons in the book, *Revolutionary Women, A Book of Stencils*:

> Some would not welcome this eulogising of their egos; some might sit uncomfortably on their page, forced into a relationship with the other women in a kind of canon of revolutionaries, even though they may have very little in common with each other and have completely opposing viewpoints. I hope they can all taste the sweet satire of our icon-style brushing of them with Ché Guevara glam; our massive nod to them; and the ways in which we are at the same time capping the knees of that cultural drive to make heroes when the real work is done by community, by people helping each other out. (*Queen of the Neighbourhood*, 2010, p. 9)

As we attempt to have a well-rounded repertoire of women represented, we are confronted by challenges. We all live within a framework built on colonialism and neo-colonialism, which results in both unfair privilege and exploitation. Because of the impacts of colonialism on the Canadian public education system, the histories most of us have been taught have been biased and incomplete. Do we not have a responsibility to question those dominant histories and respond to colonialism's ongoing effects with education and activism? *Wall of Femmes* continues to evolve by looking at the past and present sociological, political, and economic climate in Canada and around the world. As we learn about women who are more difficult to locate in textbooks and in popular culture, we have a desire to include them in our project so that others may also be exposed to their works and ideas. The more we learn, the more we are driven to interject these counter-narratives into the public domain.

Another challenge arises when researching the stories of women we would like to highlight. Before we endorse a specific individual and their work, we go through a process of informing ourselves by seeking out a variety of sources of information and analysis. Occasionally, there will be some conflict, where an individual we would like to highlight represented some ideas we support, but others that cannot be endorsed. This comes up more frequently when considering the work of feminists of previous generations, whose ideas naturally reflected the context of their own time and place rather than our own. Jessica Yee (a self-described Two Spirit multi-racial Indigenous hip hop feminist reproductive-justice freedom fighter) illustrated this problem in a 2011 interview with Toronto's *Eye Weekly* magazine:

> Look at the first wave of feminism and suffragettes, in the early 1900s. There's a statue of Emily Murphy in Ottawa, with the Famous Five, the group who argued that women were "persons" under the law. What they don't tell you about the Famous Five is that they were really racist. Emily Murphy published this eugenics book called The Black Candle, which basically talks about how Anglo-Saxon society should rule and anybody who doesn't belong to the Anglo-Saxon society is dangerous and shouldn't be trusted. She simultaneously helped pass the Residential School Act and the Indian Act, and I'm supposed to thank her for gender equality? What she wanted was more white people to vote (Wall of Femmes, 2011).

As the project evolves, and we learn to seek out diverse perspectives on ideas we had previously left unquestioned and had accepted at face value, we have trained our eyes and ears to be more critical and to question the ideas presented to us by educational and mainstream media institutions.

We are also concerned with our use of depictions of the women in the art-making process, since we have not sought authorization to use their names or likenesses, or to group them with others in the project. We have considered both the implications of using their likenesses, and the idea of asking permission from their families to acknowledge the contributions the women have made to society. However, we hope that taking to the streets autonomously allows us to consider the women who inspire us not as idols, but as peers, who also acted without permission.

Wall of Femmes deliberately calls attention to what is absent in our public spaces. Through the project, we demonstrate how we have power to announce our identity in the community in a way that challenges those who contribute to systems of oppression. We are attracted to making street art, because it is an avenue to assert our power and voice in society; we did not need to be granted that power from an authority figure. Through the project, we have learned how street art can powerfully expose both artists and viewers to a critical understanding of power structures embedded in society, and offer opportunities for self-reflection (Christen, 2003).

We routinely engage in reflexive conversations about the project, and we also imagine the possibilities for its development. We hope to offer a discussion that is rooted in practice—practice that we use to negotiate and grapple with pressing questions that we encounter in our public spaces. Self-produced art and messages inserted into public spaces can draw attention to, and counter, already existing dominant messages. Stencils and other forms of street art offer a public alternative, and are a reflection of a potent form of agency. They can be compelling, not only for their form, but also for their placement in public spaces. Through these actions, people have an opportunity to see the possibilities that exist for themselves to engage with their community in creative ways.

Conclusion

The *Wall of Femmes* project is an illustration of how people can use street art as one avenue to express ideas and perspectives that are alternative to those promoted by mass-media industries. For members of the collective, *Wall of Femmes* has become a vehicle for social action, a space for sharing and learning new skills, and for engaging with other local projects of mutual interest. An idea that originated as a side project among friends has become an integral part of our lives.

Since street art is anonymous and quick to execute, it can play a unique role in documenting and reflecting on current events and social issues by expressing solidarity with a particular viewpoint. As more and more people begin to use the street as a forum for expression, communication, and debate, street art proliferates as a powerful tool of expression for those denied more traditional platforms. Although street art does not always have an overtly political message, it often comes from a need to establish some sense of ownership over public space and the visual landscape. In this way, even without a political message, engaging in street art is a highly political act.

Unsanctioned public art helps to counteract the cultural hegemony promoted by the dominant groups who control the media and advertising that otherwise appear in our public spaces. In our increasingly homogenized world, where the same advertisements and logos of the same brands have saturated cities across the globe, engaging in street art is a way for all members of civil society to assert their agency by embedding their own images and stories into the visual and cultural landscape of the environments in which they live. In this way, our cities become more reflective and representative of the rich variety of individuals who call these unique places home. At the same time, the street has become a forum for a much needed public discourse and social commentary among citizens.

The status quo is maintained in part by the acceptance of the dominant ideology through cultural hegemony. As an act of resistance against the manifestation of this hegemony through our public spaces, the *Wall of Femmes* collective developed a grassroots, feminist, social-action project which aims to challenge these structures and reclaim our public spaces from corporatization. We hope that by amplifying the work and ideas of the courageous women featured in our stencils, individuals who view them may be inspired to follow their examples and create avenues of their own to work towards more equitable communities for all people.

Figure 45.2

References

Baltodano, C., Choudry, A., Hanley, J., Jordan, S., Shragge, E., & Stiegman, M. (2007). Becoming an immigrant worker: Learning in everyday life. *Canadian Journal for the Study of Adult Education, 20*(2), 99–113.

Berger, D., & Dixon, C. (2009). Navigating the crisis: A study groups roundtable. *Upping the Anti: A Journal of Theory and Action, 8,* 159–177.

Castells, M. (1989). *The informational city: Information technology, economic restructuring, and the urban-regional process.* Oxford, UK: Blackwell.

Christen, R. S. (2003). Hip hop learning: Graffiti as an educator of urban teenagers. *Educational Foundations, 17*(4), 57–82.

Deutsch N. L., & Theodorou, E. (2010). Aspiring, consuming, becoming: Youth identity in a culture of consumption. *Youth and Society, 42*(2), 229–254.

Duncum, P. (1999). A case for an art education of everyday aesthetic experiences. *Studies in Art Education, 40*(4), 295–311.

Foley, G. (1999). *Learning in social action: A contribution to understanding informal education.* London, UK: Zed Books.

Gramsci, A. (1971). *Selections from the prison notebooks of Antonio Gramsci.* New York, NY: International.

Hill, J. (2011). Endangered childhoods: How consumerism is impacting child and youth identity. *Media, Culture & Society, 33*(3), 347–362.

Kinsman, G. (2006). Mapping social relations of struggle: Activism, ethnography, social organization. In C. Frampton, G. Kinsman, A. K. Thompson, & K. Tilleczek (Eds.), *Sociology for changing the world: Social movements/social research* (pp. 133–156). Black Point, Nova Scotia, Canada: Fernwood.

Lorde, A. (1984). *Sister outsider: Essays and speeches.* Freedom, CA: Crossing Press.

Queen of the Neighbourhood. (2010). *Revolutionary women: A Book of Stencils.* Oakland, CA: PM Press.

Schultz, D. (Writer & Director). (2012). *Audre Lorde: The Berlin years 1984–1992.* USA: Third World Newsreel.

Tokuhama, C. (2011). Consumption, a modern affliction: Branding culture, youth identity and college admission. *Journal of College Admission, 210*, 32–38.

Tuchman, G., Daniels, A. K., & Benét, J. (Eds.). (1978). *Hearth and home: Images of women in the mass media.* New York, NY: Oxford University Press.

Voronkova, L., & Pachenkov, O. (2011). Public spaces in modern cities. *Berkeley Planning Journal, 24*(1), 197–207.

Wall of Femmes. (2011, April 25). *Jessica Yee: Multiracial two spirit indigenous hip hop feminist reproductive-justice freedom fighter.* Retrieved from http://www.walloffemmes.org/2011/04/jessica-yee-multiracial-two-spirit.html

CHAPTER 46

From a Culture of Refusal to a Culture of Renewal

Criticalizing Muslim Youths' Lives Through Calls to Collective Action

Brett Elizabeth Blake and Rohany Nayan

Introduction

"Let it NOT be a Muslim…." This was the first thought and prayer uttered by many Muslims in America and around the world on the morning of Monday, April 15, 2013, after the news release that there was an explosion near the finish line at the Boston Marathon. The bombs killed three people, injured 264 others and inflicted around $333 million in damages to the city's infrastructure, care for the 70 hospitalized victims, retail sales, and local economy, according to rough estimates reported in news outlets. Even before the dust from the collapsed infrastructures settled, the media and news outlets were abuzz with speculations on who the villains were: a "dark-skinned suspect," a 17-year-old Moroccan high-school track star who attended the marathon carrying a black bag and seen fleeing the scene, and a 21-year-old Saudi "jihadi," a student whose crime was to run away from a violent explosion. Following these reports, a conservative columnist (and sometime Fox News guest), Erik Rush, tweeted a *call to collective action*, calling on Americans to murder all Muslims, whom he described as "all evil."

Later, the suspects were identified as brothers Tamerlan and Dzhokhar Tsarnaev, ethnic Chechens, born in Kyrgyzstan, and who had lived in America for several years. These brothers are literally Caucasian, since their family came from the northern Caucus region. These brothers were good-looking young men, definitely not dark-skinned, bearded, or "Saudi," as speculated in the media circus. The alleged life story of these brothers as constructed by the media—of older brother Tamerlan Tsarnaev, 26, and younger brother Dzhokhar, 19—reflects a typical narrative of immigrants who emigrated to the US seeking the "American Dream." Anzor Tsarnaev, their father, an ethnic Chechen who grew up in Kyrgyzstan, emigrated to Boston a decade ago with his wife, two daughters, and two sons. This family reportedly has a broken family dynamic. David Remnick (2013), in his article, described the Tsarnaev family history as riddled with conflicts and violence caused by the "harrowed land of their ancestors," noting that they had experienced the strife of displacement, exile, and emigration. When news and photos of these brothers were splashed across media outlets as the bombing suspects, friends and family members were shocked, shaken, and mystified. How could these two "nice," and "cool" young ethnic Chechens who grew up in the US but with a strong attachment to their homeland, do such a horrific act? Why would Dzhokhar—described as an "angel" by his dad and a successful and popular "scholarship student," and whose friends described him as someone "with a good sense of humor"—kill innocent people? What drove these brothers to commit such atrocities?

At a glance, both brothers seemed to be doing well in their lives in their adopted home. However, upon deeper examination of the interactions and narratives they shared with family and friends, and the texts they produced on social-media outlets, we get to learn about Tamerlan's alienation, disaffection with, and disconnection from the American way of life. Dzhokhar's Twitter feed—@J_tsar—revealed his numerous bewildering thoughts, jokes, resentments, prejudices, faith, and desires (Remnick, 2013). Further investigations suggest that Tamerlan's growing extremism may be due to "the toxic combination of high-minded zealotry and the curdled disappointments of young men." Tamerlan and Dzhokhar Tsarnaev, painted as feeling alienated, disconnected, wronged, and victimized, may have used the bombings as an outlet to validate and sanctify their feelings of rage against the USA. The bombing acts by the Tsarnaev brothers can be seen as not only a "refusal" of everything American, but also *a call for collective action*—in this case, negative, dangerous, and destructive—calls by extremist zealots whose ideologies aim to derail the sense and composure of the superpower by calling for violence against America, perceived as a big bully, occupier, and oppressor of Muslims worldwide.

A deeper examination and study of this abhorrent phenomenon is crucial. We need to find out the reasons, understand the motivations, and listen to the grievances of these people who call themselves Muslims and commit violence in the name of Islam. The increasing process of radicalization and extremism on both sides, both Muslims and Americans, must be interrupted and disrupted. The US must not focus on becoming a fortress, and it should not continue targeting and treating its Muslim citizens as a suspect community. In recent times, discussions like this have become crucial in order to counter negative attitudes, discrimination, and bullying incidents that are on the rise in schools toward immigrant students, especially Muslim students, due to the rise of anti-Muslim sentiments that have permeated into school communities. Of late, Muslim Americans have again become the subject of much conversation in the United States, especially with regard to their ability, as individuals and as a community, to be truly "American." In this chapter, we answer a call to criticalize the field of "youth studies" by *re-conceptualizing* several theories that have influenced our research and practice enormously, and by synthesizing with and/or connecting them to our work with Muslim adolescents in schools. We develop this criticalization by first reviewing these theories: a culture of refusal, literacy and identity, and critical narrative theory. We then present data that Blake collected from over three years of work among Muslim middle-school students in New York City, offering both our and the students' interpretations and categorizations of meaning of their written narratives. Finally, we discuss implications that help us move from "refusal" to "renewal" among our multiply-marginalized—here, in particular, Muslim youth—as they potentially learn to raise their voices in a "call for positive collective action" in our schools, and ultimately, then, in our society.

Preliminary findings enabled us to highlight adolescent Muslim students' salient identities through their literacy practices, and in doing so provided us with a continuation of the immigrant narrative that in large part defines the United States. Similar to other religious and multiethnic groups before them, however, (who also faced significant social stigma and racism), Muslim adolescents revealed themselves in different and new ways—their sense of hope and community, and *lack* of "refusal," for example, has led us to emphasize a major point of this reconceptualization: no group of adolescents is alike, and we must take great care, especially in our schools, not to essentialize them in any way—through language, culture, or religion.

Theoretical Perspectives

Research on human learning and educational contexts has indicated that the notions of identity and culture are intricately intertwined. Many researchers and theorists have noted that culture is at the heart of meaning-making and is central to our very perception of reality. Knowing and doing are products of sociocultural processes (Lave & Wenger, 1991; Rogoff, 2003; Vygotsky, 1978) where knowledge is socially mediated and all socialization is rooted in culture and cultural identity (Ferdman, 1990). Families often use religious identity to strengthen family bonds and make sense of kaleidoscopic complexities of their life's struggles. Identities that students ascribe to, chosen or prescribed, often emerge in their literacy acts through their speech acts or written texts (Nayan, 2012; Peek, 2005). Aside from these sociocultural theories, we also use narrative inquiry to study the stories that the research participants shared with us (Blake & Blake, 2012), providing us with a lens through which we can better focus on human experience by examining the ways in which these participants experience their worlds through the stories they tell in the texts they produced.

Identity

Sociocultural theorists on identity and literacy have pointed out that both identity and literacy are fluid and dynamic, not fixed, unified, or static. In defining identity, Côté and Levine (2002) described it as the way we see ourselves, the way others see us, and the way we fit into the communities to which we belong. We often make claims about who we are by aligning and contrasting ourselves with people around us. Identity construction in cultural and social spaces is an ongoing process, with constant construction and re-construction (Holland, Lachicotte, Skinner, & Cain, 1998), with a continual process of negotiation and renegotiation between children and the social spaces within which they are embedded (Gee, 1999; Wenger, 1999).

Muslim Americans are members of a particular cultural group that has a particular historical background; that is to say, they are not all of one particular ethnic or linguistic group (much like Hispanics and/or Latinos around the world). The literature reviewed indicates that the identities that Muslim Americans, especially Muslim immigrant children and adults, enact are *dynamic, multiple, positioned, fluid, contested,* and *changing,* as they are dependent on particular social and cultural contexts (Gregory, 2002; Gregory & Williams, 2000; Merry, 2007; Nayan, 2012; Wallace, 2008) across time and space (Pahl & Rowsell, 2005; Sensoy & Stonebanks, 2009; Sirin & Fine, 2008). The multiple identities enacted were visible through the literacy practices that individuals engaged in, which were based on their lived experiences embedded in religious and cultural beliefs that were categorized through gender, race, belief systems, and class (Nayan, 2012; Pahl & Rowsell, 2005; Sarroub, 2005; Sirin & Fine, 2008; Wallace, 2008). Research using a sociocultural lens recognizes significant connections between learners and the cultural worlds that surround them (Gee, 2008; Street, 1984; Vygotsky, 1978).

Literacy

Literacy traditionally has been linked closely to the notion of being *literate* that can lead an individual to become *successful* in life. However, what it means to be *literate* and *successful* varies in different cultures, different languages, and different communities that have their own beliefs and practices (Blake & Blake, 2005). For many Muslims, to be literate means having the *Qur'anic* knowledge for character building in order to "be a good Muslim" (Rosowsky, 2008; Syed, 2001; Wagner, 1993). This means that Muslims have to acquire the Arabic language, especially Qur'anic Arabic, and Islamic literacies that are used in daily prayers and other ritualized practices. Muslims in general see the acquisition of literacy and education as part of their religious duty as a Muslim, due to the importance placed upon seeking knowledge, as revealed in the *Qur'an.*

In the past few decades, literacy research has illustrated that students' identities are enacted through their literacy practices that contain layers of their lived histories. Distinct identities often emerged in the stories students told about themselves and the artifacts they produced that were historically and socially situated (Bartlett, 2007; Pahl & Rowsell, 2005). Rohany Nayan (2012), in her study of three young Muslim immigrants from Morocco, Indonesia, and Somalia in KG–3rd grade, revealed that the children were aware of their multiple identities prescribed by their parents, teachers, and peers: religious, cultural, academic, and familial. They negotiated these identities smoothly in different domains of their lives at school, home, and in their communities. These younger children engaged actively in diverse literacy practices such as watching, listening, repeating, echoing, requesting help, asking questions, following directions, imitating, challenging, and experimenting. These practices were incorporated during their literacy acts, such as reading, writing, producing texts, artifacts (i.e., drawing, notes, messages), and engaging in e-Mersion (i.e., using the computer and the Internet). Older siblings or children in the immigrant families generally enacted their learning through "modeling, guiding, demonstrating, instructing, coaxing, looking after, comforting and socializing younger children as well as generally practicing their existing skills" (Gregory, 2008, p. 91). The literacy practices that these children engaged in reflected the multiple paths to acquiring literacy that takes place within environments that are socially and culturally situated.

Many studies on literacy have revealed that children of Muslim immigrants engage in multiple literacies, due to the expectations and roles they assume in their family and community. Similar to other immigrant children, children of Muslim immigrants, such as the Yemeni Americans (Sarroub, 2005), Somali Americans (Ajrouch & Kusow, 2007; Bigelow, 2007, 2010), and from other ethnic backgrounds (Khan, 2009; Fine & Sirin, 2007; Sensoy & Stonebanks, 2009), often have to shoulder responsibilities as the "translator," "reader," "writer," and "scribe" of their families, especially when their parents are illiterate or have a low level of print literacy. These studies support the notion that immigrant children contribute to their families in a variety of tangible ways—by babysitting, translating, completing paperwork, and sometimes, by working part-time jobs that supplement the family income (Bigelow, 2010; Sarroub, 2005; Sirin & Fine, 2008). Poor immigrant children also become the family expert on the ways of the new society (Orellana, 2009). It is crucial for us to recognize that immigrant children shoulder different expectations at different age levels, and they vary significantly from one cultural context to another. These expectations are often further intensified by the necessities generated by migration, and are dependent upon each family's needs.

The literacy practices of children of Muslim immigrants are often hybridized and syncretized. In the UK, research in London showed that Muslim immigrant children engaged in hybridized literacy practice where different cultural forms interact in the same space. The children blended the knowledge learned at school into knowledge practiced at home and in the community that were reflected through play, dialogue, artifact creation (writing, drawing), and the identities they assumed when given a choice to do so (Gregory & Williams, 2000; Kenner, 2004; Wallace, 2008). They also created further hybridity through the making of texts, which represent their complex cultural and religious backgrounds. Syncretism refers to a more complex process of hybridity, which results in the creation of new forms of practices with an emphasis on "the fluid and creative interaction of words, ideas, and practices to create a dynamic, fruitful and positive whole" (Gregory, Long, & Volk, 2004, p. 5). Gregory (2008) described how the Muslim immigrant children in her study produced syncretic literacy practices when they assumed their identity as English-language speakers and used the English language often mixed in with their native language(s) in their "play school" games with their friends or siblings at home. Studies on Muslim youth revealed that teens engage in diverse syncretic literacy practices, especially in using multimodal literacies, narratives, and technology to develop their "voices" to talk back to the Islamophobia discourse and microaggressions that surround them daily (Fine & Sirin, 2007; Sensoy & Stonebanks, 2009).

There are also other studies that suggest that immigrant children engage in "glocal" literacy practices, a description for the economic phenomena where people use local and global connections to adapt and adopt new literacies (Blake, 2004; Fine & Sirin, 2007; Sarroub, 2008). Through participating in global literacy practices, people create opportunities for interconnectedness by intertwining local and global cultural, social, and academic knowledge and experiences. Hybridity and syncretism in immigrant children's literacy and identity are distinctly visible in today's contemporary world as a result of migration and technological advancements in travel, media, and communication.

There are multiple paths to literacy acquisition and varying degrees of expertise within individuals' and groups' communicative repertoires (Martin-Jones & Jones, 2000). Some of these paths to literacy acquisition include self-instruction, home or mosque affiliation, and bilingual education materials development. Immigrant children engage in literacy activities at home and in their community based on their contacts with the adults in their life who are their literacy mediators (Gregory, 2001, 2008; Gregory & Williams, 2000; Pahl & Rowsell, 2005; Wallace, 2008). Muslim youth, especially children of immigrants, often used their multilingual knowledge in their literacy acts at school and home to make links with their unique life experiences. Their literacy practices support the notion that literacy consists of "multi-layered history of experience with language and content, cutting across many contexts" (Langer, 2001, p. 838).

Critical Narrative Theory

Identities can be conjured through the stories told (Blake & Blake, 2012). Temporally speaking, stories provide a vehicle for oscillating between the past, present, and future. As we tell and retell stories about who we were in the past, who we are in the present, and who we would like to be in the future, we mediate and transform our identities through the stories told (and retold) that may actually be real, fictional, or hypothetical and are reported orally, in print, or in combination of oral, print, and artistic expressions. Storytelling, in many societies, is regarded as an activity that includes the creation of fictional stories, passing on community histories, and sharing personal stories with others. Telling stories is a part of identity performances that is illustrative, and it is important to recognize that the stories told are indicative of the ways in which the individuals resist, relate to, respond to, and engage in literacy practices (Perry, 2007). In education and educational research, narrative inquiry can be a powerful tool to transfer, share, or examine knowledge, as emphasized by Connelly and Clandinin (2009), who stated that the study of narrative is the study of lived experiences and the ways humans experience the world. The artifacts developed from these experiences become both the content and method of investigation (Clandinin & Huber, 2002). Blake and Blake (2012) also highlighted that when teachers use narrative in their classrooms (as inquiry, as text), they also learn to bridge theory with the practices of their own teaching—to create a professional stance—reconstructing what we all know is good teaching and learning; what we know works in spite of standardized testing and accountability measures that declare the opposite.

Narratives are important tools for revealing and sharing with the readers or listeners the importance and influence of a particular experience on oneself. Solórzano and Yosso (2002) provided four functions of personal narratives:

- Personal narratives build community along the margins of society;

- Personal narratives challenge the perceived wisdom of the center;

- Personal narratives present the realities of those at the margins;

- Personal narratives teach others by combining the story with current reality.

Further research has also shown (Blake & Blake, 2012) that storytelling or narrative writing has many benefits, both in and out of school, particularly for adolescents, who often struggle with identity and literacy as prescribed by schools.

Adolescent Theory and a Culture of Refusal

The onset of adolescence is a critical period of biological, psychological, and social change for every child, involving dramatic transitions in one's physical as well as one's cultural and social environment. These "transitions" have become even more difficult in recent years, as a combination of socioeconomic and political factors has led to an erosion of the traditional, so-called support networks (schools, family, community, government) upon which our youth have so desperately depended, especially those who are of color, poor, and/or have recently immigrated to the United States, i.e., the "multiply-marginalized" (Ayers, 1997). And yet, even if we acknowledge that little, if any, work done on adolescence prior to the 1980s focused on the implications of the loss of these support systems, the real surprise is that little work has been done since the turn of the 21st century that takes into account the dramatic effects that gender, race, class, ethnicity, sexual orientation, and/or religion have on adolescence *coupled* with the loss of these support systems. Further, few have critically examined these intersections within the context of our rapidly changing, increasingly violent, politicized, and standardized school and/or social environments (a notable exception is DeVitis & Irwin-DeVitis, 2010). This critical examination is at a "breaking point," as both left- and right-leaning voters push politicians and policymakers to continue to make decisions about our youth, particularly decisions related to what constitutes "best" teaching methods and assessments in schools. Many of these mandates are guided by faulty and dangerous research based on a "deficit" model; one of the very models traditionally used to effectively sort and categorize those whose first language was not English, for example, or those whose parents had a "foreign-sounding" surname.

A culture of refusal

The term, "culture of refusal," was coined several years ago by Brett Elizabeth Blake (2004) when she worked with and studied incarcerated youth in their jail pre-GED and GED classroom settings. Designed as a way to name the discourse around these students' complete rejection of anything that traditional school or society had to offer, the term also came to represent the countless years of institutionalized racism by the various support systems—school and society—that were supposed to help them. Even the so-called "rehabilitative education" programs they were required to attend during their incarceration often did nothing more than remind them of their multiply-marginalized status and the hopelessness that accompanies it. When schooling, the resources of the local community, and the needs of the larger society in today's global, technological workplace become at odds—where the school is not providing the extra support missing from the family, the community is not providing the extra support missing from both the family and the school, and the larger society offers no support in the form of work—multiply-marginalized adolescents, in particular, become engulfed in the incongruence of their lives. This incongruence leads, then, precipitously, to a culture of refusal, where the youth themselves believe that the lack of support systems are unnecessary, unwanted, and certainly undermining of their true needs and desires.

Undoubtedly, school remains a pivotal institution in adolescents' lives. Along with the other major factors (e.g., family and community) that strongly influence adolescents' transition into adulthood, schools, too, remain notoriously ineffective in attending to the "ethnicity and the identity development of minority adolescents" (Takanishi, 1993, p. 56). Multiply-marginalized youth, like all youth, are "avid seekers of moral authenticity" (Ayers, 1997, p. 139), and yet they come face-to-face with a society and school systems that disdain them (or, in the case of incarcerated youth, throw them away). These support systems do not legitimize their understandings of themselves and their perspectives of their social

world—their identity—and so they learn to separate their formal learning experiences from more powerful, out-of-school learning experiences, taking their voices, their literacies, their cultural spaces, and
their identities underground, to the place Blake (2004) called a "culture of refusal."

It is in this period of turmoil that we hope to re-examine and to "criticalize" the theoretical under-
pinnings and understandings of youth and/or adolescent culture, and in turn find ways in which we
can, as educators, parents, and concerned citizens, help them ride that treacherous roller coaster from
adolescence into adulthood. This becomes critically important as immigrant patterns have significantly
changed in the US—indeed one in five school-aged children now speaks a language other than English
at home—and schools have returned to an era of increased standardization and a one-size-fits-all curriculum. Coupled with a society that increasingly distrusts anything and *everything* foreign, the moment
is upon us to move in new directions in searching for more equitable education opportunities for all
our youth, but particularly for our Muslim adolescent students, often the most distrusted in our schools
and society today.

Methodology and Data Source

Data for this chapter were taken from a larger ethnographic study that Blake conducted among Muslim adolescent students in private middle and secondary schools in New York City. It was originally
thought that all aspects of a "culture of refusal" could be applied to this immigrant group—indeed,
among all multiply-marginalized students—but the use of critical narrative theory (and a reexamina-
tion of other important theories, as discussed above) has shifted that focus.

A major tenet of critical narrative theory is to take care not to essentialize—not to impose our
(culturally bound) narrative stance and interpretations onto our students' work—effectively negating
the potential of using narrative as a means of excavating our students' voices (Blake & Blake, 2012). To
do this, then, we need to be hyper-vigilant in recognizing that in different cultures, life-identity stories
(narrative), for example, may not even exist as a genre, and if they do, are not constructed and/or told in
the same way we might expect in our own classrooms. And of course, each language has its own unique
structure, carrying within it its own cultural signifiers—and so we must take care that we do not automatically impose our internalized understandings of the structure of the English language—Standard
English—for example, onto our students' meanings and interpretations.

Advocating for the use of a critical narrative stance as a conceptual and/or educational framework
becomes more powerful, as it can not only help us to uncover and explore students' lives, but it also
helps us to reflect upon how these narratives can lead to a better understanding of students' literacy
practices and identities—a crucial task in arguing for a "call to collective action" and a "culture of
renewal." This, in turn, we believe, has the practical (and perhaps unintended) consequence of helping
our immigrant students to meet new state and federal mandates in what and/or how they learn and
how they are assessed.

From a Culture of Refusal to a Culture of Renewal: Preliminary Findings

A closer examination of the narratives students shared here generally revealed that through the ups and
downs of their experiences as immigrants (or children of immigrants), they continued to build communities, reimagine their distinct ethnic and religious backgrounds, and develop a uniquely American
mode(s) of living out of their multiple identities. Despite many similarities to other religious immigrant
groups, Muslim immigrants indeed are distinct in that, as a community, they are often multilingual,
have significant transnational ties, worship in highly diverse, multiethnic congregations, and are relatively upwardly mobile when compared to other religious groups.

Specifically, on a closer look, student narratives in this study revealed three distinct, major themes:
prejudice/fear, reflection/hope/identity, and *advocacy/renewal.* Most surprisingly, perhaps, was that even
though many students wrote about prejudice and fear (of war, for example), there was always a sense of

hope lingering within and among their words; a distinction not seen as clearly (or at all) in other studies Blake has conducted among adolescents (Blake, 1997, 2004). We elaborate:

Prejudice and fear

In this first group of collected narratives, fifth- and sixth-grade students were asked to write personal narratives about their "experience with prejudice." A follow-up assignment directed these same students to "write about what you might tell others to change the prejudice that happened to you." [Students' narratives have been left in their original, unedited form(s) except where meaning would be lost.]

A young girl writes:

My experience is when I was going to manhatten with my mom. I got to the train station … when I was about to sit down I tripped over a womens shoe. She said "What's your problem watch were your going" I was about to cry but my mom said don't cry and stay strong. Their were two women next to her that laughed at me. I think they were prejudice because I was wearing Hijab at that time.

She follows up with:

To help someone you can give them advice such as telling them to ignore who ever tells you something mean. If someone is raciest or saying something mean to you then describe your feelings to them or tell them how you feel. When someone is still acting the same then tell a grown-up and they will deal with them. The whole point is no matter what someone does to you just beliven in Allah.

Another narrative assignment included "I Am" and "I Wonder" poems, modeled by their teacher. A Muslim woman herself, the teacher wrote about why she gave this particular assignment:

Giving them this assignment made me aware of my own experiences and what I felt like as a Muslim American born kid growing up in Queens…. It reminded me of how important it is for my students to feel accepted and appreciated through encouragement and motivation. Sometimes the school environment is the students' escape into a promising hopeful world.

One young boy writes:

I am funny and active
I hear quietness
I see Paradise
I worry about my relatives, in Egypt
I cry when there's depression in the world
I am funny and active.

While a young girl writes:

I wonder about my future
I hear happiness
I pretend I can fly
I touch the sky
I cry about not having peace
I dream of a different world
I hope there will always be peace
I worry about the future

And finally, from another boy:

I wonder if war is going to end
I see God

I want peace in the world
I feel God's hands
I worry about war
I cry when people die
I understand that there will never be peace
I dream about peace

Teachers like her are a critical cog in the "narrative tool" that allows students to feel this hope, faith, and a view for a better world. As a teacher, she too, was able to criticalize her own experiences growing up Muslim in America, and as she modeled the activities for her students based on this criticalization, she, too, highlighted the need for all people to find hope and peace. The teacher states:

> When I was growing up as a child I had already been subjected to different treatment. When I was a freshman in high school, the first day …, I was standing with mom … I was looking around and noticed a girl staring at me. Her parent moved her daughter away when I smiled at her. When we became friends, she later told me, her mom thought I had some disease and was concerned for her safety. She had never seen a Muslim female covering her hair.

Reflection/hope/identity

In another classroom, seventh- and eighth-grade students were asked not only to write about their homelands through poetry, but also to express to President Obama and then-Secretary of State, Hillary Clinton, their hopes for the future. When asked to write about their homelands, these middle-school students clearly understood the strife in their native countries, while acknowledging that their adopted country, the US, was the best "favor" to be given to them.

Bangladesh My Bangladesh

You are very small but still
Very crowded
So many people getting
Killed everyday
But peace is yet to come

With all the Bengalis,
We can make a difference
It will bring peace to
Our Country
And make a big change.

And from another student:

Yemen My Yemen

my dearest country
you are the best in the whole wide century
very nice people helping
and caring
united with peace and love
is what they're sharing
the president Ali is
a big fool
making the country worse
oh how cruel
killing the protestors

who have a right to live
leaving the country
is the best favor
he can ever give
but we'll never stop
till we get what we want
he'll be driven out, this
is something we can grant
Don't worry Yemen,
You have strong me
Who will be your backbone
Every now and then.

Advocacy/renewal

It was not until these middle-school students, having been given the chance to reflect on their identities through poetry, that we saw great strides of advocacy bursting forth. It was as if, having had the chance to wrestle with other important issues around identity, immigration, war, etc., they now could focus on moving forward—renewing, as it were—in both physical and spiritual ways. The following essays seem to highlight this renewal:

Help Stop Global Warming!

Global warming is a very serious problem that effects everyone and everything! If global warming continues it could put the whole world in danger. What global warming does is it starts to make everything go out of whack. It's created by different kinds of polutions like air pollution. Greenhouse gases also add to the global warming problem.

Global warming could end the world, the polar ice caps could melt and start a flood. Or the winter days will get hotter or it could start snowing in the summer. If it continues everything we fought for in the past wouldn't matter if there won't [be] any future, like when women's rights were fought for, what the Civil War was started for, or anything else that helped to make our present time better. Global warming isn't stopped then the future won't happen.

If global warming continues the kids of today won't have a future to look forward to. Everyone could do something to stop this from happening. No matter how little or old a person is they could still help out. People could help plant more trees, on Earth day we could copy what the French do and not use cars or buses that day, or just turn off lights when were not in a room. It really doesn't matter what we do as long as we do something to help the Earth and make sure the future happens. So please help out the kids of today and the children of tomorrow, Mr. Obama.

And finally:

To the Senator Hillary Clinton:

Racism

Racism is a major problem in this country. I think a law should be passed to restrict racism and get cops to arrest anyone who is being racious. Still, this might not fix the problem, so there are alternatives.

One thing that should be done is to teach young kids from an early age why racism is bad and what should be done to help get rid of it. This will end up stopping racism dramaticly.

Another useful tactic to stop racism would be to show how each of us are different and unique but it should be known as a amazing thing, not a bad thing. This might help people change or have a change of heart.

Making shows or programs on people uniting and coming together regardless of race might help those confused if it's okay to do or not. If this program could go national, it will greatly help in encouraging a non-racist society.

Helping people who are already racists might help also. I suggest asking them why they are racious and how they feel about it. Next, show them something that shows how racism affects all of us not just one person.

I conclude by saying I think racism is one of if not the worst problem in the country. It's also a major problem around the world as well. I hope, somehow, racism will be abolished in the near future.

So, getting direction, support, and hope not only from teachers—"be strong"—from their families—"go tell an adult"—from their faith—"believe in Allah"—but also from their leaders—Obama and Clinton—these youth seem to be on firm ground vis-à-vis identity—vis–à-vis homeland, language, and religion—firm ground in understanding, calling for collective action, and moving forward to renewal—crucial aspects in an adolescent's life that shape who they are both in and out of school.

Conclusion: Theoretical and Pedagogical Implications

A culture of renewal?

A preliminary analysis of the students' narratives here seems to highlight not only an understanding of the existence of fear and prejudice, but also of the potential of renewal. The students accomplish this through a collective, positive call for action—whether to depose Yemen's president, admonish adults for being racist, educate others about Hijab, or by writing directly to President Obama and Mrs. Clinton with suggestions for how to move their adopted land and their adopted challenges of this land toward renewal. Further research here may help us connect our work to Freire's "trilogy of pedagogy," moving from being "oppressed" to "hope," and finally, to "freedom" (Freire, 1998).

Interestingly, what we do not yet fully understand, as teachers and researchers, is *how* this happens among this group of "multiply-marginalized" students and not necessarily among others [particularly, for example, among the incarcerated African American adolescents with whom Blake (2004) worked]. And yet, in envisioning a new movement in youth studies, we would suggest that a criticalization of the kind we have seen here is paramount if we are to move the field forward. That is, there are many, many factors at play among this group of adolescents; despite constant fear and prejudice, there does not seem to be a sense of despair, of hopelessness, of refusal, that we have seen (and that has been so dangerously portrayed in the media) among other groups of adolescents. Simply said, without calls to positive collective action, whether by family, teachers, and institutions, or the entire community where adolescents grow, play, and learn, a *culture of refusal develops and is perpetrated by schools and society as a whole.*

Cultures of renewal differ from cultures of refusal in the following ways:

Culture of Refusal	Calls to Collective Action	Culture of Renewal
Alienation	leads to	Inclusion
Subjugation		Liberation
Disempowerment		Empowerment
Culture erasure		Culture affirmation
Resistance/Exclusion		Acceptance/Inclusion
We vs. Them		Us & Our
Loneliness		Community
Destroy		Build

Culture of Refusal	Calls to Collective Action	Culture of Renewal
Reduction		Multiplication
Rejection		Acceptance
Anger & Resentment		Acknowledgment & Peace
Misunderstanding		Empathy
Animosity		Compassion
Extreme		Moderate

Calls for collective action through narrative exploration (e.g., poetry, structured as in "I am" or unstructured; letters to politicians; personal essays) can be used as a pedagogical tool for teaching both students and teachers: clean up the lunchroom, help the elderly during a storm, set up recycling centers, brainstorm and debate about racism, write a school newsletter. There are limitless opportunities to turn it into something positive. Again, this may not only be crucial for our society as a whole, but also for our schools; whereas immigrant populations become more fluid and dynamic, national educational mandates become more fixed and rigid.

Much more work needs to be done here, and many more questions challenge us. And yet, we do know that working with *all* of our adolescent students today demands that we counter this rigidity and essentialization, and begs us to look for ways, as shown through these youths' narratives, to move away from victimization and "refusal" toward collective action and renewal.

References

Ajrouch, K., & Kusow, A. (2007). Racial and religious contexts: Situational identities among Lebanese and Somali Muslim immigrants. *Ethnic and Racial Studies, 30*(1), 72–94.

Ayers, W. (1997). *A kind and just parent: The children of juvenile court.* Boston, MA: Beacon Press.

Bartlett, L. (2007). To seem and to feel: Situated identities and literacy practices. *Teachers College Record, 109*(1), 51–69.

Bigelow, M. (2007). Social and cultural capital at school: The case of a Somali teenage girl with limited formal schooling. In N. R. Faux (Ed.), *Low-educated adult second language and literacy acquisition: Proceedings of inaugural symposium* (pp. 7–22). Richmond, VA: Literacy Institute at Virginia Commonwealth University.

Bigelow, M. (2010). *Mogadishu on the Mississippi: Language, racialized identity, and education in a new land.* New York, NY: Wiley-Blackwell.

Blake, B. E. (1997). *She say, he say: Urban girls write their lives.* Albany, NY: State University of New York Press.

Blake, B. E. (2004). *A culture of refusal: The lives and literacies of out-of-school adolescents.* New York, NY: Peter Lang.

Blake, B. E. & Blake, R. W. (2005). *Literacy.* New York, NY: Peter Lang.

Blake, R. W., & Blake, B. E. (2012). *Becoming a teacher: Using narrative as reflective practice.* New York, NY: Peter Lang.

Block, D. (2008). Multilingual identities and language practices in a global city: Four London case studies. *Journal of Language, Identity & Education, 7*(1), 1–4.

Clandinin, D. J., & Huber, J. (2002). Ethical dilemmas in relational narrative inquiry with children. *Qualitative Inquiry, 8*(6), 785–803.

Connelly, F. M., & Clandinin, D. J. (2009). Stories of experience and narrative inquiry. *Educational Research, 19*(5), 2–14.

Côté, J. E., & Levine, C. G. (2002). *Identity formation, agency, and culture: A social psychological synthesis.* Mahwah, NJ: Lawrence Erlbaum.

Dedman, B., & Schoen, J. (2013, April 30). *Adding up the financial costs of the Boston bombings.* Retrieved from http://usnews.nbcnews.com/_news/2013/04/30/17975443-adding-up-the-financial-costs-of-the-boston-bombings?lite

DeVitis, J. L., & Irwin-DeVitis, L. (Eds). (2010). *Adolescent education: A reader.* New York, NY: Peter Lang.

Ferdman, B. M. (1990). Literacy and cultural identity. *Harvard Educational Review, 60*(2), 181–204.

Fine, M., & Sirin, S. R. (2007). Theorizing hyphenated selves: Researching youth development in and across contentious political contexts. *Social and Personality Psychology Compass, 1*(1), 16–38.

Freire, P. (1998). *Pedagogy of freedom: Ethics, democracy, and civic courage.* Lanham, MD: Rowman& Littlefield.

Gee, J. P. (1999). *An introduction to discourse analysis theory and method* (2nd ed.). New York, NY: Routledge.

Gee, J. P. (2008). *Social linguistics and literacies: Ideology in discourses* (3rd ed.). New York, NY: Falmer Press.

Gregory, E. (2001). *Many ways of knowing: Creating classroom cultures in London's East End.* London, UK: Goldsmiths' College.

Gregory, E. (2002, July). *Getting to know strangers: A sociocultural approach to reading, language, and literacy.* Paper presented at the Multilanguage Literacy Symposium, Edinburgh, Scotland. Retrieved from http://www.readingonline.org/international/inter_index.asp?HREF=edinburgh/gregory/index.html

Gregory, E. (2008). *Learning to read in a new language: Making sense of words and worlds.* Los Angeles, CA: Sage.

Gregory, E., Long, S., & Volk, D. (2004). *Many pathways to literacy: Young children learning with siblings, grandparents, peers, and communities.* New York, NY: RoutledgeFalmer.

Gregory, E., & Williams, A. (2000). *City literacies: Learning to read across generations and cultures.* London, UK: Routledge.

Holland, D., Lachicotte, W., Skinner, D., & Cain, C. (1998). *Identity and agency in cultural worlds.* Cambridge, MA: Harvard University Press.

Kenner, C. (2004). Living in simultaneous worlds: Difference and integration in bilingual script learning. *International Journal of Bilingual Education and Bilingualism, 7*(1), 43–61.

Khan, M. Z. (2009). *Attitudes toward Muslim Americans post 9/11* (Unpublished master's thesis). California State University, Sacramento, CA.

Kincheloe, J., & McLaren, P. (2005). Rethinking critical theory and qualitative research. In N. Denzin & Y. Lincoln (Eds.), *The Sage handbook of qualitative research* (3rd ed., pp. 303–342). Thousand Oaks, CA: Sage.

Langer, J. A. (2001). Beating the odds: Teaching middle and high school students to read and write well. *American Educational Research Journal, 38*(4), 837–880.

Lave, J., & Wenger, E. (1991). *Situated learning: Legitimate peripheral participation.* Cambridge, UK: Cambridge University Press.

Martin-Jones, M., & Jones, K. (Eds.). (2000). *Multilingual literacies: Reading and writing different worlds.* Amsterdam, The Netherlands: J. Benjamins.

McLaren, P. (1993). Moral panic, schooling and gay identity: Critical pedagogy and the politics of resistance. *High School Journal, 77*(1–2), 157–168.

Merry, M. S. (2007). *Culture, identity and Islamic schooling: A philosophical approach.* New York, NY: Palgrave Macmillan.

Nayan, R. (2012). *Reading jihad: The identity enactment and literacy practices of Muslim immigrant children in the United States.* Retrieved from ProQuest Dissertation & Thesis. (3524017).

Orellana, M. F. (2009). *Translating childhoods: Immigrant youth, language and culture.* New Brunswick, NJ: Rutgers University Press.

Pahl, K., & Rowsell, J. (2005). *Literacy and education: Understanding the new literacy studies in the classroom.* London, UK: Paul Chapman.

Peek, L. (2005). Becoming Muslim: The development of a religious identity. *Sociology of Religion, 66*(3), 215–242.

Perry, K. (2007). Sharing stories, linking lives: Literacy practices among Sudanese refugees. In V. Purcell-Gates (Ed.), *Cultural practices of literacy: Case studies of language, literacy, social practice and power.* Mahwah, NJ: Lawrence Erlbaum.

Remnick, D. (2013, April 29). The culprits. *The New Yorker.* Retrieved from http://www.newyorker.com/talk/2013/04/29/130429ta_talk_remnick

Rogoff, B. (2003). *The cultural nature of human development.* New York, NY: Oxford University Press.

Rosowsky, A. (2008). *Heavenly readings: Liturgical literacy in a multilingual context.* Bristol, UK: Multilingual Matters.

Sarroub, L. K. (2005). *All American Yemeni girls: Being Muslim in a public school.* Philadelphia, PA: University of Pennsylvania Press.

Sarroub, L. K. (2008). Living "glocally" with literacy success in the Midwest. *Theory Into Practice, 47*(1), 59–66.

Sensoy, Ö., & Stonebanks, C. D. (2009). *Muslim voices in school: Narratives of identity and pluralism.* Boston, MA: Sense.

Sirin, S. R., & Fine, M. (2008). *Muslim American youth: Understanding hyphenated identities through multiple methods.* New York, NY: New York University Press.

Solórzano, D., & Yosso, T. J. (2002). Critical race methodology: Counter-storytelling as an analytical framework for education research. *Qualitative Inquiry, 8*(1), 23–44.

Street, B. V. (1984). *Literacy in theory and practice.* Cambridge, UK: Cambridge University Press.

Syed, I. B. (2001). *Education of Muslim children—Challenges and opportunities.* Islamic Research Foundation. Retrieved from http://www.islamfortoday.com/syed07.htm

Takanishi, R. (1993). *Adolescence in the 1990s: Risk and opportunity.* New York, NY: Teachers College Press.

Vygotsky, L. S. (1978). *Mind in society.* Cambridge, MA: Harvard University Press.

Wagner, D. A. (1993). *Literacy, culture and development: Becoming literate in Morocco.* New York, NY: Cambridge University Press.

Wallace, C. (2008). Literacy and identity: A view from the bridge in two multilingual London schools. *Journal of Language, Identity and Education, 7*(1), 61–80.

Wenger, E. (1999). Communities of practice: The key to a knowledge strategy. *Knowledge Directions, 1*(2), 48–63. Reprinted in E. Lesser, M. Fontaine, & J. Slusher (2000), *Knowledge and communities* (pp. 3–20). Boston, MA: Butterworth-Heinemann.

CHAPTER 47

LGBTQ Youth and the Hidden Curriculum of Citizenship Education

A "Day of Silence" in a Suburban High School

Joe Wegwert

I must have passed by the 8½ x11-inch announcement posted on the stairway wall more than a few times without note. Indeed, it was probably the attached wad of chewed gum that finally drew my attention.

Beyond this unique addition—one that conveyed its own symbolic message of disdain about the posted announcement itself—this particular sign blended into the eclectic array of posters and artwork hawking a variety of student meetings, fundraisers, and events so common in the hallways of American high schools and no less so in this one. By appearances, then, this one sheet of paper was not dramatically different from those surrounding it: the words on the page echoed the ubiquitous call to participate in the Covington Woods High School[1] (CWHS) community, yet the central message could not have been more different.

The advertised event—the upcoming "Day of Silence" sponsored by the "Gay-Straight Alliance"—was far from familiar and drew into sharp relief both the notion of participation and the nature of community in the culture of CWHS. The bottom of the announcement named Mrs. Susman, in room 206, as the person to contact for more information. I made my way to Mrs. Susman's room that day after school.

I looked through the window in the partially opened door at posters and magazine pictures of Greek and Roman cities and classical architecture, interspersed with quotes of ancient wisdom, adorning the walls of the classroom. For just a moment, I watched—a researcher/voyeur—as she stacked papers and straightened desks. I stood there thinking, on the one hand, about the busyness of all teachers' lives—the thousands of mundane details that go into their practice and, often, manage to dominate it—and, on the other hand, the rich potential in all teachers' lives—the opportunities, seized by some, to offer themselves more completely in pedagogical relationships grounded in meaningful purpose.

I wondered if this teacher on the other side of the door practiced her craft beyond or within the mundane. I wondered how many of Mrs. Susman's colleagues could be counted as allies in her efforts of support and recognition. I wondered to what extent LGBTQ-identified students in this school feel safety or fear as they sat in classrooms, walked through hallways, talked around lunch tables, or entered gendered and, historically, homophobic and frequently violent locker room and bathroom environments. I wondered, too, if room 206 served as a counterhegemonic space, a place where the socialized, mediated, and surveilled adolescent "self" might be re-imagined and re-enacted in safety and solidarity, outside the normalizing discourses of gender identity and sexual orientation.

With these thoughts and questions foremost in my mind, I knocked lightly on Mrs. Susman's classroom door. She looked up, startled away from her focus on the immediate tasks of routine. She walked over and greeted me with a curious smile. I introduced myself and hurriedly tried to connect my standard explanation about my research study of citizenship and social studies to the seemingly distant topic of the Gay-Straight Alliance and the impending Day of Silence event. Her welcoming smile diminished a bit, changing to courteous and then to cautious as I awkwardly struggled to make that connection. It took a few long minutes for the warmth to return to her face as I worked to lay out the reasoned and serious relationship between the Gay-Straight Alliance and my larger project and to simultaneously embed in my words and demeanor a discernable and credible sense of comradeship as an ally of LGBTQ students.

Mrs. Susman's caution reflected her own serious commitments to LGBTQ students and their allies—as well as an astute understanding of their location within the larger school culture. Mrs. Susman's protective and cautious demeanor toward an unknown classroom visitor was understandable. Yet, while teacher allies existed at CWHS, those same concerns extended to a good many of her own colleagues. She understood that, for the Gay-Straight Alliance students, the usual bureaucratic notions of student privacy and confidentiality took on very real and immediate importance regarding personal safety—even in the hallways, classrooms, and offices of CWHS.

The Civic Curriculum and the Day of Silence

Drawing on data and analysis from a broader research study,[2] this chapter offers a critical analysis of the "hidden curriculum" of sexual and gender identity embedded in a more expansive "civic curriculum" at this largely white, suburban, Midwestern, middle class high school. The data in this larger study came from discussions, interviews and observations regarding the civic curriculum at CWHS, including events around the Pledge of Allegiance ritual, as taught and performed in the school at large and in the context of social studies classrooms and of the social studies curriculum, in particular. The lessons that surfaced in this study pointed to what I call a *civic curriculum of the middle class promise*—a curriculum with a distinctly middle class notion of compliance that acknowledges choice, promotes self-interest, reifies privilege (Lukacs, 1971), frames common sense, and offers success. Jean Anyon's (1980, 1981) work on social class and schools suggests ways in which the varying ecologies of schooling contribute toward different educational experiences for students from working, middle, and affluent professional social classes.

In Anyon's account, these schooling experiences reflect the relations of production that shape the work lives of a given social class: on the one hand, students in working class communities often come face-to-face and go toe-to-toe with a curriculum of obedience that marginalizes, alienates, silences and threatens students in middle class schools, on the other hand, frequently encounter a curriculum of compliance that reflects back to them the images and discourses that validate family patterns, cultural and religious practices, and ideological beliefs (Anyon, 1980, 1981; Brantlinger, 2003). Students, like those at CWHS, encounter socialization into relations of production that posit middle class attachments to autonomous individualism, meritocracy, and institutional neutrality (Agostinone-Wilson, 2006)—affirmations of their own cultural system of common sense (Geertz, 1975).

Within the context of this suburban school, CWHS, the curriculum of compliance was embedded in a *middle class promise* that offered *success* through an ideologically proscribed pedagogy. The teachers observed in this larger study taught—and modeled—the importance of *navigating the middle* in a corporatized institution where *rituals and discourses of distance* shaped students' encounters with the epistemological and ontological meanings and implications of citizenship in the American polity. Consequently, students at CWHS encountered pedagogical practices that contained powerful curricular messages—a curriculum of pedagogy that supported and actualized the lessons embedded in the *middle class promise*.

The civic curriculum that emerged in this study was not a curriculum of citizenship in any democratic sense of the word; rather, it was a curriculum of membership: a curriculum steeped in the lessons of privilege, entitlement, moderation, and exclusion that define middle class identity in American culture. The civic curriculum of membership communicated lessons of inclusion and exclusion that provided sanction for an institutional culture of intolerance. It is here, then, in the intersections between the civic curriculum of success (through compliance, neutrality, and passivity) and its concomitant curriculum of exclusion (through normalizing discourses of civility) that gay, lesbian, bisexual, transgender, queer, and questioning students at Covington Woods High School encountered cultural, curricular, and institutional messages of normalization, marginalization, and non-recognition (Gutmann, 1987; Young, 1990, 2000).

The Gay-Straight Alliance (GSA) Day of Silence event at Covington Woods High School advertised by the flier described earlier provided another opportunity to examine the operationalized civic curriculum of the *middle class promise*—in this case, a curriculum of compliance around "compulsory heterosexuality" (Rich, 1980)—or, compulsory *heteronormativity*. Mrs. Susman's protective caution regarding the Gay-Straight Alliance members was a revealing and bittersweet artifact of an institutional culture of *membership*—an *exclusionary membership*—shaped by the regulating discourses of professionally proscribed neutrality and normalizing compliance, thinly veiled under a rhetorical and public relations trope of *tolerance*.

The GSA at Covington Woods High School

While certainly not the only LGBTQ-friendly staff member at CWHS, Mrs. Susman was clearly a central "go to" person for support and encouragement. She became the "unofficial" faculty advisor when the English teacher across the hall, overscheduled with the after-school demands of the theater program, asked her to provide a room and supervision for the Gay-Straight Alliance to meet. The "unofficial" qualifier reflected the lack of formal recognition by the school and district administration. Mrs. Susman believed that official recognition for the GSA was unlikely at any time in the near future. This sensibility served to strengthen Mrs. Susman's commitment to LGBTQ students/allies and made efforts on their behalf all the more critical.

Within an institutional culture of marginalization, oppression, and non-recognition of LGBTQ students/allies, the opportunity for GSA members to come together every Wednesday afternoon in room 206 to meet and talk openly was a dramatic and affirming step toward *self*-recognition and helped, at least partially, to fill the social void in the lives of LGBTQ students/allies at CWHS.

The Day of Silence at Covington Woods High School

Laying the Day of Silence Foundation: Teachers and Administration

Several days before the scheduled Day of Silence event, the CWHS Gay-Straight Alliance president, Jake Martin, provided teachers with a packet of information that included a letter "to request your support of students who will participate in the Day of Silence on Wednesday, April 26." The letter described the purpose of the upcoming Day of Silence event, its relationship to the context of the culture of CWHS, and the potential learning outcomes for both student participants and the entire staff:

> The Day of Silence is a national student-led day of action to raise awareness of the discrimination, harassment, and abuse—in effect, the silencing—that lesbian, gay, bisexual, and transgender (LGBT) individuals and their allies face daily. On the Day of Silence, students at high schools and colleges across the country take a vow of silence and distribute "speaking cards" explaining their participation. The Day of Silence at our school is particularly relevant because it will encourage the [Covington Woods High School] community to see the intolerance and discrimination that has not only become

apparent, but socially acceptable. The Day of Silence is an opportunity for students to take the initiative to teach one another about diversity, respect, and safety for all students. Students gain leadership skills, provide a valuable service to the school community and empower themselves by realizing their ability to make a difference in their school. I hope the entire [Covington Woods] staff will support the Day of Silence.

Jake's letter also explained the nature and conditions of student involvement in the Day of Silence, anticipating teachers' potential concerns about students' lack of verbal participation in classroom activities and offering possible alternatives:

Day of Silence participants can meet their academic responsibilities without speaking in numerous ways. With the support of teachers, students could lead or take part in a "silent lesson" or complete a written assignment. Students participating will be wearing a shirt that says "Day of Silence" and/or they will have red masking tape over their mouths. Students and staff members who support the day, but who will not remain silent, will either wear the Day of Silence shirt and/or display a red tape armband. I will be giving you a list of students participating in the Day of Silence as soon as possible. Please contact me if you would like a T-shirt or red tape to show your support of the event.

The packet Jake sent to staff also contained a summary of "Key Findings" and "Conclusions" from the GLSEN's (Gay, Lesbian, Straight Education Network) *2003 National School Climate Survey*. These "Findings" and "Conclusions" spoke of the level of homophobic remarks and physical victimization experienced by students in American high schools and specifically pointed to the important role of school personnel in providing support to mitigate and reduce the pervasive negative climate faced by LGBT students. The information packet sent to staff at CWHS included the following data from the GLSEN Survey:

- 84% of LGBT students report being verbally harassed (name calling, threats, etc.) because of their sexual orientation.

- 91.5% of LGBT students report hearing homophobic remarks, such as "faggot," "dyke" or the expression "that's so gay" frequently or often.

- 82.9% of LGBT students report that faculty or staff never intervened or intervened only some of the time when present and homophobic remarks were made.

- LGBT students unable to identify supportive teachers or staff were more than twice as likely not to plan to continue their education after secondary school: 24.1% of LGBT students with no supportive faculty or staff say they do not intend to go to college. Only 10.1% of LGBT students who did report having one or more supportive faculty or staff member say they will not go to college.

- LGBT students who can identify supportive faculty or staff do better in school than those who cannot, with grade point averages more than 10% higher than their peers: Average GPA for LGBT students who cannot identify any supportive faculty or staff: 2.8. Average GPA for LGBT students who can identify one or more supportive faculty or staff member: 3.1.

- LGBT students in schools with GSAs were more likely to feel safe in school than students whose schools do not have a GSA: 68.3% of LGBT students who report their schools do not have a GSA say they feel unsafe in their schools because of their sexual orientation. Students who said their school had a (GSA) were less likely to report feeling unsafe at school for the same reason (60.9%).

Silence About the Day of Silence: The Non-Announcement Announcement

In preparation for the Day of Silence, the GSA leadership met with the two assistant principals to draft an announcement for the morning of the event. Morning announcements at CWHS were typically read over the intercom at the beginning of first period. The two assistant principals coached the GSA president in preparing the announcement, gave their approval, and then obtained the principal's consent. From the perspective of the GSA president and advisors, this was a prudent and appropriate way to lay the groundwork for a successful launching of the Day of Silence event.

Despite these efforts no announcement was heard. The principal unilaterally and in contradiction to his earlier approval of the announcement draft decided to cut off the morning announcements before the GSA statement could be read. Instead, the principal sent out an early morning email to the teaching staff outlining his view of the Day of Silence event and the options teachers had in responding to the event and its participants. While district policies claim legal privilege over the contents of the literal email, Principal Anderson described the email message during a research interview—a description that was confirmed through interview comments from numerous staff members. Citing legislation that allowed non-school sponsored groups access to school facilities, the principal communicated in the email that the event would take place that day at CWHS. When asked in the research interview about the Day of Silence event the principal stated,

> You're right [the Day of Silence] is not a school sponsored event. My personal feeling is we're not going to make it a school-sponsored event. Schools can only go so far. But I don't want [the school] to be the stomping grounds for every social issue out there. [The Day of Silence] organizers saw me [and] told me what they wanted to do. Could I have stopped them? It would have been ugly. It's a national day—okay, fine. They can do that. They knew what the circumstances were. I communicated those guidelines with the staff by email. This is—you know—it's not school sponsored, however, it's a national day. And basically it wasn't just for gay/straight alliance it was protesting, it was bringing a bunch, all forms of injustice—religious, social, etc. So, we allowed them to do that.

Mrs. Susman (and other staff) confirmed that the email sent by Principal Anderson communicated to teachers that, while students were permitted to participate in the Day of Silence, teachers were within their rights to require verbal participation in class and could impose academic consequences on those who did not meet that requirement. Mrs. Susman reported the following experience that occurred during her lunch break on the Day of Silence:

> There was one Spanish teacher who [normally] required … each student to participate in at least ten minutes of Spanish conversation [during a class period]. And she was going to hold those [Day of Silence] students accountable for that. And I got the sense that she thought it was a ridiculous thing that the event was taking place and it was a bother to her….And I always say "let me play devil's advocate"… and [I asked] "what if the child had laryngitis or if they came in emotionally upset over something, would you still put them on the spot and require them to participate?" And I don't think I got an answer from her. Nobody else at the [lunch] table—and there might have been three or four other teachers—spoke up pro or con about what was taking place that day.

Mrs. Susman was clear that the principal's decision to send an email to faculty and to omit the informational morning announcement for the student body significantly impacted the type of experience the GSA students and their allies encountered:

> If [Principal] Anderson had made that announcement it would have been, you know, verbal validation on his part for the validity of the event itself …. By him not saying anything that morning and retracting [the] announcement, I think it was a personal statement on his part not to validate the gay community at the school …. And if he had made the announcement … I think the day would have just been—much kinder.

While a number of staff members saw the email as neutral, several others indicated that the lack of an announcement, in combination with the email that was sent, conveyed a message of marginalization, distain, discrimination and, potentially, threats to student safety. Most notable in this latter group was Melissa Randall, the assistant principal who had helped the GSA leadership prepare the ill-fated morning announcement:

> That day there were 200 students that had signed up and said that they wanted to participate [in the Day of Silence]…but only about 50 of the students actually wore shirts, put the tape over their mouths if they chose to.…Many students chose to back out of it and not participate because they were fearful of retribution.…The context of the email as I read it, and as many staff members read it, I would agree that they got the view that they did not need to support the piece that did not require verbal participation, that they could enforce students to verbally participate but that there were penalties for [non-participation in class].

Like Mrs. Susman, Assistant Principal Randall was clear that the principal's strategy negatively impacted the experience of the Day of Silence participants and, additionally, directly resulted in negative behaviors:

> [That] email was only sent to the adult members in this school … It wasn't communicated to other students the purpose of the activity and what was going on. It opened a can of worms as far as I'm concerned as an Administrator because students then engaged in unacceptable behavior throughout the day. There was no clear explanation. So the members of this particular organization did not experience a positive day in school, from my perspective, to the extent that there was some discussion that kids did not feel safe.

One long-time social studies teacher, David Kimball, a strong GSA ally, connected his critique of the principal's email to the larger context of strategic administrative hostility to the GSA:

> I don't know of any such email sent out [about] any other group in the years that I have worked here— telling teachers to essentially disregard, if that is their opinion, what this group is doing.… It is not a school sponsored group, but has wished to become a school sponsored group.…They were thrown into a category that was described as a religious group and therefore they did not have access, under separation of church and state, to morning announcements. It was a very clever way of putting them in a position where they would therefore not have the right to express their [views] or even announce their meetings. It is one more incidence of the power structure—or should I call it the "football ideology"—in this building favoring some things and not favoring other things.

Social Studies Teachers, Citizenship, the Pledge of Allegiance, and the Day of Silence

The responses of a number of the social studies teachers to the Day of Silence events at CWHS strongly paralleled their responses to the Pledge of Allegiance issue that emerged in the larger research study noted earlier. The broader study of citizenship in the context of the school culture and in the curriculum and interactions in social studies classrooms at CWHS found a contradictory pattern between what social studies teachers described as the necessary skills of democratic citizenship and what those teachers actually taught and emphasized. In interview after interview, the members of the social studies department called for student engagement around controversial issues and for pedagogical strategies of class discussion and debate, yet many of them presented or revealed the recurrent—and circular— argument that students did not have adequate background information or communication skills to engage in more complex, open-ended classroom discussions around controversial issues. Their enacted classroom curriculum and pedagogy reflected an *avoidance of controversial issues* and a *causal relationship between compliance and success*—patterns that clearly surfaced in the social studies teachers' responses to the Day of Silence.

Lynn Milton, a mid-career social studies teacher who taught the department's only sections of AP Psychology, noted that during the Day of Silence some of the GSA students and allies were "called nasty names [and] spat at." She also noted that there were some faculty members who were "aggressively anti-gay." Yet, her sense that these events and conditions were "really sad," appeared to be mitigated by her assertion that "putting a piece of red duct tape over your mouth is a confrontational action. Even though they were being silent, they were bringing attention to a [controversial] issue." Indeed, Principal Anderson suggested that the GSA strategy of red tape was analogous to wearing the Confederate flag in a largely African American high school.[3] He added, "When you do things like this, when you bring yourself out in the open and you're making a public statement somebody's going to have an opposite opinion." Lynn Milton made a similar comparison to race when she suggested the issue of gay rights is not "as conveniently legitimized as civil rights. I don't see it as the same thing."

Many of the social studies teachers interviewed about the Day of Silence appeared distanced from the event. Some, actually, had difficulty acknowledging that students in their own classrooms were involved or impacted by the events of the day. For example, Tyler Benson, a government teacher who taught the yearlong AP Government course, repeatedly asserted that the Day of Silence issue "never came up." His explanation reveals the observed tension between the stated commitment to engage students in contemporary and controversial issues and the practice of strategic avoidance:

> I only had one student the whole day, and that was in my seventh period, who participated in it. So it … it never came up. I mean I had some students say stuff just in passing—like, "I can't believe they're dong that" or just stuff like that. But it never was … it never really became an issue in my class.… Just more in passing. No, we didn't discuss it. If it would have come up in class, yeah, we would've talked about it. And, probably because it didn't come up in my class, I didn't really think about it. So it's partly my own ignorance of not bringing it up to talk about it. But I think that it's something you need to talk about [in class].

So, despite disparaging comments throughout the day and the physical presence of at least one participating student in at least one class, Tyler Benson was comfortable with stating that the issues around the Day of Silence "never came up."

The GSA members themselves, however, were very clear about the very real events of the day. In a meeting after school to de-brief the Day of Silence, GSA members and allies confirmed the pattern of inappropriate behavior that Assistant Principal Randall had noted and the offensive remarks cited by Lynn Milton and Tyler Benson. As an example of the type of comments and interactions that the Day of Silence participants experienced, the GSA president reported that a student in the lunchroom requested a piece of red tape to support the Day of Silence event. After he received a piece of tape the student yelled across the cafeteria, "Look! I have a piece of fag tape!" Other GSA members and allies reported similar episodes including several examples of teachers threatening to take points off for lack of participation and examples, also, of teachers reading the principal's email out loud to support their demands for participation. Jake noted, and many GSA members agreed, that the Day of Silence activity surfaced more hostility and homophobic remarks at CWHS than ever before.

Seemingly oblivious to these events, Becky Thornton, a young teacher in her third year in the CWHS Social Studies Department, put forward an argument that rationalized her lack of investment in the Day of Silence. She noted that she was unclear about the purpose of the event and suggested that more information from the student group would have been helpful. When asked if she had received the information packet from the GSA she acknowledged she had and, then, she shifted her critique to suggest that the GSA information did not address the student body. Unlike Assistant Principal Randall, Becky Thornton's critique made no mention of the administrative responsibility to offer information to the student body regarding a schoolwide event; nor did she appear to feel empowered or obligated to *teach* her students the information provided by the GSA as a way to contextualize the Day of Silence event.

The Aftermath: "I Survived Gay Day!"

The backlash against the GSA students and their allies did not end as school let out on the Day of Silence. The homophobic slurs that characterized the Day of Silence itself continued. Principal Anderson offered this summary—and commentary:

> The next day we had about four sophomores who had some t-shirts that said, "I Survived Gay Day" and "God Created Adam and Eve, Not Adam and Steve" [and] whether I agree with that or not—and I got a chuckle out of that one—[we] made them take the shirts off because it wasn't a really good dialogue. It was more of a slap in the face.

Given his tolerant attitude toward the offending students' intolerance—and his propensity for understatement—Principal Anderson's explanation of the civic culture at CWHS is instructive:

> For the most part, if you sit back and watch our kids interact, they interact pretty well and with a crowded building the first things you have concerns about are stairwells. And our stairwells … we don't have problems in our stairwells. We don't have problems like some other people have pushing up stairwells or pushing down stairwells. They're pretty calm, they're pretty orderly, they're pretty tolerant of each other. I don't care if it's black, white, rich or poor they take their time to get up the stairwells.

Assistant Principal Randall had a more deliberative and direct response about acceptable civic behavior and had no difficulty drawing the connection to the events of the Day of Silence. She was quick to point out "philosophical differences" with the principal and suggested that, "I don't think, as an Administrator, I [can] sit here and pick and choose which groups and which kinds of kids I wish to be supportive of. You know? I'm employed to be supportive of them all." She clearly felt that not only had the principal failed to support the GSA students and allies, he then purposefully communicated that lack of support to the staff. The result, she claimed, was a day characterized by "Little jabs and little events I consider bullying behavior, intolerant behavior … Those kids were victims of what I would say, in the real world, almost bordered [on] hate crimes." In reflecting back on this event, Assistant Principal Randall expressed the hope that the GSA students and allies would not be discouraged and that the school staff would have another chance to respond with support: "I think as educators we missed a great opportunity. So, how do I make that better next year? I'm more vocal about my position."

David Kimball, the only social studies teacher I encountered who was a clear ally of the GSA and friends, suggested that the students involved in the Day of Silence recognized their marginal place within the institution and were striving to alter their environments, to empower themselves:

> They were … trying in their small way to have some control in their work place, over their destiny, over the rules of a place [where there is] clear statistical evidence, from numerous studies, that the kids in that age who are gay have the highest suicide rates of any group of kids in society. One would hope that the administration could find it within themselves to allow something to happen that might lessen that possibility.

In this sense, the GSA students and allies were responding to a school culture that sought to silence, marginalize and discipline students who resisted the core lessons of the middle class promise—the *heteronormative*, middle class promise.

Heteronormativity, Citizenship, and the Lessons of the Day of Silence

Avoidance of Controversy

The themes that emerged from teacher interviews and observations around the Day of Silence, again, paralleled the discourses and practices around the Pledge of Allegiance ritual found in the larger study of the civic curriculum at CWHS. In both cases, most social studies teachers employed a number of strategies to *avoid controversy*. Most of these teachers simply ignored dissenting views about the Pledge and ignored the controversies embedded in the Day of Silence. In the case of the Pledge ritual, a number of social studies teachers and the principal himself suggested that dissenters in the classroom were "in danger." The potential for harassment of dissenting students by others who might be, as the principal said, "very offended if a kid doesn't stand [for the Pledge]" was indicated by a number of social studies teachers who described bullying behaviors with words like "verbally abusive," "ostracism," "drawing fire," "resentment," and "intimidation." Nevertheless, several social studies teachers argued that opening space to discuss a dissenting student's rationale for resistance to the Pledge put *that* student at risk. By refusing, or failing, to provide space for class discussion, however, social studies teachers at CWHS left unchallenged and uninterrogated dominant beliefs about the range of legitimate responses to the Pledge ritual.

Parallel conditions manifested for the Day of Silence. GSA members and friends anticipated reprisals and acted on those fears—leading to a seventy-five percent drop in participation, as noted by Assistant Principal Randall. The principal himself argued that student participation would likely draw out negative reaction, and although he framed possible responses as simply "another opinion," Assistant Principal Randall suggested many of those responses looked more like "hate crimes." All this suggests that, as with the Pledge, the unwillingness to address controversial issues in the classroom context did not make the "issue" go away; rather, it allowed unexamined prejudices to seep into—and dominate—other public spaces in school (Loutzenheiser & MacIntosh, 2004).

Consequently, when teachers suggested that students who expressed dissenting views were endangered—vulnerable to bullying from other students—by open discussion of those views but then rejected the possibility of using discussion to surface, interrogate, and remediate the broader culture of intolerance, they were considering and responding to a civic culture bounded by the walls of their own classroom. That is, most of the social studies teachers expressed, in one regard or another, the centrality of their own individual role in maintaining a classroom culture of civility and control.

At CWHS, the middle class culture of interpersonal civility and neoliberal compliance combined to produce and preserve an institutional culture of bullying and justifiable intolerance. Cris Mayo (2002) reminds us "The first problem with civility may be its almost necessary presumption that everything is fine thereby justifying the behavior of ignoring even the most blatant conflict" (p. 83). In this sense, civility is operationalized as a "distancing strategy, whereby the codified social practices impede rather than facilitate, social interaction and association" (ibid., p. 85). No wonder, then, that merely the visible, if not vocal, presence of GSA students and allies during the Day of Silence violated the norm of civility.

By bringing LGBTQ issues "out of the closet," the Day of Silence brought the curriculum of compulsory heteronormativity "out of the closet." Drawing on Sedgwick (1980), Mayo (1996) writes that, "The moment that heterosexuals have to assert themselves as 'heterosexual'...the universalizing discourse creeps in; heterosexuality is no longer alone in the public eye and imagination" (n.p.). By bringing the curriculum of compulsory heteronormativity out of the closet, the events of the Day of Silence also threatened the normative curriculum of citizenship. That is, it was NOT part of the formal curriculum at CWHS to explore LGBTQ issues or concerns; however, it WAS part of the formal curriculum to frame students' understandings of citizenship. Therefore, it was crucial that the LGBTQ issues be separated from those understandings. Ignoring the normative, controversial and *civic* issues around the Day of Silence was consistent with the imperatives of a formal curriculum where "the challenge for queer youth is that of navigating ones' subjectivity within the boundaries of culturally normalizing stereotypes" (Loutzenheiser & MacIntosh, 2004, p. 152).

Compliance Means Success

At CWHS, most social studies teachers used discursive, pedagogical, and curricular devices to empha-size the *causal relationship between compliance and success*. In the case of the Pledge, this relationship was often implied, embedded in the historical and cultural narrative about *civic membership* (Abowitz & Wegwert, 2003) and the responsibilities and obligations—and benefits—that accompany adhering to dominant expectations. In the case of the Day of Silence, this relationship between compliance and success was much more explicit as *all* students gained immediate feedback—as GSA members and allies received public insults hurled from peers and public grade threats made by teachers—directly tied to participation or non-participation in an activity that challenged a curriculum of *compulsory heteronormativity*.

The relationship between *compliance* and *success* is central in a school curriculum that teaches stu-dents the importance of the *middle class promise*—an ontological view in which citizens were revealed as individual agents operating from the same neo-liberal assumptions that frame the role of middle class professionals in the corporate culture. The *middle class promise*, then, as with all hegemonic dis-courses, is grounded in what Michel Foucault views as "'structures of intelligibility,' or regimes of truth that regulate—in a given history—the thinkable, the recognizable, the limits, and the transgressions discursively codified through legal, medical and educational structures" (Britzman, 1995, p. 156). As the discursive and performative limits of exclusion set the limits of inclusion (Britzman, 1995), the culture of *compliance* at CWHS demanded visibility (participation) in the Pledge ritual of citizenship as it demanded invisibility (silence) in the curriculum of compulsory heteronormativity. Compliance during the Day of Silence event was a performative dividend of "the heterosexual bribe" (Halley, 1993, cited in Sumara & Davis, 1999, p. 192): "That is, the cultural rewards afforded those whose public per-formances of self are contained with the narrow band of behaviors considered proper to a heterosexual identity" (Sumara & Davis, 1999, p. 192).

Conclusion

While the Day of Silence event at CWHS certainly served as an artifact of student and teacher agency on behalf of LGBTQ students and their allies, it did so amidst other, more powerful, artifacts of intolerance and hostility. Schools, particularly middle class schools, now play a critically important role and hegemonic function in preparing students to seamlessly enter and quietly function in the neo-liberal corporate workplace. In the suburban, middle class context of CWHS, the lesson of compliance offered to students was located in their anticipated role as employees of the "corporation" (Quantz, 2003; Giroux, 2004; Schmidt, 2000). Social studies teachers at CWHS, like middle class professionals in other corporatist institutions, played a significant role in providing the ideological glue that holds together the neo-liberal worldview. Social studies teachers worked to weave a curricular web that served to bind and normalize the *curriculum without controversy* and *democracy without dialogue* nexus, and the reproductive structures of privilege and marginalization.

As civic education, a curriculum of compliance is a recipe for passivity. Students are routinely distanced from their understandings of the world around them and the contexts of their own lives, are offered trivialized and truncated versions of the meanings of democracy, and are marginalized and disciplined—or watch as others are marginalized and disciplined—for displaying signs of civic agency, democratic sensibility, and authentic identity. Many of the social studies teachers at CWHS actively worked to convince themselves and others that the curriculum of neo-liberal compliance was not incompatible with democratic citizenship, efforts requiring exhausting and, ultimately, ineffectual discursive and intellectual gymnastics.

For teachers and students in the middle class school, the "logic of the marketplace" reinforces the ideology of neutrality so pervasive in classrooms and curricula (Howley et al., 1995; Apple, 2001a).

Schutz (2008) points out that, "Organizations dominated by middle class professionals tend to embody the 'values, ideas, expectations, and assumptions' of 'successful professionals'" (p. 427). Accordingly, such organizational cultures operate to both privilege and reproduce—to reify—the contexts, conditions, and social imagination of the middle class. The *middle class promise of success* at CWHS actively excluded LGBTQ students and many of their allies. They were denied the *privileges of membership*. Instead, they were left with an impoverished mode of citizenship where, in a school—and society—of compulsory heteronormativity, the rights to safety, recognition, and agency fall beyond discussion—and beyond reach.

Notes

1. All of the names of individuals and places (school and school district) in this chapter are pseudonyms.
2. See Joseph C. Wegwert (2008) Democracy Without Dialogue: A Civic Curriculum of "The Middle Class Promise" for Citizens of the Corporation, Unpublished Ph.D. Dissertation, Miami University, Oxford, Ohio. The data around the Gay-Straight Alliance and the Day of Silence discussed in this chapter emerged during the research but were not used in the dissertation itself.
3. Here Principal Anderson specifically referred to a school in the area where he had worked prior to coming to CWHS.

References

Abowitz, K. & Wegwert, J. (2007). J. Veteran's Day in a U.S. public high school: Lessons for nationalistic loyalty. In K. Roth and N. Burbules (Eds.), *Changing Notions of Citizenship in Contemporary Nation-states*. Rotterdam: Sense Publishers.

Agostinone-Wilson, F. (2006). Downsized discourse: Classroom management, neoliberalism, and the shaping of correct workplace attitude. *Journal for Critical Education Policy Studies*, 4(2), Available online at http://www.jceps.com/?pageID=article&articleID=69

Anyon, J. (1980). Social class and the hidden curriculum of work. *Journal of Education*, 162(1), 67–92.

Anyon, J. (1981). Social class and school knowledge. *Curriculum Inquiry*, 11, 3–42.

Apple, M. (2001a). *Educating the "right" way: Markets, standards, God, and inequality*. New York: RoutledgeFalmer.

Britzman, D. P. (1995). Is there a queer pedagogy? Or, stop reading straight. *Educational Theory*, 45(2), 151–165.

Brantlinger, E. (2003). *Dividing classes: How the middle class negotiates and rationalizes school advantage*. New York: Routledge-Falmer.

Geertz, C. (1975). Common sense as a cultural system. *Antioch Review*, 33, 5–26.

Giroux, H. A. (2004). *The terror of neo-liberalism: Authoritarianism and the eclipse of democracy*. Boulder, CO: Paradigm Publishers.

Gutmann, A. (1987). *Democratic education*. Princeton, NJ: Princeton University Press.

Halley, J. E. (1993). The construction of heterosexuality. In M. Warner (Ed.), *Fear of a queer planet*. Minneapolis, MN: University of Minnesota Press.

Howley, C., Howley, A., & Pendarvis E. (1995). *Out of our minds: Anti-intellectualism and talent development in American schooling*. New York: Teachers College Press.

Loutzenheiser, L. W. & MacIntosh, L. B. (2004). Citizenships, sexualities, and eduction. *Theory into Practice*, 43(2), 151–158.

Lukacs, G. *History and class consciousness*. London: Merlin Press.

Mayo, C. (1996). Performance anxiety: Sexuality and school controversy. *Philosophy of Education Yearbook*.

Mayo, C. (2002). Education by association: The shortcomings of discourses of privacy and civility in anti-homophobia education. In R. M. Kissen (Ed.), *Getting ready for Benjamin: Preparing teachers for sexual diversity in the classroom*. Lanham, MD: Rowman & Littlefield.

Quantz, R. A. (2003). The Puzzlemasters: Performing the mundane, searching for intellect, and living in the belly of the corporation. *The Review of Education, Pedagogy, and Cultural Studies*, 25, 95–137.

Rich, A. (1980). Compulsory heterosexuality and lesbian existence. *Signs: Journal of Women in Culture and Society*, 5(8), 3–32.

Schmidt, J. (2000). *Disciplined minds*. Lanham, MD: Rowman & Littlefield.

Schutz, A. (2008). Social class and social action: The middle-class bias of democratic theory in education. *Teachers College Record*, 110(2), 405–442.

Sedgwick, E. (1980). *Epistemology of the closet*. Berkeley, CA: University of California Press.

Sumara, D., & Davis, B. (1999). Interrupting heteronormativity: Toward a queer curriculum theory. *Curriculum Inquiry*, 29(2), 191–208.

Young, I. M. (1990). *Justice and the politics of difference*. Princeton: Princeton University Press.

Young, I. M. (2000). *Inclusion and democracy*. New York: Oxford University Press.

CHAPTER 48

Epistemology of Emancipation
Contemporary Student Movements
and the Politics of Knowledge

Noah De Lissovoy

Knowing, like living, grows up out of the dirt and the cracked pavement—through the fences and around the corners. It reveals itself in uninvited and miraculous shoots that spring up everywhere that people live and struggle. This living knowledge of experimentation and protest, of assertion and critique, ubiquitously presses outward into its surroundings. Anchored in the lives of ordinary people, and drawing on marginalized perspectives and struggles, the production of this knowledge enlarges the circle of knowers beyond the professional intellectuals that have claimed authority even within many critical and alternative traditions. On the basis of a consideration of two recent youth and student political mobilizations, I argue here that youth movements represent an incipient and systematic knowledge project that fuses politics, theory, and culture. I call this an *epistemology of emancipation*, and argue that it challenges several common theoretical assumptions: that knowing and being are separate; that the body is external to the understanding; and that the analyses of young people are necessarily incomplete or unformed relative to those of their elders.

After constructing a theoretical framework for my discussion that draws on contemporary critical and decolonial work in political theory and cultural studies, I focus in this chapter on two exemplary recent struggles: the movement against racist and xenophobic state legislation in Arizona, and the struggle against austerity and tuition hikes in the public higher education system of California. I limit my discussion to these two cases in order to give texture and depth to my analysis. While workers, university faculty, and community members more broadly have also been active in both of these struggles, my focus here is on the participation of young people, whose independent initiatives and analyses have given both movements their creative and militant character, and who have been at the vanguard in both cases. It is not accidental that the struggles I consider have primarily, though not exclusively, focused on education. Not only are youth touched in a special way by cutbacks and reactionary reforms on this terrain; in addition, the occasion of education provides a special opportunity for the creativity of young people to be exercised, as the movements they construct work toward the imagination of new and more empowering forms of teaching, learning, and school itself. In this way, my argument foregrounds what we might call the *epistemological agency* of youth. At the same time, the conclusions it draws regarding politics and knowledge have implications for critical theory and praxis more broadly.

Understanding and Emancipation

Critical philosophy has historically valorized popular and situated sources of understanding. In particular, for *standpoint* epistemology, which is both a Marxist and feminist tradition, knowledge projects are rooted in the historical experiences of an oppressed or marginalized class, and then systematically developed from that starting point (Harding, 1993). These experiences, it is argued, are privileged with regard to the validity of the accounts of the world that can be built from them, since groups and classes that are oppressed know intimately from experience the crucial social facts and processes (in particular, *exploitation* as the secret of social reproduction) that are systematically concealed or invisible from the official and dominant perspective (Lukács, 1971). At the same time, in living simultaneously within their own resistant intuitions and the official narrative of reality, such groups are in a unique position to overcome the contradictions that plague dominant worldviews, which are incapable of this perspective on the social whole (Hartsock, 1983). For example, the determination of social reality and our common senses for understanding it by the historical fact of patriarchy is for the most part invisible to men, for whom this androcentric common sense and the official knowledges that codify it appear as universally valid and trans-historical. In more recent versions of standpoint theory, an effective critical epistemology is thought of as a dynamic shuttling between multiple oppositional and decolonizing consciousnesses (Sandoval, 2000), as a raced-gendered perspective that emphasizes communities of color as holding and creating knowledge on their own terms (Delgado Bernal, 2002), or as the unique vantage point of the simultaneously included and marginalized "outsider within" (Collins, 2000).

For these epistemologies, the connection between knowledge and social experience is axiomatic, in the sense that understanding always begins from some collective historical subject. The social experience and identity of this historical subject are taken as offering the indispensable resources for the development of a meaningful knowledge project (Harding, 1998). In this way, feminist research should organize the experiences and understandings of oppression and resistance that have occurred to women throughout the history of (patriarchal) society. The job of the critical philosopher is to develop the potentials of the historical experience of the oppressed and marginalized, to systematize their insights, and to isolate coherent principles from the raw material of original memories and impulses. In this effort, it is thought, these impulses become self-conscious, enter into dialogue (and contention) with dominant understandings, and return to oppressed groups a powerful tool for building more sophisticated analyses in the pursuit of their social and political interests. For the alternative epistemologies described above, the vernacular has value ultimately as a kind of inspiration and provocation. Systematic knowledge comes from the working through by intellectuals of the raw experiences of workers, women, youth, and other oppressed groups. It is argued that while there may be a certain truth in these original experiences that philosophy refines, there is not yet *knowledge* in a *systematic* sense. The latter is a function of professional intellectual work.

This critical epistemological tradition is an indispensable resource for thinking about how knowledge can be built from the experiences of those who have been oppressed. However, the standpoint tradition stops short before an even more radical idea: that the power of even critical-theoretical reconstructions of popular understandings and experiences is strictly a function of the echoes of the voice of the vernacular subject within them. In other words, radical and emancipatory knowledge is in the first instance an apparently illegitimate *announcement of being* against indifference and domination. In fact, oppressed groups have proven the authority of their analyses in the very moment of striking out against the forces that subjugate them. For instance, in the history of political walkouts by young people from school—from Soweto to Los Angeles—in resistance to apartheid, language discrimination, and other forms of structural violence, students have not awaited certification of their analyses by official intellectuals or activists before demonstrating these analyses to be both valid and effective. An epistemology of emancipation crucially uncovers the ubiquitous curiosity and competence of everyone, including youth, and their essential equality as human intelligences (Rancière, 1991). In this way, "everyone is a philosopher," not just in Gramsci's political and historical sense, but also in the larger sense that everyone is capable of original conceptual thought about the world. Power preserves its hegemony through persistent slander of this general competence in judgment and imagination. But in fact regular people, and young people in particular, do not fail to think and act in their homes and on their streets, and they do not fail to know and name their surroundings, even at the global level.

Important in this regard is recent work in decolonial theory which uncovers the depth of the cultural, material, and symbolic violence of Eurocentrism, and which begins, against this violence, to frame philosophies oriented to survival and healing (Maldonado-Torres, 2008; Mignolo, 2005; Smith, 1999). Decolonial accounts reject the fundamental dehumanization of non-European cultures that has underwritten Western epistemology—as well as its determined ignorance with regard to the geopolitics of knowledge—and they recognize indigenous and oppressed peoples as full subjects of knowledge, in possession of their own sciences, in spite of and against the depredations of colonialism. From a decolonial perspective, ordinary people and experience do not lack any theoretical capacity or competency. Furthermore, this perspective recognizes the inseparability of being and knowing. The ordeals of the body are not just starting points for understanding, but already represent a kind of incipient understanding. As Anzaldúa (1987) described, the work of identity and survival, and the complexity of feeling and being that it gives rise to, is also a kind of theorizing. With regard to youth, this means a more thoroughgoing rejection of the deficit discourses that consistently construct young people as lacking, and a sensitivity to their persistent capacity for resistance even "in tight spaces" (Cruz, 2011); this is a resistance at once materially and epistemologically agentic. Decolonial theory challenges progressive traditions to go beyond the limits that they set for the meaning of knowing, and to recognize the capacity in everyone for original and anti-dominative knowledge production.

These theoretical considerations have important implications for research on youth culture and movements. Theorists of youth culture have shown how independent and underground cultural idioms such as punk rock and hip hop have creatively challenged the forms and meanings of popular music, and in so doing, have opened up alternative possibilities of signification for popular culture (Dimitriadis, 2001; Hebdige, 1988). But youth subcultures have always been much more than musical idioms. They have also involved significant radical political conversations and praxes. From walkouts to protests to forms of critical research from the ground up, the political work of young people has been a crucial element in the history of social movements, especially those concerned with education (Marable, 1984; Muñoz, 1989). One might say that the point of both resistant youth culture and political mobilization has been to refuse the limits of reified and conventional understandings and social relationships, and to discover in the commonplace, cast-off, and even despised, the openings to livelier and more democratic possibilities. Within education, scholars of resistance have recently been concerned to emphasize the radical agency, dignity, and generativity of young people (Ginwright, Noguera, & Cammarota, 2006; Tuck & Yang, 2011); I believe this ethical starting point has important epistemological implications. In this way, in their organized political challenges to a contemporary "punishing state" fundamentally hostile to young people (Giroux, 2009), youth have been engaged not only in a challenge to social structures, but also in the production of knowledge from the ground up.

Against Coloniality: Youth Struggles in Arizona

One important recent context in the US for mobilization by youth is the struggle against anti-immigrant and anti-Latino politics and initiatives. Nowhere has this battle been fought out more dramatically than in the state of Arizona. A state with a notorious racist legacy, including the refusal until 1992 to recognize Martin Luther King, Jr. Day as a holiday, Arizona has recently been the site of efforts to strip immigrants without documents of basic rights, as well as attacks on ethnic-studies curricula supporting the development and academic success of Mexican American students. Arizona Senate Bill 1070 (SB 1070), signed into law in 2010, requires law enforcement officers to check the immigration status of those whom they suspect of being undocumented, clearing the way for widespread and state-sanctioned racial profiling of the Mexican American community. SB 1070 has called forth massive protests, including state and national demonstrations, as well as a boycott of the state. Young people have been at the vanguard of this struggle, organizing walkouts, protests, and civil disobedience. Another crucial flashpoint in the fight over the politics of race in the state has been the effort by conservative politicians to shut down the Mexican American Studies (MAS) program of the Tucson Unified School District. Recognized for its critical, culturally relevant, and empowering curriculum, which foregrounds indigenous perspectives and ethics, this program became another target in the state's battle against its own Mexican American community. Putting into practice important lessons in civic engagement from the MAS program itself, students did not passively stand by as this attack unfolded, but rather mobilized to defend the program and the educational opportunities it afforded. Both of these struggles have garnered national and international attention, exposing both the racist character of the state's political establishment as well as the agency and determination of youth.

As struggles over culture and identity, these battles have clear epistemological stakes. Arizona's clampdown on immigrant communities and ethnic studies is as much an effort to police understandings of history, politics, and democracy as it is an effort to safeguard a material order of racial domination. As their own testimony makes clear, conservative White elites are terrified by the possibility of an alternative reading of US history and hegemony. For instance, Tom Horne (former Arizona State Superintendent of Public Instruction and then Attorney General) has publicly denounced the MAS program, marshaling a slick color-blind racism in his portrayal of the clampdown on ethnic studies as a continuation of the civil rights movement and as an intervention against intolerance. For Horne and other conservatives, the official narrative of progress and opportunity in the US is universal and unimpeachable. However, the protests that followed in the wake of SB 1070 and the attack on the MAS program have revealed a huge reservoir of resistance to the official story, and the fact that *other knowledges* of US cultural politics are alive in the community. The Tucson ethnic-studies curriculum itself proposes a different standpoint for students from which to make sense of their world, grounded in an emphatic insistence on Chicana/o experience and identity as a legitimate epistemic starting point (Serna, 2013). In this sense, the cultural politics underlying the battles in Arizona clearly involve a politics of knowledge as well.

On the one hand, we might say that the racial profiling required by SB 1070 is a clear example of an official and dominative *knowledge of bodies*—their meanings, differences, and potentials. On the other hand, the book banning set in motion by the state's termination of the MAS program (the district actually confiscated key texts from the classrooms) is an even more obvious effort to police the boundaries of understanding—and the words and texts that are allowed to construct it. However, I also want to suggest that there are epistemological dimensions to the *modes of engagement* themselves that young people have explored and invented in their struggles against the state. In other words, the politics of knowledge here is a matter of form as well as content. In particular, in taking dramatic action to challenge the terms of the debate around culture and curriculum, youth at the same time have demonstrated the implication of the body itself in struggles over knowledge.

Even in the context of one of the most reactionary backlashes in the US, youth have organized protests of remarkable courage and militancy (Rodríguez, 2013). In nonviolent, civil-disobedience actions that they have undertaken to protest the state's anti-immigrant legislation, young people have put their bodies on the line and raised their voices, not just to demand justice, but also to interrupt the sham decorum and fake consensus of official decision-making procedures. In one especially dramatic action, in April of 2011, students from Tucson's MAS program took over a school-board meeting, chaining themselves to board members' chairs just as the meeting was set to begin. Pounding on the desks in front of them, and chanting loudly ("Our education is under attack; what do we do? Fight back!"), the youth asserted an emphatic claim on the space and conversation of education policy.[1] Allowing their anger and excitement to be felt in the halls of power, they also refused the epistemological contract that demands that the body and emotion be banished from deliberation, and which claims that reason can only be heard in the bland and measured tones of the technocrat.

As Dr. Cintli Rodríguez (2013) has reported, facing off against a highly militarized police force, including helicopters, sharpshooters, and bomb squads, students protesting in Arizona have exposed themselves to violent repression from the state, and to specific instances of police brutality, including severe beatings.[2] Althusser's (1971) observation that the ideological superstructure of society is anchored "in the last instance" in the material base is confirmed here in a different way—as struggles over knowledge and identity are fought out ultimately in the space between the exposed bodies of youth and the armored bodies of the agents of the state. In this way, we might say, *the body learns power*: both the shape of dominative power, as well as the possibilities for a power from below. Decolonial lessons on embodiment and the geopositionality of knowledge (Anzaldúa, 1987; Mignolo, 2011) are taught here through a severe object lesson: Challenging the violence that undergirds the "reasoned" surface of power invites not just criticism, but physical repression. At the same time, this is also a learning of possibility, as youth literally explore new spaces that were previously off-limits to the imagination. Thousands of students walked out of their schools as part of the protests against SB 1070, in the process discovering a knowledge that comes from breaking out of the limits of schooling and settled senses of "responsible" behavior. As Isabel García, a student participant in these protests, put it: "The youth are fearless, the youth have a political analysis that few adults have" (Hing, 2010).

On the basis of this audacious experimentation with the politics of knowledge, more organized educational experiences can be undertaken. In a video extra for *Precious Knowledge* (Palos & McGinnis, 2011), a documentary that tells the story of the battle over the MAS program in Tucson, we can see how the program opened up the possibility for explorations of the cultural wealth (Yosso, 2005) of the Mexican American community to become learning experiences. The face of Nacho Vejar, a student in the program, lights up as he describes organizing a community car show and performing as part of a mariachi. Significantly, not only does popular culture become an essential occasion for learning for Nacho, but furthermore, the educational experience moves decisively beyond the terrain of the school, while also breaking down the boundaries between knowing and being. "I don't think they should get rid of these classes," he says at the conclusion of his interview, "because there's a lot of love being shared. You can't get rid of love."

Perhaps an even more radical educational experiment is described by Cabrera, Meza, Romero, and Rodríguez (2013), in which the UNIDOS student movement (United Non-Discriminatory Individuals Demanding Our Studies, organized to defend the MAS program) established the first session of their own School of Ethnic Studies to coincide with a walkout in support of the MAS program in January of 2012. This alternative educational space involved professors, community members, and musicians. Moving beyond education as critique, events such as these propose alternative educational models, under the epistemological authority of youth themselves. It may be that as state officials target the MAS program, they are actually overlooking the most revolutionary educational moments and possibilities to which it has given rise—moments in which the limits even of the institution of schooling and adult pedagogical authority are exceeded.

A powerful "epistemological curiosity" (Freire, 1998) can also be cultivated as the contradictions of formal schooling itself become sites for critical inquiry. In *Precious Knowledge* (Palos & McGinnis, 2011), students reflect on the difference between experiences in the MAS program and other experiences they have had in school. This gap can become the starting point for a critical theory of schooling which builds from the lived realities of students—and it appears that reflection on this gap importantly moves students to action in the film. A critical theory of schooling has been an important part of the intellectual framework for radical praxis among young people as many movements demonstrate, from the blowouts of the 1960s to contemporary struggles. Indeed, as Cammarota and Aguilera (2012) have shown, the difficult itineraries of their own educational pathways can become for Mexican American students crucial *generative themes* (Freire, 1996) for critical investigation. This points to the importance of a heightened reflexivity, in epistemological terms, for teachers and students alike. The power of Tucson's Raza Studies program is demonstrated in the way it has broken through the deadening and authoritarian epistemology that has often shaped even progressive educational projects. This imaginativeness has also made it a target for elites.

The struggle against racism in Arizona has asserted a different discourse about immigrant and Chicana/o youth: As opposed to the mainstream demonization and pathologization of young people from these communities, the movements against anti-immigrant legislation and in favor of ethnic studies have proposed a discourse of youth as engaged, agentic, assertive, and militant. In this process, these movements have taken up a standpoint from within the "colonial wound," in Mignolo's (2005) terms, and have refused the dominant narration of youth identity. Young people themselves have played a crucial role in this transformation. At stake here is not just a particular curriculum, but what it *means to be a child, and what it means to learn and grow.* For example, a crucial counterhegemonic "text" of the movement is a widely disseminated poster image created by Ernesto Yerena and Shepard Fairey for the Alto Arizona campaign, which supports the struggle against SB 1070.[3] This poster depicts a young child, one hand gripping a bunch of roses, the other curled in a fist. The mountains and saguaros of Arizona are in the background. The child is smiling, fearless, and determined. While power seeks to construct Brown youth as powerless, marginal, and voiceless, this image counters with a radical confidence, indeed a threat to power. The artists' move in this work is not just to indicate a protest against a dehumanizing racial climate, but even to subvert our very understanding of youth. Breaking free from a liberal, paternalist pedagogy, this image proposes a decolonial rendering of young people as politically powerful. Here, as elsewhere in the movements I have discussed, politics, praxis, and knowledge come together in a radical challenge to the violent modes of being of power and Whiteness.

Whose University? Student Mobilization on California's Higher Education Campuses

Another important front for youth and student movement in the present, and for the production of the epistemology of emancipation that I describe in this chapter, is the global movement against austerity and privatization in higher education. Students throughout the world have pushed back against rising tuition (or the charging of tuition for the first time), the mortgaging of students' futures through excessive debt, and the privatization and corporate enclosure of public universities. One place where this struggle has played out dramatically is California, starting with a series of protests on the campuses of the state's public university systems [the University of California (UC) system and the California State University (CSU) system] that took place from the fall of 2009 in response to major tuition hikes approved by the UC Regents and CSU Trustees, to actions that took place on campuses beginning in 2011 as part of the global Occupy movement, and up to the present. These protests have included walk-outs, demonstrations, teach-ins, sit-ins, and occupations, and have precipitated an intense and sometimes violent police response. At the same time that this series of movements has involved demonstrations against austerity in higher education, it has also been an occasion for radical experimentation with autonomous forms of education and organizing. Challenging the top-down rule of the university in terms of policy, it has also opened up possibilities for new ways of knowing.

The presentation of information is vital to capitalism, (then continue with communication, and "immaterial labor" communication, and "immaterial labor" (Hardt & Negri, 2004). Theorists have pointed to the way in which globalization, technology, and the Internet have contributed to making the commod-ification of knowledge and communication central to the reproduction of capitalism. Struggles over this "cognitive capital" (Vercellone, 2009) make schooling and the university a crucial political battleground, as well as a space for experimentation with forms of knowing and being together. At the same time, however, I argue that contemporary student struggles in higher education reveal essential links between knowledge and physical space—between the virtual and the material. Protests by students have been met in many cases by brute police violence. The most notorious example of this repression is the unprovoked pepper-spraying of nonviolent students protesting in solidarity with the Occupy movement at the University of California, Davis on November 18, 2011. In this incident, a university police officer suddenly sprayed at close range, and without warning, a number of students staging a sit-in. This and other instances show that hegemony depends, in the last instance, on the control of space, and on the ability to intimidate and discipline bodies.

This coincidence of the politics of knowledge, space, and property is central to this struggle. The chant, "Whose university? Our university!" which has been heard around the country during the campus-based Occupy movements, gets to the crux of the matter: To whom do the spaces of higher education, and their potential for collaboration, learning, and production belong? In challenging the claim to ownership of ostensibly public university systems by banks, corporate sponsors, and the elite campus administrations that collaborate with them, students have asserted their right to the space of learning, and their ownership of their own futures. Importantly, they have done so through direct occupations of campuses, and not simply through demonstrations. At UC Berkeley's Wheeler Hall, for instance, on November 20, 2009, forty protesters barricaded themselves inside to protest the UC Board of Regents' thirty-two percent tuition hike of the previous day. Besieged and taunted by police, the students remained steadfast throughout the day ("After the Fall," 2010; Dongallo & Panzar, 2009). Occupations also took place in this same period at UC Davis, UCLA, Cal State Fresno, UC Santa Cruz, and San Francisco State. At UC Santa Cruz, in a statement following a brief occupation in October, students explicitly pointed to the centrality of the struggle over space within the larger fight over the university itself:

> Why have students begun to barricade the doors of buildings that we claim as our own? To carve out material spaces of resistance and emancipation…. The spaces in which we are free are those that we take and hold by force. That is the hard lesson we all have to learn. ("After the Fall," 2010, p. 13)

Furthermore, in the process of forming alliances between systematically divided sectors of higher education—students, workers, staff, lecturers, and tenure-track faculty—this movement has ques-tioned not only the structure of differential compensation, but even the hierarchical organization of the institution itself. In the production of knowledge *about the struggle*, the intellectual hierarchy of the uni-versity has been destabilized, as students themselves have become authorities on processes of cutbacks, privatization, and resistance. This is evident in independent media coverage and in the interpretation that students have offered of the movement (*Democracy Now!*, 2009a; Edwards, 2009). This movement poses a radical challenge not just to higher-education governance and finance, but also to the politics of knowledge that defines the university. In the course of the struggle, a different kind of learning begins to take place. The symbolic economy of education is opened to interrogation along with the crises of the material economy that provoked the protests in the first place. One participating student puts it this way:

> This is about solidarity. This is about not only students, but it's about faculty members, it's about work-ers, and it's about all of us being fed up with this crisis of priorities that there is. They say that it is a financial crisis, but that's not the truth. It is what they value and honor within the education system that is the problem. We are fighting for a public good. (unidentified student, *Democracy Now!*, 2009b)

What is the knowledge project being elaborated here? In the first instance, one can think of these moments as representing the emergence of a systematic view that "starts off" from marginalized lives (Harding, 1993), the tendrils of an organized representation of the interested knowledge of the oppressed—in this case, working-class students, staff, and their communities. But perhaps a more radical reconceptualization of knowledge is proposed in such moments. In the first place, the partial suspension of systems of status and authority temporarily makes the student the epistemological equal of the professor. In the second place, a new intellectual project for making sense of power and society begins to emerge which draws on diverse subjects and sources: student organizations, youth culture and activism, academic scholarship, and trade-union strategy and analysis. In this flux, a truly radical knowledge project can begin to be seen, one which does not defer to the authority of professional academic work, but nevertheless respects and incorporates it (Edu-factory Collective, 2009). This emancipatory project intervenes in the sense, order, and organization of the university.

The praxis of California's struggles over the university implicitly connects a material struggle over a public resource, an intellectual struggle over the meaning of education, and a political struggle over the right to speak and to be heard. Young people have been at the center of this organic working through of the contradictions of the neoliberal university. As it unfolds, this struggle constructs an alternative epistemology—what I call here an epistemology of emancipation—within which a different knower is foregrounded: no longer the official narrator of the elite consensus, nor the familiar authoritative intellectual, but rather the militant practitioner of occupation, refusal, and resistance. In this process, students reframe the immaturity that is supposed to characterize their relationship to knowledge and to the adult world of work and responsibility as a powerful resource—exposing the arbitrary character of the social habits and norms that we generally experience as a settled "reality." Dewey (1944/1997) celebrated the *plasticity* of young people's understandings, describing it as an asset rather than a lack; in struggles over the university, students expose the plasticity of the social itself, as they demonstrate the possibility of a radical rethinking of the categories of the public, education, and knowledge. As Dyer-Witheford (2007) has pointed out, the politicization of students tracks the larger trajectory of what Marx called "species-being"—humanity's special ability to transform its conditions of existence through conscious activity—and signals that the future is decidedly not the property of the rulers.

Conclusion

Youth and student movements offer more than the mere preconditions for radical or alternative understandings; in their assessments, analyses, and actions, these struggles are *already* incipient knowledge projects. A genuinely emancipatory epistemology challenges the limits of power, which includes a confrontation with the limits of power's definition of knowledge itself. More than a widening of knowledge, this is a perspective anchored in erased and (for power) unintelligible experiences, movements, and identities. In this context, this epistemology recognizes the ways that vernacular knowledge production proposes crucially different senses and coherences for the world. These senses are specific and dangerous, as in the radically "thick description" of the neoliberal university that emerges from the accounts of students in the midst of the struggle, as I have described above. Unsanctioned and unrecognized, a learning and knowing from the outside begins to take shape in these contexts.

Furthermore, the cases I have discussed show that young people in particular are at the front lines not only of political-economic and cultural battles, but also of contemporary efforts to imagine and struggle for different ways of knowing and being together. Student struggles on the terrain of higher education have opened the urgent question of what the university is and what it might be. Youth movements against racism and xenophobia, at the same time as they have developed a critique of contemporary cultural politics, have also proposed—in their own practice—autonomous and decolonial models of community and education. The cases that I have considered here show that young people are not simply in a relationship of apprenticeship to the political and epistemological leadership of their elders, but are, rather, at the forefront of contemporary efforts to rethink and remake social life beyond neoliberalism and coloniality. As I have argued elsewhere (De Lissovoy, 2008), activists and intellectuals going forward will need to learn from youth, and look to them for crucial leadership of oppositional and emancipatory social movements.

Importantly, the movements I have discussed highlight the essential link not just between power and knowledge, but also between knowledge and *geography*—the geography of spaces, states, and bodies. In the first place, these struggles expose the social positionality of understandings (Mignolo, 2011). Thus, against the assimilative discourse of White elites, students defending the MAS program in Arizona insist on the implication of knowledge in history, and in the history of different communities. The Tucson ethnic studies program works to recover erased and marginalized knowledge, tied to the history and struggles of the Chicana/o community. The students have risen up in defense not only of the program itself and the information it imparts, but also of this crucial meta-epistemology, which is aware of learning and knowing as terrains of struggle with different material and symbolic stakes for differently situated communities. Secondly, struggles over knowledge and understanding are ultimately anchored in and fought out in very concrete spaces, and between very specific individual bodies. Truth does not descend from the heavens, but is *decided in pitched battles* between police and protestors, and is paid for with intimidation and blows to the body. The evidence of these struggles shows a double sense in which the understanding has a social positionality: Not only are knowledges tied to different histories, but different knowledges are secured by different bodies, and put these bodies differently at risk.

To argue for a democratic broadening of the field of legitimate knowledge means complicating our sense of what knowledge is. This means recognizing that knowledge is always lived, rather than simply made and owned. But in addition, as I argue here, being and knowing cannot ultimately be coherently separated. Starting from this insight, I have argued here that emancipatory political interventions, specifically contemporary youth movements, are inherently *arguments* that build a characteristic account of the world, rather than mere action or execution of already given analyses. In this way, my interrogation of the limits of familiar alternative epistemologies also reflects a return to the question of being, under the sign of emancipation. This means challenging the distinction, in familiar descriptions of praxis, between the moments of reflection and action. As my argument suggests here, "structures of feeling" (Williams, 1980)—and action—are at the same time structures of knowing. The possibility of a general, social emancipation depends in large part on the continued commitment of young people to a radical *knowing in action*, on the terrain of education and elsewhere, that challenges the limits even of the critical imagination.

Notes

1. A video clip of this event (by Pan Left Productions) can be seen at http://www.youtube.com/watch?v=JBWv-VTaLUg&feature=related
2. For instance, Rodríguez described an incident at the Tucson district headquarters in May of 2011 in which police tossed a protesting student 10–12 feet through the air, injuring her wrists.
3. An image of this poster can be seen at http://www.aiga.org/culturestrike-design-activism-to-impact-immigration-reform/

References

After the fall: Communiqués from occupied California. (2010). Retrieved from http://afterthefallcommuniques.info

Althusser, L. (1971). Ideology and ideological state apparatuses (notes towards an investigation) (B. Brewster, Trans.). In L. Althusser, *Lenin and philosophy and other essays* (pp. 85–126). New York, NY: Monthly Review Press.

Anzaldúa, G. (1987). *Borderlands/la frontera: The new mestiza*. San Francisco, CA: Aunt Lute.

Cabrera, N. L., Meza, E. L., Romero, A. J., & Rodríguez, R. C. (2013). "If there is no struggle, there is no progress": Transformative youth activism and the school of ethnic studies. *Urban Review, 45*(1), 7–22.

Cammarota, J., & Aguilera, M. (2012). "By the time I get to Arizona": Race, language, and education in America's racist state. *Race, Ethnicity and Education, 15*(4), 485–500.

Collins, P. H. (2000). *Black feminist thought: Knowledge, consciousness, and the politics of empowerment*. New York, NY: Routledge.

Cruz, C. (2011). LGBTQ street youth talk back: A meditation on resistance and witnessing. *International Journal of Qualitative Studies in Education, 24*(5), 547–558.

Delgado Bernal, D. (2002). Critical race theory, Latino critical theory, and critical raced-gendered epistemologies; Recognizing students of color as holders and creators of knowledge. *Qualitative Inquiry, 8*(1), 105–126.

De Lissovoy, N. (2008). *Power, crisis, and education for liberation: Rethinking critical pedagogy.* New York, NY: Palgrave Macmillan.

Democracy Now! (2009a, November 17). University of California students and staff prepare for system-wide strike to protest cuts. Retrieved from http://www.democracynow.org/2009/11/17

Democracy Now! (2009b, November 24). A report from inside the takeover of Wheeler Hall. Retrieved from http://www.democracynow.org/2009/11/24

Dewey, J. (1997). *Democracy and education.* New York, NY: Free Press.

Dimitriadis, G. (2001). Pedagogy and performance in Black popular culture. *Cultural Studies <=> Critical Methodologies, 1*(1), 24–35.

Dongallo, A., & Panzar, J. (2009, November 22). Protesters occupy Wheeler Hall. *The Daily Californian.* Retrieved from http://archive.dailycal.org/article/107627/

Dyer-Witheford, N. (2007). Teaching and tear gas: The university in the era of general intellect. In M. Coté, R. J. F. Day, & G. de Peuter (Eds.), *Utopian pedagogy: Radical experiments against neoliberal globalization* (pp. 43–63). Toronto, Canada: University of Toronto Press.

Edu-factory Collective. (2009). *Toward a global autonomous university: Cognitive labor, the production of knowledge, and exodus from the education factory.* New York, NY: Autonomedia.

Edwards, H. (2009, November 24). Protesters stage sit-in at UCOP in latest demonstration. *The Daily Californian,* pp. 1, 3.

Freire, P. (1996). *Pedagogy of the oppressed* (M. B. Ramos, Trans.). New York, NY: Continuum.

Freire, P. (1998). *Pedagogy of freedom: Ethics, democracy, and civic courage* (P. Clarke, Trans.). Lanham, MD: Rowman & Littlefield.

Ginwright, S., Noguera, P., & Cammarota, J. (Eds.). (2006). *Beyond resistance! Youth activism and community change.* New York, NY: Routledge.

Giroux, H. A. (2009). *Youth in a suspect society: Democracy or disposability?* New York, NY: Palgrave Macmillan.

Harding, S. (1993). Rethinking standpoint epistemology: "What is Strong Objectivity"? In L. Alcoff & E. Potter (Eds.), *Feminist epistemologies* (pp. 49–82). New York, NY: Routledge.

Harding, S. (1998). *Is science multicultural? Postcolonialisms, feminisms, and epistemologies.* Bloomington, IN: Indiana University Press.

Hardt, M., & Negri, A. (2004). *Multitude: War and democracy in the age of empire.* New York, NY: Penguin.

Hartsock, N. (1983). The feminist standpoint: Developing the ground for a specifically feminist historical materialism. In S. Harding & M. B. Hintikka (Eds.), *Discovering reality: Feminist perspectives on epistemology, metaphysics, methodology, and philosophy of science* (pp. 283–310). Dordrecht, The Netherlands: D. Reidel.

Hebdige, D. (1988). *Subculture: The meaning of style.* London, UK: Routledge.

Hing, J. (2010, April 23). Young people at the front of pro-migrant movement, SB 1070 protests. *Colorlines.* Retrieved from http://colorlines.com/archives/2010/04/young_people_at_the_front_lines_of_pro-migrant_movement_sb1070_protests.html

Lukács, G. (1971). *History and class consciousness* (R. Livingstone, Trans.). Cambridge, MA: MIT Press.

Maldonado-Torres, N. (2008). *Against war: Views from the underside of modernity.* Durham, NC: Duke University Press.

Marable, M. (1984). *Race, reform and rebellion: The second reconstruction in Black America, 1945–1982.* Jackson, MS: University Press of Mississippi.

Mignolo, W. D. (2005). *The idea of Latin America.* Malden, MA: Blackwell.

Mignolo, W. D. (2011). *The darker side of Western modernity: Global futures, decolonial options.* Durham, NC: Duke University Press.

Muñoz, C. (1989). *Youth, identity, power: The Chicano movement.* London, UK: Verso.

Palos, A. L. (Producer and Director), & McGinnis, E. I. (Producer). (2011). *Precious knowledge: Arizona's battle over ethnic studies.* [Motion picture] Tucson, AZ: Dos Vatos.

Rancière, J. (1991). *The ignorant schoolmaster: Five lessons in intellectual emancipation* (K. Ross, Trans.). Stanford, CA: Stanford University Press.

Rodríguez, R. C. (2013). The fight for Raza studies in Tucson, Arizona. Retrieved from http://drcintli.blogspot.com/2013/04/on-receiving-ella-bakerseptima-clark.html

Sandoval, C. (2000). *Methodology of the oppressed.* Minneapolis, MN: University of Minnesota Press.

Serna, E. (2013). Tempest, Arizona: Criminal epistemologies and the rhetorical possibilities of Raza studies. *Urban Review, 45*(1), 41–57.

Smith, L. T. (1999). *Decolonizing methodologies: Research and indigenous peoples.* London, UK: Zed Books/University of Otago Press.

Tuck, E., & Yang, W. K. (2011). Youth resistance revisited: New theories of youth negotiations of educational injustices. *International Journal of Qualitative Studies in Education, 24*(5), 521–530.

Vercellone, C. (2009). Cognitive capitalism and models for the regulation of wage relations: Lessons from the anti-CPE movement. In Edu-factory Collective (Ed.), *Toward a global autonomous university* (pp. 119–124). New York, NY: Autonomedia.

Williams, R. (1980). *Problems in materialism and culture.* London, UK: Verso.

Yosso, T. (2005). Whose culture has capital? A critical race theory discussion of community cultural wealth. *Race, Ethnicity and Education, 8*(1), 69–91.

21ˢᵗ & aMTRAK

Aurielle Marie

at 3:27/ laughter/ Barrels from the cave of his throat/ Three times before I can finish my sentence
This is the way/ strangers should always make love
Teeth glistening in heat/ Mouths parted/ Eyes quick
Hands moving rapidly/ As if air was flesh

We hold our own bodies,
To house the riots of our chests

Your lips embrace words like an old friend
My poetry/ Consumed in the lines of your smile
You laugh/ Absorbed in the enamel of my speech
Four hours fly like a loved one's last breath
I fold images of him into my luggage/ for safe keeping
You are all of Sampson, the morning after Delilah sheared his crown/ defiance

You lark like flight/ We laugh like light.
When the earth exhales all dewy and sultry like
And the pavement leaps out to melt our backs
When the tension warms like stale Budweiser/ and curry
When intimacy becomes some lofty bird who sheds her feathers
In the quiet jungle of an African convenience store
And us foreigners/ we laugh and clap each other's backs
Marvel at the way Americans carry their tongues/ heavy baggage

"you speak like a weary traveler"/ She says/ "and don't know no better, and don't want to learn, either"
You Press your tongue and vowel sounds/ To the roof of your mouth/ Hoping to change your heritage

When the heavens drop their scars and steam/ When the waiting room feels like a living room floor
When the clock strikes 4:48 and we must become strangers once more
I am reminded of all the august evenings
When my smile felt like an American tongue/
Before I learned lazy speech sounds much better than silence,
I tuck away my concrete teeth/ And grin all the more fiercely.

Aurielle Marie, Atlanta, GA

"K'Lee" Gill

What are dreams exactly?
are dreams the things you see in your sleep of the things you daydream during the day?
or are they random thoughts and pictures your brain shows you?
or are they a defense mechanism for ones emotional state?
like a band aid on a scare from falling really hard onto the concrete by showing you things that make you happy
or are they just things you see on tv?
things you don't have?
the things these rappers or singers try to sell you?
I think dreams consists of all these things.
but most of all, I think dreams give you something to look forward to
a way for God to talk to you and still remain a mystery.
a way to map out your future by seeing what can happen if you make the right moves.
or maybe even a way to see what will happen whether you make moves or not
so are dreams equal to fate?
destiny?
our purpose in life?
or maybe its God showing us the path that we're on and if it brings us closer to him?
Idk … But until I know for sure
I guess I'll keep dreaming…

"K'Lee" Gill (19), SLAM HIGH, Rochester, NY
Shout out to my family friends and everyone in Rochester, NY who are trying to be the best they can be. I'd like to tell them to be good to others and themselves.

About the Contributors

Saba Alvi has a doctorate in Education, with a specialization in society, culture and literacies. Her research interests include cultural studies, anti-racism, issues affecting Muslim youth, representation and pubic pedagogies. Her current research explores how youth subcultures use fashion to inform identity.

Tasha Ausman is a doctoral student in Education at the University of Ottawa and a full-time high school teacher with Western Quebec School Board in Gatineau, Quebec. Her research areas include curriculum theory, popular culture, films, and postcolonial studies.

Jon Austin is associate professor and director of research in the Centre for Australian Indigenous Knowledges at the University of Southern Queensland. A former early childhood teacher, his work centers on anti-racist and critical pedagogies and whiteness studies in teacher education. His focus of work at present is on indigenous ways of knowing and indigenous research methods. He is the senior editor of *Taboo: The Journal of Culture and Education.*

Susan Beierling is a doctoral student in Education at the University of Calgary. Turning a life-long struggle with body image into an academic journey, Susan is interested in areas such as hermeneutics, interpretive inquiry, guided conversations, critical and interpretive theories, body image, identity and belonging.

Brett Elizabeth Blake is professor in the department of curriculum and instruction at St. John's University in Queens, NY, where she also is a senior research fellow for the Vincentian Center for Social Justice and Poverty. Brett has written several articles and books that highlight the inequitable learning opportunities available for diverse student populations, including incarcerated youth and urban ELLs. She is the author of several books on literacy and youth including, *She Say, He Say: Urban Girls Write Their Lives.*

Dennis Carlson is professor of curriculum and the cultural studies of education in the Department of Educational Leadership at Miami University, Oxford, OH. He is the author and co-editor of a number of books in the cultural studies of education and past president of the American Educational Studies Association. He is the author of several books, including *Volunteers of America: The Journey of a Peace Corps Teacher* and co-editor of *The Sexuality Curriculum in Youth Culture* with Donyell Roseboro.

Lynn Corcoran is a registered nurse engaged in doctoral studies in the Faculty of Education at the University of Calgary. Her research interest is intimate partner violence. She has an enduring interest in all issues related to women's health. Lynn teaches in the undergraduate nursing program at Athabasca University.

Marcel Danesi is professor of linguistic anthropology and semiotics at the University of Toronto. He teaches a course on youth culture and has published a number of books on the topic, from *Cool: The Signs and Meanings of Adolescence* (1994) to *Forever Young: The Teen-aging of Modern Culture* (2002) and *Geeks, Goths, and Gangstas: Youth Culture and the Evolution of Modern Society* (2011).

Noah De Lissovoy is assistant professor of Cultural Studies in Education at the University of Texas at Austin. He is the author *of Power, Crisis, and Education for Liberation: Rethinking Critical Pedagogy* (2011) and co-author of *Towards a New Common School Movement* (2013).

Dwayne Donald is Pahpahscîs Cree, his Blackfoot name is **Aipioomahkaa**; he is associate professor in Education at the University of Alberta in Edmonton. His career as an educator began in the Mathare Valley slums of Nairobi, Kenya, working alongside Kenyans with the Mathare Youth Sports Association while living in Nairobi. In 1993, he taught at Kainai High School on the Kainai (Blood) Reserve.

Maria Sylvia Edouard-Gundowry is a Mauritian journalist living in the UK. She is investigating acculturation and identity experiences of Mauritian-Chagossian teenagers in the UK. People of Chagossian origin in the UK have a history of forced displacement from their Chagos Islands by the UK government to make way for a military base on Diego Garcia.

Rosa Maria Bueno Fischer is a journalist and a professor at the School of Education at the Federal University of Rio Grande do Sul in Brazil.

L. A. Gabay holds a doctorate in Urban Education and teaches incarcerated students in Brooklyn. He is the author of many scholarly articles and chapters, and he regularly contributes to *SLAM Magazine*. You can see him on the Lower East Side of Manhattan or at Knicks games wearing Pro-Keds.

Donna Gaines is a sociologist, journalist, social worker, and holistic health practitioner. Her work has appeared in the *Village Voice, Rolling Stone Magazine, SPIN*, in scholarly journals, textbooks and fanzines. The author of *Teenage Wasteland: Suburbia's Dead End Kids*, and *A Misfit's Manifesto: The Sociological Journey of a Rock & Roll Heart*, Gaines is a professor of Community and Human Services and Youth Studies at Empire State College of the State University of New York at Old Westbury. A coastal community activist, Gaines lives on Long Island.

Henry A. Giroux currently holds the Global TV Network Chair Professorship at McMaster University in the English and Cultural Studies Department and a Distinguished Visiting Professorship at Ryerson University. His most recent books include: *Youth in Revolt: Reclaiming a Democratic Future; The Educational Deficit and the War on Youth; America's Disimagination Machine; Higher Education After Neoliberalism; Zombie Politics in the Age of Casino Capitalism;* and *Education and the Crisis of Public*

Values: Challenging the Assault on Teachers, Students & Public Education. He is a member of Truthout. org's board of directors. Website: www.henryagiroux.com.

Nichole E. Grant is a doctoral student in Society, Culture, and Literacies in Education Foundations at the University of Ottawa. She researches anti-racism education, including processes of racialized knowledge production, discourses of race and racisms, youth digital culture, and antiracist methodologies in education.

Jill Guy is completing her doctorate at the University of Southern Queensland, where she is exploring the educational lifeworlds of Australian Aboriginal students. She teaches within the Faculty of Education at the University of Southern Queensland as well as Tertiary Preparation courses at the Centre for Australian Indigenous Knowledges.

Michelle Harazny collaborates with the Montreal-based collective Wall of Femmes on art/action projects. She has organized and facilitated art workshops for youth in Saskatchewan. She holds a Master of Arts in Education and Society from McGill University, having completed a project on literacy for women learning French.

Dana Hasson is a doctoral candidate at McGill University in the Department of Integrated Studies in Education. Her research interests include media, disability studies, education, and critical youth studies. The focus of her work deals primarily with representations of disability in the media.

Awad Ibrahim is professor of Education, University of Ottawa. He is a curriculum theorist with special interest in cultural studies, Hip Hop, youth, and Black popular culture, social foundations (philosophy, history, and sociology of education), social justice and community service learning, diasporic and continental African identities, ethnography, and applied linguistics. He has researched and published widely in these areas. Among his books are *The Rhizome of Blackness: A Critical Ethnography of Hip Hop Culture, Language, Identity and the Politics of Becoming* (Peter Lang, 2014); *Provoking Curriculum Studies: Strong Poetry and the Arts of the Possible* (2014) with Nicholas Ng-A-Fook and Giuliano Reis; *Global Linguistic Flows: Hip Hop Cultures, Youth Identities and the Politics of Language* (2009) with Samy Alim and Alastair Pennycook).

Valerie J. Janesick is professor of Educational Leadership and Policy Studies, University of South Florida. She teaches qualitative research methods, curriculum theory and inquiry, critical pedagogy, ethics, and leadership. She has written numerous articles and books in these areas including her recently completed 3ʳᵈ edition of *Stretching Exercises for Qualitative Researchers*, which is reorganized around habits of mind and includes new sections on Internet inquiry and constructing poetry from interview data.

Robert Jones formerly taught at New York University. The author of various articles on computer gaming, he is the vice president of Digital Strategy at Edelman Digital, previously at Machinima.com.

Tracy D. Keats is a doctoral student at the University of Calgary and a sports medicine-physical education, and leadership teacher at a Calgary high school. She is a UC Dinos Volleyball alumna and was a member of Team Canada Volleyball before beginning a coaching career that includes several provincial and national championship titles. Her research interests are social justice, youth studies, and peer leadership in team sports.

Douglas Kellner is the George Kneller Chair in the Philosophy of Education at UCLA and is author of many books on social theory, politics, history, and culture, including *Media Culture, Guys and Guns*

Amok, Cinema Wars, and *Media Spectacle and the Crisis in Democracy; Media Spectacle and Insurrection, 2011: From the Arab Uprisings to Occupy Everywhere.*

Mandy Krahn is a doctoral student and teacher educator working in the Faculty of Education at the University of Alberta in Edmonton. Her research is focused on the holistic well-being of children and youth.

Virginia Lea is associate professor of Critical Multicultural Education at the University of Wisconsin-Stout. She directs the Hegemony Project at UW-Stout, which promotes research, collaboration, and dialogue into the ways hegemony, including whiteness, reproduces and exacerbates inequities in and through education. It aims to contribute counter-hegemonic solutions supporting a more socio-economically just and caring world. She is the co-author of *Identifying Race and Transforming Whiteness in the Classroom* with Judy Hefland and *Undoing Whiteness in the Classroom: Critical Educultural Teaching Approaches for Social Justice Activism* with Erma Jean Sims.

Haidee Smith Lefebvre is a doctoral student in Education, McGill University. She studies the ways Indigenous girls and young women form their own enlightened counter culture through 'indigenizing' HipHop. Her areas of interest are youth and gender; breaking and youth culture; and arts-based, participatory methodologies.

Carl Leggo is a poet and professor at the University of British Columbia. His books include: *Come-By-Chance; Teaching to Wonder: Responding to Poetry in the Secondary Classroom; Lifewriting as Literary Métissage and an Ethos for Our Times* (co-authored with Erika Hasebe-Ludt and Cynthia Chambers); and *Sailing in a Concrete Boat: A Teacher's Journey.*

Nancy Lesko teaches in the areas of curriculum, youth studies, gender/sexuality, and immigration at Teachers College. Recent books include: *Keywords in Youth Studies* and *Act Your Age! A Cultural Construction of Adolescence.* Current research projects involve a three-country study of beginning teachers and LGBTQ students and a high school initiative that uses storytelling to move beyond the discourse of victims and bullying.

Angel Lin is associate professor of Education at the University of Hong Kong. Well respected for her versatile interdisciplinary scholarship in language and identity studies, bilingual education, and youth cultural studies, she has published six research books and over eighty research articles.

Bettina L. Love is assistant professor in the Department of Educational Theory & Practice at the University of Georgia. She is the author of *Hip Hop's Li'l Sistas Speak: Negotiating Hip Hop Identities and Politics in the New South.* Her work has appeared in numerous books and journals.

Michael B. MacDonald is an assistant professor of music at MacEwan University, Faculty of Fine Arts and Communications, western Canada's only BMus program in Jazz and Contemporary Popular Music. He teaches courses in popular music, jazz, western art music, electro-acoustic music, and the music industry and publishes on popular music, critical youth studies, cultural studies of aesthetics, and ethnomusicology.

Curry Malott is assistant professor at West Chester University. A critical and interdisciplinary scholar, his books include *Punk Rockers' Revolution: A Pedagogy of Race, Class, and Gender* with Milagros Pena (Peter Lang, 2004), and *Policy and Research in Education: A Critical Pedagogy for Educational Leadership* (Peter Lang, 2010).

Fabiola Martinez is a graduate student at California State University, Northridge. She has had the privilege of tutoring migrant students grades K–12 and teaching at an early care and education center serving migrant families. Her desire to work for programs supporting the children of low-income families is the cornerstone of her future goals.

Kerri Mesner is a doctoral candidate and Liu Scholar in the Centre for Cross Faculty Inquiry in Education at the University of British Columbia and a minister with Metropolitan Community Churches. Kerri's research interests include performative autoethnography, queer theology, and anti-oppressive education in addressing religiously rooted anti-queer violence.

Elizabeth J. Meyer is assistant professor in the School of Education at California Polytechnic State University in San Luis Obispo. She is the author of *Gender, Bullying, and Harassment: Strategies to End Sexism and Homophobia in Schools* (2009) and *Gender and Sexual Diversity in Schools* (2010). She blogs for *Psychology Today* and you can follow her on Twitter: @lizjmeyer.

sj Miller is an award-winning author and associate professor in Secondary Literature. He has published on young adult literature, anti-bullying, challenging the gender binary, applications of popular culture, and cultivating socio-spatial justice dispositions with pre-service English teachers. Recent books include *Change Matters: Critical Essays on Moving Social Justice Research from Theory to Policy* (2010); and *Generation BULLIED 2.0: Prevention and Intervention Strategies for Our Most Vulnerable Students* (2013).

Rohany Nayan is a researcher and educator located in Charlotte, NC. Her work as a teacher, principal, ESL lecturer, and educational researcher focuses on immigrant children's experiences in their adopted country and how the interwoven issues of culture and meaning-making act upon their identity and literacy development.

Joshua I. Newman is the director of the Center for Physical Cultural Studies and associate professor of media, politics, and cultural studies in the Sport Management Department at Florida State University. Josh has published numerous articles and chapters, his most recent books are *Embodying Dixie: Studies in the Body Pedagogics of Southern Whiteness* (2010) and *Sport, Spectacle;* and *NASCAR Nation: Consumption and the Cultural Politics of Neoliberalism* with M. Giardina (2011).

Nicholas Ng-A-Fook is associate professor of Curriculum Studies in Education at the University of Ottawa. He works with Mobilizing a Global Citizenship Perspective with Educators: Curriculum Development, Equity and Community Partnerships, funded by the Knowledge Network for Applied Education Research; also with social action curriculum projects with the teachers and students at the Kikinamadinan Elementary School within the Kitigan Zibi Algonquin reserve near Maniwaki, Quebec.

Michael O'Loughlin is a professor in the School of Education and clinical and research supervisor in the doctoral program in Clinical Psychology at Adelphi University. He published *The Subject of Childhood* in 2009 and edited *Imagining Children Otherwise: Theoretical and Critical Perspectives on Childhood Subjectivity* with Richard Johnson in 2010. He is co-editor of *Psychodynamic Psychotherapy in Contemporary South Africa: Contexts, Theories, and Applications* (2013), and in 2013 he edited two books on children's emotions.

Jeff Park is associate professor at the University of Saskatchewan, teaching curriculum theory, as well as various ELA and drama methodology courses. His research includes writing theory, curriculum, literacy, critical pedagogy, and creativity. He writes in a number of genres, including poetry, short stories, and drama. His collection of jazz poems, *The Cellophane Sky*, was a major award-winner in 2012. He has also published a book on writing theory and narrative, *Writing at the Edge* (2005).

Brad Porfilio is associate professor at Lewis University. His research interests include critical pedagogy, critical theory, philosophy, and social theories. He has published many articles and chapters and has co-edited several books including *Youth Culture, Education and Resistance: Subverting the Commercial Ordering of Life* (2012) with Paul Carr and *The New Politics of the Textbook: Problematizing the Portrayal of Marginalized Groups in Textbooks* (2012) with Heather Hickman.

Elizabeth Quintero has worked as a teacher, curriculum specialist, and university teacher educator. Her passion is programs serving families in multilingual communities representing a rich culture and history. She is a professor of Early Childhood Studies at California State University, Channel Islands. Publications include *Critical Literacy in Early Childhood Education: Artful Story and the Integrated Curriculum* (2009) and *Refugee and Immigrant Family Voices: Experience and Education* (2009).

Linda Radford is adjunct professor in Education at Bishop's University. Her research looks at the pedagogical impact of teachers' reading practices in relation to youth fiction. Ongoing research addresses curriculum policy and renewal, digital storytelling with beginning teachers to foster self-reflexive reading practices, and the empowerment of marginalized youth through development of reading situations to engage literacies.

William M. Reynolds teaches in the Department of Curriculum, Foundations and Reading at Georgia Southern University. He has published numerous books including *Curriculum: A River Runs Through It* (2003), *Expanding Curriculum Theory: Dis/positions and Lines of Flight* (2004); *The Civic Gospel: A Political Cartography of Christianity* (2009); *A Curriculum of Place: Understandings Emerging Through the Southern Mist* (2013). His most recent book is *Critical Studies of Southern Place* (2014). His research addresses curriculum, the politics of education, and critical and cultural studies.

Donyell L. Roseboro is an associate professor in the Watson College of Education, UNC Wilmington, NC. She teaches courses in foundations of education and qualitative research. Her publications examine the ways that race, class, and gender shape educational experiences. She has also written about the ways South African township schools teach about democracy. She is the co-editor of *The Sexuality Curriculum in Youth Culture* with Dennis Carlson, and the author of *Jacques Lacan and Education: A Critical Introduction*.

Kelsey Catherine Schmitz is a doctoral candidate at the University of Ottawa. She explores the impact of digital media on culture. Her research focuses on life stories within the digital identity of gamers of video games by interacting with their narratives and digital representations in the world of gaming.

Suzana Feldens Schwertner is a psychologist. She has been a professor at Centro Universitário Univates (Lajeado, RS, Brazil) since 2011.

Marlon Simmons is a postdoctoral scholar at the Werklund Foundation Centre for Youth Leadership Education at the University of Calgary. He holds a doctorate of sociology of education from the Department of Sociology and Equity Studies at the Ontario Institute for Studies in Education. His current research and teaching interests include race and ethnicity, diaspora and youth, cultural studies, and Indigenous studies.

John Smyth is professor of education, an educational sociologist, and research theme leader at University of Ballarat, Australia. A former high school teacher, he has received several awards from the American Educational Research Association. The author of many books and articles on social justice and educational policy, he is a critic of the damaging direction of educational reforms on teachers and students. His recent works are: *Living on the Edge: Re-thinking Poverty, Class and Schooling* (2013) and in 2014, *The Socially Just School: Making Space for Youth to Speak Back and Doing Critical Educational Research: A Conversation with the Research of John Smyth.*

Nathan Snaza teaches modern fiction, feminist and queer theory, and educational foundations at the University of Richmond. His writings have appeared in journals such as the *Journal of Curriculum and Pedagogy, Educational Researcher, InterActions,* the *Journal for Critical Animal Studies,* and *Bad Subjects.*

Lisa Sproull is an artist and designer and member of the Montreal-based Wall of Femmes collective. She relocated to Montreal after earning her BSc (Psychology) from the University of New Brunswick in 2005. As a feminist and activist, she is interested in the social impact of unsanctioned and independently produced cultural content such as zines and street art.

Timothy J. Stanley is professor of Antiracism Education and Education Foundations, Faculty of Education, and vice-dean, Faculty of Graduate and Postdoctoral Studies, University of Ottawa. He has published extensively on anti-racism education and the histories of racism, including his award-winning book, *Contesting White Supremacy* (2011).

Shirley R. Steinberg is Research Professor of Youth Studies at the University of Calgary, and the first director of the Werklund Centre for Youth Leadership Education. Her most recent books include: *Critical Qualitative Research Reader* (2012); *Kinderculture: The Corporate Construction of Childhood* (2011); *Teaching Against Islamophobia* (2011); *19 Urban Questions: Teaching in the City* (2010); and the award-winning *Contemporary Youth Culture: An International Encyclopedia* with Priya Parmar and Birgit Richard (2005). She is a national columnist for CTV News Channel's *Culture Shock* and a regular contributor to CBC Radio One, CTV, *The Toronto Globe and Mail, The Montreal Gazette,* and the Canadian press. The organizer of The International Institute for Critical Pedagogy and Transformative Leadership, she is committed to a global community of transformative educators and community workers engaged in social justice, and the situating of power within social and cultural contexts. Freire-project.org

Susan Talburt is a professor and director of the Institute for Women's, Gender, and Sexuality Studies at Georgia State University. She has published in education, youth studies, and queer studies. Most recently, she is the co-editor, with Nancy Lesko, of *Keywords in Youth Studies: Tracing Affects, Movements, Knowledges* (2012).

Eloise Tan is a lecturer and academic developer at Dublin City University in the area of Higher Education Pedagogy. She has co-edited a special issue of *International Journal of Critical Pedagogy* on critical Hip Hop pedagogies and has published in the *Journal of Black Masculinity* and *Intercultural Education.* Her dissertation was a critical ethnography of informal learning processes and identity construction among Montreal Hip Hop artists.

Cathryn Teasley is interim assistant professor of Curriculum, Instruction, and School Organization at the University of A Coruña, Spain. She focuses on promoting cross-cultural justice through critical anti-bias teacher education, and is co-editor of the book *Transnational Perspectives on Culture, Policy and Education: Redirecting Cultural Studies in Neoliberal Times* (2008).

Cat Terleski is a graduate student in Education at McGill University and a member of the Wall of Femmes collective in Montreal. As an educator, she organizes community and social action programs for youth. A social justice framework informs her research and practice.

P. L. Thomas is associate professor of Education at Furman University and taught high school English in South Carolina before moving to teacher education. He is currently a column editor for *English Journal* (National Council of Teachers of English) and author of *Ignoring Poverty in the U.S.* (2012).

Kate Tilleczek is the Canada Research Chair in Youth Cultures and Transitions and a professor of Education/Sociology at the University of Prince Edward Island. She is adjunct research scientist at the Hospital for Sick Children in Toronto, Ontario. Kate is working on international projects relating to the impacts of globalization, inequality and technology on the social and educational lives of youth, addressing issues of equity in public education and mental health.

P. Taylor Van Zile IV is a doctoral candidate at the Derner Institute. His primary research interests are children's studies, creativity, autism, and the unsymbolized. Currently, Taylor resides in Brooklyn, NY, where he works with children diagnosed with autism.

John A. Weaver is professor of Curriculum Studies at Georgia Southern University. His most recent book is *Educating the Posthuman* (2010). He is currently working with Nathan Snaza on an edited book dealing with posthumanism and his own book on religion, economics, science, and homophobia.

Joe Wegwert is assistant professor in the Department of Teaching and Learning, Northern Arizona University. Dr. Wegwert taught high school social studies for 22 years. His research interests include constructions of civic identity in school contexts, queer issues in education, and social justice in teacher education.

Renee K. L. Wikaire is a graduate fellow in the Center for Physical Cultural Studies at Florida State University. Her current research looks at how a Native American worldview can be utilized to foster sport for development programs. Prior to this, she completed a Bachelor of Physical Education with Honors at the University of Otago, New Zealand.

Paul Willis is lecturer with rank of professor at Princeton University and editor and founder of the international journal *Ethnography*. He has published widely on work, culture, education, and method. Among his many works, his seminal books are *Learning to Labor: How Working Class Kids Get Working Class Jobs* (1977) and *The Ethnographic Imagination* (2000). After studying literature at Cambridge, he received a PhD in 1972 from the Centre for Contemporary Cultural Studies at Birmingham University. At present, he teaches seminars for juniors and seniors in research methods and the sociology of work.

Cover
Artist: Shalak Attack
Mural: "I am Hip Hop", Spraypaint, Montreal, 2009.
Cover Design: Name of designer (Original photo: Indiefotog)

Shalak Attack is an emerging Canadian-Chilean visual artist dedicated to painting, muralism, graffiti urban art, and canvases. Ever since graduating from Concordia University, Shalak has manifested her artistic expression on urban walls across the world. She shares her passion for freedom of expression, and has facilitated visual art workshops to youth of under-privileged communities and prisoners in various countries across the Americas, Europe, the Middle East and Africa.
www.shalakattack.com